DOCUMENTS SUPPLEM

INTERNATIONAL B TRANSACTIONS: A PROBLEM-ORIENTED COURSEBOOK

Twelfth Edition

and

INTERNATIONAL BUSINESS TRANSACTIONS: TRADE AND ECONOMIC RELATIONS

Twelfth Edition

■ ■ ■

by

Ralph H. Folsom
Professor of Law
University of San Diego School of Law

Michael Wallace Gordon
Professor of Law Emeritus
University of Florida Frederic G. Levin College of Law

Michael P. Van Alstine
Professor of Law
University of Maryland
Francis King Carey School of Law

Michael D. Ramsey
Hugh and Hazel Darling Foundation Professor of Law
Director of International and Comparative Law Programs
University of San Diego School of Law

AMERICAN CASEBOOK SERIES®

WEST ACADEMIC PUBLISHING

Mat #41675008

444 Cedar Street, Suite 700
St. Paul, MN 55101
1-877-888-1330

Printed in the United States of America

ISBN: 978-1-62810-223-9

PREFACE

The 2015 edition of this Documents Supplement is designed to accompany the Twelfth Edition of our West Academic Publishing problem-oriented IBT course book, **International Business Transactions** (2015). It also accompanies the Twelfth Edition of our paperback course book **IBT: Trade and Economic Relations**. Nearly every Problem in these course books involves the application of documentary law. This Supplement provides primary legal authorities indispensable to resolution of the issues raised in each Problem.

This Documents Supplement reflects the latest changes in IBT law. Some materials formerly in the text, notably concerning IBT Dispute Settlement, now appear in this Supplement. All of the documents have been alphabetized for easier access and edited to apply to the Problems in our course books.

Three Glossaries commence this Supplement. These are designed to assist understanding of trade acronyms (such as LCDs or less developed countries), trade organizations (such as the WTO or World Trade Organization), and trade law terminology (such as CVDs or countervailing duties).

Your suggestions concerning this Documents Supplement and our IBT course books are most welcome.

RALPH H. FOLSOM
rfolsom@sandiego.edu

MICHAEL W. GORDON
gordon@law.ufl.edu

MICHAEL P. VAN ALSTINE
mvanalstine@law.umaryland.edu

MICHAEL D. RAMSEY
mramsey@sandiego.edu

March 2015

TABLE OF CONTENTS

PART D. REGIONAL LAW—THE NORTH AMERICAN FREE TRADE AGREEMENT (NAFTA)

PART E. UNITED STATES LAW

Part One. General Trade Law Statutes

Part Two. Trade Law Statutes Directed to Regions

Part Three. Trade Related Laws

Part Four. Other Federal Statutes

Part Five. Uniform State Laws and Restatements of the Law

TABLE OF CONTENTS

DOCUMENTS SUPPLEMENT FOR

INTERNATIONAL BUSINESS TRANSACTIONS: A PROBLEM-ORIENTED COURSEBOOK

Twelfth Edition

and

INTERNATIONAL BUSINESS TRANSACTIONS: TRADE AND ECONOMIC RELATIONS

Twelfth Edition

PART A

GLOSSARIES

■ ■ ■

1. GLOSSARY OF INTERNATIONAL TRADE ACRONYMS*

ACDA	Arms Control And Disarmament Agency
ACTN	Advisory Committee on Trade Policy Negotiations
Ad Val	Ad Valorem Tariff Rate
AD	Anti-Dumping
ADB	Asian Development Bank ADS Agent
A/DS	Agent Distributor Service (Commerce Department)
AECA	Arms Export Control Act
AFDB	African Development Bank
AID	Agency for International Development
ANDEAN	Andean Pact Countries
APCAC	Asia-Pacific Council of American Chambers of Commerce
APEC	Asian-Pacific Economic Cooperation
APTA	Automotive Products Trade Act
ASEAN	Association of Southeast Asian Nations
ATACs	Agricultural Technical Advisory Committee
ATCA	Agreement on Trade in Civil Aircraft
ATPI	Andean Trade Preference Initiative
AUI	ASEAN-U.S. Initiative

* Source: Business America, November 19, 1990.

AVE	AD Valorem Equivalent
BEA	Bureau of Economic Analysis (Commerce Department)
BFC	Business Facilitation Center (Commerce Department)
BITS	Bilateral Investment Treaties
BNC	Binational Commission
BOND	Business Outreach to New Democracies Program
BOP	Balance of Payments
BSP	Business Sponsored or Between Show Promotion
BXA	Bureau of Export Administration (Commerce Department)
C & F	Cost and Freight
CACM	Central America Common Market
CAD/CAM	Computer Aided Design/Computer Aided Manufacturing
CAP	Country Action Plan or Common Agricultural Policy (EC)
CARIBCAN	Canadian-Caribbean Basin Initiative
CARICOM	Caribbean Common Market
CASE	Council of American States in Europe
CBERA	Caribbean Basin Economic Recovery Act
CBI	Caribbean Basin Initiative
CCC	Commodity Cooperation Council or Commodity Credit Corporation
CCCN	Customs Cooperation Council Nomenclature
CCL	Commodity Control List
CCNAA	Coordination Council for North American Affairs
CCPIT	China Council for the Promotion of International Trade
CEO	Cultural Exchange Officer or Chief Executive Officer

CET	Common External Tariff
CFIUS	Committee on Foreign Investment in the U.S.
CFR	Cost and Freight
CG	Consul General, Consulate General
CG–18	Consultative Group of Eighteen (GATT)
CHG	Charge d'Affaires
CIF	Cost, Insurance and Freight
CIME	Committee on International Investment and Multinational Enterprises
CIMS	Commercial Information Management System (Commerce Department)
CIT	Court of International Trade
CITA	Committee for the Implementation of Textile Agreement
CITIC	China International Trust and Investment Corp.
CMP	Country Marketing Plan
CNUSA	*Commercial News USA* (Commerce Department)
COCOM	Coordination Committee on Multilateral Export Controls
COE	Council of Europe
CON	Consul, Consular Section
COP	Cost of Production
CPAC	Commodity Policy Advisory Committee
CSCE	Conference on Security and Cooperation in Europe
CSIS	Center for Strategic and International Studies
CSS	Comparison Shopping Service (Commerce Department)
CTA	Committee on Trade in Agriculture (GATT)
CTF	Certified Trade Fair (Commerce Department)

CV	Constructed Value
CVD	Countervailing Duty
DAC	Development Assistance Committee
DAV	Domestic Added Value
DCs	Developed Countries
DEC	District Export Council
DF	Duty Free
DISC	Domestic International Sales Corporation
DO	District Office (Commerce Department)
DOC	U.S. Department of Commerce
DPACT	Defense Policy Advisory Committee on Trade
DRAM	Dynamic Random Access Memory
EAA	Export Administration Act
EC	European Community
ECE	Economic Commission For Europe
ECLS	Export Contact List Services (Commerce Department)
ECO/COM	Economic/Commercial Section
EDA	Economic Development Administration (Commerce Department)
EDO	Export Development Officer
EEBIC	Eastern Europe Business Information Center (Commerce Department)
EEC	European Economic Committee
EFTA	European Free Trade Association
EITCA	U.S.–Soviet Union Agreement to Facilitate Economic, Industrial and Technical Cooperation

EMS	European Monetary System
EMU	European Monetary Unit
EOD	Entrance on Duty
EPC	Economic Policy Council
EPROM	Electronically Programmable Read-Only Memory
EPS	Export Promotion Services
ESA	European Space Agency
ESCMIA	Education, Scientific and Cultural Material Import Act
ETC	Export Trading Company
ETSI	European Telecommunications Standards Institute
EU	European Union
EXIM BANK	Export-Import Bank of the United States
FAM	Foreign Affairs Manual
FAS	Foreign Agriculture Service (Agriculture Department)
FBP	Foreign Buyer Program (Commerce Department)
FCIA	Foreign Credit Insurance Association
FCO	Foreign Commonwealth Office
FCPA	Foreign Corrupt Practices Act
FCS	Foreign Commercial Service (Commerce Department)
FDIUS	Foreign Direct Investment in the U.S.
FET	*Foreign Economics Trends* Report (Commerce Department)
FIRA	Foreign Investment Review Corporation
FMC	Federal Maritime Commission
FMS	Foreign Military Sales

FMSCR	Foreign Military Sales Credit
FMV	Foreign Market Value
FOB	Free on Board
FOGS	Functioning of the GATT System
FOIA	Freedom of Information Act
FR	Federal Register
FSC	Foreign Sales Corporation
FSN	Foreign Service National
FSO	Foreign Service Officer
FTA	Free Trade Area or Free Trade Agreement
FTS	Federal Telecommunications System
FTZ	Foreign Trade Zone
FTZ-board	Federal Trade Zones Board
FTZ-SZ	FTZ-Subzone
FUPDOL	Foreign Unit Price in Dollars
FV	Fair Value
FX	Foreign Exchange Service
GATT	General Agreement on Tariffs and Trade
GDP	Gross Domestic Product
GNG	Group of Negotiations on Goods
GNP	Gross National Product
GNS	Group of Negotiations on Services
GP-zones	General Purpose FTZs
GSP	Generalized System of Preferences
HM	Home Market

HTS	Harmonized Tariff Schedule Nomenclature
IA	Import Administration (Commerce Department)
IC	Integrated Circuit or Industry Committee of the OECD
ICA	International Coffee Agreement or International Cocoa Agreement
ICAO	International Civil Aviation Organization
ICB	International Commodity Bodies
ICC	International Chamber of Commerce
ICO	International Coffee Organization
IDA	International Development Association
IDB	Inter-American Development Bank
IDCA	International Development Bank
IEP	International Economic Policy (Commerce Department)
IEPG	Independent European Program Group
IESC	International Executive Service Corps
IFA	International Franchise Assn.
IFAC	Industry Functional Advisory Committee
IFC	International Finance Corporation
IFI	International Finance Institution
IMF	International Monetary Fund
INR	Initial Negotiating Right
INRA	International Natural Rubber Agreement
INRO	International Natural Rubber Organization
INTELSAT	International Telecommunication Satellite Organization
IOGA	Industry-Organized Government-Approved

IOS	International Organization for Standardization
IPAC	Industry Policy Advisory Committee
IPC	Integrated Program for Commodities
IPR	Intellectual Property Rights
ISA	International Sugar Agreement
ISAC	Industry Sector Advisory Committee
ISO	International Standards Organization
ITA	International Trade Administration (Commerce Department)
ITA	International Tin Agreement
ITC	International Trade Commission
JCCT	(U.S.–Mexico) Joint Commission on Commerce and Trade
JCP	Japan Corporate Program
JETRO	Japan External Trade Organization
LAFTA	Latin America Free Trade Area
LC	Letter of Credit
LDC	Less Developed Country
LDDC	Least (or Lesser) Developed Countries
LTA	Long-Term Arrangement
LTFV	Less Than Fair Value
MDB	Multilateral Development Banks
MFA	Multi-Fiber Arrangement
MFN	Most Favored Nation
MITI	Ministry of International Trade and Industry (Japan)
MKR	Matchmaker Program (Commerce Department)

MNC	Multinational Corporation
MOCP	Market Oriented Cooperation Plan
MOFERT	Ministry of Foreign Economic Relations and Trade (PRC)
MOSS	Market-Oriented Sector-Selective (U.S.-Japan)
MOU	Memorandum of Understanding
MPT	Ministry of Post and Telecommunication
MT	Metric Tons
MTN	Multilateral Trade Negotiations
NCUSCT	National Council for U.S.–China Trade
NIC	Newly Industrialized Country
NME	Non-Market Economy
NOAA	National Oceanic and Atmospheric Administration (Commerce Department)
NP	Nairobi Protocol
NPIS	New Product Information Services
NSC	National Security Council
NTB	Non-Tariff Barrier
NTDB	National Trade Data Bank
NTE	New to Export
NTIA	National Telecommunications and Information Administration (Commerce Department)
NTIS	National Technical Information Service (Commerce Department)
NTM	New to Market
NTM	Non-Tariff Measure
NTS	Non-Traffic Sensitive Costs

NTT	Nippon Telephone and Telegraph Co.
OAS	Organization of American States
OBR	*Overseas Business Report* (Commerce Department)
OECD	Organization for Economic Cooperation and Development
OEM	Original Equipment Manufacturers
OMA	Orderly Marketing Agreement
OPIC	Overseas Private Investment Corporation
OTA	Office of Technology Assessment (Congress)
OTCA	Omnibus Trade and Competitiveness Act of 1988
P.L. 480	Public Law—Agricultural Trade and Assistance
PAS	Paris Air Show
PEC	President's Export Council
PL	Public Law
PRC	People's Republic of China
PSI	Pre-Shipment Inspection
QR	Quantitative Restriction
R & D	Research & Development
RBP	Restrictive Business Practices
REDO	Regional Export Development Office
SB	Surveillance Body
SBA	Small Business Administration
SCO	Senior Commercial Officer
SDR	Special Drawing Rights
SEED	Support for East European Democracy
SFO	Solo Fair Washington-recruited

SHAPE	Supreme Headquarters Allied Powers Europe
SIC	Standard Industrial Classification
SII	Structural Impediments Initiative
SIMIS	Single Internal Market Information Systems
SIMS	Single Internal Market Service
SIPS	Statutory Import Program Staff (Commerce Department)
SITC	Standard International Trade Classification
SM	Seminar Mission (Commerce Department)
SOGA	State-Organized Government-Approved
SP	Exporter Sales Price
STC	Security Trade Control
STE	State Trading Enterprises
TAA	Trade Adjustment Assistance Program
TAAC	Trade Adjustment Assistance Centers
TBAG	Technical Business Assistance Working Group
TD	Trade Development (Commerce Department)
TDP	Trade and Development Program
TELMEX	Telefono de Mexico
TFC	Trade Fair Certification
TFO	Trade Fair, Overseas-recruited
TFW	Trade Fair, Washington-recruited
TIMS	Textiles Information Management System
TM	Trade Mission
TNC	Trade Negotiations Committee
TOP	Trade Opportunity Program (Commerce Department)

TPC	Trade Policy Committee
TPCC	Trade Promotion Coordinating Committee
TPIS	Trade Policy Information System
TPM	Trigger Price Mechanism
TPRG	Trade Policy Review Group
TPRM	Trade Policy Review Mechanism
TPSC	Trade Policy Staff Committee or Trade Policy Sub Committee
TRA	Trade Adjustment Allowance
TRIM	Trade-Related Investment Measure
TRIP	Trade-Related Aspects of Intellectual Property Rights
TS	Trade Specialist
TSB	Textile Surveillance Body
TSUS	Tariff Schedule of the U.S.
TWA	Trade-Weighted Average
UNCTAD	United Nations Conference on Trade and Development
UNCTC	United Nations Centre on Transnational Corporations
UNEP	United Nations Environment Program
UNESCO	United Nations Educational, Scientific and Cultural Organization
UNIDO	United Nations Industrial Development Organization
USDIA	U.S. Direct Investment Abroad
US & FCS	U.S. & Foreign Commercial Service
USC	U.S. Code
USCITCA	U.S.-China Industrial Technological Cooperation Accord
USCJCCT	U.S.-China Joint Commission on Commerce and Trade

USDOC	U.S. Department of Commerce
USEC	US Mission to European Communities
USITC	U.S. International Trade Commission
USKJCCC	U.S.–Korea Joint Committee on Commercial Cooperation
USOECD	US Mission to the Organization for Economic Cooperation and Development
USP	United States Price
USTCC	U.S.–Thailand Commercial Commission
USTR	United States Trade Representative
USTTA	United States Travel and Tourism Administration (Commerce Department)
USUN	US Mission to the United Nations
VARs	Value-Added Resellers
VAT	Value-Added Tax
VC	Video Catalog Show (Commerce Department)
VER	Voluntary Export Restraint
VRA	Voluntary Restraint Agreement
WEPZA	World Export Processing Zones Association
WIPO	World Intellectual Property Organization

2. GLOSSARY OF INTERNATIONAL TRADE TERMS*

Ad Valorem Tariff. A tariff calculated as a percentage of the value of goods cleared through customs, e.g., 15 percent ad valorem means 15 percent of the value.

Adjustment Assistance. Financial, training and reemployment technical assistance to workers and technical assistance to firms and industries to help them cope with adjustment difficulties arising from increased import competition. The objective of the assistance is usually to help an industry

* Source: Business America, September 29, 1986.

to become more competitive in the same line of production, or to move into other economic activities. The aid to workers can take the form of training (to qualify the affected individuals for employment in new or expanding industries), relocation allowances (to help them move from areas characterized by high unemployment to areas where employment may be available) or unemployment compensation (to tide them over while they are searching for new jobs). The aid to firms can take the form of technical assistance through Trade Adjustment Assistance Centers located throughout the United States. Industry-wide technical assistance also is available through the Trade Adjustment Assistance program. The benefits of increased trade to an importing country generally exceed the costs of adjustment, but the benefits are widely shared and the adjustment costs are sometimes narrowly—and some would say unfairly—concentrated on a few domestic producers and communities. Both import restraints and adjustment assistance can be designed to reduce these hardships but adjustment assistance—unlike import restraints—allows the economy to enjoy the full benefits of lower-cost imported goods. Adjustment assistance can also be designed to facilitate structural shifts of resources from less productive to more productive industries, contributing further to greater economic efficiency and improved standards of living.

ATA Carnet. An international customs document that is recognized as an internationally valid guarantee and may be used in lieu of national customs documents and as security for import duties and taxes to cover the temporary admission of goods and sometimes the transit of goods. The ATA ("Admission Temporaire—Temporary Admission") Convention of 1961 authorized the ATA Carnet to replace the ECS ("Echantillons Commerciaux—Commercial Samples") Carnet that was created by a 1956 convention sponsored by the Customs Cooperation Council. ATA Carnets are issued by National Chambers of Commerce affiliated with the International Chamber of Commerce, which also guarantees payment of duties in the event of failure to re-export. A carnet does not replace an export license.

Balance of Payments. A tabulation of a country's credit and debit transactions with other countries and international institutions. These transactions are divided into two broad groups: Current Account and Capital Account. The Current Account includes exports and imports of goods, services (including investment income), and unilateral transfers. The Capital Account includes financial flows related to international direct investment, investment in government and private securities, international bank transactions, and changes in official gold holdings and foreign exchange reserves.

Balance of Trade. A component of the balance of payments, or the surplus or deficit that results from comparing a country's expenditures on merchandise imports and receipts derived from its merchandise exports.

Barter. The direct exchange of goods for other goods, without the use of money as a medium of exchange and without the involvement of a third party.

Beggar-Thy-Neighbor Policy. A course of action through which a country tries to reduce unemployment and increase domestic output by raising tariffs and instituting non-tariff barriers that impede imports, or by accomplishing the same objective through competitive devaluation. Countries that pursued such policies in the early 1930s found that other countries retaliated by raising their own barriers against imports, which, by reducing export markets, tended to worsen the economic difficulties that precipitated the initial protectionist action. The Smoot-Hawley Tariff Act of 1930 is often cited as a conspicuous example of this approach.

Bilateral Trade Agreement. A formal or informal agreement involving commerce between two countries. Such agreements sometimes list the quantities of specific goods that may be exchanged between participating countries within a given period.

Bounties or Grants. Payments by governments to producers of goods, often to strengthen their competitive position.

Boycott. A refusal to deal commercially or otherwise with a person, firm or country.

CIF. An abbreviation used in some international sales contracts under which the selling price includes all "costs, insurance and freight" for the goods sold ("charge in full"), meaning that the seller arranges and pays for all relevant expenses involved in shipping goods from their point of exportation to a given point of importation. In import statistics, "CIF value" means that all figures are calculated on this basis, regardless of the nature of individual transactions.

Codes of Conduct. International instruments that indicate standards of behavior by nation states or multi-national corporations deemed desirable by the international community. For private enterprises, the United Nations, for example, has supported the adoption of voluntary codes of conduct, including ones that seek to specify the rights and obligations of transnational corporations. In international trade, "codes of conduct" commonly refers to the six agreements negotiated during the Tokyo Round of GATT negotiations to liberalize and harmonize domestic measures that might impede or distort trade. These codes in large measure were replaced by specific binding Agreements during the Uruguay Round of negotiations completed in 1994.

Commodity. Broadly defined, any article exchanged in trade, but most commonly used to refer to raw materials, including such minerals as tin, copper and manganese, and bulk-produced agricultural products such as coffee, tea and rubber.

Common External Tariff (CXT). A tariff rate uniformly applied by a common market or customs union, such as the European Community, to imports from countries outside the union. For example, the European internal market is based on the principle of a free internal trade area with a common external tariff (sometimes referred to in French as the Tarif Exterieur Commun—TEC) applied to products imported from non-member countries. "Free trade areas" do not necessarily have common external tariffs.

Comparative Advantage. A central concept in international trade theory which holds that a country or a region should specialize in the production and export of those goods and services that it can produce relatively more efficiently than other goods and services, and import those goods and services in which it has a comparative disadvantage. This theory was first propounded by David Ricardo in 1817 as a basis for increasing the economic welfare of a population through international trade. The comparative advantage theory normally favors specialized production in a country based on intensive utilization of those factors of production in which the country is relatively well endowed (such as raw materials, fertile land or skilled labor), and perhaps also the accumulation of physical capital and the pace of research.

Countertrade. A reciprocal trading arrangement. Countertrade transactions include:

A) Counterpurchase obligates the foreign supplier to purchase from the buyer goods and services unrelated to the goods and services sold, usually with a one- to five-year period.

B) Reverse countertrade contracts require the importer (a U.S. buyer of machine tools from Eastern Europe, for example) to export goods equivalent in value to a specified percentage of the value of the imported goods—an obligation that can be sold to an exporter in a third country;

C) Buyback arrangements obligate the foreign supplier of plant, machinery, or technology to buy from the importer a portion of the resultant production during a 5–25 year period.

D) Clearing agreements between two countries that agree to purchase specific amounts of each other's products over a specified period of time, using a designated "clearing currency" in the transactions;

E) "Switch" arrangements that permit the sale of unpaid balances in a clearing account to be sold to a third party, usually at a discount, that may be used for producing goods in the country holding the balance;

F) Swap schemes through which products from different locations are traded to save transportation costs;

G) Barter arrangements through which two parties directly exchange goods deemed to be of approximately equivalent value without any flow of money taking place.

Countervailing Duties. Special duties imposed on imports to offset the benefits of subsidies to producers or exporters in the exporting country. GATT Article VI, and the 1994 WTO Agreement on Subsidies and Countervailing Measures (SCM Agreement), permit the use of such duties. The Executive Branch of the U.S. Government has been legally empowered since the 1890s to impose countervailing duties in amounts equal to any "bounties" or "grants" reflected in products imported into the United States. Under U.S. law and the SCM Agreement, a wide range of practices are recognized as constituting subsidies that may be offset through the imposition of countervailing duties. The Trade Agreements Act of 1979, through amendments to the Tariff Act of 1930, established rigorous procedures and deadlines for determining the existence of subsidies in response to petitions filed by interested parties such as domestic producers of competitive products and their workers. In all cases involving subsidized products from countries that are parties to the SCM Agreement, or countries which have assumed obligations substantially equivalent to those under the Agreement, U.S. law requires that countervailing duties may be imposed only after the U.S. International Trade Commission has determined that the imports are causing or threatening to cause material injury to an industry in the United States.

Current Account. That portion of a country's balance of payments that records current (as opposed to capital) transactions, including visible trade (exports and imports), invisible trade (income and expenditures for services), profits earned from foreign operations, interest and transfer payments.

Customs Classification. The particular category in a tariff nomenclature in which a product is classified for tariff purposes, or the procedure for determining the appropriate tariff category in a country's nomenclature system used for the classification, coding and description of internationally traded goods. Most important trading nations—except for the United States and Canada—classify imported goods in conformity with the Customs Cooperation Council Nomenclature (CCCN), formerly known as the Brussels Tariff Nomenclature (BTN).

Customs Cooperation Council Nomenclature (CCCN). A system for classifying goods for customs purposes, formerly known as the Brussels Tariff Nomenclature (BTN).

Customs Harmonization. International efforts to increase the uniformity of customs nomenclatures and procedures in cooperating countries. The principal effort in this regard is the Harmonized System, a uniform system of tariff classification adopted by most major trading countries in recent years. Further efforts are generally coordinated by the Customs Cooperation Council (CCC), an international organization with a secretariat in Brussels, Belgium. The CCC is also involved in developing international standards for the exchange of trade data and for determining international rules of origin and related international customs technical questions.

Devaluation. The lowering of the value of a national currency in terms of the currency of another nation. Devaluation tends to reduce domestic demand for imports in a country by raising their prices in terms of the devalued currency and to raise foreign demand for the country's exports by reducing their prices in terms of foreign currencies. Devaluation can therefore help to correct a balance of payments deficit and sometimes provide a short-term basis for economic adjustment of a national economy.

Developed Countries. A term used to distinguish the more industrialized nations from "developing"—or less developed—countries. The developed countries are sometimes collectively designated as the "North," because most of them are in the Northern Hemisphere.

Developing Countries (LCDs). A broad range of countries that generally lack a high degree of industrialization, infrastructure and other capital investment, sophisticated technology, widespread literacy, and advanced living standards among their populations as a whole. The developing countries are sometimes collectively designated as the "South," because a large number of them are in the Southern Hemisphere. All of the countries of Africa, Asia and Oceania (except Australia, Japan and New Zealand), Latin America, and the Middle East are generally considered "developing countries," as are a few European countries (Cyprus, Malta, and Turkey, for example). Some experts differentiate four sub-categories of developing countries as having different economic needs and interests: 1) A few relatively wealthy OPEC countries—sometimes referred to as oil exporting developing countries—share a particular interest in a financially sound international economy and open capital markets; 2) Newly Industrializing Countries (NICs) have a growing stake in an open international trading system; 3) A number of middle income countries—principally commodity exporters—have shown a particular interest in commodity stabilization schemes; and 4) More than 30 very poor countries ("least developed countries") are predominantly agricultural, have sharply limited development prospects during the near future, and tend to be heavily dependent on official development assistance.

Dispute Settlement. Resolution of conflict, usually through a compromise between opposing claims, sometimes facilitated through the efforts of an intermediary. GATT Article XXII and XXIII, and the WTO Dispute Settlement Understanding, set out consultation procedures a Contracting

Party may follow to obtain legal redress if it believes its benefits under various WTO Agreements are impaired.

Domestic International Sales Corporation (Interest Charge DISC). A special U.S. corporation authorized by the U.S. Revenue Act of 1971, as amended by the Tax Reform Act of 1984, to borrow from the U.S. Treasury at the average one-year Treasury bill interest rate to the extent of income tax liable on 94 percent of its annual corporate income. To qualify, the corporation must derive 95 percent of its income from U.S. exports; also, at least 95 percent of its gross assets, such as working capital, inventories, building and equipment, must be export-related. Such a corporation can buy and sell independently, or can operate as a subsidiary of another corporation. It can maintain sales and service facilities outside the United States to promote and market its goods.

Drawback. Import duties or taxes repaid by a government, in whole or in part, when the imported goods are re-exported or used in the manufacture of exported goods.

Dumping. Under U.S. law, the sale of an imported commodity in the United States at "less than fair value," usually considered to be a price lower than that at which it is sold within the exporting country or to third countries. "Fair value" can also be the constructed value of the merchandise, which includes a mandatory 8 percent profit margin plus cost of production. Dumping is generally recognized as an unfair trade practice that can disrupt markets and injure producers of competitive products in the importing country. Article VI of GATT, and the 1994 WTO Antidumping Agreement, permit the imposition of special Anti-Dumping Duties against "dumped" goods equal to the difference between their export price and their normal value in the exporting country. The U.S. Antidumping Law of 1921, as amended, considered dumping as constituting "sales at less than fair value," combined with injury, the likelihood of injury, or the prevention of the establishment of a competitive industry in the United States. The U.S. implemented its obligations under the Antidumping Agreement as part of the Uruguay Round Agreements Act in 1994.

Embargo. A prohibition upon exports or imports, either with respect to specific products or specific countries. Historically, embargoes have been ordered most frequently in time of war, but they may also be applied for political, economic or sanitary purposes. Embargoes imposed against an individual country by the United Nations—or a group of nations—in an effort to influence its conduct or its policies are sometimes called "sanctions."

Escape Clause. A provision in a bilateral or multilateral commercial agreement permitting a signatory nation to suspend tariff or other concessions when imports threaten serious harm to the producers of competitive domestic goods. GATT Article XIX, and the 1994 WTO Safeguards Agreement, sanction such "safeguard" provisions to help firms and workers adversely affected by a relatively sudden surge of imports adjust to the rising level of import competition. Section 201 of the U.S. Trade Act of 1974 requires the U.S. International Trade Commission to investigate complaints formally known as "petitions" filed by domestic industries or workers claiming that they have been injured or are threatened with injury as a consequence of rapidly rising imports and to complete any such investigation within six months. Section 203 of the Act provides that if the Commission finds that a domestic industry has been seriously injured or threatened with serious injury, it may recommend that the President grant relief to the industry in the form of adjustment assistance or temporary import restrictions in the form of tariffs, quotas, or tariff quotas. The President must then take action pursuant to the Commission's recommendations within 60 days, but he may accept, modify or reject them, according to his assessment of the national interest. The Congress can, through the majority vote in both the Senate and the House of Representatives within 90 legislative days, override a Presidential decision not to implement the Commission's recommendations. The law permits the President to impose import restrictions for an initial period of five years and to extend them for a maximum additional period of three years.

Exchange Controls. The rationing of foreign currencies, bank drafts, and other instruments for settling international financial obligations by countries seeking to ameliorate acute balance of payments difficulties. When such measures are imposed, importers must apply for prior authorization from the government to obtain the foreign currency required to bring in designated amounts and types of goods. Since such measures have the effect of restricting imports, they are considered non-tariff barriers to trade.

Exchange Rate. The price (or rate) at which one currency is exchanged for another currency, for gold, or for Special Drawing Rights (SDRs).

Excise Tax. A selective tax—sometimes called a consumption tax—on certain goods produced within or imported into a country.

Export Quotas. Specific restrictions or ceilings imposed by an exporting country on the value or volume of certain imports, designed to protect domestic producers and consumers from temporary shortages of the goods affected or to bolster their prices in world markets. Some International Commodity Agreements explicitly indicate when producers should apply such restraints. Export quotas are also often applied in Orderly Marketing Agreements and Voluntary Restraint Agreements, and to promote domestic processing of raw materials in countries that produce them.

Export Restraints. Quantitative restrictions imposed by exporting countries to limit exports to specified foreign markets, usually pursuant to a formal or informal agreement concluded at the request of the importing countries.

Export Subsidies. Government payments or other financially quantifiable benefits provided to domestic producers or exporters contingent on the export of their goods or services. GATT Article XVI recognizes that subsidies in general, and especially export subsidies, distort normal commercial activities and hinder the achievement of GATT objectives. The 1994 WTO Agreement on Subsidies and Countervailing Measures negotiated during the Uruguay Round strengthened the GATT rules on export subsidies and provided for an outright prohibition of export subsidies by developed countries for manufactured and semi-manufactured products. The Agreement also established a special committee to oversee implementation of the Agreement. Under certain conditions, the Agreement allows developing countries to use export subsidies on manufactured and semi-manufactured products, and on primary products as well, provided that the subsidies do not result in more than an equitable share of world exports of the product for the country.

Export Trading Company. A corporation or other business unit organized and operated principally for the purpose of exporting goods and services, or of providing export related services to other companies. The Export Trading Company Act of 1982 exempts authorized trading companies from certain provisions of U.S. anti-trust laws.

FAS. The term "Free Alongside Ship," in international trade, refers to the point of embarkation from which the vessel or plane selected by the buyer will transport the goods. Under this system, the seller is obligated to pay the costs and assume all risks for transporting the goods from his place of business to the FAS point. In trade statistics, "FAS value" means that the import or export figures are calculated on this basis, regardless of the nature of individual transactions reflected in the statistics.

FOB. An abbreviation used in some international sales contracts, when imports are valued at a designated point, as agreed between buyer and seller, that is considered "Free on Board." In such contracts, the seller is obligated to have the goods packaged and ready for shipment from the agreed point, whether his own place of business or some intermediate point, and the buyer normally assumes the burden of all inland transportation costs and risks in the exporting country, as well as all subsequent transportation costs, including the costs of loading the merchandise on the vessel. However, if the contract stipulates "FOB vessel" the seller bears all transportation costs to the vessel named by the buyer, as well as the costs of loading the goods on to that vessel. The same principle applies to the abbreviations "FOR" ("Free on Rail") and "FOT" ("Free on Truck").

Foreign Sales Corporation (FSC). A firm incorporated in Guam, the U.S. Virgin Islands, the Commonwealth of the Northern Mariana Islands, American Samoa, or any foreign country that has a satisfactory exchange-of-information agreement with the United States and elects to be taxed as a U.S. corporation, except for the fact that it exempts from taxable income a portion of the combined net income of the FSC and its affiliated supplier on the export of U.S. products.

Free Trade. A theoretical concept that assumes international trade unhampered by government measures such as tariffs or non-tariff barriers. The objective of trade liberalization is to achieve "freer trade" rather than "free trade," it being generally recognized among trade policy officials that some restrictions on trade are likely to remain in effect for the foreseeable future.

Free Trade Area. A group of two or more countries that have eliminated tariff and most non-tariff barriers affecting trade among themselves, while each participating country applies its own independent schedule of tariffs to imports from countries that are not members. The best known example is the European Free Trade Association (EFTA)—and the free trade area for manufactured goods that has been created through the trade agreements that have been concluded between the European Community and the individual EFTA countries. GATT Article XXIV spells out the meaning of a free trade area in GATT and specifies the applicability of other GATT provisions to free trade areas.

Free Zone. An area within a country (a seaport, airport, warehouse or any designated area) regarded as being outside its customs territory. Importers may therefore bring goods of foreign origin into such an area without paying customs duties and taxes, pending their eventual processing, transshipment or re-exportation. Free zones were numerous and prosperous during an earlier period when tariffs were high. Some still exist in capital cities, transport junctions and major seaports, but their number and prominence have declined as tariffs have fallen in recent years. Free zones may also be known as "free ports," "free warehouses," and "foreign trade zones."

Generalized System of Preferences (GSP). A concept developed within UNCTAD to encourage the expansion of manufactured and semimanufactured exports from developing countries by making goods more competitive in developed country markets through tariff preferences. The GSP reflects international agreement, negotiated at UNCTAD-II in New Delhi in 1968, that a temporary and non-reciprocal grant of preferences by developed countries to developing countries would be equitable and, in the long term, mutually beneficial.

Government Procurement Policies and Practices. The means and mechanisms through which official government agencies purchase goods and services. Government procurement policies and practices are non-tariff barriers to trade, if they discriminate in favor of domestic suppliers when competitive imported goods are cheaper or of better quality. The United States pressed for an international agreement during the Tokyo Round to ensure that government purchase of goods entering into international trade should be based on specific published regulations that prescribe open procedures for submitting bids, as had been the traditional practice in the United States. Most governments had traditionally awarded such contracts on the basis of bids solicited from selected domestic suppliers, or through private negotiations with suppliers that involved little, if any, competition. Other countries, including the United States, gave domestic suppliers a specified preferential margin, as compared with foreign suppliers. The 1994 WTO Agreement Government Procurement negotiated during the Uruguay Round sought to reduce, if not eliminate, the "Buy National" bias underlying such practices by improving transparency and equity in national procurement practices and by ensuring effective recourse to dispute settlement procedures.

Graduation. The presumption that individual developing countries are capable of assuming greater responsibilities and obligations in the international community—within GATT or the World Bank, for example—as their economies advance, as through industrialization, export development, and rising living standards. In this sense, graduation implies that donor countries may remove the more advanced developing countries from eligibility for all or some products under the Generalized System of Preferences. Within the World Bank, graduation moves a country from dependence on concessional grants to non-concessional loans from international financial institutions and private banks.

Import Substitution. An attempt by a country to reduce imports (and hence foreign exchange expenditures) by encouraging the development of domestic industries.

Industrial Policy. Encompasses traditional government policies intended to provide a favorable economic climate for the development of industry in general or specific industrial sectors. Instruments of industrial policy may include tax incentives to promote investments or exports, direct or indirect subsidies, special financing arrangements, protection against foreign competition, worker training programs, regional development programs, assistance for research and development, and measures to help small business firms. Historically, the term industrial policy has been associated with at least some degree of centralized economic planning or indicative planning, but this connotation is not always intended by its contemporary advocates.

Infant Industry Argument. The view that "temporary protection" for a new industry or firm in a particular country through tariff and non-tariff barriers to imports can help it to become established and eventually competitive in world markets. Historically, new industries that are soundly based and efficiently operated have experienced declining costs as output expands and production experience is acquired. However, industries that have been established and operated with heavy dependence on direct or indirect government subsidies have sometimes found it difficult to relinquish that support. The rationale underlying the Generalized System of Preferences is comparable to that of the infant industry argument.

Intellectual Property. Ownership conferring the right to possess, use, or dispose of products created by human ingenuity, including patents, trademarks and copyrights.

Investment Performance Requirements. Special conditions imposed on direct foreign investment by recipient governments, sometimes requiring commitments to export a certain percentage of the output, to purchase given supplies locally, or to ensure the employment of a specified percentage of local labor and management.

Invisible Trade. Items such as freight, insurance, and financial services that are included in a country's balance of payments accounts (in the "current" account), even though they are not recorded as physically visible exports and imports.

Joint Venture. A form of business partnership involving joint management and the sharing of risks and profits as between enterprises based in different countries. If joint ownership of capital is involved the partnership is known as an equity joint venture.

Least Developed Countries (LDCs). Some 36 of the world's poorest countries, considered by the United Nations to be the least developed of the less developed countries. Most of them are small in terms of area and population, and some are land-locked or small island countries. They are generally characterized by low per capita incomes, literacy levels, and medical standards; subsistence agriculture; and a lack of exploitable minerals and competitive industries. Many suffer from aridity, floods, hurricanes, and excessive animal and plant pests, and most are situated in the zone 10 to 30 degrees north latitude. These countries have little prospect of rapid economic development in the foreseeable future and are likely to remain heavily dependent upon official development assistance for many years. Most are in Africa, but a few, such as Bangladesh, Afghanistan, Laos, and Nepal, are in Asia. Haiti is the only country in the Western Hemisphere classified by the United Nations as "least developed." See developing countries.

Liberal. When referring to trade policy, "liberal" usually means relatively free of import controls or restraints and/or a preference for reducing existing barriers to trade, often contrasted with the protectionist preference for retaining or raising selected barriers to imports.

Mercantilism. A prominent economic philosophy in the 16th and 17th centuries that equated the accumulation and possession of gold and other international monetary assets, such as foreign currency reserves, with national wealth. Although this point of view is generally discredited among 20th century economists and trade policy experts, some contemporary politicians still favor policies designed to create trade "surpluses," such as import substitution and tariff protection for domestic industries, as essential to national economic strength.

Mixed Credits. Exceptionally liberal financing terms for an export sale, ostensibly provided for a foreign aid purpose.

Most-Favored-Nation Treatment (MFN). The policy of non-discrimination in trade policy that provides to all trading partners the same customs and tariff treatment given to the so-called "Most-Favored-Nation." This fundamental principle was a feature of U.S. trade policy as early as 1778. Since 1923 the United States has incorporated an "unconditional" Most-Favored-Nation clause in its trade agreements, binding the contracting governments to confer upon each other all the most favorable trade concessions that either may grant to any other country subsequent to the signing of the agreement. The United States now applies this provision to its trade with all of its trading partners except for those specifically excluded by law. The MFN principle has also provided the foundation of the world trading system since the end of World War II. All Contracting Parties to GATT apply MFN treatment to one another under Article I of GATT.

Multi–Fiber Arrangement Regarding International Trade in Textiles (MFA). An international compact under GATT that allows an importing signatory country to apply quantitative restrictions on textiles imports when it considers them necessary to prevent market disruption. The MFA provides a framework for regulating international trade in textiles and apparel with the objectives of achieving "orderly marketing" of such products, and of avoiding "market disruption" in importing countries. It provides a basis on which major importers, such as the United States and the European Community, may negotiate bilateral agreements or, if necessary, impose restraints on imports from low-wage producing countries. It provides, among other things, standards for determining market disruption, minimum levels of import restraints, and annual growth of imports. Since an importing country may impose such quotas unilaterally to restrict rapidly rising textiles imports, many important textiles-exporting countries consider it advantageous to enter into bilateral agreements with the principal textiles-importing countries. The MFA went into effect on Jan. 1, 1974, was renewed in December 1977, in December

1981, and again in July 1986, for five years. It succeeded the Long-term Agreement on International Trade in Cotton Textiles ("The LTA"), which had been in effect since 1962. Whereas the LTA applied only to cotton textiles, the MFA now applies to wool, man-made (synthetic) fiber, silk blend and other vegetable fiber textiles and apparel.

Multilateral Agreement. An international compact involving three or more parties. For example, GATT has been, since its establishment in 1947, seeking to promote trade liberalization through multilateral negotiations.

Multilateral Trade Negotiations (MTN). Seven Rounds of "Multilateral Trade Negotiations" have been held under the auspices of GATT since 1947. Each Round represented a discrete and lengthy series of interacting bargaining sessions among the participating Contracting Parties in search of mutually beneficial agreements looking toward the reduction of barriers to world trade. The agreements ultimately reached at the conclusion of each Round became new GATT commitments and thus amounted to an important step in the evolution of the world trading system.

Newly Industrializing Countries (NICs). Relatively advanced developing countries whose industrial production and exports have grown rapidly in recent years. Examples include Brazil, Hong Kong, Korea, Mexico, Singapore, and Taiwan.

Non–Market Economy. A national economy or a country in which the government seeks to determine economic activity largely through a mechanism of central planning, in contrast to a market economy that depends heavily upon market forces to allocate productive resources. In a "non-market" economy, production targets, prices, costs, investment allocations, raw materials, labor, international trade, and most other economic aggregates are manipulated within a national economic plan drawn up by a central planning authority, and hence the public sector makes the major decisions affecting demand and supply within the national economy.

Non–Tariff Barriers (NTBs). Government measures other than tariffs that restrict imports. Such measures have become relatively more conspicuous impediments to trade as tariffs have been reduced during the period since World War II.

Orderly Marketing Agreements (OMAs). International agreements negotiated between two or more governments, in which the trading partners agree to restrain the growth of trade in specified "sensitive" products, usually through the imposition of import quotas. Orderly Marketing Agreements are intended to ensure that future trade increases will not disrupt, threaten or impair competitive industries or their workers in importing countries.

Paris Club. A popular designation for meetings between representatives of a developing country that wishes to renegotiate its "official" debt (normally excluding debts owned by and to the private sector without official guarantees) and representatives of the relevant creditor governments and international institutions. Such meetings normally take place at the initiative of a debtor country that wishes to consolidate all or part of its debt service payments falling due over a specified period. The meetings are traditionally chaired by a senior official of the French Treasury Department. Comparable meetings occasionally take place in London and in New York for countries that wish to renegotiate repayment terms for their debts to private banks. Such meetings are sometimes called "creditors clubs."

Par Value. The official fixed exchange rate between two currencies or between a currency and a specific weight of gold or a basket of currencies.

Peril Point. A hypothetical limit beyond which a reduction in tariff protection would cause serious injury to a domestic industry. U.S. legislation in 1949 that extended the Trade Agreements Act of 1934 required the Tariff Commission to establish such "peril points" for U.S. industries, and for the President to submit specific reasons to Congress if and when any U.S. tariff was reduced below those levels. This requirement, which was an important constraint on U.S. negotiating positions in early GATT tariff-cutting Rounds, was eliminated by the Trade Expansion Act of 1962.

Protectionism. The deliberate use or encouragement of restrictions on imports to enable relatively inefficient domestic producers to compete successfully with foreign producers.

Quantitative Restrictions (QRs). Explicit limits, or quotas, on the physical amounts of particular commodities that can be imported or exported during a specified time period, usually measured by volume but sometimes by value. The quota may be applied on a "selective" basis, with varying limits set according to the country of origin, or on a quantitative global basis that only specifies the total limit and thus tends to benefit more efficient suppliers. Quotas are frequently administered through a system of licensing. GATT Article XI generally prohibits the use of quantitative restrictions, except under conditions specified by other GATT articles; Article XIX permits quotas to safeguard certain industries from damage by rapidly rising imports; Articles XII and XVIII provide that quotas may be imposed for balance of payments reasons under circumstances laid out in Article XV; Article XX permits special measures to apply to public health, gold stocks, items of archeological or historic interest, and several other categories of goods; and Article XXI recognizes the overriding importance of national security. Article XII provides that quantitative restrictions, whenever applied, should be non-discriminatory.

Reciprocity. The practice by which governments extend similar concessions to each other, as when one government lowers its tariffs or other barriers impeding its imports in exchange for equivalent concessions from a trading partner on barriers affecting its exports (a "balance of concessions"). Reciprocity has traditionally been a principal objective of negotiators in GATT "Rounds." Reciprocity is also defined as "mutuality of benefits," "quid pro quo," and "equivalence" of advantages. GATT Part IV (especially GATT Article XXXVI) exempts developing countries from the rigorous application of reciprocity in their negotiations with developed countries, subject to certain requirements and limitations.

Retaliation. Action taken by a country to restrain its imports from a country that has increased a tariff or imposed other measures that adversely affect its exports in a manner inconsistent with GATT. The GATT, in certain circumstances, permits such reprisal, although this has very rarely been practiced. The value of trade affected by such retaliatory measures should, in theory, approximately equal the value affected by the initial import restriction.

Round of Trade Negotiations. A cycle of multilateral trade negotiations under the aegis of GATT, culminating in simultaneous trade agreements among participating countries to reduce tariff and non-tariff barriers to trade. Eight "Rounds" have been completed thus far: Geneva, 1947–48; Annecy, France, 1949; Torquay, England, 1950–51; Geneva, 1956; Geneva, 1960–62 (the Dillon Round); Geneva, 1963–67 (the Kennedy Round); Geneva, 1973–79 (the Tokyo Round); and Marrakesh, 1986–1994 (Uruguay Round).

Section 301 (of the Trade Act of 1974). Provision of U.S. law that enables the President to withdraw concessions or restrict imports from countries that discriminate against U.S. exports, subsidize their own exports to the United States, or engage in other unjustifiable or unreasonable practices that burden or discriminate against U.S. trade.

Services. Economic activities—such as transportation, banking, insurance, tourism, space launching telecommunications, advertising, entertainment, data processing, consulting and the licensing of intellectual property—that are usually of an intangible character and often consumed as they are produced. Service industries have become increasingly important since the 1920s. Services now account for more than two-thirds of the economic activity of the United States and about 25 percent of world trade. This subject is now regulated by the 1994 WTO General Agreement on Trade in Services.

Smoot–Hawley Tariff Act of 1930. U.S. protectionist legislation that raised tariff rates on most articles imported by the United States, triggering comparable tariff increases by U.S. trading partners. The Tariff Act of 1930 is also known as the Smoot–Hawley Tariff.

Special Drawing Rights (SDRs). Created in 1969 by the International Monetary Fund as a supplemental international monetary reserve asset. SDRs are available to governments through the Fund and may be used in transactions between the Fund and member governments. IMF member countries have agreed to regard SDRs as complementary to gold and reserve currencies in settling their international accounts. The unit value of an SDR reflects the foreign exchange value of a "basket" of currencies of several major trading countries (the U.S. dollar, the German mark, the French franc, the Japanese yen, and the British pound). The SDR has become the unit of account used by the Fund and several national currencies are pegged to it. Some commercial banks accept deposits denominated in SDRs (although they are unofficial and not the same units transacted among governments and the fund).

State Trading Nations. Countries such as the People's Republic of China and Cuba that rely heavily on government entities, instead of the private sector, to conduct trade with other countries. Some of these countries, (e.g., Cuba) have long been Contracting Parties to GATT, whereas others (e.g., China), became Contracting Parties later under special Protocols of Accession. The different terms and conditions under which these countries acceded to GATT were designed in each case to ensure steady expansion of the country's trade with other GATT countries, taking into account the relative insignificance of tariffs on imports into state trading nations.

Subsidy. An economic benefit granted by a government to producers of goods, often to strengthen their competitive position. The subsidy may be direct (a cash grant) or indirect (low-interest export credits guaranteed by a government agency, for example).

Tariff. A duty (or tax) levied upon goods transported from one customs area to another. Tariffs raise the prices of imported goods, thus making them less competitive within the market of the importing country. After seven "Rounds" of GATT trade negotiations that focused heavily on tariff reductions, tariffs are less important measures of protection than they used to be. The term "tariff" often refers to a comprehensive list or "schedule" of merchandise with the rate of duty to be paid to the government for importing products listed.

Terms of Trade. The volume of exports that can be traded for a given volume of imports. Changes in the terms of trade are generally measured by comparing changes in the ratio of export prices to import prices. The terms of trade are considered to have improved when a given volume of exports can be exchanged for a larger volume of imports. Some economists have discerned an overall deteriorating trend in this ratio for developing countries as a whole. Other economists maintain that whereas the terms of trade may have become less favorable for certain countries during certain periods—and even for all developing countries during some periods—the same terms of trade have improved for other developing countries in the same periods and perhaps for most developing countries during other periods.

Tied Loan. A loan made by a government agency that requires a foreign borrower to spend the proceeds in the lender's country.

Trade Policy Committee (TPC). A senior inter-agency committee of the U.S. Government, chaired by the U.S. Trade Representative, that provides broad guidance to the President on trade policy issues. Members include the Secretaries of Commerce, State, Treasury, Agriculture, and Labor.

Transfer of Technology. The movement of modern or scientific methods of production or distribution from one enterprise, institution or country to another, as through foreign investment, international trade licensing of patent rights, technical assistance or training.

Transparency. Visibility and clarity of laws and regulations. Some of the codes of conduct negotiated during the Tokyo Round sought to increase the transparency of non-tariff barriers that impede trade.

Trigger Price Mechanism (TPM). A U.S. system for monitoring imported steel to identify imports that are possibly being "dumped" in the United States or subsidized by the governments of exporting countries. The minimum price under this system is based on the estimated landed cost at a U.S. port of entry of steel produced by the world's most efficient producers. Imported steel entering the United States below that price may "trigger" formal anti-dumping investigations by the Department of Commerce and the U.S. International Trade Commission. The TPM was in effect between early 1978 and March 1980. It was reinstated in October 1980 and suspended for all products except for stainless steel wire in January 1982.

Turnkey Contract. A compact under which the contractor assumes responsibility to the client for constructing productive installations and ensuring that they operate effectively before turning them over to the client. By centering responsibility for the contributions of all participants in the project in his own hands, the contractor is often able to arrange more favorable financing terms than the client could. The responsibility of the contractor ends when he hands the completed installation over to the client.

Unfair Trade Practices. Unusual government support to firms—such as export subsidies—or certain anti-competitive practices by firms themselves—such as dumping, boycotts or discriminatory shipping arrangements—that result in competitive advantages for the benefiting firms in international trade.

Valuation. The appraisal of the worth of imported goods by customs officials for the purpose of determining the amount of duty payable in the importing country. The GATT Customs Valuation Code obligates governments that sign it to use the "transaction value" of imported goods—or the price actually paid or payable for them—as the principal basis for valuing the goods for customs purposes.

Value Added Tax (VAT). An indirect tax on consumption that is levied at each discrete point in the chain of production and distribution, from the raw material stage to final consumption. Each processor or merchant pays a tax proportional to the amount by which he increases the value of the goods he purchases for resale after making his own contribution. The Value Added Tax is imposed throughout the European Union and EFTA countries, but the tax rates have not been harmonized among those countries.

Voluntary Restraint Agreements (VRAs). Informal arrangements through which exporters voluntarily restrain certain exports, usually through export quotas, to avoid economic dislocation in an importing country, and to avert the possible imposition of mandatory import restrictions. Such arrangements do not normally entail "compensation" for the exporting country.

3. ORGANIZATIONS INVOLVED IN INTERNATIONAL TRADE*

Agency for International Development (AID). The unit within the U.S. Government responsible for the administration of U.S. bilateral development assistance programs. AID also participates actively in the development of other U.S. policies and programs related to Third World economic development.

Coordinating Committee for Multilateral Export Controls (COCOM). A committee established in 1951 by NATO member countries to coordinate their policies relating to the restriction of exports of products and technical data of potential strategic value to the Soviet Union and certain other countries. To date, it consists of NATO countries plus Japan, minus Iceland.

Customs Cooperation Council (CCC). An intergovernmental organization created in 1953 and headquartered in Brussels, through which customs officials of participating countries seek to simplify, standardize, and conciliate customs procedures. The Council has sponsored a standardized product classification, a set of definitions of commodities for customs purposes, a standardized definition of value and a number of recommendations designed to facilitate customs procedures.

European Community (EC) and European Union (EU). A popular term for the European Communities that resulted from the 1967 "Treaty

* Source: Business America, September 29, 1986.

of Fusion" that merged the secretariat (the "Commission") and the intergovernmental executive body (the "Council") of the older European Economic Community (EEC) with those of the European Coal and Steel Community (ECSC) and the European Atomic Energy Community ("EURATOM"), which was established to develop nuclear fuel and power for civilian purposes. The EEC first came into operation on Jan. 1, 1958, based on the Treaty of Rome, with six participating member states (France, Italy, the Federal Republic of Germany, Belgium, the Netherlands and Luxembourg). From the beginning, a principal objective of the Community was the establishment of a customs union, other forms of economic integration, and political cooperation among member countries. The Treaty of Rome provided for the gradual elimination of customs duties and other internal trade barriers, the establishment of a common external tariff, and guarantees of free movement of labor and capital within the Community. The European Community is now part of a broader institutional framework known as the European Union (EU) that came into being through the Maastricht Treaty of 1993. The EU is headquartered in Brussels. The Council of the EU meets several times a year at the Foreign Minister level, and occasionally at the Heads of State level. Technical experts from EU capitals meet regularly to deal with specialized issues in such areas as agriculture, transportation, or trade policy.

European Free Trade Association (EFTA). A regional grouping established in 1960 by the Stockholm Convention, headquartered in Geneva, now comprising Iceland, Liechtenstein, Norway, and Switzerland. EFTA member countries have gradually eliminated tariffs of manufactured goods originating and traded within EFTA. Agricultural products, for the most part, are not included on the EFTA schedule for internal tariff reductions. Each member country maintains its own external tariff schedule and each has concluded a trade agreement with the European Community that provides for the mutual elimination of tariffs for most manufactured goods except for a few sensitive products. As a result, the European Community and EFTA form a de facto free trade area.

Export–Import Bank of the United States (Eximbank). A public corporation created by executive order of the President in 1934 and given a statutory basis in 1945. The Bank makes guarantees and insures loans to help finance U.S. exports, particularly for equipment to be used in capital improvement projects. The Bank also provides short-term insurance for both commercial and political risks, either directly or in cooperation with U.S. commercial banks.

Foreign Credit Insurance Association (FCIA). An agency established in the United States in 1961 to offer insurance facilities in partnership with the Export–Import Bank of the United States for U.S. exporters.

General Agreement on Tariffs and Trade (GATT). A multilateral trade agreement aimed at expanding international trade as a means of raising world welfare. GATT rules reduce uncertainty in connection with commercial transactions across national borders. The GATT is the principal agreement in the World Trade Organization set of agreements. One hundred fifty three countries are Member States to the WTO. The WTO also provides a framework within which international negotiations—known as "Rounds"—are conducted to lower tariffs and other barriers to trade, and a consultative mechanism that may be invoked by governments seeking to protect their trade interests. The cornerstone of the GATT is the Most-Favored-Nation clause (Article I of the General Agreement). For the United States, the 1994 GATT and the various other 1994 WTO Agreements were implemented by the Uruguay Round Agreements Act of 1994.

International Monetary Fund (IMF). An international financial institution proposed at the 1944 Bretton Woods Conference and established in 1946 that seeks to stabilize the international monetary system as a sound basis for the orderly expansion of international trade. Specifically, among other things, the Fund monitors exchange rate policies of member countries, lends them foreign exchange resources to support their adjustment policies when they experience balance of payments difficulties, and provides them financial assistance through a special "compensatory financing facility" when they experience temporary shortfalls in commodity export earnings.

International Trade Administration (ITA). The trade unit of the U.S. Department of Commerce, ITA carries out the U.S. Government's nonagricultural foreign trade activities. It encourages and promotes U.S. exports of manufactured goods, administers U.S. statutes and agreements dealing with foreign trade, and advises on U.S. international trade and commercial policy.

Organization for Economic Cooperation and Development (OECD). An organization based in Paris with a membership of the 34 developed countries. Their basic aims are: to achieve the highest sustainable economic growth and employment while maintaining financial stability; and to contribute to sound economic expansion worldwide and to the expansion of world trade on a multilateral, non-discriminatory basis. The OECD succeeded the Organization for European Economic Corporation (OEEC) in 1961, after the post-World War II economic reconstruction of Europe had been largely accomplished.

Organization of Petroleum Exporting Countries (OPEC). A cartel comprising leading oil producing countries that seek to coordinate oil production and pricing policies.

United Nations Conference on Trade and Development (UNCTAD). A subsidiary organ of the United Nations General Assembly that seeks to focus international attention on economic measures that might accelerate Third World development. The Conference was first convened (UNCTAD–I) in Geneva in 1964.

U.S. International Trade Commission (USITC). Formerly the U.S. Tariff Commission, which was created in 1916 by an Act of Congress. Its mandate was broadened and its name changed by the Trade Act of 1974. It is an independent factfinding agency of the U.S. Government that studies the effects of tariffs and other restraints to trade on the U.S. economy. It conducts public hearings to assist in determining whether particular U.S. industries are injured or threatened with injury by dumping, export subsidies in other countries, or rapidly rising imports. It also studies the probable economic impact on specific U.S. industries of proposed reductions in U.S. tariffs and non-tariff barriers to imports. Its six members are appointed by the President with the advice and consent of the U.S. Senate for nine-year terms (six-year terms prior to 1974).

United States Trade Representative (USTR). A cabinet-level official with the rank of Ambassador who is the principal adviser to the U.S. President on international trade policy. The U.S. Trade Representative is concerned with the expansion of U.S. exports, U.S. participation in GATT, commodity issues, East–West and North–South trade, and direct investment related to trade. As Chairman of the U.S. Trade Policy Committee, he is also the primary official responsible for U.S. participation in all international trade negotiations. Prior to the Trade Agreements Act of 1979, which created the Office of the U.S. Trade Representative, the comparable official was known as the President's Special Representative for Trade Negotiations (STR), a position first established by the Trade Expansion Act of 1962.

World Bank. The International Bank for Reconstruction and Development (IBRD), commonly referred to as the World Bank, is an intergovernmental financial institution located in Washington, D.C. Its objectives are to help raise productivity and incomes and reduce poverty in developing countries. It was established in December 1945 on the basis of a plan developed at the Bretton Woods Conference of 1944. The Bank loans financial resources to credit worthy developing countries. It raises most of its funds by selling bonds in the world's major capital markets. Its bonds have, over the years, earned a quality rating enjoyed only by sound governments and leading corporations. Projects supported by the World Bank normally receive high priority within recipient governments and are usually well planned and supervised. The World Bank earns a profit, which is plowed back into its capital.

World Intellectual Property Organization (WIPO). A specialized agency of the United Nations system that seeks to promote international cooperation in the protection of intellectual property. WIPO administers the International Union for the Protection of Industrial Property (the "Paris Union"), which was founded in 1883 to reduce discrimination in national patent practices, the International Union for the Protection of Literary and Artistic Works (the "Bern Union"), which was founded in 1886 to provide analogous functions with respect to copyrights, and other treaties, conventions and agreements concerned with intellectual property.

World Trade Organization (WTO). The WTO reflects a single institutional framework that resulted from the successful completion of the Uruguay Round of trade negotiations in 1994 and replaced the former GATT institutional structure. As an institution, the WTO came into being pursuant to the 1994 Agreement Establishing the World Trade Organization. The WTO has over 150 members and its headquarters are located in Geneva, Switzerland. Its principal function is to oversee the implementation and operation of the various Agreements that resulted from the Uruguay Round of trade negotiations, most of which are now mandatory for all members. Like the GATT organization that it replaced, the WTO also provides a forum for multilateral trade negotiations and dispute settlement, conducts reviews of member country trade policies, and cooperates with other UN institutions in global economic policy-making.

PART B

INTERNATIONAL LAW—GENERAL

■ ■ ■

DOCUMENT 1

HAGUE CONVENTION ON THE SERVICE ABROAD OF JUDICIAL AND EXTRAJUDICIAL DOCUMENTS IN CIVIL OR COMMERCIAL MATTERS (1965) (ENTERED INTO FORCE AS TO THE UNITED STATES 1969)*

■ ■ ■

20 U.S.T. 361, 1969 WL 97765 (U.S. Treaty), T.I.A.S. No. 6638

Article 1

The present Convention shall apply in all cases, in civil or commercial matters, where there is occasion to transmit a judicial or extrajudicial document for service abroad.

This Convention shall not apply where the address of the person to be served with the document is not known.

CHAPTER I—JUDICIAL DOCUMENTS

Article 2

Each contracting State shall designate a Central Authority which will undertake to receive requests for service coming from other contracting States and to proceed in conformity with the provisions of articles 3 to 6.

Each State shall organise the Central Authority in conformity with its own law.

Article 3

The authority or judicial officer competent under the law of the State in which the documents originate shall forward to the Central Authority of the State addressed a request conforming to the model annexed to the present Convention, without any requirement of legalisation or other equivalent formality.

---

* Parties to the Convention, and any Declarations or Reservations they have entered, are set forth in the Status Table maintained at the website of the Hague Conference on Private International Law, http://www.hcch.net/index_en.php?act=conventions.status&cid=17.

The document to be served or a copy thereof shall be annexed to the request. The request and the document shall both be furnished in duplicate.

Article 4

If the Central Authority considers that the request does not comply with the provisions of the present Convention it shall promptly inform the applicant and specify its objections to the request.

Article 5

The Central Authority of the State addressed shall itself serve the document or shall arrange to have it served by an appropriate agency, either—

(a) by a method prescribed by its internal law for the service of documents in domestic actions upon persons who are within its territory, or

(b) by a particular method requested by the applicant, unless such a method is incompatible with the law of the State addressed.

Subject to sub-paragraph (b) of the first paragraph of this article, the document may always be served by delivery to an addressee who accepts it voluntarily.

If the document is to be served under the first paragraph above, the Central Authority may require the document to be written in, or translated into, the official language or one of the official languages of the State addressed.

That part of the request, in the form attached to the present Convention, which contains a summary of the document to be served, shall be served with the document.

Article 6

The Central Authority of the State addressed or any authority which it may have designated for that purpose, shall complete a certificate in the form of the model annexed to the present Convention.

The certificate shall state that the document has been served and shall include the method, the place and the date of service and the person to whom the document was delivered. If the document has not been served, the certificate shall set out the reasons which have prevented service.

The applicant may require that a certificate not completed by a Central Authority or by a judicial authority shall be countersigned by one of these authorities.

The certificate shall be forwarded directly to the applicant.

Article 7

The standard terms in the model annexed to the present Convention shall in all cases be written either in French or in English. They may also be written in the official language, or in one of the official languages, of the State in which the documents originate.

The corresponding blanks shall be completed either in the language of the State addressed or in French or in English.

Article 8

Each contracting State shall be free to effect service of judicial documents upon persons abroad, without application of any compulsion, directly through its diplomatic or consular agents.

Any State may declare that it is opposed to such service within its territory, unless the document is to be served upon a national of the State in which the documents originate.

Article 9

Each contracting State shall be free, in addition, to use consular channels to forward documents, for the purpose of service, to those authorities of another contracting State which are designated by the latter for this purpose.

Each contracting State may, if exceptional circumstances so require, use diplomatic channels for the same purpose.

Article 10

Provided the State of destination does not object, the present Convention shall not interfere with—

(a) the freedom to send judicial documents, by postal channels, directly to persons abroad,

(b) the freedom of judicial officers, officials or other competent persons of the State of origin to effect service of judicial documents directly through the judicial officers, officials or other competent persons of the State of destination,

(c) the freedom of any person interested in a judicial proceeding to effect service of judicial documents directly through the judicial officers, officials or other competent persons of the State of destination.

Article 11

The present Convention shall not prevent two or more contracting States from agreeing to permit, for the purpose of service of judicial documents, channels of transmission other than those provided for in the preceding articles and, in particular, direct communication between their respective authorities.

Article 12

The service of judicial documents coming from a contracting State shall not give rise to any payment or reimbursement of taxes or costs for the services rendered by the State addressed.

The applicant shall pay or reimburse the costs occasioned by—

(a) the employment of a judicial officer or of a person competent under the law of the State of destination,

(b) the use of a particular method of service.

Article 13

Where a request for service complies with the terms of the present Convention, the State addressed may refuse to comply therewith only if it deems that compliance would infringe its sovereignty or security.

It may not refuse to comply solely on the ground that, under its internal law, it claims exclusive jurisdiction over the subject-matter of the action or that its internal law would not permit the action upon which the application is based.

The Central Authority shall, in case of refusal, promptly inform the applicant and state the reasons for the refusal.

Article 14

Difficulties which may arise in connection with the transmission of judicial documents for service shall be settled through diplomatic channels.

Article 15

Where a writ of summons or an equivalent document had to be transmitted abroad for the purpose of service, under the provisions of the present Convention, and the defendant has not appeared, judgment shall not be given until it is established that—

(a) the document was served by a method prescribed by the internal law of the State addressed for the service of documents in domestic actions upon persons who are within its territory, or

(b) the document was actually delivered to the defendant or to his residence by another method provided for by this Convention,

and that in either of these cases the service or the delivery was effected in sufficient time to enable the defendant to defend.

Each contracting State shall be free to declare that the judge, notwithstanding the provisions of the first paragraph of this article, may give judgment even if no certificate of service or delivery has been received, if all the following conditions are fulfilled—

(a) the document was transmitted by one of the methods provided for in this Convention,

(b) a period of time of not less than six months, considered adequate by the judge in the particular case, has elapsed since the date of the transmission of the document,

(c) no certificate of any kind has been received, even though every reasonable effort has been made to obtain it through the competent authorities of the State addressed.

Notwithstanding the provisions of the preceding paragraphs the judge may order, in case of urgency, any provisional or protective measures.

Article 16

When a writ of summons or an equivalent document had to be transmitted abroad for the purpose of service, under the provisions of the present Convention, and a judgment has been entered against a defendant who has not appeared, the judge shall have the power to relieve the defendant from the effects of the expiration of the time for appeal from the judgment if the following conditions are fulfilled—

(a) the defendant, without any fault on his part, did not have knowledge of the document in sufficient time to defend, or knowledge of the judgment in sufficient time to appeal, and

(b) the defendant has disclosed a prima facie defence to the action on the merits.

An application for relief may be filed only within a reasonable time after the defendant has knowledge of the judgment.

Each contracting State may declare that the application will not be entertained if it is filed after the expiration of a time to be stated in the declaration, but which shall in no case be less than one year following the date of the judgment.

This article shall not apply to judgments concerning status or capacity of persons.

CHAPTER II—EXTRAJUDICIAL DOCUMENTS

Article 17

Extrajudicial documents emanating from authorities and judicial officers of a contracting State may be transmitted for the purpose of service in another contracting State by the methods and under the provisions of the present Convention.

CHAPTER III—GENERAL CLAUSES

Article 18

Each contracting State may designate other authorities in addition to the Central Authority and shall determine the extent of their competence.

The applicant shall, however, in all cases, have the right to address a request directly to the Central Authority.

Federal States shall be free to designate more than one Central Authority.

Article 19

To the extent that the internal law of a contracting State permits methods of transmission, other than those provided for in the preceding articles, of documents coming from abroad, for service within its territory, the present Convention shall not affect such provisions.

Article 20

The present Convention shall not prevent an agreement between any two or more contracting States to dispense with—

(a) the necessity for duplicate copies of transmitted documents as required by the second paragraph of article 3,

(b) the language requirements of the third paragraph of article 5 and article 7,

(c) the provisions of the fourth paragraph of article 5,

(d) the provisions of the second paragraph of article 12.

Article 21

Each contracting State shall, at the time of the deposit of its instrument of ratification or accession, or at a later date, inform the Ministry of Foreign Affairs of the Netherlands of the following—

(a) the designation of authorities, pursuant to articles 2 and 18,

(b) the designation of the authority competent to complete the certificate pursuant to article 6,

(c) the designation of the authority competent to receive documents transmitted by consular channels, pursuant to article 9.

Each contracting State shall similarly inform the Ministry, where appropriate, of—

(a) opposition to the use of methods of transmission pursuant to articles 8 and 10,

(b) declarations pursuant to the second paragraph of article 15 and the third paragraph of article 16,

(c) all modifications of the above designations, oppositions and declarations.

* * *

Designations and Declarations Made on the Part of the United States in Connection with the Deposit of the United States Ratification

1. In accordance with Article 2, the United States Department of State is designated as the Central Authority to receive requests for service from other Contracting States and to proceed in conformity with Articles 3 to 6.

FORMS (REQUEST AND CERTIFICATE)
SUMMARY OF THE DOCUMENT TO BE SERVED
(annexes provided for Articles 3, 5, 6 and 7)

ANNEX TO THE CONVENTION
Forms
REQUEST FOR SERVICE ABROAD OF JUDICIAL OR EXTRAJUDICIAL DOCUMENTS

Convention on the Service Abroad of Judicial and Extrajudicial Documents in Civil or Commercial Matters,
signed at The Hague, the 15th of November 1965.

Identity and address of the applicant	Address of receiving authority

The undersigned applicant has the honour to transmit - in duplicate - the documents listed below and, in conformity with Article 5 of the above-mentioned Convention, requests prompt service of one copy thereof on the addressee, *i.e.*,

(identity and address) ....

a) in accordance with the provisions of sub-paragraph *(a)* of the first paragraph of Article 5 of the Convention*.

b) in accordance with the following particular method (sub-paragraph *(b)* of the first paragraph of Article 5)*: ....

c) by delivery to the addressee, if he accepts it voluntarily (second paragraph of Article 5)*.

The authority is requested to return or to have returned to the applicant a copy of the documents - and of the annexes* - with a certificate as provided on the reverse side.

List of documents

....

....

....

....

....

....

Done at . . . . , the . . . .

Signature and/or stamp.

* Delete if inappropriate.

Reverse of the request
CERTIFICATE

The undersigned authority has the honour to certify, in conformity with Article 6 of the Convention,

1) that the document has been served*

- the (date)

....

- at (place, street, number)

....

....

- in one of the following methods authorised by Article 5:

a) in accordance with the provisions of sub-paragraph *(a)* of the first paragraph of Article 5 of the Convention*.

b) in accordance with the following particular method*:

....

....

c) by delivery to the addressee, who accepted it voluntarily* .

The documents referred to in the request have been delivered to:

- (identity and description of person)
- ....

....

- relationship to the addressee (family, business or other):
- ....

....

....

2) that the document has not been served, by reason of the following facts*:

....

....

....

In conformity with the second paragraph of Article 12 of the Convention, the applicant is requested to pay or reimburse the expenses detailed in the attached statement*.

Annexes

Documents returned: ....

....

....

In appropriate cases, documents establishing the service:

....

....

Done at . . . . , the . . . .

Signature and/or stamp.

* Delete if inappropriate.

SUMMARY OF THE DOCUMENT TO BE SERVED
Convention on the Service Abroad of Judicial and Extrajudicial Documents in Civil or Commercial Matters,
signed at The Hague, the 15th of November 1965.
(Article 5, fourth paragraph)

Name and address of the requesting authority:

....

....

Particulars of the parties*:

....

....

JUDICIAL DOCUMENT**

Nature and purpose of the document:

....

....

Nature and purpose of the proceedings and, where appropriate, the amount in dispute:

....

....

Date and place for entering appearance**:

....

....

Court which has given judgment**:

....

....

Date of judgment**:

....

Time-limits stated in the document**:

....

....

EXTRAJUDICIAL DOCUMENT**

Nature and purpose of the document:

....

....

Time-limits stated in the document**:

....

....

* If appropriate, identity and address of the person interested in the transmission of the document.

** Delete if inappropriate.

DOCUMENT 2

HAGUE CONVENTION ON THE TAKING OF EVIDENCE ABROAD IN CIVIL OR COMMERCIAL MATTERS (1970; ENTERED INTO FORCE AS TO THE UNITED STATES, 1972) (INCLUDING SELECTED ARTICLE 23 DECLARATIONS AND MODEL LETTERS OF REQUEST)*

■ ■ ■

23 U.S.T. 2555, 1972 WL 122493 (U.S. Treaty), T.I.A.S. No. 7444

CHAPTER I—LETTERS OF REQUEST

Article 1

In civil or commercial matters a judicial authority of a Contracting State may, in accordance with the provisions of the law of that State, request the competent authority of another Contracting State, by means of a Letter of Request, to obtain evidence, or to perform some other judicial act.

A Letter shall not be used to obtain evidence which is not intended for use in judicial proceedings, commenced or contemplated.

The expression "other judicial act" does not cover the service of judicial documents or the issuance of any process by which judgments or orders are executed or enforced, or orders for provisional or protective measures.

Article 2

A Contracting State shall designate a Central Authority which will undertake to receive Letters of Request coming from a judicial authority of another Contracting State and to transmit them to the authority competent to execute them. Each State shall organize the Central Authority in accordance with its own law.

---

* Parties to the Convention, and any Declarations or Reservations they have entered, are set forth in the Status Table maintained at the website of the Hague Conference on Private International Law, http://www.hcch.net/index_en.php?act=conventions.status&cid=82.

Letters shall be sent to the Central Authority of the State of execution without being transmitted through any other authority of that State.

Article 3

A Letter of Request shall specify—

(a) the authority requesting its execution and the authority requested to execute it, if known to the requesting authority;

(b) the names and addresses of the parties to the proceedings and their representatives, if any;

(c) the nature of the proceedings for which the evidence is required, giving all necessary information in regard thereto;

(d) the evidence to be obtained or other judicial act to be performed.

Where appropriate, the Letter shall specify, inter alia—

(e) the names and addresses of the persons to be examined;

(f) the questions to be put to the persons to be examined or a statement of the subject-matter about which they are to be examined;

(g) the documents or other property, real or personal, to be inspected;

(h) any requirement that the evidence is to be given on oath or affirmation, and any special form to be used;

(i) any special method or procedure to be followed under Article 9.

A Letter may also mention any information necessary for the application of Article 11.

No legalization or other like formality may be required.

Article 4

A Letter of Request shall be in the language of the authority requested to execute it or be accompanied by a translation into that language.

Nevertheless, a Contracting State shall accept a Letter in either English or French, or a translation into one of these languages, unless it has made the reservation authorized by Article 33.

A Contracting State which has more than one official language and cannot, for reasons of internal law, accept Letters in one of these languages for the whole of its territory, shall, by declaration, specify the language in which the Letter or translation thereof shall be expressed for execution in the specified parts of its territory. In case of failure to comply with this declaration, without justifiable excuse, the costs of translation into the required language shall be borne by the State of origin.

A Contracting State may, by declaration, specify the language or languages other than those referred to in the preceding paragraphs, in which a Letter may be sent to its Central Authority.

Any translation accompanying a Letter shall be certified as correct, either by a diplomatic officer or consular agent or by a sworn translator or by any other person so authorized in either State.

Article 5

If the Central Authority considers that the request does not comply with the provisions of the present Convention, it shall promptly inform the authority of the State of origin which transmitted the Letter of Request, specifying the objections to the Letter.

Article 6

If the authority to whom a Letter of Request has been transmitted is not competent to execute it, the Letter shall be sent forthwith to the authority in the same State which is competent to execute it in accordance with the provisions of its own law.

Article 7

The requesting authority shall, if it so desires, be informed of the time when, and the place where, the proceedings will take place, in order that the parties concerned, and their representatives, if any, may be present. This information shall be sent directly to the parties or their representatives when the authority of the State of origin so requests.

Article 8

A Contracting State may declare that members of the judicial personnel of the requesting authority of another Contracting State may be present at the execution of a Letter of Request. Prior authorization by the competent authority designated by the declaring State may be required.

Article 9

The judicial authority which executes a Letter of Request shall apply its own law as to the methods and procedures to be followed.

However, it will follow a request of the requesting authority that a special method or procedure be followed, unless this is incompatible with the internal law of the State of execution or is impossible of performance by reason of its internal practice and procedure or by reason of practical difficulties.

A Letter of Request shall be executed expeditiously.

Article 10

In executing a Letter of Request the requested authority shall apply the appropriate measures of compulsion in the instances and to the same extent as are provided by its internal law for the execution of orders issued by the authorities of its own country or of requests made by parties in internal proceedings.

Article 11

In the execution of a Letter of Request the person concerned may refuse to give evidence in so far as he has a privilege or duty to refuse to give the evidence—

(a) under the law of the State of execution; or

(b) under the law of the State of origin, and the privilege or duty has been specified in the Letter, or, at the instance of the requested authority, has been otherwise confirmed to that authority by the requesting authority.

A Contracting State may declare that, in addition, it will respect privileges and duties existing under the law of States other than the State of origin and the State of execution, to the extent specified in that declaration.

Article 12

The execution of a Letter of Request may be refused only to the extent that—

(a) in the State of execution the execution of the Letter does not fall within the functions of the judiciary; or

(b) the State addressed considers that its sovereignty or security would be prejudiced thereby.

Execution may not be refused solely on the ground that under its internal law the State of execution claims exclusive jurisdiction over the subject-matter of the action or that its internal law would not admit a right of action on it.

Article 13

The documents establishing the execution of the Letter of Request shall be sent by the requested authority to the requesting authority by the same channel which was used by the latter.

In every instance where the Letter is not executed in whole or in part, the requesting authority shall be informed immediately through the same channel and advised of the reasons.

Article 14

The execution of the Letter of Request shall not give rise to any reimbursement of taxes or costs of any nature.

Nevertheless, the State of execution has the right to require the State of origin to reimburse the fees paid to experts and interpreters and the costs occasioned by the use of a special procedure requested by the State of origin under Article 9, paragraph 2.

The requested authority whose law obliges the parties themselves to secure evidence, and which is not able itself to execute the Letter, may, after having obtained the consent of the requesting authority, appoint a suitable person to do so. When seeking this consent the requested authority shall indicate the approximate costs which would result from this procedure. If the requesting authority gives its consent it shall reimburse any costs incurred; without such consent the requesting authority shall not be liable for the costs.

CHAPTER II—TAKING OF EVIDENCE BY DIPLOMATIC OFFICERS, CONSULAR AGENTS AND COMMISSIONERS

Article 15

In a civil or commercial matter, a diplomatic officer or consular agent of a Contracting State may, in the territory of another Contracting State and within the area where he exercises his functions, take the evidence without compulsion of nationals of a State which he represents in aid of proceedings commenced in the courts of a State which he represents.

A Contracting State may declare that evidence may be taken by a diplomatic officer or consular agent only if permission to that effect is given upon application made by him or on his behalf to the appropriate authority designated by the declaring State.

Article 16

A diplomatic officer or consular agent of a Contracting State may, in the territory of another Contracting State and within the area where he exercises his functions, also take the evidence, without compulsion, of nationals of the State in which he exercises his functions or of a third State, in aid of proceedings commenced in the courts of a State which he represents, if-

(a) a competent authority designated by the State in which he exercises his functions has given its permission either generally or in the particular case, and

(b) he complies with the conditions which the competent authority has specified in the permission.

A Contracting State may declare that evidence may be taken under this Article without its prior permission.

Article 17

In a civil or commercial matter, a person duly appointed as a commissioner for the purpose may, without compulsion, take evidence in the territory of a Contracting State in aid of proceedings commenced in the courts of another Contracting State if—

(a) a competent authority designated by the State where the evidence is to be taken has given its permission either generally or in the particular case; and

(b) he complies with the conditions which the competent authority has specified in the permission.

A Contracting State may declare that evidence may be taken under this Article without its prior permission.

Article 18

A Contracting State may declare that a diplomatic officer, consular agent or commissioner authorized to take evidence under Articles 15, 16 or 17, may apply to the competent authority designated by the declaring State for appropriate assistance to obtain the evidence by compulsion. The declaration may contain such conditions as the declaring State may see fit to impose.

If the authority grants the application it shall apply any measures of compulsion which are appropriate and are prescribed by its law for use in internal proceedings.

Article 19

The competent authority, in giving the permission referred to in Articles 15, 16 or 17, or in granting the application referred to in Article 18, may lay down such conditions as it deems fit, inter alia, as to the time and place of the taking of the evidence. Similarly it may require that it be given reasonable advance notice of the time, date and place of the taking of the evidence; in such a case a representative of the authority shall be entitled to be present at the taking of the evidence.

Article 20

In the taking of evidence under any Article of this Chapter persons concerned may be legally represented.

Article 21

Where a diplomatic officer, consular agent or commissioner is authorized under Articles 15, 16 or 17 to take evidence—

(a) he may take all kinds of evidence which are not incompatible with the law of the State where the evidence is taken or contrary to any permission granted pursuant to the above Articles, and shall have power within such limits to administer an oath or take an affirmation;

(b) a request to a person to appear or to give evidence shall, unless the recipient is a national of the State where the action is pending, be drawn up in the language of the place where the evidence is taken or be accompanied by a translation into such language;

(c) the request shall inform the person that he may be legally represented and, in any State that has not filed a declaration under Article 18, shall also inform him that he is not compelled to appear or to give evidence;

(d) the evidence may be taken in the manner provided by the law applicable to the court in which the action is pending provided that such manner is not forbidden by the law of the State where the evidence is taken;

(e) a person requested to give evidence may invoke the privileges and duties to refuse to give the evidence contained in Article 11.

Article 22

The fact that an attempt to take evidence under the procedure laid down in this Chapter has failed, owing to the refusal of a person to give evidence, shall not prevent an application being subsequently made to take the evidence in accordance with Chapter I.

CHAPTER III—GENERAL CLAUSES

Article 23

A Contracting State may at the time of signature, ratification or accession, declare that it will not execute Letters of Request issued for the purpose of obtaining pre-trial discovery of documents as known in Common Law countries.

Article 24

A Contracting State may designate other authorities in addition to the Central Authority and shall determine the extent of their competence. However, Letters of Request may in all cases be sent to the Central Authority.

Federal States shall be free to designate more than one Central Authority.

Article 25

A Contracting State which has more than one legal system may designate the authorities of one of such systems, which shall have exclusive competence to execute Letters of Request pursuant to this Convention.

Article 26

A Contracting State, if required to do so because of constitutional limitations, may request the reimbursement by the State of origin of fees and costs, in connection with the execution of Letters of Request, for the service of process necessary to compel the appearance of a person to give evidence, the costs of attendance of such persons, and the cost of any transcript of the evidence.

Where a State has made a request pursuant to the above paragraph, any other Contracting State may request from that State the reimbursement of similar fees and costs.

Article 27

The provisions of the present Convention shall not prevent a Contracting State from—

(a) declaring that Letters of Request may be transmitted to its judicial authorities through channels other than those provided for in Article 2;

(b) permitting, by internal law or practice, any act provided for in this Convention to be performed upon less restrictive conditions;

(c) permitting, by internal law or practice, methods of taking evidence other than those provided for in this Convention.

Article 28

The present Convention shall not prevent an agreement between any two or more Contracting States to derogate from—

(a) the provisions of Article 2 with respect to methods of transmitting Letters of Request;

(b) the provisions of Article 4 with respect to the languages which may be used;

(c) the provisions of Article 8 with respect to the presence of judicial personnel at the execution of Letters;

(d) the provisions of Article 11 with respect to the privileges and duties of witnesses to refuse to give evidence;

(e) the provisions of Article 13 with respect to the methods of returning executed Letters to the requesting authority;

(f) the provisions of Article 14 with respect to fees and costs;

(g) the provisions of Chapter II.

* * *

Article 33

A State may, at the time of signature, ratification or accession exclude, in whole or in part, the application of the provisions of paragraph 2 of Article 4 and of Chapter II. No other reservation shall be permitted.

Each Contracting State may at any time withdraw a reservation it has made; the reservation shall cease to have effect on the sixtieth day after notification of the withdrawal.

When a State has made a reservation, any other State affected thereby may apply the same rule against the reserving State.

Article 34

A State may at any time withdraw or modify a declaration.

Article 35

A Contracting State shall, at the time of the deposit of its instrument of ratification or accession, or at a later date, inform the Ministry of Foreign Affairs of the Netherlands of the designation of authorities, pursuant to Articles 2, 8, 24 and 25.

A Contracting State shall likewise inform the Ministry, where appropriate, of the following—

(a) the designation of the authorities to whom notice must be given, whose permission may be required, and whose assistance may be invoked in the taking of evidence by diplomatic officers and consular agents, pursuant to Articles 15, 16 and 18 respectively;

(b) the designation of the authorities whose permission may be required in the taking of evidence by commissioners pursuant to Article 17 and of those who may grant the assistance provided for in Article 18;

(c) declarations pursuant to Articles 4, 8, 11, 15, 16, 17, 18, 23 and 27;

(d) any withdrawal or modification of the above designations and declarations;

(e) the withdrawal of any reservation.

Article 36

Any difficulties which may arise between Contracting States in connection with the operation of this Convention shall be settled through diplomatic channels.

* * *

HAGUE EVIDENCE CONVENTION

Declarations pursuant to Article 23

German Declaration (made in substantially similar form by most states except the United States):

The Federal Republic of Germany declares in pursuance of Article 23 of the Convention that it will not, in its territory, execute Letters of Request issued for the purpose of obtaining pre-trial discovery of documents as known in Common Law countries.

British Declaration:

In accordance with Article 23 Her Majesty's Government declare that the United Kingdom will not execute Letters of Request issued for the purpose of obtaining pre-trial discovery of documents. Her Majesty's Government further declare that Her Majesty's Government understand "Letters of Request issued for the purpose of obtaining pre-trial discovery of documents" for the purposes of the foregoing Declaration as including any Letter of Request which requires a person:—

a. to state what documents relevant to the proceedings to which the Letter of Request relates are, or have been, in his possession, custody, or power; or

b. to produce any documents other than particular documents specified in the Letter of Request as being documents appearing to the requesting court to be, or to be likely to be, in his possession, custody or power.

MODEL FOR LETTERS OF REQUEST RECOMMENDED FOR USE IN APPLYING THE HAGUE CONVENTION OF 18 MARCH 1970 ON THE TAKING OF EVIDENCE ABROAD IN CIVIL OR COMMERCIAL MATTERS

Request for International Judicial Assistance Pursuant to the Hague Convention of 18 March 1970 on the Taking of Evidence in Civil or Commercial Matters

N.B. Under the first paragraph of article 4, the Letter of Request shall be in the language of the authority requested to execute it or be accompanied by a translation into that language. However, the provisions of the second and third paragraphs may permit use of other languages.

In order to avoid confusion, please spell out the name of the month in each date.

---

1. Sender ____*(identity and address)*
   ____

2. Central Authority of the Requested State ____*(identity and address)*
   ____

3. Person to whom the executed request is to be returned ____*(identity and address)*
   ____

4. Specification of the date by which the requesting authority requires receipt of the response to the Letter of Request ________________
   ____
   ____

Date ____________________

Reason for Urgency* ____________________

____

____

In conformity with article 3 of the Convention, the undersigned applicant has the honour to submit the following request:

5. a. Requesting judicial authority (article 3, a) ____*(identity and address)* ____________________

b. To the competent authority of (article 3, a) ____*(the requested State)* ____________________

c. Names of the case and any identifying number ____________________

6. Names and addresses of the parties and their representatives (including representatives in the requesting state*) (article 3, b) ____________________

____

____

____

a. Plaintiff ____________________

b. Defendant ____________________

c. Other parties ____________________

____

7. a. Nature of the proceedings (divorce, paternity, breach of contract, product liability, etc.) (article 3, c) ____________________

____

____

b. Summary of complaint ____________________

____

c. Summary of defence and counterclaim* ____________________

____

---

* Omit if not applicable.

* Omit if not applicable.

d. Other necessary information or documents* ____________________

____

8. a. Evidence to be obtained or other judicial act to be performed (article 3, d) ____________________

____

b. Purpose of the evidence or judicial act sought ____________________

____

DOCUMENT 3

OECD CONVENTION ON COMBATING BRIBERY OF FOREIGN PUBLIC OFFICIALS IN INTERNATIONAL BUSINESS TRANSACTIONS (1997)

■ ■ ■

(Adopted by the U.S. and used as a basis to amend the Foreign Corrupt Practices Act)

Preamble

The Parties,

Considering that bribery is a widespread phenomenon in international business transactions, including trade and investment, which raises serious moral and political concerns, undermines good governance and economic development, and distorts international competitive conditions;

Considering that all countries share a responsibility to combat bribery in international business transactions;

Having regard to the Revised Recommendation on Combating Bribery in International Business Transactions, adopted by the Council of the Organisation for Economic Co-operation and Development (OECD) on 23 May 1997, C(97)123/FINAL, which, *inter alia,* called for effective measures to deter, prevent and combat the bribery of foreign public officials in connection with international business transactions, in particular, the prompt criminalisation of such bribery in an effective and coordinated manner and in conformity with the agreed common elements set out in that Recommendation and with the jurisdictional and other basic legal principles of each country;

Welcoming other recent developments which further advance international understanding and co-operation in combating bribery of public officials, including actions of the United Nations, the World Bank, the International Monetary Fund, the World Trade Organisation, the Organisation of American States, the Council of Europe and the European Union;

Welcoming the efforts of companies, business organisations, trade unions as well as other non-governmental organisations to combat bribery;

Recognising the role of governments in the prevention of solicitation of bribes from individuals and enterprises in international business transactions;

Recognising that achieving progress in this field requires not only efforts on a national level but also multilateral co-operation, monitoring and follow-up;

Recognising that achieving equivalence among the measures to be taken by the Parties is an essential object and purpose of the Convention, which requires that the Convention be ratified without derogations affecting this equivalence;

Have agreed as follows:

Article 1

The Offence of Bribery of Foreign Public Officials

1. Each Party shall take such measures as may be necessary to establish that it is a criminal offence under its law for any person intentionally to offer, promise or give any undue pecuniary or other advantage, whether directly or through intermediaries, to a foreign public official, for that official or for a third party, in order that the official act or refrain from acting in relation to the performance of official duties, in order to obtain or retain business or other improper advantage in the conduct of international business.

2. Each Party shall take any measures necessary to establish that complicity in, including incitement, aiding and abetting, or authorisation of an act of bribery of a foreign public official shall be a criminal offence. Attempt and conspiracy to bribe a foreign public official shall be criminal offences to the same extent as attempt and conspiracy to bribe a public official of that Party.

3. The offences set out in paragraphs 1 and 2 above are hereinafter referred to as "bribery of a foreign public official".

4. For the purpose of this Convention:

   "foreign public official" means any person holding a legislative, administrative or judicial office of a foreign country, whether appointed or elected; any person exercising a public function for a foreign country, including for a public agency or public enterprise; and any official or agent of a public international organisation;

   "foreign country" includes all levels and subdivisions of government, from national to local;

   "act or refrain from acting in relation to the performance of official duties" includes any use of the public official's position, whether or not within the official's authorised competence.

Article 2

Responsibility of Legal Persons

Each party shall take such measures as may be necessary, in accordance with its legal principles, to establish the liability of legal persons for the bribery of a foreign public official.

Article 3

Sanctions

1. The bribery of a foreign public official shall be punishable by effective, proportionate and dissuasive criminal penalties. The range of penalties shall be comparable to those applicable to the bribery of the Party's own public officials and shall, in the case of natural persons, include deprivation of liberty sufficient to enable effective mutual legal assistance and extradition.

2. In the event that, under the legal system of a Party, criminal responsibility is not applicable to legal persons, that Party shall ensure that legal persons shall be subject to effective, proportionate and dissuasive non-criminal sanctions, including monetary sanctions, for bribery of foreign public officials.

3. Each Party shall take such measures as may be necessary to provide that the bribe and the proceeds of the bribery of a foreign public official, or property the value of which corresponds to that of such proceeds, are subject to seizure and confiscation or that monetary sanctions of comparable effect are applicable.

4. Each Party shall consider the imposition of additional civil or administrative sanctions upon a person subject to sanctions for the bribery of a foreign public official.

Article 4

Jurisdiction

1. Each Party shall take such measures as may be necessary to establish its jurisdiction over the bribery of a foreign public official when the offence is committed in whole or in part in its territory.

2. Each Party which has jurisdiction to prosecute its nationals for offences committed abroad shall take such measures as may be necessary to establish its jurisdiction to do so in respect of the bribery of a foreign public official, according to the same principles.

3. When more than one Party has jurisdiction over an alleged offence described in this Convention, the Parties involved shall, at the request of one of them, consult with a view to determining the most appropriate jurisdiction for prosecution.

4. Each Party shall review whether its current basis for jurisdiction is effective in the fight against the bribery of foreign public officials and, if it is not, shall take remedial steps.

Article 5

Enforcement

Investigation and prosecution of the bribery of a foreign public official shall be subject to the applicable rules and principles of each Party. They shall not be influenced by considerations of national economic interest, the potential effect upon relations with another State or the identity of the natural persons or legal entities involved.

Article 6

Statute of Limitations

Any statute of limitations applicable to the offence of bribery of a foreign public official shall allow an adequate period of time for the investigation and prosecution of this offence.

Article 7

Money Laundering

Each Party which has made bribery of its own public official a predicate offence for the purpose of the application of its money laundering legislation shall do so on the same terms for the bribery of a foreign public official, without regard to the place where the bribery occurred.

Article 8

Accounting

1. In order to combat bribery of foreign public officials effectively, each Party shall take such measures as may be necessary, within the framework of its laws and regulations regarding the maintenance of books and records, financial statement disclosures, and accounting and auditing standards, to prohibit the establishment of off-the-books accounts, the making of off-the-books or inadequately identified transactions, the recording of non-existent expenditures, the entry of liabilities with incorrect identification of their object, as well as the use of false documents, by companies subject to those laws and regulations, for the purpose of bribing foreign public officials or of hiding such bribery.

2. Each Party shall provide effective, proportionate and dissuasive civil, administrative or criminal penalties for such omissions and falsifications in respect of the books, records, accounts and financial statements of such companies.

Article 9

Mutual Legal Assistance

1. Each Party shall, to the fullest extent possible under its laws and relevant treaties and arrangements, provide prompt and effective legal assistance to another Party for the purpose of criminal investigations and proceedings brought by a Party concerning offences within the scope of this Convention and for non-criminal proceedings within the scope of this Convention brought by a Party against a legal person. The requested Party shall inform the requesting Party, without delay, of any additional information or documents needed to support the request for assistance and, where requested, of the status and outcome of the request for assistance.

2. Where a Party makes mutual legal assistance conditional upon the existence of dual criminality, dual criminality shall be deemed to exist if the offence for which the assistance is sought is within the scope of this Convention.

3. A Party shall not decline to render mutual legal assistance for criminal matters within the scope of this Convention on the ground of bank secrecy.

Article 10

Extradition

1. Bribery of a foreign public official shall be deemed to be included as an extraditable offence under the laws of the Parties and the extradition treaties between them.

2. If a Party which makes extradition conditional on the existence of an extradition treaty receives a request for extradition from another Party with which it has no extradition treaty, it may consider this Convention to be the legal basis for extradition in respect of the offence of bribery of a foreign public official.

3. Each Party shall take any measures necessary to assure either that it can extradite its nationals or that it can prosecute its nationals for the offence of bribery of a foreign public official. A Party which declines a request to extradite a person for bribery of a foreign public official solely on the ground that the person is its national shall submit the case to its competent authorities for the purpose of prosecution.

4. Extradition for bribery of a foreign public official is subject to the conditions set out in the domestic law and applicable treaties and arrangements of each Party. Where a Party makes extradition conditional upon the existence of dual criminality, that condition shall be deemed to be fulfilled if the offence for which extradition is sought is within the scope of Article 1 of this Convention.

Article 11

Responsible Authorities

For the purposes of Article 4, paragraph 3, consultation, Article 9, mutual legal assistance and Article 10, extradition, each Party shall notify to the Secretary-General of the OECD an authority or authorities responsible for making and receiving requests, which shall serve as channel of communication for these matters for that Party, without prejudice to other arrangements between Parties.

Article 12

Monitoring and Follow-up

The Parties shall co-operate in carrying out a programme of systematic follow-up to monitor and promote the full implementation of this Convention. Unless otherwise decided by a consensus of the Parties, this shall be done in the framework of the OECD Working Group on Bribery in International Business Transactions and according to its terms of reference, or within the framework and terms of reference of any successor to its functions, and Parties shall bear the costs of the programme in accordance with the rules applicable to that body.

Article 13

Signature and Accession

1. Until its entry into force, this Convention shall be open for signature by OECD members and by non-members which have become or have been invited to become full participants in its Working Group on Bribery in International Business Transactions.

2. Subsequent to its entry into force, this Convention shall be open to accession by any non-signatory which is a member of or has become a full participant in the Working Group on Bribery in International Business Transactions or any successor to its functions.

Article 14

Ratification and Depositary

1. This Convention is subject to acceptance, approval or ratification by the Signatories, in accordance with their respective laws.

2. Instruments of acceptance, approval, ratification or accession shall be deposited with the Secretary-General of the OECD, who shall serve as Depositary of this Convention.

Article 15

Entry into Force

1. This convention shall enter into force on the sixtieth day following the date upon which five of the countries which have the ten largest export

shares set out in document DAFFE/IME/BR(97)18, and which represent by themselves at least sixty percent of the combined total exports of those ten countries, have deposited their instruments of acceptance, approval, or ratification. For each state depositing its instrument after such entry into force, the Convention shall enter into force on the sixtieth day after deposit of its instrument.

2. If, by 31 December 1998, the Convention has not entered into force under paragraph 1 above, any state which has deposited its instrument of ratification may declare to the depositary its readiness to accept entry into force of this convention under this paragraph 2. The Convention shall enter into force for such a state on the sixtieth day following the date upon which such declarations have been deposited by at least two states. For each state depositing its declaration after such entry into force, the Convention shall enter into force on the sixtieth day following the date of deposit.

Article 16

Amendment

Any Party may propose the amendment of this Convention. A proposed amendment shall be submitted to the Depositary which shall communicate it to the other Parties at least sixty days before convening a meeting of the Parties to consider the proposed amendment. An amendment adopted by consensus of the parties, or by such other means as the Parties may determine by consensus, shall enter into force sixty days after the deposit of an instrument of ratification, acceptance or approval by all of the Parties, or in such other circumstances as may be specified by the Parties at the time of adoption of the amendment.

Article 17

Withdrawal

A Party may withdraw from this Convention by submitting written notification to the Depositary. Such withdrawal shall be effective one year after the date of the receipt of the notification. After withdrawal, co-operation shall continue between the Parties and the State which has withdrawn on all requests for assistance and extradition made before the effective date of withdrawal which remain pending.

DOCUMENT 4

UNITED NATIONS CONVENTION ON CONTRACTS FOR THE INTERNATIONAL SALE OF GOODS (CISG) (1980)

■ ■ ■

[This Convention (CISG) was prepared by the United Nations Commission on International Trade Law (UNCITRAL) and issued for signature through a United Nations Diplomatic Conference in Vienna in 1980. As its Final Clauses (Articles 89–101) indicate, CISG became effective as a multilateral treaty on January 1, 1988, twelve months after ten nations ratified it. On December 11, 1986, China, Italy and the United States became the ninth, tenth, and eleventh nations to ratify the Convention. Thus, CISG became effective for transactions within its scope of application (see Article 1) on January 1, 1988. It governs all international sales contracts within Article 1 concluded after that date, although the parties may expressly "opt out" of its coverage under Article 6.

As of February 1, 2015, the following 83 countries are Contracting States to CISG: Albania, Argentina, Armenia, Australia, Austria, Bahrain, Belarus, Belgium, Benin, Bosnia and Herzegovina, Brazil, Bulgaria, Burundi, Canada, Chile, China, Colombia, Congo (Republic of), Croatia, Cuba, Cyprus, Czech Republic, Denmark, Dominican Republic, Ecuador, Egypt, El Salvador, Estonia, Finland, France, Gabon, Georgia, Germany, Greece, Guinea, Guyana, Honduras, Hungary, Iceland, Iraq, Israel, Italy, Japan, Korea (Republic of), Kyrgyzstan, Latvia, Lebanon, Lesotho, Liberia, Lithuania, Luxembourg, Macedonia, Madagascar, Mauritania, Mexico, Moldova, Mongolia, Montenegro, the Netherlands, New Zealand, Norway, Paraguay, Peru, Poland, , Romania, Russian Federation, Saint Vincent and Grenadines, San Marino, Serbia, Singapore, Slovakia, Slovenia, Spain, Sweden, Switzerland, Syria, Turkey, Uganda, Ukraine, United States, Uruguay, Uzbekistan, and Zambia.

In the United States, CISG is considered a self-executing treaty, so no domestic federal legislation was enacted or is necessary. Courts may apply the Convention directly to the issues raised by individual litigants who are parties to international sales contracts covered by Article 1.]

THE STATES PARTIES TO THIS CONVENTION

BEARING IN MIND the broad objectives in the resolutions adopted by the sixth special session of the General Assembly of the United Nations on the establishment of a New International Economic Order,

CONSIDERING that the development of international trade on the basis of equality and mutual benefit is an important element in promoting friendly relations among States,

BEING OF THE OPINION that the adoption of uniform rules which govern contracts for the international sale of goods and take into account the different social, economic and legal systems would contribute to the removal of legal barriers in international trade and promote the development of international trade,

HAVE AGREED as follows:

PART I. SPHERE OF APPLICATION AND GENERAL PROVISIONS

CHAPTER I. SPHERE OF APPLICATION

Article 1

(1) This Convention applies to contracts of sale of goods between parties whose places of business are in different States:

(a) when the States are Contracting States; or

(b) when the rules of private international law lead to the application of the law of a Contracting State.

(2) The fact that the parties have their places of business in different States is to be disregarded whenever this fact does not appear either from the contract or from any dealings between, or from information disclosed by, the parties at any time before or at the conclusion of the contract.

(3) Neither the nationality of the parties nor the civil or commercial character of the parties or of the contract is to be taken into consideration in determining the application of this Convention.

[The United States has declared a reservation under Article 95, and therefore is not bound by Article 1(1)(b).]

Article 2

This Convention does not apply to sales:

(a) of goods bought for personal, family or household use, unless the seller, at any time before or at the conclusion of the contract, neither knew nor ought to have known that the goods were bought for any such use;

(b) by auction;

(c) on execution or otherwise by authority of law;

(d) of stocks, shares, investment securities, negotiable instruments or money;

(e) of ships, vessels, hovercraft or aircraft;

(f) of electricity.

Article 3

(1) Contracts for the supply of goods to be manufactured or produced are to be considered sales unless the party who orders the goods undertakes to supply a substantial part of the materials necessary for such manufacture or production.

(2) This Convention does not apply to contracts in which the preponderant part of the obligations of the party who furnishes the goods consists in the supply of labour or other services.

Article 4

This Convention governs only the formation of the contract of sale and the rights and obligations of the seller and the buyer arising from such a contract. In particular, except as otherwise expressly provided in this Convention, it is not concerned with:

(a) the validity of the contract or of any of its provisions or of any usage;

(b) the effect which the contract may have on the property in the goods sold.

Article 5

This Convention does not apply to the liability of the seller for death or personal injury caused by the goods to any person.

Article 6

The parties may exclude the application of this Convention or, subject to article 12, derogate from or vary the effect of any of its provisions.

CHAPTER II. GENERAL PROVISIONS

Article 7

(1) In the interpretation of this Convention, regard is to be had to its international character and to the need to promote uniformity in its application and the observance of good faith in international trade.

(2) Questions concerning matters governed by this Convention which are not expressly settled in it are to be settled in conformity with the general principles on which it is based or, in the absence of such principles, in conformity with the law applicable by virtue of the rules of private international law.

Article 8

(1) For the purposes of this Convention statements made by and other conduct of a party are to be interpreted according to his intent where the other party knew or could not have been unaware what that intent was.

(2) If the preceding paragraph is not applicable, statements made by and other conduct of a party are to be interpreted according to the understanding that a reasonable person of the same kind as the other party would have had in the same circumstances.

(3) In determining the intent of a party or the understanding a reasonable person would have had, due consideration is to be given to all relevant circumstances of the case including the negotiations, any practices which the parties have established between themselves, usages and any subsequent conduct of the parties.

Article 9

(1) The parties are bound by any usage to which they have agreed and by any practices which they have established between themselves.

(2) The parties are considered, unless otherwise agreed, to have impliedly made applicable to their contract or its formation a usage of which the parties knew or ought to have known and which in international trade is widely known to, and regularly observed by, parties to contracts of the type involved in the particular trade concerned.

Article 10

For the purposes of this Convention:

(a) if a party has more than one place of business, the place of business is that which has the closest relationship to the contract and its performance, having regard to the circumstances known to or contemplated by the parties at any time before or at the conclusion of the contract;

(b) if a party does not have a place of business, reference is to be made to his habitual residence.

Article 11

A contract of sale need not be concluded in or evidenced by writing and is not subject to any other requirement as to form. It may be proved by any means, including witnesses.

Article 12

Any provision of article 11, article 29 or Part II of this Convention that allows a contract of sale or its modification or termination by agreement or any offer, acceptance or other indication of intention to be made in any form other than in writing does not apply where any party has his place of business in a Contracting State which has made a declaration under article

96 of this Convention. The parties may not derogate from or vary the effect of this article.

Article 13

For the purposes of this Convention "writing" includes telegram and telex.

PART II. FORMATION OF THE CONTRACT

Article 14

(1) A proposal for concluding a contract addressed to one or more specific persons constitutes an offer if it is sufficiently definite and indicates the intention of the offeror to be bound in case of acceptance. A proposal is sufficiently definite if it indicates the goods and expressly or implicitly fixes or makes provision for determining the quantity and the price.

(2) A proposal other than one addressed to one or more specific persons is to be considered merely as an invitation to make offers, unless the contrary is clearly indicated by the person making the proposal.

* * *

Article 17

An offer, even if it is irrevocable, is terminated when a rejection reaches the offeror.

Article 18

(1) A statement made by or other conduct of the offeree indicating assent to an offer is an acceptance. Silence or inactivity does not in itself amount to acceptance.

(2) An acceptance of an offer becomes effective at the moment the indication of assent reaches the offeror. An acceptance is not effective if the indication of assent does not reach the offeror within the time he has fixed or, if no time is fixed, within a reasonable time, due account being taken of the circumstances of the transaction, including the rapidity of the means of communication employed by the offeror. An oral offer must be accepted immediately unless the circumstances indicate otherwise.

(3) However, if, by virtue of the offer or as a result of practices which the parties have established between themselves or of usage, the offeree may indicate assent by performing an act, such as one relating to the dispatch of the goods or payment of the price, without notice to the offeror, the acceptance is effective at the moment the act is performed, provided that the act is performed within the period of time laid down in the preceding paragraph.

Article 19

(1) A reply to an offer which purports to be an acceptance but contains additions, limitations or other modifications is a rejection of the offer and constitutes a counter-offer.

(2) However, a reply to an offer which purports to be an acceptance but contains additional or different terms which do not materially alter the terms of the offer constitutes an acceptance, unless the offeror, without undue delay, objects orally to the discrepancy or dispatches a notice to that effect. If he does not so object, the terms of the contract are the terms of the offer with the modifications contained in the acceptance.

(3) Additional or different terms relating, among other things, to the price, payment, quality and quantity of the goods, place and time of delivery, extent of one party's liability to the other or the settlement of disputes are considered to alter the terms of the offer materially.

* * *

PART III. SALE OF GOODS

CHAPTER I. GENERAL PROVISIONS

Article 25

A breach of contract committed by one of the parties is fundamental if it results in such detriment to the other party as substantially to deprive him of what he is entitled to expect under the contract, unless the party in breach did not foresee and a reasonable person of the same kind in the same circumstances would not have foreseen such a result.

Article 26

A declaration of avoidance of the contract is effective only if made by notice to the other party.

* * *

Article 28

If, in accordance with the provisions of this Convention, one party is entitled to require performance of any obligation by the other party, a court is not bound to enter a judgment for specific performance unless the court would do so under its own law in respect of similar contracts of sale not governed by this Convention.

Article 29

(1) A contract may be modified or terminated by the mere agreement of the parties.

(2) A contract in writing which contains a provision requiring any modification or termination by agreement to be in writing may not be

otherwise modified or terminated by agreement. However, a party may be precluded by his conduct from asserting such a provision to the extent that the other party has relied on that conduct.

CHAPTER II. OBLIGATIONS OF THE SELLER

Article 30

The seller must deliver the goods, hand over any documents relating to them and transfer the property in the goods, as required by the contract and this Convention.

Section I.

Delivery of the Goods and Handing Over of Documents

Article 31

If the seller is not bound to deliver the goods at any other particular place, his obligation to deliver consists:

(a) if the contract of sale involves carriage of the goods—in handing the goods over to the first carrier for transmission to the buyer;

(b) if, in cases not within the preceding subparagraph, the contract relates to specific goods, or unidentified goods to be drawn from a specific stock or to be manufactured or produced, and at the time of the conclusion of the contract the parties knew that the goods were at, or were to be manufactured or produced at, a particular place—in placing the goods at the buyer's disposal at that place;

(c) in other cases—in placing the goods at the buyer's disposal at the place where the seller had his place of business at the time of the conclusion of the contract.

Article 32

(1) If the seller, in accordance with the contract or this Convention, hands the goods over to a carrier and if the goods are not clearly identified to the contract by markings on the goods, by shipping documents or otherwise, the seller must give the buyer notice of the consignment specifying the goods.

(2) If the seller is bound to arrange for carriage of the goods, he must make such contracts as are necessary for carriage to the place fixed by means of transportation appropriate in the circumstances and according to the usual terms for such transportation.

(3) If the seller is not bound to effect insurance in respect of the carriage of the goods, he must, at the buyer's request, provide him with all available information necessary to enable him to effect such insurance.

Article 33

The seller must deliver the goods:

(a) if a date is fixed by or determinable from the contract, on that date;

(b) if a period of time is fixed by or determinable from the contract, at any time within that period unless circumstances indicate that the buyer is to choose a date; or

(c) in any other case, within a reasonable time after the conclusion of the contract.

Article 34

If the seller is bound to hand over documents relating to the goods, he must hand them over at the time and place and in the form required by the contract. If the seller has handed over documents before that time, he may, up to that time, cure any lack of conformity in the documents, if the exercise of this right does not cause the buyer unreasonable inconvenience or unreasonable expense. However, the buyer retains any right to claim damages as provided for in this Convention.

Section II.
Conformity of the Goods and Third Party Claims

Article 35

(1) The seller must deliver goods which are of the quantity, quality and description required by the contract and which are contained or packaged in the manner required by the contract.

(2) Except where the parties have agreed otherwise, the goods do not conform with the contract unless they:

(a) are fit for the purposes for which goods of the same description would ordinarily be used;

(b) are fit for any particular purpose expressly or impliedly made known to the seller at the time of the conclusion of the contract, except where the circumstances show that the buyer did not rely, or that it was unreasonable for him to rely, on the seller's skill and judgement;

(c) possess the qualities of goods which the seller has held out to the buyer as a sample or model;

(d) are contained or packaged in the manner usual for such goods or, where there is no such manner, in a manner adequate to preserve and protect the goods.

(3) The seller is not liable under subparagraphs (a) to (d) of the preceding paragraph for any lack of conformity of the goods if at the time

of the conclusion of the contract the buyer knew or could not have been unaware of such lack of conformity.

Article 36

(1) The seller is liable in accordance with the contract and this Convention for any lack of conformity which exists at the time when the risk passes to the buyer, even though the lack of conformity becomes apparent only after that time.

(2) The seller is also liable for any lack of conformity which occurs after the time indicated in the preceding paragraph and which is due to a breach of any of his obligations, including a breach of any guarantee that for a period of time the goods will remain fit for their ordinary purpose or for some particular purpose or will retain specified qualities or characteristics.

Article 37

If the seller has delivered goods before the date for delivery, he may, up to that date, deliver any missing part or make up any deficiency in the quantity of the goods delivered, or deliver goods in replacement of any nonconforming goods delivered or remedy any lack of conformity in the goods delivered, provided that the exercise of this right does not cause the buyer unreasonable inconvenience or unreasonable expense. However, the buyer retains any right to claim damages as provided for in this Convention.

Article 38

(1) The buyer must examine the goods, or cause them to be examined, within as short a period as is practicable in the circumstances.

(2) If the contract involves carriage of the goods, examination may be deferred until after the goods have arrived at their destination.

(3) If the goods are redirected in transit or redispatched by the buyer without a reasonable opportunity for examination by him and at the time of the conclusion of the contract the seller knew or ought to have known of the possibility of such redirection or redispatch, examination may be deferred until after the goods have arrived at the new destination.

Article 39

(1) The buyer loses the right to rely on a lack of conformity of the goods if he does not give notice to the seller specifying the nature of the lack of conformity within a reasonable time after he has discovered it or ought to have discovered it.

(2) In any event, the buyer loses the right to rely on a lack of conformity of the goods if he does not give the seller notice thereof at the latest within a period of two years from the date on which the goods were actually handed over to the buyer, unless this time-limit is inconsistent with a contractual period of guarantee.

* * *

Article 42

(1) The seller must deliver goods which are free from any right or claim of a third party based on industrial property or other intellectual property, of which at the time of the conclusion of the contract the seller knew or could not have been unaware, provided that the right or claim is based on industrial property or other intellectual property:

(a) under the law of the State where the goods will be resold or otherwise used, if it was contemplated by the parties at the time of the conclusion of the contract that the goods would be resold or otherwise used in that State; or

(b) in any other case, under the law of the State where the buyer has his place of business.

(2) The obligation of the seller under the preceding paragraph does not extend to cases where:

(a) at the time of the conclusion of the contract the buyer knew or could not have been unaware of the right or claim; or

(b) the right or claim results from the seller's compliance with technical drawings, designs, formulae or other such specifications furnished by the buyer.

Article 43

(1) The buyer loses the right to rely on the provisions of article 41 or article 42 if he does not give notice to the seller specifying the nature of the right or claim of the third party within a reasonable time after he has become aware or ought to have become aware of the right or claim.

(2) The seller is not entitled to rely on the provisions of the preceding paragraph if he knew of the right or claim of the third party and the nature of it.

Article 44

Notwithstanding the provisions of paragraph (1) of article 39 and paragraph (1) of article 43, the buyer may reduce the price in accordance with article 50 or claim damages, except for loss of profit, if he has a reasonable excuse for his failure to give the required notice.

Section III.

Remedies for Breach of Contract by the Seller

Article 45

(1) If the seller fails to perform any of his obligations under the contract or this Convention, the buyer may:

(a) exercise the rights provided in articles 46 to 52;

(b) claim damages as provided in articles 74 to 77.

(2) The buyer is not deprived of any right he may have to claim damages by exercising his right to other remedies.

* * *

Article 46

(1) The buyer may require performance by the seller of his obligations unless the buyer has resorted to a remedy which is inconsistent with this requirement.

(2) If the goods do not conform with the contract, the buyer may require delivery of substitute goods only if the lack of conformity constitutes a fundamental breach of contract and a request for substitute goods is made either in conjunction with notice given under article 39 or within a reasonable time thereafter.

* * *

Article 47

(1) The buyer may fix an additional period of time of reasonable length for performance by the seller of his obligations.

(2) Unless the buyer has received notice from the seller that he will not perform within the period so fixed, the buyer may not, during that period, resort to any remedy for breach of contract. However, the buyer is not deprived thereby of any right he may have to claim damages for delay in performance.

Article 48

(1) Subject to article 49, the seller may, even after the date for delivery, remedy at his own expense any failure to perform his obligations, if he can do so without unreasonable delay and without causing the buyer unreasonable inconvenience or uncertainty of reimbursement by the seller of expenses advanced by the buyer. However, the buyer retains any right to claim damages as provided for in this Convention.

(2) If the seller requests the buyer to make known whether he will accept performance and the buyer does not comply with the request within a reasonable time, the seller may perform within the time indicated in his request. The buyer may not, during that period of time, resort to any remedy which is inconsistent with performance by the seller.

(3) A notice by the seller that he will perform within a specified period of time is assumed to include a request, under the preceding paragraph, that the buyer make known his decision.

(4) A request or notice by the seller under paragraph (2) or (3) of this article is not effective unless received by the buyer.

Article 49

(1) The buyer may declare the contract avoided:

(a) if the failure by the seller to perform any of his obligations under the contract or this Convention amounts to a fundamental breach of contract; or

(b) in case of non-delivery, if the seller does not deliver the goods within the additional period of time fixed by the buyer in accordance with paragraph (1) of article 47 or declares that he will not deliver within the period so fixed.

* * *

Article 50

If the goods do not conform with the contract and whether or not the price has already been paid, the buyer may reduce the price in the same proportion as the value that the goods actually delivered had at the time of the delivery bears to the value that conforming goods would have had at that time. However, if the seller remedies any failure to perform his obligations in accordance with article 37 or article 48 or if the buyer refuses to accept performance by the seller in accordance with those articles, the buyer may not reduce the price.

Article 51

(1) If the seller delivers only a part of the goods or if only a part of the goods delivered is in conformity with the contract, articles 46 to 50 apply in respect of the part which is missing or which does not conform.

(2) The buyer may declare the contract avoided in its entirety only if the failure to make delivery completely or in conformity with the contract amounts to a fundamental breach of the contract.

* * *

CHAPTER III. OBLIGATIONS OF THE BUYER

Article 53

The buyer must pay the price for the goods and take delivery of them as required by the contract and this Convention.

Section I.

Payment of the Price

Article 54

The buyer's obligation to pay the price includes taking such steps and complying with such formalities as may be required under the contract or any laws and regulations to enable payment to be made.

* * *

Article 57

(1) If the buyer is not bound to pay the price at any other particular place, he must pay it to the seller:

(a) at the seller's place of business; or

(b) if the payment is to be made against the handing over of the goods or of documents, at the place where the handing over takes place.

(2) The seller must bear any increase in the expenses incidental to payment which is caused by a change in his place of business subsequent to the conclusion of the contract.

Article 58

(1) If the buyer is not bound to pay the price at any other specific time, he must pay it when the seller places either the goods or documents controlling their disposition at the buyer's disposal in accordance with the contract and this Convention. The seller may make such payment a condition for handing over the goods or documents.

(2) If the contract involves carriage of the goods, the seller may dispatch the goods on terms whereby the goods, or documents controlling their disposition, will not be handed over to the buyer except against payment of the price.

(3) The buyer is not bound to pay the price until he has had an opportunity to examine the goods, unless the procedures for delivery or payment agreed upon by the parties are inconsistent with his having such an opportunity.

* * *

Section III.

Remedies for Breach of Contract by the Buyer

Article 61

(1) If the buyer fails to perform any of his obligations under the contract or this Convention, the seller may:

(a) exercise the rights provided in articles 62 to 65;

(b) claim damages as provided in articles 74 to 77.

(2) The seller is not deprived of any right he may have to claim damages by exercising his right to other remedies.

* * *

Article 62

The seller may require the buyer to pay the price, take delivery or perform his other obligations, unless the seller has resorted to a remedy which is inconsistent with this requirement.

Article 63

(1) The seller may fix an additional period of time of reasonable length for performance by the buyer of his obligations.

(2) Unless the seller has received notice from the buyer that he will not perform within the period so fixed, the seller may not, during that period, resort to any remedy for breach of contract. However, the seller is not deprived thereby of any right he may have to claim damages for delay in performance.

Article 64

(1) The seller may declare the contract avoided:

(a) if the failure by the buyer to perform any of his obligations under the contract or this Convention amounts to a fundamental breach of contract; or

(b) if the buyer does not, within the additional period of time fixed by the seller in accordance with paragraph (1) of article 63, perform his obligation to pay the price or take delivery of the goods, or if he declares that he will not do so within the period so fixed.

* * *

CHAPTER IV. PASSING OF RISK

Article 66

Loss of or damage to the goods after the risk has passed to the buyer does not discharge him from his obligation to pay the price, unless the loss or damage is due to an act or omission of the seller.

Article 67

(1) If the contract of sale involves carriage of the goods and the seller is not bound to hand them over at a particular place, the risk passes to the buyer when the goods are handed over to the first carrier for transmission to the buyer in accordance with the contract of sale. If the seller is bound to hand the goods over to a carrier at a particular place, the risk does not

pass to the buyer until the goods are handed over to the carrier at that place. The fact that the seller is authorized to retain documents controlling the disposition of the goods does not affect the passage of the risk.

(2) Nevertheless, the risk does not pass to the buyer until the goods are clearly identified to the contract, whether by markings on the goods, by shipping documents, by notice given to the buyer or otherwise.

* * *

Article 70

If the seller had committed a fundamental breach of contract, articles 67, 68 and 69 do not impair the remedies available to the buyer on account of the breach.

CHAPTER V. PROVISIONS COMMON TO THE OBLIGATIONS OF THE SELLER AND OF THE BUYER

Section I.

Anticipatory Breach and Instalment Contracts

Article 71

(1) A party may suspend the performance of his obligations if, after the conclusion of the contract, it becomes apparent that the other party will not perform a substantial part of his obligations as a result of:

(a) a serious deficiency in his ability to perform or in his creditworthiness; or

(b) his conduct in preparing to perform or in performing the contract.

(2) If the seller has already dispatched the goods before the grounds described in the preceding paragraph become evident, he may prevent the handing over of the goods to the buyer even though the buyer holds a document which entitles him to obtain them. The present paragraph relates only to the rights in the goods as between the buyer and the seller.

(3) A party suspending performance, whether before or after dispatch of the goods, must immediately give notice of the suspension to the other party and must continue with performance if the other party provides adequate assurance of his performance.

Article 72

(1) If prior to the date for performance of the contract it is clear that one of the parties will commit a fundamental breach of contract, the other party may declare the contract avoided.

(2) If time allows, the party intending to declare the contract avoided must give reasonable notice to the other party in order to permit him to provide adequate assurance of his performance.

(3) The requirements of the preceding paragraph do not apply if the other party has declared that he will not perform his obligations.

Article 73

(1) In the case of a contract for delivery of goods by instalments, if the failure of one party to perform any of his obligations in respect of any instalment constitutes a fundamental breach of contract with respect to that instalment, the other party may declare the contract avoided with respect to that instalment.

(2) If one party's failure to perform any of his obligations in respect of any instalment gives the other party good grounds to conclude that a fundamental breach of contract will occur with respect to future instalments, he may declare the contract avoided for the future, provided that he does so within a reasonable time.

(3) A buyer who declares the contract avoided in respect of any delivery may, at the same time, declare it avoided in respect of deliveries already made or of future deliveries if, by reason of their interdependence, those deliveries could not be used for the purpose contemplated by the parties at the time of the conclusion of the contract.

Section II.

Damages

Article 74

Damages for breach of contract by one party consist of a sum equal to the loss, including loss of profit, suffered by the other party as a consequence of the breach. Such damages may not exceed the loss which the party in breach foresaw or ought to have foreseen at the time of the conclusion of the contract, in the light of the facts and matters of which he then knew or ought to have known, as a possible consequence of the breach of contract.

Article 75

If the contract is avoided and if, in a reasonable manner and within a reasonable time after avoidance, the buyer has bought goods in replacement or the seller has resold the goods, the party claiming damages may recover the difference between the contract price and the price in the substitute transaction as well as any further damages recoverable under article 74.

Article 76

(1) If the contract is avoided and there is a current price for the goods, the party claiming damages may, if he has not made a purchase or resale under article 75, recover the difference between the price fixed by the contract and the current price at the time of avoidance as well as any further damages recoverable under article 74. If, however, the party

claiming damages has avoided the contract after taking over the goods, the current price at the time of such taking over shall be applied instead of the current price at the time of avoidance.

(2) For the purpose of the preceding paragraph, the current price is the price prevailing at the place where delivery of the goods should have been made or, if there is no current price at that place, the price at such other place as serves as a reasonable substitute, making due allowance for differences in the cost of transporting the goods.

Article 77

A party who relies on a breach of contract must take such measures as are reasonable in the circumstances to mitigate the loss, including loss of profit, resulting from the breach. If he fails to take such measures, the party in breach may claim a reduction in the damages in the amount by which the loss should have been mitigated.

* * *

Section IV.

Exemptions

Article 79

(1) A party is not liable for a failure to perform any of his obligations if he proves that the failure was due to an impediment beyond his control and that he could not reasonably be expected to have taken the impediment into account at the time of the conclusion of the contract or to have avoided or overcome it or its consequences.

(2) If the party's failure is due to the failure by a third person whom he has engaged to perform the whole or a part of the contract, that party is exempt from liability only if:

(a) he is exempt under the preceding paragraph; and

(b) the person whom he has so engaged would be so exempt if the provisions of that paragraph were applied to him.

(3) The exemption provided by this article has effect for the period during which the impediment exists.

(4) The party who fails to perform must give notice to the other party of the impediment and its effects on his ability to perform. If the notice is not received by the other party within a reasonable time after the party who fails to perform knew or ought to have known of the impediment, he is liable for damages resulting from such non-receipt.

(5) Nothing in this article prevents either party from exercising any right other than to claim damages under this Convention.

* * *

Section V.

Effects of Avoidance

Article 81

(1) Avoidance of the contract releases both parties from their obligations under it, subject to any damages which may be due. Avoidance does not affect any provision of the contract for the settlement of disputes or any other provision of the contract governing the rights and obligations of the parties consequent upon the avoidance of the contract.

(2) A party who has performed the contract either wholly or in part may claim restitution from the other party of whatever the first party has supplied or paid under the contract. If both parties are bound to make restitution, they must do so concurrently.

Article 82

(1) The buyer loses the right to declare the contract avoided or to require the seller to deliver substitute goods if it is impossible for him to make restitution of the goods substantially in the condition in which he received them.

(2) The preceding paragraph does not apply:

(a) if the impossibility of making restitution of the goods or of making restitution of the goods substantially in the condition in which the buyer received them is not due to his act or omission;

(b) if the goods or part of the goods have perished or deteriorated as a result of the examination provided for in article 38; or

(c) if the goods or part of the goods have been sold in the normal course of business or have been consumed or transformed by the buyer in the course of normal use before he discovered or ought to have discovered the lack of conformity.

* * *

PART IV. FINAL PROVISIONS

* * *

Article 92

(1) A Contracting State may declare at the time of signature, ratification, acceptance, approval or accession that it will not be bound by Part II of this Convention or that it will not be bound by Part III of this Convention.

(2) A Contracting State which makes a declaration in accordance with the preceding paragraph in respect of Part II or Part III of this Convention is not to be considered a Contracting State within paragraph (1) of article

1 of this Convention in respect of matters governed by the Part to which the declaration applies.

Article 93

(1) If a Contracting State has two or more territorial units in which, according to its constitution, different systems of law are applicable in relation to the matters dealt with in this Convention, it may, at the time of signature, ratification, acceptance, approval or accession, declare that this Convention is to extend to all its territorial units or only to one or more of them, and may amend its declaration by submitting another declaration at any time.

* * *

Article 94

(1) Two or more Contracting States which have the same or closely related legal rules on matters governed by this Convention may at any time declare that the Convention is not to apply to contracts of sale or to their formation where the parties have their places of business in those States. Such declarations may be made jointly or by reciprocal unilateral declarations.

(2) A Contracting State which has the same or closely related legal rules on matters governed by this Convention as one or more non-Contracting States may at any time declare that the Convention is not to apply to contracts of sale or to their formation where the parties have their places of business in those States.

* * *

Article 95

Any State may declare at the time of the deposit of its instrument of ratification, acceptance, approval or accession that it will not be bound by subparagraph (1)(b) of article 1 of this Convention.

[The United States has declared a reservation to CISG under Article 95].

Article 96

A Contracting State whose legislation requires contracts of sale to be concluded in or evidenced by writing may at any time make a declaration in accordance with article 12 that any provision of article 11, article 29, or Part II of this Convention, that allows a contract of sale or its modification or termination by agreement or any offer, acceptance, or other indication of intention to be made in any form other than in writing, does not apply where any party has his place of business in that State.

* * *

DOCUMENT 5

UNITED NATIONS CONVENTION AGAINST CORRUPTION (2003)

■ ■ ■

Chapter V

Asset recovery

Article 51. General provision

The return of assets pursuant to this chapter is a fundamental principle of this Convention, and States Parties shall afford one another the widest measure of cooperation and assistance in this regard.

* * *

Article 53. Measures for direct recovery of property

Each State Party shall, in accordance with its domestic law:

(a) Take such measures as may be necessary to permit another State Party to initiate civil action in its courts to establish title to or ownership of property acquired through the commission of an offence established in accordance with this Convention;

(b) Take such measures as may be necessary to permit its courts to order those who have committed offences established in accordance with this Convention to pay compensation or damages to another State Party that has been harmed by such offences; and

(c) Take such measures as may be necessary to permit its courts or competent authorities, when having to decide on confiscation, to recognize another State Party's claim as a legitimate owner of property acquired through the commission of an offence established in accordance with this Convention.

Article 54. Mechanisms for recovery of property through international cooperation in confiscation

1. Each State Party, in order to provide mutual legal assistance pursuant to article 55 of this Convention with respect to property acquired through or involved in the commission of an offence established in accordance with this Convention, shall, in accordance with its domestic law:

(a) Take such measures as may be necessary to permit its competent authorities to give effect to an order of confiscation issued by a court of another State Party;

(b) Take such measures as may be necessary to permit its competent authorities, where they have jurisdiction, to order the confiscation of such property of foreign origin by adjudication of an offence of money-laundering or such other offence as may be within its jurisdiction or by other procedures authorized under its domestic law; and

(c) Consider taking such measures as may be necessary to allow confiscation of such property without a criminal conviction in cases in which the offender cannot be prosecuted by reason of death, flight or absence or in other appropriate cases.

2. Each State Party, in order to provide mutual legal assistance upon a request made pursuant to paragraph 2 of article 55 of this Convention, shall, in accordance with its domestic law:

(a) Take such measures as may be necessary to permit its competent authorities to freeze or seize property upon a freezing or seizure order issued by a court or competent authority of a requesting State Party that provides a reasonable basis for the requested State Party to believe that there are sufficient grounds for taking such actions and that the property would eventually be subject to an order of confiscation for purposes of paragraph 1 (a) of this article;

(b) Take such measures as may be necessary to permit its competent authorities to freeze or seize property upon a request that provides a reasonable basis for the requested State Party to believe that there are sufficient grounds for taking such actions and that the property would eventually be subject to an order of confiscation for purposes of paragraph 1 (a) of this article; and

(c) Consider taking additional measures to permit its competent authorities to preserve property for confiscation, such as on the basis of a foreign arrest or criminal charge related to the acquisition of such property.

Article 55. International cooperation for purposes of confiscation

1. A State Party that has received a request from another State Party having jurisdiction over an offence established in accordance with this Convention for confiscation of proceeds of crime, property, equipment or other instrumentalities referred to in article 31, paragraph 1, of this Convention situated in its territory shall, to the greatest extent possible within its domestic legal system:

(a) Submit the request to its competent authorities for the purpose of obtaining an order of confiscation and, if such an order is granted, give effect to it; or

(b) Submit to its competent authorities, with a view to giving effect to it to the extent requested, an order of confiscation issued by a court in the territory of the requesting State Party in accordance with articles 31, paragraph 1, and 54, paragraph 1 (a), of this Convention insofar as it relates to proceeds of crime, property, equipment or other instrumentalities referred to in article 31, paragraph 1, situated in the territory of the requested State Party.

2. Following a request made by another State Party having jurisdiction over an offence established in accordance with this Convention, the requested State Party shall take measures to identify, trace and freeze or seize proceeds of crime, property, equipment or other instrumentalities referred to in article 31, paragraph 1, of this Convention for the purpose of eventual confiscation to be ordered either by the requesting State Party or, pursuant to a request under paragraph 1 of this article, by the requested State Party.

3. The provisions of article 46 of this Convention are applicable, mutatis mutandis, to this article. In addition to the information specified in article 46, paragraph 15, requests made pursuant to this article shall contain:

(a) In the case of a request pertaining to paragraph 1 (a) of this article, a description of the property to be confiscated, including, to the extent possible, the location and, where relevant, the estimated value of the property and a statement of the facts relied upon by the requesting State Party sufficient to enable the requested State Party to seek the order under its domestic law;

(b) In the case of a request pertaining to paragraph I (b) of this article, a legally admissible copy of an order of confiscation upon which the request is based issued by the requesting State Party, a statement of the facts and information as to the extent to which execution of the order is requested, a statement specifying the measures taken by the requesting State Party to provide adequate notification to bona fide third parties and to ensure due process and a statement that the confiscation order is final;

(c) In the case of a request pertaining to paragraph 2 of this article, a statement of the facts relied upon by the requesting State Party and a description of the actions requested and, where available, a legally admissible copy of an order on which the request is based.

4. The decisions or actions provided for in paragraphs 1 and 2 of this article shall be taken by the requested State Party in accordance with and subject to the provisions of its domestic law and its procedural rules or any

bilateral or multilateral agreement or arrangement to which it may be bound in relation to the requesting State Party.

5. Each State Party shall furnish copies of its laws and regulations that give effect to this article and of any subsequent changes to such laws and regulations or a description thereof to the Secretary-General of the United Nations.

6. If a State Party elects to make the taking of the measures referred to in paragraphs 1 and 2 of this article conditional on the existence of a relevant treaty, that State Party shall consider this Convention the necessary and sufficient treaty basis.

7. Cooperation under this article may also be refused or provisional measures lifted if the requested State Party does not receive sufficient and timely evidence or if the property is of a *de minimis* value.

8. Before lifting any provisional measure taken pursuant to this article, the requested State Party shall, wherever possible, give the requesting State Party an opportunity to present its reasons in favour of continuing the measure.

9. The provisions of this article shall not be construed as prejudicing the rights of bona fide third parties.

* * *

Article 57. Return and disposal of assets

1. Property confiscated by a State Party pursuant to article 31 or 55 of this Convention shall be disposed of, including by return to its prior legitimate owners, pursuant to paragraph 3 of this article, by that State Party in accordance with the provisions of this Convention and its domestic law.

2. Each State Party shall adopt such legislative and other measures, in accordance with the fundamental principles of its domestic law, as may be necessary to enable its competent authorities to return confiscated property, when acting on the request made by another State Party, in accordance with this Convention, taking into account the rights of bona fide third parties.

3. In accordance with articles 46 and 55 of this Convention and paragraphs 1 and 2 of this article, the requested State Party shall:

(a) In the case of embezzlement of public funds or of laundering of embezzled public funds as referred to in articles 17 and 23 of this Convention, when confiscation was executed in accordance with article 55 and on the basis of a final judgement in the requesting State Party, a requirement that can be waived by the requested State Party, return the confiscated property to the requesting State Party;

(b) In the case of proceeds of any other offence covered by this Convention, when the confiscation was executed in accordance with article 55 of this Convention and on the basis of a final judgement in the requesting State Party, a requirement that can be waived by the requested State Party, return the confiscated property to the requesting State Party, when the requesting State Party reasonably establishes its prior ownership of such confiscated property to the requested State Party or when the requested State Party recognizes damage to the requesting State Party as a basis for returning the confiscated property;

(c) In all other cases, give priority consideration to returning confiscated property to the requesting State Party, returning such property to its prior legitimate owners or compensating the victims of the crime.

4. Where appropriate, unless States Parties decide otherwise, the requested State Party may deduct reasonable expenses incurred in investigations, prosecutions or judicial proceedings leading to the return or disposition of confiscated property pursuant to this article.

5. Where appropriate, States Parties may also give special consideration to concluding agreements or mutually acceptable arrangements, on a case-by-case basis, for the final disposal of confiscated property.

* * *

DOCUMENT 6

UNITED NATIONS CONVENTION ON INDEPENDENT GUARANTEES AND STAND-BY LETTERS OF CREDIT (1995)*

■ ■ ■

CHAPTER I. SCOPE OF APPLICATION

Article 1. Scope of application

(1) This Convention applies to an international undertaking referred to in article 2:

(a) If the place of business of the guarantor/issuer at which the undertaking is issued is in a Contracting State, or

(b) If the rules of private international law lead to the application of the law of a Contracting State, unless the undertaking excludes the application of the Convention.

(2) This Convention applies also to an international letter of credit not falling within article 2 if it expressly states that it is subject to this Convention.

(3) The provisions of articles 21 and 22 apply to international undertakings referred to in article 2 independently of paragraph (1) of this article.

Article 2. Undertaking

(1) For the purposes of this Convention, an undertaking is an independent commitment, known in international practice as an independent guarantee or as a stand-by letter of credit, given by a bank or other institution or person ("guarantor/issuer") to pay to the beneficiary a certain or determinable amount upon simple demand or upon demand accompanied by other documents, in conformity with the terms and any documentary conditions of the undertaking, indicating, or from which it is to be inferred, that payment is due because of a default in the performance of an obligation, or because of another contingency, or for money borrowed or advanced, or on account of any mature indebtedness undertaken by the principal/applicant or another person.

(2) The undertaking may be given:

---

* In force. There are eight Contracting States: Belarus, Ecuador, El Salvador, Gabon, Kuwait, Liberia, Panama and Tunisia.

(a) At the request or on the instruction of the customer ("principal/applicant") of the guarantor/issuer;

(b) On the instruction of another bank, institution or person ("instructing party") that acts at the request of the customer ("principal/applicant") of that instructing party; or

(c) On behalf of the guarantor/issuer itself.

* * *

Article 3. Independence of undertaking

For the purposes of this Convention, an undertaking is independent where the guarantor/issuer's obligation to the beneficiary is not:

(a) Dependent upon the existence or validity of any underlying transaction, or upon any other undertaking (including stand-by letters of credit or independent guarantees to which confirmations or counter-guarantees relate); or

(b) Subject to any term or condition not appearing in the undertaking, or to any future, uncertain act or event except presentation of documents or another such act or event within a guarantor/issuer's sphere of operations.

Article 4. Internationality of undertaking

(1) An undertaking is international if the places of business, as specified in the undertaking, of any two of the following persons are in different States: guarantor/issuer, beneficiary, principal/applicant, instructing party, confirmer.

(2) For the purposes of the preceding paragraph:

(a) If the undertaking lists more than one place of business for a given person, the relevant place of business is that which has the closest relationship to the undertaking;

(b) If the undertaking does not specify a place of business for a given person but specifies its habitual residence, that residence is relevant for determining the international character of the undertaking.

CHAPTER II. INTERPRETATION

Article 5. Principles of interpretation

In the interpretation of this Convention, regard is to be had to its international character and to the need to promote uniformity in its application and the observance of good faith in the international practice of independent guarantees and stand-by letters of credit.

Article 6. Definitions

For the purposes of this Convention and unless otherwise indicated in a provision of this Convention or required by the context:

(a) "Undertaking" includes "counter-guarantee" and "confirmation of an undertaking";

(b) "Guarantor/issuer" includes "counter-guarantor" and "confirmer";

(c) "Counter-guarantee" means an undertaking given to the guarantor/issuer of another undertaking by its instructing party and providing for payment upon simple demand or upon demand accompanied by other documents, in conformity with the terms and any documentary conditions of the undertaking, indicating, or from which it is to be inferred, that payment under that other undertaking has been demanded from, or made by, the person issuing that other undertaking;

(d) "Counter-guarantor" means the person issuing a counter-guarantee;

(e) "Confirmation" of an undertaking means an undertaking added to that of the guarantor/issuer, and authorized by the guarantor/issuer, providing the beneficiary with the option of demanding payment from the confirmer instead of from the guarantor/issuer, upon simple demand or upon demand accompanied by other documents, in conformity with the terms and any documentary conditions of the confirmed undertaking, without prejudice to the beneficiary's right to demand payment from the guarantor/issuer;

(f) "Confirmer" means the person adding a confirmation to an undertaking;

(g) "Document" means a communication made in a form that provides a complete record thereof.

CHAPTER III. FORM AND CONTENT OF UNDERTAKING

Article 7. Issuance, form and irrevocability of undertaking

(1) Issuance of an undertaking occurs when and where the undertaking leaves the sphere of control of the guarantor/issuer concerned.

(2) An undertaking may be issued in any form which preserves a complete record of the text of the undertaking and provides authentication of its source by generally accepted means or by a procedure agreed upon by the guarantor/issuer and the beneficiary.

(3) From the time of issuance of an undertaking, a demand for payment may be made in accordance with the terms and conditions of the undertaking, unless the undertaking stipulates a different time.

(4) An undertaking is irrevocable upon issuance, unless it stipulates that it is revocable.

* * *

Article 11. Cessation of right to demand payment

(1) The right of the beneficiary to demand payment under the undertaking ceases when:

(a) The guarantor/issuer has received a statement by the beneficiary of release from liability in a form referred to in paragraph (2) of article 7;

(b) The beneficiary and the guarantor/issuer have agreed on the termination of the undertaking in the form stipulated in the undertaking or, failing such stipulation, in a form referred to in paragraph (2) of article 7;

(c) The amount available under the undertaking has been paid, unless the undertaking provides for the automatic renewal or for an automatic increase of the amount available or otherwise provides for continuation of the undertaking;

(d) The validity period of the undertaking expires in accordance with the provisions of article 12.

(2) The undertaking may stipulate, or the guarantor/issuer and the beneficiary may agree elsewhere, that return of the document embodying the undertaking to the guarantor/issuer, or a procedure functionally equivalent to the return of the document in the case of the issuance of the undertaking in non-paper form, is required for the cessation of the right to demand payment, either alone or in conjunction with one of the events referred to in subparagraphs (a) and (b) of paragraph (1) of this article. However, in no case shall retention of any such document by the beneficiary after the right to demand payment ceases in accordance with subparagraph (c) or (d) of paragraph (1) of this article preserve any rights of the beneficiary under the undertaking.

Article 12. Expiry

The validity period of the undertaking expires:

(a) At the expiry date, which may be a specified calendar date or the last day of a fixed period of time stipulated in the undertaking, provided that, if the expiry date is not a business day at the place of business of the guarantor/issuer at which the undertaking is issued, or of another person or at another place stipulated in the undertaking for presentation of the demand for payment, expiry occurs on the first business day which follows;

(b) If expiry depends according to the undertaking on the occurrence of an act or event not within the guarantor/issuer's sphere of operations, when the guarantor/issuer is advised that the act or event has occurred by presentation of the document specified for that purpose in the undertaking or, if no such document is specified, of a certification by the beneficiary of the occurrence of the act or event;

(c) If the undertaking does not state an expiry date, or if the act or event on which expiry is stated to depend has not yet been established by presentation of the required document and an expiry date has not been stated in addition, when six years have elapsed from the date of issuance of the undertaking.

CHAPTER IV. RIGHTS, OBLIGATIONS AND DEFENCES

Article 13. Determination of rights and obligations

(1) The rights and obligations of the guarantor/issuer and the beneficiary arising from the undertaking are determined by the terms and conditions set forth in the undertaking, including any rules, general conditions or usages specifically referred to therein, and by the provisions of this Convention.

(2) In interpreting terms and conditions of the undertaking and in settling questions that are not addressed by the terms and conditions of the undertaking or by the provisions of this Convention, regard shall be had to generally accepted international rules and usages of independent guarantee or stand-by letter of credit practice.

Article 14. Standard of conduct and liability of guarantor/issuer

(1) In discharging its obligations under the undertaking and this Convention, the guarantor/issuer shall act in good faith and exercise reasonable care having due regard to generally accepted standards of international practice of independent guarantees or stand-by letters of credit.

(2) A guarantor/issuer may not be exempted from liability for its failure to act in good faith or for any grossly negligent conduct.

Article 15. Demand

(1) Any demand for payment under the undertaking shall be made in a form referred to in paragraph (2) of article 7 and in conformity with the terms and conditions of the undertaking.

(2) Unless otherwise stipulated in the undertaking, the demand and any certification or other document required by the undertaking shall be presented, within the time that a demand for payment may be made, to the guarantor/issuer at the place where the undertaking was issued.

(3) The beneficiary, when demanding payment, is deemed to certify that the demand is not in bad faith and that none of the elements referred to in subparagraphs (a), (b) and (c) of paragraph (1) of article 19 are present.

Article 16. Examination of demand and accompanying documents

(1) The guarantor/issuer shall examine the demand and any accompanying documents in accordance with the standard of conduct referred to in paragraph (1) of article 14. In determining whether documents are in facial conformity with the terms and conditions of the undertaking, and are consistent with one another, the guarantor/issuer shall have due regard to the applicable international standard of independent guarantee or stand-by letter of credit practice.

(2) Unless otherwise stipulated in the undertaking or elsewhere agreed by the guarantor/issuer and the beneficiary, the guarantor/issuer shall have reasonable time, but not more than seven business days following the day of receipt of the demand and any accompanying documents, in which to:

(a) Examine the demand and any accompanying documents;

(b) Decide whether or not to pay;

(c) If the decision is not to pay, issue notice thereof to the beneficiary.

The notice referred to in subparagraph (c) above shall, unless otherwise stipulated in the undertaking or elsewhere agreed by the guarantor/issuer and the beneficiary, be made by teletransmission or, if that is not possible, by other expeditious means and indicate the reason for the decision not to pay.

Article 17. Payment

(1) Subject to article 19, the guarantor/issuer shall pay against a demand made in accordance with the provisions of article 15. Following a determination that a demand for payment so conforms, payment shall be made promptly, unless the undertaking stipulates payment on a deferred basis, in which case payment shall be made at the stipulated time.

(2) Any payment against a demand that is not in accordance with the provisions of article 15 does not prejudice the rights of the principal/applicant.

* * *

Article 19. Exception to payment obligation

(1) If it is manifest and clear that:

(a) Any document is not genuine or has been falsified;

(b) No payment is due on the basis asserted in the demand and the supporting documents; or

(c) Judging by the type and purpose of the undertaking, the demand has no conceivable basis, the guarantor/issuer, acting in good faith, has a right, as against the beneficiary, to withhold payment.

(2) For the purposes of subparagraph (c) of paragraph (1) of this article, the following are types of situations in which a demand has no conceivable basis:

(a) The contingency or risk against which the undertaking was designed to secure the beneficiary has undoubtedly not materialized;

(b) The underlying obligation of the principal/applicant has been declared invalid by a court or arbitral tribunal, unless the undertaking indicates that such contingency falls within the risk to be covered by the undertaking;

(c) The underlying obligation has undoubtedly been fulfilled to the satisfaction of the beneficiary;

(d) Fulfilment of the underlying obligation has clearly been prevented by wilful misconduct of the beneficiary;

(e) In the case of a demand under a counter-guarantee, the beneficiary of the counter-guarantee has made payment in bad faith as guarantor/issuer of the undertaking to which the counter-guarantee relates.

(3) In the circumstances set out in subparagraphs (a), (b) and (c) of paragraph (1) of this article, the principal/applicant is entitled to provisional court measures in accordance with article 20.

CHAPTER V. PROVISIONAL COURT MEASURES

Article 20. Provisional court measures

(1) Where, on an application by the principal/applicant or the instructing party, it is shown that there is a high probability that, with regard to a demand made, or expected to be made, by the beneficiary, one of the circumstances referred to in subparagraphs (a), (b) and (c) of paragraph (1) of article 19 is present, the court, on the basis of immediately available strong evidence, may:

(a) Issue a provisional order to the effect that the beneficiary does not receive payment, including an order that the guarantor/issuer hold the amount of the undertaking, or

(b) Issue a provisional order to the effect that the proceeds of the undertaking paid to the beneficiary are blocked, taking into account whether in the absence of such an order the principal/applicant would be likely to suffer serious harm.

(2) The court, when issuing a provisional order referred to in paragraph (1) of this article, may require the person applying therefor to furnish such form of security as the court deems appropriate.

(3) The court may not issue a provisional order of the kind referred to in paragraph (1) of this article based on any objection to payment other than those referred to in subparagraphs (a), (b) and (c) of paragraph (1) of article 19, or use of the undertaking for a criminal purpose.

CHAPTER VI. CONFLICT OF LAWS

Article 21. Choice of applicable law

The undertaking is governed by the law the choice of which is:

(a) Stipulated in the undertaking or demonstrated by the terms and conditions of the undertaking; or

(b) Agreed elsewhere by the guarantor/issuer and the beneficiary.

Article 22. Determination of applicable law

Failing a choice of law in accordance with article 21, the undertaking is governed by the law of the State where the guarantor/issuer has that place of business at which the undertaking was issued.

CHAPTER VII. FINAL CLAUSES

Article 23. Depositary

The Secretary-General of the United Nations is the depositary of this Convention.

Article 24. Signature, ratification, acceptance, approval, accession

(1) This Convention is open for signature by all States at the Headquarters of the United Nations, New York, until 11 December 1997.

* * *

Article 25. Application to territorial units

(1) If a State has two or more territorial units in which different systems of law are applicable in relation to the matters dealt with in this Convention, it may, at the time of signature, ratification, acceptance, approval or accession, declare that this Convention is to extend to all its territorial units or only one or more of them, and may at any time substitute another declaration for its earlier declaration.

* * *

Article 27. Reservations

No reservations may be made to this Convention.

Article 28. Entry into force

(1) This Convention enters into force on the first day of the month following the expiration of one year from the date of the deposit of the fifth instrument of ratification, acceptance, approval or accession.

(2) For each State which becomes a Contracting State to this Convention after the date of the deposit of the fifth instrument of ratification, acceptance, approval or accession, this Convention enters into force on the first day of the month following the expiration of one year after the date of the deposit of the appropriate instrument on behalf of that State.

(3) This Convention applies only to undertakings issued on or after the date when the Convention enters into force in respect of the Contracting State referred to in subparagraph (a) or the Contracting State referred to in subparagraph (b) of paragraph (1) of article 1.

Article 29. Denunciation

(1) A Contracting State may denounce this Convention at any time by means of a notification in writing addressed to the depositary.

* * *

DOCUMENT 7

UNITED NATIONS CONVENTION ON THE RECOGNITION AND ENFORCEMENT OF FOREIGN ARBITRAL AWARDS (NEW YORK CONVENTION) (1958; ENTERED INTO FORCE AS TO THE UNITED STATES, 1970)

■ ■ ■

Article I

1. This Convention shall apply to the recognition and enforcement of arbitral awards made in the territory of a State other than the State where the recognition and enforcement of such awards are sought, and arising out of differences between persons, whether physical or legal. It shall also apply to arbitral awards not considered as domestic awards in the State where their recognition and enforcement are sought.

2. The term "arbitral awards" shall include not only awards made by arbitrators appointed for each case but also those made by permanent arbitral bodies to which the parties have submitted.

3. When signing, ratifying or acceding to this Convention, or notifying extension under article X hereof, any State may on the basis of reciprocity declare that it will apply the Convention to the recognition and enforcement of awards made only in the territory of another Contracting State. It may also declare that it will apply the Convention only to differences arising out of legal relationships, whether contractual or not, which are considered as commercial under the national law of the State making such declaration.

Article II

1. Each Contracting State shall recognize an agreement in writing under which the parties undertake to submit to arbitration all or any differences which have arisen or which may arise between them in respect of a defined legal relationship, whether contractual or not, concerning a subject matter capable of settlement by arbitration.

2. The term "agreement in writing" shall include an arbitral clause in a contract or an arbitration agreement, signed by the parties or contained in an exchange of letters or telegrams.

3. The court of a Contracting State, when seized of an action in a matter in respect of which the parties have made an agreement within the meaning of this article, shall, at the request of one of the parties, refer the parties to arbitration, unless it finds that the said agreement is null and void, inoperative or incapable of being performed.

Article III

Each Contracting State shall recognize arbitral awards as binding and enforce them in accordance with the rules of procedure of the territory where the award is relied upon, under the conditions laid down in the following articles. There shall not be imposed substantially more onerous conditions or higher fees or charges on the recognition or enforcement of arbitral awards to which this Convention applies than are imposed on the recognition or enforcement of domestic arbitral awards.

Article IV

1. To obtain the recognition and enforcement mentioned in the preceding article, the party applying for recognition and enforcement shall, at the time of the application, supply:

(a) The duly authenticated original award or a duly certified copy thereof;

(b) The original agreement referred to in article II or a duly certified copy thereof.

2. If the said award or agreement is not made in an official language of the country in which the award is relied upon, the party applying for recognition and enforcement of the award shall produce a translation of these documents into such language. The translation shall be certified by an official or sworn translator or by a diplomatic or consular agent.

Article V

1. Recognition and enforcement of the award may be refused, at the request of the party against whom it is invoked, only if that party furnishes to the competent authority where the recognition and enforcement is sought, proof that:

(a) The parties to the agreement referred to in article II were, under the law applicable to them, under some incapacity, or the said agreement is not valid under the law to which the parties have subjected it or, failing any indication thereon, under the law of the country where the award was made; or

(b) The party against whom the award is invoked was not given proper notice of the appointment of the arbitrator or of the arbitration proceedings or was otherwise unable to present his case; or

(c) The award deals with a difference not contemplated by or not falling within the terms of the submission to arbitration, or it contains decisions on matters beyond the scope of the submission to arbitration, provided that, if the decisions on matters submitted to arbitration can be separated from those not so submitted, that part of the award which contain decisions on matters submitted to arbitration may be recognized and enforced; or

(d) The composition of the arbitral authority or the arbitral procedure was not in accordance with the agreement of the parties, or, failing such agreement, was not in accordance with the law of the country where the arbitration took place; or

(e) The award has not yet become binding on the parties, or has been set aside or suspended by a competent authority of the country in which, or under the law of which, that award was made.

2. Recognition and enforcement of an arbitral award may also be refused if the competent authority in the country where recognition and enforcement is sought finds that:

(a) The subject matter of the difference is not capable of settlement by arbitration under the law of that country; or

(b) The recognition or enforcement of the award would be contrary to the public policy of that country.

Article VI

If an application for the setting aside or suspension of the award has been made to a competent authority referred to in article V(1)(e), the authority before which the award is sought to be relied upon may, if it considers it proper, adjourn the decision on the enforcement of the award and may also, on the application of the party claiming enforcement of the award, order the other party to give suitable security.

* * *

Article XIV

A Contracting State shall not be entitled to avail itself of the present Convention against other Contracting States except to the extent that it is itself bound to apply the Convention.

* * *

Article XVI

1. This Convention, of which the Chinese, English, French, Russian and Spanish texts shall be equally authentic, shall be deposited in the archives of the United Nations.

2. The Secretary-General of the United Nations shall transmit a certified copy of this Convention to the States contemplated in article VIII.

Done at New York June 10, 1958: entered into force for the United States December 29, 1970, subject to declarations.

U.S. Declarations:

The United States of America will apply the Convention, on the basis of reciprocity, to the recognition and enforcement of only those awards made in the territory of another Contracting State.

The United States of America will apply the Convention only to differences arising out of legal relationships, whether contractual or not, which are considered as commercial under the national law of the United States.

The Convention applies to all of the territories for the international relations of which the United States of America is responsible.

DOCUMENT 8

UNITED NATIONS CONVENTION ON THE USE OF ELECTRONIC COMMUNICATIONS IN INTERNATIONAL CONTRACTS (2005)

■ ■ ■

CHAPTER I. SPHERE OF APPLICATION

Article 1. Scope of Application

1. This Convention applies to the use of electronic communications in connection with the formation or performance of a contract between parties whose places of business are in different States.

2. The fact that the parties have their places of business in different States is to be disregarded whenever this fact does not appear either from the contract or from any dealings between the parties or from information disclosed by the parties at any time before or at the conclusion of the contract.

3. Neither the nationality of the parties nor the civil or commercial character of the parties or of the contract is to be taken into consideration in determining the application of this Convention.

Article 2. Exclusions

1. This Convention does not apply to electronic communications relating to any of the following:

(a) Contracts concluded for personal, family or household purposes;

(b) (i) Transactions on a regulated exchange; (ii) foreign exchange transactions; (iii) inter-bank payment systems, inter-bank payment agreements or clearance and settlement systems relating to securities or other financial assets or instruments; (iv) the transfer of security rights in sale, loan or holding of or agreement to repurchase securities or other financial assets or instruments held with an intermediary.

2. This Convention does not apply to bills of exchange, promissory notes, consignment notes, bills of lading, warehouse receipts or any transferable document or instrument that entitles the bearer or beneficiary to claim the delivery of goods or the payment of a sum of money.

Article 3. Party Autonomy

The parties may exclude the application of this Convention or derogate from or vary the effect of any of its provisions.

CHAPTER II. GENERAL PROVISIONS

Article 4. Definitions

For the purposes of this Convention:

(a) "Communication" means any statement, declaration, demand, notice or request, including an offer and the acceptance of an offer, that the parties are required to make or choose to make in connection with the formation or performance of a contract;

(b) "Electronic communication" means any communication that the parties make by means of data messages;

(c) "Data message" means information generated, sent, received or stored by electronic, magnetic, optical or similar means, including, but not limited to, electronic data interchange, electronic mail, telegram, telex or telecopy;

(d) "Originator" of an electronic communication means a party by whom, or on whose behalf, the electronic communication has been sent or generated prior to storage, if any, but it does not include a party acting as an intermediary with respect to that electronic communication;

(e) "Addressee" of an electronic communication means a party who is intended by the originator to receive the electronic communication, but does not include a party acting as an intermediary with respect to that electronic communication;

(f) "Information system" means a system for generating, sending, receiving, storing or otherwise processing data messages;

(g) "Automated message system" means a computer program or an electronic or other automated means used to initiate an action or respond to data messages or performances in whole or in part, without review or intervention by a natural person each time an action is initiated or a response is generated by the system;

(h) "Place of business" means any place where a party maintains a nontransitory establishment to pursue an economic activity other than the temporary provision of goods or services out of a specific location.

Article 5. Interpretation

1. In the interpretation of this Convention, regard is to be had to its international character and to the need to promote uniformity in its application and the observance of good faith in international trade.

2. Questions concerning matters governed by this Convention which are not expressly settled in it are to be settled in conformity with the general principles on which it is based or, in the absence of such principles, in conformity with the law applicable by virtue of the rules of private international law.

Article 6. Location of the Parties

1. For the purposes of this Convention, a party's place of business is presumed to be the location indicated by that party, unless another party demonstrates that the party making the indication does not have a place of business at that location.

2. If a party has not indicated a place of business and has more than one place of business, then the place of business for the purposes of this Convention is that which has the closest relationship to the relevant contract, having regard to the circumstances known to or contemplated by the parties at any time before or at the conclusion of the contract.

3. If a natural person does not have a place of business, reference is to be made to the person's habitual residence.

4. A location is not a place of business merely because that is: (a) where equipment and technology supporting an information system used by a party in connection with the formation of a contract are located; or (b) where the information system may be accessed by other parties.

5. The sole fact that a party makes use of a domain name or electronic mail address connected to a specific country does not create a presumption that its place of business is located in that country.

Article 7. Information Requirements

Nothing in this Convention affects the application of any rule of law that may require the parties to disclose their identities, places of business or other information, or relieves a party from the legal consequences of making inaccurate, incomplete or false statements in that regard.

CHAPTER III. USE OF ELECTRONIC COMMUNICATIONS IN INTERNATIONAL CONTRACTS

Article 8. Legal Recognition of Electronic Communications

1. A communication or a contract shall not be denied validity or enforceability on the sole ground that it is in the form of an electronic communication.

2. Nothing in this Convention requires a party to use or accept electronic communications, but a party's agreement to do so may be inferred from the party's conduct.

Article 9. Form Requirements

1. Nothing in this Convention requires a communication or a contract to be made or evidenced in any particular form.

2. Where the law requires that a communication or a contract should be in writing, or provides consequences for the absence of a writing, that requirement is met by an electronic communication if the information contained therein is accessible so as to be usable for subsequent reference.

3. Where the law requires that a communication or a contract should be signed by a party, or provides consequences for the absence of a signature, that requirement is met in relation to an electronic communication if:

(a) A method is used to identify the party and to indicate that party's intention in respect of the information contained in the electronic communication; and

(b) The method used is either:

(i) As reliable as appropriate for the purpose for which the electronic communication was generated or communicated, in the light of all the circumstances, including any relevant agreement; or

(ii) Proven in fact to have fulfilled the functions described in subparagraph (a) above, by itself or together with further evidence.

4. Where the law requires that a communication or a contract should be made available or retained in its original form, or provides consequences for the absence of an original, that requirement is met in relation to an electronic communication if:

(a) There exists a reliable assurance as to the integrity of the information it contains from the time when it was first generated in its final form, as an electronic communication or otherwise; and

(b) Where it is required that the information it contains be made available, that information is capable of being displayed to the person to whom it is to be made available.

5. For the purposes of paragraph 4 (a):

(a) The criteria for assessing integrity shall be whether the information has remained complete and unaltered, apart from the addition of any endorsement and any change that arises in the normal course of communication, storage and display; and

(b) The standard of reliability required shall be assessed in the light of the purpose for which the information was generated and in the light of all the relevant circumstances.

Article 10. Time and Place of Dispatch and Receipt of Electronic Communications

1. The time of dispatch of an electronic communication is the time when it leaves an information system under the control of the originator or of the party who sent it on behalf of the originator or, if the electronic communication has not left an information system under the control of the originator or of the party who sent it on behalf of the originator, the time when the electronic communication is received.

2. The time of receipt of an electronic communication is the time when it becomes capable of being retrieved by the addressee at an electronic address designated by the addressee. The time of receipt of an electronic communication at another electronic address of the addressee is the time when it becomes capable of being retrieved by the addressee at that address and the addressee becomes aware that the electronic communication has been sent to that address. An electronic communication is presumed to be capable of being retrieved by the addressee when it reaches the addressee's electronic address.

3. An electronic communication is deemed to be dispatched at the place where the originator has its place of business and is deemed to be received at the place where the addressee has its place of business, as determined in accordance with article 6.

4. Paragraph 2 of this article applies notwithstanding that the place where the information system supporting an electronic address is located may be different from the place where the electronic communication is deemed to be received under paragraph 3 of this article.

Article 11. Invitations to Make offers

A proposal to conclude a contract made through one or more electronic communications which is not addressed to one or more specific parties, but is generally accessible to parties making use of information systems, including proposals that make use of interactive applications for the placement of orders through such information systems, is to be considered as an invitation to make offers, unless it clearly indicates the intention of the party making the proposal to be bound in case of acceptance.

Article 12. Use of Automated Message Systems for Contract Formation

A contract formed by the interaction of an automated message system and a natural person, or by the interaction of automated message systems, shall not be denied validity or enforceability on the sole ground that no natural person reviewed or intervened in each of the individual actions carried out by the automated message systems or the resulting contract.

Article 13. Availability of Contract Terms

Nothing in this Convention affects the application of any rule of law that may require a party that negotiates some or all of the terms of a contract through the exchange of electronic communications to make available to the other party those electronic communications which contain the contractual terms in a particular manner, or relieves a party from the legal consequences of its failure to do so.

Article 14. Error in Electronic Communications

1. Where a natural person makes an input error in an electronic communication exchanged with the automated message system of another party and the automated message system does not provide the person with an opportunity to correct the error, that person, or the party on whose behalf that person was acting, has the right to withdraw the portion of the electronic communication in which the input error was made if:

(a) The person, or the party on whose behalf that person was acting, notifies the other party of the error as soon as possible after having learned of the error and indicates that he or she made an error in the electronic communication; and

(b) The person, or the party on whose behalf that person was acting, has not used or received any material benefit or value from the goods or services, if any, received from the other party.

2. Nothing in this article affects the application of any rule of law that may govern the consequences of any error other than as provided for in paragraph 1.

CHAPTER IV. FINAL PROVISIONS

* * *

Article 16. Signature, Ratification, Acceptance or Approval

1. This Convention is open for signature by all States at United Nations Headquarters in New York from 16 January 2006 to 16 January 2008.

2. This Convention is subject to ratification, acceptance or approval by the signatory States.

3. This Convention is open for accession by all States that are not signatory States as from the date it is open for signature.

4. Instruments of ratification, acceptance, approval and accession are to be deposited with the Secretary-General of the United Nations.

Article 17. Participation by Regional Economic Integration Organizations

1. A regional economic integration organization that is constituted by sovereign States and has competence over certain matters governed by this Convention may similarly sign, ratify, accept, approve or accede to this Convention. The regional economic integration organization shall in that case have the rights and obligations of a Contracting State, to the extent that that organization has competence over matters governed by this Convention. Where the number of Contracting States is relevant in this Convention, the regional economic integration organization shall not count as a Contracting State in addition to its member States that are Contracting States.

* * *

4. This Convention shall not prevail over any conflicting rules of any regional economic integration organization as applicable to parties whose respective places of business are located in States members of any such organization, as set out by declaration made in accordance with article 21.

* * *

Article 19. Declarations on the Scope of Application

1. Any Contracting State may declare, in accordance with article 21, that it will apply this Convention only:

(a) When the States referred to in article 1, paragraph 1, are Contracting States to this Convention; or

(b) When the parties have agreed that it applies.

2. Any Contracting State may exclude from the scope of application of this Convention the matters it specifies in a declaration made in accordance with article 21.

Article 20. Communications Exchanged Under Other International Conventions

1. The provisions of this Convention apply to the use of electronic communications in connection with the formation or performance of a contract to which any of the following international conventions, to which a Contracting State to this Convention is or may become a Contracting State, apply:

Convention on the Recognition and Enforcement of Foreign Arbitral Awards (New York, 10 June 1958);

Convention on the Limitation Period in the International Sale of Goods (New York, 14 June 1974) and Protocol thereto (Vienna, 11 April 1980);

United Nations Convention on Contracts for the International Sale of Goods (Vienna, 11 April 1980);

* * *

United Nations Convention on Independent Guarantees and Stand-by Letters of Credit (New York, 11 December 1995);

* * *

2. The provisions of this Convention apply further to electronic communications in connection with the formation or performance of a contract to which another international convention, treaty or agreement not specifically referred to in paragraph 1 of this article, and to which a Contracting State to this Convention is or may become a Contracting State, applies, unless the State has declared, in accordance with article 21, that it will not be bound by this paragraph.

3. A State that makes a declaration pursuant to paragraph 2 of this article may also declare that it will nevertheless apply the provisions of this Convention to the use of electronic communications in connection with the formation or performance of any contract to which a specified international convention, treaty or agreement applies to which the State is or may become a Contracting State.

4. Any State may declare that it will not apply the provisions of this Convention to the use of electronic communications in connection with the formation or performance of a contract to which any international convention, treaty or agreement specified in that State's declaration, to which the State is or may become a Contracting State, applies, including any of the conventions referred to in paragraph 1 of this article, even if such State has not excluded the application of paragraph 2 of this article by a declaration made in accordance with article 21.

Article 21. Procedure and Effects of Declarations

1. Declarations under article 17, paragraph 4, article 19, paragraphs 1 and 2, and article 20, paragraphs 2, 3 and 4, may be made at any time. Declarations made at the time of signature are subject to confirmation upon ratification, acceptance or approval.

* * *

3. A declaration takes effect simultaneously with the entry into force of this Convention in respect of the State concerned. However, a declaration of which the depositary receives formal notification after such entry into force takes effect on the first day of the month following the expiration of six months after the date of its receipt by the depositary.

4. Any State that makes a declaration under this Convention may modify or withdraw it at any time by a formal notification in writing

addressed to the depositary. The modification or withdrawal is to take effect on the first day of the month following the expiration of six months after the date of the receipt of the notification by the depositary.

Article 22. Reservations

No reservations may be made under this Convention.

Article 23. Entry Into Force

1. This Convention enters into force on the first day of the month following the expiration of six months after the date of deposit of the third instrument of ratification, acceptance, approval or accession.

2. When a State ratifies, accepts, approves or accedes to this Convention after the deposit of the third instrument of ratification, acceptance, approval or accession, this Convention enters into force in respect of that State on the first day of the month following the expiration of six months after the date of the deposit of its instrument of ratification, acceptance, approval or accession.

Article 24. Time of Application

This Convention and any declaration apply only to electronic communications that are made after the date when the Convention or the declaration enters into force or takes effect in respect of each Contracting State.

* * *

PART C

INTERNATIONAL LAW—GATT AND THE WORLD TRADE ORGANIZATION

■ ■ ■

DOCUMENT 9

GENERAL AGREEMENT ON TARIFFS AND TRADE (1947, AS AMENDED)

■ ■ ■

The following provisions are selected sections from the General Agreement on Tariffs and Trade as enacted in 1947 and as amended and in force in 1994, when the Uruguay Round proposals were enacted. The original GATT 1947 is reproduced in 55 U.N.T.S. 194. It is also reproduced in the GATT Documents, "Basic Instruments and Selected Documents", also referred to as B.I.S.D. B.I.S.D. also includes the GATT as amended and in force in 1994.

Notes and supplementary provisions have been included at the end of each Article and Paragraph to which they apply.

Table of Contents

THE GENERAL AGREEMENT ON TARIFFS AND TRADE

The Governments of the Commonwealth of Australia, the Kingdom of Belgium, the United States of Brazil, Burma, Canada, Ceylon, the Republic of Chile, the Republic of China, the Republic of Cuba, the Czechoslovak Republic, the French Republic, India, Lebanon, the Grand-Duchy of Luxemburg, the Kingdom of the Netherlands, New Zealand, the Kingdom of Norway, Pakistan, Southern Rhodesia, Syria, the Union of South Africa, the United Kingdom of Great Britain and Northern Ireland, and the United States of America:

Recognizing that their relations in the field of trade and economic endeavour should be conducted with a view to raising standards of living, ensuring full employment and a large and steadily growing volume of real income and effective demand, developing the full use of the resources of the world and expanding the production and exchange of goods,

Being desirous of contributing to these objectives by entering into reciprocal and mutually advantageous arrangements directed to the substantial reduction of tariffs and other barriers to trade and to the elimination of discriminatory treatment in international commerce,

Have through their Representatives agreed as follows:

PART I

ARTICLE I. GENERAL MOST-FAVOURED-NATION TREATMENT

1. With respect to customs duties and charges of any kind imposed on or in connection with importation or exportation or imposed on the international transfer of payments for imports or exports, and with respect to the method of levying such duties and charges, and with respect to all rules and formalities in connection with importation and exportation, and with respect to all matters referred to in paragraphs 2 and 4 of Article III, any advantage, favour, privilege or immunity granted by any contracting party to any product originating in or destined for any other country shall be accorded immediately and unconditionally to the like product originating in or destined for the territories of all other contracting parties.

Ad *Article I*

Paragraph 1

The obligations incorporated in paragraph 1 of Article I by reference to paragraphs 2 and 4 of Article III and those incorporated in paragraph 2(b) of Article II by reference to Article VI shall be considered as falling within Part II for the purposes of the Protocol of Provisional Application.

The cross-references, in the paragraph immediately above and in paragraph 1 of Article I, to paragraphs 2 and 4 of Article III shall only apply after Article III has been modified by the entry into force of the amendment provided for in the Protocol Modifying Part II and Article XXVI of the General Agreement on Tariffs and Trade, dated September 14, 1948.

---

2. The provisions of paragraph 1 of this Article shall not require the elimination of any preferences in respect of import duties or charges which do not exceed the levels provided for in paragraph 4 of this Article and which fall within the following descriptions:

(a) Preferences in force exclusively between two or more of the territories listed in Annex A, subject to the conditions set forth therein;

* * *

ARTICLE II. SCHEDULES OF CONCESSIONS

1. (a) Each contracting party shall accord to the commerce of the other contracting parties treatment no less favourable than that provided for in the appropriate Part of the appropriate Schedule annexed to this Agreement.

(b) The products described in Part I of the Schedule relating to any contracting party, which are the products of territories of other contracting parties, shall, on their importation into the territory to which the Schedule relates, and subject to the terms, conditions or qualifications set forth in that Schedule, be exempt from ordinary customs duties in excess of those set forth and provided for therein. Such products shall also be exempt from all other duties or charges of any kind imposed on or in connection with importation in excess of those imposed on the date of this Agreement or those directly and mandatorily required to be imposed thereafter by legislation in force in the importing territory on that date.

(c) The products described in Part II of the Schedule relating to any contracting party which are the products of territories entitled under Article I to receive preferential treatment upon importation into the territory to which the Schedule relates shall, on their importation into such territory, and subject to the terms, conditions or qualifications set forth in that Schedule, be exempt from ordinary customs duties in excess of those set forth and provided for in Part II of that Schedule. Such products shall also be exempt from all other duties or charges of any kind imposed on or in connection with importation in excess of those imposed on the date of this Agreement or those directly and mandatorily required to be imposed thereafter by legislation in force in the importing territory on that date. Nothing in this Article shall prevent any contracting party from maintaining its requirements existing on the date of this Agreement as to the eligibility of goods for entry at preferential rates of duty.

2. Nothing in this Article shall prevent any contracting party from imposing at any time on the importation of any product:

(a) a charge equivalent to an internal tax imposed consistently with the provisions of paragraph 2 of Article III in respect of the like domestic product or in respect of an article from which the imported product has been manufactured or produced in whole or in part;

Ad *Article II*

Paragraph 2(a)

The cross-reference, in paragraph 2(a) of Article II, to paragraph 2 of Article III shall only apply after Article III has been modified by the entry into force of the amendment provided for in the Protocol Modifying Part II and Article XXVI of the General Agreement on Tariffs and Trade, dated September 14, 1948.

(b) any anti-dumping or countervailing duty applied consistently with the provisions of Article VI;

Ad *Article II*

Paragraph 2(b)

See the note relating to paragraph 1 of Article I.

(c) fees or other charges commensurate with the cost of services rendered.

3. No contracting party shall alter its method of determining dutiable value or of converting currencies so as to impair the value of any of the concessions provided for in the appropriate Schedule annexed to this Agreement.

4. If any contracting party establishes, maintains or authorizes, formally or in effect, a monopoly of the importation of any product described in the appropriate Schedule annexed to this Agreement, such monopoly shall not, except as provided for in that Schedule or as otherwise agreed between the parties which initially negotiated the concession, operate so as to afford protection on the average in excess of the amount of protection provided for in that Schedule. The provisions of this paragraph shall not limit the use by contracting parties of any form of assistance to domestic producers permitted by other provisions of this Agreement.

Ad *Article II*

Paragraph 4

Except where otherwise specifically agreed between the contracting parties which initially negotiated the concession, the provisions of this paragraph will be applied in the light of the provisions of Article 31 of the Havana Charter.

---

5. If any contracting party considers that a product is not receiving from another contracting party the treatment which the first contracting party believes to have been contemplated by a concession provided for in the appropriate Schedule annexed to this Agreement, it shall bring the matter directly to the attention of the other contracting party. If the latter agrees that the treatment contemplated was that claimed by the first contracting party, but declares that such treatment cannot be accorded because a court or other proper authority has ruled to the effect that the product involved cannot be classified under the tariff laws of such contracting party so as to permit the treatment contemplated in this Agreement, the two contracting parties, together with any other contracting parties substantially interested, shall enter promptly into further negotiations with a view to a compensatory adjustment of the matter.

* * *

PART II

ARTICLE III. NATIONAL TREATMENT ON INTERNAL TAXATION AND REGULATION

Ad *Article III*

Any internal tax or other internal charge, or any law, regulation or requirement of the kind referred to in paragraph 1 which applies to an imported product and to the like domestic product and is collected or enforced in the case of the imported product at the time or point of importation, is nevertheless to be regarded as an internal tax or other internal charge, or a law, regulation or requirement of the kind referred to in paragraph 1, and is accordingly subject to the provisions of Article III.

---

1. The contracting parties recognize that internal taxes and other internal charges, and laws, regulations and requirements affecting the internal sale, offering for sale, purchase, transportation, distribution or use of products, and internal quantitative regulations requiring the mixture, processing or use of products in specified amounts or proportions, should not be applied to imported or domestic products so as to afford protection to domestic production.

Ad *Article III*

Paragraph 1

The application of paragraph 1 to internal taxes imposed by local governments and authorities within the territory of a contracting party is subject to the provisions of the final paragraph of Article XXIV. The term "reasonable measures" in the last-mentioned paragraph would not require, for example, the repeal of existing national legislation authorizing local governments to impose internal taxes which, although technically inconsistent with the letter of Article III, are not in fact inconsistent with its spirit, if such repeal would result in a serious financial hardship for the local governments or authorities concerned. With regard to taxation by local governments or authorities which is inconsistent with both the letter and spirit of Article III, the term "reasonable measures" would permit a contracting party to eliminate the inconsistent taxation gradually over a transition period, if abrupt action would create serious administrative and financial difficulties.

---

2. The products of the territory of any contracting party imported into the territory of any other contracting party shall not be subject, directly or indirectly, to internal taxes or other internal charges of any kind in excess of those applied, directly or indirectly, to like domestic products. Moreover, no contracting party shall otherwise apply internal taxes or other internal charges to imported or domestic products in a manner contrary to the principles set forth in paragraph 1.

Ad *Article III*

Paragraph 2

A tax conforming to the requirements of the first sentence of paragraph 2 would be considered to be inconsistent with the provisions of the second sentence only in cases where competition was involved between, on the one hand, the taxed product and, on the other hand, a directly competitive or substitutable product which was not similarly taxed.

---

3. With respect to any existing internal tax which is inconsistent with the provisions of paragraph 2, but which is specifically authorized under a trade agreement, in force on April 10, 1947, in which the import duty on the taxed product is bound against increase, the contracting party imposing the tax shall be free to postpone the application of the provisions of paragraph 2 to such tax until such time as it can obtain release from the obligations of such trade agreement in order to permit the increase of such duty to the extent necessary to compensate for the elimination of the protective element of the tax.

4. The products of the territory of any contracting party imported into the territory of any other contracting party shall be accorded treatment no less favourable than that accorded to like products of national origin in respect of all laws, regulations and requirements affecting their internal sale, offering for sale, purchase, transportation, distribution or use. The provisions of this paragraph shall not prevent the application of differential internal transportation charges which are based exclusively on the economic operation of the means of transport and not on the nationality of the product.

5. No contracting party shall establish or maintain any internal quantitative regulation relating to the mixture, processing or use of products in specified amounts or proportions which requires, directly or indirectly, that any specified amount or proportion of any product which is the subject of the regulation must be supplied from domestic sources. Moreover, no contracting party shall otherwise apply internal quantitative regulations in a manner contrary to the principles set forth in paragraph 1.

Ad *Article III*

Paragraph 5

Regulations consistent with the provisions of the first sentence of paragraph 5 shall not be considered to be contrary to the provisions of the second sentence in any case in which all of the products subject to the regulations are produced domestically in substantial quantities. A regulation cannot be justified as being consistent with the provisions of the second sentence on the ground that the proportion or amount allocated to each of the products which are the subject of the regulation constitutes an equitable relationship between imported and domestic products.

---

* * *

8. (a) The provisions of this Article shall not apply to laws, regulations or requirements governing the procurement by governmental agencies of products purchased for governmental purposes and not with a view to commercial resale or with a view to use in the production of goods for commercial sale.

(b) The provisions of this Article shall not prevent the payment of subsidies exclusively to domestic producers, including payments to domestic producers derived from the proceeds of internal taxes or charges applied consistently with the provisions of this Article and subsidies effected through governmental purchases of domestic products.

9. The contracting parties recognize that internal maximum price control measures, even though conforming to the other provisions of this Article, can have effects prejudicial to the interests of contracting parties supplying imported products. Accordingly, contracting parties applying such measures shall take account of the interests of exporting contracting parties with a view to avoiding to the fullest practicable extent such prejudicial effects.

* * *

ARTICLE IV. SPECIAL PROVISIONS RELATING TO CINEMATOGRAPH FILMS

* * *

ARTICLE V. FREEDOM OF TRANSIT

* * *

ARTICLE VI. ANTI-DUMPING AND COUNTERVAILING DUTIES

1. The contracting parties recognize that dumping, by which products of one country are introduced into the commerce of another country at less than the normal value of the products, is to be condemned if it causes or threatens material injury to an established industry in the territory of a contracting party or materially retards the establishment of a domestic industry. For the purposes of this Article, a product is to be considered as being introduced into the commerce of an importing country at less than its normal value, if the price of the product exported from one country to another

(a) is less than the comparable price, in the ordinary course of trade, for the like product when destined for consumption in the exporting country, or,

(b) in the absence of such domestic price, is less than either

(i) the highest comparable price for the like product for export to any third country in the ordinary course of trade, or

(ii) the cost of production of the product in the country of origin plus a reasonable addition for selling cost and profit.

Due allowance shall be made in each case for differences in conditions and terms of sale, for differences in taxation, and for other differences affecting price comparability.

Ad *Article VI*

Paragraph 1

1. Hidden dumping by associated houses (that is, the sale by an importer at a price below that corresponding to the price invoiced by an exporter with whom the importer is associated, and also below the price in the exporting country) constitutes a form of price dumping with respect to which the margin of dumping may be calculated on the basis of the price at which the goods are resold by the importer.

2. It is recognized that, in the case of imports from a country which has a complete or substantially complete monopoly of its trade and where all domestic prices are fixed by the State, special difficulties may exist in determining price comparability for the purposes of paragraph 1, and in such cases importing contracting parties may find it necessary to take into account the possibility that a strict comparison with domestic prices in such a country may not always be appropriate.

---

2. In order to offset or prevent dumping, a contracting party may levy on any dumped product an anti-dumping duty not greater in amount than the margin of dumping in respect of such product. For the purposes of this Article, the margin of dumping is the price difference determined in accordance with the provisions of paragraph 1.

3. No countervailing duty shall be levied on any product of the territory of any contracting party imported into the territory of another contracting party in excess of an amount equal to the estimated bounty or subsidy determined to have been granted, directly or indirectly, on the manufacture, production or export of such product in the country of origin or exportation, including any special subsidy to the transportation of a particular product. The term "countervailing duty" shall be understood to mean a special duty levied for the purpose of offsetting any bounty or subsidy bestowed, directly or indirectly, upon the manufacture, production or export of any merchandise.

Ad *Article VI*

Paragraphs 2 and 3

1. As in many other cases in customs administration, a contracting party may require reasonable security (bond or cash deposit) for the payment of anti-dumping or countervailing duty pending final determination of the facts in any case of suspected dumping or subsidization.

2. Multiple currency practices can in certain circumstances constitute a subsidy to exports which may be met by countervailing duties under paragraph 3 or can constitute a form of dumping by means of a partial depreciation of a country's currency which may be met by action under paragraph 2. By "multiple currency practices" is meant practices by governments or sanctioned by governments.

4. No product of the territory of any contracting party imported into the territory of any other contracting party shall be subject to anti-dumping or countervailing duty by reason of the exemption of such product from duties or taxes borne by the like product when destined for consumption in the country of origin or exportation, or by reason of the refund of such duties or taxes.

5. No product of the territory of any contracting party imported into the territory of any other contracting party shall be subject to both anti-dumping and countervailing duties to compensate for the same situation of dumping or export subsidization.

6. (a) No contracting party shall levy any anti-dumping or countervailing duty on the importation of any product of the territory of another contracting party unless it determines that the effect of the dumping or subsidization, as the case may be, is such as to cause or threaten material injury to an established domestic industry, or is such as to retard materially the establishment of a domestic industry.

(b) The CONTRACTING PARTIES may waive the requirement of subparagraph (a) of this paragraph so as to permit a contracting party to levy an anti-dumping or countervailing duty on the importation of any product for the purpose of offsetting dumping or subsidization which causes or threatens material injury to an industry in the territory of another contracting party exporting the product concerned to the territory of the importing contracting party. The CONTRACTING PARTIES shall waive the requirements of sub-paragraph (a) of this paragraph, so as to permit the levying of a countervailing duty, in cases in which they find that a subsidy is causing or threatening material injury to an industry in the territory of another contracting party exporting the product concerned to the territory of the importing contracting party.

Ad *Article VI*

Paragraph 6(b)

Waivers under the provisions of this sub-paragraph shall be granted only on application by the contracting party proposing to levy an anti-dumping or countervailing duty, as the case may be.

(c) In exceptional circumstances, however, where delay might cause damage which would be difficult to repair, a contracting party may levy a countervailing duty for the purpose referred to in subparagraph (b) of this paragraph without the prior approval of the CONTRACTING PARTIES; *Provided* that such action shall be reported immediately to the CONTRACTING PARTIES and that the countervailing duty shall be withdrawn promptly if the CONTRACTING PARTIES disapprove.

7. A system for the stabilization of the domestic price or of the return to domestic producers of a primary commodity, independently of the movements of export prices, which results at times in the sale of the commodity for export at a price lower than the comparable price charged for the like commodity to buyers in the domestic market, shall be presumed not to result in material injury within the meaning of paragraph 6 if it is determined by consultation among the contracting parties substantially interested in the commodity concerned that:

(a) the system has also resulted in the sale of the commodity for export at a price higher than the comparable price charged for the like commodity to buyers in the domestic market, and

(b) the system is so operated, either because of the effective regulation of production, or otherwise, as not to stimulate exports unduly or otherwise seriously prejudice the interests of other contracting parties.

ARTICLE VII. VALUATION FOR CUSTOMS PURPOSES

1. The contracting parties recognize the validity of the general principles of valuation set forth in the following paragraphs of this Article, and they undertake to give effect to such principles, in respect of all products subject to duties or other charges or restrictions on importation and exportation based upon or regulated in any manner by value. Moreover, they shall, upon a request by another contracting party review the operation of any of their laws or regulations relating to value for customs purposes in the light of these principles. The CONTRACTING PARTIES may request from contracting parties reports on steps taken by them in pursuance of the provisions of this Article.

Ad *Article VII*

Paragraph 1

The expression "or other charges" is not to be regarded as including internal taxes or equivalent charges imposed on or in connexion with imported products.

---

2. (a) The value for customs purposes of imported merchandise should be based on the actual value of the imported merchandise on which

duty is assessed, or of like merchandise, and should not be based on the value of merchandise of national origin or on arbitrary or fictitious values.

(b) "Actual value" should be the price at which, at a time and place determined by the legislation of the country of importation, such or like merchandise is sold or offered for sale in the ordinary course of trade under fully competitive conditions. To the extent to which the price of such or like merchandise is governed by the quantity in a particular transaction, the price to be considered should uniformly be related to either (i) comparable quantities, or (ii) quantities not less favourable to importers than those in which the greater volume of the merchandise is sold in the trade between the countries of exportation and importation.

(c) When the actual value is not ascertainable in accordance with sub-paragraph (b) of this paragraph, the value for customs purposes should be based on the nearest ascertainable equivalent of such value.

Ad *Article VII*

Paragraph 2

1. It would be in conformity with Article VII to presume that "actual value" may be represented by the invoice price, plus any non-included charges for legitimate costs which are proper elements of "actual value" and plus any abnormal discount or other reduction from the ordinary competitive price.

2. It would be in conformity with Article VII, paragraph 2(b), for a contracting party to construe the phrase "in the ordinary course of trade * * * under fully competitive conditions", as excluding any transaction wherein the buyer and seller are not independent of each other and price is not the sole consideration.

3. The standard of "fully competitive conditions" permits a contracting party to exclude from consideration prices involving special discounts limited to exclusive agents.

4. The wording of sub-paragraphs (a) and (b) permits a contracting party to determine the value for customs purposes uniformly either (1) on the basis of a particular exporter's prices of the imported merchandise, or (2) on the basis of the general price level of like merchandise.

---

3. The value for customs purposes of any imported product should not include the amount of any internal tax, applicable within the country of origin or export, from which the imported product has been exempted or has been or will be relieved by means of refund.

4. (a) Except as otherwise provided for in this paragraph, where it is necessary for the purposes of paragraph 2 of this Article for a contracting

party to convert into its own currency a price expressed in the currency of another country, the conversion rate of exchange to be used shall be based, for each currency involved, on the par value as established pursuant to the Articles of Agreement of the International Monetary Fund or on the rate of exchange recognized by the Fund, or on the par value established in accordance with a special exchange agreement entered into pursuant to Article XV of this Agreement.

(b) Where no such established par value and no such recognized rate of exchange exist, the conversion rate shall reflect effectively the current value of such currency in commercial transactions.

(c) The CONTRACTING PARTIES, in agreement with the International Monetary Fund, shall formulate rules governing the conversion by contracting parties of any foreign currency in respect of which multiple rates of exchange are maintained consistently with the Articles of Agreement of the International Monetary Fund. Any contracting party may apply such rules in respect of such foreign currencies for the purposes of paragraph 2 of this Article as an alternative to the use of par values. Until such rules are adopted by the CONTRACTING PARTIES, any contracting party may employ, in respect of any such foreign currency, rules of conversion for the purposes of paragraph 2 of this Article which are designed to reflect effectively the value of such foreign currency in commercial transactions.

(d) Nothing in this paragraph shall be construed to require any contracting party to alter the method of converting currencies for customs purposes which is applicable in its territory on the date of this Agreement, if such alteration would have the effect of increasing generally the amounts of duty payable.

5. The bases and methods for determining the value of products subject to duties or other charges or restrictions based upon or regulated in any manner by value should be stable and should be given sufficient publicity to enable traders to estimate, with a reasonable degree of certainty, the value for customs purposes.

ARTICLE VIII. FEES AND FORMALITIES CONNECTED WITH IMPORTATION AND EXPORTATION

1. (a) All fees and charges of whatever character (other than import and export duties and other than taxes within the purview of Article III) imposed by contracting parties on or in connexion with importation or exportation shall be limited in amount to the approximate cost of services rendered and shall not represent an indirect protection to domestic products or a taxation of imports or exports for fiscal purposes.

* * *

ARTICLE IX. MARKS OF ORIGIN

1. Each contracting party shall accord to the products of the territories of other contracting parties treatment with regard to marking requirements no less favourable than the treatment accorded to like products of any third country.

2. The contracting parties recognize that, in adopting and enforcing laws and regulations relating to marks of origin, the difficulties and inconveniences which such measures may cause to the commerce and industry of exporting countries should be reduced to a minimum, due regard being had to the necessity of protecting consumers against fraudulent or misleading indications.

3. Whenever it is administratively practicable to do so, contracting parties should permit required marks of origin to be affixed at the time of importation.

4. The laws and regulations of contracting parties relating to the marking of imported products shall be such as to permit compliance without seriously damaging the products, or materially reducing their value, or unreasonably increasing their cost.

5. As a general rule, no special duty or penalty should be imposed by any contracting party for failure to comply with marking requirements prior to importation unless corrective marking is unreasonably delayed or deceptive marks have been affixed or the required marking has been intentionally omitted.

6. The contracting parties shall co-operate with each other with a view to preventing the use of trade names in such manner as to misrepresent the true origin of a product, to the detriment of such distinctive regional or geographical names of products of the territory of a contracting party as are protected by its legislation. Each contracting party shall accord full and sympathetic consideration to such requests or representations as may be made by any other contracting party regarding the application of the undertaking set forth in the preceding sentence to names of products which have been communicated to it by the other contracting party.

ARTICLE X. PUBLICATION AND ADMINISTRATION OF TRADE REGULATIONS (omitted)

* * *

ARTICLE XI. GENERAL ELIMINATION OF QUANTITATIVE RESTRICTIONS

Ad *Articles XI, XII, XIII, XIV and XVIII*

Throughout Articles XI, XII, XIII, XIV and XVIII, the terms "import restrictions" or "export restrictions" include restrictions made effective through state-trading operations.

---

1. No prohibitions or restrictions other than duties, taxes or other charges, whether made effective through quotas, import or export licenses or other measures, shall be instituted or maintained by any contracting party on the importation of any product of the territory of any other contracting party or on the exportation or sale for export of any product destined for the territory of any other contracting party.

2. The provisions of paragraph 1 of this Article shall not extend to the following:

(a) Export prohibitions or restrictions temporarily applied to prevent or relieve critical shortages of foodstuffs or other products essential to the exporting contracting party;

(b) Import and export prohibitions or restrictions necessary to the application of standards or regulations for the classification, grading or marketing of commodities in international trade;

(c) Import restrictions on any agricultural or fisheries product, imported in any form, necessary to the enforcement of governmental measures which operate:

(i) to restrict the quantities of the like domestic product permitted to be marketed or produced, or, if there is no substantial domestic production of the like product, of a domestic product for which the imported product can be directly substituted; or

(ii) to remove a temporary surplus of the like domestic product, or, if there is no substantial domestic production of the like product, of a domestic product for which the imported product can be directly substituted, by making the surplus available to certain groups of domestic consumers free of charge or at prices below the current market level; or

(iii) to restrict the quantities permitted to be produced of any animal product the production of which is directly dependent, wholly or mainly, on the imported commodity, if the domestic production of that commodity is relatively negligible.

Ad *Article XI*

Paragraph 2(c)

The term "in any form" in this paragraph covers the same products when in an early stage of processing and still perishable, which compete directly with the fresh product and if freely imported would tend to make the restriction on the fresh product ineffective.

Any contracting party applying restrictions on the importation of any product pursuant to sub-paragraph (c) of this paragraph shall give public notice of the total quantity or value of the product permitted to be imported during a specified future period and of any change in such quantity or value. Moreover, any restrictions applied under (i) above shall not be such as will reduce the total of imports relative to the total of domestic production, as compared with the proportion which might reasonably be expected to rule between the two in the absence of restrictions. In determining this proportion, the contracting party shall pay due regard to the proportion prevailing during a previous representative period and to any special factors which may have affected or may be affecting the trade in the product concerned.

Ad *Article XI*

Paragraph 2, last sub-paragraph

The term "special factors" includes changes in relative productive efficiency as between domestic and foreign producers, or as between different foreign producers, but not changes artificially brought about by means not permitted under the Agreement.

ARTICLE XII. RESTRICTIONS TO SAFEGUARD THE BALANCE OF PAYMENTS

Ad *Articles XI, XII, XIII, XIV and XVIII*

Throughout Articles XI, XII, XIII, XIV and XVIII, the terms "import restrictions" or "export restrictions" include restrictions made effective through state-trading operations.

Ad *Article XII*

The CONTRACTING PARTIES shall make provision for the utmost secrecy in the conduct of any consultation under the provisions of this Article.

---

1. Notwithstanding the provisions of paragraph 1 of Article XI, any contracting party, in order to safeguard its external financial position and its balance of payments, may restrict the quantity or value of merchandise permitted to be imported, subject to the provisions of the following paragraphs of this Article.

2. (a) Import restrictions instituted, maintained or intensified by a contracting party under this Article shall not exceed those necessary:

(i) to forestall the imminent threat of, or to stop, a serious decline in its monetary reserves, or

(ii) in the case of a contracting party with very low monetary reserves, to achieve a reasonable rate of increase in its reserves.

Due regard shall be paid in either case to any special factors which may be affecting the reserves of such contracting party or its need for reserves, including, where special external credits or other resources are available to it, the need to provide for the appropriate use of such credits or resources.

(b) Contracting parties applying restrictions under sub-paragraph (a) of this paragraph shall progressively relax them as such conditions improve, maintaining them only to the extent that the conditions specified in that sub-paragraph still justify their application. They shall eliminate the restrictions when conditions would no longer justify their institution or maintenance under that sub-paragraph.

3. (a) Contracting parties undertake, in carrying out their domestic policies, to pay due regard to the need for maintaining or restoring equilibrium in their balance of payments on a sound and lasting basis and to the desirability of avoiding an uneconomic employment of productive resources. They recognize that, in order to achieve these ends, it is desirable so far as possible to adopt measures which expand rather than contract international trade.

(b) Contracting parties applying restrictions under this Article may determine the incidence of the restrictions on imports of different products or classes of products in such a way as to give priority to the importation of those products which are more essential.

(c) Contracting parties applying restrictions under this Article undertake:

(i) to avoid unnecessary damage to the commercial or economic interests of any other contracting party;

Ad *Article XII*

Paragraph 3(c)(i)

Contracting parties applying restrictions shall endeavour to avoid causing serious prejudice to exports of a commodity on which the economy of a contracting party is largely dependent.

(ii) not to apply restrictions so as to prevent unreasonably the importation of any description of goods in minimum commercial quantities the exclusion of which would impair regular channels of trade; and

(iii) not to apply restrictions which would prevent the importation of commercial samples or prevent compliance with patent, trade mark, copyright, or similar procedures.

(d) The contracting parties recognize that, as a result of domestic policies directed towards the achievement and maintenance of full and productive employment or towards the development of economic resources, a contracting party may experience a high level of demand for imports involving a threat to its monetary reserves of the sort referred to in paragraph 2(a) of this Article. Accordingly, a contracting party otherwise complying with the provisions of this Article shall not be required to withdraw or modify restrictions on the ground that a change in those policies would render unnecessary restrictions which it is applying under this Article.

4. (a) Any contracting party applying new restrictions or raising the general level of its existing restrictions by a substantial intensification of the measures applied under this Article shall immediately after instituting or intensifying such restrictions (or, in circumstances in which prior consultation is practicable, before doing so) consult with the CONTRACTING PARTIES as to the nature of its balance of payments difficulties, alternative corrective measures which may be available, and the possible effect of the restrictions on the economies of other contracting parties.

(b) On a date to be determined by them, the CONTRACTING PARTIES shall review all restrictions still applied under this Article on that date. Beginning one year after that date, contracting parties applying import restrictions under this Article shall enter into consultations of the type provided for in sub-paragraph (a) of this paragraph with the CONTRACTING PARTIES annually.

Ad *Article XII*

Paragraph 4(b)

It is agreed that the date shall be within ninety days after the entry into force of the amendments of this Article effected by the Protocol Amending the Preamble and Parts II and III of this Agreement. However, should the CONTRACTING PARTIES find that conditions were not suitable for the application of the provisions of this sub-paragraph at the time envisaged, they may determine a later date; *Provided* that such date is not more than thirty days after such time as the obligations of Article VIII, Sections 2, 3 and 4, of the Articles of Agreement of the International Monetary Fund become applicable to contracting parties, members of the Fund, the combined foreign trade of which constitutes at least fifty per centum of the aggregate foreign trade of all contracting parties.

(c)(i) If, in the course of consultations with a contracting party under sub-paragraph (a) or (b) above, the CONTRACTING PARTIES find that the restrictions are not consistent with the provisions of this Article or with those of Article XIII (subject to the provisions of Article XIV), they shall indicate the nature of the inconsistency and may advise that the restrictions be suitably modified.

(ii) If, however, as a result of the consultations, the CONTRACTING PARTIES determine that the restrictions are being applied in a manner involving an inconsistency of a serious nature with the provisions of this Article or with those of Article XIII (subject to the provisions of Article XIV) and that damage to the trade of any contracting party is caused or threatened thereby, they shall so inform the contracting party applying the restrictions and shall make appropriate recommendations for securing conformity with such provisions within a specified period of time. If such contracting party does not comply with these recommendations within the specified period, the CONTRACTING PARTIES may release any contracting party the trade of which is adversely affected by the restrictions from such obligations under this Agreement towards the contracting party applying the restrictions as they determine to be appropriate in the circumstances.

(d) The CONTRACTING PARTIES shall invite any contracting party which is applying restrictions under this Article to enter into consultations with them at the request of any contracting party which can establish a *prima facie* case that the restrictions are inconsistent with the provisions of this Article or with those of Article XIII (subject to the provisions of Article XIV) and that its trade is adversely affected thereby. However, no such invitation shall be issued unless the CONTRACTING PARTIES have ascertained that direct discussions between the contracting parties concerned have not been successful. If, as a result of the consultations with the CONTRACTING PARTIES, no agreement is reached and they determine that the restrictions are being applied inconsistently with such provisions, and that damage to the trade of the contracting party initiating the procedure is caused or threatened thereby, they shall recommend the withdrawal or modification of the restrictions. If the restrictions are not withdrawn or modified within such time as the CONTRACTING PARTIES may prescribe, they may release the contracting party initiating the procedure from such obligations under this Agreement towards the contracting party applying the restrictions as they determine to be appropriate in the circumstances.

(e) In proceeding under this paragraph, the CONTRACTING PARTIES shall have due regard to any special external factors adversely affecting the export trade of the contracting party applying restrictions.

Ad *Article XII*

Paragraph 4(e)

It is agreed that paragraph 4(e) does not add any new criteria for the imposition or maintenance of quantitative restrictions for balance of payments reasons. It is solely intended to ensure that all external factors such as changes in the terms of trade, quantitative restrictions, excessive tariffs and subsidies, which may be contributing to the balance of payments difficulties of the contracting party applying restrictions, will be fully taken into account.

(f) Determinations under this paragraph shall be rendered expeditiously and, if possible, within sixty days of the initiation of the consultations.

5. If there is a persistent and widespread application of import restrictions under this Article, indicating the existence of a general disequilibrium which is restricting international trade, the CONTRACTING PARTIES shall initiate discussions to consider whether other measures might be taken, either by those contracting parties the balances of payments of which are under pressure or by those the balances of payments of which are tending to be exceptionally favourable, or by any appropriate intergovernmental organization, to remove the underlying causes of the disequilibrium. On the invitation of the CONTRACTING PARTIES, contracting parties shall participate in such discussions.

ARTICLE XIII. NON-DISCRIMINATORY ADMINISTRATION OF QUANTITATIVE RESTRICTIONS

Ad *Articles XI, XII, XIII, XIV and XVIII*

Throughout Articles XI, XII, XIII, XIV and XVIII, the terms "import restrictions" or "export restrictions" include restrictions made effective through state-trading operations.

---

1. No prohibition or restriction shall be applied by any contracting party on the importation of any product of the territory of any other contracting party or on the exportation of any product destined for the territory of any other contracting party, unless the importation of the like product of all third countries or the exportation of the like product to all third countries is similarly prohibited or restricted.

2. In applying import restrictions to any product, contracting parties shall aim at a distribution of trade in such product approaching as closely as possible the shares which the various contracting parties might be expected to obtain in the absence of such restrictions, and to this end shall observe the following provisions:

(a) Wherever practicable, quotas representing the total amount of permitted imports (whether allocated among supplying countries or not) shall be fixed, and notice given of their amount in accordance with paragraph 3(b) of this Article;

(b) In cases in which quotas are not practicable, the restrictions may be applied by means of import licences or permits without a quota;

(c) Contracting parties shall not, except for purposes of operating quotas allocated in accordance with sub-paragraph (d) of this paragraph, require that import licences or permits be utilized for the importation of the product concerned from a particular country or source;

(d) In cases in which a quota is allocated among supplying countries, the contracting party applying the restrictions may seek agreement with respect to the allocation of shares in the quota with all other contracting parties having a substantial interest in supplying the product concerned. In cases in which this method is not reasonably practicable, the contracting party concerned shall allot to contracting parties having a substantial interest in supplying the product shares based upon the proportions, supplied by such contracting parties during a previous representative period, of the total quantity or value of imports of the product, due account being taken of any special factors which may have affected or may be affecting the trade in the product. No conditions or formalities shall be imposed which would prevent any contracting party from utilizing fully the share of any such total quantity or value which has been allotted to it, subject to importation being made without any prescribed period to which the quota may relate.

Ad *Article XIII*

Paragraph 2(d)

No mention was made of "commercial considerations" as a rule for the allocation of quotas because it was considered that its application by governmental authorities might not always be practicable. Moreover, in cases where it is practicable, a contracting party could apply these considerations in the process of seeking agreement, consistently with the general rule laid down in the opening sentence of paragraph 2.

---

3. (a) In cases in which import licences are issued in connection with import restrictions, the contracting party applying the restrictions shall provide, upon the request of any contracting party having an interest in the trade in the product concerned, all relevant information concerning the administration of the restrictions, the import licences granted over a recent period and the distribution of such licences among supplying countries; *Provided* that there shall be no obligation to supply information as to the names of importing or supplying enterprises.

(b) In the case of import restrictions involving the fixing of quotas, the contracting party applying the restrictions shall give public notice of the total quantity or value of the product or products which will be permitted to be imported during a specified future period and of any change in such quantity or value. Any supplies of the product in question which were *en route* at the time at which public notice was given shall not be excluded from entry; *Provided* that they may be counted so far as practicable, against the quantity permitted to be imported in the period in question, and also, where necessary, against the quantities permitted to be imported in the next following period or periods; and *Provided* further that if any contracting party customarily exempts from such restrictions products entered for consumption or withdrawn from warehouse for consumption during a period of thirty days after the day of such public notice, such practice shall be considered full compliance with this sub-paragraph.

(c) In the case of quotas allocated among supplying countries, the contracting party applying the restrictions shall promptly inform all other contracting parties having an interest in supplying the product concerned of the shares in the quota currently allocated, by quantity or value, to the various supplying countries and shall give public notice thereof.

4. With regard to restrictions applied in accordance with paragraph 2(d) of this Article or under paragraph 2(c) of Article XI, the selection of a representative period for any product and the appraisal of any special factors affecting the trade in the product shall be made initially by the contracting party applying the restriction; *Provided* that such contracting party shall, upon the request of any other contracting party having a substantial interest in supplying that product or upon the request of the CONTRACTING PARTIES, consult promptly with the other contracting party or the CONTRACTING PARTIES regarding the need for an adjustment of the proportion determined or of the base period selected, or for the reappraisal of the special factors involved, or for the elimination of conditions, formalities or any other provisions established unilaterally relating to the allocation of an adequate quota or its unrestricted utilization.

Ad *Article XIII*

Paragraph 4

See note relating to "special factors" in connexion with the last subparagraph of paragraph 2 of Article XI.

---

5. The provisions of this Article shall apply to any tariff quota instituted or maintained by any contracting party, and, in so far as applicable, the principles of this Article shall also extend to export restrictions.

ARTICLE XIV. EXCEPTIONS TO THE RULE OF NONDISCRIMINATION

Ad *Articles XI, XII, XIII, XIV and XVIII*

Throughout Articles XI, XII, XIII, XIV and XVIII, the terms "import restrictions" or "export restrictions" include restrictions made effective through state-trading operations.

---

1. A contracting party which applies restrictions under Article XII or under Section B of Article XVIII may, in the application of such restrictions, deviate from the provisions of Article XIII in a manner having equivalent effect to restrictions on payments and transfers for current

international transactions which that contracting party may at that time apply under Article VIII or XIV of the Articles of Agreement of the International Monetary Fund, or under analogous provisions of a special exchange agreement entered into pursuant to paragraph 6 of Article XV.

Ad *Article XIV*

Paragraph 1

The provisions of this paragraph shall not be so construed as to preclude full consideration by the CONTRACTING PARTIES, in the consultations provided for in paragraph 4 of Article XII and in paragraph 12 of Article XVIII, of the nature, effects and reasons for discrimination in the field of import restrictions.

---

2. A contracting party which is applying import restrictions under Article XII or under Section B of Article XVIII may, with the consent of the CONTRACTING PARTIES, temporarily deviate from the provisions of Article XIII in respect of a small part of its external trade where the benefits to the contracting party or contracting parties concerned substantially outweigh any injury which may result to the trade of other contracting parties.

Ad *Article XIV*

Paragraph 2

One of the situations contemplated in paragraph 2 is that of a contracting party holding balances acquired as a result of current transactions which it finds itself unable to use without a measure of discrimination.

---

3. The provisions of Article XIII shall not preclude a group of territories having a common quota in the International Monetary Fund from applying against imports from other countries, but not among themselves, restrictions in accordance with the provisions of Article XII or of Section B of Article XVIII on condition that such restrictions are in all other respects consistent with the provisions of Article XIII.

4. A contracting party applying import restrictions under Article XII or under Section B of Article XVIII shall not be precluded by Articles XI to XV or Section B of Article XVIII of this Agreement from applying measures to direct its exports in such a manner as to increase its earnings of currencies which it can use without deviation from the provisions of Article XIII.

5. A contracting party shall not be precluded by Articles XI to XV, inclusive, or by Section B of Article XVIII, of this Agreement from applying quantitative restrictions:

(a) having equivalent effect to exchange restrictions authorized under Section 3(*b*) of Article VII of the Articles of Agreement of the International Monetary Fund, or

(b) under the preferential arrangements provided for in Annex A of this Agreement, pending the outcome of the negotiations referred to therein.

ARTICLE XV. EXCHANGE ARRANGEMENTS

1. The CONTRACTING PARTIES shall seek co-operation with the International Monetary Fund to the end that the CONTRACTING PARTIES and the Fund may pursue a co-ordinated policy with regard to exchange questions within the jurisdiction of the Fund and questions of quantitative restrictions and other trade measures within the jurisdiction of the CONTRACTING PARTIES.

* * *

ARTICLE XVI. SUBSIDIES

Ad *Article XVI*

The exemption of an exported product from duties or taxes borne by the like product when destined for domestic consumption, or the remission of such duties or taxes in amounts not in excess of those which have accrued, shall not be deemed to be a subsidy.

Section A—Subsidies in General

1. If any contracting party grants or maintains any subsidy, including any form of income or price support, which operates directly or indirectly to increase exports of any product from, or to reduce imports of any product into, its territory, it shall notify the CONTRACTING PARTIES in writing of the extent and nature of the subsidization, of the estimated effect of the subsidization on the quantity of the affected product or products imported into or exported from its territory and of the circumstances making the subsidization necessary. In any case, in which it is determined that serious prejudice to the interests of any other contracting party is caused or threatened by any such subsidization, the contracting party granting the subsidy shall, upon request, discuss with the other contracting party or parties concerned, or with the CONTRACTING PARTIES, the possibility of limiting the subsidization.

Section B—Additional Provisions on Export Subsidies

Ad *Article XVI*

Section B

1. Nothing in Section B shall preclude the use by a contracting party of multiple rates of exchange in accordance with the Articles of Agreement of the International Monetary Fund.

2. For the purposes of Section B, a "primary product" is understood to be any product of farm, forest or fishery, or any mineral, in its natural form or which has undergone such processing as is customarily required to prepare it for marketing in substantial volume in international trade.

---

2. The contracting parties recognize that the granting by a contracting party of a subsidy on the export of any product may have harmful effects for other contracting parties, both importing and exporting, may cause undue disturbance to their normal commercial interests, and may hinder the achievement of the objectives of this Agreement.

3. Accordingly, contracting parties should seek to avoid the use of subsidies on the export of primary products. If, however, a contracting party grants directly or indirectly any form of subsidy which operates to increase the export of any primary product from its territory, such subsidy shall not be applied in a manner which results in that contracting party having more than an equitable share of world export trade in that product, account being taken of the shares of the contracting parties in such trade in the product during a previous representative period, and any special factors which may have affected or may be affecting such trade in the product.

Ad *Article XVI*

Paragraph 3

1. The fact that a contracting party has not exported the product in question during the previous representative period would not in itself preclude that contracting party from establishing its right to obtain a share of the trade in the product concerned.

2. A system for the stabilization of the domestic price or of the return to domestic producers of a primary product independently of the movements of export prices, which results at times in the sale of the product for export at a price lower than the comparable price charged for the like product to buyers in the domestic market, shall be considered not to involve a subsidy on exports within the meaning of paragraph 3 if the CONTRACTING PARTIES determine that:

(a) the system has also resulted, or is so designed as to result, in the sale of the product for export at a price higher than the comparable price charged for the like product to buyers in the domestic market; and

(b) the system is so operated, or is designed so to operate, either because of the effective regulation of production or otherwise, as not to stipulate exports unduly or otherwise seriously to prejudice the interests of other contracting parties.

Notwithstanding such determination by the CONTRACTING PARTIES, operations under such a system shall be subject to the provisions of paragraph 3 where they are wholly or partly financed out of government funds in addition to the funds collected from producers in respect of the product concerned.

---

4. Further, as from 1 January 1958 or the earliest practicable date thereafter, contracting parties shall cease to grant either directly or indirectly any form of subsidy on the export of any product other than a primary product which subsidy results in the sale of such product for export at a price lower than the comparable price charged for the like product to buyers in the domestic market. Until 31 December 1957 no contracting party shall extend the scope of any such subsidization beyond that existing on 1 January 1955 by the introduction of new, or the extension of existing, subsidies.

Ad *Article XVI*

Paragraph 4

The intention of paragraph 4 is that the contracting parties should seek before the end of 1957 to reach agreement to abolish all remaining subsidies as from 1 January 1958; or, failing this, to reach agreement to extend the application of the standstill until the earliest date thereafter by which they can expect to reach such agreement.

---

5. The CONTRACTING PARTIES shall review the operation of the provisions of this Article from time to time with a view to examining its effectiveness, in the light of actual experience, in promoting the objectives of this Agreement and avoiding subsidization seriously prejudicial to the trade or interests of contracting parties.

ARTICLE XVII. STATE TRADING ENTERPRISES

1. (a) Each contracting party undertakes that if it establishes or maintains a State enterprise, wherever located, or grants to any enterprise, formally or in effect, exclusive or special privileges, such enterprise shall, in its purchases or sales involving either imports or exports, act in a manner consistent with the general principles of nondiscriminatory

treatment prescribed in this Agreement for governmental measures affecting imports or exports by private traders.

Ad *Article XVII*

Paragraph 1

The operations of Marketing Boards, which are established by contracting parties and are engaged in purchasing or selling, are subject to the provisions of sub-paragraphs (a) and (b).

The activities of Marketing Boards which are established by contracting parties and which do not purchase or sell but lay down regulations covering private trade are governed by the relevant Articles of this Agreement.

The charging by a state enterprise of different prices for its sales of a product in different markets is not precluded by the provisions of this Article, provided that such different prices are charged for commercial reasons, to meet conditions of supply and demand in export markets.

Paragraph 1(a)

Governmental measures imposed to ensure standards of quality and efficiency in the operation of external trade, or privileges granted for the exploitation of national natural resources but which do not empower the government to exercise control over the trading activities of the enterprise in question, do not constitute "exclusive or special privileges".

(b) The provisions of sub-paragraph (a) of this paragraph shall be understood to require that such enterprises shall, having due regard to the other provisions of this Agreement, make any such purchases or sales solely in accordance with commercial considerations, including price, quality, availability, marketability, transportation and other conditions of purchase or sale, and shall afford the enterprises of the other contracting parties adequate opportunity, in accordance with customary business practice, to compete for participation in such purchases or sales.

Ad *Article XVII*

Paragraph 1(b)

A country receiving a "tied loan" is free to take this loan into account as a "commercial consideration" when purchasing requirements abroad.

(c) No contracting party shall prevent any enterprise (whether or not an enterprise described in sub-paragraph (a) of this paragraph) under its jurisdiction from acting in accordance with the principles of sub-paragraphs (a) and (b) of this paragraph.

2. The provisions of paragraph 1 of this Article shall not apply to imports of products for immediate or ultimate consumption in governmental use and not otherwise for resale or use in the production of goods for sale. With respect to such imports, each contracting party shall accord to the trade of the other contracting parties fair and equitable treatment.

Ad *Article XVII*

Paragraph 2

The term "goods" is limited to products as understood in commercial practice, and is not intended to include the purchase or sale of services.

---

3. The contracting parties recognize that enterprises of the kind described in paragraph 1(a) of this Article might be operated so as to create serious obstacles to trade; thus negotiations on a reciprocal and mutually advantageous basis designed to limit or reduce such obstacles are of importance to the expansion of international trade.

Ad *Article XVII*

Paragraph 3

Negotiations which contracting parties agree to conduct under this paragraph may be directed towards the reduction of duties and other charges on imports and exports or towards the conclusion of any other mutually satisfactory arrangement consistent with the provisions of this Agreement. (See paragraph 4 of Article II and the note to that paragraph.)

---

4. (a) Contracting parties shall notify the CONTRACTING PARTIES of the products which are imported into or exported from their territories by enterprises of the kind described in paragraph 1(a) of this Article.

(b) A contracting party establishing, maintaining or authorizing an import monopoly of a product, which is not the subject of a concession under Article II, shall, on the request of another contracting party having a substantial trade in the product concerned, inform the

CONTRACTING PARTIES of the import mark-up on the product during a recent representative period, or, when it is not possible to do so, of the price charged on the resale of the product.

Ad *Article XVII*

Paragraph 4(b)

The term "import mark-up" in this paragraph shall represent the margin by which the price charged by the import monopoly for the imported product (exclusive of internal taxes within the purview of Article III, transportation, distribution, and other expenses incident to the purchase, sale or further processing, and a reasonable margin of profit) exceeds the landed cost.

(c) The CONTRACTING PARTIES may, at the request of a contracting party which has reason to believe that its interests under this Agreement are being adversely affected by the operations of an enterprise of the kind described in paragraph 1(a), request the contracting party establishing, maintaining or authorizing such enterprise to supply information about its operations related to the carrying out of the provisions of this Agreement.

(d) The provisions of this paragraph shall not require any contracting party to disclose confidential information which would impede law enforcement or otherwise be contrary to the public interest or would prejudice the legitimate commercial interests of particular enterprises.

ARTICLE XVIII. GOVERNMENTAL ASSISTANCE TO ECONOMIC DEVELOPMENT

Ad *Articles XI, XII, XIII, XIV and XVIII*

Throughout Articles XI, XII, XIII, XIV and XVIII, the terms "import restrictions" or "export restrictions" include restrictions made effective through state-trading operations.

Ad *Article XVIII*

The CONTRACTING PARTIES and the contracting parties concerned shall preserve the utmost secrecy in respect of matters arising under this Article.

---

1. The contracting parties recognize that the attainment of the objectives of this Agreement will be facilitated by the progressive

development of their economies, particularly of those contracting parties the economies of which can only support low standards of living and are in the early stages of development.

Ad *Article XVIII*

Paragraphs 1 and 4

1. When they consider whether the economy of a contracting party "can only support low standards of living", the CONTRACTING PARTIES shall take into consideration the normal position of that economy and shall not base their determination on exceptional circumstances such as those which may result from the temporary existence of exceptionally favourable conditions for the staple export product or products of such contracting party.

2. The phrase "in the early stages of development" is not meant to apply only to contracting parties which have just started their economic development, but also to contracting parties the economics of which are undergoing a process of industrialization to correct an excessive dependence on primary production.

---

2. The contracting parties recognize further that it may be necessary for those contracting parties, in order to implement programmes and policies of economic development designed to raise the general standard of living of their people, to take protective or other measures affecting imports, and that such measures are justified in so far as they facilitate the attainment of the objectives of this Agreement. They agree, therefore, that those contracting parties should enjoy additional facilities to enable them (a) to maintain sufficient flexibility in their tariff structure to be able to grant the tariff protection required for the establishment of a particular industry and (b) to apply quantitative restrictions for balance of payments purposes in a manner which takes full account of the continued high level of demand for imports likely to be generated by their programmes of economic development.

Ad *Article XVIII*

Paragraphs 2, 3, 7, 13 and 22

The reference to the establishment of particular industries shall apply not only to the establishment of a new industry, but also to the establishment of a new branch of production in an existing industry and to the substantial transformation of an existing industry, and to the substantial expansion of an existing industry supplying a relatively small proportion of the domestic demand. It shall also cover the reconstruction of an industry destroyed or substantially damaged as a result of hostilities or natural disasters.

---

3. The contracting parties recognize finally that, with those additional facilities which are provided for in Sections A and B of this Article, the provisions of this Agreement would normally be sufficient to enable contracting parties to meet the requirements of their economic development. They agree, however, that there may be circumstances where no measure consistent with those provisions is practicable to permit a contracting party in the process of economic development to grant the governmental assistance required to promote the establishment of particular industries with a view to raising the general standard of living of its people. Special procedures are laid down in Sections C and D of this Article to deal with those cases.*

4. (a) Consequently, a contracting party the economy of which can only support low standards of living and is in the early stages of development shall be free to deviate temporarily from the provisions of the other Articles of this Agreement, as provided in Sections A, B and C of this Article.**

(b) A contracting party the economy of which is in the process of development, but which does not come within the scope of subparagraph (a) above, may submit applications to the CONTRACTING PARTIES under Section D of this Article.

5. The contracting parties recognize that the export earnings of contracting parties, the economies of which are of the type described in paragraph 4(a) and (b) above and which depend on exports of a small number of primary commodities, may be seriously reduced by a decline in the sale of such commodities. Accordingly, when the exports of primary commodities by such a contracting party are seriously affected by measures taken by another contracting party, it may have resort to the consultation provisions of Article XXII of this Agreement.

* * *

ARTICLE XIX. EMERGENCY ACTION ON IMPORTS OF PARTICULAR PRODUCTS

1. (a) If, as a result of unforeseen developments and of the effect of the obligations incurred by a contracting party under this Agreement, including tariff concessions, any product is being imported into the territory of that contracting party in such increased quantities and under such conditions as to cause or threaten serious injury to domestic producers in that territory of like or directly competitive products, the contracting party shall be free, in respect of such product, and to the extent and for such time as may be necessary to prevent or remedy such injury, to suspend the obligation in whole or in part or to withdraw or modify the concession.

* See addition to Paragraph 2.

** See addition to Paragraph 1.

(b) If any product, which is the subject of a concession with respect to a preference, is being imported into the territory of a contracting party in the circumstances set forth in sub-paragraph (a) of this paragraph, so as to cause or threaten serious injury to domestic producers of like or directly competitive products in the territory of a contracting party which receives or received such preference, the importing contracting party shall be free, if that other contracting party so requests, to suspend the relevant obligation in whole or in part or to withdraw or modify the concession in respect of the product, to the extent and for such time as may be necessary to prevent or remedy such injury.

2. Before any contracting party shall take action pursuant to the provisions of paragraph 1 of this Article, it shall give notice in writing to the CONTRACTING PARTIES as far in advance as may be practicable and shall afford the CONTRACTING PARTIES and those contracting parties having a substantial interest as exporters of the product concerned an opportunity to consult with it in respect of the proposed action. When such notice is given in relation to a concession with respect to a preference, the notice shall name the contracting party which has requested the action. In critical circumstances, where delay would cause damage which it would be difficult to repair, action under paragraph 1 of this Article may be taken provisionally without prior consultation, on the condition that consultation shall be effected immediately after taking such action.

3. (a) If agreement among the interested contracting parties with respect to the action is not reached, the contracting party which proposes to take or continue the action shall, nevertheless, be free to do so, and if such action is taken or continued, the affected contracting parties shall then be free, not later than ninety days after such action is taken, to suspend, upon the expiration of thirty days from the day on which written notice of such suspension is received by the CONTRACTING PARTIES, the application to the trade of the contracting party taking such action, or, in the case envisaged in paragraph 1(b) of this Article, to the trade of the contracting party requesting such action, of such substantially equivalent concessions or other obligations under this Agreement the suspension of which the CONTRACTING PARTIES do not disapprove.

(b) Notwithstanding the provisions of sub-paragraph (a) of this paragraph, where action is taken under paragraph 2 of this Article without prior consultation and causes or threatens serious injury in the territory of a contracting party to the domestic producers of products affected by the action, that contracting party shall, where delay would cause damage difficult to repair, be free to suspend, upon the taking of the action and throughout the period of consultation, such concessions or other obligations as may be necessary to prevent or remedy the injury.

ARTICLE XX. GENERAL EXCEPTIONS

Subject to the requirement that such measures are not applied in a manner which would constitute a means of arbitrary or unjustifiable discrimination between countries where the same conditions prevail, or a disguised restriction on international trade, nothing in this Agreement shall be construed to prevent the adoption or enforcement by any contracting party of measures:

(a) necessary to protect public morals;

(b) necessary to protect human, animal or plant life or health;

(c) relating to the importation or exportation of gold or silver;

(d) necessary to secure compliance with laws or regulations which are not inconsistent with the provisions of this Agreement, including those relating to customs enforcement, the enforcement of monopolies operated under paragraph 4 of Article II and Article XVII, the protection of patents, trade marks and copyrights, and the prevention of deceptive practices;

(e) relating to the products of prison labour;

(f) imposed for the protection of national treasures of artistic, historic or archaeological value;

(g) relating to the conservation of exhaustible natural resources if such measures are made effective in conjunction with restrictions on domestic production or consumption;

(h) undertaken in pursuance of obligations under any intergovernmental commodity agreement which conforms to criteria submitted to the CONTRACTING PARTIES and not disapproved by them or which is itself so submitted and not so disapproved;

Ad *Article XX*

Sub-paragraph (h)

The exception provided for in this sub-paragraph extends to any commodity agreement which conforms to the principles approved by the Economic and Social Council in its resolution 30(IV) of 28 March 1947.

(i) involving restrictions on exports of domestic materials necessary to ensure essential quantities of such materials to a domestic processing industry during periods when the domestic price of such materials is held below the world price as part of a governmental stabilization plan; *Provided* that such restrictions shall not operate to increase the exports of or the protection afforded to such domestic industry, and shall not depart from the provisions of this Agreement relating to non-discrimination;

(j) essential to the acquisition or distribution of products in general or local short supply; *Provided* that any such measures shall be consistent with the principle that all contracting parties are entitled to an equitable share of the international supply of such products, and that any such measures, which are inconsistent with the other provisions of this Agreement shall be discontinued as soon as the conditions giving rise to them have ceased to exist. The CONTRACTING PARTIES shall review the need for this sub-paragraph not later than 30 June 1960.

ARTICLE XXI. SECURITY EXCEPTIONS

Nothing in this Agreement shall be construed

(a) to require any contracting party to furnish any information the disclosure of which it considers contrary to its essential security interests; or

(b) to prevent any contracting party from taking any action which it considers necessary for the protection of its essential security interests

(i) relating to fissionable materials or the materials from which they are derived;

(ii) relating to the traffic in arms, ammunition and implements of war and to such traffic in other goods and materials as is carried on directly or indirectly for the purpose of supplying a military establishment;

(iii) taken in time of war or other emergency in international relations; or

(c) to prevent any contracting party from taking any action in pursuance of its obligations under the United Nations Charter for the maintenance of international peace and security.

ARTICLE XXII. CONSULTATION

1. Each contracting party shall accord sympathetic consideration to, and shall afford adequate opportunity for consultation regarding, such representations as may be made by another contracting party with respect to any matter affecting the operation of this Agreement.

2. The CONTRACTING PARTIES may, at the request of a contracting party, consult with any contracting party or parties in respect of any matter for which it has not been possible to find a satisfactory solution through consultation under paragraph 1.

ARTICLE XXIII. NULLIFICATION OR IMPAIRMENT

1. If any contracting party should consider that any benefit accruing to it directly or indirectly under this Agreement is being nullified or impaired or that the attainment of any objective of the Agreement is being impeded as the result of

(a) the failure of another contracting party to carry out its obligations under this Agreement, or

(b) the application by another contracting party of any measure, whether or not it conflicts with the provisions of this Agreement, or

(c) the existence of any other situation,

the contracting party may, with a view to the satisfactory adjustment of the matter, make written representations or proposals to the other contracting party or parties which it considers to be concerned. Any contracting party thus approached shall give sympathetic consideration to the representations or proposals made to it.

2. If no satisfactory adjustment is effected between the contracting parties concerned within a reasonable time, or if the difficulty is of the type described in paragraph 1(c) of this Article, the matter may be referred to the CONTRACTING PARTIES. The CONTRACTING PARTIES shall promptly investigate any matter so referred to them and shall make appropriate recommendations to the contracting parties which they consider to be concerned, or give a ruling on the matter, as appropriate. The CONTRACTING PARTIES may consult with contracting parties, with the Economic and Social Council of the United Nations and with any appropriate inter-governmental organization in cases where they consider such consultation necessary. If the CONTRACTING PARTIES consider that the circumstances are serious enough to justify such action, they may authorize a contracting party or parties to suspend the application to any other contracting party or parties of such concessions or other obligations under this Agreement as they determine to be appropriate in the circumstances. If the application to any contracting party of any concession or other obligation is in fact suspended, that contracting party shall then be free, not later than sixty days after such action is taken, to give written notice to the Executive Secretary to the CONTRACTING PARTIES of its intention to withdraw from this Agreement and such withdrawal shall take effect upon the sixtieth day following the day on which such notice is received by him.

PART III

ARTICLE XXIV. TERRITORIAL APPLICATION—FRONTIER TRAFFIC—CUSTOMS UNIONS AND FREE-TRADE AREAS

1. The provisions of this Agreement shall apply to the metropolitan customs territories of the contracting parties and to any other customs territories in respect of which this Agreement has been accepted under Article XXVI or is being applied under Article XXXIII or pursuant to the Protocol of Provisional Application. Each such customs territory shall, exclusively for the purposes of the territorial application of this Agreement, be treated as though it were a contracting party; *Provided* that the provisions of this paragraph shall not be construed to create any rights or

obligations as between two or more customs territories in respect of which this Agreement has been accepted under Article XXVI or is being applied under Article XXXIII or pursuant to the Protocol of Provisional Application by a single contracting party.

2. For the purposes of this Agreement a customs territory shall be understood to mean any territory with respect to which separate tariffs or other regulations of commerce are maintained for a substantial part of the trade of such territory with other territories.

3. The provisions of this Agreement shall not be construed to prevent:

(a) Advantages accorded by any contracting party to adjacent countries in order to facilitate frontier traffic;

(b) Advantages accorded to the trade with the Free Territory of Trieste by countries contiguous to that territory, provided that such advantages are not in conflict with the Treaties of Peace arising out of the Second World War.

4. The contracting parties recognize the desirability of increasing freedom of trade by the development, through voluntary agreements, of closer integration between the economies of the countries parties to such agreements. They also recognize that the purpose of a customs union or of a free-trade area should be to facilitate trade between the constituent territories and not to raise barriers to the trade of other contracting parties with such territories.

5. Accordingly, the provisions of this Agreement shall not prevent, as between the territories of contracting parties, the formation of a customs union or of a free-trade area or the adoption of an interim agreement necessary for the formation of a customs union or of a free-trade area; *Provided* that:

(a) with respect to a customs union, or an interim agreement leading to the formation of a customs union, the duties and other regulations of commerce imposed at the institution of any such union or interim agreement in respect of trade with contracting parties not parties to such union or agreement shall not on the whole be higher or more restrictive than the general incidence of the duties and regulations of commerce applicable in the constituent territories prior to the formation of such union or the adoption of such interim agreement, as the case may be;

(b) with respect to a free-trade area, or an interim agreement leading to the formation of a free-trade area, the duties and other regulations of commerce maintained in each of the constituent territories and applicable at the formation of such free-trade area or the adoption of such interim agreement to the trade of contracting parties not included in such area or not parties to such agreement shall not be higher or more restrictive than the corresponding duties and other regulations of commerce existing in the same constituent territories prior to the formation of the free-trade area, or interim agreement, as the case may be; and

(c) any interim agreement referred to in sub-paragraphs (a) and (b) shall include a plan and schedule for the formation of such a customs union or of such a free-trade area within a reasonable length of time.

6. If, in fulfilling the requirements of sub-paragraph 5(a), a contracting party proposes to increase any rate of duty inconsistently with the provisions of Article II, the procedure set forth in Article XXXVIII shall apply. In providing for compensatory adjustment, due account shall be taken of the compensation already afforded by the reductions brought about in the corresponding duty of the other constituents of the union.

7. (a) Any contracting party deciding to enter into a customs union or free-trade area, or an interim agreement leading to the formation of such a union or area, shall promptly notify the CONTRACTING PARTIES and shall make available to them such information regarding the proposed union or area as will enable them to make such reports and recommendations to contracting parties as they may deem appropriate.

(b) If, after having studied the plan and schedule included in an interim agreement referred to in paragraph 5 in consultation with the parties to that agreement and taking due account of the information made available in accordance with the provisions of sub-paragraph (a), the CONTRACTING PARTIES find that such agreement is not likely to result in the formation of a customs union or of a free-trade area within the period contemplated by the parties to the agreement or that such period is not a reasonable one, the CONTRACTING PARTIES shall make recommendations to the parties to the agreement. The parties shall not maintain or put into force, as the case may be, such agreement if they are not prepared to modify it in accordance with these recommendations.

(c) Any substantial change in the plan or schedule referred to in paragraph 5(c) shall be communicated to the CONTRACTING PARTIES, which may request the contracting parties concerned to consult with them if the change seems likely to jeopardize or delay unduly the formation of the customs union or of the free-trade area.

8. For the purposes of this Agreement:

(a) A customs union shall be understood to mean the substitution of a single customs territory for two or more customs territories, so that

(i) duties and other restrictive regulations of commerce (except, where necessary, those permitted under Articles XI, XII, XIII, XIV, XV and XX) are eliminated with respect to substantially all the trade between the constituent territories of the union or at least with respect to substantially all the trade in products originating in such territories, and,

(ii) subject to the provisions of paragraph 9, substantially the same duties and other regulations of commerce are applied by each of the members of the union to the trade of territories not included in the union;

(b) A free-trade area shall be understood to mean a group of two or more customs territories in which the duties and other restrictive regulations of commerce (except, where necessary, those permitted under Articles XI, XII, XIII, XIV, XV and XX) are eliminated on substantially all the trade between the constituent territories in products originating in such territories.

9. The preferences referred to in paragraph 2 of Article I shall not be affected by the formation of a customs union or of a free-trade area but may be eliminated or adjusted by means of negotiations with contracting parties affected. This procedure of negotiations with affected contracting parties shall, in particular, apply to the elimination of preferences required to conform with the provisions of paragraph 8(a)(i) and paragraph 8(b).

Ad *Article XXIV*

Paragraph 9

It is understood that the provisions of Article I would require that, when a product which has been imported into the territory of a member of a customs union or free-trade area at a preferential rate of duty is re-exported to the territory of another member of such union or area, the latter member should collect a duty equal to the difference between the duty already paid and any higher duty that would be payable if the product were being imported directly into its territory.

---

10. The CONTRACTING PARTIES may by a two-thirds majority approve proposals which do not fully comply with the requirements of paragraphs 5 to 9 inclusive, provided that such proposals lead to the formation of a customs union or a free-trade area in the sense of this Article.

11. Taking into account the exceptional circumstances arising out of the establishment of India and Pakistan as independent States and recognizing the fact that they have long constituted an economic unit, the contracting parties agree that the provisions of this Agreement shall not

prevent the two countries from entering into special arrangements with respect to the trade between them, pending the establishment of their mutual trade relations on a definitive basis.

Ad *Article XXIV*

Paragraph 11

Measures adopted by India and Pakistan in order to carry out definitive trade arrangements between them, once they have been agreed upon, might depart from particular provisions of this Agreement, but these measures would in general be consistent with the objectives of the Agreement.

---

12. Each contracting party shall take such reasonable measures as may be available to it to ensure observance of the provisions of this Agreement by the regional and local governments and authorities within its territory.

ARTICLE XXV. JOINT ACTION BY THE CONTRACTING PARTIES

Article XXV

Joint Action by the Contracting Parties

1. Representatives of the contracting parties shall meet from time to time for the purpose of giving effect to those provisions of this Agreement which involve joint action and, generally, with a view to facilitating the operation and furthering the objectives of this Agreement. Wherever reference is made in this Agreement to the contracting parties acting jointly they are designated as the CONTRACTING PARTIES.

2. The Secretary-General of the United Nations is requested to convene the first meeting of the CONTRACTING PARTIES, which shall take place not later than March 1, 1948.

3. Each contracting party shall be entitled to have one vote at all meetings of the CONTRACTING PARTIES.

4. Except as otherwise provided for in this Agreement, decisions of the CONTRACTING PARTIES shall be taken by a majority of the votes cast.

5. In exceptional circumstances not elsewhere provided for in this Agreement, the CONTRACTING PARTIES may waive an obligation imposed upon a contracting party by this Agreement; *Provided* that any such decision shall be approved by a two-thirds majority of the votes cast and that such majority shall comprise more than half of the contracting parties. The CONTRACTING PARTIES may also by such a vote

(i) define certain categories of exceptional circumstances to which other voting requirements shall apply for the waiver of obligations, and

(ii) prescribe such criteria as may be necessary for the application of this paragraph.

* * *

ARTICLE XXVI. ACCEPTANCE, ENTRY INTO FORCE AND REGISTRATION

1. The date of this Agreement shall be 30 October 1947.

2. This Agreement shall be open for acceptance by any contracting party which, on 1 March 1955, was a contracting party or was negotiating with a view to accession to this Agreement.

3. This Agreement, done in a single English original and in a single French original, both texts authentic, shall be deposited with the Secretary-General of the United Nations, who shall furnish certified copies thereof to all interested governments.

* * *

6. This Agreement shall enter into force, as among the governments which have accepted it, on the thirtieth day following the day on which instruments of acceptance have been deposited with the Executive Secretary* to the CONTRACTING PARTIES on behalf of governments named in Annex H, the territories of which account for 85 per centum of the total external trade of the territories of such governments, computed in accordance with the applicable column of percentages set forth therein. The instrument of acceptance of each other government shall take effect on the thirtieth day following the day on which such instrument has been deposited.

7. The United Nations is authorized to effect registration of this Agreement as soon as it enters into force.

ARTICLE XXVII. WITHHOLDING OR WITHDRAWAL OF CONCESSIONS

Any contracting party shall at any time be free to withhold or to withdraw in whole or in part any concession, provided for in the appropriate Schedule annexed to this Agreement, in respect of which such contracting party determines that it was initially negotiated with a government which has not become, or has ceased to be, a contracting party. A contracting party taking such action shall notify the CONTRACTING

* Now referred to as Director-General.

PARTIES and, upon request, consult with contracting parties which have a substantial interest in the product concerned.

ARTICLE XXVIII. MODIFICATION OF SCHEDULES

Modification of Schedules

1. On the first day of each three-year period, the first period beginning on 1 January 1958 (or on the first day of any other period* that may be specified by the CONTRACTING PARTIES by two-thirds of the votes cast) a contracting party (hereafter in this Article referred to as the "applicant contracting party") may, by negotiations and agreement with any contracting party with which such concession was initially negotiated and with any other contracting party determined by the CONTRACTING PARTIES to have a principal supplying interest* (which two preceding categories of contracting parties, together with the applicant contracting party, are in this Article hereinafter referred to as the "contracting parties primarily concerned"), and subject to consultation with any other contracting party determined by the CONTRACTING PARTIES to have a substantial interest* in such concession, modify or withdraw a concession* included in the appropriate Schedule annexed to this Agreement.

2. In such negotiations and agreement, which may include provision for compensatory adjustment with respect to other products, the contracting parties concerned shall endeavour to maintain a general level of reciprocal and mutually advantageous concessions not less favourable to trade than that provided for in this Agreement prior to such negotiations.

3. (*a*) If agreement between the contracting parties primarily concerned cannot be reached before 1 January 1958 or before the expiration of a period envisaged in paragraph 1 of this Article, the contracting party which proposes to modify or withdraw the concession shall, nevertheless, be free to do so and if such action is taken any contracting party with which such concession was initially negotiated, any contracting party determined under paragraph 1 to have a principal supplying interest and any contracting party determined under paragraph 1 to have a substantial interest shall then be free not later than six months after such action is taken, to withdraw, upon the expiration of thirty days from the day on which written notice of such withdrawal is received by the CONTRACTING PARTIES, substantially equivalent concessions initially negotiated with the applicant contracting party.

(*b*) If agreement between the contracting parties primarily concerned is reached but any other contracting party determined under paragraph 1 of this Article to have a substantial interest is not satisfied, such other contracting party shall be free, not later than six months after action under such agreement is taken, to withdraw, upon the expiration of thirty days from the day on which written notice of such withdrawal is received by the

CONTRACTING PARTIES, substantially equivalent concessions initially negotiated with the applicant contracting party.

4. The CONTRACTING PARTIES may, at any time, in special circumstances, authorize* a contracting party to enter into negotiations for modification or withdrawal of a concession included in the appropriate Schedule annexed to this Agreement subject to the following procedures and conditions:

(*a*) Such negotiations* and any related consultations shall be conducted in accordance with the provisions of paragraphs 1 and 2 of this Article.

(*b*) If agreement between the contracting parties primarily concerned is reached in the negotiations, the provisions of paragraph 3(*b*) of this Article shall apply.

(*c*) If agreement between the contracting parties primarily concerned is not reached within a period of sixty days* after negotiations have been authorized, or within such longer period as the CONTRACTING PARTIES may have prescribed, the applicant contracting party may refer the matter to the CONTRACTING PARTIES.

(*d*) Upon such reference, the CONTRACTING PARTIES shall promptly examine the matter and submit their views to the contracting parties primarily concerned with the aim of achieving a settlement. If a settlement is reached, the provisions of paragraph 3(*b*) shall apply as if agreement between the contracting parties primarily concerned had been reached. If no settlement is reached between the contracting parties primarily concerned, the applicant contracting party shall be free to modify or withdraw the concession, unless the CONTRACTING PARTIES determine that the applicant contracting party has unreasonably failed to offer adequate compensation.* If such action is taken, any contracting party with which the concession was initially negotiated, any contracting party determined under paragraph 4(*a*) to have a principal supplying interest and any contracting party determined under paragraph 4(*a*) to have a substantial interest, shall be free, not later than six months after such action is taken, to modify or withdraw, upon the expiration of thirty days from the day on which written notice of such withdrawal is received by the CONTRACTING PARTIES, substantially equivalent concessions initially negotiated with the applicant contracting party.

5. Before 1 January 1958 and before the end of any period envisaged in paragraph 1 a contracting party may elect by notifying the CONTRACTING PARTIES to reserve the right, for the duration of the next period, to modify the appropriate Schedule in accordance with the procedures of paragraphs 1 to 3. If a contracting party so elects, other

contracting parties shall have the right, during the same period, to modify or withdraw, in accordance with the same procedures, concessions initially negotiated with that contracting party.

ARTICLE XXVIII bis. TARIFF NEGOTIATIONS

1. The contracting parties recognize that customs duties often constitute serious obstacles to trade; thus negotiations on a reciprocal and mutually advantageous basis, directed to the substantial reduction of the general level of tariffs and other charges on imports and exports and in particular to the reduction of such high tariffs as discourage the importation even of minimum quantities, and conducted with due regard to the objectives of this Agreement and the varying needs of individual contracting parties, are of great importance to the expansion of international trade. The CONTRACTING PARTIES may therefore sponsor such negotiations from time to time.

2. (a) Negotiations under this Article may be carried out on a selective product-by-product basis or by the application of such multilateral procedures as may be accepted by the contracting parties concerned. Such negotiations may be directed towards the reduction of duties, the binding of duties at then existing levels or undertakings that individual duties or the average duties on specified categories of products shall not exceed specified levels. The binding against increase of low duties or of duty-free treatment shall, in principle, be recognized as a concession equivalent in value to the reduction of high duties.

(b) The contracting parties recognize that in general the success of multilateral negotiations would depend on the participation of all contracting parties which conduct a substantial proportion of their external trade with one another.

3. Negotiations shall be conducted on a basis which affords adequate opportunity to take into account:

(a) the needs of individual contracting parties and individual industries;

(b) the needs of less-developed countries for a more flexible use of tariff protection to assist their economic development and the special needs of these countries to maintain tariffs for revenue purposes; and

(c) all other relevant circumstances, including the fiscal, developmental, strategic and other needs of the contracting parties concerned.

Ad *Article XXVIII* bis

Paragraph 3

It is understood that the reference to fiscal needs would include the revenue aspect of duties and particularly duties imposed primarily for revenue purposes or duties imposed on products which can be substituted for products subject to revenue duties to prevent the avoidance of such duties.

ARTICLE XXIX. THE RELATION OF THIS AGREEMENT TO THE HAVANA CHARTER (omitted)

* * *

ARTICLE XXX. AMENDMENTS

1. Except where provision for modification is made elsewhere in this Agreement, amendments to the provisions of Part I of this Agreement or to the provisions of Article XXIX or of this Article shall become effective upon acceptance by all the contracting parties, and other amendments to this Agreement shall become effective, in respect of those contracting parties which accept them, upon acceptance by two-thirds of the contracting parties and thereafter for each other contracting party upon acceptance by it.

2. Any contracting party accepting an amendment to this Agreement shall deposit an instrument of acceptance with the Secretary-General of the United Nations within such period as the CONTRACTING PARTIES may specify. The CONTRACTING PARTIES may decide that any amendment made effective under this Article is of such a nature that any contracting party which has not accepted it within a period specified by the CONTRACTING PARTIES shall be free to withdrawn from this Agreement, or to remain a contracting party with the consent of the CONTRACTING PARTIES.

ARTICLE XXXI. WITHDRAWAL

Without prejudice to the provisions of paragraph 12 of Article XVIII, of Article XXIII or of paragraph 2 of Article XXX, any contracting party may withdraw from this Agreement, or may separately withdraw on behalf of any of the separate customs territories for which it has international responsibility and which at the time possesses full autonomy in the conduct of its external commercial relations and of the other matters provided for in this Agreement. The withdrawal shall take effect upon the expiration of six months from the day on which written notice of withdrawal is received by the Secretary-General of the United Nations.

ARTICLE XXXII. CONTRACTING PARTIES

1. The contracting parties to this Agreement shall be understood to mean those governments which are applying the provisions of this Agreement under Article XXVI or XXXIII or pursuant to the Protocol of Provisional Application.

2. At any time after the entry into force of this Agreement pursuant to paragraph 6 of Article XXVI, those contracting parties which have accepted this Agreement pursuant to paragraph 4 of Article XXVI may decide that any contracting party which has not so accepted it shall cease to be a contracting party.

ARTICLE XXXIII. ACCESSION

A government not party to this Agreement, or a government acting on behalf of a separate customs territory possessing full autonomy in the conduct of its external commercial relations and of the other matters provided for in this Agreement, may accede to this Agreement, on its own behalf or on behalf of that territory, on terms to be agreed between such government and the CONTRACTING PARTIES. Decisions of the CONTRACTING PARTIES under this paragraph shall be taken by a two-thirds majority.

ARTICLE XXXIV. ANNEXES

The annexes to this Agreement are hereby made an integral part of this Agreement.

ARTICLE XXXV. NON-APPLICATION OF THE AGREEMENT BETWEEN PARTICULAR CONTRACTING PARTIES

1. This Agreement, or alternatively Article II of this Agreement, shall not apply as between any contracting party and any other contracting party if:

(a) the two contracting parties have not entered into tariff negotiations with each other, and

(b) either of the contracting parties, at the time either becomes a contracting party, does not consent to such application.

2. The CONTRACTING PARTIES may review the operation of this Article in particular cases at the request of any contracting party and make appropriate recommendations.

PART IV. TRADE AND DEVELOPMENT

Ad *Part IV*

The words "developed contracting parties" and the words "less-developed contracting parties," as used in Part IV are to be understood to refer to developed and less-developed countries which are parties to the General Agreement on Tariffs and Trade.

ARTICLE XXXVI. PRINCIPLES AND OBJECTIVES

1. The contracting parties,

(a) recalling that the basic objectives of this Agreement include the raising of standards of living and the progressive development of the economies of all contracting parties, and considering that the attainment of these objectives is particularly urgent for less-developed contracting parties;

(b) considering that export earnings of the less-developed contracting parties can play a vital part in their economic development and that the extent of this contribution depends on the prices paid by the less-developed contracting parties for essential imports, the volume of their exports, and the prices received for these exports;

(c) noting, that there is a wide gap between standards of living in less-developed countries and in other countries;

(d) recognizing that individual and joint action is essential to further the development of the economies of less-developed contracting parties and to bring about a rapid advance in the standards of living in these countries;

(e) recognizing that international trade as a means of achieving economic and social advancement should be governed by such rules and procedures—and measures in conformity with such rules and procedures—as are consistent with the objectives set forth in this Article;

(f) noting that the CONTRACTING PARTIES may enable less-developed contracting parties to use special measures to promote their trade and development;

agree as follows.

Ad *Article XXXVI*

Paragraph 1

This Article is based upon the objectives set forth in Article I as it will be amended by Section A of paragraph 1 of the Protocol Amending Part I and Articles XXIX and XXX when that Protocol enters into force.[1]

---

[1] This Protocol was abandoned on January 1, 1968.

---

2. There is need for a rapid and sustained expansion of the export earnings of the less-developed contracting parties.

3. There is need for positive efforts designed to ensure that less-developed contracting parties secure a share in the growth in international trade commensurate with the needs of their economic development.

4. Given the continued dependence of many less-developed contracting parties on the exportation of a limited range of primary products, there is need to provide in the largest possible measure more favourable and acceptable conditions of access to world markets for these products, and wherever appropriate to devise measures designed to stabilize and improve conditions of world markets in these products, including in particular measures designed to attain stable, equitable and remunerative prices, thus permitting an expansion of world trade and demand and a dynamic and steady growth of the real export earnings of these countries so as to provide them with expanding resources for their economic development.

Ad *Article XXXVI*

Paragraph 4

The term "primary products" includes agricultural products, *vide* paragraph 2 of the note ad Article XVI, Section B.

---

5. The rapid expansion of the economies of the less-developed contracting parties will be facilitated by a diversification of the structure of their economies and the avoidance of an excessive dependence on the export of primary products. There is, therefore, need for increased access in the largest possible measure to markets under favourable conditions for processed and manufactured products currently or potentially of particular export interest to less-developed contracting parties.

Ad *Article XXXVI*

Paragraph 5

A diversification programme would generally include the intensification of activities for the processing of primary products and the development of manufacturing industries, taking into account the situation of the particular contracting party and the world outlook for production and consumption of different commodities.

---

6. Because of the chronic deficiency in the export proceeds and other foreign exchange earnings of less-developed contracting parties, there are important inter-relationships between trade and financial assistance to development. There is, therefore, need for close and continuing collaboration between the CONTRACTING PARTIES and the international lending agencies so that they can contribute most effectively to alleviating the burdens these less-developed contracting parties assume in the interest of their economic development.

7. There is need for appropriate collaboration between the CONTRACTING PARTIES, other intergovernmental bodies and the organs and agencies of the United Nations system, whose activities relate to the trade and economic development of less-developed countries.

8. The developed contracting parties do not expect reciprocity for commitments made by them in trade negotiations to reduce or remove tariffs and other barriers to the trade of less-developed contracting parties.

Ad *Article XXXVI*

Paragraph 8

It is understood that the phrase "do not expect reciprocity" means, in accordance with the objectives set forth in this Article, that the less-developed contracting parties should not be expected, in the course of trade negotiations, to make contributions which are inconsistent with their individual development, financial and trade needs, taking into consideration past trade developments.

This paragraph would apply in the event of action under Section A of Article XVII, Article XXVIII, Article XXVIII bis (Article XXIX after the amendment set forth in Section A of paragraph 1 of the Protocol Amending Part I and Articles XXIX and XXX shall have become effective), Article XXXIII, or any other procedure under this Agreement.

---

9. The adoption of measures to give effect to these principles and objectives shall be a matter of conscious and purposeful effort on the part of the contracting parties both individually and jointly.

ARTICLE XXXVII. COMMITMENTS

1. The developed contracting parties shall to the fullest extent possible—that is, except when compelling reasons, which may include legal reasons, make it impossible—give effect to the following provisions:

(a) accord high priority to the reduction and elimination of barriers to products currently or potentially of particular export interest to less-developed contracting parties, including customs duties and other restrictions which differentiate unreasonably between such products in their primary and in their processed forms;

Ad *Article XXXVII*

Paragraph 1(a)

This paragraph would apply in the event of negotiations for reduction or elimination of tariffs or other restrictive regulations of commerce under Articles XXVIII, XXVIII *bis* (XXIX after the amendment set forth in Section A of paragraph 1 of the Protocol Amending Part I and Articles XXIX and XXX shall have become effective [1]), and Article XXXIII, as well as in connexion with other action to effect such reduction or elimination which contracting parties may be able to undertake.

(b) refrain from introducing, or increasing the incidence of, customs duties or non-tariff import barriers on products currently or potentially of particular export interest to less-developed contracting parties; and

(c)(i) refrain from imposing new fiscal measures, and

(ii) in any adjustments of fiscal policy accord high priority to the reduction and elimination of fiscal measures,

which would hamper, or which hamper, significantly the growth of consumption of primary products, in raw or processed form, wholly or mainly produced in the territories of less-developed contracting parties, and which are applied specifically to those products.

2. (a) Whenever it is considered that effect is not being given to any of the provisions of sub-paragraph (a), (b) or (c) of paragraph 1, the matter shall be reported to the CONTRACTING PARTIES either by the contracting party not so giving effect to the relevant provisions or by any other interested contracting party.

(b)(i) The CONTRACTING PARTIES shall, if requested so to do by any interested contracting party, and without prejudice to any bilateral consultations that may be undertaken, consult with the contracting party concerned and all interested contracting parties with respect to the matter with a view to reaching solutions satisfactory to all contracting parties concerned in order to further the objectives set forth in Article XXXVI. In the course of these consultations, the reasons given in cases where effect was not being given to the provisions of subparagraph (a), (b) or (c) of paragraph 1 shall be examined.

(ii) As the implementation of the provisions of sub-paragraph (a), (b) or (c) of paragraph 1 by individual contracting parties may

---

[1] This Protocol was abandoned on January 1, 1968.

in some cases be more readily achieved where action is taken jointly with other developed contracting parties, such consultation might, where appropriate, be directed towards this end.

(iii) The consultations by the CONTRACTING PARTIES might also, in appropriate cases, be directed towards agreement on joint action designed to further the objectives of this Agreement as envisaged in paragraph 1 of Article XXV.

3. The developed contracting parties shall:

(a) make every effort, in cases where a government directly or indirectly determines the resale price of products wholly or mainly produced in the territories of less-developed contracting parties, to maintain trade margins at equitable levels;

(b) give active consideration to the adoption of other measures designed to provide greater scope for the development of imports from less-developed contracting parties and collaborate in appropriate international action to this end;

Ad *Article XXXVII*

Paragraph 3(b)

The other measures referred to in this paragraph might include steps to promote domestic structural changes, to encourage the consumption of particular products, or to introduce measures of trade promotion.

(c) have special regard to the trade interests of less-developed contracting parties when considering the application of other measures permitted under this Agreement to meet particular problems and explore all possibilities of constructive remedies before applying such measures where they would affect essential interests of those contracting parties.

4. Less-developed contracting parties agree to take appropriate action in implementation of the provisions of Part IV for the benefit of the trade of other less-developed contracting parties, in so far as such action is consistent with their individual present and future development, financial and trade needs taking into account past trade developments as well as the trade interests of less-developed contracting parties as a whole.

5. In the implementation of the commitments set forth in paragraphs 1 to 4 each contracting party shall afford to any other interested contracting party or contracting parties full and prompt opportunity for consultations under the normal procedures of this Agreement with respect to any matter or difficulty which may arise.

ARTICLE XXXVIII. JOINT ACTION (omitted)

* * *

ANNEX A

LIST OF TERRITORIES REFERRED TO IN PARAGRAPH 2(A) OF ARTICLE I

United Kingdom of Great Britain and Northern Ireland

Dependent territories of the United Kingdom of Great Britain and Northern Ireland

Canada

Commonwealth of Australia

Dependent territories of the Commonwealth of Australia

New Zealand

Dependent territories of New Zealand

Union of South Africa including South West Africa

Ireland

India (as of April 10, 1947)

Newfoundland

Southern Rhodesia

Burma

Ceylon

Certain of the territories listed above have two or more preferential rates in force for certain products. Any such territory may, by agreement with the other contracting parties which are principal suppliers of such products at the most-favoured-nation rate, substitute for such preferential rates a single preferential rate which shall not on the whole be less favourable to suppliers at the most-favoured-nation rate than the preferences in force prior to such substitution.

The imposition of an equivalent margin of tariff preference to replace a margin of preference in an internal tax existing on April 10, 1947 exclusively between two or more of the territories listed in this Annex or to replace the preferential quantitative arrangements described in the following paragraph, shall not be deemed to constitute an increase in a margin of tariff preference.

The preferential arrangements referred to in paragraph 5(b) of Article XIV are those existing in the United Kingdom on April 10, 1947, under contractual agreements with the Governments of Canada, Australia and New Zealand, in respect of chilled and frozen beef and veal, frozen mutton and lamb, chilled and frozen pork, and bacon. It is the intention, without prejudice to any action taken under subparagraph (h) of Article XX, that these arrangements shall be eliminated or replaced by tariff preferences, and that negotiations to this end shall take place as soon as practicable among the countries substantially concerned or involved.

The film hire tax in force in New Zealand on April 10, 1947, shall, for the purposes of this Agreement, be treated as a customs duty under Article I. The renters' film quota in force in New Zealand on April 10, 1947, shall, for the purposes of this Agreement, be treated as a screen quota under Article IV.

The Dominions of India and Pakistan have not been mentioned separately in the above list since they had not come into existence as such on the base date of April 10, 1947.

* * *

ANNEX H

Percentage Shares of Total External Trade to be Used for the Purpose of Making the Determination Referred to in Article XXVI

(based on the average of 1949–1953)

If, prior to the accession of the Government of Japan to the General Agreement, the present Agreement has been accepted by contracting parties the external trade of which under column I accounts for the percentage of such trade specified in paragraph 6 of Article XXVI, column I shall be applicable for the purposes of that paragraph. If the present Agreement has not been so accepted prior to the accession of the Government of Japan, column II shall be applicable for the purposes of that paragraph.

	Column I (Contracting parties on 1 March 1955)	*Column II* (Contracting parties on 1 March 1955 and Japan)
Australia	3.1	3.0
Austria	0.9	0.8
Belgium-Luxemburg	4.3	4.2
Brazil	2.5	2.4
Burma	0.3	0.3
Canada	6.7	6.5
Ceylon	0.5	0.5

	Column I (Contracting parties on 1 March 1955)	*Column II* (Contracting parties on 1 March 1955 and Japan)
Chile	0.6	0.6
Cuba	1.1	1.1
Czechoslovakia	1.4	1.4
Denmark	1.4	1.4
Dominican Republic	0.1	0.1
Finland	1.0	1.0
France	8.7	8.5
Germany, Federal Republic of	5.3	5.2
Greece	0.4	0.4
Haiti	0.1	0.1
India	2.4	2.4
Indonesia	1.3	1.3
Italy	2.9	2.8
Netherlands, Kingdom of the	4.7	4.6
New Zealand	1.0	1.0
Nicaragua	0.1	0.1
Norway	1.1	1.1
Pakistan	0.9	0.8
Peru	0.4	0.4
Rhodesia and Nyasaland	0.6	0.6
Sweden	2.5	2.4
Turkey	0.6	0.6
Union of South Africa	1.8	1.8
United Kingdom	20.3	19.8
United States of America	20.6	20.1
Uruguay	0.4	0.4

	Column I	*Column II*
	(Contracting parties on 1 March 1955)	(Contracting parties on 1 March 1955 and Japan)
Japan	—	2.3
	100.0	100.0

Note: These percentages have been computed taking into account the trade of all territories in respect of which the General Agreement on Tariffs and Trade is applied.

DOCUMENT 10

GENERAL AGREEMENT ON TARIFFS AND TRADE (1994)

■ ■ ■

1. The General Agreement on Tariffs and Trade 1994 ("GATT 1994") shall consist of:

(a) the provisions in the General Agreement on Tariffs and Trade, dated 30 October 1947, annexed to the Final Act Adopted at the Conclusion of the Second Session of the Preparatory Committee of the United Nations Conference on Trade and Employment (excluding the Protocol of Provisional Application), as rectified, amended or modified by the terms of legal instruments which have entered into force before the date of entry into force of the WTO Agreement;

(b) the provisions of the legal instruments set forth below that have entered into force under GATT 1947 before the date of entry into force of the WTO Agreement:

(i) protocols and certifications relating to tariff concessions;

(ii) protocols of accession (excluding the provisions (a) concerning provisional application and withdrawal of provisional application and (b) providing that Part II of GATT 1947 shall be applied provisionally to the fullest extent not inconsistent with legislation existing on the date of the Protocol);

(iii) decisions on waivers granted under Article XXV of GATT 1947 and still in force on the date of entry into force of the WTO Agreement,

(iv) other decisions of the CONTRACTING PARTIES to GATT 1947;

(c) the Understandings set forth below:

(i) Understanding on the Interpretation of Article II:1(b) of the General Agreement on Tariffs and Trade 1994;

(ii) Understanding on the Interpretation of Article XVII of the General Agreement on Tariffs and Trade 1994;

(iii) Understanding on Balance-of-Payments Provisions of the General Agreement on Tariffs and Trade 1994;

(iv) Understanding on the Interpretation of Article XXIV of the General Agreement on Tariffs and Trade 1994;

(v) Understanding in Respect of Waivers of Obligations under the General Agreement on Tariffs and Trade 1994;

(vi) Understanding on the Interpretation of Article XXVIII of the General Agreement on Tariffs and Trade 1994; and

(d) the Marrakesh Protocol to GATT 1994.

2. *Explanatory Notes*

(a) The references to "contracting party" in the provisions of GATT 1994 shall be deemed to read "Member". The references to "less-developed contracting party" and "developed contracting party" shall be deemed to read "developing country Member" and "developed country Member". The references to "Executive Secretary" shall be deemed to read "Director-General of the WTO".

(b) The references to the CONTRACTING PARTIES acting jointly in Articles XV:1, XV:2, XV:8, XXXVIII and the Notes *Ad* Article XII and XVIII; and in the provisions on special exchange agreements in Articles XV:2, XV:3, XV:6, XV:7 and XV:9 of GATT 1994 shall be deemed to be references to the WTO. The other functions that the provisions of GATT 1994 assign to the CONTRACTING PARTIES acting jointly shall be allocated by the Ministerial Conference.

(c)(i) The text of GATT 1994 shall be authentic in English, French and Spanish.

* * *

UNDERSTANDING ON THE INTERPRETATION OF ARTICLE II:1(b) OF THE GENERAL AGREEMENT ON TARIFFS AND TRADE 1994

Members hereby *agree* as follows:

1. In order to ensure transparency of the legal rights and obligations deriving from paragraph 1(b) of Article II, the nature and level of any "other duties or charges" levied on bound tariff items, as referred to in that provision, shall be recorded in the Schedules of concessions annexed to GATT 1994 against the tariff item to which they apply. It is understood that such recording does not change the legal character of "other duties or charges".

2. The date as of which "other duties or charges" are bound, for the purposes of Article II, shall be 15 April 1994. "Other duties or charges" shall therefore be recorded in the Schedules at the levels applying on this date. At each subsequent renegotiation of a concession or negotiation of a new concession the applicable date for the tariff item in question shall

become the date of the incorporation of the new concession in the appropriate Schedule. However, the date of the instrument by which a concession on any particular tariff item was first incorporated into GATT 1947 or GATT 1994 shall also continue to be recorded in column 6 of the Loose-Leaf Schedules.

3. "Other duties or charges" shall be recorded in respect of all tariff bindings.

4. Where a tariff item has previously been the subject of a concession, the level of "other duties or charges" recorded in the appropriate Schedule shall not be higher than the level obtaining at the time of the first incorporation of the concession in that Schedule. It will be open to any Member to challenge the existence of an "other duty or charge", on the ground that no such "other duty or charge" existed at the time of the original binding of the item in question, as well as the consistency of the recorded level of any "other duty or charge" with the previously bound level, for a period of three years after the date of entry into force of the WTO Agreement or three years after the date of deposit with the Director-General of the WTO of the instrument incorporating the Schedule in question into GATT 1994, if that is a later date.

5. The recording of "other duties or charges" in the Schedules is without prejudice to their consistency with rights and obligations under GATT 1994 other than those affected by paragraph 4. All Members retain the right to challenge, at any time, the consistency of any "other duty or charge" with such obligations.

6. For the purposes of this Understanding, the provisions of Articles XXII and XXIII of GATT 1994 as elaborated and applied by the Dispute Settlement Understanding shall apply.

7. "Other duties or charges" omitted from a Schedule at the time of deposit of the instrument incorporating the Schedule in question into GATT 1994 with, until the date of entry into force of the WTO Agreement, the Director-General to the CONTRACTING PARTIES to GATT 1947 or, thereafter, with the Director-General of the WTO, shall not subsequently be added to it and any "other duty or charge" recorded at a level lower than that prevailing on the applicable date shall not be restored to that level unless such additions or changes are made within six months of the date of deposit of the instrument.

8. The decision in paragraph 2 regarding the date applicable to each concession for the purposes of paragraph 1(b) of Article II of GATT 1994 supersedes the decision regarding the applicable date taken on 26 March 1980 (BISD 27S/24).

* * *

UNDERSTANDING ON THE INTERPRETATION OF ARTICLE XXIV OF THE GENERAL AGREEMENT ON TARIFFS AND TRADE 1994

Members,

Having regard to the provisions of Article XXIV of GATT 1994;

Recognizing that customs unions and free trade areas have greatly increased in number and importance since the establishment of GATT 1947 and today cover a significant proportion of world trade;

Recognizing the contribution to the expansion of world trade that may be made by closer integration between the economies of the parties to such agreements;

Recognizing also that such contribution is increased if the elimination between the constituent territories of duties and other restrictive regulations of commerce extends to all trade, and diminished if any major sector of trade is excluded;

Reaffirming that the purpose of such agreements should be to facilitate trade between the constituent territories and not to raise barriers to the trade of other Members with such territories; and that in their formation or enlargement the parties to them should to the greatest possible extent avoid creating adverse effects on the trade of other Members;

Convinced also of the need to reinforce the effectiveness of the role of the Council for Trade in Goods in reviewing agreements notified under Article XXIV, by clarifying the criteria and procedures for the assessment of new or enlarged agreements, and improving the transparency of all Article XXIV agreements;

Recognizing the need for a common understanding of the obligations of Members under paragraph 12 of Article XXIV;

Hereby *agree* as follows:

1. Customs unions, free-trade areas, and interim agreements leading to the formation of a customs union or free-trade area, to be consistent with Article XXIV, must satisfy, *inter alia,* the provisions of paragraphs 5, 6, 7 and 8 of that Article.

Article XXIV:5

2. The evaluation under paragraph 5(a) of Article XXIV of the general incidence of the duties and other regulations of commerce applicable before and after the formation of a customs union shall in respect of duties and charges be based upon an overall assessment of weighted average tariff rates and of customs duties collected. This assessment shall be based on import statistics for a previous representative period to be supplied by the customs union, on a tariff-line basis and in

values and quantities, broken down by WTO country of origin. The Secretariat shall compute the weighted average tariff rates and customs duties collected in accordance with the methodology used in the assessment of tariff offers in the Uruguay Round of Multilateral Trade Negotiations. For this purpose, the duties and charges to be taken into consideration shall be the applied rates of duty. It is recognized that for the purpose of the overall assessment of the incidence of other regulations of commerce for which quantification and aggregation are difficult, the examination of individual measures, regulations, products covered and trade flows affected may be required.

3. The "reasonable length of time" referred to in paragraph 5(c) of Article XXIV should exceed 10 years only in exceptional cases. In cases where Members parties to an interim agreement believe that 10 years would be insufficient they shall provide a full explanation to the Council for Trade in Goods of the need for a longer period.

Article XXIV:6

4. Paragraph 6 of Article XXIV establishes the procedure to be followed when a Member forming a customs union proposes to increase a bound rate of duty. In this regard Members reaffirm that the procedure set forth in Article XXVIII, as elaborated in the guidelines adopted on 10 November 1980 (BISD 27S/26–28) and in the Understanding on the Interpretation of Article XXVIII of GATT 1994, must be commenced before tariff concessions are modified or withdrawn upon the formation of a customs union or an interim agreement leading to the formation of a customs union.

5. These negotiations will be entered into in good faith with a view to achieving mutually satisfactory compensatory adjustment. In such negotiations, as required by paragraph 6 of Article XXIV, due account shall be taken of reductions of duties on the same tariff line made by other constituents of the customs union upon its formation. Should such reductions not be sufficient to provide the necessary compensatory adjustment, the customs union would offer compensation, which may take the form of reductions of duties on other tariff lines. Such an offer shall be taken into consideration by the Members having negotiating rights in the binding being modified or withdrawn. Should the compensatory adjustment remain unacceptable, negotiations should be continued. Where, despite such efforts, agreement in negotiations on compensatory adjustment under Article XXVIII as elaborated by the Understanding on the Interpretation of Article XXVIII of GATT 1994 cannot be reached within a reasonable period from the initiation of negotiations, the customs union shall, nevertheless, be free to modify or withdraw the concessions; affected Members shall then be free to withdraw substantially equivalent concessions in accordance with Article XXVIII.

6. GATT 1994 imposes no obligation on Members benefiting from a reduction of duties consequent upon the formation of a customs union, or an interim agreement leading to the formation of a customs union, to provide compensatory adjustment to its constituents.

Review of Customs Unions and Free-Trade Areas

7. All notifications made under paragraph 7(a) of Article XXIV shall be examined by a working party in the light of the relevant provisions of GATT 1994 and of paragraph 1 of this Understanding. The working party shall submit a report to the Council for Trade in Goods on its findings in this regard. The Council for Trade in Goods may make such recommendations to Members as it deems appropriate.

8. In regard to interim agreements, the working party may in its report make appropriate recommendations on the proposed time-frame and on measures required to complete the formation of the customs union or free-trade area. It may if necessary provide for further review of the agreement.

9. Members parties to an interim agreement shall notify substantial changes in the plan and schedule included in that agreement to the Council for Trade in Goods and, if so requested, the Council shall examine the changes.

10. Should an interim agreement notified under paragraph 7(a) of Article XXIV not include a plan and schedule, contrary to paragraph 5(c) of Article XXIV, the working party shall in its report recommend such a plan and schedule. The parties shall not maintain or put into force, as the case may be, such agreement if they are not prepared to modify it in accordance with these recommendations. Provision shall be made for subsequent review of the implementation of the recommendations.

11. Customs unions and constituents of free-trade areas shall report periodically to the Council for Trade in Goods, as envisaged by the CONTRACTING PARTIES to GATT 1947 in their instruction to the GATT 1947 Council concerning reports on regional agreements (BISD 18S/38), on the operation of the relevant agreement. Any significant changes and/or developments in the agreements should be reported as they occur.

Dispute Settlement

12. The provisions of Articles XXII and XXIII of GATT 1994 as elaborated and applied by the Dispute Settlement Understanding may be invoked with respect to any matters arising from the application of those provisions of Article XXIV relating to customs unions, free-trade areas or interim agreements leading to the formation of a customs union or free-trade area.

Article XXIV:12

13. Each Member is fully responsible under GATT 1994 for the observance of all provisions of GATT 1994, and shall take such reasonable measures as may be available to it to ensure such observance by regional and local governments and authorities within its territory.

14. The provisions of Articles XXII and XXIII of GATT 1994 as elaborated and applied by the Dispute Settlement Understanding may be invoked in respect of measures affecting its observance taken by regional or local governments or authorities within the territory of a Member. When the Dispute Settlement Body has ruled that a provision of GATT 1994 has not been observed, the responsible Member shall take such reasonable measures as may be available to it to ensure its observance. The provisions relating to compensation and suspension of concessions or other obligations apply in cases where it has not been possible to secure such observance.

15. Each Member undertakes to accord sympathetic consideration to and afford adequate opportunity for consultation regarding any representations made by another Member concerning measures affecting the operation of GATT 1994 taken within the territory of the former.

UNDERSTANDING IN RESPECT OF WAIVERS OF OBLIGATIONS UNDER THE GENERAL AGREEMENT ON TARIFFS AND TRADE 1994

Members hereby *agree* as follows:

1. A request for a waiver or for an extension of an existing waiver shall describe the measures which the Member proposes to take, the specific policy objectives which the Member seeks to pursue and the reasons which prevent the Member from achieving its policy objectives by measures consistent with its obligations under GATT 1994.

2. Any waiver in effect on the date of entry into force of the WTO Agreement shall terminate, unless extended in accordance with the procedures above and those of Article IX of the WTO Agreement, on the date of its expiry or two years from the date of entry into force of the WTO Agreement, whichever is earlier.

3. Any Member considering that a benefit accruing to it under GATT 1994 is being nullified or impaired as a result of:

(a) the failure of the Member to whom a waiver was granted to observe the terms or conditions of the waiver, or

(b) the application of a measure consistent with the terms and conditions of the waiver

may invoke the provisions of Article XXIII of GATT 1994 as elaborated and applied by the Dispute Settlement Understanding.

MARRAKESH PROTOCOL TO THE GENERAL AGREEMENT ON TARIFFS AND TRADE 1994

Members,

Having carried out negotiations within the framework of GATT 1947, pursuant to the Ministerial Declaration on the Uruguay Round,

Hereby *agree* as follows:

1. The schedule annexed to this Protocol relating to a Member shall become a Schedule to GATT 1994 relating to that Member on the day on which the WTO Agreement enters into force for that Member. Any schedule submitted in accordance with the Ministerial Decision on measures in favour of least-developed countries shall be deemed to be annexed to this Protocol.

2. The tariff reductions agreed upon by each Member shall be implemented in five equal rate reductions, except as may be otherwise specified in a Member's Schedule. The first such reduction shall be made effective on the date of entry into force of the WTO Agreement, each successive reduction shall be made effective on 1 January of each of the following years, and the final rate shall become effective no later than the date four years after the date of entry into force of the WTO Agreement, except as may be otherwise specified in that Member's Schedule. Unless otherwise specified in its Schedule, a Member that accepts the WTO Agreement after its entry into force shall, on the date that Agreement enters into force for it, make effective all rate reductions that have already taken place together with the reductions which it would under the preceding sentence have been obligated to make effective on 1 January of the year following, and shall make effective all remaining rate reductions on the schedule specified in the previous sentence. The reduced rate should in each stage be rounded off to the first decimal. For agricultural products, as defined in Article 2 of the Agreement on Agriculture, the staging of reductions shall be implemented as specified in the relevant parts of the schedules.

3. The implementation of the concessions and commitments contained in the schedules annexed to this Protocol shall, upon request, be subject to multilateral examination by the Members. This would be without prejudice to the rights and obligations of Members under Agreements in Annex 1A of the WTO Agreement.

4. After the schedule annexed to this Protocol relating to a Member has become a Schedule to GATT 1994 pursuant to the provisions of paragraph 1, such Member shall be free at any time to withhold or to withdraw in whole or in part the concession in such Schedule with respect to any product for which the principal supplier is any other Uruguay Round participant the schedule of which has not yet become a Schedule to GATT 1994. Such action can, however, only be taken after written notice of any

such withholding or withdrawal of a concession has been given to the Council for Trade in Goods and after consultations have been held, upon request, with any Member, the relevant schedule relating to which has become a Schedule to GATT 1994 and which has a substantial interest in the product involved. Any concessions so withheld or withdrawn shall be applied on and after the day on which the schedule of the Member which has the principal supplying interest becomes a Schedule to GATT 1994.

5. (a) Without prejudice to the provisions of paragraph 2 of Article 4 of the Agreement on Agriculture, for the purpose of the reference in paragraphs 1: (b) and 1(c) of Article II of GATT 1994 to the date of that Agreement, the applicable date in respect of each product which is the subject of a concession provided for in a schedule of concessions annexed to this Protocol shall be the date of this Protocol.

(b) For the purpose of the reference in paragraph 6(a) of Article II of GATT 1994 to the date of that Agreement, the applicable date in respect of a schedule of concessions annexed to this Protocol shall be the date of this Protocol.

6. In cases of modification or withdrawal of concessions relating to non-tariff measures as contained in Part III of the schedules, the provisions of Article XXVIII of GATT 1994 and the "Procedures for Negotiations under Article XXVIII" adopted on 10 November 1980 (BISD 27S/26–28) shall apply. This would be without prejudice to the rights and obligations of Members under GATT 1994.

7. In each case in which a schedule annexed to this Protocol results for any product in treatment less favourable than was provided for such product in the Schedules of GATT 1947 prior to the entry into force of the WTO Agreement, the Member to whom the schedule relates shall be deemed to have taken appropriate action as would have been otherwise necessary under the relevant provisions of Article XXVIII of GATT 1947 or 1994. The provisions of this paragraph shall apply only to Egypt, Peru, South Africa and Uruguay.

8. The Schedules annexed hereto are authentic in the English, French or Spanish language as specified in each Schedule.

9. The date of this Protocol is 15 April 1994.

[The agreed schedules of participants will be annexed to the Marrakesh Protocol in the treaty copy of the WTO Agreement.]

DOCUMENT 11

WTO AGREEMENT ON THE APPLICATION OF SANITARY AND PHYTOSANITARY MEASURES (SPS)

■ ■ ■

Article 1

General Provisions

1. This Agreement applies to all sanitary and phytosanitary measures which may, directly or indirectly, affect international trade. Such measures shall be developed and applied in accordance with the provisions of this Agreement.

2. For the purposes of this Agreement, the definitions provided in Annex A shall apply.

3. The annexes are an integral part of this Agreement.

4. Nothing in this Agreement shall affect the rights of Members under the Agreement on Technical Barriers to Trade with respect to measures not within the scope of this Agreement.

Article 2

Basic Rights and Obligations

1. Members have the right to take sanitary and phytosanitary measures necessary for the protection of human, animal or plant life or health, provided that such measures are not inconsistent with the provisions of this Agreement.

2. Members shall ensure that any sanitary or phytosanitary measure is applied only to the extent necessary to protect human, animal or plant life or health, is based on scientific principles and is not maintained without sufficient scientific evidence, except as provided for in paragraph 7 of Article 5.

3. Members shall ensure that their sanitary and phytosanitary measures do not arbitrarily or unjustifiably discriminate between Members where identical or similar conditions prevail, including between their own territory and that of other Members. Sanitary and phytosanitary measures shall not be applied in a manner which would constitute a disguised restriction on international trade.

4. Sanitary or phytosanitary measures which conform to the relevant provisions of this Agreement shall be presumed to be in accordance with the obligations of the Members under the provisions of GATT 1994 which relate to the use of sanitary or phytosanitary measures, in particular the provisions of Article XX(b).

Article 3

Harmonization

1. To harmonize sanitary and phytosanitary measures on as wide a basis as possible, Members shall base their sanitary or phytosanitary measures on international standards, guidelines or recommendations, where they exist, except as otherwise provided for in this Agreement, and in particular in paragraph 3.

2. Sanitary or phytosanitary measures which conform to international standards, guidelines or recommendations shall be deemed to be necessary to protect human, animal or plant life or health, and presumed to be consistent with the relevant provisions of this Agreement and of GATT 1994.

3. Members may introduce or maintain sanitary or phytosanitary measures which result in a higher level of sanitary or phytosanitary protection than would be achieved by measures based on the relevant international standards, guidelines or recommendations, if there is a scientific justification, or as a consequence of the level of sanitary or phytosanitary protection a Member determines to be appropriate in accordance with the relevant provisions of paragraphs 1 through 8 of Article 5.[2] Notwithstanding the above, all measures which result in a level of sanitary or phytosanitary protection different from that which would be achieved by measures based on international standards, guidelines or recommendations shall not be inconsistent with any other provision of this Agreement.

* * *

5. The Committee on Sanitary and Phytosanitary Measures provided for in paragraphs 1 and 4 of Article 12 (referred to in this Agreement as the "Committee") shall develop a procedure to monitor the process of international harmonization and coordinate efforts in this regard with the relevant international organizations.

---

[2] For the purposes of paragraph 3 of Article 3, there is a scientific justification if, on the basis of an examination and evaluation of available scientific information in conformity with the relevant provisions of this Agreement, a Member determines that the relevant international standards, guidelines or recommendations are not sufficient to achieve its appropriate level of sanitary or phytosanitary protection.

Article 4

Equivalence

1. Members shall accept the sanitary or phytosanitary measures of other Members as equivalent, even if these measures differ from their own or from those used by other Members trading in the same product, if the exporting Member objectively demonstrates to the importing Member that its measures achieve the importing Member's appropriate level of sanitary or phytosanitary protection. For this purpose, reasonable access shall be given, upon request, to the importing Member for inspection, testing and other relevant procedures.

* * *

Article 5

Assessment of Risk and Determination of the Appropriate Level of Sanitary or Phytosanitary Protection

1. Members shall ensure that their sanitary or phytosanitary measures are based on an assessment, as appropriate to the circumstances, of the risks to human, animal or plant life or health, taking into account risk assessment techniques developed by the relevant international organizations.

2. In the assessment of risks, Members shall take into account available scientific evidence; relevant processes and production methods; relevant inspection, sampling and testing methods; prevalence of specific diseases or pests; existence of pest- or disease-free areas; relevant ecological and environmental conditions; and quarantine or other treatment.

3. In assessing the risk to animal or plant life or health and determining the measure to be applied for achieving the appropriate level of sanitary or phytosanitary protection from such risk, Members shall take into account as relevant economic factors: the potential damage in terms of loss of production or sales in the event of the entry, establishment or spread of a pest or disease; the costs of control or eradication in the territory of the importing Member; and the relative cost-effectiveness of alternative approaches to limiting risks.

4. Members should, when determining the appropriate level of sanitary or phytosanitary protection, take into account the objective of minimizing negative trade effects.

5. With the objective of achieving consistency in the application of the concept of appropriate level of sanitary or phytosanitary protection against risks to human life or health, or to animal and plant life or health, each Member shall avoid arbitrary or unjustifiable distinctions in the levels it considers to be appropriate in different situations, if such distinctions

result in discrimination or a disguised restriction on international trade. Members shall cooperate in the Committee, in accordance with paragraphs 1, 2 and 3 of Article 12, to develop guidelines to further the practical implementation of this provision. In developing the guidelines, the Committee shall take into account all relevant factors, including the exceptional character of human health risks to which people voluntarily expose themselves.

6. Without prejudice to paragraph 2 of Article 3, when establishing or maintaining sanitary or phytosanitary measures to achieve the appropriate level of sanitary or phytosanitary protection, Members shall ensure that such measures are not more trade-restrictive than required to achieve their appropriate level of sanitary or phytosanitary protection, taking into account technical and economic feasibility.[3]

7. In cases where relevant scientific evidence is insufficient, a Member may provisionally adopt sanitary or phytosanitary measures on the basis of available pertinent information, including that from the relevant international organizations as well as from sanitary or phytosanitary measures applied by other Members. In such circumstances, Members shall seek to obtain the additional information necessary for a more objective assessment of risk and review the sanitary or phytosanitary measure accordingly within a reasonable period of time.

8. When a Member has reason to believe that a specific sanitary or phytosanitary measure introduced or maintained by another Member is constraining, or has the potential to constrain, its exports and the measure is not based on the relevant international standards, guidelines or recommendations, or such standards, guidelines or recommendations do not exist, an explanation of the reasons for such sanitary or phytosanitary measure may be requested and shall be provided by the Member maintaining the measure.

Article 6

Adaptation to Regional Conditions, Including Pest- or Disease-Free Areas and Areas of Low Pest or Disease Prevalence

1. Members shall ensure that their sanitary or phytosanitary measures are adapted to the sanitary or phytosanitary characteristics of the area—whether all of a country, part of a country, or all or parts of several countries—from which the product originated and to which the product is destined. In assessing the sanitary or phytosanitary characteristics of a region, Members shall take into account, *inter alia*, the level of prevalence of specific diseases or pests, the existence of eradication

[3] For purposes of paragraph 6 of Article 5, a measure is not more trade-restrictive than required unless there is another measure, reasonably available taking into account technical and economic feasibility, that achieves the appropriate level of sanitary or phytosanitary protection and is significantly less restrictive to trade.

or control programmes, and appropriate criteria or guidelines which may be developed by the relevant international organizations.

2. Members shall, in particular, recognize the concepts of pest- or disease-free areas and areas of low pest or disease prevalence. Determination of such areas shall be based on factors such as geography, ecosystems, epidemiological surveillance, and the effectiveness of sanitary or phytosanitary controls.

* * *

Article 7

Transparency

Members shall notify changes in their sanitary or phytosanitary measures and shall provide information on their sanitary or phytosanitary measures in accordance with the provisions of Annex B.

Article 8

Control, Inspection and Approval Procedures

Members shall observe the provisions of Annex C in the operation of control, inspection and approval procedures, including national systems for approving the use of additives or for establishing tolerances for contaminants in foods, beverages or feedstuffs, and otherwise ensure that their procedures are not inconsistent with the provisions of this Agreement.

Article 9

Technical Assistance

1. Members agree to facilitate the provision of technical assistance to other Members, especially developing country Members, either bilaterally or through the appropriate international organizations. Such assistance may be, *inter alia,* in the areas of processing technologies, research and infrastructure, including in the establishment of national regulatory bodies, and may take the form of advice, credits, donations and grants, including for the purpose of seeking technical expertise, training and equipment to allow such countries to adjust to, and comply with, sanitary or phytosanitary measures necessary to achieve the appropriate level of sanitary or phytosanitary protection in their export markets.

2. Where substantial investments are required in order for an exporting developing country Member to fulfil the sanitary or phytosanitary requirements of an importing Member, the latter shall consider providing such technical assistance as will permit the developing country Member to maintain and expand its market access opportunities for the product involved.

Article 10

Special and Differential Treatment

1. In the preparation and application of sanitary or phytosanitary measures, Members shall take account of the special needs of developing country Members, and in particular of the least-developed country Members.

2. Where the appropriate level of sanitary or phytosanitary protection allows scope for the phased introduction of new sanitary or phytosanitary measures, longer time-frames for compliance should be accorded on products of interest to developing country Members so as to maintain opportunities for their exports.

3. With a view to ensuring that developing country Members are able to comply with the provisions of this Agreement, the Committee is enabled to grant to such countries, upon request, specified, time-limited exceptions in whole or in part from obligations under this Agreement, taking into account their financial, trade and development needs.

* * *

Article 11

Consultations and Dispute Settlement

1. The provisions of Articles XXII and XXIII of GATT 1994 as elaborated and applied by the Dispute Settlement Understanding shall apply to consultations and the settlement of disputes under this Agreement, except as otherwise specifically provided herein.

* * *

Article 12

Administration

1. A Committee on Sanitary and Phytosanitary Measures is hereby established to provide a regular forum for consultations. It shall carry out the functions necessary to implement the provisions of this Agreement and the furtherance of its objectives, in particular with respect to harmonization. The Committee shall reach its decisions by consensus.

2. The Committee shall encourage and facilitate ad hoc consultations or negotiations among Members on specific sanitary or phytosanitary issues. The Committee shall encourage the use of international standards, guidelines or recommendations by all Members and, in this regard, shall sponsor technical consultation and study with the objective of increasing coordination and integration between international and national systems and approaches for approving the use of food additives or for establishing tolerances for contaminants in foods, beverages or feedstuffs.

3. The Committee shall maintain close contact with the relevant international organizations in the field of sanitary and phytosanitary protection, especially with the Codex Alimentarius Commission, the International Office of Epizootics, and the Secretariat of the International Plant Protection Convention, with the objective of securing the best available scientific and technical advice for the administration of this Agreement and in order to ensure that unnecessary duplication of effort is avoided.

4. The Committee shall develop a procedure to monitor the process of international harmonization and the use of international standards, guidelines or recommendations. For this purpose, the Committee should, in conjunction with the relevant international organizations, establish a list of international standards, guidelines or recommendations relating to sanitary or phytosanitary measures which the Committee determines to have a major trade impact. The list should include an indication by Members of those international standards, guidelines or recommendations which they apply as conditions for import or on the basis of which imported products conforming to these standards can enjoy access to their markets. For those cases in which a Member does not apply an international standard, guideline or recommendation as a condition for import, the Member should provide an indication of the reason therefor, and, in particular, whether it considers that the standard is not stringent enough to provide the appropriate level of sanitary or phytosanitary protection. If a Member revises its position, following its indication of the use of a standard, guideline or recommendation as a condition for import, it should provide an explanation for its change and so inform the Secretariat as well as the relevant international organizations, unless such notification and explanation is given according to the procedures of Annex B.

* * *

7. The Committee shall review the operation and implementation of this Agreement three years after the date of entry into force of the WTO Agreement, and thereafter as the need arises. Where appropriate, the Committee may submit to the Council for Trade in Goods proposals to amend the text of this Agreement having regard, *inter alia,* to the experience gained in its implementation.

Article 13

Implementation

Members are fully responsible under this Agreement for the observance of all obligations set forth herein. Members shall formulate and implement positive measures and mechanisms in support of the observance of the provisions of this Agreement by other than central government bodies. Members shall take such reasonable measures as may be available to them to ensure that non-governmental entities within their territories, as well as regional bodies in which relevant entities within their territories are members, comply with the relevant provisions of this Agreement. In addition, Members shall not take measures which have the effect of, directly or indirectly, requiring or encouraging such regional or non-governmental entities, or local governmental bodies, to act in a manner inconsistent with the provisions of this Agreement. Members shall ensure that they rely on the services of non-governmental entities for implementing sanitary or phytosanitary measures only if these entities comply with the provisions of this Agreement.

Article 14

Final Provisions

The least-developed country Members may delay application of the provisions of this Agreement for a period of five years following the date of entry into force of the WTO Agreement with respect to their sanitary or phytosanitary measures affecting importation or imported products. Other developing country Members may delay application of the provisions of this Agreement, other than paragraph 8 of Article 5 and Article 7, for two years following the date of entry into force of the WTO Agreement with respect to their existing sanitary or phytosanitary measures affecting importation or imported products, where such application is prevented by a lack of technical expertise, technical infrastructure or resources.

ANNEX A

DEFINITIONS

1. *Sanitary or phytosanitary measure*—Any measure applied:

(a) to protect animal or plant life or health within the territory of the Member from risks arising from the entry, establishment or spread of pests, diseases, disease-carrying organisms or disease-causing organisms;

(b) to protect human or animal life or health within the territory of the Member from risks arising from additives, contaminants, toxins or disease-causing organisms in foods, beverages or feedstuffs;

(c) to protect human life or health within the territory of the Member from risks arising from diseases carried by animals, plants or products thereof, or from the entry, establishment or spread of pests; or

(d) to prevent or limit other damage within the territory of the Member from the entry, establishment or spread of pests.

Sanitary or phytosanitary measures include all relevant laws, decrees, regulations, requirements and procedures including, *inter alia,* end product criteria; processes and production methods; testing, inspection, certification and approval procedures; quarantine treatments including relevant requirements associated with the transport of animals or plants, or with the materials necessary for their survival during transport; provisions on relevant statistical methods, sampling procedures and methods of risk assessment; and packaging and labelling requirements directly related to food safety.

2. *Harmonization*—The establishment, recognition and application of common sanitary and phytosanitary measures by different Members.

3. *International standards, guidelines and recommendations*

(a) for food safety, the standards, guidelines and recommendations established by the Codex Alimentarius Commission relating to food additives, veterinary drug and pesticide residues, contaminants, methods of analysis and sampling, and codes and guidelines of hygienic practice;

(b) for animal health and zoonoses, the standards, guidelines and recommendations developed under the auspices of the International Office of Epizootics;

(c) for plant health, the international standards, guidelines and recommendations developed under the auspices of the Secretariat of the International Plant Protection Convention in cooperation with regional organizations operating within the framework of the International Plant Protection Convention; and

(d) for matters not covered by the above organizations, appropriate standards, guidelines and recommendations promulgated by other relevant international organizations open for membership to all Members, as identified by the Committee.

4. *Risk assessment*—The evaluation of the likelihood of entry, establishment or spread of a pest or disease within the territory of an importing Member according to the sanitary or phytosanitary measures which might be applied, and of the associated potential biological and economic consequences; or the evaluation of the potential for adverse effects on human or animal health arising from the presence of additives, contaminants, toxins or disease-causing organisms in food, beverages or feedstuffs.

5. *Appropriate level of sanitary or phytosanitary protection*—The level of protection deemed appropriate by the Member establishing a sanitary or phytosanitary measure to protect human, animal or plant life or health within its territory.

NOTE: Many Members otherwise refer to this concept as the "acceptable level of risk".

ANNEX B

TRANSPARENCY OF SANITARY AND PHYTOSANITARY REGULATIONS

Notification procedures

5. Whenever an international standard, guideline or recommendation does not exist or the content of a proposed sanitary or phytosanitary regulation is not substantially the same as the content of an international standard, guideline or recommendation, and if the regulation may have a significant effect on trade of other Members, Members shall:

(a) publish a notice at an early stage in such a manner as to enable interested Members to become acquainted with the proposal to introduce a particular regulation;

(b) notify other Members, through the Secretariat, of the products to be covered by the regulation together with a brief indication of the objective and rationale of the proposed regulation. Such notifications shall take place at an early stage, when amendments can still be introduced and comments taken into account;

(c) provide upon request to other Members copies of the proposed regulation and, whenever possible, identify the parts which in substance deviate from international standards, guidelines or recommendations;

(d) without discrimination, allow reasonable time for other Members to make comments in writing, discuss these comments upon request, and take the comments and the results of the discussions into account.

6. However, where urgent problems of health protection arise or threaten to arise for a Member, that Member may omit such of the steps enumerated in paragraph 5 of this Annex as it finds necessary, provided that the Member:

(a) immediately notifies other Members, through the Secretariat, of the particular regulation and the products covered, with a brief indication of the objective and the rationale of the regulation, including the nature of the urgent problem(s);

(b) provides, upon request, copies of the regulation to other Members;

(c) allows other Members to make comments in writing, discusses these comments upon request, and takes the comments and the results of the discussions into account.

DOCUMENT 12

WTO AGREEMENT ESTABLISHING THE WORLD TRADE ORGANIZATION (1994)

■ ■ ■

The *Parties* to this Agreement,

Recognizing that their relations in the field of trade and economic endeavour should be conducted with a view to raising standards of living, ensuring full employment and a large and steadily growing volume of real income and effective demand, and expanding the production of and trade in goods and services, while allowing for the optimal use of the world's resources in accordance with the objective of sustainable development, seeking both to protect and preserve the environment and to enhance the means for doing so in a manner consistent with their respective needs and concerns at different levels of economic development,

Recognizing further that there is need for positive efforts designed to ensure that developing countries, and especially the least developed among them, secure a share in the growth in international trade commensurate with the needs of their economic development,

Being desirous of contributing to these objectives by entering into reciprocal and mutually advantageous arrangements directed to the substantial reduction of tariffs and other barriers to trade and to the elimination of discriminatory treatment in international trade relations,

Resolved, therefore, to develop an integrated, more viable and durable multilateral trading system encompassing the General Agreement on Tariffs and Trade, the results of past trade liberalization efforts, and all of the results of the Uruguay Round of Multilateral Trade Negotiations,

Determined to preserve the basic principles and to further the objectives underlying this multilateral trading system,

Agree as follows:

Article I

Establishment of the Organization

The World Trade Organization (hereinafter referred to as "the WTO") is hereby established.

Article II

Scope of the WTO

1. The WTO shall provide the common institutional framework for the conduct of trade relations among its Members in matters related to the agreements and associated legal instruments included in the Annexes to this Agreement.

2. The agreements and associated legal instruments included in Annexes 1, 2 and 3 (hereinafter referred to as "Multilateral Trade Agreements") are integral parts of this Agreement, binding on all Members.

3. The agreements and associated legal instruments included in Annex 4 (hereinafter referred to as "Plurilateral Trade Agreements") are also part of this Agreement for those Members that have accepted them, and are binding on those Members. The Plurilateral Trade Agreements do not create either obligations or rights for Members that have not accepted them.

4. The General Agreement on Tariffs and Trade 1994 as specified in Annex 1A (hereinafter referred to as "GATT 1994") is legally distinct from the General Agreement on Tariffs and Trade, dated 30 October 1947, annexed to the Final Act Adopted at the Conclusion of the Second Session of the Preparatory Committee of the United Nations Conference on Trade and Employment, as subsequently rectified, amended or modified (hereinafter referred to as "GATT 1947").

Article III

Functions of the WTO

1. The WTO shall facilitate the implementation, administration and operation, and further the objectives, of this Agreement and of the Multilateral Trade Agreements, and shall also provide the framework for the implementation, administration and operation of the Plurilateral Trade Agreements.

2. The WTO shall provide the forum for negotiations among its Members concerning their multilateral trade relations in matters dealt with under the agreements in the Annexes to this Agreement. The WTO may also provide a forum for further negotiations among its Members concerning their multilateral trade relations, and a framework for the implementation of the results of such negotiations, as may be decided by the Ministerial Conference.

3. The WTO shall administer the Understanding on Rules and Procedures Governing the Settlement of Disputes (hereinafter referred to as the "Dispute Settlement Understanding" or "DSU") in Annex 2 to this Agreement.

4. The WTO shall administer the Trade Policy Review Mechanism (hereinafter referred to as the "TPRM") provided for in Annex 3 to this Agreement.

5. With a view to achieving greater coherence in global economic policymaking, the WTO shall cooperate, as appropriate, with the International Monetary Fund and with the International Bank for Reconstruction and Development and its affiliated agencies.

Article IV

Structure of the WTO

1. There shall be a Ministerial Conference composed of representatives of all the Members, which shall meet at least once every two years. The Ministerial Conference shall carry out the functions of the WTO and take actions necessary to this effect. The Ministerial Conference shall have the authority to take decisions on all matters under any of the Multilateral Trade Agreements, if so requested by a Member, in accordance with the specific requirements for decision-making in this Agreement and in the relevant Multilateral Trade Agreement.

2. There shall be a General Council composed of representatives of all the Members, which shall meet as appropriate. In the intervals between meetings of the Ministerial Conference, its functions shall be conducted by the General Council. The General Council shall also carry out the functions assigned to it by this Agreement. The General Council shall establish its rules of procedure and approve the rules of procedure for the Committees provided for in paragraph 7.

3. The General Council shall convene as appropriate to discharge the responsibilities of the Dispute Settlement Body provided for in the Dispute Settlement Understanding. The Dispute Settlement Body may have its own chairman and shall establish such rules of procedure as it deems necessary for the fulfilment of those responsibilities.

4. The General Council shall convene as appropriate to discharge the responsibilities of the Trade Policy Review Body provided for in the TPRM. The Trade Policy Review Body may have its own chairman and shall establish such rules of procedure as it deems necessary for the fulfilment of those responsibilities.

5. There shall be a Council for Trade in Goods, a Council for Trade in Services and a Council for Trade-Related Aspects of Intellectual Property Rights (hereinafter referred to as the "Council for TRIPS"), which shall operate under the general guidance of the General Council. The Council for Trade in Goods shall oversee the functioning of the Multilateral Trade Agreements in Annex 1A. The Council for Trade in Services shall oversee the functioning of the General Agreement on Trade in Services (hereinafter referred to as "GATS"). The Council for TRIPS shall oversee

the functioning of the Agreement on Trade-Related Aspects of Intellectual Property Rights (hereinafter referred to as the "Agreement on TRIPS"). These Councils shall carry out the functions assigned to them by their respective agreements and by the General Council. They shall establish their respective rules of procedure subject to the approval of the General Council. Membership in these Councils shall be open to representatives of all Members. These Councils shall meet as necessary to carry out their functions.

* * *

Article V

Relations With Other Organizations

* * *

Article VI

The Secretariat

* * *

Article VII

Budget and Contributions

* * *

Article VIII

Status of the WTO

* * *

Article IX

Decision-Making

1. The WTO shall continue the practice of decision-making by consensus followed under GATT 1947.[1] Except as otherwise provided, where a decision cannot be arrived at by consensus, the matter at issue shall be decided by voting. At meetings of the Ministerial Conference and the General Council, each Member of the WTO shall have one vote. Where the European Communities exercise their right to vote, they shall have a number of votes equal to the number of their member States [2] which are Members of the WTO. Decisions of the Ministerial Conference and the General Council shall be taken by a majority of the votes cast, unless

[1] The body concerned shall be deemed to have decided by consensus on a matter submitted for its consideration, if no Member, present at the meeting when the decision is taken, formally objects to the proposed decision.

[2] The number of votes of the European Communities and their member States shall in no case exceed the number of the member States of the European Communities.

otherwise provided in this Agreement or in the relevant Multilateral Trade Agreement.[3]

2. The Ministerial Conference and the General Council shall have the exclusive authority to adopt interpretations of this Agreement and of the Multilateral Trade Agreements. In the case of an interpretation of a Multilateral Trade Agreement in Annex 1, they shall exercise their authority on the basis of a recommendation by the Council overseeing the functioning of that Agreement. The decision to adopt an interpretation shall be taken by a three-fourths majority of the Members. This paragraph shall not be used in a manner that would undermine the amendment provisions in Article X.

3. In exceptional circumstances, the Ministerial Conference may decide to waive an obligation imposed on a Member by this Agreement or any of the Multilateral Trade Agreements, provided that any such decision shall be taken by three fourths [4] of the Members unless otherwise provided for in this paragraph.

(a) A request for a waiver concerning this Agreement shall be submitted to the Ministerial Conference for consideration pursuant to the practice of decision-making by consensus. The Ministerial Conference shall establish a time-period, which shall not exceed 90 days, to consider the request. If consensus is not reached during the time-period, any decision to grant a waiver shall be taken by three fourths of the Members.

(b) A request for a waiver concerning the Multilateral Trade Agreements in Annexes 1A or 1B or 1C and their annexes shall be submitted initially to the Council for Trade in Goods, the Council for Trade in Services or the Council for TRIPS, respectively, for consideration during a time-period which shall not exceed 90 days. At the end of the time-period, the relevant Council shall submit a report to the Ministerial Conference.

4. A decision by the Ministerial Conference granting a waiver shall state the exceptional circumstances justifying the decision, the terms and conditions governing the application of the waiver, and the date on which the waiver shall terminate. Any waiver granted for a period of more than one year shall be reviewed by the Ministerial Conference not later than one year after it is granted, and thereafter annually until the waiver terminates. In each review, the Ministerial Conference shall examine whether the exceptional circumstances justifying the waiver still exist and

---

[3] Decisions by the General Council when convened as the Dispute Settlement Body shall be taken only in accordance with the provisions of paragraph 4 of Article 2 of the Dispute Settlement Understanding.

[4] A decision to grant a waiver in respect of any obligation subject to a transition period or a period for staged implementation that the requesting Member has not performed by the end of the relevant period shall be taken only by consensus.

whether the terms and conditions attached to the waiver have been met. The Ministerial Conference, on the basis of the annual review, may extend, modify or terminate the waiver.

5. Decisions under a Plurilateral Trade Agreement, including any decisions on interpretations and waivers, shall be governed by the provisions of that Agreement.

Article X

Amendment

1. Any Member of the WTO may initiate a proposal to amend the provisions of this Agreement or the Multilateral Trade Agreements in Annex 1 by submitting such proposal to the Ministerial Conference. The Councils listed in paragraph 5 of Article IV may also submit to the Ministerial Conference proposals to amend the provisions of the corresponding Multilateral Trade Agreements in Annex 1 the functioning of which they oversee. Unless the Ministerial Conference decides on a longer period, for a period of 90 days after the proposal has been tabled formally at the Ministerial Conference any decision by the Ministerial Conference to submit the proposed amendment to the Members for acceptance shall be taken by consensus. Unless the provisions of paragraphs 2, 5 or 6 apply, that decision shall specify whether the provisions of paragraphs 3 or 4 shall apply. If consensus is reached, the Ministerial Conference shall forthwith submit the proposed amendment to the Members for acceptance. If consensus is not reached at a meeting of the Ministerial Conference within the established period, the Ministerial Conference shall decide by a two-thirds majority of the Members whether to submit the proposed amendment to the Members for acceptance. Except as provided in paragraphs 2, 5 and 6, the provisions of paragraph 3 shall apply to the proposed amendment, unless the Ministerial Conference decides by a three-fourths majority of the Members that the provisions of paragraph 4 shall apply.

2. Amendments to the provisions of this Article and to the provisions of the following Articles shall take effect only upon acceptance by all Members:

Article IX of this Agreement;

Articles I and II of GATT 1994;

Article II:1 of GATS;

Article 4 of the Agreement on TRIPS.

3. Amendments to provisions of this Agreement, or of the Multilateral Trade Agreements in Annexes 1A and 1C, other than those listed in paragraphs 2 and 6, of a nature that would alter the rights and obligations of the Members, shall take effect for the Members that have

accepted them upon acceptance by two thirds of the Members and thereafter for each other Member upon acceptance by it. The Ministerial Conference may decide by a three-fourths majority of the Members that any amendment made effective under this paragraph is of such a nature that any Member which has not accepted it within a period specified by the Ministerial Conference in each case shall be free to withdraw from the WTO or to remain a Member with the consent of the Ministerial Conference.

4. Amendments to provisions of this Agreement or of the Multilateral Trade Agreements in Annexes 1A and 1C, other than those listed in paragraphs 2 and 6, of a nature that would not alter the rights and obligations of the Members, shall take effect for all Members upon acceptance by two thirds of the Members.

5. Except as provided in paragraph 2 above, amendments to Parts I, II and III of GATS and the respective annexes shall take effect for the Members that have accepted them upon acceptance by two thirds of the Members and thereafter for each Member upon acceptance by it. The Ministerial Conference may decide by a three-fourths majority of the Members that any amendment made effective under the preceding provision is of such a nature that any Member which has not accepted it within a period specified by the Ministerial Conference in each case shall be free to withdraw from the WTO or to remain a Member with the consent of the Ministerial Conference. Amendments to Parts IV, V and VI of GATS and the respective annexes shall take effect for all Members upon acceptance by two thirds of the Members.

6. Notwithstanding the other provisions of this Article, amendments to the Agreement on TRIPS meeting the requirements of paragraph 2 of Article 71 thereof may be adopted by the Ministerial Conference without further formal acceptance process.

7. Any Member accepting an amendment to this Agreement or to a Multilateral Trade Agreement in Annex 1 shall deposit an instrument of acceptance with the Director-General of the WTO within the period of acceptance specified by the Ministerial Conference.

8. Any Member of the WTO may initiate a proposal to amend the provisions of the Multilateral Trade Agreements in Annexes 2 and 3 by submitting such proposal to the Ministerial Conference. The decision to approve amendments to the Multilateral Trade Agreement in Annex 2 shall be made by consensus and these amendments shall take effect for all Members upon approval by the Ministerial Conference. Decisions to approve amendments to the Multilateral Trade Agreement in Annex 3 shall take effect for all Members upon approval by the Ministerial Conference.

9. The Ministerial Conference, upon the request of the Members parties to a trade agreement, may decide exclusively by consensus to add that agreement to Annex 4. The Ministerial Conference, upon the request of the Members parties to a Plurilateral Trade Agreement, may decide to delete that Agreement from Annex 4.

10. Amendments to a Plurilateral Trade Agreement shall be governed by the provisions of that Agreement.

Article XI

Original Membership

1. The contracting parties to GATT 1947 as of the date of entry into force of this Agreement, and the European Communities, which accept this Agreement and the Multilateral Trade Agreements and for which Schedules of Concessions and Commitments are annexed to GATT 1994 and for which Schedules of Specific Commitments are annexed to GATS shall become original Members of the WTO.

2. The least-developed countries recognized as such by the United Nations will only be required to undertake commitments and concessions to the extent consistent with their individual development, financial and trade needs or their administrative and institutional capabilities.

Article XII

Accession

1. Any State or separate customs territory possessing full autonomy in the conduct of its external commercial relations and of the other matters provided for in this Agreement and the Multilateral Trade Agreements may accede to this Agreement, on terms to be agreed between it and the WTO. Such accession shall apply to this Agreement and the Multilateral Trade Agreements annexed thereto.

2. Decisions on accession shall be taken by the Ministerial Conference. The Ministerial Conference shall approve the agreement on the terms of accession by a two-thirds majority of the Members of the WTO.

3. Accession to a Plurilateral Trade Agreement shall be governed by the provisions of that Agreement.

Article XIII

Non-Application of Multilateral Trade Agreements Between Particular Members

1. This Agreement and the Multilateral Trade Agreements in Annexes 1 and 2 shall not apply as between any Member and any other Member if either of the Members, at the time either becomes a Member, does not consent to such application.

2. Paragraph 1 may be invoked between original Members of the WTO which were contracting parties to GATT 1947 only where Article XXXV of that Agreement had been invoked earlier and was effective as between those contracting parties at the time of entry into force for them of this Agreement.

3. Paragraph 1 shall apply between a Member and another Member which has acceded under Article XII only if the Member not consenting to the application has so notified the Ministerial Conference before the approval of the agreement on the terms of accession by the Ministerial Conference.

4. The Ministerial Conference may review the operation of this Article in particular cases at the request of any Member and make appropriate recommendations.

5. Non-application of a Plurilateral Trade Agreement between parties to that Agreement shall be governed by the provisions of that Agreement.

Article XIV

Acceptance, Entry into Force and Deposit

1. This Agreement shall be open for acceptance, by signature or otherwise, by contracting parties to GATT 1947, and the European Communities, which are eligible to become original Members of the WTO in accordance with Article XI of this Agreement. Such acceptance shall apply to this Agreement and the Multilateral Trade Agreements annexed hereto. This Agreement and the Multilateral Trade Agreements annexed hereto shall enter into force on the date determined by Ministers in accordance with paragraph 3 of the Final Act Embodying the Results of the Uruguay Round of Multilateral Trade Negotiations and shall remain open for acceptance for a period of two years following that date unless the Ministers decide otherwise. An acceptance following the entry into force of this Agreement shall enter into force on the 30th day following the date of such acceptance.

2. A Member which accepts this Agreement after its entry into force shall implement those concessions and obligations in the Multilateral Trade Agreements that are to be implemented over a period of time starting with the entry into force of this Agreement as if it had accepted this Agreement on the date of its entry into force.

3. Until the entry into force of this Agreement, the text of this Agreement and the Multilateral Trade Agreements shall be deposited with the Director-General to the CONTRACTING PARTIES to GATT 1947. The Director-General shall promptly furnish a certified true copy of this Agreement and the Multilateral Trade Agreements, and a notification of each acceptance thereof, to each government and the European

Communities having accepted this Agreement. This Agreement and the Multilateral Trade Agreements, and any amendments thereto, shall, upon the entry into force of this Agreement, be deposited with the Director-General of the WTO.

4. The acceptance and entry into force of a Plurilateral Trade Agreement shall be governed by the provisions of that Agreement. Such Agreements shall be deposited with the Director-General to the CONTRACTING PARTIES to GATT 1947. Upon the entry into force of this Agreement, such Agreements shall be deposited with the Director-General of the WTO.

Article XV

Withdrawal

1. Any Member may withdraw from this Agreement. Such withdrawal shall apply both to this Agreement and the Multilateral Trade Agreements and shall take effect upon the expiration of six months from the date on which written notice of withdrawal is received by the Director-General of the WTO.

2. Withdrawal from a Plurilateral Trade Agreement shall be governed by the provisions of that Agreement.

Article XVI

Miscellaneous Provisions

1. Except as otherwise provided under this Agreement or the Multilateral Trade Agreements, the WTO shall be guided by the decisions, procedures and customary practices followed by the CONTRACTING PARTIES to GATT 1947 and the bodies established in the framework of GATT 1947.

2. To the extent practicable, the Secretariat of GATT 1947 shall become the Secretariat of the WTO, and the Director-General to the CONTRACTING PARTIES to GATT 1947, until such time as the Ministerial Conference has appointed a Director-General in accordance with paragraph 2 of Article VI of this Agreement, shall serve as Director-General of the WTO.

3. In the event of a conflict between a provision of this Agreement and a provision of any of the Multilateral Trade Agreements, the provision of this Agreement shall prevail to the extent of the conflict.

4. Each Member shall ensure the conformity of its laws, regulations and administrative procedures with its obligations as provided in the annexed Agreements.

5. No reservations may be made in respect of any provision of this Agreement. Reservations in respect of any of the provisions of the Multilateral Trade Agreements may only be made to the extent provided

for in those Agreements. Reservations in respect of a provision of a Plurilateral Trade Agreement shall be governed by the provisions of that Agreement.

6. This Agreement shall be registered in accordance with the provisions of Article 102 of the Charter of the United Nations.

DONE at Marrakesh this fifteenth day of April one thousand nine hundred and ninety-four, in a single copy, in the English, French and Spanish languages, each text being authentic.

DONE at Marrakesh this fifteenth day of April one thousand nine hundred and ninety-four, in a single copy, in the English, French and Spanish languages, each text being authentic.

Explanatory Notes:

The terms "country" or "countries" as used in this Agreement and the Multilateral Trade Agreements are to be understood to include any separate customs territory Member of the WTO.

In the case of a separate customs territory Member of the WTO, where an expression in this Agreement and the Multilateral Trade Agreements is qualified by the term "national", such expression shall be read as pertaining to that customs territory, unless otherwise specified.

LIST OF ANNEXES

ANNEX 1

ANNEX 1A: Multilateral Agreements on Trade in Goods

General Agreement on Tariffs and Trade 1994

Agreement on Agriculture

Agreement on the Application of Sanitary and Phytosanitary Measures

Agreement on Textiles and Clothing

Agreement on Technical Barriers to Trade

Agreement on Trade-Related Investment Measures

Agreement on Implementation of Article VI of the General Agreement on Tariffs and Trade 1994

Agreement on Implementation of Article VII of the General Agreement on Tariffs and Trade 1994

Agreement on Preshipment Inspection

Agreement on Rules of Origin

Agreement on Import Licensing Procedures

Agreement on Subsidies and Countervailing Measures

Agreement on Safeguards

ANNEX 1B: General Agreement on Trade in Services and Annexes

ANNEX 1C: Agreement on Trade-Related Aspects of Intellectual Property Rights

ANNEX 2

Understanding on Rules and Procedures Governing the Settlement of Disputes

ANNEX 3

Trade Policy Review Mechanism

ANNEX 4

Plurilateral Trade Agreements

Agreement on Trade in Civil Aircraft

Agreement on Government Procurement

International Dairy Agreement

International Bovine Meat Agreement

ANNEX 1A

MULTILATERAL AGREEMENTS ON TRADE IN GOODS

General interpretative note to Annex 1A:

In the event of conflict between a provision of the General Agreement on Tariffs and Trade 1994 and a provision of another agreement in Annex 1A to the Agreement Establishing the World Trade Organization (referred to in the agreements in Annex 1A as the "WTO Agreement"), the provision of the other agreement shall prevail to the extent of the conflict.

DOCUMENT 13

WTO AGREEMENT ON GOVERNMENT PROCUREMENT

■ ■ ■

Article I

Scope and Coverage

1. This Agreement applies to any law, regulation, procedure or practice regarding any procurement by entities covered by this Agreement, as specified in Appendix I.[1]

2. This Agreement applies to procurement by any contractual means, including through such methods as purchase or as lease, rental or hire purchase, with or without an option to buy, including any combination of products and services.

3. Where entities, in the context of procurement covered under this Agreement, require enterprises not included in Appendix I to award contracts in accordance with particular requirements, Article III shall apply *mutatis mutandis* to such requirements.

4. This Agreement applies to any procurement contract of a value of not less than the relevant threshold specified in Appendix I.

Article II

Valuation of Contracts

1. The following provisions shall apply in determining the value of contracts[2] for purposes of implementing this Agreement.

---

1 For each party, Appendix I is divided into five Annexes:

— Annex 1 contains central government entities.

— Annex 2 contains sub-central government entities.

— Annex 3 contains all other entities that procure in accordance with the provisions of this Agreement.

— Annex 4 specifies services, whether listed positively or negatively, covered by this Agreement.

— Annex 5 specifies covered construction services.

Relevant thresholds are specified in each Party's Annexes.

2 This Agreement shall apply to any procurement contract for which the contract value is estimated to equal or exceed the threshold at the time of publication of the notice in accordance with Article IX.

2. Valuation shall take into account all forms of remuneration, including any premiums, fees, commissions and interest receivable.

3. The selection of the valuation method by the entity shall not be used, nor shall any procurement requirement be divided, with the intention of avoiding the application of this Agreement.

4. If an individual requirement for a procurement results in the award of more than one contract, or in contracts being awarded in separate parts, the basis for valuation shall be either:

(a) the actual value of similar recurring contracts concluded over the previous fiscal year or 12 months adjusted, where possible, for anticipated changes in quantity and value over the subsequent 12 months; or

(b) the estimated value of recurring contracts in the fiscal year or 12 months subsequent to the initial contract.

5. In cases of contracts for the lease, rental or hire purchase of products or services, or in the case of contracts which do not specify a total price, the basis for valuation shall be:

(a) in the case of fixed term contracts, where their term is 12 months or less, the total contract value for their duration, or, where their term exceeds 12 months, their total value including the estimated residual value;

(b) in the case of contracts for an indefinite period, the monthly instalment multiplied by 48.

If there is any doubt, the second basis for valuation, namely (b), is to be used.

6. In cases where an intended procurement specifies the need for option clauses, the basis for valuation shall be the total value of the maximum permissible procurement, inclusive of optional purchases.

Article III

National Treatment and Non-discrimination

1. With respect to all laws, regulations, procedures and practices regarding government procurement covered by this Agreement, each Party shall provide immediately and unconditionally to the products, services and suppliers of other Parties offering products or services of the Parties, treatment no less favourable than:

(a) that accorded to domestic products, services and suppliers; and

(b) that accorded to products, services and suppliers of any other Party.

2. With respect to all laws, regulations, procedures and practices regarding government procurement covered by this Agreement, each Party shall ensure:

(a) that its entities shall not treat a locally-established supplier less favourably than another locally established supplier on the basis of degree of foreign affiliation or ownership; and

(b) that its entities shall not discriminate against locally-established suppliers on the basis of the country of production of the good or service being supplied, provided that the country of production is a Party to the Agreement in accordance with the provisions of Article IV.

3. The provisions of paragraphs 1 and 2 shall not apply to customs duties and charges of any kind imposed on or in connection with importation, the method of levying such duties and charges, other import regulations and formalities, and measures affecting trade in services other than laws, regulations, procedures and practices regarding government procurement covered by this Agreement.

Article IV

Rules of Origin

1. A Party shall not apply rules of origin to products or services imported or supplied for purposes of government procurement covered by this Agreement from other Parties, which are different from the rules of origin applied in the normal course of trade and at the time of the transaction in question to imports or supplies of the same products or services from the same Parties.

2. Following the conclusion of the work programme for the harmonization of rules of origin for goods to be undertaken under the Agreement on Rules of Origin in Annex 1A of the Agreement Establishing the World Trade Organization (herein referred to as "WTO Agreement") and negotiations regarding trade in services, Parties shall take the results of that work programme and those negotiations into account in amending paragraph 1 as appropriate.

Article V

Special and Differential Treatment for Developing Countries Objectives

1. Parties shall, in the implementation and administration of this Agreement, through the provisions set out in this Article, duly take into account the development, financial and trade needs of developing countries, in particular least-developed countries, in their need to:

(a) safeguard their balance-of-payments position and ensure a level of reserves adequate for the implementation of programmes of economic development;

(b) promote the establishment or development of domestic industries including the development of small-scale and cottage industries in rural or backward areas; and economic development of other sectors of the economy;

(c) support industrial units so long as they are wholly or substantially dependent on government procurement; and

(d) encourage their economic development through regional or global arrangements among developing countries presented to the Ministerial Conference of the World Trade Organization (hereinafter referred to as the "WTO") and not disapproved by it.

2. Consistently with the provisions of this Agreement, each Party shall, in the preparation and application of laws, regulations and procedures affecting government procurement, facilitate increased imports from developing countries, bearing in mind the special problems of least-developed countries and of those countries at low stages of economic development.

* * *

Article VI

Technical Specifications

1. Technical specifications laying down the characteristics of the products or services to be procured, such as quality, performance, safety and dimensions, symbols, terminology, packaging, marking and labelling, or the processes and methods for their production and requirements relating to conformity assessment procedures prescribed by procuring entities, shall not be prepared, adopted or applied with a view to, or with the effect of, creating unnecessary obstacles to international trade.

2. Technical specifications prescribed by procuring entities shall, where appropriate:

(a) be in terms of performance rather than design or descriptive characteristics; and

(b) be based on international standards, where such exist; otherwise, on national technical regulations,[3] recognized national standards,[4] or building codes.

---

[3] For the purposes of this Agreement, a technical regulation is a document which lays down characteristics of a product or a service or their related processes and production methods, including the applicable administrative provisions, with which compliance is mandatory. It may also include or deal exclusively with terminology, symbols, packaging, marking or labelling requirements as they apply to a product, service, process or production method.

[4] For the purpose of this Agreement, a standard is a document approved by a recognized body, that provides, for common and repeated use, rules, guidelines or characteristics for products or services or related processes and production methods, with which compliance is not mandatory.

3. There shall be no requirement or reference to a particular trademark or trade name, patent, design or type, specific origin, producer or supplier, unless there is no sufficiently precise or intelligible way of describing the procurement requirements and provided that words such as "or equivalent" are included in the tender documentation.

4. Entities shall not seek or accept, in a manner which would have the effect of precluding competition, advice which may be used in the preparation of specifications for a specific procurement from a firm that may have a commercial interest in the procurement.

Article VII

Tendering Procedures

1. Each Party shall ensure that the tendering procedures of its entities are applied in a non-discriminatory manner and are consistent with the provisions contained in Articles VII through XVI.

2. Entities shall not provide to any supplier information with regard to a specific procurement in a manner which would have the effect of precluding competition.

3. For the purposes of this Agreement:

(a) Open tendering procedures are those procedures under which all interested suppliers may submit a tender.

(b) Selective tendering procedures are those procedures under which, consistent with paragraph 3 of Article X and other relevant provisions of this Agreement, those suppliers invited to do so by the entity may submit a tender.

(c) Limited tendering procedures are those procedures where the entity contacts suppliers individually, only under the conditions specified in Article XV.

Article VIII

Qualification of Suppliers

In the process of qualifying suppliers, entities shall not discriminate among suppliers of other Parties or between domestic suppliers and suppliers of other Parties. Qualification procedures shall be consistent with the following:

(a) any conditions for participation in tendering procedures shall be published in adequate time to enable interested suppliers to initiate and, to the extent that it is compatible with efficient operation of the procurement process, complete the qualification procedures;

It may also include or deal exclusively with terminology, symbols, packaging, marking or labelling requirements as they apply to a product, service, process or production method.

(b) any conditions for participation in tendering procedures shall be limited to those which are essential to ensure the firm's capability to fulfil the contract in question. Any conditions for participation required from suppliers, including financial guarantees, technical qualifications and information necessary for establishing the financial, commercial and technical capacity of suppliers, as well as the verification of qualifications, shall be no less favourable to suppliers of other Parties than to domestic suppliers and shall not discriminate among suppliers of other Parties. The financial, commercial and technical capacity of a supplier shall be judged on the basis both of that supplier's global business activity as well as of its activity in the territory of the procuring entity, taking due account of the legal relationship between the supply organizations;

(c) the process of, and the time required for, qualifying suppliers shall not be used in order to keep suppliers of other Parties off a suppliers' list or from being considered for a particular intended procurement. Entities shall recognize as qualified suppliers such domestic suppliers or suppliers of other Parties who meet the conditions for participation in a particular intended procurement. Suppliers requesting to participate in a particular intended procurement who may not yet be qualified shall also be considered, provided there is sufficient time to complete the qualification procedure;

(d) entities maintaining permanent lists of qualified suppliers shall ensure that suppliers may apply for qualification at any time; and that all qualified suppliers so requesting are included in the lists within a reasonably short time;

(e) if, after publication of the notice under paragraph 1 of Article IX, a supplier not yet qualified requests to participate in an intended procurement, the entity shall promptly start procedures for qualification;

(f) any supplier having requested to become a qualified supplier shall be advised by the entities concerned of the decision in this regard. Qualified suppliers included on permanent lists by entities shall also be notified of the termination of any such lists or of their removal from them;

(g) each Party shall ensure that:

(i) each entity and its constituent parts follow a single qualification procedure, except in cases of duly substantiated need for a different procedure; and

(ii) efforts be made to minimize differences in qualification procedures between entities.

(h) nothing in subparagraphs (a) through (g) shall preclude the exclusion of any supplier on grounds such as bankruptcy or false declarations, provided that such an action is consistent with the national treatment and non-discrimination provisions of this Agreement.

Article IX

Invitation to Participate Regarding Intended Procurement

* * *

Article X

Selection Procedures

1. To ensure optimum effective international competition under selective tendering procedures, entities shall, for each intended procurement, invite tenders from the maximum number of domestic suppliers and suppliers of other Parties, consistent with the efficient operation of the procurement system. They shall select the suppliers to participate in the procedure in a fair and non-discriminatory manner.

2. Entities maintaining permanent lists of qualified suppliers may select suppliers to be invited to tender from among those listed. Any selection shall allow for equitable opportunities for suppliers on the lists.

3. Suppliers requesting to participate in a particular intended procurement shall be permitted to submit a tender and be considered, provided, in the case of those not yet qualified, there is sufficient time to complete the qualification procedure under Articles VIII and IX. The number of additional suppliers permitted to participate shall be limited only by the efficient operation of the procurement system.

4. Requests to participate in selective tendering procedures may be submitted by telex, telegram or facsimile.

Article XI

Time-Limits for Tendering and Delivery

* * *

Article XII

Tender Documentation

* * *

Article XIII

Submission, Receipt and Opening of Tenders and Awarding of Contracts

* * *

Article XVI

Offsets

1. Entities shall not, in the qualification and selection of suppliers, products, or services, or in the evaluation of tenders and award of contract, impose, seek or consider offsets.[5]

2. Nevertheless, having regard to general policy considerations, including those relating to development, a developing country may at the time of accession negotiate conditions for the use of offsets, such as requirements for the incorporation of domestic content. Such requirements shall be used only for qualification to participate in the procurement process and not as criteria for awarding contracts. Conditions shall be objective, clearly defined and non-discriminatory. They shall be set forth in the country's Appendix I and may include precise limitations on the imposition of offsets in any contract subject to this Agreement. The existence of such conditions shall be notified to the Committee and included in the notice of intended procurement and other documentation.

Article XVII

Transparency

1. Each Party shall encourage entities to indicate the terms and conditions, including any deviations from competitive tendering procedures or access to challenge procedures, under which tenders will be entertained from suppliers situated in countries not Parties to this Agreement but which, with a view to creating transparency in their own contract awards, nevertheless:

(a) specify their contracts in accordance with Article VI (technical specifications);

(b) publish the procurement notices referred to in Article IX, including, in the version of the notice referred to in paragraph 8 of Article IX (summary of the notice of intended procurement) which is published in an official language of the WTO, an indication of the terms and conditions under which tenders shall be entertained from suppliers situated in countries Parties to this Agreement;

(c) are willing to ensure that their procurement regulations shall not normally change during a procurement and, in the event that such change proves unavoidable, to ensure the availability of a satisfactory means of redress.

---

[5] Offsets in government procurement are measures used to encourage local development or improve the balance-of-payments accounts by means of domestic content, licensing of technology, investment requirements, counter-trade or similar requirements.

2. Governments not Parties to the Agreement which comply with the conditions specified in paragraphs 1(a) through 1(c), shall be entitled if they so inform the Parties to participate in the Committee as observers.

Article XVIII

Information and Review as Regards Obligations of Entities

1. Entities shall publish a notice in the appropriate publication listed in Appendix II not later than 72 days after the award of each contract under Articles XIII through XV. These notices shall contain:

(a) the nature and quantity of products or services in the contract award;

(b) the name and address of the entity awarding the contract;

(c) the date of award;

(d) the name and address of winning tenderer;

(e) the value of the winning award or the highest and lowest offer taken into account in the award of the contract;

(f) where appropriate, means of identifying the notice issued under paragraph 1 of Article IX or justification according to Article XV for the use of such procedure; and

(g) the type of procedure used.

2. Each entity shall, on request from a supplier of a Party, promptly provide;

(a) an explanation of its procurement practices and procedures;

(b) pertinent information concerning the reasons why the supplier's application to qualify was rejected, why its existing qualification was brought to an end and why it was not selected; and

(c) to an unsuccessful tenderer, pertinent information concerning the reasons why its tender was not selected and on the characteristics and relative advantages of the tender selected as well as the name of the winning tenderer.

3. Entities shall promptly inform participating suppliers of decisions on contract awards and, upon request, in writing.

4. However, entities may decide that certain information on the contract award, contained in paragraphs 1 and 2(c), be withheld where release of such information would impede law enforcement or otherwise be contrary to the public interest or would prejudice the legitimate commercial interest of particular enterprises, public or private, or might prejudice fair competition between suppliers.

* * *

Article XX

Challenge Procedures

Consultations

1. In the event of a complaint by a supplier that there has been a breach of this Agreement in the context of a procurement, each Party shall encourage the supplier to seek resolution of its complaint in consultation with the procuring entity. In such instances the procuring entity shall accord impartial and timely consideration to any such complaint, in a manner that is not prejudicial to obtaining corrective measures under the challenge system.

Challenge

2. Each Party shall provide non-discriminatory, timely, transparent and effective procedures enabling suppliers to challenge alleged breaches of the Agreement arising in the context of procurements in which they have, or have had, an interest.

3. Each Party shall provide its challenge procedures in writing and make them generally available.

4. Each Party shall ensure that documentation relating to all aspects of the process concerning procurements covered by this Agreement shall be retained for three years.

5. The interested supplier may be required to initiate a challenge procedure and notify the procuring entity within specified time-limits from the time when the basis of the complaint is known or reasonably should have been known, but in no case within a period of less than 10 days.

6. Challenges shall be heard by a court or by an impartial and independent review body with no interest in the outcome of the procurement and the members of which are secure from external influence during the term of appointment. A review body which is not a court shall either be subject to judicial review or shall have procedures which provide that:

(a) participants can be heard before an opinion is given or a decision is reached;

(b) participants can be represented and accompanied;

(c) participants shall have access to all proceedings;

(d) proceedings can take place in public;

(e) opinions or decisions are given in writing with a statement describing the basis for the opinions or decisions;

(f) witnesses can be presented;

(g) documents are disclosed to the review body.

7. Challenge procedures shall provide for:

(a) rapid interim measures to correct breaches of the Agreement and to preserve commercial opportunities. Such action may result in suspension of the procurement process. However, procedures may provide that overriding adverse consequences for the interests concerned, including the public interest, may be taken into account in deciding whether such measures should be applied. In such circumstances, just cause for not acting shall be provided in writing;

(b) an assessment and a possibility for a decision on the justification of the challenge;

(c) correction of the breach of the Agreement or compensation for the loss or damages suffered, which may be limited to costs for tender preparation or protest.

8. With a view to the preservation of the commercial and other interests involved, the challenge procedure shall normally be completed in a timely fashion.

Article XXI

Institutions

1. A Committee on Government Procurement composed of representatives from each of the Parties shall be established. This Committee shall elect its own Chairman and Vice-Chairman and shall meet as necessary but not less than once a year for the purpose of affording Parties the opportunity to consult on any matters relating to the operation of this Agreement or the furtherance of its objectives, and to carry out such other responsibilities as may be assigned to it by the Parties.

2. The Committee may establish working parties or other subsidiary bodies which shall carry out such functions as may be given to them by the Committee.

Article XXII

Consultations and Dispute Settlement

1. The provisions of the Understanding on Rules and Procedures Governing the Settlement of Disputes under the WTO Agreement (hereinafter referred to as the "Dispute Settlement Understanding") shall be applicable except as otherwise specifically provided below.

2. If any Party considers that any benefit accruing to it, directly or indirectly, under this Agreement is being nullified or impaired, or that the attainment of any objective of this Agreement is being impeded as the result of the failure of another Party or Parties to carry out its obligations under this Agreement, or the application by another Party or Parties of any measure, whether or not it conflicts with the provisions of this Agreement, it may with a view to reaching a mutually satisfactory resolution of the

matter, make written representations or proposals to the other Party or Parties which it considers be concerned. Such action shall be promptly notified to the Dispute Settlement Body established under the Dispute Settlement Understanding (hereinafter referred to as "DSB"), as specified below. Any Party thus approached shall give sympathetic consideration to the representations or proposals made to it.

3. The DSB shall have the authority to establish panels, adopt panel and Appellate Body reports, make recommendations or give rulings on the matter, maintain surveillance of implementation of rulings and recommendations, and authorize suspension of concessions and other obligations under this Agreement or consultations regarding remedies when withdrawal of measures found to be in contravention of the Agreement is not possible, provided that only Members of the WTO Party to this Agreement shall participate in decisions or actions taken by the DAB with respect to disputes under this Agreement.

4. Panels shall have the following terms of reference unless the parties to the dispute agree otherwise within 20 days of the establishment of the panel:

> "To examine, in the light of the relevant provisions of this Agreement and of (name of any other covered Agreement cited by the parties to the dispute), the matter referred to the DSB by (name of party) in document . . . and to make such findings as will assist the DSB in making the recommendations or in giving the rulings provided for in this Agreement."

In the case of a dispute in which provisions both of this Agreement and of one or more other Agreements listed in Appendix 1 of the Dispute Settlement Understanding are invoked by one of the parties to the dispute, paragraph 3 shall apply only to those parts of the panel report concerning the interpretation and application of this Agreement.

5. Panels established by the DSB to examine disputes under this Agreement shall include persons qualified in the area of government procurement.

6. Every effort shall be made to accelerate the proceedings to the greatest extent possible. Notwithstanding the provisions of paragraphs 8 and 9 of Article 12 of the Dispute Settlement Understanding, the panel shall attempt to provide its final report to the parties to the dispute not later than four months, and in case of delay not later than seven months, after the date on which the composition and terms of reference of the panel are agreed. Consequently, every effort shall be made to reduce also the periods foreseen in paragraph 1 of Article 20 and paragraph 4 of Article 21 of the Dispute Settlement Understanding by two months. Moreover, notwithstanding the provisions of paragraph 5 of Article 21 of the Dispute Settlement Understanding, the panel shall attempt to issue its decision, in

case of a disagreement as to the existence or consistency with a covered Agreement of measures taken to comply with the recommendations and rulings, within 60 days.

7. Notwithstanding paragraph 2 of Article 22 of the Dispute Settlement Understanding, any dispute arising under any Agreement listed in Appendix 1 to the Dispute Settlement Understanding other than this Agreement shall not result in the suspension of concessions or other obligations under this Agreement, and any dispute arising under this Agreement shall not result in the suspension of concessions or other obligations under any other Agreement listed in the said Appendix 1.

Article XXIII

Exceptions to the Agreement

1. Nothing in this Agreement shall be construed to prevent any Party from taking any action or not disclosing any information which it considers necessary for the protection of its essential security interests relating to the procurement of arms, ammunition or war materials, or to procurement indispensable for national security or for national defense purposes.

2. Subject to the requirement that such measures are not applied in a manner which would constitute a means of arbitrary or unjustifiable discrimination between countries where the same conditions prevail or a disguised restriction on international trade, nothing in this Agreement shall be construed to prevent any Party from imposing or enforcing measures: necessary to protect public morals, order or safety, human, animal or plant life or health or intellectual property; or relating to the products or services of handicapped persons, of philanthropic institutions or of prison labour.

DOCUMENT 14

WTO AGREEMENT ON IMPLEMENTATION OF ARTICLE VI OF THE GENERAL AGREEMENT ON TARIFFS AND TRADE 1994 (WTO ANTIDUMPING AGREEMENT)

■ ■ ■

PART I

Article 1

Principles

An anti-dumping measure shall be applied only under the circumstances provided for in Article VI of GATT 1994 and pursuant to investigations initiated[1] and conducted in accordance with the provisions of this Agreement. The following provisions govern the application of Article VI of GATT 1994 in so far as action is taken under anti-dumping legislation or regulations.

Article 2

Determination of Dumping

2.1 For the purpose of this Agreement, a product is to be considered as being dumped, i.e. introduced into the commerce of another country at less than its normal value, if the export price of the product exported from one country to another is less than the comparable price, in the ordinary course of trade, for the like product when destined for consumption in the exporting country.

2.2 When there are no sales of the like product in the ordinary course of trade in the domestic market of the exporting country or when, because of the particular market situation or the low volume of the sales in the domestic market of the exporting country,[2] such sales do not permit a

---

[1] The term "initiated" as used in this Agreement means the procedural action by which a Member formally commences an investigation as provided in Article 5.

[2] Sales of the like product destined for consumption in the domestic market of the exporting country shall normally be considered a sufficient quantity for the determination of the normal value if such sales constitute 5 per cent or more of the sales of the product under consideration to the importing Member, provided that a lower ratio should be acceptable where the evidence

proper comparison, the margin of dumping shall be determined by comparison with a comparable price of the like product when exported to an appropriate third country, provided that this price is representative, or with the cost of production in the country of origin plus a reasonable amount for administrative, selling and general costs and for profits.

2.2.1 Sales of the like product in the domestic market of the exporting country or sales to a third country at prices below per unit (fixed and variable) costs of production plus administrative, selling and general costs may be treated as not being in the ordinary course of trade by reason of price and may be disregarded in determining normal value only if the authorities[3] determine that such sales are made within an extended period of time[4] in substantial quantities[5] and are at prices which do not provide for the recovery of all costs within a reasonable period of time. If prices which are below per unit costs at the time of sale are above weighted average per unit costs for the period of investigation, such prices shall be considered to provide for recovery of costs within a reasonable period of time.

2.2.1.1 For the purpose of paragraph 2, costs shall normally be calculated on the basis of records kept by the exporter or producer under investigation, provided that such records are in accordance with the generally accepted accounting principles of the exporting country and reasonably reflect the costs associated with the production and sale of the product under consideration. Authorities shall consider all available evidence on the proper allocation of costs, including that which is made available by the exporter or producer in the course of the investigation provided that such allocations have been historically utilized by the exporter or producer, in particular in relation to establishing appropriate amortization and depreciation periods and allowances for capital expenditures and other development costs. Unless already reflected in the cost allocations under this sub-paragraph, costs shall be adjusted appropriately for those non-recurring items of cost which benefit future and/or current

---

demonstrates that domestic sales at such lower ratio are nonetheless of sufficient magnitude to provide for a proper comparison.

[3] When in this Agreement the term "authorities" is used, it shall be interpreted as meaning authorities at an appropriate senior level.

[4] The extended period of time should normally be one year but shall in no case be less than six months.

[5] Sales below per unit costs are made in substantial quantities when the authorities establish that the weighted average selling price of the transactions under consideration for the determination of the normal value is below the weighted average per unit costs, or that the volume of sales below per unit costs represents not less than 20 per cent of the volume sold in transactions under consideration for the determination of the normal value.

production, or for circumstances in which costs during the period of investigation are affected by start-up operations.[6]

2.2.2 For the purpose of paragraph 2, the amounts for administrative, selling and general costs and for profits shall be based on actual data pertaining to production and sales in the ordinary course of trade of the like product by the exporter or producer under investigation. When such amounts cannot be determined on this basis, the amounts may be determined on the basis of:

(i) the actual amounts incurred and realized by the exporter or producer in question in respect of production and sales in the domestic market of the country of origin of the same general category of products;

(ii) the weighted average of the actual amounts incurred and realized by other exporters or producers subject to investigation in respect of production and sales of the like product in the domestic market of the country of origin;

(iii) any other reasonable method, provided that the amount for profit so established shall not exceed the profit normally realized by other exporters or producers on sales of products of the same general category in the domestic market of the country of origin.

2.3 In cases where there is no export price or where it appears to the authorities concerned that the export price is unreliable because of association or a compensatory arrangement between the exporter and the importer or a third party, the export price may be constructed on the basis of the price at which the imported products are first resold to an independent buyer, or if the products are not resold to an independent buyer, or not resold in the condition as imported, on such reasonable basis as the authorities may determine.

2.4 A fair comparison shall be made between the export price and the normal value. This comparison shall be made at the same level of trade, normally at the ex-factory level, and in respect of sales made at as nearly as possible the same time. Due allowance shall be made in each case, on its merits, for differences which affect price comparability, including differences in conditions and terms of sale, taxation, levels of trade, quantities, physical characteristics, and any other differences which are also demonstrated to affect price comparability.[7] In the cases referred to in paragraph 3, allowances for costs, including duties and taxes, incurred

[6] The adjustment made for start-up operations shall reflect the costs at the end of the start-up period or, if that period extends beyond the period of investigation, the most recent costs which can reasonably be taken into account by the authorities during the investigation.

[7] It is understood that some of the above factors may overlap, and authorities shall ensure that they do not duplicate adjustments that have been already made under this provision.

between importation and resale, and for profits accruing, should also be made. If in these cases price comparability has been affected, the authorities shall establish the normal value at a level of trade equivalent to the level of trade of the constructed export price, or shall make due allowance as warranted under this paragraph. The authorities shall indicate to the parties in question what information is necessary to ensure a fair comparison and shall not impose an unreasonable burden of proof on those parties.

2.4.1 When the comparison under paragraph 4 requires a conversion of currencies, such conversion should be made using the rate of exchange on the date of sale,[8] provided that when a sale of foreign currency on forward markets is directly linked to the export sale involved, the rate of exchange in the forward sale shall be used. Fluctuations in exchange rates shall be ignored and in an investigation the authorities shall allow exporters at least 60 days to have adjusted their export prices to reflect sustained movements in exchange rates during the period of investigation.

2.4.2 Subject to the provisions governing fair comparison in paragraph 4, the existence of margins of dumping during the investigation phase shall normally be established on the basis of a comparison of a weighted average normal value with a weighted average of prices of all comparable export transactions or by a comparison of normal value and export prices on a transaction-to-transaction basis. A normal value established on a weighted average basis may be compared to prices of individual export transactions if the authorities find a pattern of export prices which differ significantly among different purchasers, regions or time periods, and if an explanation is provided as to why such differences cannot be taken into account appropriately by the use of a weighted average-to-weighted average or transaction-to-transaction comparison.

2.5 In the case where products are not imported directly from the country of origin but are exported to the importing Member from an intermediate country, the price at which the products are sold from the country of export to the importing Member shall normally be compared with the comparable price in the country of export. However, comparison may be made with the price in the country of origin, if, for example, the products are merely transshipped through the country of export, or such products are not produced in the country of export, or there is no comparable price for them in the country of export.

2.6 Throughout this Agreement the term "like product" ("produit similaire") shall be interpreted to mean a product which is identical, i.e.

---

[8] Normally, the date of sale would be the date of contract, purchase order, order confirmation, or invoice, whichever establishes the material terms of sale.

alike in all respects to the product under consideration, or in the absence of such a product, another product which, although not alike in all respects, has characteristics closely resembling those of the product under consideration.

2.7 This Article is without prejudice to the second Supplementary Provision to paragraph 1 of Article VI in Annex I to GATT 1994.

Article 3

Determination of Injury[9]

3.1 A determination of injury for purposes of Article VI of GATT 1994 shall be based on positive evidence and involve an objective examination of both *(a)* the volume of the dumped imports and the effect of the dumped imports on prices in the domestic market for like products, and *(b)* the consequent impact of these imports on domestic producers of such products.

3.2 With regard to the volume of the dumped imports, the investigating authorities shall consider whether there has been a significant increase in dumped imports, either in absolute terms or relative to production or consumption in the importing Member. With regard to the effect of the dumped imports on prices, the investigating authorities shall consider whether there has been a significant price undercutting by the dumped imports as compared with the price of a like product of the importing Member, or whether the effect of such imports is otherwise to depress prices to a significant degree or prevent price increases, which otherwise would have occurred, to a significant degree. No one or several of these factors can necessarily give decisive guidance.

3.3 Where imports of a product from more than one country are simultaneously subject to anti-dumping investigations, the investigating authorities may cumulatively assess the effects of such imports only if they determine that *(a)* the margin of dumping established in relation to the imports from each country is more than *de minimis* as defined in paragraph 8 of Article 5 and the volume of imports from each country is not negligible and *(b)* a cumulative assessment of the effects of the imports is appropriate in light of the conditions of competition between the imported products and the conditions of competition between the imported products and the like domestic product.

3.4 The examination of the impact of the dumped imports on the domestic industry concerned shall include an evaluation of all relevant economic factors and indices having a bearing on the state of the industry, including actual and potential decline in sales, profits, output, market share, productivity, return on investments, or utilization of capacity;

[9] Under this Agreement the term "injury" shall, unless otherwise specified, be taken to mean material injury to a domestic industry, threat of material injury to a domestic industry or material retardation of the establishment of such an industry and shall be interpreted in accordance with the provisions of this Article.

factors affecting domestic prices; the magnitude of the margin of dumping; actual and potential negative effects on cash flow, inventories, employment, wages, growth, ability to raise capital or investments. This list is not exhaustive, nor can one or several of these factors necessarily give decisive guidance.

3.5 It must be demonstrated that the dumped imports are, through the effects of dumping, as set forth in paragraphs 2 and 4, causing injury within the meaning of this Agreement. The demonstration of a causal relationship between the dumped imports and the injury to the domestic industry shall be based on an examination of all relevant evidence before the authorities. The authorities shall also examine any known factors other than the dumped imports which at the same time are injuring the domestic industry, and the injuries caused by these other factors must not be attributed to the dumped imports. Factors which may be relevant in this respect include, *inter alia,* the volume and prices of imports not sold at dumping prices, contraction in demand or changes in the patterns of consumption, trade restrictive practices of and competition between the foreign and domestic producers, developments in technology and the export performance and productivity of the domestic industry.

3.6 The effect of the dumped imports shall be assessed in relation to the domestic production of the like product when available data permit the separate identification of that production on the basis of such criteria as the production process, producers' sales and profits. If such separate identification of that production is not possible, the effects of the dumped imports shall be assessed by the examination of the production of the narrowest group or range of products, which includes the like product, for which the necessary information can be provided.

3.7 A determination of a threat of material injury shall be based on facts and not merely on allegation, conjecture or remote possibility. The change in circumstances which would create a situation in which the dumping would cause injury must be clearly foreseen and imminent.[10] In making a determination regarding the existence of a threat of material injury, the authorities should consider, *inter alia,* such factors as:

(i) a significant rate of increase of dumped imports into the domestic market indicating the likelihood of substantially increased importation;

(ii) sufficient freely disposable, or an imminent, substantial increase in, capacity of the exporter indicating the likelihood of substantially increased dumped exports to the importing Member's

---

[10] One example, though not an exclusive one, is that there is convincing reason to believe that there will be, in the near future, substantially increased importation of the product at dumped prices.

market, taking into account the availability of other export markets to absorb any additional exports;

(iii) whether imports are entering at prices that will have a significant depressing or suppressing effect on domestic prices, and would likely increase demand for further imports; and

(iv) inventories of the product being investigated.

No one of these factors by itself can necessarily give decisive guidance but the totality of the factors considered must lead to the conclusion that further dumped exports are imminent and that, unless protective action is taken, material injury would occur.

3.8 With respect to cases where injury is threatened by dumped imports, the application of anti-dumping measures shall be considered and decided with special care.

Article 4

Definition of Domestic Industry

4.1 For the purposes of this Agreement, the term "domestic industry" shall be interpreted as referring to the domestic producers as a whole of the like products or to those of them whose collective output of the products constitutes a major proportion of the total domestic production of those products, except that:

(i) when producers are related[11] to the exporters or importers or are themselves importers of the allegedly dumped product, the term "domestic industry" may be interpreted as referring to the rest of the producers;

(ii) in exceptional circumstances the territory of a Member may, for the production in question, be divided into two or more competitive markets and the producers within each market may be regarded as a separate industry if *(a)* the producers within such market sell all or almost all of their production of the product in question in that market, and *(b)* the demand in that market is not to any substantial degree supplied by producers of the product in question located elsewhere in the territory. * * *

4.2 When the domestic industry has been interpreted as referring to the producers in a certain area, i.e. a market as defined in paragraph 1(ii), anti-dumping duties shall be levied only on the products in question

---

[11] For the purpose of this paragraph, producers shall be deemed to be related to exporters or importers only if *(a)* one of them directly or indirectly controls the other; or *(b)* both of them are directly or indirectly controlled by a third person; or *(c)* together they directly or indirectly control a third person, provided that there are grounds for believing or suspecting that the effect of the relationship is such as to cause the producer concerned to behave differently from non-related producers. For the purpose of this paragraph, one shall be deemed to control another when the former is legally or operationally in a position to exercise restraint or direction over the latter.

consigned for final consumption to that area. When the constitutional law of the importing Member does not permit the levying of anti-dumping duties on such a basis, the importing Member may levy the anti-dumping duties without limitation only if *(a)* the exporters shall have been given an opportunity to cease exporting at dumped prices to the area concerned or otherwise give assurances pursuant to Article 8 and adequate assurances in this regard have not been promptly given, and *(b)* such duties cannot be levied only on products of specific producers which supply the area in question.

4.3 Where two or more countries have reached under the provisions of paragraph 8(a) of Article XXIV of GATT 1994 such a level of integration that they have the characteristics of a single, unified market, the industry in the entire area of integration shall be taken to be the domestic industry referred to in paragraph 1.

4.4 The provisions of paragraph 6 of Article 3 shall be applicable to this Article.

Article 5

Initiation and Subsequent Investigation

5.1 Except as provided for in paragraph 6, an investigation to determine the existence, degree and effect of any alleged dumping shall be initiated upon a written application by or on behalf of the domestic industry.

5.2 An application under paragraph 1 shall include evidence of *(a)* dumping, *(b)* injury within the meaning of Article VI of GATT 1994 as interpreted by this Agreement and *(c)* a causal link between the dumped imports and the alleged injury. Simple assertion, unsubstantiated by relevant evidence, cannot be considered sufficient to meet the requirements of this paragraph. The application shall contain such information as is reasonably available to the applicant on the following:

(i) the identity of the applicant and a description of the volume and value of the domestic production of the like product by the applicant. Where a written application is made on behalf of the domestic industry, the application shall identify the industry on behalf of which the application is made by a list of all known domestic producers of the like product (or associations of domestic producers of the like product) and, to the extent possible, a description of the volume and value of domestic production of the like product accounted for by such producers;

(ii) a complete description of the allegedly dumped product, the names of the country or countries of origin or export in question, the identity of each known exporter or foreign producer and a list of known persons importing the product in question;

(iii) information on prices at which the product in question is sold when destined for consumption in the domestic markets of the country or countries of origin or export (or, where appropriate, information on the prices at which the product is sold from the country or countries of origin or export to a third country or countries, or on the constructed value of the product) and information on export prices or, where appropriate, on the prices at which the product is first resold to an independent buyer in the territory of the importing Member;

(iv) information on the evolution of the volume of the allegedly dumped imports, the effect of these imports on prices of the like product in the domestic market and the consequent impact of the imports on the domestic industry, as demonstrated by relevant factors and indices having a bearing on the state of the domestic industry, such as those listed in paragraphs 2 and 4 of Article 3.

5.3 The authorities shall examine the accuracy and adequacy of the evidence provided in the application to determine whether there is sufficient evidence to justify the initiation of an investigation.

5.4 An investigation shall not be initiated pursuant to paragraph 1 unless the authorities have determined, on the basis of an examination of the degree of support for, or opposition to, the application expressed by domestic producers of the like product, that the application has been made by or on behalf of the domestic industry.[12] The application shall be considered to have been made "by or on behalf of the domestic industry" if it is supported by those domestic producers whose collective output constitutes more than 50 per cent of the total production of the like product produced by that portion of the domestic industry expressing either support for or opposition to the application. However, no investigation shall be initiated when domestic producers expressly supporting the application account for less than 25 per cent of total production of the like product produced by the domestic industry.

* * *

5.6 If, in special circumstances, the authorities concerned decide to initiate an investigation without having received a written application by or on behalf of a domestic industry for the initiation of such investigation, they shall proceed only if they have sufficient evidence of dumping, injury and a causal link, as described in paragraph 2, to justify the initiation of an investigation.

* * *

[12] Members are aware that in the territory of certain Members employees of domestic producers of the like product or representatives of those employees may make or support an application for an investigation under paragraph 1.

Article 6

Evidence

6.1 All interested parties in an anti-dumping investigation shall be given notice of the information which the authorities require and ample opportunity to present in writing all evidence which they consider relevant in respect of the investigation in question.

6.1.1 Exporters or foreign producers receiving questionnaires used in an anti-dumping investigation shall be given at least 30 days for reply. Due consideration should be given to any request for an extension of the 30–day period and, upon cause shown, such an extension should be granted whenever practicable.

6.1.2 Subject to the requirement to protect confidential information, evidence presented in writing by one interested party shall be made available promptly to other interested parties participating in the investigation.

6.1.3 As soon as an investigation has been initiated, the authorities shall provide the full text of the written application received under paragraph 1 of Article 5 to the known exporters and to the authorities of the exporting Member and shall make it available, upon request, to other interested parties involved. Due regard shall be paid to the requirement for the protection of confidential information, as provided for in paragraph 5.

6.2 Throughout the anti-dumping investigation all interested parties shall have a full opportunity for the defence of their interests. To this end, the authorities shall, on request, provide opportunities for all interested parties to meet those parties with adverse interests, so that opposing views may be presented and rebuttal arguments offered. Provision of such opportunities must take account of the need to preserve confidentiality and of the convenience to the parties. There shall be no obligation on any party to attend a meeting, and failure to do so shall not be prejudicial to that party's case. Interested parties shall also have the right, on justification, to present other information orally.

* * *

6.5 Any information which is by nature confidential (for example, because its disclosure would be of significant competitive advantage to a competitor or because its disclosure would have a significantly adverse effect upon a person supplying the information or upon a person from whom that person acquired the information), or which is provided on a confidential basis by parties to an investigation shall, upon good cause shown, be treated as such by the authorities. Such information shall not be disclosed without specific permission of the party submitting it.

6.5.1 The authorities shall require interested parties providing confidential information to furnish non-confidential summaries thereof. These summaries shall be in sufficient detail to permit a reasonable understanding of the substance of the information submitted in confidence. In exceptional circumstances, such parties may indicate that such information is not susceptible of summary. In such exceptional circumstances, a statement of the reasons why summarization is not possible must be provided.

6.5.2 If the authorities find that a request for confidentiality is not warranted and if the supplier of the information is either unwilling to make the information public or to authorize its disclosure in generalized or summary form, the authorities may disregard such information unless it can be demonstrated to their satisfaction from appropriate sources that the information is correct.

6.6 Except in circumstances provided for in paragraph 8, the authorities shall during the course of an investigation satisfy themselves as to the accuracy of the information supplied by interested parties upon which their findings are based.

6.7 In order to verify information provided or to obtain further details, the authorities may carry out investigations in the territory of other Members as required, provided they obtain the agreement of the firms concerned and notify the representatives of the government of the Member in question, and unless that Member objects to the investigation. * * *

6.8 In cases in which any interested party refuses access to, or otherwise does not provide, necessary information within a reasonable period or significantly impedes the investigation, preliminary and final determinations, affirmative or negative, may be made on the basis of the facts available. The provisions of Annex II shall be observed in the application of this paragraph.

* * *

6.10 The authorities shall, as a rule, determine an individual margin of dumping for each known exporter or producer concerned of the product under investigation. In cases where the number of exporters, producers, importers or types of products involved is so large as to make such a determination impracticable, the authorities may limit their examination either to a reasonable number of interested parties or products by using samples which are statistically valid on the basis of information available to the authorities at the time of the selection, or to the largest percentage of the volume of the exports from the country in question which can reasonably be investigated.

6.10.1 Any selection of exporters, producers, importers or types of products made under this paragraph shall preferably be chosen in consultation with and with the consent of the exporters, producers or importers concerned.

6.10.2 In cases where the authorities have limited their examination, as provided for in this paragraph, they shall nevertheless determine an individual margin of dumping for any exporter or producer not initially selected who submits the necessary information in time for that information to be considered during the course of the investigation, except where the number of exporters or producers is so large that individual examinations would be unduly burdensome to the authorities and prevent the timely completion of the investigation. Voluntary responses shall not be discouraged.

* * *

6.12 The authorities shall provide opportunities for industrial users of the product under investigation, and for representative consumer organizations in cases where the product is commonly sold at the retail level, to provide information which is relevant to the investigation regarding dumping, injury and causality.

6.13 The authorities shall take due account of any difficulties experienced by interested parties, in particular small companies, in supplying information requested, and shall provide any assistance practicable.

* * *

Article 7

Provisional Measures

7.1 Provisional measures may be applied only if:

(i) an investigation has been initiated in accordance with the provisions of Article 5, a public notice has been given to that effect and interested parties have been given adequate opportunities to submit information and make comments;

(ii) a preliminary affirmative determination has been made of dumping and consequent injury to a domestic industry; and

(iii) the authorities concerned judge such measures necessary to prevent injury being caused during the investigation.

7.2 Provisional measures may take the form of a provisional duty or, preferably, a security—by cash deposit or bond—equal to the amount of the anti-dumping duty provisionally estimated, being not greater than the provisionally estimated margin of dumping. Withholding of appraisement is an appropriate provisional measure, provided that the normal duty and the estimated amount of the anti-dumping duty be indicated and as long as the withholding of appraisement is subject to the same conditions as other provisional measures.

7.3 Provisional measures shall not be applied sooner than 60 days from the date of initiation of the investigation.

7.4 The application of provisional measures shall be limited to as short a period as possible, not exceeding four months or, on decision of the authorities concerned, upon request by exporters representing a significant percentage of the trade involved, to a period not exceeding six months. When authorities, in the course of an investigation, examine whether a duty lower than the margin of dumping would be sufficient to remove injury, these periods may be six and nine months, respectively.

7.5 The relevant provisions of Article 9 shall be followed in the application of provisional measures.

Article 8

Price Undertakings

8.1 Proceedings may[19] be suspended or terminated without the imposition of provisional measures or anti-dumping duties upon receipt of satisfactory voluntary undertakings from any exporter to revise its prices or to cease exports to the area in question at dumped prices so that the authorities are satisfied that the injurious effect of the dumping is eliminated. Price increases under such undertakings shall not be higher than necessary to eliminate the margin of dumping. It is desirable that the price increases be less than the margin of dumping if such increases would be adequate to remove the injury to the domestic industry.

8.2 Price undertakings shall not be sought or accepted from exporters unless the authorities of the importing Member have made a preliminary affirmative determination of dumping and injury caused by such dumping.

8.3 Undertakings offered need not be accepted if the authorities consider their acceptance impractical, for example, if the number of actual or potential exporters is too great, or for other reasons, including reasons of general policy. Should the case arise and where practicable, the authorities shall provide to the exporter the reasons which have led them to consider acceptance of an undertaking as inappropriate, and shall, to the extent possible, give the exporter an opportunity to make comments thereon.

8.4 If an undertaking is accepted, the investigation of dumping and injury shall nevertheless be completed if the exporter so desires or the authorities so decide. In such a case, if a negative determination of dumping or injury is made, the undertaking shall automatically lapse,

---

[19] The word "may" shall not be interpreted to allow the simultaneous continuation of proceedings with the implementation of price undertakings except as provided in paragraph 4.

except in cases where such a determination is due in large part to the existence of a price undertaking. In such cases, the authorities may require that an undertaking be maintained for a reasonable period consistent with the provisions of this Agreement. In the event that an affirmative determination of dumping and injury is made, the undertaking shall continue consistent with its terms and the provisions of this Agreement.

8.5 Price undertakings may be suggested by the authorities of the importing Member, but no exporter shall be forced to enter into such undertakings. The fact that exporters do not offer such undertakings, or do not accept an invitation to do so, shall in no way prejudice the consideration of the case. However, the authorities are free to determine that a threat of injury is more likely to be realized if the dumped imports continue.

8.6 Authorities of an importing Member may require any exporter from whom an undertaking has been accepted to provide periodically information relevant to the fulfilment of such an undertaking and to permit verification of pertinent data. In case of violation of an undertaking, the authorities of the importing Member may take, under this Agreement in conformity with its provisions, expeditious actions which may constitute immediate application of provisional measures using the best information available. In such cases, definitive duties may be levied in accordance with this Agreement on products entered for consumption not more than 90 days before the application of such provisional measures, except that any such retroactive assessment shall not apply to imports entered before the violation of the undertaking.

Article 9

Imposition and Collection of Anti-Dumping Duties

9.1 The decision whether or not to impose an anti-dumping duty in cases where all requirements for the imposition have been fulfilled, and the decision whether the amount of the anti-dumping duty to be imposed shall be the full margin of dumping or less, are decisions to be made by the authorities of the importing Member. It is desirable that the imposition be permissive in the territory of all Members, and that the duty be less than the margin if such lesser duty would be adequate to remove the injury to the domestic industry.

9.2 When an anti-dumping duty is imposed in respect of any product, such anti-dumping duty shall be collected in the appropriate amounts in each case, on a non-discriminatory basis on imports of such product from all sources found to be dumped and causing injury, except as to imports from those sources from which price undertakings under the terms of this Agreement have been accepted. The authorities shall name the supplier or suppliers of the product concerned. If, however, several suppliers from the same country are involved, and it is impracticable to name all these suppliers, the authorities may name the supplying country concerned. If several suppliers from more than one country are involved, the authorities may name either all the suppliers involved, or, if this is impracticable, all the supplying countries involved.

9.3 The amount of the anti-dumping duty shall not exceed the margin of dumping as established under Article 2.

* * *

Article 10

Retroactivity

10.1 Provisional measures and anti-dumping duties shall only be applied to products which enter for consumption after the time when the decision taken under paragraph 1 of Article 7 and paragraph 1 of Article 9, respectively, enters into force, subject to the exceptions set out in this Article.

* * *

Article 11

Duration and Review of Anti-Dumping Duties and Price Undertakings

11.1 An anti-dumping duty shall remain in force only as long as and to the extent necessary to counteract dumping which is causing injury.

11.2 The authorities shall review the need for the continued imposition of the duty, where warranted, on their own initiative or, provided that a reasonable period of time has elapsed since the imposition of the definitive anti-dumping duty, upon request by any interested party which submits positive information substantiating the need for a review. Interested parties shall have the right to request the authorities to examine whether the continued imposition of the duty is necessary to offset dumping, whether the injury would be likely to continue or recur if the duty were removed or varied, or both. If, as a result of the review under this paragraph, the authorities determine that the anti-dumping duty is no longer warranted, it shall be terminated immediately.

11.3 Notwithstanding the provisions of paragraphs 1 and 2, any definitive anti-dumping duty shall be terminated on a date not later than five years from its imposition (or from the date of the most recent review under paragraph 2 if that review has covered both dumping and injury, or under this paragraph), unless the authorities determine, in a review initiated before that date on their own initiative or upon a duly substantiated request made by or on behalf of the domestic industry within a reasonable period of time prior to that date, that the expiry of the duty would be likely to lead to continuation or recurrence of dumping and injury. The duty may remain in force pending the outcome of such a review.

11.4 The provisions of Article 6 regarding evidence and procedure shall apply to any review carried out under this Article. Any such review shall be carried out expeditiously and shall normally be concluded within 12 months of the date of initiation of the review.

11.5 The provisions of this Article shall apply *mutatis mutandis* to price undertakings accepted under Article 8.

Article 12

Public Notice and Explanation of Determinations

12.1 When the authorities are satisfied that there is sufficient evidence to justify the initiation of an anti-dumping investigation pursuant to Article 5, the Member or Members the products of which are subject to such investigation and other interested parties known to the investigating authorities to have an interest therein shall be notified and a public notice shall be given.

12.1.1 A public notice of the initiation of an investigation shall contain, or otherwise make available through a separate report, adequate information on the following:

(i) the name of the exporting country or countries and the product involved;

(ii) the date of initiation of the investigation;

(iii) the basis on which dumping is alleged in the application;

(iv) a summary of the factors on which the allegation of injury is based;

(v) the address to which representations by interested parties should be directed;

(vi) the time-limits allowed to interested parties for making their views known.

12.2 Public notice shall be given of any preliminary or final determination, whether affirmative or negative, of any decision to accept an undertaking pursuant to Article 8, of the termination of such an undertaking, and of the termination of a definitive anti-dumping duty. * * *

12.2.1 A public notice of the imposition of provisional measures shall set forth, or otherwise make available through a separate report, sufficiently detailed explanations for the preliminary determinations on dumping and injury and shall refer to the matters of fact and law which have led to arguments being accepted or rejected. Such a notice or report shall, due regard being paid to the requirement for the protection of confidential information, contain in particular:

(i) the names of the suppliers, or when this is impracticable, the supplying countries involved;

(ii) a description of the product which is sufficient for customs purposes;

(iii) the margins of dumping established and a full explanation of the reasons for the methodology used in the establishment and comparison of the export price and the normal value under Article 2;

(iv) considerations relevant to the injury determination as set out in Article 3;

(v) the main reasons leading to the determination.

12.2.2 A public notice of conclusion or suspension of an investigation in the case of an affirmative determination providing for the imposition of a definitive duty or the acceptance of a price undertaking shall contain, or otherwise make available through a separate report, all relevant information on the matters of fact and law and reasons which have led to the imposition of final measures or the acceptance of a price undertaking, due regard being paid to the requirement for the protection of confidential information. In particular, the notice or report shall contain the information described in subparagraph 2.1, as well as the reasons for the acceptance or rejection of relevant arguments or claims made by the exporters and importers, and the basis for any decision made under subparagraph 10.2 of Article 6.

12.2.3 A public notice of the termination or suspension of an investigation following the acceptance of an undertaking pursuant to Article 8 shall include, or otherwise make available through a separate report, the non-confidential part of this undertaking.

12.3 The provisions of this Article shall apply *mutatis mutandis* to the initiation and completion of reviews pursuant to Article 11 and to decisions under Article 10 to apply duties retroactively.

Article 13

Judicial Review

Each Member whose national legislation contains provisions on anti-dumping measures shall maintain judicial, arbitral or administrative tribunals or procedures for the purpose, *inter alia,* of the prompt review of administrative actions relating to final determinations and reviews of determinations within the meaning of Article 11. Such tribunals or procedures shall be independent of the authorities responsible for the determination or review in question.

Article 14

Anti-Dumping Action on Behalf of a Third Country

14.1 An application for anti-dumping action on behalf of a third country shall be made by the authorities of the third country requesting action.

14.2 Such an application shall be supported by price information to show that the imports are being dumped and by detailed information to show that the alleged dumping is causing injury to the domestic industry concerned in the third country. The government of the third country shall afford all assistance to the authorities of the importing country to obtain any further information which the latter may require.

14.3 In considering such an application, the authorities of the importing country shall consider the effects of the alleged dumping on the industry concerned as a whole in the third country; that is to say, the injury shall not be assessed in relation only to the effect of the alleged dumping on the industry's exports to the importing country or even on the industry's total exports.

14.4 The decision whether or not to proceed with a case shall rest with the importing country. If the importing country decides that it is prepared to take action, the initiation of the approach to the Council for Trade in Goods seeking its approval for such action shall rest with the importing country.

Article 15

Developing Country Members

It is recognized that special regard must be given by developed country Members to the special situation of developing country Members when considering the application of anti-dumping measures under this Agreement. Possibilities of constructive remedies provided for by this Agreement shall be explored before applying anti-dumping duties where they would affect the essential interests of developing country Members.

PART II

* * *

Article 17

Consultation and Dispute Settlement

17.1 Except as otherwise provided herein, the Dispute Settlement Understanding is applicable to consultations and the settlement of disputes under this Agreement.

17.2 Each Member shall afford sympathetic consideration to, and shall afford adequate opportunity for consultation regarding, representations made by another Member with respect to any matter affecting the operation of this Agreement.

17.3 If any Member considers that any benefit accruing to it, directly or indirectly, under this Agreement is being nullified or impaired, or that the achievement of any objective is being impeded, by another Member or Members, it may, with a view to reaching a mutually satisfactory resolution of the matter, request in writing consultations with the Member or Members in question. Each Member shall afford sympathetic consideration to any request from another Member for consultation.

17.4 If the Member that requested consultations considers that the consultations pursuant to paragraph 3 have failed to achieve a mutually agreed solution, and if final action has been taken by the administering authorities of the importing Member to levy definitive anti-dumping duties or to accept price undertakings, it may refer the matter to the Dispute Settlement Body ("DSB"). When a provisional measure has a significant impact and the Member that requested consultations considers that the measure was taken contrary to the provisions of paragraph 1 of Article 7, that Member may also refer such matter to the DSB.

17.5 The DSB shall, at the request of the complaining party, establish a panel to examine the matter based upon:

(i) a written statement of the Member making the request indicating how a benefit accruing to it, directly or indirectly, under this Agreement has been nullified or impaired, or that the achieving of the objectives of the Agreement is being impeded, and

(ii) the facts made available in conformity with appropriate domestic procedures to the authorities of the importing Member.

17.6 In examining the matter referred to in paragraph 5:

(i) in its assessment of the facts of the matter, the panel shall determine whether the authorities' establishment of the facts was proper and whether their evaluation of those facts was unbiased and objective. If the establishment of the facts was proper and the evaluation was unbiased and objective, even though the panel might have reached a different conclusion, the evaluation shall not be overturned;

(ii) the panel shall interpret the relevant provisions of the Agreement in accordance with customary rules of interpretation of public international law. Where the panel finds that a relevant provision of the Agreement admits of more than one permissible interpretation, the panel shall find the authorities' measure to be in conformity with the Agreement if it rests upon one of those permissible interpretations.

* * *

ANNEX II

BEST INFORMATION AVAILABLE IN TERMS OF PARAGRAPH 8 OF ARTICLE 6

1. As soon as possible after the initiation of the investigation, the investigating authorities should specify in detail the information required from any interested party, and the manner in which that information should be structured by the interested party in its response. The authorities should also ensure that the party is aware that if information is not supplied within a reasonable time, the authorities will be free to make determinations on the basis of the facts available, including those contained in the application for the initiation of the investigation by the domestic industry.

2. The authorities may also request that an interested party provide its response in a particular medium (e.g. computer tape) or computer language. * * *

3. All information which is verifiable, which is appropriately submitted so that it can be used in the investigation without undue difficulties, which is supplied in a timely fashion, and, where applicable, which is supplied in a medium or computer language requested by the authorities, should be taken into account when determinations are made. If a party does not respond in the preferred medium or computer language but the authorities find that the circumstances set out in paragraph 2 have been satisfied, the failure to respond in the preferred medium or computer language should not be considered to significantly impede the investigation.

4. Where the authorities do not have the ability to process information if provided in a particular medium (e.g. computer tape), the information should be supplied in the form of written material or any other form acceptable to the authorities.

5. Even though the information provided may not be ideal in all respects, this should not justify the authorities from disregarding it, provided the interested party has acted to the best of its ability.

6. If evidence or information is not accepted, the supplying party should be informed forthwith of the reasons therefor, and should have an opportunity to provide further explanations within a reasonable period, due account being taken of the time-limits of the investigation. If the explanations are considered by the authorities as not being satisfactory, the reasons for the rejection of such evidence or information should be given in any published determinations.

7. If the authorities have to base their findings, including those with respect to normal value, on information from a secondary source, including the information supplied in the application for the initiation of the

investigation, they should do so with special circumspection. In such cases, the authorities should, where practicable, check the information from other independent sources at their disposal, such as published price lists, official import statistics and customs returns, and from the information obtained from other interested parties during the investigation. It is clear, however, that if an interested party does not cooperate and thus relevant information is being withheld from the authorities, this situation could lead to a result which is less favourable to the party than if the party did cooperate.

DOCUMENT 15

WTO AGREEMENT ON IMPLEMENTATION OF ARTICLE VII OF THE GENERAL AGREEMENT ON TARIFFS AND TRADE 1994 (CUSTOMS VALUATION)

■ ■ ■

GENERAL INTRODUCTORY COMMENTARY

1. The primary basis for customs value under this Agreement is "transaction value" as defined in Article 1. Article 1 is to be read together with Article 8 which provides, *inter alia,* for adjustments to the price actually paid or payable in cases where certain specific elements which are considered to form a part of the value for customs purposes are incurred by the buyer but are not included in the price actually paid or payable for the imported goods. Article 8 also provides for the inclusion in the transaction value of certain considerations which may pass from the buyer to the seller in the form of specified goods or services rather than in the form of money. Articles 2 through 7 provide methods of determining the customs value whenever it cannot be determined under the provisions of Article 1.

2. Where the customs value cannot be determined under the provisions of Article 1 there should normally be a process of consultation between the customs administration and importer with a view to arriving at a basis of value under the provisions of Article 2 or 3. It may occur, for example, that the importer has information about the customs value of identical or similar imported goods which is not immediately available to the customs administration in the port of importation. On the other hand, the customs administration may have information about the customs value of identical or similar imported goods which is not readily available to the importer. A process of consultation between the two parties will enable information to be exchanged, subject to the requirements of commercial confidentiality, with a view to determining a proper basis of value for customs purposes.

3. Articles 5 and 6 provide two bases for determining the customs value where it cannot be determined on the basis of the transaction value of the imported goods or of identical or similar imported goods. Under paragraph 1 of Article 5 the customs value is determined on the basis of the price at which the goods are sold in the condition as imported to an

unrelated buyer in the country of importation. The importer also has the right to have goods which are further processed after importation valued under the provisions of Article 5 if the importer so requests. Under Article 6 the customs value is determined on the basis of the computed value. Both these methods present certain difficulties and because of this the importer is given the right, under the provisions of Article 4, to choose the order of application of the two methods.

4. Article 7 sets out how to determine the customs value in cases where it cannot be determined under the provisions of any of the preceding Articles.

DOCUMENT 16

WTO AGREEMENT ON RULES OF ORIGIN

■ ■ ■

PART I

DEFINITIONS AND COVERAGE

Article 1

Rules of Origin

1. For the purposes of Parts I to IV of this Agreement, rules of origin shall be defined as those laws, regulations and administrative determinations of general application applied by any Member to determine the country of origin of goods provided such rules of origin are not related to contractual or autonomous trade regimes leading to the granting of tariff preferences going beyond the application of paragraph 1 of Article I of GATT 1994.

2. Rules of origin referred to in paragraph 1 shall include all rules of origin used in non-preferential commercial policy instruments, such as in the application of: most-favoured-nation treatment under Articles I, II, III, XI and XIII of GATT 1994; anti-dumping and countervailing duties under Article VI of GATT 1994; safeguard measures under Article XIX of GATT 1994; origin marking requirements under Article IX of GATT 1994; and any discriminatory quantitative restrictions or tariff quotas. They shall also include rules of origin used for government procurement and trade statistics.[1]

PART II

DISCIPLINES TO GOVERN THE APPLICATION OF RULES OF ORIGIN

Article 2

Disciplines During the Transition Period

Until the work programme for the harmonization of rules of origin set out in Part IV is completed, Members shall ensure that:

---

[1] It is understood that this provision is without prejudice to those determinations made for purposes of defining "domestic industry" or "like products of domestic industry" or similar terms wherever they apply.

(a) when they issue administrative determinations of general application, the requirements to be fulfilled are clearly defined. In particular:

(i) in cases where the criterion of change of tariff classification is applied, such a rule of origin, and any exceptions to the rule, must clearly specify the subheadings or headings within the tariff nomenclature that are addressed by the rule;

(ii) in cases where the ad valorem percentage criterion is applied, the method for calculating this percentage shall also be indicated in the rules of origin;

(iii) in cases where the criterion of manufacturing or processing operation is prescribed, the operation that confers origin on the good concerned shall be precisely specified;

(b) notwithstanding the measure or instrument of commercial policy to which they are linked, their rules of origin are not used as instruments to pursue trade objectives directly or indirectly;

(c) rules of origin shall not themselves create restrictive, distorting, or disruptive effects on international trade. They shall not pose unduly strict requirements or require the fulfilment of a certain condition not related to manufacturing or processing, as a prerequisite for the determination of the country of origin. However, costs not directly related to manufacturing or processing may be included for the purposes of the application of an ad valorem percentage criterion consistent with subparagraph (a);

(d) the rules of origin that they apply to imports and exports are not more stringent than the rules of origin they apply to determine whether or not a good is domestic and shall not discriminate between other Members, irrespective of the affiliation of the manufacturers of the good concerned[2];

(e) their rules of origin are administered in a consistent, uniform, impartial and reasonable manner;

(f) their rules of origin are based on a positive standard. Rules of origin that state what does not confer origin (negative standard) are permissible as part of a clarification of a positive standard or in individual cases where a positive determination of origin is not necessary;

(g) their laws, regulations, judicial decisions and administrative rulings of general application relating to rules of origin are published

---

[2] With respect to rules of origin applied for the purposes of government procurement, this provision shall not create obligations additional to those already assumed by Members under GATT 1994.

as if they were subject to, and in accordance with, the provisions of paragraph 1 of Article X of GATT 1994;

(h) upon the request of an exporter, importer or any person with a justifiable cause, assessments of the origin they would accord to a good are issued as soon as possible but no later than 150 days after a request for such an assessment provided that all necessary elements have been submitted. Requests for such assessments shall be accepted before trade in the good concerned begins and may be accepted at any later point in time. Such assessments shall remain valid for three years provided that the facts and conditions, including the rules of origin, under which they have been made remain comparable. Provided that the parties concerned are informed in advance, such assessments will no longer be valid when a decision contrary to the assessment is made in a review as referred to in subparagraph (j). Such assessments shall be made publicly available subject to the provisions of subparagraph (k);

(i) when introducing changes to their rules of origin or new rules of origin, they shall not apply such changes retroactively as defined in, and without prejudice to, their laws or regulations;

(j) any administrative action which they take in relation to the determination of origin is reviewable promptly by judicial, arbitral or administrative tribunals or procedures, independent of the authority issuing the determination, which can effect the modification or reversal of the determination;

(k) all information that is by nature confidential or that is provided on a confidential basis for the purpose of the application of rules of origin is treated as strictly confidential by the authorities concerned, which shall not disclose it without the specific permission of the person or government providing such information, except to the extent that it may be required to be disclosed in the context of judicial proceedings.

Article 3

Disciplines After the Transition Period

Taking into account the aim of all Members to achieve, as a result of the harmonization work programme set out in Part IV, the establishment of harmonized rules of origin, Members shall ensure, upon the implementation of the results of the harmonization work programme, that:

(a) they apply rules of origin equally for all purposes as set out in Article 1;

(b) under their rules of origin, the country to be determined as the origin of a particular good is either the country where the good has been wholly obtained or, when more than one country is concerned in the production of the good, the country where the last substantial transformation has been carried out;

(c) the rules of origin that they apply to imports and exports are not more stringent than the rules of origin they apply to determine whether or not a good is domestic and shall not discriminate between other Members, irrespective of the affiliation of the manufacturers of the good concerned;

(d) the rules of origin are administered in a consistent, uniform, impartial and reasonable manner;

* * *

Article 8

Dispute Settlement

The provisions of Article XXIII of GATT 1994, as elaborated and applied by the Dispute Settlement Understanding, are applicable to this Agreement.

PART IV

HARMONIZATION OF RULES OF ORIGIN

Article 9

Objectives and Principles

1. With the objectives of harmonizing rules of origin and, *inter alia*, providing more certainty in the conduct of world trade, the Ministerial Conference shall undertake the work programme set out below in conjunction with the CCC, on the basis of the following principles:

(a) rules of origin should be applied equally for all purposes as set out in Article 1;

(b) rules of origin should provide for the country to be determined as the origin of a particular good to be either the country where the good has been wholly obtained or, when more than one country is concerned in the production of the good, the country where the last substantial transformation has been carried out;

(c) rules of origin should be objective, understandable and predictable;

(d) notwithstanding the measure or instrument to which they may be linked, rules of origin should not be used as instruments to pursue trade objectives directly or indirectly. They should not themselves create restrictive, distorting or disruptive effects on international trade. They should not pose unduly strict requirements or require the fulfilment of a certain condition not relating to manufacturing or processing as a prerequisite for the determination of the country of origin. However, costs not directly related to manufacturing or processing may be included for purposes of the application of an ad valorem percentage criterion;

(e) rules of origin should be administrable in a consistent, uniform, impartial and reasonable manner;

(f) rules of origin should be coherent;

(g) rules of origin should be based on a positive standard. Negative standards may be used to clarify a positive standard.

Work Programme

2. (a) The work programme shall be initiated as soon after the entry into force of the WTO Agreement as possible and will be completed within three years of initiation.

(b) The Committee and the Technical Committee provided for in Article 4 shall be the appropriate bodies to conduct this work.

(c) To provide for detailed input by the CCC, the Committee shall request the Technical Committee to provide its interpretations and opinions resulting from the work described below on the basis of the principles listed in paragraph 1. To ensure timely completion of the work programme for harmonization, such work shall be conducted on a product sector basis, as represented by various chapters or sections of the Harmonized System (HS) nomenclature.

(i) *Wholly Obtained and Minimal Operations or Processes*

The Technical Committee shall develop harmonized definitions of:

— the goods that are to be considered as being wholly obtained in one country. This work shall be as detailed as possible;

— minimal operations or processes that do not by themselves confer origin to a good.

The results of this work shall be submitted to the Committee within three months of receipt of the request from the Committee.

(ii) *Substantial Transformation—Change in Tariff Classification*

— The Technical Committee shall consider and elaborate upon, on the basis of the criterion of substantial transformation, the use of change in tariff subheading or heading when developing rules of origin for particular products or a product sector and, if appropriate, the minimum change within the nomenclature that meets this criterion.

— The Technical Committee shall divide the above work on a product basis taking into account the chapters or sections of the HS nomenclature, so as to submit results of its work to the Committee at least on a quarterly basis. The Technical Committee shall complete the above work within one year and three months from receipt of the request of the Committee.

(iii) *Substantial Transformation—Supplementary Criteria*

Upon completion of the work under subparagraph (ii) for each product sector or individual product category where the exclusive use of the HS nomenclature does not allow for the expression of substantial transformation, the Technical Committee:

— shall consider and elaborate upon, on the basis of the criterion of substantial transformation, the use, in a supplementary or exclusive manner, of other requirements, including ad valorem percentages[3] and/or manufacturing or processing operations,[4] when developing rules of origin for particular products or a product sector;

— may provide explanations for its proposals;

— shall divide the above work on a product basis taking into account the chapters or sections of the HS nomenclature, so as to submit results of its work to the Committee at least on a quarterly basis. The Technical Committee shall complete the above work within two years and three months of receipt of the request from the Committee.

Role of the Committee

3. On the basis of the principles listed in paragraph 1:

(a) the Committee shall consider the interpretations and opinions of the Technical Committee periodically in accordance with the time-frames provided in subparagraphs (i), (ii) and (iii) of paragraph 2(c) with a view to endorsing such interpretations and opinions. The Committee may request the Technical Committee to refine or elaborate its work and/or to develop new approaches. To assist the Technical Committee, the Committee should provide its reasons for requests for additional work and, as appropriate, suggest alternative approaches;

(b) upon completion of all the work identified in subparagraphs (i), (ii) and (iii) of paragraph 2(c), the Committee shall consider the results in terms of their overall coherence.

Results of the Harmonization Work Programme and Subsequent Work

4. The Ministerial Conference shall establish the results of the harmonization work programme in an annex as an integral part of this

---

[3] If the ad valorem criterion is prescribed, the method for calculating this percentage shall also be indicated in the rules of origin.

[4] If the criterion of manufacturing or processing operation is prescribed, the operation that confers origin on the product concerned shall be precisely specified.

Agreement.[5] The Ministerial Conference shall establish a time-frame for the entry into force of this annex.

[5] At the same time, consideration shall be given to arrangements concerning the settlement of disputes relating to customs classification.

DOCUMENT 17

WTO AGREEMENT ON SUBSIDIES AND COUNTERVAILING MEASURES (SCM AGREEMENT)

■ ■ ■

PART I: GENERAL PROVISIONS

Article 1

Definition of a Subsidy

1.1 For the purpose of this Agreement, a subsidy shall be deemed to exist if:

(a)(1) there is a financial contribution by a government or any public body within the territory of a Member (referred to in this Agreement as "government"), i.e. where:

(i) a government practice involves a direct transfer of funds (e.g. grants, loans, and equity infusion), potential direct transfers of funds or liabilities (e.g. loan guarantees);

(ii) government revenue that is otherwise due is foregone or not collected (e.g. fiscal incentives such as tax credits)[1];

(iii) a government provides goods or services other than general infrastructure, or purchases goods;

(iv) a government makes payments to a funding mechanism, or entrusts or directs a private body to carry out one or more of the type of functions illustrated in (i) to (iii) above which would normally be vested in the government and the practice, in no real sense, differs from practices normally followed by governments;

or

(a)(2) there is any form of income or price support in the sense of Article XVI of GATT 1994;

and

---

[1] In accordance with the provisions of Article XVI of GATT 1994 (Note to Article XVI) and the provisions of Annexes I through III of this Agreement, the exemption of an exported product from duties or taxes borne by the like product when destined for domestic consumption, or the remission of such duties or taxes in amounts not in excess of those which have accrued, shall not be deemed to be a subsidy.

(b) a benefit is thereby conferred.

1.2 A subsidy as defined in paragraph 1 shall be subject to the provisions of Part II or shall be subject to the provisions of Part III or V only if such a subsidy is specific in accordance with the provisions of Article 2.

Article 2

Specificity

2.1 In order to determine whether a subsidy, as defined in paragraph 1 of Article 1, is specific to an enterprise or industry or group of enterprises or industries (referred to in this Agreement as "certain enterprises") within the jurisdiction of the granting authority, the following principles shall apply:

(a) Where the granting authority, or the legislation pursuant to which the granting authority operates, explicitly limits access to a subsidy to certain enterprises, such subsidy shall be specific.

(b) Where the granting authority, or the legislation pursuant to which the granting authority operates, establishes objective criteria or conditions[2] governing the eligibility for, and the amount of, a subsidy, specificity shall not exist, provided that the eligibility is automatic and that such criteria and conditions are strictly adhered to. The criteria or conditions must be clearly spelled out in law, regulation, or other official document, so as to be capable of verification.

(c) If, notwithstanding any appearance of non-specificity resulting from the application of the principles laid down in subparagraphs (a) and (b), there are reasons to believe that the subsidy may in fact be specific, other factors may be considered. Such factors are: use of a subsidy programme by a limited number of certain enterprises, predominant use by certain enterprises, the granting of disproportionately large amounts of subsidy to certain enterprises, and the manner in which discretion has been exercised by the granting authority in the decision to grant a subsidy.[3] In applying this subparagraph, account shall be taken of the extent of diversification of economic activities within the jurisdiction of the granting authority, as well as of the length of time during which the subsidy programme has been in operation.

2.2 A subsidy which is limited to certain enterprises located within a designated geographical region within the jurisdiction of the granting

---

[2] Objective criteria or conditions, as used herein, mean criteria or conditions which are neutral, which do not favour certain enterprises over others, and which are economic in nature and horizontal in application, such as number of employees or size of enterprise.

[3] In this regard, in particular, information on the frequency with which applications for a subsidy are refused or approved and the reasons for such decisions shall be considered.

authority shall be specific. It is understood that the setting or change of generally applicable tax rates by all levels of government entitled to do so shall not be deemed to be a specific subsidy for the purposes of this Agreement.

2.3 Any subsidy falling under the provisions of Article 3 shall be deemed to be specific.

2.4 Any determination of specificity under the provisions of this Article shall be clearly substantiated on the basis of positive evidence.

PART II: PROHIBITED SUBSIDIES

Article 3

Prohibition

3.1 Except as provided in the Agreement on Agriculture, the following subsidies, within the meaning of Article 1, shall be prohibited:

(a) subsidies contingent, in law or in fact,[4] whether solely or as one of several other conditions, upon export performance, including those illustrated in Annex I[5];

(b) subsidies contingent, whether solely or as one of several other conditions, upon the use of domestic over imported goods.

3.2 A Member shall neither grant nor maintain subsidies referred to in paragraph 1.

Article 4

Remedies

4.1 Whenever a Member has reason to believe that a prohibited subsidy is being granted or maintained by another Member, such Member may request consultations with such other Member.

* * *

4.4 If no mutually agreed solution has been reached within 30 days[6] of the request for consultations, any Member party to such consultations may refer the matter to the Dispute Settlement Body ("DSB") for the immediate establishment of a panel, unless the DSB decides by consensus not to establish a panel.

---

[4] This standard is met when the facts demonstrate that the granting of a subsidy, without having been made legally contingent upon export performance, is in fact tied to actual or anticipated exportation or export earnings. The mere fact that a subsidy is granted to enterprises which export shall not for that reason alone be considered to be an export subsidy within the meaning of this provision.

[5] Measures referred to in Annex I as not constituting export subsidies shall not be prohibited under this or any other provision of this Agreement.

[6] Any time-periods mentioned in this Article may be extended by mutual agreement.

4.5 Upon its establishment, the panel may request the assistance of the Permanent Group of Experts (referred to in this Agreement as the "PGE") with regard to whether the measure in question is a prohibited subsidy. If so requested, the PGE shall immediately review the evidence with regard to the existence and nature of the measure in question and shall provide an opportunity for the Member applying or maintaining the measure to demonstrate that the measure in question is not a prohibited subsidy. The PGE shall report its conclusions to the panel within a time-limit determined by the panel. The PGE's conclusions on the issue of whether or not the measure in question is a prohibited subsidy shall be accepted by the panel without modification.

4.6 The panel shall submit its final report to the parties to the dispute. The report shall be circulated to all Members within 90 days of the date of the composition and the establishment of the panel's terms of reference.

4.7 If the measure in question is found to be a prohibited subsidy, the panel shall recommend that the subsidizing Member withdraw the subsidy without delay. In this regard, the panel shall specify in its recommendation the time-period within which the measure must be withdrawn.

4.8 Within 30 days of the issuance of the panel's report to all Members, the report shall be adopted by the DSB unless one of the parties to the dispute formally notifies the DSB of its decision to appeal or the DSB decides by consensus not to adopt the report.

4.9 Where a panel report is appealed, the Appellate Body shall issue its decision within 30 days from the date when the party to the dispute formally notifies its intention to appeal. When the Appellate Body considers that it cannot provide its report within 30 days, it shall inform the DSB in writing of the reasons for the delay together with an estimate of the period within which it will submit its report. In no case shall the proceedings exceed 60 days. The appellate report shall be adopted by the DSB and unconditionally accepted by the parties to the dispute unless the DSB decides by consensus not to adopt the appellate report within 20 days following its issuance to the Members.

4.10 In the event the recommendation of the DSB is not followed within the time-period specified by the panel, which shall commence from the date of adoption of the panel's report or the Appellate Body's report, the DSB shall grant authorization to the complaining Member to take appropriate countermeasures, unless the DSB decides by consensus to reject the request.

4.11 In the event a party to the dispute requests arbitration under paragraph 6 of Article 22 of the Dispute Settlement Understanding ("DSU"), the arbitrator shall determine whether the countermeasures are appropriate.

4.12 For purposes of disputes conducted pursuant to this Article, except for time-periods specifically prescribed in this Article, time-periods applicable under the DSU for the conduct of such disputes shall be half the time prescribed therein.

PART III: ACTIONABLE SUBSIDIES

Article 5

Adverse Effects

No Member should cause, through the use of any subsidy referred to in paragraphs 1 and 2 of Article 1, adverse effects to the interests of other Members, i.e.:

(a) injury to the domestic industry of another Member;

(b) nullification or impairment of benefits accruing directly or indirectly to other Members under GATT 1994 in particular the benefits of concessions bound under Article II of GATT 1994;

(c) serious prejudice to the interests of another Member.

This Article does not apply to subsidies maintained on agricultural products as provided in Article 13 of the Agreement on Agriculture.

Article 6

Serious Prejudice

[Note: The provisions of Art. 6(1) have "sunset" under Art. 31, and have not been renewed.]

6.2 Notwithstanding the provisions of paragraph 1, serious prejudice shall not be found if the subsidizing Member demonstrates that the subsidy in question has not resulted in any of the effects enumerated in paragraph 3.

6.3 Serious prejudice in the sense of paragraph (c) of Article 5 may arise in any case where one or several of the following apply:

(a) the effect of the subsidy is to displace or impede the imports of a like product of another Member into the market of the subsidizing Member;

(b) the effect of the subsidy is to displace or impede the exports of a like product of another Member from a third country market;

(c) the effect of the subsidy is a significant price undercutting by the subsidized product as compared with the price of a like product of another Member in the same market or significant price suppression, price depression or lost sales in the same market;

(d) the effect of the subsidy is an increase in the world market share of the subsidizing Member in a particular subsidized primary product or commodity[17] as compared to the average share it had during the previous period of three years and this increase follows a consistent trend over a period when subsidies have been granted.

6.4 For the purpose of paragraph 3(b), the displacement or impeding of exports shall include any case in which, subject to the provisions of paragraph 7, it has been demonstrated that there has been a change in relative shares of the market to the disadvantage of the non-subsidized like product (over an appropriately representative period sufficient to demonstrate clear trends in the development of the market for the product concerned, which, in normal circumstances, shall be at least one year). "Change in relative shares of the market" shall include any of the following situations: (*a*) there is an increase in the market share of the subsidized product; (*b*) the market share of the subsidized product remains constant in circumstances in which, in the absence of the subsidy, it would have declined; (*c*) the market share of the subsidized product declines, but at a slower rate than would have been the case in the absence of the subsidy.

6.5 For the purpose of paragraph 3(c), price undercutting shall include any case in which such price undercutting has been demonstrated through a comparison of prices of the subsidized product with prices of a non-subsidized like product supplied to the same market. The comparison shall be made at the same level of trade and at comparable times, due account being taken of any other factor affecting price comparability. However, if such a direct comparison is not possible, the existence of price undercutting may be demonstrated on the basis of export unit values.

6.6 Each Member in the market of which serious prejudice is alleged to have arisen shall, subject to the provisions of paragraph 3 of Annex V, make available to the parties to a dispute arising under Article 7, and to the panel established pursuant to paragraph 4 of Article 7, all relevant information that can be obtained as to the changes in market shares of the parties to the dispute as well as concerning prices of the products involved.

6.7 Displacement or impediment resulting in serious prejudice shall not arise under paragraph 3 where any of the following circumstances exist[18] during the relevant period:

(a) prohibition or restriction on exports of the like product from the complaining Member or on imports from the complaining Member into the third country market concerned;

(b) decision by an importing government operating a monopoly of trade or state trading in the product concerned to shift, for non-

---

[17] Unless other multilaterally agreed specific rules apply to the trade in the product or commodity in question.

[18] The fact that certain circumstances are referred to in this paragraph does not, in itself, confer upon them any legal status in terms of either GATT 1994 or this Agreement. These circumstances must not be isolated, sporadic or otherwise insignificant.

commercial reasons, imports from the complaining Member to another country or countries;

(c) natural disasters, strikes, transport disruptions or other *force majeure* substantially affecting production, qualities, quantities or prices of the product available for export from the complaining Member;

(d) existence of arrangements limiting exports from the complaining Member;

(e) voluntary decrease in the availability for export of the product concerned from the complaining Member (including, *inter alia,* a situation where firms in the complaining Member have been autonomously reallocating exports of this product to new markets);

(f) failure to conform to standards and other regulatory requirements in the importing country.

6.8 In the absence of circumstances referred to in paragraph 7, the existence of serious prejudice should be determined on the basis of the information submitted to or obtained by the panel, including information submitted in accordance with the provisions of Annex V.

6.9 This Article does not apply to subsidies maintained on agricultural products as provided in Article 13 of the Agreement on Agriculture.

Article 7

Remedies

7.1 Except as provided in Article 13 of the Agreement on Agriculture, whenever a Member has reason to believe that any subsidy referred to in Article 1, granted or maintained by another Member, results in injury to its domestic industry, nullification or impairment or serious prejudice, such Member may request consultations with such other Member.

* * *

7.4 If consultations do not result in a mutually agreed solution within 60 days, any Member party to such consultations may refer the matter to the DSB for the establishment of a panel, unless the DSB decides by consensus not to establish a panel. The composition of the panel and its terms of reference shall be established within 15 days from the date when it is established.

7.5 The panel shall review the matter and shall submit its final report to the parties to the dispute. The report shall be circulated to all Members within 120 days of the date of the composition and establishment of the panel's terms of reference.

7.6 Within 30 days of the issuance of the panel's report to all Members, the report shall be adopted by the DSB unless one of the parties to the dispute formally notifies the DSB of its decision to appeal or the DSB decides by consensus not to adopt the report.

* * *

7.9 In the event the Member has not taken appropriate steps to remove the adverse effects of the subsidy or withdraw the subsidy within six months from the date when the DSB adopts the panel report or the Appellate Body report, and in the absence of agreement on compensation, the DSB shall grant authorization to the complaining Member to take countermeasures, commensurate with the degree and nature of the adverse effects determined to exist, unless the DSB decides by consensus to reject the request.

* * *

PART IV: NON-ACTIONABLE SUBSIDIES

Article 8

Identification of Non-actionable Subsidies

[Note: The provisions of Arts. 8 and 9 have "sunset" under Art. 31, and have not been renewed.]

* * *

Article 9

Consultations and Authorized Remedies

[Note: The provisions of Art. 8 and 9 have "sunset" under Art. 31, and have not been renewed.]

PART V: COUNTERVAILING MEASURES

Article 10

Application of Article VI of GATT 1994[35]

[35] The provisions of Part II or III may be invoked in parallel with the provisions of Part V; however, with regard to the effects of a particular subsidy in the domestic market of the importing Member, only one form of relief (either a countervailing duty, if the requirements of Part V are met, or a countermeasure under Articles 4 or 7) shall be available. The provisions of Parts III and V shall not be invoked regarding measures considered non-actionable in accordance with the provisions of Part IV. However, measures referred to in paragraph 1(a) of Article 8 may be investigated in order to determine whether or not they are specific within the meaning of Article 2. In addition, in the case of a subsidy referred to in paragraph 2 of Article 8 conferred pursuant to a programme which has not been notified in accordance with paragraph 3 of Article 8, the provisions of Part III or V may be invoked, but such subsidy shall be treated as non-actionable if it is found to conform to the standards set forth in paragraph 2 of Article 8.

Members shall take all necessary steps to ensure that the imposition of a countervailing duty[36] on any product of the territory of any Member imported into the territory of another Member is in accordance with the provisions of Article VI of GATT 1994 and the terms of this Agreement. Countervailing duties may only be imposed pursuant to investigations initiated and conducted in accordance with the provisions of this Agreement and the Agreement on Agriculture.

Article 11

Initiation and Subsequent Investigation

11.1 Except as provided in paragraph 6, an investigation to determine the existence, degree and effect of any alleged subsidy shall be initiated upon a written application by or on behalf of the domestic industry.

11.2 An application under paragraph 1 shall include sufficient evidence of the existence of *(a)* a subsidy and, if possible, its amount, (b) injury within the meaning of Article VI of GATT 1994 as interpreted by this Agreement, and *(c)* a causal link between the subsidized imports and the alleged injury. Simple assertion, unsubstantiated by relevant evidence, cannot be considered sufficient to meet the requirements of this paragraph. The application shall contain such information as is reasonably available to the applicant on the following:

(i) the identity of the applicant and a description of the volume and value of the domestic production of the like product by the applicant. Where a written application is made on behalf of the domestic industry, the application shall identify the industry on behalf of which the application is made by a list of all known domestic producers of the like product (or associations of domestic producers of the like product) and, to the extent possible, a description of the volume and value of domestic production of the like product accounted for by such producers;

(ii) a complete description of the allegedly subsidized product, the names of the country or countries of origin or export in question, the identity of each known exporter or foreign producer and a list of known persons importing the product in question;

(iii) evidence with regard to the existence, amount and nature of the subsidy in question;

(iv) evidence that alleged injury to a domestic industry is caused by subsidized imports through the effects of the subsidies; this evidence includes information on the evolution of the volume of the allegedly subsidized imports, the effect of these imports on prices of

[36] The term "countervailing duty" shall be understood to mean a special duty levied for the purpose of offsetting any subsidy bestowed directly or indirectly upon the manufacture, production or export of any merchandise, as provided for in paragraph 3 of Article VI of GATT 1994.

the like product in the domestic market and the consequent impact of the imports on the domestic industry, as demonstrated by relevant factors and indices having a bearing on the state of the domestic industry, such as those listed in paragraphs 2 and 4 of Article 15.

11.3 The authorities shall review the accuracy and adequacy of the evidence provided in the application to determine whether the evidence is sufficient to justify the initiation of an investigation.

11.4 An investigation shall not be initiated pursuant to paragraph 1 unless the authorities have determined, on the basis of an examination of the degree of support for, or opposition to, the application expressed[38] by domestic producers of the like product, that the application has been made by or on behalf of the domestic industry.[39] The application shall be considered to have been made "by or on behalf of the domestic industry" if it is supported by those domestic producers whose collective output constitutes more than 50 per cent of the total production of the like product produced by that portion of the domestic industry expressing either support for or opposition to the application. However, no investigation shall be initiated when domestic producers expressly supporting the application account for less than 25 per cent of total production of the like product produced by the domestic industry.

* * *

11.6 If, in special circumstances, the authorities concerned decide to initiate an investigation without having received a written application by or on behalf of a domestic industry for the initiation of such investigation, they shall proceed only if they have sufficient evidence of the existence of a subsidy, injury and causal link, as described in paragraph 2, to justify the initiation of an investigation.

* * *

11.9 An application under paragraph 1 shall be rejected and an investigation shall be terminated promptly as soon as the authorities concerned are satisfied that there is not sufficient evidence of either subsidization or of injury to justify proceeding with the case. There shall be immediate termination in cases where the amount of a subsidy is *de minimis*, or where the volume of subsidized imports, actual or potential, or the injury, is negligible. For the purpose of this paragraph, the amount of the subsidy shall be considered to be *de minimis* if the subsidy is less than 1 per cent ad valorem.

---

[38] In the case of fragmented industries involving an exceptionally large number of producers, authorities may determine support and opposition by using statistically valid sampling techniques.

[39] Members are aware that in the territory of certain Members employees of domestic producers of the like product or representatives of those employees may make or support an application for an investigation under paragraph 1.

* * *

Article 12

Evidence

12.1 Interested Members and all interested parties in a countervailing duty investigation shall be given notice of the information which the authorities require and ample opportunity to present in writing all evidence which they consider relevant in respect of the investigation in question.

12.1.1 Exporters, foreign producers or interested Members receiving questionnaires used in a countervailing duty investigation shall be given at least 30 days for reply. Due consideration should be given to any request for an extension of the 30–day period and, upon cause shown, such an extension should be granted whenever practicable.

12.1.2 Subject to the requirement to protect confidential information, evidence presented in writing by one interested Member or interested party shall be made available promptly to other interested Members or interested parties participating in the investigation.

* * *

12.4 Any information which is by nature confidential (for example, because its disclosure would be of significant competitive advantage to a competitor or because its disclosure would have a significantly adverse effect upon a person supplying the information or upon a person from whom the supplier acquired the information), or which is provided on a confidential basis by parties to an investigation shall, upon good cause shown, be treated as such by the authorities. Such information shall not be disclosed without specific permission of the party submitting it.

12.4.1 The authorities shall require interested Members or interested parties providing confidential information to furnish non-confidential summaries thereof. These summaries shall be in sufficient detail to permit a reasonable understanding of the substance of the information submitted in confidence. In exceptional circumstances, such Members or parties may indicate that such information is not susceptible of summary.

In such exceptional circumstances, a statement of the reasons why summarization is not possible must be provided.

12.4.2 If the authorities find that a request for confidentiality is not warranted and if the supplier of the information is either unwilling to make the information public or to authorize its disclosure in generalized or summary form, the authorities may disregard such information unless it can be demonstrated to their satisfaction from appropriate sources that the information is correct.

12.5 Except in circumstances provided for in paragraph 7, the authorities shall during the course of an investigation satisfy themselves as to the accuracy of the information supplied by interested Members or interested parties upon which their findings are based.

12.6 The investigating authorities may carry out investigations in the territory of other Members as required, provided that they have notified in good time the Member in question and unless that Member objects to the investigation. Further, the investigating authorities may carry out investigations on the premises of a firm and may examine the records of a firm if *(a)* the firm so agrees and *(b)* the Member in question is notified and does not object. * * *

12.7 In cases in which any interested Member or interested party refuses access to, or otherwise does not provide, necessary information within a reasonable period or significantly impedes the investigation, preliminary and final determinations, affirmative or negative, may be made on the basis of the facts available.

* * *

12.10 The authorities shall provide opportunities for industrial users of the product under investigation, and for representative consumer organizations in cases where the product is commonly sold at the retail level, to provide information which is relevant to the investigation regarding subsidization, injury and causality.

12.11 The authorities shall take due account of any difficulties experienced by interested parties, in particular small companies, in supplying information requested, and shall provide any assistance practicable.

* * *

Article 13
Consultations

13.1 As soon as possible after an application under Article 11 is accepted, and in any event before the initiation of any investigation, Members the products of which may be subject to such investigation shall be invited for consultations with the aim of clarifying the situation as to the matters referred to in paragraph 2 of Article 11 and arriving at a mutually agreed solution.

13.2 Furthermore, throughout the period of investigation, Members the products of which are the subject of the investigation shall be afforded a reasonable opportunity to continue consultations, with a view to clarify the factual situation and to arriving at a mutually agreed solution.[44]

* * *

Article 14

Calculation of the Amount of a Subsidy in Terms of the Benefit to the Recipient

For the purpose of Part V, any method used by the investigating authority to calculate the benefit to the recipient conferred pursuant to paragraph 1 of Article 1 shall be provided for in the national legislation or implementing regulations of the Member concerned and its application to each particular case shall be transparent and adequately explained. Furthermore, any such method shall be consistent with the following guidelines:

(a) government provision of equity capital shall not be considered as conferring a benefit, unless the investment decision can be regarded as inconsistent with the usual investment practice (including for the provision of risk capital) of private investors in the territory of that Member;

(b) a loan by a government shall not be considered as conferring a benefit, unless there is a difference between the amount that the firm receiving the loan pays on the government loan and the amount the firm would pay on a comparable commercial loan which the firm could actually obtain on the market. In this case the benefit shall be the difference between these two amounts;

(c) a loan guarantee by a government shall not be considered as conferring a benefit, unless there is a difference between the amount that the firm receiving the guarantee pays on a loan guaranteed by the government and the amount that the firm would pay on a comparable commercial loan absent the government guarantee. In this case the benefit shall be the difference between these two amounts adjusted for any differences in fees;

(d) the provision of goods or services or purchase of goods by a government shall not be considered as conferring a benefit unless the provision is made for less than adequate remuneration, or the purchase is made for more than adequate remuneration. The adequacy of remuneration shall be determined in relation to prevailing market conditions for the good or service in question in the country of provision

---

[44] It is particularly important, in accordance with the provisions of this paragraph, that no affirmative determination whether preliminary or final be made without reasonable opportunity for consultations having been given. Such consultation may establish the basis for proceeding under the provisions of Part II, III, or X.

or purchase (including price, quality, availability, marketability, transportation and other conditions of purchase or sale).

Article 15

Determination of Injury[45]

15.1 A determination of injury for purposes of Article VI of GATT 1994 shall be based on positive evidence and involve an objective examination of both *(a)* the volume of the subsidized imports and the effect of the subsidized imports on prices in the domestic market for like products[46] and *(b)* the consequent impact of these imports on the domestic producers of such products.

15.2 With regard to the volume of the subsidized imports, the investigating authorities shall consider whether there has been a significant increase in subsidized imports, either in absolute terms or relative to production or consumption in the importing Member. With regard to the effect of the subsidized imports on prices, the investigating authorities shall consider whether there has been a significant price undercutting by the subsidized imports as compared with the price of a like product of the importing Member, or whether the effect of such imports is otherwise to depress prices to a significant degree or to prevent price increases, which otherwise would have occurred, to a significant degree. No one or several of these factors can necessarily give decisive guidance.

15.3 Where imports of a product from more than one country are simultaneously subject to countervailing duty investigations, the investigating authorities may cumulatively assess the effects of such imports only if they determine that *(a)* the amount of subsidization established in relation to the imports from each country is more than *de minimis* as defined in paragraph 9 of Article 11 and the volume of imports from each country is not negligible and *(b)* a cumulative assessment of the effects of the imports is appropriate in light of the conditions of competition between the imported products and the conditions of competition between the imported products and the like domestic product.

15.4 The examination of the impact of the subsidized imports on the domestic industry shall include an evaluation of all relevant economic factors and indices having a bearing on the state of the industry, including actual and potential decline in output, sales, market share, profits, productivity, return on investments, or utilization of capacity; factors

---

[45] Under this Agreement the term "injury" shall, unless otherwise specified, be taken to mean material injury to a domestic industry, threat of material injury to a domestic industry or material retardation of the establishment of such an industry and shall be interpreted in accordance with the provisions of this Article.

[46] Throughout this Agreement the term "like product" ("produit similaire") shall be interpreted to mean a product which is identical, i.e. alike in all respects to the product under consideration, or in the absence of such a product, another product which, although not alike in all respects, has characteristics closely resembling those of the product under consideration.

affecting domestic prices; actual and potential negative effects on cash flow, inventories, employment, wages, growth, ability to raise capital or investments and, in the case of agriculture, whether there has been an increased burden on government support programmes. This list is not exhaustive, nor can one or several of these factors necessarily give decisive guidance.

15.5 It must be demonstrated that the subsidized imports are, through the effects[47] of subsidies, causing injury within the meaning of this Agreement. The demonstration of a causal relationship between the subsidized imports and the injury to the domestic industry shall be based on an examination of all relevant evidence before the authorities. The authorities shall also examine any known factors other than the subsidized imports which at the same time are injuring the domestic industry, and the injuries caused by these other factors must not be attributed to the subsidized imports. Factors which may be relevant in this respect include, *inter alia,* the volumes and prices of non-subsidized imports of the product in question, contraction in demand or changes in the patterns of consumption, trade restrictive practices of and competition between the foreign and domestic producers, developments in technology and the export performance and productivity of the domestic industry.

15.6 The effect of the subsidized imports shall be assessed in relation to the domestic production of the like product when available data permit the separate identification of that production on the basis of such criteria as the production process, producers' sales and profits. If such separate identification of that production is not possible, the effects of the subsidized imports shall be assessed by the examination of the production of the narrowest group or range of products, which includes the like product, for which the necessary information can be provided.

15.7 A determination of a threat of material injury shall be based on facts and not merely on allegation, conjecture or remote possibility. The change in circumstances which would create a situation in which the subsidy would cause injury must be clearly foreseen and imminent. In making a determination regarding the existence of a threat of material injury, the investigating authorities should consider, *inter alia,* such factors as:

(i) nature of the subsidy or subsidies in question and the trade effects likely to arise therefrom;

(ii) a significant rate of increase of subsidized imports into the domestic market indicating the likelihood of substantially increased importation;

---

[47] As set forth in paragraphs 2 and 4.

(iii) sufficient freely disposable, or an imminent, substantial increase in, capacity of the exporter indicating the likelihood of substantially increased subsidized exports to the importing Member's market, taking into account the availability of other export markets to absorb any additional exports;

(iv) whether imports are entering at prices that will have a significant depressing or suppressing effect on domestic prices, and would likely increase demand for further imports; and

(v) inventories of the product being investigated.

No one of these factors by itself can necessarily give decisive guidance but the totality of the factors considered must lead to the conclusion that further subsidized exports are imminent and that, unless protective action is taken, material injury would occur.

15.8 With respect to cases where injury is threatened by subsidized imports, the application of countervailing measures shall be considered and decided with special care.

Article 16

Definition of Domestic Industry

16.1 For the purposes of this Agreement, the term "domestic industry" shall, except as provided in paragraph 2, be interpreted as referring to the domestic producers as a whole of the like products or to those of them whose collective output of the products constitutes a major proportion of the total domestic production of those products, except that when producers are related[48] to the exporters or importers or are themselves importers of the allegedly subsidized product or a like product from other countries, the term "domestic industry" may be interpreted as referring to the rest of the producers.

16.2 In exceptional circumstances, the territory of a Member may, for the production in question, be divided into two or more competitive markets and the producers within each market may be regarded as a separate industry if *(a)* the producers within such market sell all or almost all of their production of the product in question in that market, and *(b)* the demand in that market is not to any substantial degree supplied by producers of the product in question located elsewhere in the territory. In such circumstances, injury may be found to exist even where a major portion of the total domestic industry is not injured, provided there is a

[48] For the purpose of this paragraph, producers shall be deemed to be related to exporters or importers only if *(a)* one of them directly or indirectly controls the other; or *(b)* both of them are directly or indirectly controlled by a third person; or *(c)* together they directly or indirectly control a third person, provided that there are grounds for believing or suspecting that the effect of the relationship is such as to cause the producer concerned to behave differently from non-related producers. For the purpose of this paragraph, one shall be deemed to control another when the former is legally or operationally in a position to exercise restraint or direction over the latter.

concentration of subsidized imports into such an isolated market and provided further that the subsidized imports are causing injury to the producers of all or almost all of the production within such market.

16.3 When the domestic industry has been interpreted as referring to the producers in a certain area, i.e. a market as defined in paragraph 2, countervailing duties shall be levied only on the products in question consigned for final consumption to that area. When the constitutional law of the importing Member does not permit the levying of countervailing duties without limitation only if *(a)* the exporters shall have been given an opportunity to cease exporting at subsidized prices to the area concerned or otherwise give assurances pursuant to Article 18, and adequate assurances in this regard have not been promptly given, and *(b)* such duties cannot be levied only on products of specific producers which supply the area in question.

16.4 Where two or more countries have reached under the provisions of paragraph 8(a) of Article XXIV of GATT 1994 such a level of integration that they have the characteristics of a single, unified market, the industry in the entire area of integration shall be taken to be the domestic industry referred to in paragraphs 1 and 2.

16.5 The provisions of paragraph 6 of Article 15 shall be applicable to this Article.

Article 17

Provisional Measures

17.1 Provisional measures may be applied only if:

(a) an investigation has been initiated in accordance with the provisions of Article 11, a public notice has been given to that effect and interested Members and interested parties have been given adequate opportunities to submit information and make comments;

(b) a preliminary affirmative determination has been made that a subsidy exists and that there is injury to a domestic industry caused by subsidized imports; and

(c) the authorities concerned judge such measures necessary to prevent injury being caused during the investigation.

17.2 Provisional measures may take the form of provisional countervailing duties guaranteed by cash deposits or bonds equal to the amount of the provisionally calculated amount of subsidization.

17.3 Provisional measures shall not be applied sooner than 60 days from the date of initiation of the investigation.

17.4 The application of provisional measures shall be limited to as short a period as possible, not exceeding four months.

17.5 The relevant provisions of Article 19 shall be followed in the application of provisional measures.

Article 18

Undertakings

18.1 Proceedings may[49] be suspended or terminated without the imposition of provisional measures or countervailing duties upon receipt of satisfactory voluntary undertakings under which:

(a) the government of the exporting Member agrees to eliminate or limit the subsidy or take other measures concerning its effects; or

(b) the exporter agrees to revise its prices so that the investigating authorities are satisfied that the injurious effect of the subsidy is eliminated. Price increases under such undertakings shall not be higher than necessary to eliminate the amount of the subsidy. It is desirable that the price increases be less than the amount of the subsidy if such increases would be adequate to remove the injury to the domestic industry.

18.2 Undertakings shall not be sought or accepted unless the authorities of the importing Member have made a preliminary affirmative determination of subsidization and injury caused by such subsidization and, in case of undertakings from exporters, have obtained the consent of the exporting Member.

18.3 Undertakings offered need not be accepted if the authorities of the importing Member consider their acceptance impractical, for example if the number of actual or potential exporters is too great, or for other reasons, including reasons of general policy. Should the case arise and where practicable, the authorities shall provide to the exporter the reasons which have led them to consider acceptance of an undertaking as inappropriate, and shall, to the extent possible, give the exporter an opportunity to make comments thereon.

18.4 If an undertaking is accepted, the investigation of subsidization and injury shall nevertheless be completed if the exporting Member so desires or the importing Member so decides. In such a case, if a negative determination of subsidization or injury is made, the undertaking shall automatically lapse, except in cases where such a determination is due in large part to the existence of an undertaking. In such cases, the authorities concerned may require that an undertaking be maintained for a reasonable period consistent with the provisions of this Agreement. In the event that an affirmative determination of subsidization and injury is made, the

[49] The word "may" shall not be interpreted to allow the simultaneous continuation of proceedings with the implementation of undertakings, except as provided in paragraph 4.

undertaking shall continue consistent with its terms and the provisions of this Agreement.

18.5 Price undertakings may be suggested by the authorities of the importing Member, but no exporter shall be forced to enter into such undertakings. The fact that governments or exporters do not offer such undertakings, or do not accept an invitation to do so, shall in no way prejudice the consideration of the case. However, the authorities are free to determine that a threat of injury is more likely to be realized if the subsidized imports continue.

18.6 Authorities of an importing Member may require any government or exporter from whom an undertaking has been accepted to provide periodically information relevant to the fulfilment of such an undertaking, and to permit verification of pertinent data. In case of violation of an undertaking, the authorities of the importing Member may take, under this Agreement in conformity with its provisions, expeditious actions which may constitute immediate application of provisional measures using the best information available. In such cases, definitive duties may be levied in accordance with this Agreement on products entered for consumption not more than 90 days before the application of such provisional measures, except that any such retroactive assessment shall not apply to imports entered before the violation of the undertaking.

Article 19

Imposition and Collection of Countervailing Duties

19.1 If, after reasonable efforts have been made to complete consultations, a Member makes a final determination of the existence and amount of the subsidy and that, through the effects of the subsidy, the subsidized imports are causing injury, it may impose a countervailing duty in accordance with the provisions of this Article unless the subsidy or subsidies are withdrawn.

19.2 The decision whether or not to impose a countervailing duty in cases where all requirements for the imposition have been fulfilled, and the decision whether the amount of the countervailing duty to be imposed shall be the full amount of the subsidy or less, are decisions to be made by the authorities of the importing Member. It is desirable that the imposition should be permissive in the territory of all Members, that the duty should be less than the total amount of the subsidy if such lesser duty would be adequate to remove the injury to the domestic industry, and that procedures should be established which would allow the authorities concerned to take due account of representations made by domestic interested parties[50] whose interests might be adversely affected by the imposition of a countervailing duty.

19.3 When a countervailing duty is imposed in respect of any product, such countervailing duty shall be levied, in the appropriate amounts in each case, on a non-discriminatory basis on imports of such product from all sources found to be subsidized and causing injury, except as to imports from those sources which have renounced any subsidies in question or from which undertakings under the terms of this Agreement have been accepted. Any exporter whose exports are subject to a definitive countervailing duty but who was not actually investigated for reasons other than a refusal to cooperate, shall be entitled to an expedited review in order that the investigating authorities promptly establish an individual countervailing duty rate for that exporter.

19.4 No countervailing duty shall be levied on any imported product in excess of the amount of the subsidy found to exist, calculated in terms of subsidization per unit of the subsidized and exported product.

Article 20

Retroactivity

20.1 Provisional measures and countervailing duties shall only be applied to products which enter for consumption after the time when the decision under paragraph 1 of Article 17 and paragraph 1 of Article 19, respectively, enters into force, subject to the exceptions set out in this Article.

* * *

Article 21

Duration and Review of Countervailing Duties and Undertakings

21.1 A countervailing duty shall remain in force only as long as and to the extent necessary to counteract subsidization which is causing injury.

21.2 The authorities shall review the need for the continued imposition of the duty, where warranted, on their own initiative or, provided that a reasonable period of time has elapsed since the imposition of the definitive countervailing duty, upon request by any interested party which submits positive information substantiating the need for a review. Interested parties shall have the right to request the authorities to examine whether the continued imposition of the duty is necessary to offset subsidization, whether the injury would be likely to continue or recur if the duty were removed or varied, or both. If, as a result of the review under

---

[50] For the purpose of this paragraph, the term "domestic interested parties" shall include consumers and industrial users of the imported product subject to investigation.

this paragraph, the authorities determine that the countervailing duty is no longer warranted, it shall be terminated immediately.

21.3 Notwithstanding the provisions of paragraphs 1 and 2, any definitive countervailing duty shall be terminated on a date not later than five years from its imposition (or from the date of the most recent review under paragraph 2 if that review has covered both subsidization and injury, or under this paragraph), unless the authorities determine, in a review initiated before that date on their own initiative or upon a duly substantiated request made by or on behalf of the domestic industry within a reasonable period of time prior to that date, that the expiry of the duty would be likely to lead to continuation or recurrence of subsidization and injury. The duty may remain in force pending the outcome of such a review.

21.4 The provisions of Article 12 regarding evidence and procedure shall apply to any review carried out under this Article. Any such review shall be carried out expeditiously and shall normally be concluded within 12 months of the date of initiation of the review.

21.5 The provisions of this Article shall apply *mutatis mutandis* to undertakings accepted under Article 18.

Article 22

Public Notice and Explanation of Determinations

22.1 When the authorities are satisfied that there is sufficient evidence to justify the initiation of an investigation pursuant to Article 11, the Member or Members the products of which are subject to such investigation and other interested parties known to the investigating authorities to have an interest therein shall be notified and a public notice shall be given.

22.2 A public notice of the initiation of an investigation shall contain, or otherwise make available through a separate report, adequate information on the following:

(i) the name of the exporting country or countries and the product involved;

(ii) the date of initiation of the investigation;

(iii) a description of the subsidy practice or practices to be investigated;

(iv) a summary of the factors on which the allegation of injury is based;

(v) the address to which representations by interested Members and interested parties should be directed; and

(vi) the time-limits allowed to interested Members and interested parties for making their views known.

22.3 Public notice shall be given of any preliminary or final determination, whether affirmative or negative, of any decision to accept an undertaking pursuant to Article 18, of the termination of such an undertaking, and of the termination of a definitive countervailing duty.
* * *

22.4 A public notice of the imposition of provisional measures shall set forth, or otherwise make available through a separate report, sufficiently detailed explanations for the preliminary determinations on the existence of a subsidy and injury and shall refer to the matters of fact and law which have led to arguments being accepted or rejected. Such a notice or report shall, due regard being paid to the requirement for the protection of confidential information, contain in particular:

(i) the names of the suppliers or, when this is impracticable, the supplying countries involved;

(ii) a description of the product which is sufficient for customs purposes;

(iii) the amount of subsidy established and the basis on which the existence of a subsidy has been determined;

(iv) considerations relevant to the injury determination as set out in Article 15;

(v) the main reasons leading to the determination.

22.5 A public notice of conclusion or suspension of an investigation in the case of an affirmative determination providing for the imposition of a definitive duty or the acceptance of an undertaking shall contain, or otherwise make available through a separate report, all relevant information on the matters of fact and law and reasons which have led to the imposition of final measures or the acceptance of an undertaking, due regard being paid to the requirement for the protection of confidential information. In particular, the notice or report shall contain the information described in paragraph 4, as well as the reasons for the acceptance or rejection of relevant arguments or claims made by interested Members and by the exporters and importers.

22.6 A public notice of the termination or suspension of an investigation following the acceptance of an undertaking pursuant to Article 18 shall include, or otherwise make available through a separate report, the non-confidential part of this undertaking.

22.7 The provisions of this Article shall apply *mutatis mutandis* to the initiation and completion of reviews pursuant to Article 21 and to decisions under Article 20 to apply duties retroactively.

Article 23

Judicial Review

Each Member whose national legislation contains provisions on countervailing duty measures shall maintain judicial, arbitral or administrative tribunals or procedures for the purpose, *inter alia,* of the prompt review of administrative actions relating to final determinations and reviews of determinations within the meaning of Article 21. Such tribunals or procedures shall be independent of the authorities responsible for the determination or review in question, and shall provide all interested parties who participated in the administrative proceeding and are directly and individually affected by the administrative actions with access to review.

* * *

PART VII: NOTIFICATION AND SURVEILLANCE

Article 25

Notifications

25.1 Members agree that, without prejudice to the provisions of paragraph 1 of Article XVI of GATT 1994, their notifications of subsidies shall be submitted not later than 30 June of each year and shall conform to the provisions of paragraphs 2 through 6.

25.2 Members shall notify any subsidy as defined in paragraph 1 of Article 1, which is specific within the meaning of Article 2, granted or maintained within their territories.

25.3 The content of notifications should be sufficiently specific to enable other Members to evaluate the trade effects and to understand the operation of notified subsidy programmes. * * *

25.6 Members which consider that there are no measures in their territories requiring notification under paragraph 1 of Article XVI of GATT 1994 and this Agreement shall so inform the Secretariat in writing.

* * *

25.10 Any Member which considers that any measure of another Member having the effects of a subsidy has not been notified in accordance with the provisions of paragraph 1 of Article XVI of GATT 1994 and this Article may bring the matter to the attention of such other Member. If the alleged subsidy is not thereafter notified promptly, such Member may itself bring the alleged subsidy in question to the notice of the Committee.

25.11 Members shall report without delay to the Committee all preliminary or final actions taken with respect to countervailing duties. Such reports shall be available in the Secretariat for inspection by other Members. Members shall also submit, on a semi-annual basis, reports on any counter-vailing duty actions taken within the preceding six months. The semi-annual reports shall be submitted on an agreed standard form.

* * *

PART VIII: DEVELOPING COUNTRY MEMBERS

Article 27

Special and Differential Treatment of Developing Country Members

27.1 Members recognize that subsidies may play an important role in economic development programmes of developing country Members.

27.2 The prohibition of paragraph 1(a) of Article 3 shall not apply to:

(a) developing country Members referred to in Annex VII.

(b) other developing country Members for a period of eight years from the date of entry into force of the WTO Agreement, subject to compliance with the provisions in paragraph 4.

27.3 The prohibition of paragraph 1(b) of Article 3 shall not apply to developing country Members for a period of five years, and shall not apply to least developed country Members for a period of eight years, from the date of entry into force of the WTO Agreement.

27.4 Any developing country Member referred to in paragraph 2(b) shall phase out its export subsidies within the eight-year period, preferably in a progressive manner. * * *

* * *

PART X: DISPUTE SETTLEMENT

Article 30

The provisions of Articles XXII and XXIII of GATT 1994 as elaborated and applied by the Dispute Settlement Understanding shall apply to consultations and the settlement of disputes under this Agreement, except as otherwise specifically provided herein.

PART XI: FINAL PROVISIONS

Article 31

Provisional Application

The provisions of paragraph 1 of Article 6 and the provisions of Article 8 and Article 9 shall apply for a period of five years, beginning with the date of entry into force of the WTO Agreement. Not later than 180 days before the end of this period, the Committee shall review the operation of those provisions, with a view to determining whether to extend their application, either as presently drafted or in a modified form, for a further period.

* * *

ANNEX I

ILLUSTRATIVE LIST OF EXPORT SUBSIDIES

(a) The provision by governments of direct subsidies to a firm or an industry contingent upon export performance.

(b) Currency retention schemes or any similar practices which involve a bonus on exports.

(c) Internal transport and freight charges on export shipments, provided or mandated by governments, on terms more favourable than for domestic shipments.

(d) The provision by governments or their agencies either directly or indirectly through government-mandated schemes, of imported or domestic products or services for use in the production of exported goods, on terms or conditions more favourable than for provision of like or directly competitive products or services for use in the production of goods for domestic consumption, if (in the case of products) such terms or conditions are more favourable than those commercially available[57] on world markets to their exporters.

(e) The full or partial exemption remission, or deferral specifically related to exports, of direct taxes[58] or social welfare charges paid or payable by industrial or commercial enterprises.[59]

---

[57] The term "commercially available" means that the choice between domestic and imported products is unrestricted and depends only on commercial considerations.

[58] For the purpose of this Agreement:

The term "direct taxes" shall mean taxes on wages, profits, interests, rents, royalties, and all other forms of income, and taxes on the ownership of real property;

The term "import charges" shall mean tariffs, duties, and other fiscal charges not elsewhere enumerated in this note that are levied on imports;

The term "indirect taxes" shall mean sales, excise, turnover, value added, franchise, stamp, transfer, inventory and equipment taxes, border taxes and all taxes other than direct taxes and import charges;

"Prior-stage" indirect taxes are those levied on goods or services used directly or indirectly in making the product;

"Cumulative" indirect taxes are multi-staged taxes levied where there is no mechanism for subsequent crediting of the tax if the goods or services subject to tax at one stage of production are used in a succeeding stage of production;

"Remission" of taxes includes the refund or rebate of taxes;

"Remission or drawback" includes the full or partial exemption or deferral of import charges.

[59] The Members recognize that deferral need not amount to an export subsidy where, for example, appropriate interest charges are collected. The Members reaffirm the principle that prices for goods in transactions between exporting enterprises and foreign buyers under their or under the same control should for tax purposes be the prices which would be charged between independent enterprises acting at arm's length. Any Member may draw the attention of another Member to administrative or other practices which may contravene this principle and which result in a significant saving of direct taxes in export transactions. In such circumstances the Members shall normally attempt to resolve their differences using the facilities of existing bilateral tax

(f) The allowance of special deductions directly related to exports or export performance, over and above those granted in respect to production for domestic consumption, in the calculation of the base on which direct taxes are charged.

(g) The exemption or remission, in respect of the production and distribution of exported products, of indirect taxes in excess of those levied in respect of the production and distribution of like products when sold for domestic consumption.

(h) The exemption, remission or deferral of prior-stage cumulative indirect taxes on goods or services used in the production of exported products in excess of the exemption, remission or deferral of like prior-stage cumulative indirect taxes on goods or services used in the production of like products when sold for domestic consumption; provided, however, that prior-stage cumulative indirect taxes may be exempted, remitted or deferred on exported products even when not exempted, remitted or deferred on like products when sold for domestic consumption, if the prior-stage cumulative indirect taxes are levied on inputs that are consumed in the production of the exported product (making normal allowance for waste).[60] This item shall be interpreted in accordance with the guidelines on consumption of inputs in the production process contained in Annex II.

(i) The remission or drawback of import charges in excess of those levied on imported inputs that are consumed in the production of the exported product (making normal allowance for waste); provided, however, that in particular cases a firm may use a quantity of home market inputs equal to, and having the same quality and characteristics as, the imported inputs as a substitute for them in order to benefit from this provision if the import and the corresponding export operations both occur within a reasonable time period, not to exceed two years. This item shall be interpreted in accordance with the guidelines on consumption of inputs in the production process contained in Annex II and the guidelines in the determination of substitution drawback systems as export subsidies contained in Annex III.

(j) The provision by governments (or special institutions controlled by governments) of export credit guarantee or insurance programmes, of insurance or guarantee programmes against increases in the cost of exported products or of exchange risk programmes, at premium rates

---

treaties or other specific international mechanisms, without prejudice to the rights and obligations of Members under GATT 1994, including the right of consultation created in the preceding sentence.

Paragraph (e) is not intended to limit a Member from taking measures to avoid the double taxation of foreign-source income earned by its enterprises or the enterprises of another Member.

[60] Paragraph (h) does not apply to value-added tax systems and border-tax adjustment in lieu thereof; the problem of the excessive remission of value-added taxes is exclusively covered by paragraph (g).

which are inadequate to cover the long-term operating costs and losses of the programmes.

(k) The grant by governments (or special institutions controlled by and/or acting under the authority of governments) of export credits at rates below those which they actually have to pay for the funds so employed (or would have to pay if they borrowed on international capital markets in order to obtain funds of the same maturity and other credit terms and denominated in the same currency as the export credit), or the payment by them of all or part of the costs incurred by exporters or financial institutions in obtaining credits, in so far as they are used to secure a material advantage in the field of export credit terms.

Provided, however, that if a Member is a party to an international undertaking on official export credits to which at least twelve original Members to this Agreement are parties as of 1 January 1979 (or a successor undertaking which has been adopted by those original Members), or if in practice a Member applies the interest rates provisions of the relevant undertaking, an export credit practice which is in conformity with those provisions shall not be considered an export subsidy prohibited by this Agreement.

(*l*) Any other charge on the public account constituting an export subsidy in the sense of Article XVI of GATT 1994.

* * *

ANNEX IV

CALCULATION OF THE TOTAL AD VALOREM SUBSIDIZATION (PARAGRAPH 1(A) OF ARTICLE 6)

1. Any calculation of the amount of a subsidy for the purpose of paragraph 1(a) of Article 6 shall be done in terms of the cost to the granting government.

2. Except as provided in paragraphs 3 through 5, in determining whether the overall rate of subsidization exceeds 5 per cent of the value of the product, the value of the product shall be calculated as the total value of the recipient firm's sales in the most recent 12–month period, for which sales data is available, preceding the period in which the subsidy is granted.

3. Where the subsidy is tied to the production or sale of a given product, the value of the product shall be calculated as the total value of the recipient firm's sales of that product in the most recent 12–month period, for which sales data is available, preceding the period in which the subsidy is granted.

4. Where the recipient firm is in a start-up situation, serious prejudice shall be deemed to exist if the overall rate of subsidization

exceeds 15 per cent of the total funds invested. For purposes of this paragraph, a start-up period will not extend beyond the first year of production.

5. Where the recipient firm is located in an inflationary economy country, the value of the product shall be calculated as the recipient firm's total sales (or sales of the relevant product, if the subsidy is tied) in the preceding calendar year indexed by the rate of inflation experienced in the 12 months preceding the month in which the subsidy is to be given.

6. In determining the overall rate of subsidization in a given year, subsidies given under different programmes and by different authorities in the territory of a Member shall be aggregated.

7. Subsidies granted prior to the date of entry into force of the WTO Agreement, the benefits of which are allocated to future production, shall be included in the overall rate of subsidization.

8. Subsidies which are non-actionable under relevant provisions of this Agreement shall not be included in the calculation of the amount of a subsidy for the purpose of paragraph 1(a) of Article 6.

ANNEX V

PROCEDURES FOR DEVELOPING INFORMATION CONCERNING SERIOUS PREJUDICE

1. Every Member shall cooperate in the development of evidence to be examined by a panel in procedures under paragraphs 4 through 6 of Article 7. The parties to the dispute and any third-country Member concerned shall notify to the DSB, as soon as the provisions of paragraph 4 of Article 7 have been invoked, the organization responsible for administration of this provision within its territory and the procedures to be used to comply with requests for information.

2. In cases where matters are referred to the DSB under paragraph 4 of Article 7, the DSB shall, upon request, initiate the procedure to obtain such information from the government of the subsidizing Member as necessary to establish the existence and amount of subsidization, the value of total sales of the subsidized firms, as well as information necessary to analyze the adverse effects caused by the subsidized product.[66] This process may include, where appropriate, presentation of questions to the government of the subsidizing Member and of the complaining Member to collect information, as well as to clarify and obtain elaboration of information available to the parties to a dispute through the notification procedures set forth in Part VII.[67]

---

[66] In cases where the existence of serious prejudice has to be demonstrated.

[67] The information-gathering process by the DSB shall take into account the need to protect information which is by nature confidential or which is provided on a confidential basis by any Member involved in this process.

3. In the case of effects in third-country markets, a party to a dispute may collect information, including through the use of questions to the government of the third-country Member, necessary to analyse adverse effects, which is not otherwise reasonably available from the complaining Member or the subsidizing Member. This requirement should be administered in such a way as not to impose an unreasonable burden on the third-country Member. In particular, such a Member is not expected to make a market or price analysis specially for that purpose. The information to be supplied is that which is already available or can be readily obtained by this Member (e.g. most recent statistics which have already been gathered by relevant statistical services but which have not yet been published, customs data concerning imports and declared values of the products concerned, etc.). However, if a party to a dispute undertakes a detailed market analysis at its own expense, the task of the person or firm conducting such an analysis shall be facilitated by the authorities of the third-country Member and such a person or firm shall be given access to all information which is not normally maintained confidential by the government.

4. The DSB shall designate a representative to serve the function of facilitating the information-gathering process. The sole purpose of the representative shall be to ensure the timely development of the information necessary to facilitate expeditious subsequent multilateral review of the dispute. In particular, the representative may suggest ways to most efficiently solicit necessary information as well as encourage the cooperation of the parties.

5. The information-gathering process outlined in paragraphs 2 through 4 shall be completed within 60 days of the date on which the matter has been referred to the DSB under paragraph 4 of Article 7. The information obtained during this process shall be submitted to the panel established by the DSB in accordance with the provisions of Part X. This information should include, *inter alia,* data concerning the amount of the subsidy in question (and, where appropriate, the value of total sales of the subsidized firms), prices of the subsidized product, prices of the non-subsidized product, prices of other suppliers to the market, changes in the supply of the subsidized product to the market in question and changes in market shares. It should also include rebuttal evidence, as well as such supplemental information as the panel deems relevant in the course of reaching its conclusions.

6. If the subsidizing and/or third-country Member fails to cooperate in the information-gathering process, the complaining Member will present its case of serious prejudice, based on evidence available to it, together with facts and circumstances of the non-cooperation of the subsidizing and/or third-country Member. Where information is unavailable due to non-cooperation by the subsidizing and/or third-country Member, the panel

may complete the record as necessary relying on best information otherwise available.

7. In making its determination, the panel should draw adverse inferences from instances of non-cooperation by any party involved in the information-gathering process.

8. In making a determination to use either best information available or adverse inferences, the panel shall consider the advice of the DSB representative nominated under paragraph 4 as to the reasonableness of any requests for information and the efforts made by parties to comply with these requests in a cooperative and timely manner.

9. Nothing in the information-gathering process shall limit the ability of the panel to seek such additional information it deems essential to a proper resolution to the dispute, and which was not adequately sought or developed during that process. However, ordinarily the panel should not request additional information to complete the record where the information would support a particular party's position and the absence of that information in the record is the result of unreasonable non-cooperation by that party in the information-gathering process.

* * *

DOCUMENT 18

WTO AGREEMENT ON TECHNICAL BARRIERS TO TRADE (STANDARDS CODE)

■ ■ ■

Article 1

General Provisions

1.1 General terms for standardization and procedures for assessment of conformity shall normally have the meaning given to them by definitions adopted within the United Nations system and by international standardizing bodies taking into account their context and in the light of the object and purpose of this Agreement.

1.2 However, for the purposes of this Agreement the meaning of the terms given in Annex 1 applies.

1.3 All products, including industrial and agricultural products, shall be subject to the provisions of this Agreement.

1.4 Purchasing specifications prepared by governmental bodies for production or consumption requirements of governmental bodies are not subject to the provisions of this Agreement but are addressed in the Agreement on Government Procurement, according to its coverage.

1.5 The provisions of this Agreement do not apply to sanitary and phytosanitary measures as defined in Annex A of the Agreement on the Application of Sanitary and Phytosanitary Measures.

1.6 All references in this Agreement to technical regulations, standards and conformity assessment procedures shall be construed to include any amendments thereto and any additions to the rules or the product coverage thereof, except amendments and additions of an insignificant nature.

TECHNICAL REGULATIONS AND STANDARDS

Article 2

Preparation, Adoption and Application of Technical Regulations by Central Government Bodies

With respect to their central government bodies:

2.1 Members shall ensure that in respect of technical regulations, products imported from the territory of any Member shall be accorded treatment no less favourable than that accorded to like products of national origin and to like products originating in any other country.

2.2 Members shall ensure that technical regulations are not prepared, adopted or applied with a view to or with the effect of creating unnecessary obstacles to international trade. For this purpose, technical regulations shall not be more trade-restrictive than necessary to fulfil a legitimate objective, taking account of the risks non-fulfilment would create. Such legitimate objectives are, *inter alia*: national security requirements; the prevention of deceptive practices; protection of human health or safety, animal or plant life or health, or the environment. In assessing such risks, relevant elements of consideration are, *inter alia*: available scientific and technical information, related processing technology or intended end-uses of products.

2.3 Technical regulations shall not be maintained if the circumstances or objectives giving rise to their adoption no longer exist or if the changed circumstances or objectives can be addressed in a less trade-restrictive manner.

2.4 Where technical regulations are required and relevant international standards exist or their completion is imminent, Members shall use them, or the relevant parts of them, as a basis for their technical regulations except when such international standards or relevant parts would be an ineffective or inappropriate means for the fulfilment of the legitimate objectives pursued, for instance because of fundamental climatic or geographical factors or fundamental technological problems.

2.5 A Member preparing, adopting or applying a technical regulation which may have a significant effect on trade of other Members shall, upon the request of another Member, explain the justification for that technical regulation in terms of the provisions of paragraphs 2 to 4. Whenever a technical regulation is prepared, adopted or applied for one of the legitimate objectives explicitly mentioned in paragraph 2, and is in accordance with relevant international standards, it shall be rebuttably presumed not to create an unnecessary obstacle to international trade.

* * *

2.7 Members shall give positive consideration to accepting as equivalent technical regulations of other Members, even if these regulations differ from their own, provided they are satisfied that these regulations adequately fulfil the objectives of their own regulations.

2.8 Wherever appropriate, Members shall specify technical regulations based on product requirements in terms of performance rather than design or descriptive characteristics.

2.9 Whenever a relevant international standard does not exist or the technical content of a proposed technical regulation is not in accordance with the technical content of relevant international standards, and if the technical regulation may have a significant effect on trade of other Members, Members shall:

2.9.1 publish a notice in a publication at an early appropriate stage, in such a manner as to enable interested parties in other Members to become acquainted with it, that they propose to introduce a particular technical regulation;

2.9.2 notify other Members through the Secretariat of the products to be covered by the proposed technical regulation, together with a brief indication of its objective and rationale. Such notifications shall take place at an early appropriate stage, when amendments can still be introduced and comments taken into account;

2.9.3 upon request, provide to other Members particulars or copies of the proposed technical regulation and, whenever possible, identify the parts which in substance deviate from relevant international standards;

2.9.4 without discrimination, allow reasonable time for other Members to make comments in writing, discuss these comments upon request, and take these written comments and the results of these discussions into account.

* * *

Article 3

Preparation, Adoption and Application of Technical Regulations by Local Government Bodies and Non-Governmental Bodies

With respect to their local government and non-governmental bodies within their territories:

3.1 Members shall take such reasonable measures as may be available to them to ensure compliance by such bodies with the provisions of Article 2, with the exception of the obligation to notify as referred to in paragraphs 9.2 and 10.1 of Article 2.

3.2 Members shall ensure that the technical regulations of local governments on the level directly below that of the central government in Members are notified in accordance with the provisions of paragraphs 9.2 and 10.1 of Article 2, noting that notification shall not be required for technical regulations the technical content of which is substantially the same as that of previously notified technical regulations of central government bodies of the Member concerned.

3.3 Members may require contact with other Members, including the notifications, provision of information, comments and discussions referred to in paragraphs 9 and 10 of Article 2, to take place through the central government.

3.4 Members shall not take measures which require or encourage local government bodies or non-governmental bodies within their territories to act in a manner inconsistent with the provisions of Article 2.

3.5 Members are fully responsible under this Agreement for the observance of all provisions of Article 2. Members shall formulate and implement positive measures and mechanisms in support of the observance of the provisions of Article 2 by other than central government bodies.

Article 4

Preparation, Adoption and Application of Standards

4.1 Members shall ensure that their central government standardizing bodies accept and comply with the Code of Good Practice for the Preparation, Adoption and Application of Standards in Annex 3 to this Agreement (referred to in this Agreement as the "Code of Good Practice"). They shall take such reasonable measures as may be available to them to ensure that local government and non-governmental standardizing bodies within their territories, as well as regional standardizing bodies of which they or one or more bodies within their territories are members, accept and comply with this Code of Good Practice. In addition, Members shall not take measures which have the effect of, directly or indirectly, requiring or encouraging such standardizing bodies to act in a manner inconsistent with the Code of Good Practice. The obligations of Members with respect to compliance of standardizing bodies with the provisions of the Code of Good Practice shall apply irrespective of whether or not a standardizing body has accepted the Code of Good Practice.

4.2 Standardizing bodies that have accepted and are complying with the Code of Good Practice shall be acknowledged by the Members as complying with the principles of this Agreement.

CONFORMITY WITH TECHNICAL REGULATIONS AND STANDARDS

Article 5

Procedures for Assessment of Conformity by Central Government Bodies

5.1 Members shall ensure that, in cases where a positive assurance of conformity with technical regulations or standards is required, their central government bodies apply the following provisions to products originating in the territories of other Members:

5.1.1 conformity assessment procedures are prepared, adopted and applied so as to grant access for suppliers of like products originating in the territories of other Members under conditions no less favourable than those accorded to suppliers of like products of national origin or originating in any other country, in a comparable situation; access entails suppliers' right to an assessment of conformity under the rules of the procedure, including, when foreseen by this procedure, the possibility to have conformity assessment activities undertaken at the site of facilities and to receive the mark of the system;

5.1.2 conformity assessment procedures are not prepared, adopted or applied with a view to or with the effect of creating unnecessary obstacles to international trade. This means, *inter alia,* that conformity assessment procedures shall not be more strict or be applied more strictly than is necessary to give the importing Member adequate confidence that products conform with the applicable technical regulations or standards, taking account of the risks non-conformity would create.

* * *

5.4 In cases where a positive assurance is required that products conform with technical regulations or standards, and relevant guides or recommendations issued by international standardizing bodies exist or their completion is imminent, Members shall ensure that central government bodies use them, or the relevant parts of them, as a basis for their conformity assessment procedures, except where, as duly explained upon request, such guides or recommendations or relevant parts are inappropriate for the Members concerned, for, *inter alia,* such reasons as: national security requirements; the prevention of deceptive practices; protection of human health or safety, animal or plant life or health, or the environment; fundamental climatic or other geographical factors; fundamental technological or infrastructural problems.

* * *

5.6 Whenever a relevant guide or recommendation issued by an international standardizing body does not exist or the technical content of a proposed conformity assessment procedure is not in accordance with relevant guides and recommendations issued by international standardizing bodies, and if the conformity assessment procedure may have a significant effect on trade of other Members, Members shall:

5.6.1 publish a notice in a publication at an early appropriate stage, in such a manner as to enable interested parties in other Members to become acquainted with it, that they propose to introduce a particular conformity assessment procedure;

5.6.2 notify other Members through the Secretariat of the products to be covered by the proposed conformity assessment procedure, together with a brief indication of its objective and rationale. Such notifications shall take place at an early appropriate stage, when amendments can still be introduced and comments taken into account;

5.6.3 upon request, provide to other Members particulars or copies of the proposed procedure and, whenever possible, identify the parts which in substance deviate from relevant guides or recommendations issued by international standardizing bodies;

5.6.4 without discrimination, allow reasonable time for other Members to make comments in writing, discuss these comments upon request, and take these written comments and the results of these discussions into account.

* * *

Article 6

Recognition of Conformity Assessment by Central Government Bodies

With respect to their central government bodies:

6.1 Without prejudice to the provisions of paragraphs 3 and 4, Members shall ensure, whenever possible, that results of conformity assessment procedures in other Members are accepted, even when those procedures differ from their own, provided they are satisfied that those procedures offer an assurance of conformity with applicable technical regulations or standards equivalent to their own procedures. It is recognized that prior consultations may be necessary in order to arrive at a mutually satisfactory understanding regarding, in particular:

6.1.1 adequate and enduring technical competence of the relevant conformity assessment bodies in the exporting Member, so that confidence in the continued reliability of their conformity assessment results can exist; in this regard, verified compliance, for instance through accreditation, with relevant guides or recommendations issued by international standardizing bodies shall be taken into account as an indication of adequate technical competence;

6.1.2 limitation of the acceptance of conformity assessment results to those produced by designated bodies in the exporting Member.

* * *

Article 7

Procedures for Assessment of Conformity by Local Government Bodies

With respect to their local government bodies within their territories:

7.1 Members shall take such reasonable measures as may be available to them to ensure compliance by such bodies with the provisions of Articles 5 and 6, with the exception of the obligation to notify as referred to in paragraphs 6.2 and 7.1 of Article 5.

7.2 Members shall ensure that the conformity assessment procedures of local governments on the level directly below that of the central government in Members are notified in accordance with the provisions of paragraphs 6.2 and 7.1 of Article 5, noting that notifications shall not be required for conformity assessment procedures the technical content of which is substantially the same as that of previously notified conformity assessment procedures of central government bodies of the Members concerned.

7.3 Members may require contact with other Members, including the notifications, provision of information, comments and discussions referred to in paragraphs 6 and 7 of Article 5, to take place through the central government.

7.4 Members shall not take measures which require or encourage local government bodies within their territories to act in a manner inconsistent with the provisions of Articles 5 and 6.

7.5 Members are fully responsible under this Agreement for the observance of all provisions of Articles 5 and 6. Members shall formulate and implement positive measures and mechanisms in support of the observance of the provisions of Articles 5 and 6 by other than central government bodies.

Article 12

Special and Differential Treatment of Developing Country Members

12.1 Members shall provide differential and more favourable treatment to developing country Members to this Agreement, through the following provisions as well as through the relevant provisions of other Articles of this Agreement.

12.2 Members shall give particular attention to the provisions of this Agreement concerning developing country Members' rights and obligations and shall take into account the special development, financial and trade needs of developing country Members in the implementation of this Agreement, both nationally and in the operation of this Agreement's institutional arrangements.

12.3 Members shall, in the preparation and application of technical regulations, standards and conformity assessment procedures, take account of the special development, financial and trade needs of developing country Members, with a view to ensuring that such technical regulations, standards and conformity assessment procedures do not create unnecessary obstacles to exports from developing country Members.

12.4 Members recognize that, although international standards, guides or recommendations may exist, in their particular technological and socio-economic conditions, developing country Members adopt certain technical regulations, standards or conformity assessment procedures aimed at preserving indigenous technology and production methods and processes compatible with their development needs. Members therefore recognize that developing country Members should not be expected to use international standards as a basis for their technical regulations or standards, including test methods, which are not appropriate to their development, financial and trade needs.

* * *

Article 14

Consultation and Dispute Settlement

14.1 Consultations and the settlement of disputes with respect to any matter affecting the operation of this Agreement shall take place under the auspices of the Dispute Settlement Body and shall follow, *mutatis mutandis,* the provisions of Articles XXII and XXIII of GATT 1994, as elaborated and applied by the Dispute Settlement Understanding.

* * *

14.4 The dispute settlement provisions set out above can be invoked in cases where a Member considers that another Member has not achieved satisfactory results under Articles 3, 4, 7, 8 and 9 and its trade interests are significantly affected. In this respect, such results shall be equivalent to those as if the body in question were a Member.

FINAL PROVISIONS

Article 15

Final Provisions

Reservations

15.1 Reservations may not be entered in respect of any of the provisions of this Agreement without the consent of the other Members.

Review

15.2 Each Member shall, promptly after the date on which the WTO Agreement enters into force for it, inform the Committee of measures in existence or taken to ensure the implementation and administration of this Agreement. Any changes of such measures thereafter shall also be notified to the Committee.

15.3 The Committee shall review annually the implementation and operation of this Agreement taking into account the objectives thereof.

15.4 Not later than the end of the third year from the date of entry into force of the WTO Agreement and at the end of each three-year period thereafter, the Committee shall review the operation and implementation of this Agreement, including the provisions relating to transparency, with a view to recommending an adjustment of the rights and obligations of this Agreement where necessary to ensure mutual economic advantage and balance of rights and obligations, without prejudice to the provisions of Article 12. Having regard, *inter alia,* to the experience gained in the implementation of the Agreement, the Committee shall, where appropriate, submit proposals for amendments to the text of this Agreement to the Council for Trade in Goods.

Annexes

15.5 The annexes to this Agreement constitute an integral part thereof.

ANNEX 1

TERMS AND THEIR DEFINITIONS FOR THE PURPOSE OF THIS AGREEMENT

The terms presented in the sixth edition of the ISO/IEC Guide 2: 1991, General Terms and Their Definitions Concerning Standardization and Related Activities, shall, when used in this Agreement, have the same meaning as given in the definitions in the said Guide taking into account that services are excluded from the coverage of this Agreement.

For the purpose of this Agreement, however, the following definitions shall apply:

1. *Technical regulation*

Document which lays down product characteristics or their related processes and production methods, including the applicable administrative provisions, with which compliance is mandatory. It may also include or deal exclusively with terminology, symbols, packaging, marking or labelling requirements as they apply to a product, process or production method.

Explanatory note

The definition in ISO/IEC Guide 2 is not self-contained, but based on the so-called "building block" system.

2. *Standard*

Document approved by a recognized body, that provides, for common and repeated use, rules, guidelines or characteristics for products or related processes and production methods, with which compliance is not mandatory. It may also include or deal exclusively with terminology, symbols, packaging, marking or labelling requirements as they apply to a product, process or production method.

Explanatory note

The terms as defined in ISO/IEC Guide 2 cover products, processes and services. This Agreement deals only with technical regulations, standards and conformity assessment procedures related to products or processes and production methods. Standards as defined by ISO/IEC Guide 2 may be mandatory or voluntary. For the purpose of this Agreement standards are defined as voluntary and technical regulations as mandatory documents. Standards prepared by the international standardization community are based on consensus. This Agreement covers also documents that are not based on consensus.

3. *Conformity assessment procedures*

Any procedure used, directly or indirectly, to determine that relevant requirements in technical regulations or standards are fulfilled.

Explanatory note

Conformity assessment procedures include, *inter alia,* procedures for sampling, testing and inspection; evaluation, verification and assurance of conformity; registration, accreditation and approval as well as their combinations.

4. *International body or system*

Body or system whose membership is open to the relevant bodies of at least all Members.

5. *Regional body or system*

Body or system whose membership is open to the relevant bodies of only some of the Members.

6. *Central government body*

Central government, its ministries and departments or any body subject to the control of the central government in respect of the activity in question.

Explanatory note

In the case of the European Communities the provisions governing central government bodies apply. However, regional bodies or conformity assessment systems may be established within the European Communities, and in such cases would be subject to the provisions of this Agreement on regional bodies or conformity assessment systems.

7. *Local government body*

Government other than a central government (e.g. states, provinces, Länder, cantons, municipalities, etc.), its ministries or departments or any body subject to the control of such a government in respect of the activity in question.

8. *Non-governmental body*

Body other than a central government body or a local government body, including a non-governmental body which has legal power to enforce a technical regulation.

ANNEX 3

CODE OF GOOD PRACTICE FOR THE PREPARATION, ADOPTION AND APPLICATION OF STANDARDS

General Provisions

A. For the purposes of this Code the definitions in Annex 1 of this Agreement shall apply.

B. This Code is open to acceptance by any standardizing body within the territory of a Member of the WTO, whether a central government body, a local government body, or a non-governmental body; to any governmental regional standardizing body one or more members of which are Members of the WTO; and to any non-governmental regional standardizing body one or more members of which are situated within the territory of a Member of the WTO (referred to in this Code collectively as "standardizing bodies" and individually as "the standardizing body").

C. Standardizing bodies that have accepted or withdrawn from this Code shall notify this fact to the ISO/IEC Information Centre in Geneva. The notification shall include the name and address of the body concerned and the scope of its current and expected standardization activities. The notification may be sent either directly to the ISO/IEC Information Centre, or through the national member body of ISO/IEC or, preferably, through the relevant national member or international affiliate of ISONET, as appropriate.

SUBSTANTIVE PROVISIONS

D. In respect of standards, the standardizing body shall accord treatment to products originating in the territory of any other Member of the WTO no less favourable than that accorded to like products of national origin and to like products originating in any other country.

E. The standardizing body shall ensure that standards are not prepared, adopted or applied with a view to, or with the effect of, creating unnecessary obstacles to international trade.

F. Where international standards exist or their completion is imminent, the standardizing body shall use them, or the relevant parts of them, as a basis for the standards it develops, except where such international standards or relevant parts would be ineffective or inappropriate, for instance, because of an insufficient level of protection or fundamental climatic or geographical factors or fundamental technological problems.

G. With a view to harmonizing standards on as wide a basis as possible, the standardizing body shall, in an appropriate way, play a full part, within the limits of its resources, in the preparation by relevant international standardizing bodies of international standards regarding subject matter for which it either has adopted, or expects to adopt, standards. For standardizing bodies within the territory of a Member, participation in a particular international standardization activity shall, whenever possible, take place through one delegation representing all standardizing bodies in the territory that have adopted, or expect to adopt, standards for the subject matter to which the international standardization activity relates.

H. The standardizing body within the territory of a Member shall make every effort to avoid duplication of, or overlap with, the work of other standardizing bodies in the national territory or with the work of relevant international or regional standardizing bodies. They shall also make every effort to achieve a national consensus on the standards they develop. Likewise the regional standardizing body shall make every effort to avoid duplication of, or overlap with, the work of relevant international standardizing bodies.

I. Wherever appropriate, the standardizing body shall specify standards based on product requirements in terms of performance rather than design or descriptive characteristics.

J. At least once every six months, the standardizing body shall publish a work programme containing its name and address, the standards it is currently preparing and the standards which it has adopted in the preceding period. A standard is under preparation from the moment a decision has been taken to develop a standard until that standard has been adopted. The titles of specific draft standards shall, upon request, be provided in English, French or Spanish. A notice of the existence of the work programme shall be published in a national or, as the case may be, regional publication of standardization activities.

The work programme shall for each standard indicate, in accordance with any ISONET rules, the classification relevant to the subject matter, the stage attained in the standard's development, and the references of any international standards taken as a basis. No later than at the time of publication of its work programme, the standardizing body shall notify the existence thereof to the ISO/IEC Information Centre in Geneva.

* * *

N. The standardizing body shall take into account, in the further processing of the standard, the comments received during the period for commenting. Comments received through standardizing bodies that have accepted this Code of Good Practice shall, if so requested, be replied to as promptly as possible. The reply shall include an explanation why a deviation from relevant international standards is necessary.

* * *

Q. The standardizing body shall afford sympathetic consideration to, and adequate opportunity for, consultation regarding representations with respect to the operation of this Code presented by standardizing bodies that have accepted this Code of Good Practice. It shall make an objective effort to solve any complaints.

DOCUMENT 19

WTO AGREEMENT ON TRADE-RELATED ASPECTS OF INTELLECTUAL PROPERTY RIGHTS (TRIPS)

■ ■ ■

Table of Contents

AGREEMENT ON TRADE-RELATED ASPECTS OF INTELLECTUAL PROPERTY RIGHTS

Members,

Desiring to reduce distortions and impediments to international trade, and taking into account the need to promote effective and adequate protection of intellectual property rights, and to ensure that measures and procedures to enforce intellectual property rights do not themselves become barriers to legitimate trade;

Recognizing, to this end, the need for new rules and disciplines concerning:

(a) the applicability of the basic principles of GATT 1994 and of relevant international intellectual property agreements or conventions;

(b) the provision of adequate standards and principles concerning the availability, scope and use of trade-related intellectual property rights;

(c) the provision of effective and appropriate means for the enforcement of trade-related intellectual property rights, taking into account differences in national legal systems;

(d) the provision of effective and expeditious procedures for the multilateral prevention and settlement of disputes between governments; and

(e) transitional arrangements aiming at the fullest participation in the results of the negotiations;

Recognizing the need for a multilateral framework of principles, rules and disciplines dealing with international trade in counterfeit goods;

Recognizing that intellectual property rights are private rights;

Recognizing the underlying public policy objectives of national systems for the protection of intellectual property, including developmental and technological objectives;

Recognizing also the special needs of the least-developed country Members in respect of maximum flexibility in the domestic implementation of laws and regulations in order to enable them to create a sound and viable technological base;

Emphasizing the importance of reducing tensions by reaching strengthened commitments to resolve disputes on trade-related intellectual property issues through multilateral procedures;

Desiring to establish a mutually supportive relationship between the WTO and the World Intellectual Property Organization (referred to in this

Agreement as "WIPO") as well as other relevant international organizations;

Hereby agree as follows:

PART I

GENERAL PROVISIONS AND BASIC PRINCIPLES

Article 1

Nature and Scope of Obligations

1. Members shall give effect to the provisions of this Agreement. Members may, but shall not be obliged to, implement in their law more extensive protection than is required by this Agreement, provided that such protection does not contravene the provisions of this Agreement. Members shall be free to determine the appropriate method of implementing the provisions of this Agreement within their own legal system and practice.

2. For the purposes of this Agreement, the term "intellectual property" refers to all categories of intellectual property that are the subject of Sections 1 through 7 of Part II.

3. Members shall accord the treatment provided for in this Agreement to the nationals of other Members.[1] In respect of the relevant intellectual property right, the nationals of other Members shall be understood as those natural or legal persons that would meet the criteria for eligibility for protection provided for in the Paris Convention (1967), the Berne Convention (1971), the Rome Convention and the Treaty on Intellectual Property in Respect of Integrated Circuits, were all Members of the WTO members of those conventions.[2] Any Member availing itself of the possibilities provided in paragraph 3 of Article 5 or paragraph 2 of Article 6 of the Rome Convention shall make a notification as foreseen in those provisions to the Council for Trade-Related Aspects of Intellectual Property Rights (the "Council for TRIPS").

---

1 When "nationals" are referred to in this Agreement, they shall be deemed, in the case of a separate customs territory Member of the WTO, to mean persons, natural or legal, who are domiciled or who have a real and effective industrial or commercial establishment in that customs territory.

2 In this Agreement, "Paris Convention" refers to the Paris Convention for the Protection of Industrial Property; "Paris Convention (1967)" refers to the Stockholm Act of this Convention of 14 July 1967. "Berne Convention" refers to the Berne Convention for the Protection of Literary and Artistic Works; "Berne Convention (1971)" refers to the Paris Act of this Convention of 24 July 1971. "Rome Convention" refers to the International Convention for the Protection of Performers, Producers of Phonograms and Broadcasting Organizations, adopted at Rome on 26 October 1961. "Treaty on Intellectual Property in Respect of Integrated Circuits" (IPIC Treaty) refers to the Treaty on Intellectual Property in Respect of Integrated Circuits, adopted at Washington on 26 May 1989. "WTO Agreement" refers to the Agreement Establishing the WTO.

Article 2

Intellectual Property Conventions

1. In respect of Parts II, III and IV of this Agreement, Members shall comply with Articles 1 through 12, and Article 19, of the Paris Convention (1967).

2. Nothing in Parts I to IV of this Agreement shall derogate from existing obligations that Members may have to each other under the Paris Convention, the Berne Convention, the Rome Convention and the Treaty on Intellectual Property in Respect of Integrated Circuits.

Article 3

National Treatment

1. Each Member shall accord to the nationals of other Members treatment no less favourable than that it accords to its own nationals with regard to the protection[3] of intellectual property, subject to the exceptions already provided in, respectively, the Paris Convention (1967), the Berne Convention (1971), the Rome Convention or the Treaty on Intellectual Property in Respect of Integrated Circuits. In respect of performers, producers of phonograms and broadcasting organizations, this obligation only applies in respect of the rights provided under this Agreement. Any Member availing itself of the possibilities provided in Article 6 of the Berne Convention (1971) or paragraph 1(b) of Article 16 of the Rome Convention shall make a notification as foreseen in those provisions to the Council for TRIPS.

2. Members may avail themselves of the exceptions permitted under paragraph 1 in relation to judicial and administrative procedures, including the designation of an address for service or the appointment of an agent within the jurisdiction of a Member, only where such exceptions are necessary to secure compliance with laws and regulations which are not inconsistent with the provisions of this Agreement and where such practices are not applied in a manner which would constitute a disguised restriction on trade.

Article 4

Most-Favoured-Nation Treatment

With regard to the protection of intellectual property, any advantage, favour, privilege or immunity granted by a Member to the nationals of any other country shall be accorded immediately and unconditionally to the

[3] For the purposes of Articles 3 and 4, "protection" shall include matters affecting the availability, acquisition, scope, maintenance and enforcement of intellectual property rights as well as those matters affecting the use of intellectual property rights specifically addressed in this Agreement.

nationals of all other Members. Exempted from this obligation are any advantage, favour, privilege or immunity accorded by a Member:

(a) deriving from international agreements on judicial assistance or law enforcement of a general nature and not particularly confined to the protection of intellectual property;

(b) granted in accordance with the provisions of the Berne Convention (1971) or the Rome Convention authorizing that the treatment accorded be a function not of national treatment but of the treatment accorded in another country;

(c) in respect of the rights of performers, producers of phonograms and broadcasting organizations not provided under this Agreement;

(d) deriving from international agreements related to the protection of intellectual property which entered into force prior to the entry into force of the WTO Agreement, provided that such agreements are notified to the Council for TRIPS and do not constitute an arbitrary or unjustifiable discrimination against nationals of other Members.

Article 5

Multilateral Agreements on Acquisition or Maintenance of Protection

The obligations under Articles 3 and 4 do not apply to procedures provided in multilateral agreements concluded under the auspices of WIPO relating to the acquisition or maintenance of intellectual property rights.

Article 6

Exhaustion

For the purposes of dispute settlement under this Agreement, subject to the provisions of Articles 3 and 4 nothing in this Agreement shall be used to address the issue of the exhaustion of intellectual property rights.

Article 7

Objectives

The protection and enforcement of intellectual property rights should contribute to the promotion of technological innovation and to the transfer and dissemination of technology, to the mutual advantage of producers and users of technological knowledge and in a manner conducive to social and economic welfare, and to a balance of rights and obligations.

Article 8

Principles

1. Members may, in formulating or amending their laws and regulations, adopt measures necessary to protect public health and nutrition, and to promote the public interest in sectors of vital importance

to their socio-economic and technological development, provided that such measures are consistent with the provisions of this Agreement.

2. Appropriate measures, provided that they are consistent with the provisions of this Agreement, may be needed to prevent the abuse of intellectual property rights by right holders or the resort to practices which unreasonably restrain trade or adversely affect the international transfer of technology.

PART II

STANDARDS CONCERNING THE AVAILABILITY, SCOPE AND USE OF INTELLECTUAL PROPERTY RIGHTS

SECTION 1: COPYRIGHT AND RELATED RIGHTS

Article 9

Relation to the Berne Convention

1. Members shall comply with Articles 1 through 21 of the Berne Convention (1971) and the Appendix thereto. However, Members shall not have rights or obligations under this Agreement in respect of the rights conferred under Article 6 *bis* of that Convention or of the rights derived therefrom.

2. Copyright protection shall extend to expressions and not to ideas, procedures, methods of operation or mathematical concepts as such.

Article 10

Computer Programs and Compilations of Data

1. Computer programs, whether in source or object code, shall be protected as literary works under the Berne Convention (1971).

2. Compilations of data or other material, whether in machine readable or other form, which by reason of the selection or arrangement of their contents constitute intellectual creations shall be protected as such. Such protection, which shall not extend to the data or material itself, shall be without prejudice to any copyright subsisting in the data or material itself.

Article 11

Rental Rights

In respect of at least computer programs and cinematographic works, a Member shall provide authors and their successors in title the right to authorize or to prohibit the commercial rental to the public of originals or copies of their copyright works. A Member shall be excepted from this obligation in respect of cinematographic works unless such rental has led to widespread copying of such works which is materially impairing the exclusive right of reproduction conferred in that Member on authors and their successors in title. In respect of computer programs, this obligation does not apply to rentals where the program itself is not the essential object of the rental.

Article 12

Term of Protection

Whenever the term of protection of a work, other than a photographic work or a work of applied art, is calculated on a basis other than the life of a natural person, such term shall be no less than 50 years from the end of the calendar year of authorized publication, or, failing such authorized publication within 50 years from the making of the work, 50 years from the end of the calendar year of making.

Article 13

Limitations and Exceptions

Members shall confine limitations or exceptions to exclusive rights to certain special cases which do not conflict with a normal exploitation of the work and do not unreasonably prejudice the legitimate interests of the right holder.

Article 14

Protection of Performers, Producers of Phonograms (Sound Recordings) and Broadcasting Organizations

1. In respect of a fixation of their performance on a phonogram, performers shall have the possibility of preventing the following acts when undertaken without their authorization: the fixation of their unfixed performance and the reproduction of such fixation. Performers shall also have the possibility of preventing the following acts when undertaken without their authorization: the broadcasting by wireless means and the communication to the public of their live performance.

2. Producers of phonograms shall enjoy the right to authorize or prohibit the direct or indirect reproduction of their phonograms.

3. Broadcasting organizations shall have the right to prohibit the following acts when undertaken without their authorization: the fixation, the reproduction of fixations, and the rebroadcasting by wireless means of broadcasts, as well as the communication to the public of television broadcasts of the same. Where Members do not grant such rights to broadcasting organizations, they shall provide owners of copyright in the subject matter of broadcasts with the possibility of preventing the above acts, subject to the provisions of the Berne Convention (1971).

4. The provisions of Article 11 in respect of computer programs shall apply *mutatis mutandis* to producers of phonograms and any other right holders in phonograms as determined in a Member's law. If on 15 April 1994 a Member has in force a system of equitable remuneration of right holders in respect of the rental of phonograms, it may maintain such

system provided that the commercial rental of phonograms is not giving rise to the material impairment of the exclusive rights of reproduction of right holders.

5. The term of the protection available under this Agreement to performers and producers of phonograms shall last at least until the end of a period of 50 years computed from the end of the calendar year in which the fixation was made or the performance took place. The term of protection granted pursuant to paragraph 3 shall last for at least 20 years from the end of the calendar year in which the broadcast took place.

6. Any Member may, in relation to the rights conferred under paragraphs 1, 2 and 3, provide for conditions, limitations, exceptions and reservations to the extent permitted by the Rome Convention. However, the provisions of Article 18 of the Berne Convention (1971) shall also apply, *mutatis mutandis,* to the rights of performers and producers of phonograms in phonograms.

SECTION 2: TRADEMARKS

Article 15

Protectable Subject Matter

1. Any sign, or any combination of signs, capable of distinguishing the goods or services of one undertaking from those of other undertakings, shall be capable of constituting a trademark. Such signs, in particular words including personal names, letters, numerals, figurative elements and combinations of colours as well as any combination of such signs, shall be eligible for registration as trademarks. Where signs are not inherently capable of distinguishing the relevant goods or services, Members may make registrability depend on distinctiveness acquired through use. Members may require, as a condition of registration, that signs be visually perceptible.

2. Paragraph 1 shall not be understood to prevent a Member from denying registration of a trademark on other grounds, provided that they do not derogate from the provisions of the Paris Convention (1967).

3. Members may make registrability depend on use. However, actual use of a trademark shall not be a condition for filing an application for registration. An application shall not be refused solely on the ground that intended use has not taken place before the expiry of a period of three years from the date of application.

4. The nature of the goods or services to which a trademark is to be applied shall in no case form an obstacle to registration of the trademark.

5. Members shall publish each trademark either before it is registered or promptly after it is registered and shall afford a reasonable opportunity for petitions to cancel the registration. In addition, Members

may afford an opportunity for the registration of a trademark to be opposed.

Article 16

Rights Conferred

1. The owner of a registered trademark shall have the exclusive right to prevent all third parties not having the owner's consent from using in the course of trade identical or similar signs for goods or services which are identical or similar to those in respect of which the trademark is registered where such use would result in a likelihood of confusion. In case of the use of an identical sign for identical goods or services, a likelihood of confusion shall be presumed. The rights described above shall not prejudice any existing prior rights, nor shall they affect the possibility of Members making rights available on the basis of use.

2. Article 6 *bis* of the Paris Convention (1967) shall apply, *mutatis mutandis,* to services. In determining whether a trademark is well-known, Members shall take account of the knowledge of the trademark in the relevant sector of the public, including knowledge in the Member concerned which has been obtained as a result of the promotion of the trademark.

3. Article 6 *bis* of the Paris Convention (1967) shall apply, *mutatis mutandis,* to goods or services which are not similar to those in respect of which a trademark is registered, provided that use of that trademark in relation to those goods or services would indicate a connection between those goods or services and the owner of the registered trademark and provided that the interests of the owner of the registered trademark are likely to be damaged by such use.

Article 17

Exceptions

Members may provide limited exceptions to the rights conferred by a trademark, such as fair use of descriptive terms, provided that such exceptions take account of the legitimate interests of the owner of the trademark and of third parties.

Article 18

Term of Protection

Initial registration, and each renewal of registration, of a trademark shall be for a term of no less than seven years. The registration of a trademark shall be renewable indefinitely.

Article 19

Requirement of Use

1. If use is required to maintain a registration, the registration may be cancelled only after an uninterrupted period of at least three years of

non-use, unless valid reasons based on the existence of obstacles to such use are shown by the trademark owner. Circumstances arising independently of the will of the owner of the trademark which constitute an obstacle to the use of the trademark, such as import restrictions on or other government requirements for goods or services protected by the trademark, shall be recognized as valid reasons for non-use.

2. When subject to the control of its owner, use of a trademark by another person shall be recognized as use of the trademark for the purpose of maintaining the registration.

Article 20

Other Requirements

The use of a trademark in the course of trade shall not be unjustifiably encumbered by special requirements, such as use with another trademark, use in a special form or use in a manner detrimental to its capability to distinguish the goods or services of one undertaking from those of other undertakings. This will not preclude a requirement prescribing the use of the trademark identifying the undertaking producing the goods or services along with, but without linking it to, the trademark distinguishing the specific goods or services in question of that undertaking.

Article 21

Licensing and Assignment

Members may determine conditions on the licensing and assignment of trademarks, it being understood that the compulsory licensing of trademarks shall not be permitted and that the owner of a registered trademark shall have the right to assign the trademark with or without the transfer of the business to which the trademark belongs.

SECTION 3. GEOGRAPHICAL INDICATIONS (omitted)

* * *

SECTION 4: INDUSTRIAL DESIGNS (omitted)

* * *

Requirements for Protection

SECTION 5: PATENTS

Article 27

Patentable Subject Matter

1. Subject to the provisions of paragraphs 2 and 3, patents shall be available for any inventions, whether products or processes, in all fields of technology, provided that they are new, involve an inventive step and are

capable of industrial application.[5] Subject to paragraph 4 of Article 65, paragraph 8 of Article 70 and paragraph 3 of this Article, patents shall be available and patent rights enjoyable without discrimination as to the place of invention, the field of technology and whether products are imported or locally produced.

2. Members may exclude from patentability inventions, the prevention within their territory of the commercial exploitation of which is necessary to protect *ordre public* or morality, including to protect human, animal or plant life or health or to avoid serious prejudice to the environment, provided that such exclusion is not made merely because the exploitation is prohibited by their law.

3. Members may also exclude from patentability:

(a) diagnostic, therapeutic and surgical methods for the treatment of humans or animals;

(b) plants and animals other than micro-organisms, and essentially biological processes for the production of plants or animals other than non-biological and microbiological processes. However, Members shall provide for the protection of plant varieties either by patents or by an effective *sui generis* system or by any combination thereof. The provisions of this subparagraph shall be reviewed four years after the date of entry into force of the WTO Agreement.

Article 28

Rights Conferred

1. A patent shall confer on its owner the following exclusive rights:

(a) where the subject matter of a patent is a product, to prevent third parties not having the owner's consent from the acts of: making, using, offering for sale, selling, or importing[6] for these purposes that product;

(b) where the subject matter of a patent is a process, to prevent third parties not having the owner's consent from the act of using the process, and from the acts of: using, offering for sale, selling, or importing for these purposes at least the product obtained directly by that process.

2. Patent owners shall also have the right to assign, or transfer by succession, the patent and to conclude licensing contracts.

---

[5] For the purposes of this Article, the terms "inventive step" and "capable of industrial application" may be deemed by a Member to be synonymous with the terms "non-obvious" and "useful" respectively.

[6] This right, like all other rights conferred under this Agreement in respect of the use, sale, importation or other distribution of goods, is subject to the provisions of Article 6.

Article 29

Conditions on Patent Applicants

1. Members shall require that an applicant for a patent shall disclose the invention in a manner sufficiently clear and complete for the invention to be carried out by a person skilled in the art and may require the applicant to indicate the best mode for carrying out the invention known to the inventor at the filing date or, where priority is claimed, at the priority date of the application.

2. Members may require an applicant for a patent to provide information concerning the applicant's corresponding foreign applications and grants.

Article 30

Exceptions to Rights Conferred

Members may provide limited exceptions to the exclusive rights conferred by a patent, provided that such exceptions do not unreasonably conflict with a normal exploitation of the patent and do not unreasonably prejudice the legitimate interests of the patent owner, taking account of the legitimate interests of third parties.

Article 31

Other Use Without Authorization of the Right Holder

Where the law of a Member allows for other use[7] of the subject matter of a patent without the authorization of the right holder, including use by the government or third parties authorized by the government, the following provisions shall be respected:

(a) authorization of such use shall be considered on its individual merits;

(b) such use may only be permitted if, prior to such use, the proposed user has made efforts to obtain authorization from the right holder on reasonable commercial terms and conditions and that such efforts have not been successful within a reasonable period of time. This requirement may be waived by a Member in the case of a national emergency or other circumstances of extreme urgency or in cases of public non-commercial use. In situations of national emergency or other circumstances of extreme urgency, the right holder shall, nevertheless, be notified as soon as reasonably practicable. In the case of public non-commercial use, where the government or contractor, without making a patent search, knows or has demonstrable grounds to know that a valid patent is or will be used by or for the government, the right holder shall be informed promptly;

---

[7] "Other use" refers to other than that allowed under Article 30.

(c) the scope and duration of such use shall be limited to the purpose for which it was authorized, and in the case of semi-conductor technology shall only be for public non-commercial use or to remedy a practice determined after judicial or administrative process to be anti-competitive;

(d) such use shall be non-exclusive;

(e) such use shall be non-assignable, except with that part of the enterprise or goodwill which enjoys such use;

(f) any such use shall be authorized predominantly for the supply of the domestic market of the Member authorizing such use;

(g) authorization for such use shall be liable, subject to adequate protection of the legitimate interests of the persons so authorized, to be terminated if and when the circumstances which led to it cease to exist and are unlikely to recur. The competent authority shall have the authority to review, upon motivated request, the continued existence of these circumstances;

(h) the right holder shall be paid adequate remuneration in the circumstances of each case, taking into account the economic value of the authorization;

(i) the legal validity of any decision relating to the authorization of such use shall be subject to judicial review or other independent review by a distinct higher authority in that Member;

(j) any decision relating to the remuneration provided in respect of such use shall be subject to judicial review or other independent review by a distinct higher authority in that Member;

(k) Members are not obliged to apply the conditions set forth in subparagraphs (b) and (f) where such use is permitted to remedy a practice determined after judicial or administrative process to be anti-competitive. The need to correct anti-competitive practices may be taken into account in determining the amount of remuneration in such cases. Competent authorities shall have the authority to refuse termination of authorization if and when the conditions which led to such authorization are likely to recur;

(*l*) where such use is authorized to permit the exploitation of a patent ("the second patent") which cannot be exploited without infringing another patent ("the first patent"), the following additional conditions shall apply:

(i) the invention claimed in the second patent shall involve an important technical advance of considerable economic significance in relation to the invention claimed in the first patent;

(ii) the owner of the first patent shall be entitled to a cross-licence on reasonable terms to use the invention claimed in the second patent; and

(iii) the use authorized in respect of the first patent shall be non-assignable except with the assignment of the second patent.

Article 32

Revocation/Forfeiture

An opportunity for judicial review of any decision to revoke or forfeit a patent shall be available.

Article 33

Term of Protection

The term of protection available shall not end before the expiration of a period of twenty years counted from the filing date.[8]

Article 34

Process Patents: Burden of Proof

1. For the purposes of civil proceedings in respect of the infringement of the rights of the owner referred to in paragraph 1(b) of Article 28, if the subject matter of a patent is a process for obtaining a product, the judicial authorities shall have the authority to order the defendant to prove that the process to obtain an identical product is different from the patented process. Therefore, Members shall provide, in at least one of the following circumstances, that any identical product when produced without the consent of the patent owner shall, in the absence of proof to the contrary, be deemed to have been obtained by the patented process:

(a) if the product obtained by the patented process is new;

(b) if there is a substantial likelihood that the identical product was made by the process and the owner of the patent has been unable through reasonable efforts to determine the process actually used.

2. Any Member shall be free to provide that the burden of proof indicated in paragraph 1 shall be on the alleged infringer only if the condition referred to in subparagraph (a) is fulfilled or only if the condition referred to in subparagraph (b) is fulfilled.

3. In the adduction of proof to the contrary, the legitimate interests of defendants in protecting their manufacturing and business secrets shall be taken into account.

---

[8] It is understood that those Members which do not have a system of original grant may provide that the term of protection shall be computed from the filing date in the system of original grant.

SECTION 6: LAYOUT-DESIGNS (TOPOGRAPHIES) OF INTEGRATED CIRCUITS (omitted)

* * *

SECTION 7: PROTECTION OF UNDISCLOSED INFORMATION

Article 39

1. In the course of ensuring effective protection against unfair competition as provided in Article 10 *bis* of the Paris Convention (1967), Members shall protect undisclosed information in accordance with paragraph 2 and data submitted to governments or governmental agencies in accordance with paragraph 3.

2. Natural and legal persons shall have the possibility of preventing information lawfully within their control from being disclosed to, acquired by, or used by others without their consent in a manner contrary to honest commercial practices[10] so long as such information:

(a) is secret in the sense that it is not, as a body or in the precise configuration and assembly of its components, generally known among or readily accessible to persons within the circles that normally deal with the kind of information in question;

(b) has commercial value because it is secret; and

(c) has been subject to reasonable steps under the circumstances, by the person lawfully in control of the information, to keep it secret.

3. Members, when requiring, as a condition of approving the marketing of pharmaceutical or of agricultural chemical products which utilize new chemical entities, the submission of undisclosed test or other data, the origination of which involves a considerable effort, shall protect such data against unfair commercial use. In addition, Members shall protect such data against disclosure, except where necessary to protect the public, or unless steps are taken to ensure that the data are protected against unfair commercial use.

SECTION 8: CONTROL OF ANTI-COMPETITIVE PRACTICES IN CONTRACTUAL LICENSES

Article 40

1. Members agree that some licensing practices or conditions pertaining to intellectual property rights which restrain competition may

---

[10] For the purpose of this provision, "a manner contrary to honest commercial practices" shall mean at least practices such as breach of contract, breach of confidence and inducement to breach, and includes the acquisition of undisclosed information by third parties who knew, or were grossly negligent in failing to know, that such practices were involved in the acquisition.

have adverse effects on trade and may impede the transfer and dissemination of technology.

2. Nothing in this Agreement shall prevent Members from specifying in their legislation licensing practices or conditions that may in particular cases constitute an abuse of intellectual property rights having an adverse effect on competition in the relevant market. As provided above, a Member may adopt, consistently with the other provisions of this Agreement, appropriate measures to prevent or control such practices, which may include for example exclusive grantback conditions, conditions preventing challenges to validity and coercive package licensing, in the light of the relevant laws and regulations of that Member.

3. Each Member shall enter, upon request, into consultations with any other Member which has cause to believe that an intellectual property right owner that is a national or domiciliary of the Member to which the request for consultations has been addressed is undertaking practices in violation of the requesting Member's laws and regulations on the subject matter of this Section, and which wishes to secure compliance with such legislation, without prejudice to any action under the law and to the full freedom of an ultimate decision of either Member. The Member addressed shall accord full and sympathetic consideration to, and shall afford adequate opportunity for, consultations with the requesting Member, and shall cooperate through supply of publicly available non-confidential information of relevance to the matter in question and of other information available to the Member, subject to domestic law and to the conclusion of mutually satisfactory agreements concerning the safeguarding of its confidentiality by the requesting Member.

4. A Member whose nationals or domiciliaries are subject to proceedings in another Member concerning alleged violation of that other Member's laws and regulations on the subject matter of this Section shall, upon request, be granted an opportunity for consultations by the other Member under the same conditions as those foreseen in paragraph 3.

PART III

ENFORCEMENT OF INTELLECTUAL PROPERTY RIGHTS

SECTION 1: GENERAL OBLIGATIONS

Article 41

1. Members shall ensure that enforcement procedures as specified in this Part are available under their law so as to permit effective action against any act of infringement of intellectual property rights covered by this Agreement, including expeditious remedies to prevent infringements and remedies which constitute a deterrent to further infringements. These procedures shall be applied in such a manner as to avoid the creation of

barriers to legitimate trade and to provide for safeguards against their abuse.

2. Procedures concerning the enforcement of intellectual property rights shall be fair and equitable. They shall not be unnecessarily complicated or costly, or entail unreasonable time-limits or unwarranted delays.

3. Decisions on the merits of a case shall preferably be in writing and reasoned. They shall be made available at least to the parties to the proceeding without undue delay. Decisions on the merits of a case shall be based only on evidence in respect of which parties were offered the opportunity to be heard.

4. Parties to a proceeding shall have an opportunity for review by a judicial authority of final administrative decisions and, subject to jurisdictional provisions in a Member's law concerning the importance of a case, of at least the legal aspects of initial judicial decisions on the merits of a case. However, there shall be no obligation to provide an opportunity for review of acquittals in criminal cases.

5. It is understood that this Part does not create any obligation to put in place a judicial system for the enforcement of intellectual property rights distinct from that for the enforcement of law in general, nor does it affect the capacity of Members to enforce their law in general. Nothing in this Part creates any obligation with respect to the distribution of resources as between enforcement of intellectual property rights and the enforcement of law in general.

SECTION 2: CIVIL AND ADMINISTRATIVE PROCEDURES AND REMEDIES

Article 42

Fair and Equitable Procedures

Members shall make available to right holders[11] civil judicial procedures concerning the enforcement of any intellectual property right covered by this Agreement. Defendants shall have the right to written notice which is timely and contains sufficient detail, including the basis of the claims. Parties shall be allowed to be represented by independent legal counsel, and procedures shall not impose overly burdensome requirements concerning mandatory personal appearances. All parties to such procedures shall be duly entitled to substantiate their claims and to present all relevant evidence. The procedure shall provide a means to identify and protect confidential information, unless this would be contrary to existing constitutional requirements.

[11] For the purpose of this Part, the term "right holder" includes federations and associations having legal standing to assert such rights.

Article 43

Evidence

1. The judicial authorities shall have the authority, where a party has presented reasonably available evidence sufficient to support its claims and has specified evidence relevant to substantiation of its claims which lies in the control of the opposing party, to order that this evidence be produced by the opposing party, subject in appropriate cases to conditions which ensure the protection of confidential information.

2. In cases in which a party to a proceeding voluntarily and without good reason refuses access to, or otherwise does not provide necessary information within a reasonable period, or significantly impedes a procedure relating to an enforcement action, a Member may accord judicial authorities the authority to make preliminary and final determinations, affirmative or negative, on the basis of the information presented to them, including the complaint or the allegation presented by the party adversely affected by the denial of access to information, subject to providing the parties an opportunity to be heard on the allegations or evidence.

Article 44

Injunctions

1. The judicial authorities shall have the authority to order a party to desist from an infringement, *inter alia* to prevent the entry into the channels of commerce in their jurisdiction of imported goods that involve the infringement of an intellectual property right, immediately after customs clearance of such goods. Members are not obliged to accord such authority in respect of protected subject matter acquired or ordered by a person prior to knowing or having reasonable grounds to know that dealing in such subject matter would entail the infringement of an intellectual property right.

2. Notwithstanding the other provisions of this Part and provided that the provisions of Part II specifically addressing use by governments, or by third parties authorized by a government, without the authorization of the right holder are complied with, Members may limit the remedies available against such use to payment of remuneration in accordance with subparagraph (h) of Article 31. In other cases, the remedies under this Part shall apply or, where these remedies are inconsistent with a Member's law, declaratory judgments and adequate compensation shall be available.

Article 45

Damages

1. The judicial authorities shall have the authority to order the infringer to pay the right holder damages adequate to compensate for the injury the right holder has suffered because of an infringement of that

person's intellectual property right by an infringer who knowingly, or with reasonable grounds to know, engaged in infringing activity.

2. The judicial authorities shall also have the authority to order the infringer to pay the right holder expenses, which may include appropriate attorney's fees. In appropriate cases, Members may authorize the judicial authorities to order recovery of profits and/or payment of pre-established damages even where the infringer did not knowingly, or with reasonable grounds to know, engage in infringing activity.

Article 46

Other Remedies

In order to create an effective deterrent to infringement, the judicial authorities shall have the authority to order that goods that they have found to be infringing be, without compensation of any sort, disposed of outside the channels of commerce in such a manner as to avoid any harm caused to the right holder, or, unless this would be contrary to existing constitutional requirements, destroyed. The judicial authorities shall also have the authority to order that materials and implements the predominant use of which has been in the creation of the infringing goods be, without compensation of any sort, disposed of outside the channels of commerce in such a manner as to minimize the risks of further infringements. In considering such requests, the need for proportionality between the seriousness of the infringement and the remedies ordered as well as the interests of third parties shall be taken into account. In regard to counterfeit trademark goods, the simple removal of the trademark unlawfully affixed shall not be sufficient, other than in exceptional cases, to permit release of the goods into the channels of commerce.

Article 47

Right of Information

Members may provide that the judicial authorities shall have the authority, unless this would be out of proportion to the seriousness of the infringement, to order the infringer to inform the right holder of the identity of third persons involved in the production and distribution of the infringing goods or services and of their channels of distribution.

Article 48

Indemnification of the Defendant

1. The judicial authorities shall have the authority to order a party at whose request measures were taken and who has abused enforcement procedures to provide to a party wrongfully enjoined or restrained adequate compensation for the injury suffered because of such abuse. The judicial authorities shall also have the authority to order the applicant to

pay the defendant expenses, which may include appropriate attorney's fees.

2. In respect of the administration of any law pertaining to the protection or enforcement of intellectual property rights, Members shall only exempt both public authorities and officials from liability to appropriate remedial measures where actions are taken or intended in good faith in the course of the administration of that law.

Article 49

Administrative Procedures

To the extent that any civil remedy can be ordered as a result of administrative procedures on the merits of a case, such procedures shall conform to principles equivalent in substance to those set forth in this Section.

SECTION 3: PROVISIONAL MEASURES

Article 50

1. The judicial authorities shall have the authority to order prompt and effective provisional measures:

(a) to prevent an infringement of any intellectual property right from occurring, and in particular to prevent the entry into the channels of commerce in their jurisdiction of goods, including imported goods immediately after customs clearance;

(b) to preserve relevant evidence in regard to the alleged infringement.

2. The judicial authorities shall have the authority to adopt provisional measures *inaudita altera parte* where appropriate, in particular where any delay is likely to cause irreparable harm to the right holder, or where there is a demonstrable risk of evidence being destroyed.

3. The judicial authorities shall have the authority to require the applicant to provide any reasonably available evidence in order to satisfy themselves with a sufficient degree of certainty that the applicant is the right holder and that the applicant's right is being infringed or that such infringement is imminent, and to order the applicant to provide a security or equivalent assurance sufficient to protect the defendant and to prevent abuse.

4. Where provisional measures have been adopted *inaudita altera parte,* the parties affected shall be given notice, without delay after the execution of the measures at the latest. A review, including a right to be heard, shall take place upon request of the defendant with a view to deciding, within a reasonable period after the notification of the measures, whether these measures shall be modified, revoked or confirmed.

5. The applicant may be required to supply other information necessary for the identification of the goods concerned by the authority that will execute the provisional measures.

6. Without prejudice to paragraph 4, provisional measures taken on the basis of paragraphs 1 and 2 shall, upon request by the defendant, be revoked or otherwise cease to have effect, if proceedings leading to a decision on the merits of the case are not initiated within a reasonable period, to be determined by the judicial authority ordering the measures where a Member's law so permits or, in the absence of such a determination, not to exceed 20 working days or 31 calendar days, whichever is the longer.

7. Where the provisional measures are revoked or where they lapse due to any act or omission by the applicant, or where it is subsequently found that there has been no infringement or threat of infringement of an intellectual property right, the judicial authorities shall have the authority to order the applicant, upon request of the defendant, to provide the defendant appropriate compensation for any injury caused by these measures.

8. To the extent that any provisional measure can be ordered as a result of administrative procedures, such procedures shall conform to principles equivalent in substance to those set forth in this Section.

SECTION 4: SPECIAL REQUIREMENTS RELATED TO BORDER MEASURES[12]

Article 51

Suspension of Release by Customs Authorities

Members shall, in conformity with the provisions set out below, adopt procedures[13] to enable a right holder, who has valid grounds for suspecting that the importation of counterfeit trademark or pirated copyright goods[14] may take place, to lodge an application in writing with competent

[12] Where a Member has dismantled substantially all controls over movement of goods across its border with another Member with which it forms part of a customs union, it shall not be required to apply the provisions of this Section at that border.

[13] It is understood that there shall be no obligation to apply such procedures to imports of goods put on the market in another country by or with the consent of the right holder, or to goods in transit.

[14] For the purposes of this Agreement:

(a) "counterfeit trademark goods" shall mean any goods, including packaging, bearing without authorization a trademark which is identical to the trademark validly registered in respect of such goods, or which cannot be distinguished in its essential aspects from such a trademark, and which thereby infringes the rights of the owner of the trademark in question under the law of the country of importation;

(b) "pirated copyright goods" shall mean any goods which are copies made without the consent of the right holder or person duly authorized by the right holder in the country of production and which are made directly or indirectly from an article where the making of that copy would have constituted an infringement of a copyright or a related right under the law of the country of importation.

authorities, administrative or judicial, for the suspension by the customs authorities of the release into free circulation of such goods. Members may enable such an application to be made in respect of goods which involve other infringements of intellectual property rights, provided that the requirements of this Section are met. Members may also provide for corresponding procedures concerning the suspension by the customs authorities of the release of infringing goods destined for exportation from their territories.

Article 52

Application

Any right holder initiating the procedures under Article 51 shall be required to provide adequate evidence to satisfy the competent authorities that, under the laws of the country of importation, there is *prima facie* an infringement of the right holder's intellectual property right and to supply a sufficiently detailed description of the goods to make them readily recognizable by the customs authorities. The competent authorities shall inform the applicant within a reasonable period whether they have accepted the application and, where determined by the competent authorities, the period for which the customs authorities will take action.

Article 53

Security or Equivalent Assurance

1. The competent authorities shall have the authority to require an applicant to provide a security or equivalent assurance sufficient to protect the defendant and the competent authorities and to prevent abuse. Such security or equivalent assurance shall not unreasonably deter recourse to these procedures.

2. Where pursuant to an application under this Section the release of goods involving industrial designs, patents, layout-designs or undisclosed information into free circulation has been suspended by customs authorities on the basis of a decision other than by a judicial or other independent authority, and the period provided for in Article 55 has expired without the granting of provisional relief by the duly empowered authority, and provided that all other conditions for importation have been complied with, the owner, importer, or consignee of such goods shall be entitled to their release on the posting of a security in an amount sufficient to protect the right holder for any infringement. Payment of such security shall not prejudice any other remedy available to the right holder, it being understood that the security shall be released if the right holder fails to pursue the right of action within a reasonable period of time.

Article 54

Notice of Suspension

The importer and the applicant shall be promptly notified of the suspension of the release of goods according to Article 51.

Article 55

Duration of Suspension

If, within a period not exceeding 10 working days after the applicant has been served notice of the suspension, the customs authorities have not been informed that proceedings leading to a decision on the merits of the case have been initiated by a party other than the defendant, or that the duly empowered authority has taken provisional measures prolonging the suspension of the release of the goods, the goods shall be released, provided that all other conditions for importation or exportation have been complied with; in appropriate cases, this time-limit may be extended by another 10 working days. If proceedings leading to a decision on the merits of the case have been initiated, a review, including a right to be heard, shall take place upon request of the defendant with a view to deciding, within a reasonable period, whether these measures shall be modified, revoked or confirmed. Notwithstanding the above, where the suspension of the release of goods is carried out or continued in accordance with a provisional judicial measure, the provisions of paragraph 6 of Article 50 shall apply.

Article 56

Indemnification of the Importer and of the Owner of the Goods

Relevant authorities shall have the authority to order the applicant to pay the importer, the consignee and the owner of the goods appropriate compensation for any injury caused to them through the wrongful detention of goods or through the detention of goods released pursuant to Article 55.

Article 57

Right of Inspection and Information

Without prejudice to the protection of confidential information, Members shall provide the competent authorities the authority to give the right holder sufficient opportunity to have any goods detained by the customs authorities inspected in order to substantiate the right holder's claims. The competent authorities shall also have authority to give the importer an equivalent opportunity to have any such goods inspected. Where a positive determination has been made on the merits of a case, Members may provide the competent authorities the authority to inform the right holder of the names and addresses of the consignor, the importer and the consignee and of the quantity of the goods in question.

Article 58

Ex Officio Action

Where Members require competent authorities to act upon their own initiative and to suspend the release of goods in respect of which they have acquired *prima facie* evidence that an intellectual property right is being infringed:

(a) the competent authorities may at any time seek from the right holder any information that may assist them to exercise these powers;

(b) the importer and the right holder shall be promptly notified of the suspension. Where the importer has lodged an appeal against the suspension with the competent authorities, the suspension shall be subject to the conditions, *mutatis mutandis,* set out at Article 55;

(c) Members shall only exempt both public authorities and officials from liability to appropriate remedial measures where actions are taken or intended in good faith.

Article 59

Remedies

Without prejudice to other rights of action open to the right holder and subject to the right of the defendant to seek review by a judicial authority, competent authorities shall have the authority to order the destruction or disposal of infringing goods in accordance with the principles set out in Article 46. In regard to counterfeit trademark goods, the authorities shall not allow the re-exportation of the infringing goods in an unaltered state or subject them to a different customs procedure, other than in exceptional circumstances.

Article 60

De Minimis Imports

Members may exclude from the application of the above provisions small quantities of goods of a non-commercial nature contained in travellers' personal luggage or sent in small consignments.

SECTION 5: CRIMINAL PROCEDURES

Article 61

Members shall provide for criminal procedures and penalties to be applied at least in cases of wilful trademark counterfeiting or copyright piracy on a commercial scale. Remedies available shall include imprisonment and/or monetary fines sufficient to provide a deterrent, consistently with the level of penalties applied for crimes of a corresponding gravity. In appropriate cases, remedies available shall also include the seizure, forfeiture and destruction of the infringing goods and of any materials and implements the predominant use of which has been in the commission of the offence. Members may provide for criminal procedures and penalties to be applied in other cases of infringement of intellectual property rights, in particular where they are committed wilfully and on a commercial scale.

PART IV

ACQUISITION AND MAINTENANCE OF INTELLECTUAL PROPERTY RIGHTS AND RELATED *INTER-PARTES* PROCEDURES

Article 62

1. Members may require, as a condition of the acquisition or maintenance of the intellectual property rights provided for under Sections 2 through 6 of Part II, compliance with reasonable procedures and formalities. Such procedures and formalities shall be consistent with the provisions of this Agreement.

2. Where the acquisition of an intellectual property right is subject to the right being granted or registered, Members shall ensure that the procedures for grant or registration, subject to compliance with the substantive conditions for acquisition of the right, permit the granting or registration of the right within a reasonable period of time so as to avoid unwarranted curtailment of the period of protection.

3. Article 4 of the Paris Convention (1967) shall apply *mutatis mutandis* to service marks.

4. Procedures concerning the acquisition or maintenance of intellectual property rights and, where a Member's law provides for such procedures, administrative revocation and *inter partes* procedures such as opposition, revocation and cancellation, shall be governed by the general principles set out in paragraphs 2 and 3 of Article 41.

5. Final administrative decisions in any of the procedures referred to under paragraph 4 shall be subject to review by a judicial or quasi-judicial authority. However, there shall be no obligation to provide an opportunity for such review of decisions in cases of unsuccessful opposition or administrative revocation, provided that the grounds for such procedures can be the subject of invalidation procedures.

PART V

DISPUTE PREVENTION AND SETTLEMENT

Article 63

Transparency

1. Laws and regulations, and final judicial decisions and administrative rulings of general application, made effective by a Member pertaining to the subject matter of this Agreement (the availability, scope,

acquisition, enforcement and prevention of the abuse of intellectual property rights) shall be published, or where such publication is not practicable made publicly available, in a national language, in such a manner as to enable governments and right holders to become acquainted with them. Agreements concerning the subject matter of this Agreement which are in force between the government or a governmental agency of a Member and the government or a governmental agency of another Member shall also be published.

2. Members shall notify the laws and regulations referred to in paragraph 1 to the Council for TRIPS in order to assist that Council in its review of the operation of this Agreement. The Council shall attempt to minimize the burden on Members in carrying out this obligation and may decide to waive the obligation to notify such laws and regulations directly to the Council if consultations with WIPO on the establishment of a common register containing these laws and regulations are successful. The Council shall also consider in this connection any action required regarding notifications pursuant to the obligations under this Agreement stemming from the provisions of Article 6 *ter* of the Paris Convention (1967).

3. Each Member shall be prepared to supply, in response to a written request from another Member, information of the sort referred to in paragraph 1. A Member, having reason to believe that a specific judicial decision or administrative ruling or bilateral agreement in the area of intellectual property rights affects its rights under this Agreement, may also request in writing to be given access to or be informed in sufficient detail of such specific judicial decisions or administrative rulings or bilateral agreements.

4. Nothing in paragraphs 1, 2 and 3 shall require Members to disclose confidential information which would impede law enforcement or otherwise be contrary to the public interest or would prejudice the legitimate commercial interests of particular enterprises, public or private.

Article 64

Dispute Settlement

1. The provisions of Articles XXII and XXIII of GATT 1994 as elaborated and applied by the Dispute Settlement Understanding shall apply to consultations and the settlement of disputes under this Agreement except as otherwise specifically provided herein.

2. Subparagraphs 1(b) and 1(c) of Article XXIII of GATT 1994 shall not apply to the settlement of disputes under this Agreement for a period of five years from the date of entry into force of the WTO Agreement.

3. During the time period referred to in paragraph 2, the Council for TRIPS shall examine the scope and modalities for complaints of the type provided for under subparagraphs 1(b) and 1(c) of Article XXIII of GATT

1994 made pursuant to this Agreement, and submit its recommendations to the Ministerial Conference for approval. Any decision of the Ministerial Conference to approve such recommendations or to extend the period in paragraph 2 shall be made only by consensus, and approved recommendations shall be effective for all Members without further formal acceptance process.

PART VI

TRANSITIONAL ARRANGEMENTS

Article 65

Transitional Arrangements

1. Subject to the provisions of paragraphs 2, 3 and 4, no Member shall be obliged to apply the provisions of this Agreement before the expiry of a general period of one year following the date of entry into force of the WTO Agreement.

2. A developing country Member is entitled to delay for a further period of four years the date of application, as defined in paragraph 1, of the provisions of this Agreement other than Articles 3, 4 and 5.

3. Any other Member which is in the process of transformation from a centrally-planned into a market, free-enterprise economy and which is undertaking structural reform of its intellectual property system and facing special problems in the preparation and implementation of intellectual property laws and regulations, may also benefit from a period of delay as foreseen in paragraph 2.

4. To the extent that a developing country Member is obliged by this Agreement to extend product patent protection to areas of technology not so protectable in its territory on the general date of application of this Agreement for that Member, as defined in paragraph 2, it may delay the application of the provisions on product patents of Section 5 of Part II to such areas of technology for an additional period of five years.

5. A Member availing itself of a transitional period under paragraphs 1, 2, 3 or 4 shall ensure that any changes in its laws, regulations and practice made during that period do not result in a lesser degree of consistency with the provisions of this Agreement.

Article 66

Least-Developed Country Members

1. In view of the special needs and requirements of least-developed country Members, their economic, financial and administrative constraints, and their need for flexibility to create a viable technological base, such Members shall not be required to apply the provisions of this Agreement, other than Articles 3, 4 and 5, for a period of 10 years from the date of application as defined under paragraph 1 of Article 65. The Council

for TRIPS shall, upon duly motivated request by a least-developed country Member, accord extensions of this period.

2. Developed country Members shall provide incentives to enterprises and institutions in their territories for the purpose of promoting and encouraging technology transfer to least-developed country Members in order to enable them to create a sound and viable technological base.

Article 67

Technical Cooperation

In order to facilitate the implementation of this Agreement, developed country Members shall provide, on request and on mutually agreed terms and conditions, technical and financial cooperation in favour of developing and least-developed country Members. Such cooperation shall include assistance in the preparation of laws and regulations on the protection and enforcement of intellectual property rights as well as on the prevention of their abuse, and shall include support regarding the establishment or reinforcement of domestic offices and agencies relevant to these matters, including the training of personnel.

PART VII

INSTITUTIONAL ARRANGEMENTS; FINAL PROVISIONS

(omitted)

* * *

DOCUMENT 20

WTO AGREEMENT ON TRADE-RELATED INVESTMENT MEASURES (TRIMS)

■ ■ ■

* * *

Article 1

Coverage

This Agreement applies to investment measures related to trade in goods only (referred to in this Agreement as "TRIMs").

Article 2

National Treatment and Quantitative Restrictions

1. Without prejudice to other rights and obligations under GATT 1994, no Member shall apply any TRIM that is inconsistent with the provisions of Article III or Article XI of GATT 1994.

2. An illustrative list of TRIMs that are inconsistent with the obligation of national treatment provided for in paragraph 4 of Article III of GATT 1994 and the obligation of general elimination of quantitative restrictions provided for in paragraph 1 of Article XI of GATT 1994 is contained in the Annex to this Agreement.

Article 3

Exceptions

All exceptions under GATT 1994 shall apply, as appropriate, to the provisions of this Agreement.

Article 4

Developing Country Members

A developing country Member shall be free to deviate temporarily from the provisions of Article 2 to the extent and in such a manner as Article XVIII of GATT 1994, the Understanding on the Balance-of-Payments Provisions of GATT 1994, and the Declaration on Trade Measures Taken for Balance-of-Payments Purposes adopted on 28 November 1979 (BISD 26S/205–209) permit the Member to deviate from the provisions of Articles III and XI of GATT 1994.

Article 5

Notification and Transitional Arrangements

1. Members, within 90 days of the date of entry into force of the WTO Agreement, shall notify the Council for Trade in Goods of all TRIMs they are applying that are not in conformity with the provisions of this Agreement. Such TRIMs of general or specific application shall be notified, along with their principal features.[1]

2. Each Member shall eliminate all TRIMs which are notified under paragraph 1 within two years of the date of entry into force of the WTO Agreement in the case of a developed country Member, within five years in the case of a developing country Member, and within seven years in the case of a least-developed country Member.

3. On request, the Council for Trade in Goods may extend the transition period for the elimination of TRIMs notified under paragraph 1 for a developing country Member, including a least-developed country Member, which demonstrates particular difficulties in implementing the provisions of this Agreement. In considering such a request, the Council for Trade in Goods shall take into account the individual development, financial and trade needs of the Member in question.

4. During the transition period, a Member shall not modify the terms of any TRIM which it notifies under paragraph 1 from those prevailing at the date of entry into force of the WTO Agreement so as to increase the degree of inconsistency with the provisions of Article 2. TRIMs introduced less than 180 days before the date of entry into force of the WTO Agreement shall not benefit from the transitional arrangements provided in paragraph 2.

5. Notwithstanding the provisions of Article 2, a Member, in order not to disadvantage established enterprises which are subject to a TRIM notified under paragraph 1, may apply during the transition period the same TRIM to a new investment (*i*) where the products of such investment are like products to those of the established enterprises, and (*ii*) where necessary to avoid distorting the conditions of competition between the new investment and the established enterprises. Any TRIM so applied to a new investment shall be notified to the Council for Trade in Goods. The terms of such a TRIM shall be equivalent in their competitive effect to those applicable to the established enterprises, and it shall be terminated at the same time.

---

[1] In the case of TRIMs applied under discretionary authority, each specific application shall be notified. Information that would prejudice the legitimate commercial interests of particular enterprises need not be disclosed.

Article 6

Transparency

1. Members reaffirm, with respect to TRIMs, their commitment to obligations on transparency and notification in Article X of GATT 1994, in the undertaking on "Notification" contained in the Understanding Regarding Notification, Consultation, Dispute Settlement and Surveillance adopted on 28 November 1979 and in the Ministerial Decision on Notification Procedures adopted on 15 April 1994.

2. Each Member shall notify the Secretariat of the publications in which TRIMs may be found, including those applied by regional and local governments and authorities within their territories.

3. Each Member shall accord sympathetic consideration to requests for information, and afford adequate opportunity for consultation, on any matter arising from this Agreement raised by another Member. In conformity with Article X of GATT 1994 no Member is required to disclose information the disclosure of which would impede law enforcement or otherwise be contrary to the public interest or would prejudice the legitimate commercial interests of particular enterprises, public or private.

Article 7

Committee on Trade-Related Investment Measures

1. A Committee on Trade-Related Investment Measures (referred to in this Agreement as the "Committee") is hereby established, and shall be open to all Members. The Committee shall elect its own Chairman and Vice-Chairman, and shall meet not less than once a year and otherwise at the request of any Member.

2. The Committee shall carry out responsibilities assigned to it by the Council for Trade in Goods and shall afford Members the opportunity to consult on any matters relating to the operation and implementation of this Agreement.

3. The Committee shall monitor the operation and implementation of this Agreement and shall report thereon annually to the Council for Trade in Goods.

Article 8

Consultation and Dispute Settlement

The provisions of Articles XXII and XXIII of GATT 1994, as elaborated and applied by the Dispute Settlement Understanding, shall apply to consultations and the settlement of disputes under this Agreement.

* * *

ANNEX

Illustrative List

1. TRIMs that are inconsistent with the obligation of national treatment provided for in paragraph 4 of Article III of GATT 1994 include those which are mandatory or enforceable under domestic law or under administrative rulings, or compliance with which is necessary to obtain an advantage, and which require:

(a) the purchase or use by an enterprise of products of domestic origin or from any domestic source, whether specified in terms of particular products, in terms of volume or value of products, or in terms of a proportion of volume or value of its local production; or

(b) that an enterprise's purchases or use of imported products be limited to an amount related to the volume or value of local products that it exports.

2. TRIMs that are inconsistent with the obligation of general elimination of quantitative restrictions provided for in paragraph 1 of Article XI of GATT 1994 include those which are mandatory or enforceable under domestic law or under administrative rulings, or compliance with which is necessary to obtain an advantage, and which exports;

(a) the importation by an enterprise of products used in or related to its local production, generally or to an amount related to the volume or value of local production that it exports;

(b) the importation by an enterprise of products used in or related to its local production by restricting its access to foreign exchange to an amount related to the foreign exchange inflows attributable to the enterprise; or

(c) the exportation or sale for export by an enterprise of products, whether specified in terms of particular products, in terms of volume or value of products, or in terms of a proportion of volume or value of its local production.

DOCUMENT 21

WTO DECISIONS AND DECLARATIONS RELATING TO THE AGREEMENT ON IMPLEMENTATION OF ARTICLE VI OF THE GENERAL AGREEMENT ON TARIFFS AND TRADE 1994 (ANTIDUMPING ANTI-CIRCUMVENTION)

■ ■ ■

DECISION ON ANTI-CIRCUMVENTION

Ministers,

Noting that while the problem of circumvention of anti-dumping duty measures formed part of the negotiations which preceded the Agreement on Implementation of Article VI of GATT 1994, negotiators were unable to agree on specific text,

Mindful of the desirability of the applicability of uniform rules in this area as soon as possible,

Decide to refer this matter to the Committee on Anti-Dumping Practices established under that Agreement for resolution.

DECISION ON REVIEW OF ARTICLE 17.6 OF THE AGREEMENT ON IMPLEMENTATION OF ARTICLE VI OF THE GENERAL AGREEMENT ON TARIFFS AND TRADE 1994

Ministers decide as follows:

The standard of review in paragraph 6 of Article 17 of the Agreement on Implementation of Article VI of GATT 1994 shall be reviewed after a period of three years with a view to considering the question of whether it is capable of general application.

DECLARATION ON DISPUTE SETTLEMENT PURSUANT TO THE AGREEMENT ON IMPLEMENTATION OF ARTICLE VI OF THE GENERAL AGREEMENT ON TARIFFS AND TRADE 1994 OR PART V OF THE AGREEMENT ON SUBSIDIES AND COUNTERVAILING MEASURES

Ministers recognize, with respect to dispute settlement pursuant to the Agreement on Implementation of Article VI of GATT 1994 or Part V of the

Agreement on Subsidies and Countervailing Measures, the need for the consistent resolution of disputes arising from anti-dumping and countervailing duty measures.

DOCUMENT 22

WTO DECISION ON MEASURES IN FAVOUR OF LEAST-DEVELOPED COUNTRIES (1994)

■ ■ ■

Ministers,

Recognizing the plight of the least-developed countries and the need to ensure their effective participation in the world trading system, and to take further measures to improve their trading opportunities;

Recognizing the specific needs of the least-developed countries in the area of market access where continued preferential access remains an essential means for improving their trading opportunities;

Reaffirming their commitment to implement fully the provisions concerning the least-developed countries contained in paragraphs 2(*d.*), 6 and 8 of the Decision of 28 November 1979 on Differential and More Favourable Treatment, Reciprocity and Fuller Participation of Developing Countries;

Having regard to the commitment of the participants as set out in Section B(vii) of Part I of the Punta del Este Ministerial Declaration;

1. *Decide* that, if not already provided for in the instruments negotiated in the course of the Uruguay Round, notwithstanding their acceptance of these instruments, the least-developed countries, and for so long as they remain in that category, while complying with the general rules set out in the aforesaid instruments, will only be required to undertake commitments and concessions to the extent consistent with their individual development, financial and trade needs, or their administrative and institutional capabilities. The least-developed countries shall be given additional time of one year from 15 April 1994 to submit their schedules as required in Article XI of the Agreement Establishing the World Trade Organization.

2. *Agree* that:

(i) Expeditious implementation of all special and differential measures taken in favour of least-developed countries including those taken within the context of the Uruguay Round shall be ensured through, *inter alia,* regular reviews.

(ii) To the extent possible, MFN concessions on tariff and non-tariff measures agreed in the Uruguay Round on products of export interest to the least-developed countries may be implemented autonomously, in advance and without staging. Consideration shall be given to further improve GSP and other schemes for products of particular export interest to least-developed countries.

(iii) The rules set out in the various agreements and instruments and the transitional provisions in the Uruguay Round should be applied in a flexible and supportive manner for the least-developed countries. To this effect, sympathetic consideration shall be given to specific and motivated concerns raised by the least-developed countries in the appropriate Councils and Committees.

(iv) In the application of import relief measures and other measures referred to in paragraph 3(*c*) of Article XXXVII of GATT 1947 and the corresponding provision of GATT 1994, special consideration shall be given to the export interests of least-developed countries.

(v) Least-developed countries shall be accorded substantially increased technical assistance in the development, strengthening and diversification of their production and export bases including those of services, as well as in trade promotion, to enable them to maximize the benefits from liberalized access to markets.

3. *Agree* to keep under review the specific needs of the least-developed countries and to continue to seek the adoption of positive measures which facilitate the expansion of trading opportunities in favour of these countries.

DOCUMENT 23

WTO DECISIONS RELATING TO THE AGREEMENT ON IMPLEMENTATION OF ARTICLE VII OF THE GENERAL AGREEMENT ON TARIFFS AND TRADE 1994 (CUSTOMS VALUATION)

■ ■ ■

DECISION REGARDING CASES WHERE CUSTOMS ADMINISTRATIONS HAVE REASONS TO DOUBT THE TRUTH OR ACCURACY OF THE DECLARED VALUE

Ministers invite the Committee on Customs Valuation established under the Agreement on Implementation of Article VII of GATT 1994 to take the following decision:

The Committee on Customs Valuation,

Reaffirming that the transaction value is the primary basis of valuation under the Agreement on Implementation of Article VII of GATT 1994 (hereinafter referred to as the "Agreement");

Recognizing that the customs administration may have to address cases where it has reason to doubt the truth or accuracy of the particulars or of documents produced by traders in support of a declared value;

Emphasizing that in so doing the customs administration should not prejudice the legitimate commercial interests of traders;

Taking into account Article 17 of the Agreement, paragraph 6 of Annex III to the Agreement, and the relevant decisions of the Technical Committee on Customs Valuation;

Decides as follows:

1. When a declaration has been presented and where the customs administration has reason to doubt the truth or accuracy of the particulars or of documents produced in support of this declaration, the customs administration may ask the importer to provide further explanation, including documents or other evidence, that the declared value represents the total amount actually paid or payable for the imported goods, adjusted in accordance with the provisions of Article 8. If, after receiving further information, or in the absence of a response, the customs administration

still has reasonable doubts about the truth or accuracy of the declared value, it may, bearing in mind the provisions of Article 11, be deemed that the customs value of the imported goods cannot be determined under the provisions of Article 1. Before taking a final decision, the customs administration shall communicate to the importer, in writing if requested, its grounds for doubting the truth or accuracy of the particulars or documents produced and the importer shall be given a reasonable opportunity to respond. When a final decision is made, the customs administration shall communicate to the importer in writing its decision and the grounds therefor.

2. It is entirely appropriate in applying the Agreement for one Member to assist another Member on mutually agreed terms.

DECISION ON TEXTS RELATING TO MINIMUM VALUES AND IMPORTS BY SOLE AGENTS, SOLE DISTRIBUTORS AND SOLE CONCESSIONAIRES

Ministers decide to refer the following texts to the Committee on Customs Valuation established under the Agreement on Implementation of Article VII of GATT 1994, for adoption.

I

Where a developing country makes a reservation to retain officially established minimum values within the terms of paragraph 2 of Annex III and shows good cause, the Committee shall give the request for the reservation sympathetic consideration.

Where a reservation is consented to, the terms and conditions referred to in paragraph 2 of Annex III shall take full account of the development, financial and trade needs of the developing country concerned.

II

1. A number of developing countries have a concern that problems may exist in the valuation of imports by sole agents, sole distributors and sole concessionaires. Under paragraph 1 of Article 20, developing country Members have a period of delay of up to five years prior to the application of the Agreement. In this context, developing country Members availing themselves of this provision could use the period to conduct appropriate studies and to take such other actions as are necessary to facilitate application.

2. In consideration of this, the Committee recommends that the Customs Co-operation Council assist developing country Members, in accordance with the provisions of Annex II, to formulate and conduct studies in areas identified as being of potential concern, including those relating to importations by sole agents, sole distributors and sole concessionaires.

DOCUMENT 24

WTO UNDERSTANDING ON RULES AND PROCEDURES GOVERNING THE SETTLEMENT OF DISPUTES (1994, ANNEX 2 TO THE AGREEMENT ESTABLISHING THE WORLD TRADE ORGANIZATION)

■ ■ ■

Members hereby *agree* as follows:

Article 1

Coverage and Application

1. The rules and procedures of this Understanding shall apply to disputes brought pursuant to the consultation and dispute settlement provisions of the agreements listed in Appendix 1 to this Understanding (referred to in this Understanding as the "covered agreements"). The rules and procedures of this Understanding shall also apply to consultations and the settlement of disputes between Members concerning their rights and obligations under the provisions of the Agreement Establishing the World Trade Organization (referred to in this Understanding as the "WTO Agreement") and of this Understanding taken in isolation or in combination with any other covered agreement.

2. The rules and procedures of this Understanding shall apply subject to such special or additional rules and procedures on dispute settlement contained in the covered agreements as are identified in Appendix 2 to this Understanding. To the extent that there is a difference between the rules and procedures of this Understanding and the special or additional rules and procedures set forth in Appendix 2, the special or additional rules and procedures in Appendix 2 shall prevail. In disputes involving rules and procedures under more than one covered agreement, if there is a conflict between special or additional rules and procedures of such agreements under review, and where the parties to the dispute cannot agree on rules and procedures within 20 days of the establishment of the panel, the Chairman of the Dispute Settlement Body provided for in paragraph 1 of Article 2 (referred to in this Understanding as the "DSB"), in consultation with the parties to the dispute, shall determine the rules and procedures to be followed within 10 days after a request by either

Member. The Chairman shall be guided by the principle that special or additional rules and procedures should be used where possible, and the rules and procedures set out in this Understanding should be used to the extent necessary to avoid conflict.

Article 2

Administration

1. The Dispute Settlement Body is hereby established to administer these rules and procedures and, except as otherwise provided in a covered agreement, the consultation and dispute settlement provisions of the covered agreements. Accordingly, the DSB shall have the authority to establish panels, adopt panel and Appellate Body reports, maintain surveillance of implementation of rulings and recommendations, and authorize suspension of concessions and other obligations under the covered agreements. With respect to disputes arising under a covered agreement which is a Plurilateral Trade Agreement, the term "Member" as used herein shall refer only to those Members that are parties to the relevant Plurilateral Trade Agreement. Where the DSB administers the dispute settlement provisions of a Plurilateral Trade Agreement, only those Members that are parties to that Agreement may participate in decisions or actions taken by the DSB with respect to that dispute.

2. The DSB shall inform the relevant WTO Councils and Committees of any developments in disputes related to provisions of the respective covered agreements.

3. The DSB shall meet as often as necessary to carry out its functions within the time-frames provided in this Understanding.

4. Where the rules and procedures of this Understanding provide for the DSB to take a decision, it shall do so by consensus.[1]

Article 3

General Provisions

1. Members affirm their adherence to the principles for the management of disputes heretofore applied under Articles XXII and XXIII of GATT 1947, and the rules and procedures as further elaborated and modified herein.

2. The dispute settlement system of the WTO is a central element in providing security and predictability to the multilateral trading system. The Members recognize that it serves to preserve the rights and obligations of Members under the covered agreements, and to clarify the existing provisions of those agreements in accordance with customary rules of

[1] The DSB shall be deemed to have decided by consensus on a matter submitted for its consideration, if no Member, present at the meeting of the DSB when the decision is taken, formally objects to the proposed decision.

interpretation of public international law. Recommendations and rulings of the DSB cannot add to or diminish the rights and obligations provided in the covered agreements.

3. The prompt settlement of situations in which a Member considers that any benefits accruing to it directly or indirectly under the covered agreements are being impaired by measures taken by another Member is essential to the effective functioning of the WTO and the maintenance of a proper balance between the rights and obligations of Members.

4. Recommendations or rulings made by the DSB shall be aimed at achieving a satisfactory settlement of the matter in accordance with the rights and obligations under this Understanding and under the covered agreements.

5. All solutions to matters formally raised under the consultation and dispute settlement provisions of the covered agreements, including arbitration awards, shall be consistent with those agreements and shall not nullify or impair benefits accruing to any Member under those agreements, nor impede the attainment of any objective of those agreements.

6. Mutually agreed solutions to matters formally raised under the consultation and dispute settlement provisions of the covered agreements shall be notified to the DSB and the relevant Councils and Committees, where any Member may raise any point relating thereto.

7. Before bringing a case, a Member shall exercise its judgment as to whether action under these procedures would be fruitful. The aim of the dispute settlement mechanism is to secure a positive solution to a dispute. A solution mutually acceptable to the parties to a dispute and consistent with the covered agreements is clearly to be preferred. In the absence of a mutually agreed solution, the first objective of the dispute settlement mechanism is usually to secure the withdrawal of the measures concerned if these are found to be inconsistent with the provisions of any of the covered agreements. The provision of compensation should be resorted to only if the immediate withdrawal of the measure is impracticable and as a temporary measure pending the withdrawal of the measure which is inconsistent with a covered agreement. The last resort which this Understanding provides to the Member invoking the dispute settlement procedures is the possibility of suspending the application of concessions or other obligations under the covered agreements on a discriminatory basis vis-á-vis the other Member, subject to authorization by the DSB of such measures.

8. In cases where there is an infringement of the obligations assumed under a covered agreement, the action is considered *prima facie* to constitute a case of nullification or impairment. This means that there is normally a presumption that a breach of the rules has an adverse impact

on other Members parties to that covered agreement, and in such cases, it shall be up to the Member against whom the complaint has been brought to rebut the charge.

9. The provisions of this Understanding are without prejudice to the rights of Members to seek authoritative interpretation of provisions of a covered agreement through decision-making under the WTO Agreement or a covered agreement which is a Plurilateral Trade Agreement.

10. It is understood that requests for conciliation and the use of the dispute settlement procedures should not be intended or considered as contentious acts and that, if a dispute arises, all Members will engage in these procedures in good faith in an effort to resolve the dispute. It is also understood that complaints and counter-complaints in regard to distinct matters should not be linked.

11. This Understanding shall be applied only with respect to new requests for consultations under the consultation provisions of the covered agreements made on or after the date of entry into force of the WTO Agreement. With respect to disputes for which the request for consultations was made under GATT 1947 or under any other predecessor agreement to the covered agreements before the date of entry into force of the WTO Agreement, the relevant dispute settlement rules and procedures in effect immediately prior to the date of entry into force of the WTO Agreement shall continue to apply.[2]

12. Notwithstanding paragraph 11, if a complaint based on any of the covered agreements is brought by a developing country Member against a developed country Member, the complaining party shall have the right to invoke, as an alternative to the provisions contained in Articles 4, 5, 6 and 12 of this Understanding, the corresponding provisions of the Decision of 5 April 1966 (BISD 14S/18), except that where the Panel considers that the time-frame provided for in paragraph 7 of that Decision is insufficient to provide its report and with the agreement of the complaining party, that time-frame may be extended. To the extent that there is a difference between the rules and procedures of Articles 4, 5, 6 and 12 and the corresponding rules and procedures of the Decision, the latter shall prevail.

Article 4

Consultations

1. Members affirm their resolve to strengthen and improve the effectiveness of the consultation procedures employed by Members.

2. Each Member undertakes to accord sympathetic consideration to and afford adequate opportunity for consultation regarding any representations made by another Member concerning measures affecting

---

[2] This paragraph shall also be applied to disputes on which panel reports have not been adopted or fully implemented.

the operation of any covered agreement taken within the territory of the former.[3]

3. If a request for consultations is made pursuant to a covered agreement, the Member to which the request is made shall, unless otherwise mutually agreed, reply to the request within 10 days after the date of its receipt and shall enter into consultations in good faith within a period of no more than 30 days after the date of receipt of the request, with a view to reaching a mutually satisfactory solution. If the Member does not respond within 10 days after the date of receipt of the request, or does not enter into consultations within a period of no more than 30 days, or a period otherwise mutually agreed, after the date of receipt of the request, then the Member that requested the holding of consultations may proceed directly to request the establishment of a panel.

4. All such requests for consultations shall be notified to the DSB and the relevant Councils and Committees by the Member which requests consultations. Any request for consultations shall be submitted in writing and shall give the reasons for the request, including identification of the measures at issue and an indication of the legal basis for the complaint.

5. In the course of consultations in accordance with the provisions of a covered agreement, before resorting to further action under this Understanding, Members should attempt to obtain satisfactory adjustment of the matter.

6. Consultations shall be confidential, and without prejudice to the rights of any Member in any further proceedings.

7. If the consultations fail to settle a dispute within 60 days after the date of receipt of the request for consultations, the complaining party may request the establishment of a panel. The complaining party may request a panel during the 60–day period if the consulting parties jointly consider that consultations have failed to settle the dispute.

8. In cases of urgency, including those which concern perishable goods, Members shall enter into consultations within a period of no more than 10 days after the date of receipt of the request. If the consultations have failed to settle the dispute within a period of 20 days after the date of receipt of the request, the complaining party may request the establishment of a panel.

9. In cases of urgency, including those which concern perishable goods, the parties to the dispute, panels and the Appellate Body shall make every effort to accelerate the proceedings to the greatest extent possible.

[3] Where the provisions of any other covered agreement concerning measures taken by regional or local governments or authorities within the territory of a Member contain provisions different from the provisions of this paragraph, the provisions of such other covered agreement shall prevail.

10. During consultations Members should give special attention to the particular problems and interests of developing country Members.

11. Whenever a Member other than the consulting Members considers that it has a substantial trade interest in consultations being held pursuant to paragraph 1 of Article XXII of GATT 1994, paragraph 1 of Article XXII of GATS, or the corresponding provisions in other covered agreements,[4] such Member may notify the consulting Members and the DSB, within 10 days after the date of the circulation of the request for consultations under said Article, of its desire to be joined in the consultations. Such Member shall be joined in the consultations, provided that the Member to which the request for consultations was addressed agrees that the claim of substantial interest is well-founded. In that event they shall so inform the DSB. If the request to be joined in the consultations is not accepted, the applicant Member shall be free to request consultations under paragraph 1 of Article XXII or paragraph 1 of Article XXIII of GATT 1994, paragraph 1 of Article XXII or paragraph 1 of Article XXIII of GATS, or the corresponding provisions in other covered agreements.

Article 5

Good Offices, Conciliation and Mediation

1. Good offices, conciliation and mediation are procedures that are undertaken voluntarily if the parties to the dispute so agree.

2. Proceedings involving good offices, conciliation and mediation, and in particular positions taken by the parties to the dispute during these proceedings, shall be confidential, and without prejudice to the rights of either party in any further proceedings under these procedures.

3. Good offices, conciliation or mediation may be requested at any time by any party to a dispute. They may begin at any time and be terminated at any time. Once procedures for good offices, conciliation or mediation are terminated, a complaining party may then proceed with a request for the establishment of a panel.

4. When good offices, conciliation or mediation are entered into within 60 days after the date of receipt of a request for consultations, the complaining party must allow a period of 60 days after the date of receipt

[4] The corresponding consultation provisions in the covered agreements are listed hereunder: Agreement on Agriculture, Article 19; Agreement on the Application of Sanitary and Phytosanitary Measures, paragraph 1 of Article 11; Agreement on Textiles and Clothing, paragraph 4 of Article 8; Agreement on Technical Barriers to Trade, paragraph 1 of Article 14; Agreement on Trade-Related Investment Measures, Article 8; Agreement on Implementation of Article VI of GATT 1994, paragraph 2 of Article 17; Agreement on Implementation of Article VII of GATT 1994, paragraph 2 of Article 19; Agreement on Preshipment Inspection, Article 7; Agreement on Rules of Origin, Article 7; Agreement on Import Licensing Procedures, Article 6; Agreement on Subsidies and Countervailing Measures, Article 30; Agreement on Safeguards, Article 14; Agreement on Trade-Related Aspects of Intellectual Property Rights, Article 64.1; and any corresponding consultation provisions in Plurilateral Trade Agreements as determined by the competent bodies of each Agreement and as notified to the DSB.

of the request for consultations before requesting the establishment of a panel. The complaining party may request the establishment of a panel during the 60–day period if the parties to the dispute jointly consider that the good offices, conciliation or mediation process has failed to settle the dispute.

5. If the parties to a dispute agree, procedures for good offices, conciliation or mediation may continue while the panel process proceeds.

6. The Director-General may, acting in an *ex officio* capacity, offer good offices, conciliation or mediation with the view to assisting Members to settle a dispute.

Article 6

Establishment of Panels

1. If the complaining party so requests, a panel shall be established at the latest at the DSB meeting following that at which the request first appears as an item on the DSB's agenda, unless at that meeting the DSB decides by consensus not to establish a panel.[5]

2. The request for the establishment of a panel shall be made in writing. It shall indicate whether consultations were held, identify the specific measures at issue and provide a brief summary of the legal basis of the complaint sufficient to present the problem clearly. In case the applicant requests the establishment of a panel with other than standard terms of reference, the written request shall include the proposed text of special terms of reference.

Article 7

Terms of Reference of Panels

1. Panels shall have the following terms of reference unless the parties to the dispute agree otherwise within 20 days from the establishment of the panel:

> "To examine, in the light of the relevant provisions in (name of the covered agreement(s) cited by the parties to the dispute), the matter referred to the DSB by (name of party) in document . . . and to make such findings as will assist the DSB in making the recommendations or in giving the rulings provided for in that/those agreement(s)."

2. Panels shall address the relevant provisions in any covered agreement or agreements cited by the parties to the dispute.

3. In establishing a panel, the DSB may authorize its Chairman to draw up the terms of reference of the panel in consultation with the parties

[5] If the complaining party so requests, a meeting of the DSB shall be convened for this purpose within 15 days of the request, provided that at least 10 days' advance notice of the meeting is given.

to the dispute, subject to the provisions of paragraph 1. The terms of reference thus drawn up shall be circulated to all Members. If other than standard terms of reference are agreed upon, any Member may raise any point relating thereto in the DSB.

Article 8

Composition of Panels

1. Panels shall be composed of well-qualified governmental and/or non-governmental individuals, including persons who have served on or presented a case to a panel, served as a representative of a Member or of a contracting party to GATT 1947 or as a representative to the Council or Committee of any covered agreement or its predecessor agreement, or in the Secretariat, taught or published on international trade law or policy, or served as a senior trade policy official of a Member.

2. Panel members should be selected with a view to ensuring the independence of the members, a sufficiently diverse background and a wide spectrum of experience.

3. Citizens of Members whose governments[6] are parties to the dispute or third parties as defined in paragraph 2 of Article 10 shall not serve on a panel concerned with that dispute, unless the parties to the dispute agree otherwise.

4. To assist in the selection of panelists, the Secretariat shall maintain an indicative list of governmental and non-governmental individuals possessing the qualifications outlined in paragraph 1, from which panelists may be drawn as appropriate. That list shall include the roster of non-governmental panelists established on 30 November 1984 (BISD 31S/9), and other rosters and indicative lists established under any of the covered agreements, and shall retain the names of persons on those rosters and indicative lists at the time of entry into force of the WTO Agreement. Members may periodically suggest names of governmental and non-governmental individuals for inclusion on the indicative list, providing relevant information on their knowledge of international trade and of the sectors or subject matter of the covered agreements, and those names shall be added to the list upon approval by the DSB. For each of the individuals on the list, the list shall indicate specific areas of experience or expertise of the individuals in the sectors or subject matter of the covered agreements.

5. Panels shall be composed of three panelists unless the parties to the dispute agree, within 10 days from the establishment of the panel, to a panel composed of five panelists. Members shall be informed promptly of the composition of the panel.

---

[6] In the case where customs unions or common markets are parties to a dispute, this provision applies to citizens of all member countries of the customs unions or common markets.

6. The Secretariat shall propose nominations for the panel to the parties to the dispute. The parties to the dispute shall not oppose nominations except for compelling reasons.

7. If there is no agreement on the panelists within 20 days after the date of the establishment of a panel, at the request of either party, the Director-General, in consultation with the Chairman of the DSB and the Chairman of the relevant Council or Committee, shall determine the composition of the panel by appointing the panelists whom the Director-General considers most appropriate in accordance with any relevant special or additional rules or procedures of the covered agreement or covered agreements which are at issue in the dispute, after consulting with the parties to the dispute. The Chairman of the DSB shall inform the Members of the composition of the panel thus formed no later than 10 days after the date the Chairman receives such a request.

8. Members shall undertake, as a general rule, to permit their officials to serve as panelists.

9. Panelists shall serve in their individual capacities and not as government representatives, nor as representatives of any organization. Members shall therefore not give them instructions nor seek to influence them as individuals with regard to matters before a panel.

10. When a dispute is between a developing country Member and a developed country Member the panel shall, if the developing country Member so requests, include at least one panelist from a developing country Member.

11. Panelists' expenses, including travel and subsistence allowance, shall be met from the WTO budget in accordance with criteria to be adopted by the General Council, based on recommendations of the Committee on Budget, Finance and Administration.

Article 9

Procedures for Multiple Complainants

1. Where more than one Member requests the establishment of a panel related to the same matter, a single panel may be established to examine these complaints taking into account the rights of all Members concerned. A single panel should be established to examine such complaints whenever feasible.

2. The single panel shall organize its examination and present its findings to the DSB in such a manner that the rights which the parties to the dispute would have enjoyed had separate panels examined the complaints are in no way impaired. If one of the parties to the dispute so requests, the panel shall submit separate reports on the dispute concerned. The written submissions by each of the complainants shall be made available to the other complainants, and each complainant shall have the

right to be present when any one of the other complainants presents its views to the panel.

3. If more than one panel is established to examine the complaints related to the same manner, to the greatest extent possible the same persons shall serve as panelists on each of the separate panels and the timetable for the panel process in such disputes shall be harmonized.

Article 10

Third Parties

1. The interests of the parties to a dispute and those of other Members under a covered agreement at issue in the dispute shall be fully taken into account during the panel process.

2. Any Member having a substantial interest in a matter before a panel and having notified its interest to the DSB (referred to in this Understanding as a "third party") shall have an opportunity to be heard by the panel and to make written submissions to the panel. These submissions shall also be given to the parties to the dispute and shall be reflected in the panel report.

3. Third parties shall receive the submissions of the parties to the dispute [at] the first meeting of the panel.

4. If a third party considers that a measure already the subject of a panel proceeding nullifies or impairs benefits accruing to it under any covered agreement, that Member may have recourse to normal dispute settlement procedures under this Understanding. Such a dispute shall be referred to the original panel wherever possible.

Article 11

Function of Panels

The function of panels is to assist the DSB in discharging its responsibilities under this Understanding and the covered agreements. Accordingly, a panel should make an objective assessment of the matter before it, including an objective assessment of the facts of the case and the applicability of and conformity with the relevant covered agreements, and make such other findings as will assist the DSB in making the recommendations or in giving the rulings provided for in the covered agreements. Panels should consult regularly with the parties to the dispute and give them adequate opportunity to develop a mutually satisfactory solution.

Article 12

Panel Procedures

1. Panels shall follow the Working Procedures in Appendix 3 unless the panel decides otherwise after consulting the parties to the dispute.

2. Panel procedures should provide sufficient flexibility so as to ensure high-quality panel reports, while not unduly delaying the panel process.

3. After consulting the parties to the dispute, the panelists shall, as soon as practicable and whenever possible within one week after the composition and terms of reference of the panel have been agreed upon, fix the timetable for the panel process, taking into account the provisions of paragraph 9 of Article 4, if relevant.

4. In determining the timetable for the panel process, the panel shall provide sufficient time for the parties to the dispute to prepare their submissions.

5. Panels should set precise deadlines for written submissions by the parties and the parties should respect those deadlines.

6. Each party to the dispute shall deposit its written submissions with the Secretariat for immediate transmission to the panel and to the other party or parties to the dispute. The complaining party shall submit its first submission in advance of the responding party's first submission unless the panel decides, in fixing the timetable referred to in paragraph 3 and after consultations with the parties to the dispute, that the parties should submit their first submissions simultaneously. When there are sequential arrangements for the deposit of first submissions, the panel shall establish a firm time-period for receipt of the responding party's submission. Any subsequent written submissions shall be submitted simultaneously.

7. Where the parties to the dispute have failed to develop a mutually satisfactory solution, the panel shall submit its findings in the form of a written report to the DSB. In such cases, the report of a panel shall set out the findings of fact, the applicability of relevant provisions and the basic rationale behind any findings and recommendations that it makes. Where a settlement of the matter among the parties to the dispute has been found, the report of the panel shall be confined to a brief description of the case and to reporting that a solution has been reached.

8. In order to make the procedures more efficient, the period in which the panel shall conduct its examination, from the date that the composition and terms of reference of the panel have been agreed upon until the date the final report is issued to the parties to the dispute, shall, as a general rule, not exceed six months. In cases of urgency, including those relating to perishable goods, the panel shall aim to issue its report to the parties to the dispute within three months.

9. When the panel considers that it cannot issue its report within six months, or within three months in cases of urgency, it shall inform the DSB in writing of the reasons for the delay together with an estimate of the period within which it will issue its report. In no case should the period

from the establishment of the panel to the circulation of the report to the Members exceed nine months.

10. In the context of consultations involving a measure taken by a developing country Member, the parties may agree to extend the periods established in paragraphs 7 and 8 of Article 4. If, after the relevant period has elapsed, the consulting parties cannot agree that the consultations have concluded, the Chairman of the DSB shall decide, after consultation with the parties, whether to extend the relevant period and, if so, for how long. In addition, in examining a complaint against a developing country Member, the panel shall accord sufficient time for the developing country Member to prepare and present its argumentation. The provisions of paragraph 1 of Article 20 and paragraph 4 of Article 21 are not affected by any action pursuant to this paragraph.

11. Where one or more of the parties is a developing country Member, the panel's report shall explicitly indicate the form in which account has been taken of relevant provisions on differential and more-favourable treatment for developing country Members that form part of the covered agreements which have been raised by the developing country Member in the course of the dispute settlement procedures.

12. The panel may suspend its work at any time at the request of the complaining party for a period not to exceed 12 months. In the event of such a suspension, the time-frames set out in paragraphs 8 and 9 of this Article, paragraph 1 of Article 20, and paragraph 4 of Article 21 shall be extended by the amount of time that the work was suspended. If the work of the panel has been suspended for more than 12 months, the authority for establishment of the panel shall lapse.

Article 13

Right to Seek Information

1. Each panel shall have the right to seek information and technical advice from any individual or body which it deems appropriate. However, before a panel seeks such information or advice from any individual or body within the jurisdiction of a Member it shall inform the authorities of that Member. A Member should respond promptly and fully to any request by a panel for such information as the panel considers necessary and appropriate. Confidential information which is provided shall not be revealed without formal authorization from the individual, body, or authorities of the Member providing the information.

2. Panels may seek information from any relevant source and may consult experts to obtain their opinion on certain aspects of the matter. With respect to a factual issue concerning a scientific or other technical matter raised by a party to a dispute, a panel may request an advisory report in writing from an expert review group. Rules for the establishment of such a group and its procedures are set forth in Appendix 4.

Article 14

Confidentiality

1. Panel deliberations shall be confidential.

2. The reports of panels shall be drafted without the presence of the parties to the dispute in the light of the information provided and the statements made.

3. Opinions expressed in the panel report by individual panelists shall be anonymous.

Article 15

Interim Review Stage

1. Following the consideration of rebuttal submissions and oral arguments, the panel shall issue the descriptive (factual and argument) sections of its draft report to the parties to the dispute. Within a period of time set by the panel, the parties shall submit their comments in writing.

2. Following the expiration of the set period of time for receipt of comments from the parties to the dispute, the panel shall issue an interim report to the parties, including both the descriptive sections and the panel's findings and conclusions. Within a period of time set by the panel, a party may submit a written request for the panel to review precise aspects of the interim report prior to circulation of the final report to the Members. At the request of a party, the panel shall hold a further meeting with the parties on the issues identified in the written comments. If no comments are received from any party within the comment period, the interim report shall be considered the final panel report and circulated promptly to the Members.

3. The findings of the final panel report shall include a discussion of the arguments made at the interim review stage. The interim review stage shall be conducted within the time-period set out in paragraph 8 of Article 12.

Article 16

Adoption of Panel Reports

1. In order to provide sufficient time for the Members to consider panel reports, the reports shall not be considered for adoption by the DSB until 20 days after the date they have been circulated to the Members.

2. Members having objections to a panel report shall give written reasons to explain their objections for circulation at least 10 days prior to the DSB meeting at which the panel report will be considered.

3. The parties to a dispute shall have the right to participate fully in the consideration of the panel report by the DSB, and their views shall be fully recorded.

4. Within 60 days after the date of circulation of a panel report to the Members, the report shall be adopted at a DSB meeting[7] unless a party to the dispute formally notifies the DSB of its decision to appeal or the DSB decides by consensus not to adopt the report. If a party has notified its decision to appeal, the report by the panel shall not be considered for adoption by the DSB until after completion of the appeal. This adoption procedure is without prejudice to the right of Members to express their views on a panel report.

Article 17

Appellate Review

Standing Appellate Body

1. A standing Appellate Body shall be established by the DSB. The Appellate Body shall hear appeals from panel cases. It shall be composed of seven persons, three of whom shall serve on any one case. Persons serving on the Appellate Body shall serve in rotation. Such rotation shall be determined in the working procedures of the Appellate Body.

2. The DSB shall appoint persons to serve on the Appellate Body for a four-year term, and each person may be reappointed once. However, the terms of three of the seven persons appointed immediately after the entry into force of the WTO Agreement shall expire at the end of two years, to be determined by lot. Vacancies shall be filled as they arise. A person appointed to replace a person whose term of office has not expired shall hold office for the remainder of the predecessor's term.

3. The Appellate Body shall comprise persons of recognized authority, with demonstrated expertise in law, international trade and the subject matter of the covered agreements generally. They shall be unaffiliated with any government. The Appellate Body membership shall be broadly representative of membership in the WTO. All persons serving on the Appellate Body shall be available at all times and on short notice, and shall stay abreast of dispute settlement activities and other relevant activities of the WTO. They shall not participate in the consideration of any disputes that would create a direct or indirect conflict of interest.

4. Only parties to the dispute, not third parties, may appeal a panel report. Third parties which have notified the DSB of a substantial interest in the matter pursuant to paragraph 2 of Article 10 may make written submissions to, and be given an opportunity to be heard by, the Appellate Body.

5. As a general rule, the proceedings shall not exceed 60 days from the date a party to the dispute formally notifies its decision to appeal to the

---

[7] If a meeting of the DSB is not scheduled within this period at a time that enables the requirements of paragraphs 1 and 4 of Article 16 to be met, a meeting of the DSB shall be held for this purpose.

date the Appellate Body circulates its report. In fixing its timetable the Appellate Body shall take into account the provisions of paragraph 9 of Article 4, if relevant. When the Appellate Body considers that it cannot provide its report within 60 days, it shall inform the DSB in writing of the reasons for the delay together with an estimate of the period within which it will submit its report. In no case shall the proceedings exceed 90 days.

6. An appeal shall be limited to issues of law covered in the panel report and legal interpretations developed by the panel.

7. The Appellate Body shall be provided with appropriate administrative and legal support as it requires.

8. The expenses of persons serving on the Appellate Body, including travel and subsistence allowance, shall be met from the WTO budget in accordance with criteria to be adopted by the General Council, based on recommendations of the Committee on Budget, Finance and Administration.

Procedures for Appellate Review

9. Working procedures shall be drawn up by the Appellate Body in consultation with the Chairman of the DSB and the Director-General, and communicated to the Members for their information.

10. The proceedings of the Appellate Body shall be confidential. The reports of the Appellate Body shall be drafted without the presence of the parties to the dispute and in the light of the information provided and the statements made.

11. Opinions expressed in the Appellate Body report by individuals serving on the Appellate Body shall be anonymous.

12. The Appellate Body shall address each of the issues raised in accordance with paragraph 6 during the appellate proceeding.

13. The Appellate Body may uphold, modify or reverse the legal findings and conclusions of the panel.

Adoption of Appellate Body Reports

14. An Appellate Body report shall be adopted by the DSB and unconditionally accepted by the parties to the dispute unless the DSB decides by consensus not to adopt the Appellate Body report within 30 days following its circulation to the Members.[8] This adoption procedure is without prejudice to the right of Members to express their views on an Appellate Body report.

[8] If a meeting of the DSB is not scheduled during this period, such a meeting of the DSB shall be held for this purpose.

Article 18

Communications With the Panel or Appellate Body

1. There shall be no *ex parte* communications with the panel or Appellate Body concerning matters under consideration by the panel or Appellate Body.

2. Written submissions to the panel or the Appellate Body shall be treated as confidential, but shall be made available to the parties to the dispute. Nothing in this Understanding shall preclude a party to a dispute from disclosing statements of its own positions to the public. Members shall treat as confidential information submitted by another Member to the panel or the Appellate Body which that Member has designated as confidential. A party to a dispute shall also, upon request of a Member, provide a non-confidential summary of the information contained in its written submissions that could be disclosed to the public.

Article 19

Panel and Appellate Body Recommendations

1. Where a panel or the Appellate Body concludes that a measure is inconsistent with a covered agreement, it shall recommend that the Member concerned[9] bring the measure into conformity with that agreement.[10] In addition to its recommendations, the panel or Appellate Body may suggest ways in which the Member concerned could implement the recommendations.

2. In accordance with paragraph 2 of Article 3, in their findings and recommendations, the panel and Appellate Body cannot add to or diminish the rights and obligations provided in the covered agreements.

Article 20

Time-frame for DSB Decisions

Unless otherwise agreed to by the parties to the dispute, the period from the date of establishment of the panel by the DSB until the date the DSB considers the panel or appellate report for adoption shall as a general rule not exceed nine months where the panel report is not appealed or 12 months where the report is appealed. Where either the panel or the Appellate Body has acted, pursuant to paragraph 9 of Article 12 or paragraph 5 of Article 17, to extend the time for providing its report, the additional time taken shall be added to the above periods.

---

[9] The "Member concerned" is the party to the dispute to which the panel or Appellate Body recommendations are directed.

[10] With respect to recommendations in cases not involving a violation of GATT 1994 or any other covered agreement, see Article 26.

Article 21

Surveillance of Implementation of Recommendations and Rulings

1. Prompt compliance with recommendations or rulings of the DSB is essential in order to ensure effective resolution of disputes to the benefit of all Members.

2. Particular attention should be paid to matters affecting the interests of developing country Members with respect to measures which have been subject to dispute settlement.

3. At a DSB meeting held within 30 days[11] after the date of adoption of the panel or Appellate Body report, the Member concerned shall inform the DSB of its intentions in respect of implementation of the recommendations and rulings of the DSB. If it is impracticable to comply immediately with the recommendations and rulings, the Member concerned shall have a reasonable period of time in which to do so. The reasonable period of time shall be:

(a) the period of time proposed by the Member concerned, provided that such period is approved by the DSB; or, in the absence of such approval,

(b) a period of time mutually agreed by the parties to the dispute within 45 days after the date of adoption of the recommendations and rulings; or, in the absence of such agreement,

(c) a period of time determined through binding arbitration within 90 days after the date of adoption of the recommendations and rulings.[12] In such arbitration, a guideline for the arbitrator[13] should be that the reasonable period of time to implement panel or Appellate Body recommendations should not exceed 15 months from the date of adoption of a panel or Appellate Body report. However, that time may be shorter or longer, depending upon the particular circumstances.

4. Except where the panel or the Appellate Body has extended, pursuant to paragraph 9 of Article 12 or paragraph 5 of Article 17, the time of providing its report, the period from the date of establishment of the panel by the DSB until the date of determination of the reasonable period of time shall not exceed 15 months unless the parties to the dispute agree otherwise. Where either the panel or the Appellate Body has acted to extend the time of providing its report, the additional time taken shall be added to the 15–month period; provided that unless the parties to the

---

[11] If a meeting of the DSB is not scheduled during this period, such a meeting of the DSB shall be held for this purpose.

[12] If the parties cannot agree on an arbitrator within ten days after referring the matter to arbitration, the arbitrator shall be appointed by the Director-General within ten days, after consulting the parties.

[13] The expression "arbitrator" shall be interpreted as referring either to an individual or a group.

dispute agree that there are exceptional circumstances, the total time shall not exceed 18 months.

5. Where there is disagreement as to the existence or consistency with a covered agreement of measures taken to comply with the recommendations and rulings such dispute shall be decided through recourse to these dispute settlement procedures, including wherever possible resort to the original panel. The panel shall circulate its report within 90 days after the date of referral of the matter to it. When the panel considers that it cannot provide its report within this time frame, it shall inform the DSB in writing of the reasons for the delay together with an estimate of the period within which it will submit its report.

6. The DSB shall keep under surveillance the implementation of adopted recommendations or rulings. The issue of implementation of the recommendations or rulings may be raised at the DSB by any Member at any time following their adoption. Unless the DSB decides otherwise, the issue of implementation of the recommendations or rulings shall be placed on the agenda of the DSB meeting after six months following the date of establishment of the reasonable period of time pursuant to paragraph 3 and shall remain on the DSB's agenda until the issue is resolved. At least 10 days prior to each such DSB meeting, the Member concerned shall provide the DSB with a status report in writing of its progress in the implementation of the recommendations or rulings.

7. If the matter is one which has been raised by a developing country Member, the DSB shall consider what further action it might take which would be appropriate to the circumstances.

8. If the case is one brought by a developing country Member, in considering what appropriate action might be taken, the DSB shall take into account not only the trade coverage of measures complained of, but also their impact on the economy of developing country Members concerned.

Article 22

Compensation and the Suspension of Concessions

1. Compensation and the suspension of concessions or other obligations are temporary measures available in the event that the recommendations and rulings are not implemented within a reasonable period of time. However, neither compensation nor the suspension of concessions or other obligations is preferred to full implementation of a recommendation to bring a measure into conformity with the covered agreements. Compensation is voluntary and, if granted, shall be consistent with the covered agreements.

2. If the Member concerned fails to bring the measure found to be inconsistent with a covered agreement into compliance therewith or

otherwise comply with the recommendations and rulings within the reasonable period of time determined pursuant to paragraph 3 of Article 21, such Member shall, if so requested, and no later than the expiry of the reasonable period of time, enter into negotiations with any party having invoked the dispute settlement procedures, with a view to developing mutually acceptable compensation. If no satisfactory compensation has been agreed within 20 days after the date of expiry of the reasonable period of time, any party having invoked the dispute settlement procedures may request authorization from the DSB to suspend the application to the Member concerned of concessions or other obligations under the covered agreements.

3. In considering what concessions or other obligations to suspend, the complaining party shall apply the following principles and procedures:

(a) the general principle is that the complaining party should first seek to suspend concessions or other obligations with respect to the same sector(s) as that in which the panel or Appellate Body has found a violation or other nullification or impairment;

(b) if that party considers that it is not practicable or effective to suspend concessions or other obligations with respect to the same sector(s), it may seek to suspend concessions or other obligations in other sectors under the same agreement;

(c) if that party considers that it is not practicable or effective to suspend concessions or other obligations with respect to other sectors under the same agreement, and that the circumstances are serious enough, it may seek to suspend concessions or other obligations under another covered agreement;

(d) in applying the above principles, that party shall take into account:

(i) the trade in the sector or under the agreement under which the panel or Appellate Body has found a violation or other nullification or impairment, and the importance of such trade to that party;

(ii) the broader economic elements related to the nullification or impairment and the broader economic consequences of the suspension of concessions or other obligations;

(e) if that party decides to request authorization to suspend concessions or other obligations pursuant to subparagraphs (b) or (c), it shall state the reasons therefor in its request. At the same time as the request is forwarded to the DSB, it also shall be forwarded to the relevant Councils and also, in the case of a request pursuant to subparagraph (b), the relevant sectoral bodies;

(f) for purposes of this paragraph, "sector" means:

(i) with respect to goods, all goods;

(ii) with respect to services, a principal sector as identified in the current "Services Sectoral Classification List" which identifies such sectors,[14]

(iii) with respect to trade-related intellectual property rights, each of the categories of intellectual property rights covered in Section 1, or Section 2, or Section 3, or Section 4, or Section 5, or Section 6, or Section 7 of Part II, or the obligations under Part III, or Part IV of the Agreement on TRIPS;

(g) for purposes of this paragraph, "agreement" means:

(i) with respect to goods, the agreements listed in Annex 1A of the WTO Agreement, taken as a whole as well as the Plurilateral Trade Agreements in so far as the relevant parties to the dispute are parties to these agreements;

(ii) with respect to services, the GATS;

(iii) with respect to intellectual property rights, the Agreement on TRIPS.

4. The level of the suspension of concessions or other obligations authorized by the DSB shall be equivalent to the level of the nullification or impairment.

5. The DSB shall not authorize suspension of concessions or other obligations if a covered agreement prohibits such suspension.

6. When the situation described in paragraph 2 occurs, the DSB, upon request, shall grant authorization to suspend concessions or other obligations within 30 days of the expiry of the reasonable period of time unless the DSB decides by consensus to reject the request. However, if the Member concerned objects to the level of suspension proposed, or claims that the principles and procedures set forth in paragraph 3 have not been followed where a complaining party has requested authorization to suspend concessions or other obligations pursuant to paragraph 3(b) or (c), the matter shall be referred to arbitration. Such arbitration shall be carried out by the original panel, if members are available, or by an arbitrator[15] appointed by the Director-General and shall be completed within 60 days after the date of expiry of the reasonable period of time. Concessions or other obligations shall not be suspended during the course of the arbitration.

---

[14] The list in document MTN.GNS/W/120 identifies eleven sectors.

[15] The expression "arbitrator" shall be interpreted as referring either to an individual or a group.

7. The arbitrator[16] acting pursuant to paragraph 6 shall not examine the nature of the concessions or other obligations to be suspended but shall determine whether the level of such suspension is equivalent to the level of nullification or impairment. The arbitrator may also determine if the proposed suspension of concessions or other obligations is allowed under the covered agreement. However, if the matter referred to arbitration includes a claim that the principles and procedures set forth in paragraph 3 have not been followed, the arbitrator shall examine that claim. In the event the arbitrator determines that those principles and procedures have not been followed, the complaining party shall apply them consistent with paragraph 3. The parties shall accept the arbitrator's decision as final and the parties concerned shall not seek a second arbitration. The DSB shall be informed promptly of the decision of the arbitrator and shall upon request, grant authorization to suspend concessions or other obligations where the request is consistent with the decision of the arbitrator, unless the DSB decides by consensus to reject the request.

8. The suspension of concessions or other obligations shall be temporary and shall only be applied until such time as the measure found to be inconsistent with a covered agreement has been removed, or the Member that must implement recommendations or rulings provides a solution to the nullification or impairment of benefits, or a mutually satisfactory solution is reached. In accordance with paragraph 6 of Article 21, the DSB shall continue to keep under surveillance the implementation of adopted recommendations or rulings, including those cases where compensation has been provided or concessions or other obligations have been suspended but the recommendations to bring a measure into conformity with the covered agreements have not been implemented.

9. The dispute settlement provisions of the covered agreements may be invoked in respect of measures affecting their observance taken by regional or local governments or authorities within the territory of a Member. When the DSB has ruled that a provision of a covered agreement has not been observed, the responsible Member shall take such reasonable measures as may be available to it to ensure its observance. The provisions of the covered agreements and this Understanding relating to compensation and suspension of concessions or other obligations apply in cases where it has not been possible to secure such observance.[17]

[16] The expression "arbitrator" shall be interpreted as referring either to an individual or a group or to the members of the original panel when serving in the capacity of arbitrator.

[17] Where the provisions of any covered agreement concerning measures taken by regional or local governments or authorities within the territory of a Member contain provisions different from the provisions of this paragraph, the provisions of such covered agreement shall prevail.

Article 23

Strengthening of the Multilateral System

1. When Members seek the redress of a violation of obligations or other nullification or impairment of benefits under the covered agreements or an impediment to the attainment of any objective of the covered agreements, they shall have recourse to, and abide by, the rules and procedures of this Understanding.

2. In such cases, Members shall:

(a) not make a determination to the effect that a violation has occurred, that benefits have been nullified or impaired or that the attainment of any objective of the covered agreements has been impeded, except through recourse to dispute settlement in accordance with the rules and procedures of this Understanding, and shall make any such determination consistent with the findings contained in the panel or Appellate Body report adopted by the DSB or an arbitration award rendered under this Understanding;

(b) follow the procedures set forth in Article 21 to determine the reasonable period of time for the Member concerned to implement the recommendations and rulings; and

(c) follow the procedures set forth in Article 22 to determine the level of suspension of concessions or other obligations and obtain DSB authorization in accordance with those procedures before suspending concessions or other obligations under the covered agreements in response to the failure of the Member concerned to implement the recommendations and rulings within that reasonable period of time.

Article 24

Special Procedures Involving Least-Developed Country Members

1. At all stages of the determination of the causes of a dispute and of dispute settlement procedures involving a least-developed country Member, particular consideration shall be given to the special situation of least-developed country Members. In this regard, Members shall exercise due restraint in raising matters under these procedures involving a least-developed country Member. If nullification or impairment is found to result from a measure taken by a least-developed country Member, complaining parties shall exercise due restraint in asking for compensation or seeking authorization to suspend the application of concessions or other obligations pursuant to these procedures.

2. In dispute settlement cases involving a least-developed country Member, where a satisfactory solution has not been found in the course of consultations the Director-General or the Chairman of the DSB shall, upon request by a least-developed country Member offer their good offices,

conciliation and mediation with a view to assisting the parties to settle the dispute, before a request for a panel is made. The Director-General or the Chairman of the DSB, in providing the above assistance, may consult any source which either deems appropriate.

Article 25

Arbitration

1. Expeditious arbitration within the WTO as an alternative means of dispute settlement can facilitate the solution of certain disputes that concern issues that are clearly defined by both parties.

2. Except as otherwise provided in this Understanding, resort to arbitration shall be subject to mutual agreement of the parties which shall agree on the procedures to be followed. Agreements to resort to arbitration shall be notified to all Members sufficiently in advance of the actual commencement of the arbitration process.

3. Other Members may become party to an arbitration proceeding only upon the agreement of the parties which have agreed to have recourse to arbitration. The parties to the proceeding shall agree to abide by the arbitration award. Arbitration awards shall be notified to the DSB and the Council or Committee of any relevant agreement where any Member may raise any point relating thereto.

4. Articles 21 and 22 of this Understanding shall apply *mutatis mutandis* to arbitration awards.

Article 26

1. *Non-Violation Complaints of the Type Described in Paragraph 1(b) of Article XXIII of GATT 1994*

Where the provisions of paragraph 1(b) of Article XXIII of GATT 1994 are applicable to a covered agreement, a panel or the Appellate Body may only make rulings and recommendations where a party to the dispute considers that any benefit accruing to it directly or indirectly under the relevant covered agreement is being nullified or impaired or the attainment of any objective of that Agreement is being impeded as a result of the application by a Member of any measure, whether or not it conflicts with the provisions of that Agreement. Where and to the extent that such party considers and a panel or the Appellate Body determines that a case concerns a measure that does not conflict with the provisions of a covered agreement to which the provisions of paragraph 1(b) of Article XXIII of GATT 1994 are applicable, the procedures in this Understanding shall apply, subject to the following:

(a) the complaining party shall present a detailed justification in support of any complaint relating to a measure which does not conflict with the relevant covered agreement;

(b) where a measure has been found to nullify or impair benefits under, or impede the attainment of objectives, of the relevant covered agreement without violation thereof, there is no obligation to withdraw the measure. However, in such cases, the panel or the Appellate Body shall recommend that the Member concerned make a mutually satisfactory adjustment;

(c) notwithstanding the provisions of Article 21, the arbitration provided for in paragraph 3 of Article 21, upon request of either party, may include a determination of the level of benefits which have been nullified or impaired, and may also suggest ways and means of reaching a mutually satisfactory adjustment; such suggestions shall not be binding upon the parties to the dispute;

(d) notwithstanding the provisions of paragraph 1 of Article 22, compensation may be part of a mutually satisfactory adjustment as final settlement of the dispute.

2. *Complaints of the Type Described in Paragraph 1(c) of Article XXIII of GATT 1994*

Where the provisions of paragraph 1(c) of Article XXIII of GATT 1994 are applicable to a covered agreement, a panel may only make rulings and recommendations where a party considers that any benefit accruing to it directly or indirectly under the relevant covered agreement is being nullified or impaired or the attainment of any objective of that Agreement is being impeded as a result of the existence of any situation other than those to which the provisions of paragraphs 1(a) and 1(b) of Article XXIII of GATT 1994 are applicable. Where and to the extent that such party considers and a panel determines that the matter is covered by this paragraph, the procedures of this Understanding shall apply only up to and including the point in the proceedings where the panel report has been circulated to the Members. The dispute settlement rules and procedures contained in the Decision of 12 April 1989 (BISD 36S/61–67) shall apply to consideration for adoption, and surveillance and implementation of recommendations and rulings. The following shall also apply:

(a) the complaining party shall present a detailed justification in support of any argument made with respect to issues covered under this paragraph;

(b) in cases involving matters covered by this paragraph, if a panel finds that cases also involve dispute settlement matters other than those covered by this paragraph, the panel shall circulate a report to the DSB addressing any such matters and a separate report on matters falling under this paragraph.

Article 27

Responsibilities of the Secretariat

1. The Secretariat shall have the responsibility of assisting panels, especially on the legal, historical and procedural aspects of the matters dealt with, and of providing secretarial and technical support.

2. While the Secretariat assists Members in respect of dispute settlement at their request, there may also be a need to provide additional legal advice and assistance in respect of dispute settlement to developing country Members. To this end, the Secretariat shall make available a qualified legal expert from the WTO technical cooperation services to any developing country Member which so requests. This expert shall assist the developing country Member in a manner ensuring the continued impartiality of the Secretariat.

3. The Secretariat shall conduct special training courses for interested Members concerning these dispute settlement procedures and practices so as to enable Members' experts to be better informed in this regard.

APPENDIX 1

AGREEMENTS COVERED BY THE UNDERSTANDING

(A) Agreement Establishing the World Trade Organization

(B) Multilateral Trade Agreements

Annex 1A: Multilateral Agreements on Trade in Goods

Annex 1B: General Agreement on Trade in Services

Annex 1C: Agreement on Trade-Related Aspects of Intellectual Property Rights

Annex 2: Understanding on Rules and Procedures Governing the Settlement of Disputes

(C) Plurilateral Trade Agreements

Annex 4: Agreement on Trade in Civil Aircraft

Agreement on Government Procurement

International Dairy Agreement

International Bovine Meat Agreement

The applicability of this Understanding to the Plurilateral Trade Agreements shall be subject to the adoption of a decision by the parties to each agreement setting out the terms for the application of the Understanding to the individual agreement, including any special or additional rules or procedures for inclusion in Appendix 2, as notified to the DSB.

APPENDIX 2

SPECIAL OR ADDITIONAL RULES AND PROCEDURES CONTAINED IN THE COVERED AGREEMENTS

Agreement	*Rules and Procedures*
Agreement on the Application of Sanitary and Phytosanitary Measures	11.2
Agreement on Textiles and Clothing	2.14, 2.21, 4.4, 5.2, 5.4, 5.6, 6.9, 6.10, 6.11, 8.1 through 8.12
Agreement on Technical Barriers to Trade	14.2 through 14.4, Annex 2
Agreement on Implementation of Article VI of GATT 1994	17.4 through 17.7
Agreement on Implementation of Article VII of GATT 1994	19.3 through 19.5, Annex II.2(f), 3, 9, 21
Agreement on Subsidies and Countervailing Measures	4.2 through 4.12, 6.6, 7.2 through 7.10, 8.5, footnote 35, 24.4, 27.7, Annex V
General Agreement on Trade in Services	XXII:3, XXIII:3
Annex on Financial Services	4
Annex on Air Transport Services	4
Decision on Certain Dispute Settlement Procedures for the GATS	1 through 5

The list of rules and procedures in this Appendix includes provisions where only a part of the provision may be relevant in this context.

Any special or additional rules or procedures in the Plurilateral Trade Agreements as determined by the competent bodies of each agreement and as notified to the DSB.

* * *

PART D

REGIONAL LAW—THE NORTH AMERICAN FREE TRADE AGREEMENT (NAFTA)

■ ■ ■

DOCUMENT 25

NORTH AMERICAN FREE TRADE AGREEMENT BETWEEN THE GOVERNMENT OF THE UNITED STATES OF AMERICA, THE GOVERNMENT OF CANADA AND THE GOVERNMENT OF THE UNITED MEXICAN STATES (1994)

■ ■ ■

TABLE OF CONTENTS

PART SEVEN: ADMINISTRATIVE AND INSTITUTIONAL PROVISIONS

Chapter Eighteen: Publication, Notification and Administration of Laws (omitted)

Article 1801: Contact Points (omitted)
Article 1802: Publication (omitted)
Article 1803: Notification and Provision of Information (omitted)
Article 1804: Administrative Proceedings (omitted)
Article 1805: Review and Appeal (omitted)
Article 1806: Definitions (omitted)

Chapter Nineteen: Review and Dispute Settlement in Antidumping and Countervailing Duty Matters

Article 1901: General Provisions
Article 1902: Retention of Domestic Antidumping Law and Countervailing Duty Law
Article 1903: Review of Statutory Amendments (omitted)
Article 1904: Review of Final Antidumping and Countervailing Duty Determinations
Article 1905: Safeguarding the Panel Review System
Article 1906: Prospective Application (omitted)
Article 1907: Consultations (omitted)
Article 1908: Special Secretariat Provisions (omitted)
Article 1909: Code of Conduct (omitted)
Article 1910: Miscellaneous (omitted)
Article 1911: Definitions (omitted)
Annexes

Chapter Twenty: Institutional Arrangements and Dispute Settlement Procedures

Section A—Institutions
Article 2001: The Free Trade Commission
Article 2002: The Secretariat
Section B—Dispute Settlement
Article 2003: Cooperation
Article 2004: Recourse to Dispute Settlement Procedures
Article 2005: GATT Dispute Settlement
Article 2006: Consultations
Article 2007: Commission—Good Offices, Conciliation and Mediation
Article 2008: Request for an Arbitral Panel
Article 2009: Roster
Article 2010: Qualifications of Panelists
Article 2011: Panel Selection
Article 2012: Rules of Procedure (omitted)
Article 2013: Third Party Participation (omitted)
Article 2014: Role of Experts (omitted)
Article 2015: Scientific Review Boards (omitted)
Article 2016: Initial Report (omitted)
Article 2017: Final Report
Article 2018: Implementation of Final Report
Article 2019: Non-Implementation—Suspension of Benefits

PART ONE

GENERAL PART

Chapter One

Objectives

Article 101: Establishment of the Free Trade Area

The Parties to this Agreement, consistent with Article XXIV of the *General Agreement on Tariffs and Trade,* hereby establish a free trade area.

Article 102: Objectives

1. The objectives of this Agreement, as elaborated more specifically through its principles and rules, including national treatment, most-favored-nation treatment and transparency, are to:

(a) eliminate barriers to trade in, and facilitate the cross-border movement of, goods and services between the territories of the Parties;

(b) promote conditions of fair competition in the free trade area;

(c) increase substantially investment opportunities in the territories of the Parties;

(d) provide adequate and effective protection and enforcement of intellectual property rights in each Party's territory;

(e) create effective procedures for the implementation and application of this Agreement, for its joint administration and for the resolution of disputes; and

(f) establish a framework for further trilateral, regional and multilateral cooperation to expand and enhance the benefits of this Agreement.

2. The Parties shall interpret and apply the provisions of this Agreement in the light of its objectives set out in paragraph 1 and in accordance with applicable rules of international law.

Article 103: Relation to Other Agreements

1. The Parties affirm their existing rights and obligations with respect to each other under the *General Agreement on Tariffs and Trade* and other agreements to which such Parties are party.

2. In the event of any inconsistency between this Agreement and such other agreements, this Agreement shall prevail to the extent of the inconsistency, except as otherwise provided in this Agreement.

Article 104: Relation to Environmental and Conservation Agreements

1. In the event of any inconsistency between this Agreement and the specific trade obligations set out in:

(a) the *Convention on International Trade in Endangered Species of Wild Fauna and Flora,* done at Washington, March 3, 1973, as amended June 22, 1979,

(b) the *Montreal Protocol on Substances that Deplete the Ozone Layer,* done at Montreal, September 16, 1987, as amended June 29, 1990,

(c) the *Basel Convention on the Control of Transboundary Movements of Hazardous Wastes and Their Disposal,* done at Basel, March 22, 1989, on its entry into force for Canada, Mexico and the United States, or

(d) the agreements set out in Annex 104.1,

such obligations shall prevail to the extent of the inconsistency, provided that where a Party has a choice among equally effective and reasonably available means of complying with such obligations, the Party chooses the alternative that is the least inconsistent with the other provisions of this Agreement.

* * *

Article 105: Extent of Obligations

The Parties shall ensure that all necessary measures are taken in order to give effect to the provisions of this Agreement, including their observance, except as otherwise provided in this Agreement, by state and provincial governments.

Annex 104.1

Bilateral and Other Environmental and Conservation Agreements

1. The *Agreement Between the Government of Canada and the Government of the United States of America Concerning the Transboundary Movement of Hazardous Waste,* signed at Ottawa, October 28, 1986.

2. The *Agreement Between the United States of America and the United Mexican States on Cooperation for the Protection and Improvement of the Environment in the Border Area,* signed at La Paz, Baja California Sur, August 14, 1983.

PART TWO

TRADE IN GOODS

Chapter Three

National Treatment and Market Access for Goods

* * *

Section A—National Treatment

Article 301: National Treatment

1. Each Party shall accord national treatment to the goods of another Party in accordance with Article III of the *General Agreement on Tariffs and Trade* (GATT), including its interpretative notes, and to this end Article III of the GATT and its interpretative notes, or any equivalent provision of a successor agreement to which all Parties are party, are incorporated into and made part of this Agreement.

2. The provisions of paragraph 1 regarding national treatment shall mean, with respect to a state or province, treatment no less favorable than the most favorable treatment accorded by such state or province to any like, directly competitive or substitutable goods, as the case may be, of the Party of which it forms a part.

* * *

Section B—Tariffs

Article 302: Tariff Elimination

1. Except as otherwise provided in this Agreement, no Party may increase any existing customs duty, or adopt any customs duty, on an originating good.

2. Except as otherwise provided in this Agreement, each Party shall progressively eliminate its customs duties on originating goods in accordance with its Schedule to Annex 302.2.

3. On the request of any Party, the Parties shall consult to consider accelerating the elimination of customs duties set out in their Schedules.
* * *

* * *

Article 303: Restriction on Drawback and Duty Deferral Programs

1. Except as otherwise provided in this Article, no Party may refund the amount of customs duties paid, or waive or reduce the amount of customs duties owed, on a good imported into its territory, on condition that the good is:

(a) subsequently exported to the territory of another Party,

(b) used as a material in the production of another good that is subsequently exported to the territory of another Party, or

(c) substituted by an identical or similar good used as a material in the production of another good that is subsequently exported to the territory of another Party, in an amount that exceeds the lesser of the total amount of customs duties paid or owed on the good on importation into its territory and the total amount of customs duties paid to another Party on the good that has been subsequently exported to the territory of that other Party.

2. No Party may, on condition of export, refund, waive or reduce:

(a) an antidumping or countervailing duty that is applied pursuant to a Party's domestic law and that is not applied inconsistently with Chapter Nineteen (Review and Dispute Settlement in Antidumping and Countervailing Duty Matters);

(b) a premium offered or collected on an imported good arising out of any tendering system in respect of the administration of quantitative import restrictions, tariff rate quotas or tariff preference levels;

(c) a fee applied pursuant to section 22 of the U.S. *Agricultural Adjustment Act,* subject to Chapter Seven (Agriculture and Sanitary and Phytosanitary Measures); or

(d) customs duties paid or owed on a good imported into its territory and substituted by an identical or similar good that is subsequently exported to the territory of another Party.

3. Where a good is imported into the territory of a Party pursuant to a duty deferral program and is subsequently exported to the territory of another Party, or is used as a material in the production of another good that is subsequently exported to the territory of another Party, or is substituted by an identical or similar good used as a material in the production of another good that is subsequently exported to the territory of another Party, the Party from whose territory the good is exported:

(a) shall assess the customs duties as if the exported good had been withdrawn for domestic consumption; and

(b) may waive or reduce such customs duties to the extent permitted under paragraph 1.

* * *

Article 304: Waiver of Customs Duties

1. Except as set out in Annex 304.1, no Party may adopt any new waiver of customs duties, or expand with respect to existing recipients or extend to any new recipient the application of an existing waiver of customs duties, where the waiver is conditioned, explicitly or implicitly, on the fulfillment of a performance requirement.

2. Except as set out in Annex 304.2, no Party may, explicitly or implicitly, condition on the fulfillment of a performance requirement the continuation of any existing waiver of customs duties.

3. If a waiver or a combination of waivers of customs duties granted by a Party with respect to goods for commercial use by a designated person can be shown by another Party to have an adverse impact on the commercial interests of a person of that Party, or of a person owned or controlled by a person of that Party that is located in the territory of the Party granting the waiver, or on the other Party's economy, the Party granting the waiver shall either cease to grant it or make it generally available to any importer.

4. This Article shall not apply to measures subject to Article 303.

Article 305: Temporary Admission of Goods

1. Each Party shall grant duty-free temporary admission for:

(a) professional equipment necessary for carrying out the business activity, trade or profession of a business person who qualifies for temporary entry pursuant to Chapter Sixteen (Temporary Entry for Business Persons),

(b) equipment for the press or for sound or television broadcasting and cinematographic equipment,

(c) goods imported for sports purposes and goods intended for display or demonstration, and

(d) commercial samples and advertising films,

imported from the territory of another Party, regardless of their origin and regardless of whether like, directly competitive or substitutable goods are available in the territory of the Party.

* * *

Section C—Non-Tariff Measures

Article 309: Import and Export Restrictions

1. Except as otherwise provided in this Agreement, no Party may adopt or maintain any prohibition or restriction on the importation of any good of another Party or on the exportation or sale for export of any good destined for the territory of another Party, except in accordance with Article XI of the GATT, including its interpretative notes, and to this end Article XI of the GATT and its interpretative notes, or any equivalent provision of a successor agreement to which all Parties are party, are incorporated into and made a part of this Agreement.

2. The Parties understand that the GATT rights and obligations incorporated by paragraph 1 prohibit, in any circumstances in which any other form of restriction is prohibited, export price requirements and, except as permitted in enforcement of countervailing and antidumping orders and undertakings, import price requirements.

* * *

Article 311: Country of Origin Marking

Annex 311 applies to measures relating to country of origin marking.

Article 314: Export Taxes

Except as set out in Annex 314, no Party may adopt or maintain any duty, tax or other charge on the export of any good to the territory of another Party, unless such duty, tax or charge is adopted or maintained on:

(a) exports of any such good to the territory of all other Parties; and

(b) any such good when destined for domestic consumption.

* * *

Annex 302.2

Tariff Elimination

1. Except as otherwise provided in a Party's Schedule attached to this Annex, the following staging categories apply to the elimination of customs duties by each Party pursuant to Article 302(2):

(a) duties on goods provided for in the items in staging category A in a Party's Schedule shall be eliminated entirely and such goods shall be duty-free, effective January 1, 1994;

(b) duties on goods provided for in the items in staging category B in a Party's Schedule shall be removed in five equal annual stages beginning on January 1, 1994, and such goods shall be duty-free, effective January 1, 1998;

(c) duties on goods provided for in the items in staging category C in a Party's Schedule shall be removed in 10 equal annual stages beginning on January 1, 1994, and such goods shall be duty-free, effective January 1, 2003;

(d) duties on goods provided for in the items in staging category C+ in a Party's Schedule shall be removed in 15 equal annual stages beginning on January 1, 1994, and such goods shall be duty-free, effective January 1, 2008; and

(e) goods provided for in the items in staging category D in a Party's Schedule shall continue to receive duty-free treatment.

2. The base rate of customs duty and staging category for determining the interim rate of customs duty at each stage of reduction for an item are indicated for the item in each Party's Schedule attached to this Annex. These rates generally reflect the rate of duty in effect on July 1, 1991, including rates under the U.S. Generalized System of Preferences and the General Preferential Tariff of Canada.

* * *

Annex 311

Country of Origin Marking

1. The Parties shall establish by January 1, 1994, rules for determining whether a good is a good of a Party ("Marking Rules") for purposes of this Annex, Annex 300–B and Annex 302.2, and for such other purposes as the Parties may agree.

2. Each Party may require that a good of another Party, as determined in accordance with the Marking Rules, bear a country of origin marking, when imported into its territory, that indicates to the ultimate purchaser of that good the name of its country of origin.

3. Each Party shall permit the country of origin marking of a good of another Party to be indicated in English, French or Spanish, except that a Party may, as part of its general consumer information measures, require that an imported good be marked with its country of origin in the same manner as prescribed for goods of that Party.

4. Each Party shall, in adopting, maintaining and applying any measure relating to country of origin marking, minimize the difficulties, costs and

inconveniences that the measure may cause to the commerce and industry of the other Parties.

* * *

Annex 313

Distinctive Products

1. Canada and Mexico shall recognize Bourbon Whiskey and Tennessee Whiskey, which is a straight Bourbon Whiskey authorized to be produced only in the State of Tennessee, as distinctive products of the United States. Accordingly, Canada and Mexico shall not permit the sale of any product as Bourbon Whiskey or Tennessee Whiskey, unless it has been manufactured in the United States in accordance with the laws and regulations of the United States governing the manufacture of Bourbon Whiskey and Tennessee Whiskey.

2. Mexico and the United States shall recognize Canadian Whisky as a distinctive product of Canada. Accordingly, Mexico and the United States shall not permit the sale of any product as Canadian Whisky, unless it has been manufactured in Canada in accordance with the laws and regulations of Canada governing the manufacture of Canadian Whisky for consumption in Canada.

3. Canada and the United States shall recognize Tequila and Mezcal as distinctive products of Mexico. Accordingly, Canada and the United States shall not permit the sale of any product as Tequila or Mezcal, unless it has been manufactured in Mexico in accordance with the laws and regulations of Mexico governing the manufacture of Tequila and Mezcal. This provision shall apply to Mezcal, either on the date of entry into force of this Agreement, or 90 days after the date when the official standard for this product is made obligatory by the Government of Mexico, whichever is later.

Annex 300–A

Trade and Investment in the Automotive Sector

1. Each Party shall accord to all existing producers of vehicles in its territory treatment no less favorable than it accords to any new producer of vehicles in its territory under the measures referred to in this Annex, except that this obligation shall not be construed to apply to any differences in treatment specifically provided for in the Appendices to this Annex.

* * *

Annex 300–B

Textile and Apparel Goods

Section 1: Scope and Coverage

1. This Annex applies to the textile and apparel goods set out in Appendix 1.1.

2. In the event of any inconsistency between this Agreement and the *Arrangement Regarding International Trade in Textiles* (Multifiber Arrangement), as amended and extended, including any amendment or extension after January 1, 1994, or any other existing or future agreement applicable to trade in textile or apparel goods, this Agreement shall prevail to the extent of the inconsistency, unless the Parties agree otherwise.

Section 2: Tariff Elimination

1. Except as otherwise provided in this Agreement, each Party shall progressively eliminate its customs duties on originating textile and apparel goods in accordance with its Schedule to Annex 302.2 (Tariff Elimination), and as set out for ease of reference in Appendix 2.1.

* * *

Chapter Four

Rules of Origin

Article 401: Originating Goods

Except as otherwise provided in this Chapter, a good shall originate in the territory of a Party where:

(a) the good is wholly obtained or produced entirely in the territory of one or more of the Parties, as defined in Article 415;

(b) each of the non-originating materials used in the production of the good undergoes an applicable change in tariff classification set out in Annex 401 as a result of production occurring entirely in the territory of one or more of the Parties, or the good otherwise satisfies the applicable requirements of that Annex where no change in tariff classification is required, and the good satisfies all other applicable requirements of this Chapter;

(c) the good is produced entirely in the territory of one or more of the Parties exclusively from originating materials; or

(d) except for a good provided for in Chapters 61 through 63 of the Harmonized System, the good is produced entirely in the territory of one or more of the Parties but one or more of the non-originating materials provided for as parts under the Harmonized System that are used in the production of the good does not undergo a change in tariff classification because

(i) the good was imported into the territory of a Party in an unassembled or a disassembled form but was classified as an assembled good pursuant to General Rule of Interpretation 2(a) of the Harmonized System, or

(ii) the heading for the good provides for and specifically describes both the good itself and its parts and is not further subdivided into subheadings, or the subheading for the good provides for and specifically describes both the good itself and its parts,

provided that the regional value content of the good, determined in accordance with Article 402, is not less than 60 percent where the transaction value method is used, or is not less than 50 percent where the net cost method is used, and that the good satisfies all other applicable requirements of this Chapter.

Article 402: Regional Value Content

1. Except as provided in paragraph 5, each Party shall provide that the regional value content of a good shall be calculated, at the choice of the exporter or producer of the good, on the basis of either the transaction value method set out in paragraph 2 or the net cost method set out in paragraph 3.

2. Each Party shall provide that an exporter or producer may calculate the regional value content of a good on the basis of the following transaction value method:

$$RVC = \frac{TV - VNM}{TV} \times 100$$

where

RVC is the regional value content, expressed as a percentage;

TV is the transaction value of the good adjusted to a F.O.B. basis; and

VNM is the value of non-originating materials used by the producer in the production of the good.

3. Each Party shall provide that an exporter or producer may calculate the regional value content of a good on the basis of the following net cost method:

$$RVC = \frac{NC - VNM}{NC} \times 100$$

where

RVC is the regional value content, expressed as a percentage;

NC is the net cost of the good; and

VNM is the value of non-originating materials used by the producer in the production of the good.

4. Except as provided in Article 403(1) and for a motor vehicle identified in Article 403(2) or a component identified in Annex 403.2, the value of non-originating materials used by the producer in the production of a good shall not, for purposes of calculating the regional value content of the good under paragraph 2 or 3, include the value of non-originating materials used to produce originating materials that are subsequently used in the production of the good.

5. *Net Cost Method Must be Used in Certain Cases.*—An exporter or producer shall calculate the regional value-content of a good solely on the basis of the net cost method described in paragraph (3), if—

(A) there is no transaction value for the good;

(B) the transaction value of the good is unacceptable under Article 1 of the Customs Valuation Code;

(C) the good is sold by the producer to a related person and the volume, by units of quantity, of sales of identical or similar goods to related persons during the six-month period immediately preceding the month in which the good is sold exceeds 85 percent of the producer's total sales of such goods during that period;

(D) the good is—

(i) a motor vehicle provided for in heading 8701 or 8702, subheadings 8703.21 through 8703.90, or heading 8704, 8705, or 8706;

(ii) identified in Annex 403.1 or 403.2 of the Agreement and is for use in a motor vehicle provided for in heading 8701 or 8702, subheadings 8703.21 through 8703.90, or heading 8704, 8705, or 8706;

(iii) provided for in subheadings 6401.10 through 6406.10; or

(iv) a word processing machine provided for in subheading 8469.10.00;

(E) the exporter or producer chooses to accumulate the regional value-content of the good in accordance with subsection (d); or

(F) the good is designated as an intermediate material under paragraph (10) and is subject to a regional value-content requirement.

6. *Net Cost Method Allowed for Adjustments.*—If an exporter or producer of a good calculates the regional value-content of the good on the basis of the transaction value method and a NAFTA country subsequently notifies the exporter or producer, during the course of a verification conducted in accordance with chapter 5 of the Agreement, that the transaction value of the good or the value of any material used in the production of the good must be adjusted or is unacceptable under Article 1 of the Customs Valuation Code, the exporter or producer may calculate the regional value-content of the good on the basis of the net cost method.

7. *Review of Adjustment.*—Nothing in paragraph (6) shall be construed to prevent any review or appeal available in accordance with article 510 of the Agreement with respect to an adjustment to or a rejection of—

(A) the transaction value of a good; or

(B) the value of any material used in the production of a good.

8. *Calculating Net Cost.*—The producer may, consistent with regulations implementing this section, calculate the net cost of a good under paragraph (3), by—

(A) calculating the total cost incurred with respect to all goods produced by that producer, subtracting any sales promotion, marketing and after-sales service costs, royalties, shipping and packing costs, and nonallowable interest costs that are included in the total cost of all such goods, and reasonably allocating the resulting net cost of those goods to the good;

(B) calculating the total cost incurred with respect to all goods produced by that producer, reasonably allocating the total cost to the good, and subtracting any sales promotion, marketing and after-sales service costs, royalties, shipping and packing costs, and nonallowable interest costs that are included in the portion of the total cost allocated to the good; or

(C) reasonably allocating each cost that is part of the total cost incurred with respect to the good so that the aggregate of these costs does not include any sales promotion, marketing and after-sales service costs, royalties, shipping and packing costs, or nonallowable interest costs.

9. *Value of Material Used in Production.*—Except as provided in paragraph (11), the value of a material used in the production of a good—

(A) shall—

(i) be the transaction value of the material determined in accordance with Article 1 of the Customs Valuation Code; or

(ii) in the event that there is no transaction value or the transaction value of the material is unacceptable under Article 1 of the Customs Valuation Code, be determined in accordance with Articles 2 through 7 of the Customs Valuation Code; and

(B) if not included under clause (i) or (ii) of subparagraph (A), shall include—

(i) freight, insurance, packing, and all other costs incurred in transporting the material to the location of the producer;

(ii) duties, taxes, and customs brokerage fees paid on the material in the territory of one or more of the NAFTA countries; and

(iii) the cost of waste and spoilage resulting from the use of the material in the production of the good, less the value of renewable scrap or by-product.

10. *Intermediate Material.*—Except for goods described in subsection (c)(1), any self-produced material, other than a component identified in Annex 403.2 of the Agreement, that is used in the production of a good may be designated by the producer of the good as an intermediate material for the purpose of calculating the regional value-content of the good under paragraph (2) or (3); provided that if the intermediate material is subject to a regional value-content requirement, no other self-produced material that is subject to a regional value-content requirement and is used in the production of the intermediate material may be designated by the producer as an intermediate material.

11. *Value of Intermediate Material.*—The value of an intermediate material shall be—

(A) the total cost incurred with respect to all goods produced by the producer of the good that can be reasonably allocated to the intermediate material; or

(B) the aggregate of each cost that is part of the total cost incurred with respect to the intermediate material that can be reasonably allocated to that intermediate material.

12. *Indirect Material.*—The value of an indirect material shall be based on the Generally Accepted Accounting Principles applicable in the territory of the NAFTA country in which the good is produced.

(c) Automotive Goods.—

1. *Passenger Vehicles and Light Trucks, and their Automotive Parts.*—For purposes of calculating the regional value-content under the net cost method for—

(A) a good that is a motor vehicle for the transport of 15 or fewer persons provided for in subheading 8702.10.00 or 8702.90.00, or a motor vehicle provided for in subheadings 8703.21 through 8703.90, or subheading 8704.21 or 8704.31, or

(B) a good provided for in the tariff provisions listed in Annex 403.1 of the Agreement, that is subject to a regional value-content requirement and is for use as original equipment in the production of a motor vehicle for the transport of 15 or fewer persons provided for in subheading 8702.10.00 or 8702.90.00, or a motor vehicle provided for in subheadings 8703.21 through 8703.90, or subheading 8704.21 or 8704.31,

the value of nonoriginating materials used by the producer in the production of the good shall be the sum of the values of all nonoriginating materials, determined in accordance with subsection (b)(9) at the time the nonoriginating materials are received by the first person in the territory of a NAFTA country who takes title to them, that are imported from outside the territories of the NAFTA countries under the tariff provisions listed in Annex 403.1 of the Agreement and are used in the production of the good or that are used in the production of any material used in the production of the good.

2. *Other Vehicles and their Automotive Parts.*—For purposes of calculating the regional value-content under the net cost method for a good that is a motor vehicle provided for in heading 8701, subheading 8704.10, 8704.22, 8704.23, 8704.32, or 8704.90, or heading 8705 or 8706, a motor vehicle for the transport of 16 or more persons provided for in subheading 8702.10.00 or 8702.90.00, or a component identified in Annex 403.2 of the Agreement for use as original equipment in the production of the motor vehicle, the value of nonoriginating materials used by the producer in the production of the good shall be the sum of—

(A) for each material used by the producer listed in Annex 403.2 of the Agreement, whether or not produced by the producer, at the choice of the producer and determined in accordance with subsection (b), either—

(i) the value of such material that is nonoriginating, or

(ii) the value of nonoriginating materials used in the production of such material; and

(B) the value of any other nonoriginating material used by the producer that is not listed in Annex 403.2 of the Agreement determined in accordance with subsection (b).

3. *Averaging Permitted.*—

(A) In General.—For purposes of calculating the regional value-content of a motor vehicle described in paragraph (1) or (2), the producer may average its calculation over its fiscal year, using any of the categories described in subparagraph (B), on the basis of either all motor vehicles in the category or on the basis of only the motor vehicles in the category that are exported to the territory of one or more of the other NAFTA countries.

(B) Category Described.—A category is described in this subparagraph if it is—

(i) the same model line of motor vehicles in the same class of vehicles produced in the same plant in the territory of a NAFTA country;

(ii) the same class of motor vehicles produced in the same plant in the territory of a NAFTA country;

(iii) the same model line of motor vehicles produced in the territory of a NAFTA country; or

(iv) if applicable, the basis set out in Annex 403.3 of the Agreement.

4. *Annex 403.1 and Annex 403.2.*—For purposes of calculating the regional value-content for any or all goods provided for in a tariff provision listed in Annex 403.1 of the Agreement, or a component or material identified in Annex 403.2 of the Agreement, produced in the same plant, the producer of the good may—

(A) average its calculation—

(i) over the fiscal year of the motor vehicle producer to whom the good is sold;

(ii) over any quarter or month; or

(iii) over its fiscal year, if the good is sold as an aftermarket part;

(B) calculate the average referred to in subparagraph (A) separately for any or all goods sold to one or more motor vehicle producers; or

(C) with respect to any calculation under this paragraph, make a separate calculation for goods that are exported to the territory of one or more NAFTA countries.

5. *Phase-in of Regional Value-Content Requirement.*—Notwithstanding Annex 401 of the Agreement, and except as provided in paragraph (6), the regional value-content requirement shall be—

(A) for a producer's fiscal year beginning on the day closest to January 1, 1998, and thereafter, 56 percent calculated under the net cost method, and for a producer's fiscal year beginning on the day closest to January 1, 2002, and thereafter, 62.5 percent calculated under the net cost method, for—

(i) a good that is a motor vehicle for the transport of 15 or fewer persons provided for in subheading 8702.10.00 or 8702.90.00, or a motor vehicle provided for in subheadings 8703.21 through 8703.90, or subheading 8704.21 or 8704.31; and

(ii) a good provided for in heading 8407 or 8408, or subheading 8708.40, that is for use in a motor vehicle identified in clause (i); and

(B) for a producer's fiscal year beginning on the day closest to January 1, 1998, and thereafter, 55 percent calculated under the net cost method, and for a producer's fiscal year beginning on the day closest to January 1, 2002, and thereafter, 60 percent calculated under the net cost method, for—

(i) a good that is a motor vehicle provided for in heading 8701, subheading 8704.10, 8704.22, 8704.23, 8704.32, or 8704.90, or heading 8705 or 8706, or a motor vehicle for the transport of 16 or more persons provided for in subheading 8702.10.00 or 8702.90.00;

(ii) a good provided for in heading 8407 or 8408, or subheading 8708.40 that is for use in a motor vehicle identified in clause (i); and

(iii) except for a good identified in subparagraph (A)(ii) or a good provided for in subheadings 8482.10 through 8482.80, or subheading 8483.20 or 8483.30, a good identified in Annex 403.1 of the Agreement that is subject to a regional value-content requirement and is for use in a motor vehicle identified in subparagraph (A)(i) or (B)(i).

6. *New and Refitted Plants.*—The regional value-content requirement for a motor vehicle identified in paragraph (1) or (2) shall be—

(A) 50 percent for 5 years after the date on which the first motor vehicle prototype is produced in a plant by a motor vehicle assembler, if—

(i) it is a motor vehicle of a class, or marque, or, except for a motor vehicle identified in paragraph (2), size category and underbody, not previously produced by the motor vehicle assembler in the territory of any of the NAFTA countries;

(ii) the plant consists of a new building in which the motor vehicle is assembled; and

(iii) the plant contains substantially all new machinery that is used in the assembly of the motor vehicle; or

(B) 50 percent for 2 years after the date on which the first motor vehicle prototype is produced at a plant following a refit, if it is a motor vehicle of a class, or marque, or, except for a motor vehicle identified in paragraph (2), size category and underbody, different from that assembled by the motor vehicle assembler in the plant before the refit.

* * *

Article 403: Automotive Goods

1. For purposes of calculating the regional value content under the net cost method set out in Article 402(3) for:

(a) a good that is a motor vehicle provided for in tariff item 8702.10.bb or 8702.90.bb (vehicles for the transport of 15 or fewer persons), or subheading 8703.21 through 8703.90, 8704.21 or 8704.31, or

(b) a good provided for in the tariff provisions listed in Annex 403.1 where the good is subject to a regional value-content requirement and is for use as original equipment in the production of a good provided for in tariff item 8702.10.bb or 8702.90.bb (vehicles for the transport of 15 or fewer persons), or subheading 8702.xx, 8703.21 through 8703.90, 8704.21 or 8704.31, the value of non-originating materials used by the producer in the production of the good shall be the sum of the values of non-originating materials, determined in accordance with Article 402(9) at the time the non-originating materials are received by the first person in the territory of a Party who takes title to them, that are imported from outside the territories of the Parties under the tariff provisions listed in Annex 403.1 and that are used in the production of the good or that are used in the production of any material used in the production of the good.

2. For purposes of calculating the regional value content under the net cost method set out in Article 402(3) for a good that is a motor vehicle provided for in heading 87.01, tariff item 8702.10.aa or 8702.90.aa (vehicles for the transport of 16 or more persons), subheading 8704.10, 8704.22, 8704.23, 8704.32 or 8704.90, or heading 87.05 or 87.06, or for a component identified in Annex 403.2 for use as original equipment in the production of the motor vehicle, the value of non-originating materials used by the producer in the production of the good shall be the sum of:

(a) for each material used by the producer listed in Annex 403.2, whether or not produced by the producer, at the choice of the producer and determined in accordance with Article 402, either

(i) the value of such material that is non-originating, or

(ii) the value of non-originating materials used in the production of such material; and

(b) the value of any other non-originating material used by the producer that is not listed in Annex 403.2, determined in accordance with Article 402.

3. For purposes of calculating the regional value content of a motor vehicle identified in paragraph 1 or 2, the producer may average its calculation over its fiscal year, using any one of the following categories, on the basis of either all motor vehicles in the category or only those motor vehicles in the category that are exported to the territory of one or more of the other Parties:

(a) the same model line of motor vehicles in the same class of vehicles produced in the same plant in the territory of a Party:

(b) the same class of motor vehicles produced in the same plant in the territory of a Party;

(c) the same model line of motor vehicles produced in the territory of a Party; or

(d) if applicable, the basis set out in Annex 403.3.

4. For purposes of calculating the regional value content for any or all goods provided for in a tariff provision listed in Annex 403.1, or a component or material identified in Annex 403.2, produced in the same plant, the producer of the good may:

(a) average its calculation

(i) over the fiscal year of the motor vehicle producer to whom the good is sold.

(ii) over any quarter or month, or

(iii) over its fiscal year, if the good is sold as an aftermarket part;

(b) calculate the average referred to in subparagraph (a) separately for any or all goods sold to one or more motor vehicle producers; or

(c) with respect to any calculation under this paragraph, calculate separately those goods that are exported to the territory of one or more of the Parties.

5. Notwithstanding Annex 401, and except as provided in paragraph 6, the regional value-content requirement shall be:

(a) for a producer's fiscal year beginning on the day closest to January 1, 1998 and thereafter, 56 percent under the net cost method, and for a producer's fiscal year beginning on the day closest to January 1, 2002 and thereafter, 62.5 percent under the net cost method, for

(i) a good that is a motor vehicle provided for in tariff item 8702.10.bb or 8702.90.bb (vehicles for the transport of 15 or fewer persons), or subheading 8703.21 through 8703.90, 8704.21 or 8704.31, and

(ii) a good provided for in heading 84.07 or 84.08, or subheading 8708.40, that is for use in a motor vehicle identified in subparagraph (a)(i); and

(b) for a producer's fiscal year beginning on the day closest to January 1, 1998 and thereafter, 55 percent under the net cost method, and for a producer's fiscal year beginning on the day closest to January 1, 2002 and thereafter, 60 percent under the net cost method, for

(i) a good that is a motor vehicle provided for in heading 87.01, subheading 8702.yy (vehicles for the transport of 16 or more persons), 8704.10, 8704.22, 8704.23, 8704.32 or 8704.90, or heading 87.05 or 87.06,

(ii) a good provided for in heading 84.07 or 84.08 or subheading 8708.40 that is for use in a motor vehicle identified in subparagraph (b)(i), and

(iii) except for a good identified in subparagraph (a)(ii) or provided for in subheading 8482.10 through 8482.80, 8483.20 or 8483.30, a good identified in Annex 403.1 that is subject to a regional value content requirement and that is for use in a motor vehicle identified in subparagraphs (a)(i) or (b)(i).

6. The regional value-content requirement for a motor vehicle identified in Article 403(1) or 403(2) shall be:

(a) 50 percent for five years after the date on which the first motor vehicle prototype is produced in a plant by a motor vehicle assembler, if

(i) it is a motor vehicle of a class, or marque, or, except for a motor vehicle identified in Article 403(2), size category and underbody, not previously produced by the motor vehicle assembler in the territory of any of the Parties,

(ii) the plant consists of a new building in which the motor vehicle is assembled, and

(iii) the plant contains substantially all new machinery that is used in the assembly of the motor vehicle; or

(b) 50 percent for two years after the date on which the first motor vehicle prototype is produced at a plant following a refit, if it is a different motor vehicle of a class, or marque, or, except for a motor vehicle identified in Article 403(2), size category and underbody, than was assembled by the motor vehicle assembler in the plant before the refit.

Article 404: Accumulation

1. For purposes of determining whether a good is an originating good, the production of the good in the territory of one or more of the Parties by one or more producers shall, at the choice of the exporter or producer of the good for which preferential tariff treatment is claimed, be considered to have been performed in the territory of any of the Parties by that exporter or producer, provided that:

(a) all non-originating materials used in the production of the good undergo an applicable tariff classification change set out in Annex 401, and the good satisfies any applicable regional value-content requirement, entirely in the territory of one or more of the Parties; and

(b) the good satisfies all other applicable requirements of this Chapter.

2. For purposes of Article 402(10), the production of a producer that chooses to accumulate its production with that of other producers under paragraph 1 shall be considered to be the production of a single producer.

Article 405: De Minimis

1. Except as provided in paragraphs 3 through 6, a good shall be considered to be an originating good if the value of all non-originating materials used in the production of the good that do not undergo an applicable change in tariff classification set out in Annex 401 is not more than seven percent of the transaction value of the good, adjusted to a F.O.B. basis, or, if the transaction value of the good is unacceptable under Article 1 of the Customs Valuation Code, the value of all such non-originating materials is not more than seven percent of the total cost of the good, provided that:

(a) if the good is subject to a regional value-content requirement, the value of such non-originating materials shall be taken into account in calculating the regional value content of the good; and

(b) the good satisfies all other applicable requirements of this Chapter.

* * *

Article 411: Transshipment

A good shall not be considered to be an originating good by reason of having undergone production that satisfies the requirements of Article 401 if, subsequent to that production, the good undergoes further production or any other operation outside the territories of the Parties, other than unloading, reloading or any other operation necessary to preserve it in good condition or to transport the good to the territory of a Party.

Article 412: Non-Qualifying Operations

A good shall not be considered to be an originating good merely by reason of:

(a) mere dilution with water or another substance that does not materially alter the characteristics of the good; or

(b) any production or pricing practice in respect of which it may be demonstrated, on the basis of a preponderance of evidence, that the object was to circumvent this Chapter.

Article 413: Interpretation and Application

For purposes of this Chapter:

(a) the basis for tariff classification in this Chapter is the Harmonized System;

(b) where a good referred to by a tariff item number is described in parentheses following the tariff item number, the description is provided for purposes of reference only;

(c) where applying Article 401(d), the determination of whether a heading or subheading under the Harmonized System provides for and specifically describes both a good and its parts shall be made on the basis of the nomenclature of the heading or subheading, or the General Rules of Interpretation, the Chapter Notes or the Section Notes of the Harmonized System;

(d) in applying the Customs Valuation Code under this Chapter,

(i) the principles of the Customs Valuation Code shall apply to domestic transactions, with such modifications as may be required by the circumstances, as would apply to international transactions,

(ii) the provisions of this Chapter shall take precedence over the Customs Valuation Code to the extent of any difference, and

(iii) the definitions in Article 415 shall take precedence over the definitions in the Customs Valuation Code to the extent of any difference; and

(e) all costs referred to in this Chapter shall be recorded and maintained in accordance with the Generally Accepted Accounting

Principles applicable in the territory of the Party in which the good is produced.

* * *

Chapter Five

Customs Procedures

Section A—Certification of Origin

Article 501: Certificate of Origin

1. The Parties shall establish by January 1, 1994 a Certificate of Origin for the purpose of certifying that a good being exported from the territory of a Party into the territory of another Party qualifies as an originating good, and may thereafter revise the Certificate by agreement.

2. Each Party may require that a Certificate of Origin for a good imported into its territory be completed in a language required under its law.

3. Each Party shall:

(a) require an exporter in its territory to complete and sign a Certificate of Origin for any exportation of a good for which an importer may claim preferential tariff treatment on importation of the good into the territory of another Party; and

(b) provide that where an exporter in its territory is not the producer of the good, the exporter may complete and sign a Certificate on the basis of

(i) its knowledge of whether the good qualifies as an originating good,

(ii) its reasonable reliance on the producer's written representation that the good qualifies as an originating good, or

(iii) a completed and signed Certificate for the good voluntarily provided to the exporter by the producer.

4. Nothing in paragraph 3 shall be construed to require a producer to provide a Certificate of Origin to an exporter.

5. Each Party shall provide that a Certificate of Origin that has been completed and signed by an exporter or a producer in the territory of another Party that is applicable to:

(a) a single importation of a good into the Party's territory, or

(b) multiple importations of identical goods into the Party's territory that occur within a specified period, not exceeding 12 months, set out therein by the exporter or producer,

shall be accepted by its customs administration for four years after the date on which the Certificate was signed.

Article 502: Obligations Regarding Importations

1. Except as otherwise provided in this Chapter, each Party shall require an importer in its territory that claims preferential tariff treatment for a good imported into its territory from the territory of another Party to:

(a) make a written declaration, based on a valid Certificate of Origin, that the good qualifies as an originating good;

(b) have the Certificate in its possession at the time the declaration is made;

(c) provide, on the request of that Party's customs administration, a copy of the Certificate; and

(d) promptly make a corrected declaration and pay any duties owing where the importer has reason to believe that a Certificate on which a declaration was based contains information that is not correct.

2. Each Party shall provide that, where an importer in its territory claims preferential tariff treatment for a good imported into its territory from the territory of another Party:

(a) the Party may deny preferential tariff treatment to the good if the importer fails to comply with any requirement under this Chapter; and

(b) the importer shall not be subject to penalties for the making of an incorrect declaration, if it voluntarily makes a corrected declaration pursuant to paragraph 1(d).

3. Each Party shall provide that, where a good would have qualified as an originating good when it was imported into the territory of that Party but no claim for preferential tariff treatment was made at that time, the importer of the good may, no later than one year after the date on which the good was imported, apply for a refund of any excess duties paid as the result of the good not having been accorded preferential tariff treatment, on presentation of:

(a) a written declaration that the good qualified as an originating good at the time of importation;

(b) a copy of the Certificate of Origin; and

(c) such other documentation relating to the importation of the good as that Party may require.

* * *

Section D—Review and Appeal of Origin Determinations and Advance Rulings

Article 510: Review and Appeal

1. Each Party shall grant substantially the same rights of review and appeal of marking determinations of origin, country of origin

determinations and advance rulings by its customs administration as it provides to importers in its territory to any person:

(a) who completes and signs a Certificate of Origin for a good that has been the subject of a determination of origin;

(b) whose good has been the subject of a country of origin marking determination pursuant to Article 311 (Country of Origin Marking); or

(c) who has received an advance ruling pursuant to Article 509(1).

2. Further to Articles 1804 (Administrative Proceedings) and 1805 (Review and Appeal), each Party shall provide that the rights of review and appeal referred to in paragraph 1 shall include access to:

(a) at least one level of administrative review independent of the official or office responsible for the determination under review; and

(b) in accordance with its domestic law, judicial or quasi-judicial review of the determination or decision taken at the final level of administrative review.

Section E—Uniform Regulations

* * *

Chapter Six

Energy and Basic Petrochemicals

Article 601: Principles

1. The Parties confirm their full respect for their Constitutions.

2. The Parties recognize that it is desirable to strengthen the important role that trade in energy and basic petrochemical goods plays in the free trade area and to enhance this role through sustained and gradual liberalization.

3. The Parties recognize the importance of having viable and internationally competitive energy and petrochemical sectors to further their individual national interests.

Article 602: Scope and Coverage

1. This Chapter applies to measures relating to energy and basic petrochemical goods originating in the territories of the Parties and to measures relating to investment and to the cross-border trade in services associated with such goods, as set forth in this Chapter.

* * *

Article 603: Import and Export Restrictions

1. Subject to the further rights and obligations of this Agreement, the Parties incorporate the provisions of the *General Agreement on Tariffs and Trade* (GATT), with respect to prohibitions or restrictions on trade in

energy and basic petrochemical goods. The Parties agree that this language does not incorporate their respective protocols of provisional application to the GATT.

2. The Parties understand that the provisions of the GATT incorporated in paragraph 1 prohibit, in any circumstances in which any other form of quantitative restriction is prohibited, minimum or maximum export-price requirements and, except as permitted in enforcement of countervailing and antidumping orders and undertakings, minimum or maximum import-price requirements.

3. In circumstances where a Party adopts or maintains a restriction on importation from or exportation to a non-Party of an energy or basic petrochemical good, nothing in this Agreement shall be construed to prevent the Party from:

(a) limiting or prohibiting the importation from the territory of any Party of such energy or basic petrochemical good of the non-Party; or

(b) requiring as a condition of export of such energy or basic petrochemical good of the Party to the territory of any other Party that the good be consumed within the territory of the other Party.

4. In the event that a Party adopts or maintains a restriction on imports of an energy or basic petrochemical good from non-Party countries, the Parties, on request of any Party, shall consult with a view to avoiding undue interference with or distortion of pricing, marketing and distribution arrangements in another Party.

5. Each Party may administer a system of import and export licensing for energy or basic petrochemical goods provided that such system is operated in a manner consistent with the provisions of this Agreement, including paragraph 1 and Article 1502 (Monopolies and State Enterprises).

* * *

Article 604: Export Taxes

No Party may adopt or maintain any duty, tax or other charge on the export of any energy or basic petrochemical good to the territory of another Party, unless such duty, tax or charge is adopted or maintained on:

(a) exports of any such good to the territory of all other Parties; and

(b) any such good when destined for domestic consumption.

* * *

Annex 602.3

Reservations and Special Provisions

Reservations

1. The Mexican State reserves to itself the following strategic activities, including investment in such activities and the provision of services in such activities:

(a) exploration and exploitation of crude oil and natural gas; refining or processing of crude oil and natural gas; and production of artificial gas, basic petrochemicals and their feedstocks and pipelines;

(b) foreign trade; transportation, storage and distribution, up to and including the first hand sales of the following goods:

(i) crude oil,

(ii) natural and artificial gas,

(iii) goods covered by this Chapter obtained from the refining or processing of crude oil and natural gas, and

(iv) basic petrochemicals;

(c) the supply of electricity as a public service in Mexico, including, except as provided in paragraph 5, the generation, transmission, transformation, distribution and sale of electricity; and

(d) exploration, exploitation and processing of radioactive minerals, the nuclear fuel cycle, the generation of nuclear energy, the transportation and storage of nuclear waste, the use and reprocessing of nuclear fuel and the regulation of their applications for other purposes and the production of heavy water.

In the event of an inconsistency between this paragraph and another provision of this Agreement, this paragraph shall prevail to the extent of that inconsistency.

2. Pursuant to Article 1101(2) (Investment—Scope and Coverage), private investment is not permitted in the activities listed in paragraph 1. Chapter Twelve (Cross-Border Trade in Services) shall only apply to activities involving the provision of services covered in paragraph 1 when Mexico permits a contract to be granted in respect of such activities and only to the extent of that contract.

Trade in Natural Gas and Basic Petrochemicals

3. Where end-users and suppliers of natural gas or basic petrochemical goods consider that cross-border trade in such goods may be in their interests, each Party shall permit such end-users and suppliers, and any state enterprise of that Party as may be required under its domestic law, to negotiate supply contracts.

Each Party shall leave the modalities of the implementation of any such contract to the end-users, suppliers, and any state enterprise of the Party as may be required under its domestic law, which may take the form of individual contracts between the state enterprise and each of the other entities. Such contracts may be subject to regulatory approval.

Performance Clauses

4. Each Party shall allow its state enterprises to negotiate performance clauses in their service contracts.

Activities and Investment in Electricity Generation Facilities

* * *

Chapter Seven

Agriculture and Sanitary and Phytosanitary Measures

Section A—Agriculture

Article 701: Scope and Coverage

1. This Section applies to measures adopted or maintained by a Party relating to agricultural trade.

2. In the event of any inconsistency between this Section and another provision of this Agreement, this Section shall prevail to the extent of the inconsistency.

Article 702: International Obligations

1. Annex 702.1 applies to the Parties specified in that Annex with respect to agricultural trade under certain agreements between them.

2. Prior to adopting pursuant to an intergovernmental commodity agreement, a measure that may affect trade in an agricultural good between the Parties, the Party proposing to adopt the measure shall consult with the other Parties with a view to avoiding nullification or impairment of a concession granted by that Party in its Schedule to Annex 302.2.

3. Annex 702.3 applies to the Parties specified in that Annex with respect to measures adopted or maintained pursuant to an intergovernmental coffee agreement.

Article 703: Market Access

1. The Parties shall work together to improve access to their respective markets through the reduction or elimination of import barriers to trade between them in agricultural goods.

* * *

Article 704: Domestic Support

The Parties recognize that domestic support measures can be of crucial importance to their agricultural sectors but may also have trade distorting and production effects and that domestic support reduction commitments may result from agricultural multilateral trade negotiations under the *General Agreement on Tariffs and Trade* (GATT). Accordingly, where a Party supports its agricultural producers, that Party should endeavor to work toward domestic support measures that:

(a) have minimal or no trade distorting or production effects; or

(b) are exempt from any applicable domestic support reduction commitments that may be negotiated under the GATT.

The Parties further recognize that a Party may change its domestic support measures, including those that may be subject to reduction commitments, at the Party's discretion, subject to its rights and obligations under the GATT.

Article 705: Export Subsidies

1. The Parties share the objective of the multilateral elimination of export subsidies for agricultural goods and shall cooperate in an effort to achieve an agreement under the GATT to eliminate those subsidies.

2. The Parties recognize that export subsidies for agricultural goods may prejudice the interests of importing and exporting Parties and, in particular, may disrupt the markets of importing Parties. Accordingly, in addition to the rights and obligations of the Parties specified in Annex 702.1, the Parties affirm that it is inappropriate for a Party to provide an export subsidy for an agricultural good exported to the territory of another Party where there are no other subsidized imports of that good into the territory of that other Party.

* * *

Section B—Sanitary and Phytosanitary Measures

Article 709: Scope and Coverage

In order to establish a framework of rules and disciplines to guide the development, adoption and enforcement of sanitary and phytosanitary measures, this Section applies to any such measure of a Party that may, directly or indirectly, affect trade between the Parties.

Article 710: Relation to Other Chapters

Articles 301 (National Treatment) and 309 (Import and Export Restrictions), and the provisions of Article XX(b) of the GATT as incorporated into Article 2101(1) (General Exceptions), do not apply to any sanitary or phytosanitary measure.

Article 711: Reliance on Non-Governmental Entities

Each Party shall ensure that any non-governmental entity on which it relies in applying a sanitary or phytosanitary measure acts in a manner consistent with this Section.

Article 712: Basic Rights and Obligations

Right to Take Sanitary and Phytosanitary Measures

1. Each Party may, in accordance with this Section, adopt, maintain or apply any sanitary or phytosanitary measure necessary for the protection of human, animal or plant life or health in its territory, including a measure more stringent than an international standard, guideline or recommendation.

Right to Establish Level of Protection

2. Notwithstanding any other provision of this Section, each Party may, in protecting human, animal or plant life or health, establish its appropriate levels of protection in accordance with Article 715.

Scientific Principles

3. Each Party shall ensure that any sanitary or phytosanitary measure that it adopts, maintains or applies is:

(a) based on scientific principles, taking into account relevant factors including, where appropriate, different geographic conditions;

(b) not maintained where there is no longer a scientific basis for it; and

(c) based on a risk assessment, as appropriate to the circumstances.

Non-Discriminatory Treatment

4. Each Party shall ensure that a sanitary or phytosanitary measure that it adopts, maintains or applies does not arbitrarily or unjustifiably discriminate between its goods and like goods of another Party, or between goods of another Party and like goods of any other country, where identical or similar conditions prevail.

Unnecessary Obstacles

5. Each Party shall ensure that any sanitary or phytosanitary measure that it adopts, maintains or applies is applied only to the extent necessary to achieve its appropriate level of protection, taking into account technical and economic feasibility.

Disguised Restrictions

6. No Party may adopt, maintain or apply any sanitary or phytosanitary measure with a view to, or with the effect of, creating a disguised restriction on trade between the Parties.

Article 713: International Standards and Standardizing Organizations

1. Without reducing the level of protection of human, animal or plant life or health, each Party shall use, as a basis for its sanitary and phytosanitary measures, relevant international standards, guidelines or recommendations with the objective, among others, of making its sanitary and phytosanitary measures equivalent or, where appropriate, identical to those of the other Parties.

2. A Party's sanitary or phytosanitary measure that conforms to a relevant international standard, guideline or recommendation shall be presumed to be consistent with Article 712. A measure that results in a level of sanitary or phytosanitary protection different from that which would be achieved by a measure based on a relevant international standard, guideline or recommendation shall not for that reason alone be presumed to be inconsistent with this Section.

3. Nothing in Paragraph 1 shall be construed to prevent a Party from adopting, maintaining or applying, in accordance with the other provisions of this Section, a sanitary or phytosanitary measure that is more stringent than the relevant international standard, guideline or recommendation.

4. Where a Party has reason to believe that a sanitary or phytosanitary measure of another Party is adversely affecting or may adversely affect its exports and the measure is not based on a relevant international standard, guideline or recommendation, it may request, and the other Party shall provide in writing, the reasons for the measure.

5. Each Party shall, to the greatest extent practicable, participate in relevant international and North American standardizing organizations, including the *Codex Alimentarius Commission,* the *International Office of Epizootics,* the *International Plant Protection Convention,* and the *North American Plant Protection Organization,* with a view to promoting the development and periodic review of international standards, guidelines and recommendations.

Article 714: Equivalence

1. Without reducing the level of protection of human, animal or plant life or health, the Parties shall, to the greatest extent practicable and in accordance with this Section, pursue equivalence of their respective sanitary and phytosanitary measures.

* * *

Article 715: Risk Assessment and Appropriate Level of Protection

1. In conducting a risk assessment, each Party shall take into account:

(a) relevant risk assessment techniques and methodologies developed by international or North American standardizing organizations;

(b) relevant scientific evidence;

(c) relevant processes and production methods;

(d) relevant inspection, sampling and testing methods;

(e) the prevalence of relevant diseases or pests, including the existence of pest-free or disease-free areas or areas of low pest or disease prevalence;

(f) relevant ecological and other environmental conditions; and

(g) relevant treatments, such as quarantines.

2. Further to paragraph 1, each Party shall, in establishing its appropriate level of protection regarding the risk associated with the introduction, establishment or spread of an animal or plant pest or disease, and in assessing the risk, also take into account the following economic factors, where relevant:

(a) loss of production or sales that may result from the pest or disease;

(b) costs of control or eradication of the pest or disease in its territory; and

(c) the relative cost-effectiveness of alternative approaches to limiting risks.

3. Each Party, in establishing its appropriate level of protection:

(a) should take into account the objective of minimizing negative trade effects; and

(b) shall, with the objective of achieving consistency in such levels, avoid arbitrary or unjustifiable distinctions in such levels in different circumstances, where such distinctions result in arbitrary or unjustifiable discrimination against a good of another Party or constitute a disguised restriction on trade between the Parties.

4. Notwithstanding paragraphs (1) through (3) and Article 712(3)(c), where a Party conducting a risk assessment determines that available relevant scientific evidence or other information is insufficient to complete the assessment, it may adopt a provisional sanitary or phytosanitary measure on the basis of available relevant information, including from international or North American standardizing organizations and from sanitary or phytosanitary measures of other Parties. The Party shall, within a reasonable period after information sufficient to complete the assessment is presented to it, complete its assessment, review and, where appropriate, revise the provisional measure in the light of the assessment.

5. Where a Party is able to achieve its appropriate level of protection through the phased application of a sanitary or phytosanitary measure, it may, on the request of another Party and in accordance with this Section, allow for such a phased application, or grant specified exceptions for limited periods from the measure, taking into account the requesting Party's export interests.

Article 716: Adaptation to Regional Conditions

1. Each Party shall adapt any of its sanitary or phytosanitary measures relating to the introduction, establishment or spread of an animal or plant pest or disease, to the sanitary or phytosanitary characteristics of the area where a good subject to such a measure is produced and the area in its territory to which the good is destined, taking into account any relevant conditions, including those relating to transportation and handling, between those areas. In assessing such characteristics of an area, including whether an area is, and is likely to remain, a pest-free or disease-free area or an area of low pest or disease prevalence, each Party shall take into account, among other factors:

(a) the prevalence of relevant pests or diseases in that area;

(b) the existence of eradication or control programs in that area; and

(c) any relevant international standard, guideline or recommendation.

* * *

Chapter Eight

Emergency Action

Article 801: Bilateral Actions

1. Subject to paragraphs 2 through 4 and Annex 801.1, and during the transition period only, if a good originating in the territory of a Party, as a result of the reduction or elimination of a duty provided for in this Agreement, is being imported into the territory of another Party in such increased quantities, in absolute terms, and under such conditions that the imports of the good from that Party alone constitute a substantial cause of serious injury, or threat thereof, to a domestic industry producing a like or directly competitive good, the Party into whose territory the good is being imported may, to the minimum extent necessary to remedy or prevent the injury:

(a) suspend the further reduction of any rate of duty provided for under this Agreement on the good;

(b) increase the rate of duty on the good to a level not to exceed the lesser of

(i) the most-favored-nation (MFN) applied rate of duty in effect at the time the action is taken, and

(ii) the MFN applied rate of duty in effect on the day immediately preceding the date of entry into force of this Agreement; or

(c) in the case of a duty applied to a good on a seasonal basis, increase the rate of duty to a level not to exceed the MFN applied rate of duty that was in effect on the good for the corresponding season immediately preceding the date of entry into force of this Agreement.

2. The following conditions and limitations shall apply to a proceeding that may result in emergency action under paragraph 1: (a) a Party shall, without delay, deliver to any Party that may be affected written notice of, and a request for consultations regarding, the institution of a proceeding that could result in emergency action against a good originating in the territory of a Party; (b) any such action shall be initiated no later than one year after the date of institution of the proceeding; (c) no action may be maintained (i) for a period exceeding three years, except where the good against which the action is taken is provided for in the items in staging category C+ of the Schedule to Annex 302.2 of the Party taking the action and that Party determines that the affected industry has undertaken adjustment and requires an extension of the period of relief, in which case the period of relief may be extended for one year provided that the duty applied during the initial period of relief is substantially reduced at the beginning of the extension period, or (ii) beyond the expiration of the transition period, except with the consent of the Party against whose good the action is taken; (d) no action may be taken by a Party against any particular good originating in the territory of another Party more than once during the transition period; and (e) on the termination of the action, the rate of duty shall be the rate that, according to the Party's Schedule to Annex 302.2 for the staged elimination of the tariff, would have been in effect one year after the initiation of the action, and beginning January 1 of the year following the termination of the action, at the option of the Party that has taken the action (i) the rate of duty shall conform to the applicable rate set out in its Schedule to Annex 302.2, or (ii) the tariff shall be eliminated in equal annual stages ending on the date set out in its Schedule to Annex 302.2 for the elimination of the tariff.

3. A Party may take a bilateral emergency action after the expiration of the transition period to deal with cases of serious injury, or threat thereof, to a domestic industry arising from the operation of this Agreement only with the consent of the Party against whose good the action would be taken.

4. The Party taking an action under this Article shall provide to the Party against whose good the action is taken mutually agreed trade liberalizing compensation in the form of concessions having substantially equivalent trade effects or equivalent to the value of the additional duties expected to result from the action. If the Parties concerned are unable to agree on compensation, the Party against whose good the action is taken may take tariff action having trade effects substantially equivalent to the action taken under this Article. The Party taking the tariff action shall apply the action only for the minimum period necessary to achieve the substantially equivalent effects.

5. This Article does not apply to emergency actions respecting goods covered by Annex 300–B (Textile and Apparel Goods).

Annex 801.1

Bilateral Actions

1. Notwithstanding Article 801, bilateral emergency actions between Canada and the United States on goods originating in the territory of either Party, other than goods covered by Annex 300–B (Textile and Apparel Goods), shall be governed in accordance with the terms of Article 1101 of the Canada-United States Free Trade Agreement, which is hereby incorporated into and made a part of this Agreement for such purpose.

2. For such purposes, "good originating in the territory of one Party" means "good originating in the territory of a Party" as defined in Article 805.

Article 802

Global Actions

1. Each Party retains its rights and obligations under Article XIX of the GATT or any safeguard agreement pursuant thereto except those regarding compensation or retaliation and exclusion from an action to the extent that such rights or obligations are inconsistent with this Article. Any Party taking an emergency action under Article XIX or any such agreement shall exclude imports of a good from each other Party from the action unless: (a) imports from a Party, considered individually, account for a substantial share of total imports; and (b) imports from a Party, considered individually, or in exceptional circumstances imports from Parties considered collectively, contribute importantly to the serious injury, or threat thereof, caused by imports.

2. In determining whether: (a) imports from a Party, considered individually, account for a substantial share of total imports, those imports normally shall not be considered to account for a substantial share of total imports if that Party is not among the top five suppliers of the good subject to the proceeding, measured in terms of import share during the most recent three-year period; and (b) imports from a Party or Parties contribute importantly to the serious injury, or threat thereof, the competent investigating authority shall consider such factors as the change in the import share of each Party, and the level and change in the level of imports of each Party. In this regard, imports from a Party normally shall not be deemed to contribute importantly to serious injury, or the threat thereof, if the growth rate of imports from a Party during the period in which the injurious surge in imports occurred is appreciably lower than the growth rate of total imports from all sources over the same period.

3. A Party taking such action, from which a good from another Party or Parties is initially excluded pursuant to paragraph 1, shall have the

right subsequently to include that good from the other Party or Parties in the action in the event that the competent investigating authority determines that a surge in imports of such good from the other Party or Parties undermines the effectiveness of the action.

4. A Party shall, without delay, deliver written notice to the other Parties of the institution of a proceeding that may result in emergency action under paragraph 1 or 3.

5. No Party may impose restrictions on a good in an action under paragraph 1 or 3: (a) without delivery of prior written notice to the Commission, and without adequate opportunity for consultation with the Party or Parties against whose good the action is proposed to be taken, as far in advance of taking the action is practicable; and (b) that would have the effect of reducing imports of such good from a Party below the trend of imports of the good from that Party over a recent representative base period with allowance for reasonable growth.

6. The Party taking an action pursuant to this Article shall provide to the Party or Parties against whose good the action is taken mutually agreed trade liberalizing compensation in the form of concessions having substantially equivalent trade effects or equivalent to the value of the additional duties expected to result from the action. If the Parties concerned are unable to agree on compensation, the Party against whose good the action is taken may take action having trade effects substantially equivalent to the action taken under paragraph 1 or 3.

Article 803

Administration of Emergency Action Proceedings

1. Each Party shall ensure the consistent, impartial and reasonable administration of its laws, regulations, decisions and rulings governing all emergency action proceedings.

2. Each Party shall entrust determinations of serious injury, or threat thereof, in emergency action proceedings to a competent investigating authority, subject to review by judicial or administrative tribunals, to the extent provided by domestic law. Negative injury determinations shall not be subject to modification, except by such review. The competent investigating authority empowered under domestic law to conduct such proceedings should be provided with the necessary resources to enable it to fulfill its duties.

3. Each Party shall adopt or maintain equitable, timely, transparent and effective procedures for emergency action proceedings, in accordance with the requirements set out in Annex 803.3.

4. This Article does not apply to emergency actions taken under Annex 300–B (Textile and Apparel Goods).

Annex 803.3

Administration of Emergency Action Proceedings

Institution of a Proceeding

1. An emergency action proceeding may be instituted by a petition or complaint by entities specified in domestic law. The entity filing the petition or complaint shall demonstrate that it is representative of the domestic industry producing a good like or directly competitive with the imported good.

2. A Party may institute a proceeding on its own motion or request the competent investigating authority to conduct a proceeding.

Contents of a Petition or Complaint

3. Where the basis for an investigation is a petition or complaint filed by an entity representative of a domestic industry, the petitioning entity shall, in its petition or complaint, provide the following information to the extent that such information is publicly available from governmental or other sources, or best estimates and the basis therefor if such information is not available: (a) product description—the name and description of the imported good concerned, the tariff subheading under which that good is classified, its current tariff treatment and the name and description of the like or directly competitive domestic good concerned; (b) representativeness—(i) the names and addresses of the entities filing the petition or complaint, and the locations of the establishments in which they produce the domestic good, (ii) the percentage of domestic production of the like or directly competitive good that such entities account for and the basis for claiming that they are representative of an industry, and (iii) the names and locations of all other domestic establishments in which the like or directly competitive good is produced; (c) import data—import data for each of the five most recent full years that form the basis of the claim that the good concerned is being imported in increased quantities, either in absolute terms or relative to domestic production as appropriate; (d) domestic production data—data on total domestic production of the like or directly competitive good for each of the five most recent full years; (e) data showing injury—quantitative and objective data indicating the nature and extent of injury to the concerned industry, such as data showing changes in the level of sales, prices, production, productivity, capacity utilization, market share, profits and losses, and employment; (f) cause of injury— an enumeration and description of the alleged causes of the injury, or threat thereof, and a summary of the basis for the assertion that increased imports, either actual or relative to domestic production, of the imported good are causing or threatening to cause serious injury, supported by pertinent data; and (g) criteria for inclusion—quantitative and objective data indicating the share of imports accounted for by imports from the territory of each other Party and the petitioner's views on the extent to

which such imports are contributing importantly to the serious injury, or threat thereof, caused by imports of that good.

4. Petitions or complaints, except to the extent that they contain confidential business information, shall promptly be made available for public inspection on being filed.

Notice Requirement

5. On instituting an emergency action proceeding, the competent investigating authority shall publish notice of the institution of the proceeding in the official journal of the Party. The notice shall identify the petitioner or other requester, the imported good that is the subject of the proceeding and its tariff subheading, the nature and timing of the determination to be made, the time and place of the public hearing, dates of deadlines for filing briefs, statements and other documents, the place at which the petition and any other documents filed in the course of the proceeding may be inspected, and the name, address and telephone number of the office to be contacted for more information.

6. With respect to an emergency action proceeding instituted on the basis of a petition or complaint filed by an entity asserting that it is representative of the domestic industry, the competent investigating authority shall not publish the notice required by paragraph 5 without first assessing carefully that the petition or complaint meets the requirements of paragraph 3, including representativeness.

Public Hearing

7. In the course of each proceeding, the competent investigating authority shall: (a) hold a public hearing, after providing reasonable notice, to allow all interested parties, and any association whose purpose is to represent the interests of consumers in the territory of the Party instituting the proceeding, to appear in person or by counsel, to present evidence and to be heard on the questions of serious injury, or threat thereof, and the appropriate remedy; and (b) provide an opportunity to all interested parties and any such association appearing at the hearing to cross-question interested parties making presentations at that hearing.

Confidential Information

8. The competent investigating authority shall adopt or maintain procedures for the treatment of confidential information, protected under domestic law, that is provided in the course of a proceeding, including a requirement that interested parties and consumer associations providing such information furnish non-confidential written summaries thereof, or where they indicate that the information cannot be summarized, the reasons why a summary cannot be provided.

Evidence of Injury and Causation

9. In conducting its proceeding the competent investigating authority shall gather, to the best of its ability, all relevant information appropriate to the determination it must make. It shall evaluate all relevant factors of an objective and quantifiable nature having a bearing on the situation of that industry, including the rate and amount of the increase in imports of the good concerned, in absolute and relative terms as appropriate, the share of the domestic market taken by increased imports, and changes in the level of sales, production, productivity, capacity utilization, profits and losses, and employment. In making its determination, the competent investigating authority may also consider other economic factors, such as changes in prices and inventories, and the ability of firms in the industry to generate capital.

10. The competent investigating authority shall not make an affirmative injury determination unless its investigation demonstrates, on the basis of objective evidence, the existence of a clear causal link between increased imports of the good concerned and serious injury, or threat thereof. Where factors other than increased imports are causing injury to the domestic industry at the same time, such injury shall not be attributed to increased imports.

Deliberation and Report

11. Except in critical circumstances and in global actions involving perishable agricultural goods, the competent investigating authority, before making an affirmative determination in an emergency action proceeding, shall allow sufficient time to gather and consider the relevant information, hold a public hearing and provide an opportunity for all interested parties and consumer associations to prepare and submit their views.

12. The competent investigating authority shall publish promptly a report, including a summary thereof in the official journal of the Party, setting out its findings and reasoned conclusions on all pertinent issues of law and fact. The report shall describe the imported good and its tariff item number, the standard applied and the finding made. The statement of reasons shall set out the basis for the determination, including a description of: (a) the domestic industry seriously injured or threatened with serious injury; (b) information supporting a finding that imports are increasing, the domestic industry is seriously injured or threatened with serious injury, and increasing imports are causing or threatening serious injury; and (c) if provided for by domestic law, any finding or recommendation regarding the appropriate remedy and the basis therefor.

13. In its report, the competent investigating authority shall not disclose any confidential information provided pursuant to any

undertaking concerning confidential information that may have been made in the course of the proceedings.

Article 804

Dispute Settlement in Emergency Action Matters

No Party may request the establishment of an arbitral panel under Article 2008 (Request for an Arbitral Panel) regarding any proposed emergency action.

Article 805

Definitions

For purposes of this Chapter:

competent investigating authority means the "competent investigating authority" of a Party as defined in Annex 805;

contribute importantly means an important cause, but not necessarily the most important cause;

critical circumstances means circumstances where delay would cause damage that would be difficult to repair;

domestic industry means the producers as a whole of the like or directly competitive good operating in the territory of a Party;

emergency action does not include any emergency action pursuant to a proceeding instituted prior to January 1, 1994;

good originating in the territory of a Party means an originating good, except that in determining the Party in whose territory that good originates, the relevant rules of Annex 302.2 shall apply;

serious injury means a significant overall impairment of a domestic industry;

surge means a significant increase in imports over the trend for a recent representative base period;

threat of serious injury means serious injury that, on the basis of facts and not merely on allegation, conjecture or remote possibility, is clearly imminent; and

transition period means the 10-year period beginning on January 1, 1994, except where the good against which the action is taken is provided for in the items in staging category C+ of the Schedule to Annex 302.2 of the Party taking the action, in which case the transition period shall be the period of staged tariff elimination for that good.

Annex 805

Country-Specific Definitions

For purposes of this Chapter: **competent investigating authority** means: (a) in the case of Canada, the Canadian International Trade Tribunal, or its successor; (b) in the case of Mexico, the designated authority within the Ministry of Trade and Industrial Development ("Secretaria de Comercio y Fomento Industrial"), or its successor; and (c) in the case of the United States, the U.S. International Trade Commission, or its successor.

PART THREE

TECHNICAL BARRIERS TO TRADE

Chapter Nine

Standards-Related Measures

Article 901: Scope and Coverage

1. This Chapter applies to standards-related measures of a Party, other than those covered by Section B of Chapter Seven (Sanitary and Phytosanitary Measures), that may, directly or indirectly, affect trade in goods or services between the Parties, and to measures of the Parties relating to such measures.

2. Technical specifications prepared by governmental bodies for production or consumption requirements of such bodies shall be governed exclusively by Chapter Ten (Government Procurement).

Article 902: Extent of Obligations

1. Article 105 (Extent of Obligations) does not apply to this Chapter.

2. Each Party shall seek, through appropriate measures, to ensure observance of Articles 904 through 908 by state or provincial governments and by non-governmental standardizing bodies in its territory.

Article 903: Affirmation of Agreement on Technical Barriers to Trade and Other Agreements

Further to Article 103 (Relation to Other Agreements), the Parties affirm with respect to each other their existing rights and obligations relating to standards-related measures under the *GATT Agreement on Technical Barriers to Trade* and all other international agreements, including environmental and conservation agreements, to which those Parties are party.

Article 904: Basic Rights and Obligations

Right to Take Standards-Related Measures

1. Each Party may, in accordance with this Agreement, adopt, maintain or apply any standards-related measure, including any such measure relating to safety, the protection of human, animal or plant life or health, the environment or consumers, and any measure to ensure its enforcement or implementation. Such measures include those to prohibit the importation of a good of another Party or the provision of a service by a service provider of another Party that fails to comply with the applicable requirements of those measures or to complete the Party's approval procedures.

Right to Establish Level of Protection

2. Notwithstanding any other provision of this Chapter, each Party may, in pursuing its legitimate objectives of safety or the protection of human, animal or plant life or health, the environment or consumers, establish the levels of protection that it considers appropriate in accordance with Article 907(2).

Non-Discriminatory Treatment

3. Each Party shall, in respect of its standards-related measures, accord to goods and service providers of another Party:

(a) national treatment in accordance with Article 301 (Market Access) or Article 1202 (Cross-Border Trade in Services); and

(b) treatment no less favorable than that it accords to like goods, or in like circumstances to service providers, of any other country.

Unnecessary Obstacles

4. No Party may prepare, adopt, maintain or apply any standards-related measure with a view to or with the effect of creating an unnecessary obstacle to trade between the Parties. An unnecessary obstacle to trade shall not be deemed to be created where:

(a) the demonstrable purpose of the measure is to achieve a legitimate objective; and

(b) the measure does not operate to exclude goods of another Party that meet that legitimate objective.

Article 905: Use of International Standards

1. Each Party shall use, as a basis for its standards-related measures, relevant international standards or international standards whose completion is imminent, except where such standards would be an ineffective or inappropriate means to fulfill its legitimate objectives, for example because of fundamental climatic, geographical, technological or

infrastructural factors, scientific justification or the level of protection that the Party considers appropriate.

2. A Party's standards-related measure that conforms to an international standard shall be presumed to be consistent with Article 904(3) and (4).

3. Nothing in paragraph 1 shall be construed to prevent a Party, in pursuing its legitimate objectives, from adopting, maintaining or applying any standards-related measure that results in a higher level of protection than would be achieved if the measure were based on the relevant international standard.

Article 906: Compatibility and Equivalence

1. Recognizing the crucial role of standards-related measures in achieving legitimate objectives, the Parties shall, in accordance with this Chapter, work jointly to enhance the level of safety and of protection of human, animal and plant life and health, the environment and consumers.

2. Without reducing the level of safety or of protection of human, animal or plant life or health, the environment or consumers, without prejudice to the rights of any Party under this Chapter, and taking into account international standardization activities, the Parties shall, to the greatest extent practicable, make compatible their respective standards-related measures, so as to facilitate trade in a good or service between the Parties.

3. Further to Articles 902 and 905, a Party shall, on request of another Party, seek, through appropriate measures, to promote the compatibility of a specific standard or conformity assessment procedure that is maintained in its territory with the standards or conformity assessment procedures maintained in the territory of the other Party.

4. Each importing Party shall treat a technical regulation adopted or maintained by an exporting Party as equivalent to its own where the exporting Party, in cooperation with the importing Party, demonstrates to the satisfaction of the importing Party that its technical regulation adequately fulfills the importing Party's legitimate objectives.

5. The importing Party shall provide to the exporting Party, on request, its reasons in writing for not treating a technical regulation as equivalent under paragraph 4.

6. Each Party shall, wherever possible, accept the results of a conformity assessment procedure conducted in the territory of another Party, provided that it is satisfied that the procedure offers an assurance, equivalent to that provided by a procedure it conducts or a procedure conducted in its territory the results of which it accepts, that the relevant good or service complies with the applicable technical regulation or standard adopted or maintained in the Party's territory.

7. Prior to accepting the results of a conformity assessment procedure pursuant to paragraph 6, and to enhance confidence in the continued reliability of each other's conformity assessment results, the Parties may consult on such matters as the technical competence of the conformity assessment bodies involved, including verified compliance with relevant international standards through such means as accreditation.

Article 907: Assessment of Risk

1. A Party may, in pursuing its legitimate objectives, conduct an assessment of risk. In conducting an assessment, a Party may take into account, among other factors relating to a good or service:

(a) available scientific evidence or technical information;

(b) intended end uses;

(c) processes or production, operating, inspection, sampling or testing methods; or

(d) environmental conditions.

2. Where pursuant to Article 904(2) a Party establishes a level of protection that it considers appropriate and conducts an assessment of risk, it should avoid arbitrary or unjustifiable distinctions between similar goods or services in the level of protection it considers appropriate, where the distinctions:

(a) result in arbitrary or unjustifiable discrimination against goods or service providers of another Party;

(b) constitute a disguised restriction on trade between the Parties; or

(c) discriminate between similar goods or services for the same use under the same conditions that pose the same level of risk and provide similar benefits.

3. Where a Party conducting an assessment of risk determines that available scientific evidence or other information is insufficient to complete the assessment, it may adopt a provisional technical regulation on the basis of available relevant information. The Party shall, within a reasonable period after information sufficient to complete the assessment of risk is presented to it, complete its assessment, review and, where appropriate, revise the provisional technical regulation in the light of that assessment.

Article 908: Conformity Assessment

1. The Parties shall, further to Article 906 and recognizing the existence of substantial differences in the structure, organization and operation of conformity assessment procedures in their respective territories, make compatible those procedures to the greatest extent practicable.

2. Recognizing that it should be to the mutual advantage of the Parties concerned and except as set out in Annex 908.2, each Party shall accredit, approve, license or otherwise recognize conformity assessment bodies in

the territory of another Party on terms no less favorable than those accorded to conformity assessment bodies in its territory.

3. Each Party shall, with respect to its conformity assessment procedures:

(a) not adopt or maintain any such procedure that is stricter, nor apply the procedure more strictly, than necessary to give it confidence that a good or a service conforms with an applicable technical regulation or standard, taking into account the risks that non-conformity would create;

(b) initiate and complete the procedure as expeditiously as possible;

(c) in accordance with Article 904(3), undertake processing of applications in non-discriminatory order;

(d) publish the normal processing period for each such procedure or communicate the anticipated processing period to an applicant on request;

(e) ensure that the competent body

(i) on receipt of an application, promptly examines the completeness of the documentation and informs the applicant in a precise and complete manner of any deficiency,

(ii) transmits to the applicant as soon as possible the results of the conformity assessment procedure in a form that is precise and complete so that the applicant may take any necessary corrective action,

(iii) where the application is deficient, proceeds as far as practicable with the procedure where the applicant so requests, and

(iv) informs the applicant, on request, of the status of the application and the reasons for any delay;

(f) limit the information the applicant is required to supply to that necessary to conduct the procedure and to determine appropriate fees;

(g) accord confidential or proprietary information arising from, or supplied in connection with, the conduct of the procedure for a good of another Party or for a service provided by a person of another Party

(i) the same treatment as that for a good of the Party or a service provided by a person of the Party, and

(ii) in any event, treatment that protects an applicant's legitimate commercial interests to the extent provided under the Party's law;

(h) ensure that any fee it imposes for conducting the procedure is no higher for a good of another Party or a service provider of another Party than is equitable in relation to any such fee imposed for its like goods or service providers or for like goods or service providers of any other country, taking into account communication, transportation and other related costs;

(i) ensure that the location of facilities at which a conformity assessment procedure is conducted does not cause unnecessary inconvenience to an applicant or its agent;

(j) limit the procedure, for a good or service modified subsequent to a determination that the good or service conforms to the applicable technical regulation or standard, to that necessary to determine that the good or service continues to conform to the technical regulation or standard; and

(k) limit any requirement regarding samples of a good to that which is reasonable, and ensure that the selection of samples does not cause unnecessary inconvenience to an applicant or its agent.

4. Each Party shall apply, with such modifications as may be necessary, the relevant provisions of paragraph 3 to its approval procedures.

5. Each Party shall, on request of another Party, take such reasonable measures as may be available to it to facilitate access in its territory for conformity assessment activities.

6. Each Party shall give sympathetic consideration to a request by another Party to negotiate agreements for the mutual recognition of the results of that other Party's conformity assessment procedures.

* * *

Article 915: Definitions

1. For purposes of this Chapter:

* * *

legitimate objective includes an objective such as:

(a) safety,

(b) protection of human, animal or plant life or health, the environment or consumers, including matters relating to quality and identifiability of goods or services, and

(c) sustainable development,

considering, among other things, where appropriate, fundamental climatic or other geographical factors, technological or infrastructural factors, or scientific justification but does not include the protection of domestic production;

* * *

standard means a document, approved by a recognized body, that provides, for common and repeated use, rules, guidelines or characteristics for goods or related processes and production methods, or for services or related operating methods, with which compliance is not mandatory. It may also include or deal exclusively with terminology, symbols, packaging, marking or labelling requirements as they apply to a good, process, or production or operating method;

* * *

technical regulation means a document which lays down goods' characteristics or their related processes and production methods, or services' characteristics or their related operating methods, including the applicable administrative provisions, with which compliance is mandatory. It may also include or deal exclusively with terminology, symbols, packaging, marking or labelling requirements as they apply to a good, process, or production or operating method;

* * *

PART FOUR

GOVERNMENT PROCUREMENT

Chapter Ten

Government Procurement

Section A—Scope and Coverage and National Treatment

Article 1001: Scope and Coverage

1. This Chapter applies to measures adopted or maintained by a Party relating to procurement:

(a) by a federal government entity set out in Annex 1001.1a–1, a government enterprise set out in Annex 1001.1a–2, or a state or provincial government entity set out in Annex 1001.1a–3 in accordance with Article 1024;

(b) of goods in accordance with Annex 1001.1b–1, services in accordance with Annex 1001.1b–2, or construction services in accordance with Annex 1001.1b–3; and

(c) where the value of the contract to be awarded is estimated to be equal to or greater than a threshold, calculated and adjusted according to the U.S. inflation rate as set out in Annex 1001.1c, of

(i) for federal government entities, US$50,000 for contracts for goods, services or any combination thereof, and US$6.5 million for contracts for construction services,

(ii) for government enterprises, US$250,000 for contracts for goods, services or any combination thereof, and US$8.0 million for contracts for construction services, and

(iii) for state and provincial government entities, the applicable threshold, as set out in Annex 1001.1a–3 in accordance with Article 1024.

* * *

Article 1003: National Treatment and Non-Discrimination

1. With respect to measures covered by this Chapter, each Party shall accord to goods of another Party, to the suppliers of such goods and to service suppliers of another Party, treatment no less favorable than the most favorable treatment that the Party accords to:

(a) its own goods and suppliers; and

(b) goods and suppliers of another Party.

2. With respect to measures covered by this Chapter, no Party may:

(a) treat a locally established supplier less favorably than another locally established supplier on the basis of degree of foreign affiliation or ownership; or

(b) discriminate against a locally established supplier on the basis that the goods or services offered by that supplier for the particular procurement are goods or services of another Party.

3. Paragraph 1 does not apply to measures respecting customs duties or other charges of any kind imposed on or in connection with importation, the method of levying such duties or charges or other import regulations, including restrictions and formalities.

Article 1004: Rules of Origin

No Party may apply rules of origin to goods imported from another Party for purposes of government procurement covered by this Chapter that are different from or inconsistent with the rules of origin the Party applies in the normal course of trade, which may be the Marking Rules established under Annex 311 if they become the rules of origin applied by that Party in the normal course of its trade.

Article 1005: Denial of Benefits

1. Subject to prior notification and consultation in accordance with Articles 1803 (Notification and Provision of Information) and 2006 (Consultations), a Party may deny the benefits of this Chapter to a service supplier of another Party where the Party establishes that the service is being provided by an enterprise that is owned or controlled by persons of a non-Party and that has no substantial business activities in the territory of any Party.

2. A Party may deny to an enterprise of another Party the benefits of this Chapter if nationals of a non-Party own or control the enterprise and:

(a) the circumstance set out in Article 1113(1)(a) (Denial of Benefits) is met; or

(b) the denying Party adopts or maintains measures with respect to the non-Party that prohibit transactions with the enterprise or that would be violated or circumvented if the benefits of this Chapter were accorded to the enterprise.

Article 1006: Prohibition of Offsets

Each Party shall ensure that its entities do not, in the qualification and selection of suppliers, goods or services, in the evaluation of bids or the award of contracts, consider, seek or impose offsets. For purposes of this Article, offsets means conditions imposed or considered by an entity prior to or in the course of its procurement process that encourage local development or improve its Party's balance of payments accounts, by means of requirements of local content, licensing of technology, investment, counter-trade or similar requirements.

Article 1007: Technical Specifications

1. Each Party shall ensure that its entities do not prepare, adopt or apply any technical specification with the purpose or the effect of creating unnecessary obstacles to trade.

2. Each Party shall ensure that any technical specification prescribed by its entities is, where appropriate:

(a) specified in terms of performance criteria rather than design or descriptive characteristics; and

(b) based on international standards, national technical regulations, recognized national standards, or building codes.

3. Each Party shall ensure that the technical specifications prescribed by its entities do not require or refer to a particular trademark or name, patent, design or type, specific origin or producer or supplier unless there is no sufficiently precise or intelligible way of otherwise describing the procurement requirements and provided that, in such cases, words such as "or equivalent" are included in the tender documentation.

4. Each Party shall ensure that its entities do not seek or accept, in a manner that would have the effect of precluding competition, advice that may be used in the preparation or adoption of any technical specification for a specific procurement from a person that may have a commercial interest in that procurement.

Section B—Tendering Procedures (omitted)

* * *

Section C—Bid Challenge

Article 1017: Bid Challenge

1. In order to promote fair, open and impartial procurement procedures, each Party shall adopt and maintain bid challenge procedures for procurement covered by this Chapter in accordance with the following:

(a) each Party shall allow suppliers to submit bid challenges concerning any aspect of the procurement process, which for the purposes of this Article begins after an entity has decided on its procurement requirement and continues through the contract award;

(b) a Party may encourage a supplier to seek a resolution of any complaint with the entity concerned prior to initiating a bid challenge;

(c) each Party shall ensure that its entities accord fair and timely consideration to any complaint regarding procurement covered by this Chapter;

(d) whether or not a supplier has attempted to resolve its complaint with the entity, or following an unsuccessful attempt at such a resolution, no Party may prevent the supplier from initiating a bid challenge or seeking any other relief;

(e) a Party may require a supplier to notify the entity on initiation of a bid challenge;

(f) a Party may limit the period within which a supplier may initiate a bid challenge, but in no case shall the period be less than 10 working days from the time when the basis of the complaint became known or reasonably should have become known to the supplier;

(g) each Party shall establish or designate a reviewing authority with no substantial interest in the outcome of procurements to receive bid challenges and make findings and recommendations concerning them;

(h) on receipt of a bid challenge, the reviewing authority shall expeditiously investigate the challenge;

(i) a Party may require its reviewing authority to limit its considerations to the challenge itself;

(j) in investigating the challenge, the reviewing authority may delay the awarding of the proposed contract pending resolution of the challenge, except in cases of urgency or where the delay would be contrary to the public interest;

(k) the reviewing authority shall issue a recommendation to resolve the challenge, which may include directing the entity to re-evaluate offers, terminate or re-compete the contract in question;

(*l*) entities normally shall follow the recommendations of the reviewing authority;

(m) each Party should authorize its reviewing authority, following the conclusion of a bid challenge procedure, to make additional recommendations in writing to an entity respecting any facet of the entity's procurement process that is identified as problematic during the investigation of the challenge, including recommendations for changes in the procurement procedures of the entity to bring them into conformity with this Chapter;

(n) the reviewing authority shall provide its findings and recommendations respecting bid challenges in writing and in a timely manner, and shall make them available to the Parties and interested persons;

(*o*) each Party shall specify in writing and shall make generally available all its bid challenge procedures; and

(p) each Party shall ensure that each of its entities maintains complete documentation regarding each of its procurements, including a written record of all communications substantially affecting each procurement, for at least three years from the date the contract was awarded, to allow verification that the procurement process was carried out in accordance with this Chapter.

PART FIVE

INVESTMENT, SERVICES AND RELATED MATTERS

Chapter Eleven

Investment

Section A—Investment

Article 1101: Scope and Coverage

1. This Chapter applies to measures adopted or maintained by a Party relating to:

(a) investors of another Party;

(b) investments of investors of another Party in the territory of the Party; and

(c) with respect to Articles 1106 and 1114, all investments in the territory of the Party.

2. A Party has the right to perform exclusively the economic activities set out in Annex III and to refuse to permit the establishment of investment in such activities.

3. This Chapter does not apply to measures adopted or maintained by a Party to the extent that they are covered by Chapter Fourteen (Financial Services).

4. Nothing in this Chapter shall be construed to prevent a Party from providing a service or performing a function such as law enforcement, correctional services, income security or insurance, social security or

insurance, social welfare, public education, public training, health, and child care, in a manner that is not inconsistent with this Chapter.

Article 1102: National Treatment

1. Each Party shall accord to investors of another Party treatment no less favorable than that it accords, in like circumstances, to its own investors with respect to the establishment, acquisition, expansion, management, conduct, operation, and sale or other disposition of investments.

2. Each Party shall accord to investments of investors of another Party treatment no less favorable than that it accords, in like circumstances, to investments of its own investors with respect to the establishment, acquisition, expansion, management, conduct, operation, and sale or other disposition of investments.

3. The treatment accorded by a Party under paragraphs 1 and 2 means, with respect to a state or province, treatment no less favorable than the most favorable treatment accorded, in like circumstances, by that state or province to investors, and to investments of investors, of the Party of which it forms a part.

4. For greater certainty, no Party may:

(a) impose on an investor of another Party a requirement that a minimum level of equity in an enterprise in the territory of the Party be held by its nationals, other than nominal qualifying shares for directors or incorporators of corporations; or

(b) require an investor of another Party, by reason of its nationality, to sell or otherwise dispose of an investment in the territory of the Party.

Article 1103: Most-Favored-Nation Treatment

1. Each Party shall accord to investors of another Party treatment no less favorable than that it accords, in like circumstances, to investors of any other Party or of a non-Party with respect to the establishment, acquisition, expansion, management, conduct, operation, and sale or other disposition of investments.

2. Each Party shall accord to investments of investors of another Party treatment no less favorable than that it accords, in like circumstances, to investments of investors of any other Party or of a non-Party with respect to the establishment, acquisition, expansion, management, conduct, operation, and sale or other disposition of investments.

Article 1104: Standard of Treatment

Each Party shall accord to investors of another Party and to investments of investors of another Party the better of the treatment required by Articles 1102 and 1103.

Article 1105: Minimum Standard of Treatment

1. Each Party shall accord to investments of investors of another Party treatment in accordance with international law, including fair and equitable treatment and full protection and security.

2. Without prejudice to paragraph 1 and notwithstanding Article 1108(7)(b), each Party shall accord to investors of another Party, and to investments of investors of another Party, non-discriminatory treatment with respect to measures it adopts or maintains relating to losses suffered by investments in its territory owing to armed conflict or civil strife.

3. Paragraph 2 does not apply to existing measures relating to subsidies or grants that would be inconsistent with Article 1102 but for Article 1108(7)(b).

Article 1106: Performance Requirements

1. No Party may impose or enforce any of the following requirements, or enforce any commitment or undertaking, in connection with the establishment, acquisition, expansion, management, conduct or operation of an investment of an investor of a Party or of a non-Party in its territory:

(a) to export a given level or percentage of goods or services;

(b) to achieve a given level or percentage of domestic content;

(c) to purchase, use or accord a preference to goods produced or services provided in its territory, or to purchase goods or services from persons in its territory;

(d) to relate in any way the volume or value of imports to the volume or value of exports or to the amount of foreign exchange inflows associated with such investment;

(e) to restrict sales of goods or services in its territory that such investment produces or provides by relating such sales in any way to the volume or value of its exports or foreign exchange earnings;

(f) to transfer technology, a production process or other proprietary knowledge to a person in its territory, except when the requirement is imposed or the commitment or undertaking is enforced by a court, administrative tribunal or competition authority to remedy an alleged violation of competition laws or to act in a manner not inconsistent with other provisions of this Agreement; or

(g) to act as the exclusive supplier of the goods it produces or services it provides to a specific region or world market.

2. A measure that requires an investment to use a technology to meet generally applicable health, safety or environmental requirements shall not be construed to be inconsistent with paragraph 1(f). For greater certainty, Articles 1102 and 1103 apply to the measure.

3. No Party may condition the receipt or continued receipt of an advantage, in connection with an investment in its territory of an investor of a Party or of a non-Party, on compliance with any of the following requirements:

(a) to achieve a given level or percentage of domestic content;

(b) to purchase, use or accord a preference to goods produced in its territory, or to purchase goods from producers in its territory;

(c) to relate in any way the volume or value of imports to the volume or value of exports or to the amount of foreign exchange inflows associated with such investment; or

(d) to restrict sales of goods or services in its territory that such investment produces or provides by relating such sales in any way to the volume or value of its exports or foreign exchange earnings.

4. Nothing in paragraph 3 shall be construed to prevent a Party from conditioning the receipt or continued receipt of an advantage, in connection with an investment in its territory of an investor of a Party or of a non-Party, on compliance with a requirement to locate production, provide a service, train or employ workers, construct or expand particular facilities, or carry out research and development, in its territory.

5. Paragraphs 1 and 3 do not apply to any requirement other than the requirements set out in those paragraphs.

6. Provided that such measures are not applied in an arbitrary or unjustifiable manner, or do not constitute a disguised restriction on international trade or investment, nothing in paragraph 1(b) or (c) or 3(a) or (b) shall be construed to prevent any Party from adopting or maintaining measures, including environmental measures:

(a) necessary to secure compliance with laws and regulations that are not inconsistent with the provisions of this Agreement;

(b) necessary to protect human, animal or plant life or health; or

(c) necessary for the conservation of living or non-living exhaustible natural resources.

Article 1107: Senior Management and Boards of Directors

1. No Party may require that an enterprise of that Party that is an investment of an investor of another Party appoint to senior management positions individuals of any particular nationality.

2. A Party may require that a majority of the board of directors, or any committee thereof, of an enterprise of that Party that is an investment of an investor of another Party, be of a particular nationality, or resident in the territory of the Party, provided that the requirement does not materially impair the ability of the investor to exercise control over its investment.

Article 1108: Reservation and Exceptions

1. Articles 1102, 1103, 1106 and 1107 do not apply to:

(a) any existing non-conforming measure that is maintained by

(i) a Party at the federal level, as set out in its Schedule to Annex I or III,

(ii) a state or province, for two years after the date of entry into force of this Agreement, and thereafter as set out by a Party in its Schedule to Annex I in accordance with paragraph 2, or

(iii) a local government;

(b) the continuation or prompt renewal of non-conforming measure referred to in subparagraph (a); or

(c) an amendment to any non-conforming measure referred to in subparagraph (a) to the extent that the amendment does not decrease the conformity of the measure, as it existed immediately before the amendment, with Articles 1102, 1103, 1106 and 1107.

2. Each Party may set out in its Schedule to Annex I, within two years of the date of entry into force of this Agreement, any existing non-conforming measure maintained by a state or province, not including a local government.

3. Articles 1102, 1103, 1106 and 1107 do not apply to any measure that a Party adopts or maintains with respect to sectors, subsectors or activities, as set out in its Schedule to Annex II.

4. No Party may, under any measure adopted after the date of entry into force of this Agreement and covered by its Schedule to Annex II, require an investor of another Party, by reason of its nationality, to sell or otherwise dispose of an investment existing at the time the measure becomes effective.

5. Articles 1102 and 1103 do not apply to any measure that is an exception to, or derogation from, the obligations under Article 1703 (Intellectual Property—National Treatment) as specifically provided for in that Article.

6. Article 1103 does not apply to treatment accorded by a Party pursuant to agreements, or with respect to sectors, set out in its Schedule to Annex IV.

7. Articles 1102, 1103 and 1107 do not apply to:

(a) procurement by a Party or a State enterprise; or

(b) subsidies or grants provided by a Party or a state enterprise, including government-supported loans, guarantees and insurance.

8. The provisions of:

(a) Article 1106(1)(a), (b) and (c), and (3)(a) and (b) do not apply to qualification requirements for goods or services with respect to export promotion and foreign aid programs;

(b) Article 1106(1)(b), (c) (f) and (g), and 3(a) and (b) do not apply to procurement by a Party or a state enterprise; and

(c) Article 1106(3)(a) and (b) do not apply to requirements imposed by an importing Party relating to the content of goods necessary to qualify for preferential tariffs or preferential quotas.

Article 1109: Transfers

1. Each Party shall permit all transfers relating to an investment of an investor of another Party in the territory of the Party to be made freely and without delay. Such transfers include:

(a) profits, dividends, interest, capital gains, royalty payments, management fees, technical assistance and other fees, returns in kind and other amounts derived from the investment;

(b) proceeds from the sale of all or any part of the investment or from the partial or complete liquidation of the investment;

(c) payments made under a contract entered into by the investor, or its investment, including payments made pursuant to a loan agreement;

(d) payments made pursuant to Article 1110; and

(e) payments arising under Section B.

2. Each Party shall permit transfers to be made in a freely usable currency at the market rate of exchange prevailing on the date of transfer with respect to spot transactions in the currency to be transferred.

3. No Party may require its investors to transfer, or penalize its investors that fail to transfer, the income, earnings, profits or other amounts derived from, or attributable to, investments in the territory of another Party.

4. Notwithstanding paragraphs 1 and 2, a Party may prevent a transfer through the equitable, non-discriminatory and good faith application of its laws relating to:

(a) bankruptcy, insolvency or the protection of the rights of creditors;

(b) issuing, trading or dealing in securities;

(c) criminal or penal offenses;

(d) reports of transfers of currency or other monetary instruments; or

(e) ensuring the satisfaction of judgments in adjudicatory proceedings.

5. Paragraph 3 shall not be construed to prevent a Party from imposing any measure through the equitable, non-discriminatory and good faith application of its laws relating to the matters set out in subparagraphs (a) through (e) of paragraph 4.

6. Notwithstanding paragraph 1, a Party may restrict transfers of returns in kind in circumstances where it could otherwise restrict such transfers under this Agreement, including as set out in paragraph 4.

Article 1110: Expropriation and Compensation

1. No Party may directly or indirectly nationalize or expropriate an investment of an investor of another Party in its territory or take a measure tantamount to nationalization or expropriation of such an investment ("expropriation"), except:

(a) for a public purpose;

(b) on a non-discriminatory basis;

(c) in accordance with due process of law and Article 1105(1); and

(d) on payment of compensation in accordance with paragraphs 2 through 6.

2. Compensation shall be equivalent to the fair market value of the expropriated investment immediately before the expropriation took place ("date of expropriation"), and shall not reflect any change in value occurring because the intended expropriation had become known earlier. Valuation criteria shall include going concern value, asset value including declared tax value of tangible property, and other criteria, as appropriate, to determine fair market value.

3. Compensation shall be paid without delay and be fully realizable.

4. If payment is made in a G7 currency, compensation shall include interest at a commercially reasonable rate for that currency from the date of expropriation until the date of actual payment.

5. If a Party elects to pay in a currency other than a G7 currency, the amount paid on the date of payment, if converted into a G7 currency at the market rate of exchange prevailing on that date, shall be no less than if the amount of compensation owed on the date of expropriation had been converted into that G7 currency at the market rate of exchange prevailing on that date, and interest had accrued at a commercially reasonable rate for that G7 currency from the date of expropriation until the date of payment.

6. On payment, compensation shall be freely transferable as provided in Article 1109.

7. This Article does not apply to the issuance of compulsory licenses granted in relation to intellectual property rights, or to the revocation, limitation or creation of intellectual property rights, to the extent that such issuance, revocation, limitation or creation is consistent with Chapter Seventeen (Intellectual Property).

8. For purposes of this Article and for greater certainty, a non-discriminatory measure of general application shall not be considered a

measure tantamount to an expropriation of a debt security or loan covered by this Chapter solely on the ground that the measure imposes costs on the debtor that cause it to default on the debt.

* * *

Article 1112: Relation to Other Chapters

1. In the event of any inconsistency between this Chapter and another Chapter, the other Chapter shall prevail to the extent of the inconsistency.

2. A requirement by a Party that a service provider of another Party post a bond or other form of financial security as a condition of providing a service into its territory does not of itself make this Chapter applicable to the provision of that cross-border service. This Chapter applies to that Party's treatment of the posted bond or financial security.

Article 1113: Denial of Benefits

1. A Party may deny the benefits of this Chapter to an investor of another Party that is an enterprise of such Party and to investments of such investor if investors of a non-Party own or control the enterprise and the denying Party:

(a) does not maintain diplomatic relations with the non-Party; or

(b) adopts or maintains measures with respect to the non-Party that prohibit transactions with the enterprise or that would be violated or circumvented if the benefits of this Chapter were accorded to the enterprise or to its investments.

* * *

Article 1114: Environmental Measures

1. Nothing in this Chapter shall be construed to prevent a Party from adopting, maintaining or enforcing any measure otherwise consistent with this Chapter that it considers appropriate to ensure that investment activity in its territory is undertaken in a manner sensitive to environmental concerns.

2. The Parties recognize that it is inappropriate to encourage investment by relaxing domestic health, safety or environmental measures. Accordingly, a Party should not waive or otherwise derogate from, or offer to waive or otherwise derogate from, such measures as an encouragement for the establishment, acquisition, expansion or retention in its territory of an investment of an investor. If a Party considers that another Party has offered such an encouragement, it may request consultations with the other Party and the two Parties shall consult with a view to avoiding any such encouragement.

Section B—Settlement of Disputes Between a Party and an Investor of Another Party

Article 1115: Purpose

Without prejudice to the rights and obligations of the Parties under Chapter Twenty (Institutional Arrangements and Dispute Settlement Procedures), this Section establishes a mechanism for the settlement of investment disputes that assures both equal treatment among investors of the Parties in accordance with the principle of international reciprocity and due process before an impartial tribunal.

Article 1116: Claim by an Investor of a Party on Its Own Behalf

1. An investor of a Party may submit to arbitration under this Section a claim that another Party has breached an obligation under:

(a) Section A or Article 1503(2) (State Enterprises), or

(b) Article 1502(3)(a) (Monopolies and State Enterprises) where the monopoly has acted in a manner inconsistent with the Party's obligations under Section A,

and that the investor has incurred loss or damage by reason of, or arising out of, that breach.

* * *

Article 1117: Claim by an Investor of a Party on Behalf of an Enterprise

1. An investor of a Party, on behalf of an enterprise of another Party that is a juridical person that the investor owns or controls directly or indirectly, may submit to arbitration under this Section a claim that the other Party has breached an obligation under:

(a) Section A or Article 1503(2) (State Enterprises), or

(b) Article 1502(3)(a) (Monopolies and State Enterprises) where the monopoly has acted in a manner inconsistent with the Party's obligations under Section A,

and that the enterprise has incurred loss or damage by reason of, or arising out of, that breach.

* * *

Article 1118: Settlement of a Claim through Consultation and Negotiation

The disputing parties should first attempt to settle a claim through consultation or negotiation.

* * *

Article 1120: Submission of a Claim to Arbitration

1. Except as provided in Annex 1120.1, and provided that six months have elapsed since the events giving rise to a claim, a disputing investor may submit the claim to arbitration under:

(a) the ICSID Convention, provided that both the disputing Party and the Party of the investor are parties to the Convention;

(b) the Additional Facility Rules of ICSID, provided that either the disputing Party or the Party of the investor, but not both, is a party to the ICSID Convention; or

(c) the UNCITRAL Arbitration Rules.

* * *

Article 1121: Conditions Precedent to Submission of a Claim to Arbitration

1. A disputing investor may submit a claim under Article 1116 to arbitration only if:

(a) the investor consents to arbitration in accordance with the procedures set out in this Agreement; and

(b) the investor and, where the claim is for loss or damage to an interest in an enterprise of another Party that is a juridical person that the investor owns or controls directly or indirectly, the enterprise, waive their right to initiate or continue before any administrative tribunal or court under the law of any Party, or other dispute settlement procedures, any proceedings with respect to the measure of the disputing Party that is alleged to be a breach referred to in Article 1116, except for proceedings for injunctive, declaratory or other extraordinary relief, not involving the payment of damages, before an administrative tribunal or court under the law of the disputing Party.

2. A disputing investor may submit a claim under Article 1117 to arbitration only if both the investor and the enterprise:

(a) consent to arbitration in accordance with the procedures set out in this Agreement; and

(b) waive their right to initiate or continue before any administrative tribunal or court under the law of any Party, or other dispute settlement procedures, any proceedings with respect to the measure of the disputing Party that is alleged to be a breach referred to in Article 1117, except for proceedings for injunctive, declaratory or other extraordinary relief, not involving the payment of damages, before an administrative tribunal or court under the law of the disputing Party.

* * *

Article 1122: Consent to Arbitration

1. Each Party consents to the submission of a claim to arbitration in accordance with the procedures set out in this Agreement.

* * *

Article 1123: Number of Arbitrators and Method of Appointment

Except in respect of a Tribunal established under Article 1126, and unless the disputing parties otherwise agree, the Tribunal shall comprise three arbitrators, one arbitrator appointed by each of the disputing parties and the third, who shall be the presiding arbitrator, appointed by agreement of the disputing parties.

* * *

Article 1125: Agreement to Appointment of Arbitrators

For purposes of Article 39 of the ICSID Convention and Article 7 of Schedule C to the ICSID Additional Facility Rules, and without prejudice to an objection to an arbitrator based on Article 1124(3) or on a ground other than nationality:

(a) the disputing Party agrees to the appointment of each individual member of a Tribunal established under the ICSID Convention or the ICSID Additional Facility Rules;

(b) a disputing investor referred to in Article 1116 may submit a claim to arbitration, or continue a claim, under the ICSID Convention or the ICSID Additional Facility Rules, only on condition that the disputing investor agrees in writing to the appointment of each individual member of the Tribunal; and

(c) a disputing investor referred to in Article 1117(1) may submit a claim to arbitration, or continue a claim, under the ICSID Convention or the ICSID Additional Facility Rules, only on condition that the disputing investor and the enterprise agree in writing to the appointment of each individual member of the Tribunal.

* * *

Article 1130: Place of Arbitration

Unless the disputing parties agree otherwise, a Tribunal shall hold an arbitration in the territory of a Party that is a party to the New York Convention, selected in accordance with:

(a) the ICSID Additional Facility Rules if the arbitration is under those Rules or the ICSID Convention; or

(b) the UNCITRAL Arbitration Rules if the arbitration is under those Rules.

Article 1131: Governing Law

1. A Tribunal established under this Section shall decide the issues in dispute in accordance with this Agreement and applicable rules of international law.

2. An interpretation by the Commission of a provision of this Agreement shall be binding on a Tribunal established under this Section.

* * *

Article 1135: Final Award

1. Where a Tribunal makes a final award against a Party, the Tribunal may award, separately or in combination, only:

(a) monetary damages and any applicable interest;

(b) restitution of property, in which case the award shall provide that the disputing Party may pay monetary damages and any applicable interest in lieu of restitution.

A tribunal may also award costs in accordance with the applicable arbitration rules.

2. Subject to paragraph 1, where a claim is made under Article 1117(1):

(a) an award of restitution of property shall provide that restitution be made to the enterprise;

(b) an award of monetary damages and any applicable interest shall provide that the sum be paid to the enterprise; and

(c) the award shall provide that it is made without prejudice to any right that any person may have in the relief under applicable domestic law.

3. A Tribunal may not order a Party to pay punitive damages.

Article 1136: Finality and Enforcement of an Award

1. An award made by a Tribunal shall have no binding force except between the disputing parties and in respect of the particular case.

2. Subject to paragraph 3 and the applicable review procedure for an interim award, a disputing party shall abide by and comply with an award without delay.

3. A disputing party may not seek enforcement of a final award until:

(a) in the case of a final award made under the ICSID Convention

(i) 120 days have elapsed from the date the award was rendered and no disputing party has requested revision or annulment of the award, or

(ii) revision or annulment proceedings have been completed; and

(b) in the case of a final award under the ICSID Additional Facility Rules or the UNCITRAL Arbitration Rules

(i) three months have elapsed from the date the award was rendered and no disputing party has commenced a proceeding to revise, set aside or annul the award, or

(ii) a court has dismissed or allowed an application to revise, set aside or annul the award and there is no further appeal.

4. Each Party shall provide for the enforcement of an award in its territory.

5. If a disputing Party fails to abide by or comply with a final award, the Commission, on delivery of a request by a Party whose investor was a party to the arbitration, shall establish a panel under Article 2008 (Request for an Arbitral Panel). The requesting Party may seek in such proceedings:

(a) a determination that the failure to abide by or comply with the final award is inconsistent with the obligations of this Agreement; and

(b) a recommendation that the Party abide by or comply with the final award.

6. A disputing investor may seek enforcement of an arbitration award under the ICSID Convention, the New York Convention or the Inter-American Convention regardless of whether proceedings have been taken under paragraph 5.

7. A claim that is submitted to arbitration under this Section shall be considered to arise out of a commercial relationship or transaction for purposes of Article I of the New York Convention and Article I of the Inter-American Convention.

* * *

Annex 1120.1

Submission of a Claim to Arbitration

Mexico

With respect to the submission of a claim to arbitration:

(a) an investor of another Party may not allege that Mexico has breached an obligation under:

(i) Section A or Article 1503(2) (State Enterprises), or

(ii) Article 1502(3)(a) (Monopolies and State Enterprises) where the monopoly has acted in a manner inconsistent with the Party's obligations under Section A, both in an arbitration under this

Section and in proceedings before a Mexican court or administrative tribunal; and

(b) where an enterprise of Mexico that is a juridical person that an investor of another Party owns or controls directly or indirectly alleges in proceedings before a Mexican court or administrative tribunal that Mexico has breached an obligation under:

(i) Section A or Article 1503(2) (State Enterprises), or

(ii) Article 1502(3)(a) (Monopolies and State Enterprises) where the monopoly has acted in a manner inconsistent with the Party's obligations under Section A, the investor may not allege the breach in an arbitration under this Section.

Annex 1138.2

Exclusions From Dispute Settlement

Canada

A decision by Canada following a review under the Investment Canada Act, with respect to whether or not to permit an acquisition that is subject to review, shall not be subject to the dispute settlement provisions of Section B or of Chapter Twenty (Institutional Arrangements and Dispute Settlement Procedures).

Mexico

A decision by the National Commission on Foreign Investment ("Comision Nacional de Inversiones Extranjeras") following a review pursuant to Annex I, page I-M-4, with respect to whether or not to permit an acquisition that is subject to review, shall not be subject to the dispute settlement provisions of Section B or of Chapter Twenty.

Section C—Definitions

Article 1139

Definitions

For purposes of this Chapter:

disputing investor means an investor that makes a claim under Section B;

disputing parties means the disputing investor and the disputing Party;

disputing party means the disputing investor or the disputing Party;

disputing Party means a Party against which a claim is made under Section B;

enterprise means an "enterprise" as defined in Article 201 (Definitions of General Application), and a branch of an enterprise;

enterprise of a Party means an enterprise constituted or organized under the law of a Party, and a branch located in the territory of a Party and carrying out business activities there.

equity or debt securities includes voting and non-voting shares, bonds, convertible debentures, stock options and warrants;

G7 Currency means the currency of Canada, France, Germany, Italy, Japan, the United Kingdom of Great Britain and Northern Ireland or the United States;

ICSID means the International Centre for Settlement of Investment Disputes;

ICSID Convention means the Convention on the Settlement of Investment Disputes between States and Nationals of other States, done at Washington, March 18, 1965;

Inter-American Convention means the Inter-American Convention on International Commercial Arbitration, done at Panama, January 30, 1975;

investment means: (a) an enterprise; (b) an equity security of an enterprise; (c) a debt security of an enterprise (i) where the enterprise is an affiliate of the investor, or (ii) where the original maturity of the debt security is at least three years, but does not include a debt security, regardless of original maturity, of a state enterprise; (d) a loan to an enterprise (i) where the enterprise is an affiliate of the investor, or (ii) where the original maturity of the loan is at least three years, but does not include a loan, regardless of original maturity, to a state enterprise; (e) an interest in an enterprise that entitles the owner to share in income or profits of the enterprise; (f) an interest in an enterprise that entitles the owner to share in the assets of that enterprise on dissolution, other than a debt security or a loan excluded from subparagraph (c) or (d); (g) real estate or other property, tangible or intangible, acquired in the expectation or used for the purpose of economic benefit or other business purposes; and (h) interests arising from the commitment of capital or other resources in the territory of a Party to economic activity in such territory, such as under (i) contracts involving the presence of an investor's property in the territory of the Party, including turnkey or construction contracts, or concessions, or (ii) contracts where remuneration depends substantially on the production, revenues or profits of an enterprise; but investment does not mean, (i) claims to money that arise solely from (i) commercial contracts for the sale of goods or services by a national or enterprise in the territory of a Party to an enterprise in the territory of another Party, or (ii) the extension of credit in connection with a commercial transaction, such as trade financing, other than a loan covered by subparagraph (d); or (j) any other claims to money, that do not involve the kinds of interests set out in subparagraphs (a) through (h);

investment of an investor of a Party means an investment owned or controlled directly or indirectly by an investor of such Party;

investor of a Party means a Party or state enterprise thereof, or a national or an enterprise of such Party, that seeks to make, is making or has made an investment;

investor of a non-Party means an investor other than an investor of a Party, that seeks to make, is making or has made an investment;

New York Convention means the United Nations Convention on the Recognition and Enforcement of Foreign Arbitral Awards, done at New York, June 10, 1958;

Secretary-General means the Secretary-General of ICSID;

transfers means transfers and international payments;

Tribunal means an arbitration tribunal established under Article 1120 or 1126; and

UNCITRAL Arbitration Rules means the arbitration rules of the United Nations Commission on International Trade Law, approved by the United Nations General Assembly on December 15, 1976.

Chapter Twelve

Cross-Border Trade in Services

* * *

PART SIX
INTELLECTUAL PROPERTY

Chapter Seventeen

Intellectual Property

Article 1701: Nature and Scope of Obligations

1. Each Party shall provide in its territory to the nationals of another Party adequate and effective protection and enforcement of intellectual property rights, while ensuring that measures to enforce intellectual property rights do not themselves become barriers to legitimate trade.

2. To provide adequate and effective protection and enforcement of intellectual property rights, each Party shall, at a minimum, give effect to this Chapter and to the substantive provisions of:

(a) the *Geneva Convention for the Protection of Producers of Phonograms Against Unauthorized Duplication of their Phonograms,* 1971 (Geneva Convention);

(b) the *Berne Convention for the Protection of Literary and Artistic Works,* 1971 (Berne Convention);

(c) the *Paris Convention for the Protection of Industrial Property,* 1967 (Paris Convention); and

(d) the *International Convention for the Protection of New Varieties of Plants,* 1978 (UPOV Convention), or the *International Convention for the Protection of New Varieties of Plants,* 1991 (UPOV Convention).

If a Party has not acceded to the specified text of any such Conventions on or before the date of entry into force of this Agreement, it shall make every effort to accede.

* * *

Article 1702: More Extensive Protection

A Party may implement in its domestic law more extensive protection of intellectual property rights than is required under this Agreement, provided that such protection is not inconsistent with this Agreement.

Article 1703: National Treatment

1. Each Party shall accord to nationals of another Party treatment no less favorable than that it accords to its own nationals with regard to the protection and enforcement of all intellectual property rights. In respect of sound recordings, each Party shall provide such treatment to producers and performers of another Party, except that a Party may limit rights of performers of another Party in respect of secondary uses of sound recordings to those rights its nationals are accorded in the territory of such other Party.

2. No Party may, as a condition of according national treatment under this Article, require right holders to comply with any formalities or conditions in order to acquire rights in respect of copyright and related rights.

3. A Party may derogate from paragraph 1 in relation to its judicial and administrative procedures for the protection or enforcement of intellectual property rights, including any procedure requiring a national of another Party to designate for service of process an address in the Party's territory or to appoint an agent in the Party's territory, if the derogation is consistent with the relevant Convention listed in Article 1701(2), provided that such derogation:

(a) is necessary to secure compliance with measures that are not inconsistent with this Chapter; and

(b) is not applied in a manner that would constitute a disguised restriction on trade.

4. No Party shall have any obligation under this Article with respect to procedures provided in multilateral agreements concluded under the auspices of the World Intellectual Property Organization relating to the acquisition or maintenance of intellectual property rights.

Article 1704: Control of Abusive or Anticompetitive Practices or Conditions

Nothing in this Chapter shall prevent a Party from specifying in its domestic law licensing practices or conditions that may in particular cases constitute an abuse of intellectual property rights having an adverse effect on competition in the relevant market. A Party may adopt or maintain, consistent with the other provisions of this Agreement, appropriate measures to prevent or control such practices or conditions.

Article 1705: Copyright

1. Each Party shall protect the works covered by Article 2 of the Berne Convention, including any other works that embody original expression within the meaning of that Convention. In particular:

(a) all types of computer programs are literary works within the meaning of the Berne Convention and each Party shall protect them as such; and

(b) compilations of data or other material, whether in machine readable or other form, which by reason of the selection or arrangement of their contents constitute intellectual creations, shall be protected as such.

The protection a Party provides under subparagraph (b) shall not extend to the data or material itself, or prejudice any copyright subsisting in that data or material.

2. Each Party shall provide to authors and their successors in interest those rights enumerated in the Berne Convention in respect of works covered by paragraph 1, including the right to authorize or prohibit:

(a) the importation into the Party's territory of copies of the work made without the right holder's authorization;

(b) the first public distribution of the original and each copy of the work by sale, rental or otherwise;

(c) the communication of a work to the public; and

(d) the commercial rental of the original or a copy of a computer program.

Subparagraph (d) shall not apply where the copy of the computer program is not itself an essential object of the rental. Each Party shall provide that putting the original or a copy of a computer program on the market with the right holder's consent shall not exhaust the rental right.

3. Each Party shall provide that for copyright and related rights:

(a) any person acquiring or holding economic rights may freely and separately transfer such rights by contract for purposes of their exploitation and enjoyment by the transferee; and

(b) any person acquiring or holding such economic rights by virtue of a contract, including contracts of employment underlying the creation of works and sound recordings, shall be able to exercise those rights in its own name and enjoy fully the benefits derived from those rights.

4. Each Party shall provide that, where the term of protection of a work, other than a photographic work or a work of applied art, is to be calculated on a basis other than the life of a natural person, the term shall be not less than 50 years from the end of the calendar year of the first authorized publication of the work or, failing such authorized publication within 50 years from the making of the work, 50 years from the end of the calendar year of making.

5. Each Party shall confine limitations or exceptions to the rights provided for in this Article to certain special cases that do not conflict with a normal exploitation of the work and do not unreasonably prejudice the legitimate interests of the right holder.

6. No Party may grant translation and reproduction licenses permitted under the Appendix to the Berne Convention where legitimate needs in that Party's territory for copies or translations of the work could be met by the right holder's voluntary actions but for obstacles created by the Party's measures.

* * *

Article 1708: Trademarks

1. For purposes of this Agreement, a trademark consists of any sign, or any combination of signs, capable of distinguishing the goods or services of one person from those of another, including personal names, designs, letters, numerals, colors, figurative elements, or the shape of goods or of their packaging. Trademarks shall include service marks and collective marks, and may include certification marks. A Party may require, as a condition for registration, that a sign be visually perceptible.

2. Each Party shall provide to the owner of a registered trademark the right to prevent all persons not having the owner's consent from using in commerce identical or similar signs for goods or services that are identical or similar to those goods or services in respect of which the owner's trademark is registered, where such use would result in a likelihood of confusion. In the case of the use of an identical sign for identical goods or services, a likelihood of confusion shall be presumed. The rights described above shall not prejudice any prior rights, nor shall they affect the possibility of a Party making rights available on the basis of use.

3. A Party may make registrability depend on use. However, actual use of a trademark shall not be a condition for filing an application for registration. No Party may refuse an application solely on the ground that

intended use has not taken place before the expiry of a period of three years from the date of application for registration.

4. Each Party shall provide a system for the registration of trademarks, which shall include:

(a) examination of applications;

(b) notice to be given to an applicant of the reasons for the refusal to register a trademark;

(c) a reasonable opportunity for the applicant to respond to the notice;

(d) publication of each trademark either before or promptly after it is registered; and

(e) a reasonable opportunity for interested persons to petition to cancel the registration of a trademark.

A Party may provide for a reasonable opportunity for interested persons to oppose the registration of a trademark.

5. The nature of the goods or services to which a trademark is to be applied shall in no case form an obstacle to the registration of the trademark.

6. Article 6bis of the Paris Convention shall apply, with such modifications as may be necessary, to services. In determining whether a trademark is well-known, account shall be taken of the knowledge of the trademark in the relevant sector of the public, including knowledge in the Party's territory obtained as a result of the promotion of the trademark. No Party may require that the reputation of the trademark extend beyond the sector of the public that normally deals with the relevant goods or services.

7. Each Party shall provide that the initial registration of a trademark be for a term of at least 10 years and that the registration be indefinitely renewable for terms of not less than 10 years when conditions for renewal have been met.

8. Each Party shall require the use of a trademark to maintain a registration. The registration may be canceled for the reason of non-use only after an uninterrupted period of at least two years of non-use, unless valid reasons based on the existence of obstacles to such use are shown by the trademark owner. Each Party shall recognize, as valid reasons for non-use, circumstances arising independently of the will of the trademark owner that constitute an obstacle to the use of the trademark, such as import restrictions on, or other government requirements for, goods or services identified by the trademark.

9. Each Party shall recognize use of a trademark by a person other than the trademark owner, where such use is subject to the owner's control, as use of the trademark for purposes of maintaining the registration.

10. No Party may encumber the use of a trademark in commerce by special requirements, such as a use that reduces the trademark's function as an indication of source or a use with another trademark.

11. A Party may determine conditions on the licensing and assignment of trademarks, it being understood that the compulsory licensing of trademarks shall not be permitted and that the owner of a registered trademark shall have the right to assign its trademark with or without the transfer of the business to which the trademark belongs.

12. A Party may provide limited exceptions to the rights conferred by a trademark, such as fair use of descriptive terms, provided that such exceptions take into account the legitimate interests of the trademark owner and of other persons.

13. Each Party shall prohibit the registration as a trademark of words, at least in English, French or Spanish, that generically designate goods or services or types of goods or services to which the trademark applies.

14. Each Party shall refuse to register trademarks that consist of or comprise immoral, deceptive or scandalous matter, or matter that may disparage or falsely suggest a connection with persons, living or dead, institutions, beliefs or any Party's national symbols, or bring them into contempt or disrepute.

Article 1709: Patents

1. Subject to paragraphs 2 and 3, each Party shall make patents available for any inventions, whether products or processes, in all fields of technology, provided that such inventions are new, result from an inventive step and are capable of industrial application. For purposes of this Article, a Party may deem the terms "inventive step" and "capable of industrial application" to be synonymous with the terms "non-obvious" and "useful", respectively.

2. A Party may exclude from patentability inventions if preventing in its territory the commercial exploitation of the inventions is necessary to protect *ordre public* or morality, including to protect human, animal or plant life or health or to avoid serious prejudice to nature or the environment, provided that the exclusion is not based solely on the ground that the Party prohibits commercial exploitation in its territory of the subject matter of the patent.

3. A Party may also exclude from patentability:

(a) diagnostic, therapeutic and surgical methods for the treatment of humans or animals;

(b) plants and animals other than microorganisms; and

(c) essentially biological processes for the production of plants or animals, other than non-biological and microbiological processes for such production.

Notwithstanding subparagraph (b), each Party shall provide for the protection of plant varieties through patents, an effective scheme of *sui generis* protection, or both.

4. If a Party has not made available product patent protection for pharmaceutical or agricultural chemicals commensurate with paragraph 1:

(a) as of January 1, 1992, for subject matter that relates to naturally occurring substances prepared or produced by, or significantly derived from, microbiological processes and intended for food or medicine, and

(b) as of July 1, 1991, for any other subject matter,

that Party shall provide to the inventor of any such product or its assignee the means to obtain product patent protection for such product for the unexpired term of the patent for such product granted in another Party, as long as the product has not been marketed in the Party providing protection under this paragraph and the person seeking such protection makes a timely request.

5. Each Party shall provide that:

(a) where the subject matter of a patent is a product, the patent shall confer on the patent owner the right to prevent other persons from making, using or selling the subject matter of the patent, without the patent owner's consent; and

(b) where the subject matter of a patent is a process, the patent shall confer on the patent owner the right to prevent other persons from using that process and from using, selling, or importing at least the product obtained directly by that process, without the patent owner's consent.

6. A Party may provide limited exceptions to the exclusive rights conferred by a patent, provided that such exceptions do not unreasonably conflict with a normal exploitation of the patent and do not unreasonably prejudice the legitimate interests of the patent owner, taking into account the legitimate interests of other persons.

7. Subject to paragraphs 2 and 3, patents shall be available and patent rights enjoyable without discrimination as to the field of technology, the territory of the Party where the invention was made and whether products are imported or locally produced.

8. A Party may revoke a patent only when:

(a) grounds exist that would have justified a refusal to grant the patent; or

(b) the grant of a compulsory license has not remedied the lack of exploitation of the patent.

9. Each Party shall permit patent owners to assign and transfer by succession their patents, and to conclude licensing contracts.

10. Where the law of a Party allows for use of the subject matter of a patent, other than that use allowed under paragraph 6, without the authorization of the right holder, including use by the government or other persons authorized by the government, the Party shall respect the following provisions:

(a) authorization of such use shall be considered on its individual merits;

(b) such use may only be permitted if, prior to such use, the proposed user has made efforts to obtain authorization from the right holder on reasonable commercial terms and conditions and such efforts have not been successful within a reasonable period of time. The requirement to make such efforts may be waived by a Party in the case of a national emergency or other circumstances of extreme urgency or in cases of public non-commercial use. In situations of national emergency or other circumstances of extreme urgency, the right holder shall, nevertheless, be notified as soon as reasonably practicable. In the case of public non-commercial use, where the government or contractor, without making a patent search, knows or has demonstrable grounds to know that a valid patent is or will be used by or for the government, the right holder shall be informed promptly;

(c) the scope and duration of such use shall be limited to the purpose for which it was authorized;

(d) such use shall be non-exclusive;

(e) such use shall be non-assignable, except with that part of the enterprise or goodwill that enjoys such use;

(f) any such use shall be authorized predominantly for the supply of the Party's domestic market;

(g) authorization for such use shall be liable, subject to adequate protection of the legitimate interests of the persons so authorized, to be terminated if and when the circumstances that led to it cease to exist and are unlikely to recur. The competent authority shall have the authority to review, on motivated request, the continued existence of these circumstances;

(h) the right holder shall be paid adequate remuneration in the circumstances of each case, taking into account the economic value of the authorization;

(i) the legal validity of any decision relating to the authorization shall be subject to judicial or other independent review by a distinct higher authority;

(j) any decision relating to the remuneration provided in respect of such use shall be subject to judicial or other independent review by a distinct higher authority;

(k) the Party shall not be obliged to apply the conditions set out in subparagraphs (b) and (f) where such use is permitted to remedy a practice determined after judicial or administrative process to be anticompetitive. The need to correct anticompetitive practices may be taken into account in determining the amount of remuneration in such cases. Competent authorities shall have the authority to refuse termination of authorization if and when the conditions that led to such authorization are likely to recur;

(*l*) the Party shall not authorize the use of the subject matter of a patent to permit the exploitation of another patent except as a remedy for an adjudicated violation of domestic laws regarding anticompetitive practices.

11. Where the subject matter of a patent is a process for obtaining a product, each Party shall, in any infringement proceeding, place on the defendant the burden of establishing that the allegedly infringing product was made by a process other than the patented process in one of the following situations:

(a) the product obtained by the patented process is new; or

(b) a substantial likelihood exists that the allegedly infringing product was made by the process and the patent owner has been unable through reasonable efforts to determine the process actually used.

In the gathering and evaluation of evidence, the legitimate interests of the defendant in protecting its trade secrets shall be taken into account.

12. Each Party shall provide a term of protection for patents of at least 20 years from the date of filing or 17 years from the date of grant. A Party may extend the term of patent protection, in appropriate cases, to compensate for delays caused by regulatory approval processes.

* * *

Article 1711: Trade Secrets

1. Each Party shall provide the legal means for any person to prevent trade secrets from being disclosed to, acquired by, or used by others without the consent of the person lawfully in control of the information in a manner contrary to honest commercial practices, in so far as:

(a) the information is secret in the sense that it is not, as a body or in the precise configuration and assembly of its components, generally known among or readily accessible to persons that normally deal with the kind of information in question;

(b) the information has actual or potential commercial value because it is secret; and

(c) the person lawfully in control of the information has taken reasonable steps under the circumstances to keep it secret.

2. A Party may require that to qualify for protection a trade secret must be evidenced in documents, electronic or magnetic means, optical discs, microfilms, films or other similar instruments.

3. No Party may limit the duration of protection for trade secrets, so long as the conditions in paragraph 1 exist.

4. No Party may discourage or impede the voluntary licensing of trade secrets by imposing excessive or discriminatory conditions on such licenses or conditions that dilute the value of the trade secrets.

5. If a Party requires, as a condition for approving the marketing of pharmaceutical or agricultural chemical products that utilize new chemical entities, the submission of undisclosed test or other data necessary to determine whether the use of such products is safe and effective, the Party shall protect against disclosure of the data of persons making such submissions, where the origination of such data involves considerable effort, except where the disclosure is necessary to protect the public or unless steps are taken to ensure that the data is protected against unfair commercial use.

6. Each Party shall provide that for data subject to paragraph 5 that are submitted to the Party after the date of entry into force of this Agreement, no person other than the person that submitted them may, without the latter's permission, rely on such data in support of an application for product approval during a reasonable period of time after their submission. For this purpose, a reasonable period shall normally mean not less than five years from the date on which the Party granted approval to the person that produced the data for approval to market its product, taking account of the nature of the data and the person's efforts and expenditures in producing them. Subject to this provision, there shall be no limitation on any Party to implement abbreviated approval procedures for such products on the basis of bioequivalence and bioavailability studies.

7. Where a Party relies on a marketing approval granted by another Party, the reasonable period of exclusive use of the data submitted in connection with obtaining the approval relied on shall begin with the date of the first marketing approval relied on.

* * *

Article 1714: Enforcement of Intellectual Property Rights: General Provisions

1. Each Party shall ensure that enforcement procedures, as specified in this Article and Articles 1715 through 1718, are available under its domestic law so as to permit effective action to be taken against any act of infringement of intellectual property rights covered by this Chapter, including expeditious remedies to prevent infringements and remedies to deter further infringements. Such enforcement procedures shall be applied so as to avoid the creation of barriers to legitimate trade and to provide for safeguards against abuse of the procedures.

2. Each Party shall ensure that its procedures for the enforcement of intellectual property rights are fair and equitable, are not unnecessarily complicated or costly, and do not entail unreasonable time limits or unwarranted delays.

3. Each Party shall provide that decisions on the merits of a case in judicial and administrative enforcement proceedings shall:

(a) preferably be in writing and preferably state the reasons on which the decisions are based;

(b) be made available at least to the parties in a proceeding without undue delay; and

(c) be based only on evidence in respect of which such parties were offered the opportunity to be heard.

4. Each Party shall ensure that parties in a proceeding have an opportunity to have final administrative decisions reviewed by a judicial authority of that Party and, subject to jurisdictional provisions in its domestic laws concerning the importance of a case, to have reviewed at least the legal aspects of initial judicial decisions on the merits of a case. Notwithstanding the above, no Party shall be required to provide for judicial review of acquittals in criminal cases.

* * *

Article 1715: Specific Procedural and Remedial Aspects of Civil and Administrative Procedures

1. Each Party shall make available to right holders civil judicial procedures for the enforcement of any intellectual property right provided in this Chapter. Each Party shall provide that:

(a) defendants have the right to written notice that is timely and contains sufficient detail, including the basis of the claims;

(b) parties in a proceeding are allowed to be represented by independent legal counsel;

(c) the procedures do not include imposition of overly burdensome requirements concerning mandatory personal appearances;

(d) all parties in a proceeding are duly entitled to substantiate their claims and to present relevant evidence; and

(e) the procedures include a means to identify and protect confidential information.

2. Each Party shall provide that its judicial authorities shall have the authority:

(a) where a party in a proceeding has presented reasonably available evidence sufficient to support its claims and has specified evidence relevant to the substantiation of its claims that is within the control of the opposing party, to order the opposing party to produce such evidence, subject in appropriate cases to conditions that ensure the protection of confidential information;

(b) where a party in a proceeding voluntarily and without good reason refuses access to, or otherwise does not provide relevant evidence under that party's control within a reasonable period, or significantly impedes a proceeding relating to an enforcement action, to make preliminary and final determinations, affirmative or negative, on the basis of the evidence presented, including the complaint or the allegation presented by the party adversely affected by the denial of access to evidence, subject to providing the parties an opportunity to be heard on the allegations or evidence;

(c) to order a party in a proceeding to desist from an infringement, including to prevent the entry into the channels of commerce in their jurisdiction of imported goods that involve the infringement of an intellectual property right, which order shall be enforceable at least immediately after customs clearance of such goods;

(d) to order the infringer of an intellectual property right to pay the right holder damages adequate to compensate for the injury the right holder has suffered because of the infringement where the infringer knew or had reasonable grounds to know that it was engaged in an infringing activity;

(e) to order an infringer of an intellectual property right to pay the right holder's expenses, which may include appropriate attorney's fees; and

(f) to order a party in a proceeding at whose request measures were taken and who has abused enforcement procedures to provide adequate compensation to any party wrongfully enjoined or restrained in the proceeding for the injury suffered because of such abuse and to pay that party's expenses, which may include appropriate attorney's fees.

3. With respect to the authority referred to in subparagraph 2(c), no Party shall be obliged to provide such authority in respect of protected subject matter that is acquired or ordered by a person before that person

knew or had reasonable grounds to know that dealing in that subject matter would entail the infringement of an intellectual property right.

4. With respect to the authority referred to in subparagraph 2(d), a Party may, at least with respect to copyrighted works and sound recordings, authorize the judicial authorities to order recovery of profits or payment of pre-established damages, or both, even where the infringer did not know or had no reasonable grounds to know that it was engaged in an infringing activity.

5. Each Party shall provide that, in order to create an effective deterrent to infringement, its judicial authorities shall have the authority to order that:

(a) goods that they have found to be infringing be, without compensation of any sort, disposed of outside the channels of commerce in such a manner as to avoid any injury caused to the right holder or, unless this would be contrary to existing constitutional requirements, destroyed; and

(b) materials and implements the predominant use of which has been in the creation of the infringing goods be, without compensation of any sort, disposed of outside the channels of commerce in such a manner as to minimize the risks of further infringements.

In considering whether to issue such an order, judicial authorities shall take into account the need for proportionality between the seriousness of the infringement and the remedies ordered as well as the interests of other persons. In regard to counterfeit goods, the simple removal of the trademark unlawfully affixed shall not be sufficient, other than in exceptional cases, to permit release of the goods into the channels of commerce.

6. In respect of the administration of any law pertaining to the protection or enforcement of intellectual property rights, each Party shall only exempt both public authorities and officials from liability to appropriate remedial measures where actions are taken or intended in good faith in the course of the administration of such laws.

7. Notwithstanding the other provisions of Articles 1714 through 1718, where a Party is sued with respect to an infringement of an intellectual property right as a result of its use of that right or use on its behalf, that Party may limit the remedies available against it to the payment to the right holder of adequate remuneration in the circumstances of each case, taking into account the economic value of the use.

8. Each Party shall provide that, where a civil remedy can be ordered as a result of administrative procedures on the merits of a case, such procedures shall conform to principles equivalent in substance to those set out in this Article.

Article 1716: Provisional Measures

1. Each Party shall provide that its judicial authorities shall have the authority to order prompt and effective provisional measures:

(a) to prevent an infringement of any intellectual property right, and in particular to prevent the entry into the channels of commerce in their jurisdiction of allegedly infringing goods, including measures to prevent the entry of imported goods at least immediately after customs clearance; and

(b) to preserve relevant evidence in regard to the alleged infringement.

2. Each Party shall provide that its judicial authorities shall have the authority to require any applicant for provisional measures to provide to the judicial authorities any evidence reasonably available to that applicant that the judicial authorities consider necessary to enable them to determine with a sufficient degree of certainty whether:

(a) the applicant is the right holder;

(b) the applicant's right is being infringed or such infringement is imminent; and

(c) any delay in the issuance of such measures is likely to cause irreparable harm to the right holder, or there is a demonstrable risk of evidence being destroyed.

Each Party shall provide that its judicial authorities shall have the authority to require the applicant to provide a security or equivalent assurance sufficient to protect the interests of the defendant and to prevent abuse.

3. Each Party shall provide that its judicial authorities shall have the authority to require an applicant for provisional measures to provide other information necessary for the identification of the relevant goods by the authority that will execute the provisional measures.

4. Each Party shall provide that its judicial authorities shall have the authority to order provisional measures on an *ex parte* basis, in particular where any delay is likely to cause irreparable harm to the right holder, or where there is a demonstrable risk of evidence being destroyed.

5. Each Party shall provide that where provisional measures are adopted by that Party's judicial authorities on an *ex parte* basis:

(a) a person affected shall be given notice of those measures without delay but in any event no later than immediately after the execution of the measures;

(b) a defendant shall, on request, have those measures reviewed by that Party's judicial authorities for the purpose of deciding, within a reasonable period after notice of those measures is given, whether the measures shall be modified, revoked or confirmed, and shall be given an opportunity to be heard in the review proceedings.

6. Without prejudice to paragraph 5, each Party shall provide that, on the request of the defendant, the Party's judicial authorities shall revoke or otherwise cease to apply the provisional measures taken on the basis of paragraphs 1 and 4 if proceedings leading to a decision on the merits are not initiated:

(a) within a reasonable period as determined by the judicial authority ordering the measures where the Party's domestic law so permits; or

(b) in the absence of such a determination, within a period of no more than 20 working days or 31 calendar days, whichever is longer.

7. Each Party shall provide that, where the provisional measures are revoked or where they lapse due to any act or omission by the applicant, or where the judicial authorities subsequently find that there has been no infringement or threat of infringement of an intellectual property right, the judicial authorities shall have the authority to order the applicant, on request of the defendant, to provide the defendant appropriate compensation for any injury caused by these measures.

8. Each Party shall provide that, where a provisional measure can be ordered as a result of administrative procedures, such procedures shall conform to principles equivalent in substance to those set out in this Article.

Article 1717: Criminal Procedures and Penalties

1. Each Party shall provide criminal procedures and penalties to be applied at least in cases of willful trademark counterfeiting or copyright piracy on a commercial scale. Each Party shall provide that penalties available include imprisonment or monetary fines, or both, sufficient to provide a deterrent, consistent with the level of penalties applied for crimes of a corresponding gravity.

2. Each Party shall provide that, in appropriate cases, its judicial authorities may order the seizure, forfeiture and destruction of infringing goods and of any materials and implements the predominant use of which has been in the commission of the offense.

3. A Party may provide criminal procedures and penalties to be applied in cases of infringement of intellectual property rights, other than those in paragraph 1, where they are committed wilfully and on a commercial scale.

Article 1718: Enforcement of Intellectual Property Rights at the Border

1. Each Party shall, in conformity with this Article, adopt procedures to enable a right holder, who has valid grounds for suspecting that the importation of counterfeit trademark goods or pirated copyright goods may

take place, to lodge an application in writing with its competent authorities, whether administrative or judicial, for the suspension by the customs administration of the release of such goods into free circulation. No Party shall be obligated to apply such procedures to goods in transit. A Party may permit such an application to be made in respect of goods that involve other infringements of intellectual property rights, provided that the requirements of this Article are met. A Party may also provide for corresponding procedures concerning the suspension by the customs administration of the release of infringing goods destined for exportation from its territory.

2. Each Party shall require any applicant who initiates procedures under paragraph 1 to provide adequate evidence:

(a) to satisfy that Party's competent authorities that, under the domestic laws of the country of importation, there is *prima facie* an infringement of its intellectual property right; and

(b) to supply a sufficiently detailed description of the goods to make them readily recognizable by the customs administration.

The competent authorities shall inform the applicant within a reasonable period whether they have accepted the application and, if so, the period for which the customs administration will take action.

3. Each Party shall provide that its competent authorities shall have the authority to require an applicant under paragraph 1 to provide a security or equivalent assurance sufficient to protect the defendant and the competent authorities and to prevent abuse. Such security or equivalent assurance shall not unreasonably deter recourse to these procedures.

4. Each Party shall provide that, where pursuant to an application under procedures adopted pursuant to this Article, its customs administration suspends the release of goods involving industrial designs, patents, integrated circuits or trade secrets into free circulation on the basis of a decision other than by a judicial or other independent authority, and the period provided for in paragraphs 6 through 8 has expired without the granting of provisional relief by the duly empowered authority, and provided that all other conditions for importation have been complied with, the owner, importer or consignee of such goods shall be entitled to their release on the posting of a security in an amount sufficient to protect the right holder against any infringement. Payment of such security shall not prejudice any other remedy available to the right holder, it being understood that the security shall be released if the right holder fails to pursue its right of action within a reasonable period of time.

5. Each Party shall provide that its customs administration shall promptly notify the importer and the applicant when the customs administration suspends the release of goods pursuant to paragraph 1.

6. Each Party shall provide that its customs administration shall release goods from suspension if, within a period not exceeding 10 working days after the applicant under paragraph 1 has been served notice of the suspension, the customs administration has not been informed that:

(a) a party other than the defendant has initiated proceedings leading to a decision on the merits of the case, or

(b) a competent authority has taken provisional measures prolonging the suspension,

provided that all other conditions for importation or exportation have been met. Each Party shall provide that, in appropriate cases, the customs administration may extend the suspension by another 10 working days.

7. Each Party shall provide that if proceedings leading to a decision on the merits of the case have been initiated, a review, including a right to be heard, shall take place on request of the defendant with a view to deciding, within a reasonable period, whether these measures shall be modified, revoked or confirmed.

8. Notwithstanding paragraphs 6 and 7, where the suspension of the release of goods is carried out or continued in accordance with a provisional judicial measure, Article 1716(6) shall apply.

9. Each Party shall provide that its competent authorities shall have the authority to order the applicant under paragraph 1 to pay the importer, the consignee and the owner of the goods appropriate compensation for any injury caused to them through the wrongful detention of goods or through the detention of goods released pursuant to paragraph 6.

10. Without prejudice to the protection of confidential information, each Party shall provide that its competent authorities shall have the authority to give the right holder sufficient opportunity to have any goods detained by the customs administration inspected in order to substantiate the right holder's claims. Each Party shall also provide that its competent authorities have the authority to give the importer an equivalent opportunity to have any such goods inspected. Where the competent authorities have made a positive determination on the merits of a case, a Party may provide the competent authorities the authority to inform the right holder of the names and addresses of the consignor, the importer and the consignee, and of the quantity of the goods in question.

11. Where a Party requires its competent authorities to act on their own initiative and to suspend the release of goods in respect of which they have acquired *prima facie* evidence that an intellectual property right is being infringed:

(a) the competent authorities may at any time seek from the right holder any information that may assist them to exercise these powers;

(b) the importer and the right holder shall be promptly notified of the suspension by the Party's competent authorities, and where the importer lodges an appeal against the suspension with competent authorities, the suspension shall be subject to the conditions, with such modifications as may be necessary, set out in paragraphs 6 through 8; and

(c) the Party shall only exempt both public authorities and officials from liability to appropriate remedial measures where actions are taken or intended in good faith.

12. Without prejudice to other rights of action open to the right holder and subject to the defendant's right to seek judicial review, each Party shall provide that its competent authorities shall have the authority to order the destruction or disposal of infringing goods in accordance with the principles set out in Article 1715(5). In regard to counterfeit goods, the authorities shall not allow the re-exportation of the infringing goods in an unaltered state or subject them to a different customs procedure, other than in exceptional circumstances.

13. A Party may exclude from the application of paragraphs 1 through 12 small quantities of goods of a non-commercial nature contained in travellers' personal luggage or sent in small consignments that are not repetitive.

14. Annex 1718.14 applies to the Parties specified in that Annex.

* * *

Article 1721: Definitions

1. For purposes of this Chapter:

confidential information includes trade secrets, privileged information and other materials exempted from disclosure under the Party's domestic law.

2. For purposes of this Agreement:

encrypted program-carrying satellite signal means a program-carrying satellite signal that is transmitted in a form whereby the aural or visual characteristics, or both, are modified or altered for the purpose of preventing the unauthorized reception, by persons without the authorized equipment that is designed to eliminate the effects of such modification or alteration, of a program carried in that signal;

geographical indication means any indication that identifies a good as originating in the territory of a Party, or a region or locality in that territory, where a particular quality, reputation or other characteristic of the good is essentially attributable to its geographical origin;

in a manner contrary to honest commercial practices means at least practices such as breach of contract, breach of confidence and inducement to breach, and includes the acquisition of undisclosed information by other persons who knew, or were grossly negligent in failing to know, that such practices were involved in the acquisition;

intellectual property rights refers to copyright and related rights, trademark rights, patent rights, rights in layout designs of semiconductor integrated circuits, trade secret rights, plant breeders' rights, rights in geographical indications and industrial design rights;

nationals of another Party means, in respect of the relevant intellectual property right, persons who would meet the criteria for eligibility for protection provided for in the Paris Convention (1967), the Berne Convention (1971), the Geneva Convention (1971), the International Convention for the Protection of Performers, Producers of Phonograms and Broadcasting Organizations (1961), the UPOV Convention (1978), the UPOV Convention (1991) or the *Treaty on Intellectual Property in Respect of Integrated Circuits*, as if each Party were a party to those Conventions, and with respect to intellectual property rights that are not the subject of these Conventions, "nationals of another Party" shall be understood to be at least individuals who are citizens or permanent residents of that Party and also includes any other natural person referred to in Annex 201.1 (Country-Specific Definitions);

public includes, with respect to rights of communication and performance of works provided for under Articles 11, 11*bis* (1) and 14(1)(ii) of the Berne Convention, with respect to dramatic, dramatico-musical, musical and cinematographic works, at least, any aggregation of individuals intended to be the object of, and capable of perceiving, communications or performances of works, regardless of whether they can do so at the same or different times or in the same or different places, provided that such an aggregation is larger than a family and its immediate circle of acquaintances or is not a group comprising a limited number of individuals having similarly close ties that has not been formed for the principal purpose of receiving such performances and communications of works; and

secondary uses of sound recordings means the use directly for broadcasting or for any other public communication of a sound recording.

* * *

PART SEVEN

ADMINISTRATIVE AND INSTITUTIONAL PROVISIONS

Chapter Nineteen

Review and Dispute Settlement in Antidumping and Countervailing Duty Matters

Article 1901: General Provisions

1. Article 1904 applies only with respect to goods that the competent investigating authority of the importing Party, applying the importing Party's antidumping or countervailing duty law to the facts of a specific case, determines are goods of another Party.

2. For purposes of Articles 1903 and 1904, panels shall be established in accordance with Annex 1901.2.

3. Except for Article 2203 (Entry into Force), no provision of any other Chapter of this Agreement shall be construed as imposing obligations on a Party with respect to the Party's antidumping law or countervailing duty law.

Article 1902: Retention of Domestic Antidumping Law and Countervailing Duty Law

1. Each Party reserves the right to apply its antidumping law and countervailing duty law to goods imported from the territory of any other Party. Antidumping law and countervailing duty law include, as appropriate for each Party, relevant statutes, legislative history, regulations, administrative practice and judicial precedents.

* * *

Article 1904: Review of Final Antidumping and Countervailing Duty Determinations

1. As provided in this Article, each Party shall replace judicial review of final antidumping and countervailing duty determinations with binational panel review.

2. An involved Party may request that a panel review, based on the administrative record, a final antidumping or countervailing duty determination of a competent investigating authority of an importing Party to determine whether such determination was in accordance with the antidumping or countervailing duty law of the importing Party. For this purpose, the antidumping or countervailing duty law consists of the relevant statutes, legislative history, regulations, administrative practice and judicial precedents to the extent that a court of the importing Party would rely on such materials in reviewing a final determination of the competent investigating authority. Solely for purposes of the panel review provided for in this Article, the antidumping and countervailing duty

statutes of the Parties, as those statutes may be amended from time to time, are incorporated into and made a part of this Agreement.

3. The panel shall apply the standard of review set out in Annex 1911 and the general legal principles that a court of the importing Party otherwise would apply to a review of a determination of the competent investigating authority.

* * *

8. The panel may uphold a final determination, or remand it for action not inconsistent with the panel's decision. Where the panel remands a final determination, the panel shall establish as brief a time as is reasonable for compliance with the remand, taking into account the complexity of the factual and legal issues involved and the nature of the panel's decision. In no event shall the time permitted for compliance with a remand exceed an amount of time equal to the maximum amount of time (counted from the date of the filing of a petition, complaint or application) permitted by statute for the competent investigating authority in question to make a final determination in an investigation. If review of the action taken by the competent investigating authority on remand is needed, such review shall be before the same panel, which shall normally issue a final decision within 90 days of the date on which such remand action is submitted to it.

9. The decision of a panel under this Article shall be binding on the involved Parties with respect to the particular matter between the Parties that is before the panel.

10. This Agreement shall not affect:

(a) the judicial review procedures of any Party, or

(b) cases appealed under those procedures,

with respect to determinations other than final determinations.

11. A final determination shall not be reviewed under any judicial review procedures of the importing Party if an involved Party requests a panel with respect to that determination within the time limits set out in this Article. No Party may provide in its domestic legislation for an appeal from a panel decision to its domestic courts.

12. This Article shall not apply where:

(a) neither involved Party seeks panel review of a final determination;

(b) a revised final determination is issued as a direct result of judicial review of the original final determination by a court of the importing Party in cases where neither involved Party sought panel review of that original final determination; or

(c) a final determination is issued as a direct result of judicial review that was commenced in a court of the importing Party before the date of entry into force of this Agreement.

13. Where, within a reasonable time after the panel decision is issued, an involved Party alleges that:

(a) (i) a member of the panel was guilty of gross misconduct, bias, or a serious conflict of interest, or otherwise materially violated the rules of conduct,

(ii) the panel seriously departed from a fundamental rule of procedure, or

(iii) the panel manifestly exceeded its powers, authority or jurisdiction set out in this Article, for example by failing to apply the appropriate standard of review, and

(b) any of the actions set out in subparagraph (a) has materially affected the panel's decision and threatens the integrity of the binational panel review process,

that Party may avail itself of the extraordinary challenge procedure set out in Annex 1904.13.

* * *

Article 1905: Safeguarding the Panel Review System

1. Where a Party alleges that the application of another Party's domestic law:

(a) has prevented the establishment of a panel requested by the complaining Party;

(b) has prevented a panel requested by the complaining Party from rendering a final decision;

(c) has prevented the implementation of the decision of a panel requested by the complaining Party or denied it binding force and effect with respect to the particular matter that was before the panel; or

(d) has resulted in a failure to provide opportunity for review of a final determination by a panel or court of competent jurisdiction that is independent of the competent investigating authorities, that examines the basis for the competent investigating authority's determination and whether the competent investigating authority properly applied domestic antidumping and countervailing duty law in reaching the challenged determination, and that employs the relevant standard of review identified in Article 1911,

the Party may request in writing consultations with the other Party regarding the allegations. The consultations shall begin within 15 days of the date of the request.

* * *

Annex 1901.2

Establishment of Binational Panels

1. On the date of entry into force of this Agreement, the Parties shall establish and thereafter maintain a roster of individuals to serve as panelists in disputes under this Chapter. The roster shall include judges or former judges to the fullest extent practicable. The Parties shall consult in developing the roster, which shall include at least 75 candidates. Each Party shall select at least 25 candidates, and all candidates shall be citizens of Canada, Mexico or the United States. Candidates shall be of good character, high standing and repute, and shall be chosen strictly on the basis of objectivity, reliability, sound judgment and general familiarity with international trade law. Candidates shall not be affiliated with a Party, and in no event shall a candidate take instructions from a Party. The Parties shall maintain the roster, and may amend it, when necessary, after consultations.

2. A majority of the panelists on each panel shall be lawyers in good standing. Within 30 days of a request for a panel, each involved Party shall appoint two panelists, in consultation with the other involved Party. The involved Parties normally shall appoint panelists from the roster. If a panelist is not selected from the roster, the panelist shall be chosen in accordance with and be subject to the criteria of paragraph 1. Each involved Party shall have the right to exercise four peremptory challenges, to be exercised simultaneously and in confidence, disqualifying from appointment to the panel up to four candidates proposed by the other involved Party. Peremptory challenges and the selection of alternative panelists shall occur within 45 days of the request for the panel. If an involved Party fails to appoint its members to a panel within 30 days or if a panelist is struck and no alternative panelist is selected within 45 days, such panelist shall be selected by lot on the 31st or 46th day, as the case may be, from that Party's candidates on the roster.

3. Within 55 days of the request for a panel, the involved Parties shall agree on the selection of a fifth panelist. If the involved Parties are unable to agree, they shall decide by lot which of them shall select, by the 61st day, the fifth panelist from the roster, excluding candidates eliminated by peremptory challenges.

4. On appointment of the fifth panelist, the panelists shall promptly appoint a chair from among the lawyers on the panel by majority vote of the panelists. If there is no majority vote, the chair shall be appointed by lot from among the lawyers on the panel.

5. Decisions of the panel shall be by majority vote and based on the votes of all members of the panel. The panel shall issue a written decision with reasons, together with any dissenting or concurring opinions of panelists.

* * *

Annex 1904.13

Extraordinary Challenge Procedure

1. The involved Parties shall establish an extraordinary challenge committee, comprising three members, within 15 days of a request pursuant to Article 1904(13). The members shall be selected from a 15–person roster comprised of judges or former judges of a federal judicial court of the United States or a judicial court of superior jurisdiction of Canada, or a federal judicial court of Mexico. Each Party shall name five persons to this roster. Each involved Party shall select one member from this roster and the involved Parties shall decide by lot which of them shall select the third member from the roster.

2. The Parties shall establish by the date of entry into force of the Agreement rules of procedure for committees. The rules shall provide for a decision of a committee within 90 days of its establishment.

3. Committee decisions shall be binding on the Parties with respect to the particular matter between the Parties that was before the panel. After examination of the legal and factual analysis underlying the findings and conclusions of the panel's decision in order to determine whether one of the grounds set out in Article 1904(13) has been established, and on finding that one of those grounds has been established, the committee shall vacate the original panel decision or remand it to the original panel for action not inconsistent with the committee's decision; if the grounds are not established, it shall deny the challenge and, therefore, the original panel decision shall stand affirmed. If the original decision is vacated, a new panel shall be established pursuant to Annex 1901.2.

Annex 1911

Country-Specific Definitions

For purposes of this Chapter:

antidumping statute means:

(a) in the case of Canada, the relevant provisions of the *Special Import Measures Act,* as amended, and any successor statutes;

(b) in the case of the United States, the relevant provisions of Title VII of the *Tariff Act of 1930,* as amended, and any successor statutes:

(c) in the case of Mexico, the relevant provisions of the *Foreign Trade Act Implementing Article 131 of the Constitution of the United Mexican States* ("Ley Reglamentaria del Artículo 131 de la Constitución Política de los Estados Unidos Mexicanos en Materia de Comercio Exterior"), as amended, and any successor statutes; and

(d) the provisions of any other statute that provides for judicial review of final determinations under subparagraph (a), (b) or (c), or indicates the standard of review to be applied to such determinations;

competent investigating authority means:

(a) in the case of Canada,

(i) the Canadian International Trade Tribunal, or its successor, or

(ii) the Deputy Minister of National Revenue for Customs and Excise as defined in the *Special Import Measures Act,* as amended, or the Deputy Minister's successor;

(b) in the case of the United States,

(i) the International Trade Administration of the U.S. Department of Commerce, or its successor, or

(ii) the U.S. International Trade Commission, or its successor; and

(c) in the case of Mexico, the designated authority within the Secretariat of Trade and Industrial Development ("Secretaría de Comercio y Fomento Industrial"), or its successor;

countervailing duty statute means:

(a) in the case of Canada, the relevant provisions of the *Special Import Measures Act,* as amended, and any successor statutes;

(b) in the case of the United States, section 303 and the relevant provisions of Title VII of the *Tariff Act of 1930,* as amended, and any successor statutes;

(c) in the case of Mexico, the relevant provisions of the *Foreign Trade Act Implementing Article 131 of the Constitution of the United Mexican States* ("Ley Reglamentaria del Artículo 131 de la Constitución Política de los Estados Unidos Mexicanos en Materia de Comercio Exterior"), as amended, and any successor statutes; and

(d) the provisions of any other statute that provides for judicial review of final determinations under subparagraph (a), (b) or (c), or indicates the standard of review to be applied to such determinations;

final determination means:

(a) in the case of Canada,

(i) an order or finding of the Canadian International Trade Tribunal under subsection 43(1) of the *Special Import Measures Act,*

(ii) an order by the Canadian International Trade Tribunal under subsection 76(4) of the *Special Import Measures Act,* as amended, continuing an order or finding made under subsection 43(1) of the Act with or without amendment,

(iii) a determination by the Deputy Minister of National Revenue for Customs and Excise pursuant to section 41 of the *Special Import Measures Act,* as amended,

(iv) a re-determination by the Deputy Minister pursuant to section 59 of the *Special Import Measures Act,* as amended,

(v) a decision by the Canadian International Trade Tribunal pursuant to subsection 76(3) of the *Special Import Measures Act,* as amended, not to initiate a review,

(vi) a reconsideration by the Canadian International Trade Tribunal pursuant to subsection 91(3) of the *Special Import Measures Act,* as amended, and

(vii) a review by the Deputy Minister of an undertaking pursuant to subsection 53(1) of the *Special Import Measures Act,* as amended;

(b) in the case of the United States,

(i) a final affirmative determination by the International Trade Administration of the U.S. Department of Commerce or by the U.S. International Trade Commission under section 705 or 735 of the *Tariff Act of 1930,* as amended, including any negative part of such a determination,

(ii) a final negative determination by the International Trade Administration of the U.S. Department of Commerce or by the U.S. International Trade Commission under section 705 or 735 of the *Tariff Act of 1930,* as amended, including any affirmative part of such a determination,

(iii) a final determination, other than a determination in (iv), under section 751 of the *Tariff Act of 1930,* as amended,

(iv) a determination by the U.S. International Trade Commission under section 751(b) of the *Tariff Act of 1930,* as amended, not to review a determination based on changed circumstances, and

(v) a final determination by the International Trade Administration of the U.S. Department of Commerce as to whether a particular type of merchandise is within the class or kind of merchandise described in an existing finding of dumping or antidumping or countervailing duty order; and

(c) in the case of Mexico,

(i) a final resolution regarding antidumping or countervailing duties investigations by the Secretariat of Trade and Industrial Development ("Secretaría de Comercio y Fomento Industrial"), pursuant to Article 13 of the *Foreign Trade Act Implementing Article 131 of the Constitution of the United Mexican States* ("Ley Reglamentaria del Artículo 131 de la Constitución Política de los Estados Unidos Mexicanos en Materia de Comercio Exterior"), as amended,

(ii) a final resolution regarding an annual administrative review of antidumping or countervailing duties by the Secretariat of Trade and Industrial Development ("Secretaría de Comercio y Fomento Industrial"), as described in paragraph (*o*) of its Schedule to Annex 1904.15, and

(iii) a final resolution by the Secretariat of Trade and Industrial Development ("Secretaría de Comercio y Fomento Industrial") as to whether a particular type of merchandise is within the class or kind of merchandise described in an existing antidumping or countervailing duty resolution; and

standard of review means the following standards, as may be amended from time to time by the relevant Party:

(a) in the case of Canada, the grounds set out in subsection 18.1(4) of the *Federal Court Act,* as amended, with respect to all final determinations;

(b) in the case of the United States,

(i) the standard set out in section 516A(b)(1)(B) of the *Tariff Act of 1930,* as amended, with the exception of a determination referred to in (ii), and

(ii) the standard set out in section 516A(b)(1)(A) of the *Tariff Act of 1930,* as amended, with respect to a determination by the U.S. International Trade Commission not to initiate a review pursuant to section 751(b) of the *Tariff Act of 1930,* as amended; and

(c) in the case of Mexico, the standard set out in Article 238 of the *Federal Fiscal Code* ("Código Fiscal de la Federación"), or any successor statutes, based solely on the administrative record.

Chapter Twenty

Institutional Arrangements and Dispute Settlement Procedures

Section A—Institutions

Article 2001: The Free Trade Commission

1. The Parties hereby establish the Free Trade Commission, comprising cabinet-level representatives of the Parties or their designees.

2. The Commission shall:

(a) supervise the implementation of this Agreement;

(b) oversee its further elaboration;

(c) resolve disputes that may arise regarding its interpretation or application;

(d) supervise the work of all committees and working groups established under this Agreement, referred to in Annex 2001.2; and

(e) consider any other matter that may affect the operation of this Agreement.

3. The Commission may:

(a) establish, and delegate responsibilities to, ad hoc or standing committees, working groups or expert groups;

(b) seek the advice of non-governmental persons or groups; and

(c) take such other action in the exercise of its functions as the Parties may agree.

4. The Commission shall establish its rules and procedures. All decisions of the Commission shall be taken by consensus, except as the Commission may otherwise agree.

5. The Commission shall convene at least once a year in regular session. Regular sessions of the Commission shall be chaired successively by each Party.

Article 2002: The Secretariat

1. The Commission shall establish and oversee a Secretariat comprising national Sections.

2. Each Party shall:

(a) establish a permanent office of its Section;

(b) be responsible for

(i) the operation and costs of its Section, and

(ii) the remuneration and payment of expenses of panelists and members of committees and scientific review boards established under this Agreement, as set out in Annex 2002.2;

(c) designate an individual to serve as Secretary for its Section, who shall be responsible for its administration and management; and

(d) notify the Commission of the location of its Section's office.

3. The Secretariat shall:

(a) provide assistance to the Commission;

(b) provide administrative assistance to

(i) panels and committees established under Chapter Nineteen (Review and Dispute Settlement in Antidumping and Countervailing Duty Matters), in accordance with the procedures established pursuant to Article 1908, and

(ii) panels established under this Chapter, in accordance with procedures established pursuant to Article 2012; and

(c) as the Commission may direct

(i) support the work of other committees and groups established under this Agreement, and

(ii) otherwise facilitate the operation of this Agreement.

Section B—Dispute Settlement

Article 2003: Cooperation

The Parties shall at all times endeavor to agree on the interpretation and application of this Agreement, and shall make every attempt through cooperation and consultations to arrive at a mutually satisfactory resolution of any matter that might affect its operation.

Article 2004: Recourse to Dispute Settlement Procedures

Except for the matters covered in Chapter Nineteen (Review and Dispute Settlement in Antidumping and Countervailing Duty Matters) and as otherwise provided in this Agreement, the dispute settlement provisions of this Chapter shall apply with respect to the avoidance or settlement of all disputes between the Parties regarding the interpretation or application of this Agreement or wherever a Party considers that an actual or proposed measure of another Party is or would be inconsistent with the obligations of this Agreement or cause nullification or impairment in the sense of Annex 2004.

Article 2005: GATT Dispute Settlement

1. Subject to paragraphs 2, 3 and 4, disputes regarding any matter arising under both this Agreement and the *General Agreement on Tariffs and Trade* (GATT), any agreement negotiated thereunder, or any successor

agreement, may be settled in either forum at the discretion of the complaining Party.

2. Before a Party initiates a dispute settlement proceeding in the GATT against another Party on grounds that are substantially equivalent to those available to that Party under this Agreement, that Party shall notify any third Party of its intention. If a third Party wishes to have recourse to dispute settlement procedures under this Agreement regarding the matter, it shall inform promptly the notifying Party and those Parties shall consult with a view to agreement on a single forum. If those Parties cannot agree, the dispute normally shall be settled under this Agreement.

3. In any dispute referred to in paragraph 1 where the responding Party claims that its action is subject to Article 104 (Relation to Environmental and Conservation Agreements) and requests in writing that the matter be considered under this Agreement, the complaining Party may, in respect of that matter, thereafter have recourse to dispute settlement procedures solely under this Agreement.

4. In any dispute referred to in paragraph 1 that arises under Section B of Chapter Seven (Sanitary and Phytosanitary Measures) or Chapter Nine (Standards-Related Measures):

(a) concerning a measure adopted or maintained by a Party to protect its human, animal or plant life or health, or to protect its environment, and

(b) that raises factual issues concerning the environment, health, safety or conservation, including directly related scientific matters,

where the responding Party requests in writing that the matter be considered under this Agreement, the complaining Party may, in respect of that matter, thereafter have recourse to dispute settlement procedures solely under this Agreement.

5. The responding Party shall deliver a copy of a request made pursuant to paragraph 3 or 4 to the other Parties and to its Section of the Secretariat. Where the complaining Party has initiated dispute settlement proceedings regarding any matter subject to paragraph 3 or 4, the responding Party shall deliver its request no later than 15 days thereafter. On receipt of such request, the complaining Party shall promptly withdraw from participation in those proceedings and may initiate dispute settlement procedures under Article 2007.

6. Once dispute settlement procedures have been initiated under Article 2007 or dispute settlement proceedings have been initiated under the GATT, the forum selected shall be used to the exclusion of the other, unless a Party makes a request pursuant to paragraph 3 or 4.

7. For purposes of this Article, dispute settlement proceedings under the GATT are deemed to be initiated by a Party's request for a panel, such as

under Article XXIII:2 of the *General Agreement on Tariffs and Trade 1947,* or for a committee investigation, such as under Article 20.1 of the Customs Valuation Code.

Consultations

Article 2006: Consultations

1. Any Party may request in writing consultations with any other Party regarding any actual or proposed measure or any other matter that it considers might affect the operation of this Agreement.

2. The requesting Party shall deliver the request to the other Parties and to its Section of the Secretariat.

3. Unless the Commission otherwise provides in its rules and procedures established under Article 2001(4), a third Party that considers it has a substantial interest in the matter shall be entitled to participate in the consultations on delivery of written notice to the other Parties and to its Section of the Secretariat.

4. Consultations on matters regarding perishable agricultural goods shall commence within 15 days of the date of delivery of the request.

5. The consulting Parties shall make every attempt to arrive at a mutually satisfactory resolution of any matter through consultations under this Article or other consultative provisions of this Agreement. To this end, the consulting Parties shall:

(a) provide sufficient information to enable a full examination of how the actual or proposed measure or other matter might affect the operation of this Agreement;

(b) treat any confidential or proprietary information exchanged in the course of consultations on the same basis as the Party providing the information; and

(c) seek to avoid any resolution that adversely affects the interests under this Agreement of any other Party.

Initiation of Procedures

Article 2007: Commission—Good Offices, Conciliation and Mediation

1. If the consulting Parties fail to resolve a matter pursuant to Article 2006 within:

(a) 30 days of delivery of a request for consultations,

(b) 45 days of delivery of such request if any other Party has subsequently requested or has participated in consultations regarding the same matter,

(c) 15 days of delivery of a request for consultations in matters regarding perishable agricultural goods, or

(d) such other period as they may agree,

any such Party may request in writing a meeting of the Commission.

2. A Party may also request in writing a meeting of the Commission where:

(a) it has initiated dispute settlement proceedings under the GATT regarding any matter subject to Article 2005(3) or (4), and has received a request pursuant to Article 2005(5) for recourse to dispute settlement procedures under this Chapter; or

(b) consultations have been held pursuant to Article 513 (Working Group on Rules of Origin), Article 723 (Sanitary and Phytosanitary Measures—Technical Consultations) and Article 914 (Standards-Related Measures—Technical Consultations).

3. The requesting Party shall state in the request the measure or other matter complained of and indicate the provisions of this Agreement that it considers relevant, and shall deliver the request to the other Parties and to its Section of the Secretariat.

4. Unless it decides otherwise, the Commission shall convene within 10 days of delivery of the request and shall endeavor to resolve the dispute promptly.

5. The Commission may:

(a) call on such technical advisers or create such working groups or expert groups as it deems necessary,

(b) have recourse to good offices, conciliation, mediation or such other dispute resolution procedures, or

(c) make recommendations,

as may assist the consulting Parties to reach a mutually satisfactory resolution of the dispute.

6. Unless it decides otherwise, the Commission shall consolidate two or more proceedings before it pursuant to this Article regarding the same measure. The Commission may consolidate two or more proceedings regarding other matters before it pursuant to this Article that it determines are appropriate to be considered jointly.

Panel Proceedings

Article 2008: Request for an Arbitral Panel

1. If the Commission has convened pursuant to Article 2007(4), and the matter has not been resolved within:

(a) 30 days thereafter,

(b) 30 days after the Commission has convened in respect of the matter most recently referred to it, where proceedings have been consolidated pursuant to Article 2007(6), or

(c) such other period as the consulting Parties may agree,

any consulting Party may request in writing the establishment of an arbitral panel. The requesting Party shall deliver the request to the other Parties and to its Section of the Secretariat.

2. On delivery of the request, the Commission shall establish an arbitral panel.

3. A third Party that considers it has a substantial interest in the matter shall be entitled to join as a complaining Party on delivery of written notice of its intention to participate to the disputing Parties and its Section of the Secretariat. The notice shall be delivered at the earliest possible time, and in any event no later than seven days after the date of delivery of a request by a Party for the establishment of a panel.

4. If a third Party does not join as a complaining Party in accordance with paragraph 3, it normally shall refrain thereafter from initiating or continuing:

(a) a dispute settlement procedure under this Agreement, or

(b) a dispute settlement proceeding in the GATT on grounds that are substantially equivalent to those available to that Party under this Agreement,

regarding the same matter in the absence of a significant change in economic or commercial circumstances.

5. Unless otherwise agreed by the disputing Parties, the panel shall be established and perform its functions in a manner consistent with the provisions of this Chapter.

Article 2009: Roster

1. The Parties shall establish by January 1, 1994 and maintain a roster of up to 30 individuals who are willing and able to serve as panelists. The roster members shall be appointed by consensus for terms of three years, and may be reappointed.

2. Roster members shall:

(a) have expertise or experience in law, international trade, other matters covered by this Agreement or the resolution of disputes arising under international trade agreements, and shall be chosen strictly on the basis of objectivity, reliability and sound judgment;

(b) be independent of, and not be affiliated with or take instructions from, any Party; and

(c) comply with a code of conduct to be established by the Commission.

Article 2010: Qualifications of Panelists

1. All panelists shall meet the qualifications set out in Article 2009(2).

2. Individuals may not serve as panelists for a dispute in which they have participated pursuant to Article 2007(5).

Article 2011: Panel Selection

1. Where there are two disputing Parties, the following procedures shall apply:

(a) The panel shall comprise five members.

(b) The disputing Parties shall endeavor to agree on the chair of the panel within 15 days of the delivery of the request for the establishment of the panel. If the disputing Parties are unable to agree on the chair within this period, the disputing Party chosen by lot shall select within five days as chair an individual who is not a citizen of that Party.

(c) Within 15 days of selection of the chair, each disputing Party shall select two panelists who are citizens of the other disputing Party.

(d) If a disputing Party fails to select its panelists within such period, such panelists shall be selected by lot from among the roster members who are citizens of the other disputing Party.

2. Where there are more than two disputing Parties, the following procedures shall apply:

(a) The panel shall comprise five members.

(b) The disputing Parties shall endeavor to agree on the chair of the panel within 15 days of the delivery of the request for the establishment of the panel. If the disputing Parties are unable to agree on the chair within this period, the Party or Parties on the side of the dispute chosen by lot shall select within 10 days a chair who is not a citizen of such Party or Parties.

(c) Within 15 days of selection of the chair, the Party complained against shall select two panelists, one of whom is a citizen of a complaining Party, and the other of whom is a citizen of another complaining Party. The complaining Parties shall select two panelists who are citizens of the Party complained against.

(d) If a disputing Party fails to select a panelist within such period, such panelist shall be selected by lot in accordance with the citizenship criteria of subparagraph (c).

3. Panelists shall normally be selected from the roster. Any disputing Party may exercise a peremptory challenge against any individual not on the roster who is proposed as a panelist by a disputing Party within 15 days after the individual has been proposed.

4. If a disputing Party believes that a panelist is in violation of the code of conduct, the disputing Parties shall consult and if they agree, the panelist shall be removed and a new panelist shall be selected in accordance with this Article.

* * *

Article 2017: Final Report

1. The panel shall present to the disputing Parties a final report, including any separate opinions on matters not unanimously agreed, within 30 days of presentation of the initial report, unless the disputing Parties otherwise agree.

2. No panel may, either in its initial report or its final report, disclose which panelists are associated with majority or minority opinions.

3. The disputing Parties shall transmit to the Commission the final report of the panel, including any report of a scientific review board established under Article 2015, as well as any written views that a disputing Party desires to be appended, on a confidential basis within a reasonable period of time after it is presented to them.

4. Unless the Commission decides otherwise, the final report of the panel shall be published 15 days after it is transmitted to the Commission.

Implementation of Panel Reports

Article 2018: Implementation of Final Report

1. On receipt of the final report of a panel, the disputing Parties shall agree on the resolution of the dispute, which normally shall conform with the determinations and recommendations of the panel, and shall notify their Sections of the Secretariat of any agreed resolution of any dispute.

2. Wherever possible, the resolution shall be non-implementation or removal of a measure not conforming with this Agreement or causing nullification or impairment in the sense of Annex 2004 or, failing such a resolution, compensation.

Article 2019: Non-Implementation—Suspension of Benefits

1. If in its final report a panel has determined that a measure is inconsistent with the obligations of this Agreement or causes nullification or impairment in the sense of Annex 2004 and the Party complained against has not reached agreement with any complaining Party on a mutually satisfactory resolution pursuant to Article 2018(1) within 30 days of receiving the final report, such complaining Party may suspend the application to the Party complained against of benefits of equivalent effect until such time as they have reached agreement on a resolution of the dispute.

2. In considering what benefits to suspend pursuant to paragraph 1:

(a) a complaining Party should first seek to suspend benefits in the same sector or sectors as that affected by the measure or other matter that the panel has found to be inconsistent with the obligations of this Agreement or to have caused nullification or impairment in the sense of Annex 2004; and

(b) a complaining Party that considers it is not practicable or effective to suspend benefits in the same sector or sectors may suspend benefits in other sectors.

3. On the written request of any disputing Party delivered to the other Parties and its Section of the Secretariat, the Commission shall establish a panel to determine whether the level of benefits suspended by a Party pursuant to paragraph 1 is manifestly excessive.

4. The panel proceedings shall be conducted in accordance with the Model Rules of Procedure. The panel shall present its determination within 60 days after the last panelist is selected or such other period as the disputing Parties may agree.

Section C—Domestic Proceedings and Private Commercial Dispute Settlement

Article 2020: Referrals of Matters From Judicial or Administrative Proceedings

1. If an issue of interpretation or application of this Agreement arises in any domestic judicial or administrative proceeding of a Party that any Party considers would merit its intervention, or if a court or administrative body solicits the views of a Party, that Party shall notify the other Parties and its Section of the Secretariat. The Commission shall endeavor to agree on an appropriate response as expeditiously as possible.

2. The Party in whose territory the court or administrative body is located shall submit any agreed interpretation of the Commission to the court or administrative body in accordance with the rules of that forum.

3. If the Commission is unable to agree, any Party may submit its own views to the court or administrative body in accordance with the rules of that forum.

Article 2021: Private Rights

No Party may provide for a right of action under its domestic law against any other Party on the ground that a measure of another Party is inconsistent with this Agreement.

Article 2022: Alternative Dispute Resolution

1. Each Party shall, to the maximum extent possible, encourage and facilitate the use of arbitration and other means of alternative dispute resolution for the settlement of international commercial disputes between private parties in the free trade area.

2. To this end, each Party shall provide appropriate procedures to ensure observance of agreements to arbitrate and for the recognition and enforcement of arbitral awards in such disputes.

3. A Party shall be deemed to be in compliance with paragraph 2 if it is a party to and is in compliance with the 1958 *United Nations Convention on the Recognition and Enforcement of Foreign Arbitral Awards* or the 1975 *Inter-American Convention on International Commercial Arbitration.*

4. The Commission shall establish an Advisory Committee on Private Commercial Disputes comprising persons with expertise or experience in the resolution of private international commercial disputes. The Committee shall report and provide recommendations to the Commission on general issues referred to it by the Commission respecting the availability, use and effectiveness of arbitration and other procedures for the resolution of such disputes in the free trade area.

Annex 2004

Nullification and Impairment

1. If any Party considers that any benefit it could reasonably have expected to accrue to it under any provision of:

(a) Part Two (Trade in Goods), except for those provisions of Annex 300–A (Automotive Sector) or Chapter Six (Energy) relating to investment,

(b) Part Three (Technical Barriers to Trade),

(c) Chapter Twelve (Cross-Border Trade in Services), or

(d) Part Six (Intellectual Property),

is being nullified or impaired as a result of the application of any measure that is not inconsistent with this Agreement, the Party may have recourse to dispute settlement under this Chapter.

2. A Party may not invoke:

(a) paragraph 1(a) or (b), to the extent that the benefit arises from any cross-border trade in services provision of Part Two or Three, or

(b) paragraph 1(c) or (d),

with respect to any measure subject to an exception under Article 2101 (General Exceptions).

PART EIGHT

OTHER PROVISIONS

Chapter Twenty-One

Exceptions

Article 2101: General Exceptions

1. For purposes of:

(a) Part Two (Trade in Goods), except to the extent that a provision of that Part applies to services or investment, and

(b) Part Three (Technical Barriers to Trade), except to the extent that a provision of that Part applies to services,

GATT Article XX and its interpretative notes, or any equivalent provision of a successor agreement to which all Parties are party, are incorporated into and made part of this Agreement. The Parties understand that the measures referred to in GATT Article XX(b) include environmental measures necessary to protect human, animal or plant life or health, and that GATT Article XX(g) applies to measures relating to the conservation of living and non-living exhaustible natural resources.

2. Provided that such measures are not applied in a manner that would constitute a means of arbitrary or unjustifiable discrimination between countries where the same conditions prevail or a disguised restriction on trade between the Parties, nothing in:

(a) Part Two (Trade in Goods), to the extent that a provision of that Part applies to services,

(b) Part Three (Technical Barriers to Trade), to the extent that a provision of that Part applies to services,

(c) Chapter Twelve (Cross-Border Trade in Services), and

(d) Chapter Thirteen (Telecommunications),

shall be construed to prevent the adoption or enforcement by any Party of measures necessary to secure compliance with laws or regulations that are not inconsistent with the provisions of this Agreement, including those relating to health and safety and consumer protection.

Article 2102: National Security

1. Subject to Articles 607 (Energy—National Security Measures) and 1018 (Government Procurement—Exceptions), nothing in this Agreement shall be construed:

(a) to require any Party to furnish or allow access to any information the disclosure of which it determines to be contrary to its essential security interests;

(b) to prevent any Party from taking any actions that it considers necessary for the protection of its essential security interests

(i) relating to the traffic in arms, ammunition and implements of war and to such traffic and transactions in other goods, materials, services and technology undertaken directly or indirectly for the purpose of supplying a military or other security establishment,

(ii) taken in time of war or other emergency in international relations, or

(iii) relating to the implementation of national policies or international agreements respecting the non-proliferation of nuclear weapons or other nuclear explosive devices; or

(c) to prevent any Party from taking action in pursuance of its obligations under the United Nations Charter for the maintenance of international peace and security.

Article 2103: Taxation

1. Except as set out in this Article, nothing in this Agreement shall apply to taxation measures.

* * *

Article 2104: Balance of Payments

1. Nothing in this Agreement shall be construed to prevent a Party from adopting or maintaining measures that restrict transfers where the Party experiences serious balance of payments difficulties, or the threat thereof, and such restrictions are consistent with paragraphs 2 through 4 and are:

(a) consistent with paragraph 5 to the extent they are imposed on transfers other than cross-border trade in financial services; or

(b) consistent with paragraphs 6 and 7 to the extent they are imposed on cross-border trade in financial services.

General Rules

2. As soon as practicable after a Party imposes a measure under this Article, the Party shall:

(a) submit any current account exchange restrictions to the IMF for review under Article VIII of the Articles of Agreement of the IMF;

(b) enter into good faith consultations with the IMF on economic adjustment measures to address the fundamental underlying economic problems causing the difficulties; and

(c) adopt or maintain economic policies consistent with such consultations.

3. A measure adopted or maintained under this Article shall:

(a) avoid unnecessary damage to the commercial, economic or financial interests of another Party;

(b) not be more burdensome than necessary to deal with the balance of payments difficulties or threat thereof;

(c) be temporary and be phased out progressively as the balance of payments situation improves;

(d) be consistent with paragraph 2(c) and with the Articles of Agreement of the IMF; and

(e) be applied on a national treatment or most-favored-nation treatment basis, whichever is better.

4. A Party may adopt or maintain a measure under this Article that gives priority to services that are essential to its economic program, provided that a Party may not impose a measure for the purpose of protecting a specific industry or sector unless the measure is consistent with paragraph 2(c) and with Article VIII(3) of the Articles of Agreement of the IMF.

* * *

Article 2105: Disclosure of Information

Nothing in this Agreement shall be construed to require a Party to furnish or allow access to information the disclosure of which would impede law enforcement or would be contrary to the Party's law protecting personal privacy or the financial affairs and accounts of individual customers of financial institutions.

Article 2106: Cultural Industries

Annex 2106 applies to the Parties specified in that Annex with respect to cultural industries.

Annex 2106

Cultural Industries

Notwithstanding any other provision of this Agreement, as between Canada and the United States, any measure adopted or maintained with respect to cultural industries, except as specifically provided in Article 302 (Market Access—Tariff Elimination), and any measure of equivalent commercial effect taken in response, shall be governed under this Agreement exclusively in accordance with the provisions of the *Canada—United States Free Trade Agreement*. The rights and obligations between Canada and any other Party with respect to such measures shall be identical to those applying between Canada and the United States.

Chapter Twenty-Two

Final Provisions

Article 2201: Annexes

The Annexes to this Agreement constitute an integral part of this Agreement.

Article 2202: Amendments

1. The Parties may agree on any modification of or addition to this Agreement.

2. When so agreed, and approved in accordance with the applicable legal procedures of each Party, a modification or addition shall constitute an integral part of this Agreement.

Article 2203: Entry Into Force

This Agreement shall enter into force on January 1, 1994, on an exchange of written notifications certifying the completion of necessary legal procedures.

Article 2204: Accession

1. Any country or group of countries may accede to this Agreement subject to such terms and conditions as may be agreed between such country or countries and the Commission and following approval in accordance with the applicable legal procedures of each country.

2. This Agreement shall not apply as between any Party and any acceding country or group of countries if, at the time of accession, either does not consent to such application.

Article 2205: Withdrawal

A Party may withdraw from this Agreement six months after it provides written notice of withdrawal to the other Parties. If a Party withdraws, the Agreement shall remain in force for the remaining Parties.

Article 2206: Authentic Texts

The English, French and Spanish texts of this Agreement are equally authentic.

PART E

UNITED STATES LAW

■ ■ ■

PART ONE

GENERAL TRADE LAW STATUTES

■ ■ ■

DOCUMENT 26

OMNIBUS TRADE AND COMPETITIVENESS ACT OF 1988

■ ■ ■

Pub.L. 100–418, Aug. 23, 1988, 102 Stat. 1107

This Act includes amendments to numerous American trade laws. Such amendments have been integrated into the laws that appear in this documents supplement. The following are provisions of the 1988 Act which are not amendments to earlier laws.

Table of Contents (Selected Provisions Only)

---

* See Document 47.

SUBTITLE B—TECHNOLOGY

SUBTITLE C—COMPETITIVENESS POLICY COUNCIL ACT

SUBTITLE D—FEDERAL BUDGET COMPETITIVENESS IMPACT STATEMENT

SUBTITLE E—TRADE DATA AND STUDIES

TITLE VI—EDUCATION AND TRAINING FOR AMERICAN COMPETITIVENESS [Omitted]

TITLE VII—BUY AMERICAN ACT OF 1988**

TITLE VIII—SMALL BUSINESS [Omitted]

TITLE IX—PATENTS [Omitted]

TITLE X—OCEAN AND AIR TRANSPORTATION [Omitted]

TITLE I—TRADE, CUSTOMS, AND TARIFF LAWS

SUBTITLE A—UNITED STATES TRADE AGREEMENTS

Part 1—Negotiation and Implementation of Trade Agreements

19 U.S.C. § 2901

Sec. 1101. Overall and principal trade negotiating objectives of the United States

(a) Overall trade negotiating objectives. The overall trade negotiating objectives of the United States are to obtain—

(1) more open, equitable, and reciprocal market access;

(2) the reduction or elimination of barriers and other trade-distorting policies and practices; and

(3) a more effective system of international trading disciplines and procedures.

(b) Principal trade negotiating objectives.

(1) Dispute settlement. The principal negotiating objectives of the United States with respect to dispute settlement are—

(A) to provide for more effective and expeditious dispute settlement mechanisms and procedures; and

** Integrated into Buy American Act. See Document 34.

(B) to ensure that such mechanisms within the GATT and GATT agreements provide for more effective and expeditious resolution of disputes and enable better enforcement of United States rights.

(2) Improvement of the GATT and multilateral trade negotiation agreements. The principal negotiating objectives of the United States regarding the improvement of GATT and multilateral trade negotiation agreements are—

(A) to enhance the status of the GATT;

(B) to improve the operation and extend the coverage of the GATT and such agreements and arrangements to products, sectors, and conditions of trade not adequately covered; and

(C) to expand country participation in particular agreements or arrangements, where appropriate.

(3) Transparency. The principal negotiating objective of the United States regarding transparency is to obtain broader application of the principle of transparency and clarification of the costs and benefits of trade policy actions through the observance of open and equitable procedures in trade matters by Contracting Parties to the GATT.

(4) Developing countries. The principal negotiating objectives of the United States regarding developing countries are—

(A) to ensure that developing countries promote economic development by assuming the fullest possible measure of responsibility for achieving and maintaining an open international trading system by providing reciprocal benefits and assuming equivalent obligations with respect to their import and export practices; and

(B) to establish procedures for reducing nonreciprocal trade benefits for the more advanced developing countries.

(5) Current account surpluses. The principal negotiating objective of the United States regarding current account surpluses is to develop rules to address large and persistent global current account imbalances of countries, including imbalances which threaten the stability of the international trading system, by imposing greater responsibility on such countries to undertake policy changes aimed at restoring current account equilibrium, including expedited implementation of trade agreements where feasible and appropriate.

(6) Trade and monetary coordination. The principal negotiating objective of the United States regarding trade and monetary coordination is to develop mechanisms to assure greater coordination, consistency, and cooperation between international trade and monetary systems and institutions.

(7) Agriculture. The principal negotiating objectives of the United States with respect to agriculture are to achieve, on an expedited basis to the maximum extent feasible, more open and fair conditions of trade in agricultural commodities by—

(A) developing, strengthening, and clarifying rules for agricultural trade, including disciplines on restrictive or trade-distorting import and export practices;

(B) increasing United States agricultural exports by eliminating barriers to trade (including transparent and nontransparent barriers) and reducing or eliminating the subsidization of agricultural production consistent with the United States policy of agricultural stabilization in cyclical and unpredictable markets;

(C) creating a free and more open world agricultural trading system by resolving questions pertaining to export and other trade-distorting subsidies, market pricing and market access and eliminating and reducing substantially other specific constraints to fair trade and more open market access, such as tariffs, quotas, and other nontariff practices, including unjustified phytosanitary and sanitary restrictions; and

(D) seeking agreements by which the major agricultural exporting nations agree to pursue policies to reduce excessive production of agricultural commodities during periods of oversupply, with due regard for the fact that the United States already undertakes such policies, and without recourse to arbitrary schemes to divide market shares among major exporting countries.

(8) Unfair trade practices. The principal negotiating objectives of the United States with respect to unfair trade practices are—

(A) to improve the provisions of the GATT and nontariff measure agreements in order to define, deter, discourage the persistent use of, and otherwise discipline unfair trade practices having adverse trade effects, including forms of subsidy and dumping and other practices not adequately covered such as resource input subsidies, diversionary dumping, dumped or subsidized inputs, and export targeting practices;

(B) to obtain the application of similar rules to the treatment of primary and nonprimary products in the Agreement on Interpretation and Application of Articles VI, XVI, and XXIII of the GATT (relating to subsidies and countervailing measures); and

(C) to obtain the enforcement of GATT rules against—

(i) state trading enterprises, and

(ii) the acts, practices, or policies of any foreign government which, as a practical matter, unreasonably require that—

(I) substantial direct investment in the foreign country be made,

(II) intellectual property be licensed to the foreign country or to any firm of the foreign country, or

(III) other collateral concessions be made,

as a condition for the importation of any product or service of the United States into the foreign country or as a condition for carrying on business in the foreign country.

(9) Trade in services.

(A) The principal negotiating objectives of the United States regarding trade in services are—

(i) to reduce or to eliminate barriers to, or other distortions of, international trade in services, including barriers that deny national treatment and restrictions on establishment and operation in such markets; and

(ii) to develop internationally agreed rules, including dispute settlement procedures, which—

(I) are consistent with the commercial policies of the United States, and

(II) will reduce or eliminate such barriers or distortions, and help ensure fair, equitable opportunities for foreign markets.

(B) In pursuing the negotiating objectives described in subparagraph (A), United States negotiators shall take into account legitimate United States domestic objectives including, but not limited to, the protection of legitimate health or safety, essential security, environmental, consumer or employment opportunity interests and the law and regulations related thereto.

(10) Intellectual property. The principal negotiating objectives of the United States regarding intellectual property are—

(A) to seek the enactment and effective enforcement by foreign countries of laws which—

(i) recognize and adequately protect intellectual property, including copyrights, patents, trademarks, semiconductor chip layout designs, and trade secrets, and

(ii) provide protection against unfair competition,

(B) to establish in the GATT obligations—

(i) to implement adequate substantive standards based on—

(I) the standards in existing international agreements that provide adequate protection, and

(II) the standards in national laws if international agreement standards are inadequate or do not exist,

(ii) to establish effective procedures to enforce, both internally and at the border, the standards implemented under clause (i), and

(iii) to implement effective dispute settlement procedures that improve on existing GATT procedures;

(C) to recognize that the inclusion in the GATT of—

(i) adequate and effective substantive norms and standards for the protection and enforcement of intellectual property rights, and

(ii) dispute settlement provisions and enforcement procedures,

is without prejudice to other complementary initiatives undertaken in other international organizations; and

(D) to supplement and strengthen standards for protection and enforcement in existing international intellectual property conventions administered by other international organizations, including their expansion to cover new and emerging technologies and elimination of discrimination or unreasonable exceptions or preconditions to protection.

(11) Foreign direct investment.

(A) The principal negotiating objectives of the United States regarding foreign direct investment are—

(i) to reduce or to eliminate artificial or trade-distorting barriers to foreign direct investment, to expand the principle of national treatment, and to reduce unreasonable barriers to establishment; and

(ii) to develop internationally agreed rules, including dispute settlement procedures, which—

(I) will help ensure a free flow of foreign direct investment, and

(II) will reduce or eliminate the trade distortive effects of certain trade-related investment measures.

(B) In pursuing the negotiating objectives described in subparagraph (A), United States negotiators shall take into account legitimate United States domestic objectives including, but not limited to, the protection of legitimate health or safety, essential security, environmental, consumer or employment opportunity interests and the law and regulations related thereto.

(12) Safeguards. The principal negotiating objectives of the United States regarding safeguards are—

(A) to improve and expand rules and procedures covering safeguard measures;

(B) to ensure that safeguard measures are—

(i) transparent,

(ii) temporary,

(iii) degressive, and

(iv) subject to review and termination when no longer necessary to remedy injury and to facilitate adjustment; and

(C) to require notification of, and to monitor the use by, GATT Contracting Parties of import relief actions for their domestic industries.

(13) Specific barriers. The principal negotiating objective of the United States regarding specific barriers is to obtain competitive opportunities for United States exports in foreign markets substantially equivalent to the competitive opportunities afforded foreign exports to United States markets, including the reduction or elimination of specific tariff and nontariff trade barriers, particularly—

(A) measures identified in the annual report prepared under section 181 of the Trade Act of 1974 (19 U.S.C. § 2241) and

(B) foreign tariffs and nontariff barriers on competitive United States exports when like or similar products enter the United States at low rates of duty or are duty-free, and other tariff disparities that impede access to particular export markets.

(14) Worker rights. The principal negotiating objectives of the United States regarding worker rights are—

(A) to promote respect for worker rights;

(B) to secure a review of the relationship of worker rights to GATT articles, objectives, and related instruments with a view to ensuring that the benefits of the trading system are available to all workers; and

(C) to adopt, as a principle of the GATT, that the denial of worker rights should not be a means for a country or its industries to gain competitive advantage in international trade.

(15) Access to high technology.

(A) The principal negotiating objective of the United States regarding access to high technology is to obtain the elimination or reduction of foreign barriers to, and acts, policies, or practices by foreign governments which limit equitable access by United States persons to foreign developed technology, including barriers, acts, policies, or practices which have the effect of—

(i) restricting the participation of United States persons in government-supported research and development projects;

(ii) denying equitable access by United States persons to government-held patents;

(iii) requiring the approval or agreement of government entities, or imposing other forms of government interventions, as a condition for the granting of licenses to United States persons by foreign persons (except for approval or agreement which may be necessary for national security purposes to control the export of critical military technology); and

(iv) otherwise denying equitable access by United States persons to foreign-developed technology or contributing to the inequitable flow of technology between the United States and its trading partners.

(B) In pursuing the negotiating objective described in subparagraph (A), the United States negotiators shall take into account United States Government policies in licensing or otherwise making available to foreign persons technology and other information developed by United States laboratories.

(16) Border taxes. The principal negotiating objective of the United States regarding border taxes is to obtain a revision of the GATT with respect to the treatment of border adjustments for internal taxes to redress the disadvantage to countries relying primarily for revenue on direct taxes rather than indirect taxes.

19 U.S.C. § 2902

Sec. 1102. Trade agreement negotiating authority

(a) Agreements regarding tariff barriers.

(1) Whenever the President determines that one or more existing duties or other import restrictions of any foreign country or the United States are unduly burdening and restricting the foreign trade of the United States and that the purposes, policies, and objectives of this title will be promoted thereby, the President—

(A) before June 1, 1993, may enter into trade agreements with foreign countries; and

(B) may, subject to paragraphs (2) through (5), proclaim—

(i) such modification or continuance of any existing duty,

(ii) such continuance of existing duty-free or excise treatment, or

(iii) such additional duties;

as he determines to be required or appropriate to carry out any such trade agreement.

(2) No proclamation may be made under subsection (a) that—

(A) reduces any rate of duty (other than a rate of duty that does not exceed 5 percent ad valorem on the date of enactment of this Act) to a rate which is less than 50 percent of the rate of such duty that applies on such date of enactment; or

(B) increases any rate of duty above the rate that applies on such date of enactment.

(3)(A) Except as provided in subparagraph (B), the aggregate reduction in the rate of duty on any article which is in effect on any day pursuant to a trade agreement entered into under paragraph (1) shall not exceed the aggregate reduction which would have been in effect on such day if a reduction of 3 percent ad valorem or a reduction of one-tenth of the total reduction, whichever is greater, had taken effect on the effective date of the first reduction proclaimed in paragraph (1) to carry out such agreement with respect to such article.

(B) No staging under subparagraph (A) is required with respect to a rate reduction that is proclaimed under paragraph (1) for an article of a kind that is not produced in the United States. The United States International Trade Commission shall advise the President of the identity of articles that may be exempted from staging under this subparagraph.

(4) If the President determines that such action will simplify the computation of reductions under paragraph (3), the President may round an annual reduction by the lesser of—

(A) the difference between the reduction without regard to this paragraph and the next lower whole number; or

(B) one-half of 1 percent ad valorem.

(5) No reduction in a rate of duty under a trade agreement entered into under subsection (a) on any article may take effect more than 10 years after the effective date of the first reduction under paragraph (1) that is proclaimed to carry out the trade agreement with respect to such article.

(6) A rate of duty reduction or increase that may not be proclaimed by reason of paragraph (2) may take effect only if a provision authorizing such reduction or increase is included within an implementing bill provided for under section 1103 and that bill is enacted into law.

(b) Agreements regarding nontariff barriers.

(1) Whenever the President determines that any barrier to, or other distortion of, international trade—

(A) unduly burdens or restricts the foreign trade of the United States or adversely affects the United States economy; or

(B) the imposition of any such barrier or distortion is likely to result in such a burden, restriction, or effect;

and that the purposes, policies, and objectives of this title will be promoted thereby, the President may, before June 1, 1993, enter into a trade agreement with foreign countries providing for—

(i) the reduction or elimination of such barrier or other distortion; or

(ii) the prohibition of, or limitations on the imposition of, such barrier or other distortion.

(2) A trade agreement may be entered into under this subsection only if such agreement makes progress in meeting the applicable objectives described in section 1101.

(c) Bilateral agreements regarding tariff and nontariff barriers.

(1) Before June 1, 1993, the President may enter into bilateral trade agreements with foreign countries that provide for the elimination or reduction of any duty imposed by the United States. A trade agreement entered into under this paragraph may also provide for the reduction or elimination of barriers to, or other distortions of, the international trade of the foreign country or the United States.

(2) Notwithstanding any other provision of law, no trade benefit shall be extended to any country by reason of the extension of any trade benefit to another country under a trade agreement entered into under paragraph (1) with such other country.

(3) A trade agreement may be entered into under paragraph (1) with any foreign country only if—

(A) the agreement makes progress in meeting the applicable objectives described in section 1101;

(B) such foreign country requests the negotiation of such an agreement; and

(C) the President, at least 60 days before the date notice is provided under section 1103(a)(1)(A)—

(i) provides written notice of such negotiations to the Committee on Finance of the Senate and the Committee on Ways and Means of the House of Representatives, and

(ii) consults with such committees regarding the negotiation of such agreement.

(4) The 60-day period of time described in paragraph (3)(C) shall be computed in accordance with section 1103(f).

(5) In any case in which there is an inconsistency between any provision of this Act and any bilateral free trade area agreement that entered into force and effect with respect to the United States before January 1, 1987, the provision shall not apply with respect to the foreign country that is party to that agreement.

(d) Consultation with Congress before agreements entered into.

(1) Before the President enters into any trade agreement under subsection (b) or (c), the President shall consult with—

(A) the Committee on Ways and Means of the House of Representatives and the Committee on Finance of the Senate; and

(B) each other committee of the House and the Senate, and each joint committee of the Congress, which has jurisdiction over legislation involving subject matters which would be affected by the trade agreement.

(2) The consultation under paragraph (1) shall include—

(A) the nature of the agreement;

(B) how and to what extent the agreement will achieve the applicable purposes, policies, and objectives of this title; and

(C) all matters relating to the implementation of the agreement under section 1103.

(3) If it is proposed to implement two or more trade agreements in a single implementing bill under section 1103, the consultation under paragraph (1) shall include the desirability and feasibility of such proposed implementation.

(e) Special provisions regarding Uruguay Round trade negotiations.

(1) In general

Notwithstanding the time limitations in subsections (a) and (b) of this section, if the Uruguay Round of multilateral trade negotiations under the auspices of the General Agreement on Tariffs and Trade has not resulted in trade agreements by May 31, 1993, the President may, during the period after May 31, 1993, and before April 16, 1994, enter into, under subsections (a) and (b) of this section, trade agreements resulting from such negotiations.

(2) Application of tariff proclamation authority

No proclamation under subsection (a) of this section to carry out the provisions regarding tariff barriers of a trade agreement that is entered into pursuant to paragraph (1) may take effect before the effective date of a bill that implements the provisions regarding nontariff barriers of a trade agreement that is entered into under such paragraph.

(3) Application of implementing and "fast track" procedures

Section 1103 applies to any trade agreement negotiated under subsection (b) of this section pursuant to paragraph (1), except that—

(A) in applying subsection (a)(1)(A) of section 1103 to any such agreement, the phrase "at least 120 calendar days before the day on which he enters into the trade agreement (but not later than December 15, 1993)," shall be substituted for the phrase "at least 90 calendar days before the day on which he enters into the trade agreement,"; and

(B) no provision of subsection (b) of section 1103 other than paragraph (1)(A) applies to any such agreement and in applying such paragraph, "April 16, 1994;" shall be substituted for "June 1, 1991;".

(4) Advisory committee reports

The report required under section 135(e)(1) of the Trade Act of 1974 (19 U.S.C. § 2155) regarding any trade agreement provided for under paragraph (1) shall be provided to the President, the Congress, and the United States Trade Representative not later than 30 days after the date on which the President notifies the Congress under section 1103(a)(1)(A) of this title of his intention to enter into the agreement (but before January 15, 1994).

19 U.S.C. § 2903

Sec. 1103. Implementation of trade agreements

(a) In general.

(1) Any agreement entered into under section 1102(b) or (c) shall enter into force with respect to the United States if (and only if)—

(A) the President, at least 90 calendar days before the day on which he enters into the trade agreement, notifies the House of Representatives and the Senate of his intention to enter into the agreement, and promptly thereafter publishes notice of such intention in the Federal Register;

(B) after entering into the agreement, the President submits a document to the House of Representatives and to the Senate containing a copy of the final legal text of the agreement, together with—

(i) a draft of an implementing bill,

(ii) a statement of any administrative action proposed to implement the trade agreement, and

(iii) the supporting information described in paragraph (2); and

(C) the implementing bill is enacted into law.

(2) The supporting information required under paragraph (1)(B)(iii) consists of—

(A) an explanation as to how the implementing bill and proposed administrative action will change or affect existing law; and

(B) a statement—

(i) asserting that the agreement makes progress in achieving the applicable purposes, policies, and objectives of this title,

(ii) setting forth the reasons of the President regarding—

(I) how and to what extent the agreement makes progress in achieving the applicable purposes, policies, and objectives referred to in clause (i), and why and to what extent the agreement does not achieve other applicable purposes, policies, and objectives,

(II) how the agreement serves the interests of United States commerce, and

(III) why the implementing bill and proposed administrative action is required or appropriate to carry out the agreement;

(iii) describing the efforts made by the President to obtain international exchange rate equilibrium and any effect the agreement may have regarding increased international monetary stability; and

(iv) describing the extent, if any, to which—

(I) each foreign country that is a party to the agreement maintains non-commercial state trading enterprises that may adversely affect, nullify, or impair the benefits to the United States under the agreement, and

(II) the agreement applies to or affects purchases and sales by such enterprises.

(3) To ensure that a foreign country which receives benefits under a trade agreement entered into under section 1102(b) or (c) is subject to the obligations imposed by such agreement, the President shall recommend to Congress in the implementing bill and statement of administrative action submitted with respect to such agreement that the benefits and obligations of such agreement apply solely to the parties to such agreement, if such application is consistent with the terms of such agreement. The President may also recommend with respect to any such agreement that the benefits and obligations of such agreement not apply uniformly to all parties to such agreement, if such application is consistent with the terms of such agreement.

(b) Application of Congressional "fast track" procedures to implementing bills.

(1) Except as provided in subsection (c)—

(A) the provisions of section 151 of the Trade Act of 1974 (19 U.S.C. 2191) (hereinafter in this section referred to as "fast track procedures") apply to implementing bills submitted with respect to trade agreements entered into under section 1102(b) or (c) before June 1, 1991; and

(B) such fast track procedures shall be extended to implementing bills submitted with respect to trade agreements entered into under section 1102(b) or (c) after May 31, 1991, and before June 1, 1993, if (and only if)—

(i) the President requests such extension under paragraph (2); and

(ii) neither House of the Congress adopts an extension disapproval resolution under paragraph (5) before June 1, 1991.

(2) If the President is of the opinion that the fast track procedures should be extended to implementing bills described in paragraph (1)(B), the President must submit to the Congress, no later than March 1, 1991, a written report that contains a request for such extension, together with—

(A) a description of all trade agreements that have been negotiated under section 1102(b) or (c) and the anticipated schedule for submitting such agreements to the Congress for approval;

(B) a description of the progress that has been made in multilateral and bilateral negotiations to achieve the purposes, policies, and objectives of this title, and a statement that such progress justifies the continuation of negotiations; and

(C) a statement of the reasons why the extension is needed to complete the negotiations.

(3) The President shall promptly inform the Advisory Committee for Trade Policy and Negotiations established under section 135 of the Trade Act of 1974 (19 U.S.C. 2155) of his decision to submit a report to Congress under paragraph (2). The Advisory Committee shall submit to the Congress as soon as practicable, but no later than March 1, 1991, a written report that contains—

(A) its views regarding the progress that has been made in multilateral and bilateral negotiations to achieve the purposes, policies, and objectives of this title; and

(B) a statement of its views, and the reasons therefor, regarding whether the extension requested under paragraph (2) should be approved or disapproved.

(4) The reports submitted to the Congress under paragraphs (2) and (3), or any portion of the reports, may be classified to the extent the President determines appropriate.

(5)(A) For purposes of this subsection, the term "extension disapproval resolution" means a resolution of either House of the Congress, the sole matter after the resolving clause of which is as follows: "That the disapproves the request of the President for the extension, under section 1103(b)(1)(B)(i) of the Omnibus Trade and Competitiveness Act of 1988 [subsec. (b)(1)(B)(i) of this section], of the provisions of section 151 of the Trade Act of 1974 to any implementing bill submitted with respect to any trade agreement entered into under section 1102(b) or (c) of such Act after May 31, 1991, because sufficient tangible progress has not been made in trade negotiations.", with the blank space being filled with the name of the resolving House of the Congress.

(B) Extension disapproval resolutions—

(i) may be introduced in either House of the Congress by any member of such House; and

(ii) shall be jointly referred, in the House of Representatives, to the Committee on Ways and Means and the Committee on Rules.

(C) The provisions of section 152 (d) and (e) of the Trade Act of 1974 (19 U.S.C. 2192 (d) and (e)) (relating to the floor consideration of certain resolutions in the House and Senate) apply to extension disapproval resolutions.

(D) It is not in order for—

(i) the Senate to consider any extension disapproval resolution not reported by the Committee on Finance;

(ii) the House of Representatives to consider any extension disapproval resolution not reported by the Committee on Ways and Means and the Committee on Rules; or

(iii) either House of the Congress to consider an extension disapproval resolution that is reported to such House after May 15, 1991.

(c) Limitations on use of "fast track" procedures.

(1)(A) The fast track procedures shall not apply to any implementing bill submitted with respect to a trade agreement entered into under section 1102(b) or (c) if both Houses of the Congress separately agree to procedural disapproval resolutions within any 60-day period.

(B) Procedural disapproval resolutions—

(i) in the House of Representatives—

(I) shall be introduced by the chairman or ranking minority member of the Committee on Ways and Means or the chairman or ranking minority member of the Committee on Rules,

(II) shall be jointly referred to the Committee on Ways and Means and the Committee on Rules, and

(III) may not be amended by either Committee; and

(ii) in the Senate shall be original resolutions of the Committee on Finance.

(C) The provisions of section 152(d) and (e) of the Trade Act of 1974 (19 U.S.C. 2192(d) and (e)) (relating to the floor consideration of certain resolutions in the House and Senate) apply to procedural disapproval resolutions.

(D) It is not in order for the House of Representatives to consider any procedural disapproval resolution not reported by the Committee on Ways and Means and the Committee on Rules.

(E) For purposes of this subsection, the term "procedural disapproval resolution" means a resolution of either House of the Congress, the sole matter after the resolving clause of which is as follows: "That the President has failed or refused to consult with Congress on trade negotiations and trade agreements in accordance with the provisions of the Omnibus Trade and Competitiveness Act of 1988, and, therefore, the provisions of section 151 of the Trade Act of 1974 shall not apply to any implementing bill submitted with respect to any trade agreement entered into under section 1102(b) or (c) of such Act of 1988, if, during the 60-day period beginning on the date on which this resolution is agreed to by the * * *, the * * * agrees to a procedural disapproval resolution (within the meaning of section 1103(c)(1)(E) of such Act of 1988 [subsec. (c)(1)(E) of this section])", with the first blank space being filled with the name of the resolving House of the Congress and the second blank space being filled with the name of the other House of the Congress.

(2) The fast track procedures shall not apply to any implementing bill that contains a provision approving of any trade agreement which is entered into under section 1102(c) with any foreign country if either—

(A) the requirements of section 1102(c)(3) are not met with respect to the negotiation of such agreement; or

(B) the Committee on Finance of the Senate or the Committee on Ways and Means of the House of Representatives disapproves of the negotiation of such agreement before the close of the 60-day period which begins on the date notice is provided under section 1102(c)(3)(C)(i) with respect to the negotiation of such agreement.

(d) Rules of House of Representatives and Senate. Subsections (b) and (c) are enacted by the Congress—

(1) as an exercise of the rulemaking power of the House of Representatives and the Senate, respectively, and as such is deemed a part of the rules of each House, respectively, and such procedures supersede other rules only to the extent that they are inconsistent with such other rules; and

(2) with the full recognition of the constitutional right of either House to change the rules (so far as relating to the procedures of that House) at any time, in the same manner, and to the same extent as any other rule of that House.

(e) Computation of certain periods of time. Each period of time described in subsection (c)(1) (A) and (E) and (2) of this section shall be computed without regard to—

(1) the days on which either House of Congress is not in session because of an adjournment of more than 3 days to a day certain or an adjournment of the Congress sine die; and

(2) any Saturday and Sunday, not excluded under paragraph (1), when either House of the Congress is not in session.

* * *

SUBTITLE B—IMPLEMENTATION OF THE HARMONIZED TARIFF SCHEDULE

19 U.S.C. § 3001

Sec. 1201. Purposes

The purposes of this subtitle are—

(1) to approve the International Convention on the Harmonized Commodity Description and Coding System;

(2) to implement in United States law the nomenclature established internationally by the Convention; and

(3) to provide that the Convention shall be treated as a trade agreement obligation of the United States.

19 U.S.C. § 3002

Sec. 1202. Definitions

As used in this subtitle:

(1) The term "Commission" means the United States International Trade Commission.

(2) The term "Convention" means the International Convention on the Harmonized Commodity Description and Coding System, done at Brussels on June 14, 1983, and the Protocol thereto, done at Brussels on June 24, 1986, submitted to the Congress on June 15, 1987.

(3) The term "entered" means entered, or withdrawn from warehouse for consumption, in the customs territory of the United States.

(4) The term "Federal agency" means any establishment in the executive branch of the United States Government.

(5) The term "old Schedules" means title I of the Tariff Act of 1930 (19 U.S.C. § 1202) as in effect on the day before the effective date of the amendment to such title under section 1204(a).

(6) The term "technical rectifications" means rectifications of an editorial character or minor technical or clerical changes which do not affect the substance or meaning of the text, such as—

(A) errors in spelling, numbering, or punctuation;

(B) errors in indentation;

(C) errors (including inadvertent omissions) in cross-references to headings or subheadings or notes; and

(D) other clerical or typographical errors.

19 U.S.C. § 3003

§ 3003. Congressional approval of United States accession to the Convention

(a) Congressional approval

The Congress approves the accession by the United States of America to the Convention.

* * *

§ 3004. Enactment of Harmonized Tariff Schedule

* * *

(1) The following shall be considered to be statutory provisions of law for all purposes:

(A) The provisions of the Harmonized Tariff Schedule as enacted by this chapter.

(B) Each statutory amendment to the Harmonized Tariff Schedule.

(C) Each modification or change made to the Harmonized Tariff Schedule by the President under authority of law (including section 604 of the Trade Act of 1974 [19 U.S.C.A. § 2483]).

* * *

§ 3005. Commission review of, and recommendations regarding, Harmonized Tariff Schedule

(a) In general

The Commission shall keep the Harmonized Tariff Schedule under continuous review and periodically, at such time as amendments to the Convention are recommended by the Customs Cooperation Council for adoption, and as other circumstances warrant, shall recommend to the President such modifications in the Harmonized Tariff Schedule as the Commission considers necessary or appropriate—

(1) to conform the Harmonized Tariff Schedule with amendments made to the Convention;

(2) to promote the uniform application of the Convention and particularly the Annex thereto;

(3) to ensure that the Harmonized Tariff Schedule is kept up-to-date in light of changes in technology or in patterns of international trade;

* * *

§ 3006. Presidential action on Commission recommendations

(a) In general

The President may proclaim modifications, based on the recommendations by the Commission under section 3005 of this title, to the Harmonized Tariff Schedule if the President determines that the modifications—

(1) are in conformity with United States obligations under the Convention; and

(2) do not run counter to the national economic interest of the United States.

* * *

§ 3007. Publication of Harmonized Tariff Schedule

(a) In general

The Commission shall compile and publish, at appropriate intervals, and keep up to date the Harmonized Tariff Schedule and related information in the form of printed copy; and, if, in its judgment, such format would serve the public interest and convenience—

(1) in the form of microfilm images; or

(2) in the form of electronic media.

* * *

HISTORY; ANCILLARY LAWS AND DIRECTIVES

References in text:

"The Harmonized Tariff Schedule", referred to in subsec. (a), is not published in the Code. A current version of the Harmonized Tariff Schedule is maintained and published periodically by the United States International Trade Commission and is available for sale by the Superintendent of Documents, U.S. Government Printing Office, Washington, D.C. 20402; such Schedule is also available via the Internet at http://www.customs.treas.gov.

* * *

HARMONIZED TARIFF SCHEDULE OF THE UNITED STATES

GENERAL NOTES

1. *Tariff Treatment of Imported Goods and of Vessel Equipments, Parts and Repairs.* All goods provided for in this schedule and imported into the customs territory of the United States from outside thereof, and all vessel equipments, parts, materials and repairs covered by the provisions of

subchapter XVIII to chapter 98 of this schedule, are subject to duty or exempt therefrom as prescribed in general notes 3 through 18, inclusive.

2. *Customs Territory of the United States.* The term "*customs territory of the United States*", as used in the tariff schedule, includes only the States, the District of Columbia and Puerto Rico.

3. *Rates of Duty.* The rates of duty in the "Rates of Duty" columns designated 1 ("General" and "Special") and 2 of the tariff schedule apply to goods imported into the customs territory of the United States as hereinafter provided in this note:

(a) *Rate of Duty Column 1.*

(i) Except as provided in subparagraph (iv) of this paragraph, the rates of duty in column 1 are rates which are applicable to all products other than those of countries enumerated in paragraph (b) of this note. Column 1 is divided into two subcolumns, "General" and "Special", which are applicable as provided below.

(ii) The "*General* " subcolumn sets forth the general or normal trade relations (NTR) rates which are applicable to products of those countries described in subparagraph (i) above which are not entitled to special tariff treatment as set forth below.

(iii) The "*Special* " subcolumn reflects rates of duty under one or more special tariff treatment programs described in paragraph (c) of this note and identified in parentheses immediately following the duty rate specified in such subcolumn. These rates apply to those products which are properly classified under a provision for which a special rate is indicated and for which all of the legal requirements for eligibility for such program or programs have been met. Where a product is eligible for special treatment under more than one program, the lowest rate of duty provided for any applicable program shall be imposed. Where no special rate of duty is provided for a provision, or where the country from which a product otherwise eligible for special treatment was imported is not designated as a beneficiary country under a program appearing with the appropriate provision, the rates of duty in the "General" subcolumn of column 1 shall apply.

* * *

(b) *Rate of Duty Column 2.* Notwithstanding any of the foregoing provisions of this note, the rates of duty shown in column 2 shall apply to products, whether imported directly or indirectly, of the following countries and areas pursuant to section 401 of the Tariff Classification Act of 1962, to section 231 or 257(e)(2) of the Trade Expansion Act of 1962, to section 404(a) of the Trade Act of 1974 or to any other applicable section of law, or to action taken by the President thereunder:

Cuba

North Korea

* * *

GENERAL RULES OF INTERPRETATION

Classification of goods in the tariff schedule shall be governed by the following principles:

1. The table of contents, alphabetical index, and titles of sections, chapters and sub-chapters are provided for ease of reference only; for legal purposes, classification shall be determined according to the terms of the headings and any relative section or chapter notes and, provided such headings or notes do not otherwise require, according to the following provisions:

2. (a) Any reference in a heading to an article shall be taken to include a reference to that article incomplete or unfinished, provided that, as entered, the incomplete or unfinished article has the essential character of the complete or finished article. It shall also include a reference to that article complete or finished (or failing to be classified as complete or finished by virtue of this rule), entered unassembled or disassembled.

   (b) Any reference in a heading to a material or substance shall be taken to include a reference to mixtures or combinations of that material or substance with other materials or substances. Any reference to goods of a given material or substance shall be taken to include a reference to goods consisting wholly or partly of such material or substance. The classification of goods consisting of more than one material or substance shall be according to the principles of rule 3.

3. When, by application of rule 2(b) or for any other reason, goods are, *prima facie,* classifiable under two or more headings, classification shall be effected as follows:

   (a) The heading which provides the most specific description shall be preferred to headings providing a more general description. However, when two or more headings each refer to part only of the materials or substances contained in mixed or composite goods or to part only of the items in a set put up for retail sale, those headings are to be regarded as equally specific in relation to those goods, even if one of them gives a more complete or precise description of the goods.

   (b) Mixtures, composite goods consisting of different materials or made up of different components, and goods put up in sets for retail sale, which cannot be classified by reference to 3(a), shall be classified as if they consisted of the material or component which gives them their essential character, insofar as this criterion is applicable.

(c) When goods cannot be classified by reference to 3(a) or 3(b), they shall be classified under the heading which occurs last in numerical order among those which equally merit consideration.

4. Goods which cannot be classified in accordance with the above rules shall be classified under the heading appropriate to the goods to which they are most akin.

5. In addition to the foregoing provisions, the following rules shall apply in respect of the goods referred to therein:

(a) Camera cases, musical instrument cases, gun cases, drawing instrument cases, necklace cases and similar containers, specially shaped or fitted to contain a specific article or set of articles, suitable for long-term use and entered with the articles for which they are intended, shall be classified with such articles when of a kind normally sold therewith. The rule does not, however, apply to containers which give the whole its essential character;

(b) Subject to the provisions of rule 5(a) above, packing materials and packing containers entered with the goods therein shall be classified with the goods if they are of a kind normally used for packing such goods. However, this provision is not binding when such packing materials or packing containers are clearly suitable for repetitive use.

6. For legal purposes, the classification of goods in the subheadings of a heading shall be determined according to the terms of those subheadings and any related subheading notes and, *mutatis mutandis,* to the above rules, on the understanding that only subheadings at the same level are comparable. For the purposes of this rule, the relative section, chapter and subchapter notes also apply, unless the context otherwise requires.

ADDITIONAL U.S. RULES OF INTERPRETATION

1. In the absence of special language or context which otherwise requires—

(a) a tariff classification controlled by use (other than actual use) is to be determined in accordance with the use in the United States at, or immediately prior to, the date of importation, of goods of that class or kind to which the imported goods belong, and the controlling use is the principal use;

(b) a tariff classification controlled by the actual use to which the imported goods are put in the United States is satisfied only if such use is intended at the time of importation, the goods are so used and proof thereof is furnished within 3 years after the date the goods are entered;

(c) a provision for parts of an article covers products solely or principally used as a part of such articles but a provision for "parts" or "parts and accessories" shall not prevail over a specific provision for such part or accessory; and

(d) the principles of section XI regarding mixtures of two or more textile materials shall apply to the classification of goods in any provision in which a textile material is named.

* * *

SUBTITLE C—RESPONSE TO UNFAIR INTERNATIONAL TRADE PRACTICES

Part 1—Enforcement of United States Rights Under Trade Agreements and Response to Certain Foreign Trade Practices

* * *

Part 2—Improvement in the Enforcement of the Antidumping and Countervailing Duty Laws

Part 3—Protection of Intellectual Property Rights

Part 4—Telecommunications Trade

SUBTITLE D—ADJUSTMENT TO IMPORT COMPETITION

SUBTITLE E—NATIONAL SECURITY

SUBTITLE F—TRADE AGENCIES

SUBTITLE G—TARIFF PROVISIONS

* * *

TITLE II—EXPORT ENHANCEMENT

SUBTITLE B—EXPORT ENHANCEMENT

SUBTITLE C—EXPORT PROMOTION

SUBTITLE D—EXPORT CONTROLS

Part I—Export Controls Generally

Part II—Multilateral Export Control Enhancement

Sec. 2441. Short title

This part may be cited as the "Multilateral Export Control Enhancement Amendments Act".

Sec. 2442. Findings

The Congress makes the following findings:

(1) The diversion of advanced milling machinery to the Soviet Union by the Toshiba Machine Company and Konigsberg Trading Company has had a serious impact on United States and Western security interests.

(2) United States and Western security is undermined without the cooperation of the governments and nationals of all countries participating in the group known as the Coordinating Committee (hereafter in this part referred to as "COCOM") in enforcing the COCOM agreement.

(3) It is the responsibility of all governments participating in COCOM to place in effect strong national security export control laws, to license strategic exports carefully, and to enforce those export control laws strictly, since the COCOM system is only as strong as the national laws and enforcement on which it is based.

(4) It is also important for corporations to implement effective internal control systems to ensure compliance with export control laws.

(5) In order to protect United States national security, the United States must take steps to ensure the compliance of foreign companies with COCOM controls, including, where necessary conditions have been met, the imposition of sanctions against violators of controls commensurate with the severity of the violation.

Sec. 2443. Mandatory sanctions against Toshiba and Konigsberg

(a) Sanctions against Toshiba Machine Company, Konigsberg Trading Company, and Certain other Foreign Persons. (1) The President shall impose, for a period of 3 years—

(1) a prohibition on contracting with, and procurement of products and services from—

(A) Toshiba Machine Company and Konigsberg Trading Company, and

(B) any other foreign person whom the President finds to have knowingly facilitated the diversion of advanced milling machinery by Toshiba Machine Company and Konigsberg Trading Company to the Soviet Union, by any department, agency, or instrumentality of the United States Government; and

(2) a prohibition on the importation into the United States of all products produced by Toshiba Machine Company, Konigsberg Trading Company, and any foreign person described in paragraph (1)(B).

(b) Sanctions against Toshiba Corporation and Konigsberg Vaapenfabrikk. The President shall impose, for a period of 3 years, a prohibition on contracting with, and procurement of products and services from, the Toshiba Corporation and Konigsberg Vaapenfabrikk, by any department, agency, or instrumentality of the United States Government.

(c) Exceptions. The President shall not apply sanctions under this section—

(1) in the case of procurement of defense articles or defense services—

(A) under existing contracts or subcontracts, including exercise of options for production quantities to satisfy United States operational military requirements;

(B) if the President determines that the company or foreign person to whom the sanctions would otherwise be applied is a sole source supplier of essential defense articles or services and no alternative supplier can be identified; or

(C) if the President determines that such articles or services are essential to the national security under defense coproduction agreements; or

(2) to—

(A) products or services provided under contracts or other binding agreements (as such terms are defined by the President in regulations) entered into before June 30, 1987;

(B) spare parts;

(C) component parts, but not finished products, essential to United States products or production;

(D) routine servicing and maintenance of products; or

(E) information and technology.

(d) Definitions. For purposes of this section—

(1) the term "component part" means any article which is not usable for its intended functions without being imbedded or integrated into any other product and which, if used in production of a finished product, would be substantially transformed in that process;

(2) the term "finished product" means any article which is usable for its intended functions without being imbedded in or integrated into any other product, but in no case shall such term be deemed to include an article produced by a person other than a sanctioned person that contains parts or components of the sanctioned person if the parts or components have been substantially transformed during production of the finished product; and

(3) the term "sanctioned person" means a company or other foreign person upon whom prohibitions have been imposed under subsection (a) or (b).

* * *

TITLE III—INTERNATIONAL FINANCIAL POLICY

* * *

TITLE V—FOREIGN CORRUPT PRACTICES AMENDMENTS; INVESTMENT; AND TECHNOLOGY

SUBTITLE A—FOREIGN CORRUPT PRACTICES ACT AMENDMENTS; REVIEW OF CERTAIN ACQUISITIONS

Part I—Foreign Corrupt Practices Act Amendments [included as a separate document]

Part II—Review of Certain Mergers, Acquisitions, and Takeovers

[See FINSA, Document 48]

DOCUMENT 27

TARIFF ACT OF 1930

■ ■ ■

Act of June 17, 1930, ch. 497, 46 Stat. 590, 672, 685, 19 U.S.C. §§ 1001–1677h.

The Tariff Act of 1930 has been amended numerous times, including amendments in the Trade Act of 1974, the Trade Agreements Act of 1979, the Trade and Tariff Act of 1984, the Omnibus Trade and Competitiveness Act of 1988, the Customs and Trade Act of 1990, the North American Free Trade Agreement Implementation Act of 1993, and the Uruguay Round Agreements Act of 1994. These amendments have been incorporated into the selected provisions included below.

Table of Contents

(Selected Provisions Only)

(U.S. Code Section Numbers)

(a) Finality of decisions; return of papers

(b) Finality and conclusiveness of customs officers' determinations

(c) Form, number, and amendment of protest; filing of protest

1515. Review of protests

(a) Administrative review within two years

1516. Petitions by domestic interested parties

(a) Request for classification and rate of duty; petition

(b) Determination on petition

(c) Contest by petitioner of appraised value, classification, or rate of duty

1516a. Judicial review in countervailing duty and antidumping duty proceedings

(a) Review of determination

(f) Definitions

(g) Review of countervailing duty and antidumping duty determinations involving free trade area country merchandise

1526. Merchandise bearing American trademark

(a) Importation prohibited

(b) Seizure and forfeiture

(c) Injunction and damages

(d) Exemptions; publication in Federal Register; forfeitures; rules and regulations

(e) Merchandise bearing counterfeit mark; seizure and forfeiture; disposition of seized goods

(f) Civil penalties

SUBTITLE IV

COUNTERVAILING AND ANTIDUMPING DUTIES

IMPOSITION OF COUNTERVAILING DUTIES

1671. Countervailing duties imposed

(a) General rule

(b) Subsidies Agreement country

(c) Limited disclosure of certain proprietary information under protective order

(d) Service

(f) Disclosure of proprietary intervention under protective orders issued pursuant to the North American Free Trade Agreement or the United States-Canada Agreement

1677f–1 Sampling and averaging; determination of weighted average, dumping margin and countervailable subsidy rate

(a) In general

(b) Selection of averages and samples

(c) Determination of dumping margin

(d) Determination of less than fair value

(e) Determination of countervailable subsidy rate

1677i. Downstream product monitoring

(a) Petition requesting monitoring

(d) Definitions

1677j. Prevention of circumvention of antidumping and countervailing duty orders

(a) Merchandise completed or assembled in the United States

(b) Merchandise completed or assembled in other foreign countries

(c) Minor alterations of merchandise

(d) Later-developed merchandise

1677k. Antidumping petition by third countries

(a) Filing of petition

(b) Initiation

(c) Determinations

SUBTITLE II. SPECIAL PROVISIONS

MISCELLANEOUS

UNITED STATES INTERNATIONAL TRADE COMMISSION

§ 1330. Organization of Commission

(a) Membership. The United States International Trade Commission (referred to in this title as the "Commission") shall be composed of six commissioners who shall be appointed by the President, by and with the advice and consent of the Senate. No person shall be eligible for appointment as a commissioner unless he is a citizen of the United States, and, in the judgment of the President, is possessed of qualifications requisite for developing expert knowledge of international trade problems and efficiency in administering the duties and functions of the Commission. A person who has served as a commissioner for more than 5 years (excluding service as a commissioner before the date of the enactment of the Trade Act of 1974) shall not be eligible for reappointment as a commissioner. Not more than three of the commissioners shall be members of the same political party, and in making appointments members of different political parties shall be appointed alternately as nearly as may be practicable.

(b) Terms of office. * * * The term of office of each commissioner appointed after such date shall expire 9 years from the date of the expiration of the term for which his predecessor was appointed, except that—

(1) any commissioner appointed to fill a vacancy occurring prior to the expiration of the term for which his predecessor was appointed shall be appointed for the remainder of such term, and

(2) any commissioner may continue to serve as a commissioner after an expiration of his term of office until his successor is appointed and qualified.

* * *

(d) Effect of divided vote in certain cases

(1) In a proceeding in which the Commission is required to determine—

(A) under section 202 of the Trade Act of 1974, whether increased imports of an article are a substantial cause of serious injury, or the threat thereof, as described in subsection (b)(1) of that section hereafter in this subsection referred to as "serious injury"), or

(B) under section 406 of such Act, whether market disruption exists, and the commissioners voting are equally divided with respect to such determination, then the determination agreed upon by either group of commissioners may be considered by the President as the determination of the Commission.

(2) If under section 202(b) or 406 of the Trade Act of 1974 there is an affirmative determination of the Commission, or a determination of the Commission which the President may consider an affirmative determination under paragraph (1), that serious injury or market disruption exists, respectively, and a majority of the commissioners voting are unable to agree on a finding or recommendation described in section 202(e)(1) of such Act or the finding described in section 406(a)(3) of such Act, as the case may be (hereafter in this subsection referred to as a "remedy finding"), then—

(A) if a plurality of not less than three commissioners so voting agree on a remedy finding, such remedy finding shall, for purposes of sections 202 and 203 of such Act, be treated as the remedy finding of the Commission, or

(B) if two groups, both of which include not less than 3 commissioners, each agree upon a remedy finding and the President reports under section 204(a) of such Act [that—

(i) he is taking the action agreed upon by one such group, then the remedy finding agreed upon by the other group shall, for purposes of section 203 of such Act, be treated as the remedy finding of the Commission, or

(ii) he is taking action which differs from the action agreed upon by both such groups, or that he will not take any action, then the remedy finding agreed upon by either such group may be considered by the Congress as the remedy finding of the Commission and shall, for purposes of section 203 of such Act, be treated as the remedy finding of the Commission.

(3) In any proceeding to which paragraph (1) applies in which the commissioners voting are equally divided on a determination that serious injury exists, or that market disruption exists, the Commission shall report to the President the determination of each group of commissioners. In any proceeding to which paragraph (2) applies, the Commission shall report to the President the remedy finding of each group of commissioners voting.

* * *

(5) Whenever, in any case in which the Commission is authorized to make an investigation upon its own motion, upon complaint, or upon application of any interested party, one-half of the number of commissioners voting agree that the investigation should be made, such investigation shall thereupon be carried out in accordance with the

statutory authority covering the matter in question. Whenever the Commission is authorized to hold hearings in the course of any investigation and one-half of the number of commissioners voting agree that hearings should be held, such hearings shall thereupon be held in accordance with the statutory authority covering the matter in question.

* * *

§ 1333. Testimony and production of papers

(a) Authority to obtain information. For the purposes of carrying out its functions and duties in connection with any investigation authorized by law, the commission or its duly authorized agent or agents (1) shall have access to and the right to copy any document, paper, or record, pertinent to the subject matter under investigation, in the possession of any person, firm, copartnership, corporation, or association engaged in the production, importation, or distribution of any article under investigation, (2) may summon witnesses, take testimony, and administer oaths, (3) may require any person, firm, copartnership, corporation, or association to produce books or papers relating to any matter pertaining to such investigation, and (4) may require any person, firm, copartnership, corporation, or association to furnish in writing, in such detail and in such form as the commission may prescribe, information in their possession pertaining to such investigation. Any member of the commission may sign subpoenas, and members and agents of the commission, when authorized by the commission, may administer oaths and affirmations, examine witnesses, take testimony, and receive evidence.

(b) Witnesses and evidence. Such attendance of witnesses and the production of such documentary evidence may be required from any place in the United States at any designated place of hearing. And in case of disobedience to a subpoena the commission may invoke the aid of any district or territorial court of the United States or the Supreme Court of the District of Columbia [United States District Court for the District of Columbia] in requiring the attendance and testimony of witnesses and the production of documentary evidence, and such court within the jurisdiction of which such inquiry is carried on may, in case of contumacy or refusal to obey a subpoena issued to any corporation or other person, issue an order requiring such corporation or other person to appear before the commission, or to produce documentary evidence if so ordered or to give evidence touching the matter in question; and any failure to obey such order of the court may be punished by such court as a contempt thereof.

* * *

(d) Depositions. The commission may order testimony to be taken by deposition in any proceeding or investigation pending before the commission at any stage of such proceeding or investigation. Such depositions may be taken before any person designated by the commission and having power to administer oaths. Such testimony shall be reduced to writing by the person taking the deposition, or under his direction, and shall then be subscribed by the deponent. Any person, firm, copartnership, corporation, or association, may be compelled to appear and depose and to produce documentary evidence in the same manner as witnesses may be compelled to appear and testify and produce documentary evidence before the commission, as hereinbefore provided.

§ 1337. Unfair practices in import trade

(a) Unfair methods of competition declared unlawful.

(1) Subject to paragraph (2), the following are unlawful, and when found by the Commission to exist shall be dealt with, in addition to any other provision of law, as provided in this section:

(A) Unfair methods of competition and unfair acts in the importation of articles (other than articles provided for in subparagraphs (B), (C), (D), and (E)) into the United States, or in the sale of such articles by the owner, importer, or consignee, the threat or effect of which is—

(i) to destroy or substantially injure an industry in the United States;

(ii) to prevent the establishment of such an industry; or

(iii) to restrain or monopolize trade and commerce in the United States.

(B) The importation into the United States, the sale for importation, or the sale within the United States after importation by the owner, importer, or consignee, of articles that—

(i) infringe a valid and enforceable United States patent or a valid and enforceable United States copyright registered under title 17, United States Code; or

(ii) are made, produced, processed, or mined under, or by means of, a process covered by the claims of a valid and enforceable United States patent.

(C) The importation into the United States, the sale for importation, or the sale within the United States after importation by the owner, importer, or consignee, of articles that infringe a valid and enforceable United States trademark registered under the Trademark Act of 1946.

(D) The importation into the United States, the sale for importation, or the sale within the United States after importation by the owner, importer, or consignee, of a semiconductor chip product in a manner that constitutes infringement of a mask work registered under chapter 9 of title 17, United States Code.

(E) The importation into the United States, the sale for importation, or the sale within the United States after importation by the owner, importer, or consigner, of an article that constitutes infringement of the exclusive rights in a design protected under chapter 13 of title 17, United States Code.

(2) Subparagraphs (B), (C), (D), and (E) of paragraph (1) apply only if an industry in the United States, relating to the articles protected by the patent, copyright, trademark, mask work, or design concerned, exists or is in the process of being established.

(3) For purposes of paragraph (2), an industry in the United States shall be considered to exist if there is in the United States, with respect to the articles protected by the patent, copyright, trademark, mask work, or design concerned—

(A) significant investment in plant and equipment;

(B) significant employment of labor or capital; or

(C) substantial investment in its exploitation, including engineering, research and development, or licensing.

(4) For the purposes of this section, the phrase "owner, importer, or consignee" includes any agent of the owner, importer, or consignee.

(b) Investigation of violations by Commission.

(1) The Commission shall investigate any alleged violation of this section on complaint under oath or upon its initiative. Upon commencing any such investigation, the Commission shall publish notice thereof in the Federal Register. The Commission shall conclude any such investigation and make its determination under this section at the earliest practicable time after the date of publication of notice of such investigation. To promote expeditious adjudication, the Commission shall, within 45 days after an investigation is initiated, establish a target date for its final determination.

(2) During the course of each investigation under this section, the Commission shall consult with, and seek advice and information from, the Department of Health and Human Services, the Department of Justice, the Federal Trade Commission, and such other departments and agencies as it considers appropriate.

(3) Whenever, in the course of an investigation under this section, the Commission has reason to believe, based on information before it, that a matter, in whole or in part, may come within the purview of subtitle B of title VII of this Act, it shall promptly notify the Secretary of Commerce so that such action may be taken as is otherwise authorized by such subtitle. If the Commission has reason to believe that the matter before it (A) is

based solely on alleged acts and effects which are within the purview of section 701 or 731, or (B) relates to an alleged copyright infringement with respect to which action is prohibited by section 1008 of title 17, United States Code, the Commission shall terminate, or not institute, any investigation into the matter. If the Commission has reason to believe the matter before it is based in part on alleged acts and effects which are within the purview of section 701 or 731 of this Act, and in part on alleged acts and effects which may, independently from or in conjunction with those within the purview of such section, establish a basis for relief under this section, then it may institute or continue an investigation into the matter. If the Commission notifies the Secretary or the administering authority (as defined in section 771(1) of this Act) with respect to a matter under this paragraph, the Commission may suspend its investigation during the time the matter is before the Secretary or administering authority for final decision. Any final decision by the administering authority under section 701 or 731 of this Act with respect to the matter within such section 701 or 731 of which the Commission has notified the Secretary or administering authority shall be conclusive upon the Commission with respect to the issue of less-than-fair-value sales or subsidization and the matters necessary for such decision.

(c) Determinations; review. The Commission shall determine, with respect to each investigation conducted by it under this section, whether or not there is a violation of this section, except that the Commission may, by issuing a consent order or on the basis of an agreement between the private parties to the investigation, including an agreement to present the matter for arbitration, terminate any such investigation, in whole or in part, without making such a determination. Each determination under subsection (d) or (e) shall be made on the record after notice and opportunity for a hearing in conformity with the provisions of subchapter II of chapter 5 of title 5, United States Code. All legal and equitable defenses may be presented in all cases. A respondent may raise any counterclaim in a manner prescribed by the Commission. Immediately after a counterclaim is received by the Commission, the respondent raising such counterclaim shall file a notice of removal with a United States district court in which venue for any of the counterclaims raised by the party would exist under section 1391 of title 28, United States Code. Any counterclaim raised pursuant to this section shall relate back to the date of the original complaint in the proceeding before the Commission. Action on such counterclaim shall not delay or affect the proceeding under this section, including the legal and equitable defenses that may be raised under this subsection. Any person adversely affected by a final determination of the Commission under subsection (d), (e), (f), or (g) may appeal such determination, within 60 days after the determination becomes final, to the United States Court of Appeals for the Federal Circuit for review in accordance with chapter 7 of title 5, United States Code.

Notwithstanding the foregoing provisions of this subsection, Commission determinations under subsections (d), (e), (f), and (g) with respect to its findings on the public health and welfare, competitive conditions in the United States economy, the production of like or directly competitive articles in the United States, and United States consumers, the amount and nature of bond, or the appropriate remedy shall be reviewable in accordance with section 706 of title 5, United States Code. Determinations by the Commission under subsections (e), (f), and (j) with respect to forfeiture of bonds and under subsection (h) with respect to the imposition of sanctions for abuse of discovery or abuse of process shall also be reviewable in accordance with section 706 of title 5, United States Code.

(d) Exclusion of articles from entry.

(1) If the Commission determines, as a result of an investigation under this section, that there is a violation of this section, it shall direct that the articles concerned, imported by any person violating the provision of this section, be excluded from entry into the United States, unless, after considering the effect of such exclusion upon the public health and welfare, competitive conditions in the United States economy, the production of like or directly competitive articles in the United States, and United States consumers, it finds that such articles should not be excluded from entry. The Commission shall notify the Secretary of the Treasury of its action under this subsection directing such exclusion from entry, and upon receipt of such notice, the Secretary shall, through the proper officers, refuse such entry.

(2) The authority of the Commission to order an exclusion from entry of articles shall be limited to persons determined by the Commission to be violating this section unless the Commission determines that—

(A) a general exclusion from entry of articles is necessary to prevent circumvention of an exclusion order limited to products of named persons; or

(B) there is a pattern of violation of this section and it is difficult to identify the source of infringing products.

(e) Exclusion of articles from entry during investigation except under bond.

(1) If, during the course of an investigation under this section, the Commission determines that there is reason to believe that there is a violation of this section, it may direct that the articles concerned, imported by any person with respect to whom there is reason to believe that such person is violating this section, be excluded from entry into the United States, unless, after considering the effect of such exclusion upon the public health and welfare, competitive conditions in the United States economy, the production of like or directly competitive articles in the United States, and United States consumers, it finds that such articles should not be

excluded from entry. The Commission shall notify the Secretary of the Treasury of its action under this subsection directing such exclusion from entry, and upon receipt of such notice, the Secretary shall, through the proper officers, refuse such entry, except that such articles shall be entitled to entry under bond prescribed by the Secretary in an amount determined by the Commission to be sufficient to protect the complainant from any injury. If the Commission later determines that the respondent has violated the provisions of this section, the bond may be forfeited to the complainant.

(2) A complainant may petition the Commission for the issuance of an order under this subsection. The Commission shall make a determination with regard to such petition by no later than the 90th day after the date on which the Commission's notice of investigation is published in the Federal Register. The Commission may extend the 90–day period for an additional 60 days in a case it designates as a more complicated case. The Commission shall publish in the Federal Register its reasons why it designated the case as being more complicated. The Commission may require the complainant to post a bond as a prerequisite to the issuance of an order under this subsection. If the Commission later determines that the respondent has not violated the provisions of this section, the bond may be forfeited to the respondent.

(3) The Commission may grant preliminary relief under this subsection or subsection (f) to the same extent as preliminary injunctions and temporary restraining orders may be granted under the Federal Rules of Civil Procedure.

(4) The Commission shall prescribe the terms and conditions under which bonds may be forfeited under paragraphs (1) and (2).

(f) Cease and desist orders; civil penalty for violation of orders.

(1) In addition to, or in lieu of taking action under subsection (d) or (e), the Commission may issue and cause to be served on any person violating this section, or believed to be violating this section, as the case may be, an order directing such person to cease and desist from engaging in the unfair methods or acts involved, unless after considering the effect of such order upon the public health and welfare, competitive conditions in the United States economy, the production of like or directly competitive articles in the United States, and United States consumers, it finds that such order should not be issued. The Commission may at any time, upon such notice and in such manner as it deems proper, modify or revoke any such order, and, in the case of a revocation, may take action under subsection (d) or (e), as the case may be. If a temporary cease and desist order is issued in addition to, or in lieu of, an exclusion order under subsection (e), the Commission may require the complainant to post a bond, in an amount determined by the Commission to be sufficient to protect the respondent

from any injury, as a prerequisite to the issuance of an order under this subsection. If the Commission later determines that the respondent has not violated the provisions of this section, the bond may be forfeited to the respondent. The Commission shall prescribe the terms and conditions under which the bonds may be forfeited under this paragraph.

(2) Any person who violates an order issued by the Commission under paragraph (1) after it has become final shall forfeit and pay to the United States a civil penalty for each day on which an importation of articles, or their sale, occurs in violation of the order of not more than the greater of $ 100,000 or twice the domestic value of the articles entered or sold on such day in violation of the order. Such penalty shall accrue to the United States and may be recovered for the United States in a civil action brought by the Commission in the Federal District Court for the District of Columbia or for the district in which the violation occurs. In such actions, the United States district courts may issue mandatory injunctions incorporating the relief sought by the Commission as they deem appropriate in the enforcement of such final orders of the Commission.

(g) Filing of complaint; exclusion.

(1) If—

(A) a complaint is filed against a person under this section;

(B) the complaint and a notice of investigation are served on the person;

(C) the person fails to respond to the complaint and notice or otherwise fails to appear to answer the complaint and notice;

(D) the person fails to show good cause why the person should not be found in default; and

(E) the complainant seeks relief limited solely to that person;

the Commission shall presume the facts alleged in the complaint to be true and shall, upon request, issue an exclusion from entry or a cease and desist order, or both, limited to that person unless, after considering the effect of such exclusion or order upon the public health and welfare, competitive conditions in the United States economy, the production of like or directly competitive articles in the United States, and United States consumers, the Commission finds that such exclusion or order should not be issued.

(2) In addition to the authority of the Commission to issue a general exclusion from entry of articles when a respondent appears to contest an investigation concerning a violation of the provisions of this section, a general exclusion from entry of articles, regardless of the source or importer of the articles, may be issued if—

(A) no person appears to contest an investigation concerning a violation of the provisions of this section,

(B) such a violation is established by substantial, reliable, and probative evidence, and

(C) the requirements of subsection (d)(2) are met.

(h) Sanctions for abuse of discovery and abuse of process. The Commission may by rule prescribe sanctions for abuse of discovery and abuse of process to the extent authorized by Rule 11 and Rule 37 of the Federal Rules of Civil Procedure.

(i) Forfeiture.

(1) In addition to taking action under subsection (d), the Commission may issue an order providing that any article imported in violation of the provisions of this section be seized and forfeited to the United States if—

(A) the owner, importer, or consignee of the article previously attempted to import the article into the United States;

(B) the article was previously denied entry into the United States by reason of an order issued under subsection (d); and

(C) upon such previous denial of entry, the Secretary of the Treasury provided the owner, importer, or consignee of the article written notice of—

(i) such order, and

(ii) the seizure and forfeiture that would result from any further attempt to import the article into the United States.

(2) The Commission shall notify the Secretary of the Treasury of any order issued under this subsection and, upon receipt of such notice, the Secretary of the Treasury shall enforce such order in accordance with the provisions of this section.

(3) Upon the attempted entry of articles subject to an order issued under this subsection, the Secretary of the Treasury shall immediately notify all ports of entry of the attempted importation and shall identify the persons notified under paragraph (1)(C).

(4) The Secretary of the Treasury shall provide—

(A) the written notice described in paragraph (1)(C) to the owner, importer, or consignee of any article that is denied entry into the United States by reason of an order issued under subsection (d); and

(B) a copy of such written notice to the Commission.

(j) Referral to President.

(1) If the Commission determines that there is a violation of this section, or that, for purposes of subsection (e), there is reason to believe that there is such a violation, it shall—

(A) publish such determination in the Federal Register, and

(B) transmit to the President a copy of such determination and the action taken under subsection (d), (e), (f), (g), or (i), with respect thereto, together with the record upon which such determination is based.

(2) If, before the close of the 60–day period beginning on the day after the day on which he receives a copy of such determination, the President, for policy reasons, disapproves such determination and notifies the Commission of his disapproval, then, effective on the date of such notice, such determination and the action taken under subsection (d), (e), (f), (g), or (i) with respect thereto shall have no force or effect.

(3) Subject to the provisions of paragraph (2), such determination shall, except for purposes of subsection (c), be effective upon publication thereof in the Federal Register, and the action taken under subsection (d), (e), (f), (g), or (i) with respect thereto shall be effective as provided in such subsections, except that articles directed to be excluded from entry under subsection (d) or subject to a cease and desist order under subsection (f) shall, until such determination becomes final, be entitled to entry under bond prescribed by the Secretary in an amount determined by the Commission to be sufficient to protect the complainant from any injury. If the determination becomes final, the bond may be forfeited to the complainant. The Commission shall prescribe the terms and conditions under which bonds may be forfeited under this paragraph.

(4) If the President does not disapprove such determination within such 60–day period, or if he notifies the Commission before the close of such period that he approves such determination, then, for purposes of paragraph (3) and subsection (c) such determination shall become final on the day after the close of such period or the day on which the President notifies the Commission of his approval, as the case may be.

(k) Period of effectiveness; termination of violation or modification or rescission of exclusion or order.

(1) Except as provided in subsections (f) and (j), any exclusion from entry or order under this section shall continue in effect until the Commission finds, and in the case of exclusion from entry notifies the Secretary of the Treasury, that the conditions which led to such exclusion from entry or order no longer exist.

(2) If any person who has previously been found by the Commission to be in violation of this section petitions the Commission for a determination

that the petitioner is no longer in violation of this section or for a modification or rescission of an exclusion from entry or order under subsection (d), (e), (f), (g), or (i)—

(A) the burden of proof in any proceeding before the Commission regarding such petition shall be on the petitioner; and

(B) relief may be granted by the Commission with respect to such petition—

(i) on the basis of new evidence or evidence that could not have been presented at the prior proceeding, or

(ii) on grounds which would permit relief from a judgment or order under the Federal Rules of Civil Procedure.

(*l*) Importations by or for United States. Any exclusion from entry or order under subsection (d), (e), (f), (g), or (i) in cases based on a proceeding involving a patent copyright, mask work, or design under subsection (a)(1), shall not apply to any articles imported by and for the use of the United States, or imported for, and to be used for, the United States with the authorization or consent of the Government. Whenever any article would have been excluded from entry or would not have been entered pursuant to the provisions of such subsections but for the operation of this subsection, an owner of the patent, copyright, mask work, or design adversely affected shall be entitled to reasonable and entire compensation in an action before the United States Court of Federal Claims pursuant to the procedures of section 1498 of title 28, United States Code.

(m) Definition of United States. For purposes of this section and sections 338 and 340, the term "United States" means the customs territory of the United States as defined in general note 2 of the Harmonized Tariff Schedule of the United States.

(n) Disclosure.

(1) Information submitted to the Commission or exchanged among the parties in connection with proceedings under this section which is properly designated as confidential pursuant to Commission rules may not be disclosed (except under a protective order issued under regulations of the Commission which authorizes limited disclosure of such information) to any person (other than a person described in paragraph (2)) without the consent of the person submitting it.

(2) Notwithstanding the prohibition contained in paragraph (1), information referred to in that paragraph may be disclosed to—

(A) an officer or employee of the Commission who is directly concerned with—

(i) carrying out the investigation or related proceeding in connection with which the information is submitted,

(ii) the administration of a bond posted pursuant to subsection (e), (f), or (j),

(iii) the administration or enforcement of an exclusion order issued pursuant to subsection (d), (e), or (g), a cease and desist order issued pursuant to subsection (f), or a consent order issued pursuant to subsection (c),

(iv) proceedings for the modification or rescission of a temporary or permanent order issued under subsection (d), (e), (f), (g), or (i), or a consent order issued under this section, or

(v) maintaining the administrative record of the investigation or related proceeding,

(B) an officer or employee of the United States Government who is directly involved in the review under subsection (j), or

(C) an officer or employee of the United States Customs Service who is directly involved in administering an exclusion from entry under subsection (d), (e), or (g) resulting from the investigation or related proceeding in connection with which the information is submitted.

* * *

PROMOTION OF FOREIGN TRADE

* * *

§ 1401a. Value

(a) In general

(1) Except as otherwise specifically provided for in this Act, imported merchandise shall be appraised, for the purposes of this Act, on the basis of the following:

(A) The transaction value provided for under subsection (b).

(B) The transaction value of identical merchandise provided for under subsection (c), if the value referred to in subparagraph (A) cannot be determined, or can be determined but cannot be used by reason of subsection (b)(2).

(C) The transaction value of similar merchandise provided for under subsection (c), if the value referred to in subparagraph (B) cannot be determined.

(D) The deductive value provided for under subsection (d), if the value referred to in subparagraph (C) cannot be determined and if the importer does not request alternative valuation under paragraph (2).

(E) The computed value provided for under subsection (e), if the value referred to in subparagraph (D) cannot be determined.

(F) The value provided for under subsection (f), if the value referred to in subparagraph (E) cannot be determined.

(2) If the value referred to in paragraph (1)(C) cannot be determined with respect to imported merchandise, the merchandise shall be appraised on the basis of the computed value provided for under paragraph (1)(E), rather than the deductive value provided for under paragraph (1)(D), if the importer makes a request to that effect to the customs officer concerned within such time as the Secretary shall prescribe. If the computed value of the merchandise cannot subsequently be determined, the merchandise may not be appraised on the basis of the value referred to in paragraph (1)(F) unless the deductive value of the merchandise cannot be determined under paragraph (1)(D).

(3) Upon written request therefor by the importer of merchandise, and subject to provisions of law regarding the disclosure of information, the customs officer concerned shall provide the importer with a written explanation of how the value of that merchandise was determined under this section.

(b) Transaction value of imported merchandise

(1) The transaction value of imported merchandise is the price actually paid or payable for the merchandise when sold for exportation to the United States, plus amounts equal to—

(A) the packing costs incurred by the buyer with respect to the imported merchandise;

(B) any selling commission incurred by the buyer with respect to the imported merchandise;

(C) the value, apportioned as appropriate, of any assist;

(D) any royalty or license fee related to the imported merchandise that the buyer is required to pay, directly or indirectly, as a condition of the sale of the imported merchandise for exportation to the United States; and

(E) the proceeds of any subsequent resale, disposal, or use of the imported merchandise that accrue, directly or indirectly, to the seller.

The price actually paid or payable for imported merchandise shall be increased by the amounts attributable to the items (and no others) described in subparagraphs (A) through (E) only to the extent that each such amount (i) is not otherwise included within the price actually paid or payable; and (ii) is based on sufficient information. If sufficient information is not available, for any reason, with respect to any amount referred to in the preceding sentence, the transaction value of the imported merchandise concerned shall be treated, for purposes of this section, as one that cannot be determined.

(2)(A) The transaction value of imported merchandise determined under paragraph (1) shall be the appraised value of that merchandise for the purposes of this Act only if—

(i) there are no restrictions on the disposition or use of the imported merchandise by the buyer other than restrictions that—

(I) are imposed or required by law,

(II) limit the geographical area in which the merchandise may be resold, or

(III) do not substantially affect the value of the merchandise;

(ii) the sale of, or the price actually paid or payable for, the imported merchandise is not subject to any condition or consideration for which a value cannot be determined with respect to the imported merchandise;

(iii) no part of the proceeds of any subsequent resale, disposal, or use of the imported merchandise by the buyer will accrue directly or indirectly to the seller, unless an appropriate adjustment therefor can be made under paragraph (1)(E); and

(iv) the buyer and seller are not related, or the buyer and seller are related but the transaction value is acceptable, for purposes of this subsection, under subparagraph (B).

(B) The transaction value between a related buyer and seller is acceptable for the purposes of this subsection if an examination of the circumstances of the sale of the imported merchandise indicates that the relationship between such buyer and seller did not influence the price actually paid or payable; or if the transaction value of the imported merchandise closely approximates—

(i) the transaction value of identical merchandise, or of similar merchandise, in sales to unrelated buyers in the United States; or

(ii) the deductive value or computed value for identical merchandise or similar merchandise;

but only if each value referred to in clause (i) or (ii) that is used for comparison relates to merchandise that was exported to the United States at or about the same time as the imported merchandise.

(C) In applying the values used for comparison purposes under subparagraph (B), there shall be taken into account differences with respect to the sales involved (if such differences are based on sufficient information whether supplied by the buyer or otherwise available to the customs officer concerned) in—

(i) commercial levels;

(ii) quantity levels;

(iii) the costs, commissions, values, fees, and proceeds described in paragraph (1); and

(iv) the costs incurred by the seller in sales in which he and the buyer are not related that are not incurred by the seller in sales in which he and the buyer are related.

(3) The transaction value of imported merchandise does not include any of the following, if identified separately from the price actually paid or payable and from any cost or other item referred to in paragraph (1):

(A) Any reasonable cost or charge that is incurred for—

(i) the construction, erection, assembly, or maintenance of, or the technical assistance provided with respect to, the merchandise after its importation into the United States; or

(ii) the transportation of the merchandise after such importation.

(B) The customs duties and other Federal taxes currently payable on the imported merchandise by reason of its importation, and any Federal excise tax on, or measured by the value of, such merchandise for which vendors in the United States are ordinarily liable.

(4) For purposes of this subsection—

(A) The term "price actually paid or payable" means the total payment (whether direct or indirect, and exclusive of any costs, charges, or expenses incurred for transportation, insurance, and related services incident to the international shipment of the merchandise from the country of exportation to the place of importation in the United States) made, or to be made, for imported merchandise by the buyer to, or for the benefit of, the seller.

(B) Any rebate of, or other decrease in, the price actually paid or payable that is made or otherwise effected between the buyer and seller after the date of the importation of the merchandise into the United States shall be disregarded in determining the transaction value under paragraph (1).

(c) Transaction value of identical merchandise and similar merchandise

(1) The transaction value of identical merchandise, or of similar merchandise, is the transaction value (acceptable as the appraised value

for purposes of this Act under subsection (b) but adjusted under paragraph (2) of this subsection) of imported merchandise that is—

(A) with respect to the merchandise being appraised, either identical merchandise or similar merchandise, as the case may be; and

(B) exported to the United States at or about the time that the merchandise being appraised is exported to the United States.

(2) Transaction values determined under this subsection shall be based on sales of identical merchandise or similar merchandise, as the case may be, at the same commercial level and in substantially the same quantity as the sales of the merchandise being appraised. If no such sale is found, sales of identical merchandise or similar merchandise at either a different commercial level or in different quantities, or both, shall be used, but adjusted to take account of any such difference. Any adjustment made under this paragraph shall be based on sufficient information. If in applying this paragraph with respect to any imported merchandise, two or more transaction values for identical merchandise, or for similar merchandise, are determined, such imported merchandise shall be appraised on the basis of the lower or lowest of such values.

(d) Deductive value

(1) For purposes of this subsection, the term "merchandise concerned" means the merchandise being appraised, identical merchandise, or similar merchandise.

(2)(A) The deductive value of the merchandise being appraised is whichever of the following prices (as adjusted under paragraph (3)) is appropriate depending upon when and in what condition the merchandise concerned is sold in the United States:

(i) If the merchandise concerned is sold in the condition as imported at or about the date of importation of the merchandise being appraised, the price is the unit price at which the merchandise concerned is sold in the greatest aggregate quantity at or about such date.

(ii) If the merchandise concerned is sold in the condition as imported but not sold at or about the date of importation of the merchandise being appraised, the price is the unit price at which the merchandise concerned is sold in the greatest aggregate quantity after the date of importation of the merchandise being appraised but before the close of the 90th day after the date of such importation.

(iii) If the merchandise concerned was not sold in the condition as imported and not sold before the close of the 90th day after the date of importation of the merchandise being appraised, the price is the unit price at which the merchandise being appraised, after further processing, is sold in the greatest aggregate quantity before the 180th day after the date of such importation. This clause shall apply to appraisement of merchandise only if the importer so elects and notifies the customs officer concerned of that election within such time as shall be prescribed by the Secretary.

(B) For purposes of subparagraph (A), the unit price at which merchandise is sold in the greatest aggregate quantity is the unit price at which such merchandise is sold to unrelated persons, at the first commercial level after importation (in cases to which subparagraph (A)(i) or (ii) applies) or after further processing (in cases to which subparagraph (A)(iii) applies) at which such sales take place, in a total volume that is (i) greater than the total volume sold at any other unit price, and (ii) sufficient to establish the unit price.

(3)(A) The price determined under paragraph (2) shall be reduced by an amount equal to—

(i) any commission usually paid or agreed to be paid, or the addition usually made for profit and general expenses, in connection with sales in the United States of imported merchandise that is of the same class or kind, regardless of the country of exportation, as the merchandise concerned;

(ii) the actual costs and associated costs of transportation and insurance incurred with respect to international shipments of the merchandise concerned from the country of exportation to the United States;

(iii) the usual costs and associated costs of transportation and insurance incurred with respect to shipments of such merchandise from the place of importation to the place of delivery in the United States, if such costs are not included as a general expense under clause (i);

(iv) the customs duties and other Federal taxes currently payable on the merchandise concerned by reason of its importation, and any Federal excise tax on, or measured by the value of, such merchandise for which vendors in the United States are ordinarily liable; and

(v) but only in the case of a price determined under paragraph (2)(A)(iii) the value added by the processing of the merchandise after importation to the extent that the value is based on sufficient information relating to cost of such processing.

(B) For purposes of applying paragraph (A)—

(i) the deduction made for profits and general expenses shall be based upon the importer's profits and general expenses, unless such profits and general expenses are inconsistent with those reflected in sales in the United States of imported merchandise of the same class or kind, in which case the deduction shall be based on the usual profit and general expenses reflected in such sales, as determined from sufficient information; and

(ii) any State or local tax imposed on the importer with respect to the sale of imported merchandise shall be treated as a general expense.

(C) The price determined under paragraph (2) shall be increased (but only to the extent that such costs are not otherwise included) by an amount equal to the packing costs incurred by the importer or the buyer, as the case may be, with respect to the merchandise concerned.

(D) For purposes of determining the deductive value of imported merchandise, any sale to a person who supplies any assist for use in connection with the production or sale for export of the merchandise concerned shall be disregarded.

(e) Computed value

(1) The computed value of imported merchandise is the sum of—

(A) the cost or value of the materials and the fabrication and other processing of any kind employed in the production of the imported merchandise;

(B) an amount for profit and general expenses equal to that usually reflected in sales of merchandise of the same class or kind as the imported merchandise that are made by the producers in the country of exportation for export to the United States;

(C) any assist, if its value is not included under subparagraph (A) or (B); and

(D) the packing costs.

(2) For purposes of paragraph (1)—

(A) the cost or value of materials under paragraph (1)(A) shall not include the amount of any internal tax imposed by the country of exportation that is directly applicable to the materials or their disposition if the tax is remitted or refunded upon the exportation of the merchandise in the production of which the materials were used; and

(B) the amount for profit and general expenses under paragraph (1)(B) shall be based upon the producer's profits and expenses, unless the producer's profits and expenses are inconsistent with those usually reflected in sales of merchandise of the same class or kind as the imported merchandise that are made by producers in the country of exportation for export to the United States, in which case the amount under paragraph (1)(B) shall be based on the usual profit and general expenses of such producers in such sales, as determined from sufficient information.

(f) Value if other values cannot be determined or used

(1) If the value of imported merchandise cannot be determined, or otherwise used for the purposes of this Act, under subsections (b) through (e), the merchandise shall be appraised for the purposes of this Act on the basis of a value that is derived from the methods set forth in such subsections, with such methods being reasonably adjusted to the extent necessary to arrive at a value.

(2) Imported merchandise may not be appraised, for the purposes of this Act, on the basis of—

(A) the selling price in the United States of merchandise produced in the United States;

(B) a system that provides for the appraisement of imported merchandise at the higher of two alternative values;

(C) the price of merchandise in the domestic market of the country of exportation;

(D) a cost of production, other than a value determined under subsection (e) for merchandise that is identical merchandise or similar merchandise to the merchandise being appraised;

(E) the price of merchandise for export to a country other than the United States;

(F) minimum values for appraisement; or

(G) arbitrary or fictitious values.

This paragraph shall not apply with respect to the ascertainment, determination, or estimation of foreign market value or United States price under title VII.

(g) Special Rules

(1) For purposes of this section, the persons specified in any of the following subparagraphs shall be treated as persons who are related:

(A) Members of the same family, including brothers and sisters (whether by whole or half blood), spouse, ancestors, and lineal descendants.

(B) Any officer or director of an organization and such organization.

(C) An officer or director of an organization and an officer or director of another organization, if each such individual is also an officer or director in the other organization.

(D) Partners.

(E) Employer and employee.

(F) Any person directly or indirectly owning, controlling, or holding with power to vote, 5 percent or more of the outstanding voting stock or shares of any organization and such organization.

(G) Two or more persons directly or indirectly controlling, controlled by, or under common control with, any person.

(2) For purposes of this section, merchandise (including, but not limited to, identical merchandise and similar merchandise) shall be treated as being of the same class or kind as other merchandise if it is within a group or range of merchandise produced by a particular industry or industry sector.

(3) For purposes of this section, information that is submitted by an importer, buyer, or producer in regard to the appraisement of merchandise may not be rejected by the customs officer concerned on the basis of the accounting method by which that information was prepared, if the preparation was in accordance with generally accepted accounting principles. The term "generally accepted accounting principles" refers to any generally recognized consensus or substantial authoritative support regarding—

(A) which economic resources and obligations should be recorded as assets and liabilities;

(B) which changes in assets and liabilities should be recorded;

(C) how the assets and liabilities and changes in them should be measured;

(D) what information should be disclosed and how it should be disclosed; and

(E) which financial statements should be prepared.

The applicability of a particular set of generally accepted accounting principles will depend upon the basis on which the value of the merchandise is sought to be established.

(h) Definitions. As used in this section—

(1)(A) The term "assist" means any of the following if supplied directly or indirectly, and free of charge or at reduced cost, by the buyer of imported merchandise for use in connection with the production or the sale for export to the United States of the merchandise:

(i) Materials, components, parts, and similar items incorporated in the imported merchandise.

(ii) Tools, dies, molds, and similar items used in the production of the imported merchandise.

(iii) Merchandise consumed in the production of the imported merchandise.

(iv) Engineering, development, artwork, design work, and plans and sketches that are undertaken elsewhere than in the United States and are necessary for the production of the imported merchandise.

(B) No service or work to which subparagraph (A)(iv) applies shall be treated as an assist for purposes of this section if such service or work—

(i) is performed by an individual who is domiciled within the United States;

(ii) is performed by that individual while he is acting as an employee or agent of the buyer of the imported merchandise; and

(iii) is incidental to other engineering, development, artwork, design work, or plans or sketches that are undertaken within the United States.

(C) For purposes of this section, the following apply in determining the value of assists described in subparagraph (A)(iv):

(i) The value of an assist that is available in the public domain is the cost of obtaining copies of the assist.

(ii) If the production of an assist occurred in the United States and one or more foreign countries, the value of the assist is the value thereof that is added outside the United States.

(2) The term "identical merchandise" means—

(A) merchandise that is identical in all respects to, and was produced in the same country and by the same person as, the merchandise being appraised; or

(B) if merchandise meeting the requirements under subparagraph (A) cannot be found (or for purposes of applying subsection (b)(2)(B)(i), regardless of whether merchandise meeting such requirements can be found), merchandise that is identical in all respects to, and was produced in the same country as, but not produced by the same person as, the merchandise being appraised.

Such term does not include merchandise that incorporates or reflects any engineering, development, artwork, design work, or plan or sketch that—

(I) was supplied free or at reduced cost by the buyer of the merchandise for use in connection with the production or the sale for export to the United States of the merchandise; and

(II) is not an assist because undertaken within the United States.

(3) The term "packing costs" means the cost of all containers and coverings of whatever nature and of packing, whether for labor or materials, used in placing merchandise in condition, packed ready for shipment to the United States.

(4) The term "similar merchandise" means—

(A) merchandise that—

(i) was produced in the same country and by the same person as the merchandise being appraised,

(ii) is like the merchandise being appraised in characteristics and component material, and

(iii) is commercially interchangeable with the merchandise being appraised; or

(B) if merchandise meeting the requirements under subparagraph (A) cannot be found (or for purposes of applying subsection (b)(2)(B)(i), regardless of whether merchandise meeting such requirements can be found), merchandise that—

(i) was produced in the same country as, but not produced by the same person as, the merchandise being appraised, and

(ii) meets the requirement set forth in subparagraph (A)(ii) and (iii).

Such term does not include merchandise that incorporates or reflects any engineering, development, artwork, design work, or plan or sketch that—

(I) was supplied free or at reduced cost by the buyer of the merchandise for use in connection with the production or the sale for export to the United States of the merchandise; and

(II) is not an assist because undertaken within the United States.

(5) The term "sufficient information", when required under this section for determining—

(A) any amount—

(i) added under subsection (b)(1) to the price actually paid or payable,

(ii) deducted under subsection (d)(3) as profit or general expense or value from further processing, or

(iii) added under subsection (e)(2) as profit or general expense;

(B) any difference taken into account for purposes of subsection (b)(2)(C); or

(C) any adjustment made under subsection (c)(2);

means information that establishes the accuracy of such amount, difference, or adjustment.

* * *

§ 1500. Appraisement, classification, and liquidation procedures

The Customs Service shall, under rules and regulations prescribed by the Secretary—

(a) fix the final appraisement of merchandise by ascertaining or estimating the value thereof, under section 402, by all reasonable ways and means in his power, any statement of cost or costs of production in any invoice, affidavit, declaration, other document to the contrary notwithstanding;

(b) fix the final classification and rate of duty applicable to such merchandise;

(c) fix the final amount of duty to be paid on such merchandise and determine any increased or additional duties, taxes and fees due or any excess of duties, taxes and fees deposited;

(d) liquidate the entry and reconciliation, if any, of such merchandise; and

(e) give or transmit, pursuant to an electronic data interchange system, notice of such liquidation to the importer, his consignee, or agent in such form and manner as the Secretary shall prescribe.

* * *

§ 1505. Payment of duties and fees

(a) Deposit of estimated duties, fees—Unless the entry is subject to a periodic payment referred to in this subsection or the merchandise is entered for warehouse or transportation, or under bond, the importer of record shall deposit with the Customs Service at the time of entry, or at such later time as the Secretary may prescribe by regulation (but not later than 12 working days after entry or release) the amount of duties and fees estimated to be payable on such merchandise. As soon as a periodic payment module of the Automated Commercial Environment is developed, but no later than October 1, 2004, the Secretary shall promulgate regulations, after testing the module, permitting a participating importer of record to deposit estimated duties and fees for entries of merchandise, other than merchandise entered for warehouse, transportation, or under bond, no later than the 15 working days following the month in which the merchandise is entered or released, whichever comes first.

* * *

§ 1514. Protest against decisions of the Customs Service

(a) Finality of decisions; return of papers. Except as provided in subsection (b) of this section, section 501 [*19 U.S.C. § 1501*] (relating to voluntary reliquidations), section 516 [*19 U.S.C. § 1516*] (relating to petitions by domestic interested parties[.]), section 520 (relating to refunds) [*19 U.S.C. § 1520*], and section 6501 of the Internal Revenue Code of 1986 [*26 U.S.C. § 6501*] (but only with respect to taxes imposed under chapters 51 and 52 of such Code [*26 U.S.C. §§ 5001 et seq. and 5701 et seq.*]), any clerical error, mistake of fact, or other inadvertence, whether or not resulting from or contained in an electronic transmission, adverse to the importer, in any entry, liquidation, or reliquidation, and, decisions of the Customs Service, including the legality of all orders and findings entering into the same, as to—

(1) the appraised value of merchandise;

(2) the classification and rate and amount of duties chargeable;

(3) all charges or exactions of whatever character within the jurisdiction of the Secretary of the Treasury;

(4) the exclusion of merchandise from entry or delivery or a demand for redelivery to customs custody under any provision of the customs laws, except a determination appealable under section 337 of this Act [*19 U.S.C. § 1337*];

(5) the liquidation or reliquidation of an entry, or reconciliation as to the issues contained therein, or any modification thereof, including the liquidation of an entry, pursuant to either section 500 or section 504 [*19 U.S.C. § 1500 or 1504*];

(6) the refusal to pay a claim for drawback; or

(7) the refusal to reliquidate an entry under subsection (d) of section 520 of this Act [*19 U.S.C. § 1520*];

shall be final and conclusive upon all persons (including the United States and any officer thereof) unless a protest is filed in accordance with this section, or unless a civil action contesting the denial of a protest, in whole or in part, is commenced in the United States Court of International Trade in accordance with chapter 169 of title 28 of the United States Code [*28 U.S.C. §§ 2631 et seq.*] within the time prescribed by section 2636 [*28 U.S.C. § 2636*]. When a judgment or order of the United States Court of

International Trade has become final, the papers transmitted shall be returned, together with a copy of the judgment or order to the Customs Service, which shall take action accordingly.

(b) Finality and conclusiveness of customs officers' determinations. With respect to determinations made under section 303 of this Act [*19 U.S.C. § 1303*] or title VII of this Act [*19 U.S.C. §§ 1671 et seq.*] which are reviewable under section 516A of this title [*19 U.S.C. § 1516a*], determinations of the Customs Service are final and conclusive upon all persons (including the United States and any officer thereof) unless a civil action contesting a determination listed in section 516A of this title [*19 U.S.C. § 1516a*] is commenced in the United States Court of International Trade, or review by a binational panel of a determination to which section 516A(g)(2) [*19 U.S.C. § 1516a(g)(2)*] applies is commenced pursuant to section 516A(g) [*19 U.S.C. § 1516a(g)*] and article 1904 of the North American Free Trade Agreement or the United States-Canada Free-Trade Agreement.

(c) Form, number, and amendment of protest; filing of protest.

(1) A protest of a decision made under subsection (a) shall be filed in writing, or transmitted electronically pursuant to an electronic data interchange system, in accordance with regulations prescribed by the Secretary. A protest must set forth distinctly and specifically—

(A) each decision described in subsection (a) as to which protest is made;

(B) each category of merchandise affected by each decision set forth under paragraph (1);

(C) the nature of each objection and the reasons therefor; and

(D) any other matter required by the Secretary by regulation.

Only one protest may be filed for each entry of merchandise, except that where the entry covers merchandise of different categories, a separate protest may be filed for each category. In addition, separate protests filed by different authorized persons with respect to any one category of merchandise, or with respect to a determination of origin under section 202 of the North American Free Trade Agreement Implementation Act [*19 U.S.C. § 3332*], that is the subject of a protest are deemed to be part of a single protest. Unless a request for accelerated disposition is filed under section 515(b) [*19 U.S.C. § 1515(b)*], a protest may be amended, under regulations prescribed by the Secretary, to set forth objections as to a decision or decisions described in subsection (a) which were not the subject of the original protest, in the form and manner prescribed for a protest, any time prior to the expiration of the time in which such protest could have been filed under this section. New grounds in support of objections raised by a valid protest or amendment thereto may be presented for consideration in connection with the review of such protest pursuant to section 515 of this Act [*19 U.S.C. § 1515*] at any time prior to the disposition of the protest in accordance with that section.

(2) Except as provided in sections 485(d) and 557(b) of this Act [*19 U.S.C. §§ 1485(d) and 1557(b)*], protests may be filed with respect to merchandise which is the subject of a decision specified in subsection (a) of this section by—

(A) the importers or consignees shown on the entry papers, or their sureties;

(B) any person paying any charge or exaction;

(C) any person seeking entry or delivery;

(D) any person filing a claim for drawback;

(E) with respect to a determination of origin under section 202 of the North American Free Trade Agreement Implementation Act [*19 U.S.C. § 3332*], any exporter or producer of the merchandise subject to that determination, if the exporter or producer completed and signed a NAFTA Certificate of Origin covering the merchandise; or

(F) any authorized agent of any of the persons described in clauses (A) through (E).

(3) A protest of a decision, order, or finding described in subsection (a) shall be filed with the Customs Service within 180 days after but not before—

(A) date of liquidation or reliquidation, or

(B) in circumstances where subparagraph (A) is inapplicable, the date of the decision as to which protest is made.

A protest by a surety which has an unsatisfied legal claim under its bond may be filed within 180 days from the date of mailing of notice of demand for payment against its bond. If another party has not filed a timely protest, the surety's protest shall certify that it is not being filed collusively to extend another authorized person's time to protest as specified in this subsection.

(d) Limitation on protest of reliquidation. The reliquidation of an entry shall not open such entry so that a protest may be filed against the decision of the Customs Service upon any question not involved in such reliquidation.

(e) Advance notice of certain determinations. Except as provided in subsection (f), an exporter or producer referred to in subsection (c)(2)(E) shall be provided notice in advance of an adverse determination of origin under section 202 of the North American Free Trade Agreement Implementation Act [*19 U.S.C. § 3332*]. The Secretary may, by regulations, prescribe the time period in which such advance notice shall be issued and authorize the Customs Service to provide in the notice the entry number and any other entry information considered necessary to allow the exporter or producer to exercise the rights provided by this section.

(f) Denial of preferential treatment. If the Customs Service finds indications of a pattern of conduct by an exporter or producer of false or unsupported representations that goods qualify under the rules of origin set out in section 202 of the North American Free Trade Agreement Implementation Act [*19 U.S.C. § 3332*]—

(1) the Customs Service, in accordance with regulations issued by the Secretary, may deny preferential tariff treatment to entries of identical goods exported or produced by that person; and

(2) the advance notice requirement in subsection (e) shall not apply to that person;

until the person establishes to the satisfaction of the Customs Service that its representations are in conformity with section 202 [*19 U.S.C. § 3332*].

(g) Denial of preferential tariff treatment under United States-Chile Free Trade Agreement. If the Bureau of Customs and Border Protection or the Bureau of Immigration and Customs Enforcement finds indications of a pattern of conduct by an importer of false or unsupported representations that goods qualify under the rules of origin set out in section 202 of the United States-Chile Free Trade Agreement Implementation Act [*19 U.S.C. § 3805 note*], the Bureau of Customs and Border Protection, in accordance with regulations issued by the Secretary of the Treasury, may deny preferential tariff treatment under the United States-Chile Free Trade Agreement to entries of identical goods imported by that person until the person establishes to the satisfaction of the Bureau of Customs and Border Protection that representations of that person are in conformity with such section 202.

(h) Denial of preferential tariff treatment under the Dominican Republic-Central America-United States Free Trade Agreement. If the Bureau of Customs and Border Protection or the Bureau of Immigration and Customs Enforcement finds indications of a pattern of conduct by an importer, exporter, or producer of false or unsupported representations that goods qualify under the rules of origin set out in section 203 of the Dominican Republic-Central America-United States Free Trade Agreement Implementation Act [*19 U.S.C. § 4033*], the Bureau of Customs and Border Protection, in accordance with regulations issued by the Secretary of the Treasury, may suspend preferential tariff treatment under the Dominican Republic-Central America-United States Free Trade Agreement to entries of identical goods covered by subsequent representations by that importer, exporter, or producer until the Bureau of

Customs and Border Protection determines that representations of that person are in conformity with such section 203.

(i) Denial of preferential tariff treatment under the United States-Peru Trade Promotion Agreement. If U.S. Customs and Border Protection or U.S. Immigration and Customs Enforcement of the Department of Homeland Security finds indications of a pattern of conduct by an importer, exporter, or producer of false or unsupported representations that goods qualify under the rules of origin provided for in section 203 of the United States-Peru Trade Promotion Agreement Implementation Act [*19 U.S.C. § 3805 note*], U.S. Customs and Border Protection, in accordance with regulations issued by the Secretary of the Treasury, may suspend preferential tariff treatment under the United States-Peru Trade Promotion Agreement to entries of identical goods covered by subsequent representations by that importer, exporter, or producer until U.S. Customs and Border Protection determines that representations of that person are in conformity with such section 203.

(j) Denial of preferential tariff treatment under the United States-Korea Free Trade Agreement. If U.S. Customs and Border Protection or U.S. Immigration and Customs Enforcement of the Department of Homeland Security finds indications of a pattern of conduct by an importer, exporter, or producer of false or unsupported representations that goods qualify under the rules of origin provided for in section 202 of the United States-Korea Free Trade Agreement Implementation Act [*19 U.S.C. § 3805 note*], U.S. Customs and Border Protection, in accordance with regulations issued by the Secretary of the Treasury, may suspend preferential tariff treatment under the United States-Korea Free Trade Agreement Implementation Act to entries of identical goods covered by subsequent representations by that importer, exporter, or producer until U.S. Customs and Border Protection determines that representations of that person are in conformity with such section 202.

(k) Denial of preferential tariff treatment under the United States-Colombia Trade Promotion Agreement. If U.S. Customs and Border Protection or U.S. Immigration and Customs Enforcement of the Department of Homeland Security finds indications of a pattern of conduct by an importer, exporter, or producer of false or unsupported representations that goods qualify under the rules of origin provided for in section 203 of the United States-Colombia Trade Promotion Agreement Implementation Act [*19 U.S.C. § 3805 note*], U.S. Customs and Border Protection, in accordance with regulations issued by the Secretary of the Treasury, may suspend preferential tariff treatment under the United States-Colombia Trade Promotion Agreement to entries of identical goods covered by subsequent representations by that importer, exporter, or producer until U.S. Customs and Border Protection determines that representations of that person are in conformity with such section 203.

(*l*) Denial of preferential tariff treatment under the United States-Panama Trade Promotion Agreement. If U.S. Customs and Border Protection or U.S. Immigration and Customs Enforcement of the Department of Homeland Security finds indications of a pattern of conduct by an importer, exporter, or producer of false or unsupported representations that goods qualify under the rules of origin provided for in section 203 of the United States-Panama Trade Promotion Agreement Implementation Act [*19 U.S.C. § 3805 note*], U.S. Customs and Border Protection, in accordance with regulations issued by the Secretary of the Treasury, may suspend preferential tariff treatment under the United States-Panama Trade Promotion Agreement to entries of identical goods covered by subsequent representations by that importer, exporter, or producer until U.S. Customs and Border Protection determines that representations of that person are in conformity with such section 203.

§ 1515. Review of protests

(a) Administrative review within two years

Unless a request for an accelerated disposition of a protest is filed in accordance with subsection (b) of this section the appropriate customs officer, within two years from the date a protest was filed in accordance with section 1514 of this title, shall review the protest and shall allow or deny such protest in whole or in part. Thereafter, any duties, charge, or exaction found to have been assessed or collected in excess shall be remitted or refunded and any drawback found due shall be paid. Upon the request of the protesting party, filed within the time allowed for the filing of a protest under section 1514 of this title, a protest may be subject to further review by another appropriate customs officer, under the circumstances and in the form and manner that may be prescribed by the Secretary in regulations, but subject to the two-year limitation prescribed in the first sentence of this subsection. Notice of the denial of any protest shall be mailed in the form and manner prescribed by the Secretary. Such notice shall include a statement of the reasons for the denial, as well as a statement informing the protesting party of his right to file a civil action contesting the denial of a protest under section 1514 of this title.

* * *

§ 1516. Petitions by domestic interested parties

(a) Request for classification and rate of duty; petition

(1) The Secretary shall, upon written request by an interested party furnish the classification and the rate of duty imposed upon designated imported merchandise of a class or kind manufactured, produced, or sold at wholesale by such interested party. If the interested party believes that the appraised value, the classification, or rate of duty is not correct, it may file a petition with the Secretary setting forth—

(A) a description of the merchandise,

(B) the appraised value, the classification, or the rate of duty that it believes proper, and

(C) the reasons for its belief.

(2) As used in this section, the term "interested party" means a person who is—

(A) a manufacturer, producer, or wholesaler in the United States;

(B) a certified union or recognized union or group of workers which is representative of an industry engaged in the manufacture, production, or wholesale in the United States; or

(C) a trade or business association a majority of whose members are manufacturers, producers, or wholesalers in the United States,

of goods of the same class or kind as the designated imported merchandise.—Such term includes an association, a majority of whose members is composed of persons described in subparagraph (A), (B) or (C).

(3) Any producer of a raw agricultural product who is considered under section 771(4)(E) to be part of the industry producing a processed agricultural product of the same class or kind as the designated imported merchandise shall, for purposes of this section, be treated as an interested party producing such processed agricultural product.

(b) Determination on petition. If, after receipt and consideration of a petition filed by such an interested party, the Secretary determines that the appraised value, the classification, or rate of duty is not correct, he shall determine the proper appraised value, classification, or rate of duty and shall notify the petitioner of his determination. All such merchandise entered for consumption or withdrawn from warehouse for consumption more than thirty days after the date such notice to the petitioner is published in the weekly Customs Bulletin shall be appraised, classified, or assessed as to the rate of duty in accordance with the Secretary's determination.

(c) Contest by petitioner of appraised value, classification, or rate of duty. If the Secretary determines that the appraised value, classification, or rate of duty with respect to which a petition was filed pursuant to subsection (a) of this section is correct, he shall notify the petitioner. If dissatisfied with the determination of the Secretary, the petitioner may file with the Secretary, not later than thirty days after the date of the notification, notice that it desires to contest the appraised value, classification, or rate of duty. Upon receipt of notice from the petitioner, the Secretary shall cause publication to be made of his determination as to the proper appraised value, classification, or rate of duty and of the petitioner's desire to contest, and shall thereafter furnish the petitioner with such information as to the entries and consignees of such merchandise, entered after the publication of the determination of the Secretary, at such ports of entry designated by the petitioner in his notice of desire to contest, as will enable the petitioner to contest the appraised value, classification, or rate of duty imposed upon such merchandise in the liquidation of one such entry at such port. The Secretary shall direct the appropriate customs officer at such ports to immediately notify the petitioner by mail when the first of such entries is liquidated.

§ 1516a. Judicial review in countervailing duty and antidumping duty proceedings

(a) Review of determination.

(1) Review of certain determinations. Within 30 days after the date of publication in the Federal Register of—

(A) a determination by the administering authority, under [section] 702(c) or 732(c) of this Act [*19 U.S.C. § 1671a(c)* or *1673a(c)*], not to initiate an investigation,

(B) a determination by the Commission, under section 751(b) of this Act [*19 U.S.C. § 1675(b)*], not to review a determination based upon changed circumstances,

(C) a negative determination by the Commission, under section 703(a) or 733(a) of this Act [*19 U.S.C. § 1671b(a)* or *1673b(a)*], as to whether there is reasonable indication of material injury, threat of material injury, or material retardation, or

(D) a final determination by the administering authority or the Commission under section 751(c)(3) [*19 U.S.C. §§ 1675(c)(3)*],

an interested party who is a party to the proceeding in connection with which the matter arises may commence an action in the United States Court of International Trade by filing concurrently a summons and complaint, each with the content and in the form, manner, and style prescribed by the rules of that court, contesting any factual findings or legal conclusions upon which the determination is based.

(2) Review of determinations on record.

(A) In general. Within thirty days after—

(i) the date of publication in the Federal Register of—

(I) notice of any determination described in clause (ii), (iii), (iv), (v), or (viii) of subparagraph (B),

(II) an antidumping or countervailing duty order based upon any determination described in clause (i) of subparagraph (B), or

(III) notice of the implementation of any determination described in clause (vii) of subparagraph (B), or

(ii) the date of mailing of a determination described in clause (vi) of subparagraph (B),

an interested party who is a party to the proceeding in connection with which the matter arises may commence an action in the United States Court of International Trade by filing a summons, and within thirty days thereafter a complaint, each with the content and in the form, manner, and style prescribed by the rules of that court, contesting any factual findings or legal conclusions upon which the determination is based.

(B) Reviewable determinations. The determinations which may be contested under subparagraph (A) are as follows:

(i) Final affirmative determinations by the administering authority and by the Commission under section 705 or 735 of this Act [*19 U.S.C. § 1671d* or *1673d*], including any negative part of such a determination (other than a part referred to in clause (ii)).

(ii) A final negative determination by the administering authority or the Commission under section 705 or 735 of this Act [*19 U.S.C. § 1671d* or *1673d*], including, at the option of the appellant, any part of a final affirmative determination which specifically excludes any company or product.

(iii) A final determination, other than a determination reviewable under paragraph (1), by the administering authority or the Commission under section 751 of this Act [*19 U.S.C. § 1675*].

(iv) A determination by the administering authority, under section 704 or 734 of this Act [*19 U.S.C. § 1671c* or *1673c*], to suspend an antidumping duty or a countervailing duty investigation, including any final determination resulting from a continued investigation which changes the size of the dumping margin or net countervailable subsidy calculated, or the reasoning underlying such calculations, at the time the suspension agreement was concluded.

(v) An injurious effect determination by the Commission under section 704(h) or 734(h) of this Act [*19 U.S.C. § 1671c(h)* or *1673c(h)*].

(vi) A determination by the administering authority as to whether a particular type of merchandise is within the class of kind of merchandise described in an existing finding of dumping or antidumping or countervailing duty order.

(vii) A determination by the administering authority or the Commission under section 129 of the Uruguay Round Agreements Act concerning a determination under title VII of the Tariff Act of 1930.

(viii) A determination by the Commission under section 753(a)(1) [*19 U.S.C. § 1675b(a)(1)*].

(3) Exception. Notwithstanding the limitation imposed by paragraph (2)(A)(i)(II) of this subsection, a final affirmative determination by the administering authority under section 705 or 735 of this Act [*19 U.S.C. § 1671d* or *1673d*] may be contested by commencing an action, in accordance with the provisions of paragraph (2)(A), within thirty days after the date of publication in the Federal Register of a final negative determination by the Commission under section 705 or 735 of this Act [*19 U.S.C. § 1671d* or *1673d*].

(4) Procedures and fees. The procedures and fees set forth in chapter 169, of title 28, United States Code [*28 U.S.C. §§ 2631* et seq.], apply to an action under this section.

(5) Time limits in cases involving merchandise from free trade area countries. Notwithstanding any other provision of this subsection, in the case of a determination to which the provisions of subsection (g) apply, an action under this subsection may not be commenced, and the time limits for commencing an action under this subsection shall not begin to run, until the day specified in whichever of the following subparagraphs applies:

(A) For a determination described in paragraph (1)(B) or clause (i), (ii) or (iii) of paragraph (2)(B), the 31st day after the date on which notice of the determination is published in the Federal Register.

(B) For a determination described in clause (vi) of paragraph (2)(B), the 31st day after the date on which the government of the relevant FTA country receives notice of the determination.

(C) For a determination with respect to which binational panel review has commenced in accordance with subsection (g)(8), the day after the date as of which—

(i) the binational panel has dismissed binational panel review of the determination for lack of jurisdiction, and

(ii) any interested party seeking review of the determination under paragraph (1), (2), or (3) of this subsection has provided timely notice under subsection (g)(3)(B).

If such an interested party files a summons and complaint under this subsection after dismissal by the binational panel, and if a request for an extraordinary challenge committee is made with respect to the decision by the binational panel to dismiss—

(I) judicial review under this subsection shall be stayed during consideration by the committee of the request, and

(II) the United States Court of International Trade shall dismiss the action if the committee vacates or remands the binational panel decision to dismiss.

(D) For a determination for which review by the United States Court of International Trade is provided for—

(i) under subsection (g)(12)(B), the day after the date of publication in the Federal Register of notice that article 1904 of the NAFTA has been suspended, or

(ii) under subsection (g)(12)(D), the day after the date that notice of settlement is published in the Federal Register.

(E) For a determination described in clause (vii) of paragraph (2)(B), the 31st day after the date on which notice of the implementation of the determination is published in the Federal Register.

(b) Standards of review.

(1) Remedy. The court shall hold unlawful any determination, finding, or conclusion found—

(A) in an action brought under subparagraph (A), (B), or (C) of subsection (a)(1), to be arbitrary, capricious, an abuse of discretion, or otherwise not in accordance with law, or

(B)(i) in an action brought under paragraph (2) of subsection (a), to be unsupported by substantial evidence on the record, or otherwise not in accordance with law, or

(ii) in an action brought under paragraph (1)(D) of subsection (a), to be arbitrary, capricious, an abuse of discretion, or otherwise not in accordance with law.

(2) Record for review.

(A) In general. For the purposes of this subsection, the record, unless otherwise stipulated by the parties, shall consist of—

(i) a copy of all information presented to or obtained by the Secretary, the administering authority, or the Commission during the course of the administrative proceeding, including all governmental memoranda pertaining to the case and the record of ex parte meetings required to be kept by section 777(a)(3) [*19 U.S.C. § 1677f(a)(3)*]; and

(ii) a copy of the determination, all transcripts or records of conferences or hearings, and all notices published in the Federal Register.

(B) Confidential or privileged material. The confidential or privileged status accorded to any documents, comments, or information shall be preserved in any action under this section. Notwithstanding the preceding sentence, the court may examine, in camera, the confidential or privileged material, and may disclose such material under such terms and conditions as it may order.

(3) Effect of decisions by NAFTA or United States-Canada binational panels. In making a decision in any action brought under subsection (a), a court of the United States is not bound by, but may take into consideration, a final decision of a binational panel or extraordinary challenge committee convened pursuant to article 1904 of the NAFTA or of the Agreement.

(c) Liquidation of entries.

(1) Liquidation in accordance with determination. Unless such liquidation is enjoined by the court under paragraph (2) of this subsection, entries of merchandise of the character covered by a determination of the Secretary, the administering authority, or the Commission contested under subsection (a) shall be liquidated in accordance with the determination of the Secretary, the administering authority, or the Commission, if they are entered, or withdrawn from warehouse, for consumption on or before the date of publication in the Federal Register by the Secretary or the administering authority of a notice of a decision of the United States Court of International Trade, or of the United States Court of Appeals for the Federal Circuit, not in harmony with that determination. Such notice of a decision shall be published within ten days from the date of the issuance of the court decision.

(2) Injunctive relief. In the case of a determination described in paragraph (2) of subsection (a) by the Secretary, the administering authority, or the Commission, the United States Court of International Trade may enjoin the liquidation of some or all entries of merchandise covered by a determination of the Secretary, the administering

authority, or the Commission, upon a request by an interested party for such relief and a proper showing that the requested relief should be granted under the circumstances.

(3) Remand for final disposition. If the final disposition of an action brought under this section is not in harmony with the published determination of the Secretary, the administering authority, or the Commission, the matter shall be remanded to the Secretary, the administering authority, or the Commission, as appropriate, for disposition consistent with the final disposition of the court.

(d) Standing. Any interested party who was a party to the proceeding under section 303 of this Act or title VII of this Act shall have the right to appear and be heard as a party in interest before the United States Court of International Trade. The party filing the action shall notify all such interested parties of the filing of an action under this section, in the form, manner, style, and within the time prescribed by rules of the court.

(e) Liquidation in accordance with final decision. If the cause of action is sustained in whole or in part by a decision of the United States Court of International Trade or of the United States Court of Appeals for the Federal Circuit—

(1) entries of merchandise of the character covered by the published determination of the Secretary, the administering authority, or the Commission, which is entered, or withdrawn from warehouse, for consumption after the date of publication in the Federal Register by the Secretary or the administering authority of a notice of the court decision, and

(2) entries, the liquidation of which was enjoined under subsection (c)(2),

shall be liquidated in accordance with the final court decision in the action. Such notice of the court decision shall be published within ten days from the date of the issuance of the court decision.

(f) Definitions. For purposes of this section—

(1) Administering authority. The term "administering authority" means the administering authority described in section 771(1) of this Act [*19 U.S.C. § 1677(1)*].

(2) Commission. The term "Commission" means the United States International Trade Commission.

(3) Interested party. The term "interested party" means any person described in section 771(9) of this Act [*19 U.S.C. § 1677(9)*].

(4) Secretary. The term "Secretary" means the Secretary of the Treasury.

(5) Agreement. The term "Agreement" means the United States Canada Free Trade Agreement.

(6) United States Secretary. The term "United States Secretary" means—

(A) the secretary for the United States Section referred to in article 1908 of the NAFTA, and

(B) the secretary of the United States Section provided for in article 1909 of the Agreement.

(7) Relevant FTA Secretary. The term "relevant FTA Secretary" means the Secretary—

(A) referred to in article 1908 of the NAFTA, or

(B) provided for in paragraph 5 of article 1909 of the Agreement,

of the relevant FTA country.

(8) NAFTA. The term "NAFTA" means the North American Free Trade Agreement.

(9) Relevant FTA country. The term "relevant FTA country" means the free trade area country to which an antidumping or countervailing duty proceeding pertains.

(10) Free trade area country. The term "free trade area country" means the following:

(A) Canada for such time as the NAFTA is in force with respect to, and the United States applies the NAFTA to, Canada.

(B) Mexico for such time as the NAFTA is in force with respect to, and the United States applies the NAFTA to, Mexico.

(C) Canada for such time as—

(i) it is not a free trade area country under subparagraph (A); and

(ii) the Agreement is in force with respect to, and the United States applies the Agreement to, Canada.

(g) Review of countervailing duty and antidumping duty determinations involving free trade area country merchandise.

(1) Definition of determination. For purposes of this subsection, the term "determination" means a determination described in—

(A) paragraph (1)(B) of subsection (a), or

(B) clause (i), (ii), (iii), (vi), or (vii) of paragraph (2)(B) of subsection (a), if made in connection with a proceeding regarding a class or kind of free trade area country merchandise, as determined by the administering authority.

(2) Exclusive review of determination by binational panels. If binational panel review of a determination is requested pursuant to article 1904 of the NAFTA or of the Agreement, then, except as provided in paragraphs (3) and (4)—

(A) the determination is not reviewable under subsection (a), and

(B) no court of the United States has power or jurisdiction to review the determination on any question of law or fact by an action in the nature of mandamus or otherwise.

(3) Exception to exclusive binational panel review.

(A) In general. A determination is reviewable under subsection (a) if the determination sought to be reviewed is—

(i) a determination as to which neither the United States nor the relevant FTA country requested review by a binational panel pursuant to article 1904 of the NAFTA or of the Agreement,

(ii) a revised determination issued as a direct result of judicial review, commenced pursuant to subsection (a), if neither the United States nor the relevant FTA country requested review of the original determination,

(iii) a determination issued as a direct result of judicial review that was commenced pursuant to subsection (a) prior to the entry into force of the NAFTA or of the Agreement,

(iv) a determination which a binational panel has determined is not reviewable by the binational panel,

(v) a determination as to which binational panel review has terminated pursuant to paragraph 12 of article 1905 of the NAFTA, or

(vi) a determination as to which extraordinary challenge committee review has terminated pursuant to paragraph 12 of article 1905 of the NAFTA.

(B) Special rule. A determination described in subparagraph (A)(i) or (iv) is reviewable under subsection (a) only if the party seeking to commence review has provided timely notice of its intent to commence such review to—

(i) the United States Secretary and the relevant FTA Secretary;

(ii) all interested parties who were parties to the proceeding in connection with which the matter arises; and

(iii) the administering authority or the Commission, as appropriate.

Such notice is timely provided if the notice is delivered no later than the date that is 20 days after the date described in subparagraph (A) or (B) of subsection (a)(5) that is applicable to such determination, except that, if the time for requesting binational panel review is suspended under paragraph (8)(A)(ii) of this subsection, any unexpired time for providing notice of intent to commence judicial review shall, during the pendency of any such suspension, also be suspended. Such notice shall contain such information, and be in such form, manner, and style, as the administering authority, in consultation with the Commission, shall prescribe by regulations.

(4) Exception to exclusive binational panel review for constitutional issues.

(A) Constitutionality of binational panel review system. An action for declaratory judgment or injunctive relief, or both, regarding a determination on the grounds that any provision of, or amendment made by, the North American Free Trade Agreement Implementation Act implementing the binational dispute settlement system under chapter 19 of the NAFTA, or the United States-Canada Free-Trade Agreement Implementation Act of 1988 implementing the binational panel dispute settlement system under chapter 19 of the Agreement, violates the Constitution may be brought only in the United States Court of Appeals for the District of Columbia Circuit, which shall have jurisdiction of such action.

(B) Other constitutional review. Review is available under subsection (a) with respect to a determination solely concerning a constitutional issue (other than an issue to which subparagraph (A) applies) arising under any law of the United States as enacted or applied. An action for review under this subparagraph shall be assigned to a 3-judge panel of the United States Court of International Trade.

(C) Commencement of review. Notwithstanding the time limits in subsection (a), within 30 days after the date of publication in the Federal Register of notice that binational panel review has been completed, an interested party who is a party to the proceeding in connection with which the matter arises may commence an action under subparagraph (A) or (B) by filing an action in accordance with the rules of the court.

(D) Transfer of actions to appropriate court. Whenever an action is filed in a court under subparagraph (A) or (B) and that court finds that the action should have been filed in the other court, the court in which the action was filed shall transfer the action to the other court and the action shall proceed as if it had been filed in the court to which it is transferred on the date upon which it was actually filed in the court from which it is transferred.

(E) Frivolous claims. Frivolous claims brought under subparagraph (A) or (B) are subject to dismissal and sanctions as provided under *section 1927 of title 28, United States Code*, and the Federal Rules of Civil Procedure.

(F) Security.

(i) Subparagraph (A) Actions. The security requirements of *rule 65(c) of the Federal Rules of Civil Procedure* apply with respect to actions commenced under subparagraph (A).

(ii) Subparagraph (B) Actions. No claim shall be heard, and no temporary restraining order or temporary or permanent injunction shall be issued, under an action commenced under subparagraph (B), unless the party seeking review first files an undertaking with adequate security in an amount to be fixed by the court sufficient to recompense parties affected for any loss, expense, or damage caused by the improvident or erroneous issuance of such order or injunction. If a court upholds the constitutionality of the determination in question in such action, the court shall award to a prevailing party fees and expenses, in addition to any costs incurred by that party, unless the court finds that the position of the other party was substantially justified or that special circumstances make an award unjust.

(G) Panel record. The record of proceedings before the binational panel shall not be considered part of the record for review pursuant to subparagraph (A) or (B).

(H) Appeal to Supreme Court of court orders issued in subparagraph (A) Actions. Notwithstanding any other provision of law, any final judgment of the United States Court of Appeals for the District of Columbia Circuit which is issued pursuant to an action brought under subparagraph (A) shall be reviewable by appeal directly to the Supreme Court of the United States. Any such appeal shall be taken by a notice of appeal filed within 10 days after such order is entered; and the jurisdictional statement shall be filed within 30 days after such order is entered. No stay of an order issued pursuant to an action brought under subparagraph (A) may be issued by a single Justice of the Supreme Court.

(5) Liquidation of entries.

(A) Application. In the case of a determination for which binational panel review is requested pursuant to article 1904 of the NAFTA or of the Agreement, the rules provided in this paragraph shall apply, notwithstanding the provisions of subsection (c).

(B) General rule. In the case of a determination for which binational panel review is requested pursuant to article 1904 of the NAFTA or of the Agreement, entries of merchandise covered by such determination shall be liquidated in accordance with the determination of the administering authority or the Commission, if they are entered, or withdrawn from warehouse, for consumption on or before the date of publication in the Federal Register by the administering authority of notice of a final decision of a binational panel, or of an extraordinary challenge committee, not in harmony with that determination. Such notice of a decision shall be published within 10 days of the date of the issuance of the panel or committee decision.

(C) Suspension of liquidation.

(i) In general. Notwithstanding the provisions of subparagraph (B), in the case of a determination described in clause (iii) or (vi) of subsection (a)(2)(B) for which binational panel review is requested pursuant to article 1904 of the NAFTA or of the Agreement, the administering authority, upon request of an interested party who was a party to the proceeding in connection with which the matter arises and who is a participant in the binational panel review, shall order the continued suspension of liquidation of those entries of merchandise covered by the determination that are involved in the review pending the final disposition of the review.

(ii) Notice. At the same time as the interested party makes its request to the administering authority under clause (i), that party shall serve a copy of its request on the United States Secretary, the relevant FTA Secretary, and all interested parties who were parties to the proceeding in connection with which the matter arises.

(iii) Application of suspension. If the interested party requesting continued suspension of liquidation under clause (i) is a foreign manufacturer, producer, or exporter, or a United States importer, the continued suspension of liquidation shall apply only to entries of merchandise manufactured, produced, exported, or imported by that particular manufacturer, producer, exporter, or importer. If the interested party requesting the continued suspension of liquidation under clause (i) is an interested party described in subparagraph (C), (D), (E), or (F) of section 771(9) [*19 U.S.C. § 1677(9)(C), (D), (E), or (F)*], the continued suspension of liquidation shall apply only to entries which could be affected by a decision of the binational panel convened under chapter 19 of the NAFTA or of the Agreement.

(iv) Judicial review. Any action taken by the administering authority or the United States Customs Service under this subparagraph shall not be subject to judicial review, and no court of the United States shall have power or jurisdiction to review such action on any question of law or fact by an action in the nature of mandamus or otherwise.

(6) Injunctive relief. Except for cases under paragraph (4)(B), in the case of a determination for which binational panel review is requested pursuant to article 1904 of the NAFTA or of the Agreement, the provisions of subsection (c)(2) shall not apply.

(7) Implementation of international obligations under article 1904 of the NAFTA or the Agreement.

(A) Action upon remand. If a determination is referred to a binational panel or extraordinary challenge committee under the NAFTA or the Agreement and the panel or committee makes a decision remanding the determination to the administering authority or the Commission, the administering authority or the Commission shall, within the period specified by the panel or committee, take action not inconsistent with the decision of the panel or committee. Any action taken by the administering authority or the Commission under this paragraph shall not be subject to judicial review, and no court of the United States shall have power or jurisdiction to review such action on any question of law or fact by an action in the nature of mandamus or otherwise.

(B) Application if subparagraph (A) held unconstitutional. In the event that the provisions of subparagraph (A) are held unconstitutional under the provisions of subparagraphs (A) and (H) of paragraph (4), the provisions of this subparagraph shall take effect. In such event, the President is authorized on behalf of the United States to accept, as a whole, the decision of a binational panel or extraordinary challenge committee remanding the determination to the administering authority or the Commission within the period specified by the panel or committee. Upon acceptance by the President of such a decision, the administering authority or the Commission shall, within the period specified by the panel or committee, take action not inconsistent with such decision. Any action taken by the President, the administering authority, or the Commission under this subparagraph shall not be subject to judicial review, and no court of the United States shall have power or jurisdiction to review such action on any question of law or fact by an action in the nature of mandamus or otherwise.

(8) Requests for binational panel review.

(A) Interested party requests for binational panel review.

(i) General rule. An interested party who was a party to the proceeding in which a determination is made may request binational panel review of such determination by filing a request with the United States Secretary by no later than the date that is 30 days after the date described in subparagraph (A), (B), or (E) of subsection (a)(5) that is applicable to such determination. Receipt of such request by the United States Secretary shall be deemed to be a request for binational panel review within the meaning of article 1904(4) of the NAFTA or of the Agreement. Such request shall contain such information and be in such form, manner, and style as the administering authority, in consultation with the Commission, shall prescribe by regulations.

(ii) Suspension of time to request binational panel review under the NAFTA. Notwithstanding clause (i), the time for requesting binational panel review shall be suspended during the pendency of any stay of binational panel review that is issued pursuant to paragraph 11(a) of article 1905 of the NAFTA.

(B) Service of request for binational panel review.

(i) Service by interested party. If a request for binational panel review of a determination is filed under subparagraph (A), the party making the request shall serve a copy, by mail or personal service, on any other interested party who was a party to the proceeding in connection with which the matter arises, and on the administering authority or the Commission, as appropriate.

(ii) Service by United States Secretary. If an interested party to the proceeding requests binational panel review of a determination by filing a request with the relevant FTA

Secretary, the United States Secretary shall serve a copy of the request by mail on any other interested party who was a party to the proceeding in connection with which the matter arises, and on the administering authority or the Commission, as appropriate.

(C) Limitation on request for binational panel review. Absent a request by an interested party under subparagraph (A), the United States may not request binational panel review of a determination under article 1904 of the NAFTA or the Agreement.

(9) Representation in panel proceedings. In the case of binational panel proceedings convened under chapter 19 of the NAFTA or of the Agreement, the administering authority and the Commission shall be represented by attorneys who are employees of the administering authority or the Commission, respectively. Interested parties who were parties to the proceeding in connection with which the matter arises shall have the right to appear and be represented by counsel before the binational panel.

(10) Notification of class or kind rulings. In the case of a determination which is described in paragraph (2)(B)(vi) of subsection (a) and which is subject to the provisions of paragraph (2), the administering authority, upon request, shall inform any interested person of the date on which the Government of the relevant FTA country received notice of the determination under paragraph 4 of article 1904 of the NAFTA or the Agreement.

(11) Suspension and termination of suspension of article 1904 of the NAFTA.

(A) Suspension of article 1904. If a special committee established under article 1905 of the NAFTA issues an affirmative finding, the Trade Representative may, in accordance with paragraph 8(a) or 9, as appropriate, of article 1905 of the NAFTA, suspend the operation of article 1904 of the NAFTA.

(B) Termination of suspension of article 1904. If a special committee is reconvened and makes an affirmative determination described in paragraph 10(b) of article 1905 of the NAFTA, any suspension of the operation of article 1904 of the NAFTA shall terminate.

(12) Judicial review upon termination of binational panel or committee review under the NAFTA.

(A) Notice of suspension or termination of suspension of article 1904.

(i) Upon notification by the Trade Representative or the Government of a country described in subsection (f)(10) (A) or

(B) that the operation of article 1904 of the NAFTA has been suspended in accordance with paragraph 8(a) or 9 of article 1905 of the NAFTA, the United States Secretary shall publish in the Federal Register a notice of suspension of article 1904 of the NAFTA.

(ii) Upon notification by the Trade Representative or the Government of a country described in subsection (f)(10) (A) or (B) that the suspension of the operation of article 1904 of the NAFTA is terminated in accordance with paragraph 10 of article 1905 of the NAFTA, the United States Secretary shall publish in the Federal Register a notice of termination of suspension of article 1904 of the NAFTA.

(B) Transfer of final determinations for judicial review upon suspension of article 1904. If the operation of article 1904 of the NAFTA is suspended in accordance with paragraph 8(a) or 9 of article 1905 of the NAFTA—

(i) upon the request of an authorized person described in subparagraph (C), any final determination that is the subject of a binational panel review or an extraordinary challenge committee review shall be transferred to the United States Court of International Trade (in accordance with rules issued by the Court) for review under subsection (a); or

(ii) in a case in which—

(I) a binational panel review was completed fewer than 30 days before the suspension, and

(II) extraordinary challenge committee review has not been requested,

upon the request of an authorized person described in subparagraph (C) which is made within 60 days after the completion of the binational panel review, the final determination that was the subject of the binational panel review shall be transferred to the United States Court of International Trade (in accordance with rules issued by the Court) for review under subsection (a).

(C) Persons authorized to request transfer of final determinations for judicial review. A request that a final determination be transferred to the Court of International Trade under subparagraph (B) may be made by—

(i) if the United States made an allegation under paragraph 1 of article 1905 of the NAFTA and the operation of article 1904 of the NAFTA was suspended pursuant to paragraph 8(a) of article 1905 of the NAFTA—

(I) the government of the relevant country described in subsection (f)(10) (A) or (B),

(II) an interested party that was a party to the panel or committee review, or

(III) an interested party that was a party to the proceeding in connection with which panel review was requested, but only if the time period for filing notices of appearance in the panel review has not expired, or

(ii) if a country described in subsection (f)(10) (A) or (B) made an allegation under paragraph 1 of article 1905 of the NAFTA and the operation of article 1904 of the NAFTA was suspended pursuant to paragraph 9 of article 1905 of the NAFTA—

(I) the government of that country,

(II) an interested party that is a person of that country and that was a party to the panel or committee review, or

(III) an interested party that is a person of that country and that was a party to the proceeding in connection with which panel review was requested, but only if the time period for filing notices of appearance in the panel review has not expired.

(D) Transfer for judicial review upon settlement.

(i) If the Trade Representative achieves a settlement with the government of a country described in subsection (f)(10)(A) or (B) pursuant to paragraph 7 of article 1905 of the NAFTA, and referral for judicial review is among the terms of such settlement, any final determination that is the subject of a binational panel review or an extraordinary challenge committee review shall, upon a request described in clause (ii), be transferred to the United States Court of International Trade (in accordance with rules issued by the Court) for review under subsection (a).

(ii) A request referred to in clause (i) is a request made by—

(I) the country referred to in clause (i),

(II) an interested party that was a party to the panel or committee review, or

(III) an interested party that was a party to the proceeding in connection with which panel review was requested, but only if the time for filing notices of appearance in the panel review has not expired.

* * *

§ 1526. Merchandise bearing American trademark

(a) Importation prohibited. Except as provided in subsection (d) of this section, it shall be unlawful to import into the United States any merchandise of foreign manufacture if such merchandise, or the label, sign, print, package, wrapper, or receptacle, bears a trade-mark owned by a citizen of, or by a corporation or association created or organized within, the United States, and registered in the Patent Office [Patent and Trademark Office] by a person domiciled in the United States, under the provisions of the Act entitled "An Act to authorize the registration of trade-marks used in commerce with foreign nations or among the several States or with Indian tribes, and to protect the same," approved February 20, 1905, as amended, and if a copy of the certificate of registration of such trade-mark is filed with the Secretary of the Treasury, in the manner provided in section 27 of such Act, unless written consent of the owner of such trade-mark is produced at the time of making entry.

(b) Seizure and forfeiture. Any such merchandise imported into the United States in violation of the provisions of this section shall be subject to seizure and forfeiture for violation of the customs laws.

(c) Injunction and damages. Any person dealing in any such merchandise may be enjoined from dealing therein within the United States or may be required to export or destroy such merchandise or to remove or obliterate such trade-mark and shall be liable for the same damages and profits provided for wrongful use of a trade-mark, under the provisions of such Act of February 20, 1905, as amended.

(d) Exemptions; publication in Federal Register; forfeitures; rules and regulations.

(1) The trademark provisions of this section and section 42 of the Act of July 5, 1946 (60 Stat. 440; 15 U.S.C. 1124), do not apply to the importation of articles accompanying any person arriving in the United States when such articles are for his personal use and not for sale if (A) such articles are within the limits of types and quantities determined by the Secretary pursuant to paragraph (2) of this subsection, and (B) such person has not been granted an exemption under this subsection within thirty days immediately preceding his arrival.

(2) The Secretary shall determine and publish in the Federal Register lists of the types of articles and the quantities of each which shall be entitled to the exemption provided by this subsection. In determining such quantities of particular types of trade-marked articles, the Secretary shall

give such consideration as he deems necessary to the numbers of such articles usually purchased at retail for personal use.

(3) If any article which has been exempted from the restrictions on importation of the trade-mark laws under this subsection is sold within one year after the date of importation, such article, or its value (to be recovered from the importer), is subject to forfeiture. A sale pursuant to a judicial order or in liquidation of the estate of a decedent is not subject to the provisions of this paragraph.

(4) The Secretary may prescribe such rules and regulations as may be necessary to carry out the provisions of this subsection.

(e) Merchandise bearing counterfeit mark; seizure and forfeiture; disposition of seized goods. Any such merchandise bearing a counterfeit mark (within the meaning of section 45 of the Act of July 5, 1946 (commonly referred to as the Lanham Act, 60 Stat. 427; 15 U.S.C. 1127)) imported into the United States in violation of the provisions of section 42 of the Act of July 5, 1946 (60 Stat. 440; 15 U.S.C. 1124), shall be seized and, in the absence of the written consent of the trademark owner, forfeited for violations of the customs laws. Upon seizure of such merchandise, the Secretary shall notify the owner of the trademark, and shall, after forfeiture, destroy the merchandise. Alternatively, if the merchandise is not unsafe or a hazard to health, and the Secretary has the consent of the trademark owner, the Secretary may obliterate the trademark where feasible and dispose of the goods seized—

(1) by delivery to such Federal, State, and local government agencies as in the opinion of the Secretary have a need for such merchandise,

(2) by gift to such eleemosynary institutions as in the opinion of the Secretary have a need for such merchandise, or

(3) more than 90 days after the date of forfeiture, by sale by the Customs Service at public auction under such regulations as the Secretary prescribes, except that before making any such sale the Secretary shall determine that no Federal, State, or local government agency or eleemosynary institution has established a need for such merchandise under paragraph (1) or (2).

(f) Civil penalties.

(1) Any person who directs, assists financially or otherwise, or aids and abets the importation of merchandise for sale or public distribution that is seized under subsection (e) shall be subject to a civil fine.

(2) For the first such seizure, the fine shall be not more than the value that the merchandise would have had if it were genuine, according to the manufacturer's suggested retail price, determined under regulations promulgated by the Secretary.

(3) For the second seizure and thereafter, the fine shall be not more than twice the value that the merchandise would have had if it were genuine, as determined under regulations promulgated by the Secretary.

(4) The imposition of a fine under this subsection shall be within the discretion of the Customs Service, and shall be in addition to any other civil or criminal penalty or other remedy authorized by law.

SUBTITLE IV. COUNTERVAILING AND ANTIDUMPING DUTIES

Imposition of Countervailing Duties

§ 1671. Countervailing Duties Imposed

(a) General rule. If—

(1) the administering authority determines that the government of a country or any public entity within the territory of a country is providing, directly or indirectly, a countervailable subsidy with respect to the manufacture, production, or export of a class or kind of merchandise imported, or sold (or likely to be sold) for importation, into the United States, and

(2) in the case of merchandise imported from a Subsidies Agreement country, the Commission determines that—

(A) an industry in the United States—

(i) is materially injured, or

(ii) is threatened with material injury, or

(B) the establishment of an industry in the United States is materially retarded,

by reason of imports of that merchandise or by reason of sales (or the likelihood of sales) of that merchandise for importation,

then there shall be imposed upon such merchandise a countervailing duty, in addition to any other duty imposed, equal to the amount of the net countervailable subsidy. For purposes of this subsection and § 1671d(b)(1), a reference to the sale of merchandise includes the entering into of any leasing arrangement regarding the merchandise that is equivalent to the sale of the merchandise.

(b) Subsidies Agreement country. For purposes of this title, the term "Subsidies Agreement country" means—

(1) a WTO member country,

(2) a country which the President has determined has assumed obligations with respect to the United States which are substantially equivalent to the obligations under the Subsidies Agreement, or

(3) a country with respect to which the President determines that—

(A) there is an agreement in effect between the United States and that country which—

(i) was in force on the date of the enactment of the Uruguay Round Agreements Act, and

(ii) requires unconditional most-favored-nation treatment with respect to articles imported into the United States, and

(B) the agreement described in subparagraph (A) does not expressly permit—

(i) actions required or permitted by the GATT 1947 or GATT 1994, as defined in section 2(1) of the Uruguay Round Agreements Act, or required by the Congress, or

(ii) nondiscriminatory prohibitions or restrictions on importation which are designed to prevent deceptive or unfair practices.

(c) Countervailing duty investigations involving imports not entitled to a material injury determination. In the case of any article or merchandise imported from a country which is not a Subsidies Agreement country—

(1) no determination by the Commission under §§ 1671b(a), 1671c or 1671d(b) shall be required,

(2) an investigation may not be suspended under § 1671c(c) or § 1671c(*l*),

(3) no determination as to the presence of critical circumstances shall be made under § 1671b(e) or § 1671d(a)(2),

(4) section 1671e(c) shall not apply,

(5) any reference to a determination described in paragraph (1) or (3), or to the suspension of an investigation under § 1671c(c) or § 1671c(*l*), shall be disregarded, and

(6) section 1675(c) shall not apply.

(d) Treatment of international consortia. For purposes of this subtitle, if the members (or other participating entities) of an international consortium that is engaged in the production of a class or kind of merchandise subject to a countervailing duty investigation receive subsidies from their respective home countries to assist, permit, or otherwise enable their participation in that consortium through production or manufacturing operations in their respective home countries, then the administering authority shall cumulate all such subsidies, as well as subsidies provided directly to the international consortium, in determining any countervailing duty upon such merchandise.

(e) Upstream subsidy. Whenever the administering authority has reasonable grounds to believe or suspect that an upstream subsidy, as defined in § 1677–1(a)(1), is being paid or bestowed, the administering authority shall investigate whether an upstream subsidy has in fact been paid or bestowed, and if so, shall include the amount of the upstream subsidy as provided in § 1677–1(a)(3).

(f) Applicability to proceedings involving nonmarket economy countries

(1) *In general.*

Except as provided in paragraph (2), the merchandise on which countervailing duties shall be imposed under subsection (a) includes a class or kind of merchandise imported, or sold (or likely to be sold) for importation, into the United States from a nonmarket economy country.

(2) *Exception*

A countervailing duty is not required to be imposed under subsection (a) on a class or kind of merchandise imported, or sold (or likely to be sold) for importation, into the United States from a nonmarket economy country if the administering authority is unable to identify and measure subsidies provided by the government of the nonmarket economy country or a public entity within the territory of the nonmarket economy country because the economy of that country is essentially comprised of a single entity.

§ 1671a. Procedures for initiating a countervailing duty investigation

(a) Initiation by administering authority. A countervailing duty investigation shall be initiated whenever the administering authority determines, from information available to it, that a formal investigation is warranted into the question of whether the elements necessary for the imposition of a duty under § 1671a exist.

(b) Initiation by petition

(1) Petition requirements. A countervailing duty proceeding shall be initiated whenever an interested party described in subparagraph (C), (D), (E), (F) or (G) of § 1677(9) of this title files a petition with the administering authority, on behalf of an industry, which alleges the elements necessary for the imposition of the duty imposed by § 1671(a), and which is accompanied by information reasonably available to the petitioner supporting those allegations. The petition may be amended at such time, and upon such conditions, as the administering authority and the Commission may permit.

(2) Simultaneous filing with commission. The petitioner shall file a copy of the petition with the Commission on the same day as it is filed with the administering authority.

(3) Petition based upon a derogation of an international undertaking on official export credits. If the sole basis of a petition filed under paragraph 1 of this section is the derogation of an international undertaking on official export credits, the administering authority shall immediately notify the Secretary of the Treasury who shall, in consultation with the administering authority, within 5 days after the date on which the administering authority initiates an investigation under subsection (c) determine the existence and estimated value of the derogation, if any, and shall publish such determination in the Federal Register.

(4) Action with respect to petitions.

(A) Notification of governments. Upon receipt of a petition filed under paragraph (1), the administering authority shall—

(i) notify the government of any exporting country named in the petition by delivering a public version of the petition to an appropriate representative of such country; and

(ii) provide the government of any exporting country named in the petition that is a Subsidies Agreement country an opportunity for consultations with respect to the petition.

(B) Acceptance of communications. The administering authority shall not accept any unsolicited oral or written communication from any person other than an interested party described in § 1677a(A), (C), (D), (E), (F), or (G) before the administering authority makes its decision whether to initiate an investigation, except as provided in subparagraph (A)(ii) and subsection (c)(4)(D), and except for inquiries regarding the status of the administering authority's consideration of the petition.

(C) Nondisclosure of certain information. The administering authority and the Commission shall not disclose information with regard to any draft petition submitted for review and comment before it is filed under paragraph (1).

(c) Petition determination.

(1) In general—

(A) Time for initial determination. Except as provided in subparagraph (B), within 20 days after the date on which a petition is filed under subsection (b), the administering authority shall—

(i) after examining, on the basis of sources readily available to the administering authority, the accuracy and adequacy of the evidence provided in the petition, determine whether the petition alleges the elements necessary for the imposition of a duty under § 1671(a) and contains information reasonably available to the petitioner supporting the allegations, and

(ii) determine if the petition has been filed by or on behalf of the industry.

(B) Extension of time. In any case in which the administering authority is required to poll or otherwise determine support for the petition by the industry under paragraph (4)(D), the administering authority may, in exceptional circumstances, apply subparagraph (A) by substituting "a maximum of 40 days" for "20 days".

(C) Time limits where petition involves same merchandise as an order that has been revoked. If a petition is filed under this section with respect to merchandise that was the subject merchandise of—

(i) a countervailing duty order that was revoked under § 1675(d) in the 24 months preceding the date the petition is filed, or

(ii) a suspended investigation that was terminated under § 1675(d) in the 24 months preceding the date the petition is filed, the administering authority and the Commission shall, to the maximum extent practicable, expedite any investigation initiated under this section with respect to the petition.

(2) Affirmative determinations. If the determinations under clauses (i) and (ii) of paragraph (1)(A) are affirmative, the administering authority shall initiate an investigation to determine whether a countervailable subsidy is being provided with respect to the subject merchandise.

(3) Negative determinations. If the determination under clause (i) or (ii) of paragraph (1)(A) is negative, the administering authority shall dismiss the petition, terminate the proceeding, and notify the petitioner in writing of the reasons for the determination.

(4) Determination of industry support.

(A) General rule. For purposes of this subsection, the administering authority shall determine that the petition has been filed by or on behalf of the industry, if—

(i) the domestic producers or workers who support the petition account for at least 25 percent of the total production of the domestic like product, and

(ii) the domestic producers or workers who support the petition account for more than 50 percent of the production of the domestic like product produced by that portion of the industry expressing support for or opposition to the petition.

(B) Certain positions disregarded.

(i) Producers related to foreign producers. In determining industry support under subparagraph (A), the administering authority shall disregard the position of domestic producers who oppose the petition, if such producers are related to foreign producers, as defined in § 1677(4)(B)(ii), unless such domestic producers demonstrate that their interests as domestic producers would be adversely affected by the imposition of a countervailing duty order.

(ii) Producers who are importers. The administering authority may disregard the position of domestic producers of a domestic like product who are importers of the subject merchandise.

(C) Special rule for regional industries. If the petition alleges that the industry is a regional industry, the administering authority shall determine whether the petition has been filed by or on behalf of the industry by applying subparagraph (A) on the basis of production in the region.

(D) Polling the industry. If the petition does not establish support of domestic producers or workers accounting for more than 50 percent of the total production of the domestic like product, the administering authority shall—

(i) poll the industry or rely on other information in order to determine if there is support for the petition as required by subparagraph (A), or

(ii) if there is a large number of producers in the industry, the administering authority may determine industry support for the petition by using any statistically valid sampling method to poll the industry.

(E) Comments by interested parties. Before the administering authority makes a determination with respect to initiating an investigation, any person who would qualify as an interested party under § 1677(9) if an investigation were initiated, may submit comments or information on the issue of industry support. After the administering authority makes a determination with respect to initiating an investigation, the determination regarding industry support shall not be reconsidered.

(5) Definition of domestic producers or workers. For purposes of this subsection, the term "domestic producers or workers" means those interested parties who are eligible to file a petition under subsection (b)(1)(A).

(d) Notification to Commission of determination. The administering authority shall—

(1) notify the Commission immediately of any determination it makes under subsection (a) or (c), and

(2) if the determination is affirmative, make available to the Commission such information as it may have relating to the matter under investigation, under such procedures as the administering authority and the Commission may establish to prevent disclosure, other than with the consent of the party providing it or under protective order, of any information to which confidential treatment has been given by the administering authority.

(e) Information regarding critical circumstances. If, at any time after the initiation of an investigation under this subtitle, the administering authority finds a reasonable basis to suspect that the alleged countervailable subsidy is inconsistent with the Subsidies Agreement, the administering authority may request the Commissioner of Customs to compile information on an expedited basis regarding entries of the subject merchandise. Upon receiving such request, the Commissioner of Customs shall collect information regarding the volume and value of entries of the subject merchandise and shall transmit such information to the administering authority at such times as the administering authority shall direct (at least once every 30 days), until a final determination is made under section 705(a), the investigation is terminated, or the administering authority withdraws the request.

Sec. 1671b. Preliminary Determinations

(a) Determination by Commission of reasonable indication of injury.

(1) General rule. Except in the case of a petition dismissed by the administering authority under § 1671a(c)(3), the Commission, within the time specified in paragraph (2), shall determine, based on the information available to it at the time of the determination, whether there is a reasonable indication

that—

(A) an industry in the United States

(i) is materially injured, or

(ii) is threatened with material injury, or

(B) the establishment of an industry in the United States is materially retarded, by reason of imports of the subject merchandise and that imports of the subject merchandise are not negligible. If the Commission finds that imports of the subject merchandise are negligible or otherwise makes a negative determination under this paragraph, the investigation shall be terminated.

(2) Time for commission determination. The Commission shall make the determination described in paragraph (1)—

(A) in the case of a petition filed under § 1671a(b)

(i) within 45 days after the date on which the petition is filed, or

(ii) if the time has been extended pursuant to § 1671a(c)(1)(B), within 25 days after the date on which the Commission receives notice from the administering authority of initiation of the investigation, and

(B) in the case of an investigation initiated under § 1671a(a), within 45 days after the date on which the Commission receives notice from the administering authority that an investigation has been initiated under such section.

(b) Preliminary determination by administering authority; expedited determinations; waiver of verification. (1) Within 65 days after the date on which the administering authority initiates an investigation under § 1671a(c), or an investigation is initiated under § 1671a(a), but not before an affirmative determination by the Commission under subsection (a) of this section, the administering authority shall make a determination, based upon the information available to it at the time of the determination, of whether there is a reasonable basis to believe or suspect that a countervailable subsidy is being provided with respect to the subject merchandise.

(2) Notwithstanding paragraph (1), when the petition is one subject to § 1671a(b)(3) of this Act, the administering authority shall, taking into account the nature of the countervailable subsidy concerned, make the determination required by paragraph (1) on an expedited basis and within 65 days after the date on which the administering authority initiates an investigation under § 1671a(c) unless the provisions of subsection (c) of this section apply.

(3) Preliminary determination under waiver of verification. Within 55 days after the initiation of an investigation the administering authority shall cause an official designated for such purpose to review the information concerning the case received during the first 50 days of the investigation, and, if there appears to be sufficient information available upon which the determination can reasonably be based, to disclose to the petitioner and any interested party, then a party to the proceedings that requests such disclosure, all available nonconfidential information and all other information which is disclosed pursuant to § 1677f. Within 3 days (not counting Saturdays, Sundays, or legal public holidays) after such disclosure, the petitioner and each party which is an interested party described in subparagraph (C), (D), (E), (F), or (G) of § 1677(9) to whom such disclosure was made may furnish to the administering authority an irrevocable written waiver of verification of the information received by the authority, and an agreement that it is willing to have a determination made on the basis of the record then available to the authority. If a timely

waiver and agreement have been received from the petitioner and each party which is an interested party described in subparagraph (C), (D), (E), (F), or (G) of § 1677(9) to whom the disclosure was made, and the authority finds that sufficient information is then available upon which the preliminary determination can reasonably be based, a preliminary determination shall be made on an expedited basis on the basis of the record established during the first 50 days after the investigation was initiated.

(4) De minimis countervailable subsidy.

(A) General rule. In making a determination under this subsection, the administering authority shall disregard any de minimis countervailable subsidy. For purposes of the preceding sentence, a countervailable subsidy is de minimis if the administering authority determines that the aggregate of the net countervailable subsidies is less than 1 percent ad valorem or the equivalent specific rate for the subject merchandise.

(B) Exception for developing countries. In the case of subject merchandise imported from a Subsidies Agreement country (other than a country to which subparagraph (C) applies) designated by the Trade Representative as a developing country in accordance with section § 1677(36), a countervailable subsidy is de minimis if the administering authority determines that the aggregate of the net countervailable subsidies does not exceed 2 percent ad valorem or the equivalent specific rate for the subject merchandise.

(C) Certain other developing countries. In the case of subject merchandise imported from a Subsidies Agreement country that is—

(i) a least developed country, as determined by the Trade Representative in accordance with § 1677(36), or

(ii) a developing country with respect to which the Trade Representative has notified the administering authority that the country has eliminated its export subsidies on an expedited basis within the meaning of Article 27.11 of the Subsidies Agreement, subparagraph (B) shall be applied by substituting "3 percent" for "2 percent".

(D) Limitations on application of subparagraph (c).

(i) In general. In the case of a country described in subparagraph (C)(i), the provisions of subparagraph (C) shall not apply after the date that is 8 years after the date the WTO Agreement enters into force.

(ii) Special rule for subparagraph (C)(ii) countries. In the case of a country described in subparagraph (C)(ii), the provisions of subparagraph (C) shall not apply after the earlier of—

(I) the date that is 8 years after the date the WTO Agreement enters into force, or

(II) the date on which the Trade Representative notifies the administering authority that such country is providing an export subsidy.

(5) Notification of article 8 violation. If the only subsidy under investigation is a subsidy with respect to which the administering authority received notice from the Trade Representative of a violation of Article 8 of the Subsidies Agreement, paragraph (1) shall be applied by substituting "60 days" for "65 days."

(c) Extension of period in extraordinarily complicated cases.

(1) In general. If—

(A) the petitioner makes a timely request for an extension of the period within which the determination must be made under subsection (b), or

(B) the administering authority concludes that the parties concerned are cooperating and determines that—

(i) the case is extraordinarily complicated by reason of—

(I) the number and complexity of the alleged countervailable subsidy practices;

(II) the novelty of the issues presented;

(III) the need to determine the extent to which particular countervailable subsidies are used by individual manufacturers, producers, and exporters; or

(IV) the number of firms whose activities must be investigated; and

(ii) additional time is necessary to make the preliminary determination,

then the administering authority may postpone making the preliminary determination under subsection (b) until not later than the 130th day after the date on which the administering authority initiates an investigation under § 1671a(c), or an investigation is initiated under § 1671a(a).

(2) Notice of postponement. The administering authority shall notify the parties to the investigation, not later than 20 days before the date on which the preliminary determination would otherwise be required under subsection (b), if it intends to postpone making the preliminary determination under paragraph (1). The notification shall include an explanation of the reasons for the postponement. Notice of the postponement shall be published in the Federal Register.

(d) Effect of determination by the administering authority. If the preliminary determination of the administering authority under subsection (b) is affirmative, the administering authority—

(1)(A) shall

(i) determine an estimated individual countervailable subsidy rate for each exporter and producer individually investigated, and, in accordance with § 1671d(c)(5), an estimated all-others rate for all exporters and producers not individually investigated and for new exporters and producers within the meaning of § 1675(a)(2)(B), or

(ii) if § 1677f–1(e)(2)(B) applies, determine a single estimated country-wide subsidy rate, applicable to all exporters and producers, and

(B) shall order the posting of a cash deposit, bond, or other security, as the administering authority deems appropriate, for each entry of the subject merchandise in an amount based on the estimated individual countervailable subsidy rate, the estimated all-others rate, or the estimated country-wide subsidy rate, whichever is applicable,

(2) shall order the suspension of liquidation of all entries of merchandise subject to the determination which are entered, or withdrawn from warehouse, for consumption on or after the later of

(A) the date on which notice of the determination is published in the Federal Register, or

(B) the date that is 60 days after the date on which notice of the determination to initiate the investigation is published in the Federal Register, and

(3) shall make available to the Commission all information upon which its determination was based and which the Commission considers relevant to its injury determination, under such procedures as the administering authority and the Commission may establish to prevent disclosure, other than with the consent of the party providing it or under protective order, of any information to which confidential treatment has been given by the administering authority.

The instructions of the administering authority under paragraphs (1) and (2) may not remain in effect for more than 4 months.

(e) Critical circumstances determinations.

(1) In general. If a petitioner alleges critical circumstances in its original petition, or by amendment at any time more than 20 days before the date of a final determination by the administering authority, then the administering authority shall promptly (at any time after the initiation of the investigation under this subtitle) determine, on the basis of the

information available to it at that time, whether there is a reasonable basis to believe or suspect that—

(A) the alleged countervailable subsidy is inconsistent with the Subsidies Agreement, and

(B) there have been massive imports of the subject merchandise over a relatively short period.

(2) Suspension of liquidation. If the determination of the administering authority under paragraph (1) is affirmative, then any suspension of liquidation ordered under subsection (d)(2) shall apply, or, if notice of such suspension of liquidation is already published, be amended to apply, to unliquidated entries of merchandise entered, or withdrawn from warehouse, for consumption on or after the later of

(A) the date which is 90 days before the date on which the suspension of liquidation was first ordered, or

(B) the date on which notice of the determination to initiate the investigation is published in the Federal Register.

(f) Notice of determinations. Whenever the Commission or the administering authority makes a determination under this section, the Commission or the administering authority, as the case may be, shall notify the petitioner, and other parties to the investigation, and the Commission or the administering authority (whichever is appropriate) of its determination. The administering authority shall include with such notification the facts and conclusions on which its determination is based. Not later than 5 days after the date on which the determination is required to be made under subsection (a)(2), the Commission shall transmit to the administering authority the facts and conclusions on which its determination is based.

(g) Time period where upstream subsidization involved.

(1) In general. Whenever the administering authority concludes prior to a preliminary determination under § 1671b(b), that there is a reasonable basis to believe or suspect that an upstream subsidy is being bestowed, the time period within which a preliminary determination must be made shall be extended to 250 days after the filing of a petition under § 1671a(b) or initiation of an investigation under § 1671a(a) (310 days in cases declared extraordinarily complicated under § 1671b(c)), if the administering authority concludes that such additional time is necessary to make the required determination concerning upstream subsidization.

(2) Exceptions. Whenever the administering authority concludes, after a preliminary determination under § 1671b(b), that there is a reasonable basis to believe or suspect that an upstream subsidy is being bestowed—

(A) in cases in which the preliminary determination was negative, the time period within which a final determination must be made shall be extended to 165 days or 225 days, as appropriate, under § 1671d(a)1;

(B) in cases in which the preliminary determination is affirmative, the determination concerning upstream subsidization—

(i) need not be made until the conclusion of the first annual review under § 1675 of any eventual Countervailing Duty Order, or, at the option of the petitioner, or

(ii) will be made in the investigation and the time period within which a final determination must be made shall be extended to 165 or 225 days, as appropriate, under § 1671d(a)(1), except that the suspension of liquidation ordered in the preliminary determination shall terminate at the end of 120 days from the date of publication of that determination and not be resumed unless and until the publication of a Countervailing Duty Order under § 1671e(a).

There may be an extension of time for the making of a final determination under this subsection only if the administering authority determines that such additional time is necessary to make the required determination concerning upstream subsidization.

§ 1671c. Termination or suspension of investigation

(a) Termination of investigation upon withdrawal of petition.

(1) In general.

(A) Withdrawal of petition. Except as provided in paragraphs (2) and (3), an investigation under this subtitle may be terminated by either the administering authority or the Commission, after notice to all parties to the investigation, upon withdrawal of the petition by the petitioner or by the administering authority if the investigation was initiated under section 702(a).

(B) Refiling of petition. If, within 3 months after the withdrawal of a petition under subparagraph (A), a new petition is filed seeking the imposition of duties on both the subject merchandise of the withdrawn petition and the subject merchandise from another country, the administering authority and the Commission may use in the investigation initiated pursuant to the new petition any records compiled in an investigation conducted pursuant to the withdrawn petition. This subparagraph applies only with respect to the first withdrawal of a petition.

(2) Special rules for quantitative restriction agreements.

(A) In general. Subject to subparagraphs (B) and (C), the administering authority may not terminate an investigation under paragraph (1) by accepting, with the government of the country in which the countervailable subsidy practice is alleged to occur, an understanding or other kind of agreement to limit the volume of imports into the United States of the subject merchandise unless the administering authority is satisfied that termination on the basis of that agreement is in the public interest.

(B) Public interest factors. In making a decision under subparagraph (A) regarding the public interest, the administering authority shall take into account—

(i) whether, based upon the relative impact on consumer prices and the availability of supplies of the merchandise, the agreement would have a greater adverse impact on United States consumers than the imposition of countervailing duties;

(ii) the relative impact on the international economic interests of the United States; and

(iii) the relative impact on the competitiveness of the domestic industry producing the like merchandise, including any such impact on employment and investment in that industry.

(C) Prior consultations. Before making a decision under subparagraph (A) regarding the public interest, the administering authority shall, to the extent practicable, consult with—

(i) potentially affected consuming industries; and

(ii) potentially affected producers and workers in the domestic industry producing the like merchandise, including producers and workers not party to the investigation.

(3) Limitation on termination by commission. The Commission may not terminate an investigation under paragraph (1) before a preliminary determination is made by the administering authority under § 1671b(b).

(b) Agreements to eliminate or offset completely a countervailable subsidy or to cease exports of subject merchandise. The administering authority may suspend an investigation if the government of the country in which the countervailable subsidy practice is alleged to occur agrees, or exporters who account for substantially all of the imports of the subject merchandise agree—

(1) to eliminate the countervailable subsidy completely or to offset completely the amount of the net countervailable subsidy, with respect to that merchandise exported directly or indirectly to the United States, within 6 months after the date on which the investigation is suspended, or

(2) to cease exports of that merchandise to the United States within 6 months after the date on which the investigation is suspended.

(c) Agreements eliminating injurious effect.

(1) General rule. If the administering authority determines that extraordinary circumstances are present in a case, it may suspend an investigation upon the acceptance of an agreement from a government described in subsection (b), or from exporters described in subsection (b), if the agreement will eliminate completely the injurious effect of exports to the United States of the subject merchandise.

(2) Certain additional requirements. Except in the case of an agreement by a foreign government to restrict the volume of imports of the subject merchandise into the United States, the administering authority may not accept an agreement under this subsection unless—

(A) the suppression or undercutting of price levels of domestic products by imports of that merchandise will be prevented, and

(B) at least 85 percent of the net countervailable subsidy will be offset.

(3) Quantitative restrictions agreements. The administering authority may accept an agreement with a foreign government under this subsection to restrict the volume of imports of subject merchandise into the United States, but it may not accept such an agreement with exporters.

(4) Definition of extraordinary circumstances.

(A) Extraordinary circumstances. For purposes of this subsection, the term "extraordinary circumstances" means circumstances in which—

(i) suspension of an investigation will be more beneficial to the domestic industry than continuation of the investigation, and

(ii) the investigation is complex.

(B) Complex. For purposes of this paragraph, the term "complex" means—

(i) there are a large number of alleged countervailable subsidy practices and the practices are complicated,

(ii) the issues raised are novel, or

(iii) the number of exporters involved is large.

(d) Additional rules and conditions.

(1) Public interest; monitoring. The administering authority shall not accept an agreement under subsection (b) or (c) unless—

(A) it is satisfied that suspension of the investigation is in the public interest, and

(B) effective monitoring of the agreement by the United States is practicable.

Where practicable, the administering authority shall provide to the exporters who would have been subject to the agreement the reasons for not accepting the agreement and, to the extent possible, an opportunity to submit comments thereon. In applying subparagraph (A) with respect to any quantitative restriction agreement under subsection (c), the administering authority shall take into account, in addition to such other factors as are considered necessary or appropriate, the factors set forth in subsection (a)(2)(B)(i), (ii), and (iii) as they apply to the proposed suspension and agreement, after consulting with the appropriate consuming industries, producers, and workers referred to in subsection (a)(2)(C)(i) and (ii).

(2) Exports of merchandise to United States not to increase during interim period. The administering authority may not accept any agreement under subsection (b) unless that agreement provides a means of ensuring that the quantity of the merchandise covered by that agreement exported to the United States during the period provided for elimination or offset of the countervailable subsidy or cessation of exports does not exceed the quantity of such merchandise exported to the United States during the most recent representative period determined by the administering authority.

(3) Regulations governing entry or withdrawals. In order to carry out an agreement concluded under subsection (b) or (c), the administering authority is authorized to prescribe regulations governing the entry, or withdrawal from warehouse, for consumption of merchandise covered by such agreement.

(e) Suspension of investigation procedure. Before an investigation may be suspended under subsection (b) or (c) the administering authority shall—

(1) notify the petitioner of, and consult with the petitioner concerning, its intention to suspend the investigation, and notify other parties to the investigation and the Commission not less than 30 days before the date on which it suspends the investigation,

(2) provide a copy of the proposed agreement to the petitioner at the time of the notification, together with an explanation of how the agreement will be carried out and enforced (including any action required of foreign governments), and of how the agreement will meet the requirements of subsections (b) and (d) or (c) and (d), and

(3) permit all interested parties described in § 1677(9) to submit comments and information for the record before the date on which notice of suspension of the investigation is published under subsection (f)(1)(A).

(f) Effects of suspension of investigation.

(1) In general. If the administering authority determines to suspend an investigation upon acceptance of an agreement described in subsection (b) or (c), then—

(A) it shall suspend the investigation, publish notice of suspension of the investigation, and issue an affirmative preliminary determination under § 1671b(b) with respect to the subject merchandise, unless it has previously issued such a determination in the same investigation,

(B) the Commission shall suspend any investigation it is conducting with respect to that merchandise, and

(C) the suspension of investigation shall take effect on the day on which such notice is published.

(2) Liquidation of entries.

(A) Cessation of exports; complete elimination of net countervailable subsidy. If the agreement accepted by the administering authority is an agreement described in subsection (b), then—

(i) notwithstanding the affirmative preliminary determination required under paragraph (1)(A), the liquidation of entries of subject merchandise shall not be suspended under § 1671b(d)(2),

(ii) if the liquidation of entries of such merchandise was suspended pursuant to a previous affirmative preliminary determination in the same case with respect to such merchandise, that suspension of liquidation shall terminate, and

(iii) the administering authority shall refund any cash deposit and release any bond or other security deposited under § 1671b(d)(1)(B).

(B) Other agreements. If the agreement accepted by the administering authority is an agreement described in subsection (c), then the liquidation of entries of the subject merchandise shall be suspended under § 1671b(d)(2), or, if the liquidation of entries of such merchandise was suspended pursuant to a previous affirmative preliminary determination in the same case, that suspension of liquidation shall continue in effect, subject to subsection (h)(3), but the security required under § 1617b(d)(1)(B) may be adjusted to reflect the effect of the agreement.

(3) Where investigation is continued. If, pursuant to subsection (g), the administering authority and the Commission continue an investigation in which an agreement has been accepted under subsection (b) or (c), then—

(A) if the final determination by the administering authority or the Commission under § 1671d is negative, the agreement shall have no force or effect and the investigation shall be terminated, or

(B) if the final determinations by the administering authority and the Commission under such section are affirmative, the agreement shall remain in force, but the administering authority shall not issue a countervailing duty order in the case so long as—

(i) the agreement remains in force,

(ii) the agreement continues to meet the requirements of subsections (b) and (d) or (c) and (d), and

(iii) the parties to the agreement carry out their obligations under the agreement in accordance with its terms.

(g) Investigation to be continued upon request. If the administering authority, within 20 days after the date of publication of the notice of suspension of an investigation, receives a request for the continuation of the investigation from—

(1) the government of the country in which the countervailable subsidy practice is alleged to occur, or

(2) an interested party described in subparagraph (C), (D), (E), (F), or (G) of § 1677(9) which is a party to the investigation, then the administering authority and the Commission shall continue the investigation.

(h) Review of suspension.

(1) In general. Within 20 days after the suspension of an investigation under subsection (c), an interested party which is a party to the investigation and which is described in subparagraph (C), (D), (E), (F) or (G) of § 1677(9) may, by petition filed with the Commission and with notice to the administering authority, ask for a review of the suspension.

(2) Commission investigation. Upon receipt of a review petition under paragraph (1), the Commission shall, within 75 days after the date on which the petition is filed with it, determine whether the injurious effect of imports of the subject merchandise is eliminated completely by the agreement. If the Commission's determination under this subsection is negative, the investigation shall be resumed on the date of publication of notice of such determination as if the affirmative preliminary determination under § 1671b(b) had been made on that date.

(3) Suspension of liquidation to continue during review period. The suspension of liquidation of entries of the subject merchandise shall terminate at the close of the 20–day period beginning on the day after the date on which notice of suspension of the investigation is published in the Federal Register, or, if a review petition is filed under paragraph (1) with

respect to the suspension of the investigation, in the case of an affirmative determination by the Commission under paragraph (2), the date on which notice of the affirmative determination by the Commission is published. If the determination of the Commission under paragraph (2) is affirmative, then the administering authority shall—

(A) terminate the suspension of liquidation under § 1671b(d)(2), and

(B) release any bond or other security, and refund any cash deposit, required under § 1671b(1)(B).

(i) Violation of agreement.

(1) In general. If the administering authority determines that an agreement accepted under subsection (b) or (c) is being, or has been, violated, or no longer meets the requirements of such subsection (other than the requirement, under subsection (c)(1), of elimination of injury) and subsection (d), then, on the date of publication of its determination, it shall—

(A) suspend liquidation under § 1671b(d)(2) of unliquidated entries of the merchandise made on or after the later of—

(i) the date which is 90 days before the date of publication of the notice of suspension of liquidation, or

(ii) the date on which the merchandise, the sale or export to the United States of which was in violation of the agreement, or under an agreement which no longer meets the requirements of subsections (b) and (d) or (c) and (d), was first entered, or withdrawn from warehouse, for consumption,

(B) if the investigation was not completed, resume the investigation as if its affirmative preliminary determination under § 1671b(b) were made on the date of its determination under this paragraph,

(C) if the investigation was completed under subsection (g), issue a countervailing duty order under § 1671e(a) effective with respect to entries of merchandise the liquidation of which was suspended,

(D) if it considers the violation to be intentional, notify the Commissioner of Customs who shall take appropriate action under paragraph (2), and

(E) notify the petitioner, interested parties who are or were parties to the investigation, and the Commission of its action under this paragraph.

(2) Intentional violation to be punished by civil penalty. Any person who intentionally violates an agreement accepted by the administering authority under subsection (b) or (c) shall be subject to a civil penalty

assessed in the same amount, in the same manner, and under the same procedure, as the penalty imposed for a fraudulent violation of § 1592(a) of this Act.

(j) Determination not to take agreement into account. In making a final determination under § 1671d, or in conducting a review under § 1675, in a case in which the administering authority has terminated a suspension of investigation under subsection (i)(1), or continued an investigation under subsection (g), the Commission and the administering authority shall consider all of the subject merchandise, without regard to the effect of any agreement under subsection (b) or (c).

(k) Termination of investigations initiated by administering authority. The administering authority may terminate any investigation initiated by the administering authority under § 1671a(a) after providing notice of such termination to all parties to the investigation.

(*l*) Special rule for regional industry investigations.

(1) Suspension agreements. If the Commission makes a regional industry determination under § 1677(4)(C), the administering authority shall offer exporters of the subject merchandise who account for substantially all exports of that merchandise for sale in the region concerned the opportunity to enter into an agreement described in subsection (b) or (c).

(2) Requirements for suspension agreements. Any agreement described in paragraph (1) shall be subject to all the requirements imposed under this section for other agreements under subsection (b) or (c), except that if the Commission makes a regional industry determination described in paragraph (1) in the final affirmative determination under § 1671d(b) but not in the preliminary affirmative determination under § 1671b(a), any agreement described in paragraph (1) may be accepted within 60 days after the countervailing duty order is published under § 1671e.

(3) Effect of suspension agreement on countervailing duty order. If an agreement described in paragraph (1) is accepted after the countervailing duty order is published, the administering authority shall rescind the order, refund any cash deposit and release any bond or other security deposited under § 1671b(d)(1)(B), and instruct the Customs Service that entries of the subject merchandise that were made during the period that the order was in effect shall be liquidated without regard to countervailing duties.

§ 1671d. Final Determinations

(a) Final determination by administering authority.

(1) In general. Within 75 days after the date of the preliminary determination under § 1671b(b), the administering authority shall make a final determination of whether or not a countervailable subsidy is being

provided with respect to the subject merchandise; except that when an investigation under this subtitle is initiated simultaneously with an investigation under subtitle B, which involves imports of the same class or kind of merchandise from the same or other countries, the administering authority, if requested by the petitioner, shall extend the date of the final determination under this paragraph to the date of the final determination of the administering authority in such investigation initiated under subtitle B.

(2) Critical circumstances determinations. If the final determination of the administering authority is affirmative, then that determination, in any investigation in which the presence of critical circumstances has been alleged under § 1671b(e), shall also contain a finding as to whether—

(A) the countervailable subsidy is inconsistent with the Subsidies Agreement, and

(B) there have been massive imports of the subject merchandise over a relatively short period.

Such findings may be affirmative even though the preliminary determination under § 1671b(e)(1) was negative.

(3) De minimis countervailable subsidy. In making a determination under this subsection, the administering authority shall disregard any countervailable subsidy that is de minimis as defined in § 1671b(b)(4).

(b) Final determination by Commission.

(1) In general. The Commission shall make a final determination of whether—

(A) an industry in the United States—

(i) is materially injured, or

(ii) is threatened with material injury, or

(B) the establishment of an industry in the United States is materially retarded,

by reason of imports, or sales (or the likelihood of sales) for importation, of the merchandise with respect to which the administering authority has made an affirmative determination under subsection (a). If the Commission determines that imports of the subject merchandise are negligible, the investigation shall be terminated.

(2) Period for injury determination following affirmative preliminary determination by administering authority. If the preliminary determination by the administering authority under § 1671b(b) is affirmative, then the Commission shall make the determination required by paragraph (1) before the later of—

(A) the 120th day after the day on which the administering authority makes its affirmative preliminary determination under § 1671b(b), or

(B) the 45th day after the day on which the administering authority makes its affirmative final determination under subsection (a).

(3) Period for injury determination following negative preliminary determination by administering authority. If the preliminary determination by the administering authority under § 1671b(b) is negative, and its final determination under subsection (a) is affirmative, then the final determination by the Commission under this subsection shall be made within 75 days after the date of that affirmative final determination.

(4) Certain additional findings.

(A) Commission standard for retroactive application.

(i) In general. If the finding of the administering authority under subsection (a)(2) is affirmative, then the final determination of the Commission shall include a finding as to whether the imports subject to the affirmative determination under subsection (a)(2) are likely to undermine seriously the remedial effect of the countervailing duty order to be issued under § 1671e.

(ii) Factors to consider. In making the evaluation under clause (i), the Commission shall consider, among other factors it considers relevant—

(I) the timing and the volume of the imports,

(II) any rapid increase in inventories of the imports, and

(III) any other circumstances indicating that the remedial effect of the countervailing duty order will be seriously undermined.

(B) If the final determination of the Commission is that there is no material injury but that there is threat of material injury, then its determination shall also include a finding as to whether material injury by reason of imports of the merchandise with respect to which the administering authority has made an affirmative determination under subsection (a) would have been found but for any suspension of liquidation of entries of that merchandise.

(c) Effect of final determinations.

(1) Effect of affirmative determination by the administering authority. If the determination of the administering authority under subsection (a) is affirmative, then—

(A) the administering authority shall make available to the Commission all information upon which such determination was based and which the Commission considers relevant to its determination, under such procedures as the administering authority and the Commission may establish to prevent disclosure, other than with the consent of the party providing it or under protective order, of any information to which confidential treatment has been given by the administering authority,

(B)(i) the administering authority shall—

(I) determine an estimated individual countervailable subsidy rate for each exporter and producer individually investigated, and, in accordance with paragraph (5), an estimated all-others rate for all exporters and producers not individually investigated and for new exporters and producers within the meaning of § 1675(a)(2)(B), or

(II) if § 1677f–1(e)(2)(B) applies, determine a single estimated country-wide subsidy rate, applicable to all exporters and producers,

(ii) shall order the posting of a cash deposit, bond, or other security, as the administering authority deems appropriate, for each entry of the subject merchandise in an amount based on the estimated individual countervailable subsidy rate, the estimated all-others rate, or the estimated country-wide subsidy rate, whichever is applicable, and

(C) in cases where the preliminary determination by the administering authority under § 1671b(b) was negative, the administering authority shall order the suspension of liquidation under paragraph (2) of § 1671b(d).

(2) Issuance of order; effect of negative determination. If the determinations of the administering authority and the Commission under subsections (a)(1) and (b)(1) are affirmative, then the administering authority shall issue a countervailing duty order under § 1671e(a). If either of such determinations is negative, the investigation shall be terminated upon the publication of notice of that negative determination and the administering authority shall—

(A) terminate the suspension of liquidation under § 1671b(d)(2), and

(B) release any bond or other security and refund any cash deposit required under § 1671b(d)(1)(B).

(3) Effect of negative determinations under subsections (a)(2) and (b)(4)(A). If the determination of the administering authority or the

Commission under subsection (a)(2) and (b)(4)(A), respectively, is negative, then the administering authority shall—

(A) terminate any retroactive suspension of liquidation required under paragraph (4) or § 1671b(e)(2), and

(B) release any bond or other security, and refund any cash deposit required, under § 1671b(d)(1)(B) with respect to entries of the merchandise the liquidation of which was suspended retroactively under § 1671b(e)(2).

(4) Effect of affirmative determination under subsection (a)(2). If the determination of the administering authority under subsection (a)(2) is affirmative, then the administering authority shall—

(A) in cases where the preliminary determinations by the administering authority under §§ 1671b(b) and 1671b(e)(1) were both affirmative, continue the retroactive suspension of liquidation and the posting of a cash deposit, bond, or other security previously ordered under § 1671b(e)(2);

(B) in cases where the preliminary determination by the administering authority under § 1671b(b) was affirmative, but the preliminary determination under § 1671b(e)(1) was negative, shall modify any suspension of liquidation and security requirement previously ordered under § 1671b(d) to apply to unliquidated entries of merchandise entered, or withdrawn from warehouse, for consumption on or after the date which is 90 days before the date on which suspension of liquidation was first ordered; or

(C) in cases where the preliminary determination by the administering authority under § 1671b(b) was negative, shall apply any suspension of liquidation and security requirement ordered under § 1671d(c)(1)(B) to unliquidated entries of merchandise entered, or withdrawn from warehouse, for consumption on or after the date which is 90 days before the date on which suspension of liquidation is first ordered.

(5) Method for determining the all-others rate and the country-wide subsidy rate.

(A) All-others rate.

(i) General rule. For purposes of this subsection and § 1671b(d), the all-others rate shall be an amount equal to the weighted average countervailable subsidy rates established for exporters and producers individually investigated, excluding any zero and de minimis countervailable subsidy rates, and any rates determined entirely under § 1677e.

(ii) Exception. If the countervailable subsidy rates established for all exporters and producers individually investigated are zero or de minimis rates, or are determined entirely under § 1667e, the administering authority may use any reasonable method to establish an all-others rate for exporters and producers not individually investigated, including averaging the weighted average countervailable subsidy rates determined for the exporters and producers individually investigated.

(B) Country-wide subsidy rate. The administering authority may calculate a single country-wide subsidy rate, applicable to all exporters and producers, if the administering authority limits its examination pursuant to § 1677f–1(e)(2)(B). The estimated country-wide rate determined under § 1671b(d)(1)(A)(ii) or paragraph (1)(B)(i)(II) of this subsection shall be based on industry-wide data regarding the use of subsidies determined to be countervailable.

(d) Publication of notice of determinations. Whenever the administering authority or the Commission makes a determination under this section, it shall notify the petitioner, other parties to the investigation, and the other agency of its determination and of the facts and conclusions of law upon which the determination is based, and it shall publish notice of its determination in the Federal Register.

(e) Correction of ministerial errors. The administering authority shall establish procedures for the correction of ministerial errors in final determinations within a reasonable time after the determinations are issued under this section. Such procedures shall ensure opportunity for interested parties to present their views regarding any such errors. As used in this subsection, the term "ministerial error" includes errors in addition, subtraction, or other arithmetic function, clerical errors resulting from inaccurate copying, duplication, or the like, and any other type of unintentional error which the administering authority considers ministerial.

§ 1671e. Assessment of Duty

(a) Publication of countervailing duty order. Within 7 days after being notified by the Commission of an affirmative determination under § 1671d(b), the administering authority shall publish a countervailing duty order which—

(1) directs customs officers to assess a countervailing duty equal to the amount of the net countervailable subsidy determined or estimated to exist, within 6 months after the date on which the administering authority receives satisfactory information upon which the assessment may be based, but in no event later than 12 months after the end of the annual accounting period of the manufacturer or exporter within which the merchandise is entered, or withdrawn from warehouse, for consumption,

(2) includes a description of the subject merchandise, in such detail as the administering authority deems necessary, and

(3) requires the deposit of estimated countervailing duties pending liquidation of entries of merchandise at the same time as estimated normal customs duties on that merchandise are deposited.

(b) Imposition of duties.

(1) General rule. If the Commission, in its final determination under § 1671d(b), finds material injury or threat of material injury which, but for the suspension of liquidation under § 1671b(d)(2), would have led to a finding of material injury, then entries of the merchandise subject to the countervailing duty order, the liquidation of which has been suspended under § 1671b(d)(2), shall be subject to the imposition of countervailing duties under § 1671(a).

(2) Special rule. If the Commission, in its final determination under § 1671d(b), finds threat of material injury, other than threat of material injury described in paragraph (1), or material retardation of the establishment of an industry in the United States, then merchandise subject to a countervailing duty order which is entered, or withdrawn from warehouse, for consumption on or after the date of publication of notice of an affirmative determination of the Commission under § 1671d(b) shall be subject to the imposition of countervailing duties under § 1671(a), and the administering authority shall release any bond or other security, and refund any cash deposit made, to secure the payment of countervailing duties with respect to entries of the merchandise entered, or withdrawn from warehouse, for consumption before that date.

(c) Special rule for regional industries.

(1) In general. In an investigation under this subtitle in which the Commission makes a regional industry determination under § 1677(4)(C), the administering authority shall, to the maximum extent possible, direct that duties be assessed only on the subject merchandise of the specific exporters or producers that exported the subject merchandise for sale in the region concerned during the period of investigation.

(2) Exception for new exporters and producers. After publication of the countervailing duty order, if the administering authority finds that a new exporter or producer is exporting the subject merchandise for sale in the region concerned, the administering authority shall direct that duties be assessed on the subject merchandise of the new exporter or producer consistent with the provisions of § 1675(a)(2)(B).

§ 1671f. Treatment of difference between deposit of estimated countervailing duty and final assessed duty under countervailing duty order

(a) Deposit of estimated countervailing duty under section 1671b(d)(1)(B). If the amount of a cash deposit, or the amount of any bond or other security, required as security for an estimated countervailing duty under § 1671b(d)(1)(B) is different from the amount of the countervailing duty determined under a countervailing duty order issued under § 1671e, then the difference for entries of merchandise entered, or withdrawn from warehouse, for consumption before notice of the affirmative determination of the Commission under § 1671d(b) is published shall be—

(1) disregarded, to the extent that the cash deposit, bond, or other security is lower than the duty under the order, or

(2) refunded or released, to the extent that the cash deposit, bond, or other security is higher than the duty under the order.

(b) Deposit of estimated countervailing duty under § 1671e(a)(3). If the amount of an estimated countervailing duty deposited under § 1671e(a)(3) is different from the amount of the countervailing duty determined under a countervailing duty order issued under § 1671e, then the difference for entries of merchandise entered, or withdrawn from warehouse, for consumption after notice of the affirmative determination of the Commission under § 1671d(b) is published shall be—

(1) collected, to the extent that the deposit under § 1671e(a)(3) is lower than the duty determined under the order, or

(2) refunded, to the extent that the deposit under § 1671e(a)(3) is higher than the duty determined under the order, together with interest as provided by § 1677g.

* * *

§ 1671h. Conditional payment of countervailing duty

(a) In general. For all entries, or withdrawals from warehouse, for consumption of merchandise subject to a countervailing duty order on or after the date of publication of such order, no customs officer may deliver merchandise of that class or kind to the person by whom or for whose account it was imported unless that person complies with the requirement of subsection (b) and deposits with the appropriate customs officer an estimated countervailing duty in an amount determined by the administering authority.

(b) Importer requirements. In order to meet the requirements of this subsection, a person shall—

(1) furnish, or arrange to have furnished, to the appropriate customs officer such information as the administering authority deems necessary for ascertaining any countervailing duty to be imposed under this subtitle,

(2) maintain and furnish to the customs officer such records concerning such merchandise as the administering authority, by regulation, requires, and

(3) pay, or agree to pay on demand, to the customs officer the amount of countervailing duty imposed under this subtitle on that merchandise.

Imposition of Antidumping Duties

§ 1673. Antidumping duties imposed

If—

(1) the administering authority determines that a class or kind of foreign merchandise is being, or is likely to be, sold in the United States at less than its fair value, and

(2) the Commission determines that—

(A) an industry in the United States—

(i) is materially injured, or

(ii) is threatened with material injury, or

(B) the establishment of an industry in the United States is materially retarded,

by reason of imports of that merchandise or by reason of sales (or the likelihood of sales) of that merchandise for importation, then there shall be imposed upon such merchandise an antidumping duty, in addition to any other duty imposed, in an amount equal to the amount by which the normal value exceeds the export price (or the constructed export price) for the merchandise. For purposes of this section and § 1673d(b)(1), a reference to the sale of foreign merchandise includes the entering into of any leasing arrangement regarding the merchandise that is equivalent to the sale of the merchandise.

§ 1673a. Procedures for initiating an antidumping duty investigation

(a) Initiation by administering authority

(1) In general. An antidumping duty investigation shall be initiated whenever the administering authority determines, from information available to it, that a formal investigation is warranted into the question of whether the elements necessary for the imposition of a duty under § 1673 exist.

(2) Cases involving persistent dumping.

(A) Monitoring. The administering authority may establish a monitoring program with respect to imports of a class or kind of merchandise from any additional supplier country for a period not to exceed one year if—

(i) more than one antidumping order is in effect with respect to that class or kind of merchandise;

(ii) in the judgment of the administering authority there is reason to believe or suspect an extraordinary pattern of persistent injurious dumping from one or more additional supplier countries; and

(iii) in the judgment of the administering authority this extraordinary pattern is causing a serious commercial problem for the domestic industry.

(B) If during the period of monitoring referred to in subparagraph (A), the administering authority determines that there is sufficient information to commence a formal investigation under this subsection regarding an additional supplier country, the administering authority shall immediately commence such an investigation.

(C) Definition. For purposes of this paragraph, the term "additional supplier country" means a country regarding which no antidumping investigation is currently pending, and no antidumping duty order is currently in effect, with respect to imports of the class or kind of merchandise covered by subparagraph (A).

(D) Expeditious Action. The administering authority and the Commission, to the extent practicable, shall expedite proceedings under this subtitle undertaken as a result of a formal investigation commenced under subparagraph (B).

(b) Initiation by petition

(1) Petition requirements. An antidumping proceeding shall be initiated whenever an interested party described in subparagraph (C), (D), (E), (F) or (G) of § 1677(9) files a petition with the administering authority, on behalf of an industry, which alleges the elements necessary for the imposition of the duty imposed by § 1673, and which is accompanied by information reasonably available to the petitioner supporting those allegations. The petition may be amended at such time, and upon such conditions, as the administering authority and the Commission may permit.

(2) Simultaneous filing with commission. The petitioner shall file a copy of the petition with the Commission on the same day as it is filed with the administering authority.

(c) Petition determination.

(1) In general.

(A) Time for initial determination. Except as provided in subparagraph (B), within 20 days after the date on which a petition is filed under subsection (b), the administering authority shall—

(i) after examining, on the basis of sources readily available to the administering authority, the accuracy and adequacy of the evidence provided in the petition, determine whether the petition alleges the elements necessary for the imposition of a duty under § 1673 and contains information reasonably available to the petitioner supporting the allegations, and

(ii) determine if the petition has been filed by or on behalf of the industry.

(B) Extension of time. In any case in which the administering authority is required to poll or otherwise determine support for the petition by the industry under paragraph (4)(D), the administering authority may, in exceptional circumstances, apply subparagraph (A) by substituting "a maximum of 40 days" for "20 days".

(C) Time limits where petition involves same merchandise as an order that has been revoked. If a petition is filed under this section with respect to merchandise that was the subject merchandise of—

(i) an antidumping duty order or finding that was revoked under § 1675(d) in the 24 months preceding the date the petition is filed, or

(ii) a suspended investigation that was terminated under § 1675(d) in the 24 months preceding the date the petition is filed, the administering authority and the Commission shall, to the maximum extent practicable, expedite any investigation initiated under this section with respect to the petition.

(2) Affirmative determinations. If the determinations under clauses (i) and (ii) of paragraph (1)(A) are affirmative, the administering authority shall initiate an investigation to determine whether the subject merchandise is being, or is likely to be, sold in the United States at less than its fair value.

(3) Negative determinations. If the determination under clause (i) or (ii) of paragraph (1)(A) is negative, the administering authority shall dismiss the petition, terminate the proceeding, and notify the petitioner in writing of the reasons for the determination.

(4) Determination of industry support.

(A) General rule. For purposes of this subsection, the administering authority shall determine that the petition has been filed by or on behalf of the industry, if—

(i) the domestic producers or workers who support the petition account for at least 25 percent of the total production of the domestic like product, and

(ii) the domestic producers or workers who support the petition account for more than 50 percent of the production of the domestic like product produced by that portion of the industry expressing support for or opposition to the petition.

(B) Certain positions disregarded.

(i) Producers related to foreign producers. In determining industry support under subparagraph (A), the administering authority shall disregard the position of domestic producers who oppose the petition, if such producers are related to foreign producers, as defined in § 1677(4)(B)(ii), unless such domestic producers demonstrate that their interests as domestic producers would be adversely affected by the imposition of an antidumping duty order.

(ii) Producers who are importers. The administering authority may disregard the position of domestic producers of a domestic like product who are importers of the subject merchandise.

(C) Special rule for regional industries. If the petition alleges the industry is a regional industry, the administering authority shall determine whether the petition has been filed by or on behalf of the industry by applying subparagraph (A) on the basis of production in the region.

(D) Polling the industry. If the petition does not establish support of domestic producers or workers accounting for more than 50 percent of the total production of the domestic like product, the administering authority shall—

(i) poll the industry or rely on other information in order to determine if there is support for the petition as required by subparagraph (A), or

(ii) if there is a large number of producers in the industry, the administering authority may determine industry support for the petition by using any statistically valid sampling method to poll the industry.

(E) Comments by interested parties. Before the administering authority makes a determination with respect to initiating an investigation, any person who would qualify as an interested party under § 1677(a) if an investigation were initiated, may submit comments or information on the issue of industry support. After the administering authority makes a determination with respect to initiating an investigation, the determination regarding industry support shall not be reconsidered.

(5) Definition of domestic producers or workers. For purposes of this subsection, the term "domestic producers or workers" means those interested parties who are eligible to file a petition under subsection (b)(1)(A).

(d) Notification to Commission of determination. The administering authority shall—

(1) notify the Commission immediately of any determination it makes under subsection (a) or (c), and

(2) if the determination is affirmative, make available to the Commission such information as it may have relating to the matter under investigation, under such procedures as the administering authority and the Commission may establish to prevent disclosure, other than with the consent of the party providing it or under protective order, of any information to which confidential treatment has been given by the administering authority.

(e) Information regarding critical circumstances. If, at any time after the initiation of an investigation under this subtitle, the administering authority finds a reasonable basis to suspect that—

(1) there is a history of dumping in the United States or elsewhere of the subject merchandise, or

(2) the person by whom, or for whose account, the merchandise was imported knew, or should have known, that the exporter was selling the subject merchandise at less than its fair value, the administering authority may request the Commissioner of Customs to compile information on an expedited basis regarding entries of the subject merchandise. Upon receiving such request, the Commissioner of Customs shall collect information regarding the volume and value of entries of the subject merchandise and shall transmit such information to the administering authority at such times as the administering authority shall direct (at least once every 30 days), until a final determination is made under § 1673(d)(a), the investigation is terminated, or the administering authority withdraws the request.

§ 1673b. Preliminary Determinations

(a) Determination by Commission of reasonable indication of injury.

(1) General rule. Except in the case of a petition dismissed by the administering authority under § 1673a(c)(3), the Commission, within the time specified in paragraph (2), shall determine, based on the information

available to it at the time of the determination, whether there is a reasonable indication that—

(A) an industry in the United States—

(i) is materially injured, or

(ii) is threatened with material injury, or

(B) the establishment of an industry in the United States is materially retarded, by reason of imports of the subject merchandise and that imports of the subject merchandise are not negligible. If the Commission finds that imports of the subject merchandise are negligible or otherwise makes a negative determination under this paragraph, the investigation shall be terminated.

(2) Time for commission determination. The Commission shall make the determination described in paragraph (1)

(A) in the case of a petition filed under § 1673a(b)—

(i) within 45 days after the date on which the petition is filed, or

(ii) if the time has been extended pursuant to § 1673a(c)(1)(B), within 25 days after the date on which the Commission receives notice from the administering authority of initiation of the investigation, and

(B) in the case of an investigation initiated under § 1673a(a), within 45 days after the date on which the Commission receives notice from the administering authority that an investigation has been initiated under such section.

(b) Preliminary determination by administering authority.

(1) Period of antidumping duty investigation.

(A) In general. Except as provided in subparagraph (B), within 140 days after the date on which the administering authority initiates an investigation under § 1673a(c), or an investigation is initiated under § 1673a(a), but not before an affirmative determination by the Commission under subsection (a) of this section, the administering authority shall make a determination, based upon the information available to it at the time of the determination, of whether there is a reasonable basis to believe or suspect that the merchandise is being sold, or is likely to be sold, at less than fair value.

(B) If certain short life cycle merchandise involved. If a petition filed under § 1673a(b), or an investigation initiated under § 1673a(a), concerns short life cycle merchandise that is included in a product category established under § 1673h(a), subparagraph (A) shall be applied—

(i) by substituting "100 days" for "140 days" if manufacturers that are second offenders account for a significant proportion of the merchandise under investigation, and

(ii) by substituting "80 days" for "140 days" if manufacturers that are multiple offenders account for a significant proportion of the merchandise under investigation.

(C) Definitions of offenders. For purposes of subparagraph (B)—

(i) The term "second offender" means a manufacturer that is specified in 2 affirmative dumping determinations (within the meaning of § 1673h as the manufacturer of short life cycle merchandise that is—

(I) specified in both such determinations, and

(II) within the scope of the product category referred to in subparagraph (B).

(ii) The term "multiple offender" means a manufacturer that is specified in 3 or more affirmative dumping determinations (within the meaning of § 1673h as the manufacturer of short life cycle merchandise that is—

(I) specified in each of such determinations, and

(II) within the scope of the product category referred to in subparagraph (B).

(2) Preliminary determination under waiver of verification. Within 75 days after the initiation of an investigation, the administering authority shall cause an official designated for such purpose to review the information concerning the case received during the first 60 days of the investigation, and, if there appears to be sufficient information available upon which the preliminary determination can reasonably be based, to disclose to the petitioner and any interested party, then a party to the proceedings that requests such disclosure, all available nonconfidential information and all other information which is disclosed pursuant to § 1677f. Within 3 days (not counting Saturdays, Sundays, or legal public holidays) after such disclosure, the petitioner and each party which is an interested party described in subparagraph (C), (D), (E), (F), or (G) of § 1677(a) to whom such disclosure was made may furnish to the administering authority an irrevocable written waiver of verification of the information received by the authority, and an agreement that it is willing to have a preliminary determination made on the basis of the record then available to the authority. If a timely waiver and agreement have been received from the petitioner and each party which is an interested party described in subparagraph (C), (D), (E), (F), or (G) of § 1677(a) to whom the disclosure was made, and the authority finds that sufficient information is then available upon which the preliminary determination can reasonably

be based, a preliminary determination shall be made within 90 days after the initiation of the investigation on the basis of the record established during the first 60 days after the investigation was initiated.

(3) De minimis dumping margin. In making a determination under this subsection, the administering authority shall disregard any weighted average dumping margin that is de minimis. For purposes of the preceding sentence, a weighted average dumping margin is de minimis if the administering authority determines that it is less than 2 percent ad valorem or the equivalent specific rate for the subject merchandise.

(c) Extension of period in extraordinarily complicated cases.

(1) In general. If—

(A) the petitioner makes a timely request for an extension of the period within which the determination must be made under subsection (b)(1), or

(B) the administering authority concludes that the parties concerned are cooperating and determines that—

(i) the case is extraordinarily complicated by reason of—

(I) the number and complexity of the transactions to be investigated or adjustments to be considered,

(II) the novelty of the issues presented, or

(III) the number of firms whose activities must be investigated, and

(ii) additional time is necessary to make the preliminary determination,

then the administering authority may postpone making the preliminary determination under subsection (b)(1) until not later than the 190th day after the date on which the administering authority initiates an investigation under § 1673a(c), or an investigation is initiated under § 1673a(a). No extension of a determination date may be made under this paragraph for any investigation in which a determination date provided for in subsection (b)(1)(B) applies unless the petitioner submits written notice to the administering authority of its consent to the extension.

(2) Notice of postponement. The administering authority shall notify the parties to the investigation, not later than 20 days before the date on which the preliminary determination would otherwise be required under subsection (b)(1), if it intends to postpone making the preliminary determination under paragraph (1). The notification shall include an explanation of the reasons for the postponement, and notice of the postponement shall be published in the Federal Register.

(d) Effect of determination by the administering authority. If the preliminary determination of the administering authority under subsection (b) is affirmative, the administering authority—

(1)(A) shall

(i) determine an estimated weighted average dumping margin for each exporter and producer individually investigated, and

(ii) determine, in accordance with § 1673d(c)(5), an estimated all-others rate for all exporters and producers not individually investigated, and

(B) shall order the posting of a cash deposit, bond, or other security, as the administering authority deems appropriate, for each entry of the subject merchandise in an amount based on the estimated weighted average dumping margin or the estimated all-others rate, whichever is applicable,

(2) shall order the suspension of liquidation of all entries of merchandise subject to the determination which are entered, or withdrawn from warehouse, for consumption on or after the later of

(A) the date on which notice of the determination is published in the Federal Register, or

(B) the date that is 60 days after the date on which notice of the determination to initiate the investigation is published in the Federal Register, and

(3) shall make available to the Commission all information upon which such determination was based and which the Commission considers relevant to its injury determination, under such procedures as the administering authority and the Commission may establish to prevent disclosure, other than with the consent of the party providing it or under protective order, of any information to which confidential treatment has been given by the administering authority.

The instructions of the administering authority under paragraphs (1) and (2) may not remain in effect for more than 4 months, except that the administering authority may, at the request of exporters representing a significant proportion of exports of the subject merchandise, extend that 4–month period to not more than 6 months.

(e) Critical circumstances determinations.

(1) In general. If a petitioner alleges critical circumstances in its original petition, or by amendment at any time more than 20 days before the date of a final determination by the administering authority, then the administering authority shall promptly (at any time after the initiation of the investigation under this subtitle) determine, on the basis of the

information available to it at that time, whether there is a reasonable basis to believe or suspect that—

(A)(i) there is a history of dumping and material injury by reason of dumped imports in the United States or elsewhere of the subject merchandise, or

(ii) the person by whom, or for whose account, the merchandise was imported knew or should have known that the exporter was selling the subject merchandise at less than its fair value and that there was likely to be material injury by reason of such sales, and

(B) there have been massive imports of the subject merchandise over a relatively short period.

The administering authority shall be treated as having made an affirmative determination under subparagraph (A) in any investigation to which subsection (b)(1)(B) is applied.

(2) Suspension of liquidation. If the determination of the administering authority under paragraph (1) is affirmative, then any suspension of liquidation ordered under subsection (d)(2) shall apply, or, if notice of such suspension of liquidation is already published, be amended to apply, to unliquidated entries of merchandise entered, or withdrawn from warehouse, for consumption on or after the later of

(A) the date which is 90 days before the date on which the suspension of liquidation was first ordered, or

(B) the date on which notice of the determination to initiate the investigation is published in the Federal Register.

(f) Notice of Determination. Whenever the Commission or the administering authority makes a determination under this section, the Commission or the administering authority, as the case may be, shall notify the petitioner, and other parties to the investigation, and the Commission or the administering authority (whichever is appropriate) of its determination. The administering authority shall include with such notification the facts and conclusions on which its determination is based. Not later than 5 days after the date on which the determination is required to be made under subsection (a)(2), the Commission shall transmit to the administering authority the facts and conclusions on which its determination is based.

§ 1673c. Termination or suspension of investigation

(a) Termination of investigation upon withdrawal of petition.

(1) In general.

(A) Withdrawal of petition. Except as provided in paragraphs (2) and (3), an investigation under this subtitle may be terminated by either the administering authority or the Commission, after notice to all parties to the investigation, upon withdrawal of the petition by the petitioner or by the administering authority if the investigation was initiated under § 1673a(a).

(B) Refiling of petition. If, within 3 months after the withdrawal of a petition under subparagraph (A), a new petition is filed seeking the imposition of duties on both the subject merchandise of the withdrawn petition and the subject merchandise from another country, the administering authority and the Commission may use in the investigation initiated pursuant to the new petition any records compiled in an investigation conducted pursuant to the withdrawn petition. This subparagraph applies only with respect to the first withdrawal of a petition.

(2) Special rules for quantitative restriction agreements.

(A) In general. Subject to subparagraphs (B) and (C), the administering authority may not terminate an investigation under paragraph (1) by accepting an understanding or other kind of agreement to limit the volume of imports into the United States of the subject merchandise unless the administering authority is satisfied that termination on the basis of that agreement is in the public interest.

(B) Public interest factors. In making a decision under subparagraph (A) regarding the public interest the administering authority shall take into account—

(i) whether, based upon the relative impact on consumer prices and the availability of supplies of the merchandise, the agreement would have a greater adverse impact on United States consumers than the imposition of antidumping duties;

(ii) the relative impact on the international economic interests of the United States; and

(iii) the relative impact on the competitiveness of the domestic industry producing the like merchandise, including any such impact on employment and investment in that industry.

(C) Prior consultations. Before making a decision under subparagraph (A) regarding the public interest, the administering authority shall, to the extent practicable, consult with—

(i) potentially affected consuming industries; and

(ii) potentially affected producers and workers in the domestic industry producing the like merchandise, including producers and workers not party to the investigation.

(3) Limitation on termination by commission. The Commission may not terminate an investigation under paragraph (1) before a preliminary determination is made by the administering authority under § 1673b(b).

(b) Agreements to eliminate completely sales at less than fair value or to cease exports of merchandise. The administering authority may suspend an investigation if the exporters of the subject merchandise who account for substantially all of the imports of that merchandise agree—

(1) to cease exports of the merchandise to the United States within 6 months after the date on which the investigation is suspended, or

(2) to revise their prices to eliminate completely any amount by which the normal value of the subject merchandise exceeds the export price (or the constructed export price) of that merchandise.

(c) Agreements eliminating injurious effect.

(1) General rule. If the administering authority determines that extraordinary circumstances are present in a case, it may suspend an investigation upon the acceptance of an agreement to revise prices from exporters of the subject merchandise who account for substantially all of the imports of that merchandise into the United States, if the agreement will eliminate completely the injurious effect of exports to the United States of that merchandise and if—

(A) the suppression or undercutting of price levels of domestic products by imports of that merchandise will be prevented, and

(B) for each entry of each exporter the amount by which the estimated normal value exceeds the export price (or the constructed export price) will not exceed 15 percent of the weighted average amount by which the estimated normal value exceeded the export price (or the constructed export price) for all less-than-fair-value entries of the exporter examined during the course of the investigation.

(2) Definition of extraordinary circumstances.

(A) Extraordinary circumstances. For purposes of this subsection, the term "extraordinary circumstances" means circumstances in which—

(i) suspension of an investigation will be more beneficial to the domestic industry than continuation of the investigation, and

(ii) the investigation is complex.

(B) Complex. For purposes of this paragraph, the term "complex" means—

(i) there are a large number of transactions to be investigated or adjustments to be considered,

(ii) the issues raised are novel, or

(iii) the number of firms involved is large.

(d) Additional rules and conditions. The administering authority may not accept an agreement under subsection (b) or (c) unless—

(1) it is satisfied that suspension of the investigation is in the public interest, and

(2) effective monitoring of the agreement by the United States is practicable.

Where practicable the administering authority shall provide to the exporters who would have been subject to the agreement the reasons for not accepting the agreement and, to the extent possible, an opportunity to submit comments thereon.

(e) Suspension of investigation procedure. Before an investigation may be suspended under subsection (b) or (c) the administering authority shall—

(1) notify the petitioner of, and consult with the petitioner concerning, its intention to suspend the investigation, and notify other parties to the investigation and the Commission not less than 30 days before the date on which it suspends the investigation,

(2) provide a copy of the proposed agreement to the petitioner at the time of the notification, together with an explanation of how the agreement will be carried out and enforced, and of how the agreement will meet the requirements of subsections (b) and (d) or (c) and (d), and

(3) permit all interested parties described in § 1677(9) to submit comments and information for the record before the date on which notice of suspension of the investigation is published under subsection (f)(1)(A).

(f) Effects of suspension of investigation.

(1) In general. If the administering authority determines to suspend an investigation upon acceptance of an agreement described in subsection (b) or (c), then—

(A) it shall suspend the investigation, publish notice of suspension of the investigation, and issue an affirmative preliminary determination under § 1673b(b) with respect to the subject merchandise, unless it has previously issued such a determination in the same investigation.

(B) the Commission shall suspend any investigation it is conducting with respect to that merchandise, and

(C) the suspension of investigation shall take effect on the day on which such notice is published.

(2) Liquidation of entries.

(A) Cessation of exports; complete elimination of dumping margin. If the agreement accepted by the administering authority is an agreement described in subsection (b), then—

(i) notwithstanding the affirmative preliminary determination required under paragraph (1)(A), the liquidation of entries of subject merchandise shall not be suspended under § 1673b(d)(2),

(ii) if the liquidation of entries of such merchandise was suspended pursuant to a previous affirmative preliminary determination in the same case with respect to such merchandise, that suspension of liquidation shall terminate, and

(iii) the administering authority shall refund any cash deposit and release any bond or other security deposited under § 1673b(d)(1)(B).

(B) Other agreements. If the agreement accepted by the administering authority is an agreement described in subsection (c), the liquidation of entries of the subject merchandise shall be suspended under § 1673b(d)(2); or, if the liquidation of entries of such merchandise was suspended pursuant to a previous affirmative preliminary determination in the same case, that suspension of liquidation shall continue in effect, subject to subsection (h)(3), but the security required under section § 1673b(d)(1)(B) may be adjusted to reflect the effect of the agreement.

(3) Where investigation is continued. If, pursuant to subsection (g), the administering authority and the Commission continue an investigation in which an agreement has been accepted under subsection (b) or (c), then—

(A) if the final determination by the administering authority or the Commission under § 1673d is negative, the agreement shall have no force or effect and the investigation shall be terminated, or

(B) if the final determinations by the administering authority and the Commission under such section are affirmative, the agreement shall remain in force, but the administering authority shall not issue an antidumping duty order in the case so long as—

(i) the agreement remains in force,

(ii) the agreement continues to meet the requirements of subsections (b) and (d), or (c) and (d), and

(iii) the parties to the agreement carry out their obligations under the agreement in accordance with its terms.

(g) Investigation to be continued upon request. If the administering authority, within 20 days after the date of publication of the notice of suspension of an investigation, receives a request for the continuation of the investigation from—

(1) an exporter or exporters accounting for a significant proportion of exports to the United States of the subject merchandise, or

(2) an interested party described in subparagraph (C), (D), (E), (F), or (G) of § 1677(9) which is a party to the investigation,

then the administering authority and the Commission shall continue the investigation.

(h) Review of suspension.

(1) In general. Within 20 days after the suspension of an investigation under subsection (c), an interested party which is a party to the investigation and which is described in subparagraph (C), (D), (E), (F), or (G) of § 1677(9) may, by petition filed with the Commission and with notice to the administering authority, ask for a review of the suspension.

(2) Commission investigation. Upon receipt of a review petition under paragraph (1), the Commission shall, within 75 days after the date on which the petition is filed with it, determine whether the injurious effect of imports of the subject merchandise is eliminated completely by the agreement. If the Commission's determination under this subsection is negative, the investigation shall be resumed on the date of publication of notice of such determination as if the affirmative preliminary determination under § 1673b(b) had been made on that date.

(3) Suspension of liquidation to continue during review period. The suspension of liquidation of entries of the subject merchandise shall terminate at the close of the 20–day period beginning on the day after the date on which notice of suspension of the investigation is published in the Federal Register, or, if a review petition is filed under paragraph (1) with respect to the suspension of the investigation, in the case of an affirmative determination by the Commission under paragraph (2), the date on which notice of an affirmative determination by the Commission is published. If the determination of the Commission under paragraph (2) is affirmative, then the administering authority shall—

(A) terminate the suspension of liquidation under § 1673b(d)(2), and

(B) release any bond or other security, and refund any cash deposit, required under § 1673b(d)(1)(B).

(i) Violation of agreement.

(1) In general. If the administering authority determines that an agreement accepted under subsection (b) or (c) is being, or has been, violated, or no longer meets the requirements of such subsection (other than the requirement, under subsection (c)(1), of elimination of injury) and

subsection (d), then, on the date of publication of its determination, it shall—

(A) suspend liquidation under § 1673b(d)(2) of unliquidated entries of the merchandise made on the later of—

(i) the date which is 90 days before the date of publication of the notice of suspension of liquidation, or

(ii) the date on which the merchandise, the sale or export to the United States of which was in violation of the agreement, or under an agreement which no longer meets the requirements of subsections (b) and (d), or (c) and (d), was first entered, or withdrawn from warehouse, for consumption,

(B) if the investigation was not completed, resume the investigation as if its affirmative preliminary determination were made on the date of its determination under this paragraph,

(C) if the investigation was completed under subsection (g), issue an antidumping duty order under § 1673e(a) effective with respect to entries of merchandise liquidation of which was suspended,

(D) if it considers the violation to be intentional, notify the Commissioner of Customs who shall take appropriate action under paragraph (2), and

(E) notify the petitioner, interested parties who are or were parties to the investigation, and the Commission of its action under this paragraph.

(2) Intentional violation to be punished by civil penalty. Any person who intentionally violates an agreement accepted by the administering authority under subsection (b) or (c) shall be subject to a civil penalty assessed in the same amount, in the same manner, and under the same procedures, as the penalty imposed for a fraudulent violation of § 1592(a) of this Act.

(j) Determination not to take agreement into account. In making a final determination under § 1673d, or in conducting a review under § 1675, in a case in which the administering authority has terminated a suspension of investigation under subsection (i)(1), or continued an investigation under subsection (g), the Commission and the administering authority shall consider all of the subject merchandise without regard to the effect of any agreement under subsection (b) or (c).

(k) Termination of investigation initiated by administering authority. The administering authority may terminate any investigation initiated by the administering authority under § 1673a(a) after providing notice of such termination to all parties to the investigation.

(*l*) Special rule for nonmarket economy countries.

(1) In general. The administering authority may suspend an investigation under this subtitle upon acceptance of an agreement with a nonmarket economy country to restrict the volume of imports into the United States of the merchandise under investigation only if the administering authority determines that—

(A) such agreement satisfies the requirements of subsection (d), and

(B) will prevent the suppression or undercutting of price levels of domestic products by imports of the merchandise under investigation.

(2) Failure of agreements. If the administering authority determines that an agreement accepted under this subsection no longer prevents the suppression or undercutting of domestic prices of merchandise manufactured in the United States, the provisions of subsection (i) shall apply.

(m) Special rule for regional industry investigations.

(1) Suspension agreements. If the Commission makes a regional industry determination under § 1677(4)(c), the administering authority shall offer exporters of the subject merchandise who account for substantially all exports of that merchandise for sale in the region concerned the opportunity to enter into an agreement described in subsection (b), (c), or (*l*).

(2) Requirements for suspension agreements. Any agreement described in paragraph (1) shall be subject to all the requirements imposed under this section for other agreements under subsection (b), (c), or (*l*), except that if the Commission makes a regional industry determination described in paragraph (1) in the final affirmative determination under § 1673d(b) but not in the preliminary affirmative determination under § 1673b(a), any agreement described in paragraph (1) may be accepted within 60 days after the antidumping order is published under § 1673e.

(3) Effect of suspension agreement on antidumping duty order. If an agreement described in paragraph (1) is accepted after the antidumping duty order is published, the administering authority shall rescind the order, refund any cash deposit and release any bond or other security deposited under § 1673b(d)(1)(B), and instruct the Customs Service that entries of the subject merchandise that were made during the period that the order was in effect shall be liquidated without regard to antidumping duties.

§ 1673d. Final Determinations

(a) Final determination by administering authority.

(1) General rule. Within 75 days after the date of its preliminary determination under § 1673b(b), the administering authority shall make a

final determination of whether the subject merchandise is being, or is likely to be, sold in the United States at less than its fair value.

(2) Extension of period for determination. The administering authority may postpone making the final determination under paragraph (1) until not later than the 135th day after the date on which it published notice of its preliminary determination under § 1673b(b) if a request in writing for such a postponement is made by—

(A) exporters who account for a significant proportion of exports of the merchandise which is the subject of the investigation, in a proceeding in which the preliminary determination by the administering authority under § 1673b(b) was affirmative, or

(B) the petitioner, in a proceeding in which the preliminary determination by the administering authority under § 1673b(b) was negative.

(3) Critical circumstances determinations. If the final determination of the administering authority is affirmative, then that determination, in any investigation in which the presence of critical circumstances has been alleged under § 1673b(e), shall also contain a finding of whether—

(A)(i) there is a history of dumping and material injury by reason of dumped imports in the United States or elsewhere of the subject merchandise, or

(ii) the person by whom, or for whose account, the merchandise was imported knew or should have known that the exporter was selling the subject merchandise at less than its fair value and that there would be material injury by reason of such sales, and

(B) there have been massive imports of the subject merchandise over a relatively short period.

Such findings may be affirmative even though the preliminary determination under § 1673b(e)(1) was negative.

(4) De minimis dumping margin. In making a determination under this subsection, the administering authority shall disregard any weighted average dumping margin that is de minimis as defined in § 1673b(b)(3).

(b) Final determination by Commission.

(1) In general. The Commission shall make a final determination of whether—

(A) an industry in the United States—

(i) is materially injured, or

(ii) is threatened with material injury, or

(B) the establishment of an industry in the United States is materially retarded,

by reason of imports or sales (or the likelihood of sales) for importation of the merchandise with respect to which the administering authority has made an affirmative determination under subsection (a)(1). If the Commission determines that imports of the subject merchandise are negligible, the investigation shall be terminated.

(2) Period for injury determination following affirmative preliminary determination by administering authority. If the preliminary determination by the administering authority under § 1673b(b) is affirmative, then the Commission shall make the determination required by paragraph (1) before the later of—

(A) the 120th day after the day on which the administering authority makes its affirmative preliminary determination under § 1673b(b), or

(B) the 45th day after the day on which the administering authority makes its affirmative final determination under subsection (a).

(3) Period for injury determination following negative preliminary determination by administering authority. If the preliminary determination by the administering authority under § 1673b(b) is negative, and its final determination under subsection (a) is affirmative, then the final determination by the Commission under this subsection shall be made within 75 days after the date of that affirmative final determination.

(4) Certain additional findings.

(A) Commission standard for retroactive application.

(i) In general. If the finding of the administering authority under subsection (a)(3) is affirmative, then the final determination of the Commission shall include a finding as to whether the imports subject to the affirmative determination under subsection (a)(3) are likely to undermine seriously the remedial effect of the antidumping duty order to be issued under § 1673e.

(ii) Factors to consider. In making the evaluation under clause (i), the Commission shall consider, among other factors it considers relevant—

(I) the timing and the volume of the imports,

(II) a rapid increase in inventories of the imports, and

(III) any other circumstances indicating that the remedial effect of the antidumping order will be seriously undermined.

(A) Retroactive application.

(i) In general. If the finding of the administering authority under subsection (a)(3) is affirmative, then the final determination of the Commission shall include a finding as to whether retroactive imposition of antidumping duties on the merchandise appears necessary to prevent recurrence of material injury that was caused by massive imports of the merchandise over a relatively short period of time.

(ii) Prevention of recurrence. For purposes of making its finding under clause (i), the Commission shall make an evaluation as to whether the effectiveness of the antidumping duty order would be materially impaired if such imposition did not occur.

(iii) Evaluation of effectiveness. In making the evaluation under clause (ii), the Commission shall consider, among other factors it considers relevant—

(I) the condition of the domestic industry,

(II) whether massive imports of the merchandise in a relatively short period of time can be accounted for by efforts to avoid the potential imposition of antidumping duties,

(III) whether foreign economic conditions led to the massive imports of the merchandise, and

(IV) whether the impact of the massive imports of the merchandise is likely to continue for some period after issuance of the antidumping duty order under this subtitle.

(B) If the final determination of the Commission is that there is no material injury but that there is threat of material injury, then its determination shall also include a finding as to whether material injury by reason of the imports of the merchandise with respect to which the administering authority has made an affirmative determination under subsection (a) would have been found but for any suspension of liquidation of entries of the merchandise.

(c) Effect of final determinations.

(1) Effect of affirmative determination by the administering authority. If the determination of the administering authority under subsection (a) is affirmative, then—

(A) the administering authority shall make available to the Commission all information upon which such determination was based and which the Commission considers relevant to its determination, under such procedures as the administering authority and the Commission may establish to prevent disclosure, other than with the consent of the party providing it or under protective order, of any information as to which confidential treatment has been given by the administering authority,

(B)(i) the administering authority shall

(I) determine the estimated weighted average dumping margin for each exporter and producer individually investigated, and

(II) determine, in accordance with paragraph (5), the estimated all-others rate for all exporters and producers not individually investigated, and

(ii) the administering authority shall order the posting of a cash deposit, bond, or other security as the administering authority deems appropriate, for each entry of the subject merchandise in an amount based on the estimated weighted average dumping margin or the estimated all-others rate, whichever is applicable, and

(C) in cases where the preliminary determination by the administering authority under § 1673b(b) was negative, the administering authority shall order the suspension of liquidation under § 1673b(d)(2).

(2) Issuance of order; effect of negative determination. If the determinations of the administering authority and the Commission under subsections (a)(1) and (b)(1) are affirmative, then the administering authority shall issue an antidumping duty order under § 1673e(a). If either of such determinations is negative, the investigation shall be terminated upon the publication of notice of that negative determination and the administering authority shall—

(A) terminate the suspension of liquidation under § 1673b(d)(2), and

(B) release any bond or other security, and refund any cash deposit, required under § 1673b(d)(1)(B).

(3) Effect of negative determinations under subsections (a)(3) and (b)(4)(A). If the determination of the administering authority or the Commission under subsection (a)(3) or (b)(4)(A), respectively, is negative, then the administering authority shall—

(A) terminate any retroactive suspension of liquidation required under paragraph (4) or § 1673b(e)(2), and

(B) release any bond or other security, and refund any cash deposit required, under § 1673b(d)(1)(B) with respect to entries of the merchandise the liquidation of which was suspended retroactively under § 1673b(e)(2).

(4) Effect of affirmative determination under subsection (a)(3). If the determination of the administering authority under subsection (a)(3) is affirmative, then the administering authority shall—

(A) in cases where the preliminary determinations by the administering authority under §§ 1673b(b) and 1673b(e)(1) were both affirmative, continue the retroactive suspension of liquidation and the posting of a cash deposit, bond, or other security previously ordered under § 1673b(e)(2);

(B) in cases where the preliminary determination by the administering authority under § 1673b(b) was affirmative, but the preliminary determination under § 1673b(e)(1) was negative, shall modify any suspension of liquidation and security requirement previously ordered under § 1673b(d) to apply to unliquidated entries of merchandise entered, or withdrawn from warehouse, for consumption on or after the date which is 90 days before the date on which suspension of liquidation was first ordered; or

(C) in cases where the preliminary determination by the administering authority under § 1673b(b) was negative, shall apply any suspension of liquidation and security requirement ordered under § 1673d(c)(1)(B) to unliquidated entries of merchandise entered, or withdrawn from warehouse, for consumption on or after the date which is 90 days before the date on which suspension of liquidation is first ordered.

(5) Method for determining estimated all-others rate.

(A) General rule. For purposes of this subsection and § 1673b(d), the estimated all-others rate shall be an amount equal to the weighted average of the estimated weighted average dumping margins established for exporters and producers individually investigated, excluding any zero and de minimis margins, and any margins determined entirely under § 1677e.

(B) Exception. If the estimated weighted average dumping margins established for all exporters and producers individually investigated are zero or de minimis margins, or are determined entirely under § 1677e, the administering authority may use any reasonable method to establish the estimated all-others rate for exporters and producers not individually investigated, including averaging the estimated weighted average dumping margins determined for the exporters and producers individually investigated.

(d) Publication of notice of determinations. Whenever the administering authority or the Commission makes a determination under this section, it shall notify the petitioner, other parties to the investigation, and the other agency of its determination and of the facts and conclusions of law upon which the determination is based, and it shall publish notice of its determination in the Federal Register.

(e) Correction of ministerial errors. The administering authority shall establish procedures for the correction of ministerial errors in final determinations within a reasonable time after the determinations are issued under this section. Such procedures shall ensure opportunity for interested parties to present their views regarding any such errors. As used in this subsection, the term "ministerial error" includes errors in addition, subtraction, or other arithmetic function, clerical errors resulting from inaccurate copying, duplication, or the like, and any other type of unintentional error which the administering authority considers ministerial.

§ 1673e. Assessment of duty

(a) Publication of antidumping duty order. Within 7 days after being notified by the Commission of an affirmative determination under § 1673d(b), the administering authority shall publish an antidumping duty order which—

(1) directs customs officers to assess an antidumping duty equal to the amount by which the normal value of the merchandise exceeds the export price (or the constructed export price) of the merchandise, within 6 months after the date on which the administering authority receives satisfactory information upon which the assessment may be based, but in no event later than—

(A) 12 months after the end of the annual accounting period of the manufacturer or exporter within which the merchandise is entered, or withdrawn from warehouse, for consumption, or

(B) in the case of merchandise not sold prior to its importation into the United States, 12 months after the end of the annual accounting period of the manufacturer or exporter within which it is sold in the United States to a person who is not the exporter of that merchandise,

(2) includes a description of the subject merchandise, in such detail as the administering authority deems necessary, and

(3) requires the deposit of estimated antidumping duties pending liquidation of entries of merchandise at the same time as estimated normal customs duties on that merchandise are deposited.

(b) Imposition of duty.

(1) General rule. If the Commission, in its final determination under § 1673d(b), finds material injury or threat of material injury which, but for the suspension of liquidation under § 1673b(d)(2) would have led to a finding of material injury, then entries of the subject merchandise, the

liquidation of which has been suspended under § 1673b(d)(2), shall be subject to the imposition of antidumping duties under § 1673.

(2) Special rule. If the Commission, in its final determination under § 1673d(b), finds threat of material injury, other than threat of material injury described in paragraph (1), or material retardation of the establishment of an industry in the United States, then subject merchandise which is entered, or withdrawn from warehouse, for consumption on or after the date of publication of notice of an affirmative determination of the Commission under § 1673d(b) shall be subject to the assessment of antidumping duties under section 731, and the administering authority shall release any bond or other security, and refund any cash deposit made, to secure the payment of antidumping duties with respect to entries of the merchandise entered, or withdrawn from warehouse, for consumption before that date.

(c) Security in lieu of estimated duty pending early determination of duty.

(1) Conditions for waiver of deposit of estimated duties. The administering authority may permit, for not more than 90 days after the date of publication of an order under subsection (a), the posting of a bond or other security in lieu of the deposit of estimated antidumping duties required under subsection (a)(3) if—

(A) the investigation has not been designated as extraordinarily complicated by reason of—

(i) the number and complexity of the transactions to be investigated or adjustments to be considered,

(ii) the novelty of the issues presented, or

(iii) the number of firms whose activities must be investigated,

(B) the final determination in the investigation has not been postponed under § 1673d(a)(2)(A);

(C) on the basis of information presented to the administering authority by any manufacturer, producer, or exporter in such form and within such time as the administering authority may require, the administering authority is satisfied that a determination will be made, within 90 days after the date of publication of an order under subsection (a), of the normal value and the export price (or the constructed export price) for all merchandise of such manufacturer, producer, or exporter described in that order which was entered, or withdrawn from warehouse, for consumption on or after the date of publication of—

(i) an affirmative preliminary determination by the administering authority under § 1673b(b), or

(ii) if its determination under § 1673b(b) was negative, an affirmative final determination by the administering authority under § 1673d(a),

and before the date of publication of the affirmative final determination by the Commission under § 1673d(b);

(D) the party described in subparagraph (C) provides credible evidence that the amount by which the normal value of the merchandise exceeds the export price (or the constructed export price) of the merchandise is significantly less than the amount of such excess specified in the antidumping duty order published under subsection (a); and

(E) the data concerning the normal value and the export price (or the constructed export price) apply to sales in the usual commercial quantities and in the ordinary course of trade and the number of such sales are sufficient to form an adequate basis for comparison.

(2) Notice; hearing. If the administering authority permits the posting of a bond or other security in lieu of the deposit of estimated antidumping duties under paragraph (1), it shall—

(A) publish notice of its action in the Federal Register, and

(B) upon the request of any interested party, hold a hearing in accordance with § 1677c before determining the normal value and the export price (or the constructed export price) of the merchandise.

(3) Determinations to be basis of antidumping duty. The administering authority shall publish notice in the Federal Register of the results of its determination of normal value and export price (or the constructed export price), and that determination shall be the basis for the assessment of antidumping duties on entries of merchandise to which the notice under this subsection applies and also shall be the basis for the deposit of estimated antidumping duties on future entries of merchandise of manufacturers, producers, or exporters described in paragraph (1) to which the order issued under subsection (a) applies.

(4) Provision of business proprietary information; written comments. Before determining whether to permit the posting of bond or other security under paragraph (1) in lieu of the deposit of estimated antidumping duties, the administering authority shall—

(A) make all business proprietary information supplied to the administering authority under paragraph (1) available under a protective order in accordance with § 1677f(c) to all interested parties described in subparagraph (C), (D), (E), (F), or (G) of § 1677(a), and

(B) afford all interested parties an opportunity to file written comments on whether the posting of bond or other security under paragraph (1) in lieu of the deposit of estimated antidumping duties should be permitted.

(d) Special rule for regional industries.

(1) In general. In an investigation in which the Commission makes a regional industry determination under § 1677(4)(C), the administering authority shall, to the maximum extent possible, direct that duties be assessed only on the subject merchandise of the specific exporters or producers that exported the subject merchandise for sale in the region concerned during the period of investigation.

(2) Exception for new exporters and producers. After publication of the antidumping duty order, if the administering authority finds that a new exporter or producer is exporting the subject merchandise for sale in the region concerned, the administering authority shall direct that duties be assessed on the subject merchandise of the new exporter or producer consistent with the provisions of § 1675(a)(2)(B).

§ 1673f. Treatment of Difference Between Deposit of Estimated Antidumping Duty and Final Assessed Duty Under Antidumping Duty Order

(a) Deposit of estimated antidumping duty under § 1673b(d)(1)(B). If the amount of a cash deposit collected as security for an estimated antidumping duty under § 1673b(d)(1)(B) is different from the amount of the antidumping duty determined under an antidumping duty order published under § 1673e, then the difference for entries of merchandise entered, or withdrawn from warehouse, for consumption before notice of the affirmative determination of the Commission under § 1673d(b) is published shall be—

(1) disregarded, to the extent the cash deposit collected is lower than the duty under the order, or

(2) refunded, to the extent the cash deposit is higher than the duty under the order.

(b) Deposit of estimated antidumping duty under § 1673e(a)(3). If the amount of an estimated antidumping duty deposited under § 1673e(a)(3) is different from the amount of the antidumping duty determined under an antidumping duty order published under § 1673e, then the difference for entries of merchandise entered, or withdrawn from warehouse, for consumption after notice of the affirmative determination of the Commission under § 1673d(b) is published shall be—

(1) collected, to the extent that the deposit under § 1673e(a)(3) is lower than the duty determined under the order, or

(2) refunded, to the extent that the deposit under § 1673e(a)(3) is higher than the duty determined under the order,

together with interest as provided by § 1677g.

§ 1673g. Conditional Payment of Antidumping Duty

(a) General rule. For all entries, or withdrawals from warehouse, for consumption of merchandise subject to an antidumping duty order on or after the date of publication of such order, no customs officer may deliver merchandise of that class or kind to the person by whom or for whose account it was imported unless that person complies with the requirements of subsection (b) and deposits with the appropriate customs officer an estimated antidumping duty in an amount determined by the administering authority.

(b) Importer requirements. In order to meet the requirements of this subsection, a person shall—

(1) furnish, or arrange to have furnished, to the appropriate customs officer such information as the administering authority deems necessary for determining the export price (or the constructed export price) of the merchandise imported by or for the account of that person, and such other information as the administering authority deems necessary for ascertaining any antidumping duty to be imposed under this title;

(2) maintain and furnish to the customs officer such records concerning the sale of the merchandise as the administering authority, by regulation, requires;

(3) state under oath before the customs officer that he is not an exporter, or if he is an exporter, declare under oath at the time of entry the constructed export price of the merchandise to the customs officer if it is then known, or, if not, so declare within 30 days after the merchandise has been sold, or has been made the subject of an agreement to be sold, in the United States; and

(4) pay, or agree to pay on demand, to the customs officer the amount of antidumping duty imposed under § 1673 on that merchandise.

§ 1673h. Establishment of product categories for short life cycle merchandise

(a) Establishment of product categories.

(1) Petitions.

(A) In general. An eligible domestic entity may file a petition with the Commission requesting that a product category be established with respect to short life cycle merchandise at any time after the merchandise becomes the subject of 2 or more affirmative dumping determinations.

(B) Contents. A petition filed under subparagraph (A) shall—

(i) identify the short life cycle merchandise that is the subject of the affirmative dumping determinations,

(ii) specify the short life cycle merchandise that the petitioner seeks to have included in the same product category as the merchandise that is subject to the affirmative dumping determinations,

(iii) specify any short life cycle merchandise the petitioner particularly seeks to have excluded from the product category,

(iv) provide reasons for the inclusions and exclusions specified under clauses (ii) and (iii), and

(v) identify such merchandise in terms of the designations used in the Harmonized Tariff Schedules of the United States.

(2) Determinations on sufficiency of petition. Upon receiving a petition under paragraph (1), the Commission shall—

(A) request the administering authority to confirm promptly the affirmative determinations on which the petition is based, and

(B) upon receipt of such confirmation, determine whether the merchandise covered by the confirmed affirmative determinations is short life cycle merchandise and whether the petitioner is an eligible domestic entity.

(3) Notice; hearings. If the determinations under paragraph (2)(B) are affirmative, the Commission shall—

(A) publish notice in the Federal Register that the petition has been received, and

(B) provide opportunity for the presentation of views regarding the establishment of the requested product category, including a public hearing if requested by any interested person.

(4) Determinations.

(A) In general. By no later than the date that is 90 days after the date on which a petition is filed under paragraph (1), the Commission shall determine the scope of the product category into which the short life cycle merchandise that is the subject of the affirmative dumping determinations identified in such petition shall be classified for purposes of this section.

(B) Modifications not requested by petition.

(i) In general. The Commission may, on its own initiative, make a determination modifying the scope of any product category established under subparagraph (A) at any time.

(ii) Notice and hearing. Determinations may be made under clause (i) only after the Commission has—

(I) published in the Federal Register notice of the proposed modification, and

(II) provided interested parties an opportunity for a hearing, and a period for the submission of written comments, on the classification of merchandise into the product categories to be affected by such determination.

(C) Basis of determinations. In making determinations under subparagraph (A) or (B), the Commission shall ensure that each product category consists of similar short life cycle merchandise which is produced by similar processes under similar circumstances and has similar uses.

(b) Definitions. For purposes of this section—

(1) Eligible domestic entity. The term "eligible domestic entity" means a manufacturer or producer in the United States, or a certified union or recognized union or group of workers which is representative of an industry in the United States, that manufactures or produces short life cycle merchandise that is—

(A) like or directly competitive with other merchandise that is the subject of 2 or more affirmative dumping determinations, or

(B) is similar enough to such other merchandise as to be considered for inclusion with such merchandise in a product monitoring category established under this section.

(2) Affirmative dumping determination. The term "affirmative dumping determination" means—

(A) any affirmative final determination made by the administering authority under § 1673d(a) during the 8–year period preceding the filing of the petition under this section that results in the issuance of an antidumping duty order under § 1673e which requires the deposit of estimated antidumping duties at a rate of not less than 15 percent ad valorem, or

(B) any affirmative preliminary determination that—

(i) is made by the administering authority under § 1673b(b) during the 8–year period preceding the filing of the petition under this section in the course of an investigation for which no final determination is made under § 1673d by reason of a suspension of the investigation under § 1673c, and

(ii) includes a determination that the estimated average amount by which the normal value of the merchandise exceeds the export price (or the constructed export price) of the merchandise is not less than 15 percent ad valorem.

(3) Subject of affirmative dumping determination.

(A) In general. Short life cycle merchandise of a manufacturer shall be treated as being the subject of an affirmative dumping determination only if the administering authority—

(i) makes a separate determination of the amount by which the normal value of such merchandise of the manufacturer exceeds the export price (or the constructed export price) of such merchandise of the manufacturer, and

(ii) specifically identifies the manufacturer by name with such amount in the affirmative dumping determination or in an antidumping duty order issued as a result of the affirmative dumping determination.

(B) Exclusion. Short life cycle merchandise of a manufacturer shall not be treated as being the subject of an affirmative dumping determination if—

(i) such merchandise of the manufacturer is part of a group of merchandise to which the administering authority assigns (in lieu of making separate determinations described in subparagraph (A)(i)(I)) an amount determined to be the amount by which the normal value of the merchandise in such group exceeds the export price (or the constructed export price) of the merchandise in such group, and

(ii) the merchandise and the manufacturer are not specified by name in the affirmative dumping determination or in any antidumping duty order issued as a result of such affirmative dumping determination.

(4) Short life cycle merchandise. The term "short life cycle merchandise" means any product that the Commission determines is likely to become outmoded within 4 years, by reason of technological advances, after the product is commercially available. For purposes of this paragraph, the term "out-moded" refers to a kind of style that is no longer state-of-the-art.

(c) Transitional rules.

(1) For purposes of this section and § 1673b(b)(1)(B) and (C), all affirmative dumping determinations described in subsection (b)(2)(A) that were made after December 31, 1980, and before the date of enactment of the Omnibus Trade and Competitiveness Act of 1988, and all affirmative dumping determinations described in subsection (b)(2)(B) that were made after December 31, 1984, and before the date of enactment of such Act, with

respect to each category of short life cycle merchandise of the same manufacturer shall be treated as one affirmative dumping determination with respect to that category for that manufacturer which was made on the date on which the latest of such determinations was made.

(2) No affirmative dumping determination that—

(A) is described in subsection (b)(2)(A) and was made before January 1, 1981, or

(B) is described in subsection (b)(2)(B) and was made before January 1, 1985,

may be taken into account under this section or § 1673b(b)(1)(B) and (C).

* * *

§ 1675. Administrative review of determinations

(a) Periodic review of amount of duty

(1) In general

At least once during each 12–month period beginning on the anniversary of the date of publication of a countervailing duty order under this subtitle or under section 1303 of this title, an antidumping duty order under this subtitle or a finding under the Antidumping Act, 1921, or a notice of the suspension of an investigation, the administering authority, if a request for such a review has been received and after publication of notice of such review in the Federal Register, shall—

(A) review and determine the amount of any net countervailable subsidy,

(B) review, and determine (in accordance with paragraph (2)), the amount of any antidumping duty, and

(C) review the current status of, and compliance with, any agreement by reason of which an investigation was suspended, and review the amount of any net countervailable subsidy or dumping margin involved in the agreement,

and shall publish in the Federal Register the results of such review, together with notice of any duty to be assessed, estimated duty to be deposited, or investigation to be resumed.

(2) Determination of antidumping duties

(A) In general

For the purpose of paragraph (1)(B), the administering authority shall determine—

(i) the normal value and export price (or constructed export price) of each entry of the subject merchandise, and

(ii) the dumping margin for each such entry.

(B) Determination of antidumping or countervailing duties for new exporters and producers

(i) In general

If the administering authority receives a request from an exporter or producer of the subject merchandise establishing that—

(I) such exporter or producer did not export the merchandise that was the subject of an antidumping duty or countervailing duty order to the United States (or, in the case of a regional industry, did not export the subject merchandise for sale in the region concerned) during the period of investigation, and

(II) such exporter or producer is not affiliated (within the meaning of section 1677(33) of this title) with any exporter or producer who exported the subject merchandise to the United States (or in the case of a regional industry, who exported the subject merchandise for sale in the region concerned) during that period, the administering authority shall conduct a review under this subsection to establish an individual weighted average dumping margin or an individual countervailing duty rate (as the case may be) for such exporter or producer.

(ii) Time for review under clause (i)

The administering authority shall commence a review under clause (i) in the calendar month beginning after—

(I) the end of the 6–month period beginning on the date of the countervailing duty or antidumping duty order under review, or

(II) the end of any 6–month period occurring thereafter,

if the request for the review is made during that 6–month period.

(iii) Posting bond or security

The administering authority shall, at the time a review under this subparagraph is initiated, direct the Customs Service to allow, at the option of the importer, the posting, until the completion of the review, of a bond or security in lieu of a cash deposit for each entry of the subject merchandise.

(iv) Time limits

The administering authority shall make a preliminary determination in a review conducted under this subparagraph within 180 days after the date on which the review is initiated, and a final determination within 90 days after the date the preliminary determination is issued, except that if the administering authority concludes that the case is extraordinarily complicated, it may extend the 180–day period to 300 days and may extend the 90–day period to 150 days.

(C) Results of determinations

The determination under this paragraph shall be the basis for the assessment of countervailing or antidumping duties on entries of merchandise covered by the determination and for deposits of estimated duties.

(3) Time limits

(A) Preliminary and final determinations

The administering authority shall make a preliminary determination under subparagraph (A), (B), or (C) of paragraph (1) within 245 days after the last day of the month in which occurs the anniversary of the date of publication of the order, finding, or suspension agreement for which the review under paragraph (1) is requested, and a final determination under paragraph (1) within 120 days after the date on which the preliminary determination is published. If it is not practicable to complete the review within the foregoing time, the administering authority may extend that 245–day period to 365 days and may extend that 120–day period to 180 days. The administering authority may extend the time for making a final determination without extending the time for making a preliminary determination, if such final determination is made not later than 300 days after the date on which the preliminary determination is published.

(B) Liquidation of entries

If the administering authority orders any liquidation of entries pursuant to a review under paragraph (1), such liquidation shall be made promptly and, to the greatest extent practicable, within 90 days after the instructions to Customs are issued. In any case in which liquidation has not occurred within that 90–day period, the Secretary of the Treasury shall, upon the request of the affected party, provide an explanation thereof.

(C) Effect of pending review under section 1516a

In a case in which a final determination under paragraph (1) is under review under section 1516a of this title and a liquidation of entries covered by the determination is enjoined under section

1516a(c)(2) of this title or suspended under section 1516a(g)(5)(C) of this title, the administering authority shall, within 10 days after the final disposition of the review under section 1516a of this title, transmit to the Federal Register for publication the final disposition and issue instructions to the Customs Service with respect to the liquidation of entries pursuant to the review. In such a case, the 90–day period referred to in subparagraph (B) shall begin on the day on which the administering authority issues such instructions.

(4) Absorption of antidumping duties

During any review under this subsection initiated 2 years or 4 years after the publication of an antidumping duty order under section 1673e(a) of this title, the administering authority, if requested, shall determine whether antidumping duties have been absorbed by a foreign producer or exporter subject to the order if the subject merchandise is sold in the United States through an importer who is affiliated with such foreign producer or exporter. The administering authority shall notify the Commission of its findings regarding such duty absorption for the Commission to consider in conducting a review under subsection (c) of this section.

(b) Reviews based on changed circumstances

(1) In general

Whenever the administering authority or the Commission receives information concerning, or a request from an interested party for a review of—

(A) a final affirmative determination that resulted in an antidumping duty order under this subtitle or a finding under the Antidumping Act, 1921, or in a countervailing duty order under this subtitle or section 1303 of this title,

(B) a suspension agreement accepted under section 1671c or 1673c of this title, or

(C) a final affirmative determination resulting from an investigation continued pursuant to section 1671c(g) or 1673c(g) of this title,

which shows changed circumstances sufficient to warrant a review of such determination or agreement, the administering authority or the Commission (as the case may be) shall conduct a review of the determination or agreement after publishing notice of the review in the Federal Register.

(2) Commission review

In conducting a review under this subsection, the Commission shall—

(A) in the case of a countervailing duty order or antidumping duty order or finding, determine whether revocation of the order or finding is likely to lead to continuation or recurrence of material injury,

(B) in the case of a determination made pursuant to section 1671c(h)(2) or 1673c(h)(2) of this title, determine whether the suspension agreement continues to eliminate completely the injurious effects of imports of the subject merchandise, and

(C) in the case of an affirmative determination resulting from an investigation continued under section 1671c(g) or 1673c(g) of this title, determine whether termination of the suspended investigation is likely to lead to continuation or recurrence of material injury.

(3) Burden of persuasion

During a review conducted by the Commission under this subsection—

(A) the party seeking revocation of an order or finding described in paragraph (1)(A) shall have the burden of persuasion with respect to whether there are changed circumstances sufficient to warrant such revocation, and

(B) the party seeking termination of a suspended investigation or a suspension agreement shall have the burden of persuasion with respect to whether there are changed circumstances sufficient to warrant such termination.

(4) Limitation on period for review

In the absence of good cause shown—

(A) the Commission may not review a determination made under section 1671d(b) or 1673d(b) of this title, or an investigation suspended under section 1671c or 1673c of this title, and

(B) the administering authority may not review a determination made under section 1671d(a) or 1673d(a) of this title, or an investigation suspended under section 1671c or 1673c of this title,

less than 24 months after the date of publication of notice of that determination or suspension.

(c) Five-year review

(1) In general

Notwithstanding subsection (b) of this section and except in the case of a transition order defined in paragraph (6), 5 years after the date of publication of—

(A) a countervailing duty order (other than a countervailing duty order to which subparagraph (B) applies or which was issued without an affirmative determination of injury by the Commission under section 1303 of this title), an antidumping duty order, or a notice of suspension of an investigation, described in subsection (a)(1) of this section,

(B) a notice of injury determination under section 1675b of this title with respect to a countervailing duty order, or

(C) a determination under this section to continue an order or suspension agreement,

the administering authority and the Commission shall conduct a review to determine, in accordance with section 1675a of this title, whether revocation of the countervailing or antidumping duty order or termination of the investigation suspended under section 1671c or 1673c of this title would be likely to lead to continuation or recurrence of dumping or a countervailable subsidy (as the case may be) and of material injury.

* * *

§ 1675b. Special rules for injury investigations for certain section 303 countervailing duty orders and investigations

(a) In general.—

(1) Investigation by the Commission upon request.—In the case of a countervailing duty order described in paragraph (2), which—

(A) applies to merchandise that is the product of a Subsidies Agreement country, and

(B)(i) is in effect on the date on which such country becomes a Subsidies Agreement country, or

(ii) is issued on a date that is after the date described in clause (i) pursuant to a court order in an action brought under § 1516A,

the Commission, upon receipt of a request from an interested party described in § 1677(9)(C), (D), (E), (F), or (G) for an injury investigation with respect to such order, shall initiate an investigation and shall determine whether an industry in the United States is likely to be materially injured by reason of imports of the subject merchandise if the order is revoked.

(2) Description of countervailing duty orders.—A countervailing duty order described in this paragraph is an order issued under § 1303 with respect to which the requirement of an affirmative determination of material injury under § 1303(a)(2) was not applicable at the time such order was issued.

(3) Requirements of request for investigation.—A request for an investigation under this subsection shall be submitted—

(A) in the case of an order described in paragraph (1)(B)(i), within 6 months after the date on which the country described in paragraph (1)(A) becomes a Subsidies Agreement country, or

(B) in the case of an order described in paragraph (1)(B)(ii), within 6 months after the date the order is issued.

(4) Suspension of liquidation.—With respect to entries of subject merchandise made on or after—

(A) in the case of an order described in paragraph (1)(B)(i), the date on which the country described in paragraph (1)(A) becomes a Subsidies Agreement country, or

(B) in the case of an order described in paragraph (1)(B)(ii), the date on which the order is issued,

liquidation shall be suspended at the cash deposit rate in effect on the date described in subparagraph (A) or (B) (whichever is applicable).

(b) Investigation procedure and schedule.—

(1) Commission procedure.—

(A) In general.—Except as otherwise provided in this section, the provisions of this title regarding evidence in and procedures for investigations conducted under subtitle A shall apply to investigations conducted by the Commission under this section.

(B) Time for Commission determination.—Except as otherwise provided in subparagraph (C), the Commission shall issue its determination under subsection (a)(1), to the extent possible, not later than 1 year after the date on which the investigation is initiated under this section.

(C) Special rule to permit administrative flexibility.—In the case of requests for investigations received under this section within 1 year after the date on which the WTO Agreement enters into force with respect to the United States, the Commission may, after consulting with the administering authority, initiate its investigations in a manner that results in determinations being made in all such investigations during the 4–year period beginning on such date.

(2) Net countervailable subsidy; nature of subsidy.—

(A) Net countervailable subsidy.—The administering authority shall provide to the Commission the net countervailable subsidy that is likely to prevail if the order which is the subject of the investigation is revoked. The administering authority normally shall choose a net countervailable subsidy that was determined under § 1671d or subsection (a) or (b)(1) of § 1675. If the Commission considers the magnitude of the net countervailable subsidy in making its determination under this section, the Commission shall use the net countervailable subsidy provided by the administering authority.

(B) Nature of subsidy.—The administering authority shall inform the Commission of, and the Commission, in making its determination under this section, shall consider, the nature of the countervailable subsidy and whether the countervailable subsidy is a subsidy described in Article 3 or Article 6.1 of the Subsidies Agreement.

(3) Effect of Commission determination.—

(A) Affirmative determination.—Upon being notified by the Commission that it has made an affirmative determination under subsection (a)(1)—

(i) the administering authority shall order the termination of the suspension of liquidation required pursuant to subsection (a)(4), and

(ii) the countervailing duty order shall remain in effect until revoked, in whole or in part, under § 1675(d).

For purposes of § 1675(c), a countervailing duty order described in this section shall be treated as issued on the date of publication of the Commission's determination under this subsection.

(B) Negative determination.—

(i) In general.—Upon being notified by the Commission that it has made a negative determination under subsection (a)(1), the administering authority shall revoke the countervailing duty order, and shall refund, with interest, any estimated countervailing duties collected during the period liquidation was suspended pursuant to subsection (a)(4).

(ii) Limitation on negative determination.—A determination by the Commission that revocation of the order is not likely to result in material injury to an industry by reason of imports of the subject merchandise shall not be based, in whole or in part, on any export taxes, duties, or other charges levied on the export of the subject merchandise to the United States that were specifically intended to offset the countervailable subsidy received.

(4) Countervailing duty orders with respect to which no request for injury investigation is made.—If, with respect to a countervailing duty order described in subsection (a), a request for an investigation is not made within the time required by subsection (a)(3), the Commission shall notify the administering authority that a negative determination has been made under subsection (a) and the provisions of paragraph (3)(B) shall apply with respect to the order.

(c) Pending and suspended countervailing duty investigations.—If, on the date on which a country becomes a Subsidies Agreement country, there is a countervailing duty investigation in progress or suspended under § 1303 that applies to merchandise which is a product of that country and with respect to which the requirement of an affirmative determination of material injury under § 1303(a)(2) was not applicable at the time the investigation was initiated, the Commission shall—

(1) in the case of an investigation in progress, make a final determination under § 1671d(b) within 75 days after the date of an affirmative final determination, if any, by the administering authority,

(2) in the case of a suspended investigation to which § 1671c(i)(1)(B) applies, make a final determination under § 1671d(b) within 120 days after receiving notice from the administering authority of the resumption of the investigation pursuant to § 1671c(i), or within 45 days after the date of an affirmative final determination, if any, by the administering authority, whichever is later, or

(3) in the case of a suspended investigation to which § 1671c(i)(1)(C) applies, treat the countervailing duty order issued pursuant to such section as if it were—

(A) an order issued under subsection (a)(1)(B)(ii) for purposes of subsection (a)(3); and

(B) an order issued under subsection (a)(1)(B)(i) for purposes of subsection (a)(4).

(d) Publication in Federal Register.—The administering authority or the Commission, as the case may be, shall publish in the Federal Register a notice of the initiation of any investigation, and a notice of any determination or revocation, made pursuant to this section.

(e) Request for simultaneous expedited review under § 1675(c).—

(1) General rule.—

(A) Requests for reviews.—Notwithstanding § 1675(c)(6)(A) and except as provided in subparagraph (B), an interested party may request a review of an order under § 1675(c) at the same time the party requests an investigation under subsection (a), if the order involves the same or comparable subject merchandise. Upon receipt of such request, the administering authority, after consulting with the Commission, shall initiate a review of the order under § 1675(c). The Commission shall combine such review with the investigation under this section.

(B) Exception.—If the administering authority determines that the interested party who requested an investigation under this section is a related party or an importer within the meaning of § 1677(4)(B), the administering authority may decline a request by such party to initiate a review of an order under § 1675(c) which involves the same or comparable subject merchandise.

(2) Cumulation.—If a review under § 1675(c) is initiated under paragraph (1), such review shall be treated as having been initiated on the same day as the investigation under this section, and the Commission may, in accordance with § 1677(7)(G), cumulatively assess the volume and effect of imports of the subject merchandise from all countries with respect to which such investigations are treated as initiated on the same day.

(3) Time and procedure for Commission determination.—The Commission shall render its determination in the investigation conducted under this section at the same time as the Commission's determination is made in the review under § 1675(c) that is initiated pursuant to this subsection. The Commission shall in all other respects apply the procedures and standards set forth in § 1675(c) to such § 1675(c) reviews.

General Provisions

§ 1677. Definitions; special rules

For purposes of this title—

(1) Administering authority. The term "administering authority" means the Secretary of Commerce, or any other officer of the United States to whom the responsibility for carrying out the duties of the administering authority under this title are transferred by law.

(2) Commission. The term "Commission" means the United States International Trade Commission.

(3) Country. The term "country" means a foreign country, a political subdivision, dependent territory, or possession of a foreign country, and, except for the purpose of antidumping proceedings, may include an association of 2 or more foreign countries, political subdivisions, dependent territories, or possessions of countries into a customs union outside the United States.

(4) Industry.

(A) In general. The term "industry" means the producers as a whole of a domestic like product, or those producers whose collective output of a domestic like product constitutes a major proportion of the total domestic production of that product.

(B) Related parties.

(i) If a producer of a domestic like product and an exporter or importer of the subject merchandise are related parties, or if a producer of the domestic like product is also an importer of the subject merchandise, the producer may, in appropriate circumstances, be excluded from the industry.

(ii) For purposes of clause (i), a producer and an exporter or importer shall be considered to be related parties, if—

(I) the producer directly or indirectly controls the exporter or importer,

(II) the exporter or importer directly or indirectly controls the producer,

(III) a third party directly or indirectly controls the producer and the exporter or importer, or

(IV) the producer and the exporter or importer directly or indirectly control a third party and there is reason to believe that the relationship causes the producer to act differently than a nonrelated producer.

For purposes of this subparagraph, a party shall be considered to directly or indirectly control another party if the party is legally or operationally in a position to exercise restraint or direction over the other party.

(C) Regional industries. In appropriate circumstances, the United States, for a particular product market, may be divided into 2 or more markets and the producers within each market may be treated as if they were a separate industry if—

(i) the producers within such market sell all or almost all of their production of the domestic like product in question in that market, and

(ii) the demand in that market is not supplied, to any substantial degree, by producers of the product in question located elsewhere in the United States.

In such appropriate circumstances, material injury, the threat of material injury, or material retardation of the establishment of an industry may be found to exist with respect to an industry even if the domestic industry as a whole, or those producers whose collective output of a domestic like product constitutes a major proportion of the total domestic production of that product, is not injured, if there is a concentration of dumped imports or imports of merchandise benefiting from a countervailable subsidy into such an isolated market and if the producers of all, or almost all, of the production within that market are being materially injured or threatened by material injury, or if the establishment of an industry is being materially retarded, by reason of the dumped imports or imports of merchandise benefiting from a countervailable subsidy. The term "regional industry" means the domestic producers within a region who are treated as a separate industry under this subparagraph.

(D) Product lines. The effect of dumped imports or imports of merchandise benefiting from a countervailable subsidy shall be assessed in relation to the United States production of a domestic like product if available data permit the separate identification of production in terms of such criteria as the production process or the producer's profits. If the domestic production of the domestic like product has no separate identity in terms of such criteria, then the effect of the dumped imports shall be assessed by the examination of the production of the narrowest group or range of products, which includes a domestic like product, for which the necessary information can be provided.

(E) Industry producing processed agricultural products.

(i) In general. Subject to clause (v), in an investigation involving a processed agricultural product produced from any raw agricultural product, the producers or growers of the raw agricultural product may be considered part of the industry producing the processed product if—

(I) the processed agricultural product is produced from the raw agricultural product through a single continuous line of production; and

(II) there is a substantial coincidence of economic interest between the producers or growers of the raw agricultural product and the processors of the processed agricultural product based upon relevant economic factors, which may, in the discretion of the Commission, include price, added market value, or other economic interrelationships (regardless of whether such coincidence of economic interest is based upon any legal relationship).

(ii) Processing. For purposes of this subparagraph, the processed agricultural product shall be considered to be processed from a raw agricultural product through a single continuous line of production if—

(I) the raw agricultural product is substantially or completely devoted to the production of the processed agricultural product; and

(II) the processed agricultural product is produced substantially or completely from the raw product.

(iii) Relevant economic factors. For purposes of clause (i)(II), in addition to such other factors it considers relevant to the question of coincidence of economic interest, the Commission shall—

(I) if price is taken into account, consider the degree of correlation between the price of the raw agricultural product and the price of the processed agricultural product; and

(II) if added market value is taken into account, consider whether the value of the raw agricultural product constitutes a significant percentage of the value of the processed agricultural product.

(iv) Raw agricultural product. For purposes of this subparagraph, the term "raw agricultural product" means any farm or fishery product.

(v) Termination of this subparagraph. This subparagraph shall cease to have effect if the United States Trade Representative notifies the administering authority and the Commission that the application of this subparagraph is inconsistent with the international obligations of the United States.

(5) Countervailable Subsidy.

(A) In general. Except as provided in paragraph (5B), a countervailable subsidy is a subsidy described in this paragraph which is specific as described in paragraph (5A).

(B) Subsidy described. A subsidy is described in this paragraph in the case in which an authority—

(i) provides a financial contribution,

(ii) provides any form of income or price support within the meaning of Article XVI of the GATT 1994, or

(iii) makes a payment to a funding mechanism to provide a financial contribution, or entrusts or directs a private entity to make a financial contribution, if providing the contribution would normally be vested in the government and the practice does not differ in substance from practices normally followed by governments,

to a person and a benefit is thereby conferred. For purposes of this paragraph and paragraphs (5A) and (5B), the term "authority" means a government of a country or any public entity within the territory of the country.

(C) Other factors. The determination of whether a subsidy exists shall be made without regard to whether the recipient of the subsidy is publicly or privately owned and without regard to whether the subsidy is provided directly or indirectly on the manufacture, production, or export of merchandise. The administering authority is not required to consider the effect of the subsidy in determining whether a subsidy exists under this paragraph.

(D) Financial contribution. The term "financial contribution" means—

(i) the direct transfer of funds, such as grants, loans, and equity infusions, or the potential direct transfer of funds or liabilities, such as loan guarantees,

(ii) foregoing or not collecting revenue that is otherwise due, such as granting tax credits or deductions from taxable income,

(iii) providing goods or services, other than general infrastructure, or

(iv) purchasing goods.

(E) Benefit conferred. A benefit shall normally be treated as conferred where there is a benefit to the recipient, including—

(i) in the case of an equity infusion, if the investment decision is inconsistent with the usual investment practice of private investors, including the practice regarding the provision of risk capital, in the country in which the equity infusion is made,

(ii) in the case of a loan, if there is a difference between the amount the recipient of the loan pays on the loan and the amount the recipient would pay on a comparable commercial loan that the recipient could actually obtain on the market,

(iii) in the case of a loan guarantee, if there is a difference, after adjusting for any difference in guarantee fees, between the amount the recipient of the guarantee pays on the guaranteed loan and the amount the recipient would pay for a comparable commercial loan if there were no guarantee by the authority, and

(iv) in the case where goods or services are provided, if such goods or services are provided for less than adequate remuneration, and in the case where goods are purchased, if such goods are purchased for more than adequate remuneration.

For purposes of clause (iv), the adequacy of remuneration shall be determined in relation to prevailing market conditions for the good or service being provided or the goods being purchased in the country which is subject to the investigation or review. Prevailing market conditions include price, quality, availability, marketability, transportation, and other conditions of purchase or sale.

(F) Change in ownership. A change in ownership of all or part of a foreign enterprise or the productive assets of a foreign enterprise does not by itself require a determination by the administering authority that a past countervailing subsidy received by the enterprise no longer continues to be countervailable, even if the change in ownership is accomplished through an arm's length transaction.

(5A) Specificity.

(A) In general. A subsidy is specific if it is an export subsidy described in subparagraph (B) or an import substitution subsidy described in subparagraph (C), or if it is determined to be specific pursuant to subparagraph (D).

(B) Export subsidy. An export subsidy is a subsidy that is, in law or in fact, contingent upon export performance, alone or as 1 of 2 or more conditions.

(C) Import substitution subsidy. An import substitution subsidy is a subsidy that is contingent upon the use of domestic goods over imported goods, alone or as 1 of 2 or more conditions.

(D) Domestic subsidy. In determining whether a subsidy (other than a subsidy described in subparagraph (B) or (C)) is a specific subsidy, in law or in fact, to an enterprise or industry within the jurisdiction of the authority providing the subsidy, the following guidelines shall apply:

(i) Where the authority providing the subsidy, or the legislation pursuant to which the authority operates, expressly limits access to the subsidy to an enterprise or industry, the subsidy is specific as a matter of law.

(ii) Where the authority providing the subsidy, or the legislation pursuant to which the authority operates, establishes objective criteria or conditions governing the eligibility for, and the amount of, a subsidy, the subsidy is not specific as a matter of law, if—

(I) eligibility is automatic,

(II) the criteria or conditions for eligibility are strictly followed, and

(III) the criteria or conditions are clearly set forth in the relevant statute, regulation, or other official document so as to be capable of verification.

For purposes of this clause, the term "objective criteria or conditions" means criteria or conditions that are neutral and that do not favor one enterprise or industry over another.

(iii) Where there are reasons to believe that a subsidy may be specific as a matter of fact, the subsidy is specific if one or more of the following factors exist:

(I) The actual recipients of the subsidy, whether considered on an enterprise or industry basis, are limited in number.

(II) An enterprise or industry is a predominant user of the subsidy.

(III) An enterprise or industry receives a disproportionately large amount of the subsidy.

(IV) The manner in which the authority providing the subsidy has exercised discretion in the decision to grant the subsidy indicates that an enterprise or industry is favored over others.

In evaluating the factors set forth in subclauses (I), (II), (III), and (IV), the administering authority shall take into account the extent of diversification of economic activities within the jurisdiction of the authority providing the subsidy, and the length of time during which the subsidy program has been in operation.

(iv) Where a subsidy is limited to an enterprise or industry located within a designated geographical region within the jurisdiction of the authority providing the subsidy, the subsidy is specific.

For purposes of this paragraph and paragraph (5B), any reference to an enterprise or industry is a reference to a foreign enterprise or foreign industry and includes a group of such enterprises or industries.

(5B) Categories of noncountervailable subsidies.

(A) In general. Notwithstanding the provisions of paragraphs (5) and (5A), in the case of merchandise imported from a Subsidies Agreement country, a subsidy shall be treated as noncountervailable if the administering authority determines in an investigation under subtitle A or a review under subtitle C that the subsidy meets all of the criteria described in subparagraph (B), (C), or (D), as the case may be, or the provisions of subparagraph (E)(i) apply.

[Note: The provisions in (5B)(B), (C), (D), and (E) have all "sunset" as provided in (5B)(G)(i) and have not been renewed. See Art. 31 of the WTO SCM Agreement.]

(F) Certain subsidies on agricultural products.—Domestic support measures that are provided with respect to products listed in Annex 1 to the Agreement on Agriculture, and that the administering authority determines conform fully to the provisions of Annex 2 to that Agreement, shall be treated as noncountervailable. Upon request by the administering authority, the Trade Representative shall provide advice regarding the interpretation and application of Annex 2.

(G) Provisional application.

(i) Subparagraphs (B), (C), (D), and (E) shall not apply on or after the first day of the month that is 66 months after the WTO Agreement enters into force, unless the provisions of such subparagraphs are extended pursuant to section 282(c) of the Uruguay Round Agreements Act.

(ii) Subparagraph (F) shall not apply to imports from a WTO member country at the end of the 9–year period beginning on January 1, 1995. The Trade Representative shall determine the precise termination date for each WTO member country in accordance with paragraph (i) of Article 1 of the Agreement on Agriculture and such date shall be notified to the administering authority.

(6) Net countervailable subsidy. For the purpose of determining the net countervailable subsidy, the administering authority may subtract from the gross countervailable subsidy the amount of—

(A) any application fee, deposit, or similar payment paid in order to qualify for, or to receive, the benefit of the countervailable subsidy,

(B) any loss in the value of the countervailable subsidy resulting from its deferred receipt, if the deferral is mandated by Government order, and

(C) export taxes, duties, or other charges levied on the export of merchandise to the United States specifically intended to offset the countervailable subsidy received.

(7) Material injury.

(A) In general. The term "material injury" means harm which is not inconsequential, immaterial, or unimportant.

(B) Volume and consequent impact. In making determinations under §§ 1671b(a), 1671d(b), 1673b(a), 1673d(b), the Commission, in each case—

(i) shall consider—

(I) the volume of imports of the subject merchandise,

(II) the effect of imports of that merchandise on prices in the United States for domestic like products, and

(III) the impact of imports of such merchandise on domestic producers of domestic like products, but only in the context of production operations within the United States; and

(ii) may consider such other economic factors as are relevant to the determination regarding whether there is material injury by reason of imports.

In the notification required under § 1671d(d) or § 1673d(d), as the case may be, the Commission shall explain its analysis of each factor considered under clause (i), and identify each factor considered under clause (ii) and explain in full its relevance to the determination.

(C) Evaluation of relevant factors—Evaluation of volume and of price effects. For purposes of subparagraph (B)—

(i) Volume. In evaluating the volume of imports of merchandise, the Commission shall consider whether the volume of imports of the merchandise, or any increase in that volume, either in absolute terms or relative to production or consumption in the United States, is significant.

(ii) Price. In evaluating the effect of imports of such merchandise on prices, the Commission shall consider whether—

(I) there has been significant price underselling by the imported merchandise as compared with the price of domestic like products of the United States, and

(II) the effect of imports of such merchandise otherwise depresses prices to a significant degree or prevents price increases, which otherwise would have occurred, to a significant degree.

(iii) Impact on affected domestic industry. In examining the impact required to be considered under subparagraph (B)(i)(III), the Commission shall evaluate all relevant economic factors which have a bearing on the state of the industry in the United States, including, but not limited to—

(I) actual and potential decline in output, sales, market share, profits, productivity, return on investments, and utilization of capacity,

(II) factors affecting domestic prices,

(III) actual and potential negative effects on cash flow, inventories, employment, wages, growth, ability to raise capital, and investment, and

(IV) actual and potential negative effects on the existing development and production efforts of the domestic industry, including efforts to develop a derivative or more advanced version of the domestic like product.

(V) in a proceeding under subtitle B, the magnitude of the margin of dumping.

The Commission shall evaluate all relevant economic factors described in this clause within the context of the business cycle and conditions of competition that are distinctive to the affected industry.

(iv) Captive production. If domestic producers internally transfer significant production of the domestic like product for the production of a downstream article and sell significant production of the domestic like product in the merchant market, and the Commission finds that

(I) the domestic like product produced that is internally transferred for processing into that downstream article does not enter the merchant market for the domestic like product,

(II) the domestic like product is the predominant material input in the production of that downstream article, and

(III) the production of the domestic like product sold in the merchant market is not generally used in the production of that downstream article

then the Commission, in determining market share and the factors affecting financial performance set forth in clause (iii), shall focus primarily on the merchant market for the domestic like product.

(D) Special rules for agricultural products.

(i) The Commission shall not determine that there is no material injury or threat of material injury to United States producers of an agricultural commodity merely because the prevailing market price is at or above the minimum support price.

(ii) In the case of agricultural products, the Commission shall consider any increased burden on government income or price support programs.

(E) Special rules. For purposes of this paragraph—

(i) Nature of countervailable subsidy. In determining whether there is a threat of material injury, the Commission shall consider information provided to it by the administering authority regarding the nature of the countervailable subsidy granted by a foreign country (particularly whether the countervailable subsidy is a subsidy described in Article 3 or 6.1 of the Subsidies Agreement) and the effects likely to be caused by the countervailable subsidy.

(ii) Standard for determination. The presence or absence of any factor which the Commission is required to evaluate under subparagraph (C) or (D) shall not necessarily give decisive guidance with respect to the determination by the Commission of material injury.

(F) Threat of material injury.

(i) In general. In determining whether an industry in the United States is threatened with material injury by reason of imports (or sales for importation) of the subject merchandise, the Commission shall consider, among other relevant economic factors—

(I) if a countervailable subsidy is involved, such information as may be presented to it by the administering authority as to the nature of the subsidy (particularly as to whether the countervailable subsidy is a subsidy described in Article 3 or 6.1 of the Subsidies Agreement), and whether imports of the subject merchandise are likely to increase,

(II) any existing unused production capacity or imminent, substantial increase in production capacity in the exporting country indicating the likelihood of substantially increased imports of the subject merchandise into the United States, taking into account the availability of other export markets to absorb any additional exports,

(III) a significant rate of increase of the volume or market penetration of imports of the subject merchandise indicating the likelihood of substantially increased imports,

(IV) whether imports of the subject merchandise are entering at prices that are likely to have a significant depressing or suppressing effect on domestic prices, and are likely to increase demand for further imports,

(V) inventories of the subject merchandise,

(VI) the potential for product-shifting if production facilities in the foreign country, which can be used to produce the subject merchandise, are currently being used to produce other products,

(VII) in any investigation under this title which involves imports of both a raw agricultural product (within the meaning of paragraph (4)(E)(iv)) and any product processed from such raw agricultural product, the likelihood that there will be increased imports, by reason of product shifting, if there is an affirmative determination by the Commission under § 1671d(b)(1) or § 1673d(b)(1) with respect to either the raw agricultural product or the processed agricultural product (but not both),

(VIII) the actual and potential negative effects on the existing development and production efforts of the domestic industry, including efforts to develop a derivative or more advanced version of the domestic like product, and

(IX) any other demonstrable adverse trends that indicate the probability that there is likely to be material injury by reason of imports (or sale for importation) of the subject merchandise (whether or not it is actually being imported at the time).

(ii) Basis for determination. The Commission shall consider the factors set forth in clause (i) as a whole in making a determination of whether further dumped or subsidized imports are imminent and whether material injury by reason of imports would occur unless an order is issued or a suspension agreement is accepted under this title. The presence or absence of any factor which the Commission is required to consider under clause (i) shall not necessarily give decisive guidance with respect to the determination. Such a determination may not be made on the basis of mere conjecture or supposition.

(iii) Effect of dumping in third-country markets.

(I) In general. In investigations under subtitle B, the Commission shall consider whether dumping in the markets of foreign countries (as evidenced by dumping findings or antidumping remedies in other WTO member markets against the same class or kind of merchandise manufactured or exported by the same party as under investigation) suggests a threat of material injury to the domestic industry. In the course of its investigation, the Commission shall request information from the foreign manufacturer, exporter, or United States importer concerning this issue.

(II) WTO member market. For purposes of this clause, the term "WTO member market" means the market of any country which is a WTO member.

(III) European communities. For purposes of this clause, the European Communities shall be treated as a foreign country.

(G) Cumulation for determining material injury.

(i) In general. For purposes of clauses (i) and (ii) of subparagraph (C), and subject to clause (ii), the Commission shall cumulatively assess the volume and effect of imports of the subject merchandise from all countries with respect to which—

(I) petitions were filed under § 1671a(b) or § 1673a(b) on the same day,

(II) investigations were initiated under § 1671a(a) or § 1673a(a) on the same day, or

(III) petitioners were filed under § 1671a(b) or § 1673a(b) and investigations were initiated under § 1671a(a) or § 1673a(a) on the same day,

if such imports compete with each other and with domestic like products in the United States market.

(ii) Exceptions. The Commission shall not cumulatively assess the volume and effect of imports under clause (i)—

(I) with respect to which the administering authority has made a preliminary negative determination, unless the administering authority subsequently made a final affirmative determination with respect to those imports before the Commission's final determination is made;

(II) from any country with respect to which the investigation has been terminated;

(III) from any country designated as a beneficiary country under the Caribbean Basin Economic Recovery Act (19 U.S.C. § 2701 et seq.) for purposes of making a determination with respect to that country, except that the volume and effect of imports of the subject merchandise from such country may be cumulatively assessed with imports of the subject merchandise from any other country designated as such a beneficiary country to the extent permitted by clause (i); or

(IV) from any country that is a party to an agreement with the United States establishing a free trade area, which entered into force and effect before January 1, 1987, unless the Commission determines that a domestic industry is materially injured or threatened with material injury by reason of imports from that country.

(iii) Records in final investigations. In each final determination in which it cumulatively assesses the volume and effect of imports under clause (i), the Commission shall make its determinations based on the record compiled in the first investigation in which it makes a final determination, except that when the administering authority issues its final determination in a subsequently completed investigation, the Commission shall permit the parties in the subsequent investigation to submit comments concerning the significance of the administering authority's final determination, and shall include such comments and the administering authority's final determination in the record for the subsequent investigation.

(iv) Regional industry determinations. In an investigation which involves a regional industry, and in which the Commission decides that the volume and effect of imports should be cumulatively assessed under this subparagraph, such assessment shall be based upon the volume and effect of imports into the region or regions determined by the Commission. The provisions of clause (iii) shall apply to such investigations.

(H) Cumulation for determining threat of material injury. To the extent practicable and subject to subparagraph (G)(ii), for purposes of clause (i)(III) and (IV) of subparagraph (F), the Commission may cumulatively assess the volume and price effects of imports of the subject merchandise from all countries with respect to which—

(i) petitions were filed under § 1671a(b) or § 1673a(b) on the same day,

(ii) investigations were initiated under § 1671a(a) or § 1673a(a) on the same day, or

(iii) petitions were filed under § 1671a(b) or § 1673a(b) and investigations were initiated under § 1671a(a) or § 1673a(a) on the same day,

if such imports compete with each other and with domestic like products in the United States market.

(I) Consideration of post-petition information. The Commission shall consider whether any change in the volume, price effects, or impact of imports of the subject merchandise since the filing of the petition in an investigation under subtitle A or B is related to the pendency of the investigation and, if so, the Commission may reduce the weight accorded to the data for the period after the filing of the petition in making its determination of material injury, threat of material injury, or material retardation of the establishment of an industry in the United States.

(8) Subsidies agreement; agreement on agriculture.

(A) Subsidies agreement. The term "Subsidies Agreement" means the Agreement on Subsidies and Countervailing Measures referred to in section 101(d)(12) of the Uruguay Round Agreements Act.

(B) Agreement on agriculture. The term "Agreement on Agriculture" means the Agreement on Agriculture referred to in section 101(d)(2) of the Uruguay Round Agreements Act.

(9) Interested party. The term "interested party" means—

(A) a foreign manufacturer, producer, or exporter, or the United States importer, of subject merchandise under this title or a trade or business association a majority of the members of which are importers of such merchandise,

(B) the government of a country in which such merchandise is produced or manufactured,

(C) a manufacturer, producer, or wholesaler in the United States of a domestic like product,

(D) a certified union or recognized union or group of workers which is representative of an industry engaged in the manufacture, production, or wholesale in the United States of a domestic like product,

(E) a trade or business association a majority of whose members manufacture, produce, or wholesale a domestic like product in the United States;

(F) an association, a majority of whose members is composed of interested parties described in subparagraph (C), (D), or (E) with respect to a domestic like product, and

(G) in any investigation under this title involving an industry engaged in producing a processed agricultural product, as defined in paragraph (4)(E), a coalition or trade association which is representative of either—

(i) processors,

(ii) processors and producers, or

(iii) processors and growers,

but this subparagraph shall cease to have effect if the United States Trade Representative notifies the administering authority and the Commission that the application of this subparagraph is inconsistent with the international obligations of the United States.

(10) Domestic like product. The term "domestic like product" means a product which is like, or in the absence of like, most similar in characteristics and uses with, the article subject to an investigation under this title.

(11) Affirmative determinations by divided Commission. If the Commissioners voting on a determination by the Commission including a determination under § 1675 are evenly divided as to whether the determination should be affirmative or negative, the Commission shall be deemed to have made an affirmative determination. For the purpose of

applying this paragraph when the issue before the Commission is to determine whether there is—

(A) material injury to an industry in the United States,

(B) threat of material injury to such an industry, or

(C) material retardation of the establishment of an industry in the United States,

by reason of imports of the merchandise, an affirmative vote on any of the issues shall be treated as a vote that the determination should be affirmative.

(12) Attribution of merchandise to country of manufacture or production. For purposes of subtitle A, merchandise shall be treated as the product of the country in which it was manufactured or produced without regard to whether it is imported directly from that country and without regard to whether it is imported in the same condition as when exported from that country or in a changed condition by reason of remanufacture or otherwise.

(13) Exporter. (repealed 1994)

(14) Sold or, in the absence of sales, offered for sale. The term "sold or, in the absence of sales, offered for sale" means sold or, in the absence of sales, offered—

(A) to all purchasers in commercial quantities, or

(B) in the ordinary course of trade to one or more selected purchasers in commercial quantities at a price which fairly reflects the market value of the merchandise,

without regard to restrictions as to the disposition or use of the merchandise by the purchaser except that, where such restrictions are found to affect the market value of the merchandise, adjustment shall be made therefor in calculating the price at which the merchandise is sold or offered for sale.

(15) Ordinary course of trade. The term "ordinary course of trade" means the conditions and practices which, for a reasonable time prior to the exportation of the subject merchandise, have been normal in the trade under consideration with respect to merchandise of the same class or kind. The administering authority shall consider the following sales and transactions, among others, to be outside the ordinary course of trade:

(A) Sales disregarded under § 1677(b)(1).

(B) Transactions disregarded under § 1677b(f)(2).

(16) Foreign like product. The term "foreign like product" means merchandise in the first of the following categories in respect of which a

determination for the purposes of subtitle B of this title can be satisfactorily made:

(A) The subject merchandise and other merchandise which is identical in physical characteristics with, and was produced in the same country by the same person as, that merchandise.

(B) Merchandise—

(i) produced in the same country and by the same person as the subject merchandise,

(ii) like that merchandise in component material or materials and in the purposes for which used, and

(iii) approximately equal in commercial value to that merchandise.

(C) Merchandise—

(i) produced in the same country and by the same person and of the same general class or kind as the merchandise which is the subject of the investigation,

(ii) like that merchandise in the purposes for which used, and

(iii) which the administering authority determines may reasonably be compared with that merchandise.

(17) Usual commercial quantities. The term "usual commercial quantities", in any case in which the subject merchandise is sold in the market under consideration at different prices for different quantities, means the quantities in which such merchandise is there sold at the price or prices for one quantity in an aggregate volume which is greater than the aggregate volume sold at the price or prices for any other quantity.

(18) Nonmarket economy country.

(A) In general. The term "nonmarket economy country" means any foreign country that the administering authority determines does not operate on market principles of cost or pricing structures, so that sales of merchandise in such country do not reflect the fair value of the merchandise.

(B) Factors to be considered. In making determinations under subparagraph (A) the administering authority shall take into account—

(i) the extent to which the currency of the foreign country is convertible into the currency of other countries;

(ii) the extent to which wage rates in the foreign country are determined by free bargaining between labor and management,

(iii) the extent to which joint ventures or other investments by firms of other foreign countries are permitted in the foreign country,

(iv) the extent of government ownership or control of the means of production,

(v) the extent of government control over the allocation of resources and over the price and output decisions of enterprises, and

(vi) such other factors as the administering authority considers appropriate.

(C) Determination in effect.

(i) Any determination that a foreign country is a nonmarket economy country shall remain in effect until revoked by the administering authority.

(ii) The administering authority may make a determination under subparagraph (A) with respect to any foreign country at any time.

(D) Determinations not in issue. Notwithstanding any other provision of law, any determination made by the administering authority under subparagraph (A) shall not be subject to judicial review in any investigation conducted under subtitle B.

(E) Collection of information. Upon request by the administering authority, the Commissioner of Customs shall provide the administering authority a copy of all public and proprietary information submitted to, or obtained by, the Commissioner of Customs that the administering authority considers relevant to proceedings involving merchandise from nonmarket economy countries. The administering authority shall protect proprietary information obtained under this section from public disclosure in accordance with § 1677f.

(19) Equivalency of leases to sales. In determining whether a lease is equivalent to a sale for purposes of this title, the administering authority shall consider—

(A) the terms of the lease,

(B) commercial practice within the industry,

(C) the circumstances of the transaction,

(D) whether the product subject to the lease is integrated into the operations of the lessee or importer,

(E) whether in practice there is a likelihood that the lease will be continued or renewed for a significant period of time, and

(F) other relevant factors, including whether the lease transaction would permit avoidance of antidumping or countervailing duties.

(20) Application to governmental importations.

(A) In general. Except as otherwise provided by this paragraph, merchandise imported by, or for the use of, a department or agency of the United States Government (including merchandise provided for under chapter 98 of the Harmonized Tariff Schedule of the United States) is subject to the imposition of countervailing duties or antidumping duties under this title or § 1303.

(B) Exceptions. Merchandise imported by, or for the use of, the Department of Defense shall not be subject to the imposition of countervailing or antidumping duties under this title if—

(i) the merchandise is acquired by, or for use of, such Department—

(I) from a country with which such Department had a Memorandum of Understanding which was in effect on January 1, 1988, and has continued to have a comparable agreement (including renewals) or superceding agreements, and

(II) in accordance with terms of the Memorandum of Understanding in effect at the time of importation, or

(ii) the merchandise has no substantial nonmilitary use.

* * *

(21) United States-Canada agreement. The term "United States-Canada Agreement" means the United States-Canada Free-Trade Agreement.

(22) NAFTA

The term "NAFTA" means the North American Free Trade Agreement.

(23) Entry

The term "entry" includes, in appropriate circumstances as determined by the administering authority, a reconciliation entry created under a reconciliation process, defined in section 401, that is initiated by an importer. The liability of an importer under an antidumping or countervailing duty proceeding for entries of merchandise subject to the proceeding will attach to the corresponding reconciliation entry or entries. Suspension of liquidation of the reconciliation entry or entries, for the purpose of enforcing this subtitle, is equivalent to the suspension of liquidation of the corresponding individual entries; but the suspension of liquidation of the reconciliation entry or entries for such purpose does not preclude liquidation for any other purpose.

(24) Negligible imports.

(A) In general.

(i) Less than 3 percent. Except as provided in clauses (ii) and (iv), imports from a country of merchandise corresponding to a domestic like product identified by the Commission are "negligible" if such imports account for less than 3 percent of the volume of all such merchandise imported into the United States in the most recent 12–month period for which data are available that precedes—

(I) the filing of the petition under section 702(b) or 732(b), or

(II) the initiation of the investigation, if the investigation was initiated under section 702(a) or 732(a).

(ii) Exception. Imports that would otherwise be negligible under clause (i) shall not be negligible if the aggregate volume of imports of the merchandise from all countries described in clause (i) with respect to which investigations were initiated on the same day exceeds 7 percent of the volume of all such merchandise imported into the United States during the applicable 12–month period.

(iii) Determination of aggregate volume. In determining aggregate volume under clause (ii) or (iv), the Commission shall not consider imports from any country specified in paragraph (7)(G)(ii).

(iv) Negligibility in threat analysis. Notwithstanding clauses (i) and (ii), the Commission shall not treat imports as negligible if it determines that there is a potential that imports from a country described in clause (i) will imminently account for more than 3 percent of the volume of all such merchandise imported into the United States, or that the aggregate volumes of imports from all countries described in clause (ii) will imminently exceed 7 percent of the volume of all such merchandise imported into the United States. The Commission shall consider such imports only for purposes of determining threat of material injury.

(B) Negligibility for certain countries in countervailing duty investigations. In the case of an investigation under section 701, subparagraph (A) shall be applied to imports of subject merchandise from developing countries by substituting "4 percent" for "3 percent" in subparagraph (A)(i) and by substituting "9 percent" for "7 percent" in subparagraph (A)(ii).

(C) Computation of import volumes. In computing import volumes for purposes of subparagraphs (A) and (B), the Commission may make reasonable estimates on the basis of available statistics.

(D) Regional industries. In an investigation in which the Commission makes a regional industry determination under paragraph (4)(C), the Commission's examination under subparagraphs (A) and (B) shall be based upon the volume of subject merchandise exported for sale in the regional market in lieu of the volume of all subject merchandise imported into the United States.

(25) Subject merchandise. The term "subject merchandise" means the class or kind of merchandise that is within the scope of an investigation, a review, a suspension agreement, an order under this title or § 1303, or a finding under the Antidumping Act, 1921.

(26) Section 303. The terms "section 303" and "303" mean section 303 of this Act as in effect on the day before the effective date of title II of the Uruguay Round Agreements Act.

(27) Suspension agreement. The term "suspension agreement" means an agreement described in § 1671c(b), 1671c(c), 1677c(b), 1677c(c), or 1677c(*l*).

(28) Exporter or producer. The term "exporter or producer" means the exporter of the subject merchandise, the producer of the subject merchandise, or both where appropriate. For purposes of section 773, the term "exporter or producer" includes both the exporter of the subject merchandise and the producer of the same subject merchandise to the extent necessary to accurately calculate the total amount incurred and realized for costs, expenses, and profits in connection with production and sale of that merchandise.

(29) WTO agreement. The term "WTO Agreement" means the Agreement defined in section 2(9) of the Uruguay Round Agreements Act.

(30) WTO member and WTO member country. The terms "WTO member" and "WTO member country" mean a state, or separate customs territory (within the meaning of Article XII of the WTO Agreement), with respect to which the United States applies the WTO agreement.

(31) GATT 1994. The term "GATT 1994" means the General Agreement on Tariffs and Trade annexed to the WTO Agreement.

(32) Trade representative. The term "Trade Representative" means the United States Trade Representative.

(33) Affiliated persons. The following persons shall be considered to be "affiliated" or "affiliated persons":

(A) Members of a family, including brothers and sisters (whether by the whole or half blood), spouse, ancestors, and lineal descendants.

(B) Any officer or director of an organization and such organization.

(C) Partners.

(D) Employer and employee.

(E) Any person directly or indirectly owning, controlling, or holding with power to vote, 5 percent or more of the outstanding voting stock or shares of any organization and such organization.

(F) Two or more persons directly or indirectly controlling, controlled by, or under common control with, any person.

(G) Any person who controls any other person and such other person.

For purposes of this paragraph, a person shall be considered to control another person if the person is legally or operationally in a position to exercise restraint or direction over the other person.

(34) Dumped; dumping. The terms "dumped" and "dumping" refer to the sale or likely sale of goods at less than fair value.

(35) Dumping margin; weighted average dumping margin.

(A) Dumping margin. The term "dumping margin" means the amount by which the normal value exceeds the export price or constructed export price of the subject merchandise.

(B) Weighted average dumping margin.—The term "weighted average dumping margin" is the percentage determined by dividing the aggregate dumping margins determined for a specific exporter or producer by the aggregate export prices and constructed export prices of such exporter or producer.

(C) Magnitude of the margin of dumping.—The magnitude of the margin of dumping used by the Commission shall be—

(i) in making a preliminary determination under § 1677b(a) in an investigation (including any investigation in which the Commission cumulatively assesses the volume and effect of imports under paragraph (7)(G)(i)), the dumping margin or margins published by the administering authority in its notice of initiation of the investigation;

(ii) in making a final determination under § 1677d(b), the dumping margin or margins most recently published by the administering authority prior to the closing of the Commission's administrative record;

(iii) in a review under § 1675(b)(2), the most recent dumping margin or margins determined by the administering authority under § 1676(c)(3), if any, or under § 1673b(b) or 1673d(a); and

(iv) in a review under § 1673b(b) or 1673d(a), the dumping margin or margins determined by the administering authority under § 1676(c)(3).

(36) Developing and least developed country.

(A) Developing country. The term "developing country" means a country designated as a developing country by the Trade Representative.

(B) Least developed country. The term "least developed country" means a country which the Trade Representative determines is—

(i) a country referred to as a least developed country within the meaning of paragraph (a) of Annex VII to the Subsidies Agreement, or

(ii) any other country listed in Annex VII to the Subsidies Agreement, but only if the country has a per capita gross national product of less than $1,000 per annum as measured by the most recent data available from the World Bank.

(C) Publication of list. The Trade Representative shall publish in the Federal Register, and update as necessary, a list of—

(i) developing countries that have eliminated their export subsidies on an expedited basis within the meaning of Article 27.11 of the Subsidies Agreement, and

(ii) countries determined by the Trade Representative to be least developed or developing countries.

(D) Factors to consider. In determining whether a country is a developing country under subparagraph (A), the Trade Representative shall consider such economic, trade, and other factors which the Trade Representative considers appropriate, including the level of economic development of such country (the assessment of which shall include a review of the country's per capita gross national product) and the country's share of world trade.

(E) Limitation on designation. A determination that a country is a developing or least developed country pursuant to this paragraph shall be for purposes of this title only and shall not affect the determination of a country's status as a developing or least developed country with respect to any other law.

§ 1677–1. Upstream subsidies

(a) Definition. The term "upstream subsidy" means any countervailable subsidy, other than an export subsidy, that

(1) is paid or bestowed by an authority (as defined in § 1677(5)) with respect to a product (hereafter in this section referred to as an "input

product") that is used in the same country as the authority in the manufacture or production of merchandise which is the subject of a countervailing duty proceeding;

(2) in the judgment of the administering authority bestows a competitive benefit on the merchandise; and

(3) has a significant effect on the cost of manufacturing or producing the merchandise.

In applying this subsection, an association of two or more foreign countries, political subdivisions, dependent territories, or possessions of foreign countries organized into a customs union outside the United States shall be treated as being one country if the countervailable subsidy is provided by the customs union.

(b) Determination of competitive benefit.

(1) In general. Except as provided in paragraph (2), the administering authority shall decide that a competitive benefit has been bestowed when the price for the input product referred to in subsection (a)(1) for such use is lower than the price that the manufacturer or producer of merchandise which is the subject of a countervailing duty proceeding would otherwise pay for the product in obtaining it from another seller in an arms-length transaction.

(2) Adjustments. If the administering authority has determined in a previous proceeding that a countervailable subsidy is paid or bestowed on the input product that is used for comparison under paragraph (1), the administering authority may (A) where appropriate, adjust the price that the manufacturer or producer of merchandise which is the subject of such proceeding would otherwise pay for the product to reflect the effects of the countervailable subsidy, or (B) select in lieu of that price a price from another source.

(c) Inclusion of amount of countervailable subsidy. If the administering authority decides, during the course of a countervailing duty proceeding that an upstream countervailable subsidy is being or has been paid or bestowed regarding the subject merchandise, the administering authority shall include in the amount of any countervailing duty imposed on the merchandise an amount equal to the amount of the competitive benefit referred to in subparagraph (1)(B), except that in no event shall the amount be greater than the amount of the countervailable subsidy determined with respect to the upstream product.

§ 1677–2. Calculation of countervailable subsidies on certain processed agricultural products

In the case of an agricultural product processed from a raw agricultural product in which (1) the demand for the prior stage product is substantially dependent on the demand for the latter stage product, and

(2) the processing operation adds only limited value to the raw commodity, countervailable subsidies found to be provided to either producers or processors of the product shall be deemed to be provided with respect to the manufacture, production, or exportation of the processed product.

§ 1677a. Export price and constructed export price

(a) Export price. The term "export price" means the price at which the subject merchandise is first sold (or agreed to be sold) before the date of importation by the producer or exporter of the subject merchandise outside of the United States to an unaffiliated purchaser in the United States or to an unaffiliated purchaser for exportation to the United States, as adjusted under subsection (c).

(b) Constructed export price. The term "constructed export price" means the price at which the subject merchandise is first sold (or agreed to be sold) in the United States before or after the date of importation by or for the account of the producer or exporter of such merchandise or by a seller affiliated with the producer or exporter, to a purchaser not affiliated with the producer or exporter, as adjusted under subsections (c) and (d).

(c) Adjustments for export price and constructed export price. The price used to establish export price and constructed export price shall be—

(1) increased by—

(A) when not included in such price, the cost of all containers and coverings and all other costs, charges, and expenses incident to placing the subject merchandise in condition packed ready for shipment to the United States,

(B) the amount of any import duties imposed by the country of exportation which have been rebated, or which have not been collected, by reason of the exportation of the subject merchandise to the United States, and

(C) the amount of any countervailing duty imposed on the subject merchandise under subtitle A to offset an export subsidy, and

(2) reduced by—

(A) except as provided in paragraph (1)(C), the amount, if any, included in such price, attributable to any additional costs, charges, or expenses, and United States import duties, which are incident to bringing the subject merchandise from the original place of shipment in the exporting country to the place of delivery in the United States, and

(B) the amount, if included in such price, of any export tax, duty, or other charge imposed by the exporting country on the exportation of the subject merchandise to the United States, other than an export tax, duty, or other charge described in § 1677(6)(c).

(d) Additional adjustments to constructed export price. For purposes of this section, the price used to establish constructed export price shall also be reduced by—

(1) the amount of any of the following expenses generally incurred by or for the account of the producer or exporter, or the affiliated seller in the United States, in selling the subject merchandise (or subject merchandise to which value has been added)—

(A) commissions for selling the subject merchandise in the United States;

(B) expenses that result from, and bear a direct relationship to, the sale, such as credit expenses, guarantees and warranties;

(C) any selling expenses that the seller pays on behalf of the purchaser;

(D) any selling expenses not deducted under subparagraph (A), (B), or (C);

(2) the cost of any further manufacture or assembly (including additional material and labor), except in circumstances described in subsection (e); and

(3) the profit allocated to the expenses described in paragraphs (1) and (2).

(e) Special rule for merchandise with value added after importation. Where the subject merchandise is imported by a person affiliated with the exporter or producer, and the value added in the United States by the affiliated person is likely to exceed substantially the value of the subject merchandise, the administering authority shall determine the constructed export price for such merchandise by using one of the following prices if there is a sufficient quantity of sales to provide a reasonable basis for comparison and the administering authority determines that the use of such sales is appropriate:

(1) The price of identical subject merchandise sold by the exporter or producer to an unaffiliated person.

(2) The price of other subject merchandise sold by the exporter or producer to an unaffiliated person.

If there is not a sufficient quantity of sales to provide a reasonable basis for comparison under paragraph (1) or (2), or the administering authority determines that neither of the prices described in such paragraphs is appropriate, then the constructed export price may be determined on any other reasonable basis.

(f) Special rule for determining profit.

(1) In general. For purposes of subsection (d)(3), profit shall be an amount determined by multiplying the total actual profit by the applicable percentage.

(2) Definitions. For purposes of this subsection—

(A) Applicable percentage. The term "applicable percentage" means the percentage determined by dividing the total United States expenses by the total expenses.

(B) Total United States expenses. The term "total United States expenses" means the total expenses described in subsection (d)(1) and (2).

(C) Total expenses. The term "total expenses" means all expenses in the first of the following categories which applies and which are incurred by or on behalf of the foreign producer and foreign exporter of the subject merchandise and by or on behalf of the United States seller affiliated with the producer or exporter with respect to the production and sale of such merchandise:

(i) The expenses incurred with respect to the subject merchandise sold in the United States and the foreign like product sold in the exporting country if such expenses were requested by the administering authority for the purpose of establishing normal value and constructed export price.

(ii) The expenses incurred with respect to the narrowest category of merchandise sold in the United States and the exporting country which includes the subject merchandise.

(iii) The expenses incurred with respect to the narrowest category of merchandise sold in all countries which includes the subject merchandise.

(D) Total actual profit. The term "total actual profit" means the total profit earned by the foreign producer, exporter, and affiliated parties described in subparagraph (C) with respect to the sale of the same merchandise for which total expenses are determined under such subparagraph.

§ 1677b. Normal Value

(a) Determination. In determining under this title whether subject merchandise is being, or is likely to be, sold at less than fair value, a fair comparison shall be made between the export price or constructed export price and normal value. In order to achieve a fair comparison with the export price or constructed export price, normal value shall be determined as follows:

(1) Determination of normal value.

(A) In general. The normal value of the subject merchandise shall be the price described in subparagraph (B), at a time reasonably corresponding to the time of the sale used to determine the export price or constructed export price under § 1677a(a) or (b).

(B) Price. The price referred to in subparagraph (A) is—

(i) the price at which the foreign like product is first sold (or, in the absence of a sale, offered for sale) for consumption in the exporting country, in the usual commercial quantities and in the ordinary course of trade and, to the extent practicable, at the same level of trade as the export price or constructed export price, or

(ii) in a case to which subparagraph (C) applies, the price at which the foreign like product is so sold (or offered for sale) for consumption in a country other than the exporting country or the United States, if—

(I) such price is representative,

(II) the aggregate quantity (or, if quantity is not appropriate, value) of the foreign like product sold by the exporter or producer in such other country is 5 percent or more of the aggregate quantity (or value) of the subject merchandise sold in the United States or for export to the United States, and

(III) the administering authority does not determine that the particular market situation in such other country prevents a proper comparison with the export price or constructed export price.

(C) Third country sales. This subparagraph applies when—

(i) the foreign like product is not sold (or offered for sale) for consumption in the exporting country as described in subparagraph (B)(i),

(ii) the administering authority determines that the aggregate quantity (or, if quantity is not appropriate, value) of the foreign like product sold in the exporting country is insufficient to permit a proper comparison with the sales of the subject merchandise to the United States, or

(iii) the particular market situation in the exporting country does not permit a proper comparison with the export price or constructed export price.

For purposes of clause (ii), the aggregate quantity (or value) of the foreign like product sold in the exporting country shall normally be considered to be insufficient if such quantity (or value) is less than 5 percent of the aggregate quantity (or value) of sales of the subject merchandise to the United States.

(2) Fictitious markets. No pretended sale or offer for sale, and no sale or offer for sale intended to establish a fictitious market, shall be taken into account in determining normal value. The occurrence of different movements in the prices at which different forms of the foreign like product are sold (or, in the absence of sales, offered for sale) in the exporting country after the issuance of an antidumping duty order may be considered by the administering authority as evidence of the establishment of a fictitious market for the foreign like product if the movement in such prices appears to reduce the amount by which the normal value exceeds the export price (or the constructed export price) of the subject merchandise.

(3) Exportation from an intermediate country. Where the subject merchandise is exported to the United States from an intermediate country, normal value shall be determined in the intermediate country, except that normal value may be determined in the country of origin of the subject merchandise if—

(A) the producer knew at the time of the sale that the subject merchandise was destined for exportation;

(B) the subject merchandise is merely transshipped through the intermediate country;

(C) sales of the foreign like product in the intermediate country do not satisfy the conditions of paragraph (1)(C); or

(D) the foreign like product is not produced in the intermediate country.

(4) Use of constructed value. If the administering authority determines that the normal value of the subject merchandise cannot be determined under paragraph (1)(B)(i), then, notwithstanding paragraph (1)(B)(ii), the normal value of the subject merchandise may be the constructed value of that merchandise, as determined under subsection (e).

(5) Indirect sales or offers for sale. If the foreign like product is sold or, in the absence of sales, offered for sale through an affiliated party, the prices at which the foreign like product is sold (or offered for sale) by such affiliated party may be used in determining normal value.

(6) Adjustments. The price described in paragraph (1)(B) shall be—

(A) increased by the cost of all containers and coverings and all other costs, charges, and expenses incident to placing the subject merchandise in condition packed ready for shipment to the United States;

(B) reduced by—

(i) when included in the price described in paragraph (1)(B), the cost of all containers and coverings and all other costs, charges, and expenses incident to placing the foreign like product in condition packed ready for shipment to the place of delivery to the purchaser,

(ii) the amount, if any, included in the price described in paragraph (1)(B), attributable to any additional costs, charges, and expenses incident to bringing the foreign like product from the original place of shipment to the place of delivery to the purchaser, and

(iii) the amount of any taxes imposed directly upon the foreign like product or components thereof which have been rebated, or which have not been collected, on the subject merchandise, but only to the extent that such taxes are added to or included in the price of the foreign like product, and

(C) increased or decreased by the amount of any difference (or lack thereof) between the export price or constructed export price and the price described in paragraph (1)(B) (other than a difference for which allowance is otherwise provided under this section) that is established to the satisfaction of the administering authority to be wholly or partly due to—

(i) the fact that the quantities in which the subject merchandise is sold or agreed to be sold to the United States are greater than or less than the quantities in which the foreign like product is sold, agreed to be sold, or offered for sale,

(ii) the fact that merchandise described in subparagraph (B) or (C) of § 1677(16) is used in determining normal value, or

(iii) other differences in the circumstances of sale.

(7) Additional adjustments.

(A) Level of trade. The price described in paragraph (1)(B) shall also be increased or decreased to make due allowance for any difference (or lack thereof) between the export price or constructed export price and the price described in paragraph (1)(B) (other than a difference for which allowance is otherwise made under this section) that is shown to be wholly or partly due to a difference in level of trade between the export price or constructed export price and normal value, if the difference in level of trade—

(i) involves the performance of different selling activities; and

(ii) is demonstrated to affect price comparability, based on a pattern of consistent price differences between sales at different levels of trade in the country in which normal value is determined.

In a case described in the preceding sentence, the amount of the adjustment shall be based on the price differences between the two levels of trade in the country in which normal value is determined.

(B) Constructed export price offset. When normal value is established at a level of trade which constitutes a more advanced stage of distribution than the level of trade of the constructed export price, but the data available do not provide an appropriate basis to determine under subparagraph (A)(ii) a level of trade adjustment, normal value shall be reduced by the amount of indirect selling expenses incurred in the country in which normal value is determined on sales of the foreign like product but not more than the amount of such expenses for which a deduction is made under § 1677a(d)(1)(D).

(8) Adjustments to constructed value. Constructed value as determined under subsection (e), may be adjusted, as appropriate, pursuant to this subsection.

(b) Sales at less than cost of production.

(1) Determination; sales disregarded. Whenever the administering authority has reasonable grounds to believe or suspect that sales of the foreign like product under consideration for the determination of normal value have been made at prices which represent less than the cost of production of that product, the administering authority shall determine whether, in fact, such sales were made at less than the cost of production. If the administering authority determines that sales made at less than the cost of production—

(A) have been made within an extended period of time in substantial quantities, and

(B) were not at prices which permit recovery of all costs within a reasonable period of time, such sales may be disregarded in the determination of normal value. Whenever such sales are disregarded, normal value shall be based on the remaining sales of the foreign like product in the ordinary course of trade. If no sales made in the ordinary course of trade remain, the normal value shall be based on the constructed value of the merchandise.

(2) Definitions and special rules. For purposes of this subsection—

(A) Reasonable grounds to believe or suspect. There are reasonable grounds to believe or suspect that sales of the foreign like product were made at prices that are less than the cost of production of the product, if—

(i) in an investigation initiated under § 1673a or a review conducted under § 1675, an interested party described in subparagraph (C), (D), (E), (F), or (G) of § 1677(9) provides information, based upon observed prices or constructed prices or costs, that sales of the foreign like product under consideration for the determination of normal value have been made at prices which represent less than the cost of production of the product; or

(ii) in a review conducted under § 1675 involving a specific exporter, the administering authority disregarded some or all of the exporter's sales pursuant to paragraph (1) in the investigation or if a review has been completed, in the most recently completed review.

(B) Extended period of time. The term "extended period of time" means a period that is normally 1 year, but not less than 6 months.

(C) Substantial quantities. Sales made at prices below the cost of production have been made in substantial quantities if—

(i) the volume of such sales represents 20 percent or more of the volume of sales under consideration for the determination of normal value, or

(ii) the weighted average per unit price of the sales under consideration for the determination of normal value is less than the weighted average per unit cost of production for such sales.

(D) Recovery of costs. If prices which are below the per unit cost of production at the time of sale are above the weighted average per unit cost of production for the period of investigation or review, such prices shall be considered to provide for recovery of costs within a reasonable period of time.

(3) Calculation of cost of production. For purposes of this subtitle, the cost of production shall be an amount equal to the sum of—

(A) the cost of materials and of fabrication or other processing of any kind employed in producing the foreign like product, during a period which would ordinarily permit the production of that foreign like product in the ordinary course of business;

(B) an amount for selling, general, and administrative expenses based on actual data pertaining to production and sales of the foreign like product by the exporter in question; and

(C) the cost of all containers and coverings of whatever nature, and all other expenses incidental to placing the foreign like product in condition packed ready for shipment.

For purposes of subparagraph (A), if the normal value is based on the price of the foreign like product sold for consumption in a country other than the exporting country, the cost of materials shall be determined without regard to any internal tax in the exporting country imposed on such materials or their disposition which are remitted or refunded upon exportation.

(c) Nonmarket economy countries.

(1) In general. If—

(A) the subject merchandise is exported from a nonmarket economy country, and

(B) the administering authority finds that available information does not permit the normal value of the subject merchandise to be determined under subsection (a),

the administering authority shall determine the normal value of the subject merchandise on the basis of the value of the factors of production utilized in producing the merchandise and to which shall be added an amount for general expenses and profit plus the cost of containers, coverings, and other expenses. Except as provided in paragraph (2), the valuation of the factors of production shall be based on the best available information regarding the values of such factors in a market economy country or countries considered to be appropriate by the administering authority.

(2) Exception. If the administering authority finds that the available information is inadequate for purposes of determining the normal value of subject merchandise under paragraph (1), the administering authority shall determine the normal value on the basis of the price at which merchandise that is—

(A) comparable to the subject merchandise, and

(B) produced in one or more market economy countries that are at a level of economic development comparable to that of the nonmarket economy country,

is sold in other countries, including the United States.

(3) Factors of production. For purposes of paragraph (1), the factors of production utilized in producing merchandise include, but are not limited to—

(A) hours of labor required,

(B) quantities of raw materials employed,

(C) amounts of energy and other utilities consumed, and

(D) representative capital cost, including depreciation.

(4) Valuation of factors of production. The administering authority, in valuing factors of production under paragraph (1), shall utilize, to the extent possible, the prices or costs of factors of production in one or more market economy countries that are—

(A) at a level of economic development comparable to that of the nonmarket economy country, and

(B) significant producers of comparable merchandise.

(d) Special rule for certain multinational corporations. Whenever, in the course of an investigation under this title, the administering authority determines that—

(1) subject merchandise exported to the United States is being produced in facilities which are owned or controlled, directly or indirectly, by a person, firm, or corporation which also owns or controls, directly or indirectly, other facilities for the production of the foreign like product which are located in another country or countries,

(2) subsection (a)(1)(C) applies, and

(3) the normal value of the foreign like product produced in one or more of the facilities outside the exporting country is higher than the normal value of the foreign like product produced in the facilities located in the exporting country,

it shall determine the normal value of the subject merchandise by reference to the normal value at which the foreign like product is sold in substantial quantities from one or more facilities outside the exporting country. The administering authority, in making any determination under this paragraph, shall make adjustments for the difference between the cost of production (including taxes, labor, materials, and overhead) of the foreign like product produced in facilities outside the exporting country and costs of production of the foreign like product produced in facilities in the exporting country, if such differences are demonstrated to its satisfaction. For purposes of this subsection, in determining the normal value of the foreign like product produced in a country outside of the exporting country, the administering authority shall determine its price at the time of exportation from the exporting country and shall make any adjustments required by subsection (a) for the cost of all containers and coverings and all other costs, charges, and expenses incident to placing the merchandise in condition packed ready for shipment to the United States by reference to such costs in the exporting country.

(e) Constructed value. For purposes of this title, the constructed value of imported merchandise shall be an amount equal to the sum of—

(1) the cost of materials and fabrication or other processing of any kind employed in producing the merchandise, during a period which would ordinarily permit the production of the merchandise in the ordinary course of business;

(2)(A) the actual amounts incurred and realized by the specific exporter or producer being examined in the investigation or review for selling, general, and administrative expenses, and for profits, in connection with the production and sale of a foreign like product, in the ordinary course of trade, for consumption in the foreign country, or

(B) if actual data are not available with respect to the amounts described in subparagraph (A), then—

(i) the actual amounts incurred and realized by the specific exporter or producer being examined in the investigation or review for selling, general, and administrative expenses, and for profits, in connection with the production and sale, for consumption in the foreign country, of merchandise that is in the same general category of products as the subject merchandise,

(ii) the weighted average of the actual amounts incurred and realized by exporters or producers that are subject to the investigation or review (other than the exporter or producer described in clause (i)) for selling, general, and administrative expenses, and for profits, in connection with the production and sale of a foreign like product, in the ordinary course of trade, for consumption in the foreign country, or

(iii) the amounts incurred and realized for selling, general, and administrative expenses, and for profits, based on any other reasonable method, except that the amount allowed for profit may not exceed the amount normally realized by exporters or producers (other than the exporter or producer described in clause (i)) in connection with the sale, for consumption in the foreign country, of merchandise that is in the same general category of products as the subject merchandise; and

(3) the cost of all containers and coverings of whatever nature, and all other expenses incidental to placing the subject merchandise in condition packed ready for shipment to the United States.

For purposes of paragraph (1), the cost of materials shall be determined without regard to any internal tax in the exporting country imposed on such materials or their disposition which are remitted or refunded upon exportation of the subject merchandise produced from such materials.

(f) Special rules for calculation of cost of production and for calculation of constructed value. For purposes of subsections (b) and (e)—

(1) Costs.

(A) In general. Costs shall normally be calculated based on the records of the exporter or producer of the merchandise, if such records are kept in accordance with the generally accepted accounting principles of the exporting country (or the producing country, where appropriate) and reasonably reflect the costs associated with the production and sale of the merchandise. The administering authority shall consider all available evidence on the proper allocation of costs, including that which is made available by the exporter or producer on a timely basis, if such allocations have been historically used by the exporter or producer, in particular for establishing appropriate amortization and depreciation periods, and allowances for capital expenditures and other development costs.

(B) Nonrecurring costs. Costs shall be adjusted appropriately for those nonrecurring costs that benefit current or future production, or both.

(C) Startup costs.

(i) In general. Costs shall be adjusted appropriately for circumstances in which costs incurred during the time period covered by the investigation or review are affected by startup operations.

(ii) Startup operations. Adjustments shall be made for startup operations only where—

(I) a producer is using new production facilities or producing a new product that requires substantial additional investment, and

(II) production levels are limited by technical factors associated with the initial phase of commercial production.

For purposes of subclause (II), the initial phase of commercial production ends at the end of the startup period. In determining whether commercial production levels have been achieved, the administering authority shall consider factors unrelated to startup operations that might affect the volume of production processed, such as demand, seasonality, or business cycles.

(iii) Adjustment for startup operations. The adjustment for startup operations shall be made by substituting the unit production costs incurred with respect to the merchandise at the end of the startup period for the unit production costs incurred during the startup period. If the startup period extends beyond the period of the investigation or review under this title, the administering authority shall use the most recent cost of production data that it reasonably can obtain, analyze, and verify without delaying the timely completion of the investigation or review. For purposes of this subparagraph, the startup period ends at the point at which the level of commercial production that is characteristic of the merchandise, producer, or industry concerned is achieved.

(2) Transactions disregarded. A transaction directly or indirectly between affiliated persons may be disregarded if, in the case of any element of value required to be considered, the amount representing that element

does not fairly reflect the amount usually reflected in sales of merchandise under consideration in the market under consideration. If a transaction is disregarded under the preceding sentence and no other transactions are available for consideration, the determination of the amount shall be based on the information available as to what the amount would have been if the transaction had occurred between persons who are not affiliated.

(3) Major input rule. If, in the case of a transaction between affiliated persons involving the production by one of such persons of a major input to the merchandise, the administering authority has reasonable grounds to believe or suspect that an amount represented as the value of such input is less than the cost of production of such input, then the administering authority may determine the value of the major input on the basis of the information available regarding such cost of production, if such cost is greater than the amount that would be determined for such input under paragraph (2).

§ 1677b–1. Currency conversion

(a) In general. In an antidumping proceeding under this title, the administering authority shall convert foreign currencies into United States dollars using the exchange rate in effect on the date of sale of the subject merchandise, except that, if it is established that a currency transaction on forward markets is directly linked to an export sale under consideration, the exchange rate specified with respect to such currency in the forward sale agreement shall be used to convert the foreign currency. Fluctuations in exchange rates shall be ignored.

(b) Sustained movement in foreign currency value. In an investigation under subtitle B, if there is a sustained movement in the value of the foreign currency relative to the United States dollar, the administering authority shall allow exporters at least 60 days to adjust their export prices to reflect such sustained movement.

§ 1677c. Hearings

(a) Investigation hearings

(1) In general. Except as provided in paragraph (2), the administering authority and the Commission shall each hold a hearing in the course of an investigation upon the request of any party to the investigation before making a final determination under § 1671d or 1673d.

(2) Exception. If investigations are initiated under subtitle A and subtitle B regarding the same merchandise from the same country within 6 months of each other (but before a final determination is made in either investigation), the holding of a hearing by the Commission in the course of one of the investigations shall be treated as compliance with paragraph (1) for both investigations, unless the Commission considers that special circumstances require that a hearing be held in the course of each of the

investigations. During any investigation regarding which the holding of a hearing is waived under this paragraph, the Commission shall allow any party to submit such additional written comment as it considers relevant.

(b) Procedures. Any hearing required or permitted under this title shall be conducted after notice published in the Federal Register, and a transcript of the hearing shall be prepared and made available to the public. The hearing shall not be subject to the provisions of subchapter II of chapter 5 of title 5, United States Code, or to § 702 of such title.

§ 1677d. Countervailable subsidy practices discovered during a proceeding

If, in the course of a proceeding under this title, the administering authority discovers a practice which appears to be a countervailable subsidy, but was not included in the matters alleged in a countervailing duty petition, or if the administering authority receives notice from the Trade Representative that a subsidy or subsidy program is in violation of Article 8 of the Subsidies Agreement, then the administering authority—

(1) shall include the practice, subsidy, or subsidy program in the proceeding if the practice, subsidy, or subsidy program appears to be a countervailable subsidy with respect to the merchandise which is the subject of the proceeding, or

(2) shall transfer the information (other than confidential information) concerning the practice, subsidy, or subsidy program to the library maintained under § 1677f(a)(1), if the practice, subsidy, or subsidy program appears to be a countervailable subsidy with respect to any other merchandise.

§ 1677e. Determinations on the basis of the facts available

(a) In general. If—

(1) necessary information is not available on the record, or

(2) an interested party or any other person—

(A) withholds information that has been requested by the administering authority or the Commission under this title,

(B) fails to provide such information by the deadlines for submission of the information or in the form and manner requested, subject to subsections (c)(1) and (e) of § 1677m [782 of Act],

(C) significantly impedes a proceeding under this title, or

(D) provides such information but the information cannot be verified as provided in § 1677m(i),

the administering authority and the Commission shall, subject to § 1677(d), use the facts otherwise available in reaching the applicable determination under this title.

(b) Adverse inferences. If the administering authority of the Commission (as the case may be) finds that an interested party has failed to cooperate by not acting to the best of its ability to comply with a request for information from the administering authority or the Commission, the administering authority or the Commission (as the case may be), in reaching the applicable determination under this title, may use an inference that is adverse to the interests of that party in selecting from among the facts otherwise available. Such adverse inference may include reliance on information derived from—

(1) the petition,

(2) a final determination in the investigation under this title,

(3) any previous review under § 1675 or determination under § 1675b [753 of Act], or

(4) any other information placed on the record.

(c) Corroboration of secondary information. When the administering authority or the Commission relies on secondary information rather than on information obtained in the course of an investigation or review, the administering authority or the Commission, as the case may be, shall, to the extent practicable, corroborate that information from independent sources that are reasonably at their disposal.

§ 1677f. Access to information

(a) Information generally made available

(1) Public information function. There shall be established a library of information relating to foreign subsidy practices and countervailing measures. Copies of material in the library shall be made available to the public upon payment of the costs of preparing such copies.

(2) Progress of investigation reports. The administering authority and the Commission shall, from time to time upon request, inform the parties to an investigation of the progress of that investigation.

(3) Ex parte meetings. The administering authority and the Commission shall maintain a record of any ex parte meeting between—

(A) interested parties or other persons providing factual information in connection with a proceeding, and

(B) the person charged with making the determination, or any person charged with making a final recommendation to that person, in connection with that proceeding,

if information relating to that proceeding was presented or discussed at such meeting. The record of such an ex parte meeting shall include the identity of the persons present at the meeting, the date, time, and place of the meeting, and a summary of the matters discussed or submitted. The record of the ex parte meeting shall be included in the record of the proceeding.

(4) Summaries; non-proprietary submissions. The administering authority and the Commission shall disclose—

(A) any proprietary information received in the course of a proceeding if it is disclosed in a form which cannot be associated with, or otherwise be used to identify, operations of a particular person, and

(B) any information submitted in connection with a proceeding which is not designated as proprietary by the person submitting it.

(b) Proprietary Information.

(1) Proprietary status maintained.

(A) In general. Except as provided in subsection (a)(4)(A) and subsection (c), information submitted to the administering authority or the Commission which is designated as proprietary by the person submitting the information shall not be disclosed to any person without the consent of the person submitting the information, other than—

(i) to an officer or employee of the administering authority or the Commission who is directly concerned with carrying out the investigation in connection with which the information is submitted or any review under this title covering the same subject merchandise, or

(ii) to an officer or employee of the United States Customs Service who is directly involved in conducting an investigation regarding fraud under this title.

(B) Additional requirements. The administering authority and the Commission shall require that information for which proprietary treatment is requested be accompanied by—

(i) either—

(I) a non-proprietary summary in sufficient detail to permit a reasonable understanding of the substance of the information submitted in confidence, or

(II) a statement that the information is not susceptible to summary accompanied by a statement of the reasons in support of the contention, and

(ii) either—

(I) a statement which permits the administering authority or the Commission to release under administrative protective order, in accordance with subsection (c), the information submitted in confidence, or

(II) a statement to the administering authority or the Commission that the business proprietary information is of a type that should not be released under administrative protective order.

(2) Unwarranted designation. If the administering authority or the Commission determines, on the basis of the nature and extent of the information or its availability from public sources, that designation of any information as proprietary is unwarranted, then it shall notify the person who submitted it and ask for an explanation of the reasons for the designation. Unless that person persuades the administering authority or the Commission that the designation is warranted, or withdraws the designation, the administering authority or the Commission, as the case may be, shall return it to the party submitting it. In a case in which the administering authority or the Commission returns the information to the person submitting it, the person may thereafter submit other material concerning the subject matter of the returned information if the submission is made within the time otherwise provided for submitting such material.

(3) Section 1675 reviews. Notwithstanding the provisions of paragraph (1), information submitted to the administering authority or the Commission in connection with a review under § 1675(b) or 1675(c) which is designated as proprietary by the person submitting the information may, if the review results in the revocation of an order or finding (or termination of a suspended investigation) under § 1675(d) be used by the agency to which the information was originally submitted in any investigation initiated within 2 years after the date of the revocation or termination pursuant to a petition covering the same subject merchandise.

(c) Limited disclosure of certain proprietary information under protective order.

(1) Disclosure by administering authority or commission.

(A) In general. Upon receipt of an application (before or after receipt of the information requested) which describes in general terms the information requested and sets forth the reasons for the request, the administering authority or the Commission shall make all business proprietary information presented to, or obtained by it, during a proceeding (except privileged information, classified information, and specific information of a type for which there is a clear and compelling need to withhold from disclosure) available to interested parties who are parties to the proceeding under a protective order described in subparagraph (B), regardless of when the information is submitted during a proceeding. Customer names obtained during any investigation which requires a determination under § 1671d(b) or § 1673d(b) may not be disclosed by the administering authority under protective order until either an order is published under § 1671e(a) or 1673e(a) as a result of the investigation or the investigation is suspended or terminated. The Commission may delay disclosure of customer names under protective order during any such investigation until a reasonable time prior to any hearing provided under § 1677c.

(B) Protective order. The protective order under which information is made available shall contain such requirements as the administering authority or the Commission may determine by regulation to be appropriate. The administering authority and the Commission shall provide by regulation for such sanctions as the administering authority and the Commission determine to be appropriate, including disbarment from practice before the agency.

(C) Time limitation on determinations. The administering authority or the Commission, as the case may be, shall determine whether to make information available under this paragraph—

(i) not later than 14 days (7 days if the submission pertains to a proceeding under § 1671b(a) or 1673b(a)) after the date on which the information is submitted, or

(ii) if—

(I) the person that submitted the information raises objection to its release, or

(II) the information is unusually voluminous or complex, not later than 30 days (10 days if the submission pertains to a proceeding under section § 1671b(a) or 1673b(a)) after the date on which the information is submitted.

(D) Availability after determination. If the determination under subparagraph (C) is affirmative, then—

(i) the business proprietary information submitted to the administering authority or the Commission on or before the date of the determination shall be made available, subject to the terms and conditions of the protective order, on such date; and

(ii) the business proprietary information submitted to the administering authority or the Commission after the date of the determination shall be served as required by subsection (d).

(E) Failure to disclose. If a person submitting information to the administering authority refuses to disclose business proprietary information which the administering authority determines should be released under a protective order described in subparagraph (B), the administering authority shall return the information, and any nonconfidential summary thereof, to the person submitting the information and summary and shall not consider either.

(2) Disclosure under court order. If the administering authority denies a request for information under paragraph (1), then application may be made to the United States Customs Court for an order directing the administering authority or the Commission to make the information available. After notification of all parties to the investigation and after an opportunity for a hearing on the record, the court may issue an order, under such conditions as the court deems appropriate, which shall not have the effect of stopping or suspending the investigation, directing the administering authority or the Commission to make all or a portion of the requested information described in the preceding sentence available under a protective order and setting forth sanctions for violation of such order if the court finds that, under the standards applicable in proceedings of the court, such an order is warranted, and that—

(A) the administering authority or the Commission has denied access to the information under subsection (b)(1),

(B) the person on whose behalf the information is requested is an interested party who is a party to the investigation in connection with which the information was obtained or developed, and

(C) the party which submitted the information to which the request relates has been notified, in advance of the hearing, of the request made under this section and of its right to appear and be heard.

(d) Service. Any party submitting written information, including business proprietary information, to the administering authority or the Commission during a proceeding shall, at the same time, serve the information upon all interested parties who are parties to the proceeding, if the information is covered by a protective order. The administering authority or the Commission shall not accept any such information that is not accompanied by a certificate of service and a copy of the protective order version of the document containing the information. Business proprietary information shall only be served upon interested parties who are parties to the proceeding that are subject to protective order; however, a nonconfidential summary thereof shall be served upon all other interested parties who are parties to the proceeding.

(f) Disclosure of proprietary information under protective orders issued pursuant to the North American Free Trade Agreement or the United States-Canada Agreement.

(1) Issuance of protective orders.

(A) In general. If binational panel review of a determination under this subchapter is requested pursuant to article 1904 of the NAFTA or the United States-Canada Agreement, or an extraordinary challenge committee is convened under Annex 1904.13 of the NAFTA or the United States-Canada Agreement, the administering authority or the Commission, as appropriate, may make available to authorized persons, under a protective order described in paragraph (2), a copy of all proprietary material in the administrative record made during the proceeding in question. If the administering authority or the Commission claims a privilege as to a document or portion of a document in the administrative record of the proceeding in question and a binational panel or extraordinary challenge committee finds that in camera inspection or limited disclosure of that document or portion thereof is required by United States law, the administering authority or the Commission, as appropriate, may restrict access to such document or portion thereof to the authorized persons identified by the panel or committee as requiring access and may require such persons to obtain access under a protective order described in paragraph (2).

(B) Authorized persons. For purposes of this subsection, the term "authorized persons" means—

(i) the members of, and the appropriate staff of, the binational panel or the extraordinary challenge committee, as the case may be, and the Secretariat,

(ii) counsel for parties to such panel or committee proceeding, and employees, and persons under the direction and control, of such counsel,

(iii) any officer or employee of the United States Government designated by the administering authority or the Commission, as appropriate, to whom disclosure is necessary in order to make recommendations to the Trade Representative regarding the convening of extraordinary challenge committees under chapter 19 of the NAFTA or the Agreement, and

(iv) any officer or employee of the Government of a free trade area country (as defined in § 1516a(f)(10) of this title) designated by an authorized agency of such country to whom disclosure is necessary in order to make decisions regarding the convening of extraordinary challenge committees under chapter 19 of the NAFTA or the Agreement.

(C) Review. A decision concerning the disclosure or nondisclosure of material under protective order by the administering authority or the Commission shall not be subject to judicial review, and no court of the United States shall have power or jurisdiction to review such decision on any question of law or fact by an action in the nature of mandamus or otherwise.

(2) Contents of protective order. Each protective order issued under this subsection shall be in such form and contain such requirements as the administering authority or the Commission may determine by regulation to be appropriate. The administering authority and the Commission shall ensure that regulations issued pursuant to this paragraph shall be designed to provide an opportunity for participation in the binational panel proceeding, including any extraordinary challenge, equivalent to that available for judicial review of determinations by the administering authority or the Commission that are not subject to review by a binational panel.

(3) Prohibited acts. It is unlawful for any person to violate, to induce the violation of, or knowingly to receive information the receipt of which constitutes a violation of, any provision of a protective order issued under this subsection or to violate, to induce the violation of, or knowingly to receive information the receipt of which constitutes a violation of, any provision of an undertaking entered into with an authorized agency of a free trade area country (as defined in § 1516a(f)(10) of this title) to protect proprietary material during binational panel or extraordinary challenge committee review pursuant to article 1904 of the NAFTA or the United States-Canada Agreement.

(4) Sanctions for violation of protective orders. Any person, except a judge appointed to a binational panel or an extraordinary challenge committee under section 402, who is found by the administering authority or the Commission, as appropriate, after notice and an opportunity for a hearing in accordance with section 554 of Title 5 to have committed an act prohibited by paragraph (3) shall be liable to the United States for a civil penalty and shall be subject to such other administrative sanctions, including, but not limited to, debarment from practice before the administering authority or the Commission, as the administering authority or the Commission determines to be appropriate. The amount of the civil penalty shall not exceed $100,000 for each violation. Each day of a continuing violation shall constitute a separate violation. The amount of such civil penalty and other sanctions shall be assessed by the administering authority or the Commission by written notice, except that assessment shall be made by the administering authority for violation, inducement of a violation or receipt of information with reason to know that such information was disclosed in violation, of an undertaking entered into by any person with an authorized agency of a free trade area country (as defined in § 1516a(f)(10) of this title).

(5) Review of sanctions. Any person against whom sanctions are imposed under paragraph (4) may obtain review of such sanctions by filing a notice of appeal in the United States Court of International Trade within 30 days from the date of the order imposing the sanction and by simultaneously sending a copy of such notice by certified mail to the

administering authority or the Commission, as appropriate. The administering authority or the Commission shall promptly file in such court a certified copy of the record upon which such violation was found or such sanction imposed, as provided in section 2112 of title 28, United States Code. The findings and order of the administering authority or the Commission shall be set aside by the court only if the court finds that such findings and order are not supported by substantial evidence, as provided in section 706(2) of title 5, United States Code.

(6) Enforcement of sanctions. If any person fails to pay an assessment of a civil penalty or to comply with other administrative sanctions after the order imposing such sanctions becomes a final and unappealable order, or after the United States Court of International Trade has entered final judgment in favor of the administering authority or the Commission, an action may be filed in such court to enforce the sanctions. In such action, the validity and appropriateness of the final order imposing the sanctions shall not be subject to review.

(7) Testimony and production of papers.

(A) Authority to obtain information. For the purpose of conducting any hearing and carrying out other functions and duties under this subsection, the administering authority and the Commission, or their duly authorized agents—

(i) shall have access to and the right to copy any pertinent document, paper, or record in the possession of any individual, partnership, corporation, association, organization, or other entity,

(ii) may summon witnesses, take testimony, and administer oaths,

(iii) and may require any individual or entity to produce pertinent documents, books, or records.

Any member of the Commission, and any person so designated by the administering authority, may sign subpoenas, and members and agents of the administering authority and the Commission, when authorized by the administering authority or the Commission, as appropriate, may administer oaths and affirmations, examine witnesses, take testimony, and receive evidence.

(B) Witnesses and evidence. The attendance of witnesses who are authorized to be summoned, and the production of documentary evidence authorized to be ordered, under subparagraph (A) may be required from any place in the United States at any designated place of hearing. In the case of disobedience to a subpoena issued under subparagraph (A), an action may be filed in any district or territorial court of the United States to require the attendance and testimony of witnesses and the production of documentary evidence. Such court, within the jurisdiction of which such inquiry is carried on, may, in case of contumacy or refusal to obey a subpoena issued to any individual, partnership, corporation, association, organization or other entity, issue any order requiring such individual or entity to appear before the administering authority or the Commission, or to produce documentary evidence if so ordered or to give evidence concerning the matter in question. Any failure to obey such order of the court may be punished by the court as a contempt thereof.

(C) Mandamus. Any court referred to in subparagraph (B) shall have jurisdiction to issue writs of mandamus commanding compliance with the provisions of this subsection or any order of the administering authority or the Commission made in pursuance thereof.

(D) Depositions. For purposes of carrying out any functions or duties under this subsection, the administering authority or the Commission may order testimony to be taken by deposition. Such deposition may be taken before any person designated by the administering authority or Commission and having power to administer oaths. Such testimony shall be reduced to writing by the person taking the deposition, or under the direction of such person, and shall then be subscribed by the deponent. Any individual, partnership, corporation, association, organization or other entity may be compelled to appear and depose and to produce documentary evidence in the same manner as witnesses may be compelled to appear and testify and produce documentary evidence before the administering authority or Commission, as provided in this paragraph.

(E) Fees and mileage of witnesses. Witnesses summoned before the administering authority or the Commission shall be paid the same fees and mileage that are paid witnesses in the courts of the United States.

* * *

§ 1677f–1. Sampling and averaging; determination of weighted average dumping margin and countervailable subsidy rate

(a) In general. For purposes of determining the export price (or constructed export price) under § 1677a or the normal value under § 1677b, and in carrying out reviews under § 1675, the administering authority may—

(1) use averaging and statistically valid samples, if there is a significant volume of sales of the subject merchandise or a significant number or types of products, and

(2) decline to take into account adjustments which are insignificant in relation to the price or value of the merchandise.

(b) Selection of averages and samples. The authority to select averages and statistically valid samples shall rest exclusively with the administering authority. The administering authority shall, to the greatest extent possible, consult with the exporters and producers regarding the method to be used to select exporters, producers, or types of products under this section.

(c) Determination of dumping margin.

(1) General rule. In determining weighted average dumping margins under § 1673b(d), 1673d(c), or 1675(a), the administering authority shall determine the individual weighted average dumping margin for each known exporter and producer of the subject merchandise.

(2) Exception. If it is not practicable to make individual weighted average dumping margin determinations under paragraph (1) because of the large number of exporters or producers involved in the investigation or review, the administering authority may determine the weighted average dumping margins for a reasonable number of exporters or producers by limiting its examination to—

(A) a sample of exporters, producers, or types of products that is statistically valid based on the information available to the administering authority at the time of selection, or

(B) exporters and producers accounting for the largest volume of the subject merchandise from the exporting country that can be reasonably examined.

(d) Determination of less than fair value.

(1) Investigations.

(A) In general. In an investigation under subtitle B, the administering authority shall determine whether the subject merchandise is being sold in the United States at less than fair value—

(i) by comparing the weighted average of the normal values to the weighted average of the export prices (and constructed export prices) for comparable merchandise, or

(ii) by comparing the normal values of individual transactions to the export prices (or constructed export prices) of individual transactions for comparable merchandise.

(B) Exception. The administering authority may determine whether the subject merchandise is being sold in the United States at less than fair value by comparing the weighted average of the normal values to the export prices (or constructed export prices) of individual transactions for comparable merchandise, if—

(i) there is a pattern of export prices (or constructed export prices) for comparable merchandise that differ significantly among purchasers, regions, or periods of time, and

(ii) the administering authority explains why such differences cannot be taken into account using a method described in paragraph (1)(A)(i) or (ii).

(2) Reviews. In a review under § 1675, when comparing export prices (or constructed export prices) of individual transactions to the weighted average price of sales of the foreign like product, the administering authority shall limit its averaging of prices to a period not exceeding the calendar month that corresponds most closely to the calendar month of the individual export sale.

(e) Determination of countervailable subsidy rate.

(1) General rule. In determining countervailable subsidy rates under § 1671b(d), 1671d(c), or 1675(a), the administering authority shall determine an individual countervailable subsidy rate for each known exporter or producer of the subject merchandise.

(2) Exception. If the administering authority determines that it is not practicable to determine individual countervailable subsidy rates under paragraph (1) because of the large number of exporters or producers involved in the investigation or review, the administering authority may—

(A) determine individual countervailable subsidy rates for a reasonable number of exporters or producers by limiting its examination to—

(i) a sample of exporters or producers that the administering authority determines is statistically valid based on the information available to the administering authority at the time of selection, or

(ii) exporters and producers accounting for the largest volume of the subject merchandise from the exporting country that the administering authority determines can be reasonably examined; or

(B) determine a single country-wide subsidy rate to be applied to all exporters and producers.

The individual countervailable subsidy rates determined under subparagraph (A) shall be used to determine the all-others rate under § 1671d(c)(5).

(f) Adjustment of antidumping duty in certain proceedings relating to imports from nonmarket economy countries

(1) *In general*

If the administering authority determines, with respect to a class or kind of merchandise from a nonmarket economy country for which an antidumping duty is determined using normal value pursuant to section 1677b(c) of this title, that--

(A) pursuant to section 1671(a)(1) of this title, a countervailable subsidy (other than an export subsidy referred to in section 1677a(c)(1)(C) of this title) has been provided with respect to the class or kind of merchandise,

(B) such countervail able subsidy has been demonstrated to have reduced the average price of imports of the class or kind of merchandise during the relevant period, and

(C) the administering authority can reasonably estimate the extent to which the countervailable subsidy referred to in subparagraph (B), in combination with the use of normal value determined pursuant to section 1677b(c) of this title, has increased the weighted average dumping margin for the class or kind of merchandise, the administering authority shall, except as provided in paragraph (2), reduce the antidumping duty by the amount of the increase in the weighted average dumping margin estimated by the administering authority under subparagraph (C).

(2) *Maximum reduction in antidumping duty*

The administering authority may not reduce the antidumping duty applicable to a class or kind of merchandise from a nonmarket economy country under this subsection by more than the portion of the countervailing duty rate attributable to a countervailable subsidy that is provided with respect to the class or kind of merchandise and that meets the conditions described in subparagraphs (A), (B), and (C) of paragraph (1).

* * *

§ 1677i. Downstream product monitoring

(a) Petition requesting monitoring

(1) In general. A domestic producer of an article that is like a component part or a downstream product may petition the administering authority to designate a downstream product for monitoring under subsection (b). The petition shall specify—

(A) the downstream product,

(B) the component product incorporated into such downstream product, and

(C) the reasons for suspecting that the imposition of antidumping or countervailing duties has resulted in a diversion of exports of the component part into increased production and exportation to the United States of such downstream product.

* * *

(d) Definitions. For purposes of this section—

(1) The term "component part" means any imported article that—

(A) during the 5–year period ending on the date on which the petition is filed under subsection (a), has been subject to—

(i) a countervailing or antidumping duty order issued under this title or § 1303 that requires the deposit of estimated countervailing or antidumping duties imposed at a rate of at least 15 percent ad valorem, or

(ii) an agreement entered into under § 1671c, 1673c, or § 1303 after a preliminary affirmative determination under § 1671b(b), § 1673b(b)(1) or § 1303 was made by the administering authority which included a determination that the estimated net countervailable subsidy was at least 15 percent ad valorem or that the estimated average amount by which the nominal value exceeded the export price (or the constructed export price) was at least 15 percent ad valorem, and

(B) because of its inherent characteristics, is routinely used as a major part, component, assembly, subassembly, or material in a downstream product.

(2) The term "downstream product" means any manufactured article—

(A) which is imported into the United States, and

(B) into which is incorporated any component part.

§ 1677j. Prevention of circumvention of antidumping and countervailing duty orders

(a) Merchandise completed or assembled in the United States.

(1) In general. If—

(A) merchandise sold in the United States is of the same class or kind as any other merchandise that is the subject of—

(i) an antidumping duty order issued under § 1673e,

(ii) a finding issued under the Antidumping Act, 1921, or

(iii) a countervailing duty order issued under § 1671e or § 1303,

(B) such merchandise sold in the United States is completed or assembled in the United States from parts or components produced in the foreign country with respect to which such order or finding applies,

(C) the process of assembly or completion in the United States is minor or insignificant, and

(D) the value of the parts or components referred to in subparagraph (B) is a significant portion of the total value of the merchandise,

the administering authority, after taking into account any advice provided by the Commission under subsection (e), may include within the scope of such order or finding the imported parts or components referred to in subparagraph (B) that are used in the completion or assembly of the merchandise in the United States at any time such order or finding is in effect.

(2) Determination of whether process is minor or insignificant. In determining whether the process of assembly or completion is minor or insignificant under paragraph (1)(C), the administering authority shall take into account—

(A) the level of investment in the United States,

(B) the level of research and development in the United States,

(C) the nature of the production process in the United States,

(D) the extent of production facilities in the United States, and

(E) whether the value of the processing performed in the United States represents a small proportion of the value of the merchandise sold in the United States.

(3) Factors to consider. In determining whether to include parts or components in a countervailing or antidumping duty order or finding under paragraph (1), the administering authority shall take into account such factors as—

(A) the pattern of trade, including sourcing patterns,

(B) whether the manufacturer or exporter of the parts or components is affiliated with the person who assembles or completes the merchandise sold in the United States from the parts or components produced in the foreign country with respect to which the order or finding described in paragraph (1) applies, and

(C) whether imports into the United States of the parts or components produced in such foreign country have increased after the initiation of the investigation which resulted in the issuance of such order or finding.

(b) Merchandise completed or assembled in other foreign countries.

(1) In general. If—

(A) merchandise imported into the United States is of the same class or kind as any merchandise produced in a foreign country that is the subject of—

(i) an antidumping duty order issued under § 1673e,

(ii) a finding issued under the Antidumping Act, 1921, or

(iii) a countervailing duty order issued under § 1671e or § 1303,

(B) before importation into the United States, such imported merchandise is completed or assembled in another foreign country from merchandise which—

(i) is subject to such order or finding, or

(ii) is produced in the foreign country with respect to which such order or finding applies,

(C) the process of assembly or completion in the foreign country referred to in subparagraph (B) is minor or insignificant,

(D) the value of the merchandise produced in the foreign country to which the antidumping duty order applies is a significant portion of the total value of the merchandise exported to the United States, and

(E) the administering authority determines that action is appropriate under this paragraph to prevent evasion of such order or finding,

the administering authority, after taking into account any advice provided by the Commission under subsection (e), may include such imported merchandise within the scope of such order or finding at any time such order or finding is in effect.

(2) Determination of whether process is minor or insignificant. In determining whether the process of assembly or completion is minor or insignificant under paragraph (1)(C), the administering authority shall take into account—

(A) the level of investment in the foreign country,

(B) the level or research and development in the foreign country,

(C) the nature of the production process in the foreign country,

(D) the extent of production facilities in the foreign country, and

(E) whether the value of the processing performed in the foreign country represents a small proportion of the value of the merchandise imported into the United States.

(3) Factors to consider. In determining whether to include merchandise assembled or completed in a foreign country in a countervailing duty order

or an antidumping duty order or finding under paragraph (1), the administering authority shall take into account such factors as—

(A) the pattern of trade, including sourcing patterns,

(B) whether the manufacturer or exporter of the merchandise described in paragraph (1)(B) is affiliated with the person who uses the merchandise described in paragraph (1)(B) to assemble or complete in the foreign country the merchandise that is subsequently imported into the United States, and

(C) whether imports into the foreign country of the merchandise described in paragraph (1)(B) have increased after the initiation of the investigation which resulted in the issuance of such order or finding.

(c) Minor alterations of merchandise

(1) In general. The class or kind of merchandise subject to—

(A) an investigation under this title,

(B) an antidumping duty order issued under § 1673e,

(C) a finding issued under the Antidumping Act, 1921, or

(D) a countervailing duty order issued under § 1671e or § 1303,

shall include articles altered in form or appearance in minor respects (including raw agricultural products that have undergone minor processing), whether or not included in the same tariff classification.

(2) Exception. Paragraph (1) shall not apply with respect to altered merchandise if the administering authority determines that it would be unnecessary to consider the altered merchandise within the scope of the investigation, order, or finding.

(d) Later-developed merchandise

(1) In general. For purposes of determining whether merchandise developed after an investigation is initiated under this title or § 1303 (hereafter in this paragraph referred to as the "later-developed merchandise") is within the scope of an outstanding antidumping or countervailing duty order issued under this title or § 1303 as a result of such investigation, the administering authority shall consider whether—

(A) the later-developed merchandise has the same general physical characteristics as the merchandise with respect to which the order was originally issued (hereafter in this paragraph referred to as the "earlier product"),

(B) the expectations of the ultimate purchasers of the later-developed merchandise are the same as for the earlier product,

(C) the ultimate use of the earlier product and the later-developed merchandise are the same,

(D) the later-developed merchandise is sold through the same channels of trade as the earlier product, and

(E) the later-developed merchandise is advertised and displayed in a manner similar to the earlier product.

The administering authority shall take into account any advice provided by the Commission under subsection (e) before making a determination under this subparagraph.

(2) Exclusion from orders. The administering authority may not exclude a later-developed merchandise from a countervailing or antidumping duty order merely because the merchandise—

(A) is classified under a tariff classification other than that identified in the petition or the administering authority's prior notices during the proceeding, or

(B) permits the purchaser to perform additional functions, unless such additional functions constitute the primary use of the merchandise and the cost of the additional functions constitute more than a significant proportion of the total cost of production of the merchandise.

* * *

§ 1677k. Antidumping petitions by third countries

(a) Filing of petition. The government of a WTO member may file with the Trade Representative a petition requesting that an investigation be conducted to determine if—

(1) imports from another country are being sold in the United States at less than fair value, and

(2) an industry in the petitioning country is materially injured by reason of those imports.

(b) Initiation. The Trade Representative, after consultation with the administering authority and the Commission and obtaining the approval of the WTO Council for Trade in Goods, shall determine whether to initiate an investigation described in subsection (a).

(c) Determinations. Upon initiation of an investigation under this section, the Trade Representative shall request the following determinations be made according to substantive and procedural requirements specified by the Trade Representative, notwithstanding any other provision of this title:

(1) The administering authority shall determine whether imports into the United States of the subject merchandise are being sold at less than fair value.

(2) The Commission shall determine whether an industry in the petitioning country is materially injured by reason of imports of the subject merchandise into the United States.

DOCUMENT 28

TRADE ACT OF 1974

■ ■ ■

Pub.L. 93–618, Approved January 3, 1975, 19 U.S.C. §§ 2101–2487, 88 Stat. 1978

The Trade Act of 1974 has been amended, particularly by the Trade Agreements Act of 1979, the Trade and Tariff Act of 1984, the Omnibus Trade and Competitiveness Act of 1988, the Customs and Trade Act of 1990, the North American Free Trade Agreement Implementation Act of 1993, and the Uruguay Round Agreements Act of 1994. These amendments, as well as more detailed amendments in 2004, 2009, and 2011, have been incorporated into the selected provisions included below.

Table of Contents

(Selected Provisions Only)

(Trade Act Section Numbers)

19 U.S.C. § 2102

Sec. 2. Statement of Purposes

The purposes of this Act are, through trade agreements affording mutual benefits—

(1) to foster the economic growth of and full employment in the United States and to strengthen economic relations between the United States and foreign countries through open and nondiscriminatory world trade;

(2) to harmonize, reduce, and eliminate barriers to trade on a basis which assures substantially equivalent competitive opportunities for the commerce of the United States;

(3) to establish fairness and equity in international trading relations, including reform of the General Agreement on Tariffs and Trade;

(4) to provide adequate procedures to safeguard American industry and labor against unfair or injurious import competition, and to assist industries, firms, workers, and communities to adjust to changes in international trade flows;

(5) to open up market opportunities for United States commerce in nonmarket economies; and

(6) to provide fair and reasonable access to products of less developed countries in the United States market.

TITLE I. NEGOTIATING AND OTHER AUTHORITY

CHAPTER 1. RATES OF DUTY AND OTHER TRADE BARRIERS

* * *

CHAPTER 2. OTHER AUTHORITY

* * *

CHAPTER 3. HEARINGS AND ADVICE CONCERNING NEGOTIATIONS

* * *

CHAPTER 4. OFFICE OF THE UNITED STATES TRADE REPRESENTATIVE

19 U.S.C. § 2171

Sec. 141. Structure, functions, powers, and personnel

(a) Establishment within Executive Office of the President. There is established within the Executive Office of the President the Office of United States Trade Representative (hereinafter in this section referred to as the "Office").

(b) United States Trade Representative; Deputy United States Trade Representatives.

(1) The Office shall be headed by the United States Trade Representative who shall be appointed by the President, by and with the advice and consent of the Senate. As an exercise of the rulemaking power of the Senate, any nomination of the United States Trade Representative submitted to the Senate for confirmation, and referred to a committee, shall be referred to the Committee on Finance. The United States Trade Representative shall hold office at the pleasure of the President, shall be entitled to receive the same allowances as a chief of mission, and shall have the rank of Ambassador Extraordinary and Plenipotentiary.

(2) There shall be in the Office three Deputy United States Trade Representatives and one Chief Agricultural Negotiator who shall be appointed by the President, by and with the advice and consent of the Senate. As an exercise of the rulemaking power of the Senate, any nomination of a Deputy United States Trade Representative or the Chief Agricultural Negotiator submitted to the Senate for its advice and consent, and referred to a committee, shall be referred to the Committee on Finance. Each Deputy United States Trade Representative and the Chief Agricultural Negotiator shall hold office at the pleasure of the President and shall have the rank of Ambassador.

(3) A person who has directly represented, aided, or advised a foreign entity (as defined by section 207(f)(3) of title 18, United States Code) in any trade negotiation, or trade dispute, with the United States may not be appointed as United States Trade Representative or as a Deputy United States Trade Representative.

(c) Duties of United States Trade Representative and Deputy United States Trade Representatives.

(1) The United States Trade Representative shall—

(A) have primary responsibility for developing, and for coordinating the implementation of, United States international trade policy, including commodity matters, and, to the extent they are related to international trade policy, direct investment matters;

(B) serve as the principal advisor to the President on international trade policy and shall advise the President on the impact of other policies of the United States Government on international trade;

(C) have lead responsibility for the conduct of, and shall be the chief representative of the United States for, international trade negotiations, including all negotiations on any matter considered under the auspices of the World Trade Organization, commodity and direct investment negotiations, in which the United States participates;

(D) issue and coordinate policy guidance to departments and agencies on basic issues of policy and interpretation arising in the exercise of international trade functions, including any matter considered under the auspices of the World Trade Organization, to the extent necessary to assure the coordination of international trade policy and consistent with any other law;

(E) act as the principal spokesman of the President on international trade;

(F) report directly to the President and the Congress regarding, and be responsible to the President and the Congress for the administration of, trade agreements programs;

(G) advise the President and Congress with respect to nontariff barriers to international trade, international commodity agreements, and other matters which are related to the trade agreements programs;

(H) be responsible for making reports to Congress with respect to matters referred to in subparagraphs (C) and (F);

(I) be chairman of the interagency trade organization established under section 242(a) of the Trade Expansion Act of 1962 [19 U.S.C. § 1872(a)], and shall consult with and be advised by such organization in the performance of his functions; and

(J) in addition to those functions that are delegated to the United States Trade Representative as of the date of the enactment of the Omnibus Trade and Competitiveness Act of 1988 [enacted Aug. 23, 1988], be responsible for such other functions as the President may direct.

(2) It is the sense of Congress that the United States Trade Representative should—

(A) be the senior representative on any body that the President may establish for the purpose of providing to the President advice on overall economic policies in which international trade matters predominate; and

(B) be included as a participant in all economic summit and other international meetings at which international trade is a major topic.

(3) The United States Trade Representative may—

(A) delegate any of his functions, powers, and duties to such officers and employees of the Office as he may designate; and

(B) authorize such successive redelegations of such functions, powers, and duties to such officers and employees of the Office as he may deem appropriate.

(4) Each Deputy United States Trade Representative shall have as his principal function the conduct of trade negotiations under this Act and shall have such other functions as the United States Trade Representative may direct.

(5) The principal function of the Chief Agricultural Negotiator shall be to conduct trade negotiations and to enforce trade agreements relating to United States agricultural products and services. The Chief Agricultural Negotiator shall be a vigorous advocate on behalf of United States agricultural interests. The Chief Agricultural Negotiator shall perform such other functions as the United States Trade Representative may direct.

(d) Unfair trade practices; additional duties of Representative; advisory committee; definition.

(1) In carrying out subsection (c) with respect to unfair trade practices, the United States Trade Representative shall—

(A) coordinate the application of interagency resources to specific unfair trade practice cases;

(B) identify, and refer to the appropriate Federal department or agency for consideration with respect to action, each act, policy, or practice referred to in the report required under section 181(b) [19 U.S.C. § 2241(b)], or otherwise known to the United States Trade Representative on the basis of other available information, that may be an unfair trade practice that either—

(i) is considered to be inconsistent with the provisions of any trade agreement and has a significant adverse impact on United States commerce, or

(ii) has a significant adverse impact on domestic firms or industries that are either too small or financially weak to initiate proceedings under the trade laws;

(C) identify practices having a significant adverse impact on United States commerce that the attainment of United States negotiating objectives would eliminate; and

(D) identify, on a biennial basis, those United States Government policies and practices that, if engaged in by a foreign government, might constitute unfair trade practices under United States law.

(2) For purposes of carrying out paragraph (1), the United States Trade Representative shall be assisted by an interagency unfair trade practices advisory committee composed of the Trade Representative, who shall chair the committee, and senior representatives of the following agencies, appointed by the respective heads of those agencies:

(A) The Bureau of Economics and Business Affairs of the Department of State.

(B) The United States and Foreign Commercial Services of the Department of Commerce.

(C) The International Trade Administration (other than the United States and Foreign Commercial Service) of the Department of Commerce.

(D) The Foreign Agricultural Service of the Department of Agriculture.

The United States Trade Representative may also request the advice of the United States International Trade Commission regarding the carrying out of paragraph (1).

(3) For purposes of this subsection, the term "unfair trade practice" means any act, policy, or practice that—

(A) may be a subsidy with respect to which countervailing duties may be imposed under subtitle A of title VII [*19 U.S.C. § 1671 et seq.*];

(B) may result in the sale or likely sale of foreign merchandise with respect to which antidumping duties may be imposed under subtitle B of title VII [*19 U.S.C. § 1673 et seq.*];

(C) may be either an unfair method of competition, or an unfair act in the importation of articles into the United States, that is unlawful under section 337 [*19 U.S.C. § 1337*]; or

(D) may be an act, policy, or practice of a kind with respect to which action may be taken under title III of the Trade Act of 1974 [*19 U.S.C. § 2411 et seq.*].

* * *

CHAPTER 5. CONGRESSIONAL PROCEDURES WITH RESPECT TO PRESIDENTIAL ACTIONS

19 U.S.C. § 2191

Sec. 151. Bills implementing trade agreements on nontariff barriers and resolutions approving commercial agreements with Communist countries

(a) Rules of House of Representatives and Senate.

This section and sections 2192 and 2193 of this title are enacted by the Congress—

(1) as an exercise of the rulemaking power of the House of Representatives and the Senate, respectively, and as such they are deemed a part of the rules of each House, respectively, but applicable only with respect to the procedure to be followed in that House in the case of implementing bills described in subsection (b)(1) of this section, implementing revenue bills described in subsection (b)(2) of this section, approval resolutions described in subsection (b)(3) of this section, and resolutions described in sections 2192(a) and 2193(a) of this title; and they supersede other rules only to the extent that they are inconsistent therewith; and

(2) with full recognition of the constitutional right of either House to change the rules (so far as relating to the procedure of that House) at any time, in the same manner and to the same extent as in the case of any other rule of that House.

(b) Definitions

For purposes of this section—

(1) The term "implementing bill" means only a bill of either House of Congress which is introduced as provided in subsection (c) of this section with respect to one or more trade agreements, or with respect to an extension described in section 3572(c)(3) of this title, submitted to the House of Representatives and the Senate under section 2112 of this title, section 3572 of this title, or section 3805(a)(1) of this title and which contains—

(A) a provision approving such trade agreement or agreements or such extension,

(B) a provision approving the statement of administrative action (if any) proposed to implement such trade agreement or agreements, and

(C) if changes in existing laws or new statutory authority is required to implement such trade agreement or agreements or such extension, provisions, necessary or appropriate to implement such trade agreement or agreements or such extension, either repealing or amending existing laws or providing new statutory authority.

(2) The term "implementing revenue bill or resolution" means an implementing bill, or approval resolution, which contains one or more revenue measures by reason of which it must originate in the House of Representatives.

(3) The term "approval resolution" means only a joint resolution of the two Houses of the Congress, the matter after the resolving clause of which is as follows: "That the Congress approves the extension of nondiscriminatory treatment with respect to the products of ______ transmitted by the President to the Congress on ______.", the first blank space being filled with the name of the country involved and the second blank space being filled with the appropriate date.

(c) Introduction and referral

(1) On the day on which a trade agreement or extension is submitted to the House of Representatives and the Senate under section 2112 of this title, section 3572 of this title, or section 3805(a)(1) of this title, the implementing bill submitted by the President with respect to such trade agreement or extension shall be introduced (by request) in the House by the majority leader of the House, for himself and the minority leader of the House, or by Members of the House designated by the majority leader and minority leader of the House; and shall be introduced (by request) in the Senate by the majority leader of the Senate, for himself and the minority leader of the Senate, or by Members of the Senate designated by the majority leader and minority leader of the Senate. If either House is not in session on the day on which such a trade agreement or extension is submitted, the implementing bill shall be introduced in that House, as provided in the preceding sentence, on the first day thereafter on which that House is in session. Such bills shall be referred by the Presiding Officers of the respective Houses to the appropriate committee, or, in the case of a bill containing provisions within the jurisdiction of two or more committees, jointly to such committees for consideration of those provisions within their respective jurisdictions.

(2) On the day on which a bilateral commercial agreement, entered into under subchapter IV of this chapter after January 3, 1975, is transmitted to the House of Representatives and the Senate, an approval resolution with respect to such agreement shall be introduced (by request) in the House by the majority leader of the House, for himself and the minority leader of the House, or by Members of the House designated by the majority leader and minority leader of the House; and shall be introduced (by request) in the Senate by the majority leader of the Senate, for himself and the minority leader of the Senate, or by Members of the Senate designated by the majority leader and minority leader of the

Senate. If either House is not in session on the day on which such an agreement is transmitted, the approval resolution with respect to such agreement shall be introduced in that House, as provided in the preceding sentence, on the first day thereafter on which that House is in session. The approval resolution introduced in the House shall be referred to the Committee on Ways and Means and the approval resolution introduced in the Senate shall be referred to the Committee on Finance.

(d) Amendments prohibited

No amendment to an implementing bill or approval resolution shall be in order in either the House of Representatives or the Senate; and no motion to suspend the application of this subsection shall be in order in either House, nor shall it be in order in either House for the Presiding Officer to entertain a request to suspend the application of this subsection by unanimous consent.

(e) Period for committee and floor consideration

(1) Except as provided in paragraph (2), if the committee or committees of either House to which an implementing bill or approval resolution has been referred have not reported it at the close of the 45th day after its introduction, such committee or committees shall be automatically discharged from further consideration of the bill or resolution and it shall be placed on the appropriate calendar. A vote on final passage of the bill or resolution shall be taken in each House on or before the close of the 15th day after the bill or resolution is reported by the committee or committees of that House to which it was referred, or after such committee or committees have been discharged from further consideration of the bill or resolution. If prior to the passage by one House of an implementing bill or approval resolution of that House, that House receives the same implementing bill or approval resolution from the other House, then—

(A) the procedure in that House shall be the same as if no implementing bill or approval resolution had been received from the other House, but

(B) the vote on final passage shall be on the implementing bill or approval resolution of the other House.

(2) The provisions of paragraph (1) shall not apply in the Senate to an implementing revenue bill or resolution. An implementing revenue bill or resolution received from the House shall be referred to the appropriate committee or committees of the Senate. If such committee or committees have not reported such bill or resolution at the close of the 15th day after its receipt by the Senate (or, if later, before the close of the 45th day after the corresponding implementing revenue bill or resolution was introduced in the Senate), such committee or committees shall be automatically discharged from further consideration of such bill or resolution and it shall be placed on the calendar. A vote on final passage of such bill or resolution

shall be taken in the Senate on or before the close of the 15th day after such bill or resolution is reported by the committee or committees of the Senate to which it was referred, or after such committee or committees have been discharged from further consideration of such bill or resolution.

(3) For purposes of paragraphs (1) and (2), in computing a number of days in either House, there shall be excluded any day on which that House is not in session.

(f) Floor consideration in the House

(1) A motion in the House of Representatives to proceed to the consideration of an implementing bill or approval resolution shall be highly privileged and not debatable. An amendment to the motion shall not be in order, nor shall it be in order to move to reconsider the vote by which the motion is agreed to or disagreed to.

(2) Debate in the House of Representatives on an implementing bill or approval resolution shall be limited to not more than 20 hours, which shall be divided equally between those favoring and those opposing the bill or resolution. A motion further to limit debate shall not be debatable. It shall not be in order to move to recommit an implementing bill or approval resolution or to move to reconsider the vote by which an implementing bill or approval resolution is agreed to or disagreed to.

(3) Motions to postpone, made in the House of Representatives with respect to the consideration of an implementing bill or approval resolution, and motions to proceed to the consideration of other business, shall be decided without debate.

(4) All appeals from the decisions of the Chair relating to the application of the Rules of the House of Representatives to the procedure relating to an implementing bill or approval resolution shall be decided without debate.

(5) Except to the extent specifically provided in the preceding provisions of this subsection, consideration of an implementing bill or approval resolution shall be governed by the Rules of the House of Representatives applicable to other bills and resolutions in similar circumstances.

(g) Floor consideration in the Senate

(1) A motion in the Senate to proceed to the consideration of an implementing bill or approval resolution shall be privileged and not debatable. An amendment to the motion shall not be in order, nor shall it be in order to move to reconsider the vote by which the motion is agreed to or disagreed to.

(2) Debate in the Senate on an implementing bill or approval resolution, and all debatable motions and appeals in connection therewith,

shall be limited to not more than 20 hours. The time shall be equally divided between, and controlled by, the majority leader and the minority leader or their designees.

(3) Debate in the Senate on any debatable motion or appeal in connection with an implementing bill or approval resolution shall be limited to not more than 1 hour, to be equally divided between, and controlled by, the mover and the manager of the bill or resolution, except that in the event the manager of the bill or resolution is in favor of any such motion or appeal, the time in opposition thereto, shall be controlled by the minority leader or his designee. Such leaders, or either of them, may, from time under their control on the passage of an implementing bill or approval resolution, allot additional time to any Senator during the consideration of any debatable motion or appeal.

(4) A motion in the Senate to further limit debate is not debatable. A motion to recommit an implementing bill or approval resolution is not in order.

* * *

CHAPTER 8. IDENTIFICATION OF MARKET BARRIERS AND CERTAIN UNFAIR TRADE ACTIONS

19 U.S.C. § 2241

Sec. 181. Estimates of barriers to market access

(a) National trade estimates.

(1) In general. For calendar year 1988 and for each succeeding calendar year, the United States Trade Representative, through the interagency trade organization established pursuant to section 242(a) of the Trade Expansion Act of 1962 and with the assistance of the interagency advisory committee established under section 141(d)(2) shall—

(A) identify and analyze acts, policies, or practices of each foreign country which constitute significant barriers to, or distortions of—

(i) United States exports of goods or services (including agricultural commodities; and property protected by trademarks, patents, and copyrights exported or licensed by United States persons), and

(ii) foreign direct investment by United States persons, especially if such investment has implications for trade in goods or services; and

(B) make an estimate of the trade-distorting impact on United States commerce of any act, policy, or practice identified under subparagraph (A); and

(C) make an estimate, if feasible, of—

(i) the value of additional goods and services of the United States, and

(ii) the value of additional foreign direct investment by United States persons,

that would have been exported to, or invested in, each foreign country during such calendar year if each of such acts, policies, and practices of such country did not exist.

(2) Certain factors taken into account in making analysis and estimate. In making any analysis or estimate under paragraph (1), the Trade Representative shall take into account—

(A) the relative impact of the act, policy, or practice on United States commerce;

(B) the availability of information to document prices, market shares, and other matters necessary to demonstrate the effects of the act, policy, or practice;

(C) the extent to which such act, policy, or practice is subject to international agreements to which the United States is a party; and

(D) any advice given through appropriate committees established pursuant to section 135; and

(E) the actual increase in—

(i) the value of goods and services of the United States exported to, and

(ii) the value of foreign direct investment made in, the foreign country during the calendar year for which the estimate under paragraph (1)(C) is made.

(3) Annual revisions and updates. The Trade Representative shall annually revise and update the analysis and estimate under paragraph (1).

* * *

19 U.S.C. § 2242

Sec. 182. Identification of countries that deny adequate protection, or market access, for intellectual property rights

(a) In general. By no later than the date that is 30 days after the date on which the annual report is submitted to Congressional committees under section 181(b), the United States Trade Representative (hereafter in this section referred to as the "Trade Representative") shall identify—

(1) those foreign countries that—

(A) deny adequate and effective protection of intellectual property rights, or

(B) deny fair and equitable market access to United States persons that rely upon intellectual property protection, and

(2) those foreign countries identified under paragraph (1) that are determined by the Trade Representative to be priority foreign countries.

(b) Special rules for identifications.

(1) In identifying priority foreign countries under subsection (a)(2), the Trade Representative shall only identify those foreign countries—

(A) that have the most onerous or egregious acts, policies, or practices that—

(i) deny adequate and effective intellectual property rights, or

(ii) deny fair and equitable market access to United States persons that rely upon intellectual property protection,

(B) whose acts, policies, or practices described in subparagraph (A) have the greatest adverse impact (actual or potential) on the relevant United States products, and

(C) that are not—

(i) entering into good faith negotiations, or

(ii) making significant progress in bilateral or multilateral negotiations, to provide adequate and effective protection of intellectual property rights.

(2) In identifying priority foreign countries under subsection (a)(2), the Trade Representative shall—

(A) consult with the Register of Copyrights, the Under Secretary of Commerce for Intellectual Property and Director of the United States Patent and Trademark Office, other appropriate officers of the Federal Government, and

(B) take into account information from such sources as may be available to the Trade Representative and such information as may be submitted to the Trade Representative by interested persons, including information contained in reports submitted under section 181(b) and petitions submitted under section 302.

(3) The Trade Representative may identify a foreign country under subsection (a)(1)(B) only if the Trade Representative finds that there is a factual basis for the denial of fair and equitable market access as a result of the violation of international law or agreement, or the existence of barriers, referred to in subsection (d)(3).

(4) In identifying foreign countries under paragraphs (1) and (2) of subsection (a), the Trade Representative shall take into account—

(A) the history of intellectual property laws and practices of the foreign country, including any previous identification under subsection (a)(2), and

(B) the history of efforts of the United States, and the response of the foreign country, to achieve adequate and effective protection and enforcement of intellectual property rights.

(c) Revocations and additional identifications.

(1) The Trade Representative may at any time—

(A) revoke the identification of any foreign country as a priority foreign country under this section, or

(B) identify any foreign country as a priority foreign country under this section, if information available to the Trade Representative indicates that such action is appropriate.

(2) The Trade Representative shall include in the semiannual report submitted to the Congress under section 309(3) a detailed explanation of the reasons for the revocation under paragraph (1) of the identification of any foreign country as a priority foreign country under this section.

(d) Definitions. For purposes of this section—

(1) The term "persons that rely upon intellectual property protection" means persons involved in—

(A) the creation, production or licensing of works of authorship (within the meaning of sections 102 and 103 of title 17, United States Code) that are copyrighted, or

(B) the manufacture of products that are patented or for which there are process patents.

(2) A foreign country denies adequate and effective protection of intellectual property rights if the foreign country denies adequate and effective means under the laws of the foreign country for persons who are not citizens or nationals of such foreign country to secure, exercise, and enforce rights relating to patents, process patents, registered trademarks, copyrights and mask works.

(3) A foreign country denies fair and equitable market access if the foreign country effectively denies access to a market for a product protected by a copyright or related right, patent, trademark, mask work, trade secret, or plant breeder's right, through the use of laws, procedures, practices, or regulations which—

(A) violate provisions of international law or international agreements to which both the United States and the foreign country are parties, or

(B) constitute discriminatory nontariff trade barriers.

(4) A foreign country may be determined to deny adequate and effective protection of intellectual property rights, notwithstanding the fact that the foreign country may be in compliance with the specific obligations of the Agreement on Trade-Related Aspects of Intellectual Property Rights referred to in section 101(d)(15) of the Uruguay Round Agreements Act.

(e) Publication. The Trade Representative shall publish in the Federal Register a list of foreign countries identified under subsection (a) and shall make such revisions to the list as may be required by reason of action under subsection (c).

(f) Special rule for actions affecting United States cultural industries.

(1) In general. By no later than the date that is 30 days after the date on which the annual report is submitted to Congressional committees under section 181(b), the Trade Representative shall identify any act, policy, or practice of Canada which—

(A) affects cultural industries,

(B) is adopted or expanded after December 17, 1992, and

(C) is actionable under article 2106 of the North American Free Trade Agreement.

(2) Special rules for identifications. For purposes of section 302(b)(2)(A) an act, policy, or practice identified under this subsection shall be treated as an act, policy, or practice that is the basis for identification of a country under subsection (a)(2), unless the United States has already taken action pursuant to article 2106 of the North American Free Trade Agreement in response to such act, policy, or practice. In deciding whether to identify an act, policy, or practice under paragraph (1), the Trade Representative shall—

(A) consult with and take into account the views of representatives of the relevant domestic industries, appropriate committees established pursuant to section 135, and appropriate officers of the Federal Government, and

(B) take into account the information from such sources as may be available to the Trade Representative and such information as may be submitted to the Trade Representative by interested persons, including information contained in reports submitted under section 181(b).

(3) Cultural industries. For purposes of this subsection, the term "cultural industries" means persons engaged in any of the following activities:

(A) The publication, distribution, or sale of books, magazines, periodicals, or newspapers in print or machine readable form but not including the sole activity of printing or typesetting any of the foregoing.

(B) The production, distribution, sale, or exhibition of film or video recordings.

(C) The production, distribution, sale, or exhibition of audio or video music recordings.

(D) The publication, distribution, or sale of music in print or machine readable form.

(E) Radio communications in which the transmissions are intended for direct reception by the general public, and all radio, television, and cable broadcasting undertakings and all satellite programming and broadcast network services.

(g) Annual report. The Trade Representative shall, by not later than the date by which countries are identified under subsection (a), transmit to the Committee on Ways and Means of the House of Representatives and the Committee on Finance of the Senate, a report on actions taken under this section during the 12 months preceding such report, and the reasons for such actions, including a description of progress made in achieving improved intellectual property protection and market access for persons relying on intellectual property rights.

* * *

TITLE II. RELIEF FROM INJURY CAUSED BY IMPORT COMPETITION

* * *

TITLE III. RELIEF FROM UNFAIR TRADE PRACTICES

CHAPTER 1. ENFORCEMENT OF UNITED STATES RIGHTS UNDER TRADE AGREEMENTS AND RESPONSE TO CERTAIN FOREIGN TRADE PRACTICES

19 U.S.C. § 2411

Sec. 301. Actions by United States Trade Representative

(a) Mandatory action.

(1) If the United States Trade Representative determines under section 304(a)(1) that—

(A) the rights of the United States under any trade agreement are being denied; or

(B) an act, policy, or practice of a foreign country—

(i) violates, or is inconsistent with, the provisions of, or otherwise denies benefits to the United States under, any trade agreement, or

(ii) is unjustifiable and burdens or restricts United States commerce; the Trade Representative shall take action authorized in subsection (c), subject to the specific direction, if any, of the President regarding any such action, and shall take all other appropriate and feasible action within the power of the President that the President may direct the Trade Representative to take under this subsection, to enforce such rights or to obtain the elimination of such act, policy, or practice. Actions may be taken that are within the power of the President with respect to trade in any goods or services, or with respect to any other area of pertinent relations with the foreign country.

(2) The Trade Representative is not required to take action under paragraph (1) in any case in which—

(A) the Dispute Settlement Body (as defined in section 121(5) of the Uruguay Round Agreements Act) has adopted a report, or a ruling issued under the formal dispute settlement proceeding provided under any other trade agreement finds, that—

(i) the rights of the United States under a trade agreement are not being denied, or

(ii) the act, policy, or practice—

(I) is not a violation of, or inconsistent with, the rights of the United States, or

(II) does not deny, nullify, or impair benefits to the United States under any trade agreement; or

(B) the Trade Representative finds that—

(i) the foreign country is taking satisfactory measures to grant the rights of the United States under a trade agreement,

(ii) the foreign country has—

(I) agreed to eliminate or phase out the act, policy, or practice, or

(II) agreed to an imminent solution to the burden or restriction on United States commerce that is satisfactory to the Trade Representative,

(iii) it is impossible for the foreign country to achieve the results described in clause (i) or (ii), as appropriate, but the foreign country agrees to provide to the United States compensatory trade benefits that are satisfactory to the Trade Representative,

(iv) in extraordinary cases, where the taking of action under this subsection would have an adverse impact on the United States economy substantially out of proportion to the benefits of such action, taking into account the impact of not taking such action on the credibility of the provisions of this chapter, or

(v) the taking of action under this subsection would cause serious harm to the national security of the United States.

(3) Any action taken under paragraph (1) to eliminate an act, policy, or practice shall be devised so as to affect goods or services of the foreign country in an amount that is equivalent in value to the burden or restriction being imposed by that country on United States commerce.

(b) Discretionary action. If the Trade Representative determines under section 304(a)(1) that—

(1) an act, policy, or practice of a foreign country is unreasonable or discriminatory and burdens or restricts United States commerce, and

(2) action by the United States is appropriate, the Trade Representative shall take all appropriate and feasible action authorized under subsection (c), subject to the specific direction, if any, of the President regarding any such action, and all other appropriate and feasible action within the power of the President that the President may direct the Trade Representative to take under this subsection, to obtain the elimination of that act, policy, or practice. Actions may be taken that are within the power of the President with respect to trade in any goods or services, or with respect to any other area of pertinent relations with the foreign country.

(c) Scope of authority.

(1) For purposes of carrying out the provisions of subsection (a) or (b), the Trade Representative is authorized to—

(A) suspend, withdraw, or prevent the application of, benefits of trade agreement concessions to carry out a trade agreement with the foreign country referred to in such subsection;

(B) impose duties or other import restrictions on the goods of, and, notwithstanding any other provision of law, fees or restrictions on the services of, such foreign country for such time as the Trade Representative determines appropriate;

(C) in a case in which the act, policy, or practice also fails to meet the eligibility criteria for receiving duty-free treatment under subsections (b) and (c) of section 502 of this Act, subsections (b) and (c) of section 212 of the Caribbean Basin Economic Recovery Act (19

U.S.C. 2702(b) and (c)), or subsections (c) and (d) of section 203 of the Andean Trade Preference Act (19 U.S.C. 3202(c) and (d)), withdraw, limit, or suspend such treatment under such provisions, notwithstanding the provisions of subsection (a)(3) of this section; or

(D) enter into binding agreements with such foreign country that commit such foreign country to—

(i) eliminate, or phase out, the act, policy, or practice that is the subject of the action to be taken under subsection (a) or (b),

(ii) eliminate any burden or restriction on United States commerce resulting from such act, policy, or practice, or

(iii) provide the United States with compensatory trade benefits that—

(I) are satisfactory to the Trade Representative, and

(II) meet the requirements of paragraph (4).

(2)(A) Notwithstanding any other provision of law governing any service sector access authorization, and in addition to the authority conferred in paragraph (1), the Trade Representative may, for purposes of carrying out the provisions of subsection (a) or (b)—

(i) restrict, in the manner and to the extent the Trade Representative determines appropriate, the terms and conditions of any such authorization, or

(ii) deny the issuance of any such authorization.

(B) Actions described in subparagraph (A) may only be taken under this section with respect to service sector access authorizations granted, or applications therefor pending, on or after the date on which—

(i) a petition is filed under section 302(a), or

(ii) a determination to initiate an investigation is made by the Trade Representative under section 302(b).

(C) Before the Trade Representative takes any action under this section involving the imposition of fees or other restrictions on the services of a foreign country, the Trade Representative shall, if the services involved are subject to regulation by any agency of the Federal Government or of any State, consult, as appropriate, with the head of the agency concerned.

(3) The actions the Trade Representative is authorized to take under subsection (a) or (b) may be taken against any goods or economic sector—

(A) on a nondiscriminatory basis or solely against the foreign country described in such subsection, and

(B) without regard to whether or not such goods or economic sector were involved in the act, policy, or practice that is the subject of such action.

(4) Any trade agreement described in paragraph (1)(D)(iii) shall provide compensatory trade benefits that benefit the economic sector which includes the domestic industry that would benefit from the elimination of the act, policy, or practice that is the subject of the action to be taken under subsection (a) or (b), or benefit the economic sector as closely related as possible to such economic sector, unless—

(A) the provision of such trade benefits is not feasible, or

(B) trade benefits that benefit any other economic sector would be more satisfactory than such trade benefits.

(5) If the Trade Representative determines that actions to be taken under subsection (a) or (b) are to be in the form of import restrictions, the Trade Representative shall—

(A) give preference to the imposition of duties over the imposition of other import restrictions, and

(B) if an import restriction other than a duty is imposed, consider substituting, on an incremental basis, an equivalent duty for such other import restriction.

(6) Any action taken by the Trade Representative under this section with respect to export targeting shall, to the extent possible, reflect the full benefit level of the export targeting to the beneficiary over the period during which the action taken has an effect.

(d) Definitions and special rules. For purposes of this chapter—

(1) The term "commerce" includes, but is not limited to—

(A) services (including transfers of information) associated with international trade, whether or not such services are related to specific goods, and

(B) foreign direct investment by United States persons with implications for trade in goods or services.

(2) An act, policy, or practice of a foreign country that burdens or restricts United States commerce may include the provision, directly or indirectly, by that foreign country of subsidies for the construction of vessels used in the commercial transportation by water of goods between foreign countries and the United States.

(3)(A) An act, policy, or practice is unreasonable if the act, policy, or practice, while not necessarily in violation of, or inconsistent with, the international legal rights of the United States, is otherwise unfair and inequitable.

(B) Acts, policies, and practices that are unreasonable include, but are not limited to, any act, policy, or practice, or any combination of acts, policies, or practices, which—

(i) denies fair and equitable—

(I) opportunities for the establishment of an enterprise,

(II) provision of adequate and effective protection of intellectual property rights notwithstanding the fact that the foreign country may be in compliance with the specific obligations of the Agreement on Trade-Related Aspects of Intellectual Property Rights referred to in section 101(d)(15) of the Uruguay Round Agreements Act,

(III) nondiscriminatory market access opportunities for United States persons that rely upon intellectual property protection, or

(IV) market opportunities, including the toleration by a foreign government of systematic anticompetitive activities by enterprises or among enterprises in the foreign country that have the effect of restricting, on a basis that is inconsistent with commercial considerations, access of United States goods or services to a foreign market,

(ii) constitutes export targeting, or

(iii) constitutes a persistent pattern of conduct that—

(I) denies workers the right of association,

(II) denies workers the right to organize and bargain collectively,

(III) permits any form of forced or compulsory labor,

(IV) fails to provide a minimum age for the employment of children, or

(V) fails to provide standards for minimum wages, hours of work, and occupational safety and health of workers.

(C)(i) Acts, policies, and practices of a foreign country described in subparagraph (B)(iii) shall not be treated as being unreasonable if the Trade Representative determines that—

(I) the foreign country has taken, or is taking, actions that demonstrate a significant and tangible overall advancement in providing throughout the foreign country (including any designated zone within the foreign country) the rights and other standards described in the subclauses of subparagraph (B)(iii), or

(II) such acts, policies, and practices are not inconsistent with the level of economic development of the foreign country.

(ii) The Trade Representative shall publish in the Federal Register any determination made under clause (i), together with a description of the facts on which such determination is based.

(D) For purposes of determining whether any act, policy, or practice is unreasonable, reciprocal opportunities in the United States for foreign nationals and firms shall be taken into account, to the extent appropriate.

(E) The term "export targeting" means any government plan or scheme consisting of a combination of coordinated actions (whether carried out severally or jointly) that are bestowed on a specific enterprise, industry, or group thereof, the effect of which is to assist the enterprise, industry, or group to become more competitive in the export of a class or kind of merchandise.

(F)(i) For the purposes of subparagraph (B)(i)(II), adequate and effective protection of intellectual property rights includes adequate and effective means under the laws of the foreign country for persons who are not citizens or nationals of such country to secure, exercise, and enforce rights and enjoy commercial benefits relating to patents, trademarks, copyrights and related rights, mask works, trade secrets, and plant breeder's rights.

(ii) For purposes of subparagraph (B)(i)(IV), the denial of fair and equitable nondiscriminatory market access opportunities includes restrictions on market access related to the use, exploitation, or enjoyment of commercial benefits derived from exercising intellectual property rights in protected works or fixations or products embodying protected works.

(4)(A) An act, policy, or practice is unjustifiable if the act, policy, or practice is in violation of, or inconsistent with, the international legal rights of the United States.

(B) Acts, policies, and practices that are unjustifiable include, but are not limited to, any act, policy, or practice described in subparagraph (A) which denies national or most-favored-nation treatment or the right of establishment or protection of intellectual property rights.

(5) Acts, policies, and practices that are discriminatory include, when appropriate, any act, policy, and practice which denies national or most-favored-nation treatment to United States goods, services, or investment.

(6) The term "service sector access authorization" means any license, permit, order, or other authorization, issued under the authority of Federal

law, that permits a foreign supplier of services access to the United States market in a service sector concerned.

(7) The term "foreign country" includes any foreign instrumentality. Any possession or territory of a foreign country that is administered separately for customs purposes shall be treated as a separate foreign country.

(8) The term "Trade Representative" means the United States Trade Representative.

(9) The term "interested persons", only for purposes of sections 302(a)(4)(B), 304(b)(1)(A), 306(c)(2), and 307(a)(2), includes, but is not limited to, domestic firms and workers, representatives of consumer interests, United States product exporters, and any industrial user of any goods or services that may be affected by actions taken under subsection (a) or (b).

19 U.S.C. § 2412

Sec. 302. Initiation of investigations

(a) Petitions.

(1) Any interested person may file a petition with the Trade Representative requesting that action be taken under section 301 and setting forth the allegations in support of the request.

(2) The Trade Representative shall review the allegations in any petition filed under paragraph (1) and, not later than 45 days after the date on which the Trade Representative received the petition, shall determine whether to initiate an investigation.

(3) If the Trade Representative determines not to initiate an investigation with respect to a petition, the Trade Representative shall inform the petitioner of the reasons therefor and shall publish notice of the determination, together with a summary of such reasons, in the Federal Register.

(4) If the Trade Representative makes an affirmative determination under paragraph (2) with respect to a petition, the Trade Representative shall initiate an investigation regarding the issues raised in the petition. The Trade Representative shall publish a summary of the petition in the Federal Register and shall, as soon as possible, provide opportunity for the presentation of views concerning the issues, including a public hearing—

(A) within the 30–day period beginning on the date of the affirmative determination (or on a date after such period if agreed to by the petitioner) if a public hearing within such period is requested in the petition, or

(B) at such other time if a timely request therefor is made by the petitioner or by any interested person.

(b) Initiation of investigation by means other than petition.

(1)(A) If the Trade Representative determines that an investigation should be initiated under this chapter with respect to any matter in order to determine whether the matter is actionable under section 301, the Trade Representative shall publish such determination in the Federal Register and shall initiate such investigation.

(B) The Trade Representative shall, before making any determination under subparagraph (A), consult with appropriate committees established pursuant to section 135.

(2)(A) By no later than the date that is 30 days after the date on which a country is identified under section 182(a)(2), the Trade Representative shall initiate an investigation under this chapter with respect to any act, policy, or practice of that country that—

(i) was the basis for such identification, and

(ii) is not at that time the subject of any other investigation or action under this chapter.

(B) The Trade Representative is not required under subparagraph (A) to initiate an investigation under this chapter with respect to any act, policy, or practice of a foreign country if the Trade Representative determines that the initiation of the investigation would be detrimental to United States economic interests.

(C) If the Trade Representative makes a determination under subparagraph (B) not to initiate an investigation, the Trade Representative shall submit to the Congress a written report setting forth, in detail—

(i) the reasons for the determination, and

(ii) the United States economic interests that would be adversely affected by the investigation.

(D) The Trade Representative shall, from time to time, consult with the Register of Copyrights, the Commissioner of Patents and Trademarks, and other appropriate officers of the Federal Government, during any investigation initiated under this chapter by reason of subparagraph (A).

(c) Discretion. In determining whether to initiate an investigation under subsection (a) or (b) of any act, policy, or practice that is enumerated in any provision of section 301(d), the Trade Representative shall have discretion to determine whether action under section 301 would be effective in addressing such act, policy, or practice.

19 U.S.C. § 2413

Sec. 303. Consultation upon initiation of investigation

(a) In general.

(1) On the date on which an investigation is initiated under section 302, the Trade Representative, on behalf of the United States, shall request consultations with the foreign country concerned regarding the issues involved in such investigation.

(2) If the investigation initiated under section 302 involves a trade agreement and a mutually acceptable resolution is not reached before the earlier of—

(A) the close of the consultation period, if any, specified in the trade agreement, or

(B) the 150th day after the day on which consultation was commenced,

the Trade Representative shall promptly request proceedings on the matter under the formal dispute settlement procedures provided under such agreement.

(3) The Trade Representative shall seek information and advice from the petitioner (if any) and the appropriate committees established pursuant to section 135 in preparing United States presentations for consultations and dispute settlement proceedings.

(b) Delay of request for consultations.

(1) Notwithstanding the provisions of subsection (a) of this section—

(A) the United States Trade Representative may, after consulting with the petitioner (if any), delay for up to 90 days any request for consultations under subsection (a) for the purpose of verifying or improving the petition to ensure an adequate basis for consultation, and

(B) if such consultations are delayed by reason of subparagraph (A), each time limitation under section 304 shall be extended for the period of such delay.

(2) The Trade Representative shall—

(A) publish notice of any delay under paragraph (1) in the Federal Register, and

(B) report to Congress on the reasons for such delay in the report required under section 309(a)(3).

19 U.S.C. § 2414

Sec. 304. Determinations by the Trade Representative

(a) In general.

(1) On the basis of the investigation initiated under section 302 [19 U.S.C. § 2412] and the consultations (and the proceedings, if applicable) under section 303 [19 U.S.C. § 2413], the Trade Representative shall—

(A) determine whether—

(i) the rights to which the United States is entitled under any trade agreement are being denied, or

(ii) any act, policy, or practice described in subsection (a)(1)(B) or (b)(1) of section 301 [19 U.S.C. § 2411(a)(1)(B) or (b)(1)] exists, and

(B) if the determination made under subparagraph (A) is affirmative, determine what action, if any, the Trade Representative should take under subsection (a) or (b) of section 301 [19 U.S.C. § 2411(a) or (b)].

(2) The Trade Representative shall make the determinations required under paragraph (1) on or before—

(A) in the case of an investigation involving a trade agreement, except an investigation initiated pursuant to section 302(b)(2)(A) [19 U.S.C. § 2412(b)(2)(A)] involving rights under the Agreement on Trade-Related Aspects of Intellectual Property Rights (referred to in section 101(d)(15) of the Uruguay Round Agreements Act [19 U.S.C. § 3511(d)(15)]) or the GATT 1994 (as defined in section 2(1)(B) of that Act [19 U.S.C. § 3501(1)(B)]) relating to products subject to intellectual property protection, the earlier of—

(i) the date that is 30 days after the date on which the dispute settlement procedure is concluded, or

(ii) the date that is 18 months after the date on which the investigation is initiated, or

(B) in all cases not described in subparagraph (A) or paragraph (3), the date that is 12 months after the date on which the investigation is initiated.

(3)(A) If an investigation is initiated under this chapter [19 U.S.C. §§ 2411 et seq.] by reason of section 302(b)(2) [19 U.S.C. § 2412(b)(2)] and—

(i) the Trade Representative considers that rights under the Agreement on Trade-Related Aspects of Intellectual Property Rights or the GATT 1994 relating to products subject to intellectual property protection are involved, the Trade Representative shall make the determination required under paragraph (1) not later than 30 days after the date on which the dispute settlement procedure is concluded; or

(ii) the Trade Representative does not consider that a trade agreement, including the Agreement on Trade-Related Aspects of Intellectual Property Rights, is involved or does not make a determination described in subparagraph (B) with respect to such investigation, the Trade Representative shall make the determinations required under paragraph (1) with respect to such investigation not later than the date that is 6 months after the date on which such investigation is initiated.

(B) If the Trade Representative determines with respect to an investigation initiated by reason of section 302(b)(2) [19 U.S.C. § 2412(b)(2)] (other than an investigation involving a trade agreement) that—

(i) complex or complicated issues are involved in the investigation that require additional time,

(ii) the foreign country involved in the investigation is making substantial progress in drafting or implementing legislative or administrative measures that will provide adequate and effective protection of intellectual property rights, or

(iii) such foreign country is undertaking enforcement measures to provide adequate and effective protection of intellectual property rights,

the Trade Representative shall publish in the Federal Register notice of such determination and shall make the determinations required under paragraph (1) with respect to such investigation by no later than the date that is 9 months after the date on which such investigation is initiated.

(4) In any case in which a dispute is not resolved before the close of the minimum dispute settlement period provided for in a trade agreement, the Trade Representative, within 15 days after the close of such dispute settlement period, shall submit a report to Congress setting forth the reasons why the dispute was not resolved within the minimum dispute settlement period, the status of the case at the close of the period, and the prospects for resolution. For purposes of this paragraph, the minimum dispute settlement period provided for under any such trade agreement is the total period of time that results if all stages of the formal dispute settlement procedures are carried out within the time limitations specified in the agreement, but computed without regard to any extension authorized under the agreement at any stage.

(b) Consultation before determinations.

(1) Before making the determinations required under subsection (a)(1), the Trade Representative, unless expeditious action is required—

(A) shall provide an opportunity (after giving not less than 30 days notice thereof) for the presentation of views by interested persons, including a public hearing if requested by any interested person,

(B) shall obtain advice from the appropriate committees established pursuant to section 135 [19 U.S.C. § 2155], and

(C) may request the views of the United States International Trade Commission regarding the probable impact on the economy of the United States of the taking of action with respect to any goods or service.

(2) If the Trade Representative does not comply with the requirements of subparagraphs (A) and (B) of paragraph (1) because expeditious action is required, the Trade Representative shall, after making the determinations under subsection (a)(1), comply with such subparagraphs.

(c) Publication. The Trade Representative shall publish in the Federal Register any determination made under subsection (a)(1), together with a description of the facts on which such determination is based.

19 U.S.C. § 2415

Sec. 305. Implementation of actions

(a) Actions to be taken under section 301 [19 U.S.C. § 2411].

(1) Except as provided in paragraph (2), the Trade Representative shall implement the action the Trade Representative determines under section 304(a)(1)(B) [19 U.S.C. § 2414(a)(1)(B)] to take under section 301 [19 U.S.C. § 2411], subject to the specific direction, if any, of the President regarding any such action, by no later than the date that is 30 days after the date on which such determination is made.

(2)(A) Except as otherwise provided in this paragraph, the Trade Representative may delay, by not more than 180 days, the implementation of any action that is to be taken under section 301 [19 U.S.C. § 2411]—

(i) if—

(I) in the case of an investigation initiated under section 302(a) [19 U.S.C. § 2412(a)], the petitioner requests a delay, or

(II) in the case of an investigation initiated under section 302(b)(1) [19 U.S.C. § 2412(b)(1)] or to which section 304(a)(3)(B) [19 U.S.C. § 2414(a)(3)(B)] applies, a delay is requested by a majority of the representatives of the domestic industry that would benefit from the action, or

(ii) if the Trade Representative determines that substantial progress is being made, or that a delay is necessary or desirable, to obtain United States rights or a satisfactory solution with respect to the acts, policies, or practices that are the subject of the action.

(B) The Trade Representative may not delay under subparagraph (A) the implementation of any action that is to be taken under section 301 [19 U.S.C. § 2411] with respect to any investigation to which section 304(a)(3)(A)(ii) [19 U.S.C. § 2414(a)(3)(A)(ii)] applies.

(C) The Trade Representative may not delay under subparagraph (A) the implementation of any action that is to be taken under section 301 [19 U.S.C. § 2411] with respect to any investigation to which section 304(a)(3)(B) [19 U.S.C. § 2414(a)(3)(B)] applies by more than 90 days.

(b) Alternative actions in certain cases of export targeting.

(1) If the Trade Representative makes an affirmative determination under section 304(a)(1)(A) [19 U.S.C. § 2414(a)(1)(A)] involving export targeting by a foreign country and determines to take no action under section 301 [19 U.S.C. § 2411] with respect to such affirmation determination, the Trade Representative—

(A) shall establish an advisory panel to recommend measures which will promote the competitiveness of the domestic industry affected by the export targeting,

(B) on the basis of the report of such panel submitted under paragraph (2)(B) and subject to the specific direction, if any, of the President, may take any administrative actions authorized under any other provision of law, and, if necessary, propose legislation to implement any other actions, that would restore or improve the international competitiveness of the domestic industry affected by the export targeting, and

(C) shall, by no later than the date that is 30 days after the date on which the report of such panel is submitted under paragraph (2)(B), submit a report to the Congress on the administrative actions taken, and legislative proposals made, under subparagraph (B) with respect to the domestic industry affected by the export targeting.

(2)(A) The advisory panels established under paragraph (1)(A) shall consist of individuals appointed by the Trade Representative who—

(i) earn their livelihood in the private sector of the economy, including individuals who represent management and labor in the domestic industry affected by the export targeting that is the subject of the affirmative determination made under section 304(a)(1)(A) [19 U.S.C. § 2414(a)(1)(A)], and

(ii) by education or experience, are qualified to serve on the advisory panel.

(B) By no later than the date that is 6 months after the date on which an advisory panel is established under paragraph (1)(A), the advisory panel shall submit to the Trade Representative and to the Congress a report on measures that the advisory panel recommends be taken by the United States to promote the competitiveness of the domestic industry affected by the export targeting that is the subject of the affirmative determination made under section 304(a)(1)(A) [19 U.S.C. § 2414(a)(1)(A)].

19 U.S.C. § 2416

Sec. 306. Monitoring of foreign compliance

(a) In general. The Trade Representative shall monitor the implementation of each measure undertaken, or agreement that is entered into, by a foreign country to provide a satisfactory resolution of a matter subject to investigation under this chapter or subject to dispute settlement proceedings to enforce the rights of the United States under a trade agreement providing for such proceedings.

(b) Further action.

(1) In general. If, on the basis of the monitoring carried out under subsection (a), the Trade Representative considers that a foreign country is not satisfactorily implementing a measure or agreement referred to in subsection (a), the Trade Representative shall determine what further action the Trade Representative shall take under section 301(a). For purposes of section 301, any such determination shall be treated as a determination made under section 304(a)(1).

(2) WTO dispute settlement recommendations.

(A) Failure to implement recommendation. If the measure or agreement referred to in subsection (a) concerns the implementation of a recommendation made pursuant to dispute settlement proceedings under the World Trade Organization, and the Trade Representative considers that the foreign country has failed to implement it, the Trade Representative shall make the determination in paragraph (1) no later than 30 days after the expiration of the reasonable period of time provided for such implementation under paragraph 21 of the Understanding on Rules and Procedures Governing the Settlement of Disputes that is referred to in section 101(d)(16) of the Uruguay Round Agreements Act.

(B) Revision of retaliation list and action.

(i) Except as provided in clause (ii), in the event that the United States initiates a retaliation list or takes any other action described in section 301(c)(1)(A) or (B) against the goods of a foreign country or countries because of the failure of such country or countries to implement the recommendation made pursuant to a dispute settlement proceeding under the World Trade Organization, the Trade Representative shall periodically revise the list or action to affect other goods of the country or countries that have failed to implement the recommendation.

(ii) Exception. The Trade Representative is not required to revise the retaliation list or the action described in clause (i) with respect to a country, if—

(I) the Trade Representative determines that implementation of a recommendation made pursuant to a dispute settlement proceeding described in clause (i) by the country is imminent; or

(II) the Trade Representative together with the petitioner involved in the initial investigation under this chapter (or if no petition was filed, the affected United States industry) agree that it is unnecessary to revise the retaliation list.

(C) Schedule for revising list or action. The Trade Representative shall, 120 days after the date the retaliation list or other section 301(a) action is first taken, and every 180 days thereafter, review the list or action taken and revise, in whole or in part, the list or action to affect other goods of the subject country or countries.

(D) Standards for revising list or action. In revising any list or action against a country or countries under this subsection, the Trade Representative shall act in a manner that is most likely to result in the country or countries implementing the recommendations adopted in the dispute settlement proceeding or in achieving a mutually satisfactory solution to the issue that gave rise to the dispute settlement proceeding. The Trade Representative shall consult with the petitioner, if any, involved in the initial investigation under this chapter.

(E) Retaliation list. The term "retaliation list" means the list of products of a foreign country or countries that have failed to comply with the report of the panel or Appellate Body of the WTO and with respect to which the Trade Representative is imposing duties above the level that would otherwise be imposed under the Harmonized Tariff Schedule of the United States.

(F) Requirement to include reciprocal goods on retaliation list. The Trade Representative shall include on the retaliation list, and on any revised lists, reciprocal goods of the industries affected by the failure of the foreign country or countries to implement the recommendation made pursuant to a dispute settlement proceeding under the World Trade Organization, except in cases where existing retaliation and its corresponding preliminary retaliation list do not already meet this requirement.

(c) Consultations. Before making any determination under subsection (b), the Trade Representative shall—

(1) consult with the petitioner, if any, involved in the initial investigation under this chapter and with representatives of the domestic industry concerned; and

(2) provide an opportunity for the presentation of views by interested persons.

19 U.S.C. § 2417

Sec. 307. Modification and termination of actions

(a) In general.

(1) The Trade Representative may modify or terminate any action, subject to the specific direction, if any, of the President with respect to such action, that is being taken under section 301 if—

(A) any of the conditions described in section 301(a)(2) exist,

(B) the burden or restriction on United States commerce of the denial rights, or of the acts, policies, and practices, that are the subject of such action has increased or decreased, or

(C) such action is being taken under section 301(b) and is no longer appropriate.

(2) Before taking any action under paragraph (1) to modify or terminate any action taken under section 301, the Trade Representative shall consult with the petitioner, if any, and with representatives of the domestic industry concerned, and shall provide opportunity for the presentation of views by other interested persons affected by the proposed modification or termination concerning the effects of the modification or termination and whether any modification or termination of the action is appropriate.

(b) Notice; report to Congress. The Trade Representative shall promptly publish in the Federal Register notice of, and report in writing to the Congress with respect to, any modification or termination of any action taken under section 301 and the reasons therefor.

(c) Review of necessity.

(1) If—

(A) a particular action has been taken under section 301 during any 4-year period, and

(B) neither the petitioner nor any representative of the domestic industry which benefits from such action has submitted to the Trade Representative during the last 60 days of such 4-year period a written request for the continuation of such action, such action shall terminate at the close of such 4-year period.

(2) The Trade Representative shall notify by mail the petitioner and representatives of the domestic industry described in paragraph (1)(B) of any termination of action by reason of paragraph (1) at least 60 days before the date of such termination.

(3) If a request is submitted to the Trade Representative under paragraph (1)(B) to continue taking a particular action under section 301, the Trade Representative shall conduct a review of—

(A) the effectiveness in achieving the objectives of section 301 of—

(i) such action, and

(ii) other actions that could be taken (including actions against other products or services), and

(B) the effects of such actions on the United States economy, including consumers.

19 U.S.C. § 2418

Sec. 308. Request for information

(a) In general. Upon receipt of written request therefor from any person, the Trade Representative shall make available to that person information (other than that to which confidentiality applies) concerning—

(1) the nature and extent of a specific trade policy or practice of a foreign country with respect to particular goods, services, investment, or intellectual property rights, to the extent that such information is available to the Trade Representative or other Federal agencies;

(2) United States rights under any trade agreement and the remedies which may be available under that agreement and under the laws of the United States; and

(3) past and present domestic and international proceedings or actions with respect to the policy or practice concerned.

(b) If information not available. If information that is requested by a person under subsection (a) is not available to the Trade Representative or other Federal agencies, the Trade Representative shall, within 30 days after receipt of the request—

(1) request the information from the foreign government; or

(2) decline to request the information and inform the person in writing of the reasons for refusal.

(c) Certain business information not made available.

(1) Except as provided in paragraph (2), and notwithstanding any other provision of law (including section 552 of title 5, United States Code), no information requested and received by the Trade Representative in aid of any investigation under this chapter shall be made available to any person if—

(A) the person providing such information certifies that—

(i) such information is business confidential,

(ii) the disclosure of such information would endanger trade secrets or profitability, and

(iii) such information is not generally available;

(B) the Trade Representative determines that such certification is well-founded; and

(C) to the extent required in regulations prescribed by the Trade Representative, the person providing such information provides an adequate nonconfidential summary of such information.

(2) The Trade Representative may—

(A) use such information, or make such information available (in his own discretion) to any employee of the Federal Government for use, in any investigation under this chapter, or

(B) may make such information available to any other person in a form which cannot be associated with, or otherwise identify, the person providing the information.

* * *

19 U.S.C. § 2420

Sec. 310. Identification of trade expansion priorities

(a) Identification.

(1) Within 180 days after the submission in calendar year 1995 of the report required by section 181(b), the Trade Representative shall—

(A) review United States trade expansion priorities,

(B) identify priority foreign country practices, the elimination of which is likely to have the most significant potential to increase United States exports, either directly or through the establishment of a beneficial precedent, and

(C) submit to the Committee on Finance of the Senate and the Committee on Ways and Means of the House of Representatives and publish in the Federal Register a report on the priority foreign country practices identified.

(2) In identifying priority foreign country practices under paragraph (1) of this section, the Trade Representative shall take into account all relevant factors, including—

(A) the major barriers and trade distorting practices described in the National Trade Estimate Report required under section 181(b);

(B) the trade agreements to which a foreign country is a party and its compliance with those agreements;

(C) the medium- and long-term implications of foreign government procurement plans; and

(D) the international competitive position and export potential of United States products and services.

(3) The Trade Representative may include in the report, if appropriate—

(A) a description of foreign country practices that may in the future warrant identification as priority foreign country practices; and

(B) a statement about other foreign country practices that were not identified because they are already being addressed by provisions of United States trade law, by existing bilateral trade agreements, or as part of trade negotiations with other countries and progress is being made toward the elimination of such practices.

(b) Initiation of investigations. By no later than the date which is 21 days after the date on which a report is submitted to the appropriate congressional committees under subsection (a)(1), the Trade Representative shall initiate under section 302(b)(1) investigations under this chapter with respect to all of the priority foreign country practices identified.

(c) Agreements for the elimination of barriers. In the consultations with a foreign country that the Trade Representative is required to request under section 303(a) with respect to an investigation initiated by reason of subsection (b), the Trade Representative shall seek to negotiate an agreement that provides for the elimination of the practices that are the subject of the investigation as quickly as possible or, if elimination of the practices is not feasible, an agreement that provides for compensatory trade benefits.

(d) Reports. The Trade Representative shall include in the semiannual report required by section 309 a report on the status of any investigations initiated pursuant to subsection (b) and, where appropriate, the extent to which such investigations have led to increased opportunities for the export of products and services of the United States.

TITLE IV. TRADE RELATIONS WITH COUNTRIES NOT CURRENTLY RECEIVING NONDISCRIMINATORY TREATMENT

19 U.S.C. § 2431

Sec. 401. Exception of the products of certain countries or areas

Except as otherwise provided in this title, the President shall continue to deny nondiscriminatory treatment to the products of any country, the products of which were not eligible for the rates set forth in rate column numbered 1 of the Tariff Schedules of the United States on January 3, 1975.

19 U.S.C. § 2432

Sec. 402. Freedom of emigration in East-West trade

(a) Actions of nonmarket economy countries making them ineligible for normal trade relations, programs of credits, credit guarantees, or investment guarantees, or commercial agreements. To assure the continued dedication of the United States to fundamental human rights, and notwithstanding any other provision of law, on or after the date of the enactment of this Act [enacted Jan. 3, 1975] products from any nonmarket economy country shall not be eligible to receive nondiscriminatory treatment (normal trade relations), such country shall not participate in any program of the Government of the United States which extends credits or credit guarantees or investment guarantees, directly or indirectly, and the President of the United States shall not conclude any commercial agreement with any such country, during the period beginning with the date on which the President determines that such country—

(1) denies its citizens the right or opportunity to emigrate;

(2) imposes more than a nominal tax on emigration or on the visas or other documents required for emigration, for any purpose or cause whatsoever; or

(3) imposes more than a nominal tax, levy, fine, fee, or other charge on any citizen as a consequence of the desire of such citizen to emigrate to the country of his choice,

and ending on the date on which the President determines that such country is no longer in violation of paragraph (1), (2), or (3).

(b) Presidential determination and report to Congress that nation is not violating freedom of emigration. After the date of the enactment of this Act [enacted Jan. 3, 1975], (A) products of a nonmarket economy country may be eligible to receive nondiscriminatory treatment (normal trade relations), (B) such country may participate in any program of the Government of the United States which extends credits or credit guarantees or investment guarantees, and (C) the President may conclude a commercial agreement with such country, only after the President has submitted to the Congress a report indicating that such country is not in violation of paragraph (1), (2), or (3) of subsection (a). Such report with respect to such country shall include information as to the nature and implementation of emigration laws and policies and restrictions or discrimination applied to or against persons wishing to emigrate. The report required by this subsection shall be submitted initially as provided herein and, with current information, on or before each June 30 and December 31 thereafter so long as such treatment is received, such credits or guarantees are extended, or such agreement is in effect.

(c) Waiver authority of President.

(1) During the 18-month period beginning on the date of the enactment of this Act [enacted Jan. 3, 1975], the President is authorized to waive by Executive order the application of subsections (a) and (b) with respect to any country, if he reports to the Congress that—

(A) he has determined that such waiver will substantially promote the objectives of this section; and

(B) he has received assurances that the emigration practices of that country will henceforth lead substantially to the achievement of the objectives of this section.

(2) During any period subsequent to the 18-month period referred to in paragraph (1), the President is authorized to waive by Executive order the application of subsections (a) and (b) with respect to any country, if the waiver authority granted by this subsection continues to apply to such country pursuant to subsection (d), and if he reports to the Congress that—

(A) he has determined that such waiver will substantially promote the objectives of this section; and

(B) he has received assurances that the emigration practices of that country will henceforth lead substantially to the achievement of the objectives of this section.

(3) A waiver with respect to any country shall terminate on the day after the waiver authority granted by this subsection ceases to be effective with respect to such country pursuant to subsection (d). The President may, at any time, terminate by Executive order any waiver granted under this subsection.

(d) Extension of waiver authority.

(1) If the President determines that the further extension of the waiver authority granted under subsection (c) will substantially promote the objectives of this section, he may recommend further extensions of such authority for successive 12-month periods. Any such recommendations shall—

(A) be made not later than 30 days before the expiration of such authority;

(B) be made in a document transmitted to the House of Representatives and the Senate setting forth his reasons for recommending the extension of such authority; and

(C) include, for each country with respect to which a waiver granted under subsection (c) is in effect, a determination that continuation of the waiver applicable to that country will substantially promote the objectives of this section, and a statement setting forth his reasons for such determination.

If the President recommends the further extension of such authority, such authority shall continue in effect until the end of the 12-month period following the end of the previous 12-month extension with respect to any country (except for any country with respect to which such authority has not been extended under this subsection), unless a joint resolution described in section 153(a) is enacted into law pursuant to the provisions of paragraph (2).

(2)(A) The requirements of this paragraph are met if the joint resolution is enacted under the procedures set forth in section 153, and—

(i) the Congress adopts and transmits the joint resolution to the President before the end of the 60-day period beginning on the date the waiver authority would expire but for an extension under paragraph (1), and

(ii) if the President vetoes the joint resolution, each House of Congress votes to override such veto on or before the later of the last day of the 60-day period referred to in clause (i) or the last day of the 15-day period (excluding any day described in section 154(b)) beginning on the date the Congress receives the veto message from the President.

(B) If a joint resolution is enacted into law under the provisions of this paragraph, the waiver authority applicable to any country with respect to which the joint resolution disapproves of the extension of such authority shall cease to be effective as of the day after the 60-day period beginning on the date of the enactment of the joint resolution.

(C) A joint resolution to which this subsection and section 153 apply may be introduced at any time on or after the date the President transmits to the Congress the document described in paragraph (1)(B).

(e) Countries not covered. This section shall not apply to any country the products of which are eligible for the rates set forth in rate column numbered 1 of the Tariff Schedules of the United States on the date of the enactment of this Act [enacted Jan. 3, 1975].

* * *

19 U.S.C. § 2434

Sec. 404. Extension of nondiscriminatory treatment

(a) Presidential proclamation. Subject to the provisions of section 405(c), the President may by proclamation extend nondiscriminatory treatment to the products of a foreign country which has entered into a bilateral commercial agreement referred to in section 405.

(b) Limitation on period of effectiveness. The application of nondiscriminatory treatment shall be limited to the period of effectiveness of the obligations of the United States to such country under such bilateral commercial agreement. In addition, in the case of any foreign country receiving nondiscriminatory treatment pursuant to this title which has entered into an agreement with the United States regarding the settlement of lend-lease reciprocal aid and claims, the application of such nondiscriminatory treatment shall be limited to periods during which such country is not in arrears on its obligations under such agreement.

(c) Suspension or withdrawal of extensions of nondiscriminatory treatment. The President may at any time suspend or withdraw any extension of nondiscriminatory treatment to any country pursuant to subsection (a), and thereby cause all products of such country to be dutiable at the rates set forth in rate column numbered 2 of the Harmonized Tariff Schedules for the United States.

* * *

19 U.S.C. § 2451

Sec. 421. Action to address market disruption

(a) Presidential action

If a product of the People's Republic of China is being imported into the United States in such increased quantities or under such conditions as to cause or threaten to cause market disruption to the domestic producers of a like or directly competitive product, the President shall, in accordance with the provisions of this section, proclaim increased duties or other import restrictions with respect to such product, to the extent and for such period as the President considers necessary to prevent or remedy the market disruption.

(b) Initiation of an investigation

(1) Upon the filing of a petition by an entity described in section 2252(a) of this title, upon the request of the President or the United States Trade Representative (in this part referred to as the "Trade Representative"), upon resolution of either the Committee on Ways and Means of the House of Representatives, or the Committee on Finance of the

Senate (in this part referred to as the "Committees") or on its own motion, the United States International Trade Commission (in this part referred to as the "Commission") shall promptly make an investigation to determine whether products of the People's Republic of China are being imported into the United States in such increased quantities or under such conditions as to cause or threaten to cause market disruption to the domestic producers of like or directly competitive products.

(2) The limitations on investigations set forth in section 2252(h)(1) of this title shall apply to investigations conducted under this section.

(3) The provisions of subsections (a)(8) and (i) of section 2252 of this title, relating to treatment of confidential business information, shall apply to investigations conducted under this section.

(4) Whenever a petition is filed, or a request or resolution is received, under this subsection, the Commission shall transmit a copy thereof to the President, the Trade Representative, the Committee on Ways and Means of the House of Representatives, and the Committee on Finance of the Senate, except that in the case of confidential business information, the copy may include only nonconfidential summaries of such information.

(5) The Commission shall publish notice of the commencement of any proceeding under this subsection in the Federal Register and shall, within a reasonable time thereafter, hold public hearings at which the Commission shall afford interested parties an opportunity to be present, to present evidence, to respond to the presentations of other parties, and otherwise to be heard.

(c) Market disruption

(1) For purposes of this section, market disruption exists whenever imports of an article like or directly competitive with an article produced by a domestic industry are increasing rapidly, either absolutely or relatively, so as to be a significant cause of material injury, or threat of material injury, to the domestic industry.

(2) For purposes of paragraph (1), the term "significant cause" refers to a cause which contributes significantly to the material injury of the domestic industry, but need not be equal to or greater than any other cause.

(d) Factors in determination

In determining whether market disruption exists, the Commission shall consider objective factors, including—

(1) the volume of imports of the product which is the subject of the investigation;

(2) the effect of imports of such product on prices in the United States for like or directly competitive articles; and

(3) the effect of imports of such product on the domestic industry producing like or directly competitive articles.

The presence or absence of any factor under paragraph (1), (2), or (3) is not necessarily dispositive of whether market disruption exists.

(e) Time for Commission determinations

The Commission shall make and transmit to the President and the Trade Representative its determination under subsection (b)(1) of this section at the earliest practicable time, but in no case later than 60 days (or 90 days in the case of a petition requesting relief under subsection (i) of this section) after the date on which the petition is filed, the request or resolution is received, or the motion is adopted, under subsection (b) of this section. If the Commissioners voting are equally divided with respect to its determination, then the determination agreed upon by either group of Commissioners may be considered by the President and the Trade Representative as the determination of the Commission.

(f) Recommendations of Commission on proposed remedies

If the Commission makes an affirmative determination under subsection (b) of this section, or a determination which the President or the Trade Representative may consider as affirmative under subsection (e) of this section, the Commission shall propose the amount of increase in, or imposition of, any duty or other import restrictions necessary to prevent or remedy the market disruption. Only those members of the Commission who agreed to the affirmative determination under subsection (b) of this section are eligible to vote on the proposed action to prevent or remedy market disruption. Members of the Commission who did not agree to the affirmative determination may submit, in the report required under subsection (g) of this section, separate views regarding what action, if any, should be taken to prevent or remedy market disruption.

(g) Report by Commission

(1) Not later than 20 days after a determination under subsection (b) of this section is made, the Commission shall submit a report to the President and the Trade Representative.

(2) The Commission shall include in the report required under paragraph (1) the following:

(A) The determination made under subsection (b) of this section and an explanation of the basis for the determination.

(B) If the determination under subsection (b) of this section is affirmative, or may be considered by the President or the Trade Representative as affirmative under subsection (e) of this section, the recommendations of the Commission on proposed remedies under subsection (f) of this section and an explanation of the basis for each recommendation.

(C) Any dissenting or separate views by members of the Commission regarding the determination and any recommendation referred to in subparagraphs (A) and (B).

(D) A description of—

(i) the short- and long-term effects that implementation of the action recommended under subsection (f) is likely to have on the petitioning domestic industry, on other domestic industries, and on consumers; and

(ii) the short- and long-term effects of not taking the recommended action on the petitioning domestic industry, its workers, and the communities where production facilities of such industry are located, and on other domestic industries.

(3) The Commission, after submitting a report to the President under paragraph (1), shall promptly make it available to the public (but shall not include confidential business information) and cause a summary thereof to be published in the Federal Register.

(h) Opportunity to present views and evidence on proposed measure and recommendation to the President

(1) Within 20 days after receipt of the Commission's report under subsection (g) of this section (or 15 days in the case of an affirmative preliminary determination under subsection (i)(1)(B) of this section), the Trade Representative shall publish in the Federal Register notice of any measure proposed by the Trade Representative to be taken pursuant to subsection (a) and of the opportunity, including a public hearing, if requested, for importers, exporters, and other interested parties to submit their views and evidence on the appropriateness of the proposed measure and whether it would be in the public interest.

(2) Within 55 days after receipt of the report under subsection (g) of this section (or 35 days in the case of an affirmative preliminary determination under subsection (i)(1)(B) of this section), the Trade Representative, taking into account the views and evidence received under paragraph (1) on the measure proposed by the Trade Representative, shall make a recommendation to the President concerning what action, if any, to take to prevent or remedy the market disruption.

(i) Critical circumstances

(1) When a petition filed under subsection (b) of this section alleges that critical circumstances exist and requests that provisional relief be provided under this subsection with respect to the product identified in the

petition, the Commission shall, not later than 45 days after the petition containing the request is filed—

(A) determine whether delay in taking action under this section would cause damage to the relevant domestic industry which would be difficult to repair; and

(B) if the determination under subparagraph (A) is affirmative, make a preliminary determination of whether imports of the product which is the subject of the investigation have caused or threatened to cause market disruption.

If the Commissioners voting are equally divided with respect to either of its determinations, then the determination agreed upon by either group of Commissioners may be considered by the President and the Trade Representative as the determination of the Commission.

(2) On the date on which the Commission completes its determinations under paragraph (1), the Commission shall transmit a report on the determinations to the President and the Trade Representative, including the reasons for its determinations. If the determinations under paragraph (1) are affirmative, or may be considered by the President or the Trade Representative as affirmative under paragraph (1), the Commission shall include in its report its recommendations on proposed provisional measures to be taken to prevent or remedy the market disruption. Only those members of the Commission who agreed to the affirmative determinations under paragraph (1) are eligible to vote on the proposed provisional measures to prevent or remedy market disruption. Members of the Commission who did not agree to the affirmative determinations may submit, in the report, dissenting or separate views regarding the determination and any recommendation of provisional measures referred to in this paragraph.

(3) If the determinations under paragraph (1) are affirmative, or may be considered by the President or the Trade Representative as affirmative under paragraph (1), the Trade Representative shall, within 10 days after receipt of the Commission's report, determine the amount or extent of provisional relief that is necessary to prevent or remedy the market disruption and shall provide a recommendation to the President on what provisional measures, if any, to take.

(4)(A) The President shall determine whether to provide provisional relief and proclaim such relief, if any, within 10 days after receipt of the recommendation from the Trade Representative.

(B) Such relief may take the form of

(i) the imposition of or increase in any duty;

(ii) any modification, or imposition of any quantitative restriction on the importation of an article into the United States; or

(iii) any combination of actions under clauses (i) and (ii).

(C) Any provisional action proclaimed by the President pursuant to a determination of critical circumstances shall remain in effect not more than 200 days.

(D) Provisional relief shall cease to apply upon the effective date of relief proclaimed under subsection (a), upon a decision by the President not to provide such relief, or upon a negative determination by the Commission under subsection (b) of this section.

(j) Agreements with the People's Republic of China

(1) The Trade Representative is authorized to enter into agreements for the People's Republic of China to take such action as necessary to prevent or remedy market disruption, and should seek to conclude such agreements before the expiration of the 60–day consultation period provided for under the product-specific safeguard provision of the Protocol of Accession of the People's Republic of China to the WTO, which shall commence not later than 5 days after the Trade Representative receives an affirmative determination provided for in subsection (e) of this section or a determination which the Trade Representative considers to be an affirmative determination pursuant to subsection (e) of this section.

(2) If no agreement is reached with the People's Republic of China pursuant to consultations under paragraph (1), or if the President determines than an agreement reached pursuant to such consultations is not preventing or remedying the market disruption at issue, the President shall provide import relief in accordance with subsection (a) of this section.

(k) Standard for Presidential action

(1) Within 15 days after receipt of a recommendation from the Trade Representative under subsection (h) of this section on the appropriate action, if any, to take to prevent or remedy the market disruption, the President shall provide import relief for such industry pursuant to subsection (a) of this section, unless the President determines that provision of such relief is not in the national economic interest of the United States or, in extraordinary cases, that the taking of action pursuant to subsection (a) of this section would cause serious harm to the national security of the United States.

(2) The President may determine under paragraph (1) that providing import relief is not in the national economic interest of the United States only if the President finds that the taking of such action would have an adverse impact on the United States economy clearly greater than the benefits of such action.

(*l*) Publication of decision and reports

(1) The President's decision, including the reasons therefor and the scope and duration of any action taken, shall be published in the Federal Register.

(2) The Commission shall promptly make public any report transmitted under this section, but shall not make public any information which the Commission determines to be confidential, and shall publish notice of such report in the Federal Register.

(m) Effective date of relief

Import relief under this section shall take effect not later than 15 days after the President's determination to provide such relief.

(n) Modifications of relief

(1) At any time after the end of the 6–month period beginning on the date on which relief under subsection (m) of this section first takes effect, the President may request that the Commission provide a report on the probable effect of the modification, reduction, or termination of the relief provided on the relevant industry. The Commission shall transmit such report to the President within 60 days of the request.

(2) The President may, after receiving a report from the Commission under paragraph (1), take such action to modify, reduce, or terminate relief that the President determines is necessary to continue to prevent or remedy the market disruption at issue.

(3) Upon the granting of relief under subsection (k) of this section, the Commission shall collect such data as is necessary to allow it to respond rapidly to a request by the President under paragraph (1).

(*o*) Extension of action

(1) Upon request of the President, or upon petition on behalf of the industry concerned filed with the Commission not earlier than the date which is 9 months, and not later than the date which is 6 months, before the date any relief provided under subsection (k) of this section is to terminate, the Commission shall investigate to determine whether action under this section continues to be necessary to prevent or remedy market disruption.

(2) The Commission shall publish notice of the commencement of any proceeding under this subsection in the Federal Register and shall, within a reasonable time thereafter, hold a public hearing at which the Commission shall afford interested parties and consumers an opportunity to be present, to present evidence, and to respond to the presentations of other parties and consumers, and otherwise to be heard.

(3) The Commission shall transmit to the President a report on its investigation and determination under this subsection not later than 60 days before the action under subsection (m) of this section is to terminate.

(4) The President, after receiving an affirmative determination from the Commission under paragraph (3), may extend the effective period of any action under this section if the President determines that the action continues to be necessary to prevent or remedy the market disruption.

* * *

TITLE V. GENERALIZED SYSTEM OF PREFERENCES

19 U.S.C. § 2461

Sec. 501. Authority to extend preferences

The President may provide duty-free treatment for any eligible article from any beneficiary developing country in accordance with the provisions of this title. In taking any such action, the President shall have due regard for—

(1) the effect such action will have on furthering the economic development of developing countries through the expansion of their exports;

(2) the extent to which other major developed countries are undertaking a comparable effort to assist developing countries by granting generalized preferences with respect to imports of products of such countries;

(3) the anticipated impact of such action on United States producers of like or directly competitive products; and

(4) the extent of the beneficiary developing country's competitiveness with respect to eligible articles.

19 U.S.C. § 2462

Sec. 502. Designation of beneficiary developing countries

(a) Authority to designate countries.

(1) Beneficiary developing countries. The President is authorized to designate countries as beneficiary developing countries for purposes of this title.

(2) Least-developed beneficiary developing countries. The President is authorized to designate any beneficiary developing country as a least-developed beneficiary developing country for purposes of this title, based on the considerations in section 501 and subsection (c) of this section.

(b) Countries ineligible for designation.

(1) Specific countries. The following countries may not be designated as beneficiary developing countries for purposes of this title et seq.]:

(A) Australia.

(B) Canada.

(C) European Union member states.

(D) Iceland.

(E) Japan.

(F) Monaco.

(G) New Zealand.

(H) Norway.

(I) Switzerland.

(2) Other bases for ineligibility. The President shall not designate any country a beneficiary developing country under this title if any of the following applies:

(A) Such country is a Communist country, unless—

(i) the products of such country receive nondiscriminatory treatment,

(ii) such country is a WTO Member (as such term is defined in section 2(10) of the Uruguay Round Agreements Act) (19 U.S.C. 3501(10)) and a member of the International Monetary Fund, and

(iii) such country is not dominated or controlled by international communism.

(B) Such country is a party to an arrangement of countries and participates in any action pursuant to such arrangement, the effect of which is—

(i) to withhold supplies of vital commodity resources from international trade or to raise the price of such commodities to an unreasonable level, and

(ii) to cause serious disruption of the world economy.

(C) Such country affords preferential treatment to the products of a developed country, other than the United States, which has, or is likely to have, a significant adverse effect on United States commerce.

(D)(i) Such country—

(I) has nationalized, expropriated, or otherwise seized ownership or control of property, including patents, trademarks, or copyrights, owned by a United States citizen or by a corporation, partnership, or association which is 50 percent or more beneficially owned by United States citizens,

(II) has taken steps to repudiate or nullify an existing contract or agreement with a United States citizen or a corporation, partnership, or association which is 50 percent or more beneficially owned by United States citizens, the effect of which is to nationalize, expropriate, or otherwise seize ownership or control of property, including patents, trademarks, or copyrights, so owned, or

(III) has imposed or enforced taxes or other exactions, restrictive maintenance or operational conditions, or other measures with respect to property, including patents, trademarks, or copyrights, so owned, the effect of which is to nationalize, expropriate, or otherwise seize ownership or control of such property, unless clause (ii) applies.

(ii) This clause applies if the President determines that—

(I) prompt, adequate, and effective compensation has been or is being made to the citizen, corporation, partnership, or association referred to in clause (i),

(II) good faith negotiations to provide prompt, adequate, and effective compensation under the applicable provisions of international law are in progress, or the country described in clause (i) is otherwise taking steps to discharge its obligations under international law with respect to such citizen, corporation, partnership, or association, or

(III) a dispute involving such citizen, corporation, partnership, or association over compensation for such a seizure has been submitted to arbitration under the provisions of the Convention for the Settlement of Investment Disputes, or in another mutually agreed upon forum, and the President promptly furnishes a copy of such determination to the Senate and House of Representatives.

(E) Such country fails to act in good faith in recognizing as binding or in enforcing arbitral awards in favor of United States citizens or a corporation, partnership, or association which is 50 percent or more beneficially owned by United States citizens, which have been made by arbitrators appointed for each case or by permanent arbitral bodies to which the parties involved have submitted their dispute.

(F) Such country aids or abets, by granting sanctuary from prosecution to, any individual or group which has committed an act of international terrorism or the Secretary of State makes a determination with respect to such country under section 6(j)(1)(A) of the Export Administration Act of 1979 or such country has not taken steps to support the efforts of the United States to combat terrorism.

(G) Such country has not taken or is not taking steps to afford internationally recognized worker rights to workers in the country (including any designated zone in that country).

(H) Such country has not implemented its commitments to eliminate the worst forms of child labor.

Subparagraphs (D), (E), (F), (G) and (H) (to the extent described in section 507(6)(D)) shall not prevent the designation of any country as a beneficiary developing country under this title if the President determines that such designation will be in the national economic interest of the United States and reports such determination to the Congress with the reasons therefor.

(c) Factors affecting country designation. In determining whether to designate any country as a beneficiary developing country under this title, the President shall take into account—

(1) an expression by such country of its desire to be so designated;

(2) the level of economic development of such country, including its per capita gross national product, the living standards of its inhabitants, and any other economic factors which the President deems appropriate;

(3) whether or not other major developed countries are extending generalized preferential tariff treatment to such country;

(4) the extent to which such country has assured the United States that it will provide equitable and reasonable access to the markets and basic commodity resources of such country and the extent to which such country has assured the United States that it will refrain from engaging in unreasonable export practices;

(5) the extent to which such country is providing adequate and effective protection of intellectual property rights;

(6) the extent to which such country has taken action to—

(A) reduce trade distorting investment practices and policies (including export performance requirements); and

(B) reduce or eliminate barriers to trade in services; and

(7) whether or not such country has taken or is taking steps to afford to workers in that country (including any designated zone in that country) internationally recognized worker rights.

(d) Withdrawal, suspension, or limitation of country designation.

(1) In general. The President may withdraw, suspend, or limit the application of the duty-free treatment accorded under this title with respect to any country. In taking any action under this subsection, the President shall consider the factors set forth in section 501 and subsection (c) of this section.

(2) Changed circumstances. The President shall, after complying with the requirements of subsection (f)(2), withdraw or suspend the designation of any country as a beneficiary developing country if, after such designation, the President determines that as the result of changed circumstances such country would be barred from designation as a beneficiary developing country under subsection (b)(2). Such country shall cease to be a beneficiary developing country on the day on which the President issues an Executive order or Presidential proclamation revoking the designation of such country under this title.

(3) Advice to Congress. The President shall, as necessary, advise the Congress on the application of section 501 and subsection (c) of this section, and the actions the President has taken to withdraw, to suspend, or to limit the application of duty-free treatment with respect to any country which has failed to adequately take the actions described in subsection (c).

(e) Mandatory graduation of beneficiary developing countries. If the President determines that a beneficiary developing country has become a "high income" country, as defined by the official statistics of the International Bank for Reconstruction and Development, then the President shall terminate the designation of such country as a beneficiary developing country for purposes of this title, effective on January 1 of the second year following the year in which such determination is made.

(f) Congressional notification.

(1) Notification of designation.

(A) In general. Before the President designates any country as a beneficiary developing country under this title, the President shall notify the Congress of the President's intention to make such designation, together with the considerations entering into such decision.

(B) Designation as least-developed beneficiary developing country. At least 60 days before the President designates any country as a least-developed beneficiary developing country, the President shall notify the Congress of the President's intention to make such designation.

(2) Notification of termination. If the President has designated any country as a beneficiary developing country under this title, the President

shall not terminate such designation unless, at least 60 days before such termination, the President has notified the Congress and has notified such country of the President's intention to terminate such designation, together with the considerations entering into such decision.

19 U.S.C. § 2463

Sec. 503. Designation of eligible articles

(a) Eligible articles

(1) Designation

(A) In general

Except as provided in subsection (b) of this section, the President is authorized to designate articles as eligible articles from all beneficiary developing countries for purposes of this subchapter by Executive order or Presidential proclamation after receiving the advice of the International Trade Commission in accordance with subsection (e) of this section.

(B) Least-developed beneficiary developing countries

Except for articles described in subparagraphs (A), (B), and (E) of subsection (b)(1) of this section and articles described in paragraphs (2) and (3) of subsection (b) of this section, the President may, in carrying out section 502(d) of this title [19 U.S.C. § 2462(d)(1)] and subsection (C)(1) of this section, designate articles as eligible articles only for countries designated as least-developed beneficiary developing countries under section 502(a)(2) of this title [19 U.S.C. § 2462(a)(2)] if, after receiving the advice of the International Trade Commission in accordance with subsection (e) of this section, the President determines that such articles are not import-sensitive in the context of imports from least-developed beneficiary developing countries.

(C) Three-year rule

If, after receiving the advice of the International Trade Commission under subsection (e) of this section, an article has been formally considered for designation as an eligible article under this subchapter and denied such designation, such article may not be reconsidered for such designation for a period of 3 years after such denial.

(2) Rule of origin

(A) General rule

The duty-free treatment provided under this subchapter shall apply to any eligible article which is the growth, product, or manufacture of a beneficiary developing country if—

(i) that article is imported directly from a beneficiary developing country into the customs territory of the United States; and

(ii) the sum of—

(I) the cost or value of the materials produced in the beneficiary developing country or any two or more such countries that are members of the same association of countries and are treated as one country under section 507(2) of this title [19 U.S.C. § 2467(2)], plus

(II) the direct costs of processing operations performed in such beneficiary developing country or such member countries,

is not less than 35 percent of the appraised value of such article at the time it is entered.

(B) Exclusions

An article shall not be treated as the growth, product, or manufacture of a beneficiary developing country by virtue of having merely undergone—

(i) simple combining or packaging operations, or

(ii) mere dilution with water or mere dilution with another substance that does not materially alter the characteristics of the article.

(3) Regulations

The Secretary of the Treasury, after consulting with the United States Trade Representative, shall prescribe such regulations as may be necessary to carry out paragraph (2), including, but not limited to, regulations providing that, in order to be eligible for duty-free treatment under this subchapter, an article—

(A) must be wholly the growth, product, or manufacture of a beneficiary developing country, or

(B) must be a new or different article of commerce which has been grown, produced, or manufactured in the beneficiary developing country.

(b) Articles that may not be designated as eligible articles

(1) Import-sensitive articles

The President may not designate any article as an eligible article under subsection (a) of this section if such article is within one of the following categories of import-sensitive articles:

(A) Except as provided in paragraph (4), textile and apparel articles which were not eligible articles for purposes of this subchapter on January 1, 1994, as this subchapter was in effect on such date.

(B) Watches, except those watches entered after June 30, 1989, that the President specifically determines, after public notice and comment, will not cause material injury to watch or watch band, strap, or bracelet manufacturing and assembly operations in the United States or the United States insular possessions.

(C) Import-sensitive electronic articles.

(D) Import-sensitive steel articles.

(E) Footwear, handbags, luggage, flat goods, work gloves, and leather wearing apparel which were not eligible articles for purposes of this subchapter on January 1, 1995, as this subchapter was in effect on such date.

(F) Import-sensitive semimanufactured and manufactured glass products.

(G) Any other articles which the President determines to be import-sensitive in the context of the Generalized System of Preferences.

(2) Articles against which other actions taken

An article shall not be an eligible article for purposes of this subchapter for any period during which such article is the subject of any action proclaimed pursuant to section 203 of this title [19 U.S.C. § 2253] or sections 232 or 351 of this title [19 U.S.C. §§ 1862 or 1981].

(3) Agricultural products

No quantity of an agricultural product subject to a tariff-rate quota that exceeds the in-quota quantity shall be eligible for duty-free treatment under this subchapter.

(4) Certain hand-knotted or hand-woven carpets

Notwithstanding paragraph (1)(A), the President may designate as an eligible article or articles under subsection (a) of this section carpets or rugs which are hand-loomed, hand-woven, hand-hooked, hand-tufted, or hand-knotted, and classifiable under subheading 5701.10.16, 5701.10.40, 5701.90.10, 5701.90.20, 5702.10.90, 5702.42.20, 5702.49.10, 5702.51.20, 5702.91.30, 5702.92.00, 5702.99.10, 5703. 10.00, 5703.20.10, or 5703.30.00 of the Harmonized Tariff Schedule of the United States.

(c) Withdrawal, suspension, or limitation of duty-free treatment; competitive need limitation

(1) In general

The President may withdraw, suspend, or limit the application of the duty-free treatment accorded under this subchapter with respect to any article, except that no rate of duty may be established with respect to any article pursuant to this subsection other than the rate which would apply but for this subchapter. In taking any action under this subsection, the President shall consider the factors set forth in sections 501 and 502(c) of this title [19 U.S.C. §§ 2461 and 2462(c)].

(2) Competitive need limitation

(A) Basis for withdrawal of duty-free treatment

(i) In general

Except as provided in clause (ii) and subject to subsection (d) of this section, whenever the President determines that a beneficiary developing country has exported (directly or indirectly) to the United States during any calendar year beginning after December 31, 1995—

(I) a quantity of an eligible article having an appraised value in excess of the applicable amount for the calendar year, or

(II) a quantity of an eligible article equal to or exceeding 50 percent of the appraised value of the total imports of that article into the United States during any calendar year,

the President shall, not later than July 1 of the next calendar year, terminate the duty-free treatment for that article from that beneficiary developing country.

(ii) Annual adjustment of applicable amount

For purposes of applying clause (i), the applicable amount is—

(I) for 1996, $75,000,000, and

(II) for each calendar year thereafter, an amount equal to the applicable amount in effect for the preceding calendar year plus $5,000,000.

(B) "Country" defined

For purposes of this paragraph, the term "country" does not include an association of countries which is treated as one country under section 507(2) of this title [19 U.S.C. § 2467(2)], but does include a country which is a member of any such association.

(C) Redesignations

A country which is no longer treated as a beneficiary developing country with respect to an eligible article by reason of subparagraph (A) may, subject to the considerations set forth in sections 501 and 502 of this title [19 U.S.C. §§ 2461 and 2462], be redesignated a beneficiary developing country with respect to such article if imports of such article from such country did not exceed the limitations in subparagraph (A) during the preceding calendar year.

(D) Least-developed beneficiary developing countries and beneficiary sub-Saharan African countries

Subparagraph (A) shall not apply to any least-developed beneficiary developing country or any beneficiary sub-Saharan African country.

(E) Articles not produced in the United States excluded

Subparagraph (A)(i)(II) shall not apply with respect to any eligible article if a like or directly competitive article was not produced in the United States on January 1, 1995.

(F) De minimis waivers

(i) In general

The President may disregard subparagraph (A)(i)(II) with respect to any eligible article from any beneficiary developing country if the aggregate appraised value of the imports of such article into the United States during the preceding calendar year does not exceed the applicable amount for such preceding calendar year.

(ii) Applicable amount

For purposes of applying clause (i), the applicable amount is—

(I) for calendar year 1996, $13,000,000, and

(II) for each calendar year thereafter, an amount equal to the applicable amount in effect for the preceding calendar year plus $500,000.

(d) Waiver of competitive need limitation

(1) In general

The President may waive the application of subsection (c)(2) of this section with respect to any eligible article of any beneficiary developing country if, before July 1 of the calendar year beginning after the calendar year for which a determination described in subsection (c)(2)(A) of this section was made with respect to such eligible article, the President—

(A) receives the advice of the International Trade Commission under section 332 of this title [19 U.S.C. § 1332] on whether any industry in the United States is likely to be adversely affected by such waiver,

(B) determines, based on the considerations described in sections 501 and 502(c) of this title [19 U.S.C. §§ 2461 and 2462(c)] and the advice described in subparagraph (A), that such waiver is in the national economic interest of the United States, and

(C) publishes the determination described in subparagraph (B) in the Federal Register.

(2) Considerations by the President

In making any determination under paragraph (1), the President shall give great weight to—

(A) the extent to which the beneficiary developing country has assured the United States that such country will provide equitable and reasonable access to the markets and basic commodity resources of such country, and

(B) the extent to which such country provides adequate and effective protection of intellectual property rights.

(3) Other bases for waiver

The President may waive the application of subsection (c)(2) of this section if, before July 1 of the calendar year beginning after the calendar year for which a determination described in subsection (c)(2) of this section was made with respect to a beneficiary developing country, the President determines that—

(A) there has been a historical preferential trade relationship between the United States and such country,

(B) there is a treaty or trade agreement in force covering economic relations between such country and the United States, and

(C) such country does not discriminate against, or impose unjustifiable or unreasonable barriers to, United States commerce,

and the President publishes that determination in the Federal Register.

(4) Limitations on waivers

(A) In general

The President may not exercise the waiver authority under this subsection with respect to a quantity of an eligible article entered during any calendar year beginning after 1995, the aggregate appraised value of which equals or exceeds 30 percent of the aggregate appraised value of all articles that entered duty-free under this subchapter during the preceding calendar year.

(B) Other waiver limits

(i) The President may not exercise the waiver authority provided under this subsection with respect to a quantity of an eligible article entered during any calendar year beginning after 1995, the aggregate appraised value of which exceeds 15 percent of the aggregate appraised value of all articles that have entered duty-free under this subchapter during the preceding calendar year from those beneficiary developing countries which for the preceding calendar year—

(I) had a per capita gross national product (calculated on the basis of the best available information, including that of the International Bank for Reconstruction and Development) of $5,000 or more; or

(II) had exported (either directly or indirectly) to the United States a quantity of articles that was duty-free under this subchapter that had an aggregate appraised value of more than 10 percent of the aggregate appraised value of all articles that entered duty-free under this subchapter during that year.

(ii) Not later than July 1 of each year, the President should revoke any waiver that has then been in effect with respect to an article for 5 years or more if the beneficiary developing country has exported to the United States (directly or indirectly) during the preceding calendar year a quantity of the article—

(I) having an appraised value in excess of 1.5 times the applicable amount set forth in subsection (c)(2)(A)(ii) of this section for that calendar year; or

(II) exceeding 75 percent of the appraised value of the total imports of that article into the United States during that calendar year.

(C) Calculation of limitations

There shall be counted against the limitations imposed under subparagraphs (A) and (B) for any calendar year only that value of any eligible article of any country that—

(i) entered duty-free under this subchapter during such calendar year; and

(ii) is in excess of the value of that article that would have been so entered during such calendar year if the limitations under subsection (c)(2)(A) of this section applied.

(5) Effective period of waiver

Any waiver granted under this subsection shall remain in effect until the President determines that such waiver is no longer warranted due to changed circumstances.

(e) International Trade Commission advice

Before designating articles as eligible articles under subsection (a)(1) of this section, the President shall publish and furnish the International Trade Commission with lists of articles which may be considered for designation as eligible articles for purposes of this subchapter. The provisions of sections 131, 132, 133, and 134 of this title [19 U.S.C. §§ 2151, 2152, 2153, and 2154] shall be complied with as though action under section 501 of this title [19 U.S.C. § 2461] and this section were action under section 123 of this title [19 U.S.C. § 2133] to carry out a trade agreement entered into under section 123 of this title [19 U.S.C. § 2133].

(f) Special rule concerning Puerto Rico

No action under this subchapter may affect any tariff duty imposed by the Legislature of Puerto Rico pursuant to section 319 of this title [19 U.S.C. § 1319] on coffee imported into Puerto Rico.

Sec. 504. Review and report to Congress

The President shall submit an annual report to the Congress on the status of internationally recognized worker rights within each beneficiary developing country, including the findings of the Secretary of Labor with respect to the beneficiary country's implementation of its international commitments to eliminate the worst forms of child labor.

* * *

TITLE VI. GENERAL PROVISIONS

19 U.S.C. § 2481

Sec. 601. Definitions

For purposes of this Act—

(1) The term "duty" includes the rate and form of any import duty, including but not limited to tariff-rate quotas.

(2) The term "other import restriction" includes a limitation, prohibition, charge, and exaction other than duty, imposed on importation or imposed for the regulation of importation. The term does not include any orderly marketing agreement.

(3) The term "ad valorem" includes ad valorem equivalent. Whenever any limitation on the amount by which or to which any rate of duty may be decreased or increased pursuant to a trade agreement is expressed in terms of an ad valorem percentage, the ad valorem amount taken into account for purposes of such limitation shall be determined by the President on the

basis of the value of imports of the articles concerned during the most recent representative period.

(4) The term "ad valorem equivalent" means the ad valorem equivalent of a specific rate or, in the case of a combination of rates including a specific rate, the sum of the ad valorem equivalent of the specific rate and of the ad valorem rate. The ad valorem equivalent shall be determined by the President on the basis of the value of imports of the article concerned during the most recent representative period. In determining the value of imports, the President shall utilize, to the maximum extent practicable, the standards of valuation contained in section 402 or 402a of the Tariff Act of 1930 (19 U.S.C. §§ 1401a or 1402) applicable to the article concerned during such representative period.

(5) An imported article is "directly competitive with" a domestic article at an earlier or later stage of processing, and a domestic article is "directly competitive with" an imported article at an earlier or later stage of processing, if the importation of the article has an economic effect on producers of the domestic article comparable to the effect of importation of articles in the same stage of processing as the domestic article. For purposes of this paragraph, the unprocessed article is at an earlier stage of processing.

(6) The term "modification", as applied to any duty or other import restriction, includes the elimination of any duty or other import restriction.

(7) The term "existing" means (A) when used, without the specification of any date, with respect to any matter relating to entering into or carrying out a trade agreement or other action authorized by this Act, existing on the day on which such trade agreement is entered into or such other action is taken; and (B) when used with respect to a rate of duty, the nonpreferential rate of duty (however established, and even though temporarily suspended by Act of Congress or otherwise) set forth in rate column numbered 1 of schedules 1 through 97 of the Harmonized Tariff Schedules of the United States on the date specified or (if no date is specified) on the day referred to in clause (A).

(8) A product of a country or area is an article which is the growth, produce, or manufacture of such country or area.

(9) The term "nondiscriminatory treatment" means most-favored-nation treatment.

(10) The term "commerce" includes services associated with international trade.

* * *

DOCUMENT 29

TRADE ACT OF 2002, TITLE XXI—BIPARTISAN TRADE PROMOTION AUTHORITY ACT OF 2002

■ ■ ■

Pub. L. 107–210

SEC. 2101. [19 USC 3801.] SHORT TITLE AND FINDINGS.

(a) Short Title.—This title may be cited as the "Bipartisan Trade Promotion Authority Act of 2002".

(b) Findings.—The Congress makes the following findings: (1) The expansion of international trade is vital to the national security of the United States. Trade is critical to the economic growth and strength of the United States and to its leadership in the world. Stable trading relationships promote security and prosperity. Trade agreements today serve the same purposes that security pacts played during the Cold War, binding nations together through a series of mutual rights and obligations. Leadership by the United States in international trade fosters open markets, democracy, and peace throughout the world.

(2) The national security of the United States depends on its economic security, which in turn is founded upon a vibrant and growing industrial base. Trade expansion has been the engine of economic growth. Trade agreements maximize opportunities for the critical sectors and building blocks of the economy of the United States, such as information technology, telecommunications and other leading technologies, basic industries, capital equipment, medical equipment, services, agriculture, environmental technology, and intellectual property. Trade will create new opportunities for the United States and preserve the unparalleled strength of the United States in economic, political, and military affairs. The United States, secured by expanding trade and economic opportunities, will meet the challenges of the twenty-first century.

(3) Support for continued trade expansion requires that dispute settlement procedures under international trade agreements not add to or diminish the rights and obligations provided in such agreements. Therefore—(A) the recent pattern of decisions by dispute settlement panels of the WTO and the Appellate Body to impose obligations and

restrictions on the use of antidumping, countervailing, and safeguard measures by WTO members under the Antidumping Agreement, the Agreement on Subsidies and Countervailing Measures, and the Agreement on Safeguards has raised concerns; and (B) the Congress is concerned that dispute settlement panels of the WTO and the Appellate Body appropriately apply the standard of review contained in Article 17.6 of the Antidumping Agreement, to provide deference to a permissible interpretation by a WTO member of provisions of that Agreement, and to the evaluation by a WTO member of the facts where that evaluation is unbiased and objective and the establishment of the facts is proper.

SEC. 2102. [19 USC 3802.] TRADE NEGOTIATING OBJECTIVES.

(a) Overall Trade Negotiating Objectives.—The overall trade negotiating objectives of the United States for agreements subject to the provisions of section 2103 are—(1) to obtain more open, equitable, and reciprocal market access;

(2) to obtain the reduction or elimination of barriers and distortions that are directly related to trade and that decrease market opportunities for United States exports or otherwise distort United States trade;

(3) to further strengthen the system of international trading disciplines and procedures, including dispute settlement;

(4) to foster economic growth, raise living standards, and promote full employment in the United States and to enhance the global economy;

(5) to ensure that trade and environmental policies are mutually supportive and to seek to protect and preserve the environment and enhance the international means of doing so, while optimizing the use of the world's resources;

(6) to promote respect for worker rights and the rights of children consistent with core labor standards of the ILO (as defined in section 2113(6)) and an understanding of the relationship between trade and worker rights;

(7) to seek provisions in trade agreements under which parties to those agreements strive to ensure that they do not weaken or reduce the protections afforded in domestic environmental and labor laws as an encouragement for trade;

(8) to ensure that trade agreements afford small businesses equal access to international markets, equitable trade benefits, and expanded export market opportunities, and provide for the reduction or elimination of trade barriers that disproportionately impact small businesses; and

(9) to promote universal ratification and full compliance with ILO Convention No. 182 Concerning the Prohibition and Immediate Action for the Elimination of the Worst Forms of Child Labor.

(b) Principal Trade Negotiating Objectives.—

(1) Trade barriers and distortions.—The principal negotiating objectives of the United States regarding trade barriers and other trade distortions are—

(A) to expand competitive market opportunities for United States exports and to obtain fairer and more open conditions of trade by reducing or eliminating tariff and nontariff barriers and policies and practices of foreign governments directly related to trade that decrease market opportunities for United States exports or otherwise distort United States trade; and

(B) to obtain reciprocal tariff and nontariff barrier elimination agreements, with particular attention to those tariff categories covered in section 111(b) of the Uruguay Round Agreements Act (19 U.S.C. 3521(b)).

(2) Trade in services.—The principal negotiating objective of the United States regarding trade in services is to reduce or eliminate barriers to international trade in services, including regulatory and other barriers that deny national treatment and market access or unreasonably restrict the establishment or operations of service suppliers.

(3) Foreign investment.—Recognizing that United States law on the whole provides a high level of protection for investment, consistent with or greater than the level required by international law, the principal negotiating objectives of the United States regarding foreign investment are to reduce or eliminate artificial or trade-distorting barriers to foreign investment, while ensuring that foreign investors in the United States are not accorded greater substantive rights with respect to investment protections than United States investors in the United States, and to secure for investors important rights comparable to those that would be available under United States legal principles and practice, by—

(A) reducing or eliminating exceptions to the principle of national treatment;

(B) freeing the transfer of funds relating to investments;

(C) reducing or eliminating performance requirements, forced technology transfers, and other unreasonable barriers to the establishment and operation of investments;

(D) seeking to establish standards for expropriation and compensation for expropriation, consistent with United States legal principles and practice;

(E) seeking to establish standards for fair and equitable treatment consistent with United States legal principles and practice, including the principle of due process;

(F) providing meaningful procedures for resolving investment disputes;

(G) seeking to improve mechanisms used to resolve disputes between an investor and a government through—

(i) mechanisms to eliminate frivolous claims and to deter the filing of frivolous claims;

(ii) procedures to ensure the efficient selection of arbitrators and the expeditious disposition of claims;

(iii) procedures to enhance opportunities for public input into the formulation of government positions; and

(iv) providing for an appellate body or similar mechanism to provide coherence to the interpretations of investment provisions in trade agreements; and

(H) ensuring the fullest measure of transparency in the dispute settlement mechanism, to the extent consistent with the need to protect information that is classified or business confidential, by—

(i) ensuring that all requests for dispute settlement are promptly made public;

(ii) ensuring that—

(I) all proceedings, submissions, findings, and decisions are promptly made public; and

(II) all hearings are open to the public; and

(iii) establishing a mechanism for acceptance of amicus curiae submissions from businesses, unions, and nongovernmental organizations.

(4) Intellectual property.—The principal negotiating objectives of the United States regarding trade-related intellectual property are—

(A) to further promote adequate and effective protection of intellectual property rights, including through—

(i)(I) ensuring accelerated and full implementation of the Agreement on Trade-Related Aspects of Intellectual Property Rights referred to in section 101(d)(15) of the Uruguay Round Agreements Act (19 U.S.C. 3511(d)(15)), particularly with respect to meeting enforcement obligations under that agreement; and

(II) ensuring that the provisions of any multilateral or bilateral trade agreement governing intellectual property rights that is entered into by the United States reflect a standard of protection similar to that found in United States law;

(ii) providing strong protection for new and emerging technologies and new methods of transmitting and distributing products embodying intellectual property;

(iii) preventing or eliminating discrimination with respect to matters affecting the availability, acquisition, scope, maintenance, use, and enforcement of intellectual property rights;

(iv) ensuring that standards of protection and enforcement keep pace with technological developments, and in particular ensuring that rightholders have the legal and technological means to control the use of their works through the Internet and other global communication media, and to prevent the unauthorized use of their works; and

(v) providing strong enforcement of intellectual property rights, including through accessible, expeditious, and effective civil, administrative, and criminal enforcement mechanisms;

(B) to secure fair, equitable, and nondiscriminatory market access opportunities for United States persons that rely upon intellectual property protection; and

(C) to respect the Declaration on the TRIPS Agreement and Public Health, adopted by the World Trade Organization at the Fourth Ministerial Conference at Doha, Qatar on November 14, 2001.

(5) Transparency.—The principal negotiating objective of the United States with respect to transparency is to obtain wider and broader application of the principle of transparency through—

(A) increased and more timely public access to information regarding trade issues and the activities of international trade institutions;

(B) increased openness at the WTO and other international trade fora by increasing public access to appropriate meetings, proceedings, and submissions, including with regard to dispute settlement and investment; and

(C) increased and more timely public access to all notifications and supporting documentation submitted by parties to the WTO.

(6) Anti-corruption.—The principal negotiating objectives of the United States with respect to the use of money or other things of value to influence acts, decisions, or omissions of foreign governments or officials or to secure any improper advantage in a manner affecting trade are—

(A) to obtain high standards and appropriate domestic enforcement mechanisms applicable to persons from all countries participating in the applicable trade agreement that prohibit such attempts to influence acts, decisions, or omissions of foreign governments; and

(B) to ensure that such standards do not place United States persons at a competitive disadvantage in international trade.

(7) Improvement of the wto and multilateral trade agreements.—The principal negotiating objectives of the United States regarding the improvement of the World Trade Organization, the Uruguay Round Agreements, and other multilateral and bilateral trade agreements are—

(A) to achieve full implementation and extend the coverage of the World Trade Organization and such agreements to products, sectors, and conditions of trade not adequately covered; and

(B) to expand country participation in and enhancement of the Information Technology Agreement and other trade agreements.

(8) Regulatory practices.—The principal negotiating objectives of the United States regarding the use of government regulation or other practices by foreign governments to provide a competitive advantage to their domestic producers, service providers, or investors and thereby reduce market access for United States goods, services, and investments are—

(A) to achieve increased transparency and opportunity for the participation of affected parties in the development of regulations;

(B) to require that proposed regulations be based on sound science, cost-benefit analysis, risk assessment, or other objective evidence;

(C) to establish consultative mechanisms among parties to trade agreements to promote increased transparency in developing guidelines, rules, regulations, and laws for government procurement and other regulatory regimes; and

(D) to achieve the elimination of government measures such as price controls and reference pricing which deny full market access for United States products.

(9) Electronic commerce.—The principal negotiating objectives of the United States with respect to electronic commerce are—

(A) to ensure that current obligations, rules, disciplines, and commitments under the World Trade Organization apply to electronic commerce;

(B) to ensure that—

(i) electronically delivered goods and services receive no less favorable treatment under trade rules and commitments than like products delivered in physical form; and

(ii) the classification of such goods and services ensures the most liberal trade treatment possible;

(C) to ensure that governments refrain from implementing trade-related measures that impede electronic commerce;

(D) where legitimate policy objectives require domestic regulations that affect electronic commerce, to obtain commitments that any such regulations are the least restrictive on trade, nondiscriminatory, and transparent, and promote an open market environment; and

(E) to extend the moratorium of the World Trade Organization on duties on electronic transmissions.

(10) Reciprocal trade in agriculture.—

(A) The principal negotiating objective of the United States with respect to agriculture is to obtain competitive opportunities for United States exports of agricultural commodities in foreign markets substantially equivalent to the competitive opportunities afforded foreign exports in United States markets and to achieve fairer and more open conditions of trade in bulk, specialty crop, and value-added commodities by—

(i) reducing or eliminating, by a date certain, tariffs or other charges that decrease market opportunities for United States exports—

(I) giving priority to those products that are subject to significantly higher tariffs or subsidy regimes of major producing countries; and

(II) providing reasonable adjustment periods for United States import-sensitive products, in close consultation with the Congress on such products before initiating tariff reduction negotiations;

(ii) reducing tariffs to levels that are the same as or lower than those in the United States;

(iii) reducing or eliminating subsidies that decrease market opportunities for United States exports or unfairly distort agriculture markets to the detriment of the United States;

(iv) allowing the preservation of programs that support family farms and rural communities but do not distort trade;

(v) developing disciplines for domestic support programs, so that production that is in excess of domestic food security needs is sold at world prices;

(vi) eliminating government policies that create price-depressing surpluses;

(vii) eliminating state trading enterprises whenever possible;

(viii) developing, strengthening, and clarifying rules and effective dispute settlement mechanisms to eliminate practices that unfairly decrease United States market access opportunities or distort agricultural markets to the detriment of the United States, particularly with respect to import-sensitive products, including—

(I) unfair or trade-distorting activities of state trading enterprises and other administrative mechanisms, with emphasis on requiring price transparency in the operation of state trading enterprises and such other mechanisms in order to end cross subsidization, price discrimination, and price undercutting;

(II) unjustified trade restrictions or commercial requirements, such as labeling, that affect new technologies, including biotechnology;

(III) unjustified sanitary or phytosanitary restrictions, including those not based on scientific principles in contravention of the Uruguay Round Agreements;

(IV) other unjustified technical barriers to trade; and

(V) restrictive rules in the administration of tariff rate quotas;

(ix) eliminating practices that adversely affect trade in perishable or cyclical products, while improving import relief mechanisms to recognize the unique characteristics of perishable and cyclical agriculture;

(x) ensuring that import relief mechanisms for perishable and cyclical agriculture are as accessible and timely to growers in the United States as those mechanisms that are used by other countries;

(xi) taking into account whether a party to the negotiations has failed to adhere to the provisions of already existing trade agreements with the United States or has circumvented obligations under those agreements;

(xii) taking into account whether a product is subject to market distortions by reason of a failure of a major producing country to adhere to the provisions of already existing trade agreements with the United States or by the circumvention by that country of its obligations under those agreements;

(xiii) otherwise ensuring that countries that accede to the World Trade Organization have made meaningful market liberalization commitments in agriculture;

(xiv) taking into account the impact that agreements covering agriculture to which the United States is a party, including the North American Free Trade Agreement, have on the United States agricultural industry;

(xv) maintaining bona fide food assistance programs and preserving United States market development and export credit programs; and

(xvi) striving to complete a general multilateral round in the World Trade Organization by January 1, 2005, and seeking the broadest market access possible in multilateral, regional, and bilateral negotiations, recognizing the effect that simultaneous sets of negotiations may have on United States import-sensitive commodities (including those subject to tariff-rate quotas).

(B)(i) Before commencing negotiations with respect to agriculture, the United States Trade Representative, in consultation with the Congress, shall seek to develop a position on the treatment of seasonal and perishable agricultural products to be employed in the negotiations in order to develop an international consensus on the treatment of seasonal or perishable agricultural products in investigations relating to dumping and safeguards and in any other relevant area.

(ii) During any negotiations on agricultural subsidies, the United States Trade Representative shall seek to establish the common base year for calculating the Aggregated Measurement of Support (as defined in the Agreement on

Agriculture) as the end of each country's Uruguay Round implementation period, as reported in each country's Uruguay Round market access schedule.

(iii) The negotiating objective provided in subparagraph (A) applies with respect to agricultural matters to be addressed in any trade agreement entered into under section 2103(a) or (b), including any trade agreement entered into under section 2103(a) or (b) that provides for accession to a trade agreement to which the United States is already a party, such as the North American Free Trade Agreement and the United States-Canada Free Trade Agreement.

(11) Labor and the environment.—The principal negotiating objectives of the United States with respect to labor and the environment are—

(A) to ensure that a party to a trade agreement with the United States does not fail to effectively enforce its environmental or labor laws, through a sustained or recurring course of action or inaction, in a manner affecting trade between the United States and that party after entry into force of a trade agreement between those countries;

(B) to recognize that parties to a trade agreement retain the right to exercise discretion with respect to investigatory, prosecutorial, regulatory, and compliance matters and to make decisions regarding the allocation of resources to enforcement with respect to other labor or environmental matters determined to have higher priorities, and to recognize that a country is effectively enforcing its laws if a course of action or inaction reflects a reasonable exercise of such discretion, or results from a bona fide decision regarding the allocation of resources, and no retaliation may be authorized based on the exercise of these rights or the right to establish domestic labor standards and levels of environmental protection;

(C) to strengthen the capacity of United States trading partners to promote respect for core labor standards (as defined in section 2113(6));

(D) to strengthen the capacity of United States trading partners to protect the environment through the promotion of sustainable development;

(E) to reduce or eliminate government practices or policies that unduly threaten sustainable development;

(F) to seek market access, through the elimination of tariffs and nontariff barriers, for United States environmental technologies, goods, and services; and

(G) to ensure that labor, environmental, health, or safety policies and practices of the parties to trade agreements with the United States do not arbitrarily or unjustifiably discriminate against United States exports or serve as disguised barriers to trade.

(12) Dispute settlement and enforcement.—The principal negotiating objectives of the United States with respect to dispute settlement and enforcement of trade agreements are—

(A) to seek provisions in trade agreements providing for resolution of disputes between governments under those trade agreements in an effective, timely, transparent, equitable, and reasoned manner, requiring determinations based on facts and the principles of the agreements, with the goal of increasing compliance with the agreements;

(B) to seek to strengthen the capacity of the Trade Policy Review Mechanism of the World Trade Organization to review compliance with commitments;

(C) to seek adherence by panels convened under the Dispute Settlement Understanding and by the Appellate Body to the standard of review applicable under the Uruguay Round Agreement involved in the dispute, including greater deference, where appropriate, to the fact-finding and technical expertise of national investigating authorities;

(D) to seek provisions encouraging the early identification and settlement of disputes through consultation;

(E) to seek provisions to encourage the provision of trade-expanding compensation if a party to a dispute under the agreement does not come into compliance with its obligations under the agreement;

(F) to seek provisions to impose a penalty upon a party to a dispute under the agreement that—

(i) encourages compliance with the obligations of the agreement;

(ii) is appropriate to the parties, nature, subject matter, and scope of the violation; and

(iii) has the aim of not adversely affecting parties or interests not party to the dispute while maintaining the effectiveness of the enforcement mechanism; and

(G) to seek provisions that treat United States principal negotiating objectives equally with respect to—

(i) the ability to resort to dispute settlement under the applicable agreement;

(ii) the availability of equivalent dispute settlement procedures; and

(iii) the availability of equivalent remedies.

(13) WTO extended negotiations.—The principal negotiating objectives of the United States regarding trade in civil aircraft are those set forth in section 135(c) of the Uruguay Round Agreements Act (19 U.S.C. 3355(c)) and regarding rules of origin are the conclusion of an agreement described in section 132 of that Act (19 U.S.C. 3552).

(14) Trade remedy laws.—The principal negotiating objectives of the United States with respect to trade remedy laws are—

(A) to preserve the ability of the United States to enforce rigorously its trade laws, including the antidumping, countervailing duty, and safeguard laws, and avoid agreements that lessen the effectiveness of domestic and international disciplines on unfair trade, especially dumping and subsidies, or that lessen the effectiveness of domestic and international safeguard provisions, in order to ensure that United States workers, agricultural producers, and firms can compete fully on fair terms and enjoy the benefits of reciprocal trade concessions; and

(B) to address and remedy market distortions that lead to dumping and subsidization, including overcapacity, cartelization, and market-access barriers.

(15) Border taxes.—The principal negotiating objective of the United States regarding border taxes is to obtain a revision of the WTO rules with respect to the treatment of border adjustments for internal taxes to redress the disadvantage to countries relying primarily on direct taxes for revenue rather than indirect taxes.

(16) Textile Negotiations.—The principal negotiating objectives of the United States with respect to trade in textiles and apparel articles are to obtain competitive opportunities for United States exports of textiles and apparel in foreign markets substantially equivalent to the competitive opportunities afforded foreign exports in United States markets and to achieve fairer and more open conditions of trade in textiles and apparel.

(17) Worst Forms of Child Labor.—The principal negotiating objective of the United States with respect to the trade-related aspects of the worst forms of child labor are to seek commitments by parties to trade

agreements to vigorously enforce their own laws prohibiting the worst forms of child labor.

(c) Promotion of Certain Priorities.—In order to address and maintain United States competitiveness in the global economy, the President shall—

(1) seek greater cooperation between the WTO and the ILO;

(2) seek to establish consultative mechanisms among parties to trade agreements to strengthen the capacity of United States trading partners to promote respect for core labor standards (as defined in section 2113(6)) and to promote compliance with ILO Convention No. 182 Concerning the Prohibition and Immediate Action for the Elimination of the Worst Forms of Child Labor, and report to the Committee on Ways and Means of the House of Representatives and the Committee on Finance of the Senate on the content and operation of such mechanisms;

(3) seek to establish consultative mechanisms among parties to trade agreements to strengthen the capacity of United States trading partners to develop and implement standards for the protection of the environment and human health based on sound science, and report to the Committee on Ways and Means of the House of Representatives and the Committee on Finance of the Senate on the content and operation of such mechanisms;

(4) conduct environmental reviews of future trade and investment agreements, consistent with Executive Order 13141 of November 16, 1999, and its relevant guidelines, and report to the Committee on Ways and Means of the House of Representatives and the Committee on Finance of the Senate on such reviews;

(5) review the impact of future trade agreements on United States employment, including labor markets, modeled after Executive Order 13141 to the extent appropriate in establishing procedures and criteria, report to the Committee on Ways and Means of the House of Representatives and the Committee on Finance of the Senate on such review, and make that report available to the public;

(6) take into account other legitimate United States domestic objectives including, but not limited to, the protection of legitimate health or safety, essential security, and consumer interests and the law and regulations related thereto;

(7) direct the Secretary of Labor to consult with any country seeking a trade agreement with the United States concerning that country's labor laws and provide technical assistance to that country if needed;

(8) in connection with any trade negotiations entered into under this Act, submit to the Committee on Ways and Means of the House of

Representatives and the Committee on Finance of the Senate a meaningful labor rights report of the country, or countries, with respect to which the President is negotiating, on a time frame determined in accordance with section 2107(b)(2)(E);

(9) with respect to any trade agreement which the President seeks to implement under trade authorities procedures, submit to the Congress a report describing the extent to which the country or countries that are parties to the agreement have in effect laws governing exploitative child labor;

(10) continue to promote consideration of multilateral environmental agreements and consult with parties to such agreements regarding the consistency of any such agreement that includes trade measures with existing environmental exceptions under Article XX of the GATT 1994;

(11) report to the Committee on Ways and Means of the House of Representatives and the Committee on Finance of the Senate, not later than 12 months after the imposition of a penalty or remedy by the United States permitted by a trade agreement to which this title applies, on the effectiveness of the penalty or remedy applied under United States law in enforcing United States rights under the trade agreement; and

(12) seek to establish consultative mechanisms among parties to trade agreements to examine the trade consequences of significant and unanticipated currency movements and to scrutinize whether a foreign government engaged in a pattern of manipulating its currency to promote a competitive advantage in international trade.

The report under paragraph (11) shall address whether the penalty or remedy was effective in changing the behavior of the targeted party and whether the penalty or remedy had any adverse impact on parties or interests not party to the dispute.

(d) Consultations.—

(1) Consultations with congressional advisers.—In the course of negotiations conducted under this title, the United States Trade Representative shall consult closely and on a timely basis with, and keep fully apprised of the negotiations, the Congressional Oversight Group convened under section 2107 and all committees of the House of Representatives and the Senate with jurisdiction over laws that would be affected by a trade agreement resulting from the negotiations.

(2) Consultation before agreement initialed.—In the course of negotiations conducted under this title, the United States Trade Representative shall—

(A) consult closely and on a timely basis (including immediately before initialing an agreement) with, and keep fully apprised of the negotiations, the congressional advisers for trade policy and negotiations appointed under section 161 of the Trade Act of 1974 (19 U.S.C. 2211), the Committee on Ways and Means of the House of Representatives, the Committee on Finance of the Senate, and the Congressional Oversight Group convened under section 2107; and

(B) with regard to any negotiations and agreement relating to agricultural trade, also consult closely and on a timely basis (including immediately before initialing an agreement) with, and keep fully apprised of the negotiations, the Committee on Agriculture of the House of Representatives and the Committee on Agriculture, Nutrition, and Forestry of the Senate.

(e) Adherence to Obligations Under Uruguay Round Agreements.—In determining whether to enter into negotiations with a particular country, the President shall take into account the extent to which that country has implemented, or has accelerated the implementation of, its obligations under the Uruguay Round Agreements.

SEC. 2103. [19 USC 3803.] TRADE AGREEMENTS AUTHORITY.

(a) Agreements Regarding Tariff Barriers.—

(1) In general.—Whenever the President determines that one or more existing duties or other import restrictions of any foreign country or the United States are unduly burdening and restricting the foreign trade of the United States and that the purposes, policies, priorities, and objectives of this title will be promoted thereby, the President—

(A) may enter into trade agreements with foreign countries before—

(i) June 1, 2005; or

(ii) June 1, 2007, if trade authorities procedures are extended under subsection (c); and

(B) may, subject to paragraphs (2) and (3), proclaim—

(i) such modification or continuance of any existing duty,

(ii) such continuance of existing duty-free or excise treatment, or

(iii) such additional duties, as the President determines to be required or appropriate to carry out any such trade agreement.

The President shall notify the Congress of the President's intention to enter into an agreement under this subsection.

(2) Limitations.—No proclamation may be made under paragraph (1) that—

(A) reduces any rate of duty (other than a rate of duty that does not exceed 5 percent ad valorem on the date of the enactment of this Act) to a rate of duty which is less than 50 percent of the rate of such duty that applies on such date of enactment;

(B) reduces the rate of duty below that applicable under the Uruguay Round Agreements, on any import sensitive agricultural product; or

(C) increases any rate of duty above the rate that applied on the date of the enactment of this Act.

(3) Aggregate reduction; exemption from staging.—

(A) Aggregate reduction.—Except as provided in subparagraph (B), the aggregate reduction in the rate of duty on any article which is in effect on any day pursuant to a trade agreement entered into under paragraph (1) shall not exceed the aggregate reduction which would have been in effect on such day if—

(i) a reduction of 3 percent ad valorem or a reduction of one-tenth of the total reduction, whichever is greater, had taken effect on the effective date of the first reduction proclaimed under paragraph (1) to carry out such agreement with respect to such article; and

(ii) a reduction equal to the amount applicable under clause (i) had taken effect at 1-year intervals after the effective date of such first reduction.

(B) Exemption from staging.—No staging is required under subparagraph (A) with respect to a duty reduction that is proclaimed under paragraph (1) for an article of a kind that is not produced in the United States. The United States International Trade Commission shall advise the President of the identity of articles that may be exempted from staging under this subparagraph.

(4) Rounding.—If the President determines that such action will simplify the computation of reductions under paragraph (3), the President may round an annual reduction by an amount equal to the lesser of—

(A) the difference between the reduction without regard to this paragraph and the next lower whole number; or

(B) one-half of 1 percent ad valorem.

(5) Other limitations.—A rate of duty reduction that may not be proclaimed by reason of paragraph (2) may take effect only if a provision authorizing such reduction is included within an implementing bill provided for under section 2105 and that bill is enacted into law.

(6) Other tariff modifications.—Notwithstanding paragraphs (1)(B), (2)(A), (2)(C), and (3) through (5), and subject to the consultation and layover requirements of section 115 of the Uruguay Round Agreements Act, the President may proclaim the modification of any duty or staged rate reduction of any duty set forth in Schedule XX, as defined in section 2(5) of that Act, if the United States agrees to such modification or staged rate reduction in a negotiation for the reciprocal elimination or harmonization of duties under the auspices of the World Trade Organization.

(7) Authority under uruguay round agreements act not affected.—Nothing in this subsection shall limit the authority provided to the President under section 111(b) of the Uruguay Round Agreements Act (19 U.S.C. 3521(b)).

(b) Agreements Regarding Tariff and Nontariff Barriers.—

(1) In general.—

(A) Whenever the President determines that—

(i) one or more existing duties or any other import restriction of any foreign country or the United States or any other barrier to, or other distortion of, international trade unduly burdens or restricts the foreign trade of the United States or adversely affects the United States economy, or

(ii) the imposition of any such barrier or distortion is likely to result in such a burden, restriction, or effect, and that the purposes, policies, priorities, and objectives of this title will be promoted thereby, the President may enter into a trade agreement described in subparagraph (B) during the period described in subparagraph (C).

(B) The President may enter into a trade agreement under subparagraph (A) with foreign countries providing for—

(i) the reduction or elimination of a duty, restriction, barrier, or other distortion described in subparagraph (A); or

(ii) the prohibition of, or limitation on the imposition of, such barrier or other distortion.

(C) The President may enter into a trade agreement under this paragraph before—

(i) June 1, 2005; or

(ii) June 1, 2007, if trade authorities procedures are extended under subsection (c).

(2) Conditions.—A trade agreement may be entered into under this subsection only if such agreement makes progress in meeting the applicable objectives described in section 2102(a) and (b) and the President satisfies the conditions set forth in section 2104.

(3) Bills qualifying for trade authorities procedures.—(A) The provisions of section 151 of the Trade Act of 1974 (in this title referred to as "trade authorities procedures") apply to a bill of either House of Congress which contains provisions described in subparagraph (B) to the same extent as such section 151 applies to implementing bills under that section. A bill to which this paragraph applies shall hereafter in this title be referred to as an "implementing bill".

(B) The provisions referred to in subparagraph (A) are—

(i) a provision approving a trade agreement entered into under this subsection and approving the statement of administrative action, if any, proposed to implement such trade agreement; and

(ii) if changes in existing laws or new statutory authority are required to implement such trade agreement or agreements, provisions, necessary or appropriate to implement such trade agreement or agreements, either repealing or amending existing laws or providing new statutory authority.

(c) Extension Disapproval Process for Congressional Trade Authorities Procedures.—

(1) In general.—Except as provided in section 2105(b)—

(A) the trade authorities procedures apply to implementing bills submitted with respect to trade agreements entered into under subsection (b) before July 1, 2005; and

(B) the trade authorities procedures shall be extended to implementing bills submitted with respect to trade agreements entered into under subsection (b) after June 30, 2005, and before July 1, 2007, if (and only if)—

(i) the President requests such extension under paragraph (2); and

(ii) neither House of the Congress adopts an extension disapproval resolution under paragraph (5) before June 1, 2005.

(2) Report to congress by the president.—If the President is of the opinion that the trade authorities procedures should be extended to implementing bills described in paragraph (1)(B), the President shall submit to the Congress, not later than March 1, 2005, a written report that contains a request for such extension, together with—

(A) a description of all trade agreements that have been negotiated under subsection (b) and the anticipated schedule for submitting such agreements to the Congress for approval;

(B) a description of the progress that has been made in negotiations to achieve the purposes, policies, priorities, and objectives of this title, and a statement that such progress justifies the continuation of negotiations; and

(C) a statement of the reasons why the extension is needed to complete the negotiations.

(3) Other reports to congress.—Deadlines.

(A) Report by the advisory committee.—The President shall promptly inform the Advisory Committee for Trade Policy and Negotiations established under section 135 of the Trade Act of 1974 (19 U.S.C. 2155) of the President's decision to submit a report to the Congress under paragraph (2). The Advisory Committee shall submit to the Congress as soon as practicable, but not later than May 1, 2005, a written report that contains—

(i) its views regarding the progress that has been made in negotiations to achieve the purposes, policies, priorities, and objectives of this title; and

(ii) a statement of its views, and the reasons therefor, regarding whether the extension requested under paragraph (2) should be approved or disapproved.

(B) Report by itc.—The President shall promptly inform the International Trade Commission of the President's decision to submit a report to the Congress under paragraph (2). The International Trade Commission shall submit to the Congress as soon as practicable, but not later than May 1, 2005, a written report that contains a review and analysis of the economic impact on the United States of all trade agreements implemented between the date of enactment of this Act and the date on which the President decides to seek an extension requested under paragraph (2).

(4) Status of reports.—The reports submitted to the Congress under paragraphs (2) and (3), or any portion of such reports, may be classified to the extent the President determines appropriate.

(5) Extension disapproval resolutions.—(A) For purposes of paragraph (1), the term "extension disapproval resolution" means a resolution of either House of the Congress, the sole matter after the resolving clause of which is as follows: "That the ____ disapproves the request of the President for the extension, under section 2103(c)(1)(B)(i) of the Bipartisan Trade Promotion Authority Act of 2002, of the trade authorities procedures under that Act to any implementing bill submitted with respect to any trade agreement entered into under section 2103(b) of that Act after June 30, 2005.", with the blank space being filled with the name of the resolving House of the Congress.

(B) Extension disapproval resolutions—

(i) may be introduced in either House of the Congress by any member of such House; and

(ii) shall be referred, in the House of Representatives, to the Committee on Ways and Means and, in addition, to the Committee on Rules.

(C) The provisions of section 152(d) and (e) of the Trade Act of 1974 (19 U.S.C. 2192(d) and (e)) (relating to the floor consideration of certain resolutions in the House and Senate) apply to extension disapproval resolutions.

(D) It is not in order for—

(i) the Senate to consider any extension disapproval resolution not reported by the Committee on Finance;

(ii) the House of Representatives to consider any extension disapproval resolution not reported by the Committee on Ways and Means and, in addition, by the Committee on Rules; or

(iii) either House of the Congress to consider an extension disapproval resolution after June 30, 2005.

(d) Commencement of Negotiations.—In order to contribute to the continued economic expansion of the United States, the President shall commence negotiations covering tariff and nontariff barriers affecting any industry, product, or service sector, and expand existing sectoral agreements to countries that are not parties to those agreements, in cases where the President determines that such negotiations are feasible and timely and would benefit the United States. Such sectors include agriculture, commercial services, intellectual property rights, industrial and capital goods, government procurement, information technology products, environmental technology and services, medical equipment and services, civil aircraft, and infrastructure products. In so doing, the

President shall take into account all of the principal negotiating objectives set forth in section 2102(b).

SEC. 2104. [19 USC 3804.] CONSULTATIONS AND ASSESSMENT.

(a) Notice and Consultation Before Negotiation.—The President, with respect to any agreement that is subject to the provisions of section 2103(b), shall—

(1) provide, at least 90 calendar days before initiating negotiations, written notice to the Congress of the President's intention to enter into the negotiations and set forth therein the date the President intends to initiate such negotiations, the specific United States objectives for the negotiations, and whether the President intends to seek an agreement, or changes to an existing agreement;

(2) before and after submission of the notice, consult regarding the negotiations with the Committee on Finance of the Senate and the Committee on Ways and Means of the House of Representatives, such other committees of the House and Senate as the President deems appropriate, and the Congressional Oversight group convened under section 2107; and

(3) upon the request of a majority of the members of the Congressional Oversight Group under section 2107(c), meet with the Congressional Oversight Group before initiating the negotiations or at any other time concerning the negotiations.

(b) Negotiations Regarding Agriculture.—

(1) In general.—Before initiating or continuing negotiations the subject matter of which is directly related to the subject matter under section 2102(b)(10)(A)(i) with any country, the President shall assess whether United States tariffs on agricultural products that were bound under the Uruguay Round Agreements are lower than the tariffs bound by that country. In addition, the President shall consider whether the tariff levels bound and applied throughout the world with respect to imports from the United States are higher than United States tariffs and whether the negotiation provides an opportunity to address any such disparity. The President shall consult with the Committee on Ways and Means and the Committee on Agriculture of the House of Representatives and the Committee on Finance and the Committee on Agriculture, Nutrition, and Forestry of the Senate concerning the results of the assessment, whether it is appropriate for the United States to agree to further tariff reductions based on the conclusions reached in the assessment, and how all applicable negotiating objectives will be met.

(2) Special consultations on import sensitive products.—

(A) Before initiating negotiations with regard to agriculture, and, with respect to the Free Trade Area for the Americas and negotiations with regard to agriculture under the auspices of the World Trade Organization, as soon as practicable after the enactment of this Act, the United States Trade Representative shall—

(i) identify those agricultural products subject to tariff-rate quotas on the date of enactment of this Act, and agricultural products subject to tariff reductions by the United States as a result of the Uruguay Round Agreements, for which the rate of duty was reduced on January 1, 1995, to a rate which was not less than 97.5 percent of the rate of duty that applied to such article on December 31, 1994;

(ii) consult with the Committee on Ways and Means and the Committee on Agriculture of the House of Representatives and the Committee on Finance and the Committee on Agriculture, Nutrition, and Forestry of the Senate concerning—

(I) whether any further tariff reductions on the products identified under clause (i) should be appropriate, taking into account the impact of any such tariff reduction on the United States industry producing the product concerned;

(II) whether the products so identified face unjustified sanitary or phytosanitary restrictions, including those not based on scientific principles in contravention of the Uruguay Round Agreements; and

(III) whether the countries participating in the negotiations maintain export subsidies or other programs, policies, or practices that distort world trade in such products and the impact of such programs, policies, and practices on United States producers of the products;

(iii) request that the International Trade Commission prepare an assessment of the probable economic effects of any such tariff reduction on the United States industry producing the product concerned and on the United States economy as a whole; and

(iv) upon complying with clauses (i), (ii), and (iii), notify the Committee on Ways and Means and the Committee on Agriculture of the House of Representatives and the Committee on Finance and the Committee on Agriculture,

Nutrition, and Forestry of the Senate of those products identified under clause (i) for which the Trade Representative intends to seek tariff liberalization in the negotiations and the reasons for seeking such tariff liberalization.

(B) If, after negotiations described in subparagraph (A) are commenced—

(i) the United States Trade Representative identifies any additional agricultural product described in subparagraph (A)(i) for tariff reductions which were not the subject of a notification under subparagraph (A)(iv), or

(ii) any additional agricultural product described in subparagraph (A)(i) is the subject of a request for tariff reductions by a party to the negotiations, the Trade Representative shall, as soon as practicable, notify the committees referred to in subparagraph (A)(iv) of those products and the reasons for seeking such tariff reductions.

(3) Negotiations regarding the fishing industry.—Before initiating, or continuing, negotiations which directly relate to fish or shellfish trade with any country, the President shall consult with the Committee on Ways and Means and the Committee on Resources of the House of Representatives, and the Committee on Finance and the Committee on Commerce, Science, and Transportation of the Senate, and shall keep the Committees apprised of negotiations on an ongoing and timely basis.

(c) Negotiations Regarding Textiles.—Before initiating or continuing negotiations the subject matter of which is directly related to textiles and apparel products with any country, the President shall assess whether United States tariffs on textile and apparel products that were bound under the Uruguay Round Agreements are lower than the tariffs bound by that country and whether the negotiation provides an opportunity to address any such disparity. The President shall consult with the Committee on Ways and Means of the House of Representatives and the Committee on Finance of the Senate concerning the results of the assessment, whether it is appropriate for the United States to agree to further tariff reductions based on the conclusions reached in the assessment, and how all applicable negotiating objectives will be met.

(d) Consultation With Congress Before Agreements Entered Into.—

(1) Consultation.—Before entering into any trade agreement under section 2103(b), the President shall consult with—

(A) the Committee on Ways and Means of the House of Representatives and the Committee on Finance of the Senate;

(B) each other committee of the House and the Senate, and each joint committee of the Congress, which has jurisdiction over legislation involving subject matters which would be affected by the trade agreement; and

(C) the Congressional Oversight Group convened under section 2107.

(2) Scope.—The consultation described in paragraph (1) shall include consultation with respect to—

(A) the nature of the agreement;

(B) how and to what extent the agreement will achieve the applicable purposes, policies, priorities, and objectives of this title; and

(C) the implementation of the agreement under section 2105, including the general effect of the agreement on existing laws.

(3) Report regarding United States trade remedy laws.—

(A) Changes in certain trade laws.—The President, at least 180 calendar days before the day on which the President enters into a trade agreement under section 2103(b), shall report to the Committee on Ways and Means of the House of Representatives and the Committee on Finance of the Senate—

(i) the range of proposals advanced in the negotiations with respect to that agreement, that may be in the final agreement, and that could require amendments to title VII of the Tariff Act of 1930 or to chapter 1 of title II of the Trade Act of 1974; and

(ii) how these proposals relate to the objectives described in section 2102(b)(14).

(B) Certain agreements.—With respect to a trade agreement entered into with Chile or Singapore, the report referred to in subparagraph (A) shall be submitted by the President at least 90 calendar days before the day on which the President enters into that agreement.

(C) Resolutions.—

(i) At any time after the transmission of the report under subparagraph (A), if a resolution is introduced with respect to that report in either House of Congress, the procedures set forth in clauses (iii) through (vi) shall apply to that resolution if—

(I) no other resolution with respect to that report has previously been reported in that House of Congress by the Committee on Ways and Means or the Committee on Finance, as the case may be, pursuant to those procedures; and

(II) no procedural disapproval resolution under section 2105(b) introduced with respect to a trade agreement entered into pursuant to the negotiations to which the report under subparagraph (A) relates has previously been reported in that House of Congress by the Committee on Ways and Means or the Committee on Finance, as the case may be.

(ii) For purposes of this subparagraph, the term "resolution" means only a resolution of either House of Congress, the matter after the resolving clause of which is as follows: "That the ____ finds that the proposed changes to United States trade remedy laws contained in the report of the President transmitted to the Congress on ____ under section 2104(d)(3) of the Bipartisan Trade Promotion Authority Act of 2002 with respect to ____, are inconsistent with the negotiating objectives described in section 2102(b)(14) of that Act.", with the first blank space being filled with the name of the resolving House of Congress, the second blank space being filled with the appropriate date of the report, and the third blank space being filled with the name of the country or countries involved.

(iii) Resolutions in the House of Representatives—

(I) may be introduced by any Member of the House;

(II) shall be referred to the Committee on Ways and Means and, in addition, to the Committee on Rules; and

(III) may not be amended by either Committee.

(iv) Resolutions in the Senate—

(I) may be introduced by any Member of the Senate;

(II) shall be referred to the Committee on Finance; and

(III) may not be amended.

(iv) It is not in order for the House of Representatives to consider any resolution that is not reported by the Committee on Ways and Means and, in addition, by the Committee on Rules.

(v) It is not in order for the Senate to consider any resolution that is not reported by the Committee on Finance.

(vi) The provisions of section 152(d) and (e) of the Trade Act of 1974 (19 U.S.C. 2192(d) and (e)) (relating to floor consideration of certain resolutions in the House and Senate) shall apply to resolutions.

(e) Advisory Committee Reports.—The report required under section 135(e)(1) of the Trade Act of 1974 regarding any trade agreement entered into under section 2103(a) or (b) of this Act shall be provided to the President, the Congress, and the United States Trade Representative not later than 30 days after the date on which the President notifies the Congress under section 2103(a)(1) or 2105(a)(1)(A) of the President's intention to enter into the agreement.

(f) ITC Assessment.—

(1) In general.—The President, at least 90 calendar days before the day on which the President enters into a trade agreement under section 2103(b), shall provide the International Trade Commission (referred to in this subsection as "the Commission") with the details of the agreement as it exists at that time and request the Commission to prepare and submit an assessment of the agreement as described in paragraph (2). Between the time the President makes the request under this paragraph and the time the Commission submits the assessment, the President shall keep the Commission current with respect to the details of the agreement.

(2) ITC assessment.—Not later than 90 calendar days after the President enters into the agreement, the Commission shall submit to the President and the Congress a report assessing the likely impact of the agreement on the United States economy as a whole and on specific industry sectors, including the impact the agreement will have on the gross domestic product, exports and imports, aggregate employment and employment opportunities, the production, employment, and competitive position of industries likely to be significantly affected by the agreement, and the interests of United States consumers.

(3) Review of empirical literature.—In preparing the assessment, the Commission shall review available economic assessments regarding the agreement, including literature regarding any substantially equivalent proposed agreement, and shall provide in its assessment a description of the analyses used and conclusions drawn in such literature, and a discussion of areas of consensus and divergence between the various analyses and conclusions, including those of the Commission regarding the agreement.

SEC. 2105. [19 USC 3805.] IMPLEMENTATION OF TRADE AGREEMENTS.

(a) In General.—

(1) Notification and submission.—Any agreement entered into under section 2103(b) shall enter into force with respect to the United States if (and only if)—

(A) the President, at least 90 calendar days before the day on which the President enters into the trade agreement, notifies the House of Representatives and the Senate of the President's intention to enter into the agreement, and promptly thereafter publishes notice of such intention in the Federal Register;

(B) within 60 days after entering into the agreement, the President submits to the Congress a description of those changes to existing laws that the President considers would be required in order to bring the United States into compliance with the agreement;

(C) after entering into the agreement, the President submits to the Congress, on a day on which both Houses of Congress are in session, a copy of the final legal text of the agreement, together with—

(i) a draft of an implementing bill described in section 2103(b)(3);

(ii) a statement of any administrative action proposed to implement the trade agreement; and

(iii) the supporting information described in paragraph (2); and

(D) the implementing bill is enacted into law.

(2) Supporting information.—The supporting information required under paragraph (1)(C)(iii) consists of—

(A) an explanation as to how the implementing bill and proposed administrative action will change or affect existing law; and

(B) a statement—

(i) asserting that the agreement makes progress in achieving the applicable purposes, policies, priorities, and objectives of this title; and

(ii) setting forth the reasons of the President regarding—

(I) how and to what extent the agreement makes progress in achieving the applicable purposes, policies, and objectives referred to in clause (i);

(II) whether and how the agreement changes provisions of an agreement previously negotiated;

(III) how the agreement serves the interests of United States commerce;

(IV) how the implementing bill meets the standards set forth in section 2103(b)(3); and

(V) how and to what extent the agreement makes progress in achieving the applicable purposes, policies, and objectives referred to in section 2102(c) regarding the promotion of certain priorities.

(3) Reciprocal benefits.—In order to ensure that a foreign country that is not a party to a trade agreement entered into under section 2103(b) does not receive benefits under the agreement unless the country is also subject to the obligations under the agreement, the implementing bill submitted with respect to the agreement shall provide that the benefits and obligations under the agreement apply only to the parties to the agreement, if such application is consistent with the terms of the agreement. The implementing bill may also provide that the benefits and obligations under the agreement do not apply uniformly to all parties to the agreement, if such application is consistent with the terms of the agreement.

(4) Disclosure of commitments.—Any agreement or other understanding with a foreign government or governments (whether oral or in writing) that—

(A) relates to a trade agreement with respect to which the Congress enacts an implementing bill under trade authorities procedures, and

(B) is not disclosed to the Congress before an implementing bill with respect to that agreement is introduced in either House of Congress, shall not be considered to be part of the agreement approved by the Congress and shall have no force and effect under United States law or in any dispute settlement body.

(b) Limitations on Trade Authorities Procedures.—

(1) For lack of notice or consultations.—

(A) In general.—The trade authorities procedures shall not apply to any implementing bill submitted with respect to a trade agreement or trade agreements entered into under section 2103(b) if during the 60-day period beginning on the date that one House of Congress agrees to a procedural disapproval resolution for lack of notice or consultations with respect to such trade agreement or agreements, the other House separately agrees to a procedural disapproval resolution with respect to such trade agreement or agreements.

(B) Procedural disapproval resolution.—(i) For purposes of this paragraph, the term "procedural disapproval resolution" means a resolution of either House of Congress, the sole matter after the resolving clause of which is as follows: "That the President has failed or refused to notify or consult in accordance with the Bipartisan Trade Promotion Authority Act of 2002 on negotiations with respect to ____________ and, therefore, the trade authorities procedures under that Act shall not apply to any implementing bill submitted with respect to such trade agreement or agreements.", with the blank space being filled with a description of the trade agreement or agreements with respect to which the President is considered to have failed or refused to notify or consult.

(ii) For purposes of clause (i), the President has "failed or refused to notify or consult in accordance with the Bipartisan Trade Promotion Authority Act of 2002" on negotiations with respect to a trade agreement or trade agreements if—

(I) the President has failed or refused to consult (as the case may be) in accordance with section 2104 or 2105 with respect to the negotiations, agreement, or agreements;

(II) guidelines under section 2107(b) have not been developed or met with respect to the negotiations, agreement, or agreements;

(III) the President has not met with the Congressional Oversight Group pursuant to a request made under section 2107(c) with respect to the negotiations, agreement, or agreements; or

(IV) the agreement or agreements fail to make progress in achieving the purposes, policies, priorities, and objectives of this title.

(2) Procedures for considering resolutions.—

(A) Procedural disapproval resolutions—

(i) in the House of Representatives—

(I) may be introduced by any Member of the House;

(II) shall be referred to the Committee on Ways and Means and, in addition, to the Committee on Rules; and

(III) may not be amended by either Committee; and

(ii) in the Senate—

(I) may be introduced by any Member of the Senate;

(II) shall be referred to the Committee on Finance; and

(III) may not be amended.

(B) The provisions of section 152(d) and (e) of the Trade Act of 1974 (19 U.S.C. 2192(d) and (e)) (relating to the floor consideration of certain resolutions in the House and Senate) apply to a procedural disapproval resolution introduced with respect to a trade agreement if no other procedural disapproval resolution with respect to that trade agreement has previously been reported in that House of Congress by the Committee on Ways and Means or the Committee on Finance, as the case may be, and if no resolution described in section 2104(d)(3)(C)(ii) with respect to that trade agreement has been reported in that House of Congress by the Committee on Ways and Means or the Committee on Finance, as the case may be, pursuant to the procedures set forth in clauses (iii) through (vi) of such section 2104(d)(3)(C).

(C) It is not in order for the House of Representatives to consider any procedural disapproval resolution not reported by the Committee on Ways and Means and, in addition, by the Committee on Rules.

(D) It is not in order for the Senate to consider any procedural disapproval resolution not reported by the Committee on Finance.

(3) For failure to meet other requirements.—

Not later than December 31, 2002, the Secretary of Commerce, in consultation with the Secretary of State, the Secretary of the Treasury, the Attorney General, and the United States Trade Representative, shall transmit to the Congress a report setting forth the strategy of the executive branch to address concerns of the Congress regarding whether dispute settlement panels and the Appellate Body of the WTO have added to obligations, or diminished rights, of the United States, as described in section 2101(b)(3). Trade authorities procedures shall not apply to any implementing bill with respect to an agreement negotiated under the auspices of the WTO unless the Secretary of Commerce has issued such report in a timely manner.

(c) Rules of House of Representatives and Senate.—Subsection (b) of this section, section 2103(c), aand section 2104(d)(3)(C) are enacted by the Congress—

(1) as an exercise of the rulemaking power of the House of Representatives and the Senate, respectively, and as such are deemed a part of the rules of each House, respectively, and such procedures supersede other rules only to the extent that they are inconsistent with such other rules; and

(2) with the full recognition of the constitutional right of either House to change the rules (so far as relating to the procedures of that House) at any time, in the same manner, and to the same extent as any other rule of that House.

SEC. 2106. [19 USC 3806.] TREATMENT OF CERTAIN TRADE AGREEMENTS FOR WHICH NEGOTIATIONS HAVE ALREADY BEGUN.

(a) Certain Agreements.—Notwithstanding the prenegotiation notification and consultation requirement described in section 2104(a), if an agreement to which section 2103(b) applies—

(1) is entered into under the auspices of the World Trade Organization,

(2) is entered into with Chile,

(3) is entered into with Singapore, or

(4) establishes a Free Trade Area for the Americas, and results from negotiations that were commenced before the date of the enactment of this Act, subsection (b) shall apply.

(b) Treatment of Agreements.—In the case of any agreement to which subsection (a) applies—

(1) the applicability of the trade authorities procedures to implementing bills shall be determined without regard to the requirements of section 2104(a) (relating only to 90 days notice prior to initiating negotiations), and any procedural disapproval resolution under section 2105(b)(1)(B) shall not be in order on the basis of a failure or refusal to comply with the provisions of section 2104(a); and

(2) the President shall, as soon as feasible after the enactment of this Act—

(A) notify the Congress of the negotiations described in subsection (a), the specific United States objectives in the negotiations, and whether the President is seeking a new agreement or changes to an existing agreement; and

(B) before and after submission of the notice, consult regarding the negotiations with the committees referred to in section 2104(a)(2) and the Congressional Oversight Group convened under section 2107.

SEC. 2107. [19 USC 3807.] CONGRESSIONAL OVERSIGHT GROUP.

(a) Members and Functions.—

(1) In general.—By not later than 60 days after the date of the enactment of this Act, and not later than 30 days after the convening of each Congress, the chairman of the Committee on Ways and Means

of the House of Representatives and the chairman of the Committee on Finance of the Senate shall convene the Congressional Oversight Group.

(2) Membership from the house.—In each Congress, the Congressional Oversight Group shall be comprised of the following Members of the House of Representatives:

(A) The chairman and ranking member of the Committee on Ways and Means, and 3 additional members of such Committee (not more than 2 of whom are members of the same political party).

(B) The chairman and ranking member, or their designees, of the committees of the House of Representatives which would have, under the Rules of the House of Representatives, jurisdiction over provisions of law affected by a trade agreement negotiations for which are conducted at any time during that Congress and to which this title would apply.

(3) Membership from the senate.—In each Congress, the Congressional Oversight Group shall also be comprised of the following members of the Senate:

(A) The chairman and ranking member of the Committee on Finance and 3 additional members of such Committee (not more than 2 of whom are members of the same political party).

(B) The chairman and ranking member, or their designees, of the committees of the Senate which would have, under the Rules of the Senate, jurisdiction over provisions of law affected by a trade agreement negotiations for which are conducted at any time during that Congress and to which this title would apply.

(4) Accreditation.—Each member of the Congressional Oversight Group described in paragraph (2)(A) and (3)(A) shall be accredited by the United States Trade Representative on behalf of the President as an official adviser to the United States delegation in negotiations for any trade agreement to which this title applies. Each member of the Congressional Oversight Group described in paragraph (2)(B) and (3)(B) shall be accredited by the United States Trade Representative on behalf of the President as an official adviser to the United States delegation in the negotiations by reason of which the member is in the Congressional Oversight Group. The Congressional Oversight Group shall consult with and provide advice to the Trade Representative regarding the formulation of specific objectives, negotiating strategies and positions, the development of the applicable trade agreement, and compliance and enforcement of the negotiated commitments under the trade agreement.

(5) Chair.—The Congressional Oversight Group shall be chaired by the Chairman of the Committee on Ways and Means of the House of Representatives and the Chairman of the Committee on Finance of the Senate.

(b) Guidelines.—

(1) Purpose and revision.—The United States Trade Representative, in consultation with the chairmen and ranking minority members of the Committee on Ways and Means of the House of Representatives and the Committee on Finance of the Senate—

(A) shall, within 120 days after the date of the enactment of this Act, develop written guidelines to facilitate the useful and timely exchange of information between the Trade Representative and the Congressional Oversight Group convened under this section; and

(B) may make such revisions to the guidelines as may be necessary from time to time.

(2) Content.—The guidelines developed under paragraph (1) shall provide for, among other things—

(A) regular, detailed briefings of the Congressional Oversight Group regarding negotiating objectives, including the promotion of certain priorities referred to in section 2102(c), and positions and the status of the applicable negotiations, beginning as soon as practicable after the Congressional Oversight Group is convened, with more frequent briefings as trade negotiations enter the final stage;

(B) access by members of the Congressional Oversight Group, and staff with proper security clearances, to pertinent documents relating to the negotiations, including classified materials;

(C) the closest practicable coordination between the Trade Representative and the Congressional Oversight Group at all critical periods during the negotiations, including at negotiation sites;

(D) after the applicable trade agreement is concluded, consultation regarding ongoing compliance and enforcement of negotiated commitments under the trade agreement; and

(E) the time frame for submitting the report required under section 2102(c)(8).

(c) Request for Meeting.—Upon the request of a majority of the Congressional Oversight Group, the President shall meet with the Congressional Oversight Group before initiating negotiations with respect to a trade agreement, or at any other time concerning the negotiations.

SEC. 2108. [19 USC 3808.] ADDITIONAL IMPLEMENTATION AND ENFORCEMENT REQUIREMENTS.

(a) In General.—At the time the President submits to the Congress the final text of an agreement pursuant to section 2105(a)(1)(C), the President shall also submit a plan for implementing and enforcing the agreement. The implementation and enforcement plan shall include the following:

(1) Border personnel requirements.—A description of additional personnel required at border entry points, including a list of additional customs and agricultural inspectors.

(2) Agency staffing requirements.—A description of additional personnel required by Federal agencies responsible for monitoring and implementing the trade agreement, including personnel required by the Office of the United States Trade Representative, the Department of Commerce, the Department of Agriculture (including additional personnel required to implement sanitary and phytosanitary measures in order to obtain market access for United States exports), the Department of the Treasury, and such other agencies as may be necessary.

(3) Customs infrastructure requirements.—A description of the additional equipment and facilities needed by the United States Customs Service.

(4) Impact on state and local governments.—A description of the impact the trade agreement will have on State and local governments as a result of increases in trade.

(5) Cost analysis.—An analysis of the costs associated with each of the items listed in paragraphs (1) through (4).

(b) Budget Submission.—The President shall include a request for the resources necessary to support the plan described in subsection (a) in the first budget that the President submits to the Congress after the submission of the plan.

SEC. 2109. [19 USC 3809.] COMMITTEE STAFF.

The grant of trade promotion authority under this title is likely to increase the activities of the primary committees of jurisdiction in the area of international trade. In addition, the creation of the Congressional Oversight Group under section 2107 will increase the participation of a broader number of Members of Congress in the formulation of United States trade policy and oversight of the international trade agenda for the United States. The primary committees of jurisdiction should have adequate staff to accommodate these increases in activities.

SEC. 2110. CONFORMING AMENDMENTS.

(a) In General.—Title I of the Trade Act of 1974 (19 U.S.C. 2111 et seq.) is amended as follows:

(1) Implementing bill.—

(A) Section 151(b)(1) (19 U.S.C. 2191(b)(1)) is amended by striking "section 1103(a)(1) of the Omnibus Trade and Competitiveness Act of 1988, or section 282 of the Uruguay Round Agreements Act" and inserting "section 282 of the Uruguay Round Agreements Act, or section 2105(a)(1) of the Bipartisan Trade Promotion Authority Act of 2002".

(B) Section 151(c)(1) (19 U.S.C. 2191(c)(1)) is amended by striking "or section 282 of the Uruguay Round Agreements Act" and inserting ", section 282 of the Uruguay Round Agreements Act, or section 2105(a)(1) of the Bipartisan Trade Promotion Authority Act of 2002".

(2) Advice from international trade commission.—Section 131 (19 U.S.C. 2151) is amended—

(A) in subsection (a)—

(i) in paragraph (1), by striking "section 123 of this Act or section 1102 (a) or (c) of the Omnibus Trade and Competitiveness Act of 1988," and inserting "section 123 of this Act or section 2103(a) or (b) of the Bipartisan Trade Promotion Authority Act of 2002,"; and

(ii) in paragraph (2), by striking "section 1102 (b) or (c) of the Omnibus Trade and Competitiveness Act of 1988" and inserting "section 2103(b) of the Bipartisan Trade Promotion Authority Act of 2002";

(B) in subsection (b), by striking "section 1102(a)(3)(A)" and inserting "section 2103(a)(3)(A) of the Bipartisan Trade Promotion Authority Act of 2002"; and

(C) in subsection (c), by striking "section 1102 of the Omnibus Trade and Competitiveness Act of 1988," and inserting "section 2103 of the Bipartisan Trade Promotion Authority Act of 2002,".

(3) Hearings and advice.—Sections 132, 133(a), and 134(a) (19 U.S.C. 2152, 2153(a), and 2154(a)) are each amended by striking "section 1102 of the Omnibus Trade and Competitiveness Act of 1988," each place it appears and inserting "section 2103 of the Bipartisan Trade Promotion Authority Act of 2002,".

(4) Prerequisites for offers.—Section 134(b) (19 U.S.C. 2154(b)) is amended by striking "section 1102 of the Omnibus Trade and

Competitiveness Act of 1988" and inserting "section 2103 of the Bipartisan Trade Promotion Authority Act of 2002".

(5) Advice from private and public sectors.—Section 135 (19 U.S.C. 2155) is amended—

(A) in subsection (a)(1)(A), by striking "section 1102 of the Omnibus Trade and Competitiveness Act of 1988" and inserting "section 2103 of the Bipartisan Trade Promotion Authority Act of 2002";

(B) in subsection (e)(1)—

(i) by striking "section 1102 of the Omnibus Trade and Competitiveness Act of 1988" each place it appears and inserting "section 2103 of the Bipartisan Trade Promotion Authority Act of 2002"; and

(ii) by striking "section 1103(a)(1)(A) of such Act of 1988" and inserting "section 2105(a)(1)(A) of the Bipartisan Trade Promotion Authority Act of 2002"; and

(C) in subsection (e)(2), by striking "section 1101 of the Omnibus Trade and Competitiveness Act of 1988" and inserting "section 2102 of the Bipartisan Trade Promotion Authority Act of 2002".

(6) Transmission of agreements to congress.—Section 162(a) (19 U.S.C. 2212(a)) is amended by striking "or under section 1102 of the Omnibus Trade and Competitiveness Act of 1988" and inserting "or under section 2103 of the Bipartisan Trade Promotion Authority Act of 2002".

(b) Application of Certain Provisions.—For purposes of applying sections 125, 126, and 127 of the Trade Act of 1974 (19 U.S.C. 2135, 2136(a), and 2137)—

(1) any trade agreement entered into under section 2103 shall be treated as an agreement entered into under section 101 or 102, as appropriate, of the Trade Act of 1974 (19 U.S.C. 2111 or 2112); and

(2) any proclamation or Executive order issued pursuant to a trade agreement entered into under section 2103 shall be treated as a proclamation or Executive order issued pursuant to a trade agreement entered into under section 102 of the Trade Act of 1974.

SEC. 2111. [19 USC 3811.] REPORT ON IMPACT OF TRADE PROMOTION AUTHORITY.

(a) In General.—Not later than 1 year after the date of enactment of this Act, the International Trade Commission shall report to the Committee on Finance of the Senate and the Committee on Ways and Means of the House of Representatives regarding the economic impact on the United States of the trade agreements described in subsection (b).

(b) Agreements.—The trade agreements described in this subsection are the following:

(1) The United States-Israel Free Trade Agreement.

(2) The United States-Canada Free Trade Agreement.

(3) The North American Free Trade Agreement.

(4) The Uruguay Round Agreements.

(5) The Tokyo Round of Multilateral Trade Negotiations.

SEC. 2112. [19 USC 3812.] INTERESTS OF SMALL BUSINESS.

The Assistant United States Trade Representative for Industry and Telecommunications shall be responsible for ensuring that the interests of small business are considered in all trade negotiations in accordance with the objective described in section 2102(a)(8). It is the sense of the Congress that the small business functions should be reflected in the title of the Assistant United States Trade Representative assigned the responsibility for small business.

SEC. 2113. [19 USC 3813.] DEFINITIONS.

In this title:

(1) Agreement on agriculture.—The term "Agreement on Agriculture" means the agreement referred to in section 101(d)(2) of the Uruguay Round Agreements Act (19 U.S.C. 3511(d)(2)).

(2) Agreement on safeguards.—The term "Agreement on Safeguards means the agreement referred to in section 101(d)(12) of the Uruguay Round Agreements Act (19 U.S.C. 3511(d)(12)).

(2) Agreement on subsidies and countervailing measures.—The term "Agreement on Subsidies and Countervailing Measures" means the agreement referred to in section 101(d)(13) of the Uruguay Round Agreements Act (19 U.S.C. 3511(d)(13)).

(4) Antidumping agreement.—The term "Antidumping Agreement" means the Agreement on Implementation of Article VI of the General Agreement on Tariffs and Trade 1994 referred to in section 101(d)(7) of the Uruguay Round Agreements Act (19 U.S.C. 3511(d)(7)).

(5) Appellate body.—The term "Appellate Body" means the Appellate Body established under Article 17.1 of the Dispute Settlement Understanding.

(6) Core labor standards.—The term "core labor standards" means—

(A) the right of association;

(B) the right to organize and bargain collectively;

(C) a prohibition on the use of any form of forced or compulsory labor;

(D) a minimum age for the employment of children; and

(E) acceptable conditions of work with respect to minimum wages, hours of work, and occupational safety and health.

(7) Dispute settlement understanding.—The term "Dispute Settlement Understanding" means the Understanding on Rules and Procedures Governing the Settlement of Disputes referred to in section 101(d)(16) of the Uruguay Round Agreements Act.

(8) GATT 1994.—The term "GATT 1994" has the meaning given that term in section 2 of the Uruguay Round Agreements Act (19 U.S.C. 3501).

(9) ILO.—The term "ILO" means the International Labor Organization.

(10) Import sensitive agricultural product.—The term "import sensitive agricultural product" means an agricultural product—

(A) with respect to which, as a result of the Uruguay Round Agreements the rate of duty was the subject of tariff reductions by the United States and, pursuant to such Agreements, was reduced on January 1, 1995, to a rate that was not less than 97.5 percent of the rate of duty that applied to such article on December 31, 1994; or

(B) which was subject to a tariff-rate quota on the date of the enactment of this Act.

(11) United states person.—The term "United States person" means—

(A) a United States citizen;

(B) a partnership, corporation, or other legal entity organized under the laws of the United States; and

(C) a partnership, corporation, or other legal entity that is organized under the laws of a foreign country and is controlled by entities described in subparagraph (B) or United States citizens, or both.

(12) Uruguay round agreements.—The term "Uruguay Round Agreements" has the meaning given that term in section 2(7) of the Uruguay Round Agreements Act (19 U.S.C. 3501(7)).

(13) World trade organization; wto.—The terms "World Trade Organization" and "WTO" mean the organization established pursuant to the WTO Agreement.

(14) WTO agreement.—The term "WTO Agreement" means the Agreement Establishing the World Trade Organization entered into on April 15, 1994.

(15) WTO member.—The term "WTO member" has the meaning given that term in section 2(10) of the Uruguay Round Agreements Act (19 U.S.C. 3501(10)).

DOCUMENT 30

TRADE AGREEMENTS ACT OF 1979

■ ■ ■

Pub.L. 96–39, Approved July 26, 1979, 93 Stat. 144 as amended Pub.L. 100–418, Aug. 23, 1988, 102 Stat. 1107

This Act included amendments to both the Tariff Act of 1930 and the Trade Act of 1974. Such amendments have been integrated into those acts. The following include provisions of the Act which are not amendments to earlier laws.

Table of Contents Selected Provisions Only

---

* These amendments have been integrated into the Tariff Act of 1930.

TITLE III. GOVERNMENT PROCUREMENT

19 U.S.C. § 2511

Sec. 301. General authority to modify discriminatory purchasing requirements

(a) Presidential waiver of discriminatory purchasing requirements. Subject to subsection (f) of this section, the President may waive, in whole or in part, with respect to eligible products of any foreign country or instrumentality designated under subsection (b), and suppliers of such products, the application of any law, regulation, procedure, or practice regarding Government procurement that would, if applied to such products and suppliers, result in treatment less favorable than that accorded—

(1) to United States products and suppliers of such products; or

(2) to eligible products of another foreign country or instrumentality which is a party to the Agreement and suppliers of such products.

(b) Designation of eligible countries and instrumentalities. The President may designate a foreign country or instrumentality for purposes of subsection (a) only if he determines that such country or instrumentality—

(1) is a country or instrumentality which (A) has become a party to the Agreement or the North American Free Trade Agreement, and (B) will

provide appropriate reciprocal competitive government procurement opportunities to United States products and suppliers of such products;

(2) is a country or instrumentality, other than a major industrial country, which (A) will otherwise assume the obligations of the Agreement, and (B) will provide such opportunities to such products and suppliers;

(3) is a country or instrumentality, other than a major industrial country, which will provide such opportunities to such products and suppliers; or

(4) is a least developed country.

(c) Modification or withdrawal of waivers and designations. The President may modify or withdraw any waiver granted pursuant to subsection (a) or designation made pursuant to subsection (b).

(d) [Terminated].

(e) Procurement procedures by certain Federal agencies. Notwithstanding any other provision of law, the President may direct any agency of the United States listed in Annex 1001.1a–2 of the North American Free Trade Agreement to procure eligible products in compliance with the procedural provisions of chapter 10 of such Agreement.

(f) Small business and minority preferences. The authority of the President under subsection (a) of this section to waive any law, regulation, procedure, or practice regarding Government procurement does not authorize the waiver of any small business or minority preference.

19 U.S.C. § 2518

Sec. 308. Definitions

As used in this title—

(1) Agreement. The term "Agreement" means the Agreement on Government Procurement referred to in section 101(d)(17) of the Uruguay Round Agreements Act, as submitted to the Congress, but including rectifications, modifications, and amendments which are accepted by the United States.

(2) Civil aircraft. The term "civil aircraft and related articles" means—

(A) all aircraft other than aircraft to be purchased for use by the Department of Defense or the United States Coast Guard;

(B) the engines (and parts and components for incorporation therein) of such aircraft;

(C) any other parts, components, and subassemblies for incorporation in such aircraft; and

(D) any ground flight simulators, and parts and components thereof, for use with respect to such aircraft, whether to be purchased for use as original or replacement equipment in the manufacture, repair, maintenance, rebuilding, modification, or conversion of such aircraft, and without regard to whether such aircraft or articles receive duty-free treatment pursuant to section 601(a)(2).

(3) Developed countries. The term "developed countries" means countries so designated by the President.

(4)(A) In general. The term "eligible product" means, with respect to any foreign country or instrumentality that is—

(i) a party to the Agreement, a product or service of that country or instrumentality which is covered under the Agreement for procurement by the United States; or

(ii) a party to the North American Free Trade Agreement, a product or service of that country or instrumentality which is covered under the North American Free Trade Agreement for procurement by the United States.

(B) Rule of origin. An article is a product of a country or instrumentality only if (i) it is wholly the growth, product, or manufacture of that country or instrumentality, or (ii) in the case of an article which consists in whole or in part of materials from another country or instrumentality, it has been substantially transformed into a new and different article of commerce with a name, character, or use distinct from that of the article or articles from which it was so transformed.

(C) Lowered threshold for certain products as a consequence of United States-Israel Free Trade Area provisions. The term "eligible product" includes a product or service of Israel for which the United States is obligated to waive Buy National restrictions under—

(i) the Agreement on the Establishment of a Free Trade Area between the Government of the United States of America and the Government of Israel, regardless of the thresholds provided for in the Agreement (as defined in paragraph (1)), or

(ii) any subsequent agreement between the United States and Israel which lowers on a reciprocal basis the applicable threshold for entities covered by the Agreement.

(D) Lowered threshold for certain products as a consequence of United States-Canada Free-Trade Agreement. Except as otherwise agreed by the United States and Canada under paragraph 3 of article 1304 of the United States-Canada Free-Trade Agreement, the term "eligible product" includes a product or service of Canada having a contract value of $ 25,000 or more that would be covered for procurement by the United States under the Agreement (as defined in paragraph (1)), but for the thresholds provided for in the Agreement.

(5) Instrumentality. The term "instrumentality" shall not be construed to include an agency or division of the government of a country, but may be construed to include such arrangements as the European Economic Community.

(6) Least developed country. The term "least developed country" means any country on the United Nations General Assembly list of least developed countries.

(7) Major industrial country. The term "major industrial country" means any such country as defined in section 126 of the Trade Act of 1974 and any instrumentality of such a country.

* * *

TITLE IV. TECHNICAL BARRIERS TO TRADE (STANDARDS)

Subtitle A

Obligations of the United States

19 U.S.C. § 2531

Sec. 401. Certain standards-related activities

(a) No bar to engaging in standards activity. Nothing in this title may be construed

(1) to prohibit a Federal agency from engaging in activity related to standards-related measures, including any such measure relating to safety, the protection of human, animal, or plant life or health, the environment, or consumers; or

(2) to limit the authority of a Federal agency to determine the level it considers appropriate of safety or of protection of human, animal, or plant life or health, the environment, or consumers.

(b) Unnecessary obstacles. Nothing in this title may be construed as prohibiting any private person, Federal agency, or State agency from engaging in standards-related activities that do not create unnecessary obstacles to the foreign commerce of the United States. No standards-related activity of any private person, Federal agency, or State agency shall be deemed to constitute an unnecessary obstacle to the foreign commerce of the United States if the demonstrable purpose of the standards-related activity is to achieve a legitimate domestic objective including, but not limited to, the protection of legitimate health or safety, essential security, environmental, or consumer interests and if such activity does not operate to exclude imported products which fully meet the objectives of such activity.

19 U.S.C. § 2532

Sec. 402. Federal standards-related activities

No Federal agency may engage in any standards-related activity that creates unnecessary obstacles to the foreign commerce of the United States, including, but not limited to, standards-related activities that violate any of the following requirements:

(1) Nondiscriminatory treatment. Each Federal agency shall ensure, in applying standards-related activities with respect to any imported product, that such product is treated no less favorably than are like domestic or imported products, including, but not limited to, when applying tests or test methods, no less favorable treatment with respect to—

(A) the acceptance of the product for testing in comparable situations;

(B) the administration of the tests in comparable situations;

(C) the fees charged for tests;

(D) the release of test results to the exporter, importer, or agents;

(E) the siting of testing facilities and the selection of samples for testing; and

(F) the treatment of confidential information pertaining to the product.

(2) Use of international standards.

(A) In general. Except as provided in subparagraph (B)(ii), each Federal agency, in developing standards, shall take into consideration international standards and shall, if appropriate, base the standards on international standards.

(B) Application of requirement. For purposes of this paragraph, the following apply:

(i) International standards not appropriate. The reasons for which the basing of a standard on an international standard may not be appropriate include, but are not limited to, the following:

(I) National security requirements.

(II) The prevention of deceptive practices.

(III) The protection of human health or safety, animal or plant life or health, or the environment.

(IV) Fundamental climatic or other geographical factors.

(V) Fundamental technological problems.

(ii) Regional standards. In developing standards, a Federal agency may, but is not required to, take into consideration any international standard promulgated by an international standards organization the membership of which is described in section 451(6)(A)(ii).

(3) Performance criteria. Each Federal agency shall, if appropriate, develop standards based on performance criteria, such as those relating to the intended use of a product and the level of performance that the product must achieve under defined conditions, rather than on design criteria, such as those relating to the physical form of the product or the types of material of which the product is made.

(4) Certification access for foreign suppliers. Each Federal agency shall, with respect to any certification system used by it, permit access for obtaining certification under that system to foreign suppliers of a product on the same basis as access is permitted to suppliers of like products, whether of domestic or other foreign origin.

19 U.S.C. § 2533

Sec. 403. State and private standards-related activities

(a) In general. It is the sense of the Congress that no State agency and no private person should engage in any standards-related activity that creates unnecessary obstacles to the foreign commerce of the United States.

(b) Presidential action. The President shall take such reasonable measures as may be available to promote the observance by State agencies and private persons, in carrying out standards-related activities, of requirements equivalent to those imposed on Federal agencies under section 402, and of procedures that provide for notification, participation, and publication with respect to such activities.

Subtitle D

Definitions and Miscellaneous Provisions

19 U.S.C. § 2571

Sec. 451. Definitions

As used in this title—

(1) Agreement. The term "Agreement" means the Agreement on Technical Barriers to Trade referred to in section 101(d)(5) of the Uruguay Round Agreements Act.

(2) Conformity assessment procedure. The term "conformity assessment procedure" means any procedure used, directly or indirectly, to determine that relevant requirements in technical regulations or standards are fulfilled.

Such term also includes any modification of, or change to, any such system.

(3) Federal agency. The term "Federal agency" means any of the following within the meaning of chapter 2 of part I of title 5, United States Code:

(A) Any executive department.

(B) Any military department.

(C) Any Government corporation.

(D) Any Government-controlled corporation.

(E) Any independent establishment.

(4) International certification system. The term "international certification system" means a certification system that is adopted by an international standards organization.

(5) International standard. The term "international standard" means any standard that is promulgated by an international standards organization.

(6) International standards organization. The term "international standards organization" means any organization—

(A) the membership of which is open to representatives, whether public or private, of the United States and at least all members.

(B) that is engaged in international standards-related activities.

(7) International standards-related activity. The term "international standards-related activity" means the negotiation, development, or promulgation of, or any amendment or change to, an international standard, or an international certification system, or both.

(8) Member. The term "Member" means a WTO member as defined in section 2(10) of the Uruguay Round Agreements Act.

(9) Private person. The term "private person" means—

(A) any individual who is a citizen or national of the United States; and

(B) any corporation, partnership, association, or other legal entity organized or existing under the law of any State, whether for profit or not for profit.

(10) Product. The term "product" means any natural or manufactured item.

(11) Secretary concerned. The term "Secretary concerned" means the Secretary of Commerce with respect to functions under this title relating to nonagricultural products, and the Secretary of Agriculture with respect to functions under this title relating to agricultural products.

(12) Trade representative. The term "Trade Representative" means the United States Trade Representative.

(13) Standard. The term "standard" means a document approved by a recognized body, that provides, for common and repeated use, rules, guidelines, or characteristics for products or related processes and productive methods, with which compliance is not mandatory. Such term may also include or deal exclusively with terminology, symbols, packaging, marking, or labeling requirements as they apply to a product, process, or production method.

(14) Standards-related activity. The term "standards-related activity" means the development, adoption, or application of any standard technical regulation, or conformity assessment procedure.

(15) State. The term "State" means any of the several States, the District of Columbia, the Commonwealth of Puerto Rico, the Virgin Islands, American Samoa, Guam and any other Commonwealth, territory, or possession of the United States.

(16) State agency. The term "State agency" means any department, agency, or other instrumentality of the government of any State or of any political subdivision of any State.

(17) Technical regulation. The term "technical regulation" means a document which lays down product characteristics or their related processes and production methods, including the applicable administrative provisions, with which compliance is mandatory. Such term may also include or deal exclusively with terminology, symbols, packaging, marking, or labeling requirements as they apply to a product, process, or production method.

(18) United States. The term "United States", when used in a geographical context, means all States.

19 U.S.C. § 2572

Sec. 452. Exemptions under title

This title does not apply to—

(1) any standards activity engaged in by any Federal agency or State agency for the use (including, but not limited to, use with respect to research and development, production, or consumption) of that agency or the use of another such agency; or

(2) any standards activity engaged in by any private person solely for use in the production or consumption of products by that person.

* * *

Subtitle E

Standards and Measures Under the North American Free Trade Agreement

Chapter 1

Sanitary and Phytosanitary Measures

19 U.S.C. § 2575

Sec. 461. General

Nothing in this chapter may be construed—

(1) to prohibit a Federal agency or State agency from engaging in activity related to sanitary or phytosanitary measures to protect human, animal, or plant life or health; or

(2) to limit the authority of a Federal agency or State agency to determine the level of protection of human, animal, or plant life or health the agency considers appropriate.

19 U.S.C. § 2575a

Sec. 462. Inquiry point

The standards information center maintained under section 414 shall, in addition to the functions specified therein, make available to the public relevant documents, at such reasonable fees as the Secretary of Commerce may prescribe, and information regarding—

(1) any sanitary or phytosanitary measure of general application, including any control or inspection procedure or approval procedure proposed, adopted, or maintained by a Federal or State agency;

(2) the procedures of a Federal or State agency for risk assessment, and factors the agency considers in conducting the assessment and in establishing the levels of protection that the agency considers appropriate;

(3) the membership and participation of the Federal Government and State governments in international and regional sanitary and phytosanitary organizations and systems, and in bilateral and multilateral arrangements regarding sanitary and phytosanitary measures, and the provisions of those systems and arrangements; and

(4) the location of notices of the type required under article 719 of the NAFTA, or where the information contained in such notices can be obtained.

19 U.S.C. § 2575b

Sec. 463. Chapter definitions

Notwithstanding section 451, for purposes of this chapter—

(1) Animal. The term "animal" includes fish, bees, and wild fauna.

(2) Approval procedure. The term "approval procedure" means any registration, notification, or other mandatory administrative procedure for—

(A) approving the use of an additive for a stated purpose or under stated conditions, or

(B) establishing a tolerance for a stated purpose or under stated conditions for a contaminant,

in a food, beverage, or feedstuff prior to permitting the use of the additive or the marketing of a food, beverage, or feedstuff containing the additive or contaminant.

(3) Contaminant. The term "contaminant" includes pesticide and veterinary drug residues and extraneous matter.

(4) Control or inspection procedure. The term "control or inspection procedure" means any procedure used, directly or indirectly, to determine that a sanitary or phytosanitary measure is fulfilled, including sampling, testing, inspection, evaluation, verification, monitoring, auditing, assurance of conformity, accreditation, registration, certification, or other procedure involving the physical examination of a good, of the packaging of a good, or of the equipment or facilities directly related to production, marketing, or use of a good, but does not mean an approval procedure.

(5) Plant. The term "plant" includes wild flora.

(6) Risk assessment. The term "risk assessment" means an evaluation of—

(A) the potential for the introduction, establishment or spread of a pest or disease and associated biological and economic consequences; or

(B) the potential for adverse effects on human or animal life or health arising from the presence of an additive, contaminant, toxin or disease-causing organism in a food, beverage, or feedstuff.

(7) Sanitary or phytosanitary measure.

(A) In general. The term "sanitary or phytosanitary measure" means a measure to—

(i) protect animal or plant life or health in the United States from risks arising from the introduction, establishment, or spread of a pest or disease;

(ii) protect human or animal life or health in the United States from risks arising from the presence of an additive, contaminant, toxin, or disease-causing organism in a food, beverage, or feedstuff;

(iii) protect human life or health in the United States from risks arising from a disease-causing organism or pest carried by an animal or plant, or a product thereof; or

(iv) prevent or limit other damage in the United States arising from the introduction, establishment, or spread of a pest.

(B) Form. The form of a sanitary or phytosanitary measure includes—

(i) end product criteria;

(ii) a product-related processing or production method;

(iii) a testing, inspection, certification, or approval procedure;

(iv) a relevant statistical method;

(v) a sampling procedure;

(vi) a method of risk assessment;

(vii) a packaging and labeling requirement directly related to food safety; and

(viii) a quarantine treatment, such as a relevant requirement associated with the transportation of animals or plants or with material necessary for their survival during transportation.

Chapter 2

Standards and Related Measures

19 U.S.C. § 2576

Sec. 471. General

(a) No bar to engaging in standards activity. Nothing in this chapter shall be construed—

(1) to prohibit a Federal agency from engaging in activity related to standards-related measures, including any such measure relating to safety, the protection of human, animal, or plant life or health, the environment or consumers; or

(2) to limit the authority of a Federal agency to determine the level it considers appropriate of safety or of protection of human, animal, or plant life or health, the environment or consumers.

(b) Exclusion. This chapter does not apply to—

(1) technical specifications prepared by a Federal agency for production or consumption requirements of the agency; or

(2) sanitary or phytosanitary measures under chapter 1.

19 U.S.C. § 2576a

Sec. 472. Inquiry point

The standards information center maintained under section 414 shall, in addition to the functions specified therein, make available to the public relevant documents, at such reasonable fees as the Secretary of Commerce may prescribe, and information regarding—

(1) the membership and participation of the Federal Government, State governments, and relevant nongovernmental bodies in the United States in international and regional standardizing bodies and conformity assessment systems, and in bilateral and multilateral arrangements regarding standards-related measures, and the provisions of those systems and arrangements;

(2) the location of notices of the type required under article 909 of the NAFTA, or where the information contained in such notice can be obtained; and

(3) the Federal agency procedures for assessment of risk, and factors the agency considers in conducting the assessment and establishing the levels of protection that the agency considers appropriate.

19 U.S.C. § 2576b

Sec. 473. Chapter definitions

Notwithstanding section 451, for purposes of this chapter—

(1) Approval procedure. The term "approval procedure" means any registration, notification, or other mandatory administrative procedure for granting permission for a good or service to be produced, marketed, or used for a stated purpose or under stated conditions.

(2) Conformity assessment procedure. The term "conformity assessment procedure" means any procedure used, directly or indirectly, to determine that a technical regulation or standard is fulfilled, including sampling, testing, inspection, evaluation, verification, monitoring, auditing, assurance of conformity, accreditation, registration, or approval used for such a purpose, but does not mean an approval procedure.

(3) Objective. The term "objective" includes—

(A) safety,

(B) protection of human, animal, or plant life or health, the environment or consumers, including matters relating to quality and identifiability of goods or services, and

(C) sustainable development,

but does not include the protection of domestic production.

(4) Service. The term "service" means a land transportation service or a telecommunications service.

(5) Standard. The term "standard" means—

(A) characteristics for a good or a service,

(B) characteristics, rules, or guidelines for—

(i) processes or production methods relating to such good, or

(ii) operating methods relating to such service, and

(C) provisions specifying terminology, symbols, packaging, marking, or labeling for—

(i) a good or its related process or production methods, or

(ii) a service or its related operating methods,

for common and repeated use, including explanatory and other related provisions set out in a document approved by a standardizing body, with which compliance is not mandatory.

(6) Standards-related measure. The term "standards-related measure" means a standard, technical regulation, or conformity assessment procedure.

(7) Technical regulation. The term "technical regulation" means—

(A) characteristics or their related processes and production methods for a good,

(B) characteristics for a service or its related operating methods, or

(C) provisions specifying terminology, symbols, packaging, marking, or labeling for—

(i) a good or its related process or production method, or

(ii) a service or its related operating methods,

set out in a document, including applicable administrative, explanatory, and other related provisions, with which compliance is mandatory.

(8) Telecommunications service. The term "telecommunications service" means a service provided by means of the transmission and reception of signals by any electromagnetic means, but does not mean the cable, broadcast, or other electromagnetic distribution of radio or television programming to the public generally.

TITLE XI. MISCELLANEOUS PROVISIONS

19 U.S.C. § 2581

Sec. 1102. Auction of import licenses

(a) In general. Notwithstanding any other provision of law, the President may sell import licenses at public auction under such terms and conditions as he deems appropriate. Regulations prescribed under this subsection shall, to the extent practicable and consistent with efficient and fair administration, insure against inequitable sharing of imports by a relatively small number of the larger importers.

(b) Definition of import license. For purposes of this section, the term "import license" means any documentation used to administer a quantitative restriction imposed or modified after the date of enactment of this Act under—

(1) section 125, 203, 301, or 406 of the Trade Act of 1974 (19 U.S.C. §§ 2135, 2253, 2411, or 2436),

(2) the International Emergency Economic Powers Act (50 U.S.C.App. §§ 1701–1706),

(3) authority under the notes of the Harmonized Tariff Schedules of the United States, but not including any quantitative restriction imposed under section 22 of the Agricultural Adjustment Act of 1934 (7 U.S.C. § 624),

(4) the Trading With the Enemy Act (50 U.S.C.App. §§ 1–44),

(5) section 204 of the Agricultural Act of 1956 (7 U.S.C. § 1854) other than for meat or meat products, or

(6) any Act enacted explicitly for the purpose of implementing an international agreement to which the United States is a party, including such agreements relating to commodities, but not including any agreement relating to cheese or dairy products.

PART TWO

TRADE LAW STATUTES DIRECTED TO REGIONS

■ ■ ■

DOCUMENT 31

CARIBBEAN BASIN ECONOMIC RECOVERY ACT (1983)

■ ■ ■

Pub.L. 98–67, Title II, Approved August 5, 1983, 19 U.S.C. §§ 2701–2707, 97 Stat. 384, as amended.

§ 2701. Authority to Grant Duty-free Treatment

The President may proclaim duty-free treatment (or other preferential treatment) for all eligible articles from any beneficiary country in accordance with the provisions of this chapter.

§ 2702. Beneficiary country

(a) Definitions; termination of designation.

(1) For purposes of this title—

(A) The term "beneficiary country" means any country listed in subsection (b) with respect to which there is in effect a proclamation by the President designating such country as a beneficiary country for purposes of this title. Before the President designates any country as a beneficiary country for purposes of this title, he shall notify the House of Representatives and the Senate of his intention to make such designation, together with the considerations entering into such decision.

(B) The term "entered" means entered, or withdrawn from warehouse for consumption, in the customs territory of the United States.

(C) The term "HTS" means Harmonized Tariff Schedule of the United States (*19 U.S.C. 1202*).

(D) The term "NAFTA" means the North American Free Trade Agreement entered into between the United States, Mexico, and Canada on December 17, 1992.

(E) The terms "WTO" and "WTO member"' have the meanings given those terms in section 2 of the Uruguay Round Agreements Act (*19 U.S.C. 3501*).

(F) The term "former beneficiary country" means a country that ceases to be designated as a beneficiary country under this title [for full classification, consult USCS Tables volumes] because the country has become a party to a free trade agreement with the United States.

(2) If the President has designated any country as a beneficiary country for purposes of this title, he shall not terminate such designation (either by issuing a proclamation for that purpose or by issuing a proclamation which has the effect of terminating such designation) unless, at least sixty days before such termination, he has notified the House of Representatives and the Senate and has notified such country of his intention to terminate such designation, together with the considerations entering into such decision.

(b) Countries eligible for designation as beneficiary countries; conditions. In designating countries as "beneficiary countries" under this title the President shall consider only the following countries and territories or successor political entities:

Anguilla

Antigua and Barbuda

Bahamas, The

Barbados

Belize

Dominica

Grenada

Guyana

Haiti

Jamaica

Panama

Saint Lucia

Saint Vincent and the Grenadines

Suriname

Trinidad and Tobago

Cayman Islands

Montserrat

Netherlands Antilles

Saint Christopher-Nevis

Turks and Caicos Islands

Virgin Islands, British

In addition, the President shall not designate any country a beneficiary country under this title—

(1) if such country is a Communist country;

(2) if such country—

(A) has nationalized, expropriated or otherwise seized ownership or control of property owned by a United States citizen or by a corporation, partnership, or association which is 50 per centum or more beneficially owned by United States citizens,

(B) has taken steps to repudiate or nullify—

(i) any existing contract or agreement with, or

(ii) any patent, trademark, or other intellectual property of,

a United States citizen or a corporation, partnership, or association which is 50 per centum or more beneficially owned by United States citizens, the effect of which is to nationalize, expropriate, or otherwise seize ownership or control of property so owned, or

(C) has imposed or enforced taxes or other exactions, restrictive maintenance or operational conditions, or other measures with respect to property so owned, the effect of which is to nationalize, expropriate, or otherwise seize ownership or control of such property, unless the President determines that—

(i) prompt, adequate, and effective compensation has been or is being made to such citizen, corporation, partnership, or association,

(ii) good-faith negotiations to provide prompt, adequate, and effective compensation under the applicable provisions of international law are in progress, or such country is otherwise taking steps to discharge its obligations under international law with respect to such citizen, corporation, partnership, or association, or

(iii) a dispute involving such citizen, corporation, partnership, or association, over compensation for such a seizure has been submitted to arbitration under the provisions of the Convention for the Settlement of Investment Disputes, or in another mutually agreed upon forum, and promptly furnishes a copy of such determination to the Senate and House of Representatives;

(3) if such country fails to act in good faith in recognizing as binding or in enforcing arbitral awards in favor of United States citizens or a corporation, partnership or association which is 50 per

centum or more beneficially owned by United States citizens, which have been made by arbitrators appointed for each case or by permanent arbitral bodies to which the parties involved have submitted their dispute;

(4) if such country affords preferential treatment to the products of a developed country, other than the United States, which has, or is likely to have, a significant adverse effect on United States commerce, unless the President has received assurances satisfactory to him that such preferential treatment will be eliminated or that action will be taken to assure that there will be no such significant adverse effect, and he reports those assurances to the Congress;

(5) if a government-owned entity in such country engages in the broadcast of copyrighted material, including films or television material, belonging to United States copyright owners without their express consent;

(6) unless such country is a signatory to a treaty, convention, protocol, or other agreement regarding the extradition of United States citizens; and

(7) if such country has not or is not taking steps to afford internationally recognized worker rights (as defined in section 507(4) of the Trade Act of 1974 [*19 USC § 2467(4)*]) to workers in the country (including any designated zone in that country).

Paragraphs (1), (2), (3), (5), and (7) shall not prevent the designation of any country as a beneficiary country under this Act if the President determines that such designation will be in the national economic or security interest of the United States and reports such determination to the Congress with his reasons therefor.

(c) Factors determining designation. In determining whether to designate any country a beneficiary country under this title, the President shall take into account—

(1) an expression by such country of its desire to be so designated;

(2) the economic conditions in such country, the living standards of its inhabitants, and any other economic factors which he deems appropriate;

(3) the extent to which such country has assured the United States it will provide equitable and reasonable access to the markets and basic commodity resources of such country;

(4) the degree to which such country follows the accepted rules of international trade provided for under the WTO Agreement and the multilateral trade agreements (as such terms are defined in

paragraphs (9) and (4), respectively, of section 2 of the Uruguay Round Agreements Act [*19 USC § 3501(9)* and (4)]);

(5) the degree to which such country uses export subsidies or imposes export performance requirements or local content requirements which distort international trade;

(6) the degree to which the trade policies of such country as they relate to other beneficiary countries are contributing to the revitalization of the region;

(7) the degree to which such country is undertaking self-help measures to promote its own economic development;

(8) whether or not such country has taken or is taking steps to afford to workers in that country (including any designated zone in that country) internationally recognized worker rights.[;]

(9) the extent to which such country provides under its law adequate and effective means for foreign nationals to secure, exercise, and enforce exclusive rights in intellectual property, including patent, trademark, and copyright rights;

(10) the extent to which such country prohibits its nationals from engaging in the broadcast of copyrighted material, including films or television material, belonging to United States copyright owners without their express consent; and

(11) the extent to which such country is prepared to cooperate with the United States in the administration of the provisions of this title.

(d) [Omitted]

(e) Withdrawal or suspension of duty-free treatment to specific articles.

(1)(A) The President may, after the requirements of subsection (a)(2) and paragraph (2) have been met—

(i) withdraw or suspend the designation of any country as a beneficiary country, or

(ii) withdraw, suspend, or limit the application of duty-free treatment under this subtitle to any article of any country, if, after such designation, the President determines that as a result of changed circumstances such country would be barred from designation as a beneficiary country under subsection (b).

(B) The President may, after the requirements of subsection (a)(2) and paragraph (2) have been met—

(i) withdraw or suspend the designation of any country as a CBTPA beneficiary country; or

(ii) withdraw, suspend, or limit the application of preferential treatment under section 213(b)(2) and (3) [*19 USC § 2703(b)(2)* and (3)] to any article of any country,

if, after such designation, the President determines that, as a result of changed circumstances, the performance of such country is not satisfactory under the criteria set forth in section 213(b)(5)(B) [*19 USC § 2703(b)(5)(B)*].

(2) (A) The President shall publish in the Federal Register notice of the action the President proposes to take under paragraph (1) at least 30 days prior to taking such action.

(B) The United States Trade Representative shall, within the 30-day period beginning on the date on which the President publishes under subparagraph (A) notice of proposed action—

(i) accept written comments from the public regarding such proposed action,

(ii) hold a public hearing on such proposed action, and

(iii) publish in the Federal Register—

(I) notice of the time and place of such hearing prior to the hearing, and

(II) the time and place at which such written comments will be accepted.

(3) If preferential treatment under section 213(b)(2) and (3) [*19 USC § 2703(b)(2)* and (3)] is withdrawn, suspended, or limited with respect to a CBTPA beneficiary country, such country shall not be deemed to be a "party" for the purposes of applying section 213(b)(5)(C) [*19 USC § 2703(b)(5)(C)*] to imports of articles for which preferential treatment has been withdrawn, suspended, or limited with respect to such country.

(f) Reporting requirements.

(1) In general. Not later than December 31, 2001, and every 2 years thereafter during the period this title is in effect, the United States Trade Representative shall submit to Congress a report regarding the operation of this title, including—

(A) with respect to subsections (b) and (c), the results of a general review of beneficiary countries based on the considerations described in such subsections; and

(B) the performance of each beneficiary country or CBTPA beneficiary country, as the case may be, under the criteria set forth in section 213(b)(5)(B) [*19 USC § 2703(b)(5)(B)*].

(2) Public comment. Before submitting the report described in paragraph (1), the United States Trade Representative shall publish a notice in the Federal Register requesting public comments on whether beneficiary countries are meeting the criteria listed in section 213(b)(5)(B) [*19 USC § 2703(b)(5)(B)*].

§ 2703. Eligible Articles

(a) Growth, product, or manufacture of beneficiary countries.

(1) Unless otherwise excluded from eligibility by this title, and subject to section 423 of the Tax Reform Act of 1986 [note to this section], and except as provided in subsection (b)(2) and (3), the duty-free treatment provided under this title shall apply to any article which is the growth, product, or manufacture of a beneficiary country if—

(A) that article is imported directly from a beneficiary country into the customs territory of the United States; and

(B) the sum of (i) the cost or value of the materials produced in a beneficiary country or two or more beneficiary countries, plus (ii) the direct costs of processing operations performed in a beneficiary country or countries is not less than 35 per centum of the appraised value of such article at the time it is entered.

For purposes of determining the percentage referred to in subparagraph (B), the term "beneficiary country" includes the Commonwealth of Puerto Rico, the United States Virgin Islands, and any former beneficiary country. If the cost or value of materials produced in the customs territory of the United States (other than the Commonwealth of Puerto Rico) is included with respect to an article to which this paragraph applies, an amount not to exceed 15 per centum of the appraised value of the article at the time it is entered that is attributed to such United States cost or value may be applied toward determining the percentage referred to in subparagraph (B).

(2) The Secretary of the Treasury shall prescribe such regulations as may be necessary to carry out this subsection including, but not limited to, regulations providing that, in order to be eligible for duty-free treatment under this title, an article must be wholly the growth, product, or manufacture of a beneficiary country, or must be a new or different article of commerce which has been grown, produced, or manufactured in the beneficiary country; but no article or material of a beneficiary country shall be eligible for such treatment by virtue of having merely undergone—

(A) simple combining or packaging operations, or

(B) mere dilution with water or mere dilution with another substance that does not materially alter the characteristics of the article.

(3) As used in this subsection, the phrase "direct costs of processing operations" includes, but is not limited to—

(A) all actual labor costs involved in the growth, production, manufacture, or assembly of the specific merchandise, including fringe benefits, on-the-job training and the cost of engineering, supervisory, quality control, and similar personnel; and

(B) dies, molds, tooling, and depreciation on machinery and equipment which are allocable to the specific merchandise.

Such phrase does not include costs which are not directly attributable to the merchandise concerned or are not costs of manufacturing the product, such as (i) profit, and (ii) general expenses of doing business which are either not allocable to the specific merchandise or are not related to the growth, production, manufacture, or assembly of the merchandise, such as administrative salaries, casualty and liability insurance, advertising, and salesmen's salaries, commissions or expenses.

(4) Notwithstanding section 311 of the Tariff Act of 1930 [*19 USC § 1311*], the products of a beneficiary country which are imported directly from any beneficiary country into Puerto Rico may be entered under bond for processing or use in manufacturing in Puerto Rico. No duty shall be imposed on the withdrawal from warehouse of the product of such processing or manufacturing if, at the time of such withdrawal, such product meets the requirements of paragraph (1)(B).

(5) The duty-free treatment provided under this title shall apply to an article (other than an article listed in subsection (b)) which is the growth, product, or manufacture of the Commonwealth of Puerto Rico if—

(A) the article is imported directly from the beneficiary country into the customs territory of the United States,

(B) the article was by any means advanced in value or improved in condition in a beneficiary country, and

(C) if any materials are added to the article in a beneficiary country, such materials are a product of a beneficiary country or the United States.

(6) Notwithstanding paragraph (1), the duty-free treatment provided under this title shall apply to liqueurs and spirituous beverages produced in the territory of Canada from rum if—

(A) such rum is the growth, product, or manufacture of a beneficiary country or of the Virgin Islands of the United States;

(B) such rum is imported directly from a beneficiary country or the Virgin Islands of the United States into the territory of Canada, and such liqueurs and spirituous beverages are imported directly from the territory of Canada into the customs territory of the United States;

(C) when imported into the customs territory of the United States, such liqueurs and spirituous beverages are classified in subheading 2208.90 or 2208.40 of the HTS; and

(D) such rum accounts for at least 90 percent by volume of the alcoholic content of such liqueurs and spirituous beverages.

(b) Import-sensitive articles.

(1) In general. Subject to paragraphs (2) through (5), the duty-free treatment provided under this title does not apply to—

(A) textile and apparel articles which were not eligible articles for purposes of this title on January 1, 1994, as this title was in effect on that date;

(B) footwear provided for in any of subheadings 6401.10.00, 6401.91.00, 6401.92.90, 6401.99.30, 6401.99.60, 6401.99.90, 6402.30.50, 6402.30.70, 6402.30.80, 6402.91.50, 6402.91.80, 6402.91.90, 6402.99.20, 6402.99.80, 6402.99.90, 6403.59.60, 6403.91.30, 6403.99.60, 6403.99.90, 6404.11.90, and 6404.19.20 of the HTS that was not designated at the time of the effective date of this title as eligible articles for the purpose of the generalized system of preferences under title V of the Trade Act of 1974 [*19 USCS §§ 2461* et seq.];

(C) tuna, prepared or preserved in any manner, in airtight containers;

(D) petroleum, or any product derived from petroleum, provided for in headings 2709 and 2710 of the HTS;

(E) watches and watch parts (including cases, bracelets, and straps), of whatever type including, but not limited to, mechanical, quartz digital or quartz analog, if such watches or watch parts contain any material which is the product of any country with respect to which HTS column 2 rates of duty apply; or

(F) articles to which reduced rates of duty apply under subsection (h).

(2) Transition period treatment of certain textile and apparel articles.

(A) Articles covered. During the transition period, the preferential treatment described in subparagraph (B) shall apply to the following articles:

(i) Apparel articles assembled in one or more CBTPA beneficiary countries. Apparel articles sewn or otherwise assembled in one or more CBTPA beneficiary countries from fabrics wholly formed and cut, or from components knit-to-shape, in the United States from yarns wholly formed in the United States, or both (including fabrics not formed from yarns, if such fabrics are classifiable under heading 5602 or 5603 of the HTS and are wholly formed and cut in the United States) that are—

(I) entered under subheading 9802.00.80 of the HTS; or

(II) entered under chapter 61 or 62 of the HTS, if, after such assembly, the articles would have qualified for entry under subheading 9802.00.80 of the HTS but for the fact that the articles were embroidered or subjected to stone-washing, enzyme-washing, acid washing, perma-pressing, oven-baking, bleaching, garment-dyeing, screen printing, or other similar processes.

Apparel articles entered on or after September 1, 2002, shall qualify under the preceding sentence only if all dyeing, printing, and finishing of the fabrics from which the articles are assembled, if the fabrics are knit fabrics, is carried out in the United States. Apparel articles entered on or after September 1, 2002, shall qualify under the first sentence of this clause only if all dyeing, printing, and finishing of the fabrics from which the articles are assembled, if the fabrics are woven fabrics, is carried out in the United States.

(ii) Other apparel articles assembled in one or more CBTPA beneficiary countries. Apparel articles sewn or otherwise assembled in one or more CBTPA beneficiary countries with thread formed in the United States from fabrics wholly formed in the United States and cut in one or more CBTPA beneficiary countries from yarns wholly formed in the United States, or from components knit-to-shape in the United States from yarns wholly formed in the United States, or both (including fabrics not formed from yarns, if such fabrics are classifiable under heading 5602 or 5603 of the HTS and are wholly formed in the United States). Apparel articles entered on or after September 1, 2002, shall qualify under the preceding sentence only if all dyeing, printing, and finishing of the fabrics from which the articles are assembled, if the fabrics are knit fabrics, is carried out in the United States. Apparel articles entered on or after September 1, 2002, shall qualify under the first sentence of this clause only if all dyeing, printing, and finishing of the fabrics from which the articles are assembled, if the fabrics are woven fabrics, is carried out in the United States.

(iii) Certain knit apparel articles.

(I) Apparel articles knit to shape (other than socks provided for in heading 6115 of the HTS) in a CBTPA beneficiary country from yarns wholly formed in the United States, and knit apparel articles (other than t-shirts described in subclause (III)) cut and wholly assembled in one or more CBTPA beneficiary countries from fabric formed in one or more CBTPA beneficiary countries or the United States from yarns wholly formed in the United States (including fabrics not formed from yarns, if such fabrics are classifiable under heading 5602 or 5603 of the HTS and are formed in one or more CBTPA beneficiary countries), in an amount not exceeding the amount set forth in subclause (II).

(II) The amount referred to in subclause (I) is as follows:

(aa) 500,000,000 square meter equivalents during the 1-year period beginning on October 1, 2002.

(bb) 850,000,000 square meter equivalents during the 1-year period beginning on October 1, 2003.

(cc) 970,000,000 square meter equivalents in each succeeding 1-year period through September 30, 2008.

(III) T-shirts, other than underwear, classifiable under subheadings 6109.10.00 and 6109.90.10 of the HTS, made in one or more CBTPA beneficiary countries from fabric formed in one or more CBTPA beneficiary countries from yarns wholly formed in the United States, in an amount not exceeding the amount set forth in subclause (IV).

(IV) The amount referred to in subclause (III) is as follows:

(aa) 4,872,000 dozen during the 1-year period beginning on October 1, 2001.

(bb) 9,000,000 dozen during the 1-year period beginning on October 1, 2002.

(cc) 10,000,000 dozen during the 1-year period beginning on October 1, 2003.

(dd) 12,000,000 dozen in each succeeding 1-year period through September 30, 2008.

(V) It is the sense of the Congress that the Congress should determine, based on the record of expansion of exports from the United States as a result of the preferential treatment of articles under this clause, the percentage by which the amount provided in subclauses (II) and (IV) should be compounded for the 1-year periods occurring after the 1-year period ending on September 30, 2004.

(iv) Certain other apparel articles.

(I) General rule. Subject to subclause (II), any apparel article classifiable under subheading 6212.10 of the HTS, except for articles entered under clause (i), (ii), (iii), (v), or (vi), if the article is both cut and sewn or otherwise assembled in the United States, or one or more CBTPA beneficiary countries, or both.

(II) Limitation. During the 1-year period beginning on October 1, 2001, and during each of the 6 succeeding 1-year periods, apparel articles described in subclause (I) of a producer or an entity controlling production shall be eligible for preferential treatment under subparagraph (B) only if the aggregate cost of fabrics (exclusive of all findings and trimmings) formed in the United States that are used in the production of all such articles of that producer or entity that are entered and eligible under this clause during the preceding 1-year period is at least 75 percent of the aggregate declared customs value of the fabric (exclusive of all findings and trimmings) contained in all such articles of that producer or entity that are entered and eligible under this clause during the preceding 1-year period.

(III) Development of procedure to ensure compliance. The United States Customs Service shall develop and implement methods and procedures to ensure ongoing compliance with the requirement set forth in subclause (II). If the Customs Service finds that a producer or an entity controlling production has not satisfied such requirement in a 1-year period, then apparel articles described in subclause (I) of that producer or entity shall be ineligible for preferential treatment under subparagraph (B) during any succeeding 1-year period until the aggregate cost of fabrics (exclusive of all findings and trimmings) formed in the United States that are used in the production of such articles of that producer or entity entered during the preceding 1-year period is at least 85 percent of the aggregate declared customs value of the fabric (exclusive of all findings and trimmings) contained in all such articles of that producer or entity that are entered and eligible under this clause during the preceding 1-year period.

(v) Apparel articles assembled from fabrics or yarn not widely available in commercial quantities.

(I) Apparel articles that are both cut (or knit-to-shape) and sewn or otherwise assembled in one or more CBTPA beneficiary countries, to the extent that apparel articles of such fabrics or yarn would be eligible for preferential treatment, without regard to the source of the fabrics or yarn, under Annex 401 of the NAFTA.

(II) At the request of any interested party, the President is authorized to proclaim additional fabrics and yarn as eligible for preferential treatment under subclause (I) if—

(aa) the President determines that such fabrics or yarn cannot be supplied by the domestic industry in commercial quantities in a timely manner;

(bb) the President has obtained advice regarding the proposed action from the appropriate advisory committee established under section 135 of the Trade Act of 1974 (*19 U.S.C. 2155*) and the United States International Trade Commission;

(cc) within 60 days after the request, the President has submitted a report to the Committee on Ways and Means of the House of Representatives and the Committee on Finance of the Senate that sets forth the action proposed to be proclaimed and the reasons for such actions, and the advice obtained under division (bb);

(dd) a period of 60 calendar days, beginning with the first day on which the President has met the requirements of division (cc), has expired; and (ee) the President has consulted with such committees regarding the proposed action during the period referred to in division (cc).

(III) If the President determines that any fabric or yarn was determined to be eligible for preferential treatment under subclause (I) on the basis of fraud, the President is authorized to remove that designation from that fabric or yarn with respect to articles entered after such removal.

(vi) Handloomed, handmade, and folklore articles. A handloomed, handmade, or folklore article of a CBTPA beneficiary country identified under subparagraph (C) that is certified as such by the competent authority of such beneficiary country.

(vii) Special rules.

(I) Exception for findings and trimmings.

(aa) An article otherwise eligible for preferential treatment under this paragraph shall not be ineligible for such treatment because the article contains findings or trimmings of foreign origin, if such findings and trimmings do not exceed 25 percent of the cost of the components of the assembled product. Examples of findings and trimmings are sewing thread, hooks and eyes, snaps, buttons, "bow buds", decorative lace, trim, elastic strips, zippers, including zipper tapes and labels, and other similar products. Elastic strips are considered findings or trimmings only if they are each less than 1 inch in width and are used in the production of brassieres.

(bb) In the case of an article described in clause (ii) of this subparagraph, sewing thread shall not be treated as findings or trimmings under this subclause.

(II) Certain interlining.

(aa) An article otherwise eligible for preferential treatment under this paragraph shall not be ineligible for such treatment because the article contains certain interlinings of foreign origin, if the value of such interlinings (and any findings and trimmings) does not exceed 25 percent of the cost of the components of the assembled article.

(bb) Interlinings eligible for the treatment described in division (aa) include only a chest type plate, "hymo" piece, or "sleeve header", of woven or weft-inserted warp knit construction and of coarse animal hair or man-made filaments.

(cc) The treatment described in this subclause shall terminate if the President makes a determination that United States manufacturers are producing such interlinings in the United States in commercial quantities.

(III) De minimis rule. An article that would otherwise be ineligible for preferential treatment under this paragraph because the article contains fibers or yarns not wholly formed in the United States or in one or more CBTPA beneficiary countries shall not be ineligible for such treatment if the total weight of all such fibers or yarns is not more than 7 percent of the total weight of the good. Notwithstanding the preceding sentence, an apparel article containing elastomeric yarns shall be eligible for preferential treatment under this paragraph only if such yarns are wholly formed in the United States.

(IV) Special origin rule. An article otherwise eligible for preferential treatment under clause (i), (ii), or (ix) of this subparagraph shall not be ineligible for such treatment because the article contains nylon filament yarn (other than elastomeric yarn) that is classifiable under subheading 5402.10.30, 5402.10.60, 5402.31.30, 5402.31.60, 5402.32.30, 5402.32.60, 5402.41.10, 5402.41.90, 5402.51.00, or 5402.61.00 of the HTS duty-free from a country that is a party to an agreement with the United States establishing a free trade area, which entered into force before January 1, 1995.

(V) Thread. An article otherwise eligible for preferential treatment under this paragraph shall not be ineligible for such treatment because the thread used to assemble the article is dyed, printed, or finished in one or more CBTPA beneficiary countries.

(viii) Textile luggage. Textile luggage—

(I) assembled in a CBTPA beneficiary country from fabric wholly formed and cut in the United States, from yarns wholly formed in the United States, that is entered under subheading 9802.00.80 of the HTS; or

(II) assembled from fabric cut in a CBTPA beneficiary country from fabric wholly formed in the

United States from yarns wholly formed in the United States.

(ix) Apparel articles assembled in one or more CBTPA beneficiary countries from United States and CBTPA beneficiary country components. Apparel articles sewn or otherwise assembled in one or more CBTPA beneficiary countries with thread formed in the United States from components cut in the United States and in one or more CBTPA beneficiary countries from fabric wholly formed in the United States from yarns wholly formed in the United States, or from components knit-to-shape in the United States and one or more CBTPA beneficiary countries from yarns wholly formed in the United States, or both (including fabrics not formed from yarns, if such fabrics are classifiable under heading 5602 or 5603 of the HTS). Apparel articles shall qualify under this clause only if they meet the requirements of clause (i) or (ii) (as the case may be) with respect to dyeing, printing, and finishing of knit and woven fabrics from which the articles are assembled.

(B) Preferential treatment. Except as provided in subparagraph (E), during the transition period, the articles to which this subparagraph applies shall enter the United States free of duty and free of any quantitative restrictions, limitations, or consultation levels.

(C) Handloomed, handmade, and folklore articles. For purposes of subparagraph (A)(vi), the President shall consult with representatives of the CBTPA beneficiary countries concerned for the purpose of identifying particular textile and apparel goods that are mutually agreed upon as being handloomed, handmade, or folklore goods of a kind described in section 2.3(a), (b), or (c) of the Annex or Appendix 3.1.B.11 of the Annex.

(D) Penalties for transshipments.

(i) Penalties for exporters. If the President determines, based on sufficient evidence, that an exporter has engaged in transshipment with respect to textile or apparel articles from a CBTPA beneficiary country, then the President shall deny all benefits under this title to such exporter, and any successor of such exporter, for a period of 2 years.

(ii) Penalties for countries. Whenever the President finds, based on sufficient evidence, that transshipment has occurred, the President shall request that the CBTPA beneficiary country or countries through whose territory the transshipment has occurred take all necessary and appropriate actions to prevent such transshipment. If the President determines that a country is not taking such actions, the President shall reduce the quantities of textile and apparel articles that may be imported into the United States from such country by the quantity of the transshipped articles multiplied by 3, to the extent consistent with the obligations of the United States under the WTO.

(iii) Transshipment described. Transshipment within the meaning of this subparagraph has occurred when preferential treatment under subparagraph (B) has been claimed for a textile or apparel article on the basis of material false information concerning the country of origin, manufacture, processing, or assembly of the article or any of its components. For purposes of this clause, false information is material if disclosure of the true information would mean or would have meant that the article is or was ineligible for preferential treatment under subparagraph (B).

(E) Bilateral emergency actions.

(i) In general. The President may take bilateral emergency tariff actions of a kind described in section 4 of the Annex with respect to any apparel article imported from a CBTPA beneficiary country if the application of tariff treatment under subparagraph (B) to such article results in conditions that would be cause for the taking of such actions under such section 4 with respect to a like article described in the same 8-digit subheading of the HTS that is imported from Mexico.

(ii) Rules relating to bilateral emergency action. For purposes of applying bilateral emergency action under this subparagraph—

(I) the requirements of paragraph (5) of section 4 of the Annex (relating to providing compensation) shall not apply;

(II) the term "transition period" in section 4 of the Annex shall have the meaning given that term in paragraph (5)(D) of this subsection; and

(III) the requirements to consult specified in section 4 of the Annex shall be treated as satisfied if the President requests consultations with the CBTPA beneficiary country in question and the country does not agree to consult within the time period specified under section 4.

(3) Transition period treatment of certain other articles originating in beneficiary countries.

(A) Equivalent tariff treatment.

(i) In general. Subject to clauses (ii) and (iii), the tariff treatment accorded at any time during the transition period to any article referred to in any of subparagraphs (B) through (F) of paragraph (1) that is a CBTPA originating good shall be identical to the tariff treatment that is accorded at such time under Annex 302.2 of the NAFTA to an article described in the same 8-digit subheading of the HTS that is a good of Mexico and is imported into the United States.

(ii) Exception. Clause (i) does not apply to any article accorded duty-free treatment under U.S. Note 2(b) to subchapter II of chapter 98 of the HTS.

(iii) Certain footwear. Notwithstanding paragraph (1)(B) and clause (i) of this subparagraph, footwear provided for in any of subheadings 6403.59.60, 6403.91.30, 6403.99.60, and 6403.99.90 of the HTS shall be eligible for the duty-free treatment provided for under this title if—

(I) the article of footwear is the growth, product, or manufacture of a CBTPA beneficiary country; and

(II) the article otherwise meets the requirements of subsection (a), except that in applying such subsection, "CBTPA beneficiary country" shall be substituted for "beneficiary country" each place it appears.

(B) Relationship to subsection (h) duty reductions. If at any time during the transition period the rate of duty that would (but for action taken under subparagraph (A)(i) in regard to such period) apply with respect to any article under subsection (h) is a rate of duty that is lower than the rate of duty resulting from such action, then such lower rate of duty shall be applied for the purposes of implementing such action.

(4) Customs procedures.

(A) In general.

(i) Regulations. Any importer that claims preferential treatment under paragraph (2) or (3) shall comply with customs procedures similar in all material respects to the requirements of Article 502(1) of the NAFTA as implemented pursuant to United States law, in accordance with regulations promulgated by the Secretary of the Treasury.

(ii) Determination.

(I) In general. In order to qualify for the preferential treatment under paragraph (2) or (3) and for a Certificate of Origin to be valid with respect to any article for which such treatment is claimed, there shall be in effect a determination by the President that each country described in subclause (II)—

(aa) has implemented and follows; or

(bb) is making substantial progress toward implementing and following,

procedures and requirements similar in all material respects to the relevant procedures and requirements under chapter 5 of the NAFTA.

(II) Country described. A country is described in this subclause if it is a CBTPA beneficiary country—

(aa) from which the article is exported; or

(bb) in which materials used in the production of the article originate or in which the article or such materials undergo production that contributes to a claim that the article is eligible for preferential treatment under paragraph (2) or (3).

(B) Certificate of Origin. The Certificate of Origin that otherwise would be required pursuant to the provisions of subparagraph (A) shall not be required in the case of an article imported under paragraph (2) or (3) if such Certificate of Origin would not be required under Article 503 of the NAFTA (as implemented pursuant to United States law), if the article were imported from Mexico.

(C) Report by USTR on cooperation of other countries concerning circumvention. The United States Commissioner of Customs shall conduct a study analyzing the extent to which each CBTPA beneficiary country—

(i) has cooperated fully with the United States, consistent with its domestic laws and procedures, in instances of circumvention or alleged circumvention of existing quotas on imports of textile and apparel goods, to establish necessary relevant facts in the places of import, export, and, where applicable, transshipment, including investigation of circumvention practices, exchanges of documents, correspondence, reports, and other relevant information, to the extent such information is available;

(ii) has taken appropriate measures, consistent with its domestic laws and procedures, against exporters and importers involved in instances of false declaration concerning fiber content, quantities, description, classification, or origin of textile and apparel goods; and

(iii) has penalized the individuals and entities involved in any such circumvention, consistent with its domestic laws and procedures, and has worked closely to seek the cooperation of any third country to prevent such circumvention from taking place in that third country.

The Trade Representative shall submit to Congress, not later than October 1, 2001, a report on the study conducted under this subparagraph.

(5) Definitions and special rules. For purposes of this subsection—

(A) Annex. The term "the Annex" means Annex 300–B of the NAFTA.

(B) CBTPA beneficiary country. The term "CBTPA beneficiary country" means any "beneficiary country", as defined in section 212(a)(1)(A) of this title [*19 USC § 2702(a)(1)(A)*], which the President designates as a CBTPA beneficiary country, taking into account the criteria contained in subsections (b) and (c) of section 212 [*19 USC § 2702*] and other appropriate criteria, including the following:

(i) Whether the beneficiary country has demonstrated a commitment to—

(I) undertake its obligations under the WTO, including those agreements listed in section 101(d) of the Uruguay Round Agreements Act [*19 USC § 3511(d)*], on or ahead of schedule; and

(II) participate in negotiations toward the completion of the FTAA or another free trade agreement.

(ii) The extent to which the country provides protection of intellectual property rights consistent with or greater than the protection afforded under the Agreement on Trade-Related Aspects of Intellectual Property Rights described in section 101(d)(15) of the Uruguay Round Agreements Act [*19 USC § 3511(d)(15)*].

(iii) The extent to which the country provides internationally recognized worker rights, including—

(I) the right of association;

(II) the right to organize and bargain collectively;

(III) a prohibition on the use of any form of forced or compulsory labor;

(IV) a minimum age for the employment of children; and

(V) acceptable conditions of work with respect to minimum wages, hours of work, and occupational safety and health;

(iv) Whether the country has implemented its commitments to eliminate the worst forms of child labor, as defined in section 507(6) of the Trade Act of 1974 [*19 USC § 2467(6)*].

(v) The extent to which the country has met the counter-narcotics certification criteria set forth in section 490 of the Foreign Assistance Act of 1961 (*22 U.S.C. 2291j*) for eligibility for United States assistance.

(vi) The extent to which the country has taken steps to become a party to and implements the Inter-American Convention Against Corruption.

(vii) The extent to which the country—

(I) applies transparent, nondiscriminatory, and competitive procedures in government procurement equivalent to those contained in the Agreement on Government Procurement described in section 101(d)(17) of the Uruguay Round Agreements Act [*19 USC § 3511(d)(17)*]; and

(II) contributes to efforts in international fora to develop and implement international rules in transparency in government procurement.

(C) CBTPA originating good.

(i) In general. The term "CBTPA originating good" means a good that meets the rules of origin for a good set forth in chapter 4 of the NAFTA as implemented pursuant to United States law.

(ii) Application of chapter 4. In applying chapter 4 of the NAFTA with respect to a CBTPA beneficiary country for purposes of this subsection—

(I) no country other than the United States and a CBTPA beneficiary country may be treated as being a party to the NAFTA;

(II) any reference to trade between the United States and Mexico shall be deemed to refer to trade between the United States and a CBTPA beneficiary country;

(III) any reference to a party shall be deemed to refer to a CBTPA beneficiary country or the United States; and

(IV) any reference to parties shall be deemed to refer to any combination of CBTPA beneficiary countries or to the United States and one or more CBTPA beneficiary countries (or any combination thereof).

(D) Transition period. The term "transition period" means, with respect to a CBTPA beneficiary country, the period that begins on October 1, 2000, and ends on the earlier of—

(i) September 30, 2008; or

(ii) the date on which the FTAA or another free trade agreement that makes substantial progress in achieving the negotiating objectives set forth in [section] 108(b)(5) of Public Law 103–182 (*19 U.S.C. 3317(b)(5)*) enters into force with respect to the United States and the CBTPA beneficiary country.

(E) CBTPA. The term "CBTPA" means the United States-Caribbean Basin Trade Partnership Act.

(F) FTAA. The term "FTAA" means the Free Trade Area of the Americas.

(G) Former CBTPA beneficiary country. The term "former CBTPA beneficiary country" means a country that ceases to be designated as a CBTPA beneficiary country under this title because the country has become a party to a free trade agreement with the United States.

(H) Articles that undergo production in a CBTPA beneficiary country and a former CBTPA beneficiary country.

(i) For purposes of determining the eligibility of an article for preferential treatment under paragraph (2) or (3), references in either such paragraph, and in subparagraph (C) of this paragraph to—

(I) a "CBTPA beneficiary country" shall be considered to include any former CBTPA beneficiary country, and

(II) "CBTPA beneficiary countries" shall be considered to include former CBTPA beneficiary countries, if the article, or a good used in the production of the article, undergoes production in a CBTPA beneficiary country.

(ii) An article that is eligible for preferential treatment under clause (i) shall not be ineligible for such treatment because the article is imported directly from a former CBTPA beneficiary country.

(iii) Notwithstanding clauses (i) and (ii), an article that is a good of a former CBTPA beneficiary country for purposes of section 304 of the Tariff Act of 1930 (*19 U.S.C. 1304*) or section 334 of the Uruguay Round Agreements Act (*19 U.S.C. 3592*), as the case may be, shall not be eligible for preferential treatment under paragraph (2) or (3), unless—

(I) it is an article that is a good of the Dominican Republic under either such section 304 or 334; and

(II) the article, or a good used in the production of the article, undergoes production in Haiti.

(c) Sugar and beef products; stable food production plan; suspension of duty-free treatment; monitoring.

(1) As used in this subsection—

(A) The term "sugar and beef products" means—

(i) sugars, sirups, and molasses provided for in subheadings 1701.11.00, 1701.12.00, 1701.91.20, 1701.99.00, 1702.90.30, 1806.10.40, and 2106.90.10 of the Harmonized Tariff Schedule of the United States, and

(ii) articles of beef or veal, however provided for in chapters 2 and 16 of the Harmonized Tariff Schedule of the United States.

(B) The term "Plan" means a stable food production plan that consists of measures and proposals designed to ensure that the present level of food production in, and the nutritional level of the population of, a beneficiary country will not be adversely affected by changes in land use and land ownership that will result if increased production of sugar and beef products is undertaken in response to the duty-free treatment extended under this title to such products. A Plan must specify such facts regarding, and such proposed actions by, a beneficiary country as the President deems necessary for purposes of carrying out this subsection, including but not limited to—

(i) the current levels of food production and nutritional health of the population;

(ii) current level of production and export of sugar and beef products;

(iii) expected increases in production and export of sugar and beef products as a result of the duty-free access to the United States market provided under this title;

(iv) measures to be taken to ensure that the expanded production of those products because of such duty-free access will not occur at the expense of stable food production; and

(v) proposals for a system to monitor the impact of such duty-free access on stable food production and land use and land ownership patterns.

(2) Duty-free treatment extended under this title to sugar and beef products that are the product of a beneficiary country shall be suspended by the President under this subsection if—

(A) the beneficiary country, within the ninety-day period beginning on the date of its designation as such a country under section 212 [*19 USC § 2702*], does not submit a Plan to the President for evaluation;

(B) on the basis of his evaluation, the President determines that the Plan of a beneficiary country does not meet the criteria set forth in paragraph (1)(B); or

(C) as a result of the monitoring of the operation of the Plan under paragraph (5), the President determines that a beneficiary country is not making a good faith effort to implement its Plan, or that the measures and proposals in the Plan, although being implemented, are not achieving their purposes.

(3) Before the President suspends duty-free treatment by reason of paragraph (2)(A), (B), or (C) to the sugar and beef products of a beneficiary country, he must offer to enter into consultation with the beneficiary country for purposes of formulating appropriate remedial action which may be taken by that country to avoid such suspension. If the beneficiary country thereafter enters into consultation within a reasonable time and undertakes to formulate remedial action in good faith, the President shall withhold the suspension of duty-free treatment on the condition that the remedial action agreed upon be appropriately implemented by that country.

(4) The President shall monitor on a biennial basis the operation of the Plans implemented by beneficiary countries, and shall submit a written report to Congress by March 15 following the close of each biennium, that—

(A) specifies the extent to which each Plan, and remedial actions, if any, agreed upon under paragraph (4), have been implemented; and

(B) evaluates the results of such implementation.

(5) The President shall terminate any suspension of duty-free treatment imposed under this subsection if he determines that the beneficiary country has taken appropriate action to remedy the factors on which the suspension was based.

(d) Tariff-rate quotas. No quantity of an agricultural product subject to a tariff-rate quota that exceeds the in-quota quantity shall be eligible for duty-free treatment under this title.

(e) Proclamations suspending duty-free treatment.

(1) The President may by proclamation suspend the duty-free treatment provided by this title with respect to any eligible article and may proclaim a duty rate for such article if such action is provided under chapter 1 of title II of the Trade Act of 1974 [*19 USC §§ 2251* et seq.] or *section 232* of the Trade Expansion Act of 1962 [*19 USC § 1862*].

(2) In any report by the International Trade Commission to the President under section 202(f) of the Trade Act of 1974 [*19 USC § 2252(f)*] regarding any article for which duty-free treatment has been proclaimed by the President pursuant to this title, the Commission shall state whether and to what extent its findings and recommendations apply to such article when imported from beneficiary countries.

(3) For purposes of [subsections] section 203 of the Trade Act of 1974 [*19 USC § 2253*], the suspension of the duty-free treatment provided by this title shall be treated as an increase in duty.

(4) No proclamation which provides solely for a suspension referred to in paragraph (3) of this subsection with respect to any article shall be taken under section 203 of the Trade Act of 1974 [*19 USC § 2253*] unless the United States International Trade Commission, in addition to making an affirmative determination with respect to such article under section 202(b) of the Trade Act of 1974 [*19 USC § 2252(b)*], determines in the course of its investigation under such section that the serious injury (or threat thereof) substantially caused by imports to the domestic industry producing a like or directly competitive article results from the duty-free treatment provided by this title.

(5) (A) Any action taken under section 203 of the Trade Act of 1974 [*19 USC § 2253*] that is in effect when duty-free treatment pursuant

to section 101 of this title is proclaimed shall remain in effect until modified or terminated.

(B) If any article is subject to any such action at the time duty-free treatment is proclaimed pursuant to section 211 [*19 USC § 2701*], the President may reduce or terminate the application of such action to the importation of such article from beneficiary countries prior to the otherwise scheduled date on which such reduction or termination would occur pursuant to the criteria and procedures of section 203 of the Trade Act of 1974 [*19 USC § 2253*].

(f) Petitions to International Trade Commission.

(1) If a petition is filed with the International Trade Commission pursuant to the provisions of section 201 of the Trade Act of 1974 [*19 USC § 2251*] regarding a perishable product and alleging injury from imports from beneficiary countries, then the petition may also be filed with the Secretary of Agriculture with a request that emergency relief be granted pursuant to paragraph (3) of this subsection with respect to such article.

(2) Within fourteen days after the filing of a petition under paragraph (1) of this subsection—

(A) if the Secretary of Agriculture has reason to believe that a perishable product from a beneficiary country is being imported into the United States in such increased quantities as to be a substantial cause of serious injury, or the threat thereof, to the domestic industry producing a perishable product like or directly competitive with the imported product and that emergency action is warranted, he shall advise the President and recommend that the President take emergency action; or

(B) the Secretary of Agriculture shall publish a notice of his determination not to recommend the imposition of emergency action and so advise the petitioner.

(3) Within seven days after the President receives a recommendation from the Secretary of Agriculture to take emergency action pursuant to paragraph (2) of this subsection, he shall issue a proclamation withdrawing the duty-free treatment provided by this title or publish a notice of his determination not to take emergency action.

(4) The emergency action provided by paragraph (3) of this subsection shall cease to apply—

(A) upon the taking of action under section 203 of the Trade Act of 1974 [*19 USC § 2253*],

(B) on the day a determination by the President not to take action under section 203 of such Act [*19 USC § 2253*] [not to take action] becomes final,

(C) in the event of a report of the United States International Trade Commission containing a negative finding, on the day the Commission's report is submitted to the President, or

(D) whenever the President determines that because of changed circumstances such relief is no longer warranted.

(5) For purposes of this subsection, the term "perishable product" means—

(A) live plants and fresh cut flowers provided for in chapter 6 of the HTS;

(B) fresh or chilled vegetables provided for in headings 0701 through 0709 (except subheading 0709.52.00 and heading 0714 of the HTS;

(C) fresh fruit provided for in subheadings 0804.20 through 0810.90 (except citrons of subheading 0810.90.20, and cashew apples, mameyes colorados, sapodillas, soursops and sweetsop of subheading 0810,90) of the HTS; and

(D) concentrated citrus fruit juice provided for in subheadings 2009.11.00, 2009.19.40, 2009.20.40, 2009.30.20, and 2009.30.60 of the HTS.

(g) Fees not affected by proclamation

No proclamation issued pursuant to this chapter shall affect fees imposed pursuant to section 624 of Title 7.

(h) Duty reduction for certain leather-related products

(1) Subject to paragraph (2), the President shall proclaim reduction in the rates of duty on handbags, luggage, flat goods, work gloves, and leather wearing apparel that—

(A) are the product of any beneficiary country; and

(B) were not designated on August 5, 1983, as eligible articles for purposes of the generalized system of preferences under title V of the Trade Act of 1974 [*19 U.S.C. § 2461 et. seq.*].

(2) The reduction required under paragraph (1) in the rate of duty on any article shall—

(A) result in a rate that is equal to 80 percent of the rate of duty that applies to the article on December 31, 1991, except that, subject to the limitations in paragraph (3), the reduction may not exceed 2.5 percent ad valorem; and

(B) be implemented in 5 equal annual stages with the first one-fifth of the aggregate reduction in the rate of duty being applied to entries, or withdrawals from warehouse for consumption, of the article on or after January 1, 1992.

(3) The reduction required under this subsection with respect to the rate of duty on any article is in addition to any reduction in the rate of duty on that article that may be proclaimed by the President as being required or appropriate to carry out any trade agreement entered into under the Uruguay Round of trade negotiations; except that if the reduction so proclaimed—

(A) is less than 1.5 percent ad valorem, the aggregate of such proclaimed reduction and the reduction under this subsection may not exceed 3.5 percent ad valorem, or

(B) is 1.5 percent ad valorem or greater, the aggregate of such proclaimed reduction and the reduction under this subsection may not exceed the proclaimed reduction plus 1 percent ad valorem.

DOCUMENT 32

NORTH AMERICAN FREE TRADE AGREEMENT IMPLEMENTATION ACT (1993)

■ ■ ■

PUBLIC LAW 103–182 of December 8, 1993, 107 Stat. 2060

An Act to implement the North American Free Trade Agreement.

Be it enacted by the Senate and House of Representatives of the United States of America in Congress assembled,

SECTION 1. SHORT TITLE AND TABLE OF CONTENTS.

19 U.S.C. § 3301 NOTE

(a) Short Title.—This Act may be cited as the "North American Free Trade Agreement Implementation Act". (omitted)

(b) Table of Contents. (omitted)

* * *

19 U.S.C. § 3301

Sec. 2. Definitions

For purposes of this Act:

(1) Agreement.—The term "Agreement" means the North American Free Trade Agreement approved by the Congress under section 101(a).

(2) HTS.—The term "HTS" means the Harmonized Tariff Schedule of the United States.

(3) Mexico.—Any reference to Mexico shall be considered to be a reference to the United Mexican States.

(4) NAFTA Country.—Except as provided in section 202, the term "NAFTA country" means—

(A) Canada for such time as the Agreement is in force with respect to, and the United States applies the Agreement to, Canada; and

(B) Mexico for such time as the Agreement is in force with respect to, and the United States applies the Agreement to, Mexico.

(5) International Trade Commission.—The term "International Trade Commission" means the United States International Trade Commission.

(6) Trade Representative.—The term "Trade Representative" means the United States Trade Representative.

TITLE I—APPROVAL OF, AND GENERAL PROVISIONS RELATING TO, THE NORTH AMERICAN FREE TRADE AGREEMENT

19 U.S.C. § 3311

Sec. 101. Approval and Entry into Force of the North American Free Trade Agreement

(a) Approval of agreement and statement of administrative action.—Pursuant to section 1103 of the Omnibus Trade and Competitiveness Act of 1988 (19 U.S.C. § 2903) and section 151 of the Trade Act of 1974 (19 U.S.C. § 2191), the Congress approves—

(1) the North American Free Trade Agreement entered into on December 17, 1992, with the Governments of Canada and Mexico and submitted to the Congress on November 4, 1993; * * *

19 U.S.C. § 3312

Sec. 102. Relationship of the Agreement to United States and State law

(a) Relationship of Agreement to United States Law.—

(1) United States law to Prevail in Conflict.—No provision of the Agreement, nor the application of any such provision to any person or circumstance, which is inconsistent with any law of the United States shall have effect.

(2) Construction.—Nothing in this Act shall be construed—

(A) to amend or modify any law of the United States, including any law regarding—

(i) the protection of human, animal, or plant life or health,

(ii) the protection of the environment, or

(iii) motor carrier or worker safety; or

(B) to limit any authority conferred under any law of the United States, including section 301 of the Trade Act of 1974;

unless specifically provided for in this Act.

(b) Relationship of Agreement to State Law.—

(1) Federal-State Consultation.—

(A) In General.—Upon the enactment of this Act, the President shall, through the intergovernmental policy advisory committees on trade established under section 306(c)(2)(A) of the Trade and Tariff Act of 1984, consult with the States for the purpose of achieving conformity of State laws and practices with the Agreement.

(B) Federal-State Consultation Process.—The Trade Representative shall establish within the Office of the United States Trade Representative a Federal-State consultation process for addressing issues relating to the Agreement that directly relate to, or will potentially have a direct impact on, the States. The Federal-State consultation process shall include procedures under which—

(i) the Trade Representative will assist the States in identifying those State laws that may not conform with the Agreement but may be maintained under the Agreement by reason of being in effect before the Agreement entered into force;

(ii) the States will be informed on a continuing basis of matters under the Agreement that directly relate to, or will potentially have a direct impact on, the States;

(iii) the States will be provided opportunity to submit, on a continuing basis, to the Trade Representative information and advice with respect to matters referred to in clause (ii);

(iv) the Trade Representative will take into account the information and advice received from the States under clause (iii) when formulating United States positions regarding matters referred to in clause (ii); and

(v) the States will be involved (including involvement through the inclusion of appropriate representatives of the States) to the greatest extent practicable at each stage of the development of United States positions regarding matters referred to in clause (ii) that will be addressed by committees, subcommittees, or working groups established under the Agreement or through dispute settlement processes provided for under the Agreement.

The Federal Advisory Committee Act (5 U.S.C.App.) shall not apply to the Federal-State consultation process established by this paragraph.

(2) Legal Challenge.—No State law, or the application thereof, may be declared invalid as to any person or circumstance on the ground that the provision or application is inconsistent with the Agreement, except in an action brought by the United States for the purpose of declaring such law or application invalid.

(3) Definition of State law.—For purposes of this subsection, the term "State law" includes—

(A) any law of a political subdivision of a State; and

(B) any State law regulating or taxing the business of insurance.

(c) Effect of Agreement with Respect to Private Remedies.—No person other than the United States—

(1) shall have any cause of action or defense under—

(A) the Agreement or by virtue of Congressional approval thereof, or

(B) the North American Agreement on Environmental Cooperation or the North American Agreement on Labor Cooperation; or

(2) may challenge, in any action brought under any provision of law, any action or inaction by any department, agency, or other instrumentality of the United States, any State, or any political subdivision of a State on the ground that such action or inaction is inconsistent with the Agreement, the North American Agreement on Environmental Cooperation, or the North American Agreement on Labor Cooperation.

* * *

TITLE II—CUSTOMS PROVISIONS

19 U.S.C. § 3331

Sec. 201. Tariff Modifications

(a) Tariff Modifications Provided for in the Agreement.—

(1) Proclamation Authority.—The President may proclaim—

(A) such modifications or continuation of any duty,

(B) such continuation of duty-free or excise treatment, or

(C) such additional duties,

as the President determines to be necessary or appropriate to carry out or apply articles 302, 305, 307, 308, and 703 and Annexes 302.2, 307.1, 308.1, 308.2, 300–B, 703.2, and 703.3 of the Agreement.

(2) Effect on Mexican GSP Status.—Notwithstanding section 502(a)(2) of the Trade Act of 1974 (19 U.S.C. § 2462(a)(2)), the President shall terminate the designation of Mexico as a beneficiary developing country for purposes of title V of the Trade Act of 1974 on the date of entry into force of the Agreement between the United States and Mexico.

* * *

19 U.S.C. § 3332

Sec. 202. Rules of Origin

(a) Originating Goods.—

(1) In General.—For purposes of implementing the tariff treatment and quantitative restrictions provided for under the Agreement, except as otherwise provided in this section, a good originates in the territory of a NAFTA country if—

(A) the good is wholly obtained or produced entirely in the territory of one or more of the NAFTA countries;

(B)(i) each nonoriginating material used in the production of the good—

(I) undergoes an applicable change in tariff classification set out in Annex 401 of the Agreement as a result of production occurring entirely in the territory of one or more of the NAFTA countries; or

(II) where no change in tariff classification is required, the good otherwise satisfies the applicable requirements of such Annex; and

(ii) the good satisfies all other applicable requirements of this section;

(C) the good is produced entirely in the territory of one or more of the NAFTA countries exclusively from originating materials; or

(D) except for a good provided for in chapters 61 through 63 of the HTS, the good is produced entirely in the territory of one or more of the NAFTA countries, but one or more of the nonoriginating materials, that are provided for as parts under the HTS and are used in the production of the good, does not undergo a change in tariff classification because—

(i) the good was imported into the territory of a NAFTA country in an unassembled or a disassembled form but was classified as an assembled good pursuant to General Rule of Interpretation 2(a) of the HTS; or

(ii)(I) the heading for the good provides for and specifically describes both the good itself and its parts and is not further subdivided into subheadings; or

(II) the subheading for the good provides for and specifically describes both the good itself and its parts.

(2) Special Rules.—

(A) Foreign-Trade Zones.—Subparagraph (B) of paragraph (1) shall not apply to a good produced in a foreign-trade zone or subzone (established pursuant to the Act of June 18, 1934, commonly known as the Foreign Trade Zones Act) that is entered for consumption in the customs territory of the United States.

(B) Regional Value-Content Requirement.—For purposes of subparagraph (D) of paragraph (1), a good shall be treated as originating in a NAFTA country if the regional value-content of the good, determined in accordance with subsection (b), is not less than 60 percent where the transaction value method is used, or not less than 50 percent where the net cost method is used, and the good satisfies all other applicable requirements of this section.

(b) Regional Value-Content.—

(1) In General.—Except as provided in paragraph (5), the regional value-content of a good shall be calculated, at the choice of the exporter or producer of the good, on the basis of—

(A) the transaction value method described in paragraph (2); or

(B) the net cost method described in paragraph (3).

(2) Transaction Value Method.—

(A) In General.—An exporter or producer may calculate the regional value-content of a good on the basis of the following transaction value method:

$$RVC = \frac{TV - VNM}{TV} \times 100$$

(B) Definitions.—For purposes of subparagraph (A):

(i) The term "RVC" means the regional value-content, expressed as a percentage.

(ii) The term "NC" means the net cost of the good.

(iii) The term "VNM" means the value of nonoriginating materials used by the producer in the production of the good.

(4) Value of Nonoriginating Materials Used in Originating Materials.—Except as provided in subsection (c)(1), and for a motor vehicle identified in subsection (c)(2) or a component identified in Annex 403.2 of the Agreement, the value of nonoriginating materials used by the producer in the production of a good shall not, for purposes of calculating the regional value-content of the good under paragraph (2) or (3), include the value of nonoriginating materials used to produce originating materials that are subsequently used in the production of the good.

(5) Net Cost Method Must be Used in Certain Cases.—An exporter or producer shall calculate the regional value-content of a good solely on the basis of the net cost method described in paragraph (3), if—

(A) there is no transaction value for the good;

(B) the transaction value of the good is unacceptable under Article 1 of the Customs Valuation Code;

(C) the good is sold by the producer to a related person and the volume, by units of quantity, of sales of identical or similar goods to related persons during the six-month period immediately preceding the month in which the good is sold exceeds 85 percent of the producer's total sales of such goods during that period;

(D) the good is—

(i) a motor vehicle provided for in heading 8701 or 8702, subheadings 8703.21 through 8703.90, or heading 8704, 8705, or 8706;

(ii) identified in Annex 403.1 or 403.2 of the Agreement and is for use in a motor vehicle provided for in heading 8701 or 8702, subheadings 8703.21 through 8703.90, or heading 8704, 8705, or 8706;

(iii) provided for in subheadings 6401.10 through 6406.10; or

(iv) a word processing machine provided for in subheading 8469.10.00;

(E) the exporter or producer chooses to accumulate the regional value-content of the good in accordance with subsection (d); or

(F) the good is designated as an intermediate material under paragraph (10) and is subject to a regional value-content requirement.

(6) Net Cost Method Allowed for Adjustments.—If an exporter or producer of a good calculates the regional value-content of the good on the basis of the transaction value method and a NAFTA country subsequently notifies the exporter or producer, during the course of a verification conducted in accordance with chapter 5 of the Agreement, that the transaction value of the good or the value of any material used in the production of the good must be adjusted or is unacceptable under Article 1 of the Customs Valuation Code, the exporter or producer may calculate the regional value-content of the good on the basis of the net cost method.

(7) Review of Adjustment.—Nothing in paragraph (6) shall be construed to prevent any review or appeal available in accordance with article 510 of the Agreement with respect to an adjustment to or a rejection of—

(A) the transaction value of a good; or

(B) the value of any material used in the production of a good.

(8) Calculating Net Cost.—The producer may, consistent with regulations implementing this section, calculate the net cost of a good under paragraph (3), by—

(A) calculating the total cost incurred with respect to all goods produced by that producer, subtracting any sales promotion, marketing and after-sales service costs, royalties, shipping and packing costs, and nonallowable interest costs that are included in the total cost of all such goods, and reasonably allocating the resulting net cost of those goods to the good;

(B) calculating the total cost incurred with respect to all goods produced by that producer, reasonably allocating the total cost to the good, and subtracting any sales promotion, marketing and after-sales service costs, royalties, shipping and packing costs, and nonallowable interest costs that are included in the portion of the total cost allocated to the good; or

(C) reasonably allocating each cost that is part of the total cost incurred with respect to the good so that the aggregate of these costs does not include any sales promotion, marketing and after-sales service costs, royalties, shipping and packing costs, or nonallowable interest costs.

(9) Value of Material Used in Production.—Except as provided in paragraph (11), the value of a material used in the production of a good—

(A) shall—

(i) be the transaction value of the material determined in accordance with Article 1 of the Customs Valuation Code; or

(ii) in the event that there is no transaction value or the transaction value of the material is unacceptable under Article 1 of the Customs Valuation Code, be determined in accordance with Articles 2 through 7 of the Customs Valuation Code; and

(B) if not included under clause (i) or (ii) of subparagraph (A), shall include—

(i) freight, insurance, packing, and all other costs incurred in transporting the material to the location of the producer;

(ii) duties, taxes, and customs brokerage fees paid on the material in the territory of one or more of the NAFTA countries; and

(iii) the cost of waste and spoilage resulting from the use of the material in the production of the good, less the value of renewable scrap or by-product.

(10) Intermediate Material.—Except for goods described in subsection (c)(1), any self-produced material, other than a component identified in Annex 403.2 of the Agreement, that is used in the production of a good may be designated by the producer of the good as an intermediate material for the purpose of calculating the regional value-content of the good under paragraph (2) or (3); provided that if the intermediate material is subject to a regional value-content requirement, no other self-produced material that is subject to a regional value-content requirement, and is used in the production of the intermediate material may be designated by the producer as an intermediate material.

(11) Value of Intermediate Material.—The value of an intermediate material shall be—

(A) the total cost incurred with respect to all goods produced by the producer of the good that can be reasonably allocated to the intermediate material; or

(B) the aggregate of each cost that is part of the total cost incurred with respect to the intermediate material that can be reasonably allocated to that intermediate material.

(12) Indirect Material.—The value of an indirect material shall be based on the Generally Accepted Accounting Principles applicable in the territory of the NAFTA country in which the good is produced.

(c) Automotive Goods.—

* * *

(m) Interpretation and Application.—For purposes of this section:

(1) The basis for any tariff classification is the HTS.

(2) Except as otherwise expressly provided, whenever in this section there is a reference to a heading or subheading such reference shall be a reference to a heading or subheading of the HTS.

(3) In applying subsection (a)(4), the determination of whether a heading or subheading under the HTS provides for and specifically describes both a good and its parts shall be made on the basis of the nomenclature of the heading or subheading, the rules of interpretation, or notes of the HTS.

(4) In applying the Customs Valuation Code—

(A) the principles of the Customs Valuation Code shall apply to domestic transactions, with such modifications as may be required by the circumstances, as would apply to international transactions;

(B) the provisions of this section shall take precedence over the Customs Valuation Code to the extent of any difference; and

(C) the definitions in subsection (*o*) shall take precedence over the definitions in the Customs Valuation Code to the extent of any difference.

(5) All costs referred to in this section shall be recorded and maintained in accordance with the Generally Accepted Accounting Principles applicable in the territory of the NAFTA country in which the good is produced.

* * *

TITLE IV—DISPUTE SETTLEMENT IN ANTIDUMPING AND COUNTERVAILING DUTY CASES

Subtitle A—Organizational, Administrative, and Procedural Provisions Regarding the Implementation of Chapter 19 of the Agreement

* * *

19 U.S.C. § 3432

Sec. 402. Organizational and Administrative Provisions

(a) Criteria for Selection of Individuals to Serve on Panels and Committees.—

(1) In General.—The selection of individuals under this section for—

(A) placement on lists prepared by the interagency group under subsection (c)(2)(B)(i) and (ii);

(B) placement on preliminary candidate lists under subsection (c)(3)(A);

(C) placement on final candidate lists under subsection (c)(4)(A);

(D) placement by the Trade Representative on the rosters described in paragraph 1 of Annex 1901.2 and paragraph 1 of Annex 1904.13; and

(E) appointment by the Trade Representative for service on the panels and committees convened under chapter 19;

shall be made on the basis of the criteria provided in paragraph 1 of Annex 1901.2 and paragraph 1 of Annex 1904.13 and shall be made without regard to political affiliation.

(2) Additional Criteria for Roster Placements and Appointments Under Paragraph 1 of Annex 1901.2.—Rosters described in paragraph 1 of Annex 1901.2 shall include, to the fullest extent practicable, judges and former judges who meet the criteria referred to in paragraph (1). The Trade Representative shall, subject to subsection (b), appoint judges to binational panels convened under chapter 19, extraordinary challenge committees convened under chapter 19, and special committees established under article 1905, where such judges offer and are available to serve and such service is authorized by the chief judge of the court on which they sit.

(b) Selection of Certain Judges to Serve on Panels and Committees.—

(1) Applicability.—This subsection applies only with respect to the selection of individuals for binational panels convened under chapter 19, extraordinary challenge committees convened under chapter 19, and special committees established under article 1905, who are judges of courts created under article III of the Constitution of the United States.

(2) Consultation with Chief Judges.—The Trade Representative shall consult, from time to time, with the chief judges of the Federal judicial circuits regarding the interest in, and availability for, participation in binational panels, extraordinary challenge committees, and special committees, of judges within their respective circuits. If the chief judge of a Federal judicial circuit determines that it is appropriate for one or more judges within that circuit to be included on a roster described in subsection (a)(1)(D), the chief judge shall identify all such judges for the Chief Justice of the United States who may, upon his or her approval, submit the names of such judges to the Trade Representative. The Trade Representative shall include the names of such judges on the roster.

(3) Submission of Lists to Congress.—The Trade Representative shall submit to the Committee on the Judiciary and the Committee on Ways and Means of the House of Representatives and to the Committee on Finance and the Committee on the Judiciary of the Senate a list of all judges

included on a roster under paragraph (2). Such list shall be submitted at the same time as the final candidate lists are submitted under subsection (c)(4)(A) and the final forms of amendments are submitted under subsection (c)(4)(C)(iv).

(4) Appointment of Judges to Panels or Committees.—At such time as the Trade Representative proposes to appoint a judge described in paragraph (1) to a binational panel, an extraordinary challenge committee, or a special committee, the Trade Representative shall consult with that judge in order to ascertain whether the judge is available for such appointment.

(c) Selection of Other Candidates.—

(1) Applicability.—This subsection applies only with respect to the selection of individuals for binational panels convened under chapter 19, extraordinary challenge committees convened under chapter 19, and special committees established under article 1905, other than those individuals to whom subsection (b) applies.

(2) Interagency Group.—

(A) Establishment.—There is established within the interagency organization established under section 242 of the Trade Expansion Act of 1962 (19 U.S.C. § 1872) an interagency group which shall—

(i) be chaired by the Trade Representative; and

(ii) consist of such officers (or the designees thereof) of the United States Government as the Trade Representative considers appropriate.

(B) Functions.—The interagency group established under subparagraph (A) shall, in a manner consistent with chapter 19—

(i) prepare by January 3 of each calendar year—

(I) a list of individuals who are qualified to serve as members of binational panels convened under chapter 19; and

(II) a list of individuals who are qualified to serve on extraordinary challenge committees convened under chapter 19 and special committees established under article 1905;

(ii) if the Trade Representative makes a request under paragraph (4)(C)(i) with respect to a final candidate list during any calendar year, prepare by July 1 of such calendar year a list of those individuals who are qualified to be added to that final candidate list;

(iii) exercise oversight of the administration of the United States Section that is authorized to be established under section 105; and

(iv) make recommendations to the Trade Representative regarding the convening of extraordinary challenge committees and special committees under chapter 19.

(3) Preliminary Candidate Lists.—

(A) In General.—The Trade Representative shall select individuals from the respective lists prepared by the interagency group under paragraph (2)(B)(i) for placement on—

(i) a preliminary candidate list of individuals eligible to serve as members of binational panels under Annex 1901.2; and

(ii) a preliminary candidate list of individuals eligible for selection as members of extraordinary challenge committees under Annex 1904.13 and special committees under article 1905.

(B) Submission of Lists to Congressional Committees.—

(i) In General.—No later than January 3 of each calendar year, the Trade Representative shall submit to the Committee on Finance of the Senate and the Committee on Ways and Means of the House of Representatives (hereafter in this section referred to as the "appropriate Congressional Committees") the preliminary candidate lists of those individuals selected by the Trade Representative under subparagraph (A) to be candidates eligible to serve on panels or committees convened pursuant to chapter 19 during the 1–year period beginning on April 1 of such calendar year.

(ii) Additional Information.—At the time the candidate lists are submitted under clause (i), the Trade Representative shall submit for each individual on the list a statement of professional qualifications.

(C) Consultation.—Upon submission of the preliminary candidate lists under subparagraph (B) to the appropriate Congressional Committees, the Trade Representative shall consult with such Committees with regard to the individuals included on the preliminary candidate lists.

(D) Revision of Lists.—The Trade Representative may add and delete individuals from the preliminary candidate lists submitted under subparagraph (B) after consultation with the appropriate Congressional Committees regarding the additions and deletions. The Trade Representative shall provide to the appropriate Congressional Committees written notice of any addition or deletion of an individual from the preliminary candidate lists, along with the information described in subparagraph (B)(ii) with respect to any proposed addition.

(4) Final Candidate Lists.—

(A) Submission of Lists to Congressional Committees.—No later than March 31 of each calendar year, the Trade Representative shall submit to the appropriate Congressional Committees the final candidate lists of those individuals selected by the Trade Representative to be candidates eligible to serve on panels and committees convened under chapter 19 during the 1–year period beginning on April 1 of such calendar year. An individual may be included on a final candidate list only if such individual was included in the preliminary candidate list or if written notice of the addition of such individual to the preliminary candidate list was submitted to the appropriate Congressional Committees at least 15 days before the date on which that final candidate list is submitted to such Committees under this subparagraph.

(B) Finality of Lists.—Except as provided in subparagraph (C), no additions may be made to the final candidate lists after the final candidate lists are submitted to the appropriate Congressional Committees under subparagraph (A).

(C) Amendment of Lists.—

(i) In General.—If, after the Trade Representative has submitted the final candidate lists to the appropriate Congressional Committees under subparagraph (A) for a calendar year and before July 1 of such calendar year, the Trade Representative determines that additional individuals need to be added to a final candidate list, the Trade Representative shall—

(I) request the interagency group established under paragraph (2)(A) to prepare a list of individuals who are qualified to be added to such candidate list;

(II) select individuals from the list prepared by the interagency group under paragraph (2)(B)(ii) to be included in a proposed amendment to such final candidate list; and

(III) by no later than July 1 of such calendar year, submit to the appropriate Congressional Committees the proposed amendments to such final candidate list developed by the Trade Representative under subclause (II), along with the information described in paragraph (3)(B)(ii).

(ii) Consultation with Congressional Committees. Upon submission of a proposed amendment under clause (i)(III) to the appropriate Congressional Committees, the Trade Representative shall consult with the appropriate Congressional Committees with regard to the individuals included in the proposed amendment.

(iii) Adjustment of Proposed Amendment.—The Trade Representative may add and delete individuals from any proposed amendment submitted under clause (i)(III) after consulting with the appropriate Congressional Committees with regard to the additions and deletions. The Trade Representative shall provide to the appropriate Congressional Committees written notice of any addition or deletion of an individual from the proposed amendment.

(iv) Final Amendment.—

(I) In General.—If the Trade Representative submits under clause (i)(III) in any calendar year a proposed amendment to a final candidate list, the Trade Representative shall, no later than September 30 of such calendar year, submit to the appropriate Congressional Committees the final form of such amendment. On October 1 of such calendar year, such amendment shall take effect and, subject to subclause (II), the individuals included in the final form of such amendment shall be added to the final candidate list.

(II) Inclusion of Individuals.—An individual may be included in the final form of an amendment submitted under subclause (I) only if such individual was included in the proposed form of such amendment or if written notice of the addition of such individual to the proposed form of such amendment was submitted to the appropriate Congressional Committees at least 15 days before the date on which the final form of such amendment is submitted to such Committees under subclause (I).

(III) Eligibility for Service.—Individuals added to a final candidate list under subclause (I) shall be eligible to serve on panels or committees convened under chapter 19 during the 6–month period beginning on October 1 of the calendar year in which such addition occurs.

(IV) Finality of Amendment.—No additions may be made to the final form of an amendment described in subclause (I) after the final form of such amendment is submitted to the appropriate Congressional Committees under subclause (I).

(5) Treatment of Responses.—For purposes of applying section 1001 of title 18, United States Code, the written or oral responses of individuals to inquiries of the interagency group established under paragraph (2)(A) or of

the Trade Representative regarding their personal and professional qualifications, and financial and other relevant interests, that bear on their suitability for the placements and appointments described in subsection (a)(1), shall be treated as matters within the jurisdiction of an agency of the United States.

(d) Selection and Appointment.—

(1) Authority of Trade Representative.—The Trade Representative is the only officer of the United States Government authorized to act on behalf of the United States Government in making any selection or appointment of an individual to—

(A) the rosters described in paragraph 1 of Annex 1901.2 and paragraph 1 of Annex 1904.13; or

(B) the panels or committees convened under chapter 19;

that is to be made solely or jointly by the United States Government under the terms of the Agreement.

(2) Restrictions on Selection and Appointment.—Except as provided in paragraph (3)—

(A) the Trade Representative may—

(i) select an individual for placement on the rosters described in paragraph 1 of Annex 1901.2 and paragraph 1 of Annex 1904.13 during the 1–year period beginning on April 1 of any calendar year;

(ii) appoint an individual to serve as one of those members of any panel or committee convened under chapter 19 during such 1–year period who, under the terms of the Agreement, are to be appointed solely by the United States Government; or

(iii) act to make a joint appointment with the Government of a NAFTA country, under the terms of the Agreement, of any individual who is a citizen or national of the United States to serve as any other member of such a panel or committee;

only if such individual is on the appropriate final candidate list that was submitted to the appropriate Congressional Committees under subsection (c)(4)(A) during such calendar year or on such list as it may be amended under subsection (c)(4)(C)(iv)(I), or on the list submitted under subsection (b)(3) to the congressional committees referred to in such subsection; and

(B) no individual may—

(i) be selected by the United States Government for placement on the rosters described in paragraph 1 of Annex 1901.2 and paragraph 1 of Annex 1904.13; or

(ii) be appointed solely or jointly by the United States Government to serve as a member of a panel or committee convened under chapter 19;

during the 1–year period beginning on April 1 of any calendar year for which the Trade Representative has not met the requirements of subsection (a), and of subsection (b) or (c) (as the case may be).

(3) Exceptions.—Notwithstanding subsection (c)(3) (other than subparagraph (B)), (c)(4), or paragraph (2)(A) of this subsection, individuals included on the preliminary candidate lists submitted to the appropriate Congressional Committees under subsection (c)(3)(B) may—

(A) be selected by the Trade Representative for placement on the rosters described in paragraph 1 of Annex 1901.2 and paragraph 1 of Annex 1904.13 during the 3–month period beginning on the date on which the Agreement enters into force with respect to the United States; and

(B) be appointed solely or jointly by the Trade Representative under the terms of the Agreement to serve as members of panels or committees that are convened under chapter 19 during such 3–month period.

(e) Transition.—If the Agreement enters into force between the United States and a NAFTA country after January 3, 1994, the provisions of subsection (c) shall be applied with respect to the calendar year in which such entering into force occurs—

(1) by substituting "the date that is 30 days after the date on which the Agreement enters into force with respect to the United States" for "January 3 of each calendar year" in subsections (c)(2)(B)(i) and (c)(3)(B)(i); and

(2) by substituting "the date that is 3 months after the date on which the Agreement enters into force with respect to the United States" for "March 31 of each calendar year" in subsection (c)(4)(A).

(f) Immunity.—With the exception of acts described in section 777(f)(3) of the Tariff Act of 1930 (19 U.S.C. § 1677f(f)(3)), individuals serving on panels or committees convened pursuant to chapter 19, and individuals designated to assist the individuals serving on such panels or committees, shall be immune from suit and legal process relating to acts performed by such individuals in their official capacity and within the scope of their functions as such panelists or committee members or assistants to such panelists or committee members.

(g) Regulations.—The administering authority under title VII of the Tariff Act of 1930, the International Trade Commission, and the Trade Representative may promulgate such regulations as are necessary or appropriate to carry out actions in order to implement their respective responsibilities under chapter 19. Initial regulations to carry out such functions shall be issued before the date on which the Agreement enters into force with respect to the United States.

(h) Report to Congress.—At such time as the final candidate lists are submitted under subsection (c)(4)(A) and the final forms of amendments are submitted under subsection (c)(4)(C)(iv), the Trade Representative shall submit to the Committee on the Judiciary and the Committee on Ways and Means of the House of Representatives, and to the Committee on Finance and the Committee on the Judiciary of the Senate, a report regarding the efforts made to secure the participation of judges and former judges on binational panels, extraordinary challenge committees, and special committees established under chapter 19.

19 U.S.C. § 3433

Sec. 403. Testimony and Production of Papers in Extraordinary Challenges

(a) Authority of Extraordinary Challenge Committee to Obtain Information.—If an extraordinary challenge committee (hereafter in this section referred to as the "committee") is convened under paragraph 13 of article 1904, and the allegations before the committee include a matter referred to in paragraph 13(a)(i) of article 1904, for the purposes of carrying out its functions and duties under Annex 1904.13, the committee—

(1) shall have access to, and the right to copy, any document, paper, or record pertinent to the subject matter under consideration, in the possession of any individual, partnership, corporation, association, organization, or other entity;

(2) may summon witnesses, take testimony, and administer oaths;

(3) may require any individual, partnership, corporation, association, organization, or other entity to produce documents, books, or records relating to the matter in question; and

(4) may require any individual, partnership, corporation, association, organization, or other entity to furnish in writing, in such detail and in such form as the committee may prescribe, information in its possession pertaining to the matter.

Any member of the committee may sign subpoenas, and members of the committee, when authorized by the committee, may administer oaths and affirmations, examine witnesses, take testimony, and receive evidence.

(b) Witnesses and Evidence.—The attendance of witnesses who are authorized to be summoned, and the production of documentary evidence authorized to be ordered, under subsection (a) may be required from any place in the United States at any designated place of hearing. In the case of disobedience to a subpoena authorized under subsection (a), the committee may request the Attorney General of the United States to invoke the aid of any district or territorial court of the United States in requiring the attendance and testimony of witnesses and the production of documentary evidence. Such court, within the jurisdiction of which such inquiry is carried on, may, in case of contumacy or refusal to obey a subpoena issued to any individual, partnership, corporation, association, organization, or other entity, issue an order requiring such individual or entity to appear before the committee, or to produce documentary evidence if so ordered or to give evidence concerning the matter in question. Any failure to obey such order of the court may be punished by such court as a contempt thereof.

(c) Mandamus.—Any court referred to in subsection (b) shall have jurisdiction to issue writs of mandamus commanding compliance with the provisions of this section or any order of the committee made in pursuance thereof.

(d) Depositions.—The committee may order testimony to be taken by deposition at any stage of the committee review. Such deposition may be taken before any person designated by the committee and having power to administer oaths. Such testimony shall be reduced to writing by the person taking the deposition, or under the direction of such person, and shall then be subscribed by the deponent. Any individual, partnership, corporation, association, organization, or other entity may be compelled to appear and be deposed and to produce documentary evidence in the same manner as witnesses may be compelled to appear and testify and produce documentary evidence before the committee, as provided in this section.

19 U.S.C. § 3434

Sec. 404. Requests for Review of Determinations by Competent Investigating Authorities of NAFTA Countries

(a) Definitions.—As used in this section:

(1) Competent Investigating Authority.—The term "competent investigating authority" means the competent investigating authority, as defined in article 1911, of a NAFTA country.

(2) United States Secretary.—The term "United States Secretary" means that officer of the United States referred to in article 1908.

(b) Requests for Review by the United States.—In the case of a final determination of a competent investigating authority, requests by the United States for binational panel review of such determination under article 1904 shall be made by the United States Secretary.

(c) Requests for Review by a Person.—In the case of a final determination of a competent investigating authority, a person, within the meaning of paragraph 5 of article 1904, may request a binational panel review of such determination by filing such a request with the United States Secretary within the time limit provided for in paragraph 4 of article

1904. The receipt of such request by the United States Secretary shall be deemed to be a request for binational panel review within the meaning of article 1904. The request for such panel review shall be without prejudice to any challenge before a binational panel of the basis for a particular request for review.

(d) Service of Request for Review.—Whenever binational panel review of a final determination made by a competent investigating authority is requested under this section, the United States Secretary shall serve a copy of the request on all persons who would otherwise be entitled under the law of the importing country to commence proceedings for judicial review of the determination.

19 U.S.C. § 3435

Sec. 405. Rules of Procedure for Panels and Committees

(a) Rules of Procedure for Binational Panels.—The administering authority shall prescribe rules, negotiated in accordance with paragraph 14 of article 1904, governing, with respect to binational panel reviews—

* * *

(b) Rules of Procedure for Extraordinary Challenge Committees.—The administering authority shall prescribe rules, negotiated in accordance with paragraph 2 of Annex 1904.13, governing the procedures for reviews by extraordinary challenge committees.

(c) Rules of Procedure for Safeguarding the Panel Review System.—The administering authority shall prescribe rules, negotiated in accordance with Annex 1905.6, governing the procedures for special committees described in such Annex.

* * *

DOCUMENT 33

URUGUAY ROUND AGREEMENTS ACT (1993)

■ ■ ■

Pub.L. 103–465, 108 Stat. 4809

19 U.S.C. § 3501

Sec. 1. Short Title and Table of Contents

(a) Short Title.—This Act may be cited as the "Uruguay Round Agreements Act".

(b) Table of Contents.

Sec. 2. Definitions

For purposes of this Act:

(1) GATT 1947; GATT 1994.

(A) GATT 1947.—The term "GATT 1947" means the General Agreement on Tariffs and Trade, dated October 30, 1947, annexed to the Final Act Adopted at the Conclusion of the Second Session of the Preparatory Committee of the United Nations Conference on Trade and Employment, as subsequently rectified, amended, or modified by the terms of legal instruments which have entered into force before the date of entry into force of the WTO Agreement.

(B) GATT 1994.—The term "GATT 1994" means the General Agreement on Tariffs and Trade annexed to the WTO Agreement.

(2) HTS.—The term "HTS" means the Harmonized Tariff Schedule of the United States.

(3) International trade commission.—The term "International Trade Commission" means the United States International Trade Commission.

(4) Multilateral trade agreement.—The term "multilateral trade agreement" means an agreement described in section 101(d) of this Act (other than an agreement described in paragraph (17) or (18) of such section).

(5) Schedule xx.—The term "Schedule XX" means Schedule XX—United States of America annexed to the Marrakesh Protocol to the GATT 1994.

(6) Trade representative.—The term "Trade Representative" means the United States Trade Representative.

(7) Uruguay round agreements.—The term "Uruguay Round Agreements" means the agreements approved by the Congress under section 101(a)(1).

(8) World trade organization and WTO.—The terms "World Trade Organization" and "WTO" mean the organization established pursuant to the WTO Agreement.

(9) WTO agreement.—The term "WTO Agreement" means the Agreement Establishing the World Trade Organization entered into on April 15, 1994.

(10) WTO member and WTO member country.—The terms "WTO member" and "WTO member country" mean a state, or separate customs territory (within the meaning of Article XII of the WTO Agreement), with respect to which the United States applies the WTO Agreement.

TITLE I—APPROVAL OF, AND GENERAL PROVISIONS RELATING TO, THE URUGUAY ROUND AGREEMENTS

Subtitle A—Approval of Agreements and Related Provisions

19 U.S.C. § 3511

Sec. 101. Approval and Entry into Force of the Uruguay Round Agreements

(a) Approval of Agreements and Statement of Administrative Action.—Pursuant to section 1103 of the Omnibus Trade and Competitiveness Act of 1988 (19 U.S.C. § 2903) and section 151 of the Trade Act of 1974 (19 U.S.C. § 2191), the Congress approves

(1) the trade agreements described in subsection (d) resulting from the Uruguay Round of multilateral trade negotiations under the auspices of the General Agreement on Tariffs and Trade, * * *; and

* * *

(b) Entry Into Force.—At such time as the President determines that a sufficient number of foreign countries are accepting the obligations of the Uruguay Round Agreements, in accordance with article XIV of the WTO Agreement, to ensure the effective operation of, and adequate benefits for the United States under, those Agreements, the President may accept the Uruguay Round Agreements and implement article VIII of the WTO Agreement.

(c) Authorization of Appropriations.—There are authorized to be appropriated annually such sums as may be necessary for the payment by the United States of its share of the expenses of the WTO.

(d) Trade Agreements to Which This Act Applies.—Subsection (a) applies to the WTO Agreement and to the following agreements annexed to that Agreement:

(1) The General Agreement on Tariffs and Trade 1994.

(2) The Agreement on Agriculture.

(3) The Agreement on the Application of Sanitary and Phytosanitary Measures.

(4) The Agreement on Textiles and Clothing.

(5) The Agreement on Technical Barriers to Trade.

(6) The Agreement on Trade-Related Investment Measures.

(7) The Agreement on Implementation of Article VI of the General Agreement on Tariffs and Trade 1994.

(8) The Agreement on Implementation of Article VII of the General Agreement on Tariffs and Trade 1994.

(9) The Agreement on Preshipment Inspection.

(10) The Agreement on Rules of Origin.

(11) The Agreement on Import Licensing Procedures.

(12) The Agreement on Subsidies and Countervailing Measures.

(13) The Agreement on Safeguards.

(14) The General Agreement on Trade in Services.

(15) The Agreement on Trade-Related Aspects of Intellectual Property Rights.

(16) The Understanding on Rules and Procedures Governing the Settlement of Disputes.

(17) The Agreement on Government Procurement.

(18) The International Bovine Meat Agreement.

19 U.S.C. § 3512

Sec. 102. Relationship of the Agreements to United States Law and State Law

(a) Relationship of Agreements to United States Law.

(1) United States law to prevail in conflict.—No provision of any of the Uruguay Round Agreements, nor the application of any such provision to any person or circumstance, that is inconsistent with any law of the United States shall have effect.

(2) Construction.—Nothing in this Act shall be construed

(A) to amend or modify any law of the United States, including any law relating to

(i) the protection of human, animal, or plant life or health,

(ii) the protection of the environment, or

(iii) worker safety, or

(B) to limit any authority conferred under any law of the United States, including section 301 of the Trade Act of 1974,

unless specifically provided for in this Act.

(b) Relationship of Agreements to State Law.

(1) Federal-state consultation.

(A) In general.—Upon the enactment of this Act, the President shall, through the intergovernmental policy advisory committees on trade established under section 306(c)(2)(A) of the Trade and Tariff Act of 1984 (19 U.S.C. § 2114c(2)(A)), consult with the States for the purpose of achieving conformity of State laws and practices with the Uruguay Round Agreements.

(B) Federal-state consultation process.—The Trade Representative shall establish within the Office of the United States Trade Representative a Federal-State consultation process for addressing issues relating to the Uruguay Round Agreements that directly relate to, or will potentially have a direct effect on, the States. The Federal-State consultation process shall include procedures under which

(i) the States will be informed on a continuing basis of matters under the Uruguay Round Agreements that directly relate to, or will potentially have a direct impact on, the States;

(ii) the States will be provided an opportunity to submit, on a continuing basis, to the Trade Representative information and advice with respect to matters referred to in clause (i); and

(iii) the Trade Representative will take into account the information and advice received from the States under clause (ii) when formulating United States positions regarding matters referred to in clause (i).

The Federal Advisory Committee Act (5 U.S.C.App.) shall not apply to the Federal-State consultation process established by this paragraph.

(C) Federal-state cooperation in dispute settlement.

(i) When a WTO member requests consultations with the United States under Article 4 of the Understanding on Rules and Procedures Governing the Settlement of Disputes referred to in section 101(d)(16) (hereafter in this subsection referred to as the "Dispute Settlement Understanding") concerning whether the law of a State is inconsistent with the obligations undertaken by the United States in any of the Uruguay Round Agreements, the Trade Representative shall notify the Governor of the State or the Governor's designee, and the chief legal officer of the jurisdiction whose law is the subject of the consultations, as soon as possible after the request is received, but in no event later than 7 days thereafter.

(ii) Not later than 30 days after receiving such a request for consultations, the Trade Representative shall consult with representatives of the State concerned regarding the matter. If the consultations involve the laws of a large number of States, the Trade Representative may consult with an appropriate group of representatives of the States concerned, as determined by those States.

(iii) The Trade Representative shall make every effort to ensure that the State concerned is involved in the development of the position of the United States at each stage of the consultations and each subsequent stage of dispute settlement proceedings regarding the matter. In particular, the Trade Representative shall

(I) notify the State concerned not later than 7 days after a WTO member requests the establishment of a dispute settlement panel or gives notice of the WTO member's decision to appeal a report by a dispute settlement panel regarding the matter; and

(II) provide the State concerned with the opportunity to advise and assist the Trade Representative in the preparation of factual information and argumentation for any written or oral presentations by the United States in consultations or in proceedings of a panel or the Appellate Body regarding the matter.

(iv) If a dispute settlement panel or the Appellate Body finds that the law of a State is inconsistent with any of the Uruguay Round Agreements, the Trade Representative shall consult with the State concerned in an effort to develop a mutually agreeable response to the report of the panel or the Appellate Body and shall make every effort to ensure that the State concerned is involved in the development of the United States position regarding the response.

(D) Notice to states regarding consultations on foreign subcentral government laws.

(i) Subject to clause (ii), the Trade Representative shall, at least 30 days before making a request for consultations under Article 4 of the Dispute Settlement Understanding regarding a subcentral government measure of another member, notify, and solicit the views of, appropriate representatives of each State regarding the matter.

(ii) In exigent circumstances clause (i) shall not apply, in which case the Trade Representative shall notify the appropriate representatives of each State not later than 3 days after making the request for consultations referred to in clause (i).

(2) Legal challenge.

(A) In general.—No State law, or the application of such a State law, may be declared invalid as to any person or circumstance on the ground that the provision or application is inconsistent with any of the Uruguay Round Agreements, except in an action brought by the

United States for the purpose of declaring such law or application invalid.

(B) Procedures governing action.—In any action described in subparagraph (A) that is brought by the United States against a State or any subdivision thereof

(i) a report of a dispute settlement panel or the Appellate Body convened under the Dispute Settlement Understanding regarding the State law, or the law of any political subdivision thereof, shall not be considered as binding or otherwise accorded deference;

(ii) the United States shall have the burden of proving that the law that is the subject of the action, or the application of that law, is inconsistent with the agreement in question;

(iii) any State whose interests may be impaired or impeded in the action shall have the unconditional right to intervene in the action as a party, and the United States shall be entitled to amend its complaint to include a claim or cross-claim concerning the law of a State that so intervenes; and

(iv) any State law that is declared invalid shall not be deemed to have been invalid in its application during any period before the court's judgment becomes final and all timely appeals, including discretionary review, of such judgment are exhausted.

(C) Reports to congressional committees.—At least 30 days before the United States brings an action described in subparagraph (A), the Trade Representative shall provide a report to the Committee on Ways and Means of the House of Representatives and the Committee on Finance of the Senate

(i) describing the proposed action;

(ii) describing efforts by the Trade Representative to resolve the matter with the State concerned by other means; and

(iii) if the State law was the subject of consultations under the Dispute Settlement Understanding, certifying that the Trade Representative has substantially complied with the requirements of paragraph (1)(C) in connection with the matter.

Following the submission of the report, and before the action is brought, the Trade Representative shall consult with the committees referred to in the preceding sentence concerning the matter.

(3) Definition of state law.—For purposes of this subsection

(A) the term "State law" includes

(i) any law of a political subdivision of a State; and

(ii) any State law regulating or taxing the business of insurance; and

(B) the terms "dispute settlement panel" and "Appellate Body" have the meanings given those terms in section 121.

(c) Effect of Agreement With Respect to Private Remedies.

(1) Limitations.—No person other than the United States

(A) shall have any cause of action or defense under any of the Uruguay Round Agreements or by virtue of congressional approval of such an agreement, or

(B) may challenge, in any action brought under any provision of law, any action or inaction by any department, agency, or other instrumentality of the United States, any State, or any political subdivision of a State on the ground that such action or inaction is inconsistent with such agreement.

(2) Intent of congress.—It is the intention of the Congress through paragraph (1) to occupy the field with respect to any cause of action or defense under or in connection with any of the Uruguay Round Agreements, including by precluding any person other than the United States from bringing any action against any State or political subdivision thereof or raising any defense to the application of State law under or in connection with any of the Uruguay Round Agreements

(A) on the basis of a judgment obtained by the United States in an action brought under any such agreement; or

(B) on any other basis.

(d) Statement of Administrative Action.—The statement of administrative action approved by the Congress under section 101(a) shall be regarded as an authoritative expression by the United States concerning the interpretation and application of the Uruguay Round Agreements and this Act in any judicial proceeding in which a question arises concerning such interpretation or application.

* * *

Subtitle B—Tariff Modifications

19 U.S.C. § 3531

Sec. 121. Definitions

For purposes of this subtitle:

(1) *Administering authority*.—The term "administering authority" has the meaning given that term in section 771(1) of the Tariff Act of 1930.

(2) *Appellate body.*—The term "Appellate Body" means the Appellate Body established under Article 17.1 of the Dispute Settlement Understanding.

(3) *Appropriate congressional committees; congressional committees.*

(A) Appropriate congressional committees.—The term "appropriate congressional committees" means the committees referred to in subparagraph (B) and any other committees of the Congress that have jurisdiction involving the matter with respect to which consultations are to be held.

(B) Congressional committees.—The term "congressional committees" means the Committee on Ways and Means of the House of Representatives and the Committee on Finance of the Senate.

(4) *Dispute settlement panel; panel.*—The terms "dispute settlement panel" and "panel" mean a panel established pursuant to Article 6 of the Dispute Settlement Understanding.

(5) *Dispute settlement body.*—The term "Dispute Settlement Body" means the Dispute Settlement Body administering the rules and procedures set forth in the Dispute Settlement Understanding.

(6) *Dispute settlement understanding.*—The term "Dispute Settlement Understanding" means the Understanding on Rules and Procedures Governing the Settlement of Disputes referred to in section 101(d)(16).

(7) *General council.*—The term "General Council" means the General Council established under paragraph 2 of Article IV of the Agreement.

(8) *Ministerial conference.*—The term "Ministerial Conference" means the Ministerial Conference established under paragraph 1 of Article IV of the Agreement.

(9) *Other terms.*—The terms "Antidumping Agreement", "Agreement on Subsidies and Countervailing Measures", and "Safeguards Agreement" mean the agreements referred to in section 101(d)(7), (12), and (13), respectively.

* * *

19 U.S.C. § 3533

Sec. 123. Dispute Settlement Panels and Procedures

(a) Review by President.—The President shall review annually the panel roster and shall include the panel roster and the list of persons serving on the Appellate Body in the annual report submitted by the President under section 163(a) of the Trade Act of 1974.

(b) Qualifications of Appointees to Panels.—The Trade Representative shall

(1) seek to ensure that persons appointed to the panel roster are well-qualified, and that the roster includes persons with expertise in the subject areas covered by the Uruguay Round Agreements; and

(2) inform the President of persons nominated to the roster by other member countries.

(c) Rules Governing Conflicts of Interest.—The Trade Representative shall seek the establishment by the General Council and the Dispute Settlement Body of rules governing conflicts of interest by persons serving on panels and members of the Appellate Body and shall describe, in the annual report submitted under section 124, any progress made in establishing such rules.

(d) Notification of Disputes.—Promptly after a dispute settlement panel is established to consider the consistency of Federal or State law with any of the Uruguay Round Agreements, the Trade Representative shall notify the appropriate congressional committees of

(1) the nature of the dispute, including the matters set forth in the request for the establishment of the panel, the legal basis of the complaint, and the specific measures, in particular any State or Federal law cited in the request for establishment of the panel;

(2) the identity of the persons serving on the panel; and

(3) whether there was any departure from the rule of consensus with respect to the selection of persons to serve on the panel.

(e) Notice of Appeals of Panel Reports.—If an appeal is taken of a report of a panel in a proceeding described in subsection (d), the Trade Representative shall, promptly after the notice of appeal is filed, notify the appropriate congressional committees of

(1) the issues under appeal; and

(2) the identity of the persons serving on the Appellate Body who are reviewing the report of the panel.

(f) Actions upon Circulation of Reports.—Promptly after the circulation of a report of a panel or of the Appellate Body to members in a proceeding described in subsection (d), the Trade Representative shall

(1) notify the appropriate congressional committees of the report;

(2) in the case of a report of a panel, consult with the appropriate congressional committees concerning the nature of any appeal that may be taken of the report; and

(3) if the report is adverse to the United States, consult with the appropriate congressional committees concerning whether to implement the report's recommendation and, if so, the manner of such implementation and the period of time needed for such implementation.

(g) Requirements for Agency Action.

(1) Changes in agency regulations or practice.—In any case in which a dispute settlement panel or the Appellate Body finds in its report that a regulation or practice of a department or agency of the United States is inconsistent with any of the Uruguay Round Agreements, that regulation or practice may not be amended, rescinded, or otherwise modified in the implementation of such report unless and until

(A) the appropriate congressional committees have been consulted under subsection (f);

(B) the Trade Representative has sought advice regarding the modification from relevant private sector advisory committees established under section 135 of the Trade Act of 1974 (19 U.S.C. § 2155);

(C) the head of the relevant department or agency has provided an opportunity for public comment by publishing in the Federal Register the proposed modification and the explanation for the modification;

(D) the Trade Representative has submitted to the appropriate congressional committees a report describing the proposed modification, the reasons for the modification, and a summary of the advice obtained under subparagraph (B) with respect to the modification;

(E) the Trade Representative and the head of the relevant department or agency have consulted with the appropriate congressional committees on the proposed contents of the final rule or other modification; and

(F) the final rule or other modification has been published in the Federal Register.

(2) Effective date of modification.—A final rule or other modification to which paragraph (1) applies may not go into effect before the end of the 60-day period beginning on the date on which consultations under paragraph (1)(E) begin, unless the President determines that an earlier effective date is in the national interest.

(3) Vote by congressional committees.—During the 60-day period described in paragraph (2), the Committee on Ways and Means of the House of Representatives and the Committee on Finance of the Senate may vote to indicate the agreement or disagreement of the committee with the proposed contents of the final rule or other modification. Any such vote shall not be binding on the department or agency which is implementing the rule or other modification.

(4) Inapplicability to ITC.—This subsection does not apply to any regulation or practice of the International Trade Commission.

(h) Consultations Regarding Review of WTO Rules and Procedures.—Before the review is conducted of the dispute settlement rules and procedures WTO that is provided for in the Decision on the Application of the Understanding on Rules and Procedures Governing the Settlement of Disputes, as such decision is set forth in the Ministerial Declarations and Decisions adopted on April 15, 1994, together with the Uruguay Round Agreements, the Trade Representative shall consult with the congressional committees regarding the policy of the United States concerning the review.

19 U.S.C. § 3534

Sec. 124. Annual Report on the WTO

Not later than March 1 of each year beginning in 1996, the Trade Representative shall submit to the Congress a report describing, for the preceding fiscal year of the WTO—

(1) the major activities and work programs of the WTO, including the functions and activities of the committees established under article IV of the Agreement, and the expenditures made by the WTO in connection with those activities and programs;

(2) the percentage of budgetary assessments by the WTO that were accounted for by each WTO member country, including the United States;

(3) the total number of personnel employed or retained by the Secretariat of the WTO, and the number of professional, administrative, and support staff of the WTO;

(4) for each personnel category described in paragraph (3), the number of citizens of each country, and the average salary of the personnel, in that category;

(5) each report issued by a panel or the Appellate Body in a dispute settlement proceeding regarding Federal or State law, and any efforts by the Trade Representative to provide for implementation of the recommendations contained in a report that is adverse to the United States;

(6) each proceeding before a panel or the Appellate Body that was initiated during that fiscal year regarding Federal or State law, the status of the proceeding, and the matter at issue;

(7) the status of consultations with any State whose law was the subject of a report adverse to the United States that was issued by a panel or the Appellate Body; and

(8) any progress achieved in increasing the transparency of proceedings of the Ministerial Conference and the General Council, and of

dispute settlement proceedings conducted pursuant to the Dispute Settlement Understanding.

19 U.S.C. § 3535

Sec. 125. Review of Participation in the WTO

(a) Report on the Operation of the WTO.—The first annual report submitted to the Congress under section 124

(1) after the end of the 5-year period beginning on the date on which the WTO Agreement enters into force with respect to the United States, and

(2) after the end of every 5-year period thereafter,

shall include an analysis of the effects of the WTO Agreement on the interests of the United States, the costs and benefits to the United States of its participation in the WTO, and the value of the continued participation of the United States in the WTO.

(b) Congressional Disapproval of U.S. Participation in the WTO.

(1) General rule.—The approval of the Congress, provided under section 101(a), of the WTO Agreement shall cease to be effective if, and only if, a joint resolution described in subsection (c) is enacted into law pursuant to the provisions of paragraph (2).

(2) Procedural provisions.—

(A) The requirements of this paragraph are met if the joint resolution is enacted under subsection (c), and

(i) the Congress adopts and transmits the joint resolution to the President before the end of the 90-day period (excluding any day described in section 154(b) of the Trade Act of 1974), beginning on the date on which the Congress receives a report referred to in subsection (a), and

(ii) if the President vetoes the joint resolution, each House of Congress votes to override that veto on or before the later of the last day of the 90-day period referred to in clause (i) or the last day of the 15-day period (excluding any day described in section 154(b) of the Trade Act of 1974) beginning on the date on which the Congress receives the veto message from the President.

(B) A joint resolution to which this section applies may be introduced at any time on or after the date on which the President transmits to the Congress a report described in subsection (a), and before the end of the 90-day period referred to in subparagraph (A).

(c) Joint Resolutions.

(1) Joint Resolutions.—For purposes of this section, the term "joint resolution" means only a joint resolution of the 2 Houses of Congress, the matter after the resolving clause of which is as follows: "That the Congress withdraws its approval, provided under section 101(a) of the Uruguay Round Agreements Act, of the WTO Agreement as defined in section 2(9) of that Act."

* * *

19 U.S.C. § 3537

Sec. 127. Access to the WTO Dispute Settlement Process

(a) In General.—Whenever the United States is a party before a dispute settlement panel established pursuant to Article 6 of the Dispute Settlement Understanding, the Trade Representative shall, at each stage of the proceeding before the panel or the Appellate Body, consult with the appropriate congressional committees, the petitioner (if any) under section 302(a) of the Trade Act of 1974 (19 U.S.C. § 2412) with respect to the matter that is the subject of the proceeding, and relevant private sector advisory committees established under section 135 of the Trade Act of 1974 (19 U.S.C. § 2155), and shall consider the views of representatives of appropriate interested private sector and nongovernmental organizations concerning the matter.

(b) Notice and Public Comment.—In any proceeding described in subsection (a), the Trade Representative shall

(1) promptly after requesting the establishment of a panel, or receiving a request from another WTO member country for the establishment of a panel, publish a notice in the Federal Register

(A) identifying the initial parties to the dispute,

(B) setting forth the major issues raised by the country requesting the establishment of a panel and the legal basis of the complaint,

(C) identifying the specific measures, including any State or Federal law cited in the request for establishment of the panel, and

(D) seeking written comments from the public concerning the issues raised in the dispute; and

(2) take into account any advice received from appropriate congressional committees and relevant private sector advisory committees referred to in subsection (a), and written comments received pursuant to paragraph (1)(D), in preparing United States submissions to the panel or the Appellate Body.

(c) Access to Documents.—In each proceeding described in subsection (a), the Trade Representative shall

(1) make written submissions by the United States referred to in subsection (b) available to the public promptly after they are submitted to the panel or Appellate Body, except that the Trade Representative is authorized to withhold from disclosure any information contained in such submissions identified by the provider of the information as proprietary information or information treated as confidential by a foreign government;

(2) request each other party to the dispute to permit the Trade Representative to make that party's written submissions to the panel or the Appellate Body available to the public; and

(3) make each report of the panel or the Appellate Body available to the public promptly after it is circulated to WTO members, and inform the public of such availability.

(d) Requests for Nonconfidential Summaries.—In any dispute settlement proceeding conducted pursuant to the Dispute Settlement Understanding, the Trade Representative shall request each party to the dispute to provide nonconfidential summaries of its written submissions, if that party has not made its written submissions public, and shall make those summaries available to the public promptly after receiving them.

(e) Public File.—The Trade Representative shall maintain a file accessible to the public on each dispute settlement proceeding to which the United States is a party that is conducted pursuant to the Dispute Settlement Understanding. The file shall include all United States submissions in the proceeding and a listing of any submissions to the Trade Representative from the public with respect to the proceeding, as well as the report of the dispute settlement panel and the report of the Appellate Body.

* * *

19 U.S.C. § 3538

Sec. 129. Administrative Action Following WTO Panel Reports

(a) Action by United States International Trade Commission.

(1) Advisory report.—If a dispute settlement panel finds in an interim report under Article 15 of the Dispute Settlement Understanding, or the Appellate Body finds in a report under Article 17 of that Understanding, that an action by the International Trade Commission in connection with a particular proceeding is not in conformity with the obligations of the United States under the Antidumping Agreement, the Safeguards Agreement, or the Agreement on Subsidies and Countervailing Measures, the Trade Representative may request the Commission to issue an advisory report on whether title VII of the Tariff Act of 1930 or title II of the Trade Act of 1974, as the case may be, permits the Commission to take steps in connection with the particular proceeding that would render its action not

inconsistent with the findings of the panel or the Appellate Body concerning those obligations. The Trade Representative shall notify the congressional committees of such request.

* * *

(b) Action by Administering Authority.

(1) Consultations with administering authority and congressional committees.—Promptly after a report by a dispute settlement panel or the Appellate body is issued that contains findings that an action by the administering authority in a proceeding under title VII of the Tariff Act of 1930 is not in conformity with the obligations of the United States under the Antidumping Agreement or the Agreement on Subsidies and Countervailing Measures, the Trade Representative shall consult with the administering authority and the congressional committees on the matter.

(2) Determination by administering authority.—Notwithstanding any provision of the Tariff Act of 1930, the administering authority shall, within 180 days after receipt of a written request from the Trade Representative, issue a determination in connection with the particular proceeding that would render the administering authority's action described in paragraph (1) not inconsistent with the findings of the panel or the Appellate Body.

(3) Consultations before implementation.—Before the administering authority implements any determination under paragraph (2), the Trade Representative shall consult with the administering authority and the congressional committees with respect to such determination.

(4) Implementation of determination.—The Trade Representative may, after consulting with the administering authority and the congressional committees under paragraph (3), direct the administering authority to implement, in whole or in part, the determination made under paragraph (2).

* * *

TITLE II—ANTIDUMPING AND COUNTERVAILING DUTY PROVISIONS

Subtitle D—Related Provisions

* * *

PART 4—ENFORCEMENT OF UNITED STATES RIGHTS UNDER THE SUBSIDIES AGREEMENT

19 U.S.C. § 3571

Sec. 281. Subsidies Enforcement

(a) Assistance Regarding Multilateral Subsidy Remedies.—The administering authority shall provide information to the public upon request, and, to the extent feasible, assistance and advice to interested parties concerning

(1) remedies and benefits available under relevant provisions of the Subsidies Agreement, and

(2) the procedures relating to such remedies and benefits.

(b) Prohibited Subsidies

(1) Notification of trade representative.—If the administering authority determines pursuant to title VII of the Tariff Act of 1930 that a class or kind of merchandise is benefiting from a subsidy which is prohibited under Article 3 of the Subsidies Agreement, the administering authority shall notify the Trade Representative and shall provide the Trade Representative with the information upon which the administering authority based its determination.

(2) Request by interested party regarding prohibited subsidy.—An interested party may request that the administering authority determine if there is reason to believe that merchandise produced in a WTO member country is benefiting from a subsidy which is prohibited under Article 3 of the Subsidies Agreement. The request shall contain such information as the administering authority may require to support the allegations contained in the request. If the administering authority, after analyzing the request and other information reasonably available to the administering authority, determines that there is reason to believe that such merchandise is benefiting from a subsidy which is prohibited under Article 3 of the Subsidies Agreement, the administering authority shall so notify the Trade Representative, and shall include supporting information with the notification.

(c) Subsidies Actionable Under the Agreement

(1) In general.—If the administering authority determines pursuant to title VII of the Tariff Act of 1930 that a class or kind of merchandise is benefiting from a subsidy described in Article 6.1 of the Subsidies Agreement, the administering authority shall notify the Trade Representative, and shall provide the Trade Representative with the information upon which the administering authority based its determination.

(2) Request by interested party regarding adverse effects.—An interested party may request the administering authority to determine if there is reason to believe that a subsidy which is actionable under the Subsidies Agreement is causing adverse effects. The request shall contain such information as the administering authority may require to support the allegations contained in the request. At the request of the administering authority, the Commission shall assist the administering authority in analyzing the information pertaining to the existence of such adverse effects. If the administering authority, after analyzing the request and other information reasonably available to the administering authority, determines that there is reason to believe that a subsidy which is actionable under the Subsidies Agreement is causing adverse effects, the administering authority shall so notify the Trade Representative, and shall include supporting information with the notification.

(d) Initiation of Section 301 Investigation.—On the basis of the notification and information provided by the administering authority pursuant to subsection (b) or (c), such other information as the Trade Representative may have or obtain, and where applicable, after consultation with an interested party referred to in subsection (b)(2) or (c)(2), the Trade Representative shall, unless such interested party objects, determine as expeditiously as possible, in accordance with the procedures in section 302(b)(1) of the Trade Act of 1974 (19 U.S.C. § 2412(b)(1)), whether to initiate an investigation pursuant to title III of that Act (19 U.S.C. § 2411 et seq.). At the request of the Trade Representative, the administering authority and the Commission shall assist the Trade Representative in an investigation initiated pursuant to this subsection.

* * *

(f) Notification, Consultation, and Publication

* * *

(g) Cooperation of Other Agencies. * * *

(h) Definitions.—For purposes of this section

(1) Adverse effects.—The term "adverse effects" has the meaning given that term in Articles 5(a) and 5(c) of the Subsidies Agreement.

(2) Administering authority.—The term "administering authority" has the meaning given that term in section 771(1) of the Tariff Act of 1930 (19 U.S.C. § 1677(1)).

(3) Commission.—The term "Commission" means the United States International Trade Commission.

(4) Interested party.—The term "interested party" means a party described in subparagraph (C), (D), (E), (F), or (G) of section 771(9) of the Tariff Act of 1930 (19 U.S.C. § 1677(9)(A), (C), (D), (E), (F), or (G)).

(5) Nonactionable subsidy.—The term "nonactionable subsidy" means a subsidy described in Article 8.1(b) of the Subsidies Agreement.

(6) Notified subsidy program.—The term "notified subsidy program" means a subsidy program which has been notified pursuant to Article 8.3 of the Subsidies Agreement.

(7) Serious adverse effects.—The term "serious adverse effects" has the meaning given that term in Article 9.1 of the Subsidies Agreement.

(8) Subsidies agreement.—The term "Subsidies Agreement" means the Agreement on Subsidies and Countervailing Measures described in section 771(8) of the Tariff Act of 1930 (19 U.S.C. § 1677(8)).

(9) Subsidies committee.—The term "Subsidies Committee" means the committee established pursuant to Article 24 of the Subsidies Agreement.

(10) Subsidy.—The term "subsidy" has the meaning given that term in Article 1 of the Subsidies Agreement.

(11) Trade representative.—The term "Trade Representative" means the United States Trade Representative.

(12) Violation of Article 8.—The term "violation of Article 8" means the failure of a notified subsidy program or an individual subsidy granted pursuant to a notified subsidy program to meet the applicable conditions and criteria described in Article 8.2 of the Subsidies Agreement.

(i) Treatment of Proprietary Information.—Notwithstanding any other provision of law, the administering authority may provide the Trade Representative with a copy of proprietary information submitted to, or obtained by, the administering authority that the Trade Representative considers relevant in carrying out its responsibilities under this part. The Trade Representative shall protect from public disclosure proprietary information obtained from the administering authority under this part.

19 U.S.C. § 3572

Sec. 282. Review of Subsidies Agreement

(a) General Objectives.—The general objectives of the United States under this part are

(1) to ensure that parts II and III of the Agreement on Subsidies and Countervailing Measures referred to in section 101(d)(12) (hereafter in this section referred to as the "Subsidies Agreement") are effective in disciplining the use of subsidies and in remedying the adverse effects of subsidies, and

(2) to ensure that part IV of the Subsidies Agreement does not undermine the benefits derived from any other part of that Agreement.

(b) Specific Objective.—The specific objective of the United States under this part shall be to create a mechanism which will provide for an ongoing review of the operation of part IV of the Subsidies Agreement.

(c) Sunset of Noncountervailable Subsidies Provisions.

(1) In general.—Subparagraphs (B), (C), (D), and (E) of section 771(5B) of the Tariff Act of 1930 shall cease to apply as provided in subparagraph (G)(i) of such section, unless, before the date referred to in such subparagraph (G)(i).

(A) the Subsidies Committee determines to extend Articles 6.1, 8, and 9 of the Subsidies Agreement as in effect on the date on which the Subsidies Agreement enters into force or in a modified form, in accordance with Article 31 of such Agreement,

(B) the President consults with the Congress in accordance with paragraph (2), and

(C) an implementing bill is submitted and enacted into law in accordance with paragraphs (3) and (4).

(2) Consultation with congress before subsidies committee agrees to extend.—Before a determination is made by the Subsidies Committee to extend Articles 6.1, 8, and 9 of the Subsidies Agreement, the President shall consult with the Committee on Ways and Means of the House of Representatives and the Committee on Finance of the Senate regarding such extension.

(3) Implementation of extension.

(A) Notification and submission.—Any extension of subparagraphs (B), (C), (D), and (E) of section 771(5B) of the Tariff Act of 1930 shall take effect if (and only if)

(i) after the Subsidies Committee determines to extend Articles 6.1, 8, and 9 of the Subsidies Agreement, the President submits to the committees referred to in paragraph (2) a copy of the document describing the terms of such extension, together with

(I) a draft of an implementing bill,

(II) a statement of any administrative action proposed to implement the extension, and

(III) the supporting information described in subparagraph (C); and

(ii) the implementing bill is enacted into law.

(B) Implementing bill.—The implementing bill referred to in subparagraph (A) shall contain only those provisions that are necessary or appropriate to implement an extension of the provisions of section 771(5B)(B), (C), (D), and (E) of the Tariff Act of 1930 as in effect on the day before the date of the enactment of the implementing bill or as modified to reflect the determination of the Subsidies Committee to extend Articles 6.1, 8, and 9 of the Subsidies Agreement.

(C) Supporting information.—The supporting information required under subparagraph (A)(i)(III) consists of

(i) an explanation as to how the implementing bill and proposed administrative action will change or affect existing law; and

(ii) a statement regarding

(I) how the extension serves the interests of United States commerce, and

(II) why the implementing bill and proposed administrative action is required or appropriate to carry out the extension. * * *

(5) Report by the trade representative.—Not later than the date referred to in section 771(5B)(G)(i) of the Tariff Act of 1930, the Trade Representative shall submit to the Congress a report setting forth the provisions of law which were enacted to implement Articles 6.1, 8, and 9 of the Subsidies Agreement and should be repealed or modified if such provisions are not extended.

Part Three

Trade Related Laws

■ ■ ■

Document 34

Buy American Act of 1933

■ ■ ■

Act of March 3, 1933, 47 Stat. 1520, 41 U.S.C. §§ 10a–10d as amended Pub.L. 100–418, Title VII, Aug. 23, 1988, 102 Stat. 1107

§ 10a. American materials required for public use

Notwithstanding any other provision of law, and unless the head of the department or independent establishment concerned shall determine it to be inconsistent with the public interest, or the cost to be unreasonable, only such unmanufactured articles, materials, and supplies as have been mined or produced in the United States, and only such manufactured articles, materials, and supplies as have been manufactured in the United States substantially all from articles, materials, or supplies mined, produced, or manufactured, as the case may be, in the United States, shall be acquired for public use. This section shall not apply with respect to articles, materials, or supplies for use outside the United States, or if articles, materials, or supplies of the class or kind to be used or the articles, materials, or supplies from which they are manufactured are not mined, produced, or manufactured, as the case may be, in the United States in sufficient and reasonably available commercial quantities and of a satisfactory quality. This section shall not apply to manufactured articles, materials, or supplies procured under any contract the award value of which is less than or equal to the micro-purchase threshold under section 32 of the Office of Federal Procurement Policy Act.

§ 10b. Contracts for public works; specification for use of American materials; blacklisting contractors violating requirements

(a) Every contract for the construction, alteration, or repair of any public building or public work in the United States growing out of an appropriation heretofore made or hereafter to be made shall contain a provision that in the performance of the work the contractor, subcontractors, material men, or suppliers, shall use only such unmanufactured articles, materials, and supplies as have been mined or produced in the United States, and only such manufactured articles, materials, and supplies as have been manufactured in the United States substantially all from articles, materials, or supplies mined, produced, or manufactured, as the case may be, in the United States except as provided in section 10a of this title: *Provided, however,* That if the head of the department or independent establishment making the contract shall find that in respect to some particular articles, materials, or supplies it is impracticable to make such requirement or that it would unreasonably increase the cost, an exception shall be noted in the specifications as to that particular article, material, or supply, and a public record made of the findings which justified the exception.

(b) If the head of a department, bureau, agency, or independent establishment which has made any contract containing the provision required by subsection (a) of this section finds that in the performance of such contract there has been a failure to comply with such provisions, he shall make public his findings, including therein the name of the contractor obligated under such contract, and no other contract for the construction, alteration, or repair of any public building or public work in the United States or elsewhere shall be awarded to such contractor, subcontractors, material men, or suppliers with which such contractor is associated or affiliated, within a period of three years after such finding is made public.

* * *

§ 10d. Clarification of Congressional intent regarding sections 10a and 10b(a) [1949]

In order to clarify the original intent of Congress, hereafter, section 10a of this title and that part of section 10b(a) of this title preceding the words "*Provided, however,*" shall be regarded as requiring the purchase, for public use within the United States, of articles, materials, or supplies manufactured in the United States in sufficient and reasonably available commercial quantities and of a satisfactory quality, unless the head of the department or independent establishment concerned shall determine their purchase to be inconsistent with the public interest or their cost to be unreasonable.

* * *

DOCUMENT 35

CUBAN ASSETS CONTROL REGULATIONS (31 C.F.R.)

■ ■ ■

31 C.F.R. Part 515

§ 515.204 Importation of and dealings in certain merchandise

(a) Except as specifically authorized by the Secretary of the Treasury (or any person, agency, or instrumentality designated by him) by means of regulations, rulings, instructions, licenses, or otherwise, no person subject to the jurisdiction of the United States may purchase, transport, import, or otherwise deal in or engage in any transaction with respect to any merchandise outside the United States if such merchandise:

(1) Is of Cuban origin; or

(2) Is or has been located in or transported from or through Cuba; or

(3) Is made or derived in whole or in part of any article which is the growth, produce or manufacture of Cuba.

* * *

§ 515.305 Designated national

For the purposes of this part, the term *designated national* shall mean Cuba and any national thereof including any person who is a specially designated national.

§ 515.306 Specially designated national

(a) The term *specially designated national* shall mean:

(1) Any person who is determined by the Secretary of the Treasury to be a specially designated national,

(2) Any person who on or since the "effective date" has acted for or on behalf of the Government or authorities exercising control over a designated foreign country, or

(3) Any partnership, association, corporation or other organization which on or since the "effective date" has been owned or controlled directly or indirectly by the Government or authorities exercising control over a designated foreign country or by any specially designated national.

(b) [Reserved].

Note to § 515.306: Please refer to the appendices at the end of this chapter for listings of persons designated pursuant to this part. Section 501.807 of this chapter sets forth the procedures to be followed by persons seeking administrative reconsideration of their designation or that of a vessel as blocked, or who wish to assert that the circumstances resulting in the designation are no longer applicable.

§ 515.559 Transactions by U.S.-owned or controlled foreign firms with Cuba

(a) Effective October 23, 1992, no specific licenses will be issued pursuant to paragraph (b) of this section for transactions between U.S.-owned or controlled firms in third countries and Cuba for the exportation to Cuba of commodities produced in the authorized trade zone or for the importation of goods of Cuban origin into countries in the authorized trade zone, unless, in addition to meeting all requirements of paragraph (b), one or more of the following conditions are satisfied:

(1) The contract underlying the proposed transaction was entered into prior to October 23, 1992;

(2) The transaction is for the exportation of medicine or medical supplies from a third country to Cuba, which shall not be restricted:

(i) Except to the extent such restrictions would be permitted under section 5(m) of the Export Administration Act of 1979 or section 203(b)(2) of the International Emergency Economic Powers Act if the exportation were subject to these provisions;

(ii) Except in a case in which there is a reasonable likelihood that the item to be exported will be used for purposes of torture or other human rights abuses;

(iii) Except in a case in which there is a reasonable likelihood that the item to be exported will be reexported; or

(iv) Except in a case in which the item to be exported could be used in the production of any biotechnological product; and

(v) Except in a case where it is determined that the United States Government is unable to verify, by on-site inspection or other means, that the item to be exported will be used for the purpose for which it was intended and only for the use and benefit of the Cuban people, but this exception shall not apply to donations for humanitarian purposes to a nongovernmental organization in Cuba.

(3) The transaction is for the exportation of telecommunications equipment from a third country, when the equipment is determined to be necessary for efficient and adequate telecommunications service between the United States and Cuba.

(b) Specific licenses will be issued in appropriate cases for certain categories of transactions between U.S.-owned or controlled firms in third countries and Cuba, where local law requires, or policy in the third country favors, trade with Cuba. The categories include:

(1) Exportation to Cuba of commodities produced in the authorized trade territory, provided:

(i) The commodities to be exported are non-strategic;

(ii) United States-origin technical data (other than maintenance, repair and operations data) will not be transferred;

(iii) If any U.S.-origin parts and components are included therein, such inclusion has been authorized by the Department of Commerce;

(iv) If any U.S.-origin spares are to be reexported to Cuba in connection with a licensed transaction, such reexport has been authorized by the Department of Commerce;

(v) No U.S. dollar accounts are involved; and

(vi) Any financing or other extension of credit by a U.S.-owned or controlled firm is granted on normal short-term conditions which are appropriate for the commodity to be exported.

(2) [Reserved]

(3) Importation of goods of Cuban origin into countries in the authorized trade territory.

(c) The term *strategic goods* means any item, regardless of origin, of a type included in the Commodity Control List of the U.S. Department of Commerce (15 CFR part 399) and identified by the code letter "A" following the Export Control Commodity Numbers, or of a type the unauthorized exportation of which from the United States is prohibited by regulations issued under the Arms Export Control Act of 1976, 22 U.S.C. 2778, or under the Atomic Energy Act of 1954, 42 U.S.C. 2011, *et seq.*, or successor acts restricting the export of strategic goods.

(d) Specific licenses issued pursuant to the policies set forth in this section do not authorize any person within the United States to engage in, participate in, or be involved in a licensed transactions with Cuba or Cuban nationals. Such involvement includes, but is not limited to, assistance or participation by a U.S. parent firm, or any officer or employee thereof, in the negotiation or performance of a transaction which is the subject of a license application. Such participation is a ground for denial of a license application, or for revocation of a license. To be eligible for a license under this section, the affiliate must be generally independent, in the conduct of transactions of the type for which the license is being sought, in such matters as decision-making, risk-taking, negotiation, financing or arranging of financing, and performance.

DOCUMENT 36

CUBAN DEMOCRACY ACT OF 1992

■ ■ ■

P.L. 102–484, 106 Stat. 2575

Sec. 1701. Short Title

This title may be cited as the "Cuban Democracy Act of 1992".

Sec. 1702. Findings [omitted]

Sec. 1703. Statement of Policy

It should be the policy of the United States—

(1) to seek a peaceful transition to democracy and a resumption of economic growth in Cuba through the careful application of sanctions directed at the Castro government and support for the Cuban people;

(2) to seek the cooperation of other democratic countries in this policy;

(3) to make clear to other countries that, in determining its relations with them, the United States will take into account their willingness to cooperate in such a policy;

* * *

(6) to maintain sanctions on the Castro regime so long as it continues to refuse to move toward democratization and greater respect for human rights;

(7) to be prepared to reduce the sanctions in carefully calibrated ways in response to positive developments in Cuba;

(8) to encourage free and fair elections to determine Cuba's political future;

* * *

Sec. 1704. International Cooperation

(a) Cuban Trading Partners.—The President should encourage the governments of countries that conduct trade with Cuba to restrict their trade and credit relations with Cuba in a manner consistent with the purposes of this title.

(b) Sanctions Against Countries Assisting Cuba.—

(1) Sanctions.—The President may apply the following sanctions to any country that provides assistance to Cuba:

(A) The government of such country shall not be eligible for assistance under the Foreign Assistance Act of 1961 or assistance or sales under the Arms Export Control Act.

(B) Such country shall not be eligible, under any program, for forgiveness or reduction of debt owed to the United States Government.

* * *

(g) Assistance to Support Democracy in Cuba.—The United States Government may provide assistance, through appropriate nongovernmental organizations, for the support of individuals and organizations to promote nonviolent democratic change in Cuba.

* * *

Sec. 1706. Sanctions

(a) Prohibition on Certain Transactions Between Certain United States Firms and Cuba.—

(1) Prohibition.—Notwithstanding any other provision of law, no license may be issued for any transaction described in section 515.559 of title 31, Code of Federal Regulations, as in effect on July 1, 1989.

DOCUMENT 37

CUBAN LIBERTY AND DEMOCRATIC SOLIDARITY (LIBERTAD) ACT OF 1996 (HELMS-BURTON ACT)

■ ■ ■

Pub. L. 104–114, 110 Stat. 785, 22 U.S.C. §§ 6021–6091

Table of Contents

Sec.

---

§ 6023. Definitions

As used in this Act, the following terms have the following meanings:

(1) Agency or Instrumentality of a Foreign State.—The term "agency or instrumentality of a foreign state" has the meaning given that term in section 1603(b) of title 28, United States Code.

* * *

(3) Commercial Activity.—The term "commercial activity" has the meaning given that term in section 1603(d) of title 28, United States Code.[a]

(4) Confiscated.—As used in titles I and III, the term "confiscated" refers to—

(A) the nationalization, expropriation, or other seizure by the Cuban Government of ownership or control of property, on or after January 1, 1959—

---

[a] These are the definitions in the Foreign Sovereign Immunities Act, which is included in this Documents Supplement.

(i) without the property having been returned or adequate and effective compensation provided; or

(ii) without the claim to the property having been settled pursuant to an international claims settlement agreement or other mutually accepted settlement procedure; and

(B) the repudiation by the Cuban Government of, the default by the Cuban Government on, or the failure of the Cuban Government to pay, on or after January 1, 1959—

(i) a debt of any enterprise which has been nationalized, expropriated, or otherwise taken by the Cuban Government;

(ii) a debt which is a charge on property nationalized, expropriated, or otherwise taken by the Cuban Government; or

(iii) a debt which was incurred by the Cuban Government in satisfaction or settlement of a confiscated property claim.

* * *

(9) Knowingly.—The term "knowingly" means with knowledge or having reason to know.

* * *

(12) Property.—(A) The term "property" means any property (including patents, copyrights, trademarks, and any other form of intellectual property), whether real, personal, or mixed, and any present, future, or contingent right, security, or other interest therein, including any leasehold interest.

(B) For purposes of title III of this Act, the term "property" does not include real property used for residential purposes unless, as of the date of the enactment of this Act—

(i) the claim to the property is held by a United States national and the claim has been certified under title V of the International Claims Settlement Act of 1949; or

(ii) the property is occupied by an official of the Cuban Government or the ruling political party in Cuba.

(13) Traffics.—(A) As used in title III, and except as provided in subparagraph (B), a person "traffics" in confiscated property if that person knowingly and intentionally—

(i) sells, transfers, distributes, dispenses, brokers, manages, or otherwise disposes of confiscated property, or purchases, leases, receives, possesses, obtains control of, manages, uses, or otherwise acquires or holds an interest in confiscated property,

(ii) engages in a commercial activity using or otherwise benefiting from confiscated property, or

(iii) causes, directs, participates in, or profits from, trafficking (as described in clause (i) or (ii)) by another person, or otherwise engages in trafficking (as described in clause (i) or (ii)) through another person,

without the authorization of any United States national who holds a claim to the property.

* * *

TITLE I—STRENGTHENING INTERNATIONAL SANCTIONS AGAINST THE CASTRO GOVERNMENT

§ 6032. Enforcement of the Economic Embargo of Cuba

(a) Policy.—

(1) Restrictions by other countries.—The Congress hereby reaffirms section 1704(a) of the Cuban Democracy Act of 1992, which states that the President should encourage foreign countries to restrict trade and credit relations with Cuba in a manner consistent with the purposes of that Act.

(2) Sanctions on other countries.—The Congress further urges the President to take immediate steps to apply the sanctions described in section 1704(b)(1) of that Act against countries assisting Cuba.

(b) Diplomatic Efforts.—The Secretary of State should ensure that United States diplomatic personnel abroad understand and, in their contacts with foreign officials, are communicating the reasons for the United States economic embargo of Cuba, and are urging foreign governments to cooperate more effectively with the embargo.

(c) Existing Regulations.—The President shall instruct the Secretary of the Treasury and the Attorney General to enforce fully the Cuban Assets Control Regulations set forth in part 515 of title 31, Code of Federal Regulations.

* * *

(h) Codification of Economic Embargo.—The economic embargo of Cuba, as in effect on March 1, 1996, including all restrictions under part 515 of title 31, Code of Federal Regulations, shall be in effect upon the enactment of this Act, and shall remain in effect, subject to section 204 [22 U.S.C. § 6064] of this Act.

* * *

§ 6038. Reports on Commerce With, and Assistance to, Cuba From Other Foreign Countries

(a) Reports Required.—Not later than 90 days after the date of the enactment of this Act, and by January 1 of each year thereafter until the President submits a determination under section 203(c)(1), the President shall submit a report to the appropriate congressional committees on commerce with, and assistance to, Cuba from other foreign countries during the preceding 12–month period.

* * *

§ 6040. Importation Safeguard Against Certain Cuban Products

(a) Prohibition on Import of and Dealings in Cuban Products.—The Congress notes that section 515.204 of title 31, Code of Federal Regulations, prohibits the entry of, and dealings outside the United States in, merchandise that—

(1) is of Cuban origin;

(2) is or has been located in or transported from or through Cuba; or

(3) is made or derived in whole or in part of any article which is the growth, produce, or manufacture of Cuba.

(b) Effect of NAFTA.—The Congress notes that United States accession to the North American Free Trade Agreement does not modify or alter the United States sanctions against Cuba. The statement of administrative action accompanying that trade agreement specifically states the following:

(1) "The NAFTA rules of origin will not in any way diminish the Cuban sanctions program. . . . Nothing in the NAFTA would operate to override this prohibition.".

(2) "Article 309(3) [of the NAFTA] permits the United States to ensure that Cuban products or goods made from Cuban materials are not imported into the United States from Mexico or Canada and that United States products are not exported to Cuba through those countries.".

(c) Restriction of Sugar Imports.—The Congress notes that section 902(c) of the Food Security Act of 1985 (Public Law 99–198) requires the President not to allocate any of the sugar import quota to a country that is a net importer of sugar unless appropriate officials of that country verify to the President that the country does not import for reexport to the United States any sugar produced in Cuba.

(d) Assurances Regarding Sugar Products.—Protection of essential security interests of the United States requires assurances that sugar products that are entered, or withdrawn from warehouse for consumption, into the customs territory of the United States are not products of Cuba.

* * *

§ 6046. Condemnation of Cuban Attack on American Aircraft

(a) Findings.—The Congress makes the following findings:

(1) Brothers to the Rescue is a Miami-based humanitarian organization engaged in searching for and aiding Cuban refugees in the Straits of Florida, and was engaged in such a mission on Saturday, February 24, 1996.

(2) The members of Brothers to the Rescue were flying unarmed and defenseless planes in a mission identical to hundreds they have flown since 1991 and posed no threat whatsoever to the Cuban Government, the Cuban military, or the Cuban people.

(3) Statements by the Cuban Government that Brothers to the Rescue has engaged in covert operations, bombing campaigns, and commando operations against the Government of Cuba have no basis in fact.

(4) The Brothers to the Rescue aircraft notified air traffic controllers as to their flight plans, which would take them south of the 24th parallel and close to Cuban airspace.

(5) International law provides a nation with airspace over the 12–mile territorial sea.

(6) The response of Fidel Castro's dictatorship to Saturday's afternoon flight was to scramble 2 fighter jets from a Havana airfield.

(7) At approximately 3:24 p.m., the pilot of one of the Cuban MiGs received permission and proceeded to shoot down one Brothers to the Rescue airplane more than 6 miles north of the Cuban exclusion zone, or 18 miles from the Cuban coast.

(8) Approximately 7 minutes later, the pilot of the Cuban fighter jet received permission and proceeded to shoot down the second Brothers to the Rescue airplane almost 18.5 miles north of the Cuban exclusion zone, or 30.5 miles from the Cuban coast.

(9) The Cuban dictatorship, if it truly felt threatened by the flight of these unarmed aircraft, could have and should have pursued other peaceful options as required by international law.

(10) The response chosen by Fidel Castro, the use of lethal force, was completely inappropriate to the situation presented to the Cuban Government, making such actions a blatant and barbaric violation of international law and tantamount to cold-blooded murder.

(11) There were no survivors of the attack on these aircraft, and the crew of a third aircraft managed to escape this criminal attack by Castro's Air Force.

(12) The crew members of the destroyed planes, Pablo Morales, Carlos Costa, Mario de la Pena, and Armando Alejandre, were United States citizens from Miami flying with Brothers to the Rescue on a voluntary basis.

(13) It is incumbent upon the United States Government to protect the lives and livelihoods of United States citizens as well as the rights of free passage and humanitarian missions.

(14) This premeditated act took place after a week-long wave of repression by the Cuban Government against Concilio Cubano, an umbrella organization of human rights activists, dissidents, independent economists, and independent journalists, among others.

(15) The wave of repression against Concilio Cubano, whose membership is committed to peaceful democratic change in Cuba, included arrests, strip searches, house arrests, and in some cases sentences to more than 1 year in jail.

(b) Statements by the Congress.—(1) The Congress strongly condemns the act of terrorism by the Castro regime in shooting down the Brothers to the Rescue aircraft on February 24, 1996.

(2) The Congress extends its condolences to the families of Pablo Morales, Carlos Costa, Mario de la Pena, and Armando Alejandre, the victims of the attack.

(3) The Congress urges the President to seek, in the International Court of Justice, indictment for this act of terrorism by Fidel Castro.

TITLE II—ASSISTANCE TO A FREE AND INDEPENDENT CUBA

§ 6061. Policy Toward a Transition Government and a Democratically Elected Government in Cuba

The policy of the United States is as follows:

* * *

(6) Through . . . assistance, to facilitate a peaceful transition to representative democracy and a market economy in Cuba and to consolidate democracy in Cuba.

(7) To deliver . . . assistance to the Cuban people only through a transition government in Cuba, through a democratically elected government in Cuba, through United States Government organizations, or through United States, international, or indigenous nongovernmental organizations.

* * *

(12) To be prepared to enter into negotiations with a democratically elected government in Cuba either to return the United States Naval Base at Guantanamo to Cuba or to renegotiate the present agreement under mutually agreeable terms.

(13) To consider the restoration of diplomatic recognition and support the reintegration of the Cuban Government into Inter-American organizations when the President determines that there exists a democratically elected government in Cuba.

(14) To take steps to remove the economic embargo of Cuba when the President determines that a transition to a democratically elected government in Cuba has begun.

* * *

§ 6064. Termination of the Economic Embargo of Cuba

(a) Presidential Actions.—Upon submitting a determination to the appropriate congressional committees under section 203(c)(1) [22 U.S.C. § 6063(c)(1)] that a transition government in Cuba is in power, the President, after consultation with the Congress, is authorized to take steps to suspend the economic embargo of Cuba and to suspend the right of action created in section 302 [22 U.S.C. § 6082] with respect to actions thereafter filed against the Cuban Government, to the extent that such steps contribute to a stable foundation for a democratically elected government in Cuba.

(b) Suspension of Certain Provisions of Law.—In carrying out subsection (a), the President may suspend the enforcement of—

* * *

(3) sections 1704, 1705(d), and 1706 of the Cuban Democracy Act of 1992 (22 U.S.C. 6003, 6004(d), and 6005);

* * *

(5) the prohibitions on transactions described in part 515 of title 31, Code of Federal Regulations.

(c) Additional Presidential Actions.—Upon submitting a determination to the appropriate congressional committees under section 203(c)(3) [22 U.S.C. § 6063(c)(3)] that a democratically elected government in Cuba is in power, the President shall take steps to terminate the economic embargo of Cuba, including the restrictions under part 515 of title 31, Code of Federal Regulations.

(d) Conforming Amendments.—On the date on which the President submits a determination under section 203(c)(3) [22 U.S.C. § 6063(c)(3)]—

* * *

(3) sections 1704, 1705(d), and 1706 of the Cuban Democracy Act of 1992 (22 U.S.C. 6003, 6004(d), and 6005) are repealed; and

* * *

(e) Review of Suspension of Economic Embargo.—

(1) Review.—If the President takes action under subsection (a) to suspend the economic embargo of Cuba, the President shall immediately so notify the Congress. The President shall report to the Congress no less frequently than every 6 months thereafter, until he submits a determination under section 203(c)(3) [22 U.S.C. § 6063(c)(3)] that a democratically elected government in Cuba is in power, on the progress being made by Cuba toward the establishment of such a democratically elected government. The action of the President under subsection (a) shall cease to be effective upon the enactment of a joint resolution described in paragraph (2).

* * *

§ 6065. Requirements and Factors for Determining a Transition Government

(a) Requirements.—For the purposes of this Act, a transition government in Cuba is a government that—

(1) has legalized all political activity;

(2) has released all political prisoners and allowed for investigations of Cuban prisons by appropriate international human rights organizations;

(3) has dissolved the present Department of State Security in the Cuban Ministry of the Interior, including the Committees for the Defense of the Revolution and the Rapid Response Brigades; and

(4) has made public commitments to organizing free and fair elections for a new government—

(A) to be held in a timely manner within a period not to exceed 18 months after the transition government assumes power;

(B) with the participation of multiple independent political parties that have full access to the media on an equal basis, including (in the case of radio, television, or other telecommunications media) in terms of allotments of time for such access and the times of day such allotments are given; and

(C) to be conducted under the supervision of internationally recognized observers, such as the Organization of American States, the United Nations, and other election monitors;

(5) has ceased any interference with Radio Marti or Television Marti broadcasts;

(6) makes public commitments to and is making demonstrable progress in—

(A) establishing an independent judiciary;

(B) respecting internationally recognized human rights and basic freedoms as set forth in the Universal Declaration of Human Rights, to which Cuba is a signatory nation;

(C) allowing the establishment of independent trade unions as set forth in conventions 87 and 98 of the International Labor Organization, and allowing the establishment of independent social, economic, and political associations;

(7) does not include Fidel Castro or Raul Castro; and

(8) has given adequate assurances that it will allow the speedy and efficient distribution of assistance to the Cuban people.

(b) Additional Factors.—In addition to the requirements in subsection (a), in determining whether a transition government in Cuba is in power, the President shall take into account the extent to which that government—

(1) is demonstrably in transition from a communist totalitarian dictatorship to representative democracy;

(2) has made public commitments to, and is making demonstrable progress in—

(A) effectively guaranteeing the rights of free speech and freedom of the press, including granting permits to privately owned media and telecommunications companies to operate in Cuba;

(B) permitting the reinstatement of citizenship to Cuban-born persons returning to Cuba;

(C) assuring the right to private property; and

(D) taking appropriate steps to return to United States citizens (and entities which are 50 percent or more beneficially owned by United States citizens) property taken by the Cuban Government from such citizens and entities on or after January 1, 1959, or to provide equitable compensation to such citizens and entities for such property;

(3) has extradited or otherwise rendered to the United States all persons sought by the United States Department of Justice for crimes committed in the United States; and

(4) has permitted the deployment throughout Cuba of independent and unfettered international human rights monitors.

§ 6066. Requirements for Determining a Democratically Elected Government

For purposes of this Act, a democratically elected government in Cuba, in addition to meeting the requirements of section 205(a) [22 U.S.C. § 6065], is a government which—

(1) results from free and fair elections—

* * *

(3) is substantially moving toward a market-oriented economic system based on the right to own and enjoy property;

* * *

(6) has made demonstrable progress in returning to United States citizens (and entities which are 50 percent or more beneficially owned by United States citizens) property taken by the Cuban Government from such citizens and entities on or after January 1, 1959, or providing full compensation for such property in accordance with international law standards and practice.

§ 6067. Settlement of Outstanding United States Claims to Confiscated Property in Cuba

(a) Report to Congress.—Not later than 180 days after the date of the enactment of this Act, the Secretary of State shall provide a report to the appropriate congressional committees containing an assessment of the property dispute question in Cuba, including—

(1) an estimate of the number and amount of claims to property confiscated by the Cuban Government that are held by United States nationals in addition to those claims certified under section 507 of the International Claims Settlement Act of 1949;

(2) an assessment of the significance of promptly resolving confiscated property claims to the revitalization of the Cuban economy;

(3) a review and evaluation of technical and other assistance that the United States could provide to help either a transition government in Cuba or a democratically elected government in Cuba establish mechanisms to resolve property questions;

(4) an assessment of the role and types of support the United States could provide to help resolve claims to property confiscated by the Cuban Government that are held by United States nationals who did not receive or qualify for certification under section 507 of the International Claims Settlement Act of 1949; and

(5) an assessment of any areas requiring legislative review or action regarding the resolution of property claims in Cuba prior to a change of government in Cuba.

(b) Sense of Congress.—It is the sense of the Congress that the satisfactory resolution of property claims by a Cuban Government recognized by the United States remains an essential condition for the full resumption of economic and diplomatic relations between the United States and Cuba.

TITLE III—PROTECTION OF PROPERTY RIGHTS OF UNITED STATES NATIONALS

§ 6081. Findings

The Congress makes the following findings:

* * *

(2) The wrongful confiscation or taking of property belonging to United States nationals by the Cuban Government, and the subsequent exploitation of this property at the expense of the rightful owner, undermines the comity of nations, the free flow of commerce, and economic development.

* * *

(5) The Cuban Government is offering foreign investors the opportunity to purchase an equity interest in, manage, or enter into joint ventures using property and assets some of which were confiscated from United States nationals.

(6) This "trafficking" in confiscated property provides badly needed financial benefit, including hard currency, oil, and productive investment and expertise, to the current Cuban Government and thus undermines the foreign policy of the United States—

* * *

(7) The United States Department of State has notified other governments that the transfer to third parties of properties confiscated by the Cuban Government "would complicate any attempt to return them to their original owners".

(8) The international judicial system, as currently structured, lacks fully effective remedies for the wrongful confiscation of property and for unjust enrichment from the use of wrongfully confiscated property by governments and private entities at the expense of the rightful owners of the property.

(9) International law recognizes that a nation has the ability to provide for rules of law with respect to conduct outside its territory that has or is intended to have substantial effect within its territory.

(10) The United States Government has an obligation to its citizens to provide protection against wrongful confiscations by foreign nations and their citizens, including the provision of private remedies.

(11) To defer trafficking in wrongfully confiscated property, United States nationals who were the victims of these confiscations should be endowed with a judicial remedy in the courts of the United States that would deny traffickers any profits from economically exploiting Castro's wrongful seizures.

§ 6082. Liability for Trafficking in Confiscated Property Claimed by United States Nationals

(a) Civil Remedy.—

(1) Liability for Trafficking.—(A) Except as otherwise provided in this section, any person that, after the end of the 3–month period beginning on the effective date of this title, traffics in property which was confiscated by the Cuban Government on or after January 1, 1959, shall be liable to any United States national who owns the claim to such property for money damages in an amount equal to the sum of—

(i) the amount which is the greater of—

(I) the amount, if any, certified to the claimant by the Foreign Claims Settlement Commission under the International Claims Settlement Act of 1949, plus interest;

(II) the amount determined under section 303(a)(2) [22 U.S.C. § 6083(a)(2)], plus interest; or

(III) the fair market value of that property, calculated as being either the current value of the property, or the value of the property when confiscated plus interest, whichever is greater; and

(ii) court costs and reasonable attorneys' fees.

* * *

(3) Increased Liability.—

(A) Any person that traffics in confiscated property for which liability is incurred under paragraph (1) shall, if a United States national owns a claim with respect to that property which was certified by the Foreign Claims Settlement Commission under title V of the International Claims Settlement Act of 1949, be liable for damages computed in accordance with subparagraph (C).

(B) If the claimant in an action under this subsection (other than a United States national to whom subparagraph (A) applies) provides, after the end of the 3–month period described in paragraph (1) notice to—

(i) a person against whom the action is to be initiated, or

(ii) a person who is to be joined as a defendant in the action,

at least 30 days before initiating the action or joining such person as a defendant, as the case may be, and that person, after the end of the 30–day period beginning on the date the notice is provided, traffics in the confiscated property that is the subject of the action, then that person shall be liable to that claimant for damages computed in accordance with subparagraph (C).

(C) Damages for which a person is liable under subparagraph (A) or subparagraph (B) are money damages in an amount equal to the sum of—

(i) the amount determined under paragraph (1)(A)(ii), and

(ii) 3 times the amount determined applicable under paragraph (1)(A)(i).

* * *

(4) Applicability.—(A) Except as otherwise provided in this paragraph, actions may be brought under paragraph (1) with respect to property confiscated before, on, or after the date of the enactment of this Act.

(B) In the case of property confiscated before the date of the enactment of this Act, a United States national may not bring an action under this section on a claim to the confiscated property unless such national acquires ownership of the claim before such date of enactment.

(C) In the case of property confiscated on or after the date of the enactment of this Act, a United States national who, after the property is confiscated, acquires ownership of a claim to the property by assignment for value, may not bring an action on the claim under this section.

(5) Treatment of Certain Actions.—

* * *

(C) A United States national, other than a United States national bringing an action under this section on a claim certified under title V of the International Claims Settlement Act of 1949, may not bring an action on a claim under this section before the end of the 2–year period beginning on the date of the enactment of this Act.

* * *

(6) Inapplicability of Act of State Doctrine.—No court of the United States shall decline, based upon the act of state doctrine, to make a determination on the merits in an action brought under paragraph (1).

* * *

(b) Amount in Controversy.—An action may be brought under this section by a United States national only where the amount in controversy exceeds the sum or value of $50,000, exclusive of interest, costs, and attorneys' fees. . . .

* * *

(d) Enforceability of Judgments Against Cuban Government.—In an action brought under this section, any judgment against an agency or instrumentality of the Cuban Government shall not be enforceable against an agency or instrumentality of either a transition government in Cuba or a democratically elected government in Cuba.

* * *

§ 6083. Proof of Ownership of Claims to Confiscated Property

(a) Evidence of Ownership.—

(1) Conclusiveness of Certified Claims.—In any action brought under this title, the court shall accept as conclusive proof of ownership of an interest in property a certification of a claim to ownership of that interest that has been made by the Foreign Claims Settlement Commission under title V of the International Claims Settlement Act of 1949 (22 U.S.C. § 1643 and following).

(2) Claims not Certified.—If in an action under this title a claim has not been so certified by the Foreign Claims Settlement Commission, the court may appoint a special master, including the Foreign Claims Settlement Commission, to make determinations regarding the amount and ownership of the claim. . . .

* * *

§ 6085. Effective Date

* * *

(c) Other Authorities.—

(1) Suspension.—After this title and the amendments of this title have taken effect—

* * *

(B) the President may suspend the right to bring an action under this title with respect to confiscated property for a period of not more than 6 months if the President determines and reports in writing to the appropriate congressional committees at least 15 days before the suspension takes effect that such suspension is necessary to the national interests of the United States and will expedite a transition to democracy in Cuba.

(2) Additional Suspensions.—The President may suspend the right to bring an action under this title for additional periods of not more than 6 months each, each of which shall begin on the day after the last day of the period during which a suspension is in effect under this subsection, if the President determines and reports in writing to the appropriate congressional committees at least 15 days before the date on which the additional suspension is to begin that the suspension is necessary to the national interests of the United States and will expedite a transition to democracy in Cuba.

* * *

TITLE IV—EXCLUSION OF CERTAIN ALIENS

§ 6091. Exclusion From the United States of Aliens Who Have Confiscated Property of United States Nationals or Who Traffic in Such Property

(a) Grounds for Exclusion.—The Secretary of State shall deny a visa to, and the Attorney General shall exclude from the United States, any alien who the Secretary of State determines is a person who, after the date of the enactment of this Act—

(1) has confiscated, or has directed or overseen the confiscation of, property a claim to which is owned by a United States national, or converts or has converted for personal gain confiscated property, a claim to which is owned by a United States national;

(2) traffics in confiscated property, a claim to which is owned by a United States national;

(3) is a corporate officer, principal, or shareholder with a controlling interest of an entity which has been involved in the confiscation of property or trafficking in confiscated property, a claim to which is owned by a United States national; or

(4) is a spouse, minor child, or agent of a person excludable under paragraph (1), (2), or (3).

* * *

(b) Definitions.—

* * *

(2) Traffics.—(A) . . . a person "traffics" in confiscated property if that person knowingly and intentionally—

(i)(I) transfers, distributes, dispenses, brokers, or otherwise disposes of confiscated property,

(II) purchases, receives, obtains control of, or otherwise acquires confiscated property, or

(III) improves (other than for routine maintenance), invests in (by contribution of funds or anything of value, other than for routine maintenance), or begins after the date of the enactment of this Act to manage, lease, possess, use, or hold an interest in confiscated property,

(ii) enters into a commercial arrangement using or otherwise benefiting from confiscated property, or

(iii) causes, directs, participates in, or profits from, trafficking (as described in clause (i) or (ii)) by another person, or otherwise engages in trafficking (as described in clause (i) or (ii)) through another person,

without the authorization of any United States national who holds a claim to the property.

* * *

DOCUMENT 38

EXECUTIVE ORDER 10582 (1954)

■ ■ ■

PRESCRIBING UNIFORM PROCEDURES FOR CERTAIN DETERMINATIONS UNDER THE BUY-AMERICAN ACT

December 17, 1954

WHEREAS in the administration of the act of March 3, 1933, 47 Stat. 1520, 41 U. S. C. 10a–10c; 41 U. S. C. 10d, commonly known as the Buy-American Act, and other laws requiring the application of the Buy-American Act, the heads of executive agencies are required to determine, as a condition precedent to the purchase by their agencies of materials of foreign origin for public use within the United States, (a) that the price of like materials of domestic origin is unreasonable, or (b) that the purchase of like materials of domestic origin is inconsistent with the public interest; and

WHEREAS it is desirable and in the public interest that such determinations be made on as uniform a basis as possible:

NOW, THEREFORE, by virtue of the authority vested in me as President of the United States, it is hereby ordered as follows:

SEC. 1. As used in this order, (a) the term 'materials' includes articles and supplies, (b) the term 'executive agency' includes executive department, independent establishment, and other instrumentality of the executive branch of the Government, and (c) the term 'bid or offered price of materials of foreign origin' means the bid or offered price of such materials delivered at the place specified in the invitation to bid including applicable duty and all costs incurred after arrival in the United States.

SEC. 2. (a) For the purposes of this order materials shall be considered to be of foreign origin if the cost of the foreign products used in such materials constitutes fifty per centum or more of the cost of all the products used in such materials.

(b) For the purposes of the said act of March 3, 1933, and the other laws referred to in the first paragraph of the preamble of this order, the bid or offered price of materials of domestic origin shall be deemed to be unreasonable, or the purchase of such materials shall be deemed to be inconsistent with the public interest, if the bid or offered price thereof exceeds the sum of the bid or offered price of like materials of foreign origin and a differential computed as provided in subsection (c) of this section.

(c) The executive agency concerned shall in each instance determine the amount of the differential referred to in subsection (b) of this section on the basis of one of the following-described formulas, subject to the terms thereof:

(1) The sum determined by computing six per centum of the bid or offered price of materials of foreign origin.

(2) The sum determined by computing ten per centum of the bid or offered price of materials of foreign origin exclusive of applicable duty and all costs incurred after arrival in the United States: provided that when the bid or offered price of materials of foreign origin amounts to less than $25,000, the sum shall be determined by computing ten per centum of such price exclusive only of applicable duty.

SEC. 3. Nothing in this order shall affect the authority or responsibility of an executive agency:

(a) To reject any bid or offer for reasons of the national interest not described or referred to in this order; or

(b) To place a fair proportion of the total purchases with small business concerns in accordance with section 302(b) of the Federal Property and Administrative Services Act of 1949, as amended, section 2(b) of the Armed Services Procurement Act of 1947, as amended, and section 202 of the Small Business Act of 1953; or

(c) To reject a bid or offer to furnish materials of foreign origin in any situation in which the domestic supplier offering the lowest price for furnishing the desired materials undertakes to produce substantially all of such materials in areas of substantial unemployment, as determined by the Secretary of Labor in accordance with such appropriate regulations as he may establish and during such period as the President may determine that it is in the national interest to provide to such areas preference in the award of Government contracts:

Provided, that nothing in this section shall prevent the rejection of a bid or offered price which is excessive; or

(d) To reject any bid or offer for materials of foreign origin if such rejection is necessary to protect essential national-security interests after receiving advice with respect thereto form the President or from any officer of the Government designated by the President to furnish such advice.

SEC. 4. The head of each executive agency shall issue such regulations as may be necessary to insure that procurement practices under his jurisdiction conform to the provisions of this order.

SEC. 5. This order shall apply only to contracts entered into after the date hereof. In any case in which the head of an executive agency proposing to purchase domestic materials determines that a greater differential than that provided in this order between the cost of such materials of domestic origin and materials of foreign origin is not unreasonable or that the purchase of materials of domestic origin is not inconsistent with the public interest, this order shall not apply. A written report of the facts of each case in which such a determination is made shall be submitted to the President through the Director of the Bureau of the Budget by the official making the determination within 30 days thereafter.

DOCUMENT 39

EXPORT ADMINISTRATION ACT OF 1979

■ ■ ■

Pub.L. 96–72, Approved September 29, 1979, 93 Stat. 503, as amended, Pub.L. 97–145, December 29, 1981, 95 Stat. 1727

Pub.L. 99–64, July 12, 1985, 99 Stat. 120 and Pub.L. 100–418, Aug. 23, 1988, 102 Stat. 1107

[Note: The EAA expired in 1994, but it survives by periodic presidential extensions under the authority of the IEEPA.]

50 App. U.S.C. § 2402

Congressional Declaration of Policy

The Congress makes the following declarations:

(1) It is the policy of the United States to minimize uncertainties in export control policy and to encourage trade with all countries with which the United States has diplomatic or trading relations, except those countries with which such trade has been determined by the President to be against the national interest.

(2) It is the policy of the United States to use export controls only after full consideration of the impact on the economy of the United States and only to the extent necessary—

(A) to restrict the export of goods and technology which would make a significant contribution to the military potential of any other country or combination of countries which would prove detrimental to the national security of the United States;

(B) to restrict the export of goods and technology where necessary to further significantly the foreign policy of the United States or to fulfill its declared international obligations; and

(C) to restrict the export of goods where necessary to protect the domestic economy from the excessive drain of scarce materials and to reduce the serious inflationary impact of foreign demand.

(3) It is the policy of the United States (A) to apply any necessary controls to the maximum extent possible in cooperation with all nations, and (B) to encourage observance of a uniform export control policy by all nations with which the United States has defense treaty commitments or common strategic objectives.

(4) It is the policy of the United States to use its economic resources and trade potential to further the sound growth and stability of its economy as well as to further its national security and foreign policy objectives.

(5) It is the policy of the United States—

(A) to oppose restrictive trade practices or boycotts fostered or imposed by foreign countries against other countries friendly to the United States or against any United States person;

(B) to encourage and, in specified cases, require United States persons engaged in the export of goods or technology or other information to refuse to take actions, including furnishing information or entering into or implementing agreements, which have the effect of furthering or supporting the restrictive trade practices or boycotts fostered or imposed by any foreign country against a country friendly to the United States or against any United States person; and

(C) to foster international cooperation and the development of international rules and institutions to assure reasonable access to world supplies.

(6) It is the policy of the United States that the desirability of subjecting, or continuing to subject, particular goods or technology or other information to United States export controls should be subjected to review by and consultation with representatives of appropriate United States Government agencies and private industry.

(7) It is the policy of the United States to use export controls, including license fees, to secure the removal by foreign countries of restrictions on access to supplies where such restrictions have or may have a serious domestic inflationary impact, have caused or may cause a serious domestic shortage, or have been imposed for purposes of influencing the foreign policy of the United States. In effecting this policy, the President shall make reasonable and prompt efforts to secure the removal or reduction of such restrictions, policies, or actions through international cooperation and agreement before imposing export control. No action taken in fulfillment of the policy set forth in this paragraph shall apply to the export of medicine or medical supplies.

(8) It is the policy of the United States to use export controls to encourage other countries to take immediate steps to prevent the use of their territories or resources to aid, encourage, or give sanctuary to those persons involved in directing, supporting, or participating in acts of international terrorism. To achieve this objective, the President shall make reasonable and prompt efforts to secure the removal or reduction of such assistance to international terrorists through international cooperation and agreement before imposing export controls.

(9) It is the policy of the United States to cooperate with other countries with which the United States has defense treaty commitments or common strategic objectives in restricting the export of goods and technology which would make a significant contribution to the military potential of any country or combination of countries which would prove detrimental to the security of the United States and of those countries with which the United States has defense treaty commitments or common strategic objectives, and to encourage other friendly countries to cooperate in restricting the sale of goods and technology that can harm the security of the United States.

(10) It is the policy of the United States that export trade by United States citizens be given a high priority and not be controlled except when such controls (A) are necessary to further fundamental national security, foreign policy, or short supply objectives, (B) will clearly further such objectives, and (C) are administered consistent with basic standards of due process.

(11) It is the policy of the United States to minimize restrictions on the export of agricultural commodities and products.

(12) It is the policy of the United States to sustain vigorous scientific enterprise. To do so involves sustaining the ability of scientists and other scholars freely to communicate research findings, in accordance with applicable provisions of law, by means of publication, teaching, conferences, and other forms of scholarly exchange.

(13) It is the policy of the United States to control the export of goods and substances banned or severely restricted for use in the United States in order to foster public health and safety and to prevent injury to the foreign policy of the United States as well as to the credibility of the United States as a responsible trading partner.

(14) It is the policy of the United States to cooperate with countries which are allies of the United States and countries which share common strategic objectives with the United States in minimizing dependence on imports of energy and other critical resources from potential adversaries and in developing alternative supplies of such resources in order to minimize strategic threats posed by excessive hard currency earnings derived from such resource exports by countries with policies adverse to the security interests of the United States.

(15) It is the policy of the United States, particularly in light of the Soviet massacre of innocent men, women, and children aboard Korean Air Lines flight 7, to continue to object to exceptions to the International Control List for the Union of Soviet Socialist Republics, subject to periodic review by the President.

* * *

50 App. U.S.C. § 2407

Foreign Boycotts

(a) Prohibitions and exceptions.

(1) For the purpose of implementing the policies set forth in subparagraph (A) or (B) of paragraph (5) of section 3 of this Act [section 2402(5)(A) or (B) of this Appendix], the President shall issue regulations prohibiting any United States person, with respect to his activities in the interstate or foreign commerce of the United States, from taking or knowingly agreeing to take any of the following actions with intent to comply with, further, or support any boycott fostered or imposed by a foreign country against a country which is friendly to the United States and which is not itself the object of any form of boycott pursuant to United States law or regulation:

(A) Refusing, or requiring any other person to refuse, to do business with or in the boycotted country, with any business concern organized under the laws of the boycotted country, with any national or resident of the boycotted country, or with any other person, pursuant to an agreement with, a requirement of, or a request from or on behalf of the boycotting country. The mere absence of a business relationship with or in the boycotted country with any business concern organized under the laws of the boycotted country, with any national or resident of the boycotted country, or with any other person, does not indicate the existence of the intent required to establish a violation of regulations issued to carry out this subparagraph.

(B) Refusing, or requiring any other person to refuse, to employ or otherwise discriminating against any United States person on the basis of race, religion, sex, or national origin of that person or of any owner, officer, director, or employee of such person.

(C) Furnishing information with respect to the race, religion, sex, or national origin of any United States person or of any owner, officer, director, or employee of such person.

(D) Furnishing information about whether any person has, has had, or proposes to have any business relationship (including a relationship by way of sale, purchase, legal or commercial representation, shipping or other transport, insurance, investment, or supply) with or in the boycotted country, with any business concern organized under the laws of the boycotted country, with any national or resident of the boycotted country, or with any other person which is known or believed to be restricted from having any business relationship with or in the boycotting country. Nothing in this paragraph shall prohibit the furnishing of normal business information in a commercial context as defined by the Secretary.

(E) Furnishing information about whether any person is a member of, has made contributions to, or is otherwise associated with or involved in the activities of any charitable or fraternal organization which supports the boycotted country.

(F) Paying, honoring, confirming, or otherwise implementing a letter of credit which contains any condition or requirement compliance with which is prohibited by regulations issued pursuant to this paragraph, and no United States person shall, as a result of the application of this paragraph, be obligated to pay or otherwise honor or implement such letter of credit.

(2) Regulations issued pursuant to paragraph (1) shall provide exceptions for—

(A) complying or agreeing to comply with requirements (i) prohibiting the import of goods or services from the boycotted country or goods produced or services provided by any business concern organized under the laws of the boycotted country or by nationals or residents of the boycotted country, or (ii) prohibiting the shipment of goods to the boycotting country on a carrier of the boycotted country, or by a route other than that prescribed by the boycotting country or the recipient of the shipment;

(B) complying or agreeing to comply with import and shipping document requirements with respect to the country of origin, the name of the carrier and route of shipment, the name of the supplier of the shipment or the name of the provider of other services, except that no information knowingly furnished or conveyed in response to such requirements may be stated in negative, blacklisting, or similar exclusionary terms, other than with respect to carriers or route of shipment as may be permitted by such regulations in order to comply with precautionary requirements protecting against war risks and confiscation;

(C) complying or agreeing to comply in the normal course of business with the unilateral and specific selection by a boycotting country, or national or resident thereof, of carriers, insurers, suppliers of services to be performed within the boycotting country or specific goods which, in the normal course of business, are identifiable by source when imported into the boycotting country;

(D) complying or agreeing to comply with export requirements of the boycotting country relating to shipments or transshipments of exports to the boycotted country, to any business concern of or organized under the laws of the boycotted country, or to any national or resident of the boycotted country;

(E) compliance by an individual or agreement by an individual to comply with the immigration or passport requirements of any country with respect to such individual or any member of such individual's family or with requests for information regarding requirements of employment of such individual within the boycotting country; and

(F) compliance by a United States person resident in a foreign country or agreement by such person to comply with the laws of that country with respect to his activities exclusively therein, and such regulations may contain exceptions for such resident complying with the laws or regulations of that foreign country governing imports into such country of trademarked, trade named, or similarly specifically identifiable products, or components of products for his own use, including the performance of contractual services within that country, as may be defined by such regulations.

(3) Regulations issued pursuant to paragraphs (2)(C) and (2)(F) shall not provide exceptions from paragraphs (1)(B) and (1)(C).

(4) Nothing in this subsection may be construed to supersede or limit the operation of the antitrust or civil rights laws of the United States.

(5) This section shall apply to any transaction or activity undertaken, by or through a United States person or any other person, with intent to evade the provisions of this section as implemented by the regulations issued pursuant to this subsection, and such regulations shall expressly provide that the exceptions set forth in paragraph (2) shall not permit activities or agreements (expressed or implied by a course of conduct, including a pattern of responses) otherwise prohibited, which are not within the intent of such exceptions.

(b) Foreign policy controls.

* * *

(2) Such regulations shall require that any United States person receiving a request for the furnishing of information, the entering into or implementing of agreements, or the taking of any other action referred to in section 3(5) [section 2402(5) of this Appendix] shall report that fact to the Secretary, together with such other information concerning such request as the Secretary may require for such action as the Secretary considers appropriate for carrying out the policies of that section. Such person shall also report to the Secretary whether such person intends to comply and whether such person has complied with such request. Any report filed pursuant to this paragraph shall be made available promptly for public inspection and copying, except that information regarding the quantity, description, and value of any goods or technology to which such report relates may be kept confidential if the Secretary determines that disclosure thereof would place the United States person involved at a competitive disadvantage. The Secretary shall periodically transmit summaries of the information contained in such reports to the Secretary of

State for such action as the Secretary of State, in consultation with the Secretary, considers appropriate for carrying out the policies set forth in section 3(5) of this Act [section 2402(5) of this Appendix].

* * *

50 App. U.S.C. § 2410

Violations

(a) In general.

Except as provided in subsection (b) of this section, whoever knowingly violates or conspires to or attempts to violate any provision of this Act [sections 2401 to 2420 of this Appendix] or any regulation, order, or license issued thereunder shall be fined not more than five times the value of the exports involved or $50,000, whichever is greater, or imprisoned not more than 5 years, or both.

(b) Willful violations.

(1) Whoever willfully violates or conspires to or attempts to violate any provision of this Act [sections 2401 to 2420 of this Appendix] or any regulation, order, or license issued thereunder, with knowledge that the exports involved will be used for the benefit of, or that the destination or intended destination of the goods or technology involved is, any controlled country or any country to which exports are controlled for foreign policy purposes—

(A) except in the case of an individual, shall be fined not more than five times the value of the exports involved or $1,000,000, whichever is greater; and

(B) in the case of an individual, shall be fined not more than $250,000, or imprisoned not more than 10 years, or both.

(2) Any person who is issued a validated license under this Act [sections 2401 to 2420 of this Appendix] for the export of any good or technology to a controlled country and who, with knowledge that such a good or technology is being used by such controlled country for military or intelligence gathering purposes contrary to the conditions under which the license was issued, willfully fails to report such use to the Secretary of Defense—

(A) except in the case of an individual, shall be fined not more than five times the value of the exports involved or $1,000,000, whichever is greater; and

(B) in the case of an individual, shall be fined not more than $250,000, or imprisoned not more than 5 years, or both.

(3) Any person who possesses any goods or technology—

(A) with the intent to export such goods or technology in violation of an export control imposed under section 5 or 6 of this Act [section 2404 or 2405 of this Appendix] or any regulation, order, or license issued with respect to such control, or

(B) knowing or having reason to believe that the goods or technology would be so exported,

shall, in the case of a violation of an export control imposed under section 5 [section 2404 of this Appendix] (or any regulation, order, or license issued with respect to such control), be subject to the penalties set forth in paragraph (1) of this subsection and shall, in the case of a violation of an export control imposed under section 6 [section 2405 of this Appendix] (or any regulation, order, or license issued with respect to such control), be subject to the penalties set forth in subsection (a).

(4) Any person who takes any action with the intent to evade the provisions of this Act [sections 2401 to 2420 of this Appendix] or any regulation, order, or license issued under this Act [sections 2401 to 2420 of this Appendix] shall be subject to the penalties set forth in subsection (a), except that in the case of an evasion of an export control imposed under section 5 or 6 of this Act (or any regulation, order, or license issued with respect to such control), such person shall be subject to the penalties set forth in paragraph (1) of this subsection.

* * *

(c) Civil penalties; administrative sanctions.

(1) The Secretary (and officers and employees of the Department of Commerce specifically designated by the Secretary) may impose a civil penalty not to exceed $10,000 for each violation of this Act [sections 2401 to 2420 of this Appendix] or any regulation, order, or license issued under this Act [sections 2401 to 2420 of this Appendix], either in addition to or in lieu of any other liability or penalty which may be imposed, except that the civil penalty for each such violation involving national security controls imposed under section 5 of this Act [section 2404 of this Appendix] or controls imposed on the export of defense articles and defense services under section 38 of the Arms Export Control Act [section 2778 of Title 22] may not exceed $100,000.

(2) The authority under this Act [sections 2401 to 2440] to suspend or revoke the authority of any United States person to export goods or technology may be used with respect to any violation of the regulations issued pursuant to section 8(a) of this Act [section 2407(a)].

* * *

(g) Forfeiture of property interest and proceeds.

(1) Any person who is convicted under subsection (a) or (b) of a violation of an export control imposed under section 5 of this Act [section 2404 of this Appendix] (or any regulation, order, or license issued with respect to such control) shall, in addition to any other penalty, forfeit to the United States—

(A) any of that person's interest in, security of, claim against, or property or contractual rights of any kind in the goods or tangible items that were the subject of the violation;

(B) any of that person's interest in, security of, claim against, or property or contractual rights of any kind in tangible property that was used in the export or attempt to export that was the subject of the violation; and

(C) any of that person's property constituting, or derived from, any proceeds obtained directly or indirectly as a result of the violation.

* * *

50 App. U.S.C. § 2415

Definitions

As used in this Act—

(1) the term "person" includes the singular and the plural and any individual, partnership, corporation, or other form of association, including any government or agency thereof;

(2) the term "United States person" means any United States resident or national (other than an individual resident outside the United States and employed by other than a United States person), any domestic concern (including any permanent domestic establishment of any foreign concern) and any foreign subsidiary or affiliate (including any permanent foreign establishment) of any domestic concern which is controlled in fact by such domestic concern, as determined under regulations of the President;

(3) the term "good" means any article, natural or manmade substance, material, supply or manufactured product, including inspection and test equipment, and excluding technical data;

(4) the term "technology" means the information and know-how (whether in tangible form, such as models, prototypes, drawings, sketches, diagrams, blueprints, or manuals, or in intangible form, such as training or technical services) that can be used to design, produce, manufacture, utilize, or reconstruct goods, including computer software and technical data, but not the goods themselves;

(5) the term "export" means—

(A) an actual shipment, transfer, or transmission of goods or technology out of the United States;

(B) a transfer of goods or technology in the United States to an embassy or affiliate of a controlled country; or

(C) a transfer to any person of goods or technology either within the United States or outside of the United States with the knowledge or intent that the goods or technology will be shipped, transferred, or transmitted to an unauthorized recipient;

(6) the term "controlled country" means a controlled country under section 5(b)(1) of this Act;

(7) the term "United States" means the States of the United States, the District of Columbia, and any commonwealth, territory, dependency, or possession of the United States, and includes the Outer Continental Shelf, as defined in section 2(a) of the Outer Continental Shelf Lands Act (43 U.S.C. § 1331(a)); and

(8) the term "Secretary" means the Secretary of Commerce.

DOCUMENT 40

EXPORT ADMINISTRATION REGULATIONS (15 C.F.R.)

■ ■ ■

§ 730.2 Statutory Authority.

The EAR have been designed primarily to implement the Export Administration Act of 1979, as amended, 50 U.S.C. app. 2401–2420 (EAA). There are numerous other legal authorities underlying the EAR. These are listed in the *Federal Register* documents promulgating the EAR and at the beginning of each part of the EAR in the Code of Federal Regulations (CFR). From time to time, the President has exercised authority under the International Emergency Economic Powers Act with respect to the EAR (50 U.S.C. 1701–1706 (IEEPA)). The EAA is not permanent legislation, and when it has lapsed, Presidential executive orders under IEEPA have directed and authorized the continuation in force of the EAR.

§ 730.3 Dual use exports.

The convenient term "dual use" is sometimes used to distinguish the types of items covered by the EAR from those that are covered by the regulations of certain other U.S. government departments and agencies with export licensing responsibilities. In general, the term dual use serves to distinguish EAR-controlled items that can be used both in military and other strategic uses (e.g., nuclear) and commercial applications. In general, the term dual use serves to distinguish EAR-controlled items that can be used both in military and other strategic uses and in civil applications from those that are weapons and military related use or design and subject to the controls of the Department of State or subject to the nuclear related controls of the Department of Energy or the Nuclear Regulatory Commission. Note, however, that although the short-hand term dual use may be employed to refer to the entire scope of the EAR, the EAR also apply to some items that have solely civil uses.

§ 730.4 Other Control Agencies and Departments.

In addition to the departments and agencies mentioned in § 730.3 of this part, other departments and agencies have jurisdiction over certain narrower classes of exports and reexports. These include the Department of Treasury's Office of Foreign Assets Control (OFAC), which administers controls against certain countries that are the object of sanctions affecting not only exports and reexports, but also imports and financial dealings. For your convenience, Supplement No. 3 to part 730 identifies other departments and agencies with regulatory jurisdiction over certain types of exports and reexports. This is not a comprehensive list, and the brief descriptions are only generally indicative of the types of controls administered and/or enforced by each agency.

§ 730.5 Coverage of more than exports.

The core of the export control provisions of the EAR concerns exports from the United States. You will find, however, that some provisions give broad meaning to the term "export," apply to transactions outside of the United States, or apply to activities other than exports.

(a) Reexports. Commodities, software, and technology that have been exported from the United States are generally subject to the EAR with respect to reexport. Many such reexports, however, may go to many destinations without a license or will qualify for an exception from licensing requirements.

(b) Foreign products. In some cases, authorization to export technology from the United States will be subject to assurances that items produced abroad that are the direct product of that technology will not be exported to certain destinations without authorization from BIS.

(c) Scope of "exports". Certain actions that you might not regard as an "export" in other contexts do constitute an export subject to the EAR. The release of technology to a foreign national in the United States through such means as demonstration or oral briefing is deemed an export. Other examples of exports under the EAR include the return of foreign equipment to its country of origin after repair in the United States, shipments from a U.S. foreign trade zone, and the electronic transmission of non-public data that will be received abroad.

(d) U.S. person activities. To counter the proliferation of weapons of mass destruction, the EAR restrict the involvement of "United States persons" anywhere in the world in exports of foreign-origin items, or in providing services or support, that may contribute to such proliferation.

PART 732—STEPS FOR USING THE EAR

§ 732.1 Steps overview.

(a)(1) *Introduction*. . . . A flow chart describing these steps is contained in Supplement No. 1 to part 732. By cross-references to the relevant provisions of the EAR, this part describes the suggested steps for you to determine applicability of the following:

(i) The scope of the EAR (part 734 of the EAR);

(ii) Each of the general prohibitions (part 736 of the EAR);

(iii) The License Exceptions (part 740 of the EAR); and

(iv) Other requirements such as clearing your export with the U.S. Customs Service, keeping records, and completing and documenting license applications.

(2) These steps describe the organization of the EAR, the relationship among the provisions of the EAR, and the appropriate order for you to consider the various provisions of the EAR.

(b) *Facts about your transaction.* The following five types of facts determine your obligations under the EAR and will be of help to you in reviewing these steps:

(1) *What is it?* What an item is, for export control purposes, depends on its *classification*, which is its place on the Commerce Control List (see part 774 of the EAR).

(2) *Where is it going?* The *country of ultimate destination* for an export or reexport also determines licensing requirements (see parts and 738 and 774 of the EAR).

(3) *Who will receive it?* The *ultimate end-user* of your item cannot be a bad end-user. . . .

(4) *What will they do with it?* The *ultimate end-use* of your item cannot be a bad end-use. . . .

(5) *What else do they do?* Conduct such as contracting, financing, and freight forwarding in support of a proliferation project (as described in § 744.6 of the EAR) may prevent you from dealing with someone.

(c) *Are your items and activities subject to the EAR?* You should first determine whether your commodity, software, or technology is subject to the EAR (see part 734 of the EAR concerning scope), and Steps 1 through 6 help you do that. For exports from the United States, only Steps 1 and 2 are relevant. If you already know that your item or activity is subject to the EAR, you should go on to consider the ten general prohibitions in part 736 of the EAR. If your item or activity is not subject to the EAR, you have no obligations under the EAR and may skip the remaining steps.

(d) *Does your item or activity require a license under one or more of the ten general prohibitions?*

(1) Brief summary of the ten general prohibitions. The general prohibitions are found in part 736 of the EAR and referred to in these steps. They consist, very briefly, of the following:

(i) General Prohibition One (Exports and Reexports): Export and reexport of controlled items to listed countries.

(ii) General Prohibition Two (Parts and Components Reexports): Reexport and export from abroad of foreign-made items incorporating more than a de minimis amount of controlled U.S. content.

(iii) General Prohibition Three (Foreign-produced Direct Product Reexports): Reexport and export from abroad of the foreign-produced direct product of U.S. technology and software.

(iv) General Prohibition Four (Denial Orders): Engaging in actions prohibited by a denial order.

(v) General Prohibition Five (End-Use End-User): Export or reexport to prohibited end-user or end-users.

(vi) General Prohibition Six (Embargo): Export or reexport to embargoed destinations.

(vii) General Prohibition Seven (U.S. Person Proliferation Activity): Support of proliferation activities.

(viii) General Prohibition Eight (In-Transit): In-transit shipments and items to be unladen from vessels and aircraft.

(ix) General Prohibition Nine (Orders, Terms and Conditions): Violation of any orders, terms, or conditions.

(x) General Prohibition Ten (Knowledge Violation to Occur): Proceeding with transactions with knowledge that a violation has occurred or is about to occur.

(2) *Controls on items on the Commerce Control List (CCL).* If your item or activity is subject to the EAR, you should determine whether any one or more of the ten general prohibitions require a license for your export, reexport, or activity. Steps 7 through 11 refer to classification of your item on the Commerce Control List (CCL) (part 774 of the EAR) and how to use the Country Chart (Supplement No. 1 to part 738 of the EAR) to determine whether a license is required based upon the classification of your item. . . .

(3) *Controls on activities.* Steps 12 through 18 refer to General Prohibitions Four through Ten. Those general prohibitions apply to all items subject to the EAR, not merely those items listed on the CCL in part 774 of the EAR. . . .

(4) *General prohibitions.* If none of the ten general prohibitions applies, you should skip the steps concerning License Exceptions and for exports from the United States, review Steps 27 through 29 concerning Shipper's Export Declarations to be filed with the U.S. Customs Service, Destination Control Statements for export control documents, and recordkeeping requirements.

(e) *Is a License Exception available to overcome the license requirement?* If you decide by reviewing the CCL in combination with the Country Chart that a license is required for your destination, you should determine whether a License Exception will except you from that requirement. Steps 20 through 24 help you determine whether a License

Exception is available. . . . If a License Exception is not available, go on to Steps 25 through 29.

§ 732.2 Steps regarding scope of the EAR.

Steps 1 through 6 are designed to aid you in determining the scope of the EAR. A flow chart describing these steps is contained in Supplement No. 2 to part 732.

(a) *Step 1: Items subject to the exclusive jurisdiction of another Federal agency.* This step is relevant for both exports and reexports. Determine whether your item is subject to the exclusive jurisdiction of another Federal Agency as provided in § 734.3 of the EAR.

* * *

(2) If your item is not subject to the exclusive jurisdiction of another federal agency, then proceed to Step 2 in paragraph (b) of this section.

(b) *Step 2: Publicly available technology and software.* This step is relevant for both exports and reexports. Determine if your technology or software is publicly available as defined and explained at part 734 of the EAR. . .

(1) If your technology or software is publicly available, and therefore outside the scope of the EAR, you may proceed with the export or reexport if you are not a U.S. person subject to General Prohibition Seven. . . . If you are a U.S. person and General Prohibition Seven concerning proliferation activity of U.S. persons does not apply, then you may proceed with the export or reexport of your publicly available technology or software. Note that all U.S. persons are subject to the provisions of General Prohibition Seven.

(2) If your technology or software is not publicly available and you are exporting from the United States, skip to Step 7 in § 732.3(b) of this part concerning the general prohibitions.

(3) If you are exporting items from a foreign country, you should then proceed Step 3 in paragraph (c) of this section and the other steps concerning the scope of the EAR.

* * *

(d) *Step 4: Foreign-made items incorporating controlled U.S. origin items.* This step is appropriate only for items that are made outside the United States and not currently in the United States. Special requirements and restrictions apply to items that incorporate U.S. origin encryption items (see § 734.4(a)(2)(b) and (g) of the EAR).

(1) Determining whether your foreign made item is subject to the EAR. Using the guidance provided Supplement No. 2 to part 734 of the EAR,

determine whether controlled U.S. origin items are incorporated into the foreign made item and are above the level set forth in § 734.4 of the EAR.

(2) If no U.S. parts, components or materials are incorporated or if the incorporated U.S. parts, components, and materials are equal or below the de minimis level described in § 734.4 of the EAR, then the foreign-made item is not subject to the EAR by reason of the de minimis rules, and you should go on to consider Step 6 regarding the foreign-produced direct product rule.

(3) If the foreign made item incorporates more than the de minimis level of U.S. origin items, then that item is subject to the EAR and you should go on to Step 7 at § 732.2 of this part and consider the steps regarding all other general prohibitions, license exceptions, and other requirements to determine the applicability of these provisions to the foreign made item.

* * *

(f) Step 6: Foreign made items produced with certain U.S. technology for export to specified destinations. This step is appropriate for foreign made items in foreign countries.

(1) If your foreign-produced item is described in an entry on the CCL and the Country Chart requires a license to your export or reexport destination for national security reasons, you should determine whether your item is subject to General Prohibition Three (Foreign-Produced Direct Product Reexports) (§ 736.2(b)(3) of the EAR). . . .

(2) License Exceptions. Each License Exception described in part 740 of the EAR overcomes this General Prohibition Three if all terms and conditions of a given License Exception are met by the exporter or reexporter.

(3) Subject to the EAR. If your item is captured by the foreign-produced direct product control at General Prohibition Three, then your export from abroad is subject to the EAR. You should next consider the steps regarding all other general prohibitions, License Exceptions, and other requirements. If your item is not captured by General Prohibition Three, then your export from abroad is not subject to the EAR. You have completed the steps necessary to determine whether your transaction is subject to the EAR, and you may skip the remaining steps. Note that in summary, items in foreign countries are subject to the EAR when they are:

(i) U.S.-origin commodities, software and technology unless controlled for export exclusively by another Federal agency or unless publicly available;

(ii) Foreign-origin commodities, software, and technology that are within the scope of General Prohibition Two (Parts and Components

Reexports), or General Prohibition Three (Foreign-Produced Direct Product Reexports). (However, such foreign-made items are also outside the scope of the EAR if they are controlled for export exclusively by another Federal Agency or publicly available.)

§ 732.3 Steps regarding the ten general prohibitions.

(a) *Introduction.* If your item or activity is subject to the scope of the EAR, you should then consider each of the ten general prohibitions listed in part 736 of the EAR. General Prohibitions One (Exports and Reexports), Two (Parts and Components Reexports), and Three (Foreign-Produced Direct Product Reexports) (§ 736.2(b)(1), (2), and (3) of the EAR) are product controls that are shaped and limited by parameters specified on the CCL and Country Chart. General Prohibitions Four through Ten are prohibitions on certain activities that are not allowed without authorization from BISBIS, and these prohibitions apply to all items subject to the EAR unless otherwise specified (§ 736.2(b)(4) through (10) of the EAR).

(b) *Step 7: Classification.*

(1) You should classify your items in the relevant entry on the CCL, and you may do so on your own without the assistance of BISS. You are responsible for doing so correctly, and your failure to correctly classify your items does not relieve you of the obligation to obtain a license when one is required by the EAR.

(2) You have a right to request the applicable classification of your item from BIS, and BIS has a duty to provide that classification to you. . . .

(3) For items subject to the EAR but not listed on the CCL, the proper classification is EAR99. This number is a "basket" for items not specified under any CCL entry and appears at the end of each Category on the CCL.

(c) *Step 8: Country of ultimate destination.* You should determine the country of ultimate destination. The country of destination determines the applicability of several general prohibitions, License Exceptions, and other requirements. . . .

(d) *Step 9: Reason for control and the Country Chart.*

(1) *Reason for control and column identifier within the Export Control Classification Number (ECCN).* Once you have determined that your item is controlled by a specific ECCN, you must use information contained in the "License Requirements" section of that ECCN in combination with the Country Chart to decide whether a license is required under General Prohibitions One, Two, or Three to a particular destination. The CCL and the Country Chart are taken together to define these license requirements. The applicable ECCN will indicate the reason or reasons for control for items within that ECCN. For example, ECCN 6A007 is controlled for national security, missile technology, and anti-terrorism reasons.

(2) *Reason for control within the Country Chart.* With each of the applicable Country Chart column identifiers noted in the correct ECCN, turn to the Country Chart. Locate the correct Country Chart column identifier on the horizontal axis, and determine whether an "X" is marked in the cell next to the destination in question. Consult § 738.4 of the EAR for comprehensive instructions on using the Country Chart and a detailed example.

(i) An "X" in the cell or cells for the relevant country and reason(s) for control column indicates that a license is required for General Prohibitions One (Exports and Reexports in the Form Received), Two (Parts and Components Reexports), and Three (Foreign-Produced Direct Product Reexports). . . .

(ii) If one or more cells have an "X" in the relevant column, a license is required unless you qualify for a License Exception described in part 740 of the EAR. If a cell does not contain an "X" for your destination in one or more relevant columns, a license is not required under the CCL and the Country Chart.

(iii) Additional controls may apply to your export. You must go on to steps 12 through 18 described in paragraphs (g) to (m) of this section to determine whether additional limits described in General Prohibition Two (Parts and Components Reexports) and General Prohibition Three (Foreign-Produced Direct Product Reexports) apply to your proposed transaction. If you are exporting an item from the United States, you should skip Step 10 and Step 11. Proceed directly to Step 12 in paragraph (g) of this section.

* * *

(4) Destinations subject to embargo provisions. The Country Chart does not apply to Cuba, Iran, and North Korea; and for those countries you should review the embargo provisions at part 746 of the EAR and may skip this step concerning the Country Chart. For Iraq and Rwanda, the Country Chart provides for certain license requirements, and part 746 of the EAR provides additional requirements.

(5) Items subject to the EAR but not on the CCL. Items subject to the EAR that are not on the CCL are properly classified EAR99. For such items, you may skip this step and proceed directly with Step 12 in paragraph (g) of this section.

(e) *Step 10: Foreign-made items incorporating U.S.-origin items and the de minimis rule.*

(1) De minimis rules. If your foreign made item abroad is a foreign made commodity that incorporates U.S. origin commodities, a foreign made commodity that is "bundled" with controlled U.S. origin software, foreign made software that is commingled with controlled U.S. origin software, or

foreign made technology that is commingled with controlled U.S. origin technology, then it is subject to the EAR if the U.S. origin controlled content exceeds the de minimis levels described in § 734.4 of the EAR.

* * *

(g) *Step 12: Persons denied export privileges.*

(1) Determine whether your transferee, ultimate end user, any intermediate consignee, or any other party to a transaction is a person denied export privileges. . . . It is a violation of the EAR to engage in any activity that violates the terms or conditions of a denial order. . .

(2) There are no License Exceptions to General Prohibition Four (Denial Orders). The prohibition concerning persons denied export privileges may be overcome only by a specific authorization from BIS, something that is rarely granted.

(h) *Step 13: Prohibited end-uses and end-users*

(1) Review the end-uses and end-users prohibited under General Prohibition Five (End-Use End-User) . . . described in part 744 of the EAR. Part 744 of the EAR contains all the end-use and end-user license requirements, and those are in addition to the license requirements under General Prohibitions One (Exports and Reexports), Two (Parts and Components Reexports), and Three (Foreign-produced Direct Product Reexports). Unless otherwise indicated, the license requirements of General Prohibition Five (End-Use End-User) described in part 744 of the EAR apply to all items subject to the EAR, i.e. both items on the CCL and within EAR99. Moreover, the requirements of General Prohibition Five (End-Use and End-User) are in addition to various end-use and end-user limitations placed on certain License Exceptions.

(2) Under License Exception TSU (§ 740.13 of the EAR), operation technology and software, sales technology, and software updates overcome General Prohibition Five (End-Use and End-User) (§ 736.2(b)(5) of the EAR) if all terms and conditions of these provisions are met by the exporter or reexporter.

(i) *Step 14: Embargoed countries and special destinations*

If your destination for any item is Cuba, Iran, Iraq, North Korea, or Rwanda you must consider the requirements of parts 742 and 746 of the EAR. Unless otherwise indicated, General Prohibition Six (Embargo) applies to all items subject to the EAR, i.e. both items on the CCL and within EAR99. You may not make an export or reexport contrary to the provisions of part 746 of the EAR without a license unless:

(1) You are exporting or reexporting only publicly available technology or software or other items outside the scope of the EAR, or

(2) You qualify for a License Exception referenced in part 746 of the EAR concerning embargoed destinations. You may not use a License Exception described in part 740 of the EAR to overcome General Prohibition Six (Embargo) (§ 736.2(b)(6) of the EAR) unless it is specifically authorized in part 746 of the EAR. Note that part 754 of the EAR concerning short supply controls is self-contained and is the only location in the EAR for both the prohibitions and exceptions applicable to short supply controls.

(j) *Step 15: Proliferation activity of U.S. persons unrelated to exports and reexports*

(1) Review the scope of activity prohibited by General Prohibition Seven (U.S. Person Proliferation Activity) (§ 736.2(b)(7) of the EAR) as that activity is described in § 744.6 of the EAR. Keep in mind that such activity is not limited to exports and reexports and is not limited to items subject to General Prohibition One (Exports and Reexports), Two (Parts and Components Reexports), and Three (Foreign-Produced Direct Product Reexports). Moreover, such activity extends to services and dealing in wholly foreign-origin items in support of the specified proliferation activity and is not limited to items listed on the CCL or included in EAR99.

(2) Review the definition of U.S. Person in part 744 of the EAR.

* * *

(m) *Step 18: Review the "Know Your Customer" Guidance and General Prohibition Ten (Knowledge Violation to Occur)*

License requirements under the EAR are determined solely by the classification, end-use, end-user, ultimate destination, and conduct of U.S. persons. Supplement No. 1 to part 732 of the EAR is intended to provide helpful guidance regarding the process for the evaluation of information about customers, end-uses, and end-users. General Prohibition Ten (Knowledge Violation to Occur) prohibits anyone from proceeding with a transaction with knowledge that a violation of the EAR has occurred or is about to occur. It also prohibits related shipping, financing, and other services. General Prohibition Ten applies to all items subject to the EAR, i.e. both items on the CCL and within EAR99.

(n) *Step 19: Complete the review of the general prohibitions.* After completion of Steps described in this section and review of all ten general prohibitions in part 736 of the EAR, including cross-referenced regulations in the EAR, you will know which, if any, of the ten general prohibitions of the EAR apply to you and your contemplated transaction or activity.

(1) If none of the ten general prohibitions is applicable to your export from the United States, no license from BIS is required, you do not need to qualify for a License Exception under part 740 of the EAR. You should skip the Steps in § 732.4 of this part regarding License Exceptions and proceed

directly to the Steps in § 732.5 of this part regarding recordkeeping, clearing the U.S. Customs Service with the appropriate Shipper's Export Declaration, and using the required Destination Control Statement.

(2) If none of the ten general prohibitions is applicable to your reexport or export from abroad, no license is required and you should skip all remaining Steps.

(3) If one or more of the ten general prohibitions are applicable, continue with the remaining steps.

§ 732.4 Steps regarding License Exceptions.

(a) *Introduction to Steps for License Exceptions.* If your export or reexport is subject to the EAR and is subject to General Prohibitions One (Exports and Reexports), Two (Parts and Components Reexports), or Three (Foreign-Produced Direct Product Reexports), consider the steps listed in paragraph (b) of this section. . . .

(b) *Steps for License Exceptions.*

(1) *Step 20: Applicability of General Prohibitions.* Determine whether any one or more of the general prohibitions described in § 736.2(b) of the EAR apply to your export or reexport. . . .

(2) *Step 21: Applicability of restrictions on all License Exceptions.* Determine whether any one or more of the restrictions in § 740.2 of the EAR applies to your export or reexport. If any one or more of these restrictions apply, there are no License Exceptions available to you, and you must either obtain a license or refrain from the export or reexport.

(3) *Step 22: Terms and conditions of the License Exceptions.*

(i) If none of the restrictions in § 740.2 of the EAR applies, then review each of the License Exceptions to determine whether any one of them authorizes your export or reexport. Eligibility for License Exceptions is based on the item, the country of ultimate destination, the end-use, and the end-user, along with any special conditions imposed within a specific License Exception.

* * *

(4) *Step 23: Scope of License Exceptions.* Some License Exceptions are limited by country or by type of item.

(i) Countries are arranged in country groups for ease of reference. For a listing of country groups, please refer to Supplement No. 1 to part 740 of the EAR. . . .

(5) *Step 24: Compliance with all terms and conditions.* If a License Exception is available, you may proceed with your export or reexport. However, you must meet all the terms and conditions required by the License Exception that you determined authorized your export or reexport.

You must also consult part 758 and 762 of the EAR to determine your recordkeeping and documentation requirements.

(6) *Step 25: License requirements.* If no License Exception is available, then you must either obtain a license before proceeding with your export or reexport or you must refrain from the proposed export or reexport.

(7) *Step 26: License applications.* If you are going to file a license application with BIS, you should first review the requirements at part 748 of the EAR. Exporters, reexporters, and exporters from abroad should review the instructions concerning applications and required support documents prior to submitting an application for a license.

§ 732.5 Steps regarding Shipper's Export Declaration, Destination Control Statements, record keeping, license applications, and other requirements.

(a) *Step 27: Shipper's Export Declaration (SED) or Automated Export System (AES) record*

Exporters or agents authorized to complete the Shipper's Export Declaration (SED), or to file SED information electronically using the Automated Export System (AES), should review § 758.1 of the EAR to determine when an SED is required and what export control information should be entered on the SED or AES record. . . .

(1) Entering license authority. You must enter the correct license authority for your export on the SED or AES record (License number, License Exception symbol, or No License Required designator "NLR") as appropriate. . . .

(i) License number and expiration date. If you are exporting under the authority of a license, you must enter the license number on the SED or AES record. The expiration date must be entered on paper versions of the SED only.

(ii) License Exception. If you are exporting under the authority of a License Exception, you must enter the correct License Exception symbol (*e.g.*, LVS, GBS, CIV) on the SED or AES record. . . .

(iii) NLR. If you are exporting items for which no license is required, you must enter the designator NLR. You should use the NLR designator in two circumstances: first, when the items to be exported are subject to the EAR but not listed on the Commerce Control List (CCL) (*i.e.*, items that are classified as EAR99), and second, when the items to be exported are listed on the CCL but do not require a license. Use of the NLR designator is also a representation that no license is required under any of the General Prohibitions set forth in part 736 of the EAR.

* * *

(c) *Step 29: Recordkeeping*

Records of transactions subject to the EAR must be maintained for five years in accordance with the recordkeeping provisions of part 762 of the EAR.

§ 732.6 Steps For Other Requirements

Sections 732.1 through 732.4 of this part are useful in determining the license requirements that apply to you. Other portions of the EAR impose other obligations and requirements. Some of them are:

(a) Requirements relating to the use of a license in § 758.4 of the EAR.

(b) Obligations of carriers, forwarders, exporters and others to take specific steps and prepare and deliver certain documents to assure that items subject to the EAR are delivered to the destination to which they are licensed or authorized by a License Exception or some other provision of the regulations in § 758.1 through § 758.6 of the EAR.

(c) Duty of carriers to return or unload shipments at the direction of U.S. Government officials (see § 758.8 of the EAR).

(d) Specific obligations imposed on parties to Special Comprehensive licenses in part 752 of the EAR.

(e) Recordkeeping requirements imposed in part 762 of the EAR.

(f) Requirements of part 764 of the EAR to disclose facts that may come to your attention after you file a license application or make other statements to the government concerning a transaction or proposed transaction that is subject to the EAR.

(g) Certain obligations imposed by part 760 of the EAR on parties who receive requests to take actions related to foreign boycotts and prohibits certain actions relating to those boycotts.

* * *

Supplement No. 1 to part 732

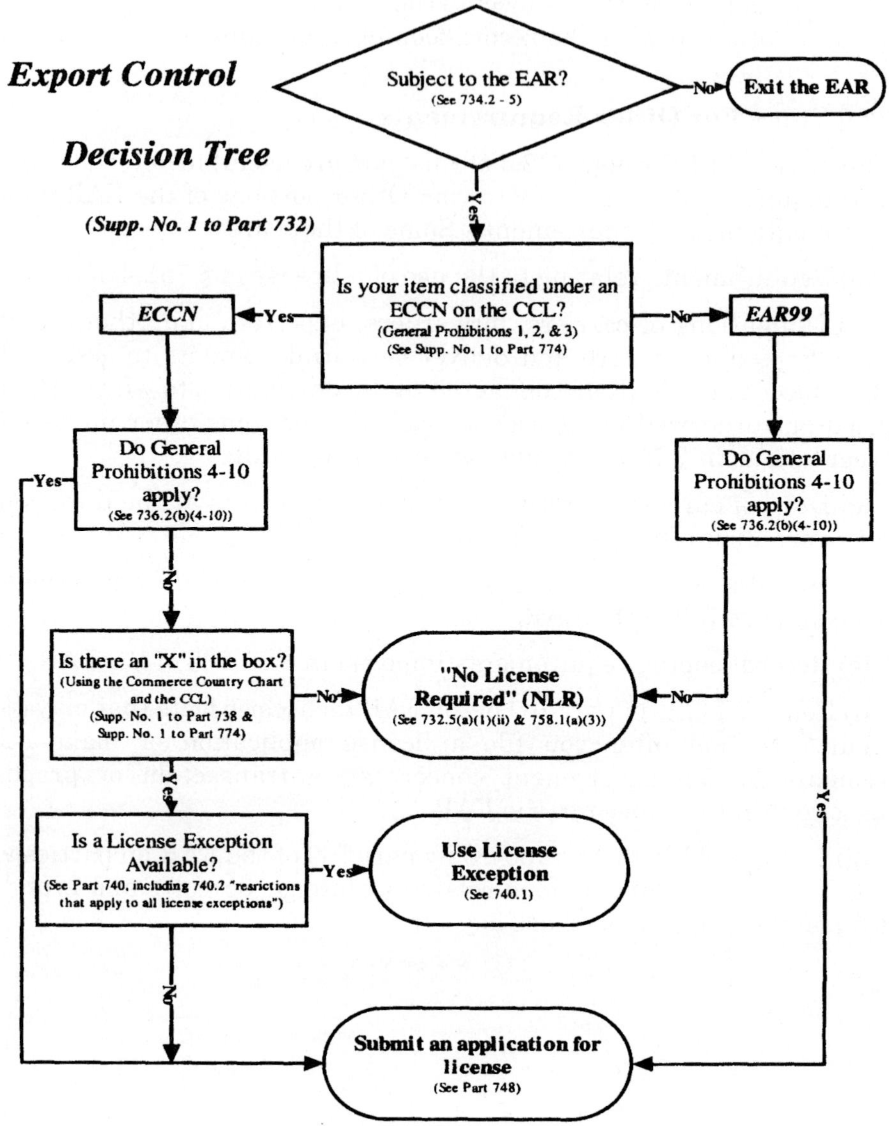

SUPPLEMENT NO. 2 TO PART 732

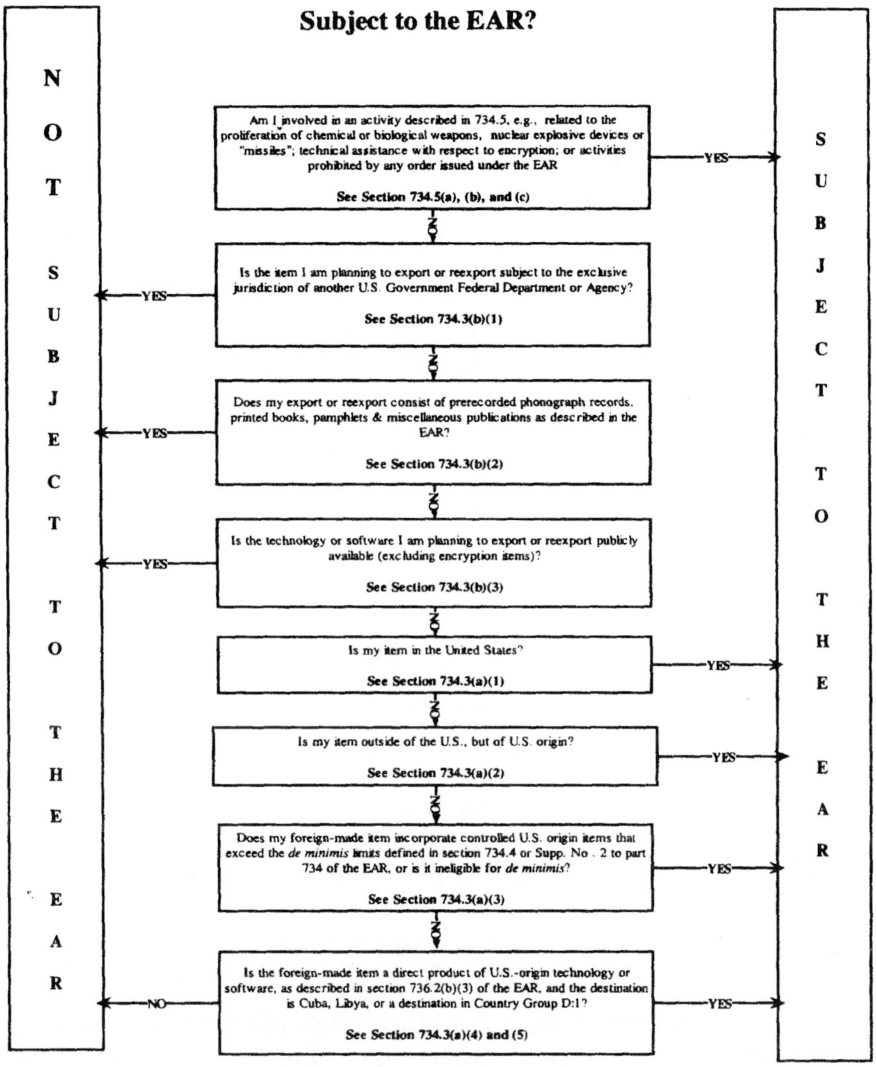

Supplement No. 3 to Part 732

BIS "KNOW YOUR CUSTOMER" GUIDANCE

Various requirements of the EAR are dependent upon a person's knowledge of the end-use, end-user, ultimate destination, or other facts relating to a transaction or activity. These provisions include the nonproliferation-related "catch-all" sections and the prohibition against proceeding with a transaction with knowledge that a violation of the EAR has occurred or is about to occur.

(a) BIS provides the following guidance on how individuals and firms should act under this knowledge standard. This guidance does not change or interpret the EAR.

(1) *Decide whether there are "red flags".* Take into account any abnormal circumstances in a transaction that indicate that the export may be destined for an inappropriate end-use, end-user, or destination. Such circumstances are referred to as "red flags". Included among examples of red flags are orders for items that are inconsistent with the needs of the purchaser, a customer declining installation and testing when included in the sales price or when normally requested, or requests for equipment configurations that are incompatible with the stated destination (e.g., 120 volts in a country with 220 volts). Commerce has developed lists of such red flags that are not all-inclusive but are intended to illustrate the types of circumstances that should cause reasonable suspicion that a transaction will violate the EAR.

(2) *If there are "red flags", inquire.* If there are no "red flags" in the information that comes to your firm, you should be able to proceed with a transaction in reliance on information you have received. That is, absent "red flags" (or an express requirement in the EAR), there is no affirmative duty upon exporters to inquire, verify, or otherwise "go behind" the customer's representations. However, when "red flags" are raised in information that comes to your firm, you have a duty to check out the suspicious circumstances and inquire about the end-use, end-user, or ultimate country of destination. The duty to check out "red flags" is not confined to the use of License Exceptions affected by the "know" or "reason to know" language in the EAR. Applicants for licenses are required by part 748 of the EAR to obtain documentary evidence concerning the transaction, and misrepresentation or concealment of material facts is prohibited, both in the licensing process and in all export control documents. You can rely upon representations from your customer and repeat them in the documents you file unless red flags oblige you to take verification steps.

(3) *Do not self-blind.* Do not cut off the flow of information that comes to your firm in the normal course of business. For example, do not instruct the sales force to tell potential customers to refrain from discussing the actual end-use, end-user, and ultimate country of destination for the product your firm is seeking to sell. Do not put on blinders that prevent the learning of relevant information. An affirmative policy of steps to avoid "bad" information would not insulate a company from liability, and it would usually be considered an aggravating factor in an enforcement proceeding.

(4) *Employees need to know how to handle "red flags".* Knowledge possessed by an employee of a company can be imputed to a firm so as to make it liable for a violation. This makes it important for firms to establish clear policies and effective compliance procedures to ensure that such

knowledge about transactions can be evaluated by responsible senior officials. Failure to do so could be regarded as a form of self-blinding.

(5) *Reevaluate all the information after the inquiry.* The purpose of this inquiry and reevaluation is to determine whether the "red flags" can be explained or justified. If they can, you may proceed with the transaction. If the "red flags" cannot be explained or justified and you proceed, you run the risk of having had "knowledge" that would make your action a violation of the EAR.

(6) *Refrain from the transaction or advise BIS and wait.* If you continue to have reasons for concern after your inquiry, then you should either refrain from the transaction or submit all the relevant information to BIS in the form of an application for a license or in such other form as BIS may specify.

(b) Industry has an important role to play in preventing exports and reexports contrary to the national security and foreign policy interests of the United States. BIS will continue to work in partnership with industry to make this front line of defense effective, while minimizing the regulatory burden on exporters. . .

RED FLAGS

Possible indicators that an unlawful diversion might be planned by your customer include the following:

1.— The customer or purchasing agent is reluctant to offer information about the end-use of a product.

2.— The product's capabilities do not fit the buyer's line of business; for example, a small bakery places an order for several sophisticated lasers.

3.— The product ordered is incompatible with the technical level of the country to which the product is being shipped. For example, semiconductor manufacturing equipment would be of little use in a country without an electronics industry.

4.— The customer has little or no business background.

5.— The customer is willing to pay cash for a very expensive item when the terms of the sale call for financing.

6.— The customer is unfamiliar with the product's performance characteristics but still wants the product.

7.— Routine installation, training or maintenance services are declined by the customer.

8.— Delivery dates are vague, or deliveries are planned for out-of-the-way destinations.

9.— A freight forwarding firm is listed as the product's final destination.

10.— The shipping route is abnormal for the product and destination.

11.— Packaging is inconsistent with the stated method of shipment or destination.

12.— When questioned, the buyer is evasive or unclear about whether the purchased product is for domestic use, export or reexport.

PART 734—SCOPE OF THE EXPORT ADMINISTRATION REGULATIONS

§ 734.2 Important EAR terms and principles

(a) Subject to the EAR—Definition

(1) "Subject to the EAR" is a term used in the EAR to describe those items and activities over which BIS exercises regulatory jurisdiction under the EAR. Conversely, items and activities that are *not* subject to the EAR are outside the regulatory jurisdiction of the EAR and are not affected by these regulations. . . . Publicly available technology and software not subject to the EAR are described in § 734.7 through § 734.11 and Supplement No. 1 to this part.

(2) Items and activities subject to the EAR may also be controlled under export-related programs administered by other agencies. Items and activities subject to the EAR are not necessarily exempted from the control programs of other agencies. . . . [I]n some instances you may have to comply with more than one regulatory program.

(3) The term "subject to the EAR" should not be confused with licensing or other requirements imposed in other parts of the EAR. Just because an item or activity is subject to the EAR does not mean that a license or other requirement automatically applies. A license or other requirement applies only in those cases where other parts of the EAR impose a licensing or other requirement on such items or activities.

(b) Export and reexport

(1) Definition of export. "Export" means an actual shipment or transmission of items subject to the EAR out of the United States, or release of technology or software subject to the EAR to a foreign national in the United States, as described in paragraph (b)(2)(ii) of this section. . . .

(2) Export of technology or software. . . . "Export" of technology or software, excluding encryption software subject to "EI" controls, includes:

(i) Any release of technology or software subject to the EAR in a foreign country; or

(ii) Any release of technology or source code subject to the EAR to a foreign national. Such release is deemed to be an export to the home country or countries of the foreign national. This deemed export rule does not apply to persons lawfully admitted for permanent residence in the United States and does not apply to persons who are protected individuals under the Immigration and Naturalization Act (8 U.S.C. 1324b(a)(3)). Note that the release of any item to any party with knowledge a violation is about to occur is prohibited by § 736.2(b)(10) of the EAR.

(3) Definition of "release" of technology or software. Technology or software is "released" for export through:

(i) Visual inspection by foreign nationals of U.S.-origin equipment and facilities;

(ii) Oral exchanges of information in the United States or abroad; or

(iii) The application to situations abroad of personal knowledge or technical experience acquired in the United States.

(4) Definition of reexport. "Reexport" means an actual shipment or transmission of items subject to the EAR from one foreign country to another foreign country; or release of technology or software subject to the EAR to a foreign national outside the United States, as described in paragraph (b)(5) of this section.

(5) Reexport of technology or software. Any release of technology or source code subject to the EAR to a foreign national of another country is a deemed reexport to the home country or countries of the foreign national. However, this deemed reexport definition does not apply to persons lawfully admitted for permanent residence. The term "release" is defined in paragraph (b)(3) of this section. Note that the release of any item to any party with knowledge or reason to know a violation is about to occur is prohibited by § 736.2(b)(10) of the EAR.

§ 734.3 Items subject to the EAR.

(a) Except for items excluded in paragraph (b) of this section, the following items are subject to the EAR:

(1) All items in the United States, including in a U.S. Foreign Trade Zone or moving intransit through the United States from one foreign country to another;

(2) All U.S. origin items wherever located;

(3) Foreign made commodities that incorporate controlled U.S. origin commodities, foreign made commodities that are 'bundled' with controlled U.S. origin software, foreign made software that is commingled with controlled U.S. origin software, and foreign made technology that is commingled with controlled U.S. origin technology:

(i) In any quantity, as described in § 734.4(a) of this part; or

(ii) In quantities exceeding *de minimis* levels as described in § 734.4(c) or 734.4(d) of this part;

(4) Certain foreign-made direct products of U.S. origin technology or software, as described in § 736.2(b)(3) of the EAR. The term "direct product"

means the immediate product (including processes and services) produced directly by the use of technology or software; and

(5) Certain commodities produced by any plant or major component of a plant located outside the United States that is a direct product of U.S.-origin technology or software, as described in § 736.2(b)(3) of the EAR.

(b) The following items are not subject to the EAR:

(1) Items that are exclusively controlled for export or reexport by the following departments and agencies of the U.S. Government which regulate exports or reexports for national security or foreign policy purposes:

(i) *Department of State.* The International Traffic in Arms Regulations (22 CFR part 121) administered by the Office of Defense Trade Controls relate to defense articles and defense services on the U.S. Munitions List. Section 38 of the Arms Export Control Act (22 U.S.C. 2778).

(ii) *Treasury Department, Office of Foreign Assets Control (OFAC).* Regulations administered by OFAC implement broad controls and embargo transactions with certain foreign countries.

* * *

(3) Publicly available technology and software, except software controlled for EI reasons under ECCN 5D002 on the Commerce Control List List and mass market encryption software with symmetric key length exceeding 64-bits controlled under ECCN 5D992.

* * *

(4) Foreign made items that have less than the *de minimis* percentage of controlled U.S. content based on the principles described in § 734.4 of this part.

(c) "Items subject to the EAR" consist of the items listed on the Commerce Control List (CCL) in part 774 of the EAR and all other items which meet the definition of that term. For ease of reference and classification purposes, items subject to the EAR which are not listed on the CCL are designated as "EAR99."

§ 734.4 De Minimis U.S. Content

(c) 10% De Minimis Rule. . . the following reexports are note subject to the EAR when made to any country in the world. . .

(1) Reexports of a foreign made commodity incorporated controlled U.S. origin commodities or 'bundled' with U.S. origin software valued at 10% or less of the total value of the foreign made commodity . . .

(2) Reexports of foreign made software incorporating controlled U.S. origin software valued at 10% or less of the total value of the foreign made software; or

(3) Reexports of foreign technology comingled with controlled U.S. origin technology valued at 10% or less of the total value of the foreign technology . . .

(d) 25% De Minimis Rule. . . the following reexports are note subject to the EAR when made to countries other than those listed in Country Group E:1 of Supplement No. 1 to part 740 of the EAR . . .

> (1) Reexports of a foreign made commodity incorporated controlled U.S. origin commodities or 'bundled' with U.S. origin software valued at 25% or less of the total value of the foreign made commodity . . .
>
> (2) Reexports of foreign made software incorporating controlled U.S. origin software valued at 25% or less of the total value of the foreign made software; or
>
> (3) Reexports of foreign technology comingled with controlled U.S. origin technology valued at 25% or less of the total value of the foreign technology . . .

§ 734.7 Published information and software.

(a) Information is "published" when it becomes generally accessible to the interested public in any form, including:

(1) Publication in periodicals, books, print, electronic, or any other media available for general distribution to any member of the public or to a community of persons interested in the subject matter, such as those in a scientific or engineering discipline, either free or at a price that does not exceed the cost of reproduction and distribution . . . ;

(2) Ready availability at libraries open to the public or at university libraries . . . ;

(3) Patents and open (published) patent applications available at any patent office; and

(4) Release at an open conference, meeting, seminar, trade show, or other open gathering.

> (i) A conference or gathering is "open" if all technically qualified members of the public are eligible to attend and attendees are permitted to take notes or otherwise make a personal record (not necessarily a recording) of the proceedings and presentations.
>
> (ii) All technically qualified members of the public may be considered eligible to attend a conference or other gathering notwithstanding a registration fee reasonably related to cost and reflecting an intention that all interested and technically qualified

persons be able to attend, or a limitation on actual attendance, as long as attendees either are the first who have applied or are selected on the basis of relevant scientific or technical competence, experience, or responsibility. . . .

(iii) "Publication" includes submission of papers to domestic or foreign editors or reviewers of journals, or to organizers of open conferences or other open gatherings, with the understanding that the papers will be made publicly available if favorably received. . .

(b) Software and information is published when it is available for general distribution either for free or at a price that does not exceed the cost of reproduction and distribution . . .

(c) Notwithstanding paragraphs (a) and (b) of this section, note that encryption software controlled under ECCN 5D002 for "EI" reasons on the Commerce Control List and mass market encryption software with symmetric key length exceeding 64-bits controlled under ECCN 5D992 remain subject to the EAR . . .

§ 734.8 Information Resulting From Fundamental Research

(a) *Fundamental research.* Paragraphs (b) through (d) of this section and § 734.11 of this part provide specific rules that will be used to determine whether research in particular institutional contexts qualifies as "fundamental research". The intent behind these rules is to identify as "fundamental research" basic and applied research in science and engineering, where the resulting information is ordinarily published and shared broadly within the scientific community. Such research can be distinguished from proprietary research and from industrial development, design, production, and product utilization, the results of which ordinarily are restricted for proprietary reasons or specific national security reasons as defined in § 734.11(b) of this part. . . .

(b) *University based research*

(1) Research conducted by scientists, engineers, or students at a university normally will be considered fundamental research, as described in paragraphs (b)(2) through (6) of this section. ("University" means any accredited institution of higher education located in the United States.)

(2) Prepublication review by a sponsor of university research solely to insure that the publication would not inadvertently divulge proprietary information that the sponsor has furnished to the researchers does not change the status of the research as fundamental research. However, release of information from a corporate sponsor to university researchers where the research results are subject to prepublication review, is subject to the EAR. . . .

(3) Prepublication review by a sponsor of university research solely to ensure that publication would not compromise patent rights does not

change the status of fundamental research, so long as the review causes no more than a temporary delay in publication of the research results.

(4) The initial transfer of information from an industry sponsor to university researchers is subject to the EAR where the parties have agreed that the sponsor may withhold from publication some or all of the information so provided. . . .

(5) University based research is not considered "fundamental research" if the university or its researchers accept (at the request, for example, of an industrial sponsor) other restrictions on publication of scientific and technical information resulting from the project or activity. Scientific and technical information resulting from the research will nonetheless qualify as fundamental research once all such restrictions have expired or have been removed. . . .

* * *

(d) *Corporate research*

(1) Research conducted by scientists or engineers working for a business entity will be considered "fundamental research" at such time and to the extent that the researchers are free to make scientific and technical information resulting from the research publicly available without restriction or delay based on proprietary concerns or specific national security controls as defined in § 734.11(b) of this part.

(2) Prepublication review by the company solely to ensure that the publication would compromise no proprietary information provided by the company to the researchers is not considered to be a proprietary restriction under paragraph (d)(1) of this section. However, paragraph (d)(1) of this section does not authorize the release of information to university researchers where the research results are subject to prepublication review. . . .

(3) Prepublication review by the company solely to ensure that publication would compromise no patent rights will not be considered a proprietary restriction for this purpose, so long as the review causes no more than a temporary delay in publication of the research results.

(4) However, the initial transfer of information from a business entity to researchers is not authorized under the "fundamental research" provision where the parties have agreed that the business entity may withhold from publication some or all of the information so provided.

(e) *Research based elsewhere.* Research conducted by scientists or engineers who are not working for any of the institutions described in paragraphs (b) through (d) of this section will be treated as corporate research, as described in paragraph (d) of this section. . . .

* * *

§ 734.12 Effect On Foreign Laws And Regulations

Any person who complies with any of the license or other requirements of the EAR is not relieved of the responsibility of complying with applicable foreign laws and regulations. Conversely, any person who complies with the license or other requirements of a foreign law or regulation is not relieved of the responsibility of complying with U.S. laws and regulations, including the EAR.

PART 736—GENERAL PROHIBITIONS

§ 736.1 Introduction.

. . . A person may undertake transactions subject to the EAR without a license or other authorization, unless the regulations affirmatively state such a requirement. As such, if an export, reexport, or activity is subject to the EAR, the general prohibitions contained in this part and the License Exceptions specified in part 740 of the EAR must be reviewed to determine if a license is necessary. . . .

* * *

§ 736.2 General prohibitions and determination of applicability.

* * *

(b) *General prohibitions.* The following ten general prohibitions describe certain exports, reexports, and other conduct, subject to the scope of the EAR, in which you may not engage unless you either have a license from the Bureau of Industry and Security (BIS) or qualify under part 740 of the EAR for a License Exception from each applicable general prohibition in this paragraph. The License Exceptions at part 740 of the EAR apply only to General Prohibitions One (Exports and Reexports in the Form Received), Two (Parts and Components Reexports), and Three (Foreign-Produced Direct Product Reexports); . . .

(1) *General Prohibition One—Export and reexport of controlled items to listed countries (Exports and Reexports).* You may not, without a license or License Exception, export any item subject to the EAR to another country or reexport any item of U.S.-origin if each of the following is true:

(i) The item is controlled for a reason indicated in the applicable Export Control Classification Number (ECCN), and

(ii) Export to the country of destination requires a license for the control reason as indicated on the Country Chart at part 738 of the EAR. (The scope of this prohibition is determined by the correct classification of your item and the ultimate destination as that combination is reflected on the Country Chart.) Note that each License Exception described at part 740 of the EAR supersedes General Prohibition One if all terms and conditions of a given License Exception are met by the exporter or reexporter.

* * *

(4) *General Prohibition Four (Denial Orders)—Engaging in actions prohibited by a denial order.* (i) You may not take any action that is prohibited by a denial order issued under part 766 of the EAR, Administrative Enforcement Proceedings. . . .

* * *

(10) *General Prohibition Ten—Proceeding with transactions with knowledge that a violation has occurred or is about to occur (Knowledge Violation to Occur).* You may not sell, transfer, export, reexport, finance, order, buy, remove, conceal, store, use, loan, dispose of, transfer, transport, forward, or otherwise service, in whole or in part, any item subject to the EAR and exported or to be exported with knowledge that a violation of the Export Administration Regulations, the Export Administration Act or any order, license, License Exception, or other authorization issued thereunder has occurred, is about to occur, or is intended to occur in connection with the item. Nor may you rely upon any license or License Exception after notice to you of the suspension or revocation of that license or exception. There are no License Exceptions to this General Prohibition Ten in part 740 of the EAR.

PART 738—COMMERCE CONTROL LIST OVERVIEW AND THE COUNTRY CHART

§ 738.1 Introduction.

(a) *Commerce Control List scope.* The Bureau of Industry and Security (BIS) maintains the Commerce Control List (CCL) within the Export Administration Regulations (EAR), which includes items (i.e., commodities, software, and technology) subject to the export licensing authority of BXA. The CCL does not include those items exclusively controlled for export or reexport by another department or agency of the U.S. Government. In instances where agencies other than the Department of Commerce administer controls over related items, entries in the CCL contain a reference to these controls.

* * *

(b) *Commerce Country Chart scope.* BIS also maintains the Commerce Country Chart. The Commerce Country Chart, located in Supplement No. 1 to part, contains licensing requirements based on destination and Reason for Control. In combination with the CCL, the Commerce Country Chart allows you to determine whether a license is required for items on the CCL to any country in the world.

§ 738.2 Commerce Control List (CCL) structure.

(a) *Categories.* The CCL is divided into 10 categories, numbered as follows:

0—Nuclear Materials, Facilities and Equipment and Miscellaneous

1—Materials, Chemicals, "Microorganisms," and Toxins

2—Materials Processing

3—Electronics

4—Computers

5—Telecommunications and Information Security

6—Lasers and Sensors

7—Navigation and Avionics

8—Marine

9—Propulsion Systems, Space Vehicles and Related Equipment

(b) *Groups.* Within each category, items are arranged by group. Each category contains the same five groups. Each Group is identified by the letters A through E, as follows:

A—Equipment, Assemblies and Components

B—Test, Inspection and Production Equipment

C—Materials

D—Software

E—Technology

(c) *Order of review.* In order to classify your item against the CCL, you should begin with a review of the general characteristics of your item. This will usually guide you to the appropriate category on the CCL. Once the appropriate category is identified, you should match the particular characteristics and functions of your item to a specific ECCN. If the ECCN contains a list under the "*Items*" heading, you should review the list to determine within which subparagraph(s) your items are identified.

(d) *Entries.* (1) *Composition of an entry.* Within each group, individual items are identified by an Export Control Classification Number (ECCN). Each number consists of a set of digits and a letter. The first digit identifies the general category within which the entry falls (e.g., 3*A*001). The letter immediately following this first digit identifies under which of the five groups the item is listed (e.g., *3* A001). The second digit differentiates individual entries by identifying the type of controls associated with the items contained in the entry (e.g., 3A001). Listed below are the Reasons for Control associated with this second digit.

0: National Security reasons (including Dual Use and International Munitions List) and Items on the NSG Dual Use Annex and Trigger List

1: Missile Technology reasons

2: Nuclear Nonproliferation reasons

3: Chemical & Biological Weapons reasons

9: Anti-terrorism, Crime Control, Regional Stability, Short Supply, UN Sanctions, etc.

(i) Since Reasons for Control are not mutually exclusive, numbers are assigned in order of precedence. As an example, if an item is controlled for both National Security and Missile Technology reasons, the entry's third digit will be a "0". If the item is controlled only for Missile Technology the third digit will be "1".

(ii) The numbers in either the second or third digit (e.g., 3A001) serve to differentiate between multilateral and unilateral entries. An entry with the number "9" as the second digit, identifies the entire entry as controlled for a unilateral concern (e.g., 2B991 for antiterrorism reasons). If the number "9" appears as the third digit, the item is controlled for unilateral purposes based on a proliferation concern (e.g., 2A292 is controlled for unilateral purposes based on nuclear nonproliferation concerns).

(iii) The last digit within each entry (e.g., 3A001) is used for the sequential numbering of ECCNs to differentiate between entries on the CCL.

(2) *Reading an ECCN.* A brief description is provided next to each ECCN. Following this description is the actual entry containing "License Requirements," "License Exceptions," and "List of Items Controlled" sections. A brief description of each section and its use follows:

(i) *License Requirements.* This section contains a separate line identifying all possible Reasons for Control in order of precedence, and two columns entitled "Control(s)" and "Country Chart".

(A) The "Controls" header identifies all applicable Reasons for Control, in order of restrictiveness, and to what extent each applies (e.g., to the entire entry or only to certain subparagraphs). Those requiring licenses for a larger number of countries and/or items are listed first. As you read down the list the number of countries and/or items requiring a license declines. Since Reasons for Control are not mutually exclusive, items controlled within a particular ECCN may be controlled for more than one reason. The following is a list of all possible Reasons for Control:

AT Anti-Terrorism

CB Chemical & Biological Weapons

CC Crime Control

CW Chemical Weapons Convention

EI Encryption Items

FC Firearms Convention

MT Missile Technology

NS National Security

NP Nuclear Nonproliferation

RS Regional Stability

SS Short Supply

UN United Nations Embargo

SI Significant Items

SL Surreptitious Listening

(B) The "Country Chart" header identifies, for each applicable Reason for Control, a column name and number (e.g., CB Column 1). These column identifiers are used to direct you from the CCL to the appropriate column identifying the countries requiring a license. Consult part 742 of the EAR for an indepth discussion of the licensing requirements and policies applicable to each Country Chart column.

(ii) *License Exceptions.* This section provides a brief eligibility statement for each ECCN-driven License Exception that may be applicable to your transaction, and should be consulted only AFTER you have determined a license is required based on an analysis of the entry and the Country Chart. The brief eligibility statement in this section is provided to assist you in deciding which ECCN-driven License Exception related to your particular item and destination you should explore prior to submitting an application. The term "Yes" (followed in some instances by the scope of Yes) appears next to each available ECCN-driven License Exception. The term "N/A" will be noted for License Exceptions that are not available within a particular entry. If one or more License Exceptions appear to apply to your transaction, you must consult part 740 of the EAR to review the conditions and restrictions applicable to each available License Exception. The list of License Exceptions contained within each ECCN is not an all-exclusive list. Other License Exceptions, not based on particular ECCNs, may be available. Consult part 740 of the EAR to determine eligibility for non-ECCN-driven License Exceptions.

(iii) *List of Items Controlled*—(A) *Units.* The unit of measure applicable to each entry is identified in the "Units" header. Most measurements used in the CCL are expressed in metric units with an inch-pound conversion where appropriate. Note that in some ECCNs the inch-pound unit will be listed first. In instances where other units are in general usage or specified by law, these will be used instead of metric. Generally, when there is a difference between the metric and inch-pound figures, the metric standard will be used for classification and licensing purposes.

(B) *Related definitions.* This header identifies, where appropriate, definitions or parameters that apply to all items controlled by the entry. The information provided in this section is unique to the entry, and hence not listed in the definitions contained in part 772 of the EAR.

(C) *Related controls.* If another U.S. government agency or department has export licensing authority over items related to those controlled by an entry, a statement is included identifying the agency or department along with the applicable regulatory cite. An additional cross-reference may be included in instances where the scope of controls differs between a CCL entry and its corresponding entry on list maintained by the European Union. This information is provided to assist readers who use both lists.

(D) *Items.* This header contains a positive list of all items controlled by a particular entry and must be reviewed to determine whether your item is controlled by that entry. In some entries, the list is contained within the entry heading. In these entries a note is included to direct you to the entry heading.

§ 738.3 Commerce Country Chart structure.

(a) *Scope.* The Commerce Country Chart (Country Chart) allows you to determine, based on the Reason(s) for Control associated with your item, if you need a license to export or reexport your item to a particular destination. . . .

* * *

(b) *Countries.* The first column of the Country Chart lists all countries in alphabetical order. There are a number of destinations that are not listed in the Country Chart contained in Supplement No. 1 to part. If your destination is not listed on the Country Chart and such destination is a territory, possession, or department of a country included on the Country Chart, the EAR accords your destination the same licensing treatment as the country of which it is a territory, possession, or department. For example, if your destination is the Cayman Islands, a dependent territory of the United Kingdom, consult the United Kingdom on the Country Chart for licensing requirements.

(c) *Columns.* Stretching out to the right are horizontal headers identifying the various Reasons for Control. Under each Reason for Control header are diagonal column identifiers capping individual columns. Each column identifier consists of the two letter Reason for Control and a column number. (e.g., CB Column 1). The column identifiers correspond to those listed in the "Country Chart" header within the "License Requirements" section of each ECCN.

(d) *Cells.* The symbol "X" is used to denote licensing requirements on the Country Chart. If an "X" appears in a particular cell, transactions subject to that particular Reason for Control/Destination combination require a license. There is a direct correlation between the number of "X"s applicable to your transaction and the number of licensing reviews your application will undergo.

§ 738.4 Determining whether a license is required.

(a) *Using the CCL and the Country Chart*—(1) *Overview.* Once you have determined that your item is controlled by a specific ECCN, you must use information contained in the "License Requirements" section of that ECCN in combination with the Country Chart to decide whether a license is required.

(2) *License decision making process.* The following decision making process must be followed in order to determine whether a license is required to export or reexport a particular item to a specific destination:

(i) *Examine the appropriate ECCN in the CCL.* Is the item you intend to export or reexport controlled for a single Reason for Control?

(A) If yes, identify the single Reason for Control and the relevant Country Chart column identifier (e.g., CB Column 1).

(B) If no, identify the Country Chart column identifier for each applicable Reason for Control (e.g., NS Column 1, NP Column 1, etc.).

(ii) *Review the Country Chart.* With each of the applicable Country Chart Column identifiers noted, turn to the Country Chart (Supplement No. 1 to part). Locate the correct Country Chart column identifier on the diagonal headings, and determine whether an "X" is marked in the cell next to the country in question for each Country Chart column identified in the applicable ECCN. If your item is subject to more than one reason for control, repeat this step using each unique Country Chart column identifier.

(A) If yes, a license application must be submitted based on the particular reason for control and destination, unless a License Exception applies. If "Yes" is noted next to any of the listed License Exceptions, you should consult part 740 of the EAR to determine whether you can use any of the available ECCN-driven License Exceptions to effect your shipment, rather than applying for a license. Each affirmative license requirement must be overcome by a License Exception. If you are unable to qualify for a License Exception based on each license requirement noted on the Country Chart, you must apply for a license. Note that other License Exceptions, not related to the CCL, may also apply to your transaction (See part 740 of the EAR).

(B) If no, a license is not required based on the particular reason for control and destination. Provided General Prohibitions Four through Ten do not apply to your proposed transaction, you may effect your shipment using the symbol "NLR". Proceed to parts 758 and 762 of the EAR for information on export clearance procedures and recordkeeping requirements. Note that although you may stop after determining a license is required based on the first Reason for Control, it is best to work through each applicable Reason for Control. A full analysis of every possible licensing requirement based on each applicable Reason for Control is required to determine the most advantageous License Exception available for your particular transaction and, if a license is required, ascertain the scope of review conducted by BIS on your license application.

(b) *Sample analysis using the CCL and Country Chart*—(1) *Scope.* The following sample entry and related analysis is provided to illustrate the type of thought process you must complete in order to determine whether a license is required to export or reexport a particular item to a specific destination using the CCL in combination with the Country Chart.

(2) *Sample CCL entry.*

2AOOO: Entry heading.

LICENSE REQUIREMENTS

Reason for Control: NS, NP, AT

Control(s)	Country Chart
NS applies to entire entry	NS Column 2
NP applies to 2A000.b	NP Column 1
AT applies to entire entry	AT Column 1

LICENSE EXCEPTIONS

LVS: $5,000

GBS: Yes

CIV: N/A

LIST OF ITEMS CONTROLLED

Unit: Number

Related Definition: N/A

Related Controls: N/A

Items:

a. Having x.

b. Having y.

(3) *Sample analysis:* After consulting the CCL, I determine my item, valued at $10,000, is classified under ECCN 2A000.a. I read that the entire

entry is controlled for national security, and anti-terrorism reasons. Since my item is classified under paragraph .a, and not .b, I understand that though nuclear nonproliferation controls apply to a portion the entry, they do not apply to my item. I note that the appropriate Country Chart column identifiers are NS Column 2 and AT Column 1. Turning to the Country Chart, I locate my specific destination, India, and see that an "X" appears in the NS Column 2 cell for India, but not in the AT Column 1 cell. I understand that a license is required, unless my transaction qualifies for a License Exception or Special Comprehensive License. From the License Exception LVS value listed, I know immediately that my proposed transaction exceeds the value limitation associated with LVS. Noting that License Exception GBS is "Yes" for this entry, I turn to part 740 of the EAR to review the provisions related to use of GBS.

Supplement No. 1 to Part 738 * * *

Commerce Country Chart

Reason for Control

Countries	Chemical & Biological Weapons			Nuclear Nonproliferation		National Security		Missile Tech	Regional Stability		Firearms Convention	Crime Control			Anti-Terrorism	
	CB 1	CB 2	CB 3	NP 1	NP 2	NS 1	NS 2	MT 1	RS 1	RS 2	FC 1	CC 1	CC 2	CC 3	AT 1	AT 2
Afghanistan	X	X	X	X		X	X	X	X	X		X		X		
Germany	X					X		X	X							
Iran	See part 746 of the EAR to determine whether a license is required in order to export or reexport to this destination.															
Iraq[1]	X	X	X	X	X	X	X	X	X	X		X	X			
Ireland	X					X		X	X	X		X		X		
Israel	X	X	X	X	X	X	X	X	X	X		X		X		
Switzerland	X					X		X	X	X		X		X		
Syria	X	X	X	X		X	X	X	X	X		X		X	X	
Taiwan	X	X	X	X		X	X	X	X	X		X		X		

[1] This country is subject to sanctions implemented by the United Nations Security Council. See part 746 for additional information and licensing requirements that apply to exports and reexports to the countries so marked. See also §746.3 for license requirements for exports and reexports to Iraq or transfers within Iraq. Although most items controlled only for AT reasons do not require a license to Iraq, some items do require a license. See §746.8 for license requirements for exports and reexports to Rwanda.

* * *

PART 740—LICENSE EXCEPTIONS

§ 740.1 Introduction.

(a) *Scope.* A "License Exception" is an authorization contained in this part that allows you to export or reexport under stated conditions, items subject to the Export Administration Regulations (EAR) that would otherwise require a license under General Prohibition One, Two, or Three, as indicated under one or more of the Export Control Classification Numbers (ECCNs) in the Commerce Control List (CCL) in Supplement No. 1 to part 774 of the EAR. . . .

(b) *Certification.* By using any of the License Exceptions you are certifying that the terms, provisions, and conditions for the use of the License Exception described in the EAR have been met. . . .

(c) *License Exception symbols.* Each License Exception bears a three letter symbol that will be used for export clearance purposes. . .

§ 740.2 Restrictions on all License Exceptions.

(a) You may not use *any* License Exception if *any* one or more of the following apply:

(1) Your authorization to use a License Exception has been suspended or revoked, or your intended export does not qualify for a License Exception.

(2) The export or reexport is subject to one of the ten General Prohibitions, is not eligible for a License Exception, and has not been authorized by BIS. . . .

§ 740.3 Shipments of Limited Value (LVS)

(a) *Scope.*

License Exception LVS authorizes the export and reexport in a single shipment of eligible commodities as identified by "LVS—$(value limit)" on the CCL.

(b) *Eligible Destinations.*

This License Exception is available for all destinations in Country Group B (see Supplement No. 1 to part 740), provided that the net value of the commodities included in the same order and controlled under the same ECCN entry on the CCL does not exceed the amount specified in the LVS paragraph for that entry.

* * *

(e) *Reexports*

Commodities may be reexported under this License Exception, provided that they could be exported from the United States to the new country of destination under LVS.

* * *

§ 740.6 Technology and Software Under Restriction (TSR)

(a) *Scope* License Exception TSR permits exports and reexports of technology and software where the Commerce Country Chart (Supplement No. 1 to part 738 of the EAR) indicates a license requirement to the ultimate destination for national security reasons only and identified by "TSR—Yes" in entries on the CCL, provided the software or technology is destined to Country Group B. (See Supplement No. 1 to part 740.) A written assurance is required from the consignee before exporting under this License Exception.

(1) Required assurance for export of technology. You may not export or reexport technology under this License Exception until you have received from the importer a written assurance that, without a BIS license or License Exception, the importer will not:

(i) Reexport or release the technology to a national of a country in Country Groups D:1 or E:2; or

(ii) Export to Country Groups D:1 or E:2 the direct product of the technology, if such foreign produced direct product is subject to national security controls as identified on the CCL (See General Prohibition Three, § 736.2(b)(3) of the EAR); or

(iii) If the direct product of the technology is a complete plant or any major component of a plant, export to Country Groups D:1 or E:2 the direct product of the plant or major component thereof, if such foreign produced direct product is subject to national security controls as identified on the CCL or is subject to State Department controls under the U.S. Munitions List (22 CFR part 121).

(2) Required assurance for export of software. You may not export or reexport software under this License Exception until you have received from the importer a written assurance that, without a BIS license or License Exception, the importer will neither:

(i) Reexport or release the software or the source code for the software to a national of a country in Country Groups D:1 or E:2; nor

(ii) Export to Country Groups D:1 or E:2 the direct product of the software, if such foreign produced direct product is subject to national security controls as identified on the CCL. (See General Prohibition Three, § 736.2(b)(3) of the EAR).

(3) Form of written assurance. The required assurance may be made in the form of a letter or any other written communication from the importer, including communications via facsimile, or the assurance may be incorporated into a licensing agreement that specifically includes the assurances. An assurance included in a licensing agreement is acceptable only if the agreement specifies that the assurance will be honored even after the expiration date of the licensing agreement. If such a written assurance is not received, License Exception TSR is not applicable and a license is required. The license application must include a statement explaining why assurances could not be obtained.

* * *

SUPPLEMENT NO. 1 TO PART 740—COUNTRY GROUPS

COUNTRY GROUP A

Country	[A:1]	[A:2] Missile technology control regime	[A:3] Australia group	[A:4] Nuclear suppliers group
Argentina		X	X	X
Australia	X	X	X	X
Austria [1]		X	X	X
Belarus				X
Belgium	X	X	X	X
Brazil		X		X
Bulgaria		X	X	X
Canada	X	X	X	X
Croatia			X	
Cyprus			X	X
Czech Republic		X	X	X
Denmark	X	X	X	X
Estonia			X	
Finland [1]		X	X	X
France	X	X	X	X
Germany	X	X	X	X
Greece	X	X	X	X
Hong Kong [1]				
Hungary		X	X	X
Iceland		X	X	
Ireland [1]		X	X	X
Italy	X	X	X	X
Japan	X	X	X	X
Kazakhstan				X
Korea, South [1]		X	X	X
Latvia			X	X
Lithuania			X	
Luxembourg	X	X	X	X
Malta			X	
Netherlands	X	X	X	X
New Zealand [1]		X	X	X
Norway	X	X	X	X
Poland		X	X	X
Portugal	X	X	X	X
Romania			X	X
Russia		X		X
Slovakia			X	X
Slovenia			X	X
South Africa		X		X
Spain	X	X	X	X
Sweden [1]		X	X	X
Switzerland [1]		X	X	X
Turkey	X	X	X	X
Ukraine		X	X	X
United Kingdom	X	X	X	X
United States	X	X	X	X

[1] Cooperating Countries.

COUNTRY GROUP B—COUNTRIES

Afghanistan
Algeria
Andorra
Angola
Antigua and Barbuda
Argentina
Aruba
Australia
Austria
The Bahamas
Bahrain
Bangladesh
Barbados
Belgium
Belize
Benin
Bhutan
Bolivia
Bosnia & Herzegovina
Botswana
Brazil
Brunei
Bulgaria
Burkina Faso
Burundi
Cameroon
Canada
Cape Verde
Central African Republic
Chad
Chile
Colombia
Comoros
Congo (Democratic Republic of the)
Congo (Republic of the)
Costa Rica
Cote d'Ivoire
Croatia
Cyprus
Czech Republic
Denmark
Djibouti
Dominica
Dominican Republic
East Timor
Ecuador
Egypt
El Salvador
Equatorial Guinea
Eritrea
Estonia
Ethiopia
Fiji
Finland
France
Gabon
Gambia, The
Germany
Ghana
Greece
Grenada
Guatemala
Guinea
Guinea-Bissau
Guyana
Haiti
Honduras
Hong Kong
Hungary
Iceland
India
Indonesia
Ireland
Israel
Italy
Jamaica
Japan
Jordan
Kenya
Kiribati
Korea, South
Kuwait
Latvia
Lebanon
Lesotho
Liberia
Liechtenstein
Lithuania
Luxembourg
Macedonia, The Former Yugoslav Republic of
Madagascar
Malawi
Malaysia
Maldives
Mali
Malta
Marshall Islands
Mauritania
Mauritius
Mexico
Micronesia, Federated States of
Monaco
Montenegro
Morocco
Mozambique
Namibia
Nauru
Nepal
Netherlands Antilles
Netherlands
New Zealand
Nicaragua
Niger
Nigeria
Norway
Oman
Pakistan
Palau
Panama
Papua New Guinea
Paraguay
Peru
Philippines
Poland
Portugal
Qatar
Romania
Rwanda
Saint Kitts & Nevis
Saint Lucia
Saint Vincent and the Grenadines
Samoa
San Marino
Sao Tome & Principe
Saudi Arabia
Senegal
Serbia
Seychelles
Sierra Leone
Singapore
Slovakia
Slovenia
Solomon Islands
Somalia
South Africa
Spain
Sri Lanka
Surinam
Swaziland
Sweden
Switzerland
Taiwan
Tanzania
Thailand
Togo
Tonga
Trinidad & Tobago
Tunisia
Turkey
Tuvalu
Uganda
United Arab Emirates
United Kingdom
United States
Uruguay
Vanuatu
Vatican City
Venezuela
Western Sahara
Yemen
Zambia
Zimbabwe

COUNTRY GROUP D

Country	[D: 1] National Security	[D: 2] Nuclear	[D: 3] Chemical & Biological	[D: 4] Missile Technology
Afghanistan			X	
Albania	X			
Algeria.				
Andorra.				
Armenia	X		X	
Azerbaijan	X		X	
Bahrain			X	X
Belarus	X		X	
Burma	X		X	
Cambodia	X			
China (PRC)	X		X	X
Comoros.				
Cuba		X	X	
Djibouti.				
Egypt			X	X
Georgia	X		X	
India		X	X	X
Iran		X	X	X
Iraq	X	X	X	X
Israel		X	X	X
Jordan			X	X
Kazakhstan	X		X	
Korea, North	X	X	X	X
Kuwait			X	X
Kyrgyzstan	X		X	
Laos	X			
Lebanon			X	X
Libya	X	X	X	X
Macau	X		X	X
Micronesia, Federated States of.				
Moldova	X		X	
Mongolia	X		X	
Oman			X	X
Pakistan		X	X	X
Qatar			X	X
Russia	X		X	
Saudi Arabia			X	X
Syria			X	X
Taiwan			X	
Tajikstan	X		X	
Turkmenistan	X		X	
Ukraine	X			
United Arab Emirates			X	X
Uzbekistan	X		X	
Vanuatu.				
Vietnam	X		X	
Yemen			X	X

COUNTRY GROUP E[1]

Country	[E:1] Terrorist supporting countries[2]	[E:2] Unilateral embargo
Cuba	X	X
Iran	X	
Korea, North	X	
Sudan	X	
Syria	X	

[1] In addition to the controls maintained by the Bureau of Industry and Security pursuant to the EAR, note that the Department of the Treasury administers:

(a) A comprehensive embargo against Cuba, Iran, and Sudan; and

(b) An embargo against certain persons, e.g., Specially Designated Terrorists (SDT), Foreign Terrorist Organizations (FTO), Specially Designated Global Terrorists (SDGT), and Specially Designated Narcotics Traffickers (SDNT). Please see part 744 of the EAR for controls maintained by the Bureau of Industry and Security on these and other persons.

[2] The President made inapplicable with respect to Iraq provisions of law that apply to countries that have supported terrorism.

PART 744—CONTROL POLICY: END-USER AND END-USE BASED

§ 744.1 General Provisions

(a) *Introduction.*

(1) . . . This part contains prohibitions against exports, reexports, and selected transfers to certain end-users and end-uses as introduced under General Prohibition Five (End-use/End-users) and Nine (Orders, Terms, and Conditions), unless authorized by BIS. Sections 744.2, 744.3, 744.4 and 744.5 prohibit exports and reexports of items subject to the EAR to defined nuclear, missile, chemical and biological activities and nuclear maritime end-uses. Section 744.6 prohibits certain activities by U.S. persons in support of certain nuclear, missile, chemical, or biological end-uses regardless of whether that support involves the export or reexport of items subject to the EAR. . . . Sections 744.12, 744.13 and 744.14 prohibit exports and reexports of any item subject to the EAR to persons designated as Specially Designated Global Terrorists, Specially Designated Terrorists, or Foreign Terrorist Organizations, respectively. . . . Section 744.15 describes restrictions on exports and reexports to persons named in general orders. In addition, these sections include license review standards for export license applications submitted as required by these sections. It should also be noted that part 764 of the EAR prohibits exports, reexports and certain in-country transfers of items subject to the EAR to denied parties.

(2) If controls set forth under more than one section of part 744 apply to a person, the license requirements for such a person will be determined based on the requirements of all applicable sections of part 744, and license applications will be reviewed under all applicable licensing policies.

(b) *Steps.* The following are steps you should follow in using the provisions of this part:

(1) *Review end-use and end-user prohibitions.* First, review each end-use and end-user prohibition described in this part to learn the scope of these prohibitions.

(2) *Determine applicability.* Second, determine whether any of the end-use and end-user prohibitions described in this part are applicable to your planned export, reexport, or other activity. See Supplement No. 1 to part 732 for guidance.

(c) A list of entities is included in Supplement No. 4 to this part 744 of the EAR (Entity List). The public is hereby informed that these entities are ineligible to receive any items subject to the EAR without a license to the extent specified in the supplement. . . .

§ 744.2 Restrictions On Certain Nuclear End-Uses

(a) *General prohibition.* In addition to the license requirements for items specified on the CCL, you may not export or reexport to any destination, other than countries in the Supplement No. 3 to this part, any item subject to the EAR without a license if at the time of the export or reexport you know the item will be used directly or indirectly in any one or more of the following activities described in paragraphs (a)(1), (a)(2), and (a)(3) of this section:

(1) *Nuclear explosive activities.* . . .

(2) *Unsafeguarded nuclear activities.* . . .

(3) *Safeguarded and unsafeguarded nuclear activities.* . . .

(b) *Additional prohibition on exporters or reexporters informed by BIS.* BIS may inform an exporter or reexporter, either individually by specific notice or through amendment to the EAR, that a license is required for export or reexport of specified items to specified end-users, because BIS has determined that there is an unacceptable risk of use in, or diversion to, any of the activities described in paragraph (a) of this section. Specific notice is to be given only by, or at the direction of, the Deputy Assistant Secretary for Export Administration. When such notice is provided orally, it will be followed by a written notice within two working days signed by the Deputy Assistant Secretary for Export Administration. The absence of any such notification does not excuse the exporter or reexporter from compliance with the license requirements of paragraph (a) of this section.

* * *

§ 744.3 Restrictions On Certain Rocket Systems (Including Ballistic Missile Systems And Space Launch Vehicles And Sounding Rockets) And Unmanned Air Vehicles (Including Cruise

Missile Systems, Target Drones And Reconnaissance Drones) End-Uses

(a) *General prohibition.* In addition to the license requirements for items specified on the CCL, you may not export, reexport, or transfer (in-country) an item subject to the EAR, without a license if at the time of the export, reexport or transfer you know the item:

(1) Will be used in the design, development, production or use of rocket systems or unmanned air vehicles capable of a range of at least 300 kilometers in or by a country listed in Country Group D:4 of Supplement No. 1 to part 740 of the EAR.

(2) Will be used, anywhere in the world except by governmental programs for nuclear weapons delivery of NPT Nuclear Weapons States that are also members of NATO, in rocket systems or unmanned air vehicles, regardless of range capabilities, for the delivery of chemical, biological, or nuclear weapons; or

(3) Will be used in the design, development, production or use of any rocket systems or unmanned air vehicles in or by a country listed in Country Group D:4, but you are unable to determine [the precise characteristics or use of the system]. . . .

(b) *Additional prohibition.* BIS may inform, either individually, by specific notice, or generally through amendment to the EAR, that a license is required for a specific export, reexport or transfer of specified items to a certain end-user, anywhere in the world, because there is an unacceptable risk of use in or diversion to activities described in paragraphs (a)(1) or (a)(2) of this section. Specific notice is to be given only by, or at the direction of, the Deputy Assistant Secretary for Export Administration. When such notice is provided orally, it will be followed by a written notice within two working days signed by the Deputy Assistant Secretary for Export Administration. However, the absence of any such notification does not excuse non-compliance with the license requirements of paragraphs (a)(1), (a)(2), or (a)(3) of this section.

* * *

§ 744.4 Restrictions On Certain Chemical And Biological Weapons End-Uses

(a) *General prohibition.* In addition to the license requirements for items specified on the CCL, you may not export or reexport an item subject to the EAR without a license if at the time of the export or reexport you know the item will be used in the design, development, production, stockpiling, or use of chemical or biological weapons in or by any country or destination, worldwide.

(b) *Additional prohibition on exporters informed by BIS.* BIS may inform persons, either individually by specific notice or through amendment to the EAR, that a license is required for a specific export,reexport, or transfer (in country), for export, reexport, or transfer (in country) of specified items to a certain end-user, because there is an unacceptable risk of use in or diversion to the activities, specified in paragraph (a) of this section, anywhere in the world. Specific notice is to be given only by, or at the direction of, the Deputy Assistant Secretary for Export Administration. When such notice is provided orally, it will be followed by a written notice within two working days signed by the Deputy Assistant Secretary for Export Administration. However, the absence of any such notification does not excuse the exporter from compliance with the license requirements of paragraph (a) of this section.

* * *

§ 744.6 Restrictions on Certain Activities of U.S. Persons

(a) *General prohibitions*

(1) Activities related to exports

(i) No U.S. person as defined in paragraph (c) of this section may, without a license from BIS, export, reexport, or transfer to or in any country any item where that person knows that such items:

(A) Will be used in the design, development, production, or use of nuclear explosive devices in or by a country listed in Country Group D:2 (see Supplement No. 1 to part 740 of the EAR).

(B) Will be used in the design, development, production, or use of missiles in or by a country listed in Country Group D:4 (see Supplement No. 1 to part 740 of the EAR); or

(C) Will be used in the design, development, production, stockpiling, or use of chemical or biological weapons in or by any country worldwide.

(ii) No U.S. person shall, without a license from BIS, knowingly support an export, reexport, or transfer that does not have a license as required by this section. Support means any action, including financing, transportation, and freight forwarding, by which a person facilitates an export, reexport, or transfer without being the actual exporter or reexporter.

(2) *Other activities unrelated to exports.* No U.S. person shall, without a license from BIS:

(i) Perform any contract, service, or employment that the U.S. person knows will directly assist in the design, development, production, or use of missiles in or by a country listed in Country Group D:4 (see Supplement No. 1 to part 740 of the EAR); or

(ii) Perform any contract, service, or employment that the U.S. person knows directly will directly assist in the design, development, production, stockpiling, or use of chemical or biological weapons in or by any country worldwide.

* * *

(b) *Additional prohibitions on U.S. persons informed by BIS.* BIS may inform U.S. persons, either individually or through amendment to the EAR, that a license is required because an activity could involve the types of participation and support described in paragraph (a) of this section anywhere in the world. Specific notice is to be given only by, or at the direction of, the Deputy Assistant Secretary for Export Administration. When such notice is provided orally, it will be followed by a written notice within two working days signed by the Deputy Assistant Secretary for Export Administration. However, the absence of any such notification does not excuse the exporter from compliance with the license requirements of paragraph (a) of this section.

(c) *Definition of U.S. person.*For purposes of this section, the term U.S. person includes:

(1) Any individual who is a citizen of the United States, a permanent resident alien of the United States, or a protected individual as defined by 8 U.S.C. 1324b(a)(3);

(2) Any juridical person organized under the laws of the United States or any jurisdiction within the United States, including foreign branches; and

(3) Any person in the United States.

(d) *Exceptions.* No License Exceptions apply to the prohibitions described in paragraphs (a) and (b) of this section.

* * *

Supplement No. 4 to Part 744

Entity List

This Supplement lists certain entities subject to license requirements for specified items under this part 744 of the EAR. License requirements for these entities includes exports and reexports, unless otherwise stated. This list of entities is revised and updated on a periodic basis in this Supplement by adding new or amended notifications and deleting notifications no longer in effect.

* * *

§ 758.3 Responsibilities of the Parties to the Transaction

All parties that participate in transactions subject to the EAR must comply with the EAR. Parties are free to structure transactions as they wish, and to delegate functions and tasks as they deem necessary, as long as the transaction complies with the EAR. However, acting through a forwarding or other agent, or delegating or redelegating authority, does not in and of itself relieve anyone of responsibility for compliance with the EAR.

* * *

PART 760—RESTRICTIVE TRADE PRACTICES OR BOYCOTTS

* * *

§ 760.2 Prohibitions

PROHIBITIONS

(a) Refusals to Do Business

PROHIBITION AGAINST REFUSALS TO DO BUSINESS

(1) No United States person may: refuse, knowingly agree to refuse, require any other person to refuse, or knowingly agree to require any other person to refuse, to do business with or in a boycotted country, with any business concern organized under the laws of a boycotted country, with any national or resident of a boycotted country, or with any other person, when such refusal is pursuant to an agreement with the boycotting country, a requirement of the boycotting country, or a request from or on behalf of the boycotting country.

(2) Generally, a refusal to do business under this section consists of action that excludes a person or country from a transaction for boycott reasons. This includes a situation in which a United States person chooses or selects one person over another on a boycott basis or takes action to carry out another person's boycott-based selection when he knows or has reason to know that the other person's selection is boycott-based.

(3) Refusals to do business which are prohibited by this section include not only specific refusals, but also refusals implied by a course or pattern of conduct. There need not be a specific offer and refusal to constitute a refusal to do business; a refusal may occur when a United States person has a financial or commercial opportunity and declines for boycott reasons to consider or accept it.

(4) A United States person's use of either a boycott-based list of persons with whom he will not deal (a so-called "blacklist") or a boycott-based list of persons with whom he will deal (a so-called "whitelist") constitutes a refusal to do business.

(5) An agreement by a United States person to comply generally with the laws of the boycotting country with which it is doing business or an agreement that local laws of the boycotting country shall apply or govern is not, in and of itself, a refusal to do business. Nor, in and of itself, is use of a contractual clause explicitly requiring a person to assume the risk of loss of non-delivery of his products a refusal to do business with any person who will not or cannot comply with such a clause. (But see § 769.4 on "Evasion.")

(6) If, for boycott reasons, a United States general manager chooses one supplier over another, or enters into a contract with one supplier over another, or advises its client to do so, then the general manager's actions constitute a refusal to do business under this section. However, it is not a refusal to do business under this section for a United States person to provide management, procurement, or other pre-award services for another person so long as (a) the provision of such pre-award services is customary for that firm (or industry of which the firm is a part), without regard to the boycotting or non-boycotting character of the countries in which they are performed, and (b) the United States person, in providing such services, does not act to exclude a person or country from the transaction for boycott reasons, or otherwise take actions that are boycott-based. For example, a United States person under contract to provide general management services in connection with a construction project in a boycotting country may compile lists of qualified bidders for the client if that service is a customary one and if persons who are qualified are not excluded from that list because they are blacklisted.

(7) With respect to post-award services, if a client makes a boycott-based selection, actions taken by the United States general manager or contractor to carry out the client's choice are themselves refusals to do business if the United States contractor knows or has reason to know that the client's choice was boycott-based. (It is irrelevant whether the United States contractor also provided pre-award services.) Such actions include entering into a contract with the selected supplier, notifying the supplier of the client's choice, executing a contract on behalf of the client, arranging for inspection and shipment of the supplier's goods, or taking any other action to effect the client's choice. (But see § 769.3(c) on "Compliance with Unilateral Selection" as it may apply to post-award services.)

(8) An agreement is not a prerequisite to a violation of this section since the prohibition extends to actions taken pursuant not only to agreements but also to requirements of, and requests from or on behalf of, a boycotting country.

(9) Agreements under this section may be either express or implied by a course or pattern of conduct. There need not be a direct request from a boycotting country for action by a United States person to have been taken pursuant to an agreement with or requirement of a boycotting country.

(10) This prohibition, like all others, applies only with respect to a United States person's activities in the interstate or foreign commerce of the United States and only when such activities are undertaken with intent to comply with, further, or support an unsanctioned foreign boycott. The mere absence of a business relationship with or in the boycotted country, with any business concern organized under the laws of the boycotted country, with national(s) or resident(s) of the boycotted country, or with any other person does not indicate the existence of the required intent.

EXAMPLES OF REFUSALS AND AGREEMENTS TO REFUSE TO DO BUSINESS

The following examples are intended to give guidance in determining the circumstances in which, in a boycott situation, a refusal to do business or an agreement to refuse to do business is prohibited. They are illustrative, not comprehensive.[a]

REFUSALS TO DO BUSINESS

(i) A, a U.S. manufacturer, receives an order for its products from boycotting country Y. To fill that order, A solicits bids from U.S. companies B and C, manufacturers of components used in A's products. A does not, however, solicit bids from U.S. companies D or E, which also manufacture such components, because it knows that D and E are restricted from doing business in Y and that their products are, therefore, not importable into that country.

Company A may not refuse to solicit bids from D and E for boycott reasons, because to do so would constitute a refusal to do business with those persons.

* * *

(iv) U.S. company A exports goods to boycotting country Y. In selecting vessels to transport the goods to Y, A chooses only from among carriers which call at ports in Y.

A's action is not a refusal to do business with carriers which do not call at ports in Y.

* * *

(vi) A, a U.S. company that manufactures office equipment, has been restricted from doing business in boycotting country Y because of its business dealings with boycotted country X. In an effort to have itself removed from Y's blacklist, A ceases its business in X.

A's action constitutes a refusal to do business in boycotted country X.

[a] The examples have been edited. The full list of examples is extensive.

(vii) A, a U.S. computer company, does business in boycotting country Y. A decides to explore business opportunities in boycotted country X. After careful analysis of possible business opportunities in X, A decides, solely for business reasons, not to market its products in X.

A's decision not to proceed is not a refusal to do business, because it is not based on boycott considerations. A has no affirmative obligation to do business in X.

(viii) A, a U.S. oil company with operations in boycotting country Y, has regularly purchased equipment from U.S. petroleum equipment suppliers B, C, and D, none of whom is on the blacklist of Y. Because of its satisfactory relationship with B, C, and D, A has not dealt with other suppliers, including supplier E, who is blacklisted by Y.

A's failure affirmatively to seek or secure business with blacklisted supplier E is not a refusal to do business with E.

* * *

(x) A, a U.S. construction company, enters into a contract to build an office complex in boycotting country Y. A receives bids from B and C, U.S. companies that are equally qualified suppliers of electrical cable for the project. A knows that B is blacklisted by Y and that C is not. A accepts C's bid, in part because C is as qualified as the other potential supplier and in part because C is not blacklisted.

A's decision to select supplier C instead of blacklisted supplier B is a refusal to do business, because the boycott was one of the reasons for A's decision.

* * *

(xiii) A, a U.S. engineering and construction company, contracts with a government agency in boycotting country Y to perform a variety of services in connection with the construction of a large industrial facility in Y. Pursuant to this contract, A analyzes the market of prospective suppliers, compiles a suggested bidders list, analyzes the bids received, and makes recommendations to the client. The client independently selects and awards the contract to supplier C for boycott reasons. All of A's services are performed without regard to Y's blacklist or any other boycott considerations, and are the type of services A provides clients in both boycotting and non-boycotting countries.

A's actions do not constitute a refusal to do business, because, in the provision of pre-award services, A has not excluded the other bidders and because A customarily provides such services to its clients.

(xiv) Same as (xiii), except that in compiling a list of prospective suppliers, A deletes suppliers he knows his client will refuse to select because they are blacklisted. A knows that including the names of blacklisted suppliers will neither enhance their chances of being selected nor provide his client with a useful service, the function for which he has been retained.

A's actions, which amount to furnishing a so-called "whitelist," constitute refusals to do business, because A's pre-award services have not been furnished without regard to boycott considerations.

(xv) A, a U.S. construction firm, provides its boycotting country client with a permissible list of prospective suppliers, B, C, D, and E. The client independently selects and awards the contract to C, for boycott reasons, and then requests A to advise C of his selection, negotiate the contract with C, arrange for the shipment, and inspect the goods upon arrival. A knows that C was chosen by the client for boycott reasons.

A's action in complying with his client's direction is a refusal to do business, because A's post-award actions carry out his client's boycott-based decision. (Note: Whether A's action comes within the unilateral selection exception depends upon factors discussed in § 769.3(c).)

* * *

(xvii) A, a U.S. exporter of machine tools, receives an order for drill presses from boycotting country Y. The cover letter from Y's procurement official states that A was selected over other U.S. manufacturers in part because A is not on Y's blacklist.

A's action in filling this order is not a refusal to do business, because A has not excluded anyone from the transaction.

(xviii) A, a U.S. engineering firm under contract to construct a dam in boycotting country Y, compiles, on a non-boycott basis, a list of potential heavy equipment suppliers, including information on their qualifications and prior experience. A then solicits bids from the top three firms on its list—B, C, and D—because they are the best qualified.

None of them happens to be blacklisted. A does not solicit bids from E, F, or G, the next three firms on the list, one of whom is on Y's blacklist.

A's decision to solicit bids from only B, C, and D, is not a refusal to do business with any person, because the solicited bidders were not selected for boycott reasons.

(xix) U.S. bank A receives a letter of credit in favor of U.S. beneficiary B. The letter of credit requires B to certify that he is not blacklisted. B meets all other conditions of the letter of credit but refuses to certify as to his blacklist status. A refuses to pay B on the letter of credit solely because B refuses to certify as to his blacklist status.

A has refused to do business with another person pursuant to a boycott requirement or request.

* * *

(xxiii) U.S. bank A receives a letter of credit in favor of U.S. beneficiary B. The letter of credit requires B to certify that he is not blacklisted. B fails to provide such a certification when he presents the documents to A for payment. A notifies B that the certification has not been submitted.

A has not refused to do business with another person pursuant to a boycott requirement by notifying B of the omitted certificate. A may not refuse to pay on the letter of credit, however, if B states that B will not provide such a certificate.

(xxiv) U.S. bank A receives a letter of credit in favor of U.S. beneficiary B from the issuing bank for the purpose of confirmation, negotiation or payment. The letter of credit requires B to certify that he is not blacklisted. A notifies B that it is contrary to the policy of A to handle letters of credit containing this condition and that, unless an amendment is obtained deleting this condition, A will not implement the letter of credit.

A has not refused to do business with another person pursuant to a boycott requirement, because A has indicated its policy against implementing the letter of credit containing the term without regard to B's ability or willingness to furnish such a certificate.

AGREEMENTS TO REFUSE TO DO BUSINESS

* * *

(ii) A, a U.S. manufacturer of commercial refrigerators and freezers, receives an invitation to bid from boycotting country Y. The tender states that the bidder must agree not to deal with companies on Y's blacklist. A does not know which companies are on the blacklist, and A's bid makes no commitment regarding not dealing with certain companies. A's bid in response to the tender is accepted.

At the point when A's bid is accepted, A has agreed to refuse to do business with blacklisted persons, because the terms of Y's tender are part of the contract between Y and A.

(iii) A, a U.S. construction firm, is offered a contract to perform engineering and construction services in connection with a project located in boycotting country Y. The contract contains a clause stating that, in the event of a contract dispute, the laws of Y will apply.

A may enter into the contract. Agreement that the laws of boycotting country Y will control in resolving a contract dispute is not an agreement to refuse to do business.

(iv) Same as (iii), except that the contract contains a clause that A and its employees will comply with the laws of boycotting country Y. A knows that Y has a number of boycott laws.

Such an agreement is not, in and of itself, an agreement to refuse to do business. If, however, A subsequently refuses to do business with someone because of the laws of Y, A's action would be a refusal to do business.

(v) Same as (iv) except that the contract contains a clause that A and its employees will comply with the laws of boycotting country Y, "including boycott laws".

A's agreeing, without qualification, to comply with local boycott laws constitutes an agreement to refuse to do business.

(vi) Same as (v), except that A inserts a proviso "except insofar as Y's laws conflict with U.S. laws", or words to that effect.

Such an agreement is not an agreement to refuse to do business.

(vii) A, a U.S. general contractor, is retained to construct a pipeline in boycotting country Y. A provision in the proposed contract stipulates that in purchasing equipment, supplies, and services A must give preference to companies located in host country Y.

A may agree to this contract provision. Agreeing to a "buy local" contract provision is not an agreement to refuse to do business, because A's agreement is not made for boycott reasons.

* * *

(c) Furnishing information about race, religion, sex, or national origin.

PROHIBITION AGAINST FURNISHING INFORMATION ABOUT RACE, RELIGION, SEX, OR NATIONAL ORIGIN

(1) No United States person may:

(i) Furnish information about the race, religion, sex, or national origin of any United States person;

(ii) Furnish information about the race, religion, sex, or national origin of any owner, officer, director, or employee of any corporation or other organization which is a United States person;

(iii) Knowingly agree to furnish information about the race, religion, sex, or national origin of any United States person; or

(iv) Knowingly agree to furnish information about the race, religion, sex, or national origin of any owner, officer, director, or employee of any corporation or other organization which is a United States person.

(2) This prohibition shall apply whether the information is specifically requested or is offered voluntarily by the United States person. It shall also

apply whether the information requested or volunteered is stated in the affirmative or the negative.

(3) Information about the place of birth of or the nationality of the parents of a United States person comes within this prohibition, as does information in the form of code words or symbols which could identify a United States person's race, religion, sex, or national origin.

(4) This prohibition, like all others, applies only with respect to a United States person's activities in the interstate or foreign commerce of the United States and only when such activities are undertaken with intent to comply with, further, or support an unsanctioned foreign boycott.

EXAMPLES OF THE PROHIBITION AGAINST FURNISHING DISCRIMINATORY INFORMATION

The following examples are intended to give guidance in determining the circumstances in which the furnishing of discriminatory information is prohibited. They are illustrative, not comprehensive.

(i) U.S. company A receives a boycott questionnaire from boycotting country Y asking whether it is owned or controlled by persons of a particular faith, whether it has any persons on its board of directors who are of that faith, and what the national origin of its president is. The information is sought for purposes of enforcing Y's boycott against country X, and A knows or has reason to know that the information is sought for that reason.

A may not answer the questionnaire, because A would be furnishing information about the religion and national origin of U.S. persons for purposes of complying with or supporting Y's boycott against X.

* * *

(d) Furnishing information about business relationships with boycotted countries or blacklisted persons.

PROHIBITION AGAINST FURNISHING INFORMATION ABOUT BUSINESS RELATIONSHIPS WITH BOYCOTTED COUNTRIES OR BLACKLISTED PERSONS

(1) No United States person may furnish or knowingly agree to furnish information concerning his or any other person's past, present or proposed business relationships:

(i) With or in a boycotted country;

(ii) With any business concern organized under the laws of a boycotted country;

(iii) With any national or resident of a boycotted country; or

(iv) With any other person who is known or believed to be restricted from having any business relationship with or in a boycotting country.

(2) This prohibition shall apply:

(i) Whether the information pertains to a business relationship involving a sale, purchase, or supply transaction; legal or commercial representation; shipping or other transportation transaction; insurance; investment; or any other type of business transaction or relationship; and

(ii) Whether the information is directly or indirectly requested or is furnished on the initiative of the United States person.

(3) This prohibition does not apply to the furnishing of normal business information in a commercial context. Normal business information may relate to factors such as financial fitness, technical competence, or professional experience, and may be found in documents normally available to the public such as annual reports, disclosure statements concerning securities, catalogues, promotional brochures, and trade and business handbooks. Such information may also appear in specifications or statements of experience and qualifications.

(4) Normal business information furnished in a commercial context does not cease to be such simply because the party soliciting the information may be a boycotting country or a national or resident thereof. If the information is of a type which is generally sought for a legitimate business purpose (such as determining financial fitness, technical competence, or professional experience), the information may be furnished even if the information could be used, or without the knowledge of the person supplying the information is intended to be used, for boycott purposes. However, no information about business relationships with blacklisted persons or boycotted countries, their residents or nationals, may be furnished in response to a boycott request, even if the information is publicly available. Requests for such information from a boycott office will be presumed to be boycott-based.

(5) This prohibition, like all others, applies only with respect to a United States person's activities in the interstate or foreign commerce of the United States and only when such activities are undertaken with intent to comply with, further, or support an unsanctioned foreign boycott.

EXAMPLES CONCERNING FURNISHING OF INFORMATION

The following examples are intended to give guidance in determining the circumstances in which the furnishing of information is prohibited. They are illustrative, not comprehensive.

* * *

(ii) U.S. contractor A is considering bidding for a contract to construct a school in boycotting country Y. Each bidder is required to submit copies of its annual report with its bid. Since A's annual report describes A's worldwide operations, including the countries in which it does business, it necessarily discloses whether A has business relations with boycotted country X. A has no reason to know that its report is being sought for boycott purposes.

A, in furnishing its annual report, is supplying ordinary business information in a commercial context.

(iii) Same as (ii), except that accompanying the invitation to bid is a questionnaire from country Y's boycott office asking each bidder to supply a copy of its annual report.

A may not furnish the annual report despite its public availability, because it would be furnishing information in response to a questionnaire from a boycott office.

* * *

(vii) U.S. company A, in seeking to expand its exports to boycotting country Y, sends a sales representative to Y for a one week trip. During a meeting in Y with trade association representatives, A's representative desires to explain that neither A nor any companies with which A deals has any business relationship with boycotted country X. The purpose of supplying such information is to ensure that A does not get blacklisted.

A's representative may not volunteer this information even though A, for reasons unrelated to the boycott, does not deal with X, because A's representative would be volunteering information about A's business relationships with X for boycott reasons.

(viii) U.S. company A is asked by boycotting country Y to furnish information concerning its business relationships with boycotted country X. A, knowing that Y is seeking the information for boycott purposes, refuses to furnish the information asked for directly, but proposes to respond by supplying a copy of its annual report which lists the countries with which A is presently doing business. A does not happen to be doing business with X.

A may not respond to Y's request by supplying its annual report, because A knows that it would be responding to a boycott-based request for information about its business relationships with X.

* * *

(x) U.S. company A, in the course of negotiating a sale of its goods to a buyer in boycotting country Y, is asked to certify that its supplier is not on Y's blacklist.

A may not furnish the information about its supplier's blacklist status, because this is information about A's business relationships with another person who is believed to be restricted from having any business relationship with or in a boycotting country.

* * *

(xiv) U.S. oil company A distributes to potential customers promotional brochures and catalogues which give background information on A's past projects. A does not have business dealings with boycotted country X. The brochures, which are identical to those which A uses throughout the world, list those countries in which A does or has done business. In soliciting potential customers in boycotting country Y, A desires to distribute copies of its brochures.

A may do so, because this is furnishing normal business information, in a commercial context, relating to professional experience.

(xv) U.S. company A is interested in doing business with boycotting country Y. A wants to ask Y's Ministry of Trade whether, and if so why, A is on Y's blacklist or is otherwise restricted for boycott reasons from doing business with Y.

A may take this limited inquiry, because it does not constitute furnishing information.

* * *

PART 764—ENFORCEMENT AND PROTECTIVE MEASURES

§ 764.2 Violations.

(a) *Engaging in prohibited conduct.* No person may engage in any conduct prohibited by or contrary to, or refrain from engaging in any conduct required by, the EAA, the EAR, or any order, license or authorization issued thereunder.

(b) *Causing, aiding, or abetting a violation.* No person may cause or aid, abet, counsel, command, induce, procure, or permit the doing of any act prohibited, or the omission of any act required, by the EAA, the EAR, or any order, license or authorization issued thereunder.

(c) *Solicitation and attempt.* No person may solicit or attempt a violation of the EAA, the EAR, or any order, license or authorization issued thereunder.

(d) *Conspiracy.* No person may conspire or act in concert with one or more persons in any manner or for any purpose to bring about or to do any act that constitutes a violation of the EAA, the EAR, or any order, license or authorization issued thereunder.

(e) *Acting with knowledge of a violation.* No person may order, buy, remove, conceal, store, use, sell, loan, dispose of, transfer, transport, finance, forward, or otherwise service, in whole or in part, any item exported or to be exported from the United States, or that is otherwise subject to the EAR, with knowledge that a violation of the EAA, the EAR, or any order, license or authorization issued thereunder, has occurred, is about to occur, or is intended to occur in connection with the item.

* * *

(g) *Misrepresentation and concealment of facts*

(1) No person may make any false or misleading representation, statement, or certification, or falsify or conceal any material fact, either directly to BIS, the United States Customs Service, or an official of any other United States agency, or indirectly through any other person:

(i) In the course of an investigation or other action subject to the EAR; or

(ii) In connection with the preparation, submission, issuance, use, or maintenance of any export control document or restrictive trade practice or boycott request report, as defined in § 760.6 of the EAR; or

(iii) For the purpose of or in connection with effecting an export, reexport or other activity subject to the EAR.

(2) All representations, statements, and certifications made by any person are deemed to be continuing in effect. Every person who has made any representation, statement, or certification must notify BIS and any other relevant agency, in writing, of any change of any material fact or intention from that previously represented, stated, or certified, immediately upon receipt of any information that would lead a reasonably prudent person to know that a change of material fact or intention has occurred or may occur in the future.

(h) *Evasion.* No person may engage in any transaction or take any other action with intent to evade the provisions of the EAA, the EAR, or any order, license or authorization issued thereunder.

(i) *Failure to comply with reporting, recordkeeping requirements.* No person may fail or refuse to comply with any reporting or recordkeeping requirement of the EAR or of any order, license or authorization issued thereunder.

* * *

§ 764.3 Sanctions.

(a) *Administrative.* Violations of the EAA, the EAR, or any order, license or authorization issued thereunder are subject to the administrative sanctions described in this section and to any other liability, sanction, or penalty available under law. The protective administrative measures that are described in § 764.6 of this part are distinct from administrative sanctions.

(1) *Civil penalty.* (i) A civil penalty not to exceed $10,000 may be imposed for each violation, except that a civil penalty not to exceed $100,000 may be imposed for each violation involving national security controls imposed under section 5 of the EAA.

* * *

(2) *Denial of export privileges.* An order may be issued that restricts the ability of the named persons to engage in export and reexport transactions involving items subject to the EAR, or that restricts access by named persons to items subject to the EAR. An order denying export privileges may be imposed either as a sanction for a violation specified in this part or as a protective administrative measure described in § 764.6(c) or (d) of this part. An order denying export privileges may suspend or revoke any or all outstanding licenses issued under the EAR to a person named in the denial order or in which such person has an interest, may deny or restrict exports and reexports by or to such person of any item subject to the EAR, and may restrict dealings in which that person may benefit from any export or reexport of such items.

* * *

(3) *Exclusion from practice.* Any person acting as an attorney, accountant, consultant, freight forwarder, or in any other representative capacity for any license application or other matter before BIS may be excluded by order from any or all such activities before BIS.

(b) *Criminal.* (1) *General.* Except as provided in paragraph (b)(2) of this section, whoever knowingly violates or conspires to or attempts to violate the EAA, EAR, or any order or license issued thereunder, shall be fined not more than five times the value of the exports or reexports involved or $50,000, whichever is greater, or imprisoned not more than five years, or both.

(2) *Willful violations.* (i) Whoever willfully violates or conspires to or attempts to violate any provision of the EAA, the EAR, or any order or license issued thereunder, with knowledge that the exports involved will be used for the benefit of, or that the destination or intended destination of items involved is, any controlled country or any country to which exports or reexports are controlled for foreign policy purposes, except in the case of an individual, shall be fined not more than five times the value of the export or reexport involved or $1,000,000, whichever is greater; and, in the case of an individual, shall be fined not more than $250,000, or imprisoned not more than 10 years, or both.

(ii) Any person who is issued a license under the EAA or the EAR for the export or reexport of any items to a controlled country and who, with knowledge that such export or reexport is being used by such controlled country for military or intelligence gathering purposes contrary to the conditions under which the license was issued, willfully fails to report such use to the Secretary of Defense, except in the case of an individual, shall be fined not more than five times the value of the exports or reexports involved or $1,000,000, whichever is greater; and in the case of an individual, shall be fined not more than $250,000, or imprisoned not more than five years or both.

PART 772—DEFINITIONS OF TERMS

§ 772.1 Definitions of Terms As Used in the Export Administration Regulations (EAR)

The following are definitions of terms as used in the Export Administration Regulations (EAR). In this part, references to the EAR are references to 15 CFR chapter VII, subchapter C. . . .

* * *

Know. See "knowledge."

Knowledge. Knowledge of a circumstance (the term may be a variant, such as "know," "reason to know," or "reason to believe") includes not only positive knowledge that the circumstance exists or is substantially certain to occur, but also an awareness of a high probability of its existence or future occurrence. Such awareness is inferred from evidence of the conscious disregard of facts known to a person and is also inferred from a person's willful avoidance of facts. This definition does not apply to part 760 of the EAR (Restrictive Trade Practices or Boycotts).

* * *

PART 774—THE COMMERCE CONTROL LIST

* * *

Supplement No. 1 to Part 774
The Commerce Control List

* * *

CATEGORY 2—MATERIALS PROCESSING

Note: *For quiet running bearings, see the U.S. Munitions List.*

A. SYSTEMS, EQUIPMENT AND COMPONENTS

2A001 Anti-friction bearings and bearing systems, as follows, (see List of Items Controlled) and components therefor.

License Requirements

Reason for Control: NS, MT, AT

Control(s)	*Country Chart*
NS applies to entire entry	NS Column 2
MT applies to radial ball bearings having all tolerances specified in accordance with ISO 492 Tolerance Class 2 (or ANSI/ABMA Std 20 Tolerance Class ABEC–9, or other national equivalents) or better and having all the following characteristics: an inner ring bore diameter between 12 and 50 mm; an outer ring outside diameter between 25 and 100mm; and a width between 10 and 20 mm.	MT Column 1
AT applies to entire entry	AT Column 1

License Exceptions

LVS:	$3000 NA for MT
GBS:	Yes, for 2A001.a and 2A001.b NA for MT
CIV:	Yes, for 2A001.a and 2A001.b NA for MT

List of Items Controlled

Unit: $ value

Related Controls: (1) See also 2A991. (2) Quiet running bearings are subject to the export licensing authority of the Department of State, Directorate of Defense Trade Controls. (See 22 CFR part 121.)

Related Definitions: Annular Bearing Engineers Committee (ABEC).

Items:

Note: *2A001 does not control balls with tolerance specified by the manufacturer in accordance with ISO 3290 as grade 5 or worse.*

Note: *2A001 does not control balls with tolerance specified by the manufacturer in accordance with ISO 3290 as grade 5 or worse.*

a. Ball bearings and solid roller bearings having all tolerances specified by the manufacturer in accordance with ISO 492 Tolerance Class 4 (or ANSI/ABMA Std 20 Tolerance Class ABEC–7 or RBEC–7, or other national equivalents), or better, and having both rings and rolling elements (ISO 5593) made from monel or beryllium;

Note: *2A001.a does not control tapered roller bearings.*

b. Other ball bearings and solid roller bearings having all tolerances specified by the manufacturer in accordance with ISO 492 Tolerance Class 2 (or ANSI/ABMA Std 20 Tolerance Class ABEC–9 or RBEC–9, or other national equivalents), or better;

Note: *2A001.b does not control tapered roller bearings.*

c. Active magnetic bearing systems using any of the following:

c.1. Materials with flux densities of 2.0 T or greater and yield strengths greater than 414 MPa;

c.2. All-electromagnetic 3D homopolar bias designs for actuators; *or*

c.3. High temperature (450 K (177°C) and above) position sensors.

* * *

E. TECHNOLOGY

2E001 "Technology" according to the General Technology Note for the "development" of equipment or "software" controlled by 2A (except 2A983, 2A991, or 2A994), 2B (except 2B991, 2B993, 2B996, 2B997, or 2B998), or 2D (except 2D983, 2D991, 2D992, or 2D994).

License Requirements

Reason for Control: NS, MT, NP, CB, AT

Control(s)	*Country Chart*

NS applies to "technology" for items controlled by 2A001, 2B001 to 2B009, 2D001 or 2D002	NS Column 1
MT applies to "technology" for items controlled by 2B004, 2B009, 2B018, 2B104, 2B105, 2B109, 2B116, 2B117, 2B119 to 2B122, 2D001, or 2D101 for MT reasons	MT Column 1
NP applies to "technology" for items controlled by 2A225, 2A226, 2B001, 2B004, 2B006, 2B007, 2B009, 2B104, 2B109, 2B116, 2B201, 2B204, 2B206, 2B207, 2B209, 2B225 to 2B232, 2D001, 2D002, 2D101, 2D201 or 2D202 for NP reasons	NP Column 1
NP applies to "technology" for items controlled by 2A290 to 2A293, 2B290, or 2D290 for NP reasons	NP Column 2
CB applies to "technology" for equipment controlled	CB Column 3

by 2B350 to 2B352 and for valves controlled by 2A226 or 2A292 having the characteristics of those controlled by 2B350.g

AT applies to entire entry AT Column 1

License Requirement Notes: See § 743.1 of the EAR for reporting requirements for exports under License Exceptions.

License Exceptions

CIV: N/A

TSR: Yes, except N/A for MT

List of Items Controlled

Unit: N/A

Related Controls: See also 2E101, 2E201, and 2E301

Related Definitions: N/A

Items:

The list of items controlled is contained in the ECCN heading.

* * *

EAR99 Items subject to the EAR that are *not* elsewhere controlled by this CCL Category *or* in any other category in the CCL are designated by the number *EAR99*.

PART FOUR

OTHER FEDERAL STATUTES

■ ■ ■

DOCUMENT 41

ALIEN TORT STATUTE (ATS)

■ ■ ■

28 U.S.C. § 1350

§ 1350. Alien's action for tort

The district courts shall have original jurisdiction of any civil action by an alien for a tort only, committed in violation of the law of nations or a treaty of the United States.

TORTURE VICTIM PROTECTION ACT (TVPA)

■ ■ ■

Pub. L. 102–256, Mar. 12, 1992, 106 Stat. 73 (codified at 28 U.S.C. § 1350 Note)

Section 1. Short Title.

This Act may be cited as the 'Torture Victim Protection Act of 1991'.

Section 2. Establishment of Civil Action.

(a) Liability.—An individual who, under actual or apparent authority, or color of law, of any foreign nation—

(1) subjects an individual to torture shall, in a civil action, be liable for damages to that individual; or

(2) subjects an individual to extrajudicial killing shall, in a civil action, be liable for damages to the individual's legal representative, or to any person who may be a claimant in an action for wrongful death.

(b) Exhaustion of remedies.—A court shall decline to hear a claim under this section if the claimant has not exhausted adequate and available remedies in the place in which the conduct giving rise to the claim occurred.

(c) Statute of limitations.—No action shall be maintained under this section unless it is commenced within 10 years after the cause of action arose.

Section 3. Definitions.

(a) Extrajudicial killing.—For the purposes of this Act, the term 'extrajudicial killing' means a deliberated killing not authorized by a previous judgment pronounced by a regularly constituted court affording all the judicial guarantees which are recognized as indispensable by civilized peoples. Such term, however, does not include any such killing that, under international law, is lawfully carried out under the authority of a foreign nation.

(b) Torture.—For the purposes of this Act—

(1) the term 'torture' means any act, directed against an individual in the offender's custody or physical control, by which severe pain or suffering (other than pain or suffering arising only from or inherent in, or incidental to, lawful sanctions), whether physical or mental, is intentionally inflicted on that individual for such purposes as obtaining from that individual or a third person information or a confession, punishing that individual for an act that individual or a third person has committed or is suspected of having committed, intimidating or coercing that individual or a third person, or for any reason based on discrimination of any kind; and

(2) mental pain or suffering refers to prolonged mental harm caused by or resulting from—

(A) the intentional infliction or threatened infliction of severe physical pain or suffering;

(B) the administration or application, or threatened administration or application, of mind altering substances or other procedures calculated to disrupt profoundly the senses or the personality;

(C) the threat of imminent death; or

(D) the threat that another individual will imminently be subjected to death, severe physical pain or suffering, or the administration or application of mind altering substances or other procedures calculated to disrupt profoundly the senses or personality."

DOCUMENT 42

CARRIAGE OF GOODS BY SEA ACT (COGSA) AND HARTER ACT

■ ■ ■

THE HARTER ACT

46 U.S.C. § 30701. Definition

In this chapter, the term "carrier" means the owner, manager, charterer, agent, or master of a vessel.

Revision Note: This chapter codifies the Act of February 13, 1893 (ch. 105, 27 Stat. 445) (commonly known as the Harter Act). Changes are made to simplify, clarify, and modernize the language and style, but the intent is that these changes should not result in changes in substance.

46 U.S.C. § 30702. Application

(a) In general.—Except as otherwise provided, this chapter applies to a carrier engaged in the carriage of goods to or from any port in the United States.

* * *

46 U.S.C. § 30704. Loading, stowage, custody, care, and delivery

A carrier may not insert in a bill of lading or shipping document a provision avoiding its liability for loss or damage arising from negligence or fault in loading, stowage, custody, care, or proper delivery. Any such provision is void.

46 U.S.C. § 30705. Seaworthiness

(a) Prohibition.—A carrier may not insert in a bill of lading or shipping document a provision lessening or avoiding its obligation to exercise due diligence to—

(1) make the vessel seaworthy; and

(2) properly man, equip, and supply the vessel.

(b) Voidness.—A provision described in subsection (a) is void.

CARRIAGE OF GOODS BY SEA ACT (COGSA)

[*Authors' Note: In 2006, Congress moved COGSA from the formal text of the United States Code to an appendix to 46 U.S.C. § 30701. This move did not alter the substance or effectiveness of COGSA.*]

* * *

Sec. 3. Responsibilities and liabilities of carrier and ship

(1) Seaworthiness

The carrier shall be bound, before and at the beginning of the voyage, to exercise due diligence to—

(a) Make the ship seaworthy;

(b) Properly man, equip, and supply the ship;

(c) Make the holds, refrigerating and cooling chambers, and all other parts of the ship in which goods are carried, fit and safe for their reception, carriage, and preservation.

(2) Cargo

The carrier shall properly and carefully load, handle, stow, carry, keep, care for, and discharge the goods carried.

(3) Contents of bill

After receiving the goods into his charge the carrier, or the master or agent of the carrier, shall, on demand of the shipper, issue to the shipper a bill of lading showing among other things—

(a) The leading marks necessary for identification of the goods as the same are furnished in writing by the shipper before the loading of such goods starts, provided such marks are stamped or otherwise shown clearly upon the goods if uncovered, or on the cases or coverings in which such goods are contained, in such a manner as should ordinarily remain legible until the end of the voyage.

(b) Either the number of packages or pieces, or the quantity or weight, as the case may be, as furnished in writing by the shipper.

(c) The apparent order and condition of the goods: Provided, That no carrier, master, or agent of the carrier, shall be bound to state or show in the bill of lading any marks, number, quantity, or weight which he has reasonable ground for suspecting not accurately to represent the goods actually received, or which he has had no reasonable means of checking.

(4) Bill as prima facie evidence

Such a bill of lading shall be prima facie evidence of the receipt by the carrier of the goods as therein described in accordance with paragraphs (3)(a), (b), and (c), of this section: Provided, That nothing in this chapter shall be construed as repealing or limiting the application of any part of chapter 801 of title 49.

(5) Guaranty of statements

The shipper shall be deemed to have guaranteed to the carrier the accuracy at the time of shipment of the marks, number, quantity, and weight, as furnished by him; and the shipper shall indemnify the carrier against all loss, damages, and expenses arising or resulting from inaccuracies in such particulars. The right of the carrier to such indemnity shall in no way limit his responsibility and liability under the contract of carriage to any person other than the shipper.

(6) Notice of loss or damage; limitation of actions

Unless notice of loss or damage and the general nature of such loss or damage be given in writing to the carrier or his agent at the port of discharge before or at the time of the removal of the goods into the custody of the person entitled to delivery thereof under the contract of carriage, such removal shall be prima facie evidence of the delivery by the carrier of the goods as described in the bill of lading. If the loss or damage is not apparent, the notice must be given within three days of the delivery.

Said notice of loss or damage may be endorsed upon the receipt for the goods given by the person taking delivery thereof.

The notice in writing need not be given if the state of the goods has at the time of their receipt been the subject of joint survey or inspection.

In any event the carrier and the ship shall be discharged from all liability in respect of loss or damage unless suit is brought within one year after delivery of the goods or the date when the goods should have been delivered: Provided, That if a notice of loss or damage, either apparent or concealed, is not given as provided for in this section, that fact shall not affect or prejudice the right of the shipper to bring suit within one year after the delivery of the goods or the date when the goods should have been delivered.

In the case of any actual or apprehended loss or damage the carrier and the receiver shall give all reasonable facilities to each other for inspecting and tallying the goods.

(7) "Shipped" bill of lading

After the goods are loaded the bill of lading to be issued by the carrier, master, or agent of the carrier to the shipper shall, if the shipper so demands, be a "shipped" bill of lading: Provided, That if the shipper shall have previously taken up any document of title to such goods, he shall surrender the same as against the issue of the "shipped" bill of lading, but at the option of the carrier such document of title may be noted at the port of shipment by the carrier, master, or agent with the name or names of the ship or ships upon which the goods have been shipped and the date or dates of shipment, and when so noted the same shall for the purpose of this section be deemed to constitute a "shipped" bill of lading.

(8) Limitation of liability for negligence

Any clause, covenant, or agreement in a contract of carriage relieving the carrier or the ship from liability for loss or damage to or in connection with the goods, arising from negligence, fault, or failure in the duties and obligations provided in this section, or lessening such liability otherwise than as provided in this chapter, shall be null and void and of no effect. A benefit of insurance in favor of the carrier, or similar clause, shall be deemed to be a clause relieving the carrier from liability.

Sec. 4. Rights and Immunities of Carrier and Ship

* * *

(5) Amount of liability; valuation of cargo

Neither the carrier nor the ship shall in any event be or become liable for any loss or damage to or in connection with the transportation of goods in an amount exceeding $500 per package lawful money of the United States, or in case of goods not shipped in packages, per customary freight unit, or the equivalent of that sum in other currency, unless the nature and value of such goods have been declared by the shipper before shipment and inserted in the bill of lading. This declaration, if embodied in the bill of lading, shall be prima facie evidence, but shall not be conclusive on the carrier.

By agreement between the carrier, master, or agent of the carrier, and the shipper another maximum amount than that mentioned in this paragraph may be fixed: Provided, That such maximum shall not be less than the figure above named. In no event shall the carrier be liable for more than the amount of damage actually sustained.

Neither the carrier nor the ship shall be responsible in any event for loss or damage to or in connection with the transportation of the goods if the nature or value thereof has been knowingly and fraudulently misstated by the shipper in the bill of lading.

(Apr. 16, 1936, ch. 229, title I, § 3, 49 Stat. 1208.)

Codification

In par. (4), "chapter 801 of title 49" substituted for "the Act of August 29, 1916, commonly known as the 'Pomerene Bills of Lading Act' [49 App. U.S.C. § 81 et seq.]" on authority of Pub. L. 103–272, § 6(b), July 5, 1994, 108 Stat. 1378, the first section of which enacted subtitles II, III, and V to X of Title 49, Transportation.

DOCUMENT 43

ELECTRONIC SIGNATURES IN GLOBAL AND NATIONAL COMMERCE ACT (2000) (E-SIGN)

■ ■ ■

Section 1. Short Title.

This Act may be cited as the 'Electronic Signatures in Global and National Commerce Act'.

TITLE I—ELECTRONIC RECORDS AND SIGNATURES IN COMMERCE

15 U.S.C. § 7001

Sec. 101. General Rule of Validity.

(a) In General—Notwithstanding any statute, regulation, or other rule of law (other than this title and title II), with respect to any transaction in or affecting interstate or foreign commerce—

(1) a signature, contract, or other record relating to such transaction may not be denied legal effect, validity, or enforceability solely because it is in electronic form; and

(2) a contract relating to such transaction may not be denied legal effect, validity, or enforceability solely because an electronic signature or electronic record was used in its formation.

(b) Preservation of Rights and Obligations—This title does not—

(1) limit, alter, or otherwise affect any requirement imposed by a statute, regulation, or rule of law relating to the rights and obligations of persons under such statute, regulation, or rule of law other than a requirement that contracts or other records be written, signed, or in nonelectronic form; or

(2) require any person to agree to use or accept electronic records or electronic signatures, other than a governmental agency with respect to a record other than a contract to which it is a party.

(c) Consumer Disclosures—

(1) Consent to Electronic Records—Notwithstanding subsection (a), if a statute, regulation, or other rule of law requires that

information relating to a transaction or transactions in or affecting interstate or foreign commerce be provided or made available to a consumer in writing, the use of an electronic record to provide or make available (whichever is required) such information satisfies the requirement that such information be in writing if—

(A) the consumer has affirmatively consented to such use and has not withdrawn such consent;

(B) the consumer, prior to consenting, is provided with a clear and conspicuous statement—

(i) informing the consumer of (I) any right or option of the consumer to have the record provided or made available on paper or in nonelectronic form, and (II) the right of the consumer to withdraw the consent to have the record provided or made available in an electronic form and of any conditions, consequences (which may include termination of the parties' relationship), or fees in the event of such withdrawal;

(ii) informing the consumer of whether the consent applies (I) only to the particular transaction which gave rise to the obligation to provide the record, or (II) to identified categories of records that may be provided or made available during the course of the parties' relationship;

(iii) describing the procedures the consumer must use to withdraw consent as provided in clause (i) and to update information needed to contact the consumer electronically; and

(iv) informing the consumer (I) how, after the consent, the consumer may, upon request, obtain a paper copy of an electronic record, and (II) whether any fee will be charged for such copy;

(C) the consumer—

(i) prior to consenting, is provided with a statement of the hardware and software requirements for access to and retention of the electronic records; and

(ii) consents electronically, or confirms his or her consent electronically, in a manner that reasonably demonstrates that the consumer can access information in the electronic form that will be used to provide the information that is the subject of the consent; and

(D) after the consent of a consumer in accordance with subparagraph (A), if a change in the hardware or software requirements needed to access or retain electronic records creates a material risk that the consumer will not be able to access or retain a subsequent electronic record that was the subject of the consent, the person providing the electronic record—

(i) provides the consumer with a statement of (I) the revised hardware and software requirements for access to and retention of the electronic records, and (II) the right to withdraw consent without the imposition of any fees for such withdrawal and without the imposition of any condition or consequence that was not disclosed under subparagraph (B)(i); and

(ii) again complies with subparagraph (C).

(2) Other Rights—

(A) Preservation of Consumer Protections—Nothing in this title affects the content or timing of any disclosure or other record required to be provided or made available to any consumer under any statute, regulation, or other rule of law.

(B) Verification or Acknowledgment—If a law that was enacted prior to this Act expressly requires a record to be provided or made available by a specified method that requires verification or acknowledgment of receipt, the record may be provided or made available electronically only if the method used provides verification or acknowledgment of receipt (whichever is required).

(3) Effect of Failure to Obtain Electronic Consent or Confirmation of Consent—The legal effectiveness, validity, or enforceability of any contract executed by a consumer shall not be denied solely because of the failure to obtain electronic consent or confirmation of consent by that consumer in accordance with paragraph (1)(C)(ii).

(4) Prospective Effect—Withdrawal of consent by a consumer shall not affect the legal effectiveness, validity, or enforceability of electronic records provided or made available to that consumer in accordance with paragraph (1) prior to implementation of the consumer's withdrawal of consent. A consumer's withdrawal of consent shall be effective within a reasonable period of time after receipt of the withdrawal by the provider of the record. Failure to comply with paragraph (1)(D) may, at the election of the consumer, be treated as a withdrawal of consent for purposes of this paragraph.

(5) Prior consent—This subsection does not apply to any records that are provided or made available to a consumer who has consented prior to the effective date of this title to receive such records in electronic form as permitted by any statute, regulation, or other rule of law.

(6) Oral Communications—An oral communication or a recording of an oral communication shall not qualify as an electronic record for purposes of this subsection except as otherwise provided under applicable law.

(d) Retention of Contracts and Records—

(1) Accuracy and Accessibility—If a statute, regulation, or other rule of law requires that a contract or other record relating to a transaction in or affecting interstate or foreign commerce be retained, that requirement is met by retaining an electronic record of the information in the contract or other record that—

(A) accurately reflects the information set forth in the contract or other record; and

(B) remains accessible to all persons who are entitled to access by statute, regulation, or rule of law, for the period required by such statute, regulation, or rule of law, in a form that is capable of being accurately reproduced for later reference, whether by transmission, printing, or otherwise.

(2) Exception—A requirement to retain a contract or other record in accordance with paragraph (1) does not apply to any information whose sole purpose is to enable the contract or other record to be sent, communicated, or received.

(3) Originals—If a statute, regulation, or other rule of law requires a contract or other record relating to a transaction in or affecting interstate or foreign commerce to be provided, available, or retained in its original form, or provides consequences if the contract or other record is not provided, available, or retained in its original form, that statute, regulation, or rule of law is satisfied by an electronic record that complies with paragraph (1).

(4) Checks—If a statute, regulation, or other rule of law requires the retention of a check, that requirement is satisfied by retention of an electronic record of the information on the front and back of the check in accordance with paragraph (1).

(e) Accuracy and Ability to Retain Contracts and Other Records—Notwithstanding subsection (a), if a statute, regulation, or other rule of law requires that a contract or other record relating to a transaction in or affecting interstate or foreign commerce be in writing, the legal effect, validity, or enforceability of an electronic record of such contract or other record may be denied if such electronic record is not in a form that is capable of being retained and accurately reproduced for later reference by all parties or persons who are entitled to retain the contract or other record.

(f) Proximity—Nothing in this title affects the proximity required by any statute, regulation, or other rule of law with respect to any warning, notice, disclosure, or other record required to be posted, displayed, or publicly affixed.

(g) Notarization and Acknowledgment—If a statute, regulation, or other rule of law requires a signature or record relating to a transaction in or affecting interstate or foreign commerce to be notarized, acknowledged, verified, or made under oath, that requirement is satisfied if the electronic signature of the person authorized to perform those acts, together with all other information required to be included by other applicable statute, regulation, or rule of law, is attached to or logically associated with the signature or record.

(h) Electronic Agents—A contract or other record relating to a transaction in or affecting interstate or foreign commerce may not be denied legal effect, validity, or enforceability solely because its formation, creation, or delivery involved the action of one or more electronic agents so long as the action of any such electronic agent is legally attributable to the person to be bound.

* * *

15 U.S.C. § 7002

Sec. 102. Exemption to Preemption.

(a) In General—A State statute, regulation, or other rule of law may modify, limit, or supersede the provisions of section 101 with respect to State law only if such statute, regulation, or rule of law—

(1) constitutes an enactment or adoption of the Uniform Electronic Transactions Act as approved and recommended for enactment in all the States by the National Conference of Commissioners on Uniform State Laws in 1999, except that any exception to the scope of such Act enacted by a State under section 3(b)(4) of such Act shall be preempted to the extent such exception is inconsistent with this title or title II, or would not be permitted under paragraph (2)(A)(ii) of this subsection; or

(2) (A) specifies the alternative procedures or requirements for the use or acceptance (or both) of electronic records or electronic signatures to establish the legal effect, validity, or enforceability of contracts or other records, if—

(i) such alternative procedures or requirements are consistent with this title and title II; and

(ii) such alternative procedures or requirements do not require, or accord greater legal status or effect to, the implementation or application of a specific technology or technical specification for performing the functions of creating, storing, generating, receiving, communicating, or authenticating electronic records or electronic signatures; and

(B) if enacted or adopted after the date of the enactment of this Act, makes specific reference to this Act.

(b) Exceptions for Actions by States as Market Participants—Subsection (a)(2)(A)(ii) shall not apply to the statutes, regulations, or other rules of law governing procurement by any State, or any agency or instrumentality thereof.

(c) Prevention of Circumvention—Subsection (a) does not permit a State to circumvent this title or title II through the imposition of nonelectronic delivery methods under section 8(b)(2) of the Uniform Electronic Transactions Act.

* * *

15 U.S.C. § 7006

Sec. 106. Definitions.

For purposes of this title:

(1) Consumer—The term 'consumer' means an individual who obtains, through a transaction, products or services which are used primarily for personal, family, or household purposes, and also means the legal representative of such an individual.

(2) Electronic—The term 'electronic' means relating to technology having electrical, digital, magnetic, wireless, optical, electromagnetic, or similar capabilities.

(3) Electronic Agent—The term 'electronic agent' means a computer program or an electronic or other automated means used independently to initiate an action or respond to electronic records or performances in whole or in part without review or action by an individual at the time of the action or response.

(4) Electronic Record—The term 'electronic record' means a contract or other record created, generated, sent, communicated, received, or stored by electronic means.

(5) Electronic Signature—The term 'electronic signature' means an electronic sound, symbol, or process, attached to or logically associated with a contract or other record and executed or adopted by a person with the intent to sign the record.

(6) Federal Regulatory Agency—The term 'Federal regulatory agency' means an agency, as that term is defined in section 552(f) of title 5, United States Code.

(7) Information—The term 'information' means data, text, images, sounds, codes, computer programs, software, databases, or the like.

(8) Person—The term 'person' means an individual, corporation, business trust, estate, trust, partnership, limited liability company, association, joint venture, governmental agency, public corporation, or any other legal or commercial entity.

(9) Record—the term 'record' means information that is inscribed on a tangible medium or that is stored in an electronic or other medium and is retrievable in perceivable form.

(10) Requirement—The term 'requirement' includes a prohibition.

(11) Self-Regulatory Organization—The term "self-regulatory organization" means an organization or entity that is not a Federal regulatory agency or a State, but that is under the supervision of a Federal regulatory agency and is authorized under Federal law to adopt and administer rules applicable to its members that are enforced by such organization or entity, by a Federal regulatory agency, or by another self-regulatory organization.

(12) State—The term "State" includes the District of Columbia and the territories and possessions of the United States.

(13) Transaction—The term 'transaction' means an action or set of actions relating to the conduct of business, consumer, or commercial affairs between two or more persons, including any of the following types of conduct—

(A) the sale, lease, exchange, licensing, or other disposition of (i) personal property, including goods and intangibles, (ii) services, and (iii) any combination thereof; and

(B) the sale, lease, exchange, or other disposition of any interest in real property, or any combination thereof.

DOCUMENT 44

FEDERAL ARBITRATION ACT (IMPLEMENTATION OF THE NEW YORK CONVENTION)

Pub.L. 91–368, Approved July 31, 1970, 9 U.S.C. §§ 201–208, 84 Stat. 692

■ ■ ■

§ 201. Enforcement of Convention

The Convention on the Recognition and Enforcement of Foreign Arbitral Awards of June 10, 1958, shall be enforced in United States courts in accordance with this chapter.

§ 202. Agreement or Award Falling Under the Convention

An arbitration agreement or arbitral award arising out of a legal relationship, whether contractual or not, which is considered as commercial, including a transaction, contract, or agreement described in section 2 of this title, falls under the Convention. An agreement or award arising out of such a relationship which is entirely between citizens of the United States shall be deemed not to fall under the Convention unless that relationship involves property located abroad, envisages performance or enforcement abroad, or has some other reasonable relation with one or more foreign states. For the purpose of this section a corporation is a citizen of the United States if it is incorporated or has its principal place of business in the United States.

§ 203. Jurisdiction; Amount in Controversy

An action or proceeding falling under the Convention shall be deemed to arise under the laws and treaties of the United States. The district courts of the United States (including the courts enumerated in section 460 of title 28) shall have original jurisdiction over such an action or proceeding, regardless of the amount in controversy.

§ 204. Venue

An action or proceeding over which the district courts have jurisdiction pursuant to section 203 of this title may be brought in any such court in which save for the arbitration agreement an action or proceeding with respect to the controversy between the parties could be brought, or in such court for the district and division which embraces the place designated in the agreement as the place of arbitration if such place is within the United States.

§ 205. Removal of Cases from State Courts

Where the subject matter of an action or proceeding pending in a State court relates to an arbitration agreement or award falling under the Convention, the defendant or the defendants may, at any time before the trial thereof, remove such action or proceeding to the district court of the United States for the district and division embracing the place where the action or proceeding is pending. The procedure for removal of causes otherwise provided by law shall apply, except that the ground for removal provided in this section need not appear on the face of the complaint but may be shown in the petition for removal. For the purposes of Chapter 1 of this title any action or proceeding removed under this section shall be deemed to have been brought in the district court to which it is removed.

§ 206. Order to Compel Arbitration; Appointment of Arbitrators

A court having jurisdiction under this chapter may direct that arbitration be held in accordance with the agreement at any place therein provided for, whether that place is within or without the United States. Such court may also appoint arbitrators in accordance with the provisions of the agreement.

§ 207. Award of Arbitrators; Confirmation; Jurisdiction; Proceeding

Within three years after an arbitral award falling under the Convention is made, any party to the arbitration may apply to any court having jurisdiction under this chapter for an order confirming the award as against any other party to the arbitration. The court shall confirm the award unless it finds one of the grounds for refusal or deferral of recognition or enforcement of the award specified in the said Convention.

§ 208. Chapter 1; Residual Application

Chapter 1 applies to actions and proceedings brought under this chapter to the extent that that chapter is not in conflict with this chapter or the Convention as ratified by the United States.

DOCUMENT 45

FEDERAL BILLS OF LADING ACT

■ ■ ■

CHAPTER 801

49 U.S.C. § 80101. Definitions

In this chapter—

(1) "consignee" means the person named in a bill of lading as the person to whom the goods are to be delivered.

(2) "consignor" means the person named in a bill of lading as the person from whom the goods have been received for shipment.

(3) "goods" means merchandise or personal property that has been, is being, or will be transported.

(4) "holder" means a person having possession of, and a property right in, a bill of lading.

(5) "order" means an order by indorsement on a bill of lading.

(6) "purchase" includes taking by mortgage or pledge.

(7) "State" means a State of the United States, the District of Columbia, and a territory or possession of the United States.

49 U.S.C. § 80102. Application

This chapter applies to a bill of lading when the bill is issued by a common carrier for the transportation of goods—

(1) between a place in the District of Columbia and another place in the District of Columbia;

(2) between a place in a territory or possession of the United States and another place in the same territory or possession;

(3) between a place in a State and a place in another State;

(4) between a place in a State and a place in the same State through another State or a foreign country; or

(5) from a place in a State to a place in a foreign country.

49 U.S.C. § 80103. Negotiable and nonnegotiable bills

(a) Negotiable bills.—(1) A bill of lading is negotiable if the bill—

(A) states that the goods are to be delivered to the order of a consignee; and

(B) does not contain on its face an agreement with the shipper that the bill is not negotiable.

(2) Inserting in a negotiable bill of lading the name of a person to be notified of the arrival of goods—

(A) does not limit its negotiability; and

(B) is not notice to the purchaser of the goods of a right the named person has to the goods.

(b) Nonnegotiable bills.—(1) A bill of lading is nonnegotiable if the bill states that the goods are to be delivered to a consignee. The indorsement of a nonnegotiable bill does not—

(A) make the bill negotiable; or

(B) give the transferee any additional right.

(2) A common carrier issuing a nonnegotiable bill of lading must put "nonnegotiable" or "not negotiable" on the bill. This paragraph does not apply to an informal memorandum or acknowledgment.

49 U.S.C. § 80104. Form and requirements for negotiation

(a) General Rules.—(1) A negotiable bill of lading may be negotiated by indorsement. An indorsement may be made in blank or to a specified person. If the goods are deliverable to the order of a specified person, then the bill must be indorsed by that person.

(2) A negotiable bill of lading may be negotiated by delivery when the common carrier, under the terms of the bill, undertakes to deliver the goods to the order of a specified person and that person or a subsequent indorsee has indorsed the bill in blank.

(3) A negotiable bill of lading may be negotiated by a person possessing the bill, regardless of the way in which the person got possession, if—

(A) a common carrier, under the terms of the bill, undertakes to deliver the goods to that person; or

(B) when the bill is negotiated, it is in a form that allows it to be negotiated by delivery.

(b) Validity not affected.— The validity of a negotiation of a bill of lading is not affected by the negotiation having been a breach of duty by the person making the negotiation, or by the owner of the bill having been deprived of possession by fraud, accident, mistake, duress, loss, theft, or conversion, if the person to whom the bill is negotiated, or a person to whom the bill is subsequently negotiated, gives value for the bill in good faith and without notice of the breach of duty, fraud, accident, mistake, duress, loss, theft, or conversion.

(c) Negotiation by seller, mortgagor, or pledgor to person without notice.— When goods for which a negotiable bill of lading has been issued are in a common carrier's possession, and the person to whom the bill has been issued retains possession of the bill after selling, mortgaging, or pledging the goods or bill, the subsequent negotiation of the bill by that person to another person receiving the bill for value, in good faith, and without notice of the prior sale, mortgage, or pledge has the same effect as if the first purchaser of the goods or bill had expressly authorized the subsequent negotiation.

49 U.S.C. § 80105. Title and rights affected by negotiation

(a) Title.—When a negotiable bill of lading is negotiated—

(1) the person to whom it is negotiated acquires the title to the goods that—

(A) the person negotiating the bill had the ability to convey to a purchaser in good faith for value; and

(B) the consignor and consignee had the ability to convey to such a purchaser; and

(2) the common carrier issuing the bill becomes obligated directly to the person to whom the bill is negotiated to hold possession of the goods under the terms of the bill the same as if the carrier had issued the bill to that person.

(b) Superiority of rights.—When a negotiable bill of lading is negotiated to a person for value in good faith, that person's right to the goods for which the bill was issued is superior to a seller's lien or to a right to stop the transportation of the goods. This subsection applies whether the negotiation is made before or after the common carrier issuing the bill receives notice of the seller's claim. The carrier may deliver the goods to an unpaid seller only if the bill first is surrendered for cancellation.

(c) Mortgagee and lien holder rights not affected.—Except as provided in subsection (b) of this section, this chapter does not limit a right of a mortgagee or lien holder having a mortgage or lien on goods against a person that purchased for value in good faith from the owner, and got possession of the goods immediately before delivery to the common carrier.

* * *

49 U.S.C. § 80107. Warranties and liability

(a) General rule.—Unless a contrary intention appears, a person negotiating or transferring a bill of lading for value warrants that—

(1) the bill is genuine;

(2) the person has the right to transfer the bill and the title to the goods described in the bill;

(3) the person does not know of a fact that would affect the validity or worth of the bill; and

(4) the goods are merchantable or fit for a particular purpose when merchantability or fitness would have been implied if the agreement of the parties had been to transfer the goods without a bill of lading.

(b) Security for debt.—A person holding a bill of lading as security for a debt and in good faith demanding or receiving payment of the debt from another person does not warrant by the demand or receipt—

(1) the genuineness of the bill; or

(2) the quantity or quality of the goods described in the bill.

(c) Duplicates.—A common carrier issuing a bill of lading, on the face of which is the word "duplicate" or another word indicating that the bill is not an original bill, is liable the same as a person that represents and warrants that the bill is an accurate copy of an original bill properly issued. The carrier is not otherwise liable under the bill.

(d) Indorser liability.—Indorsement of a bill of lading does not make the indorser liable for failure of the common carrier or a previous indorser to fulfill its obligations.

* * *

49 U.S.C. § 80110. Duty to deliver goods

(a) General rules.—Except to the extent a common carrier establishes an excuse provided by law, the carrier must deliver goods covered by a bill of lading on demand of the consignee named in a nonnegotiable bill or the holder of a negotiable bill for the goods when the consignee or holder—

(1) offers in good faith to satisfy the lien of the carrier on the goods;

(2) has possession of the bill and, if a negotiable bill, offers to indorse and give the bill to the carrier; and

(3) agrees to sign, on delivery of the goods, a receipt for delivery if requested by the carrier.

(b) Persons to whom goods may be delivered.—Subject to section 80111 of this title, a common carrier may deliver the goods covered by a bill of lading to—

(1) a person entitled to their possession;

(2) the consignee named in a nonnegotiable bill; or

(3) a person in possession of a negotiable bill if—

(A) the goods are deliverable to the order of that person; or

(B) the bill has been indorsed to that person or in blank by the consignee or another indorsee.

(c) Common carrier claims of title and possession.—A claim by a common carrier that the carrier has title to goods or right to their possession is an excuse for nondelivery of the goods only if the title or right is derived from—

(1) a transfer made by the consignor or consignee after the shipment; or

(2) the carrier's lien.

(d) Adverse claims.—If a person other than the consignee or the person in possession of a bill of lading claims title to or possession of goods and the common carrier knows of the claim, the carrier is not required to deliver the goods to any claimant until the carrier has had a reasonable time to decide the validity of the adverse claim or to bring a civil action to require all claimants to interplead.

(e) Interpleader.—If at least 2 persons claim title to or possession of the goods, the common carrier may—

(1) bring a civil action to interplead all known claimants to the goods; or

(2) require those claimants to interplead as a defense in an action brought against the carrier for nondelivery.

(f) Third person claims not a defense.—Except as provided in subsections (b), (d), and (e) of this section, title or a right of a third person is not a defense to an action brought by the consignee of a nonnegotiable bill of lading or by the holder of a negotiable bill against the common carrier for failure to deliver the goods on demand unless enforced by legal process.

49 U.S.C. § 80111. Liability for delivery of goods

(a) General rules.—A common carrier is liable for damages to a person having title to, or right to possession of, goods when—

(1) the carrier delivers the goods to a person not entitled to their possession unless the delivery is authorized under section 80110(b)(2) or (3) of this title;

(2) the carrier makes a delivery under section 80110(b)(2) or (3) of this title after being requested by or for a person having title to, or right to possession of, the goods not to make the delivery; or

(3) at the time of delivery under section 80110(b)(2) or (3) of this title, the carrier has information it is delivering the goods to a person not entitled to their possession.

(b) Effectiveness of request or information.—A request or information is effective under subsection (a)(2) or (3) of this section only if—

(1) an officer or agent of the carrier, whose actual or apparent authority includes acting on the request or information, has been given the request or information; and

(2) the officer or agent has had time, exercising reasonable diligence, to stop delivery of the goods.

(c) Failure to take and cancel bills.—Except as provided in subsection (d) of this section, if a common carrier delivers goods for which a negotiable bill of lading has been issued without taking and canceling the bill, the carrier is liable for damages for failure to deliver the goods to a person purchasing the bill for value in good faith whether the purchase was before or after delivery and even when delivery was made to the person entitled to the goods. The carrier also is liable under this paragraph if part of the goods are delivered without taking and canceling the bill or plainly noting on the bill that a partial delivery was made and generally describing the goods or the remaining goods kept by the carrier.

(d) Exceptions to liability.—A common carrier is not liable for failure to deliver goods to the consignee or owner of the goods or a holder of the bill if—

(1) a delivery described in subsection (c) of this section was compelled by legal process;

(2) the goods have been sold lawfully to satisfy the carrier's lien;

(3) the goods have not been claimed; or

(4) the goods are perishable or hazardous.

* * *

49 U.S.C. § 80113. Liability for nonreceipt, misdescription, and improper loading

(a) Liability for nonreceipt and misdescription.—Except as provided in this section, a common carrier issuing a bill of lading is liable for damages caused by nonreceipt by the carrier of any part of the goods by the date shown in the bill or by failure of the goods to correspond with the description contained in the bill. The carrier is liable to the owner of goods transported under a nonnegotiable bill (subject to the right of stoppage in transit) or to the holder of a negotiable bill if the owner or holder gave value in good faith relying on the description of the goods in the bill or on the shipment being made on the date shown in the bill.

(b) Nonliability of carriers.—A common carrier issuing a bill of lading is not liable under subsection (a) of this section—

(1) when the goods are loaded by the shipper;

(2) when the bill—

(A) describes the goods in terms of marks or labels, or in a statement about kind, quantity, or condition; or

(B) is qualified by "contents or condition of contents of packages unknown", "said to contain", "shipper's weight, load, and count", or words of the same meaning; and

(3) to the extent the carrier does not know whether any part of the goods were received or conform to the description.

(c) Liability for improper loading.—A common carrier issuing a bill of lading is not liable for damages caused by improper loading if—

(1) the shipper loads the goods; and

(2) the bill contains the words "shipper's weight, load, and count", or words of the same meaning indicating the shipper loaded the goods.

(d) Carrier's duty to determine kind, quantity, and number.—(1) When bulk freight is loaded by a shipper that makes available to the common carrier adequate facilities for weighing the freight, the carrier must determine the kind and quantity of the freight within a reasonable time after receiving the written request of the shipper to make the determination. In that situation, inserting the words "shipper's weight" or words of the same meaning in the bill of lading has no effect.

(2) When goods are loaded by a common carrier, the carrier must count the packages of goods, if package freight, and determine the kind and quantity, if bulk freight. In that situation, inserting in the bill of lading or in a notice, receipt, contract, rule, or tariff, the words "shipper's weight, load, and count" or words indicating that the shipper described and loaded the goods, has no effect except for freight concealed by packages.

DOCUMENT 46

FEDERAL RULES OF CIVIL PROCEDURE, RULE 4

■ ■ ■

* * *

(e) SERVING AN INDIVIDUAL WITHIN A JUDICIAL DISTRICT OF THE UNITED STATES. Unless federal law provides otherwise, an individual—other than a minor, an incompetent person, or a person whose waiver has been filed—may be served in a judicial district of the United States by:

(1) following state law for serving a summons in an action brought in courts of general jurisdiction in the state where the district court is located or where service is made; or

(2) doing any of the following:

(A) delivering a copy of the summons and of the complaint to the individual personally;

(B) leaving a copy of each at the individual's dwelling or usual place of abode with someone of suitable age and discretion who resides there; or

(C) delivering a copy of each to an agent authorized by appointment or by law to receive service of process.

(f) SERVING AN INDIVIDUAL IN A FOREIGN COUNTRY. Unless federal law provides otherwise, an individual—other than a minor, an incompetent person, or a person whose waiver has been filed—may be served at a place not within any judicial district of the United States:

(1) by any internationally agreed means of service that is reasonably calculated to give notice, such as those authorized by the Hague Convention on the Service Abroad of Judicial and Extrajudicial Documents;

(2) if there is no internationally agreed means, or if an international agreement allows but does not specify other means, by a method that is reasonably calculated to give notice:

(A) as prescribed by the foreign country's law for service in that country in an action in its courts of general jurisdiction;

(B) as the foreign authority directs in response to a letter rogatory or letter of request; or

(C) unless prohibited by the foreign country's law, by:

(i) delivering a copy of the summons and of the complaint to the individual personally; or

(ii) using any form of mail that the clerk addresses and sends to the individual and that requires a signed receipt; or

(3) by other means not prohibited by international agreement, as the court orders.

* * *

(h) SERVING A CORPORATION, PARTNERSHIP, OR ASSOCIATION. Unless federal law provides otherwise or the defendant's waiver has been filed, a domestic or foreign corporation, or a partnership or other unincorporated association that is subject to suit under a common name, must be served:

(1) in a judicial district of the United States:

(A) in the manner prescribed by Rule 4(e)(1) for serving an individual; or

(B) by delivering a copy of the summons and of the complaint to an officer, a managing or general agent, or any other agent authorized by appointment or by law to receive service of process and—if the agent is one authorized by statute and the statute so requires—by also mailing a copy of each to the defendant; . . .

(2) at a place not within any judicial district of the United States, in any manner prescribed by Rule 4(f) for serving an individual, except personal delivery under (f)(2)(C)(i).

DOCUMENT 47

FOREIGN CORRUPT PRACTICES ACT OF 1977 (AS AMENDED) (FCPA)

■ ■ ■

Pub. L. 95–213, 91 Stat. 1494, Dec. 19, 1977 (amending the Securities Exchange Act of 1934, 15 U.S.C.A. §§ 78q(b), 78dd, 78ff(a) (1976)); as amended by Pub. L. 100–418, 102 Stat. 1107, Aug. 23, 1988; as amended by Pub. L. 105–366, Nov. 10, 1998 (International Anti-Bribery & Fair Competition Act)

15 U.S.C. § 78m. Periodical and other reports

* * *

(b) Form of report; books, records, and internal accounting[.]

* * *

(2) Every issuer which has a class of securities registered pursuant to section 78*l* of this title and every issuer which is required to file reports pursuant to section 78*o*(d) of this title shall—

(A) make and keep books, records, and accounts, which, in reasonable detail, accurately and fairly reflect the transactions and dispositions of the assets of the issuer;

(B) devise and maintain a system of internal accounting controls sufficient to provide reasonable assurances that—

(i) transactions are executed in accordance with management's general or specific authorization;

(ii) transactions are recorded as necessary (I) to permit preparation of financial statements in conformity with generally accepted accounting principles or any other criteria applicable to such statements, and (II) to maintain accountability for assets;

(iii) access to assets is permitted only in accordance with management's general or specific authorization; and

(iv) the recorded accountability for assets is compared with the existing assets at reasonable intervals and appropriate action is taken with respect to any differences[.]

* * *

(4) No criminal liability shall be imposed for failing to comply with the requirements of paragraph (2) of this subsection except as provided in paragraph (5) of this subsection.

(5) No person shall knowingly circumvent or knowingly fail to implement a system of internal accounting controls or knowingly falsify any book, record, or account described in paragraph (2).

(6) Where an issuer which has a class of securities registered pursuant to section 78*l* of this title or an issuer which is required to file reports pursuant to section 78*o*(d) of this title holds 50 per centum or less of the voting power with respect to a domestic or foreign firm, the provisions of paragraph (2) require only that the issuer proceed in good faith to use its influence, to the extent reasonable under the issuer's circumstances, to cause such domestic or foreign firm to devise and maintain a system of internal accounting controls consistent with paragraph (2). Such circumstances include the relative degree of the issuer's ownership of the domestic or foreign firm and the laws and practices governing the business operations of the country in which such firm is located. An issuer which demonstrates good faith efforts to use such influence shall be conclusively presumed to have complied with the requirements of paragraph (2).

(7) For the purpose of paragraph (2) of this subsection, the terms "reasonable assurances" and "reasonable detail" mean such level of detail and degree of assurance as would satisfy prudent officials in the conduct of their own affairs.

* * *

15 U.S.C. § 78dd–1. Prohibited foreign trade practices by issuers

(a) Prohibition

It shall be unlawful for any issuer which has a class of securities registered pursuant to section 78*l* of this title or which is required to file reports under section 78*o*(d) of this title, or for any officer, director, employee, or agent of such issuer or any stockholder thereof acting on behalf of such issuer, to make use of the mails or any means or instrumentality of interstate commerce corruptly in furtherance of an offer, payment, promise to pay, or authorization of the payment of any money, or offer, gift, promise to give, or authorization of the giving of anything of value to—

(1) any foreign official for purposes of—

(A)(i) influencing any act or decision of such foreign official in his official capacity, (ii) inducing such foreign official to do or omit to do any act in violation of the lawful duty of such official, or (iii) securing any improper advantage; or

(B) inducing such foreign official to use his influence with a foreign government or instrumentality thereof to affect or influence any act or decision of such government or instrumentality, in order to assist such issuer in obtaining or retaining business for or with, or directing business to, any person;

(2) any foreign political party or official thereof or any candidate for foreign political office for purposes of—

(A)(i) influencing any act or decision of such party, official, or candidate in its or his official capacity, (ii) inducing such party, official, or candidate to do or omit to do an act in violation of the lawful duty of such party, official, or candidate, or (iii) securing any improper advantage; or

(B) inducing such party, official, or candidate to use its or his influence with a foreign government or instrumentality thereof to affect or influence any act or decision of such government or instrumentality.

in order to assist such issuer in obtaining or retaining business for or with, or directing business to, any person; or

(3) any person, while knowing that all or a portion of such money or thing of value will be offered, given, or promised, directly or indirectly, to any foreign official, to any foreign political party or official thereof, or to any candidate for foreign political office, for purposes of—

(A)(i) influencing any act or decision of such foreign official, political party, party official, or candidate in his or its official capacity, (ii) inducing such foreign official, political party, party official, or candidate to do or omit to do any act in violation of the lawful duty of such foreign official, political party, party official, or candidate, or (iii) securing any improper advantage; or

(B) inducing such foreign official, political party, party official, or candidate to use his or its influence with a foreign government or instrumentality thereof to affect or influence any act or decision of such government or instrumentality,

in order to assist such issuer in obtaining or retaining business for or with, or directing business to, any person.

(b) Exception for routine governmental action

Subsections (a) and (g) of this section shall not apply to any facilitating or expediting payment to a foreign official, political party, or party official the purpose of which is to expedite or to secure the performance of a routine governmental action by a foreign official, political party, or party official.

(c) Affirmative defenses

It shall be an affirmative defense to actions under subsection (a) or (g) of this section that—

(1) the payment, gift, offer, or promise of anything of value that was made, was lawful under the written laws and regulations of the foreign official's, political party's, party official's, or candidate's country; or

(2) the payment, gift, offer, or promise of anything of value that was made, was a reasonable and bona fide expenditure, such as travel and lodging expenses, incurred by or on behalf of a foreign official, party, party official, or candidate and was directly related to—

(A) the promotion, demonstration, or explanation of products or services; or

(B) the execution or performance of a contract with a foreign government or agency thereof.

(d) Guidelines by Attorney General

[T]he Attorney General, after consultation with the Commission, the Secretary of Commerce, the United States Trade Representative, the Secretary of State, and the Secretary of the Treasury, and after obtaining the views of all interested persons through public notice and comment procedures, shall determine to what extent compliance with this section would be enhanced and the business community would be assisted by further clarification of the preceding provisions of this section and may, based on such determination and to the extent necessary and appropriate, issue—

(1) guidelines describing specific types of conduct, associated with common types of export sales arrangements and business contracts, which for purposes of the Department of Justice's present enforcement policy, the Attorney General determines would be in conformance with the preceding provisions of this section; and

(2) general precautionary procedures which issuers may use on a voluntary basis to conform their conduct to the Department of Justice's present enforcement policy regarding the preceding provisions of this section.

* * *

(e) Opinions of Attorney General

(1) The Attorney General, after consultation with appropriate departments and agencies of the United States and after obtaining the views of all interested persons through public notice and comment procedures, shall establish a procedure to provide responses to specific inquiries by issuers concerning conformance of their conduct with the Department of Justice's present enforcement policy regarding the

preceding provisions of this section. The Attorney General shall, within 30 days after receiving such a request, issue an opinion in response to that request. The opinion shall state whether or not certain specified prospective conduct would, for purposes of the Department of Justice's present enforcement policy, violate the preceding provisions of this section. * * *

(f) Definitions

For purposes of this section:

(1)(A) The term "foreign official" means any officer or employee of a foreign government or any department, agency, or instrumentality thereof, or of a public international organization, or any person acting in an official capacity for or on behalf of any such government or department, agency, or instrumentality, or for or on behalf of any such public international organization.

(B) For purposes of subparagraph (A), the term "public international organization" means—

(i) an organization that is designated by Executive order pursuant to section 1 of the International Organizations Immunities Act (22 U.S.C. § 288); or

(ii) any other international organization that is designated by the President by Executive order for the purposes of this section, effective as of the date of publication of such order in the Federal Register.

(2)(A) A person's state of mind is "knowing" with respect to conduct, a circumstance, or a result if—

(i) such person is aware that such person is engaging in such conduct, that such circumstance exists, or that such result is substantially certain to occur; or

(ii) such person has a firm belief that such circumstance exists or that such result is substantially certain to occur.

(B) When knowledge of the existence of a particular circumstance is required for an offense, such knowledge is established if a person is aware of a high probability of the existence of such circumstance, unless the person actually believes that such circumstance does not exist.

(3)(A) The term "routine governmental action" means only an action which is ordinarily and commonly performed by a foreign official in—

(i) obtaining permits, licenses, or other official documents to qualify a person to do business in a foreign country;

(ii) processing governmental papers, such as visas and work orders;

(iii) providing police protection, mail pick-up and delivery, or scheduling inspections associated with contract performance or inspections related to transit of goods across country;

(iv) providing phone service, power and water supply, loading and unloading cargo, or protecting perishable products or commodities from deterioration; or

(v) actions of a similar nature.

(B) The term "routine governmental action" does not include any decision by a foreign official whether, or on what terms, to award new business to or to continue business with a particular party, or any action taken by a foreign official involved in the decision-making process to encourage a decision to award new business to or continue business with a particular party.

(g) Alternative jurisdiction

(1) It shall also be unlawful for any issuer organized under the laws of the United States, or a State, territory, possession, or commonwealth of the United States or a political subdivision thereof and which has a class of securities registered pursuant to section 78l of this title or which is required to file reports under section 78*o*(d) of this title, or for any United States person that is an officer, director, employee, or agent of such issuer or a stockholder thereof acting on behalf of such issuer, to corruptly do any act outside the United States in furtherance of an offer, payment, promise to pay, or authorization of the payment of any money, or offer, gift, promise to give, or authorization of the giving of anything of value to any of the persons or entities set forth in paragraphs (1), (2), and (3) of subsection (a) of this section for the purposes set forth therein, irrespective of whether such issuer or such officer, director, employee, agent, or stockholder makes use of the mails or any means or instrumentality of interstate commerce in furtherance of such offer, gift, payment, promise, or authorization.

(2) As used in this subsection, the term "United States person" means a national of the United States (as defined in section 101 of the Immigration and Nationality Act (8 U.S.C. § 1101)) or any corporation, partnership, association, joint-stock company, business trust, unincorporated organization, or sole proprietorship organized under the laws of the United States or any State, territory, possession, or commonwealth of the United States, or any political subdivision thereof.

15 U.S.C. § 78dd–2. Prohibited foreign trade practices by domestic concerns

(a) Prohibition

It shall be unlawful for any domestic concern, other than an issuer which is subject to section 78dd–1 of this title, or for any officer, director, employee, or agent of such domestic concern or any stockholder thereof acting on behalf of such domestic concern * * *

[Subsection 78dd–2(a) then continues with the same test for a prohibited payment to a foreign official as in § 78dd–1.]

[Subsection 78dd–2(b) contains the same exception for a "routine governmental action" as in § 78dd–1(b).]

[Subsections 78dd–2(c) contains the same affirmative defenses as in § 78dd–1(c).]

* * *

(d) Injunctive relief

(1) When it appears to the Attorney General that any domestic concern to which this section applies, or officer, director, employee, agent, or stockholder thereof, is engaged, or about to engage, in any act or practice constituting a violation of subsection (a) or (i) of this section, the Attorney General may, in his discretion, bring a civil action in an appropriate district court of the United States to enjoin such act or practice, and upon a proper showing, a permanent injunction or a temporary restraining order shall be granted without bond.

* * *

(e) Guidelines by Attorney General *[This subsection contains the same language as in § 78dd–1(d).]*

(f) Opinions of Attorney General *[This subsection contains the same language as in § 78dd–1(e).]*

(g) Penalties

(1)(A) Any domestic concern that is not a natural person and that violates subsection (a) or (i) of this section shall be fined not more than $2,000,000.

(B) Any domestic concern that is not a natural person and that violates subsection (a) or (i) of this section shall be subject to a civil penalty of not more than $10,000 imposed in an action brought by the Attorney General.

(2)(A) Any natural person that is an officer, director, employee, or agent of a domestic concern, or stockholder acting on behalf of such domestic concern, who willfully violates subsection (a) or (i) of this section shall be fined not more than $100,000 or imprisoned not more than 5 years, or both.

(B) Any natural person that is an officer, director, employee, or agent of a domestic concern, or stockholder acting on behalf of such domestic concern, who violates subsection (a) or (i) of this section shall be subject to a civil penalty of not more than $10,000 imposed in an action brought by the Attorney General.

(3) Whenever a fine is imposed under paragraph (2) upon any officer, director, employee, agent, or stockholder of a domestic concern, such fine may not be paid, directly or indirectly, by such domestic concern.

(h) Definitions

For purposes of this section:

(1) The term "domestic concern" means—

(A) any individual who is a citizen, national, or resident of the United States; and

(B) any corporation, partnership, association, joint-stock company, business trust, unincorporated organization, or sole proprietorship which has its principal place of business in the United States, or which is organized under the laws of a State of the United States or a territory, possession, or commonwealth of the United States.

[Subsections 78dd–2(h)(2)–(4) then contain the same definitions of "foreign official," "public international organization," "knowing" and "routine governmental action" as in § 78dd–1(f).]

(5) The term "interstate commerce" means trade, commerce, transportation, or communication among the several States, or between any foreign country and any State or between any State and any place or ship outside thereof, and such term includes the intrastate use of—

(A) a telephone or other interstate means of communication, or

(B) any other interstate instrumentality.

(i) Alternative jurisdiction

(1) It shall also be unlawful for any United States person to corruptly do any act outside the United States in furtherance of an offer, payment, promise to pay, or authorization of the payment of any money, or offer, gift, promise to give, or authorization of the giving of anything of value to any of the persons or entities set forth in

paragraphs (1), (2), and (3) of subsection (a), for the purposes set forth therein, irrespective of whether such United States person makes use of the mails or any means or instrumentality of interstate commerce in furtherance of such offer, gift, payment, promise, or authorization.

(2) As used in this subsection, the term "United States person" means a national of the United States (as defined in section 101 of the Immigration and Nationality Act (8 U.S.C. § 101)) or any corporation, partnership, association, joint-stock company, business trust, unincorporated organization, or sole proprietorship organized under the laws of the United States or any State, territory, possession, or commonwealth of the United States, or any political subdivision thereof.

15 U.S.C. § 78dd–3. Prohibited foreign trade practices by persons other than issuers or domestic concerns

(a) Prohibition

It shall be unlawful for any person other than an issuer that is subject to section 78dd–1 of this title or a domestic concern (as defined in section 78dd–2 of this title), or for any officer, director, employee, or agent of such person or any stockholder thereof acting on behalf of such person, while in the territory of the United States, * * *

[Subsection 78dd–3(a) then continues with the same test for a prohibited payment to a foreign official as in §§ 78dd–1 and 78dd–2.]

[Subsection 78dd–3(b) contains the same exception for a "routine governmental action" as in § 78dd–1(b).]

[Subsections 78dd–3(c) contains the same affirmative defenses as in § 78dd–1(c).]

[Subsection 78dd–3(d) contains the same basic provision on injunctive relief as in § 78dd–2(d).]

(e) Penalties

(1)(A) Any juridical person that violates subsection (a) of this section shall be fined not more than $2,000,000.

(B) Any juridical person that violates subsection (a) of this section shall be subject to a civil penalty of not more than $10,000 imposed in an action brought by the Attorney General.

(2)(A) Any natural person who willfully violates subsection (a) of this section shall be fined not more than $100,000 or imprisoned not more than 5 years, or both.

(B) Any natural person who violates subsection (a) of this section shall be subject to a civil penalty of not more than $10,000 imposed in an action brought by the Attorney General.

(3) Whenever a fine is imposed under paragraph (2) upon any officer, director, employee, agent, or stockholder of a person, such fine may not be paid, directly or indirectly, by such person.

(f) Definitions

For purposes of this section:

(1) The term "person", when referring to an offender, means any natural person other than a national of the United States (as defined in section 101 of the Immigration and Nationality Act (8 U.S.C. § 1101)) or any corporation, partnership, association, joint-stock company, business trust, unincorporated organization, or sole proprietorship organized under the law of a foreign nation or a political subdivision thereof.

[Subsections 78dd–3(f)(2)–(5) then contain the same definitions of "foreign official," "public international organization," "knowing," and "routine governmental action" as in § 78dd–1(f), and the same definition of "interstate commerce" as in § 78dd–2(h)(5).]

* * *

15 U.S.C. § 78ff. Penalties

(a) Willful violations; false and misleading statements

Any person who willfully violates any provision of this chapter (other than section 78dd–1 of this title), or any rule or regulation thereunder the violation of which is made unlawful or the observance of which is required under the terms of this chapter, or any person who willfully and knowingly makes, or causes to be made, any statement in any application, report, or document required to be filed under this chapter or any rule or regulation thereunder or any undertaking contained in a registration statement as provided in subsection (d) of section 78*o* of this title, or by any self-regulatory organization in connection with an application for membership or participation therein or to become associated with a member thereof, which statement was false or misleading with respect to any material fact, shall upon conviction be fined not more than $5,000,000, or imprisoned not more than 20 years, or both, except that when such person is a person other than a natural person, a fine not exceeding $25,000,000 may be imposed; but no person shall be subject to imprisonment under this section for the violation of any rule or regulation if he proves that he had no knowledge of such rule or regulation.

* * *

(c) Violations by issuers, officers, directors, stockholders, employees, or agents of issuers

(1)(A) Any issuer that violates subsection (a) or (g) of section 78dd–1 of this title shall be fined not more than $2,000,000.

(B) Any issuer that violates subsection (a) or (g) of section 78dd–1 of this title shall be subject to a civil penalty of not more than $10,000 imposed in an action brought by the Commission.

(2)(A) Any officer, director, employee, or agent of an issuer, or stockholder acting on behalf of such issuer, who willfully violates subsection (a) or (g) of section 78dd–1 of this title shall be fined not more than $100,000, or imprisoned not more than 5 years, or both.

(B) Any officer, director, employee, or agent of an issuer, or stockholder acting on behalf of such issuer, who violates subsection (a) or (g) of section 78dd–1 of this title shall be subject to a civil penalty of not more than $10,000 imposed in an action brought by the Commission.

(3) Whenever a fine is imposed under paragraph (2) upon any officer, director, employee, agent, or stockholder of an issuer, such fine may not be paid, directly or indirectly, by such issuer.

DOCUMENT 48

FOREIGN INVESTMENT AND NATIONAL SECURITY ACT OF 2007 (FINSA)

■ ■ ■

Amending Section 721 of the Defense Production Act of 1950 (50 U.S.C. App. 2170)

SEC. 1. SHORT TITLE; TABLE OF CONTENTS.

(a) Short Title—This Act may be cited as the 'Foreign Investment and National Security Act of 2007'.

(b) Table of Contents—* * *

SEC. 2. UNITED STATES SECURITY IMPROVEMENT AMENDMENTS; CLARIFICATION OF REVIEW AND INVESTIGATION PROCESS.

Section 721 of the Defense Production Act of 1950 (50 U.S.C. App. 2170) is amended by striking subsections (a) and (b) and inserting the following:

'(a) Definitions—For purposes of this section, the following definitions shall apply:

'(1) COMMITTEE; CHAIRPERSON—The terms 'Committee' and 'chairperson' mean the Committee on Foreign Investment in the United States and the chairperson thereof, respectively.

'(2) CONTROL—The term 'control' has the meaning given to such term in regulations which the Committee shall prescribe.

'(3) COVERED TRANSACTION—The term 'covered transaction' means any merger, acquisition, or takeover that is proposed or pending after August 23, 1988, by or with any foreign person which could result in foreign control of any person engaged in interstate commerce in the United States.

'(4) FOREIGN GOVERNMENT-CONTROLLED TRANSACTION—The term 'foreign government—controlled transaction' means any covered transaction that could result in the control of any person engaged in interstate commerce in the United States by a foreign government or an entity controlled by or acting on behalf of a foreign government.

'(5) CLARIFICATION—The term 'national security' shall be construed so as to include those issues relating to 'homeland security', including its application to critical infrastructure.

'(6) CRITICAL INFRASTRUCTURE—The term 'critical infrastructure' means, subject to rules issued under this section, systems and assets, whether physical or virtual, so vital to the United States that the incapacity or destruction of such systems or assets would have a debilitating impact on national security.

'(7) CRITICAL TECHNOLOGIES—The term 'critical technologies' means critical technology, critical components, or critical technology items essential to national defense, identified pursuant to this section, subject to regulations issued at the direction of the President, in accordance with subsection (h).

'(8) LEAD AGENCY—The term 'lead agency' means the agency, or agencies, designated as the lead agency or agencies pursuant to subsection (k)(5) for the review of a transaction.

'(b) National Security Reviews and Investigations—

'(1) NATIONAL SECURITY REVIEWS—

'(A) IN GENERAL—Upon receiving written notification under subparagraph (C) of any covered transaction, or pursuant to a unilateral notification initiated under subparagraph (D) with respect to any covered transaction, the President, acting through the Committee—

'(i) shall review the covered transaction to determine the effects of the transaction on the national security of the United States; and

'(ii) shall consider the factors specified in subsection (f) for such purpose, as appropriate.

'(B) CONTROL BY FOREIGN GOVERNMENT—If the Committee determines that the covered transaction is a foreign government—controlled transaction, the Committee shall conduct an investigation of the transaction under paragraph (2).

'(C) WRITTEN NOTICE—

'(i) IN GENERAL—Any party or parties to any covered transaction may initiate a review of the transaction under this paragraph by submitting a written notice of the transaction to the Chairperson of the Committee. * * *

'(D) UNILATERAL INITIATION OF REVIEW—Subject to subparagraph (F), the President or the Committee may initiate a review under subparagraph (A) of—

'(i) any covered transaction;

'(ii) any covered transaction that has previously been reviewed or investigated under this section, if any party to the transaction submitted false or misleading material information to the Committee in connection with the review or investigation or omitted material information, including material documents, from information submitted to the Committee; or

'(iii) any covered transaction that has previously been reviewed or investigated under this section, if—

'(I) any party to the transaction or the entity resulting from consummation of the transaction intentionally materially breaches a mitigation agreement or condition described in subsection (*l*)(1)(A);

'(II) such breach is certified to the Committee by the lead department or agency monitoring and enforcing such agreement or condition as an intentional material breach; and

'(III) the Committee determines that there are no other remedies or enforcement tools available to address such breach.

'(E) TIMING—Any review under this paragraph shall be completed before the end of the 30–day period beginning on the date of the acceptance of written notice under subparagraph (C) by the chairperson, or beginning on the date of the initiation of the review in accordance with subparagraph (D), as applicable.

'(F) LIMIT ON DELEGATION OF CERTAIN AUTHORITY—The authority of the Committee to initiate a review under subparagraph (D) may not be delegated to any person, other than the Deputy Secretary or an appropriate Under Secretary of the department or agency represented on the Committee.

'(2) NATIONAL SECURITY INVESTIGATIONS—

'(A) IN GENERAL—In each case described in subparagraph (B), the Committee shall immediately conduct an investigation of the effects of a covered transaction on the national security of the United States, and take any necessary actions in connection with the transaction to protect the national security of the United States.

'(B) APPLICABILITY—Subparagraph (A) shall apply in each case in which—

'(i) a review of a covered transaction under paragraph (1) results in a determination that—

'(I) the transaction threatens to impair the national security of the United States and that threat has not been mitigated during or prior to the review of a covered transaction under paragraph (1);

'(II) the transaction is a foreign government—controlled transaction; or

'(III) the transaction would result in control of any critical infrastructure of or within the United States by or on behalf of any foreign person, if the Committee determines that the transaction could impair national security, and that such impairment to national security has not been mitigated by assurances provided or renewed with the approval of the Committee, as described in subsection (*l*), during the review period under paragraph (1); or

'(ii) the lead agency recommends, and the Committee concurs, that an investigation be undertaken.

'(C) TIMING—Any investigation under subparagraph (A) shall be completed before the end of the 45–day period beginning on the date on which the investigation commenced.

'(D) EXCEPTION—

'(i) IN GENERAL—Notwithstanding subparagraph (B)(i), an investigation of a foreign government—controlled transaction described in subclause (II) of subparagraph (B)(i) or a transaction involving critical infrastructure described in subclause (III) of subparagraph (B)(i) shall not be required under this paragraph, if the Secretary of the Treasury and the head of the lead agency jointly determine, on the basis of the review of the transaction under paragraph (1), that the transaction will not impair the national security of the United States.

* * *

'(E) GUIDANCE ON CERTAIN TRANSACTIONS WITH NATIONAL SECURITY IMPLICATIONS—The Chairperson shall, not later than 180 days after the effective date of the Foreign Investment and National Security Act of 2007, publish in the Federal Register guidance on the types of transactions that the Committee has reviewed and that have presented national security considerations, including transactions that may constitute covered transactions that would result in control of critical infrastructure relating to United States national security by a foreign government or an entity controlled by or acting on behalf of a foreign government.

'(3) CERTIFICATIONS TO CONGRESS—

'(A) CERTIFIED NOTICE AT COMPLETION OF REVIEW—Upon completion of a review under subsection (b) that concludes action under this section, the chairperson and the head of the lead agency shall transmit a certified notice to the members of Congress. . . .

'(B) CERTIFIED REPORT AT COMPLETION OF INVESTIGATION—As soon as is practicable after completion of an investigation under subsection (b) that concludes action under this section, the chairperson and the head of the lead agency shall transmit to the members of Congress. . . .

* * *

'(4) ANALYSIS BY DIRECTOR OF NATIONAL INTELLIGENCE—

'(A) IN GENERAL—The Director of National Intelligence shall expeditiously carry out a thorough analysis of any threat to the national security of the United States posed by any covered transaction. The Director of National Intelligence shall also seek and incorporate the views of all affected or appropriate intelligence agencies with respect to the transaction.

'(B) TIMING—The analysis required under subparagraph (A) shall be provided by the Director of National Intelligence to the Committee not later than 20 days after the date on which notice of the transaction is accepted by the Committee. . . .

'(C) INTERACTION WITH INTELLIGENCE COMMUNITY—The Director of National Intelligence shall ensure that the intelligence community remains engaged in the collection, analysis, and dissemination to the Committee of any additional relevant information that may become available during the course of any investigation conducted under subsection (b) with respect to a transaction.

'(D) INDEPENDENT ROLE OF DIRECTOR—The Director of National Intelligence shall be a nonvoting, ex officio member of the Committee, and shall be provided with all notices received by the Committee . . . regarding covered transactions, but shall serve no policy role on the Committee, other than to provide analysis under subparagraphs (A) and (C) in connection with a covered transaction.

* * *

SEC. 3. STATUTORY ESTABLISHMENT OF THE COMMITTEE ON FOREIGN INVESTMENT IN THE UNITED STATES.

'(1) ESTABLISHMENT—The Committee on Foreign Investment in the United States, established pursuant to Executive Order No. 11858, shall be a multi agency committee to carry out this section and such other assignments as the President may designate.

'(2) MEMBERSHIP—The Committee shall be comprised of the following members or the designee of any such member:

'(A) The Secretary of the Treasury.

'(B) The Secretary of Homeland Security.

'(C) The Secretary of Commerce.

'(D) The Secretary of Defense.

'(E) The Secretary of State.

'(F) The Attorney General of the United States.

'(G) The Secretary of Energy.

'(H) The Secretary of Labor (nonvoting, ex officio).

'(I) The Director of National Intelligence (nonvoting, ex officio).

'(J) The heads of any other executive department, agency, or office, as the President determines appropriate, generally or on a case-by-case basis.

'(3) CHAIRPERSON—The Secretary of the Treasury shall serve as the chairperson of the Committee.

'(4) ASSISTANT SECRETARY FOR THE DEPARTMENT OF THE TREASURY—There shall be established an additional position of Assistant Secretary of the Treasury, who shall be appointed by the President, by and with the advice and consent of the Senate. The Assistant Secretary appointed under this paragraph shall report directly to the Undersecretary of the

Treasury for International Affairs. The duties of the Assistant Secretary shall include duties related to the Committee on Foreign Investment in the United States, as delegated by the Secretary of the Treasury under this section.

'(5) DESIGNATION OF LEAD AGENCY—The Secretary of the Treasury shall designate, as appropriate, a member or members of the Committee to be the lead agency or agencies on behalf of the Committee—

'(A) for each covered transaction, and for negotiating any mitigation agreements or other conditions necessary to protect national security; and

'(B) for all matters related to the monitoring of the completed transaction, to ensure compliance with such agreements or conditions and with this section.

'(6) OTHER MEMBERS—The chairperson shall consult with the heads of such other Federal departments, agencies, and independent establishments in any review or investigation under subsection (a), as the chairperson determines to be appropriate, on the basis of the facts and circumstances of the covered transaction under review or investigation (or the designee of any such department or agency head).

* * *

SEC. 4. ADDITIONAL FACTORS FOR CONSIDERATION.

* * * '(6) the potential national security—related effects on United States critical infrastructure, including major energy assets;

'(7) the potential national security-related effects on United States critical technologies;

'(8) whether the covered transaction is a foreign government—controlled transaction, as determined under subsection (b)(1)(B);

* * *

'(10) the long-term projection of United States requirements for sources of energy and other critical resources and material; * * *

SEC. 5. MITIGATION, TRACKING, AND POSTCONSUMMATION MONITORING AND ENFORCEMENT.

' * * *(1) MITIGATION—

'(A) IN GENERAL—The Committee or a lead agency may, on behalf of the Committee, negotiate, enter into or impose, and enforce any agreement or condition with any party to the covered transaction in order to mitigate any threat to the national security of the United States that arises as a result of the covered transaction.

'(B) RISK-BASED ANALYSIS REQUIRED—Any agreement entered into or condition imposed under subparagraph (A) shall be based on a risk-based analysis, conducted by the Committee, of the threat to national security of the covered transaction.

* * *

SEC. 6. ACTION BY THE PRESIDENT.

* * *

'(1) IN GENERAL—Subject to paragraph (4), the President may take such action for such time as the President considers appropriate to suspend or prohibit any covered transaction that threatens to impair the national security of the United States.

'(2) ANNOUNCEMENT BY THE PRESIDENT—The President shall announce the decision on whether or not to take action pursuant to paragraph (1) not later than 15 days after the date on which an investigation described in subsection (b) is completed.

'(3) ENFORCEMENT—The President may direct the Attorney General of the United States to seek appropriate relief, including divestment relief, in the district courts of the United States, in order to implement and enforce this subsection.

'(4) FINDINGS OF THE PRESIDENT—The President may exercise the authority conferred by paragraph (1), only if the President finds that—

'(A) there is credible evidence that leads the President to believe that the foreign interest exercising control might take action that threatens to impair the national security; and

'(B) provisions of law, other than this section and the International Emergency Economic Powers Act, do not, in the judgment of the President, provide adequate and appropriate authority for the President to protect the national security in the matter before the President.

'(5) FACTORS TO BE CONSIDERED—For purposes of determining whether to take action under paragraph (1), the President shall consider, among other factors each of the factors described in subsection (f), as appropriate.

'(e) Actions and Findings Nonreviewable—The actions of the President under paragraph (1) of subsection (d) and the findings of the President under paragraph (4) of subsection (d) shall not be subject to judicial review.'.

SEC. 7. INCREASED OVERSIGHT BY CONGRESS.

(g) Additional Information to Congress; Confidentiality—

'(1) BRIEFING REQUIREMENT ON REQUEST—The Committee shall, upon request from any Member of Congress specified in subsection (b)(3)(C)(iii), provide briefings on a covered transaction for which all action has concluded under this section, or on compliance with a mitigation agreement or condition imposed with respect to such transaction, on a classified basis, if deemed necessary by the sensitivity of the information. Briefings under this paragraph may be provided to the congressional staff of such a Member of Congress having appropriate security clearance.

'(2) APPLICATION OF CONFIDENTIALITY PROVISIONS—

'(A) IN GENERAL—The disclosure of information under this subsection shall be consistent with the requirements of subsection (c). Members of Congress and staff of either House of Congress or any committee of Congress, shall be subject to the same limitations on disclosure of information as are applicable under subsection (c).

'(B) PROPRIETARY INFORMATION—Proprietary information which can be associated with a particular party to a covered transaction shall be furnished in accordance with subparagraph (A) only to a committee of Congress, and only when the committee provides assurances of confidentiality, unless such party otherwise consents in writing to such disclosure.'

* * *

'(m) Annual Report to Congress—

(1) IN GENERAL—The chairperson shall transmit a report to the chairman and ranking member of the committee of jurisdiction in the Senate and the House of Representatives, before July 31 of each year on all of the reviews and investigations of covered transactions completed . . . during the 12–month period covered by the report.

* * *

(3) CONTENTS OF REPORT RELATING TO CRITICAL TECHNOLOGIES—

'(A) IN GENERAL—In order to assist Congress in its oversight responsibilities with respect to this section, the President and such agencies as the President shall designate shall include in the annual report submitted under paragraph (1)—

'(i) an evaluation of whether there is credible evidence of a coordinated strategy by 1 or more countries or companies to acquire United States companies involved in research, development, or production of critical technologies for which the United States is a leading producer; and

'(ii) an evaluation of whether there are industrial espionage activities directed or directly assisted by foreign governments against private United States companies aimed at obtaining commercial secrets related to critical technologies.

'(B) RELEASE OF UNCLASSIFIED STUDY—All appropriate portions of the annual report under paragraph (1) may be classified. An unclassified version of the report, as appropriate, consistent with safeguarding national security and privacy, shall be made available to the public.'.

(c) Study and Report—

(1) STUDY REQUIRED—Before the end of the 120–day period beginning on the date of enactment of this Act and annually thereafter, the Secretary of the Treasury, in consultation with the Secretary of State and the Secretary of Commerce, shall conduct a study on foreign direct investments in the United States, especially investments in critical infrastructure and industries affecting national security, by—

(A) foreign governments, entities controlled by or acting on behalf of a foreign government, or persons of foreign countries which comply with any boycott of Israel; or

(B) foreign governments, entities controlled by or acting on behalf of a foreign government, or persons of foreign countries which do not ban organizations designated by the Secretary of State as foreign terrorist organizations.

* * *

DOCUMENT 49

FOREIGN SOVEREIGN IMMUNITIES ACT OF 1976, AS AMENDED (FSIA)

■ ■ ■

28 U.S.C. §§ 1330, 1391, 1441, 1602–1611

28 U.S.C. § 1330. Actions against Foreign States

(a) The district courts shall have original jurisdiction without regard to amount in controversy of any nonjury civil action against a foreign state as defined in section 1603(a) of this title as to any claim for relief in personam with respect to which the foreign state is not entitled to immunity either under sections 1605–1607 of this title or under any applicable international agreement.

(b) Personal jurisdiction over a foreign state shall exist as to every claim for relief over which the district courts have jurisdiction under subsection (a) where service has been made under section 1608 of this title.

(c) For purposes of subsection (b), an appearance by a foreign state does not confer personal jurisdiction with respect to any claim for relief not arising out of any transaction or occurrence enumerated in sections 1605–1607 of this title.

28 U.S.C. § 1391 [Venue] * * *

(f) A civil action against a foreign state as defined in section 1603(a) of this title may be brought—

(1) in any judicial district in which a substantial part of the events or omissions giving rise to the claim occurred, or a substantial part of property that is the subject of the action is situated;

(2) in any judicial district in which the vessel or cargo of a foreign state is situated, if the claim is asserted under section 1605(b) of this title;

(3) in any judicial district in which the agency or instrumentality is licensed to do business or is doing business, if the action is brought against an agency or instrumentality of a foreign state as defined in section 1603(b) of this title; or

(4) in the United States District Court for the District of Columbia if the action is brought against a foreign state or political subdivision thereof."

28 U.S.C. § 1441 [Removal] * * *

(d) Any civil action brought in a State court against a foreign state as defined in section 1603(a) of this title may be removed by the foreign state to the district court of the United States for the district and division embracing the place where such action is pending. Upon removal the action shall be tried by the court without jury. Where removal is based upon this subsection, the time limitations of section 1446(b) of this chapter may be enlarged at any time for cause shown.

CHAPTER 97—JURISDICTIONAL IMMUNITIES OF FOREIGN STATES

§ 1602. Findings and Declaration of Purpose

The Congress finds that the determination by United States courts of the claims of foreign states to immunity from the jurisdiction of such courts would serve the interests of justice and would protect the rights of both foreign states and litigants in United States courts. Under international law, states are not immune from the jurisdiction of foreign courts insofar as their commercial activities are concerned, and their commercial property may be levied upon for the satisfaction of judgments rendered against them in connection with their commercial activities. Claims of foreign states to immunity should henceforth be decided by courts of the United States and of the States in conformity with the principles set forth in this chapter.

§ 1603. Definitions

For purposes of this chapter—

(a) A 'foreign state' except as used in section 1608 of this title, includes a political subdivision of a foreign state or an agency or instrumentality of a foreign state as defined in subsection (b).

(b) An 'agency or instrumentality of a foreign state' means any entity—

(1) which is a separate legal person, corporate or otherwise, and

(2) which is an organ of a foreign state or political subdivision thereof, or a majority of whose shares or other ownership interest is owned by a foreign state or political subdivision thereof, and

(3) which is neither a citizen of a State of the United States as defined in section 1332(c) and (d) of this title, nor created under the laws of any third country.

(c) The 'United States' includes all territory and waters, continental or insular, subject to the jurisdiction of the United States.

(d) A 'commercial activity' means either a regular course of commercial conduct or a particular commercial transaction or act. The commercial character of an activity shall be determined by reference to the nature of the course of conduct or particular transaction or act, rather than by reference to its purpose.

(e) A 'commercial activity carried on in the United States by a foreign state' means commercial activity carried on by such state and having substantial contact with the United States.

§ 1604. Immunity of a Foreign State from Jurisdiction

Subject to existing international agreements to which the United States is a party at the time of enactment of this Act a foreign state shall be immune from the jurisdiction of the courts of the United States and of the States except as provided in sections 1605 to 1607 of this chapter.

§ 1605. General Exceptions to the Jurisdictional Immunity of a Foreign State

(a) A foreign state shall not be immune from the jurisdiction of courts of the United States or of the States in any case—

(1) in which the foreign state has waived its immunity either explicitly or by implication, notwithstanding any withdrawal of the waiver which the foreign state may purport to effect except in accordance with the terms of the waiver;

(2) in which the action is based upon a commercial activity carried on in the United States by the foreign state; or upon an act performed in the United States in connection with a commercial activity of the foreign state elsewhere; or upon an act outside the territory of the United States in connection with a commercial activity of the foreign state elsewhere and that act causes a direct effect in the United States;

(3) in which rights in property taken in violation of international law are in issue and that property or any property exchanged for such property is present in the United States in connection with a commercial activity carried on in the United States by the foreign state; or that property or any property exchanged for such property is owned or operated by an agency or instrumentality of the foreign state and that agency or instrumentality is engaged in a commercial activity in the United States;

(4) in which rights in property in the United States acquired by succession or gift or rights in immovable property situated in the United States are in issue;

(5) not otherwise encompassed in paragraph (2) above, in which money damages are sought against a foreign state for personal injury or death, or damage to or loss of property, occurring in the United

States and caused by the tortious act or omission of that foreign state or of any official or employee of that foreign state while acting within the scope of his office or employment; except this paragraph shall not apply to—

(A) any claim based upon the exercise or performance or the failure to exercise or perform a discretionary function regardless of whether the discretion be abused, or

(B) any claim arising out of malicious prosecution, abuse of process, libel, slander, misrepresentation, deceit, or interference with contract rights;

(6) in which the action is brought, either to enforce an agreement made by the foreign State with or for the benefit of a private party to submit to arbitration all or any differences which have arisen or which may arise between the parties with respect to a defined legal relationship, whether contractual or not, concerning a subject matter capable of settlement by arbitration under the laws of the United States, or to confirm an award made pursuant to such an agreement to arbitrate, if (A) the arbitration takes place or is intended to take place in the United States, (B) the agreement or award is or may be governed by a treaty or other international agreement in force for the United States calling for the recognition and enforcement of arbitral awards, (C) the underlying claim, save for the agreement to arbitrate, could have been brought in a United States court under this section or section 1607, or (D) paragraph (1) of this subsection is otherwise applicable.

* * *

§ 1605A. Terrorism Exception to the Jurisdictional Immunity of a Foreign State

(a) In General.—

(1) No immunity.— A foreign state shall not be immune from the jurisdiction of courts of the United States or of the States in any case not otherwise covered by this chapter in which money damages are sought against a foreign state for personal injury or death that was caused by an act of torture, extrajudicial killing, aircraft sabotage, hostage taking, or the provision of material support or resources for such an act if such act or provision of material support or resources is engaged in by an official, employee, or agent of such foreign state while acting within the scope of his or her office, employment, or agency.

(2) Claim heard.— The court shall hear a claim under this section if—(A)(i)

(I) the foreign state was designated as a state sponsor of terrorism at the time the act described in paragraph (1) occurred, or was so designated as a result of such act, and, subject to subclause (II), either remains so designated when the claim is filed under this section or was so designated within the 6-month period before the claim is filed under this section; * * * [and]

(ii) the claimant or the victim was, at the time the act described in paragraph (1) occurred—(I) a national of the United States;

(II) a member of the armed forces; or (III) otherwise an employee of the Government of the United States, or of an individual performing a contract awarded by the United States Government, acting within the scope of the employee's employment; and

(iii) in a case in which the act occurred in the foreign state against which the claim has been brought, the claimant has afforded the foreign state a reasonable opportunity to arbitrate the claim in accordance with the accepted international rules of arbitration; * * *

(c) Private Right of Action.— A foreign state that is or was a state sponsor of terrorism as described in subsection (a)(2)(A)(i), and any official, employee, or agent of that foreign state while acting within the scope of his or her office, employment, or agency, shall be liable to—

(1) a national of the United States,

(2) a member of the armed forces,

(3) an employee of the Government of the United States, or of an individual performing a contract awarded by the United States Government, acting within the scope of the employee's employment, or

(4) the legal representative of a person described in paragraph (1), (2), or (3), for personal injury or death caused by acts described in subsection (a)(1) of that foreign state, or of an official, employee, or agent of that foreign state, for which the courts of the United States may maintain jurisdiction under this section for money damages. * * *

(h) Definitions.— For purposes of this section—

(1) the term "aircraft sabotage" has the meaning given that term in Article 1 of the Convention for the Suppression of Unlawful Acts Against the Safety of Civil Aviation;

(2) the term "hostage taking" has the meaning given that term in Article 1 of the International Convention Against the Taking of Hostages;

(3) the term "material support or resources" has the meaning given that term in section 2339A of title 18;

(4) the term "armed forces" has the meaning given that term in section 101 of title 10;

(5) the term "national of the United States" has the meaning given that term in section 101(a)(22) of the Immigration and Nationality Act (8 U.S.C. 1101 (a)(22));

(6) the term "state sponsor of terrorism" means a country the government of which the Secretary of State has determined * * * is a government that has repeatedly provided support for acts of international terrorism; and

(7) the terms "torture" and "extrajudicial killing" have the meaning given those terms in section 3 of the Torture Victim Protection Act of 1991 (28 U.S.C. 1350 note).

§ 1606. Extent of Liability

As to any claim for relief with respect to which a foreign state is not entitled to immunity under section 1605 or 1607 of this chapter, the foreign state shall be liable in the same manner and to the same extent as a private individual under like circumstances; but a foreign state except for an agency or instrumentality thereof shall not be liable for punitive damages; if, however, in any case wherein death was caused, the law of the place where the action or omission occurred provides, or has been construed to provide, for damages only punitive in nature, the foreign state shall be liable for actual or compensatory damages measured by the pecuniary injuries resulting from such death which were incurred by the persons for whose benefit the action was brought.

§ 1607. Counterclaims

In any action brought by a foreign state, or in which a foreign state intervenes, in a court of the United States or of a State, the foreign state shall not be accorded immunity with respect to any counterclaim—

(a) for which a foreign state would not be entitled to immunity under section 1605 or 1605A of this chapter had such claim been brought in a separate action against the foreign state; or

(b) arising out of the transaction or occurrence that is the subject matter of the claim of the foreign state; or

(c) to the extent that the counterclaim does not seek relief exceeding in amount or differing in kind from that sought by the foreign state.

* * *

§ 1609. Immunity from Attachment and Execution of Property of a Foreign State

Subject to existing international agreements to which the United States is a party at the time of enactment of this Act the property in the United States of a foreign state shall be immune from attachment arrest and execution except as provided in sections 1610 and 1611 of this chapter.

§ 1610. Exceptions to the Immunity from Attachment or Execution

(a) The property in the United States of a foreign state, as defined in section 1603(a) of this chapter, used for a commercial activity in the United States, shall not be immune from attachment in aid of execution, or from execution, upon a judgment entered by a court of the United States or of a State after the effective date of this Act, if—

(1) the foreign state has waived its immunity from attachment in aid of execution or from execution either explicitly or by implication, notwithstanding any withdrawal of the waiver the foreign state may purport to effect except in accordance with the terms of the waiver, or

(2) the property is or was used for the commercial activity upon which the claim is based, or

(3) the execution relates to a judgment establishing rights in property which has been taken in violation of international law or which has been exchanged for property taken in violation of international law, or

(4) the execution relates to a judgment establishing rights in property—

(A) which is acquired by succession or gift, or

(B) which is immovable and situated in the United States: *Provided,* That such property is not used for purposes of maintaining a diplomatic or consular mission or the residence of the Chief of such mission, or

(5) the property consists of any contractual obligation or any proceeds from such a contractual obligation to indemnify or hold harmless the foreign state or its employees under a policy of automobile or other liability or casualty insurance covering the claim which merged into the judgment;

(6) the judgment is based on an order confirming an arbitral award rendered against the foreign State, provided that attachment in aid of execution, or execution, would not be inconsistent with any provision in the arbitral agreement, or

(7) the judgment relates to a claim for which the foreign state is not immune under section 1605A or 1605(a)(7), regardless of whether

the property is or was involved with the act upon which the claim is based.

(b) In addition to subsection (a), any property in the United States of an agency or instrumentality of a foreign state engaged in commercial activity in the United States shall not be immune from attachment in aid of execution, or from execution, upon a judgment entered by a court of the United States or of a State after the effective date of this Act, if—

(1) the agency or instrumentality has waived its immunity from attachment in aid of execution or from execution either explicitly or implicitly, notwithstanding any withdrawal of the waiver the agency or instrumentality may purport to effect except in accordance with the terms of the waiver, or

(2) the judgment relates to a claim for which the agency or instrumentality is not immune by virtue of section 1605(a)(2), (3), or (5) or 1605(b) of this chapter, regardless of whether the property is or was used for the activity upon which the claim is based; or

(3) the judgment relates to a claim for which the agency or instrumentality is not immune by virtue of section 1605A of this chapter * * * regardless of whether the property is or was involved in the act upon which the claim is based.

(c) No attachment or execution referred to in subsections (a) and (b) of this section shall be permitted until the court has ordered such attachment and execution after having determined that a reasonable period of time has elapsed following the entry of judgment and the giving of any notice required under section 1608(e) of this chapter.

(d) The property of a foreign state, as defined in section 1603(a) of this chapter, used for a commercial activity in the United States, shall not be immune from attachment prior to the entry of judgment in any action brought in a court of the United States or of a State, or prior to the elapse of the period of time provided in subsection (c) of this section, if—

(1) the foreign state has explicitly waived its immunity from attachment prior to judgment, notwithstanding any withdrawal of the waiver the foreign state may purport to effect except in accordance with the terms of the waiver, and

(2) the purpose of the attachment is to secure satisfaction of a judgment that has been or may ultimately be entered against the foreign state, and not to obtain jurisdiction.

* * *

§ 1611. Certain Types of Property Immune from Execution

(a) Notwithstanding the provisions of section 1610 of this chapter, the property of those organizations designated by the President as being entitled to enjoy the privileges, exemptions and immunities provided by the International Organizations Immunities Act shall not be subject to attachment or any other judicial process impeding the disbursement of funds to, or on the order of, a foreign state as the result of an action brought in the courts of the United States or of the States.

(b) Notwithstanding the provisions of section 1610 of this chapter, the property of a foreign state shall be immune from attachment and from execution, if—

(1) the property is that of a foreign central bank or monetary authority held for its own account, unless such bank or authority, or its parent foreign government, has explicitly waived its immunity from attachment in aid of execution, or from execution, notwithstanding any withdrawal of the waiver which the bank, authority or government may purport to effect except in accordance with the terms of the waiver; or

(2) the property is, or is intended to be, used in connection with a military activity and

(A) is of a military character, or

(B) is under the control of a military authority or defense agency.

(c) Notwithstanding the provisions of section 1610 of this chapter, the property of a foreign state shall be immune from attachment and from execution in an action brought under section 302 of the Cuban Liberty and Democratic Solidarity (LIBERTAD) Act of 1996 to the extent that the property is a facility or installation used by an accredited diplomatic mission for official purposes.

DOCUMENT 50

SHERMAN ACT (1890), AS AMENDED BY THE FOREIGN TRADE ANTITRUST IMPROVEMENTS ACT (1982)

■ ■ ■

5 U.S.C. § 1, 2 and 7.

An act to protect trade and commerce against unlawful restraints and monopolies.

Sec. 1. Every contract, combination in the form of trust or otherwise, or conspiracy, in restraint of trade or commerce among the several States, or with foreign nations, is declared to be illegal. Every person who shall make any contract or engage in any combination or conspiracy hereby declared to be illegal shall be deemed guilty of a felony and, on conviction thereof, shall be punished by fine not exceeding $10,000,000 if a corporation, or, if any other person, $350,000, or by imprisonment not exceeding three years, or by both said punishments, in the discretion of the court.

Sec. 2. Every person who shall monopolize, or attempt to monopolize, or combine or conspire with any other person or persons, to monopolize any part of the trade or commerce among the several States, or with foreign nations, shall be deemed guilty of a felony, and, on conviction thereof, shall be punished by fine not exceeding $10,000,000 if a corporation, or, if any other person, $350,000, or by imprisonment not exceeding three years, or by both said punishments, in the discretion of the court.

* * *

Sec. 7. [FTAIA*] This Act shall not apply to conduct involving trade or commerce (other than import trade or import commerce) with foreign nations unless—

(1) such conduct has a direct, substantial, and reasonably foreseeable effect—

(A) on trade or commerce which is not trade or commerce with foreign nations, or on import trade or import commerce with foreign nations; or

* Foreign Trade Antitrust Improvements Act of 1982.

(B) on export trade or export commerce with foreign nations, of a person engaged in such trade or commerce in the United States; and

(2) such effect gives rise to a claim under the provisions of this Act, other than this section.

If this Act applies to such conduct only because of the operation of paragraph (1)(B), then this Act shall apply to such conduct only for injury to export business in the United States.

PART FIVE

UNIFORM STATE LAWS AND RESTATEMENTS OF THE LAW

DOCUMENT 51

RESTATEMENT (FIRST) OF CONFLICT OF LAWS (1934)

■ ■ ■

Chapter 8. Contracts

§ 332 Law Governing Validity of Contract

The law of the place of contracting determines the validity and effect of a promise with respect to

(a) capacity to make the contract;

(b) the necessary form, if any, in which the promise must be made;

(c) the mutual assent or consideration, if any, required to make a promise binding;

(d) any other requirements for making a promise binding;

(e) fraud, illegality, or any other circumstances which make a promise void or voidable;

(f) except as stated in § 358, the nature and extent of the duty for the performance of which a party becomes bound;

(g) the time when and the place where the promise is by its terms to be performed;

(h) the absolute or conditional character of the promise.

* * *

§ 358 Law Governing Performance

The duty for the performance of which a party to a contract is bound will be discharged by compliance with the law of the place of performance of the promise with respect to:

(a) the manner of performance;

(b) the time and locality of performance;

(c) the person or persons by whom or to whom performance shall be made or rendered;

(d) the sufficiency of performance;

(e) excuse for non-performance.

[comment b]. Practical line separating question of obligation from question of performance. While the law of the place of performance is applicable to determine the manner and sufficiency and conditions under which performance is to be made, it is not applicable to the point where the substantial obligation of the parties is materially altered. * * * [T]here is no logical line which separates questions of the obligation of the contract, which is determined by the law of the place of contracting, from questions of performance, determined by the law of the place of performance. There is, however, a practical line which is drawn in every case by the particular circumstances thereof. When the application of the law of the place of contracting would extend to the determination of the minute details of the manner, method, time and sufficiency of performance so that it would be an unreasonable regulation of acts in the place of performance, the law of the place of contracting will cease to control and the law of the place of performance will be applied. On the other hand, when the application of the law of the place of performance would extend to a regulation of the substance of the obligation to which the parties purported to bind themselves so that it would unreasonably determine the effect of an agreement made in the place of contracting, the law of the place of performance will give way to the law of the place of contracting.

* * *

Chapter 9. Wrongs

§ 377 The Place of Wrong

The place of wrong is in the state where the last event necessary to make an actor liable for an alleged tort takes place.

§ 378 Law Governing Plaintiff's Injury

The law of the place of wrong determines whether a person has sustained a legal injury.

§ 379 Law Governing Liability-Creating Conduct

* * * [T]the law of the place of wrong determines

(a) whether a person is responsible for harm he has caused only if he intended it,

(b) whether a person is responsible for unintended harm he has caused only if he was negligent.

(c) whether a person is responsible for harm he has caused irrespective of his intention or the care which he has exercised.

* * *

§ 384 Recognition of Foreign Cause of Action

(1) If a cause of action in tort is created at the place of wrong, a cause of action will be recognized in other states.

(2) If no cause of action is created at the place of wrong, no recovery in tort can be had in any other State.

* * *

Chapter 12. Procedure

§ 612 Action Contrary to Public Policy

No action can be maintained upon a cause of action created in another state the enforcement of which is contrary to the strong public policy of the forum.

DOCUMENT 52

RESTATEMENT (SECOND) OF CONFLICT OF LAWS (1971)

■ ■ ■

Chapter 1. Introduction

§ 6 Choice-of-Law Principles

(1) A court, subject to constitutional restrictions, will follow a statutory directive of its own state on choice of law.

(2) When there is no such directive, the factors relevant to the choice of the applicable rule of law include

(a) the needs of the interstate and international systems,

(b) the relevant policies of the forum,

(c) the relevant policies of other interested states and the relative interests of those states in the determination of the particular issue,

(d) the protection of justified expectations,

(e) the basic policies underlying the particular field of law,

(f) certainty, predictability and uniformity of result, and

(g) ease in the determination and application of the law to be applied.

[Comment c:]

Legislatures usually legislate, and courts usually adjudicate, only with the local situation in mind. They rarely give thought to the extent to which the laws they enact, and the common law rules they enunciate, should apply to out-of-state facts. When there are no adequate directives in the statute or in the case law, the court will take account of the factors listed in this Subsection in determining the state whose local law will be applied to determine the issue at hand. It is not suggested that this list of factors is exclusive. Undoubtedly, a court will on occasion give consideration to other factors in deciding a question of choice of law. Also it is not suggested that the factors mentioned are listed in the order of their relative importance. Varying weight will be given to a particular factor, or to a group of factors, in different areas of choice of law. * * *

At least some of the factors mentioned in this Subsection will point in different directions in all but the simplest case. Hence any rule of choice of law, like any other common law rule, represents an accommodation of conflicting values. Those chapters in the Restatement of this Subject which are concerned with choice of law state the rules which the courts have evolved in accommodation of the factors listed in this Subsection. * * * In [some] areas, such as in Wrongs (Chapter 7) and Contracts (Chapter 8), the difficulties and complexities involved have as yet prevented the courts from formulating a precise rule, or series of rules, which provide a satisfactory accommodation of the underlying factors in all of the situations which may arise. All that can presently be done in these areas is to state a general principle, such as application of the local law "of the state of most significant relationship", which provides some clue to the correct approach but does not furnish precise answers. In these areas, the courts must look in each case to the underlying factors themselves in order to arrive at a decision which will best accommodate them.

Statement of precise rules in many areas of choice of law is made even more difficult by the great variety of situations and of issues, by the fact that many of these situations and issues have not been thoroughly explored by the courts, by the generality of statement frequently used by the courts in their opinions, and by the new grounds of decision stated in many of the more recent opinions.

§ 10 Interstate and International Conflict of Laws

The rules in the Restatement of this Subject apply to cases with elements in one or more States of the United States and are generally applicable to cases with elements in one or more foreign nations. There may, however, be factors in a particular international case which call for a result different from that which would be reached in an interstate case.

Chapter 8. Contracts

Topic 1. Validity of Contracts and Rights Created Thereby

§ 187 Law of the State Chosen by the Parties

(1) The law of the state chosen by the parties to govern their contractual rights and duties will be applied if the particular issue is one which the parties could have resolved by an explicit provision in their agreement directed to that issue.

(2) The law of the state chosen by the parties to govern their contractual rights and duties will be applied, even if the particular issue is one which the parties could not have resolved by an explicit provision in their agreement directed to that issue, unless either

(a) the chosen state has no substantial relationship to the parties or the transaction and there is no other reasonable basis for the parties' choice, or

(b) application of the law of the chosen state would be contrary to a fundamental policy of a state which has a materially greater interest than the chosen state in the determination of the particular issue and which, under the rule of § 188, would be the state of the applicable law in the absence of an effective choice of law by the parties.

(3) In the absence of a contrary indication of intention, the reference is to the local law of the state of the chosen law.

§ 188 Law Governing in Absence of Effective Choice by the Parties

(1) The rights and duties of the parties with respect to an issue in contract are determined by the local law of the state which, with respect to that issue, has the most significant relationship to the transaction and the parties under the principles stated in § 6.

(2) In the absence of an effective choice of law by the parties (see § 187), the contacts to be taken into account in applying the principles of § 6 to determine the law applicable to an issue include:

(a) the place of contracting,

(b) the place of negotiation of the contract,

(c) the place of performance,

(d) the location of the subject matter of the contract, and

(e) the domicil, residence, nationality, place of incorporation and place of business of the parties.

These contacts are to be evaluated according to their relative importance with respect to the particular issue.

(3) If the place of negotiating the contract and the place of performance are in the same state, the local law of this state will usually be applied * * *.

Chapter 7. Wrongs

§ 145 The General Principle

(1) The rights and liabilities of the parties with respect to an issue in tort are determined by the local law of the state which, with respect to that issue, has the most significant relationship to the occurrence and the parties under the principles stated in§ 6.

(2) Contacts to be taken into account in applying the principles of § 6 to determine the law applicable to an issue include:

(a) the place where the injury occurred,

(b) the place where the conduct causing the injury occurred,

(c) the domicil, residence, nationality, place of incorporation and place of business of the parties, and

(d) the place where the relationship, if any, between the parties is centered.

These contacts are to be evaluated according to their relative importance with respect to the particular issue.

§ 146 Personal Injuries

In an action for a personal injury, the local law of the state where the injury occurred determines the rights and liabilities of the parties, unless, with respect to the particular issue, some other state has a more significant relationship under the principles stated in § 6 to the occurrence and the parties, in which event the local law of the other state will be applied.

§ 147 Injuries to Tangible Things

In an action for an injury to land or other tangible thing, the local law of the state where the injury occurred determines the rights and liabilities of the parties unless, with respect to the particular issue, some other state has a more significant relationship under the principles stated in § 6 to the occurrence, the thing and the parties, in which event the local law of the other state will be applied.

§ 156 Tortious Character of Conduct

(1) The law selected by application of the rule of § 145 determines whether the actor's conduct was tortious.

(2) The applicable law will usually be the local law of the state where the injury occurred.

* * *

DOCUMENT 53

UNIFORM COMMERCIAL CODE*

■ ■ ■

Table of Contents

Article 1. General Provisions

ARTICLE 1. GENERAL PROVISIONS

§ 1–103. Construction of uniform commercial code to promote its purposes and policies; applicability of supplemental principles of law

(a) The uniform commercial code must be liberally construed and applied to promote its underlying purposes and policies, which are:

(1) To simplify, clarify, and modernize the law governing commercial transactions;

(2) to permit the continued expansion of commercial practices through custom, usage and agreement of the parties; and

(3) to make uniform the law among the various jurisdictions.

(b) Unless displaced by the particular provisions of the uniform commercial code, the principles of law and equity, including the law merchant and the law relative to capacity to contract, principal and agent, estoppel, fraud, misrepresentation, duress, coercion, mistake, bankruptcy, and other validating or invalidating cause supplement its provisions.

Official Comments

1. The Uniform Commercial Code is drawn to provide flexibility so that, since it is intended to be a semi-permanent and infrequently-amended piece of legislation, it will provide its own machinery for expansion of commercial practices. It is intended to make it possible for the law embodied in the Uniform Commercial Code to be applied by the courts in the light of unforeseen and new circumstances and practices. The proper construction of the Uniform Commercial Code requires, of course, that its interpretation and application be limited to its reason.

* * *

The Uniform Commercial Code should be construed in accordance with its underlying purposes and policies. The text of each section should be read in the light of the purpose and policy of the rule or principle in question, as also of the Uniform Commercial Code as a whole, and the application of the language should be construed narrowly or broadly, as the case may be, in conformity with the purposes and policies involved.

[§ 1–105—See Authors' Note for § 1–301 below.]

§ 1–201. General Definitions

(a) Unless the context otherwise requires, words or phrases defined in this section, or in the additional definitions contained in other articles of the uniform commercial code that apply to particular articles or parts thereof, have the meanings stated.

* * *

(6) "Bill of lading" means a document of title evidencing the receipt of goods for shipment issued by a person engaged in the business of directly or indirectly transporting or forwarding goods.

* * *

(31) "Record" means information that is inscribed on a tangible medium or that is stored in an electronic or other medium and is retrievable in perceivable form.

* * *

(37) "Signed" includes using any symbol executed or adopted with present intention to adopt or accept a writing.

* * *

(43) "Writing" includes printing, typewriting, or any other intentional reduction to tangible form. "Written" has a corresponding meaning.

Official Comments

6. "Bill of Lading". * * * A bill of lading is one type of document of title * * *.

* * *

37. "Signed." * * * This provision refers only to writings, because the term "signed," as used in some articles, refers only to writings. This provision also makes it clear that, as the term "signed" is used in the Uniform Commercial Code, a complete signature is not necessary. The symbol may be printed, stamped or written; it may be by initials or by thumbprint. It may be on any part of the document and in appropriate cases may be found in a billhead or letterhead. No catalog of possible situations can be complete and the court must use common sense and commercial experience in passing upon these matters. The question always is whether the symbol was executed or adopted by the party with present intention to adopt or accept the writing.

* * *

[*Authors' Note on § 1–301: Although as of 2015 forty-six states have adopted revised Article 1, all have rejected the proposed provision on choice-of-law in § 1–301. Instead, they have reenacted the substance of the original § 1–105 and renumbered that provision as § 1–301. The Uniform Law Commission subsequently revised the official version of § 1–301 accordingly. The text below thus sets forth the re-adoption of original § 1–105 as well as the now Official Comments to that section.*]

§ 1–301. Territorial Application of the Act; Parties' Power to Choose Applicable Law

(1) Except as provided hereafter in this section, when a transaction bears a reasonable relation to this state and also to another state or nation the parties may agree that the law either of this state or of such other state or nation shall govern their rights and duties.

(2) In the absence of an agreement effective under subsection (a) * * *, the uniform commercial code applies to transactions bearing an appropriate relation to this state.

* * *

Official Comments

1. Subsection (1) states affirmatively the right of the parties to a multi-state transaction or a transaction involving foreign trade to choose their own law. That right is subject to the firm rules stated in the five sections listed in subsection (2), and is limited to jurisdictions to which the transaction bears a "reasonable relation." In general, the test of "reasonable relation" is similar to that laid down by the Supreme Court in Seeman v. Philadelphia Warehouse Co., 274 U.S. 403, 47 S.Ct. 626, 71 L.Ed. 1123 (1927). Ordinarily the law chosen must be that of a jurisdiction where a significant enough portion of the making

or performance of the contract is to occur or occurs. But an agreement as to choice of law may sometimes take effect as a shorthand expression of the intent of the parties as to matters governed by their agreement, even though the transaction has no significant contact with the jurisdiction chosen.

2. Where there is no agreement as to the governing law, the Act is applicable to any transaction having an "appropriate" relation to any state which enacts it. Of course, the Act applies to any transaction which takes place in its entirety in a state which has enacted the Act. But the mere fact that suit is brought in a state does not make it appropriate to apply the substantive law of that state. Cases where a relation to the enacting state is not "appropriate" include, for example, those where the parties have clearly contracted on the basis of some other law, as where the law of the place of contracting and the law of the place of contemplated performance are the same and are contrary to the law under the Code.

3. Where a transaction has significant contacts with a state which has enacted the Act and also with other jurisdictions, the question what relation is "appropriate" is left to judicial decision. In deciding that question, the court is not strictly bound by precedents established in other contexts. Thus a conflict-of-laws decision refusing to apply a purely local statute or rule of law to a particular multi-state transaction may not be valid precedent for refusal to apply the Code in an analogous situation. Application of the Code in such circumstances may be justified by its comprehensiveness, by the policy of uniformity, and by the fact that it is in large part a reformulation and restatement of the law merchant and of the understanding of a business community which transcends state and even national boundaries. Compare Global Commerce Corp. v. Clark-Babbitt Industries, Inc., 239 F.2d 716, 719 (2d Cir. 1956). In particular, where a transaction is governed in large part by the Code, application of another law to some detail of performance because of an accident of geography may violate the commercial understanding of the parties.

4. The Act does not attempt to prescribe choice-of-law rules for states which do not enact it, but this section does not prevent application of the Act in a court of such a state. Common-law choice of law often rests on policies of giving effect to agreements and of uniformity of result regardless of where suit is brought. To the extent that such policies prevail, the relevant considerations are similar in such a court to those outlined above.

5. Subsection (2) spells out essential limitations on the parties' right to choose the applicable law. Especially in Article 9 parties taking a security interest or asked to extend credit which may be subject to a security interest must have sure ways to find out whether and where to file and where to look for possible existing filings.

6. Section 9–103 should be consulted as to the rules for perfection of security interests and the effects of perfection and nonperfection.

* * *

§ 1–302. Variation by agreement

(a) Except as otherwise provided in subsection (b) or elsewhere in the uniform commercial code, the effect of provisions of the uniform commercial code may be varied by agreement.

(b) The obligations of good faith, diligence, reasonableness, and care prescribed by the uniform commercial code may not be disclaimed by agreement. The parties, by agreement, may determine the standards by which the performance of those obligations is to be measured if those standards are not manifestly unreasonable. Whenever the uniform commercial code requires an action to be taken within a reasonable time, a time that is not manifestly unreasonable may be fixed by agreement.

(c) The presence in certain provisions of the uniform commercial code of the phrase "unless otherwise agreed", or words of similar import, does not imply that the effect of other provisions may not be varied by agreement under this section.

Official Comments

Source: Former Sections 1–102(3)–(4) and 1–204(1).

Changes: This section combines the rules from subsections (3) and (4) of former Section 1–102 and subsection (1) of former Section 1–204. No substantive changes are made.

1. Subsection (a) states affirmatively at the outset that freedom of contract is a principle of the Uniform Commercial Code: "the effect" of its provisions may be varied by "agreement." The meaning of the statute itself must be found in its text, including its definitions, and in appropriate extrinsic aids; it cannot be varied by agreement. * * * But an agreement can change the legal consequences that would otherwise flow from the provisions of the Uniform Commercial Code. "Agreement" here includes the effect given to course of dealing, usage of trade and course of performance by Sections 1–201 and 1–303; the effect of an agreement on the rights of third parties is left to specific provisions of the Uniform Commercial Code and to supplementary principles applicable under Section 1–103. The rights of third parties under Section 9–317 when a security interest is unperfected, for example, cannot be destroyed by a clause in the security agreement.

This principle of freedom of contract is subject to specific exceptions found elsewhere in the Uniform Commercial Code and to the general exception stated here. The specific exceptions vary in explicitness: the statute of frauds found in Section 2–201, for example, does not explicitly preclude oral waiver of the requirement of a writing, but a fair reading denies enforcement to such a waiver as part of the "contract" made unenforceable; Section 9–602, on the other hand, is a quite explicit limitation on freedom of contract. Under the exception for "the obligations of good faith, diligence, reasonableness and care prescribed by [the Uniform Commercial Code]," provisions of the Uniform Commercial Code prescribing such obligations are not to be disclaimed.

However, the section also recognizes the prevailing practice of having agreements set forth standards by which due diligence is measured and explicitly provides that, in the absence of a showing that the standards manifestly are unreasonable, the agreement controls. In this connection, Section 1–303 incorporating into the agreement prior course of dealing and usages of trade is of particular importance.

Subsection (b) also recognizes that nothing is stronger evidence of a reasonable time than the fixing of such time by a fair agreement between the parties. However, provision is made for disregarding a clause which whether by inadvertence or overreaching fixes a time so unreasonable that it amounts to eliminating all remedy under the contract. The parties are not required to fix the most reasonable time but may fix any time which is not obviously unfair as judged by the time of contracting.

2. An agreement that varies the effect of provisions of the Uniform Commercial Code may do so by stating the rules that will govern in lieu of the provisions varied. Alternatively, the parties may vary the effect of such provisions by stating that their relationship will be governed by recognized bodies of rules or principles applicable to commercial transactions. Such bodies of rules or principles may include, for example, those that are promulgated by intergovernmental authorities such as UNCITRAL or Unidroit (*see, e.g.*, Unidroit Principles of International Commercial Contracts), or non-legal codes such as trade codes.

3. Subsection (c) is intended to make it clear that, as a matter of drafting, phrases such as "unless otherwise agreed" have been used to avoid controversy as to whether the subject matter of a particular section does or does not fall within the exceptions to subsection (b), but absence of such words contains no negative implication since under subsection (b) the general and residual rule is that the effect of all provisions of the Uniform Commercial Code may be varied by agreement.

§ 1–303. Course of performance, course of dealing, and usage of trade

(a) A "course of performance" is a sequence of conduct between the parties to a particular transaction that exists if:

(1) The agreement of the parties with respect to the transaction involves repeated occasions for performance by a party; and

(2) the other party, with knowledge of the nature of the performance and opportunity for objection to it, accepts the performance or acquiesces in it without objection.

(b) A "course of dealing" is a sequence of conduct concerning previous transactions between the parties to a particular transaction that is fairly to be regarded as establishing a common basis of understanding for interpreting their expressions and other conduct.

(c) A "usage of trade" is any practice or method of dealing having such regularity of observance in a place, vocation, or trade as to justify an expectation that it will be observed with respect to the transaction in question. The existence and scope of such a usage must be proved as facts. If it is established that such a usage is embodied in a trade code or similar record, the interpretation of the record is a question of law.

(d) A course of performance or course of dealing between the parties or usage of trade in the vocation or trade in which they are engaged or of which they are or should be aware is relevant in ascertaining the meaning of the parties' agreement, may give particular meaning to specific terms of the agreement, and may supplement or qualify the terms of the agreement. A usage of trade applicable in the place in which part of the performance under the agreement is to occur may be so utilized as to that part of the performance.

(e) Except as otherwise provided in subsection (f), the express terms of an agreement and any applicable course of performance, course of dealing, or usage of trade must be construed whenever reasonable as consistent with each other. If such a construction is unreasonable:

(1) Express terms prevail over course of performance, course of dealing, and usage of trade;

(2) course of performance prevails over course of dealing and usage of trade; and

(3) course of dealing prevails over usage of trade.

(f) Subject to Section 2–209 * * *, a course of performance is relevant to show a waiver or modification of any term inconsistent with the course of performance.

(g) Evidence of a relevant usage of trade offered by one party is not admissible unless that party has given the other party notice that the court finds sufficient to prevent unfair surprise to the other party.

Official Comments

1. The Uniform Commercial Code rejects both the "lay-dictionary" and the "conveyancer's" reading of a commercial agreement. Instead the meaning of the agreement of the parties is to be determined by the language used by them and by their action, read and interpreted in the light of commercial practices and other surrounding circumstances. The measure and background for interpretation are set by the commercial context, which may explain and supplement even the language of a formal or final writing.

2. "Course of dealing," as defined in subsection (b), is restricted, literally, to a sequence of conduct between the parties previous to the agreement. A sequence of conduct after or under the agreement, however, is a "course of performance." "Course of dealing" may enter the agreement either by explicit provisions of the agreement or by tacit recognition.

3. The Uniform Commercial Code deals with "usage of trade" as a factor in reaching the commercial meaning of the agreement that the parties have made. The language used is to be interpreted as meaning what it may fairly be expected to mean to parties involved in the particular commercial transaction in a given locality or in a given vocation or trade. By adopting in this context the term "usage of trade," the Uniform Commercial Code expresses its intent to reject those cases which see evidence of "custom" as representing an effort to displace or negate "established rules of law." A distinction is to be drawn between mandatory rules of law such as the Statute of Frauds provisions of Article 2 on Sales whose very office is to control and restrict the actions of the parties, and which cannot be abrogated by agreement, or by a usage of trade, and those rules of law (such as those in Part 3 of Article 2 on Sales) which fill in points which the parties have not considered and in fact agreed upon. The latter rules hold "unless otherwise agreed" but yield to the contrary agreement of the parties. Part of the agreement of the parties to which such rules yield is to be sought for in the usages of trade which furnish the background and give particular meaning to the language used, and are the framework of common understanding controlling any general rules of law which hold only when there is no such understanding.

4. A usage of trade under subsection (c) must have the "regularity of observance" specified. The ancient English tests for "custom" are abandoned in this connection. Therefore, it is not required that a usage of trade be "ancient or immemorial," "universal," or the like. Under the requirement of subsection (c) full recognition is thus available for new usages and for usages currently observed by the great majority of decent dealers, even though dissidents ready to cut corners do not agree. There is room also for proper recognition of usage agreed upon by merchants in trade codes.

* * *

6. Subsection (d), giving the prescribed effect to usages of which the parties "are or should be aware," reinforces the provision of subsection (c) requiring not universality but only the described "regularity of observance" of the practice or method. This subsection also reinforces the point of subsection (c) that such usages may be either general to trade or particular to a special branch of trade.

* * *

8. In cases of a well established line of usage varying from the general rules of the Uniform Commercial Code where the precise amount of the variation has not been worked out into a single standard, the party relying on the usage is entitled, in any event, to the minimum variation demonstrated. The whole is not to be disregarded because no particular line of detail has been established. In case a dominant pattern has been fairly evidenced, the party relying on the usage is entitled under this section to go to the trier of fact on the question of whether such dominant pattern has been incorporated into the agreement.

9. Subsection (g) is intended to insure that this Act's liberal recognition of the needs of commerce in regard to usage of trade shall not be made into an instrument of abuse.

* * *

ARTICLE 2. SALES

§ 2–201. Formal Requirements; Statute of Frauds.

(1) Except as otherwise provided in this section a contract for the sale of goods for the price of $500 or more is not enforceable by way of action or defense unless there is some writing sufficient to indicate that a contract for sale has been made between the parties and signed by the party against whom enforcement is sought or by his authorized agent or broker. A writing is not insufficient because it omits or incorrectly states a term agreed upon but the contract is not enforceable under this paragraph beyond the quantity of goods shown in such writing.

(2) Between merchants if within a reasonable time a writing in confirmation of the contract and sufficient against the sender is received and the party receiving it has reason to know its contents, it satisfies the requirements of subsection (1) against such party unless written notice of objection to its contents is given within 10 days after it is received.

(3) A contract which does not satisfy the requirements of subsection (1) but which is valid in other respects is enforceable

(a) if the goods are to be specially manufactured for the buyer and are not suitable for sale to others in the ordinary course of the seller's business and the seller, before notice of repudiation is received and under circumstances which reasonably indicate that the goods are for the buyer, has made either a substantial beginning of their manufacture or commitments for their procurement; or

(b) if the party against whom enforcement is sought admits in his pleading, testimony or otherwise in court that a contract for sale was made, but the contract is not enforceable under this provision beyond the quantity of goods admitted; or

(c) with respect to goods for which payment has been made and accepted or which have been received and accepted (Sec. 2–606).

Official Comment

1. The required writing need not contain all the material terms of the contract and such material terms as are stated need not be precisely stated. All that is required is that the writing afford a basis for believing that the offered oral evidence rests on a real transaction. It may be written in lead pencil on a scratch pad. It need not indicate which party is the buyer and which the seller. The only term which must appear is the quantity term which need not be accurately stated but recovery is limited to the amount stated. The price,

time and place of payment or delivery, the general quality of the goods, or any particular warranties may all be omitted.

Special emphasis must be placed on the permissibility of omitting the price term in view of the insistence of some courts on the express inclusion of this term even where the parties have contracted on the basis of a published price list. In many valid contracts for sale the parties do not mention the price in express terms, the buyer being bound to pay and the seller to accept a reasonable price which the trier of the fact may well be trusted to determine. Again, frequently the price is not mentioned since the parties have based their agreement on a price list or catalogue known to both of them and this list serves as an efficient safeguard against perjury. Finally, "market" prices and valuations that are current in the vicinity constitute a similar check. Thus if the price is not stated in the memorandum it can normally be supplied without danger of fraud. Of course if the "price" consists of goods rather than money the quantity of goods must be stated.

Only three definite and invariable requirements as to the memorandum are made by this subsection. First, it must evidence a contract for the sale of goods; second, it must be "signed", a word which includes any authentication which identifies the party to be charged; and third, it must specify a quantity.

2. "Partial performance" as a substitute for the required memorandum can validate the contract only for the goods which have been accepted or for which payment has been made and accepted.

* * *

3. Between merchants, failure to answer a written confirmation of a contract within ten days of receipt is tantamount to a writing under subsection (2) and is sufficient against both parties under subsection (1). The only effect, however, is to take away from the party who fails to answer the defense of the Statute of Frauds; the burden of persuading the trier of fact that a contract was in fact made orally prior to the written confirmation is unaffected. Compare the effect of a failure to reply under Section 2–207.

4. Failure to satisfy the requirements of this section does not render the contract void for all purposes, but merely prevents it from being judicially enforced in favor of a party to the contract. For example, a buyer who takes possession of goods as provided in an oral contract which the seller has not meanwhile repudiated, is not a trespasser. Nor would the Statute of Frauds provisions of this section be a defense to a third person who wrongfully induces a party to refuse to perform an oral contract, even though the injured party cannot maintain an action for damages against the party so refusing to perform.

5. The requirement of "signing" is discussed in the comment to Section 1–201.

6. It is not necessary that the writing be delivered to anybody. It need not be signed or authenticated by both parties but it is, of course, not sufficient

against one who has not signed it. Prior to a dispute no one can determine which party's signing of the memorandum may be necessary but from the time of contracting each party should be aware that to him it is signing by the other which is important.

* * *

§ 2–207. Additional Terms in Acceptance or Confirmation.

(1) A definite and seasonable expression of acceptance or a written confirmation which is sent within a reasonable time operates as an acceptance even though it states terms additional to or different from those offered or agreed upon, unless acceptance is expressly made conditional on assent to the additional or different terms.

(2) The additional terms are to be construed as proposals for addition to the contract. Between merchants such terms become part of the contract unless:

(a) the offer expressly limits acceptance to the terms of the offer;

(b) they materially alter it; or

(c) notification of objection to them has already been given or is given within a reasonable time after notice of them is received.

(3) Conduct by both parties which recognizes the existence of a contract is sufficient to establish a contract for sale although the writings of the parties do not otherwise establish a contract. In such case the terms of the particular contract consist of those terms on which the writings of the parties agree, together with any supplementary terms incorporated under any other provisions of this Act.

Official Comment

1. This section is intended to deal with two typical situations. The one is the written confirmation, where an agreement has been reached either orally or by informal correspondence between the parties and is followed by one or both of the parties sending formal memoranda embodying the terms so far as agreed upon and adding terms not discussed. The other situation is offer and acceptance, in which a wire or letter expressed and intended as an acceptance or the closing of an agreement adds further minor suggestions or proposals such as "ship by Tuesday," "rush," "ship draft against bill of lading inspection allowed," or the like. A frequent example of the second situation is the exchange of printed purchase order and acceptance (sometimes called "acknowledgment") forms. Because the forms are oriented to the thinking of the respective drafting parties, the terms contained in them often do not correspond. Often the seller's form contains terms different from or additional to those set forth in the buyer's form. Nevertheless, the parties proceed with the transaction. [Comment 1 was amended in 1966.]

2. Under this Article a proposed deal which in commercial understanding has in fact been closed is recognized as a contract. Therefore, any additional matter contained in the confirmation or in the acceptance falls within subsection (2) and must be regarded as a proposal for an added term unless the acceptance is made conditional on the acceptance of the additional or different terms. [Comment 2 was amended in 1966.]

3. Whether or not additional or different terms will become part of the agreement depends upon the provisions of subsection (2). If they are such as materially to alter the original bargain, they will not be included unless expressly agreed to by the other party. If, however, they are terms which would not so change the bargain they will be incorporated unless notice of objection to them has already been given or is given within a reasonable time.

4. Examples of typical clauses which would normally "materially alter" the contract and so result in surprise or hardship if incorporated without express awareness by the other party are: a clause negating such standard warranties as that of merchantability or fitness for a particular purpose in circumstances in which either warranty normally attaches; a clause requiring a guaranty of 90% or 100% deliveries in a case such as a contract by cannery, where the usage of the trade allows greater quantity leeways; a clause reserving to the seller the power to cancel upon the buyer's failure to meet any invoice when due; a clause requiring that complaints be made in a time materially shorter than customary or reasonable.

5. Examples of clauses which involve no element of unreasonable surprise and which therefore are to be incorporated in the contract unless notice of objection is seasonably given are: a clause setting forth and perhaps enlarging slightly upon the seller's exemption due to supervening causes beyond his control, similar to those covered by the provision of this Article on merchant's excuse by failure of presupposed conditions or a clause fixing in advance any reasonable formula of proration under such circumstances; a clause fixing a reasonable time for complaints within customary limits, or in the case of a purchase for sub-sale, providing for inspection by the sub-purchaser; a clause providing for interest on overdue invoices or fixing the seller's standard credit terms where they are within the range of trade practice and do not limit any credit bargained for; a clause limiting the right of rejection for defects which fall within the customary trade tolerances for acceptance "with adjustment" or otherwise limiting remedy in a reasonable manner (see Sections 2–718 and 2–719).

6. If no answer is received within a reasonable time after additional terms are proposed, it is both fair and commercially sound to assume that their inclusion has been assented to. Where clauses on confirming forms sent by both parties conflict each party must be assumed to object to a clause of the other conflicting with one on the confirmation sent by himself. As a result the requirement that there be notice of objection which is found in subsection (2) is satisfied and the conflicting terms do not become a part of the contract. The contract then consists of the terms originally expressly agreed to, terms on

which the confirmations agree, and terms supplied by this Act, including subsection (2). The written confirmation is also subject to Section 2–201. Under that section a failure to respond permits enforcement of a prior oral agreement; under this section a failure to respond permits additional terms to become part of the agreement. [Comment 6 was amended in 1966.]

7. In many cases, as where goods are shipped, accepted and paid for before any dispute arises, there is no question whether a contract has been made. In such cases, where the writings of the parties do not establish a contract, it is not necessary to determine which act or document constituted the offer and which the acceptance. See Section 2–204. The only question is what terms are included in the contract, and subsection (3) furnishes the governing rule. [Comment 7 was added in 1966.]

* * *

§ 2–305. Open Price Term.

(1) The parties if they so intend can conclude a contract for sale even though the price is not settled. In such a case the price is a reasonable price at the time for delivery if

(a) nothing is said as to price; or

(b) the price is left to be agreed by the parties and they fail to agree; or

(c) the price is to be fixed in terms of some agreed market or other standard as set or recorded by a third person or agency and it is not so set or recorded.

(2) A price to be fixed by the seller or by the buyer means a price for him to fix in good faith.

(3) When a price left to be fixed otherwise than by agreement of the parties fails to be fixed through fault of one party the other may at his option treat the contract as cancelled or himself fix a reasonable price.

(4) Where, however, the parties intend not to be bound unless the price be fixed or agreed and it is not fixed or agreed there is no contract. In such a case the buyer must return any goods already received or if unable so to do must pay their reasonable value at the time of delivery and the seller must return any portion of the price paid on account.

Official Comment

1. This section applies when the price term is left open on the making of an agreement which is nevertheless intended by the parties to be a binding agreement. This Article rejects in these instances the formula that "an agreement to agree is unenforceable" if the case falls within subsection (1) of this section, and rejects also defeating such agreements on the ground of "indefiniteness". Instead this Article recognizes the dominant intention of the parties to have the deal continue to be binding upon both. As to future

performance, since this Article recognizes remedies such as cover (Section 2–712), resale (Section 2–706) and specific performance (Section 2–716) which go beyond any mere arithmetic as between contract price and market price, there is usually a "reasonably certain basis for granting an appropriate remedy for breach" so that the contract need not fail for indefiniteness.

2. Under some circumstances the postponement of agreement on price will mean that no deal has really been concluded, and this is made express in the preamble of subsection (1) ("The parties *if they so intend*") and in subsection (4). Whether or not this is so is, in most cases, a question to be determined by the trier of fact.

3. Subsection (2), dealing with the situation where the price is to be fixed by one party rejects the uncommercial idea that an agreement that the seller may fix the price means that he may fix any price he may wish by the express qualification that the price so fixed must be fixed in good faith. Good faith includes observance of reasonable commercial standards of fair dealing in the trade if the party is a merchant. (Section 2–103). But in the normal case a "posted price" or a future seller's or buyer's "given price," "price in effect," "market price," or the like satisfies the good faith requirement.

* * *

§ 2–306. Output, Requirements and Exclusive Dealings.

(1) A term which measures the quantity by the output of the seller or the requirements of the buyer means such actual output or requirements as may occur in good faith, except that no quantity unreasonably disproportionate to any stated estimate or in the absence of a stated estimate to any normal or otherwise comparable prior output or requirements may be tendered or demanded.

(2) A lawful agreement by either the seller or the buyer for exclusive dealing in the kind of goods concerned imposes unless otherwise agreed an obligation by the seller to use best efforts to supply the goods and by the buyer to use best efforts to promote their sale.

Official Comment

1. Subsection (1) of this section, in regard to output and requirements, applies to this specific problem the general approach of this Act which requires the reading of commercial background and intent into the language of any agreement and demands good faith in the performance of that agreement. It applies to such contracts of nonproducing establishments such as dealers or distributors as well as to manufacturing concerns.

2. Under this Article, a contract for output or requirements is not too indefinite since it is held to mean the actual good faith output or requirements of the particular party. Nor does such a contract lack mutuality of obligation since, under this section, the party who will determine quantity is required to operate his plant or conduct his business in good faith and according to

commercial standards of fair dealing in the trade so that his output or requirements will approximate a reasonably foreseeable figure. Reasonable elasticity in the requirements is expressly envisaged by this section and good faith variations from prior requirements are permitted even when the variation may be such as to result in discontinuance. A shut-down by a requirements buyer for lack of orders might be permissible when a shut-down merely to curtail losses would not. The essential test is whether the party is acting in good faith. Similarly, a sudden expansion of the plant by which requirements are to be measured would not be included within the scope of the contract as made but normal expansion undertaken in good faith would be within the scope of this section. One of the factors in an expansion situation would be whether the market price had risen greatly in a case in which the requirements contract contained a fixed price. Reasonable variation of an extreme sort is exemplified in Southwest Natural Gas Co. v. Oklahoma Portland Cement Co., 102 F.2d 630 (C.C.A.10, 1939). This Article takes no position as to whether a requirements contract is a provable claim in bankruptcy.

3. If an estimate of output or requirements is included in the agreement, no quantity unreasonably disproportionate to it may be tendered or demanded. Any minimum or maximum set by the agreement shows a clear limit on the intended elasticity. In similar fashion, the agreed estimate is to be regarded as a center around which the parties intend the variation to occur.

* * *

5. Subsection (2), on exclusive dealing, makes explicit the commercial rule embodied in this Act under which the parties to such contracts are held to have impliedly, even when not expressly, bound themselves to use reasonable diligence as well as good faith in their performance of the contract. Under such contracts the exclusive agent is required, although no express commitment has been made, to use reasonable effort and due diligence in the expansion of the market or the promotion of the product, as the case may be. The principal is expected under such a contract to refrain from supplying any other dealer or agent within the exclusive territory. An exclusive dealing agreement brings into play all of the good faith aspects of the output and requirement problems of subsection (1). It also raises questions of insecurity and right to adequate assurance under this Article.

* * *

§ 2–314. Implied Warranty: Merchantability; Usage of Trade.

(1) Unless excluded or modified (Section 2–316), a warranty that the goods shall be merchantable is implied in a contract for their sale if the seller is a merchant with respect to goods of that kind. Under this section the serving for value of food or drink to be consumed either on the premises or elsewhere is a sale.

(2) Goods to be merchantable must be at least such as

(a) pass without objection in the trade under the contract description; and

(b) in the case of fungible goods, are of fair average quality within the description; and

(c) are fit for the ordinary purposes for which such goods are used; and

(d) run, within the variations permitted by the agreement, of even kind, quality and quantity within each unit and among all units involved; and

(e) are adequately contained, packaged, and labeled as the agreement may require; and

(f) conform to the promise or affirmations of fact made on the container or label if any.

(3) Unless excluded or modified (Section 2–316) other implied warranties may arise from course of dealing or usage of trade.

Official Comment

* * *

3. A specific designation of goods by the buyer does not exclude the seller's obligation that they be fit for the general purposes appropriate to such goods. A contract for the sale of second-hand goods, however, involves only such obligation as is appropriate to such goods for that is their contract description. A person making an isolated sale of goods is not a "merchant" within the meaning of the full scope of this section and, thus, no warranty of merchantability would apply. His knowledge of any defects not apparent on inspection would, however, without need for express agreement and in keeping with the underlying reason of the present section and the provisions on good faith, impose an obligation that known material but hidden defects be fully disclosed.

* * *

8. Fitness for the ordinary purposes for which goods of the type are used is a fundamental concept of the present section and is covered in paragraph (c). As stated above, merchantability is also a part of the obligation owing to the purchaser for use. Correspondingly, protection, under this aspect of the warranty, of the person buying for resale to the ultimate consumer is equally necessary, and merchantable goods must therefore be "honestly" resalable in the normal course of business because they are what they purport to be.

* * *

11. Exclusion or modification of the warranty of merchantability, or of any part of it, is dealt with in the section to which the text of the present section makes explicit precautionary references. That section must be read with

particular reference to its subsection (4) on limitation of remedies. The warranty of merchantability, wherever it is normal, is so commonly taken for granted that its exclusion from the contract is a matter threatening surprise and therefore requiring special precaution.

12. Subsection (3) is to make explicit that usage of trade and course of dealing can create warranties and that they are implied rather than express warranties and thus subject to exclusion or modification under Section 2–316. A typical instance would be the obligation to provide pedigree papers to evidence conformity of the animal to the contract in the case of a pedigreed dog or blooded bull.

§ 2–315. Implied Warranty: Fitness for Particular Purpose.

Where the seller at the time of contracting has reason to know any particular purpose for which the goods are required and that the buyer is relying on the seller's skill or judgment to select or furnish suitable goods, there is unless excluded or modified under the next section an implied warranty that the goods shall be fit for such purpose.

Official Comment

1. Whether or not this warranty arises in any individual case is basically a question of fact to be determined by the circumstances of the contracting. Under this section the buyer need not bring home to the seller actual knowledge of the particular purpose for which the goods are intended or of his reliance on the seller's skill and judgment, if the circumstances are such that the seller has reason to realize the purpose intended or that the reliance exists. The buyer, of course, must actually be relying on the seller.

2. A "particular purpose" differs from the ordinary purpose for which the goods are used in that it envisages a specific use by the buyer which is peculiar to the nature of his business whereas the ordinary purposes for which goods are used are those envisaged in the concept of merchantability and go to uses which are customarily made of the goods in question. For example, shoes are generally used for the purpose of walking upon ordinary ground, but a seller may know that a particular pair was selected to be used for climbing mountains.

A contract may of course include both a warranty of merchantability and one of fitness for a particular purpose.

The provisions of this Article on the cumulation and conflict of express and implied warranties must be considered on the question of inconsistency between or among warranties. In such a case any question of fact as to which warranty was intended by the parties to apply must be resolved in favor of the warranty of fitness for particular purpose as against all other warranties except where the buyer has taken upon himself the responsibility of furnishing the technical specifications.

3. In connection with the warranty of fitness for a particular purpose the provisions of this Article on the allocation or division of risks are

particularly applicable in any transaction in which the purpose for which the goods are to be used combines requirements both as to the quality of the goods themselves and compliance with certain laws or regulations. How the risks are divided is a question of fact to be determined, where not expressly contained in the agreement, from the circumstances of contracting, usage of trade, course of performance and the like, matters which may constitute the "otherwise agreement" of the parties by which they may divide the risk or burden.

* * *

6. The specific reference forward in the present section to the following section on exclusion or modification of warranties is to call attention to the possibility of eliminating the warranty in any given case. However it must be noted that under the following section the warranty of fitness for a particular purpose must be excluded or modified by a conspicuous writing.

§ 2–316. Exclusion or Modification of Warranties.

(1) Words or conduct relevant to the creation of an express warranty and words or conduct tending to negate or limit warranty shall be construed wherever reasonable as consistent with each other; but subject to the provisions of this Article on parol or extrinsic evidence (Section 2–202) negation or limitation is inoperative to the extent that such construction is unreasonable.

(2) Subject to subsection (3), to exclude or modify the implied warranty of merchantability or any part of it the language must mention merchantability and in case of a writing must be conspicuous, and to exclude or modify any implied warranty of fitness the exclusion must be by a writing and conspicuous. Language to exclude all implied warranties of fitness is sufficient if it states, for example, that "There are no warranties which extend beyond the description on the face hereof."

(3) Notwithstanding subsection (2)

(a) unless the circumstances indicate otherwise, all implied warranties are excluded by expressions like "as is", "with all faults" or other language which in common understanding calls the buyer's attention to the exclusion of warranties and makes plain that there is no implied warranty; and

(b) when the buyer before entering into the contract has examined the goods or the sample or model as fully as he desired or has refused to examine the goods there is no implied warranty with regard to defects which an examination ought in the circumstances to have revealed to him; and

(c) an implied warranty can also be excluded or modified by course of dealing or course of performance or usage of trade.

(4) Remedies for breach of warranty can be limited in accordance with the provisions of this Article on liquidation or limitation of damages and on contractual modification of remedy (Sections 2–718 and 2–719).

Official Comment

1. This section is designed principally to deal with those frequent clauses in sales contracts which seek to exclude "all warranties, express or implied." It seeks to protect a buyer from unexpected and unbargained language of disclaimer by denying effect to such language when inconsistent with language of express warranty and permitting the exclusion of implied warranties only by conspicuous language or other circumstances which protect the buyer from surprise.

* * *

3. Disclaimer of the implied warranty of merchantability is permitted under subsection (2), but with the safeguard that such disclaimers must mention merchantability and in case of a writing must be conspicuous.

4. Unlike the implied warranty of merchantability, implied warranties of fitness for a particular purpose may be excluded by general language, but only if it is in writing and conspicuous.

5. Subsection (2) presupposes that the implied warranty in question exists unless excluded or modified. Whether or not language of disclaimer satisfies the requirements of this section, such language may be relevant under other sections to the question whether the warranty was ever in fact created. Thus, unless the provisions of this Article on parol and extrinsic evidence prevent, oral language of disclaimer may raise issues of fact as to whether reliance by the buyer occurred and whether the seller had "reason to know" under the section on implied warranty of fitness for a particular purpose.

6. The exceptions to the general rule set forth in paragraphs (a), (b) and (c) of subsection (3) are common factual situations in which the circumstances surrounding the transaction are in themselves sufficient to call the buyer's attention to the fact that no implied warranties are made or that a certain implied warranty is being excluded.

* * *

9. The situation in which the buyer gives precise and complete specifications to the seller is not explicitly covered in this section, but this is a frequent circumstance by which the implied warranties may be excluded. The warranty of fitness for a particular purpose would not normally arise since in such a situation there is usually no reliance on the seller by the buyer. The warranty of merchantability in such a transaction, however, must be considered in connection with the next section on the cumulation and conflict of warranties. Under paragraph (c) of that section in case of such an inconsistency the implied warranty of merchantability is displaced by the express warranty that the goods will comply with the specifications. Thus,

where the buyer gives detailed specifications as to the goods, neither of the implied warranties as to quality will normally apply to the transaction unless consistent with the specifications.

* * *

§ 2–319. F.O.B. and F.A.S. Terms.

(1) Unless otherwise agreed the term F.O.B. (which means "free on board") at a named place, even though used only in connection with the stated price, is a delivery term under which

(a) when the term is F.O.B. the place of shipment, the seller must at that place ship the goods in the manner provided in this Article (Section 2–504) and bear the expense and risk of putting them into the possession of the carrier; or

(b) when the term is F.O.B. the place of destination, the seller must at his own expense and risk transport the goods to that place and there tender delivery of them in the manner provided in this Article (Section 2–503);

(c) when under either (a) or (b) the term is also F.O.B. vessel, car or other vehicle, the seller must in addition at his own expense and risk load the goods on board. If the term is F.O.B. vessel the buyer must name the vessel and in an appropriate case the seller must comply with the provisions of this Article on the form of bill of lading (Section 2–323).

(2) Unless otherwise agreed the term F.A.S. vessel (which means "free alongside") at a named port, even though used only in connection with the stated price, is a delivery term under which the seller must

(a) at his own expense and risk deliver the goods alongside the vessel in the manner usual in that port or on a dock designated and provided by the buyer; and

(b) obtain and tender a receipt for the goods in exchange for which the carrier is under a duty to issue a bill of lading.

(3) Unless otherwise agreed in any case falling within subsection (1)(a) or (c) or subsection (2) the buyer must seasonably give any needed instructions for making delivery, including when the term is F.A.S. or F.O.B. the loading berth of the vessel and in an appropriate case its name and sailing date. The seller may treat the failure of needed instructions as a failure of cooperation under this Article (Section 2–311). He may also at his option move the goods in any reasonable manner preparatory to delivery or shipment.

(4) Under the term F.O.B. vessel or F.A.S. unless otherwise agreed the buyer must make payment against tender of the required documents and

the seller may not tender nor the buyer demand delivery of the goods in substitution for the documents.

Official Comment

1. This section is intended to negate the uncommercial line of decision which treats an "F.O.B." term as "merely a price term." The distinctions taken in subsection (1) handle most of the issues which have on occasion led to the unfortunate judicial language just referred to. Other matters which have led to sound results being based on unhappy language in regard to F.O.B. clauses are dealt with in this Act by Section 2–311(2) (seller's option re arrangements relating to shipment) and Sections 2–614 and 615 (substituted performance and seller's excuse).

2. Subsection (1)(c) not only specifies the duties of a seller who engages to deliver "F.O.B. vessel," or the like, but ought to make clear that no agreement is soundly drawn when it looks to reshipment from San Francisco or New York, but speaks merely of "F.O.B." the place.

3. The buyer's obligations stated in subsection (1)(c) and subsection (3) are, as shown in the text, obligations of cooperation. The last sentence of subsection (3) expressly, though perhaps unnecessarily, authorizes the seller, pending instructions, to go ahead with such preparatory moves as shipment from the interior to the named point of delivery. The sentence presupposes the usual case in which instructions "fail"; a prior repudiation by the buyer, giving notice that breach was intended, would remove the reason for the sentence, and would normally bring into play, instead, the second sentence of Section 2–704, which duly calls for lessening damages.

4. The treatment of "F.O.B. vessel" in conjunction with F.A.S. fits, in regard to the need for payment against documents, with standard practice and case-law; but "F.O.B. vessel" is a term which by its very language makes express the need for an "on board" document. In this respect, that term is stricter than the ordinary overseas "shipment" contract (C.I.F., etc., Section 2–320).

§ 2–320. C.I.F. and C. & F. Terms.

(1) The term C.I.F. means that the price includes in a lump sum the cost of the goods and the insurance and freight to the named destination. The term C. & F. or C.F. means that the price so includes cost and freight to the named destination.

(2) Unless otherwise agreed and even though used only in connection with the stated price and destination, the term C.I.F. destination or its equivalent requires the seller at his own expense and risk to

(a) put the goods into the possession of a carrier at the port for shipment and obtain a negotiable bill or bills of lading covering the entire transportation to the named destination; and

(b) load the goods and obtain a receipt from the carrier (which may be contained in the bill of lading) showing that the freight has been paid or provided for; and

(c) obtain a policy or certificate of insurance, including any war risk insurance, of a kind and on terms then current at the port of shipment in the usual amount, in the currency of the contract, shown to cover the same goods covered by the bill of lading and providing for payment of loss to the order of the buyer or for the account of whom it may concern; but the seller may add to the price the amount of the premium for any such war risk insurance; and

(d) prepare an invoice of the goods and procure any other documents required to effect shipment or to comply with the contract; and

(e) forward and tender with commercial promptness all the documents in due form and with any indorsement necessary to perfect the buyer's rights.

(3) Unless otherwise agreed the term C. & F. or its equivalent has the same effect and imposes upon the seller the same obligations and risks as a C.I.F. term except the obligation as to insurance.

(4) Under the term C.I.F. or C. & F. unless otherwise agreed the buyer must make payment against tender of the required documents and the seller may not tender nor the buyer demand delivery of the goods in substitution for the documents.

Official Comment

1. The C.I.F. contract is not a destination but a shipment contract with risk of subsequent loss or damage to the goods passing to the buyer upon shipment if the seller has properly performed all his obligations with respect to the goods. Delivery to the carrier is delivery to the buyer for purposes of risk and "title". Delivery of possession of the goods is accomplished by delivery of the bill of lading, and upon tender of the required documents the buyer must pay the agreed price without awaiting the arrival of the goods and if they have been lost or damaged after proper shipment he must seek his remedy against the carrier or insurer. The buyer has no right of inspection prior to payment or acceptance of the documents.

2. The seller's obligations remain the same even though the C.I.F. term is "used only in connection with the stated price and destination".

3. The insurance stipulated by the C.I.F. term is for the buyer's benefit, to protect him against the risk of loss or damage to the goods in transit. A clause in a C.I.F. contract "insurance—for the account of sellers" should be viewed in its ordinary mercantile meaning that the sellers must pay for the insurance and not that it is intended to run to the seller's benefit.

4. A bill of lading covering the entire transportation from the port of shipment is explicitly required but the provision on this point must be read in the light of its reason to assure the buyer of as full protection as the conditions of shipment reasonably permit, remembering always that this type of contract is designed to move the goods in the channels commercially available. To enable the buyer to deal with the goods while they are afloat the bill of lading must be one that covers only the quantity of goods called for by the contract. The buyer is not required to accept his part of the goods without a bill of lading because the latter covers a larger quantity, nor is he required to accept a bill of lading for the whole quantity under a stipulation to hold the excess for the owner. Although the buyer is not compelled to accept either goods or documents under such circumstances he may of course claim his rights in any goods which have been identified to his contract.

* * *

6. The requirement that unless otherwise agreed the seller must procure insurance "of a kind and on terms then current at the port for shipment in the usual amount, in the currency of the contract, sufficiently shown to cover the same goods covered by the bill of lading", applies to both marine and war risk insurance. As applied to marine insurance, it means such insurance as is usual or customary at the port for shipment with reference to the particular kind of goods involved, the character and equipment of the vessel, the route of the voyage, the port of destination and any other considerations that affect the risk. It is the substantial equivalent of the ordinary insurance in the particular trade and on the particular voyage and is subject to agreed specifications of type or extent of coverage. The language does not mean that the insurance must be adequate to cover all risks to which the goods may be subject in transit. There are some types of loss or damage that are not covered by the usual marine insurance and are excepted in bills of lading or in applicable statutes from the causes of loss or damage for which the carrier or the vessel is liable. Such risks must be borne by the buyer under this Article.

Insurance secured in compliance with a C.I.F. term must cover the entire transportation of the goods to the named destination.

7. An additional obligation is imposed upon the seller in requiring him to procure customary war risk insurance at the buyer's expense. This changes the common law on the point. The seller is not required to assume the risk of including in the C.I.F. price the cost of such insurance, since it often fluctuates rapidly, but is required to treat it simply as a necessary for the buyer's account. What war risk insurance is "current" or usual turns on the standard forms of policy or rider in common use.

8. The C.I.F. contract calls for insurance covering the value of the goods at the time and place of shipment and does not include any increase in market value during transit or any anticipated profit to the buyer on a sale by him.

The contract contemplates that before the goods arrive at their destination they may be sold again and again on C.I.F. terms and that the original policy of insurance and bill of lading will run with the interest in the goods by being transferred to each successive buyer. A buyer who becomes the seller in such an intermediate contract for sale does not thereby, if his sub-buyer knows the circumstances, undertake to insure the goods again at an increased price fixed in the new contract or to cover the increase in price by additional insurance, and his buyer may not reject the documents on the ground that the original policy does not cover such higher price. If such a sub-buyer desires additional insurance he must procure it for himself.

* * *

12. Under a C.I.F. contract the buyer, as under the common law, must pay the price upon tender of the required documents without first inspecting the goods, but his payment in these circumstances does not constitute an acceptance of the goods nor does it impair his right of subsequent inspection or his options and remedies in the case of improper delivery. All remedies and rights for the seller's breach are reserved to him. The buyer must pay before inspection and assert his remedy against the seller afterward unless the nonconformity of the goods amounts to a real failure of consideration, since the purpose of choosing this form of contract is to give the seller protection against the buyer's unjustifiable rejection of the goods at a distant port of destination which would necessitate taking possession of the goods and suing the buyer there.

13. A valid C.I.F. contract may be made which requires part of the transportation to be made on land and part on the sea, as where the goods are to be brought by rail from an inland point to a seaport and thence transported by vessel to the named destination under a "through" or combination bill of lading issued by the railroad company. In such a case shipment by rail from the inland point within the contract period is a timely shipment notwithstanding that the loading of the goods on the vessel is delayed by causes beyond the seller's control.

14. Although subsection (2) stating the legal effects of the C.I.F. term is an "unless otherwise agreed" provision, the express language used in an agreement is frequently a precautionary, fuller statement of the normal C.I.F. terms and hence not intended as a departure or variation from them. Moreover, the dominant outlines of the C.I.F. term are so well understood commercially that any variation should, whenever reasonably possible, be read as falling within those dominant outlines rather than as destroying the whole meaning of a term which essentially indicates a contract for proper shipment rather than one for delivery at destination. Particularly careful consideration is necessary before a printed form or clause is construed to mean agreement otherwise and where a C.I.F. contract is prepared on a printed form designed for some other type of contract, the C.I.F. terms must prevail over printed clauses repugnant to them.

* * *

17. It is to be remembered that in a French contract the term "C.A.F." does not mean "Cost and Freight" but has exactly the same meaning as the term "C.I.F." since it is merely the French equivalent of that term. The "A" does not stand for "and" but for "assurance" which means insurance.

* * *

§ 2–323. Form of Bill of Lading Required in Overseas Shipment; Overseas.

(1) Where the contract contemplates overseas shipment and contains a term C.I.F. or C. & F. or F.O.B. vessel, the seller unless otherwise agreed must obtain a negotiable bill of lading stating that the goods have been loaded on board or, in the case of a term C.I.F. or C. & F., received for shipment.

(2) Where in a case within subsection (1) a tangible bill of lading has been issued in a set of parts, unless otherwise agreed if the documents are not to be sent from abroad the buyer may demand tender of the full set; otherwise only one part of the bill of lading need be tendered. Even if the agreement expressly requires a full set

(a) due tender of a single part is acceptable within the provisions of this article on cure of improper delivery (subsection (1) of section 2–508); and

(b) even though the full set is demanded, if the documents are sent from abroad the person tendering an incomplete set may nevertheless require payment upon furnishing an indemnity which the buyer in good faith deems adequate.

(3) A shipment by water or by air or a contract contemplating such shipment is "overseas" insofar as by usage of trade or agreement it is subject to the commercial, financing, or shipping practices characteristic of international deep water commerce.

§ 2–403. Power to Transfer; Good Faith Purchase of Goods; "Entrusting".

(1) A purchaser of goods acquires all title which his transferor had or had power to transfer except that a purchaser of a limited interest acquires rights only to the extent of the interest purchased. A person with voidable title has power to transfer a good title to a good faith purchaser for value. When goods have been delivered under a transaction of purchase the purchaser has such power even though

(a) the transferor was deceived as to the identity of the purchaser, or

(b) the delivery was in exchange for a check which is later dishonored, or

(c) it was agreed that the transaction was to be a "cash sale", or

(d) the delivery was procured through fraud punishable as larcenous under the criminal law.

(2) Any entrusting of possession of goods to a merchant who deals in goods of that kind gives him power to transfer all rights of the entruster to a buyer in ordinary course of business.

(3) "Entrusting" includes any delivery and any acquiescence in retention of possession regardless of any condition expressed between the parties to the delivery or acquiescence and regardless of whether the procurement of the entrusting or the possessor's disposition of the goods have been such as to be larcenous under the criminal law.

(4) The rights of other purchasers of goods and of lien creditors are governed by the Articles on Secured Transactions (Article 9), Bulk Sales (Article 6) and Documents of Title (Article 7).

§ 2–504. Shipment by Seller.

Where the seller is required or authorized to send the goods to the buyer and the contract does not require him to deliver them at a particular destination, then unless otherwise agreed he must

(a) put the goods in the possession of such a carrier and make such a contract for their transportation as may be reasonable having regard to the nature of the goods and other circumstances of the case; and

(b) obtain and promptly deliver or tender in due form any document necessary to enable the buyer to obtain possession of the goods or otherwise required by the agreement or by usage of trade; and

(c) promptly notify the buyer of the shipment.

Failure to notify the buyer under paragraph (c) or to make a proper contract under paragraph (a) is a ground for rejection only if material delay or loss ensues.

Official Comment

1. The section is limited to "shipment" contracts as contrasted with "destination" contracts or contracts for delivery at the place where the goods are located. The general principles embodied in this section cover the special cases of F.O.B. point of shipment contracts and C.I.F. and C. & F. contracts. Under the preceding section on manner of tender of delivery, due tender by the seller requires that he comply with the requirements of this section in appropriate cases.

2. The contract to be made with the carrier under paragraph (a) must conform to all express terms of the agreement, subject to any substitution necessary because of failure of agreed facilities as provided in the later provision on substituted performance. However, under the policies of this

Article on good faith and commercial standards and on buyer's rights on improper delivery, the requirements of explicit provisions must be read in terms of their commercial and not their literal meaning. This policy is made express with respect to bills of lading in a set in the provision of this Article on form of bills of lading required in overseas shipment.

3. In the absence of agreement, the provision of this Article on options and cooperation respecting performance gives the seller the choice of any reasonable carrier, routing and other arrangements. Whether or not the shipment is at the buyer's expense the seller must see to any arrangements, reasonable in the circumstances, such as refrigeration, watering of live stock, protection against cold, the sending along of any necessary help, selection of specialized cars and the like for paragraph (a) is intended to cover all necessary arrangements whether made by contract with the carrier or otherwise. There is, however, a proper relaxation of such requirements if the buyer is himself in a position to make the appropriate arrangements and the seller gives him reasonable notice of the need to do so. It is an improper contract under paragraph (a) for the seller to agree with the carrier to a limited valuation below the true value and thus cut off the buyer's opportunity to recover from the carrier in the event of loss, when the risk of shipment is placed on the buyer by his contract with the seller.

* * *

In this connection, in the case of pool car shipments a delivery order furnished by the seller on the pool car consignee, or on the carrier for delivery out of a larger quantity, satisfies the requirements of paragraph (b) unless the contract requires some other form of document.

5. This Article, unlike the prior uniform statutory provision, makes it the seller's duty to notify the buyer of shipment in all cases. The consequences of his failure to do so, however, are limited in that the buyer may reject on this ground only where material delay or loss ensues.

A standard and acceptable manner of notification in open credit shipments is the sending of an invoice and in the case of documentary contracts is the prompt forwarding of the documents as under paragraph (b) of this section. It is also usual to send on a straight bill of lading but this is not necessary to the required notification. However, should such a document prove necessary or convenient to the buyer, as in the case of loss and claim against the carrier, good faith would require the seller to send it on request.

* * *

§ 2–513. Buyer's Right to Inspection of Goods.

(1) Unless otherwise agreed and subject to subsection (3), where goods are tendered or delivered or identified to the contract for sale, the buyer has a right before payment or acceptance to inspect them at any reasonable place and time and in any reasonable manner. When the seller is required

or authorized to send the goods to the buyer, the inspection may be after their arrival.

(2) Expenses of inspection must be borne by the buyer but may be recovered from the seller if the goods do not conform and are rejected.

(3) Unless otherwise agreed and subject to the provisions of this Article on C.I.F. contracts (subsection (3) of Section 2–321), the buyer is not entitled to inspect the goods before payment of the price when the contract provides

(a) for delivery "C.O.D." or on other like terms; or

(b) for payment against documents of title, except where such payment is due only after the goods are to become available for inspection.

(4) A place or method of inspection fixed by the parties is presumed to be exclusive but unless otherwise expressly agreed it does not postpone identification or shift the place for delivery or for passing the risk of loss. If compliance becomes impossible, inspection shall be as provided in this section unless the place or method fixed was clearly intended as an indispensable condition failure of which avoids the contract.

Official Comment

1. The buyer is entitled to inspect goods as provided in subsection (1) unless it has been otherwise agreed by the parties. The phrase "unless otherwise agreed" is intended principally to cover such situations as those outlined in subsections (3) and (4) and those in which the agreement of the parties negates inspection before tender of delivery. However, no agreement by the parties can displace the entire right of inspection except where the contract is simply for the sale of "this thing." Even in a sale of boxed goods "as is" inspection is a right of the buyer, since if the boxes prove to contain some other merchandise altogether the price can be recovered back; nor do the limitations of the provision on effect of acceptance apply in such a case.

2. The buyer's right of inspection is available to him upon tender, delivery or appropriation of the goods with notice to him. Since inspection is available to him on tender, where payment is due against delivery he may, unless otherwise agreed, make his inspection before payment of the price. It is also available to him after receipt of the goods and so may be postponed after receipt for a reasonable time. Failure to inspect before payment does not impair the right to inspect after receipt of the goods unless the case falls within subsection (4) on agreed and exclusive inspection provisions. The right to inspect goods which have been appropriated with notice to the buyer holds whether or not the sale was by sample.

3. The buyer may exercise his right of inspection at any reasonable time or place and in any reasonable manner. It is not necessary that he select the

most appropriate time, place or manner to inspect or that his selection be the customary one in the trade or locality. Any reasonable time, place or manner is available to him and the reasonableness will be determined by trade usages, past practices between the parties and the other circumstances of the case.

The last sentence of subsection (1) makes it clear that the place of arrival of shipped goods is a reasonable place for their inspection.

4. Expenses of an inspection made to satisfy the buyer of the seller's performance must be assumed by the buyer in the first instance. Since the rule provides merely for an allocation of expense there is no policy to prevent the parties from providing otherwise in the agreement. Where the buyer would normally bear the expenses of the inspection but the goods are rightly rejected because of what the inspection reveals, demonstrable and reasonable costs of the inspection are part of his incidental damage caused by the seller's breach.

5. In the case of payment against documents, subsection (3) requires payment before inspection, since shipping documents against which payment is to be made will commonly arrive and be tendered while the goods are still in transit. This Article recognizes no exception in any peculiar case in which the goods happen to arrive before the documents. However, where by the agreement payment is to await the arrival of the goods, inspection before payment becomes proper since the goods are then "available for inspection."

Where by the agreement the documents are to be held until arrival the buyer is entitled to inspect before payment since the goods are then "available for inspection". Proof of usage is not necessary to establish this right, but if inspection before payment is disputed the contrary must be established by usage or by an explicit contract term to that effect.

For the same reason, that the goods are available for inspection, a term calling for payment against storage documents or a delivery order does not normally bar the buyer's right to inspection before payment under subsection (3)(b). This result is reinforced by the buyer's right under subsection (1) to inspect goods which have been appropriated with notice to him.

* * *

§ 2–615. Excuse by Failure of Presupposed Conditions.

Except so far as a seller may have assumed a greater obligation and subject to the preceding section on substituted performance:

(a) Delay in delivery or non-delivery in whole or in part by a seller who complies with paragraphs (b) and (c) is not a breach of his duty under a contract for sale if performance as agreed has been made impracticable by the occurrence of a contingency the non-occurrence of which was a basic assumption on which the contract was made or by compliance in good faith with any applicable foreign or domestic governmental regulation or order whether or not it later proves to be invalid.

(b) Where the causes mentioned in paragraph (a) affect only a part of the seller's capacity to perform, he must allocate production and deliveries among his customers but may at his option include regular customers not then under contract as well as his own requirements for further manufacture. He may so allocate in any manner which is fair and reasonable.

(c) The seller must notify the buyer seasonably that there will be delay or non-delivery and, when allocation is required under paragraph (b), of the estimated quota thus made available for the buyer.

Official Comment

1. This section excuses a seller from timely delivery of goods contracted for, where his performance has become commercially impracticable because of unforeseen supervening circumstances not within the contemplation of the parties at the time of contracting. The destruction of specific goods and the problem of the use of substituted performance on points other than delay or quantity, treated elsewhere in this Article, must be distinguished from the matter covered by this section.

2. The present section deliberately refrains from any effort at an exhaustive expression of contingencies and is to be interpreted in all cases sought to be brought within its scope in terms of its underlying reason and purpose.

3. The first test for excuse under this Article in terms of basic assumption is a familiar one. The additional test of commercial impracticability (as contrasted with "impossibility," "frustration of performance" or "frustration of the venture") has been adopted in order to call attention to the commercial character of the criterion chosen by this Article.

4. Increased cost alone does not excuse performance unless the rise in cost is due to some unforeseen contingency which alters the essential nature of the performance. Neither is a rise or a collapse in the market in itself a justification, for that is exactly the type of business risk which business contracts made at fixed prices are intended to cover. But a severe shortage of raw materials or of supplies due to a contingency such as war, embargo, local crop failure, unforeseen shutdown of major sources of supply or the like, which either causes a marked increase in cost or altogether prevents the seller from securing supplies necessary to his performance, is within the contemplation of this section. (See Ford & Sons, Ltd., v. Henry Leetham & Sons, Ltd., 21 Com.Cas. 55 (1915, K.B.D.).)

5. Where a particular source of supply is exclusive under the agreement and fails through casualty, the present section applies rather than the provision on destruction or deterioration of specific goods. The same holds true where a particular source of supply is shown by the circumstances to have been contemplated or assumed by the parties at the time of contracting. There is no

excuse under this section, however, unless the seller has employed all due measures to assure himself that his source will not fail.

In the case of failure of production by an agreed source for causes beyond the seller's control, the seller should, if possible, be excused since production by an agreed source is without more a basic assumption of the contract. Such excuse should not result in relieving the defaulting supplier from liability nor in dropping into the seller's lap an unearned bonus of damages over. The flexible adjustment machinery of this Article provides the solution under the provision on the obligation of good faith. A condition to his making good the claim of excuse is the turning over to the buyer of his rights against the defaulting source of supply to the extent of the buyer's contract in relation to which excuse is being claimed.

6. In situations in which neither sense nor justice is served by either answer when the issue is posed in flat terms of "excuse" or "no excuse," adjustment under the various provisions of this Article is necessary, especially the sections on good faith, on insecurity and assurance and on the reading of all provisions in the light of their purposes, and the general policy of this Act to use equitable principles in furtherance of commercial standards and good faith.

7. The failure of conditions which go to convenience or collateral values rather than to the commercial practicability of the main performance does not amount to a complete excuse. However, good faith and the reason of the present section and of the preceding one may properly be held to justify and even to require any needed delay involved in a good faith inquiry seeking a readjustment of the contract terms to meet the new conditions.

8. The provisions of this section are made subject to assumption of greater liability by agreement and such agreement is to be found not only in the expressed terms of the contract but in the circumstances surrounding the contracting, in trade usage and the like. Thus the exemptions of this section do not apply when the contingency in question is sufficiently foreshadowed at the time of contracting to be included among the business risks which are fairly to be regarded as part of the dickered terms, either consciously or as a matter of reasonable, commercial interpretation from the circumstances. The exemption otherwise present through usage of trade under the present section may also be expressly negated by the language of the agreement. Generally, express agreements as to exemptions designed to enlarge upon or supplant the provisions of this section are to be read in the light of mercantile sense and reason, for this section itself sets up the commercial standard for normal and reasonable interpretation and provides a minimum beyond which agreement may not go.

Agreement can also be made in regard to the consequences of exemption as laid down in paragraphs (b) and (c) and the next section on procedure on notice claiming excuse.

* * *

Exemption of the buyer in the case of a "requirements" contract is covered by the "Output and Requirements" section both as to assumption and allocation of the relevant risks. But when a contract by a manufacturer to buy fuel or raw material makes no specific reference to a particular venture and no such reference may be drawn from the circumstances, commercial understanding views it as a general deal in the general market and not conditioned on any assumption of the continuing operation of the buyer's plant. Even when notice is given by the buyer that the supplies are needed to fill a specific contract of a normal commercial kind, commercial understanding does not see such a supply contract as conditioned on the continuance of the buyer's further contract for outlet. On the other hand, where the buyer's contract is in reasonable commercial understanding conditioned on a definite and specific venture or assumption as, for instance, a war procurement subcontract known to be based on a prime contract which is subject to termination, or a supply contract for a particular construction venture, the reason of the present section may well apply and entitle the buyer to the exemption.

10. Following its basic policy of using commercial practicability as a test for excuse, this section recognizes as of equal significance either a foreign or domestic regulation and disregards any technical distinctions between "law," "regulation," "order" and the like. Nor does it make the present action of the seller depend upon the eventual judicial determination of the legality of the particular governmental action. The seller's good faith belief in the validity of the regulation is the test under this Article and the best evidence of his good faith is the general commercial acceptance of the regulation. However, governmental interference cannot excuse unless it truly "supervenes" in such a manner as to be beyond the seller's assumption of risk. And any action by the party claiming excuse which causes or colludes in inducing the governmental action preventing his performance would be in breach of good faith and would destroy his exemption.

11. An excused seller must fulfill his contract to the extent which the supervening contingency permits, and if the situation is such that his customers are generally affected he must take account of all in supplying one. Subsections (a) and (b), therefore, explicitly permit in any proration a fair and reasonable attention to the needs of regular customers who are probably relying on spot orders for supplies. Customers at different stages of the manufacturing process may be fairly treated by including the seller's manufacturing requirements. A fortiori, the seller may also take account of contracts later in date than the one in question. The fact that such spot orders may be closed at an advanced price causes no difficulty, since any allocation which exceeds normal past requirements will not be reasonable. However, good faith requires, when prices have advanced, that the seller exercise real care in making his allocations, and in case of doubt his contract customers should be favored and supplies prorated evenly among them regardless of price. Save for the extra care thus required by changes in the market, this section seeks to leave every reasonable business leeway to the seller.

* * *

ARTICLE 4. BANK DEPOSITS AND COLLECTIONS

§ 4–104. Definitions and index of definitions

(a) In this title, unless the context otherwise requires:

* * *

(6) "Documentary draft" means a draft to be presented for acceptance or payment if specified documents, * * * statements, or the like are to be received by the drawee or other payor before acceptance or payment of the draft[.]

* * *

PART. 5. COLLECTION OF DOCUMENTARY DRAFTS

§ 4–501. Handling of documentary drafts; duty to send for presentment and to notify customer of dishonor

A bank that takes a documentary draft for collection shall present or send the draft and accompanying documents for presentment and, upon learning that the draft has not been paid or accepted in due course, shall seasonably notify its customer of the fact even though it may have discounted or bought the draft or extended credit available for withdrawal as of right.

§ 4–502. Presentment of "on arrival" drafts

If a draft or the relevant instructions require presentment "on arrival", "when goods arrive", or the like, the collecting bank need not present until in its judgment a reasonable time for arrival of the goods has expired. Refusal to pay or accept because the goods have not arrived is not dishonor; the bank must notify its transferor of the refusal but need not present the draft again until it is instructed to do so or learns of the arrival of the goods.

§ 4–503. Responsibility of presenting bank for documents and goods; report of reasons for dishonor; referee in case of need

Unless otherwise instructed and except as provided in Title 5, a bank presenting a documentary draft:

(1) Must deliver the documents to the drawee on acceptance of the draft if it is payable more than three days after presentment; otherwise, only on payment; and

(2) Upon dishonor, either in the case of presentment for acceptance or presentment for payment, may seek and follow instructions from any referee in case of need designated in the draft or if the presenting bank does not choose to utilize the referee's services, it must use diligence and good faith to ascertain the reasons for dishonor, must notify its transferor of the dishonor and of the results

of its effort to ascertain the reasons therefor, and must request instructions.

However the presenting bank is under no obligation with respect to goods represented by the documents except to follow any reasonable instructions seasonably received; it has a right to reimbursement for any expense incurred in following instructions and to prepayment of or indemnity for those expenses.

§ 4–504. Privilege of presenting bank to deal with goods; security interest for expenses

(a) A presenting bank that, following the dishonor of a documentary draft, has seasonably requested instructions but does not receive them within a reasonable time may store, sell, or otherwise deal with the goods in any reasonable manner.

(b) For its reasonable expenses incurred by action under subsection (a) the presenting bank has a lien upon the goods or their proceeds, which may be foreclosed in the same manner as an unpaid seller's lien.

ARTICLE 5. LETTERS OF CREDIT

§ 5–101. Short Title.

This article may be cited as Uniform Commercial Code—Letters of Credit.

Official Comment

The Official Comment to the original Section 5–101 was a remarkably brief inaugural address. Noting that letters of credit had not been the subject of statutory enactment and that the law concerning them had been developed in the cases, the Comment stated that Article 5 was intended "within its limited scope" to set an independent theoretical frame for the further development of letters of credit. That statement addressed accurately conditions as they existed when the statement was made, nearly half a century ago. Since Article 5 was originally drafted, the use of letters of credit has expanded and developed, and the case law concerning these developments is, in some respects, discordant.

Revision of Article 5 therefore has required reappraisal both of the statutory goals and of the extent to which particular statutory provisions further or adversely affect achievement of those goals.

The statutory goal of Article 5 was originally stated to be: (1) to set a substantive theoretical frame that describes the function and legal nature of letters of credit; and (2) to preserve procedural flexibility in order to accommodate further development of the efficient use of letters of credit. A letter of credit is an idiosyncratic form of undertaking that supports performance of an obligation incurred in a separate financial, mercantile, or other transaction or arrangement. The objectives of the original and revised Article 5 are best achieved (1) by defining the peculiar characteristics of a letter of credit that distinguish it and the legal consequences of its use from other forms of assurance such as secondary guarantees, performance bonds, and insurance policies, and from ordinary contracts, fiduciary engagements, and escrow arrangements; and (2) by preserving flexibility through variation by agreement in order to respond to and accommodate developments in custom and usage that are not inconsistent with the essential definitions and substantive mandates of the statute. No statute can, however, prescribe the manner in which such substantive rights and duties are to be enforced or imposed without risking stultification of wholesome developments in the letter of credit mechanism. Letter of credit law should remain responsive to commercial reality and in particular to the customs and expectations of the international banking and mercantile community. Courts should read the terms of this article in a manner consistent with these customs and expectations.

The subject matter in Article 5, letters of credit, may also be governed by an international convention that is now being drafted by UNCITRAL, the draft Convention on Independent Guarantees and Standby Letters of Credit. The Uniform Customs and Practice is an international body of trade practice that is commonly adopted by international and domestic letters of credit and as such is the "law of the transaction" by agreement of the parties. Article 5 is consistent with and was influenced by the rules in the existing version of the UCP. In addition to the UCP and the international convention, other bodies of law apply to letters of credit. For example, the federal bankruptcy law applies to letters of credit with respect to applicants and beneficiaries that are in bankruptcy; regulations of the Federal Reserve Board and the Comptroller of the Currency lay out requirements for banks that issue letters of credit and describe how letters of credit are to be treated for calculating asset risk and for the purpose of loan limitations. In addition there is an array of anti-boycott and other similar laws that may affect the issuance and performance of letters of credit. All of these laws are beyond the scope of Article 5, but in certain circumstances they will override Article 5.

§ 5–102. Definitions.

(a) In this article:

(1) "Adviser" means a person who, at the request of the issuer, a confirmer, or another adviser, notifies or requests another adviser to notify the beneficiary that a letter of credit has been issued, confirmed, or amended.

(2) "Applicant" means a person at whose request or for whose account a letter of credit is issued. The term includes a person who requests an issuer to issue a letter of credit on behalf of another if the person making the request undertakes an obligation to reimburse the issuer.

(3) "Beneficiary" means a person who under the terms of a letter of credit is entitled to have its complying presentation honored. The

term includes a person to whom drawing rights have been transferred under a transferable letter of credit.

(4) "Confirmer" means a nominated person who undertakes, at the request or with the consent of the issuer, to honor a presentation under a letter of credit issued by another.

(5) "Dishonor" of a letter of credit means failure timely to honor or to take an interim action, such as acceptance of a draft, that may be required by the letter of credit.

(6) "Document" means a draft or other demand, document of title, investment security, certificate, invoice, or other record, statement, or representation of fact, law, right, or opinion (i) which is presented in a written or other medium permitted by the letter of credit or, unless prohibited by the letter of credit, by the standard practice referred to in Section 5–108(e) and (ii) which is capable of being examined for compliance with the terms and conditions of the letter of credit. A document may not be oral.

(7) "Good faith" means honesty in fact in the conduct or transaction concerned.

(8) "Honor" of a letter of credit means performance of the issuer's undertaking in the letter of credit to pay or deliver an item of value. Unless the letter of credit otherwise provides, "honor" occurs

(i) upon payment,

(ii) if the letter of credit provides for acceptance, upon acceptance of a draft and, at maturity, its payment, or

(iii) if the letter of credit provides for incurring a deferred obligation, upon incurring the obligation and, at maturity, its performance.

(9) "Issuer" means a bank or other person that issues a letter of credit, but does not include an individual who makes an engagement for personal, family, or household purposes.

(10) "Letter of credit" means a definite undertaking that satisfies the requirements of Section 5–104 by an issuer to a beneficiary at the request or for the account of an applicant or, in the case of a financial institution, to itself or for its own account, to honor a documentary presentation by payment or delivery of an item of value.

(11) "Nominated person" means a person whom the issuer (i) designates or authorizes to pay, accept, negotiate, or otherwise give value under a letter of credit and (ii) undertakes by agreement or custom and practice to reimburse.

(12) "Presentation" means delivery of a document to an issuer or nominated person for honor or giving of value under a letter of credit.

(13) "Presenter" means a person making a presentation as or on behalf of a beneficiary or nominated person.

(14) "Record" means information that is inscribed on a tangible medium, or that is stored in an electronic or other medium and is retrievable in perceivable form.

(15) "Successor of a beneficiary" means a person who succeeds to substantially all of the rights of a beneficiary by operation of law, including a corporation with or into which the beneficiary has been merged or consolidated, an administrator, executor, personal representative, trustee in bankruptcy, debtor in possession, liquidator, and receiver.

* * *

Official Comment

1. Since no one can be a confirmer unless that person is a nominated person as defined in Section 5–102(a)(11), those who agree to "confirm" without the designation or authorization of the issuer are not confirmers under Article 5. Nonetheless, the undertakings to the beneficiary of such persons may be enforceable by the beneficiary as letters of credit issued by the "confirmer" for its own account or as guarantees or contracts outside of Article 5.

2. The definition of "document" contemplates and facilitates the growing recognition of electronic and other nonpaper media as "documents," however, for the time being, data in those media constitute documents only in certain circumstances. For example, a facsimile received by an issuer would be a document only if the letter of credit explicitly permitted it, if the standard practice authorized it and the letter did not prohibit it, or the agreement of the issuer and beneficiary permitted it. The fact that data transmitted in a nonpaper (unwritten) medium can be recorded on paper by a recipient's computer printer, facsimile machine, or the like does not under current practice render the data so transmitted a "document." A facsimile or S.W.I.F.T. message received directly by the issuer is in an electronic medium when it crosses the boundary of the issuer's place of business. One wishing to make a presentation by facsimile (an electronic medium) will have to procure the explicit agreement of the issuer (assuming that the standard practice does not authorize it). Where electronic transmissions are authorized neither by the letter of credit nor by the practice, the beneficiary may transmit the data electronically to its agent who may be able to put it in written form and make a conforming presentation.

3. "Good faith" continues in revised Article 5 to be defined as "honesty in fact." "Observance of reasonable standards of fair dealing" has not been added to the definition. The narrower definition of "honesty in fact" reinforces

the "independence principle" in the treatment of "fraud," "strict compliance," "preclusion," and other tests affecting the performance of obligations that are unique to letters of credit. This narrower definition—which does not include "fair dealing"—is appropriate to the decision to honor or dishonor a presentation of documents specified in a letter of credit. The narrower definition is also appropriate for other parts of revised Article 5 where greater certainty of obligations is necessary and is consistent with the goals of speed and low cost. It is important that U.S. letters of credit have continuing vitality and competitiveness in international transactions.

For example, it would be inconsistent with the "independence" principle if any of the following occurred: (i) the beneficiary's failure to adhere to the standard of "fair dealing" in the underlying transaction or otherwise in presenting documents were to provide applicants and issuers with an "unfairness" defense to dishonor even when the documents complied with the terms of the letter of credit; (ii) the issuer's obligation to honor in "strict compliance in accordance with standard practice" were changed to "reasonable compliance" by use of the "fair dealing" standard, or (iii) the preclusion against the issuer (Section 5–108(d)) were modified under the "fair dealing" standard to enable the issuer later to raise additional deficiencies in the presentation. The rights and obligations arising from presentation, honor, dishonor and reimbursement, are independent and strict, and thus "honesty in fact" is an appropriate standard.

The contract between the applicant and beneficiary is not governed by Article 5, but by applicable contract law, such as Article 2 or the general law of contracts. "Good faith" in that contract is defined by other law, such as Section 2–103(1)(b) or Restatement of Contracts 2d, § 205, which incorporate the principle of "fair dealing" in most cases, or a State's common law or other statutory provisions that may apply to that contract.

The contract between the applicant and the issuer (sometimes called the "reimbursement" agreement) is governed in part by this article (e.g., Sections 5–108(i), 5–111(b), and 5–103(c)) and partly by other law (e.g., the general law of contracts). The definition of good faith in Section 5–102(a)(7) applies only to the extent that the reimbursement contract is governed by provisions in this article; for other purposes good faith is defined by other law.

* * *

6. The label on a document is not conclusive; certain documents labelled "guarantees" in accordance with European (and occasionally, American) practice are letters of credit. On the other hand, even documents that are labelled "letter of credit" may not constitute letters of credit under the definition in Section 5–102(a). When a document labelled a letter of credit requires the issuer to pay not upon the presentation of documents, but upon the determination of an extrinsic fact such as applicant's failure to perform a construction contract, and where that condition appears on its face to be fundamental and would, if ignored, leave no obligation to the issuer under the

document labelled letter of credit, the issuer's undertaking is not a letter of credit. It is probably some form of suretyship or other contractual arrangement and may be enforceable as such. See Sections 5–102(a)(10) and 5–103(d). Therefore, undertakings whose fundamental term requires an issuer to look beyond documents and beyond conventional reference to the clock, calendar, and practices concerning the form of various documents are not governed by Article 5. Although Section 5–108(g) recognizes that certain nondocumentary conditions can be included in a letter of credit without denying the undertaking the status of letter of credit, that section does not apply to cases where the nondocumentary condition is fundamental to the issuer's obligation. The rules in Sections 5–102(a)(10), 5–103(d), and 5–108(g) approve the conclusion in Wichita Eagle & Beacon Publishing Co. v. Pacific Nat. Bank, 493 F.2d 1285 (9th Cir.1974).

A financial institution may be both the issuer and the applicant or the issuer and the beneficiary. Such letters are sometimes issued by a bank in support of the bank's own lease obligations or on behalf of one of its divisions as an applicant or to one of its divisions as beneficiary, such as an overseas branch. Because wide use of letters of credit in which the issuer and the applicant or the issuer and the beneficiary are the same would endanger the unique status of letters of credit, only financial institutions are authorized to issue them.

In almost all cases the ultimate performance of the issuer under a letter of credit is the payment of money. In rare cases the issuer's obligation is to deliver stock certificates or the like. The definition of letter of credit in Section 5–102(a)(10) contemplates those cases.

7. Under the UCP any bank is a nominated bank where the letter of credit is "freely negotiable." A letter of credit might also nominate by the following: "We hereby engage with the drawer, indorsers, and bona fide holders of drafts drawn under and in compliance with the terms of this credit that the same will be duly honored on due presentation" or "available with any bank by negotiation." A restricted negotiation credit might be "available with x bank by negotiation" or the like.

Several legal consequences may attach to the status of nominated person. First, when the issuer nominates a person, it is authorizing that person to pay or give value and is authorizing the beneficiary to make presentation to that person. Unless the letter of credit provides otherwise, the beneficiary need not present the documents to the issuer before the letter of credit expires; it need only present those documents to the nominated person. Secondly, a nominated person that gives value in good faith has a right to payment from the issuer despite fraud. Section 5–109(a)(1).

8. A "record" must be in or capable of being converted to a perceivable form. For example, an electronic message recorded in a computer memory that could be printed from that memory could constitute a record. Similarly, a tape recording of an oral conversation could be a record.

* * *

§ 5–103. Scope.

(a) This article applies to letters of credit and to certain rights and obligations arising out of transactions involving letters of credit.

(b) The statement of a rule in this article does not by itself require, imply, or negate application of the same or a different rule to a situation not provided for, or to a person not specified, in this article.

(c) With the exception of this subsection, subsections (a) and (d), Sections 5–102(a)(9) and (10), 5–106(d), and 5–114(d), and except to the extent prohibited in Sections 1–102(3) and 5–117(d), the effect of this article may be varied by agreement or by a provision stated or incorporated by reference in an undertaking. A term in an agreement or undertaking generally excusing liability or generally limiting remedies for failure to perform obligations is not sufficient to vary obligations prescribed by this article.

(d) Rights and obligations of an issuer to a beneficiary or a nominated person under a letter of credit are independent of the existence, performance, or nonperformance of a contract or arrangement out of which the letter of credit arises or which underlies it, including contracts or arrangements between the issuer and the applicant and between the applicant and the beneficiary.

Official Comment

1. Sections 5–102(a)(10) and 5–103 are the principal limits on the scope of Article 5. Many undertakings in commerce and contract are similar, but not identical to the letter of credit. Principal among those are "secondary," "accessory," or "suretyship" guarantees. Although the word "guarantee" is sometimes used to describe an independent obligation like that of the issuer of a letter of credit (most often in the case of European bank undertakings but occasionally in the case of undertakings of American banks), in the United States the word "guarantee" is more typically used to describe a suretyship transaction in which the "guarantor" is only secondarily liable and has the right to assert the underlying debtor's defenses. This article does not apply to secondary or accessory guarantees and it is important to recognize the distinction between letters of credit and those guarantees. It is often a defense to a secondary or accessory guarantor's liability that the underlying debt has been discharged or that the debtor has other defenses to the underlying liability. In letter of credit law, on the other hand, the independence principle recognized throughout Article 5 states that the issuer's liability is independent of the underlying obligation. That the beneficiary may have breached the underlying contract and thus have given a good defense on that contract to the applicant against the beneficiary is no defense for the issuer's refusal to honor. Only staunch recognition of this principle by the issuers and the courts will give letters of credit the continuing vitality that arises from the certainty and

speed of payment under letters of credit. To that end, it is important that the law not carry into letter of credit transactions rules that properly apply only to secondary guarantees or to other forms of engagement.

2. Like all of the provisions of the Uniform Commercial Code, Article 5 is supplemented by Section 1–103 and, through it, by many rules of statutory and common law. Because this article is quite short and has no rules on many issues that will affect liability with respect to a letter of credit transaction, law beyond Article 5 will often determine rights and liabilities in letter of credit transactions. Even within letter of credit law, the article is far from comprehensive; it deals only with "certain" rights of the parties. Particularly with respect to the standards of performance that are set out in Section 5–108, it is appropriate for the parties and the courts to turn to customs and practice such as the Uniform Customs and Practice for Documentary Credits, currently published by the International Chamber of Commerce as I.C.C. Pub. No. 500 (hereafter UCP). Many letters of credit specifically adopt the UCP as applicable to the particular transaction. Where the UCP are adopted but conflict with Article 5 and except where variation is prohibited, the UCP terms are permissible contractual modifications under Sections 1–102(3) and 5–103(c). See Section 5–116(c). Normally Article 5 should not be considered to conflict with practice except when a rule explicitly stated in the UCP or other practice is different from a rule explicitly stated in Article 5.

Except by choosing the law of a jurisdiction that has not adopted the Uniform Commercial Code, it is not possible entirely to escape the Uniform Commercial Code. Since incorporation of the UCP avoids only "conflicting" Article 5 rules, parties who do not wish to be governed by the nonconflicting provisions of Article 5 must normally either adopt the law of a jurisdiction other than a State of the United States or state explicitly the rule that is to govern. When rules of custom and practice are incorporated by reference, they are considered to be explicit terms of the agreement or undertaking.

Neither the obligation of an issuer under Section 5–108 nor that of an adviser under Section 5–107 is an obligation of the kind that is invariable under Section 1–102(3). Section 5–103(c) and Comment 1 to Section 5–108 make it clear that the applicant and the issuer may agree to almost any provision establishing the obligations of the issuer to the applicant. The last sentence of subsection (c) limits the power of the issuer to achieve that result by a nonnegotiated disclaimer or limitation of remedy.

What the issuer could achieve by an explicit agreement with its applicant or by a term that explicitly defines its duty, it cannot accomplish by a general disclaimer. The restriction on disclaimers in the last sentence of subsection (c) is based more on procedural than on substantive unfairness. Where, for example, the reimbursement agreement provides explicitly that the issuer need not examine any documents, the applicant understands the risk it has undertaken. A term in a reimbursement agreement which states generally that an issuer will not be liable unless it has acted in "bad faith" or committed "gross negligence" is ineffective under Section 5–103(c). On the other hand, less general terms such as terms that permit issuer reliance on an oral or electronic message believed in good faith to have been received from the applicant or terms that entitle an issuer to reimbursement when it honors a "substantially" though not "strictly" complying presentation, are effective. In each case the question is whether the disclaimer or limitation is sufficiently clear and explicit in reallocating a liability or risk that is allocated differently under a variable Article 5 provision.

Of course, no term in a letter of credit, whether incorporated by reference to practice rules or stated specifically, can free an issuer from a conflicting contractual obligation to its applicant. If, for example, an issuer promised its applicant that it would pay only against an inspection certificate of a particular company but failed to require such a certificate in its letter of credit or made the requirement only a nondocumentary condition that had to be disregarded, the issuer might be obliged to pay the beneficiary even though its payment might violate its contract with its applicant.

3. Parties should generally avoid modifying the definitions in Section 5–102. The effect of such an agreement is almost inevitably unclear. To say that something is a "guarantee" in the typical domestic transaction is to say that the parties intend that particular legal rules apply to it. By acknowledging that something is a guarantee, but asserting that it is to be treated as a "letter of credit," the parties leave a court uncertain about where the rules on guarantees stop and those concerning letters of credit begin.

* * *

§ 5–104. Formal Requirements.

A letter of credit, confirmation, advice, transfer, amendment, or cancellation may be issued in any form that is a record and is authenticated (i) by a signature or (ii) in accordance with the agreement of the parties or the standard practice referred to in Section 5–108(e).

Official Comment

1. Neither Section 5–104 nor the definition of letter of credit in Section 5–102(a)(10) requires inclusion of all the terms that are normally contained in a letter of credit in order for an undertaking to be recognized as a letter of credit under Article 5. For example, a letter of credit will typically specify the amount available, the expiration date, the place where presentation should be made, and the documents that must be presented to entitle a person to honor. Undertakings that have the formalities required by Section 5–104 and meet the conditions specified in Section 5–102(a)(10) will be recognized as letters of credit even though they omit one or more of the items usually contained in a letter of credit.

2. The authentication specified in this section is authentication only of the identity of the issuer, confirmer, or adviser.

An authentication agreement may be by system rule, by standard practice, or by direct agreement between the parties. The reference to practice is intended to incorporate future developments in the UCP and other practice rules as well as those that may arise spontaneously in commercial practice.

3. Many banking transactions, including the issuance of many letters of credit, are now conducted mostly by electronic means. For example, S.W.I.F.T. is currently used to transmit letters of credit from issuing to advising banks. The letter of credit text so transmitted may be printed at the advising bank, stamped "original" and provided to the beneficiary in that form. The printed document may then be used as a way of controlling and recording payments and of recording and authorizing assignments of proceeds or transfers of rights under the letter of credit. Nothing in this section should be construed to conflict with that practice.

To be a record sufficient to serve as a letter of credit or other undertaking under this section, data must have a durability consistent with that function. Because consideration is not required for a binding letter of credit or similar undertaking (Section 5–105) yet those undertakings are to be strictly construed (Section 5–108), parties to a letter of credit transaction are especially dependent on the continued availability of the terms and conditions of the letter of credit or other undertaking. By declining to specify any particular medium in which the letter of credit must be established or communicated, Section 5–104 leaves room for future developments.

* * *

§ 5–106. Issuance, Amendment, Cancellation, and Duration.

(a) A letter of credit is issued and becomes enforceable according to its terms against the issuer when the issuer sends or otherwise transmits it to the person requested to advise or to the beneficiary. A letter of credit is revocable only if it so provides.

(b) After a letter of credit is issued, rights and obligations of a beneficiary, applicant, confirmer, and issuer are not affected by an amendment or cancellation to which that person has not consented except to the extent the letter of credit provides that it is revocable or that the issuer may amend or cancel the letter of credit without that consent.

* * *

§ 5–107. Confirmer, Nominated Person, and Adviser.

(a) A confirmer is directly obligated on a letter of credit and has the rights and obligations of an issuer to the extent of its confirmation. The confirmer also has rights against and obligations to the issuer as if the issuer were an applicant and the confirmer had issued the letter of credit at the request and for the account of the issuer.

(b) A nominated person who is not a confirmer is not obligated to honor or otherwise give value for a presentation.

(c) A person requested to advise may decline to act as an adviser. An adviser that is not a confirmer is not obligated to honor or give value for a presentation. An adviser undertakes to the issuer and to the beneficiary accurately to advise the terms of the letter of credit, confirmation, amendment, or advice received by that person and undertakes to the beneficiary to check the apparent authenticity of the request to advise. Even if the advice is inaccurate, the letter of credit, confirmation, or amendment is enforceable as issued.

(d) A person who notifies a transferee beneficiary of the terms of a letter of credit, confirmation, amendment, or advice has the rights and obligations of an adviser under subsection (c). The terms in the notice to the transferee beneficiary may differ from the terms in any notice to the transferor beneficiary to the extent permitted by the letter of credit, confirmation, amendment, or advice received by the person who so notifies.

Official Comment

1. A confirmer has the rights and obligations identified in Section 5–108. Accordingly, unless the context otherwise requires, the terms "confirmer" and "confirmation" should be read into this article wherever the terms "issuer" and "letter of credit" appear.

A confirmer that has paid in accordance with the terms and conditions of the letter of credit is entitled to reimbursement by the issuer even if the beneficiary committed fraud (see Section 5–109(a)(1)(ii)) and, in that sense, has greater rights against the issuer than the beneficiary has. To be entitled to reimbursement from the issuer under the typical confirmed letter of credit, the confirmer must submit conforming documents, but the confirmer's presentation to the issuer need not be made before the expiration date of the letter of credit.

A letter of credit confirmation has been analogized to a guarantee of issuer performance, to a parallel letter of credit issued by the confirmer for the account of the issuer or the letter of credit applicant or both, and to a back-to-back letter of credit in which the confirmer is a kind of beneficiary of the original issuer's letter of credit. Like letter of credit undertakings, confirmations are both unique and flexible, so that no one of these analogies is perfect, but unless otherwise indicated in the letter of credit or confirmation, a confirmer should be viewed by the letter of credit issuer and the beneficiary as an issuer of a parallel letter of credit for the account of the original letter of credit issuer. Absent a direct agreement between the applicant and a confirmer, normally the obligations of a confirmer are to the issuer not the applicant, but the applicant might have a right to injunction against a confirmer under Section 5–109 or warranty claim under Section 5–110, and either might have claims against the other under Section 5–117.

2. * * * By advising or agreeing to advise a letter of credit, the adviser assumes a duty to the issuer and to the beneficiary accurately to report what it has received from the issuer, but, beyond determining the apparent

authenticity of the letter, an adviser has no duty to investigate the accuracy of the message it has received from the issuer. "Checking" the apparent authenticity of the request to advise means only that the prospective adviser must attempt to authenticate the message (e.g., by "testing" the telex that comes from the purported issuer), and if it is unable to authenticate the message must report that fact to the issuer and, if it chooses to advise the message, to the beneficiary. By proper agreement, an adviser may disclaim its obligation under this section.

3. An issuer may issue a letter of credit which the adviser may advise with different terms. The issuer may then believe that it has undertaken a certain engagement, yet the text in the hands of the beneficiary will contain different terms, and the beneficiary would not be entitled to honor if the documents it submitted did not comply with the terms of the letter of credit as originally issued. On the other hand, if the adviser also confirmed the letter of credit, then as a confirmer it will be independently liable on the letter of credit as advised and confirmed. If in that situation the beneficiary's ultimate presentation entitled it to honor under the terms of the confirmation but not under those in the original letter of credit, the confirmer would have to honor but might not be entitled to reimbursement from the issuer.

4. When the issuer nominates another person to "pay," "negotiate," or otherwise to take up the documents and give value, there can be confusion about the legal status of the nominated person. In rare cases the person might actually be an agent of the issuer and its act might be the act of the issuer itself. In most cases the nominated person is not an agent of the issuer and has no authority to act on the issuer's behalf. * * *

§ 5–108. Issuer's Rights and Obligations.

(a) Except as otherwise provided in Section 5–109, an issuer shall honor a presentation that, as determined by the standard practice referred to in subsection (e), appears on its face strictly to comply with the terms and conditions of the letter of credit. Except as otherwise provided in Section 5–113 and unless otherwise agreed with the applicant, an issuer shall dishonor a presentation that does not appear so to comply.

(b) An issuer has a reasonable time after presentation, but not beyond the end of the seventh business day of the issuer after the day of its receipt of documents:

(1) to honor,

(2) if the letter of credit provides for honor to be completed more than seven business days after presentation, to accept a draft or incur a deferred obligation, or

(3) to give notice to the presenter of discrepancies in the presentation.

(c) Except as otherwise provided in subsection (d), an issuer is precluded from asserting as a basis for dishonor any discrepancy if timely notice is not given, or any discrepancy not stated in the notice if timely notice is given.

(d) Failure to give the notice specified in subsection (b) or to mention fraud, forgery, or expiration in the notice does not preclude the issuer from asserting as a basis for dishonor fraud or forgery as described in Section 5–109(a) or expiration of the letter of credit before presentation.

(e) An issuer shall observe standard practice of financial institutions that regularly issue letters of credit. Determination of the issuer's observance of the standard practice is a matter of interpretation for the court. The court shall offer the parties a reasonable opportunity to present evidence of the standard practice.

(f) An issuer is not responsible for:

(1) the performance or nonperformance of the underlying contract, arrangement, or transaction,

(2) an act or omission of others, or

(3) observance or knowledge of the usage of a particular trade other than the standard practice referred to in subsection (e).

(g) If an undertaking constituting a letter of credit under Section 5–102(a)(10) contains nondocumentary conditions, an issuer shall disregard the nondocumentary conditions and treat them as if they were not stated.

(h) An issuer that has dishonored a presentation shall return the documents or hold them at the disposal of, and send advice to that effect to, the presenter.

(i) An issuer that has honored a presentation as permitted or required by this article:

(1) is entitled to be reimbursed by the applicant in immediately available funds not later than the date of its payment of funds;

(2) takes the documents free of claims of the beneficiary or presenter;

(3) is precluded from asserting a right of recourse on a draft under Sections 3–414 and 3–415;

(4) except as otherwise provided in Sections 5–110 and 5–117, is precluded from restitution of money paid or other value given by mistake to the extent the mistake concerns discrepancies in the documents or tender which are apparent on the face of the presentation; and

(5) is discharged to the extent of its performance under the letter of credit unless the issuer honored a presentation in which a required signature of a beneficiary was forged.

Official Comment

1. * * * Because a confirmer has the rights and duties of an issuer, this section applies equally to a confirmer and an issuer.

The standard of strict compliance governs the issuer's obligation to the beneficiary and to the applicant. By requiring that a "presentation" appear strictly to comply, the section requires not only that the documents themselves appear on their face strictly to comply, but also that the other terms of the letter of credit such as those dealing with the time and place of presentation are strictly complied with. Typically, a letter of credit will provide that presentation is timely if made to the issuer, confirmer, or any other nominated person prior to expiration of the letter of credit. Accordingly, a nominated person that has honored a demand or otherwise given value before expiration will have a right to reimbursement from the issuer even though presentation to the issuer is made after the expiration of the letter of credit. Conversely, where the beneficiary negotiates documents to one who is not a nominated person, the beneficiary or that person acting on behalf of the beneficiary must make presentation to a nominated person, confirmer, or issuer prior to the expiration date.

This section does not impose a bifurcated standard under which an issuer's right to reimbursement might be broader than a beneficiary's right to honor. However, the explicit deference to standard practice in Section 5–108(a) and (e) and elsewhere expands issuers' rights of reimbursement where that practice so provides. Also, issuers can and often do contract with their applicants for expanded rights of reimbursement. Where that is done, the beneficiary will have to meet a more stringent standard of compliance as to the issuer than the issuer will have to meet as to the applicant. Similarly, a nominated person may have reimbursement and other rights against the issuer based on this article, the UCP, bank-to-bank reimbursement rules, or other agreement or undertaking of the issuer. These rights may allow the nominated person to recover from the issuer even when the nominated person would have no right to obtain honor under the letter of credit.

The section adopts strict compliance, rather than the standard that commentators have called "substantial compliance," the standard arguably applied in Banco Español de Credito v. State Street Bank and Trust Company, 385 F.2d 230 (1st Cir.1967) and Flagship Cruises Ltd. v. New England Merchants Nat. Bank, 569 F.2d 699 (1st Cir.1978). Strict compliance does not mean slavish conformity to the terms of the letter of credit. For example, standard practice (what issuers do) may recognize certain presentations as complying that an unschooled layman would regard as discrepant. By adopting standard practice as a way of measuring strict compliance, this article indorses the conclusion of the court in New Braunfels Nat. Bank v. Odiorne, 780 S.W.2d 313 (Tex.Ct.App. 1989) (beneficiary could collect when draft requested payment on "Letter of Credit No. 86–122–5" and letter of credit specified "Letter of Credit No. 86–122–S" holding strict compliance does not demand oppressive perfectionism). The section also indorses the result in Tosco Corp. v. Federal Deposit Insurance Corp., 723 F.2d 1242 (6th Cir.1983). The letter of credit in that case called for "drafts Drawn under Bank of Clarksville Letter of Credit Number 105." The draft presented stated "drawn under Bank of Clarksville, Clarksville, Tennessee letter of Credit No. 105." The court correctly found that despite the change of upper case "L" to a lower case "l" and the use of the word "No." instead of "Number," and despite the addition of the words "Clarksville, Tennessee," the presentation conformed. Similarly a document addressed by a foreign person to General Motors as "Jeneral Motors" would strictly conform in the absence of other defects.

Identifying and determining compliance with standard practice are matters of interpretation for the court, not for the jury. As with similar rules in Sections 4A–202(c) and 2–302, it is hoped that there will be more consistency in the outcomes and speedier resolution of disputes if the responsibility for determining the nature and scope of standard practice is granted to the court, not to a jury. Granting the court authority to make these decisions will also encourage the salutary practice of courts' granting summary judgment in circumstances where there are no significant factual disputes. The statute encourages outcomes such as American Coleman Co. v. Intrawest Bank, 887 F.2d 1382 (10th Cir.1989), where summary judgment was granted.

In some circumstances standards may be established between the issuer and the applicant by agreement or by custom that would free the issuer from liability that it might otherwise have. For example, an applicant might agree that the issuer would have no duty whatsoever to examine documents on certain presentations (e.g., those below a certain dollar amount). Where the transaction depended upon the issuer's payment in a very short time period (e.g., on the same day or within a few hours of presentation), the issuer and the applicant might agree to reduce the issuer's responsibility for failure to discover discrepancies. By the same token, an agreement between the applicant and the issuer might permit the issuer to examine documents exclusively by electronic or electro-optical means. Neither those agreements nor others like them explicitly made by issuers and applicants violate the terms of Section 5–108(a) or (b) or Section 5–103(c).

2. Section 5–108(a) balances the need of the issuer for time to examine the documents against the possibility that the examiner (at the urging of the applicant or for fear that it will not be reimbursed) will take excessive time to search for defects. What is a "reasonable time" is not extended to accommodate an issuer's procuring a waiver from the applicant. See Article 14c of the UCP.

Under both the UCC and the UCP the issuer has a reasonable time to honor or give notice. The outside limit of that time is measured in business days under the UCC and in banking days under the UCP, a difference that will rarely be significant. Neither business nor banking days are defined in Article

5, but a court may find useful analogies in Regulation CC, 12 CFR 229.2, in state law outside of the Uniform Commercial Code, and in Article 4.

Examiners must note that the seven-day period is not a safe harbor. The time within which the issuer must give notice is the lesser of a reasonable time or seven business days. Where there are few documents (as, for example, with the mine run standby letter of credit), the reasonable time would be less than seven days. If more than a reasonable time is consumed in examination, no timely notice is possible. What is a "reasonable time" is to be determined by examining the behavior of those in the business of examining documents, mostly banks. Absent prior agreement of the issuer, one could not expect a bank issuer to examine documents while the beneficiary waited in the lobby if the normal practice was to give the documents to a person who had the opportunity to examine those together with many others in an orderly process. That the applicant has not yet paid the issuer or that the applicant's account with the issuer is insufficient to cover the amount of the draft is not a basis for extension of the time period.

This section does not preclude the issuer from contacting the applicant during its examination; however, the decision to honor rests with the issuer, and it has no duty to seek a waiver from the applicant or to notify the applicant of receipt of the documents. If the issuer dishonors a conforming presentation, the beneficiary will be entitled to the remedies under Section 5–111, irrespective of the applicant's views.

* * *

Failure of the issuer to act within the time permitted by subsection (b) constitutes dishonor. Because of the preclusion in subsection (c) and the liability that the issuer may incur under Section 5–111 for wrongful dishonor, the effect of such a silent dishonor may ultimately be the same as though the issuer had honored, i.e., it may owe damages in the amount drawn but unpaid under the letter of credit.

3. The requirement that the issuer send notice of the discrepancies or be precluded from asserting discrepancies is new to Article 5. It is taken from the similar provision in the UCP and is intended to promote certainty and finality.

The section thus substitutes a strict preclusion principle for the doctrines of waiver and estoppel that might otherwise apply under Section 1–103. * * *

4. To act within a reasonable time, the issuer must normally give notice without delay after the examining party makes its decision. If the examiner decides to dishonor on the first day, it would be obliged to notify the beneficiary shortly thereafter, perhaps on the same business day. This rule accepts the reasoning in cases such as Datapoint Corp. v. M & I Bank, 665 F.Supp. 722 (W.D.Wis.1987) and Esso Petroleum Canada, Div. of Imperial Oil, Ltd. v. Security Pacific Bank, 710 F.Supp. 275 (D.Or.1989).

The section deprives the examining party of the right simply to sit on a presentation that is made within seven days of expiration. The section requires the examiner to examine the documents and make a decision and, having made a decision to dishonor, to communicate promptly with the presenter. Nevertheless, a beneficiary who presents documents shortly before the expiration of a letter of credit runs the risk that it will never have the opportunity to cure any discrepancies.

5. Confirmers, other nominated persons, and collecting banks acting for beneficiaries can be presenters and, when so, are entitled to the notice provided in subsection (b). * * *

6. In many cases a letter of credit authorizes presentation by the beneficiary to someone other than the issuer. Sometimes that person is identified as a "payor" or "paying bank," or as an "acceptor" or "accepting bank," in other cases as a "negotiating bank," and in other cases there will be no specific designation. The section does not impose any duties on a person other than the issuer or confirmer, however a nominated person or other person may have liability under this article or at common law if it fails to perform an express or implied agreement with the beneficiary.

7. The issuer's obligation to honor runs not only to the beneficiary but also to the applicant. It is possible that an applicant who has made a favorable contract with the beneficiary will be injured by the issuer's wrongful dishonor. Except to the extent that the contract between the issuer and the applicant limits that liability, the issuer will have liability to the applicant for wrongful dishonor under Section 5–111 as a matter of contract law. A good faith extension of the time in Section 5–108(b) by agreement between the issuer and beneficiary binds the applicant even if the applicant is not consulted or does not consent to the extension.

The issuer's obligation to dishonor when there is no apparent compliance with the letter of credit runs only to the applicant. * * *

8. The standard practice referred to in subsection (e) includes (i) international practice set forth in or referenced by the Uniform Customs and Practice, (ii) other practice rules published by associations of financial institutions, and (iii) local and regional practice. It is possible that standard practice will vary from one place to another. Where there are conflicting practices, the parties should indicate which practice governs their rights. A practice may be overridden by agreement or course of dealing. See Section 1–205(4).

* * *

10. Subsection (f) condones an issuer's ignorance of "any usage of a particular trade"; that trade is the trade of the applicant, beneficiary, or others who may be involved in the underlying transaction. The issuer is expected to know usage that is commonly encountered in the course of document examination. For example, an issuer should know the common usage with respect to documents in the maritime shipping trade but would not be expected

to understand synonyms used in a particular trade for product descriptions appearing in a letter of credit or an invoice.

* * *

13. The last clause of Section 5–108(i)(5) deals with a special case in which the fraud is not committed by the beneficiary, but is committed by a stranger to the transaction who forges the beneficiary's signature. If the issuer pays against documents on which a required signature of the beneficiary is forged, it remains liable to the true beneficiary.

§ 5–109. Fraud and Forgery.

(a) If a presentation is made that appears on its face strictly to comply with the terms and conditions of the letter of credit, but a required document is forged or materially fraudulent, or honor of the presentation would facilitate a material fraud by the beneficiary on the issuer or applicant:

(1) the issuer shall honor the presentation, if honor is demanded by (i) a nominated person who has given value in good faith and without notice of forgery or material fraud, (ii) a confirmer who has honored its confirmation in good faith, (iii) a holder in due course of a draft drawn under the letter of credit which was taken after acceptance by the issuer or nominated person, or (iv) an assignee of the issuer's or nominated person's deferred obligation that was taken for value and without notice of forgery or material fraud after the obligation was incurred by the issuer or nominated person; and

(2) the issuer, acting in good faith, may honor or dishonor the presentation in any other case.

(b) If an applicant claims that a required document is forged or materially fraudulent or that honor of the presentation would facilitate a material fraud by the beneficiary on the issuer or applicant, a court of competent jurisdiction may temporarily or permanently enjoin the issuer from honoring a presentation or grant similar relief against the issuer or other persons only if the court finds that:

(1) the relief is not prohibited under the law applicable to an accepted draft or deferred obligation incurred by the issuer;

(2) a beneficiary, issuer, or nominated person who may be adversely affected is adequately protected against loss that it may suffer because the relief is granted;

(3) all of the conditions to entitle a person to the relief under the law of this State have been met; and

(4) on the basis of the information submitted to the court, the applicant is more likely than not to succeed under its claim of forgery

or material fraud and the person demanding honor does not qualify for protection under subsection (a)(1).

Official Comment

1. This recodification makes clear that fraud must be found either in the documents or must have been committed by the beneficiary on the issuer or applicant. See Cromwell v. Commerce & Energy Bank, 464 So.2d 721 (La.1985).

Secondly, it makes clear that fraud must be "material." Necessarily courts must decide the breadth and width of "materiality." The use of the word requires that the fraudulent aspect of a document be material to a purchaser of that document or that the fraudulent act be significant to the participants in the underlying transaction. Assume, for example, that the beneficiary has a contract to deliver 1,000 barrels of salad oil. Knowing that it has delivered only 998, the beneficiary nevertheless submits an invoice showing 1,000 barrels. If two barrels in a 1,000 barrel shipment would be an insubstantial and immaterial breach of the underlying contract, the beneficiary's act, though possibly fraudulent, is not materially so and would not justify an injunction. Conversely, the knowing submission of those invoices upon delivery of only five barrels would be materially fraudulent. The courts must examine the underlying transaction when there is an allegation of material fraud, for only by examining that transaction can one determine whether a document is fraudulent or the beneficiary has committed fraud and, if so, whether the fraud was material.

Material fraud by the beneficiary occurs only when the beneficiary has no colorable right to expect honor and where there is no basis in fact to support such a right to honor. The section indorses articulations such as those stated in Intraworld Indus. v. Girard Trust Bank, 336 A.2d 316 (Pa.1975), Roman Ceramics Corp. v. People's Nat. Bank, 714 F.2d 1207 (3d Cir.1983), and similar decisions and embraces certain decisions under Section 5–114 that relied upon the phrase "fraud in the transaction." Some of these decisions have been summarized as follows in Ground Air Transfer v. Westates Airlines, 899 F.2d 1269, 1272–73 (1st Cir.1990):

> We have said throughout that courts may not "*normally*" issue an injunction because of an important exception to the general "no injunction" rule. The exception, as we also explained in Itek, 730 F.2d at 24–25, concerns "fraud" so serious as to make it obviously pointless and unjust to permit the beneficiary to obtain the money. Where the circumstances "*plainly*" show that the underlying contract forbids the beneficiary to call a letter of credit, Itek, 730 F.2d at 24; where they show that the contract deprives the beneficiary of even a "*colorable*" right to do so, id., at 25; where the contract and circumstances reveal that the beneficiary's demand for payment has "absolutely no basis in fact," id.; see Dynamics Corp. of America, 356 F.Supp. at 999; where the beneficiary's conduct has "so vitiated the entire transaction that the legitimate purposes of the independence of the issuer's obligation would no longer be

served," Itek, 730 F.2d at 25 (quoting Roman Ceramics Corp. v. Peoples National Bank, 714 F.2d 1207, 1212 n.12, 1215 (3d Cir.1983) (quoting Intraworld Indus., 336 A.2d at 324–25)); *then* a court may enjoin payment.

2. Subsection (a)(2) makes clear that the issuer may honor in the face of the applicant's claim of fraud. The subsection also makes clear what was not stated in former Section 5–114, that the issuer may dishonor and defend that dishonor by showing fraud or forgery of the kind stated in subsection (a). Because issuers may be liable for wrongful dishonor if they are unable to prove forgery or material fraud, presumably most issuers will choose to honor despite applicant's claims of fraud or forgery unless the applicant procures an injunction. Merely because the issuer has a right to dishonor and to defend that dishonor by showing forgery or material fraud does not mean it has a duty to the applicant to dishonor. The applicant's normal recourse is to procure an injunction, if the applicant is unable to procure an injunction, it will have a claim against the issuer only in the rare case in which it can show that the issuer did not honor in good faith.

3. Whether a beneficiary can commit fraud by presenting a draft under a clean letter of credit (one calling only for a draft and no other documents) has been much debated. Under the current formulation it would be possible but difficult for there to be fraud in such a presentation. If the applicant were able to show that the beneficiary were committing material fraud on the applicant in the underlying transaction, then payment would facilitate a material fraud by the beneficiary on the applicant and honor could be enjoined. The courts should be skeptical of claims of fraud by one who has signed a "suicide" or clean credit and thus granted a beneficiary the right to draw by mere presentation of a draft.

4. The standard for injunctive relief is high, and the burden remains on the applicant to show, by evidence and not by mere allegation, that such relief is warranted. Some courts have enjoined payments on letters of credit on insufficient showing by the applicant. For example, in Griffin Cos. v. First Nat. Bank, 374 N.W.2d 768 (Minn.App.1985), the court enjoined payment under a standby letter of credit, basing its decision on plaintiff's allegation, rather than competent evidence, of fraud.

There are at least two ways to prohibit injunctions against honor under this section after acceptance of a draft by the issuer. First is to define honor (see Section 5–102(a)(8)) in the particular letter of credit to occur upon acceptance and without regard to later payment of the acceptance. Second is explicitly to agree that the applicant has no right to an injunction after acceptance—whether or not the acceptance constitutes honor.

5. Although the statute deals principally with injunctions against honor, it also cautions against granting "similar relief" and the same principles apply when the applicant or issuer attempts to achieve the same legal outcome by injunction against presentation (see Ground Air Transfer Inc. v. Westates Airlines, Inc., 899 F.2d 1269 (1st Cir.1990)), interpleader, declaratory judgment, or attachment. These attempts should face the same obstacles that

face efforts to enjoin the issuer from paying. Expanded use of any of these devices could threaten the independence principle just as much as injunctions against honor. For that reason courts should have the same hostility to them and place the same restrictions on their use as would be applied to injunctions against honor. Courts should not allow the "sacred cow of equity to trample the tender vines of letter of credit law."

6. Section 5–109(a)(1) also protects specified third parties against the risk of fraud. By issuing a letter of credit that nominates a person to negotiate or pay, the issuer (ultimately the applicant) induces that nominated person to give value and thereby assumes the risk that a draft drawn under the letter of credit will be transferred to one with a status like that of a holder in due course who deserves to be protected against a fraud defense.

7. The "loss" to be protected against—by bond or otherwise under subsection (b)(2)—includes incidental damages. Among those are legal fees that might be incurred by the beneficiary or issuer in defending against an injunction action.

§ 5–110. Warranties.

(a) If its presentation is honored, the beneficiary warrants:

(1) to the issuer, any other person to whom presentation is made, and the applicant that there is no fraud or forgery of the kind described in Section 5–109(a); and

(2) to the applicant that the drawing does not violate any agreement between the applicant and beneficiary or any other agreement intended by them to be augmented by the letter of credit.

(b) The warranties in subsection (a) are in addition to warranties arising under Article 3, 4, 7, and 8 because of the presentation or transfer of documents covered by any of those articles.

Official Comment

1. Since the warranties in subsection (a) are not given unless a letter of credit has been honored, no breach of warranty under this subsection can be a defense to dishonor by the issuer. Any defense must be based on Section 5–108 or 5–109 and not on this section. Also, breach of the warranties by the beneficiary in subsection (a) cannot excuse the applicant's duty to reimburse.

2. The warranty in Section 5–110(a)(2) assumes that payment under the letter of credit is final. It does not run to the issuer, only to the applicant. In most cases the applicant will have a direct cause of action for breach of the underlying contract. This warranty has primary application in standby letters of credit or other circumstances where the applicant is not a party to an underlying contract with the beneficiary. It is not a warranty that the statements made on the presentation of the documents presented are truthful nor is it a warranty that the documents strictly comply under Section 5–108(a).

It is a warranty that the beneficiary has performed all the acts expressly and implicitly necessary under any underlying agreement to entitle the beneficiary to honor. If, for example, an underlying sales contract authorized the beneficiary to draw only upon "due performance" and the beneficiary drew even though it had breached the underlying contract by delivering defective goods, honor of its draw would break the warranty. By the same token, if the underlying contract authorized the beneficiary to draw only upon actual default or upon its or a third party's determination of default by the applicant and if the beneficiary drew in violation of its authorization, then upon honor of its draw the warranty would be breached. In many cases, therefore, the documents presented to the issuer will contain inaccurate statements (concerning the goods delivered or concerning default or other matters), but the breach of warranty arises not because the statements are untrue but because the beneficiary's drawing violated its express or implied obligations in the underlying transaction.

* * *

§ 5–116. Choice of Law and Forum.

(a) The liability of an issuer, nominated person, or adviser for action or omission is governed by the law of the jurisdiction chosen by an agreement in the form of a record signed or otherwise authenticated by the affected parties in the manner provided in Section 5–104 or by a provision in the person's letter of credit, confirmation, or other undertaking. The jurisdiction whose law is chosen need not bear any relation to the transaction.

(b) Unless subsection (a) applies, the liability of an issuer, nominated person, or adviser for action or omission is governed by the law of the jurisdiction in which the person is located. The person is considered to be located at the address indicated in the person's undertaking. If more than one address is indicated, the person is considered to be located at the address from which the person's undertaking was issued. For the purpose of jurisdiction, choice of law, and recognition of interbranch letters of credit, but not enforcement of a judgment, all branches of a bank are considered separate juridical entities and a bank is considered to be located at the place where its relevant branch is considered to be located under this subsection.

(c) Except as otherwise provided in this subsection, the liability of an issuer, nominated person, or adviser is governed by any rules of custom or practice, such as the Uniform Customs and Practice for Documentary Credits, to which the letter of credit, confirmation, or other undertaking is expressly made subject. If (i) this article would govern the liability of an issuer, nominated person, or adviser under subsection (a) or (b), (ii) the relevant undertaking incorporates rules of custom or practice, and (iii) there is conflict between this article and those rules as applied to that undertaking, those rules govern except to the extent of any conflict with the nonvariable provisions specified in Section 5–103(c).

* * *

Official Comment

1. Although it would be possible for the parties to agree otherwise, the law normally chosen by agreement under subsection (a) and that provided in the absence of agreement under subsection (b) is the substantive law of a particular jurisdiction not including the choice of law principles of that jurisdiction. Thus, two parties, an issuer and an applicant, both located in Oklahoma might choose the law of New York. Unless they agree otherwise, the section anticipates that they wish the substantive law of New York to apply to their transaction and they do not intend that a New York choice of law principle might direct a court to Oklahoma law. By the same token, the liability of an issuer located in New York is governed by New York substantive law—in the absence of agreement—even in circumstances in which choice of law principles found in the common law of New York might direct one to the law of another State. Subsection (b) states the relevant choice of law principles and it should not be subordinated to some other choice of law rule. Within the States of the United States *renvoi* will not be a problem once every jurisdiction has enacted Section 5–116 because every jurisdiction will then have the same choice of law rule and in a particular case all choice of law rules will point to the same substantive law.

Subsection (b) does not state a choice of law rule for the "liability of an applicant." However, subsection (b) does state a choice of law rule for the liability of an issuer, nominated person, or adviser, and since some of the issues in suits by applicants against those persons involve the "liability of an issuer, nominated person, or adviser," subsection (b) states the choice of law rule for those issues. Because an issuer may have liability to a confirmer both as an issuer (Section 5–108(a), Comment 5 to Section 5–108) and as an applicant (Section 5–107(a), Comment 1 to Section 5–107, Section 5–108(i)), subsection (b) may state the choice of law rule for some but not all of the issuer's liability in a suit by a confirmer.

2. Because the confirmer or other nominated person may choose different law from that chosen by the issuer or may be located in a different jurisdiction and fail to choose law, it is possible that a confirmer or nominated person may be obligated to pay (under their law) but will not be entitled to payment from the issuer (under its law). Similarly, the rights of an unreimbursed issuer, confirmer, or nominated person against a beneficiary under Section 5–109, 5–110, or 5–117, will not necessarily be governed by the same law that applies to the issuer's or confirmer's obligation upon presentation. Because the UCP and other practice are incorporated in most international letters of credit, disputes arising from different legal obligations to honor have not been frequent. Since Section 5–108 incorporates standard

practice, these problems should be further minimized—at least to the extent that the same practice is and continues to be widely followed.

3. This section does not permit what is now authorized by the nonuniform Section 5–102(4) in New York. Under the current law in New York a letter of credit that incorporates the UCP is not governed in any respect by Article 5. Under revised Section 5–116 letters of credit that incorporate the UCP or similar practice will still be subject to Article 5 in certain respects. First, incorporation of the UCP or other practice does not override the nonvariable terms of Article 5. Second, where there is no conflict between Article 5 and the relevant provision of the UCP or other practice, both apply. Third, practice provisions incorporated in a letter of credit will not be effective if they fail to comply with Section 5–103(c). Assume, for example, that a practice provision purported to free a party from any liability unless it were "grossly negligent" or that the practice generally limited the remedies that one party might have against another. Depending upon the circumstances, that disclaimer or limitation of liability might be ineffective because of Section 5–103(c).

Even though Article 5 is generally consistent with UCP 500, it is not necessarily consistent with other rules or with versions of the UCP that may be adopted after Article 5's revision, or with other practices that may develop. Rules of practice incorporated in the letter of credit or other undertaking are those in effect when the letter of credit or other undertaking is issued. Except in the unusual cases discussed in the immediately preceding paragraph, practice adopted in a letter of credit will override the rules of Article 5 and the parties to letter of credit transactions must be familiar with practice (such as future versions of the UCP) that is explicitly adopted in letters of credit.

* * *

ARTICLE 7. DOCUMENTS OF TITLE

PART 1

GENERAL

* * *

§ 7–103. Relation of article to treaty or statute

(a) This article is subject to any treaty or statute of the United States or regulatory statute of this state to the extent the treaty, statute, or regulatory statute is applicable.

* * *

§ 7–104. Negotiable and nonnegotiable document of title

(a) Except as otherwise provided in subsection (c), a document of title is negotiable if by its terms the goods are to be delivered to bearer or to the order of a named person.

(b) A document of title other than one described in subsection (a) is nonnegotiable. A bill of lading that states that the goods are consigned to a named person is not made negotiable by a provision that the goods are to be delivered only against an order in a record signed by the same or another named person.

(c) A document of title is nonnegotiable if, at the time it is issued, the document has a conspicuous legend, however expressed, that it is nonnegotiable.

* * *

PART 4

WAREHOUSE RECEIPTS AND BILLS OF LADING: GENERAL OBLIGATIONS

* * *

§ 7–403. Obligation of Bailee to Deliver; Excuse

(a) A bailee shall deliver the goods to a person entitled under a document of title if the person complies with subsections (b) and (c), unless and to the extent that the bailee establishes any of the following:

(1) Delivery of the goods to a person whose receipt was rightful as against the claimant;

(2) damage to or delay, loss, or destruction of the goods for which the bailee is not liable;

(3) previous sale or other disposition of the goods in lawful enforcement of a lien or on a warehouse's lawful termination of storage;

* * *

(6) release, satisfaction, or any other personal defense against the claimant; or

(7) any other lawful excuse.

(b) A person claiming goods covered by a document of title shall satisfy the bailee's lien if the bailee so requests or if the bailee is prohibited by law from delivering the goods until the charges are paid.

(c) Unless a person claiming the goods is a person against which the document of title does not confer a right under Section 7–503(a):

(1) The person claiming under a document shall surrender possession or control of any outstanding negotiable document covering the goods for cancellation or indication of partial deliveries; and

(2) the bailee shall cancel the document or conspicuously indicate in the document the partial delivery or the bailee is liable to any person to which the document is duly negotiated.

* * *

PART 5

WAREHOUSE RECEIPTS AND BILLS OF LADING: NEGOTIATION AND TRANSFER

§ 7–501. Form of negotiation and requirements of due negotiation

(a) The following rules apply to a negotiable tangible document of title:

(1) If the document's original terms run to the order of a named person, the document is negotiated by the named person's indorsement and delivery. After the named person's indorsement in blank or to bearer, any person may negotiate the document by delivery alone.

(2) If the document's original terms run to bearer, it is negotiated by delivery alone.

(3) If the document's original terms run to the order of a named person and it is delivered to the named person, the effect is the same as if the document had been negotiated.

(4) Negotiation of the document after it has been indorsed to a named person requires indorsement by the named person and delivery.

(5) A document is duly negotiated if it is negotiated in the manner stated in this subsection to a holder that purchases it in good faith, without notice of any defense against or claim to it on the part of any person, and for value, unless it is established that the negotiation is not in the regular course of business or financing or involves receiving the document in settlement or payment of a monetary obligation.

* * *

(c) Indorsement of a nonnegotiable document of title neither makes it negotiable nor adds to the transferee's rights.

(d) The naming in a negotiable bill of lading of a person to be notified of the arrival of the goods does not limit the negotiability of the bill or constitute notice to a purchaser of the bill of any interest of that person in the goods.

Official Comments

Article 7 does not separately define the term "duly negotiated." However, the elements of "duly negotiated" are set forth in subsection (a)(5) for tangible documents * * *. As under former Section 7–501, in order to effect a "due negotiation" the negotiation must be in the "regular course of business or financing" in order to transfer greater rights than those held by the person negotiating. The foundation of the mercantile doctrine of good faith purchase for value has always been, as shown by the case situations, the furtherance and protection of the regular course of trade. The reason for allowing a person, in bad faith or in error, to convey away rights which are not its own has from the beginning been to make possible the speedy handling of that great run of commercial transactions which are patently usual and normal. * * *

§ 7–502. Rights acquired by due negotiation

(a) Subject to Section[ ] * * * 7–503, a holder to which a negotiable document of title has been duly negotiated acquires thereby:

(1) Title to the document;

(2) title to the goods;

(3) all rights accruing under the law of agency or estoppel, including rights to goods delivered to the bailee after the document was issued; and

(4) the direct obligation of the issuer to hold or deliver the goods according to the terms of the document free of any defense or claim by the issuer except those arising under the terms of the document or under this article * * *.

(b) Subject to Section 7–503, title and rights acquired by due negotiation are not defeated by any stoppage of the goods represented by the document of title or by surrender of the goods by the bailee and are not impaired even if:

(1) The due negotiation or any prior due negotiation constituted a breach of duty;

(2) any person has been deprived of possession of a negotiable tangible document or control of a negotiable electronic document by misrepresentation, fraud, accident, mistake, duress, loss, theft, or conversion; or

(3) a previous sale or other transfer of the goods or document has been made to a third person.

§ 7–503. Document of title to goods defeated in certain cases

(a) A document of title confers no right in goods against a person that before issuance of the document had a legal interest or a perfected security interest in the goods and that did not:

(1) Deliver or entrust the goods or any document of title covering the goods to the bailor or the bailor's nominee with:

(A) Actual or apparent authority to ship, store, or sell;

(B) power to obtain delivery under Section 7–403; or

(C) power of disposition under Section 2–403 * * * or other statute or rule of law; or

(2) acquiesce in the procurement by the bailor or its nominee of any document.

* * *

(c) Title to goods based upon a bill of lading issued to a freight forwarder is subject to the rights of any person to which a bill issued by the freight forwarder is duly negotiated. However, delivery by the carrier in accordance with Part 4 pursuant to its own bill of lading discharges the carrier's obligation to deliver.

* * *

§ 7–507. Warranties on negotiation or delivery of document of title

If a person negotiates or delivers a document of title for value, otherwise than as a mere intermediary under Section 7–508, unless otherwise agreed, the transferor, in addition to any warranty made in selling or leasing the goods, warrants to its immediate purchaser only that:

(1) The document is genuine;

(2) the transferor does not have knowledge of any fact that would impair the document's validity or worth; and

(3) the negotiation or delivery is rightful and fully effective with respect to the title to the document and the goods it represents.

§ 7–508. Warranties of collecting bank as to documents of title

A collecting bank or other intermediary known to be entrusted with documents of title on behalf of another or with collection of a draft or other claim against delivery of documents warrants by the delivery of the documents only its own good faith and authority even if the collecting bank or other intermediary has purchased or made advances against the claim or draft to be collected.

Official Comments

Purposes:

1. To state the limited warranties given with respect to the documents accompanying a documentary draft.

2. In warranting its authority a collecting bank or other intermediary only warrants its authority from its transferor. See Section 4–203. It does not warrant the genuineness or effectiveness of the document. Compare Section 7–507.

3. Other duties and rights of banks handling documentary drafts for collection are stated in Article 4, Part 5. * * *

DOCUMENT 54

UNIFORM COMPUTER INFORMATION TRANSACTIONS ACT (1999)

■ ■ ■

PART 1

GENERAL PROVISIONS

[SUBPART A. SHORT TITLE AND DEFINITIONS]

Section 101. Short Title. This [Act] may be cited as the Uniform Computer Information Transactions Act.

Section 102. Definitions.

(a) In this [Act]:

* * *

(4) "Agreement" means the bargain of the parties in fact as found in their language or by implication from other circumstances, including course of performance, course of dealing, and usage of trade as provided in this [Act].

(5) "Attribution procedure" means a procedure to verify that an electronic authentication, display, message, record, or performance is that of a particular person or to detect changes or errors in information. The term includes a procedure that requires the use of algorithms or other codes, identifying words or numbers, encryption, or callback or other acknowledgment.

(6) "Authenticate" means:

(A) to sign; or

(B) with the intent to sign a record, otherwise to execute or adopt an electronic symbol, sound, message, or process referring to, attached to, included in, or logically associated or linked with, that record.

(7) "Automated transaction" means a transaction in which a contract is formed in whole or part by electronic actions of one or both parties which are not previously reviewed by an individual in the ordinary course.

(8) "Cancellation" means the ending of a contract by a party because of breach of contract by another party.

(9) "Computer" means an electronic device that accepts information in digital or similar form and manipulates it for a result based on a sequence of instructions.

(10) "Computer information" means information in electronic form which is obtained from or through the use of a computer or which is in a form capable of being processed by a computer. The term includes a copy of the information and any documentation or packaging associated with the copy.

(11) "Computer information transaction" means an agreement or the performance of it to create, modify, transfer, or license computer information or informational rights in computer information. The term includes a support contract under Section 612. The term does not include a transaction merely because the parties' agreement provides that their communications about the transaction will be in the form of computer information.

(12) "Computer program" means a set of statements or instructions to be used directly or indirectly in a computer to bring about a certain result. The term does not include separately identifiable informational content.

(13) "Consequential damages" resulting from breach of contract includes (i) any loss resulting from general or particular requirements and needs of which the breaching party at the time of contracting had reason to know and which could not reasonably be prevented and (ii) any injury to an individual or damage to property other than the subject matter of the transaction proximately resulting from breach of warranty. The term does not include direct damages or incidental damages.

(14) "Conspicuous", with reference to a term, means so written, displayed, or presented that a reasonable person against which it is to operate ought to have noticed it. A term in an electronic record intended to evoke a response by an electronic agent is conspicuous if it is presented in a form that would enable a reasonably configured electronic agent to take it into account or react to it without review of the record by an individual. Conspicuous terms include the following:

(A) with respect to a person:

(i) a heading in capitals in a size equal to or greater than, or in contrasting type, font, or color to, the surrounding text;

(ii) language in the body of a record or display in larger or other contrasting type, font, or color or set off from the surrounding text by symbols or other marks that draw attention to the language; and

(iii) a term prominently referenced in an electronic record or display which is readily accessible or reviewable from the record or display; and

(B) with respect to a person or an electronic agent, a term or reference to a term that is so placed in a record or display that the person or electronic agent cannot proceed without taking action with respect to the particular term or reference.

(15) "Consumer" means an individual who is a licensee of information or informational rights that the individual at the time of contracting intended to be used primarily for personal, family, or household purposes. The term does not include an individual who is a licensee primarily for professional or commercial purposes, including agriculture, business management, and investment management other than management of the individual's personal or family investments.

(16) "Consumer contract" means a contract between a merchant licensor and a consumer.

(17) "Contract" means the total legal obligation resulting from the parties' agreement as affected by this [Act] and other applicable law.

(18) "Contract fee" means the price, fee, rent, or royalty payable in a contract under this [Act] or any part of the amount payable.

(19) "Contractual use term" means an enforceable term that defines or limits the use, disclosure of, or access to licensed information or informational rights, including a term that defines the scope of a license.

(20) "Copy" means the medium on which information is fixed on a temporary or permanent basis and from which it can be perceived, reproduced, used, or communicated, either directly or with the aid of a machine or device.

(21) "Course of dealing" means a sequence of previous conduct between the parties to a particular transaction which establishes a common basis of understanding for interpreting their expressions and other conduct.

(22) "Course of performance" means repeated performances, under a contract that involves repeated occasions for performance, which are accepted or acquiesced in without objection by a party having knowledge of the nature of the performance and an opportunity to object to it.

* * *

(24) "Delivery", with respect to a copy, means the voluntary physical or electronic transfer of possession or control.

* * *

(26) "Electronic" means relating to technology having electrical, digital, magnetic, wireless, optical, electromagnetic, or similar capabilities.

(27) "Electronic agent" means a computer program, or electronic or other automated means, used by a person to initiate an action, or to respond to electronic messages or performances, on the person's behalf

without review or action by an individual at the time of the action or response to the message or performance.

(28) "Electronic message" means a record or display that is stored, generated, or transmitted by electronic means for the purpose of communication to another person or electronic agent.

* * *

(32) "Good faith" means honesty in fact and the observance of reasonable commercial standards of fair dealing.

(33) "Goods" means all things that are movable at the time relevant to the computer information transaction. The term includes the unborn young of animals, growing crops, and other identified things to be severed from realty which are covered by [Section 2–107 of the Uniform Commercial Code]. The term does not include computer information, money, the subject matter of foreign exchange transactions, documents, letters of credit, letter-of-credit rights, instruments, investment property, accounts, chattel paper, deposit accounts, or general intangibles.

* * *

(35) "Information" means data, text, images, sounds, mask works, or computer programs, including collections and compilations of them.

(36) "Information processing system" means an electronic system for creating, generating, sending, receiving, storing, displaying, or processing information.

(37) "Informational content" means information that is intended to be communicated to or perceived by an individual in the ordinary use of the information, or the equivalent of that information.

(38) "Informational rights" include all rights in information created under laws governing patents, copyrights, mask works, trade secrets, trademarks, publicity rights, or any other law that gives a person, independently of contract, a right to control or preclude another person's use of or access to the information on the basis of the rights holder's interest in the information.

(39) "Knowledge", with respect to a fact, means actual knowledge of the fact.

(40) "License" means a contract that authorizes access to, or use, distribution, performance, modification, or reproduction of, information or informational rights, but expressly limits the access or uses authorized or expressly grants fewer than all rights in the information, whether or not the transferee has title to a licensed copy. The term includes an access contract, a lease of a computer program, and a consignment of a copy. The term does not include a reservation or creation of a security interest to the

extent the interest is governed by [Article 9 of the Uniform Commercial Code].

(41) "Licensee" means a person entitled by agreement to acquire or exercise rights in, or to have access to or use of, computer information under an agreement to which this [Act] applies. A licensor is not a licensee with respect to rights reserved to it under the agreement.

(42) "Licensor" means a person obligated by agreement to transfer or create rights in, or to give access to or use of, computer information or informational rights in it under an agreement to which this [Act] applies. Between the provider of access and a provider of the informational content to be accessed, the provider of content is the licensor. In an exchange of information or informational rights, each party is a licensor with respect to the information, informational rights, or access it gives.

(43) "Mass-market license" means a standard form used in a mass-market transaction.

(44) "Mass-market transaction" means a transaction that is:

(A) a consumer contract; or

(B) any other transaction with an end-user licensee if:

(i) the transaction is for information or informational rights directed to the general public as a whole, including consumers, under substantially the same terms for the same information;

(ii) the licensee acquires the information or informational rights in a retail transaction under terms and in a quantity consistent with an ordinary transaction in a retail market; and

(iii) the transaction is not:

(I) a contract for redistribution or for public performance or public display of a copyrighted work;

(II) a transaction in which the information is customized or otherwise specially prepared by the licensor for the licensee, other than minor customization using a capability of the information intended for that purpose;

(III) a site license; or

(IV) an access contract.

(45) "Merchant" means a person:

(A) that deals in information or informational rights of the kind involved in the transaction;

(B) that by the person's occupation holds itself out as having knowledge or skill peculiar to the relevant aspect of the business practices or information involved in the transaction; or

(C) to which the knowledge or skill peculiar to the practices or information involved in the transaction may be attributed by the person's employment of an agent or broker or other intermediary that by its occupation holds itself out as having the knowledge or skill.

(46) "Nonexclusive license" means a license that does not preclude the licensor from transferring to other licensees the same information, informational rights, or contractual rights within the same scope. The term includes a consignment of a copy.

(47) "Notice" of a fact means knowledge of the fact, receipt of notification of the fact, or reason to know the fact exists.

(48) "Notify", or "give notice", means to take such steps as may be reasonably required to inform the other person in the ordinary course, whether or not the other person actually comes to know of it.

(49) "Party" means a person that engages in a transaction or makes an agreement under this [Act].

(50) "Person" means an individual, corporation, business trust, estate, trust, partnership, limited liability company, association, joint venture, governmental subdivision, instrumentality, or agency, public corporation, or any other legal or commercial entity.

(51) "Published informational content" means informational content prepared for or made available to recipients generally, or to a class of recipients, in substantially the same form. The term does not include informational content that is:

(A) customized for a particular recipient by one or more individuals acting as or on behalf of the licensor, using judgment or expertise; or

(B) provided in a special relationship of reliance between the provider and the recipient.

(52) "Receipt" means:

(A) with respect to a copy, taking delivery; or

(B) with respect to a notice:

(i) coming to a person's attention; or

(ii) being delivered to and available at a location or system designated by agreement for that purpose or, in the absence of an agreed location or system:

(I) being delivered at the person's residence, or the person's place of business through which the contract was made, or at any other place held out by the person as a place for receipt of communications of the kind; or

(II) in the case of an electronic notice, coming into existence in an information processing system or at an address in that system in a form capable of being processed by or perceived from a system of that type by a recipient, if the recipient uses, or otherwise has designated or holds out, that place or system for receipt of notices of the kind to be given and the sender does not know that the notice cannot be accessed from that place.

(53) "Receive" means to take receipt.

(54) "Record" means information that is inscribed on a tangible medium or that is stored in an electronic or other medium and is retrievable in perceivable form.

(55) "Release" means an agreement by a party not to object to, or exercise any rights or pursue any remedies to limit, the use of information or informational rights which agreement does not require an affirmative act by the party to enable or support the other party's use of the information or informational rights. The term includes a waiver of informational rights.

(56) "Return", with respect to a record containing contractual terms that were rejected, refers only to the computer information and means:

(A) in the case of a licensee that rejects a record regarding a single information product transferred for a single contract fee, a right to reimbursement of the contract fee paid from the person to which it was paid or from another person that offers to reimburse that fee, on:

(i) submission of proof of purchase; and

(ii) proper redelivery of the computer information and all copies within a reasonable time after initial delivery of the information to the licensee;

(B) in the case of a licensee that rejects a record regarding an information product provided as part of multiple information products integrated into and transferred as a bundled whole but retaining their separate identity:

(i) a right to reimbursement of any portion of the aggregate contract fee identified by the licensor in the initial transaction as charged to the licensee for all bundled information products which was actually paid, on:

(I) rejection of the record before or during the initial use of the bundled product;

(II) proper redelivery of all computer information products in the bundled whole and all copies of them within a reasonable time after initial delivery of the information to the licensee; and

(III) submission of proof of purchase; or

(ii) a right to reimbursement of any separate contract fee identified by the licensor in the initial transaction as charged to the licensee for the separate information product to which the rejected record applies, on:

(I) submission of proof of purchase; and

(II) proper redelivery of that computer information product and all copies within a reasonable time after initial delivery of the information to the licensee; or

(C) in the case of a licensor that rejects a record proposed by the licensee, a right to proper redelivery of the computer information and all copies from the licensee, to stop delivery or access to the information by the licensee, and to reimbursement from the licensee of amounts paid by the licensor with respect to the rejected record, on reimbursement to the licensee of contract fees that it paid with respect to the rejected record, subject to recoupment and setoff.

(57) "Scope", with respect to terms of a license, means:

(A) the licensed copies, information, or informational rights involved;

(B) the use or access authorized, prohibited, or controlled;

(C) the geographic area, market, or location; or

(D) the duration of the license.

(58) "Seasonable", with respect to an act, means taken within the time agreed or, if no time is agreed, within a reasonable time.

(59) "Send" means, with any costs provided for and properly addressed or directed as reasonable under the circumstances or as otherwise agreed, to deposit a record in the mail or with a commercially reasonable carrier, to deliver a record for transmission to or re-creation in another location or information processing system, or to take the steps necessary to initiate transmission to or re-creation of a record in another location or information processing system. In addition, with respect to an electronic message, the message must be in a form capable of being processed by or perceived from a system of the type the recipient uses or otherwise has designated or held out as a place for the receipt of communications of the kind sent. Receipt within the time in which it would have arrived if properly sent, has the effect of a proper sending.

(60) "Standard form" means a record or a group of related records containing terms prepared for repeated use in transactions and so used in

a transaction in which there was no negotiated change of terms by individuals except to set the price, quantity, method of payment, selection among standard options, or time or method of delivery.

* * *

[SUBPART B. GENERAL SCOPE AND TERMS]

Section 103. Scope; Exclusions.

(a) This [Act] applies to computer information transactions.

(b) Except for subject matter excluded in subsection (d) and as otherwise provided in Section 104, if a computer information transaction includes subject matter other than computer information or subject matter excluded under subsection (d), the following rules apply:

(1) If a transaction includes computer information and goods, this [Act] applies to the part of the transaction involving computer information, informational rights in it, and creation or modification of it. However, if a copy of a computer program is contained in and sold or leased as part of goods, this [Act] applies to the copy and the computer program only if:

(A) the goods are a computer or computer peripheral; or

(B) giving the buyer or lessee of the goods access to or use of the program is ordinarily a material purpose of transactions in goods of the type sold or leased.

(2) In all other cases, this [Act] applies to the entire transaction if the computer information and informational rights, or access to them, is the primary subject matter, but otherwise applies only to the part of the transaction involving computer information, informational rights in it, and creation or modification of it.

(c) To the extent of a conflict between this [Act] and [Article 9 of the Uniform Commercial Code], [Article 9] governs.

(d) This [Act] does not apply to:

(1) a financial services transaction;

(2) an agreement to create, perform or perform in, include information in, acquire, use, distribute, modify, reproduce, have access to, adapt, make available, transmit, license, or display:

(A) audio or visual programming that is provided by broadcast, satellite, or cable as defined or used in the Federal Communications Act and related regulations as they existed on July 1, 1999, or by similar methods of delivering that programming; or

(B) a motion picture, sound recording, musical work, or phonorecord as defined or used in Title 17 of the United States Code as of July 1, 1999, or an enhanced sound recording.

(3) a compulsory license; or

(4) a contract of employment of an individual, other than an individual hired as an independent contractor to create or modify computer information, unless the independent contractor is a freelancer in the news reporting industry as that term is commonly understood in that industry;

(5) a contract that does not require that information be furnished as computer information or a contract in which, under the agreement, the form of the information as computer information is otherwise insignificant with respect to the primary subject matter of the part of the transaction pertaining to the information; or

(6) subject matter within the scope of [Article 3, 4, 4A, 5, [6,] 7, or 8 of the Uniform Commercial Code].

(e) As used in subsection (d)(2)(B), "enhanced sound recording" means a separately identifiable product or service the dominant character of which consists of recorded sounds but which includes (i) statements or instructions whose purpose is to allow or control the perception, reproduction, or communication of those sounds or (ii) other information so long as recorded sounds constitute the dominant character of the product or service despite the inclusion of the other information.

Section 104. Mixed Transactions: Agreement to Opt-in or Opt-Out. The parties may agree that this [Act], including contract-formation rules, governs the transaction, in whole or part, or that other law governs the transaction and this [Act] does not apply, if a material part of the subject matter to which the agreement applies is computer information or informational rights in it that are within the scope of this [Act], or is subject matter within this [Act] under Section 103(b), or is subject matter excluded by Section 103(d)(1) or (2). However, any agreement to do so is subject to the following rules:

(1) An agreement that this [Act] governs a transaction does not alter the applicability of any rule or procedure that may not be varied by agreement of the parties or that may be varied only in a manner specified by the rule or procedure, including a consumer protection statute [or administrative rule]. In addition, in a mass-market transaction, the agreement does not alter the applicability of a law applicable to a copy of information in printed form.

(2) An agreement that this [Act] does not govern a transaction:

(A) does not alter the applicability of Section 214 or 816; and

(B) in a mass-market transaction, does not alter the applicability under [this Act] of the doctrine of unconscionability or fundamental public policy or the obligation of good faith.

(3) In a mass-market transaction, any term under this section which changes the extent to which this [Act] governs the transaction must be conspicuous.

(4) A copy of a computer program contained in and sold or leased as part of goods and which is excluded from this [Act] by Section 103(b)(1) cannot provide the basis for an agreement under this section that this [Act] governs the transaction.

Section 105. Relation to Federal Law; Fundamental Public Policy; Transactions Subject to Other State Law.

(a) A provision of this [Act] which is preempted by federal law is unenforceable to the extent of the preemption.

(b) If a term of a contract violates a fundamental public policy, the court may refuse to enforce the contract, enforce the remainder of the contract without the impermissible term, or limit the application of the impermissible term so as to avoid a result contrary to public policy, in each case to the extent that the interest in enforcement is clearly outweighed by a public policy against enforcement of the term.

(c) Except as otherwise provided in subsection (d), if this [Act] or a term of a contract under this [Act] conflicts with a consumer protection statute [or administrative rule], the consumer protection statute [or rule] governs.

(d) If a law of this State in effect on the effective date of this [Act] applies to a transaction governed by this [Act], the following rules apply:

(1) A requirement that a term, waiver, notice, or disclaimer be in a writing is satisfied by a record.

(2) A requirement that a record, writing, or term be signed is satisfied by an authentication.

(3) A requirement that a term be conspicuous, or the like, is satisfied by a term that is conspicuous under this [Act].

(4) A requirement of consent or agreement to a term is satisfied by a manifestation of assent to the term in accordance with this [Act].

[(e) The following laws govern in the case of a conflict between this [Act] and the other law: [List laws establishing a digital signature and similar form of attribution procedure.]]

Legislative Note: If there are any consumer protection laws that should be excepted from the electronic commerce rules in subsection (d), those laws should be excluded from the operation of that subsection.

Section 107. Legal Recognition of Electronic Record and Authentication; Use of Electronic Agents.

(a) A record or authentication may not be denied legal effect or enforceability solely because it is in electronic form.

(b) This [Act] does not require that a record or authentication be generated, stored, sent, received, or otherwise processed by electronic means or in electronic form.

(c) In any transaction, a person may establish requirements regarding the type of authentication or record acceptable to it.

(d) A person that uses an electronic agent that it has selected for making an authentication, performance, or agreement, including manifestation of assent, is bound by the operations of the electronic agent, even if no individual was aware of or reviewed the agent's operations or the results of the operations.

Section 108. Proof and Effect of Authentication.

(a) Authentication may be proven in any manner, including a showing that a party made use of information or access that could have been available only if it engaged in conduct or operations that authenticated the record or term.

(b) Compliance with a commercially reasonable attribution procedure agreed to or adopted by the parties or established by law for authenticating a record authenticates the record as a matter of law.

Section 109. Choice of Law.

(a) The parties in their agreement may choose the applicable law. However, the choice is not enforceable in a consumer contract to the extent it would vary a rule that may not be varied by agreement under the law of the jurisdiction whose law would apply under subsections (b) and (c) in the absence of the agreement.

(b) In the absence of an enforceable agreement on choice of law, the following rules determine which jurisdiction's law governs in all respects for purposes of contract law:

(1) An access contract or a contract providing for electronic delivery of a copy is governed by the law of the jurisdiction in which the licensor was located when the agreement was entered into.

(2) A consumer contract that requires delivery of a copy on a tangible medium is governed by the law of the jurisdiction in which the copy is or should have been delivered to the consumer.

(3) In all other cases, the contract is governed by the law of the jurisdiction having the most significant relationship to the transaction.

(c) In cases governed by subsection (b), if the jurisdiction whose law governs is outside the United States, the law of that jurisdiction governs only if it provides substantially similar protections and rights to a party not located in that jurisdiction as are provided under this [Act]. Otherwise, the law of the State that has the most significant relationship to the transaction governs.

(d) For purposes of this section, a party is located at its place of business if it has one place of business, at its chief executive office if it has more than one place of business, or at its place of incorporation or primary registration if it does not have a physical place of business. Otherwise, a party is located at its primary residence.

Section 110. Contractual Choice of Forum.

(a) The parties in their agreement may choose an exclusive judicial forum unless the choice is unreasonable and unjust.

(b) A judicial forum specified in an agreement is not exclusive unless the agreement expressly so provides.

Section 111. Unconscionable Contract or Term.

(a) If a court as a matter of law finds a contract or a term thereof to have been unconscionable at the time it was made, the court may refuse to enforce the contract, enforce the remainder of the contract without the unconscionable term, or limit the application of the unconscionable term so as to avoid an unconscionable result.

(b) If it is claimed or appears to the court that a contract or term thereof may be unconscionable, the parties must be afforded a reasonable opportunity to present evidence as to its commercial setting, purpose, and effect to aid the court in making the determination.

Section 112. Manifesting Assent; Opportunity to Review.

(a) A person manifests assent to a record or term if the person, acting with knowledge of, or after having an opportunity to review the record or term or a copy of it:

(1) authenticates the record or term with intent to adopt or accept it; or

(2) intentionally engages in conduct or makes statements with reason to know that the other party or its electronic agent may infer from the conduct or statement that the person assents to the record or term.

(b) An electronic agent manifests assent to a record or term if, after having an opportunity to review it, the electronic agent:

(1) authenticates the record or term; or

(2) engages in operations that in the circumstances indicate acceptance of the record or term.

(c) If this [Act] or other law requires assent to a specific term, a manifestation of assent must relate specifically to the term.

(d) Conduct or operations manifesting assent may be proved in any manner, including a showing that a person or an electronic agent obtained or used the information or informational rights and that a procedure existed by which a person or an electronic agent must have engaged in the conduct or operations in order to do so. Proof of compliance with subsection (a)(2) is sufficient if there is conduct that assents and subsequent conduct that reaffirms assent by electronic means.

(e) With respect to an opportunity to review, the following rules apply:

(1) A person has an opportunity to review a record or term only if it is made available in a manner that ought to call it to the attention of a reasonable person and permit review.

(2) An electronic agent has an opportunity to review a record or term only if it is made available in manner that would enable a reasonably configured electronic agent to react to the record or term.

(3) If a record or term is available for review only after a person becomes obligated to pay or begins its performance, the person has an opportunity to review only if it has a right to a return if it rejects the record. However, a right to a return is not required if:

(A) the record proposes a modification of contract or provides particulars of performance under Section 305; or

(B) the primary performance is other than delivery or acceptance of a copy, the agreement is not a mass-market transaction, and the parties at the time of contracting had reason to know that a record or term would be presented after performance, use, or access to the information began.

(4) The right to a return under paragraph (3) may arise by law or by agreement.

(f) The effect of provisions of this section may be modified by an agreement setting out standards applicable to future transactions between the parties.

Section 113. variation by agreement; commercial practice.

(a) The effect of any provision of this [Act], including an allocation of risk or imposition of a burden, may be varied by agreement of the parties. However, the following rules apply:

(1) Obligations of good faith, diligence, reasonableness, and care imposed by this [Act] may not be disclaimed by agreement, but the

parties by agreement may determine the standards by which the performance of the obligation is to be measured if the standards are not manifestly unreasonable.

(2) The limitations on enforceability imposed by unconscionability under Section 111 and fundamental public policy under Section 105(b) may not be varied by agreement.

(3) Limitations on enforceability of, or agreement to, a contract, term, or right expressly stated in the sections listed in the following subparagraphs may not be varied by agreement except to the extent provided in each section:

(A) the limitations on agreed choice of law in Section 109(a);

(B) the limitations on agreed choice of forum in Section 110;

(C) the requirements for manifesting assent and opportunity for review in Section 112;

(D) the limitations on enforceability in Section 201;

(E) the limitations on a mass-market license in Section 209;

(F) the consumer defense arising from an electronic error in Section 214;

(G) the requirements for an enforceable term in Sections 303(b), 307(g), 406(b) and (c), and 804(a);

(H) the limitations on a financier in Sections 507 through 511;

(I) the restrictions on altering the period of limitations in Section 805(a) and (b); and

(J) the limitations on self-help repossession in Sections 815(b) and 816.

(b) Any usage of trade of which the parties are or should be aware and any course of dealing or course of performance between the parties are relevant to determining the existence or meaning of an agreement.

Section 114. Supplemental Principles; Good Faith; Decision for Court; Reasonable Time; Reason to Know.

(a) Unless displaced by this [Act], principles of law and equity, including the law merchant and the common law of this State relative to capacity to contract, principal and agent, estoppel, fraud, misrepresentation, duress, coercion, mistake, and other validating or invalidating cause, supplement this [Act]. Among the laws supplementing and not displaced by this [Act] are trade secret laws and unfair competition laws.

(b) Every contract or duty within the scope of this [Act] imposes an obligation of good faith in its performance or enforcement.

(c) Whether a term is conspicuous or is unenforceable under Section 105(a) or (b), 111, or 209(a) and whether an attribution procedure is commercially reasonable or effective under Section 108, 212, or 213 are questions to be determined by the court.

(d) Whether an agreement has legal consequences is determined by this [Act].

(e) Whenever this [Act] requires any action to be taken within a reasonable time, the following rules apply:

(1) What is a reasonable time for taking the action depends on the nature, purpose, and circumstances of the action.

(2) Any time that is not manifestly unreasonable may be fixed by agreement.

(f) A person has reason to know a fact if the person has knowledge of the fact or, from all the facts and circumstances known to the person without investigation, the person should be aware that the fact exists.

PART 2

FORMATION AND TERMS

[SUBPART A. FORMATION OF CONTRACT]

Section 201. Formal Requirements.

(a) Except as otherwise provided in this section, a contract requiring payment of a contract fee of $5,000 or more is not enforceable by way of action or defense unless:

(1) the party against which enforcement is sought authenticated a record sufficient to indicate that a contract has been formed and which reasonably identifies the copy or subject matter to which the contract refers; or

(2) the agreement is a license for an agreed duration of one year or less or which may be terminated at will by the party against which the contract is asserted.

(b) A record is sufficient under subsection (a) even if it omits or incorrectly states a term, but the contract is not enforceable under that subsection beyond the number of copies or subject matter shown in the record.

(c) A contract that does not satisfy the requirements of subsection (a) is nevertheless enforceable under that subsection if:

(1) a performance was tendered or the information was made available by one party and the tender was accepted or the information accessed by the other; or

(2) the party against which enforcement is sought admits in court, by pleading or by testimony or otherwise under oath, facts sufficient to indicate a contract has been made, but the agreement is not enforceable under this paragraph beyond the number of copies or the subject matter admitted.

(d) Between merchants, if, within a reasonable time, a record in confirmation of the contract and sufficient against the sender is received and the party receiving it has reason to know its contents, the record satisfies subsection (a) against the party receiving it unless notice of objection to its contents is given in a record within 10 days after the confirming record is received.

(e) An agreement that the requirements of this section need not be satisfied as to future transactions is effective if evidenced in a record authenticated by the person against which enforcement is sought.

(f) A transaction within the scope of this [Act] is not subject to a statute of frauds contained in another law of this State.

Section 202. Formation in General.

(a) A contract may be formed in any manner sufficient to show agreement, including offer and acceptance or conduct of both parties or operations of electronic agents which recognize the existence of a contract.

(b) If the parties so intend, an agreement sufficient to constitute a contract may be found even if the time of its making is undetermined, one or more terms are left open or to be agreed on, the records of the parties do not otherwise establish a contract, or one party reserves the right to modify terms.

(c) Even if one or more terms are left open or to be agreed upon, a contract does not fail for indefiniteness if the parties intended to make a contract and there is a reasonably certain basis for giving an appropriate remedy.

(d) In the absence of conduct or performance by both parties to the contrary, a contract is not formed if there is a material disagreement about a material term, including a term concerning scope.

(e) If a term is to be adopted by later agreement and the parties intend not to be bound unless the term is so adopted, a contract is not formed if the parties do not agree to the term. In that case, each party shall deliver to the other party, or with the consent of the other party destroy, all copies of information, access materials, and other materials received or made, and each party is entitled to a return with respect to any contract fee paid for which performance has not been received, has not been accepted, or has been redelivered without any benefit being retained. The parties remain bound by any restriction in a contractual use term with respect to information or copies received or made from copies received pursuant to the agreement, but the contractual use term does not apply to information or copies properly received or obtained from another source.

Section 203. Offer and Acceptance in General. Unless Otherwise Unambiguously Indicated by the Language or the Circumstances:

(1) An offer to make a contract invites acceptance in any manner and by any medium reasonable under the circumstances.

(2) An order or other offer to acquire a copy for prompt or current delivery invites acceptance by either a prompt promise to ship or a prompt or current shipment of a conforming or nonconforming copy. However, a shipment of a nonconforming copy is not an acceptance if the licensor seasonably notifies the licensee that the shipment is offered only as an accommodation to the licensee.

(3) If the beginning of a requested performance is a reasonable mode of acceptance, an offeror that is not notified of acceptance or performance within a reasonable time may treat the offer as having lapsed before acceptance.

(4) If an offer in an electronic message evokes an electronic message accepting the offer, a contract is formed:

(A) when an electronic acceptance is received; or

(B) if the response consists of beginning performance, full performance, or giving access to information, when the performance is received or the access is enabled and necessary access materials are received.

Section 204. Acceptance With Varying Terms.

(a) In this section, an acceptance materially alters an offer if it contains a term that materially conflicts with or varies a term of the offer or that adds a material term not contained in the offer.

(b) Except as otherwise provided in Section 205, a definite and seasonable expression of acceptance operates as an acceptance, even if the acceptance contains terms that vary from the terms of the offer, unless the acceptance materially alters the offer.

(c) If an acceptance materially alters the offer, the following rules apply:

(1) A contract is not formed unless:

(A) a party agrees, such as by manifesting assent, to the other party's offer or acceptance; or

(B) all the other circumstances, including the conduct of the parties, establish a contract.

(2) If a contract is formed by the conduct of both parties, the terms of the contract are determined under Section 210.

(d) If an acceptance varies from but does not materially alter the offer, a contract is formed based on the terms of the offer. In addition, the following rules apply:

(1) Terms in the acceptance which conflict with terms in the offer are not part of the contract.

(2) An additional nonmaterial term in the acceptance is a proposal for an additional term. Between merchants, the proposed additional term becomes part of the contract unless the offeror gives notice of objection before, or within a reasonable time after, it receives the proposed terms.

Section 205. Conditional Offer or Acceptance.

(a) In this section, an offer or acceptance is conditional if it is conditioned on agreement by the other party to all the terms of the offer or acceptance.

(b) Except as otherwise provided in subsection (c), a conditional offer or acceptance precludes formation of a contract unless the other party agrees to its terms, such as by manifesting assent.

(c) If an offer and acceptance are in standard forms and at least one form is conditional, the following rules apply:

(1) Conditional language in a standard term precludes formation of a contract only if the actions of the party proposing the form are consistent with the conditional language, such as by refusing to perform, refusing to permit performance, or refusing to accept the benefits of the agreement, until its proposed terms are accepted.

(2) A party that agrees, such as by manifesting assent, to a conditional offer that is effective under paragraph (1) adopts the terms of the offer under Section 208 or 209, except a term that conflicts with an expressly agreed term regarding price or quantity.

Section 206. Offer and Acceptance: Electronic Agents.

(a) A contract may be formed by the interaction of electronic agents. If the interaction results in the electronic agents' engaging in operations that under the circumstances indicate acceptance of an offer, a contract is formed, but a court may grant appropriate relief if the operations resulted from fraud, electronic mistake, or the like.

(b) A contract may be formed by the interaction of an electronic agent and an individual acting on the individual's own behalf or for another person. A contract is formed if the individual takes an action or makes a statement that the individual can refuse to take or say and that the individual has reason to know will:

(1) cause the electronic agent to perform, provide benefits, or allow the use or access that is the subject of the contract, or send instructions to do so; or

(2) indicate acceptance, regardless of other expressions or actions by the individual to which the individual has reason to know the electronic agent cannot react.

(c) The terms of a contract formed under subsection (b) are determined under Section 208 or 209 but do not include a term provided by the individual if the individual had reason to know that the electronic agent could not react to the term.

Section 207. Formation: Releases of Informational Rights.

(a) A release is effective without consideration if it is:

(1) in a record to which the releasing party agrees, such as by manifesting assent, and which identifies the informational rights released; or

(2) enforceable under estoppel, implied license, or other law.

(b) A release continues for the duration of the informational rights released if the release does not specify its duration and does not require affirmative performance after the grant of the release by:

(1) the party granting the release; or

(2) the party receiving the release, except for relatively insignificant acts.

(c) In cases not governed by subsection (b), the duration of a release is governed by Section 308.

* * *

Section 209. Mass-market License.

(a) A party adopts the terms of a mass-market license for purposes of Section 208 only if the party agrees to the license, such as by manifesting assent, before or during the party's initial performance or use of or access to the information. A term is not part of the license if:

(1) the term is unconscionable or is unenforceable under Section 105(a) or (b); or

(2) subject to Section 301, the term conflicts with a term to which the parties to the license have expressly agreed.

(b) If a mass-market license or a copy of the license is not available in a manner permitting an opportunity to review by the licensee before the licensee becomes obligated to pay and the licensee does not agree, such as by manifesting assent, to the license after having an opportunity to review, the licensee is entitled to a return under Section 112 and, in addition, to:

(1) reimbursement of any reasonable expenses incurred in complying with the licensor's instructions for returning or destroying the computer information or, in the absence of instructions, expenses incurred for return postage or similar reasonable expense in returning the computer information; and

(2) compensation for any reasonable and foreseeable costs of restoring the licensee's information processing system to reverse changes in the system caused by the installation, if:

(A) the installation occurs because information must be installed to enable review of the license; and

(B) the installation alters the system or information in it but does not restore the system or information after removal of the installed information because the licensee rejected the license.

(c) In a mass-market transaction, if the licensor does not have an opportunity to review a record containing proposed terms from the licensee before the licensor delivers or becomes obligated to deliver the information, and if the licensor does not agree, such as by manifesting assent, to those terms after having that opportunity, the licensor is entitled to a return.

* * *

Section 214. Electronic Error: Consumer Defenses.

(a) In this section, "electronic error" means an error in an electronic message created by a consumer using an information processing system if a reasonable method to detect and correct or avoid the error was not provided.

(b) In an automated transaction, a consumer is not bound by an electronic message that the consumer did not intend and which was caused by an electronic error, if the consumer:

(1) promptly on learning of the error:

(A) notifies the other party of the error; and

(B) causes delivery to the other party or, pursuant to reasonable instructions received from the other party, delivers to another person or destroys all copies of the information; and

(2) has not used, or received any benefit or value from, the information or caused the information or benefit to be made available to a third party.

(c) If subsection (b) does not apply, the effect of an electronic error is determined by other law.

Section 215. Electronic Message: When Effective; Effect of Acknowledgment.

(a) Receipt of an electronic message is effective when received even if no individual is aware of its receipt.

(b) Receipt of an electronic acknowledgment of an electronic message establishes that the message was received but by itself does not establish that the content sent corresponds to the content received.

* * *

DOCUMENT 55

UNIFORM ELECTRONIC TRANSACTIONS ACT (1999)

■ ■ ■

Section 1. Short Title. This [Act] may be cited as the Uniform Electronic Transactions Act.

Section 2. Definitions. In this [Act]:

(1) "Agreement" means the bargain of the parties in fact, as found in their language or inferred from other circumstances and from rules, regulations, and procedures given the effect of agreements under laws otherwise applicable to a particular transaction.

(2) "Automated transaction" means a transaction conducted or performed, in whole or in part, be electronic means or electronic records, in which the acts or records of one or both parties are not reviewed by an individual in the ordinary course in forming a contract, performing under an existing contract, or fulfilling an obligation required by the transaction.

(3) "Computer program" means a set of statements or instructions to be used directly or indirectly in an information processing system in order to bring about a certain result.

(4) "Contract" means the total legal obligation resulting from the parties' agreement as affected by this [Act] and other applicable law.

(5) "Electronic" means relating to technology having electrical, digital, magnetic, wireless, optical, electromagnetic, or similar capabilities.

(6) "Electronic Agent" means a computer program or an electronic or other automated means used independently to initiate an action or respond to electronic records or performances in whole or in part, without review or action by an individual.

(7) "Electronic record" means a record created, generated, sent, communicated, received, or stored by electronic means.

(8) "Electronic signature" means an electronic sound, symbol, or process attached to or logically associated with a record and executed or adopted by a person with the intent to sign the record.

(9) "Government agency" means an executive, legislative, or judicial agency, department, board, commission, authority, institution, or

instrumentality of the federal government or of a State or of a county, municipality, or other political subdivision of a State.

(10) "Information" means data, text, images, sounds, codes, computer programs, software, databases, or the like.

(11) "Information processing system" means an electronic system for creating, generating, sending, receiving, storing, displaying, or processing information.

(12) "Person" means an individual, corporation, business trust, estate, trust, partnership, limited liability company, association, joint venture, governmental agency, public corporation, or any other legal or commercial entity.

(13) "Record" means information that is inscribed on a tangible medium or that is stored in an electronic or other medium and is retrievable in perceivable form.

(14) "Security procedure" means a procedure employed for the purpose of verifying that an electronic signature, record, or performance is that of a specific person or for detecting changes or errors in the information in an electronic record. The terms includes a procedure that requires the use of algorithms or other codes, identifying words or numbers, encryption, or callback or other acknowledgment procedures.

(15) "State" means a State of the United States, the District of Columbia, Puerto Rico, the United States Virgin Islands, or any territory or insular possession subject to the jurisdiction of the United States. The term includes an Indian Tribe or band, or Alaskan native village, which is recognized by federal law or formally acknowledged by a State.

(16) "Transaction" means an action or set of actions occurring between two or more persons relating to the conduct of business, commercial, or governmental affairs.

Section 3. Scope.

(a) Except as otherwise provided in subsection (b), this [Act] applies to electronic records and electronic signatures relating to a transaction.

(b) This [Act] does not apply to a transaction to the extent it is governed by:

(1) a law governing the creation and execution of wills, codicils, or testamentary trusts;

(2) [The Uniform Commercial Code other than Sections 1–107 and 1–206, Article 2, and Article 2A];

(3) [the Uniform Computer Information Transactions Act]; and

(4) [other laws, if any, identified by State].

(c) This [Act] applies to an electronic record or electronic signature otherwise excluded from the application of this [Act] under subsection (b) to the extent it is governed by a law other than those specified in subsection (b).

(d) A transaction subject to this [Act] is also subject to other applicable substantive law.

Section 4. Prospective Application. This [Act] applies to any electronic record or electronic signature created, generated, sent, communicated, received, or stored on or after the effective date of this [Act].

Section 5. Use of Electronic Records and Electronic Signatures; Variation by Agreement.

(a) This [Act] does not require a record or signature to be created, generated, sent, communicated, received, stored, or otherwise processed or used by electronic means or in electronic form.

(b) This [Act] applies only to transactions between parties each of which has agreed to conduct transactions by electronic means. Whether the parties agree to conduct a transaction by electronic means is determined from the context and surrounding circumstances, including the parties' conduct.

(c) A party that agrees to conduct a transaction by electronic means may refuse to conduct other transactions by electronic means. The right granted by this subsection may not be waived by agreement.

(d) Except as otherwise provided in this [Act], the effect of any of its provisions may be varied by agreement. The presence in certain provisions of this [Act] of the words "unless otherwise agreed", or words of similar import, does not imply that the effect of other provisions may not be varied by agreement.

(e) Whether an electronic record or electronic signature has legal consequences is determined by this [Act] and other applicable law.

Section 6. Construction and Application. This [Act] must be construed and applied:

(1) to facilitate electronic transactions consistent with other applicable law:

(2) to be consistent with reasonable practices concerning electronic transactions and with the continued expansion of those practices; and

(3) to effectuate its general purpose to make uniform the law with respect to the subject of this [Act] among States enacting it.

Section 7. Legal Recognition of Electronic Records, Electronic Signatures, and Electronic Contracts.

(a) A record or signature may not be denied legal effect or enforceability solely because it is in electronic form.

(b) A contract may not be denied legal effect or enforceability solely because an electronic record was used in its formation.

(c) If a law requires a record to be in writing, an electronic record satisfies the law.

(d) If a law requires a signature, an electronic signature satisfies the law.

Section 8. Provision of Information in Writing: Presentation of Records.

(a) If parties have agreed to conduct a transaction by electronic means and a law requires a person to provide, send, or deliver information in writing to another person, the requirement is satisfied if the information is provided, sent, or delivered, as the case may be, in an electronic record capable of retention by the recipient at the time of receipt. An electronic record is not capable of retention by the recipient if the sender or its information processing system inhibits the ability of the recipient to print or store the electronic record.

(b) If a law other than this [Act] requires a record (i) to be posted or displayed in a certain manner, (ii) to be sent, communicated, or transmitted by a specified method, or (iii) to contain information that is formatted in a certain manner, the following rules apply:

(1) The record must be posted displayed in the manner specified in the other law.

(2) Except, as otherwise provided in subsection (d)(2), the record must be sent, communicated, or transmitted by the method specified in the other law.

(3) The record must contain the information formatted in the manner specified in the other law.

(c) If a sender inhibits the ability of a recipient to store or print an electronic record, the electronic record is not enforceable against the recipient.

(d) The requirements of this section may not be varied by agreement, but:

(1) to the extent a law other than this [Act] requires information to be provided, sent, or delivered in writing but permits that requirement to be varied by agreement, the requirement under subsection (a) that the information be in the form of an electronic record capable of retention may also be varied by agreement; and

(2) a requirement under a law other than this [Act] to send, communicate, or transmit a record by [first-class mail, postage prepaid] [regular United States mail], may be varied by agreement to the extent permitted by the other law.

Section 9. Attribution and Effect of Electronic Record and Electronic Signature.

(a) An electronic record or electronic signature is attributable to a person if it was the act of the person. The act of the person may be shown in any manner, including a showing of the efficacy of any security procedure applied to determine the person to which the electronic record or electronic signature was attributable.

(b) The effect of an electronic record or electronic signature attributed to a person under subsection (a) is determined from the context and surrounding circumstances at the time of its creation, execution, or adoption, including the parties' agreement, if any, and otherwise provided by law.

Section 10. Effect of Change or Error. If a change or error in an electronic record occurs in a transmission between parties to a transaction, the following rules apply:

(1) If the parties have agreed to use a security procedure to detect changes or errors and one party has conformed to the procedure, but the other party has not, and the nonconforming party would have detected the change or error had that party also conformed, the conforming party may avoid the effect of the changed or erroneous electronic record.

(2) In an automated transaction involving an individual, the individual may avoid the effect of an electronic record that resulted from an error made by the individual in dealing with the electronic agent of another person if the electronic did not provide an opportunity for the prevention or correction of the error and, at the time the individual learns of the error, the individual:

(A) promptly notifies the other person of the error and that the individual did not intend to be bound by the electronic record received by the other person:

(B) takes reasonable steps, including steps that conform to the other person's reasonable instructions, to return to the other person or, if instructed by the other person, to destroy the consideration received, if any, as a result of the erroneous electronic record; and

(C) has not used or received any benefit or value from the consideration, if any, received from the other person

(3) If neither paragraph (1) nor paragraph (2) applies, the change or error has the effect provided by other law, including the law of mistake, and the parties' contract, if any.

(4) Paragraphs (2) and (3) may not be varied by agreement.

Section 11. Notarization and Acknowledgment. If a law requires a signature or record to be notarized, acknowledged, verified, or made under oath, the requirement is satisfied if the electronic signature of the person authorized to perform those acts, together with all other information required to be included by other applicable law, is attached to or logically associated with the signature or record.

Section 12. Retention of Electronic Records; Originals.

(a) If a law requires that a record be retained, the requirement is satisfied by retaining an electronic record of the information in the record which:

(1) accurately reflects the information set forth in the record after it was first generated in its final form as an electronic record or otherwise; and

(2) remains accessible for later reference.

(b) A requirement to retain a record in accordance with subsection (a) does not apply to any information the sole purpose of which is to enable the record to be sent, communicated, or received.

(c) A person may satisfy subsection (a) by using the services of another person if the requirements of that subsection are satisfied.

(d) If a law requires a record to be presented or retained in its original form, or provides consequences if the record is not presented or retained in its original form, that law is satisfied by an electronic record retained in accordance with subsection (a)

(e) If a law requires retention of a check, that requirement is satisfied by retention of an electronic record of the information on the front and back of the check in accordance with subsection (a).

(f) A record retained as an electronic record in accordance with subsection (a) satisfies a law requiring a person to retain a record for evidentiary, audit, or like purposes, unless a law enacted after the effective date of this [Act] specifically prohibits the use of an electronic record for the specified purpose.

(g) This section does not preclude a governmental agency of this State from specifying additional requirements for the retention of a record subject to the agency's jurisdiction.

Section 13. Admissibility in Evidence. In a proceeding, evidence of a record or signature may not be excluded solely because it is an electronic form.

Section 14. Automated Transaction. In an automated transaction, the following rules apply:

(1) A contract may be formed by the interaction of electronic agents of the parties, even if no individual was aware of or reviewed the electronic agents' actions or the resulting terms and agreements.

(2) A contract may be formed by the interaction of an electronic agent and an individual, acting on the individual's own behalf or for another person, including by an interaction in which the individual performs actions that the individual is free to refuse to perform and which the individual knows or has reason to know will cause the electronic agent to complete the transaction or performance.

(3) The terms of the contract are determined by the substantive law applicable to it.

Section 15. Time and Place of Sending and Receipt.

(a) Unless otherwise agreed between the sender and the recipient, an electronic record is sent when it:

(1) is addressed properly or otherwise directed properly to an information processing system that the recipient has designated or uses for the purpose of receiving electronic records or information of the type sent and from which the recipient is able to retrieve the electronic record;

(2) is in a form capable of being processed by that system; and

(3) enters an information processing system outside the control of the sender or of a person that sent the electronic record on behalf of the sender or enters a region of the information processing system designated or used by the recipient which is under the control of the recipient.

(b) Unless otherwise agreed between a sender and the recipient, an electronic record is received when:

(1) it enters an information processing system that the recipient has designated or uses for the purpose of receiving electronic records or information of the type sent and from which the recipient is able to retrieve the electronic record; and

(2) it is in a form capable of being processed by that system.

(c) Subsection (b) applies even if the place the information processing system is located is different from the place the electronic record is deemed to be received under subsection (d).

(d) Unless otherwise expressly provided in the electronic record or agreed between the sender and the recipient, an electronic record is deemed to be sent from the senders place of business and to be received at the recipient's place of business, For purposes of this subsection, the following rules apply:

(1) If the sender or recipient has more than one place of business, the place of business of that person is the place having the closest relationship to the underlying transaction.

(2) If the sender or the recipient does not have a place of business, the place of business is the sender's or recipient's residence, as the case may be.

(e) An electronic record is received under subsection (b) even if no individual is aware of its receipt.

(f) Receipt of an electronic acknowledgment from an information processing system described in subsection (b) establishes that a record was received but, by itself, does not establish that the content sent corresponds to the content received.

(g) If a person is aware that an electronic record purportedly sent under subsection (a), or purportedly received under subsection (b), was not actually sent or received, the legal effect of the sending or receipt is determined by other applicable law. Except to the extent permitted by the other law, the requirements of this subsection may not be varied by agreement.

Section 16. Transferable Records

(a) In this section, "transferable record" means an electronic record that:

(1) would be a note under [Article 3 of the Uniform Commercial Code] or a document under [Article 7 of the Uniform Commercial Code] if the electronic record were in writing; and

(2) the issuer of the electronic record expressly has agreed is a transferable record.

(b) A person has control of transferable record if a system employed for evidencing the transfer of interests in the transferable record reliably establishes that person as the person to which the transferable record was issued or transferred.

(c) A system satisfies subsection (b), and a person is deemed to have control of a transferable record, if the transferable record is created, stored, and assigned in such a manner that:

(1) a single authoritative copy of the transferable record exists which is unique, identifiable, and except as otherwise provided in paragraphs (4), (5), and (6), unalterable;

(2) the authoritative copy identifies the person asserting control as:

(A) the person to which the transferable record was issued; or

(B) if the authoritative copy indicates that the transferable record has been transferred, the person to which the transferable record was most recently transferred;

(3) the authoritative copy is communicated to and maintained by the person asserting control or its designated custodian;

(4) copies or revisions that add or change an identified assignee of the authoritative copy can be made only with the consent of the person asserting control;

(5) each copy of the authoritative copy and any copy of a copy is readily identifiable as a copy that is not the authoritative copy; and

(6) any revision of the authoritative copy is readily identifiable as authorized or unauthorized.

(d) Except as otherwise agreed, a person having control of a transferable record is the holder, as defined in [Section 1–201(20) of the Uniform Commercial Code], of the transferable record and has the same rights and defenses as a holder of an equivalent record or writing under [the Uniform Commercial Code], including, if the applicable statutory requirements under [Section 3–802(a), 7–501, or 9–308 of the Uniform Commercial Code] are satisfied the rights and defenses of a holder in due course, a holder to which a negotiable document of title has been duly negotiated, or a purchaser respectively. Delivery, possession; and indorsement are not required to obtain or exercise any of the rights under this subsection.

(e) Except as otherwise agreed an obligor under a transferable record has the same rights and defenses as an equivalent obligor under equivalent records or writings under [Uniform Commercial Code].

(f) If requested by a person against which enforcement is sought, the person seeking to enforce the transferable record shall provide reasonable proof that the person is in control of the transferable record. Proof may include access to the authoritative copy of the transferable record and related business records sufficient to review the terms of the transferable record and to establish the identity of the person having control of the transferable record.

DOCUMENT 56

UNIFORM FOREIGN-COUNTRY MONEY JUDGMENTS RECOGNITION ACT (UFCMJRA) (THE "2005 ACT")*

■ ■ ■

TABLE OF CONTENTS

* Reprinted with permission of the National Conference of Commissioners on Uniform State Laws and West Group.

UNIFORM FOREIGN-COUNTRY MONEY JUDGMENTS RECOGNITION ACT

PREFATORY NOTE

This Act is a revision of the Uniform Foreign Money-Judgments Recognition Act of 1962. That Act codified the most prevalent common law rules with regard to the recognition of money judgments rendered in other countries. The hope was that codification by a state of its rules on the recognition of foreign-country money judgments, by satisfying reciprocity concerns of foreign courts, would make it more likely that money judgments rendered in that state would be recognized in other countries. Towards this end, the Act sets out the circumstances in which the courts in states that have adopted the Act must recognize foreign-country money judgments. It delineates a minimum of foreign-country judgments that must be recognized by the courts of adopting states, leaving those courts free to recognize other foreign-country judgments not covered by the Act under principles of comity or otherwise. Since its promulgation over forty years ago, the 1962 Act has been adopted in a majority of the states and has been in large part successful in carrying out it purpose of establishing uniform and clear standards under which state courts will enforce the foreign-country money judgments that come within its scope.

This Act continues the basic policies and approach of the 1962 Act. Its purpose is not to depart from the basic rules or approach of the 1962 Act, which have withstood well the test of time, but rather to update the 1962 Act, to clarify its provisions, and to correct problems created by the interpretation of the provisions of that Act by the courts over the years since its promulgation. Among the more significant issues that have arisen under the 1962 Act which are addressed in this Revised Act are (1) the need to update and clarify the definitions section; (2) the need to reorganize and clarify the scope provisions, and to allocate the burden of proof with regard to establishing application of the Act; (3) the need to set out the procedure by which recognition of a foreign-country money judgment under the Act must be sought; (4) the need to clarify and, to a limited extent, expand upon the grounds for denying recognition in light of differing interpretations of those provisions in the current case law; (5) the need to expressly allocate the burden of proof with regard to the grounds for denying recognition; and (6) the need to establish a statute of limitations for recognition actions.

In the course of drafting this Act, the drafters revisited the decision made in the 1962 Act not to require reciprocity as a condition to recognition of the foreign-country money judgments covered by the Act. After much discussion, the drafters decided that the approach of the 1962 Act continues to be the wisest course with regard to this issue. While recognition of U.S. judgments continues to be problematic in a number of foreign countries, there was insufficient evidence to establish that a reciprocity requirement would have a greater effect on encouraging foreign recognition of U.S.

judgments than does the approach taken by the Act. At the same time, the certainty and uniformity provided by the approach of the 1962 Act, and continued in this Act, creates a stability in this area that facilitates international commercial transactions.

UNIFORM FOREIGN-COUNTRY MONEY JUDGMENTS RECOGNITION ACT

SECTION 1. SHORT TITLE. This [act] may be cited as the [Uniform Foreign-Country Money Judgments Recognition Act].

COMMENT

Source: This section is an updated version of Section 9 of the Uniform Foreign Money-Judgments Recognition Act of 1962.

SECTION 2. DEFINITIONS. In this [act]:

(1) "Foreign country" means a government other than:

(A) the United States;

(B) a state, district, commonwealth, territory, or insular possession of the United States; or

(C) any other government with regard to which the decision in this state as to whether to recognize a judgment of that government's courts is initially subject to determination under the Full Faith and Credit Clause of the United States Constitution.

(2) "Foreign-country judgment" means a judgment of a court of a foreign country.

COMMENT

Source: This section is derived from Section 1 of the Uniform Foreign Money-Judgments Recognition Act of 1962.

1. The defined terms "foreign state" and "foreign judgment" in the 1962 Act have been changed to "foreign country" and "foreign-country judgment" in order to make it clear that the Act does not apply to recognition of sister-state judgments. Some courts have noted that the "foreign state" and "foreign judgment" definitions of the 1962 Act have caused confusion as to whether the Act should apply to sister-state judgments because "foreign state" and "foreign judgment" are terms of art generally used in connection with recognition and enforcement of sister-state judgments. *See, e.g.,* Eagle Leasing v. Amandus, 476 N.W.2d 35 (S.Ct. Iowa 1991) (reversing lower court's application of UFMJRA to a sister-state judgment, but noting lower court's confusion was understandable as "foreign judgment" is term of art normally applied to sister-state judgments). *See also,* Uniform Enforcement of Foreign Judgments Act § 1 (defining "foreign judgment" as the judgment of a sister state or federal court).

The 1962 Act defines a "foreign state" as "any governmental unit other than the United States, or any state, district, commonwealth, territory, insular possession thereof, or the Panama Canal Zone, the Trust Territory of the Pacific Islands, or the Ryuku Islands." Rather than simply updating the list in the 1962 Act's definition of "foreign state," the new definition of "foreign country" in this Act combines the "listing" approach of the 1962 Act's "foreign state" definition with a provision that defines "foreign country" in terms of whether the judgments of the particular government's courts are initially subject to the Full Faith and Credit Clause standards for determining whether those judgments will be recognized. Under this new definition, a governmental unit is a "foreign country" if it is (1) not the United States or a state, district, commonwealth, territory or insular possession of the United States; and (2) its judgments are not initially subject to Full Faith and Credit Clause standards.

The Full Faith and Credit Clause, Art. IV, section 1, provides that "Full Faith and Credit shall be given in each State to the public Acts, Records, and judicial Proceedings of every other State. And the Congress may by general Laws prescribe the Manner in which such Acts, Records, and Proceedings shall be proved, and the Effect thereof." Whether the judgments of a governmental unit are subject to the Full Faith and Credit Clause may be determined by judicial interpretation of the Full Faith and Credit Clause or by statute, or by a combination of these two sources. For example, pursuant to the authority granted by the second sentence of the Full Faith and Credit Clause, Congress has passed 28 U.S.C.A. § 1738, which provides *inter alia* that court records from "any State, Territory, or Possession of the United States" are entitled to full faith and credit under the Full Faith and Credit Clause. In *Stoll v. Gottlieb*, 305 U.S. 165, 170 (1938), the United States Supreme Court held that this statute also requires that full faith and credit be given to judgments of federal courts. States also have made determinations as to whether certain types of judgments are subject to the Full Faith and Credit Clause. *E.g.* Day v. Montana Dept. Of Social & Rehab. Servs., 900 P.2d 296 (Mont. 1995) (tribal court judgment not subject to Full Faith and Credit, and should be treated with same deference shown foreign-country judgments). Under the definition of "foreign country" in this Act, the determination as to whether a governmental unit's judgments are subject to full faith and credit standards should be made by reference to any relevant law, whether statutory or decisional, that is applicable "in this state."

The definition of "foreign country" in terms of those judgments not subject to Full Faith and Credit standards also has the advantage of more effectively coordinating the Act with the Uniform Enforcement of Foreign Judgments Act. That Act, which establishes a registration procedure for the enforcement of sister state and equivalent judgments, defines a "foreign judgment" as "any judgment, decree, or order of a court of the United States or of any other court which is entitled to full faith and credit in this state." Uniform Enforcement of Foreign Judgments Act, § 1 (1964). By defining "foreign country" in the Recognition Act in terms of those judgments not subject to full faith and credit standards, this Act makes it clear that the Enforcement Act and the

Recognition Act are mutually exclusive—if a foreign money judgment is subject to full faith and credit standards, then the Enforcement Act's registration procedure is available with regard to its enforcement; if the foreign money judgment is not subject to full faith and credit standards, then the foreign money judgment may not be enforced until recognition of it has been obtained in accordance with the provisions of the Recognition Act.

2. The definition of "foreign-country judgment" in this Act differs significantly from the 1962 Act's definition of "foreign judgment." The 1962 Act's definition served in large part as a scope provision for the Act. The part of the definition defining the scope of the Act has been moved to section 3, which is the scope section.

3. The definition of "foreign-country judgment" in this Act refers to "a judgment" of "a court" of the foreign country. The foreign-country judgment need not take a particular form—any order or decree that meets the requirements of this section and comes within the scope of the Act under Section 3 is subject to the Act. Similarly, any competent government tribunal that issues such a "judgment" comes within the term "court" for purposes of this Act. The judgment, however, must be a judgment of an adjudicative body of the foreign country, and not the result of an alternative dispute mechanism chosen by the parties. Thus, foreign arbitral awards and agreements to arbitrate are not covered by this Act. They are governed instead by federal law, Chapter 2 of the U.S. Arbitration Act, 9 U.S.C. §§ 201–208, implementing the United Nations Convention on the Recognition and Enforcement of Foreign Arbitral Awards and Chapter 3 of the U.S. Arbitration Act, 9 U.S.C. §§ 301–307, implementing the Inter-American Convention on International Commercial Arbitration. A judgment of a foreign court confirming or setting aside an arbitral award, however, would be covered by this Act.

4. The definition of "foreign-country judgment" does not limit foreign-country judgments to those rendered in litigation between private parties. Judgments in which a governmental entity is a party also are included, and are subject to this Act if they meet the requirements of this section and are within the scope of the Act under Section 3.

SECTION 3. APPLICABILITY.

(a) Except as otherwise provided in subsection (b), this [act] applies to a foreign-country judgment to the extent that the judgment:

(1) grants or denies recovery of a sum of money; and

(2) under the law of the foreign country where rendered, is final, conclusive, and enforceable.

(b) This [act] does not apply to a foreign-country judgment, even if the judgment grants or denies recovery of a sum of money, to the extent that the judgment is:

(1) a judgment for taxes;

(2) a fine or other penalty; or

(3) a judgment for divorce, support, or maintenance, or other judgment rendered in connection with domestic relations.

(c) A party seeking recognition of a foreign-country judgment has the burden of establishing that this [act] applies to the foreign-country judgment.

COMMENT

Source: This section is based on Section 2 of the 1962 Act. Subsection (b) contains material that was included as part of the definition of "foreign judgment" in Section 1(2) of the 1962 Act. Subsection (c) is new.

1. Like the 1962 Act, this Act sets out in subsection 3(a) two basic requirements that a foreign-country judgment must meet before it comes within the scope of this Act—the foreign-country judgment must (1) grant or deny recovery of a sum of money and (2) be final, conclusive and enforceable under the law of the foreign country where it was rendered. Subsection 3(b) then sets out three types of foreign-country judgments that are excluded from the coverage of this Act, even though they meet the criteria of subsection 3(a)—judgments for taxes, judgments constituting fines and other penalties, and judgments in domestic relations matters. These exclusions are comparable to those contained in Section 1(2) of the 1962 Act.

2. This Act applies to a foreign-country judgment only to the extent the foreign-country judgment grants or denies recovery of a sum of money. If a foreign-country judgment both grants or denies recovery of a sum money and provides for some other form of relief, this Act would apply to the portion of the judgment that grants or denies monetary relief, but not to the portion that provides for some other form of relief. The U.S. court, however, would be left free to decide to recognize and enforce the non-monetary portion of the judgment under principles of comity or other applicable law. See Section 11.

3. In order to come within the scope of this Act, a foreign-country judgment must be final, conclusive, and enforceable under the law of the foreign country in which it was rendered. This requirement contains three distinct, although inter-related concepts. A judgment is final when it is not subject to additional proceedings in the rendering court other than execution. A judgment is conclusive when it is given effect between the parties as a determination of their legal rights and obligations. A judgment is enforceable when the legal procedures of the state to ensure that the judgment debtor complies with the judgment are available to the judgment creditor to assist in collection of the judgment.

While the first two of these requirements—finality and conclusiveness—will apply with regard to every foreign-country money judgment, the requirement of enforceability is only relevant when the judgment is one granting recovery of a sum of money. A judgment denying a sum of money obviously is not subject to enforcement procedures, as there is no monetary award to enforce. This Act, however, covers both judgments granting and those denying recovery of a sum of money. Thus, the fact that a foreign-country judgment denying recovery of a sum of money is not enforceable does not mean that such judgments are not within the scope of the Act. Instead, the requirement that the judgment be enforceable should be read to mean that, if the foreign-country judgment grants recovery of a sum of money, it must be enforceable in the foreign country in order to be within the scope of the Act.

Like the 1962 Act, subsection 3(b) requires that the determinations as to finality, conclusiveness and enforceability be made using the law of the foreign country in which the judgment was rendered. Unless the foreign-country judgment is final, conclusive, and (to the extent it grants recovery of a sum of money) enforceable in the foreign country where it was rendered, it will not be within the scope of this Act.

4. Subsection 3(b) follows the 1962 Act by excluding three categories of foreign-country money judgments from the scope of the Act—judgments for taxes, judgments that constitute fines and penalties, and judgments in domestic relations matters. The domestic relations exclusion has been redrafted to make it clear that all judgments in domestic relations matters are excluded from the Act, not just judgments "for support" as provided in the 1962 Act. This is consistent with interpretation of the 1962 Act by the courts, which extended the "support" exclusion in the 1962 Act beyond its literal wording to exclude other money judgments in connection with domestic matters. *E.g.*, Wolff v. Wolff, 389 A.2d 413 (My. App. 1978) ("support" includes alimony).

Recognition and enforcement of domestic relations judgments traditionally has been treated differently from recognition and enforcement of other judgments. The considerations with regard to those judgments, particularly with regard to jurisdiction and finality, differ from those with regard to other money judgments. Further, national laws with regard to domestic relations vary widely, and recognition and enforcement of such judgments thus is more appropriately handled through comity than through use of this uniform Act. Finally, other statutes, such as the Uniform Interstate Family Support Act and the federal International Child Support Enforcement Act, 42 U.S.C. § 659a (1996), address various aspects of the recognition and enforcement of domestic relations awards. Under Section 11 of this Act, courts are free to recognize money judgments in domestic relations matters under principles of comity or otherwise, and U.S. courts routinely enforce money judgments in domestic relations matters under comity principles.

Foreign-country judgments for taxes and judgments that constitute fines or penalties traditionally have not been recognized and enforced in U.S. courts. *See, e.g.*, Restatement Third of the Foreign Relations Law of the United States § 483 (1986). Both the "revenue rule," under which the courts of one country will not enforce the revenue laws of another country, and the prohibition on enforcement of penal judgments seem to be grounded in the idea that one country does not enforce the public laws of another. *See id.* Reporters' Note 2. The exclusion of tax judgments and judgments constituting fines or penalties from the scope of the Act reflects this tradition. Under Section 11, however, courts remain free to consider whether such judgments should be recognized and enforced under comity or other principles.

A judgment for taxes is a judgment in favor of a foreign country or one of its subdivisions based on a claim for an assessment of a tax. Thus, a judgment awarding a plaintiff restitution of the purchase price paid for an item would not be considered in any part a judgment for taxes, even though one element of the recovery was the sales tax paid by the plaintiff at the time of purchase. Such a judgment would not be one designed to enforce the revenue laws of the foreign country, but rather one designed to compensate the plaintiff. Courts generally hold that the test for whether a judgment is a fine or penalty is determined by whether its purpose is remedial in nature, with its benefits accruing to private individuals, or it is penal in nature, punishing an offense against public justice. *E.g.*, Chase Manhattan Bank, N.A. v. Hoffman, 665 F.Supp 73 (D. Mass. 1987) (finding that Belgium judgment was not penal even though the proceeding forming the basis of the suit was primarily criminal where Belgium court considered damage petition a civil remedy, the judgment did not constitute punishment for an offense against public justice of Belgium, and benefit of the judgment accrued to private judgment creditor, not Belgium). Thus, a judgment that awards compensation or restitution for the benefit of private individuals should not automatically be considered penal in nature and therefore outside the scope of the Act simply because the action is brought on behalf of the private individuals by a government entity. *Cf.* U.S.-Australia Free Trade Agreement, art.14.7.2, U.S.-Austl., May 18, 2004 (providing that when government agency obtains a civil monetary judgment for purpose of providing restitution to consumers, investors, or customers who suffered economic harm due to fraud, judgment generally should not be denied recognition and enforcement on ground that it is penal or revenue in nature, or based on other foreign public law).

5. Under subsection 3(b), a foreign-country money judgment is not within the scope of this Act "to the extent" that it comes within one of the excluded categories. Therefore, if a foreign-country money judgment is only partially within one of the excluded categories, the non-excluded portion will be subject to this Act.

6. Subsection 3(c) is new. The 1962 Act does not expressly allocate the burden of proof with regard to establishing whether a foreign-country judgment is within the scope of the Act. Courts applying the 1962 Act generally have held that the burden of proof is on the person seeking recognition to establish that the judgment is final, conclusive and enforceable where rendered. *E.g.*, Mayekawa Mfg. Co. Ltd. v. Sasaki, 888 P.2d 183, 189 (Wash. App. 1995) (burden of proof on creditor to establish judgment is final, conclusive, and enforceable where rendered); Bridgeway Corp. v. Citibank, 45 F.Supp.2d 276, 285 (S.D.N.Y. 1999) (party seeking recognition must establish that there is a final judgment, conclusive and enforceable where rendered); S.C.Chimexim S.A. v. Velco Enterprises, Ltd., 36 F. Supp.2d 206, 212 (S.D.N.Y. 1999) (Plaintiff has the burden of establishing conclusive effect). Subsection (3)(c) places the burden of proof to establish whether a foreign-country

judgment is within the scope of the Act on the party seeking recognition of the foreign-country judgment with regard to both subsection (a) and subsection (b).

SECTION 4. STANDARDS FOR RECOGNITION OF FOREIGN-COUNTRY JUDGMENT.

(a) Except as otherwise provided in subsections (b) and (c), a court of this state shall recognize a foreign-country judgment to which this [act] applies.

(b) A court of this state may not recognize a foreign-country judgment if:

(1) the judgment was rendered under a judicial system that does not provide impartial tribunals or procedures compatible with the requirements of due process of law;

(2) the foreign court did not have personal jurisdiction over the defendant; or

(3) the foreign court did not have jurisdiction over the subject matter.

(c) A court of this state need not recognize a foreign-country judgment if:

(1) the defendant in the proceeding in the foreign court did not receive notice of the proceeding in sufficient time to enable the defendant to defend;

(2) the judgment was obtained by fraud that deprived the losing party of an adequate opportunity to present its case;

(3) the judgment or the [cause of action] [claim for relief] on which the judgment is based is repugnant to the public policy of this state or of the United States;

(4) the judgment conflicts with another final and conclusive judgment;

(5) the proceeding in the foreign court was contrary to an agreement between the parties under which the dispute in question was to be determined otherwise than by proceedings in that foreign court;

(6) in the case of jurisdiction based only on personal service, the foreign court was a seriously inconvenient forum for the trial of the action;

(7) the judgment was rendered in circumstances that raise substantial doubt about the integrity of the rendering court with respect to the judgment; or

(8) the specific proceeding in the foreign court leading to the judgment was not compatible with the requirements of due process of law.

(d) A party resisting recognition of a foreign-country judgment has the burden of establishing that a ground for nonrecognition stated in subsection (b) or (c) exists.

COMMENT

Source: This section is based on Section 4 of the 1962 Act.

1. This Section provides the standards for recognition of a foreign-country money judgment. Section 7 sets out the effect of recognition of a foreign-country money judgment under this Act.

2. Recognition of a judgment means that the forum court accepts the determination of legal rights and obligations made by the rendering court in the foreign country. *See, e.g.* Restatement (Second) of Conflicts of Laws, Ch. 5, Topic 3, Introductory Note (recognition of foreign judgment occurs to the extent the forum court gives the judgment "the same effect with respect to the parties, the subject matter of the action and the issues involved that it has in the state where it was rendered.") Recognition of a foreign-country judgment must be distinguished from enforcement of that judgment. Enforcement of the foreign-country judgment involves the application of the legal procedures of the state to ensure that the judgment debtor obeys the foreign-country judgment. Recognition of a foreign-country money judgment often is associated with enforcement of the judgment, as the judgment creditor usually seeks recognition of the foreign-country judgment primarily for the purpose of invoking the enforcement procedures of the forum state to assist the judgment creditor's collection of the judgment from the judgment debtor. Because the forum court cannot enforce the foreign-country judgment until it has determined that the judgment will be given effect, recognition is a prerequisite to enforcement of the foreign-country judgment. Recognition, however, also has significance outside the enforcement context because a foreign-country judgment also must be recognized before it can be given preclusive effect under res judicata and collateral estoppel principles. The issue of whether a foreign-country judgment will be recognized is distinct from both the issue of whether the judgment will be enforced, and the issue of the extent to which it will be given preclusive effect.

3. Subsection 4(a) places an affirmative duty on the forum court to recognize a foreign-country money judgment unless one of the grounds for nonrecognition stated in subsection (b) or (c) applies. Subsection (b) states three mandatory grounds for denying recognition to a foreign-country money judgment. If the forum court finds that one of the grounds listed in subsection (b) exists, then it must deny recognition to the foreign-country money judgment. Subsection (c) states eight nonmandatory grounds for denying recognition. The forum court has discretion to decide whether or not to refuse recognition based on one of these grounds. Subsection (d) places the burden of

proof on the party resisting recognition of the foreign-country judgment to establish that one of the grounds for nonrecognition exists.

4. The mandatory grounds for nonrecognition stated in subsection (b) are identical to the mandatory grounds stated in Section 4 of the 1962 Act. The discretionary grounds stated in subsection 4(c)(1) through (6) are based on subsection 4(b)(1) through (6) of the 1962 Act. The discretionary grounds stated in subsection 4(c)(7) and (8) are new.

5. Under subsection (b)(1), the forum court must deny recognition to the foreign-country money judgment if that judgment was "rendered under a judicial system that does not provide impartial tribunals or procedures compatible with the requirements of due process of law." The standard for this ground for nonrecognition "has been stated authoritatively by the Supreme Court of the United States in *Hilton v. Guyot*, 159 U.S.113, 205 (1895). As indicated in that decision, a mere difference in the procedural system is not a sufficient basis for nonrecognition. A case of serious injustice must be involved." Cmt § 4, Uniform Foreign Money-Judgment Recognition Act (1962). The focus of inquiry is not whether the procedure in the rendering country is similar to U.S. procedure, but rather on the basic fairness of the foreign-country procedure. Kam-Tech Systems, Ltd. v. Yardeni, 74 A.2d 644, 649 (N.J. App. 2001) (interpreting the comparable provision in the 1962 Act); *accord*, Society of Lloyd's v. Ashenden, 233 F.3d 473 (7th Cir. 2000) (procedures need not meet all the intricacies of the complex concept of due process that has emerged from U.S. case law, but rather must be fair in the broader international sense) (interpreting comparable provision in the 1962 Act). Procedural differences, such as absence of jury trial or different evidentiary rules are not sufficient to justify denying recognition under subsection (b)(1), so long as the essential elements of impartial administration and basic procedural fairness have been provided in the foreign proceeding. As the U.S. Supreme Court stated in *Hilton*:

> Where there has been opportunity for a full and fair trial abroad before a court of competent jurisdiction conducting the trial upon regular proceedings, after due citation or voluntary appearance of the defendant, and under a system of jurisprudence likely to secure an impartial administration of justice between the citizens of its own country and those of other countries, and there is nothing to show either prejudice in the court, or in the system of laws under which it was sitting, or fraud in procuring the judgment, or any other special reason why the comity of this nation should not allow it full effect then a foreign-country judgment should be recognized. *Hilton*, 159 U.S. at 202.

6. Under section 4(b)(2), the forum court must deny recognition to the foreign-country judgment if the foreign court did not have personal jurisdiction over the defendant. Section 5(a) lists six bases for personal jurisdiction that are adequate as a matter of law to establish that the foreign court had personal jurisdiction. Section 5(b) makes clear that other grounds for personal jurisdiction may be found sufficient.

7. Subsection 4(c)(2) limits the type of fraud that will serve as a ground for denying recognition to extrinsic fraud. This provision is consistent with the interpretation of the comparable provision in subsection 4(b)(2) of the 1962 Act by the courts, which have found that only extrinsic fraud—conduct of the prevailing party that deprived the losing party of an adequate opportunity to present its case—is sufficient under the 1962 Act. Examples of extrinsic fraud would be when the plaintiff deliberately had the initiating process served on the defendant at the wrong address, deliberately gave the defendant wrong information as to the time and place of the hearing, or obtained a default judgment against the defendant based on a forged confession of judgment. When this type of fraudulent action by the plaintiff deprives the defendant of an adequate opportunity to present its case, then it provides grounds for denying recognition of the foreign-country judgment. Extrinsic fraud should be distinguished from intrinsic fraud, such as false testimony of a witness or admission of a forged document into evidence during the foreign proceeding. Intrinsic fraud does not provide a basis for denying recognition under subsection 4(c)(2), as the assertion that intrinsic fraud has occurred should be raised and dealt with in the rendering court.

8. The public policy exception in subsection 4(c)(3) is based on the public policy exception in subsection 4(b)(3) of the 1962 Act, with one difference. The public policy exception in the 1962 Act states that the relevant inquiry is whether "the [cause of action] [claim for relief] on which the judgment is based" is repugnant to public policy. Based on this "cause of action" language, some courts interpreting the 1962 Act have refused to find that a public policy challenge based on something other than repugnancy of the foreign cause of action comes within this exception. *E.g.*, Southwest Livestock & Trucking Co., Inc. v. Ramon, 169 F.3d 317 (5th Cir. 1999) (refusing to deny recognition to Mexican judgment on promissory note with interest rate of 48% because cause of action to collect on promissory note does not violate public policy); Guinness PLC v. Ward, 955 F.2d 875 (4th Cir. 1992) (challenge to recognition based on post-judgment settlement could not be asserted under public policy exception); The Society of Lloyd's v. Turner, 303 F.3d 325 (5th Cir. 2002) (rejecting argument legal standards applied to establish elements of breach of contract violated public policy because cause of action for breach of contract itself is not contrary to state public policy); *cf.* Bachchan v. India Abroad Publications, Inc., 585 N.Y.S.2d 661 (N.Y. Sup. Ct. 1992) (judgment creditor argued British libel judgment should be recognized despite argument it violated First Amendment because New York recognizes a cause of action for libel). Subsection 4(c)(3) rejects this narrow focus by providing that the forum court may deny recognition if either the cause of action or the judgment itself violates public policy. *Cf.* Restatement (Third) of the Foreign Relations Law of the United States, § 482(2)(d) (1986) (containing a similarly-worded public policy exception to recognition).

Although subsection 4(c)(3) of this Act rejects the narrow focus on the cause of action under the 1962 Act, it retains the stringent test for finding a public policy violation applied by courts interpreting the 1962 Act. Under that test, a difference in law, even a marked one, is not sufficient to raise a public policy issue. Nor is it relevant that the foreign law allows a recovery that the forum state would not allow. Public policy is violated only if recognition or enforcement of the foreign-country judgment would tend clearly to injure the public health, the public morals, or the public confidence in the administration of law, or would undermine "that sense of security for individual rights, whether of personal liberty or of private property, which any citizen ought to feel." Hunt v. BP Exploration Co. (Libya) Ltd., 492 F. Supp. 885, 901 (N.D. Tex. 1980).

The language "or of the United States" in subsection 4(c)(3), which does not appear in the 1962 Act provision, makes it clear that the relevant public policy is that of both the State in which recognition is sought and that of the United States. This is the position taken by the vast majority of cases interpreting the 1962 public policy provision. *E.g.*, Bachchan v. India Abroad Publications, Inc., 585 N.Y.S.2d 661 (Sup.Ct. N.Y. 1992) (British libel judgment denied recognition because it violates First Amendment).

9. Subsection 4(c)(5) allows the forum court to refuse recognition of a foreign-country judgment when the parties had a valid agreement, such as a valid forum selection clause or agreement to arbitrate, providing that the relevant dispute would be resolved in a forum other than the forum issuing the foreign-country judgment. Under this provision, the forum court must find both the existence of a valid agreement and that the agreement covered the subject matter involved in the foreign litigation resulting in the foreign-country judgment.

10. Subsection 4(c)(6) authorizes the forum court to refuse recognition of a foreign-country judgment that was rendered in the foreign country solely on the basis of personal service when the forum court believes the original action should have been dismissed by the court in the foreign country on grounds of *forum non conveniens.*

11. Subsection 4(c)(7) is new. Under this subsection, the forum court may deny recognition to a foreign-country judgment if there are circumstances that raise substantial doubt about the integrity of the rendering court with respect to that judgment. It requires a showing of corruption in the particular case that had an impact on the judgment that was rendered. This provision may be contrasted with subsection 4(b)(1), which requires that the forum court refuse recognition to the foreign-country judgment if it was rendered under a judicial system that does not provide impartial tribunals. Like the comparable provision in subsection 4(a)(1) of the 1962 Act, subsection 4(b)(1) focuses on the judicial system of the foreign country as a whole, rather than on whether the particular judicial proceeding leading to the foreign-country judgment was impartial and fair. *See, e.g.*, The Society of Lloyd's v. Turner, 303 F.3d 325, 330 (5th Cir. 2002) (interpreting the 1962 Act); CIBC Mellon Trust Co. v. Mora Hotel Corp,. N.V., 743 N.Y.S.2d 408, 415 (N.Y. App. 2002) (interpreting the 1962 Act); Society of Lloyd's v. Ashenden, 233 F.3d 473, 477 (7th Cir. 2000) (interpreting the 1962 Act). On the other hand, subsection 4(c)(7) allows the court to deny recognition to the foreign-country judgment if it finds a lack of

impartiality and fairness of the tribunal in the individual proceeding leading to the foreign-country judgment. Thus, the difference is that between showing, for example, that corruption and bribery is so prevalent throughout the judicial system of the foreign country as to make that entire judicial system one that does not provide impartial tribunals versus showing that bribery of the judge in the proceeding that resulted in the particular foreign-country judgment under consideration had a sufficient impact on the ultimate judgment as to call it into question.

12. Subsection 4(c)(8) also is new. It allows the forum court to deny recognition to the foreign-country judgment if the court finds that the specific proceeding in the foreign court was not compatible with the requirements of fundamental fairness. Like subsection 4(c)(7), it can be contrasted with subsection 4(b)(1), which requires the forum court to deny recognition to the foreign-country judgment if the forum court finds that the entire judicial system in the foreign country where the foreign-country judgment was rendered does not provide procedures compatible with the requirements of fundamental fairness. While the focus of subsection 4(b)(1) is on the foreign country's judicial system as a whole, the focus of subsection 4(c)(8) is on the particular proceeding that resulted in the specific foreign-country judgment under consideration. Thus, the difference is that between showing, for example, that there has been such a breakdown of law and order in the particular foreign country that judgments are rendered on the basis of political decisions rather than the rule of law throughout the judicial system versus a showing that for political reasons the particular party against whom the foreign-country judgment was entered was denied fundamental fairness in the particular proceedings leading to the foreign-country judgment.

Subsections 4(c)(7) and (8) both are discretionary grounds for denying recognition, while subsection 4(b)(1) is mandatory. Obviously, if the entire judicial system in the foreign country fails to satisfy the requirements of impartiality and fundamental fairness, a judgment rendered in that foreign country would be so compromised that the forum court should refuse to recognize it as a matter of course. On the other hand, if the problem is evidence of a lack of integrity or fundamental fairness with regard to the particular proceeding leading to the foreign-country judgment, then there may or may not be other factors in the particular case that would cause the forum court to decide to recognize the foreign-country judgment. For example, a forum court might decide not to exercise its discretion to deny recognition despite evidence of corruption or procedural unfairness in a particular case because the party resisting recognition failed to raise the issue on appeal from the foreign-country judgment in the foreign country, and the evidence establishes that, if the party had done so, appeal would have been an adequate mechanism for correcting the transgressions of the lower court.

13. Under subsection 4(d), the party opposing recognition of the foreign-country judgment has the burden of establishing that one of the grounds for nonrecognition set out in subsection 4(b) or (c) applies. The 1962 Act was silent as to who had the burden of proof to establish a ground for nonrecognition and

courts applying the 1962 Act took different positions on the issue. *Compare* Bridgeway Corp. v. Citibank, 45 F.Supp. 2d 276, 285 (S.D.N.Y. 1999) (plaintiff has burden to show no mandatory basis under 4(a) for nonrecognition exists; defendant has burden regarding discretionary bases) *with* The Courage Co. LLC v. The ChemShare Corp., 93 S.W.3d 323, 331 (Tex. App. 2002) (party seeking to avoid recognition has burden to prove ground for nonrecognition). Because the grounds for nonrecognition in Section 4 are in the nature of defenses to recognition, the burden of proof is most appropriately allocated to the party opposing recognition of the foreign-country judgment.

SECTION 5. PERSONAL JURISDICTION.

(a) A foreign-country judgment may not be refused recognition for lack of personal jurisdiction if:

(1) the defendant was served with process personally in the foreign country;

(2) the defendant voluntarily appeared in the proceeding, other than for the purpose of protecting property seized or threatened with seizure in the proceeding or of contesting the jurisdiction of the court over the defendant;

(3) the defendant, before the commencement of the proceeding, had agreed to submit to the jurisdiction of the foreign court with respect to the subject matter involved;

(4) the defendant was domiciled in the foreign country when the proceeding was instituted or was a corporation or other form of business organization that had its principal place of business in, or was organized under the laws of, the foreign country;

(5) the defendant had a business office in the foreign country and the proceeding in the foreign court involved a [cause of action] [claim for relief] arising out of business done by the defendant through that office in the foreign country; or

(6) the defendant operated a motor vehicle or airplane in the foreign country and the proceeding involved a [cause of action] [claim for relief] arising out of that operation.

(b) The list of bases for personal jurisdiction in subsection (a) is not exclusive. The courts of this state may recognize bases of personal jurisdiction other than those listed in subsection(a) as sufficient to support a foreign-country judgment.

COMMENT

Source: This provision is based on Section 5 of the 1962 Act. Its substance is the same as that of Section 5 of the 1962 Act, except as noted in Comment 2 below with regard to subsection 5(a)(4).

1. Under section 4(b)(2), the forum court must deny recognition to the foreign-country judgment if the foreign court did not have personal jurisdiction over the defendant. Section 5(a) lists six bases for personal jurisdiction that are adequate as a matter of law to establish that the foreign court had personal jurisdiction. Section 5(b) makes it clear that these bases of personal jurisdiction are not exclusive. The forum court may find that the foreign court had personal jurisdiction over the defendant on some other basis.

2. Subsection 5(a)(4) of the 1962 Act provides that the foreign court had personal jurisdiction over the defendant if the defendant was "a body corporate" that "had its principal place of business, was incorporated, or had otherwise acquired corporate status, in the foreign state." Subsection 5(a)(4) of this Act extends that concept to forms of business organization other than corporations.

3. Subsection 5(a)(3) provides that the foreign court has personal jurisdiction over the defendant if the defendant agreed before commencement of the proceeding leading to the foreign-country judgment to submit to the jurisdiction of the foreign court with regard to the subject matter involved. Under this provision, the forum court must find both the existence of a valid agreement to submit to the foreign court's jurisdiction and that the agreement covered the subject matter involved in the foreign litigation resulting in the foreign-country judgment.

SECTION 6. PROCEDURE FOR RECOGNITION OF FOREIGN-COUNTRY JUDGMENT.

(a) If recognition of a foreign-country judgment is sought as an original matter, the issue of recognition shall be raised by filing an action seeking recognition of the foreign-country judgment.

(b) If recognition of a foreign-country judgment is sought in a pending action, the issue of recognition may be raised by counterclaim, cross-claim, or affirmative defense.

COMMENT

Source: This section is new.

1. Unlike the 1962 Act, which was silent as to the proper procedure for seeking recognition of a foreign-country judgment, Section 6 of this Act expressly sets out the ways in which the issue of recognition may be raised. Under section 6, the issue of recognition always must be raised in a court proceeding. Thus, section 6 rejects decisions under the 1962 Act holding that the registration procedure found in the Uniform Enforcement of Foreign Judgments Act could be utilized with regard to recognition of a foreign-country judgment. *E.g.* Society of Lloyd's v. Ashenden, 233 F.3d 473 (7th Cir. 2000). The Enforcement Act deals solely with the *enforcement* of sister-state judgments and other judgments entitled to full faith and credit, not with the *recognition* of foreign-country judgments.

More broadly, section 6 rejects the use of any registration procedure in the context of the foreign-country judgments covered by this Act. A registration procedure represents a balance between the interest of the judgment creditor in obtaining quick and efficient recognition and enforcement of a judgment when the judgment debtor has already been provided with an opportunity to litigate the underlying issues, and the interest of the judgment debtor in being provided an adequate opportunity to raise and litigate issues regarding whether the foreign-country judgment should be recognized. In the context of sister-state judgments, this balance favors use of a truncated procedure such as that found in the Enforcement Act. Recognition of sister-state judgments normally is mandated by the Full Faith and Credit Clause. Courts recognize only a very limited number of grounds for denying full faith and credit to a sister-state judgment—that the rendering court lacked jurisdiction, that the judgment was procured by fraud, that the judgment has been satisfied, or that the limitations period has expired. Thus, the judgment debtor with regard to a sister-state judgment normally does not have any grounds for opposing recognition and enforcement of the judgment. The extremely limited grounds for denying full faith and credit to a sister-state judgment reflect the fact such judgments will have been rendered by a court that is subject to the same due process limitations and the same overlap of federal statutory and constitutional law as the forum state's courts, and, to a large extent, the same body of court precedent and socio-economic ideas as those shaping the law of the forum state. Therefore, there is a strong presumption of fairness and competence attached to a sister-state judgment that justifies use of a registration procedure.

The balance between the benefits and costs of a registration procedure is significantly different, however, in the context of recognition and enforcement of foreign-country judgments. Unlike the limited grounds for denying full faith and credit to a sister-state judgment, this Act provides a number of grounds upon which recognition of a foreign-country judgment may be denied. Determination of whether these grounds apply requires the forum court to look behind the foreign-country judgment to evaluate the law and the judicial system under which the foreign-country judgment was rendered. The existence of these grounds for nonrecognition reflects the fact there is less expectation that foreign-country courts will follow procedures comporting with U.S. notions of fundamental fairness and jurisdiction or that those courts will apply laws viewed as substantively tolerable by U.S. standards than there is with regard to sister-state courts. In some situations, there also may be suspicions of corruption or fraud in the foreign-country proceedings. These differences between sister-state judgments and foreign-country judgments provide a justification for requiring judicial involvement in the decision whether to recognize a foreign-country judgment in all cases in which that issue is raised. Although the threshold for establishing that a foreign-country judgment is not entitled to recognition under Section 4 is high, there is a sufficiently greater likelihood that significant recognition issues will be raised so as to require a judicial proceeding.

2. This Section contemplates that the issue of recognition may be raised either as an original matter or in the context of a pending proceeding. Subsection 6(a) provides that in order to raise the issue of recognition of a foreign-country judgment as an initial matter, the party seeking recognition must file an action for recognition of the foreign-country judgment. Subsection 6(b) provides that when the recognition issue is raised in a pending proceeding, it may be raised by counterclaim, cross-claim or affirmative defense, depending on the context in which it is raised. These rules are consistent with the way the issue of recognition most often was raised in most states under the 1962 Act.

3. An action seeking recognition of a foreign-country judgment under this Section is an action on the foreign-country judgment itself, not an action on the underlying cause of action that gave rise to that judgment. The parties to an action under Section 6 may not relitigate the merits of the underlying dispute that gave rise to the foreign-country judgment.

4. While this Section sets out the ways in which the issue of recognition of a foreign-country judgment may be raised, it is not intended to create any new procedure not currently existing in the state or to otherwise effect existing state procedural requirements. The parties to an action in which recognition of a foreign-country judgment is sought under Section 6 must comply with all state procedural rules with regard to that type of action. Nor does this Act address the question of what constitutes a sufficient basis for jurisdiction to adjudicate with regard to an action under Section 6. Courts have split over the issue of whether the presence of assets of the debtor in a state is a sufficient basis for jurisdiction in light of footnote 36 of the U.S. Supreme Court decision in Shaffer v. Heitner, 433 U.S. 186, 210 n.36 (1977). This Act takes no position on that issue.

5. In states that have adopted the Uniform Foreign-Money Claims Act, that Act will apply to the determination of the amount of a money judgment recognized under this Act.

SECTION 7. EFFECT OF RECOGNITION OF FOREIGN-COUNTRY JUDGMENT. If the court in a proceeding under Section 6 finds that the foreign-country judgment is entitled to recognition under this [act] then, to the extent that the foreign-country judgment grants or denies recovery of a sum of money, the foreign-country judgment is:

(1) conclusive between the parties to the same extent as the judgment of a sister state entitled to full faith and credit in this state would be conclusive; and

(2) enforceable in the same manner and to the same extent as a judgment rendered in this state.

COMMENT

Source: The substance of subsection 7(1) is based on Section 3 of the 1962 Act. Subsection 7(2) is new.

1. Section 5 of this Act sets out the standards for the recognition of foreign-country judgments within the scope of this Act, and places an affirmative duty on the forum court to recognize any foreign-country judgment that meets those standards. Section 6 of this Act sets out the procedures by which the issue of recognition may be raised. This Section sets out the consequences of the decision by the forum court that the foreign-country judgment is entitled to recognition.

2. Under subsection 7(1), the first consequence of recognition of a foreign-country judgment is that it is treated as conclusive between the parties in the forum state. Section 7(1) does not attempt to establish directly the extent of that conclusiveness. Instead, it provides that the foreign-country judgment is treated as conclusive to the same extent that a judgment of a sister state that had been determined to be entitled to full faith and credit would be conclusive. This means that the foreign-country judgment generally will be given the same effect in the forum state that it has in the foreign country where it was rendered. Subsection 7(1), however, sets out the minimum effect that must be given to the foreign-country judgment once recognized. The forum court remains free to give the foreign-country judgment a greater preclusive effect in the forum state than the judgment would have in the foreign country where it was rendered. *Cf.* Restatement (Third) of the Foreign Relations Law of the United States, § 481 cmt *c* (1986).

3. Under subsection 7(2), the second consequence of recognition of a foreign-country judgment is that, to the extent it grants a sum of money, it is enforceable in the forum state in accordance with the procedures for enforcement in the forum state and to the same extent that a judgment of the forum state would be enforceable. *Cf.* Restatement (Third) of the Foreign Relations Law of the United States § 481 (1986) (judgment entitled to recognition is enforceable in accordance with the procedure for enforcement of judgments applicable where enforcement is sought). Thus, under subsection 7(2), once recognized, the foreign-country judgment has the same effect and is subject to the same procedures, defenses and proceedings for reopening, vacating, or staying a judgment of a comparable court in the forum state, and can be enforced or satisfied in the same manner as such a judgment of the forum state.

SECTION 8. STAY OF PROCEEDINGS PENDING APPEAL OF FOREIGN-COUNTRY JUDGMENT. If a party establishes that an appeal from a foreign-country judgment is pending or will be taken, the court may stay any proceedings with regard to the foreign-country judgment until the appeal is concluded, the time for appeal expires, or the appellant has had sufficient time to prosecute the appeal and has failed to do so.

COMMENT

Source: This section is the same substantively as section 6 of the 1962 Act, except that it adds as an additional measure for the duration of the stay "the time for appeal expires."

1. Under Section 3 of this Act, a foreign-country judgment is not within the scope of this Act unless it is conclusive and enforceable where rendered. Thus, if the effect of appeal under the law of the foreign country in which the judgment was rendered is to prevent it from being conclusive or enforceable between the parties, the existence of a pending appeal in the foreign country would prevent the application of this Act. Section 8 addresses a different situation. It deals with the situation in which either (1) the party seeking a stay has demonstrated that it intends to file an appeal in the foreign country, although the appeal has not yet been filed or (2) an appeal has been filed in the foreign country, but under the law of the foreign country filing of an appeal does not affect the conclusiveness or enforceability of the judgment. Section 8 allows the forum court in those situations to determine in its discretion that a stay of proceedings is appropriate.

SECTION 9. STATUTE OF LIMITATIONS. An action to recognize a foreign-country judgment must be commenced within the earlier of the time during which the foreign-country judgment is effective in the foreign country or 15 years from the date that the foreign-country judgment became effective in the foreign country.

COMMENT

Source: This Section is new. The 1962 Act did not contain a statute of limitations. Some courts applying the 1962 Act have used the state's general statute of limitations, *e.g.*, Vrozos v. Sarantopoulos, 552 N.E.2d 1053 (Ill. App. 1990) (as Recognition Act contains no statute of limitations, general five-year statute of limitations applies), while others have used the statute of limitations applicable with regard to enforcement of a domestic judgment, *e.g.*, La Societe Anonyme Goro v. Conveyor Accessories, Inc., 677 N.E. 2d 30 (Ill. App. 1997).

1. Under Section 3 of this Act, this Act only applies to foreign-country judgments that are conclusive, and if the judgment grants recovery of a sum of money, enforceable where rendered. Thus, if the period of effectiveness of the foreign-country judgment has expired in the foreign country where the judgment was rendered, the foreign-country judgment would not be subject to this Act. This means that the period of time during which a foreign-country judgment may be recognized under this Act normally is measured by the period of time during which that judgment is effective (that is, conclusive and, if applicable, enforceable) in the foreign country that rendered the judgment. If, however, the foreign-country judgment remains effective for more than fifteen years after the date on which it became effective in the foreign country, Section 9 places an additional time limit on recognition of a foreign-country judgment. It provides that, if the foreign-country judgment remains effective between the parties for more than fifteen years, then an action to recognize the foreign-

country judgment under this Act must be commenced within that fifteen year period.

2. Section 9 does not address the issue of whether a foreign-country judgment that can no longer be the basis of a recognition action under this Act because of the application of the fifteen-year limitations period in Section 9 may be used for other purposes. For example, a common rule with regard to judgments barred by a statute of limitations is that they still may be used defensively for purposes of offset and for their preclusive effect. The extent to which a foreign-country judgment with regard to which a recognition action is barred by Section 9 may be used for these or other purposes is left to the other law of the forum state.

SECTION 10. UNIFORMITY OF INTERPRETATION. In applying and construing this uniform act, consideration must be given to the need to promote uniformity of the law with respect to its subject matter among states that enact it.

COMMENT

Source: This Section is substantively the same as Section 8 of the 1962 Act. The section has been rewritten to reflect current NCCUSL practice.

SECTION 11. SAVING CLAUSE. This [act] does not prevent the recognition under principles of comity or otherwise of a foreign-country judgment not within the scope of this [act].

COMMENT

Source: This section is based on Section 7 of the 1962 Act.

1. Section 3 of this Act provides that this Act applies only to certain foreign-country judgments that grant or deny recovery of a sum of money. The purpose of this Act is to establish the minimum standards for recognition of those judgments. Section 11 makes clear that no negative implication should be read from the fact that this Act does not provide for recognition of other foreign-country judgments. Rather, this Act simply does not address the issue of whether foreign-country judgments not within its scope under Section 3 should be recognized. Courts are free to recognize those foreign-country judgments not within the scope of this Act under common law principles of comity or other applicable law.

SECTION 12. EFFECTIVE DATE.

[(a) This [act] takes effect _______ .]

[(b) This [act] applies to all actions commenced on or after the effective date of this [act] in which the issue of recognition of a foreign-country judgment is raised.]

Comment

Source: Subsection 12(a) is the same as Section 11 of the 1962 Act. Subsection 12(b) is new.

1. Subsection 12(b) provides that this Act will apply to all actions in which the issue of recognition of a foreign-country judgment is raised that are commenced on or after the effective date of this Act. Thus, the application of this Act is measured not from the time the original action leading to the foreign-country judgment was commenced in the foreign country, but rather from the time the action in which the issue of recognition is raised is commenced in the forum court. Subsection 12(b) does not distinguish between whether the purpose of the action commenced in the forum court was to seek recognition as an original matter under Subsection 6(a) or was an action that was already pending when the issue of recognition was raised under Subsection 6(b).

SECTION 13. REPEAL. The following [acts] are repealed:

(a) Uniform Foreign Money-Judgments Recognition Act,

* * *

Comment

Source: This Section is an updated version of Section 10 of the 1962 Act.

DOCUMENT 57

UNIFORM FOREIGN MONEY CLAIMS ACT (1989)*

■ ■ ■

Table of Contents

§ 1. Definitions

In this [Act]:

(1) "Action" means a judicial proceeding or arbitration in which a payment in money may be awarded or enforced with respect to a foreign-money claim.

(2) "Bank-offered spot rate" means the spot rate of exchange at which a bank will sell foreign money at a spot rate.

(3) "Conversion date" means the banking day next preceding the date on which money, in accordance with this [Act], is:

(i) paid to a claimant in an action or distribution proceeding;

---

* Reprinted with permission of the National Conference of Commissioners on Uniform State Laws and West Group.

(ii) paid to the official designated by law to enforce a judgment or award on behalf of a claimant; or

(iii) used to recoup, set-off, or counterclaim in different moneys in an action or distribution proceeding.

(4) "Distribution proceeding" means a judicial or nonjudicial proceeding for the distribution of a fund in which one or more foreign-money claims is asserted and includes an accounting, an assignment for the benefit of creditors, a foreclosure, the liquidation or rehabilitation of a corporation or other entity, and the distribution of an estate, trust, or other fund.

(5) "Foreign money" means money other than money of the United States of America.

(6) "Foreign-money claim" means a claim upon an obligation to pay, or a claim for recovery of a loss, expressed in or measured by a foreign money.

(7) "Money" means a medium of exchange for the payment of obligations or a store of value authorized or adopted by a government or by inter-governmental agreement.

(8) "Money of the claim" means the money determined as proper pursuant to Section 4.

(9) "Person" means an individual, a corporation, government or governmental subdivision or agency, business trust, estate, trust, joint venture, partnership, association, two or more persons having a joint or common interest, or any other legal or commercial entity.

(10) "Rate of exchange" means the rate at which money of one country may be converted into money of another country in a free financial market convenient to or reasonably usable by a person obligated to pay or to state a rate of conversion. If separate rates of exchange apply to different kinds of transactions, the term means the rate applicable to the particular transaction giving rise to the foreign-money claim.

(11) "Spot rate" means the rate of exchange at which foreign money is sold by a bank or other dealer in foreign exchange for immediate or next day availability or for settlement by immediate payment in cash or equivalent, by charge to an account, or by an agreed delayed settlement not exceeding two days.

(12) "State" means a State of the United States, the District of Columbia, the Commonwealth of Puerto Rico, or a territory or insular possession subject to the jurisdiction of the United States.

§ 2. Scope

(a) This [Act] applies only to a foreign-money claim in an action or distribution proceeding.

(b) This [Act] applies to foreign-money issues even if other law under the conflict of laws rules of this State applies to other issues in the action or distribution proceeding.

§ 3. Variation by Agreement

(a) The effect of this [Act] may be varied by agreement of the parties made before or after commencement of an action or distribution proceeding or the entry of judgment.

(b) Parties to a transaction may agree upon the money to be used in a transaction giving rise to a foreign-money claim and may agree to use different moneys for different aspects of the transaction. Stating the price in a foreign money for one aspect of a transaction does not alone require the use of that money for other aspects of the transaction.

§ 4. Determining Money of the Claim

(a) The money in which the parties to a transaction have agreed that payment is to be made is the proper money of the claim for payment.

(b) If the parties to a transaction have not otherwise agreed, the proper money of the claim, as in each case may be appropriate, is the money:

(1) regularly used between the parties as a matter of usage or course of dealing;

(2) used at the time of a transaction in international trade, by trade usage or common practice, for valuing or settling transactions in the particular commodity or service involved; or

(3) in which the loss was ultimately felt or will be incurred by the party claimant.

§ 5. Determining Amount of the Money of Certain Contract Claims

(a) If an amount contracted to be paid in a foreign money is measured by a specified amount of a different money, the amount to be paid is determined on the conversion date.

(b) If an amount contracted to be paid in a foreign money is to be measured by a different money at the rate of exchange prevailing on a date before default, that rate of exchange applies only to payments made within a reasonable time after default, not exceeding 30 days. Thereafter, conversion is made at the bank-offered spot rate on the conversion date.

(c) A monetary claim is neither usurious nor unconscionable because the agreement on which it is based provides that the amount of the debtor's obligation to be paid in the debtor's money, when received by the creditor, must equal a specified amount of the foreign money of the country of the creditor. If, because of unexcused delay in payment of a judgment or award, the amount received by the creditor does not equal the amount of the foreign money specified in the agreement, the court or arbitrator shall amend the judgment or award accordingly.

§ 6. Asserting and Defending Foreign-Money Claim

(a) A person may assert a claim in a specified foreign money. If a foreign-money claim is not asserted, the claimant makes the claim in United States dollars.

(b) An opposing party may allege and prove that a claim, in whole or in part, is in a different money than that asserted by the claimant.

(c) A person may assert a defense, set-off, recoupment, or counterclaim in any money without regard to the money of other claims.

(d) The determination of the proper money of the claim is a question of law.

§ 7. Judgments and Awards on Foreign-Money Claims; Times of Money Conversion; Form of Judgment

(a) Except as provided in subsection (c), a judgment or award on a foreign-money claim must be stated in an amount of the money of the claim.

(b) A judgment or award on a foreign-money claim is payable in that foreign money or, at the option of the debtor, in the amount of United States dollars which will purchase that foreign money on the conversion date at a bank-offered spot rate.

(c) Assessed costs must be entered in United States dollars.

(d) Each payment in United States dollars must be accepted and credited on a judgment or award on a foreign-money claim in the amount of the foreign money that could be purchased by the dollars at a bank-offered spot rate of exchange at or near the close of business on the conversion date for that payment.

(e) A judgment or award made in an action or distribution proceeding on both (i) a defense, set-off, recoupment, or counterclaim and (ii) the adverse party's claim, must be netted by converting the money of the smaller into the money of the larger, and by subtracting the smaller from the larger, and specify the rates of exchange used.

(f) A judgment substantially in the following form complies with subsection (a):

[IT IS ADJUDGED AND ORDERED, that Defendant (*insert name*) pay to Plaintiff (*insert name*) the sum of (*insert amount in the foreign money*) plus interest on that sum at the rate of (*insert rate—see Section 9*) percent a year or, at the option of the judgment debtor, the number of United States dollars which will purchase the (*insert name of foreign money*) with interest due, at a bank-offered spot rate at or near the close of business on the banking day next before the day of payment, together with assessed costs of (*insert amount*) United States dollars.]

[Note: States should insert their customary forms of judgment with appropriate modifications.]

(g) If a contract claim is of the type covered by Section 5(a) or (b), the judgment or award must be entered for the amount of money stated to measure the obligation to be paid in the money specified for payment or, at the option of the debtor, the number of United States dollars which will purchase the computed amount of the money of payment on the conversion date at a bank-offered spot rate.

(h) A judgment must be [filed] [docketed] [recorded] and indexed in foreign money in the same manner, and has the same effect as a lien, as other judgments. It may be discharged by payment.

§ 8. Conversions of Foreign Money in Distribution Proceeding

The rate of exchange prevailing at or near the close of business on the day the distribution proceeding is initiated governs all exchanges of foreign money in a distribution proceeding. A foreign-money claimant in a distribution proceeding shall assert its claim in the named foreign money and show the amount of United States dollars resulting from a conversion as of the date the proceeding was initiated.

§ 9. Pre-judgment and Judgment Interest

(a) With respect to a foreign-money claim, recovery of pre-judgment or pre-award interest and the rate of interest to be applied in the action or distribution proceeding, except as provided in subsection (b), are matters of the substantive law governing the right to recovery under the conflict-of-laws rules of this State.

(b) The court or arbitrator shall increase or decrease the amount of pre-judgment or pre-award interest otherwise payable in a judgment or award in foreign-money to the extent required by the law of this State governing a failure to make or accept an offer of settlement or offer of judgment, or conduct by a party or its attorney causing undue delay or expense.

(c) A judgment or award on a foreign-money claim bears interest at the rate applicable to judgments of this State.

§ 10. Enforcement of Foreign Judgments

(a) If an action is brought to enforce a judgment of another jurisdiction expressed in a foreign money and the judgment is recognized in this State as enforceable, the enforcing judgment must be entered as provided in Section 7, whether or not the foreign judgment confers an option to pay in an equivalent amount of United States dollars.

(b) A foreign judgment may be [filed] [docketed] [recorded] in accordance with any rule or statute of this State providing a procedure for its recognition and enforcement.

(c) A satisfaction or partial payment made upon the foreign judgment, on proof thereof, must be credited against the amount of foreign money specified in the judgment, notwithstanding the entry of judgment in this State.

(d) A judgment entered on a foreign-money claim only in United States dollars in another state must be enforced in this State in United States dollars only.

§ 11. Determining United States Dollar Value of Foreign-Money Claims for Limited Purposes

(a) Computations under this section are for the limited purposes of the section and do not affect computation of the United States dollar equivalent of the money of the judgment for the purpose of payment.

(b) For the limited purpose of facilitating the enforcement of provisional remedies in an action, the value in United States dollars of assets to be seized or restrained pursuant to a writ of attachment, garnishment, execution, or other legal process, the amount of United States dollars at issue for assessing costs, or the amount of United States dollars involved for a surety bond or other court-required undertaking, must be ascertained as provided in subsections (c) and (d).

(c) A party seeking process, costs, bond, or other undertaking under subsection (b) shall compute in United States dollars the amount of the foreign money claimed from a bank-offered spot rate prevailing at or near the close of business on the banking day next preceding the filing of a request or application for the issuance of process or for the determination of costs, or an application for a bond or other court-required undertaking.

(d) A party seeking the process, costs, bond, or other undertaking under subsection (b) shall file with each request or application an affidavit or certificate executed in good faith by its counsel or a bank officer, stating the market quotation used and how it was obtained, and setting forth the calculation. Affected court officials incur no liability, after a filing of the affidavit or certificate, for acting as if the judgment were in the amount of United States dollars stated in the affidavit or certificate.

§ 12. Effect of Currency Revalorization

(a) If, after an obligation is expressed or a loss is incurred in a foreign money, the country issuing or adopting that money substitutes a new money in place of that money, the obligation or the loss is treated as if expressed or incurred in the new money at the rate of conversion the issuing country establishes for the payment of like obligations or losses denominated in the former money.

(b) If substitution under subsection (a) occurs after a judgment or award is entered on a foreign-money claim, the court or arbitrator shall amend the judgment or award by a like conversion of the former money.

§ 13. Supplementary General Principles of Law

Unless displaced by particular provisions of this [Act], the principles of law and equity, including the law merchant, and the law relative to capacity to contract, principal and agent, estoppel, fraud, misrepresentation, duress, coercion, mistake, bankruptcy, or other validating or invalidating causes supplement its provisions.

§ 14. Uniformity of Application and Construction

This [Act] shall be applied and construed to effectuate its general purpose to make uniform the law with respect to the subject of this [Act] among states enacting it.

§ 15. Short Title

This [Act] may be cited as the Uniform Foreign-Money Claims Act.

§ 16. Severability Clause

If any provision of this [Act] or its application to any person or circumstance is held invalid, the invalidity does not affect other provisions or applications of this [Act] which can be given effect without the invalid provision or application, and to this end the provisions of this [Act] are severable.

DOCUMENT 58

UNIFORM FOREIGN MONEY JUDGMENTS RECOGNITION ACT (UFMJRA) (THE "1962 ACT")*

■ ■ ■

§ 1. [Definitions]

As used in this Act:

(1) "foreign state" means any governmental unit other than the United States, or any state, district, commonwealth, territory, insular possession thereof, or the Panama Canal Zone, the Trust Territory of the Pacific Islands, or the Ryukyu Islands;

(2) "foreign judgment" means any judgment of a foreign state granting or denying recovery of a sum of money, other than a judgment for taxes, a fine or other penalty, or a judgment for support in matrimonial or family matters.

§ 2. [Applicability]

This Act applies to any foreign judgment that is final and conclusive and enforceable where rendered even though an appeal therefrom is pending or it is subject to appeal.

§ 3. [Recognition and Enforcement]

Except as provided in section 4, a foreign judgment meeting the requirements of section 2 is conclusive between the parties to the extent that it grants or denies recovery of a sum of money. The foreign judgment is enforceable in the same manner as the judgment of a sister state which is entitled to full faith and credit.

§ 4. [Grounds for Non-recognition]

(a) A foreign judgment is not conclusive if

(1) the judgment was rendered under a system which does not provide impartial tribunals or procedures compatible with the requirements of due process of law;

---

* Reprinted with permission of the National Conference of Commissioners on Uniform State Laws and West Group.

(2) the foreign court did not have personal jurisdiction over the defendant; or

(3) the foreign court did not have jurisdiction over the subject matter.

(b) A foreign judgment need not be recognized if

(1) the defendant in the proceedings in the foreign court did not receive notice of the proceedings in sufficient time to enable him to defend;

(2) the judgment was obtained by fraud;

(3) the [cause of action] [claim for relief] on which the judgment is based is repugnant to the public policy of this state;

(4) the judgment conflicts with another final and conclusive judgment;

(5) the proceeding in the foreign court was contrary to an agreement between the parties under which the dispute in question was to be settled otherwise than by proceedings in that court; or

(6) in the case of jurisdiction based only on personal service, the foreign court was a seriously inconvenient forum for the trial of the action.

§ 5. [Personal Jurisdiction]

(a) The foreign judgment shall not be refused recognition for lack of personal jurisdiction if

(1) the defendant was served personally in the foreign state;

(2) the defendant voluntarily appeared in the proceedings, other than for the purpose of protecting property seized or threatened with seizure in the proceedings or of contesting the jurisdiction of the court over him;

(3) the defendant prior to the commencement of the proceedings had agreed to submit to the jurisdiction of the foreign court with respect to the subject matter involved;

(4) the defendant was domiciled in the foreign state when the proceedings were instituted or, being a body corporate had its principal place of business, was incorporated, or had otherwise acquired corporate status, in the foreign state;

(5) the defendant had a business office in the foreign state and the proceedings in the foreign court involved a [cause of action] [claim for relief] arising out of business done by the defendant through that office in the foreign state; or

(6) the defendant operated a motor vehicle or airplane in the foreign state and the proceedings involved a [cause of action] [claim for relief] arising out of such operation.

(b) The courts of this state may recognize other bases of jurisdiction.

§ 6. [Stay in Case of Appeal]

If the defendant satisfies the court either that an appeal is pending or that he is entitled and intends to appeal from the foreign judgment, the court may stay the proceedings until the appeal has been determined or until the expiration of a period of time sufficient to enable the defendant to prosecute the appeal.

§ 7. [Saving Clause]

This Act does not prevent the recognition of a foreign judgment in situations not covered by this Act.

§ 8. [Uniformity of Interpretation]

This Act shall be so construed as to effectuate its general purpose to make uniform the law of those states which enact it.

§ 9. [Short Title]

This Act may be cited as the Uniform Foreign Money-Judgments Recognition Act.

PART F

FOREIGN LAWS, REGULATIONS AND ORDERS

■ ■ ■

DOCUMENT 59

CANADIAN ORDER REQUIRING PERSONS IN CANADA TO GIVE NOTICE OF COMMUNICATIONS RELATING TO, AND PROHIBITING SUCH PERSONS FROM COMPLYING WITH, AN EXTRATERRITORIAL MEASURE OF THE UNITED STATES THAT ADVERSELY AFFECTS TRADE OR COMMERCE BETWEEN CANADA AND CUBA (1992)

■ ■ ■

JUS–92–777–01 (SOR/DORS)

Short Title

1. This Order may be cited as the *Foreign Extraterritorial Measures (United States) Order, 1992.*

Interpretation

2. In this Order,

"corporation" means a corporation that is registered or incorporated under the laws of Canada or of a province and that carries on business in whole or in part in Canada; (*personne morale*)

"extraterritorial measure of the United States" means the measure set out in section 1706(a)(1) of the *National Defense Authorization Act for Fiscal Year 1993*, as passed by the United States Congress on October 5, 1992, to the extent that it affects trade or commerce between Canada and Cuba. (*mesure extraterritoriale des Etats-Unis*)

Notice

3. Every corporation and every officer of a corporation who receives, in respect of any trade or commerce between Canada and Cuba, any directives, instructions, intimations of policy or other communications relating to an extraterritorial measure of the United States from a person

who is in a position to direct or influence the policies of the corporation in Canada shall give notice thereof to the Attorney General of Canada.

Prohibition

4. No corporation shall comply with an extraterritorial measure of the United States in respect of trade or commerce between Canada and Cuba or with any directives, instructions, intimations of policy or other communications relating thereto that are received from a person who is in a position to direct or influence the policies of the corporation in Canada.

DOCUMENT 60

EU UNFAIR COMMERCIAL PRACTICES DIRECTIVE NO. 2005/29

■ ■ ■

DIRECTIVE 2005/29/EC OF THE EUROPEAN PARLIAMENT AND OF THE COUNCIL

CHAPTER 1

GENERAL PROVISIONS

Article 1

Purpose

The purpose of this Directive is to contribute to the proper functioning of the internal market and achieve a high level of consumer protection by approximating the laws, regulations and administrative provisions of the Member States on unfair commercial practices harming consumers' economic interests.

Article 2

Definitions

For the purposes of this Directive:

(a) 'consumer' means any natural person who, in commercial practices covered by this Directive, is acting for purposes which are outside his trade, business, craft or profession;

(b) 'trader' means any natural or legal person who, in commercial practices covered by this Directive, is acting for purposes relating to his trade, business, craft or profession and anyone acting in the name of or on behalf of a trader;

(c) 'product' means any goods or service including immovable property, rights and obligations;

(d) 'business-to-consumer commercial practices' (hereinafter also referred to as commercial practices) means any act, omission, course of conduct or representation, commercial communication including advertising and marketing, by a trader, directly connected with the promotion, sale or supply of a product to consumers;

(e) 'to materially distort the economic behaviour of consumers' means using a commercial practice to appreciably impair the consumer's ability to make an informed decision, thereby causing the consumer to take a transactional decision that he would not have taken otherwise;

(f) 'code of conduct' means an agreement or set of rules not imposed by law, regulation or administrative provision of a Member State which defines the behaviour of traders who undertake to be bound by the code in relation to one or more particular commercial practices or business sectors;

(g) 'code owner' means any entity, including a trader or group of traders, which is responsible for the formulation and revision of a code of conduct and/or for monitoring compliance with the code by those who have undertaken to be bound by it;

(h) 'professional diligence' means the standard of special skill and care which a trader may reasonably be expected to exercise towards consumers, commensurate with honest market practice and/or the general principle of good faith in the trader's field of activity;

(i) 'invitation to purchase' means a commercial communication which indicates characteristics of the product and the price in a way appropriate to the means of the commercial communication used and thereby enables the consumer to make a purchase;

(j) 'undue influence' means exploiting a position of power in relation to the consumer so as to apply pressure, even without using or threatening to use physical force, in a way which significantly limits the consumer's ability to make an informed decision;

(k) 'transactional decision' means any decision taken by a consumer concerning whether, how and on what terms to purchase, make payment in whole or in part for, retain or dispose of a product or to exercise a contractual right in relation to the product, whether the consumer decides to act or to refrain from acting;

(*l*) 'regulated profession' means a professional activity or a group of professional activities, access to which or the pursuit of which, or one of the modes of pursuing which, is conditional, directly or indirectly, upon possession of specific professional qualifications, pursuant to laws, regulations or administrative provisions.

Article 3

Scope

1. This Directive shall apply to unfair business-to-consumer commercial practices, as laid down in Article 5, before, during and after a commercial transaction in relation to a product.

2. This Directive is without prejudice to contract law and, in particular, to the rules on the validity, formation or effect of a contract.

3. This Directive is without prejudice to Community or national rules relating to the health and safety aspects of products.

4. In the case of conflict between the provisions of this Directive and other Community rules regulating specific aspects of unfair commercial practices, the latter shall prevail and apply to those specific aspects.

5. For a period of six years from 12 June 2007, Member States shall be able to continue to apply national provisions within the field approximated by this Directive which are more restrictive or prescriptive than this Directive and which implement directives containing minimum harmonisation clauses. These measures must be essential to ensure that consumers are adequately protected against unfair commercial practices and must be proportionate to the attainment of this objective. The review referred to in Article 18 may, if considered appropriate, include a proposal to prolong this derogation for a further limited period.

6. Member States shall notify the Commission without delay of any national provisions applied on the basis of paragraph 5.

7. This Directive is without prejudice to the rules determining the jurisdiction of the courts.

8. This Directive is without prejudice to any conditions of establishment or of authorisation regimes, or to the deontological codes of conduct or other specific rules governing regulated professions in order to uphold high standards of integrity on the part of the professional, which Member States may, in conformity with Community law, impose on professionals.

9. In relation to 'financial services', as defined in Directive 2002/65/EC, and immovable property, Member States may impose requirements which are more restrictive or prescriptive than this Directive in the field which it approximates.

10. This Directive shall not apply to the application of the laws, regulations and administrative provisions of Member States relating to the certification and indication of the standard of fineness of articles of precious metal.

Article 4

Internal market

Member States shall neither restrict the freedom to provide services nor restrict the free movement of goods for reasons falling within the field approximated by this Directive.

CHAPTER 2

UNFAIR COMMERCIAL PRACTICES

Article 5

Prohibition of unfair commercial practices

1. Unfair commercial practices shall be prohibited.

2. A commercial practice shall be unfair if:

(a) it is contrary to the requirements of professional diligence, and

(b) it materially distorts or is likely to materially distort the economic behaviour with regard to the product of the average consumer whom it reaches or to whom it is addressed, or of the average member of the group when a commercial practice is directed to a particular group of consumers.

3. Commercial practices which are likely to materially distort the economic behaviour only of a clearly identifiable group of consumers who are particularly vulnerable to the practice or the underlying product because of their mental or physical infirmity, age or credulity in a way which the trader could reasonably be expected to foresee, shall be assessed from the perspective of the average member of that group. This is without prejudice to the common and legitimate advertising practice of making exaggerated statements or statements which are not meant to be taken literally.

4. In particular, commercial practices shall be unfair which:

(a) are misleading as set out in Articles 6 and 7, or

(b) are aggressive as set out in Articles 8 and 9.

5. Annex I contains the list of those commercial practices which shall in all circumstances be regarded as unfair. The same single list shall apply in all Member States and may only be modified by revision of this Directive.

Section 1

Misleading commercial practices

Article 6

Misleading actions

1. A commercial practice shall be regarded as misleading if it contains false information and is therefore untruthful or in any way, including overall presentation, deceives or is likely to deceive the average consumer, even if the information is factually correct, in relation to one or more of the following elements, and in either case causes or is likely to cause him to take a transactional decision that he would not have taken otherwise:

(a) the existence or nature of the product;

(b) the main characteristics of the product, such as its availability, benefits, risks, execution, composition, accessories, aftersale customer assistance and complaint handling, method and date of manufacture or provision, delivery, fitness for purpose, usage, quantity, specification, geographical or commercial origin or the results to be expected from its use, or the results and material features of tests or checks carried out on the product;

(c) the extent of the trader's commitments, the motives for the commercial practice and the nature of the sales process, any statement or symbol in relation to direct or indirect sponsorship or approval of the trader or the product;

(d) the price or the manner in which the price is calculated, or the existence of a specific price advantage;

(e) the need for a service, part, replacement or repair;

(f) the nature, attributes and rights of the trader or his agent, such as his identity and assets, his qualifications, status, approval, affiliation or connection and ownership of industrial, commercial or intellectual property rights or his awards and distinctions;

(g) the consumer's rights, including the right to replacement or reimbursement under Directive 1999/44/EC of the European Parliament and of the Council of 25 May 1999 on certain aspects of the sale of consumer goods and associated guarantees, or the risks he may face.

2. A commercial practice shall also be regarded as misleading if, in its factual context, taking account of all its features and circumstances, it causes or is likely to cause the average consumer to take a transactional decision that he would not have taken otherwise, and it involves:

(a) any marketing of a product, including comparative advertising, which creates confusion with any products, trade marks, trade names or other distinguishing marks of a competitor;

(b) non-compliance by the trader with commitments contained in codes of conduct by which the trader has undertaken to be bound, where:

(i) the commitment is not aspirational but is firm and is capable of being verified, and

(ii) the trader indicates in a commercial practice that he is bound by the code.

Article 7

Misleading omissions

1. A commercial practice shall be regarded as misleading if, in its factual context, taking account of all its features and circumstances and the limitations of the communication medium, it omits material information that the average consumer needs, according to the context, to take an informed transactional decision and thereby causes or is likely to cause the average consumer to take a transactional decision that he would not have taken otherwise.

2. It shall also be regarded as a misleading omission when, taking account of the matters described in paragraph 1, a trader hides or provides in an unclear, unintelligible, ambiguous or untimely manner such material information as referred to in that paragraph or fails to identify the commercial intent of the commercial practice if not already apparent from the context, and where, in either case, this causes or is likely to cause the average consumer to take a transactional decision that he would not have taken otherwise.

3. Where the medium used to communicate the commercial practice imposes limitations of space or time, these limitations and any measures taken by the trader to make the information available to consumers by other means shall be taken into account in deciding whether information has been omitted.

4. In the case of an invitation to purchase, the following information shall be regarded as material, if not already apparent from the context:

(a) the main characteristics of the product, to an extent appropriate to the medium and the product;

(b) the geographical address and the identity of the trader, such as his trading name and, where applicable, the geographical address and the identity of the trader on whose behalf he is acting;

(c) the price inclusive of taxes, or where the nature of the product means that the price cannot reasonably be calculated in advance, the manner in which the price is calculated, as well as, where appropriate, all additional freight, delivery or postal charges or, where these charges cannot reasonably be calculated in advance, the fact that such additional charges may be payable;

(d) the arrangements for payment, delivery, performance and the complaint handling policy, if they depart from the requirements of professional diligence;

(e) for products and transactions involving a right of withdrawal or cancellation, the existence of such a right.

5. Information requirements established by Community law in relation to commercial communication including advertising or marketing, a non-exhaustive list of which is contained in Annex II, shall be regarded as material.

* * *

Article 13

Penalties

Member States shall lay down penalties for infringements of national provisions adopted in application of this Directive and shall take all necessary measures to ensure that these are enforced. These penalties must be effective, proportionate and dissuasive.

* * *

ANNEX I

COMMERCIAL PRACTICES WHICH ARE IN ALL CIRCUMSTANCES CONSIDERED UNFAIR

Misleading commercial practices

1. Claiming to be a signatory to a code of conduct when the trader is not.

2. Displaying a trust mark, quality mark or equivalent without having obtained the necessary authorisation.

3. Claiming that a code of conduct has an endorsement from a public or other body which it does not have.

4. Claiming that a trader (including his commercial practices) or a product has been approved, endorsed or authorised by a public or private body when he/it has not or making such a claim without complying with the terms of the approval, endorsement or authorisation.

5. Making an invitation to purchase products at a specified price without disclosing the existence of any reasonable grounds the trader may have for believing that he will not be able to offer for supply or to procure another trader to supply, those products or equivalent products at that price for a period that is, and in quantities that are, reasonable having regard to the product, the scale of advertising of the product and the price offered (bait advertising).

6. Making an invitation to purchase products at a specified price and then:

(a) refusing to show the advertised item to consumers; or

(b) refusing to take orders for it or deliver it within a reasonable time; or

(c) demonstrating a defective sample of it, with the intention of promoting a different product (bait and switch)

7. Falsely stating that a product will only be available for a very limited time, or that it will only be available on particular terms for a very limited time, in order to elicit an immediate decision and deprive consumers of sufficient opportunity or time to make an informed choice.

8. Undertaking to provide after-sales service to consumers with whom the trader has communicated prior to a transaction in a language which is not an official language of the Member State where the trader is located and then making such service available only in another language without clearly disclosing this to the consumer before the consumer is committed to the transaction.

9. Stating or otherwise creating the impression that a product can legally be sold when it cannot.

10. Presenting rights given to consumers in law as a distinctive feature of the trader's offer.

11. Using editorial content in the media to promote a product where a trader has paid for the promotion without making that clear in the content or by images or sounds clearly identifiable by the consumer (advertorial). This is without prejudice to Council Directive 89/552/EEC (1).

12. Making a materially inaccurate claim concerning the nature and extent of the risk to the personal security of the consumer or his family if the consumer does not purchase the product.

13. Promoting a product similar to a product made by a particular manufacturer in such a manner as deliberately to mislead the consumer into believing that the product is made by that same manufacturer when it is not.

14. Establishing, operating or promoting a pyramid promotional scheme where a consumer gives consideration for the opportunity to receive compensation that is derived primarily from the introduction of other consumers into the scheme rather than from the sale or consumption of products.

15. Claiming that the trader is about to cease trading or move premises when he is not.

16. Claiming that products are able to facilitate winning in games of chance.

17. Falsely claiming that a product is able to cure illnesses, dysfunction or malformations.

18. Passing on materially inaccurate information on market conditions or on the possibility of finding the product with the intention of

inducing the consumer to acquire the product at conditions less favourable than normal market conditions.

19. Claiming in a commercial practice to offer a competition or prize promotion without awarding the prizes described or a reasonable equivalent.

20. Describing a product as 'gratis', 'free', 'without charge' or similar if the consumer has to pay anything other than the unavoidable cost of responding to the commercial practice and collecting or paying for delivery of the item.

21. Including in marketing material an invoice or similar document seeking payment which gives the consumer the impression that he has already ordered the marketed product when he has not.

22. Falsely claiming or creating the impression that the trader is not acting for purposes relating to his trade, business, craft or profession, or falsely representing oneself as a consumer.

23. Creating the false impression that after-sales service in relation to a product is available in a Member State other than the one in which the product is sold.

Aggressive commercial practices

24. Creating the impression that the consumer cannot leave the premises until a contract is formed.

25. Conducting personal visits to the consumer's home ignoring the consumer's request to leave or not to return except in circumstances and to the extent justified, under national law, to enforce a contractual obligation.

26. Making persistent and unwanted solicitations by telephone, fax, e-mail or other remote media except in circumstances and to the extent justified under national law to enforce a contractual obligation. This is without prejudice to Article 10 of Directive 97/7/EC and Directives 95/46/EC and 2002/58/EC.

27. Requiring a consumer who wishes to claim on an insurance policy to produce documents which could not reasonably be considered relevant as to whether the claim was valid, or failing systematically to respond to pertinent correspondence, in order to dissuade a consumer from exercising his contractual rights.

28. Including in an advertisement a direct exhortation to children to buy advertised products or persuade their parents or other adults to buy advertised products for them. This provision is without prejudice to Article 16 of Directive 89/552/EEC on television broadcasting.

29. Demanding immediate or deferred payment for or the return or safekeeping of products supplied by the trader, but not solicited by the

consumer except where the product is a substitute supplied in conformity with Article 7(3) of Directive 97/7/EC (inertia selling).

30. Explicitly informing a consumer that if he does not buy the product or service, the trader's job or livelihood will be in jeopardy.

31. Creating the false impression that the consumer has already won, will win, or will on doing a particular act win, a prize or other equivalent benefit, when in fact either:

— there is no prize or other equivalent benefit, or

— taking any action in relation to claiming the prize or other equivalent benefit is subject to the consumer paying money or incurring a cost.

DOCUMENT 61

EU DISTANCE SELLING DIRECTIVE NO. 1997/7

■ ■ ■

DIRECTIVE 1997/7/EC OF THE EUROPEAN PARLIAMENT AND OF THE COUNCIL

Article 1. Object

The object of this Directive is to approximate the laws, regulations and administrative provisions of the Member States concerning distance contracts between consumers and suppliers.

Article 2. Definitions

For the purposes of this Directive:

(1) 'distance contract' means any contract concerning goods or services concluded between a supplier and a consumer under an organized distance sales or service-provision scheme run by the supplier, who, for the purpose of the contract, makes exclusive use of one or more means of distance communication up to and including the moment at which the contract is concluded;

(2) 'consumer' means any natural person who, in contracts covered by this Directive, is acting for purposes which are outside his trade, business or profession;

(3) 'supplier' means any natural or legal person who, in contracts covered by this Directive, is acting in his commercial or professional capacity;

(4) 'means of distance communication' means any means which, without the simultaneous physical presence of the supplier and the consumer, may be used for the conclusion of a contract between those parties. An indicative list of the means covered by this Directive is contained in Annex I;

(5) 'operator of a means of communication' means any public or private natural or legal person whose trade, business or profession involves making one or more means of distance communication available to suppliers.

* * *

Article 4. Prior information

1. In good time prior to the conclusion of any distance contract, the consumer shall be provided with the following information:

(a) the identity of the supplier and, in the case of contracts requiring payment in advance, his address;

(b) the main characteristics of the goods or services;

(c) the price of the goods or services including all taxes;

(d) delivery costs, where appropriate;

(e) the arrangements for payment, delivery or performance;

(f) the existence of a right of withdrawal, except in the cases referred to in Article 6 (3);

(g) the cost of using the means of distance communication, where it is calculated other than at the basic rate;

(h) the period for which the offer or the price remains valid;

(i) where appropriate, the minimum duration of the contract in the case of contracts for the supply of products or services to be performed permanently or recurrently.

2. The information referred to in paragraph 1, the commercial purpose of which must be made clear, shall be provided in a clear and comprehensible manner in any way appropriate to the means of distance communication used, with due regard, in particular, to the principles of good faith in commercial transactions, and the principles governing the protection of those who are unable, pursuant to the legislation of the Member States, to give their consent, such as minors.

3. Moreover, in the case of telephone communications, the identity of the supplier and the commercial purpose of the call shall be made explicitly clear at the beginning of any conversation with the consumer.

Article 5. Written confirmation of information

1. The consumer must receive written confirmation or confirmation in another durable medium available and accessible to him of the information referred to in Article 4 (1) (a) to (f), in good time during the performance of the contract, and at the latest at the time of delivery where goods not for delivery to third parties are concerned, unless the information has already been given to the consumer prior to conclusion of the contract in writing or on another durable medium available and accessible to him.

In any event the following must be provided:

– written information on the conditions and procedures for exercising the right of withdrawal, within the meaning of Article 6, including the cases referred to in the first indent of Article 6 (3),

– the geographical address of the place of business of the supplier to which the consumer may address any complaints,

– information on after-sales services and guarantees which exist,

– the conclusion for cancelling the contract, where it is of unspecified duration or a duration exceeding one year.

2. Paragraph 1 shall not apply to services which are performed through the use of a means of distance communication, where they are supplied on only one occasion and are invoiced by the operator of the means of distance communication. Nevertheless, the consumer must in all cases be able to obtain the geographical address of the place of business of the supplier to which he may address any complaints.

Article 6. Right of withdrawal

1. For any distance contract the consumer shall have a period of at least seven working days in which to withdraw from the contract without penalty and without giving any reason. The only charge that may be made to the consumer because of the exercise of his right of withdrawal is the direct cost of returning the goods.

The period for exercise of this right shall begin:

– in the case of goods, from the day of receipt by the consumer where the obligations laid down in Article 5 have been fulfilled,

– in the case of services, from the day of conclusion of the contract or from the day on which the obligations laid down in Article 5 were fulfilled if they are fulfilled after conclusion of the contract, provided that this period does not exceed the three-month period referred to in the following subparagraph.

If the supplier has failed to fulfil the obligations laid down in Article 5, the period shall be three months. The period shall begin:

– in the case of goods, from the day of receipt by the consumer,

– in the case of services, from the day of conclusion of the contract.

If the information referred to in Article 5 is supplied within this three-month period, the seven working day period referred to in the first subparagraph shall begin as from that moment.

2. Where the right of withdrawal has been exercised by the consumer pursuant to this Article, the supplier shall be obliged to reimburse the sums paid by the consumer free of charge. The only charge that may be made to the consumer because of the exercise of his right of withdrawal is the direct cost of returning the goods. Such reimbursement must be carried out as soon as possible and in any case within 30 days.

3. Unless the parties have agreed otherwise, the consumer may not exercise the right of withdrawal provided for in paragraph 1 in respect of contracts:

– for the provision of services if performance has begun, with the consumer's agreement, before the end of the seven working day period referred to in paragraph 1,

– for the supply of goods or services the price of which is dependent on fluctuations in the financial market which cannot be controlled by the supplier,

– for the supply of goods made to the consumer's specifications or clearly personalized or which, by reason of their nature, cannot be returned or are liable to deteriorate or expire rapidly,

– for the supply of audio or video recordings or computer software which were unsealed by the consumer,

– for the supply of newspapers, periodicals and magazines,

– for gaming and lottery services.

4. The Member States shall make provision in their legislation to ensure that:

– if the price of goods or services is fully or partly covered by credit granted by the supplier, or

– if that price is fully or partly covered by credit granted to the consumer by a third party on the basis of an agreement between the third party and the supplier,

the credit agreement shall be cancelled, without any penalty, if the consumer exercises his right to withdraw from the contract in accordance with paragraph 1.

Member States shall determine the detailed rules for cancellation of the credit agreement.

Article 7. Performance

1. Unless the parties have agreed otherwise, the supplier must execute the order within a maximum of 30 days from the day following that on which the consumer forwarded his order to the supplier.

2. Where a supplier fails to perform his side of the contract on the grounds that the goods or services ordered are unavailable, the consumer must be informed of this situation and must be able to obtain a refund of any sums he has paid as soon as possible and in any case within 30 days.

3. Nevertheless, Member States may lay down that the supplier may provide the consumer with goods or services of equivalent quality and price provided that this possibility was provided for prior to the conclusion of the

contract or in the contract. The consumer shall be informed of this possibility in a clear and comprehensible manner. The cost of returning the goods following exercise of the right of withdrawal shall, in this case, be borne by the supplier, and the consumer must be informed of this. In such cases the supply of goods or services may not be deemed to constitute inertia selling within the meaning of Article 9.

Article 8. Payment by card

Member States shall ensure that appropriate measures exist to allow a consumer:

– to request cancellation of a payment where fraudulent use has been made of his payment card in connection with distance contracts covered by this Directive,

– in the event of fraudulent use, to be recredited with the sums paid or have them returned.

Article 9. Inertia selling

Member States shall take the measures necessary to:

– prohibit the supply of goods or services to a consumer without their being ordered by the consumer beforehand, where such supply involves a demand for payment,

– exempt the consumer from the provision of any consideration in cases of unsolicited supply, the absence of a response not constituting consent.

Article 10. Restrictions on the use of certain means of distance communication

1. Use by a supplier of the following means requires the prior consent of the consumer:

– automated calling system without human intervention (automatic calling machine),

– facsimile machine (fax).

2. Member States shall ensure that means of distance communication, other than those referred to in paragraph 1, which allow individual communications may be used only where there is no clear objection from the consumer.

Article 11. Judicial or administrative redress

1. Member States shall ensure that adequate and effective means exist to ensure compliance with this Directive in the interests of consumers.

2. The means referred to in paragraph 1 shall include provisions whereby one or more of the following bodies, as determined by national law,

may take action under national law before the courts or before the competent administrative bodies to ensure that the national provisions for the implementation of this Directive are applied:

(a) public bodies or their representatives;

(b) consumer organizations having a legitimate interest in protecting consumers;

(c) professional organizations having a legitimate interest in acting.

3. (a) Member States may stipulate that the burden of proof concerning the existence of prior information, written confirmation, compliance with time-limits or consumer consent can be placed on the supplier.

(b) Member States shall take the measures needed to ensure that suppliers and operators of means of communication, where they are able to do so, cease practices which do not comply with measures adopted pursuant to this Directive.

4. Member States may provide for voluntary supervision by self-regulatory bodies of compliance with the provisions of this Directive and recourse to such bodies for the settlement of disputes to be added to the means which Member States must provided to ensure compliance with the provisions of this Directive.

Article 12. Binding nature

1. The consumer may not waive the rights conferred on him by the transposition of this Directive into national law.

2. Member States shall take the measures needed to ensure that the consumer does not lose the protection granted by this Directive by virtue of the choice of the law of a non-member country as the law applicable to the contract if the latter has close connection with the territory of one or more Member States.

* * *

Article 14. Minimal clause

Member States may introduce or maintain, in the area covered by this Directive, more stringent provisions compatible with the Treaty, to ensure a higher level of consumer protection. Such provisions shall, where appropriate, include a ban, in the general interest, on the marketing of certain goods or services, particularly medicinal products, within their territory by means of distance contracts, with due regard for the Treaty.

Article 15. Implementation

1. Member States shall bring into force the laws, regulations and administrative provisions necessary to comply with this Directive no later

than three years after it enters into force. They shall forthwith inform the Commission thereof.

DOCUMENT 62

EU E-COMMERCE DIRECTIVE NO. 2000/31

■ ■ ■

DIRECTIVE 2000/31/EC OF THE EUROPEAN PARLIAMENT AND OF THE COUNCIL

GENERAL PROVISIONS

Article 1

Objective and scope

1. This Directive seeks to contribute to the proper functioning of the internal market by ensuring the free movement of information society services between the Member States.

2. This Directive approximates, to the extent necessary for the achievement of the objective set out in paragraph 1, certain national provisions on information society services relating to the internal market, the establishment of service providers, commercial communications, electronic contracts, the liability of intermediaries, codes of conduct, out-of-court dispute settlements, court actions and cooperation between Member States.

3. This Directive complements Community law applicable to information society services without prejudice to the level of protection for, in particular, public health and consumer interests, as established by Community acts and national legislation implementing them in so far as this does not restrict the freedom to provide information society services.

4. This Directive does not establish additional rules on private international law nor does it deal with the jurisdiction of Courts.

5. This Directive shall not apply to:

(a) the field of taxation;

(b) questions relating to information society services covered by Directives 95/46/EC and 97/66/EC;

(c) questions relating to agreements or practices governed by cartel law;

(d) the following activities of information society services:

– the activities of notaries or equivalent professions to the extent that they involve a direct and specific connection with the exercise of public authority,

– the representation of a client and defence of his interests before the courts,

– gambling activities which involve wagering a stake with monetary value in games of chance, including lotteries and betting transactions.

6. This Directive does not affect measures taken at Community or national level, in the respect of Community law, in order to promote cultural and linguistic diversity and to ensure the defence of pluralism.

Article 2

Definitions

For the purpose of this Directive, the following terms shall bear the following meanings:

(e) 'consumer': any natural person who is acting for purposes which are outside his or her trade, business or profession;

Article 3

Internal market

* * *

2. Member States may not, for reasons falling within the coordinated field, restrict the freedom to provide information society services from another Member State.

* * *

4. Member States may take measures to derogate from paragraph 2 in respect of a given information society service if the following conditions are fulilled:

(i) necessary for one of the following reasons:

– public policy. . . ,

– the protection of public health,

– public security, including the safeguarding of national security and defense,

– the protection of consumers, including investors;

* * *

(iii) proportionate to those objectives. . . .

CHAPTER II
PRINCIPLES

* * *

Article 5

General information to be provided

1. In addition to other information requirements established by Community law, Member States shall ensure that the service provider shall render easily, directly and permanently accessible to the recipients of the service and competent authorities, at least the following information:

(a) the name of the service provider;

(b) the geographic address at which the service provider is established;

(c) the details of the service provider, including his electronic mail address, which allow him to be contacted rapidly and communicated with in a direct and effective manner;

(d) where the service provider is registered in a trade or similar public register, the trade register in which the service provider is entered and his registration number, or equivalent means of identification in that register;

(e) where the activity is subject to an authorisation scheme, the particulars of the relevant supervisory authority;

(f) as concerns the regulated professions:

– any professional body or similar institution with which the service provider is registered,

– the professional title and the Member State where it has been granted,

– a reference to the applicable professional rules in the Member State of establishment and the means to access them;

(g) where the service provider undertakes an activity that is subject to VAT, the identification number referred to in Article 22(1) of the sixth Council Directive 77/388/EEC of 17 May 1977 on the harmonisation of the laws of the Member States relating to turnover taxes—Common system of value added tax: uniform basis of assessment.

2. In addition to other information requirements established by Community law, Member States shall at least ensure that, where information society services refer to prices, these are to be indicated clearly and unambiguously and, in particular, must indicate whether they are inclusive of tax and delivery costs.

Section 2

Commercial Communications

Article 6

Information to be provided

In addition to other information requirements established by Community law, Member States shall ensure that commercial communications which are part of, or constitute, an information society service comply at least with the following conditions:

(a) the commercial communication shall be clearly identifiable as such;

(b) the natural or legal person on whose behalf the commercial communication is made shall be clearly identifiable;

(c) promotional offers, such as discounts, premiums and gifts, where permitted in the Member State where the service provider is established, shall be clearly identifiable as such, and the conditions which are to be met to qualify for them shall be easily accessible and be presented clearly and unambiguously;

(d) promotional competitions or games, where permitted in the Member State where the service provider is established, shall be clearly identifiable as such, and the conditions for participation shall be easily accessible and be presented clearly and unambiguously.

* * *

Section 3

Contracts Concluded by Electronic Means

Article 9

Treatment of contracts

1. Member States shall ensure that their legal system allows contracts to be concluded by electronic means. Member States shall in particular ensure that the legal requirements applicable to the contractual process neither create obstacles for the use of electronic contracts nor result in such contracts being deprived of legal effectiveness and validity on account of their having been made by electronic means.

2. Member States may lay down that paragraph 1 shall not apply to all or certain contracts falling into one of the following categories:

(a) contracts that create or transfer rights in real estate, except for rental rights;

(b) contracts requiring by law the involvement of courts, public authorities or professions exercising public authority;

(c) contracts of suretyship granted and on collateral securities furnished by persons acting for purposes outside their trade, business or profession;

(d) contracts governed by family law or by the law of succession.

3. Member States shall indicate to the Commission the categories referred to in paragraph 2 to which they do not apply paragraph 1. Member States shall submit to the Commission every five years a report on the application of paragraph 2 explaining the reasons why they consider it necessary to maintain the category referred to in paragraph 2(b) to which they do not apply paragraph 1.

Article 10

Information to be provided

1. In addition to other information requirements established by Community law, Member States shall ensure, except when otherwise agreed by parties who are not consumers, that at least the following information is given by the service provider clearly, comprehensibly and unambiguously and prior to the order being placed by the recipient of the service:

(a) the different technical steps to follow to conclude the contract;

(b) whether or not the concluded contract will be filed by the service provider and whether it will be accessible;

(c) the technical means for identifying and correcting input errors prior to the placing of the order;

(d) the languages offered for the conclusion of the contract.

2. Member States shall ensure that, except when otherwise agreed by parties who are not consumers, the service provider indicates any relevant codes of conduct to which he subscribes and information on how those codes can be consulted electronically.

3. Contract terms and general conditions provided to the recipient must be made available in a way that allows him to store and reproduce them.

4. Paragraphs 1 and 2 shall not apply to contracts concluded exclusively by exchange of electronic mail or by equivalent individual communications.

Article 11

Placing of the order

1. Member States shall ensure, except when otherwise agreed by parties who are not consumers, that in cases where the recipient of the

service places his order through technological means, the following principles apply:

– the service provider has to acknowledge the receipt of the recipient's order without undue delay and by electronic means,

– the order and the acknowledgement of receipt are deemed to be received when the parties to whom they are addressed are able to access them.

2. Member States shall ensure that, except when otherwise agreed by parties who are not consumers, the service provider makes available to the recipient of the service appropriate, effective and accessible technical means allowing him to identify and correct input errors, prior to the placing of the order.

3. Paragraph 1, first indent, and paragraph 2 shall not apply to contracts concluded exclusively by exchange of electronic mail or by equivalent individual communications.

DOCUMENT 63

EU REGULATION NO. 593/2008 ON THE LAW APPLICABLE TO CONTRACTUAL OBLIGATIONS (ROME I)

■ ■ ■

Council Regulation (EC) No. 593/2008 of 17 June 2008

(Selected Provisions)

CHAPTER I. SCOPE

ARTICLE 1. MATERIAL SCOPE

1. This Regulation shall apply, in situations involving a conflict of laws, to contractual obligations in civil and commercial matters.

It shall not apply, in particular, to revenue, customs or administrative matters.

2. The following shall be excluded from the scope of this Regulation:

(a) questions involving the status or legal capacity of natural persons, without prejudice to Article 13;

(b) obligations arising out of family relationships and relationships deemed by the law applicable to such relationships to have comparable effects, including maintenance obligations;

(c) obligations arising out of matrimonial property regimes, property regimes of relationships deemed by the law applicable to such relationships to have comparable effects to marriage, and wills and succession;

(d) obligations arising under bills of exchange, cheques and promissory notes and other negotiable instruments to the extent that the obligations under such other negotiable instruments arise out of their negotiable character;

(e) arbitration agreements and agreements on the choice of court;

* * *

4. In this Regulation, the term "Member State" shall mean Member States to which this Regulation applies. However, in Article 3(4) and Article 7 the term shall mean all the Member States.

ARTICLE 2. UNIVERSAL APPLICATION

Any law specified by this Regulation shall be applied whether or not it is the law of a Member State.

CHAPTER II. UNIFORM RULES

ARTICLE 3. FREEDOM OF CHOICE

1. A contract shall be governed by the law chosen by the parties. The choice shall be made expressly or clearly demonstrated by the terms of the contract or the circumstances of the case. By their choice the parties can select the law applicable to the whole or to part only of the contract.

2. The parties may at any time agree to subject the contract to a law other than that which previously governed it, whether as a result of an earlier choice made under this Article or of other provisions of this Regulation. Any change in the law to be applied that is made after the conclusion of the contract shall not prejudice its formal validity under Article 11 or adversely affect the rights of third parties.

3. Where all other elements relevant to the situation at the time of the choice are located in a country other than the country whose law has been chosen, the choice of the parties shall not prejudice the application of provisions of the law of that other country which cannot be derogated from by agreement.

4. Where all other elements relevant to the situation at the time of the choice are located in one or more Member States, the parties' choice of applicable law other than that of a Member State shall not prejudice the application of provisions of Community law, where appropriate as implemented in the Member State of the forum, which cannot be derogated from by agreement.

5. The existence and validity of the consent of the parties as to the choice of the applicable law shall be determined in accordance with the provisions of Articles 10, 11 and 13.

ARTICLE 4. APPLICABLE LAW IN THE ABSENCE OF CHOICE

1. To the extent that the law applicable to the contract has not been chosen in accordance with Article 3 and without prejudice to Articles 5 to 8, the law governing the contract shall be determined as follows:

(a) a contract for the sale of goods shall be governed by the law of the country where the seller has his habitual residence;

(b) a contract for the provision of services shall be governed by the law of the country where the service provider has his habitual residence;

(c) a contract relating to a right in rem in immovable property or to a tenancy of immovable property shall be governed by the law of the country where the property is situated;

(d) notwithstanding point (c), a tenancy of immovable property concluded for temporary private use for a period of no more than six consecutive months shall be governed by the law of the country where the landlord has his habitual residence, provided that the tenant is a natural person and has his habitual residence in the same country;

(e) a franchise contract shall be governed by the law of the country where the franchisee has his habitual residence;

(f) a distribution contract shall be governed by the law of the country where the distributor has his habitual residence;

(g) a contract for the sale of goods by auction shall be governed by the law of the country where the auction takes place, if such a place can be determined;

* * *

2. Where the contract is not covered by paragraph 1 or where the elements of the contract would be covered by more than one of points (a) to (h) of paragraph 1, the contract shall be governed by the law of the country where the party required to effect the characteristic performance of the contract has his habitual residence.

3. Where it is clear from all the circumstances of the case that the contract is manifestly more closely connected with a country other than that indicated in paragraphs 1 or 2, the law of that other country shall apply.

4. Where the law applicable cannot be determined pursuant to paragraphs 1 or 2, the contract shall be governed by the law of the country with which it is most closely connected.

* * *

ARTICLE 6. CONSUMER CONTRACTS

1. Without prejudice to Articles 5 and 7, a contract concluded by a natural person for a purpose which can be regarded as being outside his trade or profession (the consumer) with another person acting in the exercise of his trade or profession (the professional) shall be governed by the law of the country where the consumer has his habitual residence, provided that the professional:

(a) pursues his commercial or professional activities in the country where the consumer has his habitual residence, or

(b) by any means, directs such activities to that country or to several countries including that country, and the contract falls within the scope of such activities.

2. Notwithstanding paragraph 1, the parties may choose the law applicable to a contract which fulfils the requirements of paragraph 1, in accordance with Article 3. Such a choice may not, however, have the result of depriving the consumer of the protection afforded to him by provisions that cannot be derogated from by agreement by virtue of the law which, in the absence of choice, would have been applicable on the basis of paragraph 1.

3. If the requirements in points (a) or (b) of paragraph 1 are not fulfilled, the law applicable to a contract between a consumer and a professional shall be determined pursuant to Articles 3 and 4.

4. Paragraphs 1 and 2 shall not apply to:

(a) a contract for the supply of services where the services are to be supplied to the consumer exclusively in a country other than that in which he has his habitual residence;

(b) a contract of carriage other than a contract relating to package travel within the meaning of Council Directive 90/314/EEC of 13 June 1990 on package travel, package holidays and package tours [15];

(c) a contract relating to a right in rem in immovable property or a tenancy of immovable property other than a contract relating to the right to use immovable properties on a timeshare basis within the meaning of Directive 94/47/EC; * * *

* * *

ARTICLE 9. OVERRIDING MANDATORY PROVISIONS

1. Overriding mandatory provisions are provisions the respect for which is regarded as crucial by a country for safeguarding its public interests, such as its political, social or economic organisation, to such an extent that they are applicable to any situation falling within their scope, irrespective of the law otherwise applicable to the contract under this Regulation.

2. Nothing in this Regulation shall restrict the application of the overriding mandatory provisions of the law of the forum.

3. Effect may be given to the overriding mandatory provisions of the law of the country where the obligations arising out of the contract have to be or have been performed, in so far as those overriding mandatory provisions render the performance of the contract unlawful. In considering whether to give effect to those provisions, regard shall be had to their nature and purpose and to the consequences of their application or non-application.

ARTICLE 10. CONSENT AND MATERIAL VALIDITY

1. The existence and validity of a contract, or of any term of a contract, shall be determined by the law which would govern it under this Regulation if the contract or term were valid.

2. Nevertheless, a party, in order to establish that he did not consent, may rely upon the law of the country in which he has his habitual residence if it appears from the circumstances that it would not be reasonable to determine the effect of his conduct in accordance with the law specified in paragraph 1.

ARTICLE 11. FORMAL VALIDITY

1. A contract concluded between persons who, or whose agents, are in the same country at the time of its conclusion is formally valid if it satisfies the formal requirements of the law which governs it in substance under this Regulation or of the law of the country where it is concluded.

2. A contract concluded between persons who, or whose agents, are in different countries at the time of its conclusion is formally valid if it satisfies the formal requirements of the law which governs it in substance under this Regulation, or of the law of either of the countries where either of the parties or their agent is present at the time of conclusion, or of the law of the country where either of the parties had his habitual residence at that time.

3. A unilateral act intended to have legal effect relating to an existing or contemplated contract is formally valid if it satisfies the formal requirements of the law which governs or would govern the contract in substance under this Regulation, or of the law of the country where the act was done, or of the law of the country where the person by whom it was done had his habitual residence at that time.

4. Paragraphs 1, 2 and 3 of this Article shall not apply to contracts that fall within the scope of Article 6. The form of such contracts shall be governed by the law of the country where the consumer has his habitual residence.

5. Notwithstanding paragraphs 1 to 4, a contract the subject matter of which is a right in rem in immovable property or a tenancy of immovable property shall be subject to the requirements of form of the law of the country where the property is situated if by that law:

(a) those requirements are imposed irrespective of the country where the contract is concluded and irrespective of the law governing the contract; and

(b) those requirements cannot be derogated from by agreement.

ARTICLE 12. SCOPE OF THE LAW APPLICABLE

1. The law applicable to a contract by virtue of this Regulation shall govern in particular:

(a) interpretation;

(b) performance;

(c) within the limits of the powers conferred on the court by its procedural law, the consequences of a total or partial breach of obligations, including the assessment of damages in so far as it is governed by rules of law;

(d) the various ways of extinguishing obligations, and prescription and limitation of actions;

(e) the consequences of nullity of the contract.

2. In relation to the manner of performance and the steps to be taken in the event of defective performance, regard shall be had to the law of the country in which performance takes place.

ARTICLE 13. INCAPACITY

In a contract concluded between persons who are in the same country, a natural person who would have capacity under the law of that country may invoke his incapacity resulting from the law of another country, only if the other party to the contract was aware of that incapacity at the time of the conclusion of the contract or was not aware thereof as a result of negligence.

* * *

ARTICLE 18. BURDEN OF PROOF

1. The law governing a contractual obligation under this Regulation shall apply to the extent that, in matters of contractual obligations, it contains rules which raise presumptions of law or determine the burden of proof.

2. A contract or an act intended to have legal effect may be proved by any mode of proof recognised by the law of the forum or by any of the laws referred to in Article 11 under which that contract or act is formally valid, provided that such mode of proof can be administered by the forum.

CHAPTER III. OTHER PROVISIONS

ARTICLE 19. HABITUAL RESIDENCE

1. For the purposes of this Regulation, the habitual residence of companies and other bodies, corporate or unincorporated, shall be the place of central administration.

The habitual residence of a natural person acting in the course of his business activity shall be his principal place of business.

2. Where the contract is concluded in the course of the operations of a branch, agency or any other establishment, or if, under the contract, performance is the responsibility of such a branch, agency or establishment, the place where the branch, agency or any other establishment is located shall be treated as the place of habitual residence.

3. For the purposes of determining the habitual residence, the relevant point in time shall be the time of the conclusion of the contract.

ARTICLE 20. EXCLUSION OF RENVOI

The application of the law of any country specified by this Regulation means the application of the rules of law in force in that country other than its rules of private international law, unless provided otherwise in this Regulation.

ARTICLE 21. PUBLIC POLICY OF THE FORUM

The application of a provision of the law of any country specified by this Regulation may be refused only if such application is manifestly incompatible with the public policy (ordre public) of the forum.

ARTICLE 22. STATES WITH MORE THAN ONE LEGAL SYSTEM

1. Where a State comprises several territorial units, each of which has its own rules of law in respect of contractual obligations, each territorial unit shall be considered as a country for the purposes of identifying the law applicable under this Regulation.

2. A Member State where different territorial units have their own rules of law in respect of contractual obligations shall not be required to apply this Regulation to conflicts solely between the laws of such units.

ARTICLE 23. RELATIONSHIP WITH OTHER PROVISIONS OF COMMUNITY LAW

With the exception of Article 7, this Regulation shall not prejudice the application of provisions of Community law which, in relation to particular matters, lay down conflict-of-law rules relating to contractual obligations.

ARTICLE 24. RELATIONSHIP WITH THE ROME CONVENTION

1. This Regulation shall replace the Rome Convention in the Member States, except as regards the territories of the Member States which fall within the territorial scope of that Convention and to which this Regulation does not apply pursuant to Article 299 of the Treaty.

2. In so far as this Regulation replaces the provisions of the Rome Convention, any reference to that Convention shall be understood as a reference to this Regulation.

ARTICLE 25. RELATIONSHIP WITH EXISTING INTERNATIONAL CONVENTIONS

1. This Regulation shall not prejudice the application of international conventions to which one or more Member States are parties at the time when this Regulation is adopted and which lay down conflict-of-law rules relating to contractual obligations.

2. However, this Regulation shall, as between Member States, take precedence over conventions concluded exclusively between two or more of them in so far as such conventions concern matters governed by this Regulation.

DOCUMENT 64

EU REGULATION NO. 1215/2012 ON JURISDICTION AND THE RECOGNITION AND ENFORCEMENT OF JUDGMENTS IN CIVIL AND COMMERCIAL MATTERS (RECAST) (EFFECTIVE 10 JANUARY 2015)

■ ■ ■

CHAPTER I
SCOPE AND DEFINITIONS

Article 1

1. This Regulation shall apply in civil and commercial matters whatever the nature of the court or tribunal. It shall not extend, in particular, to revenue, customs or administrative matters or to the liability of the State for acts and omissions in the exercise of State authority (*acta iure imperii*).

2. This Regulation shall not apply to:

(a) the status or legal capacity of natural persons, rights in property arising out of a matrimonial relationship or out of a relationship deemed by the law applicable to such relationship to have comparable effects to marriage;

(b) bankruptcy, proceedings relating to the winding-up of insolvent companies or other legal persons, judicial arrangements, compositions and analogous proceedings;

(c) social security;

(d) arbitration;

(e) maintenance obligations arising from a family relationship, parentage, marriage or affinity;

(f) wills and succession, including maintenance obligations arising by reason of death.

* * *

CHAPTER II

JURISDICTION

SECTION 1

General provisions

Article 4

1. Subject to this Regulation, persons domiciled in a Member State shall, whatever their nationality, be sued in the courts of that Member State.

2. Persons who are not nationals of the Member State in which they are domiciled shall be governed by the rules of jurisdiction applicable to nationals of that Member State.

Article 5

1. Persons domiciled in a Member State may be sued in the courts of another Member State only by virtue of the rules set out in Sections 2 to 7 of this Chapter.

2. In particular, the rules of national jurisdiction of which the Member States are to notify the Commission pursuant to point (a) of Article 76(1) shall not be applicable as against the persons referred to in paragraph 1.

Article 6

1. If the defendant is not domiciled in a Member State, the jurisdiction of the courts of each Member State shall, subject to Article 18(1), Article 21(2) and Articles 24 and 25, be determined by the law of that Member State.

2. As against such a defendant, any person domiciled in a Member State may, whatever his nationality, avail himself in that Member State of the rules of jurisdiction there in force, and in particular those of which the Member States are to notify the Commission pursuant to point (a) of Article 76(1), in the same way as nationals of that Member State.

SECTION 2

Special jurisdiction

Article 7

A person domiciled in a Member State may be sued in another Member State:

(1) (a) in matters relating to a contract, in the courts for the place of performance of the obligation in question;

(b) for the purpose of this provision and unless otherwise agreed, the place of performance of the obligation in question shall be:

– in the case of the sale of goods, the place in a Member State where, under the contract, the goods were delivered or should have been delivered,

– in the case of the provision of services, the place in a Member State where, under the contract, the services were provided or should have been provided;

(c) if point (b) does not apply then point (a) applies;

(2) in matters relating to tort, delict or quasi-delict, in the courts for the place where the harmful event occurred or may occur;

(3) as regards a civil claim for damages or restitution which is based on an act giving rise to criminal proceedings, in the court seised of those proceedings, to the extent that that court has jurisdiction under its own law to entertain civil proceedings;

(4) as regards a civil claim for the recovery, based on ownership, of a cultural object * * *, in the courts for the place where the cultural object is situated at the time when the court is seised;

(5) as regards a dispute arising out of the operations of a branch, agency or other establishment, in the courts for the place where the branch, agency or other establishment is situated;

(6) as regards a dispute brought against a settlor, trustee or beneficiary of a trust created by the operation of a statute, or by a written instrument, or created orally and evidenced in writing, in the courts of the Member State in which the trust is domiciled;

(7) as regards a dispute concerning the payment of remuneration claimed in respect of the salvage of a cargo or freight, in the court under the authority of which the cargo or freight in question:

(a) has been arrested to secure such payment; or

(b) could have been so arrested, but bail or other security has been given;

provided that this provision shall apply only if it is claimed that the defendant has an interest in the cargo or freight or had such an interest at the time of salvage.

Article 8

A person domiciled in a Member State may also be sued:

(1) where he is one of a number of defendants, in the courts for the place where any one of them is domiciled, provided the claims are so closely connected that it is expedient to hear and determine them together to avoid the risk of irreconcilable judgments resulting from separate proceedings;

(2) as a third party in an action on a warranty or guarantee or in any other third-party proceedings, in the court seised of the original proceedings, unless these were instituted solely with the object of removing him from the jurisdiction of the court which would be competent in his case;

(3) on a counter-claim arising from the same contract or facts on which the original claim was based, in the court in which the original claim is pending;

(4) in matters relating to a contract, if the action may be combined with an action against the same defendant in matters relating to rights *in rem* in immovable property, in the court of the Member State in which the property is situated.

Article 9

Where by virtue of this Regulation a court of a Member State has jurisdiction in actions relating to liability from the use or operation of a ship, that court, or any other court substituted for this purpose by the internal law of that Member State, shall also have jurisdiction over claims for limitation of such liability.

* * *

SECTION 4

Jurisdiction over consumer contracts

Article 17

1. In matters relating to a contract concluded by a person, the consumer, for a purpose which can be regarded as being outside his trade or profession, jurisdiction shall be determined by this Section, without prejudice to Article 6 and point 5 of Article 7, if:

(a) it is a contract for the sale of goods on instalment credit terms;

(b) it is a contract for a loan repayable by instalments, or for any other form of credit, made to finance the sale of goods; or

(c) in all other cases, the contract has been concluded with a person who pursues commercial or professional activities in the Member State of the consumer's domicile or, by any means, directs such activities to that Member State or to several States including that Member State, and the contract falls within the scope of such activities.

2. Where a consumer enters into a contract with a party who is not domiciled in a Member State but has a branch, agency or other establishment in one of the Member States, that party shall, in disputes arising out of the operations of the branch, agency or establishment, be deemed to be domiciled in that Member State.

3. This Section shall not apply to a contract of transport other than a contract which, for an inclusive price, provides for a combination of travel and accommodation.

Article 18

1. A consumer may bring proceedings against the other party to a contract either in the courts of the Member State in which that party is domiciled or, regardless of the domicile of the other party, in the courts for the place where the consumer is domiciled.

2. Proceedings may be brought against a consumer by the other party to the contract only in the courts of the Member State in which the consumer is domiciled.

3. This Article shall not affect the right to bring a counter-claim in the court in which, in accordance with this Section, the original claim is pending.

Article 19

The provisions of this Section may be departed from only by an agreement:

(1) which is entered into after the dispute has arisen;

(2) which allows the consumer to bring proceedings in courts other than those indicated in this Section; or

(3) which is entered into by the consumer and the other party to the contract, both of whom are at the time of conclusion of the contract domiciled or habitually resident in the same Member State, and which confers jurisdiction on the courts of that Member State, provided that such an agreement is not contrary to the law of that Member State.

* * *

SECTION 6

Exclusive jurisdiction

Article 24

The following courts of a Member State shall have exclusive jurisdiction, regardless of the domicile of the parties:

(1) in proceedings which have as their object rights *in rem* in immovable property or tenancies of immovable property, the courts of the Member State in which the property is situated.

However, in proceedings which have as their object tenancies of immovable property concluded for temporary private use for a maximum period of six consecutive months, the courts of the Member State in which the defendant is domiciled shall also have jurisdiction, provided that the tenant is a natural person and that the landlord and the tenant are domiciled in the same Member State;

(2) in proceedings which have as their object the validity of the constitution, the nullity or the dissolution of companies or other legal persons or associations of natural or legal persons, or the validity of the decisions of their organs, the courts of the Member State in which the company, legal person or association has its seat. In order to determine that seat, the court shall apply its rules of private international law;

(3) in proceedings which have as their object the validity of entries in public registers, the courts of the Member State in which the register is kept;

(4) in proceedings concerned with the registration or validity of patents, trade marks, designs, or other similar rights required to be deposited or registered, irrespective of whether the issue is raised by way of an action or as a defence, the courts of the Member State in which the deposit or registration has been applied for, has taken place or is under the terms of an instrument of the Union or an international convention deemed to have taken place.

Without prejudice to the jurisdiction of the European Patent Office under the Convention on the Grant of European Patents, signed at Munich on 5 October 1973, the courts of each Member State shall have exclusive jurisdiction in proceedings concerned with the registration or validity of any European patent granted for that Member State;

(5) in proceedings concerned with the enforcement of judgments, the courts of the Member State in which the judgment has been or is to be enforced.

SECTION 7

Prorogation of jurisdiction

Article 25

1. If the parties, regardless of their domicile, have agreed that a court or the courts of a Member State are to have jurisdiction to settle any disputes which have arisen or which may arise in connection with a particular legal relationship, that court or those courts shall have jurisdiction, unless the agreement is null and void as to its substantive validity under the law of that Member State. Such jurisdiction shall be exclusive unless the parties have agreed otherwise. The agreement conferring jurisdiction shall be either:

(a) in writing or evidenced in writing;

(b) in a form which accords with practices which the parties have established between themselves; or

(c) in international trade or commerce, in a form which accords with a usage of which the parties are or ought to have been aware and which in such trade or commerce is widely known to, and regularly observed by, parties to contracts of the type involved in the particular trade or commerce concerned.

2. Any communication by electronic means which provides a durable record of the agreement shall be equivalent to 'writing'.

3. The court or courts of a Member State on which a trust instrument has conferred jurisdiction shall have exclusive jurisdiction in any proceedings brought against a settlor, trustee or beneficiary, if relations between those persons or their rights or obligations under the trust are involved.

* * *

5. An agreement conferring jurisdiction which forms part of a contract shall be treated as an agreement independent of the other terms of the contract.

The validity of the agreement conferring jurisdiction cannot be contested solely on the ground that the contract is not valid.

Article 26

1. Apart from jurisdiction derived from other provisions of this Regulation, a court of a Member State before which a defendant enters an appearance shall have jurisdiction. This rule shall not apply where appearance was entered to contest the jurisdiction, or where another court has exclusive jurisdiction by virtue of Article 24.

* * *

CHAPTER III

RECOGNITION AND ENFORCEMENT

SECTION 1

Recognition

Article 36

1. A judgment given in a Member State shall be recognised in the other Member States without any special procedure being required.

2. Any interested party may, in accordance with the procedure provided for in Subsection 2 of Section 3, apply for a decision that there are no grounds for refusal of recognition as referred to in Article 45.

3. If the outcome of proceedings in a court of a Member State depends on the determination of an incidental question of refusal of recognition, that court shall have jurisdiction over that question.

Article 37

1. A party who wishes to invoke in a Member State a judgment given in another Member State shall produce:

(a) a copy of the judgment which satisfies the conditions necessary to establish its authenticity; and

(b) the certificate issued pursuant to Article 53.

2. The court or authority before which a judgment given in another Member State is invoked may, where necessary, require the party invoking it to provide, in accordance with Article 57, a translation or a transliteration of the contents of the certificate referred to in point (b) of paragraph 1. The court or authority may require the party to provide a translation of the judgment instead of a translation of the contents of the certificate if it is unable to proceed without such a translation.

Article 38

The court or authority before which a judgment given in another Member State is invoked may suspend the proceedings, in whole or in part, if:

(a) the judgment is challenged in the Member State of origin; or

(b) an application has been submitted for a decision that there are no grounds for refusal of recognition as referred to in Article 45 or for a decision that the recognition is to be refused on the basis of one of those grounds.

SECTION 2

Enforcement

Article 39

A judgment given in a Member State which is enforceable in that Member State shall be enforceable in the other Member States without any declaration of enforceability being required.

Article 40

An enforceable judgment shall carry with it by operation of law the power to proceed to any protective measures which exist under the law of the Member State addressed.

Article 41

1. Subject to the provisions of this Section, the procedure for the enforcement of judgments given in another Member State shall be governed by the law of the Member State addressed. A judgment given in a Member State which is enforceable in the Member State addressed shall be enforced there under the same conditions as a judgment given in the Member State addressed.

2. Notwithstanding paragraph 1, the grounds for refusal or of suspension of enforcement under the law of the Member State addressed shall apply in so far as they are not incompatible with the grounds referred to in Article 45.

3. The party seeking the enforcement of a judgment given in another Member State shall not be required to have a postal address in the Member State addressed. Nor shall that party be required to have an authorised representative in the Member State addressed unless such a representative is mandatory irrespective of the nationality or the domicile of the parties.

Article 42

1. For the purposes of enforcement in a Member State of a judgment given in another Member State, the applicant shall provide the competent enforcement authority with:

(a) a copy of the judgment which satisfies the conditions necessary to establish its authenticity; and

(b) the certificate issued pursuant to Article 53, certifying that the judgment is enforceable and containing an extract of the judgment as well as, where appropriate, relevant information on the recoverable costs of the proceedings and the calculation of interest.

2. For the purposes of enforcement in a Member State of a judgment given in another Member State ordering a provisional, including a protective, measure, the applicant shall provide the competent enforcement authority with:

(a) a copy of the judgment which satisfies the conditions necessary to establish its authenticity;

(b) the certificate issued pursuant to Article 53, containing a description of the measure and certifying that:

(i) the court has jurisdiction as to the substance of the matter;

(ii) the judgment is enforceable in the Member State of origin; and

(c) where the measure was ordered without the defendant being summoned to appear, proof of service of the judgment.

3. The competent enforcement authority may, where necessary, require the applicant to provide, in accordance with Article 57, a translation or a transliteration of the contents of the certificate.

4. The competent enforcement authority may require the applicant to provide a translation of the judgment only if it is unable to proceed without such a translation.

Article 43

1. Where enforcement is sought of a judgment given in another Member State, the certificate issued pursuant to Article 53 shall be served on the person against whom the enforcement is sought prior to the first enforcement measure. The certificate shall be accompanied by the judgment, if not already served on that person.

2. Where the person against whom enforcement is sought is domiciled in a Member State other than the Member State of origin, he may request a translation of the judgment in order to contest the enforcement if the judgment is not written in or accompanied by a translation into either of the following languages:

(a) a language which he understands; or

(b) the official language of the Member State in which he is domiciled or, where there are several official languages in that Member State, the official language or one of the official languages of the place where he is domiciled.

Where a translation of the judgment is requested under the first subparagraph, no measures of enforcement may be taken other than protective measures until that translation has been provided to the person against whom enforcement is sought.

This paragraph shall not apply if the judgment has already been served on the person against whom enforcement is sought in one of the languages referred to in the first subparagraph or is accompanied by a translation into one of those languages.

3. This Article shall not apply to the enforcement of a protective measure in a judgment or where the person seeking enforcement proceeds to protective measures in accordance with Article 40.

Article 44

1. In the event of an application for refusal of enforcement of a judgment pursuant to Subsection 2 of Section 3, the court in the Member State addressed may, on the application of the person against whom enforcement is sought:

(a) limit the enforcement proceedings to protective measures;

(b) make enforcement conditional on the provision of such security as it shall determine; or

(c) suspend, either wholly or in part, the enforcement proceedings.

2. The competent authority in the Member State addressed shall, on the application of the person against whom enforcement is sought, suspend the enforcement proceedings where the enforceability of the judgment is suspended in the Member State of origin.

SECTION 3

Refusal of recognition and enforcement

Subsection 1

Refusal of recognition

Article 45

1. On the application of any interested party, the recognition of a judgment shall be refused:

(a) if such recognition is manifestly contrary to public policy (ordre public) in the Member State addressed;

(b) where the judgment was given in default of appearance, if the defendant was not served with the document which instituted the proceedings or with an equivalent document in sufficient time and in such a way as to enable him to arrange for his defence, unless the defendant failed to commence proceedings to challenge

(c) if the judgment is irreconcilable with a judgment given between the same parties in the Member State addressed;

(d) if the judgment is irreconcilable with an earlier judgment given in another Member State or in a third State involving the same cause of action and between the same parties, provided that the earlier judgment fulfils the conditions necessary for its recognition in the Member State addressed; or

(e) if the judgment conflicts with:

(i) Sections 3, 4 or 5 of Chapter II where the policyholder, the insured, a beneficiary of the insurance contract, the injured party, the consumer or the employee was the defendant; or

(ii) Section 6 of Chapter II.

2. In its examination of the grounds of jurisdiction referred to in point (e) of paragraph 1, the court to which the application was submitted shall be bound by the findings of fact on which the court of origin based its jurisdiction.

3. Without prejudice to point (e) of paragraph 1, the jurisdiction of the court of origin may not be reviewed. The test of public policy referred to in point (a) of paragraph 1 may not be applied to the rules relating to jurisdiction.

4. The application for refusal of recognition shall be made in accordance with the procedures provided for in Subsection 2 and, where appropriate, Section 4.

Subsection 2

Refusal of enforcement

Article 46

On the application of the person against whom enforcement is sought, the enforcement of a judgment shall be refused where one of the grounds referred to in Article 45 is found to exist.

Article 47

1. The application for refusal of enforcement shall be submitted to the court which the Member State concerned has communicated to the Commission pursuant to point (a) of Article 75 as the court to which the application is to be submitted.

2. The procedure for refusal of enforcement shall, in so far as it is not covered by this Regulation, be governed by the law of the Member State addressed.

3. The applicant shall provide the court with a copy of the judgment and, where necessary, a translation or transliteration of it.

The court may dispense with the production of the documents referred to in the first subparagraph if it already possesses them or if it considers it unreasonable to require the applicant to provide them. In the latter case, the court may require the other party to provide those documents.

4. The party seeking the refusal of enforcement of a judgment given in another Member State shall not be required to have a postal address in the Member State addressed. Nor shall that party be required to have an authorised representative in the Member State addressed unless such a representative is mandatory irrespective of the nationality or the domicile of the parties.

Article 48

The court shall decide on the application for refusal of enforcement without delay.

Article 49

1. The decision on the application for refusal of enforcement may be appealed against by either party.

2. The appeal is to be lodged with the court which the Member State concerned has communicated to the Commission pursuant to point (b) of Article 75 as the court with which such an appeal is to be lodged.

* * *

SECTION 4

Common provisions

Article 52

Under no circumstances may a judgment given in a Member State be reviewed as to its substance in the Member State addressed.

* * *

Article 55

A judgment given in a Member State which orders a payment by way of a penalty shall be enforceable in the Member State addressed only if the amount of the payment has been finally determined by the court of origin.

* * *

DOCUMENT 65

FOREIGN INVESTMENT LAW OF THE UNITED MEXICAN STATES

■ ■ ■

Published in the Official Gazette (Diario Oficial) of the Federation on December 27, 1993 and in force as of December 28, 1993, as amended December 24, 1996

[**Authors' Note**: Major changes in Mexican foreign investment law, particularly as to the oil and gas and electricity sectors were in progress in 2014–15.]

TITLE FIRST

GENERAL PROVISIONS

Chapter I
Purpose of Law

* * *

ARTICLE 2

For purposes of this Law, the following definitions shall apply:

I. The Commission: The National Foreign Investments Commission;

II. Foreign Investment:

  a. Participation of foreign investors in any proportion in the capital of Mexican corporations;

  b. That done by Mexican corporations with majority foreign investment; and

  c. The participation by foreign investors in the activities and acts included in this Law.

III. Foreign investor: The individual or corporate person with nationality other than Mexican and foreign entities without legal status.

IV. Registry: The National Foreign Investments Registry.

V. The Secretariat: The Secretariat of Commerce and Industrial Development.

VI. Restricted Zone: The strip of Mexican territory one hundred kilometers in depth from the borders and fifty kilometers in depth from the coast lines to which Article 27, paragraph I of the Political Constitution of the United Mexican States refers; and

VII. Exclusion of Foreigners Clause: The express agreement, or pact that forms an integral part of corporate by-laws by which it is provided that the companies at hand shall not admit directly or indirectly, foreign investors nor corporations with an admission of foreigners clause.

* * *

ARTICLE 4

Foreign investment may participate in any proportion in the capital of Mexican companies, acquire fixed assets, enter new fields of economic activity or manufacture new product lines, open and operate establishments, and expand or relocate existing establishments, except as otherwise provided herein.

* * *

Chapter II
Reserved Activities

ARTICLE 5

The functions determined by the laws in the following strategic areas are reserved exclusively to the State:

I. Petroleum and other hydrocarbons;

II. Basic petrochemicals;

III. Electricity;

IV. Generation of nuclear energy;

V. Radioactive minerals;

VI. Satellite communication;

VII. Telegraph;

VIII. Radiotelegraph;

IX. Mail;

X. Railroads;

XI. Issue of currency; and

XII. Minting of coins.

XIII. Control, supervision and oversight of ports, airports, and heliports; and

XIV. Such others as are expressly stated in the applicable legal provisions.

ARTICLE 6

The following economic activities and corporations hereinafter mentioned, are reserved exclusively to Mexicans or to Mexican companies with an Exclusion of Foreigners Clause:

I. National surface transportation of passengers, tourism, and freight, excluding messenger and package delivery service;

II. Retail trade in gasoline and liquid petroleum gas;

III. Radio broadcasting service and other radio and television services different from cable television;

IV. Credit unions;

V. Development banking institutions, pursuant to the provisions of the law on the subject; and

VI. Supply of professional and technical services expressly set forth in the applicable legal provisions.

Foreign investment may not participate in the aforesaid activities and corporations in this article directly or through trusts, agreements, corporate or shareholder pacts, pyramid schemes, or any other mechanism which grants any control or equity participation whatsoever, except as provided by Title Fifth hereof.

Chapter III
Activities and Acquisitions Subject to Specific Regulation

ARTICLE 7

In the economic activities and corporations mentioned hereafter, foreign investment may participate in the following percentages:

I. Up to 10% in:

Cooperative companies for production;

II. Up to 25% in:

a. Domestic air transportation

b. Air taxi transportation; and

c. Specialized air transportation;

III. Up to 49% in:

a. Holding companies for financial groups;

b. Commercial (multiple) banking credit institutions;

c. Securities brokerage firms; and

d. Securities market specialists;

e. Insurance institutions;

f. Bonding institutions:

g. Currency exchange houses;

h. General deposit warehouses;

i. Financial leasing companies;

j. Financial factoring companies;

k. Financial companies with purpose limited to those provided for in Article 103, paragraph IV, of the Law of Credit Institutions;

l. Companies to which Article 12 Bis of the Securities Market Law refers;

m. Shares representing the fixed capital in investment companies and operating companies of investment corporations;

n. Manufacture and commercialization of explosives, firearms, cartridges, munitions and fireworks, excluding acquisition and use of explosives for industrial and extraction activities or the preparation of explosive mixtures for use in said activities;

o. Printing and publication of newspapers for circulation solely throughout Mexico;

p. Series T shares in companies that own agricultural, ranching, and forestry lands;

q. Cable television;

r. Basic telephone services;

s. Fresh water, coastal, and exclusive economic zone fishing, excluding aquaculture;

t. Comprehensive port management services;

u. Piloting port services for vessels to carry out operations of inland navigation operations in the terms of the subject law;

v. Shipping companies engaged in commercial exploitation of ships for inland and coastal navigation, excluding tourism cruisers and exploitation of marine dredging and implements for port construction, conservation and operation;

w. Services connected to the railway sector that consist of passenger service, maintenance and rehabilitation of roads, rights of way, repair shops for tractive and hauling equipment, organization and commercialization of unit trains, operation of domestic terminals for freight and railroad telecommunications; and

x. Supply of fuel and lubricants for ships, airplanes, and railway equipment;

The limitations for foreign investment participation set forth in this article may not be exceeded directly, nor through trusts, agreements, corporate or shareholder pacts, pyramid schemes or any other mechanism which grants control or equity participation greater than that established, except pursuant to Title Fifth of this Law.

ARTICLE 8

Favorable resolution by the Commission is required for foreign investment participation in a percentage greater than 49% in the economic activities and companies referred to hereafter:

I. Port services for ships to effect their inland navigation operations, such as towing, mooring and lighterage;

II. Shipping companies engaged in exploitation of ships solely for high seas traffic;

III. Management of air terminals;

IV. Private education services at the pre-school, primary, secondary, upper middle, upper, and combined levels;

V. Legal services;

VI. Credit information companies;

VII. Securities classification institutions;

VIII. Insurance agents;

IX. Cellular telephone.

X. Construction of pipeline for the transportation of petroleum and products derived therefrom; and

XI. Drilling of petroleum and gas wells; and

XII. Construction, operation and exploitation of railroads that constitute a general communication route, and rendering of the public service railroad transportation.

ARTICLE 9

Favorable resolution from the Commission is required for foreign investment to acquire assets or shares in Mexican companies, regardless of the activity they engage in only whose total asset value at the time of acquisition exceeds the amount established annually by said Commission, and provided said acquisition implies that the direct or indirect participation of foreign investment in the capital of the companies in question exceeds 49% thereof.

* * *

TITLE THIRD

COMPANIES

Creation and Modification of Companies

ARTICLE 15

A permit from the Secretariat of Foreign Relations is required for the creation of companies. The Exclusion of Foreigners Clause or the agreement provided for in Constitutional Article 27, paragraph (1) must be included in the by-laws of companies that are created.

ARTICLE 16

A permit from the Secretariat of Foreign Relations is required for companies created to change their corporate name. Companies that replace the Exclusion of Foreigners Clause with a clause for admission of foreigners shall notify the Secretariat of Foreign Relations within the following thirty business days of the replacement.

TITLE FOURTH

INVESTMENT BY FOREIGN CORPORATIONS

ARTICLE 17

Without prejudice to that established in international treaties and conventions to which Mexico is a party, the following shall obtain authorization from the Secretariat:

I. The foreign companies that intend to habitually perform commerce acts in the Republic; and

II. The persons referred to in Article 2736 of the Civil Code for the Federal District in Common Matters and for the whole Republic in Federal Matters, that intend to settle in the Republic and that are not regulated by laws other than such Code.

ARTICLE 17A

The authorization referred to in the previous paragraph will be given when the following requirements are complied with:

a. That such persons prove that they are duly established according to the laws of their country;

b. That the by-laws and other incorporation documents of such persons are not contrary to the provisions of public order set forth under Mexican Laws; and

c. The persons referred to in Section I of the previous Article are settled in the Republic or have any agency or subsidiary in it; or, the person referred to in Section II of the previous Article have a representative domiciled in its place of operation authorized to comply with any acquired obligation.

All applications to obtain authorization to which the preceding paragraph refers to which meets the above mentioned requirements must be given within the 15 business days following the date of its filing. If after such period no resolution has been issued, such application will be deemed approved.

The Secretariat shall submit to the Secretariat of Foreign Relations a copy of its requests and authorizations given according to this Article.

TITLE FIFTH

NEUTRAL INVESTMENT

Chapter I
Neutral Investment Concept

ARTICLE 18

Neutral Investment is that investment made in Mexican companies, or trusts authorized pursuant to this Title and shall not be computed to determine the percentage of foreign investment in the capital of Mexican companies.

* * *

TITLE SIXTH

NATIONAL FOREIGN INVESTMENT COMMISSION

* * *

Chapter III
Operation of the Commission

ARTICLE 28

The Commission must decide on applications submitted for its consideration within a period not to exceed 45 business days counted from the date the relevant application is filed pursuant to the Regulations to this Law.

If the Commission does not enter a resolution within the aforesaid period, the application shall be deemed approved as filed. Upon request of interested party, the Secretariat must issue the corresponding authorization.

ARTICLE 29

To evaluate the applications submitted to its consideration, the Commission shall observe the following criteria:

I. The impact on jobs and training for employees;

II. The technological contribution;

III. Compliance of environmental requirements contained in the environmental statutes applicable; and

IV. Generally, the contribution toward increasing competitiveness in the Mexican production plant.

The Commission, in deciding whether an application is appropriate, may only impose requirements that do not distort international trade.

ARTICLE 30

The Commission may prevent acquisitions by foreign investment for reasons of national security.

TITLE SEVENTH

NATIONAL FOREIGN INVESTMENTS REGISTRY

* * *

ARTICLE 32

The following must register with the Registry:

I. Mexican companies in which foreign investors participate, including those in which foreign investors participate through a trust, and neutral investment;

II. Foreign individuals or corporations who habitually undertake commercial activity in Mexico, and branches of foreign investors established in Mexico; and

III. Trusts on shares or corporate equity interests, on real estate, and on neutral investment by which rights are derived for the foreign investment.

The obligation to register falls upon the individuals and corporations to which Paragraphs I and II refer, and in the case of Paragraph III, the obligation shall correspond upon the fiduciary institution. The registration must be done within 40 business days counted from the date of the creation of the corporation or the equity participation by foreign investors; of formalization or protocolling of the documents relating to the foreign company; or of the creation of the relevant trust or granting of beneficial rights to foreign investors.

* * *

TRANSITIONAL ARTICLES

* * *

SECOND

The following are abrogated:

I. The Law to Promote Mexican Investment and to Regulate Foreign Investment, published in the Official Gazette (Diario Oficial) of the Federation, on March 9, 1973;

* * *

DOCUMENT 66

UNITED KINGDOM PROTECTION OF TRADING INTERESTS ACT 1980, CH. 11

■ ■ ■

An Act to provide protection from requirements, prohibitions and judgments imposed or given under the laws of countries outside the United Kingdom and affecting the trading or other interests of persons in the United Kingdom.

1. Overseas Measures Affecting United Kingdom Trading Interests

(1) If it appears to the Secretary of State—

(*a*) that measures have been or are proposed to be taken by or under the law of any overseas country for regulating or controlling international trade; and

(*b*) that those measures, in so far as they apply or would apply to things done or to be done outside the territorial jurisdiction of that country by persons carrying on business in the United Kingdom, are damaging or threaten to damage the trading interests of the United Kingdom,

the Secretary of State may by order direct that this section shall apply to those measures either generally or in their application to such cases as may be specified in the order.

(2) The Secretary of State may by order make provision for requiring, or enabling the Secretary of State to require, a person in the United Kingdom who carries on business there to give notice to the Secretary of State of any requirement or prohibition imposed or threatened to be imposed on that person pursuant to any measures in so far as this section applies to them by virtue of an order under subsection (I) above.

(3) The Secretary of State may give to any person in the United Kingdom who carries on business there such directions for prohibiting compliance with any such requirement or prohibition as aforesaid as he considers appropriate for avoiding damage to the trading interests of the United Kingdom.

(4) The power of the Secretary of State to make orders under subsection (I) or (2) above shall be exercisable by statutory instrument subject to annulment in pursuance of a resolution of either House of Parliament.

(5) Directions under subsection (3) above may be either general or special and may prohibit compliance with any requirement or prohibition either absolutely or in such cases or subject to such conditions as to consent or otherwise as may be specified in the directions; and general directions under that subsection shall be published in such manner as appears to the Secretary of State to be appropriate.

(6) In this section "trade" includes any activity carried on in the course of a business of any description and "trading interests" shall be construed accordingly.

2. Documents and Information Required by Overseas Courts and Authorities

(1) If it appears to the Secretary of State—

(*a*) that a requirement has been or may be imposed on a person or persons in the United Kingdom to produce to any court, tribunal or authority of an overseas country any commercial document which is not within the territorial jurisdiction of that country or to furnish any commercial information to any such court, tribunal or authority; or

(*b*) that any such authority has imposed or may impose a requirement on a person or persons in the United Kingdom to publish any such document or information,

the Secretary of State may, if it appears to him that the requirement is inadmissible by virtue of subsection (2) or (3) below, give directions for prohibiting compliance with the requirement.

(2) A requirement such as is mentioned in subsection (I)(*a*) or (*b*) above is inadmissible—

(*a*) if it infringes the jurisdiction of the United Kingdom or is otherwise prejudicial to the sovereignty of the United Kingdom; or

(*b*) if compliance with the requirement would be prejudicial to the security of the United Kingdom or to the relations of the government of the United Kingdom with the government of any other country.

(3) A requirement such as is mentioned in subsection (I)(*a*) above is also inadmissible—

(*a*) if it is made otherwise than for the purposes of civil or criminal proceedings which have been instituted in the overseas country; or

(*b*) if it requires a person to state what documents relevant to any such proceedings are or have been in his possession, custody or power or to produce for the purposes of any such proceedings any documents other than particular documents specified in the requirement.

(4) Directions under subsection (I) above may be either general or special and may prohibit compliance with any requirement either absolutely or in such cases or subject to such conditions as to consent or

otherwise as may be specified in the directions; and general directions under that subsection shall be published in such manner as appears to the Secretary of State to be appropriate.

(5) For the purposes of this section the making of a request or demand shall be treated as the imposition of a requirement if it is made in circumstances in which a requirement to the same effect could be or could have been imposed; and

(*a*) any request or demand for the supply of a document or information which, pursuant to the requirement of any court, tribunal or authority of an overseas country, is addressed to a person in the United Kingdom; or

(*b*) any requirement imposed by such a court, tribunal or authority to produce or furnish any document or information to a person specified in the requirement,

shall be treated as a requirement to produce or furnish that document or information to that court, tribunal or authority.

(6) In this section "commercial document" and "commercial information" mean respectively a document or information relating to a business of any description and "document" includes any record or device by means of which material is recorded or stored.

3. Offences Under ss. 1 and 2

(1) Subject to subsection (2) below, any person who without reasonable excuse fails to comply with any requirement imposed under subsection (2) of section I above or knowingly contravenes any directions given under subsection (3) of that section or section 2(I) above shall be guilty of an offence and liable—

(*a*) on conviction on indictment, to a fine;

(*b*) on summary conviction, to a fine not exceeding the statutory maximum.

(2) A person who is neither a citizen of the United Kingdom and Colonies nor a body corporate incorporated in the United Kingdom shall not be guilty of an offence under subsection (I) above by reason of anything done or omitted outside the United Kingdom in contravention of directions under section I(3) or 2(I) above.

(3) No proceedings for an offence under subsection (I) above shall be instituted in England, Wales or Northern Ireland except by the Secretary of State or with the consent of the Attorney General or, as the case may be, the Attorney General for Northern Ireland.

(4) Proceedings against any person for an offence under this section may be taken before the appropriate court in the United Kingdom having jurisdiction in the place where that person is for the time being.

* * *

4. Restriction of Evidence (Proceedings in Other Jurisdictions) Act 1975

A court in the United Kingdom shall not make an order under section 2 of the Evidence (Proceedings in Other Jurisdictions) Act 1975 for giving effect to a request issued by or on behalf of a court or tribunal of an overseas country if it is shown that the request infringes the jurisdiction of the United Kingdom or is otherwise prejudicial to the sovereignty of the United Kingdom; and a certificate signed by or on behalf of the Secretary of State to the effect that it infringes that jurisdiction or is so prejudicial shall be conclusive evidence of that fact.

5. Restriction on Enforcement of Certain Overseas Judgments

(1) A judgment to which this section applies shall not be registered under Part II of the Administration of Justice Act 1920 or Part I of the Foreign Judgments (Reciprocal Enforcement) Act 1933 and no court in the United Kingdom shall entertain proceedings at common law for the recovery of any sum payable under such a judgment.

(2) This section applies to any judgment given by a court of an overseas country, being—

(*a*) a judgment for multiple damages within the meaning of subsection (3) below;

(*b*) a judgment based on a provision or rule of law specified or described in an order under subsection (4) below and given after the coming into force of the order; or

(*c*) a judgment on a claim for contribution in respect of damages awarded by a judgment falling within paragraph (*a*) or (*b*) above.

(3) In subsection (2)(*a*) above a judgment for multiple damages means a judgment for an amount arrived at by doubling, trebling or otherwise multiplying a sum assessed as compensation for the loss or damage sustained by the person in whose favour the judgment is given.

(4) The Secretary of State may for the purposes of subsection (2)(*b*) above make an order in respect of any provision or rule of law which appears to him to be concerned with the prohibition or regulation of agreements, arrangements or practices designed to restrain, distort or restrict competition in the carrying on of business of any description or to be otherwise concerned with the promotion of such competition as aforesaid.

(5) The power of the Secretary of State to make orders under subsection (4) above shall be exercisable by statutory instrument subject to annulment in pursuance of a resolution of either House of Parliament.

(6) Subsection (2)(*a*) above applies to a judgment given before the date of the passing of this Act as well as to a judgment given on or after that date but this section does not affect any judgment which has been registered before that date under the provisions mentioned in subsection (I) above or in respect of which such proceedings as are there mentioned have been finally determined before that date.

6. Recovery of Awards of Multiple Damages

(1) This section applies where a court of an overseas country has given a judgment for multiple damages within the meaning of section 5(3) above against—

(*a*) a citizen of the United Kingdom and Colonies; or

(*b*) a body corporate incorporated in the United Kingdom or in a territory outside the United Kingdom for whose international relations Her Majesty's Government in the United Kingdom are responsible; or

(*c*) a person carrying on business in the United Kingdom,

(in this section referred to as a "qualifying defendant") and an amount on account of the damages has been paid by the qualifying defendant either to the party in whose favour the judgment was given or to another party who is entitled as against the qualifying defendant to contribution in respect of the damages.

(2) Subject to subsections (3) and (4) below, the qualifying defendant shall be entitled to recover from the party in whose favour the judgment was given so much of the amount referred to in subsection (I) above as exceeds the part attributable to compensation; and that part shall be taken to be such part of the amount as bears to the whole of it the same proportion as the sum assessed by the court that gave the judgment as compensation for the loss or damage sustained by that party bears to the whole of the damages awarded to that party.

(3) Subsection (2) above does not apply where the qualifying defendant is an individual who was ordinarily resident in the overseas country at the time when the proceedings in which the judgment was given were instituted or a body corporate which had its principal place of business there at that time.

(4) Subsection (2) above does not apply where the qualifying defendant carried on business in the overseas country and the proceedings in which the judgment was given were concerned with activities exclusively carried on in that country.

(5) A court in the United Kingdom may entertain proceedings on a claim under this section notwithstanding that the person against whom the proceedings are brought is not within the jurisdiction of the court.

(6) The reference in subsection (I) above to an amount paid by the qualifying defendant includes a reference to an amount obtained by execution against his property or against the property of a company which (directly or indirectly) is wholly owned by him; and references in that subsection and subsection (2) above to the party in whose favour the judgment was given or to a party entitled to contribution include references to any person in whom the rights of any such party have become vested by succession or assignment or otherwise.

(7) This section shall, with the necessary modifications, apply also in relation to any order which is made by a tribunal or authority of an overseas country and would, if that tribunal or authority were a court, be a judgment for multiple damages within the meaning of section 5(3) above.

(8) This section does not apply to any judgment given or order made before the passing of this Act.

7. Enforcement of Overseas Judgment Under Provision Corresponding to s. 6

(1) If it appears to Her Majesty that the law of an overseas country provides or will provide for the enforcement in that country of judgments given under section 6 above, Her Majesty may by Order in Council provide for the enforcement in the United Kingdom of judgments given under any provision of the law of that country corresponding to that section.

(2) An Order under this section may apply, with or without modification, any of the provisions of the Foreign Judgments (Reciprocal Enforcement) Act 1933.

* * *

DOCUMENT 67

UNITED KINGDOM PROTECTION OF TRADING INTERESTS (US CUBAN ASSETS CONTROL REGULATIONS) ORDER 1992

■ ■ ■

Whereas it appears to the Secretary of State that the measures to which this Order relates have been taken by or under the law of the United States of America ("the United States") for regulating or controlling international trade and that those measures, in so far as they apply to things done or to be done outside the territorial jurisdiction of the United States by persons carrying on business in the United Kingdom, are damaging or threaten to damage the trading interests of the United Kingdom:

Now therefore the Secretary of State, in exercise of his powers under section 1(1) of the Protection of Trading Interests Act 1980 ("the 1980 Act") and of all other powers enabling him in that behalf, hereby makes the following Order—

1. This Order may be cited as the Protection of Trading Interests (US Cuban Assets Control Regulations) Order 1992 and shall come into force [in] October 1992.

2. The Secretary of State hereby directs that section 1 of the 1980 Act shall apply to the measures taken under the law of the United States referred to in the following Article.

3. The measures to which this Order applies are those provisions of part 515 (entitled Cuban Assets Control Regulations) of title 31 of the Code of Federal Regulations which affect trading activities carried on in the United Kingdom or the import of goods to or the export of goods from the United Kingdom.

4. In this Order "trading activities" includes any activity carried on in the course of a business of any description.

EXPLANATORY NOTE

(This Note is not part of the Order)

This Order *applies section 1 of the Protection of Trading Interests Act 1980* to *Part 515* (US Cuban Assets Control Regulations) of *title 31* of the United States Code of Federal Regulations in so far as that part affects trading activities carried on in the United Kingdom or the import of goods to or the export of goods from the United Kingdom. It has been made following the passing by the United States Congress on October 5th 1992 of section 1706(a)(1) of the National Defense Authorization Act for the Fiscal Year 1993 (in the part entitled "Cuban Democracy Act of 1992") which would prohibit the granting of licences under the US Cuban Assets Control Regulations for certain transactions between US owned or controlled firms in the United Kingdom and Cuba.

Where section 1 of the 1980 Act is applied the Secretary of State may require persons in the United Kingdom who carry on business there (a) to notify him of any requirements or prohibitions imposed or threatened to be imposed on them pursuant to the measures to which section 1 has been applied, and (b) not to comply with any such requirement or prohibition—(sections 1(2) and (3) of the 1980 Act).

Protection of Trading Interests Act 1980 General Directions by the Secretary of State Under Section 1.

WHEREAS the Secretary of State:

(1) has directed that *section 1 of the Protection of Trading Interests Act 1980* (the "1980 Act") shall apply to those provisions of *Part 515* (entitled Cuban Assets Control Regulations) of *title 31* of the Code of Federal Regulations which affect trading activities carried on in the United Kingdom or the import of goods to or the export of goods from the United Kingdom (the "measures");

(2) has considered the effect of the measures on the trading interests of the United Kingdom;

(3) considers that the following direction is appropriate for avoiding damage to the trading interests of the United Kingdom:

Now, therefore, the Secretary of State in exercise of his powers under section 1(3) of the 1980 Act, hereby gives the following direction:

1. Except with the consent of the Secretary of State, no person or persons in the United Kingdom shall comply, or cause or permit compliance, whether by themselves, their officers or agents with any requirement or prohibition imposed on them pursuant to the said measures in so far as such requirement or prohibition affects trading activities carried on in the United Kingdom or the import of goods to or the export of goods from the United Kingdom.

2. In this Direction "trading activities" includes any activity carried on in the course of a business of any description.

3. This Direction shall come into operation at 11:40 on 14th October 1992.

14TH OCTOBER 1992
MINISTER FOR TRADE
DEPARTMENT OF TRADE AND INDUSTRY